SUPPLEMENTS PREVIEW

FOURTH EDITION

Linda Julian • Patricia Kelvin • Scott Leonard •
Laurel Black • Cynthia Myers • Edgar Roberts

STRATEGIES & RESOURCES
FOR TEACHING WRITING
with the

SIMON &
SCHUSTER
HANDBOOK
for WRITERS

Lynn Quitman Troyka

H EDITION

Ann O. Gebhard
TEACHING WRITING
ACROSS THE CURRICULUM

SIMON &
SCHUSTER
HANDBOOK
for WRITERS

Lynn Quitman Troyka

Strategies & Resources for Teaching Writing with the Simon & Schuster Handbook for Writers, Fourth Edition

*by Linda Julian, Patricia Kelvin, Scott Leonard,
Laurel Black, Cynthia Myers, and Edgar Roberts*

This comprehensive, spiral-bound manual includes *Strategies for Teaching Writing* by Linda Julian, Furman University, along with extensive, special sections on the following issues and approaches to writing: *Teaching Collaborative Writing* by Patricia Kelvin and Scott A. Leonard, Youngstown State University; *Portfolios* by Laurel Black, St. John Fisher College; *ESL Writers in the Composition Class* by Cynthia L. Myers, Iowa State University; *Reading and Writing About Literature* by Edgar V. Roberts, Lehman College of CUNY; and *Workplace Writing* by Linda Julian. This resource guide also includes the answer key to the handbook. This supplement is free to adopters. (0-13-455411-6)

Teaching Writing Across the Curriculum

by Ann O. Gebhard, SUNY Cortland

Designed specifically for instructors in disciplines other than English, this supplement offers guidelines for integrating writing assignments into their courses to promote more effective learning and critical thinking. This supplement is free to adopters. (0-13-455429-9)

Computers and Writing

by Dawn Rodrigues, Kennesaw State College

This guide by Dawn Rodrigues provides an overview of the possibilities for computer use in English departments. It is aimed not only at faculty who are currently using technology in teaching, but also those who are just beginning to consider it and those who merely want to learn about the possibilities.

Computers and Writing is free to adopters. (0-13-435934-8)

Teaching Writing

by Phyllis Hastings, Saginaw Valley State University

This manual provides guidance on teaching writing for both new and experienced teachers. Topics include student-teacher interaction, class dynamics, course plans, and the evaluation of student work.

Teaching Writing is free to adopters. (0-13-435942-9)

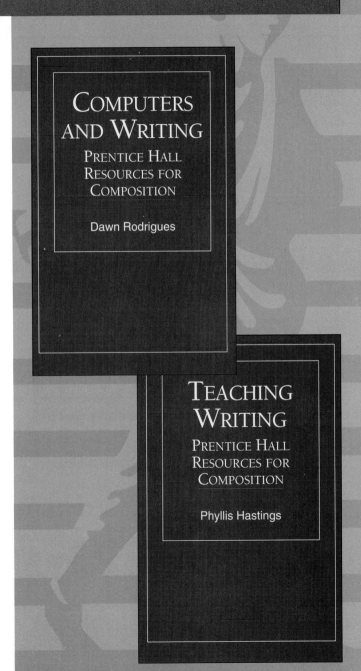

COMPUTERS
AND WRITING
PRENTICE HALL
RESOURCES FOR
COMPOSITION

Dawn Rodrigues

TEACHING
WRITING
PRENTICE HALL
RESOURCES FOR
COMPOSITION

Phyllis Hastings

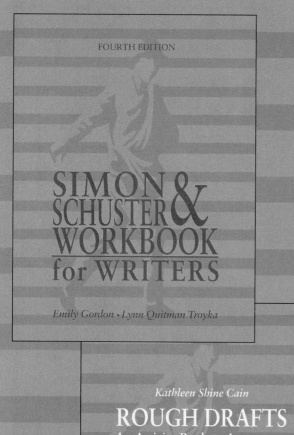

Simon & Schuster Workbook for Writers, Fourth Edition

by Emily Gordon and Lynn Quitman Troyka

Useful as a supplement to the handbook or as a primary text for freshman composition or basic writing courses, the workbook offers instruction and exercises on everything from punctuation to planning an essay. The workbook's organization parallels that of the handbook, making it easy to use the books in concert. ESL material has been incorporated into this edition of the workbook. This workbook is available as a for-sale item. (0-13-455396-9)

A Workbook Answer Key is free to instructors upon adoption. (0-13-456245-3)

Rough Drafts: An Activity Book to Accompany the Simon & Schuster Handbook for Writers, Fourth Edition

by Kathleen Shine Cain, Merrimack College

This supplement first offers invention exercises, then passages for editing and correction. It also includes full rough drafts of essays for students to revise. The exercises are keyed to the handbook. Professors may copy this supplement or parts of it for free, or students may purchase it at a nominal cost. (0-13-438441-5)

Preparing for the TASP with the Simon & Schuster Handbook for Writers, Fourth Edition

by Matilda Delgado Saenz, Northlake College

This booklet suggests ways that the handbook can be used to teach students the competencies tested in the writing sample and objective portions of the Texas Academic Skills Program Exam. Sample exams follow the format of the TASP examination. This booklet may be copied free upon adoption of the handbook, or students may purchase it for a nominal price. (0-13-455437-X)

Preparing for the CLAST with the Simon & Schuster Handbook for Writers, Fourth Edition

by Sybil Patterson, Hillsborough Community College

Students are taught how to study for the objective English language skills test and the essay portions of Florida's College Level Academic Skills Test. The competencies tested during CLAST are correlated with the handbook, and two sample tests in the format of the actual CLAST are included. The booklet may be copied free upon adoption of the handbook, or students may purchase it for a nominal price. (0-13-455446-9)

FOURTH EDITION

Matilda Delgado Saenz
PREPARING FOR THE TASP
with the

SIMON &
SCHUSTER
HANDBOOK
for WRITERS

Lynn Quitman Troyka

Sybil Patterson
PREPARING FOR THE CLAST
with the

SIMON &
SCHUSTER
HANDBOOK
for WRITERS

Lynn Quitman Troyka

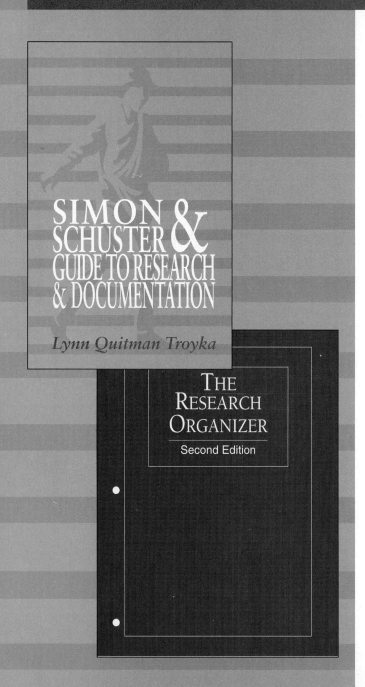

Simon & Schuster Guide to Research and Documentation

Lynn Quitman Troyka

This handy supplement not only includes the most up-to-date information on documentation in MLA, APA, CBE, and CM formats, but also covers the entire research process. This item is available to students for a nominal fee. (0-13-438433-4)

The Research Organizer, Second Edition

by Sue D. Hopke, Broward Community College

This convenient tool is designed to help students assemble their research paper notes and drafts in an organized and efficient manner. It offers guidance on the research process and provides space for students to record their search strategy, notes, citations, outlines, and drafts. This supplement will make preparing for a research paper easier and more efficient by allowing students to keep the majority of their materials in one place.

Professors may copy this supplement or parts of it for free, or students may purchase it at a nominal cost. (0-13-813957-1)

The Prentice Hall Critical Thinking Audio Study Cassette

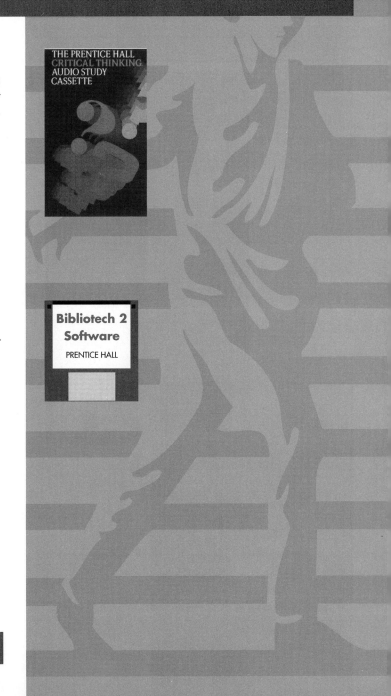

This 60-minute cassette helps students develop their critical thinking skills—from asking the right questions about material they are reading or hearing, to helpful tips on how to study, take effective notes, and become a more effective learner.

This cassette is free to adopters of and can be shrinkwrapped for students to the qualifying text for a nominal fee.

If you prefer, Prentice Hall will provide adopting departments with up to ten cassettes free of charge. (0-13-678335-X)

Bibliotech 2

Using this computerized bibliography generator, students follow prompts to format their bibliography in either MLA, APA or CBE documentation style. Students can print the bibliography directly from the program or save it to an ASCII file from which it can then be converted to a word processing file of their choice. This program is free to adopters with permission to make multiple copies for students. Available in IBM (0-13-008582-0) and Macintosh (0-13-228560-6) versions.

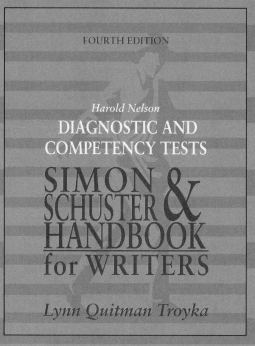

Diagnostic and Competency Tests

by Harold Nelson, Minot State University

This supplement contains several reproducible objective tests that can be used for pre-, mid-, or post-course evaluation. Now includes two ESL diagnostic tests. Answers to all the test items are keyed to sections of the handbook. (0-13-453094-2)

Correction Chart

When marking student papers, instructors can use this convenient stand-up chart—with correction symbols on one side and the handbook's table of contents on the other—to refer students to the appropriate handbook chapter and section. This item is free to adopters. (0-13-438425-3)

Supplementary Essays for Writers

by Gary D. Schmidt

This rhetorically arranged reader provides a collection of 31 classic essays by well-known professional writers. Each essay is accompanied by questions for discussion and writing, and each rhetorical section ends with several writing suggestions.

Supplementary Essays for Writers is free to adopters, with permission to reproduce individual essays for students. This reader is also salable to students for a nominal fee. (0-13-101338-6)

Webster's Dictionary Offers

Webster's New World Dictionary, Third College Edition or *Webster's New World Compact School & Office Dictionary* may be shrinkwrapped to the handbook at a discounted price.

The Prentice Hall/New York Times "Themes of the Times" Program

The Themes of the Times program, cosponsored by Prentice Hall and The New York Times, gives you and your students a newspaper supplement containing a recent collection of articles that provides students with timely examples of rhetorical principles and springboards for writing. The New York Times supplement is free to adopters. (0-13-437559-9)

6-4

Springboard for Writing: FINDING THE RIGHT WORD

Ernest Stock, "Marathon Dancers"

You may be familiar with the dance marathons held during the Great Depression if you have seen the movie "They Shoot Horses, Don't They?" Although we normally associate dance with joy and grace, these marathons were almost desperate parodies of that joy: couples danced non-stop for hours, hoping to outlast all the others in order to win a cash prize. Here Ernest Stock tries to capture the dark side of the dance marathon, while at the same time suggesting something of the human drama behind it.

The Prentice Hall / Simon & Schuster Transparencies for Writers

by Duncan Carter, Portland State University

This set of 100 two- and four-color transparencies features exercises, examples, and suggestions for student writing that focus on all aspects of the writing process—from generating ideas and shaping an outline to preparing a final draft and revising, editing, and documenting the final paper. These transparencies also cover grammar, punctuation, and mechanics via overlays that show how sentence and paragraph errors can be corrected most effectively.

Each section also contains a transparency of a work of fine art that is intended to serve as a springboard for student writing. (0-13-703209-9)

"Profiles of a Writer" Video Series

This professionally produced video series documents the lives and work of twelve renowned authors: Jorge Luis Borges, Jean Cocteau, Agatha Christie, Jules Feiffer, Joseph Heller, Patricia Highsmith, Anthony Burgess on D.H. Lawrence, Norman Mailer, Evan Hunter is Ed McBain, Alberto Moravia, Toni Morrison, and Gore Vidal. The segments in this series were produced by such organizations as BBC and by gifted contemporary film-makers. The average playing time for each tape is 50 minutes. Available free upon adoption based on number of texts purchased. Contact your local Prentice Hall representative for details.

ABC News/Prentice Hall Video Library: Composition, Volume 2

Through an exclusive agreement between ABC News and Prentice Hall, you can keep your classroom discussions lively and current with thematically arranged video clips from news programs such as 20/20, World News Tonight, and PrimeTime Live. Updated periodically, these clips, specifically chosen for use in composition courses, serve as visual representations of rhetorical strategies, springboards for discussion, critical thinking, and writing. There is a limit of 5 videos in any one term.

Video Clips

1) Lyme Disease—Nightline, 7/13/89, 20:56
2) Jack Smith's Vietnam Diary—Nightline, 1/21/94, 9:30
3) Prozac—American Agenda, 1/4/94, 5:03
4) Smart Cars and Highways are Key to Environment's Future—American Agenda, 11/24/92, 4:05
5) Teaching Values in the Schools—American Agenda, 12/14/93, 5:01
6) Teens Confront Prejudices—American Agenda, 9/8/93, 4:55
7) Political Correctness on US Campuses—Nightline, 5/13/91, 7:56
8) Maya Angelou, Inaugural Poetess—World News Tonight, 1/22/93, 4:48
9) Crime and Punishment Issues and Politics—Nightline, 1/26/94, 8:18

ISBN: 0-13-149030-3

These transparencies and videos are free to adopters based on the following schedule:
  up to 100 copies: 1 set
  100-250 copies: 2 sets
  251-500 copies: 3 sets
  501-750 copies: 4 sets
  751-1000 copies: 5 sets

Blue Pencil
Software

PRENTICE HALL

The On-Line Handbook

The On-Line Handbook is a condensed version of the *Simon & Schuster Handbook for Writers,* Fourth Edition on disk, which can be installed on a computer and accessed by using a hot key or, in the case of the Windows version, an icon. The main menu parallels the main parts of the handbook; the sub menus correspond to chapters within the parts. This software is free to adopters with permission to use in a networked environment or to copy for students. Available in three formats: IBM 3.5″ (0-13-453102-7) or 5.25″ (0-13-453078-0), Macintosh (0-13-453136-1), and Windows (0-13-453169-8).

Blue Pencil

by Bob Bator

This computerized interactive editing program allows students to practice their writing skills by making revisions in paragraph-length passages. The program is organized around the following skill categories: capitalization and internal punctuation; modifiers; commas; fragments; comma splices, run-on sentences; quotation marks and end punctuation; subject/verb agreement; usage; verbs; and pronouns. A counter at the bottom of the screen keeps track of corrections that remain to be made. A final exercise reviews all skill categories together. This software is free to adopters with permission to use in a networked environment or to copy for students. Available for IBM 3.5″ (0-13-453177-9) or 5.25″ (0-13-453185-X) and Macintosh (0-13-438417-2).

America On-Line®— Connect to a whole new world!

We'll help you get started. Adopt this textbook and we'll waive the America Online membership fee for the first two months! Use this introductory membership to access a wide range of interactive services and educational information including a fast and easy gateway to the Internet. All you need is a computer and a modem. We'll make it easy for your students to get started too! What's more, Simon & Schuster Higher Education Group has developed COLLEGE Online, an online service specifically for college and university faculty and student use! Ask your local representative for more details.

Here are just some of the growing resources available through COLLEGE Online:

- Faculty Resources
- College Talk
- Student Success
- Internet & New Media

Microsoft Bookshelf®

Through an exciting agreement with Microsoft, Prentice Hall can offer Bookshelf '95, an award winning CD-Rom reference product. Qualified adopters can enjoy Roget's Thesaurus, The American Heritage Dictionary, The Concise Columbia Encyclopedia, Hammond Intermediate World Atlas, The World Almanac, The People's Chronology and The Columbia Dictionary of Quotations. Please see your local Prentice Hall representative for further details.

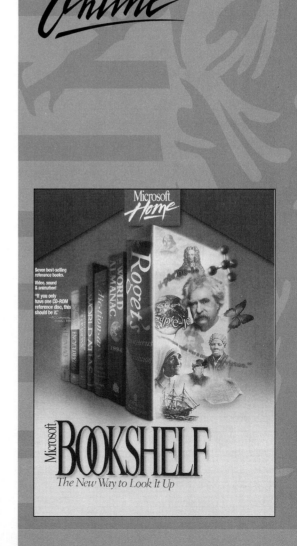

INDEX OF TITLES

ANNOTATED
INSTRUCTOR'S EDITION

FOURTH EDITION

SIMON & SCHUSTER HANDBOOK
for WRITERS

*Lynn Quitman Troyka
with Judith A. Stanford,
Ann B. Dobie, and
Emily R. Gordon*

Prentice Hall
Upper Saddle River, New Jersey 07458

For David,
who makes it all great fun

President, Humanities and Social Sciences: J. Philip Miller
Development Editor: Joyce Perkins
Assistant Development Editor: Kara Hado
Production Editor: Andrew Roney
Executive Editor: Alison Reeves
Creative Design Director: Leslie Osher
Interior Design and Page Layout: Susan Walrath
Cover Design: Leslie Osher and Susan Walrath
Supervisor of Production Services: Lori Kane
Prepress and Manufacturing Buyer: Mary Ann Gloriande

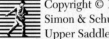 Copyright © 1996, 1993, 1990, 1987 by Lynn Quitman Troyka
Simon & Schuster/ A Viacom Company
Upper Saddle River, New Jersey 07458

Printed in the United States of America

10 9 8 7 6 5 4 3 2 1

ISBN 0-13-455015-3

Prentice-Hall International (UK) Limited, *London*
Prentice-Hall of Australia Pty. Limited, *Sydney*
Prentice-Hall Canada Inc., *Toronto*
Prentice-Hall Hispanoamericana, S.A., *Mexico*
Prentice-Hall of India Private Limited, *New Delhi*
Prentice-Hall of Japan, Inc., *Tokyo*
Simon & Schuster Asia Pte. Ltd., *Singapore*
Editora Prentice-Hall do Brasil, Ltda., *Rio de Janeiro*

Contents

Preface to the Annotated Instructor's Edition

I have designed the *Annotated Instructor's Edition (AIE)* of the *Simon & Schuster Handbook for Writers, Fourth Edition* to carry two major messages as it serves as a catalyst for faculty, including teaching assistants, part-time faculty, and new and experienced full-time faculty.

First, this *AIE* seeks to set forth the theoretical grounding that supports the structure, content, and approaches found in the *Handbook*. Foremost, these contexts are described by five comprehensive bibliography essays at the front of the *AIE*. They survey scholarship in the history of rhetoric, the writing process, English as a second language, writing across the curriculum, and essay testing. I am indebted to the author of each essay for undertaking the specially commissioned research and for the writing entailed, for as a group they help me deliver my message that the teaching of writing relies upon an intellectual tradition and current knowledge about language and learning.

The second message of this *AIE* is that all teaching decisions in composition classrooms derive from an informed, cohesive vision of goals and strategies. Teaching is not the result of a "grab bag" of what "might work on Monday morning." Therefore, the margins of this *AIE*, which run alongside each page of the student edition, duplicated exactly, include: background information as rationales, teaching tips based on respected research and proven practice, quotations about writing and its related activities, annotated bibliographic citations to stimulate further reading, and explicit links between the text and the wealth of supplementary materials that Prentice Hall/Simon & Schuster makes available for student and for faculty use (a 14-page description of all supplements is now included in the *AIE*).

Along with these resources are answers to exercises and, of paramount importance, the exact coverage of each item in each exercise. At a glance, teachers can tell what section each item relates to, so that they can identify student strengths and weaknesses instantly.

No project as huge and complex as this *AIE* could be done alone. Many colleagues have contributed their ideas informally as this *AIE* has evolved over editions. My co-authors on the *AIE* were headed up for the Fourth Edition by Judith A. Stanford, River College, who brought her efficiency, industry, and special grace to the project. I thank her enthusiastically. Key people in the prior editions included Ann B. Dobie, University of Southwestern Louisiana; Emily R. Gordon, Queensborough Community College; James MacDonald, University of Southwestern Louisiana; and Patricia Morgan, Louisiana State University. I am grateful to each.

At Prentice Hall/Simon & Schuster, I was fortunate to work with a top team. Alison Reeves, Executive Editor, spearheaded the editorial effort with a strong, hands-on commitment to quality and consistency; Kara Hado, Assistant Development Editor, oversaw the daily, myriad details of coordination with unfailing intelligence; Joyce F. Perkins, Senior Development Editor, kept her keen eye on the project with comforting good will; Andrew Roney, Senior Project Manager, brought order and efficiency to a production challenge on a tight schedule that would have daunted most—all the while gentling us with his wry humor. Others whose support were indispensable include Phil Miller, President of Humanities and Social Sciences; Gina Sluss, Executive Marketing Manager; Leslie Osher, Creative Design Director; Susan Walrath, Designer; Lori Kane, Supervisor of Production Services; Mary Ann Gloriande, Manufacturing Buyer; and Kane Tung, Editorial Assistant.

Lynn Quitman Troyka

The Composing Process: An Overview

Josephine Koster Tarvers

On the surface, rhetoricians used to suppose, the composing process looked easy to explain. All we had to do was to explain how ideas got into a writer's head, and from there onto paper. But more than three decades of research into the composing process have convinced us that this process is far more complex than we initially thought. In this essay, I discuss briefly some of the major theories about the composing process, to show you not only where these theories intersect but also where they differ, and conclude with suggestions about applying these theories to your teaching.

First of all, when we speak of the "composing process," we are amalgamating a number of processes, both psychological and physical, both for discovering ideas and actually committing them to writing. Research suggests that each person's writing process is different and that it changes with the writer's age, experience, level of knowledge about the subject, and particular writing situation. It also depends on the environment a writer is working in, the culture that writer grew up in, and the people who give that writer feedback about a particular piece of writing. So when you see a book or article like this talk about "the writing process" or "the composing process," you must begin by remembering that it is radically compressing a complex group of actions and decisions.

Until the mid-1960s, few writing books or writing theorists even talked about a writing process, for writing was a *product* you generated, not a group of actions. But in that decade, for the first time rhetoricians began to talk about writing as an activity that had distinct stages (what we now call a stage-model theory). Most variations acknowledged some shared stages of the process: a period of gathering information and noting down ideas, one

of "roughing out" those ideas, and one in which the information is reshaped and adjusted according to the writer's intentions and certain conventions of linguistic etiquette. We call these stages *planning* or *prewriting; drafting* or *writing;* and *revising* or *editing.* The stage-model theories, though, attempt to narrow, rather than broaden the focus of composing.

D. Gordon Rohman and Albert O. Wlecke are credited with the first exploration of the stage-model theory. In *Pre-Writing* [25], they argue that a pre-assimilation of ideas occurs in the mind before writing, and that writers must learn to "picture the process" in order to imitate it consciously. They suggest techniques such as keeping journals, writing meditations, and developing analogies as ways for students to discover their messages. They also insist on the separation from and primacy of prewriting over other stages of the composing process, and that the composing process is essentially linear, views that have been assailed by later theorists.

JOSEPHINE KOSTER TARVERS teaches writing and literature and directs the Writing Center at Winthrop University, Rock Hill, SC. She is also president of In*Scribe Communications, a consulting firm that works with writers in the workplace. She has taught writing, grammar theory, history of the language, and other courses in language, gender, and medieval literature at Rutgers and the University of North Carolina at Chapel Hill. Her recent publications include *Teaching Writing: Theories and Practices,* 4th edition (1994) and *Learned Books and Lewd Women: Literacy, Gender, and Rhetoric in Late Medieval Literature* (forthcoming).

Another noted stage-model theorist is Peter Elbow. In *Writing Without Teachers* [8], he promotes the technique of *freewriting,* which encourages writers to record ideas quickly and continuously, without the premature editing for spelling, punctuation, and word choice that so often interrupts or destroys the writer's train of thought. One major criticism of systems like Elbow's, however, is that they privilege the initial stages of the writing process over the others. As a result, students enamored with prewriting may give scant attention to later stages, and produce less satisfactory results. Donald Murray attempts to counter this imbalance through use of a preliminary or "discovery" draft, where writers learn what other kinds of plans and explorations they might make before beginning the formal writing process. [22] But like Elbow, Murray emphasizes prewriting; revision in his scheme is the repetition of the prewriting stages of collecting, planning and developing as many times as is needed until the text is ready for editing.

As rhetoricians became more aware of the "holes" in stage-model theory, they turned more to psychology to learn how writers' minds may work. James Moffett, for instance, has based his work on the theories of Jean Piaget [2], who divided all childhood learning experiences into four stages, based on the behaviors children can learn in each stage (assimilation) and the changes they can make in those behaviors (adaptation). At each stage in Moffett's composing process [20], students are encouraged to return to the previous ones for help in planning and developing, so that their writing processes are not separate and linear but recursive, hierarchic, and spiraling, drawing on earlier knowledge to produce new kinds of writing for new audiences. In other words, they are encouraged to make *cognitive plans* [21].

The construction of cognitive plans is also central to the research in composing conducted by Linda Flower, John R. Hayes, and their many associates [14]. They base their conclusions on the study of "writing protocols," chronological descriptions of all the activities a writer uses in composing a text and transcripts of the writer narrating his or her decisions and choices in those activities. Flower and Hayes postulate a complex model of the composing process based on planning, translating, and reviewing texts. Planning involves probing one's own memory, organizing that information, and making an initial plan for producing a text. In translation, the writer puts sentences on paper, leading to a draft; in review the writer improves problem areas in the draft. This process is recursive: students might plan, generate, and revise one paragraph before moving on to another, or plan the whole essay, generate a draft, and revise globally, or use some combination of these processes. Composing is goal-directed, and students use different kinds of strategic knowledge in setting these goals and evaluating how effectively they have been realized. [11]

Flower and Hayes use their model to explain how writers solve the problems of moving from the planning to generating stages by juggling, discarding, or subdividing the constraints on their writing; by drawing on routines or familiar procedures (such as the five-paragraph theme); and by readjusting their goals and hypotheses. This latter stage, revision, has recently been investigated in more detail. More than a decade ago, Nancy Sommers [27,28] found that student writers frequently confuse revising with correcting, focusing only on "mistakes," whereas more experienced writers reconsider audience and purpose, paying attention to global issues. Sommers suggested that learning to distinguish between revising and editing in the composing process produces better student writing. Many scholars, following in Sommers's and Flower and Hayes's footsteps, have recently begun publishing their conclusions about *how* writers juggle the stages of composing, learning to move between the elements productively, to take advantage of their pauses, and to use heuristic planning strategies. [10, 24, 26]

The chief criticism of cognitive theories of the composing process is that they make writers too isolated; that is, such theories usually picture writers working alone, and ignore or downplay the social nature of writing and the writer's place in a community or communities of readers and writers. Such critics have developed a *social-constructionist* theory of the writing process, which argues that the writer, at whatever stage of a piece of writing, is working within the constraints and demands of the communities she or he belongs to.

Thus, social constructionist views of the writing process are heavily influenced by the writer's purpose and audience. Richard Gebhardt [12] has suggested, in fact, that there are two large classes of composing processes, one in which the writer is relatively certain about audience, purpose, and the information these require, and one in which the writer discovers the relationship among these three elements. More recently, Maxine Hairston has proposed a three-category continuum [13] among these elements, calling the categories "message writing" needed to conduct well-understood business between writer and reader; "self-limiting writing" where the writer knows audience and purpose, and has the necessary information at hand; and "extended reflective writing," where the writer discovers information, purpose, and sometimes even the audience through the composing process.

Theorists like Kenneth Bruffee [4], Patricia Bizzell [3], and David Bartholmae [1] have expanded our knowledge of how communities influence writers; it is, in fact, safe to say that "social construction" and its paired term, "collaborative learning," are the watchwords for rhetorical theory in the early 1990s. Whether they will remain so is open to question, since evolving an understanding of the writing process is in itself an evolving process. Recently, even our notions of what defines a "community" have been called into question [19]; it's clear, then, that we still haven't pinned down the composing process, nor are we likely to in the near future.

Although no competing theories completely agree on descriptions of or labels for the composing process, most theorists agree in many respects about what is important in it:

- The composing process contains several distinct stages. Each is important, and, depending on the kind of writing, the purpose, the writer's available fund of information, and the audience, each will require different amounts of attention for any particular writing task. No one stage is intrinsically "more important" than any other. As teachers, we must help our students gain experience in handling each stage, and overcome our instincts to emphasize the stage(s) most important to us.

- Composing processes are recursive, not linear; only in the ideal world of textbooks do writers blithely choose an idea, make a neat outline, develop it, write about it, and make final cosmetic changes before presenting it to an audience. In reality, writers struggle, chew their pencils, cross out, go back, pause, reconsider, find other information, rack their brains, stare at the screen, juggle ideas, fling curses, and even start over from scratch in the process of composing a text. All of these may be positive actions in creating a text. We can help our students appreciate the recursive nature of writing by sharing our own drafts with them; when students see our corrections and stacks of paper, they are more likely to believe that such challenges face *all* writers, not just inexperienced ones.

- Writing takes many forms, depending in each case on the writer's purpose and audience. Although writers may develop certain writing habits, their composing processes will vary with every writing occasion. We need to discuss with our students how those processes may change from professor to professor or boss to boss, or from routine memo to lab report to application letter to literary analysis.

- Many techniques can stimulate the composing process; none are inherently "better" than others. Writers need to find the strategy or strategies which work best for them in each kind of writing situation they face. This means not only providing them with a repertoire of strategies to try, but also with the time to practice them.

- Before writers actually begin *writing,* they need to find subjects and gather ideas and information to write about. The time this takes will be determined by the writer's purpose, audience, and existing fund of knowledge. By varying our assignments, we can help them learn to manipulate these variables.

- The need to put ideas on paper "correctly" may inhibit writers. By drafting quickly and suspending editing until a text is nearly complete, many writers can compose more successful early drafts. Demonstrating techniques like freewriting and discovery drafts, for instance, can help students gain the courage to set aside the rules dinned in by previous teachers.

■ Many inexperienced writers do not distinguish between revising and editing. Revision allows writers to test drafts against their intentions and to add, delete, and rearrange what they have produced until it suits their purpose and audience. Working together as a class and then in small groups to revise pieces of student and professional writing will help students master true revising skills.

■ Editing is an act of social etiquette, in which writers decide how closely they wish their texts to conform to the audience's accepted conventions of language, and adjust their texts accordingly. Writers who choose to violate these conventions take their audience and purpose into account, and accept the consequences. Asking students to react to well- and poorly-edited copies of the same texts, and to answer questions such as "Which deserves the better grade? Which writer would you hire?" helps students see some of the real advantages of editing once a well-written document has been constructed.

Knowing what we do, then, about the composing process, how can we incorporate this knowledge into our teaching? We can encourage students to write frequently—and not always for grades—to make their own discoveries about the composing process. We can allow regular time in class for writing to help students develop the habit of writing. Students need to learn many different strategies to facilitate their composing. By introducing them to many planning and drafting strategies (not all at once!), we can help them become more productive writers. Questions of grammar, spelling, punctuation, and "where to start the next paragraph"

often hinder students' attempts to produce texts; we can encourage them to postpone those worries and decisions until the editing stage, where they can be productively addressed. Students also need to learn to revise their papers to suit their purposes and audiences; by scheduling draft review sessions, encouraging peer editing, and holding conferences, we can direct students' attention away from "error-hunting" to more substantive questions.

Since students must also learn to write for audiences outside the classroom and in forms other than essay writing, we can provide them with practice by varying the design of our assignments. We can include other possibilities and other audiences, give students time in class not only to write, but to plan, discuss, reflect on, and generate ideas that prompt writing. We can work with our colleagues in other disciplines to provide writing across and throughout the curriculum, for many audiences and purposes. We can encourage students to practice these activities by collecting their notes and drafts along with the finished products. (Of course, the preliminary materials shouldn't be marked or graded, but we can examine them to help our students.)

And we shouldn't wait until *after* the student completes a document to offer our suggestions; rather, as Robert Zoellner has suggested [30], we need to intervene *during* the writing process, in a *talk-write* manner, so that students get maximum guidance. Zoellner uses a telling analogy: he says ski instructors don't tell novice skiers, "Ski down this slope, and I'll come back in about a week or so, look at the marks you made that still remain in the snow, and tell you what you should have done."[15] Rather, we need to be active coaches, helping writers through the process, giving them feedback, encouragement, and education. Above all, we can make our students more conscious of themselves as *writers*, people who have composing processes; teach them skills that let them work more effectively as writers; and help them realize that their texts are not merely products, but journeys—journeys of discovery, growth, and sometimes of liberation.

Annotated Bibliography of Suggested Readings

Below I list a number of works which deal, in part or totally, with the views of the writing process discussed above. This is by no means a complete bibliography, but will provide you with plenty of information and leads to follow. Abbreviations used are *CCC, College Composition and Communication; CE, College English;* NCTE, National Council of Teachers of English; *RTE, Research in the Teaching of English.*

1. Bartholmae, David. "Inventing the University." *When a Writer Can't Write: Research on Writer's Block and Other Writing Process Problems.* Ed. Mike Rose. NY: Guilford, 1986.

   Argues that students are often unaware of the conventions required by the academic community and must be familiarized with those if they are to succeed as writers.

2. Beard, Ruth M. *An Outline of Piaget's Developmental Psychology for Students and Teachers.* NY: NAL, 1969.

   Contains sections on the development of intelligence, on each of Piaget's four stages of cognitive growth, and on the implications of these theories for teachers.

3. Bizzell, Patricia. "Cognition, Convention, and Certainty: What We Need to Know about Writing." PRE/TEXT 3 (1983): 213–43.

   One of the first statements of the social-constructionist composing position, with a critique of other positions.

4. Bruffee, Kenneth. "Social Construction, Language, and the Authority of Knowledge." *CE* 48 (1986): 773–90.

   The theory and proposed practices underlying social construction.

5. Connors, Robert, and Cheryl Glenn. *The St. Martin's Guide to Teaching Writing.* 2nd ed. NY: St. Martin's, 1992.

   Overview to the profession, with an excellent chapter on the composing process and implications for your teaching.

6. Cooper, Charles R., and Lee Odell, eds. *Research on Composing: Points of Departure.* Urbana, IL: NCTE, 1978.

   Ten essays on the composing process by well-known specialists.

7. Elbow, Peter. *Writing With Power.* NY: Oxford UP, 1981.

   Emphasizes writing as a way of controlling one's world; discusses freewriting, revision, and peer editing, with many teaching suggestions.

8. ———, *Writing Without Teachers.* NY: Oxford UP, 1973.

   Encourages writers to break away from traditional practices (such as outlining) and to use other prewriting methods (especially freewriting) to discover new information.

9. Faigley, Lester, et al. *Assessing Writers' Knowledge and Processes of Composing.* Norwood, NJ: Ablex,1985.

   Surveys the cognitive backgrounds of composing and the applications of this knowledge in pedagogy and theory.

10. ———, and Stephen Witte. "Analyzing Revision." *CE* 32 (1981): 400–14.

    There are two kinds of revision, surface (correcting minor flaws) and text-based (addressing larger concerns). The latter must be taught to students as an integral part of composing.

11. Flower, Linda. "The Construction of Purpose in Writing and Reading." *CE* 50 (1988): 528–50.

    A critique of earlier studies of writing, and of using protocols, and an elegant presentation of the Flower-Hayes theories.

12. Gebhardt, Richard C. "Initial Plans and Spontaneous Composition: Toward a Comprehensive Theory of the Writing Process." *CE* 44 (1982): 620–27.

    Identifies two relatively large groups of composing processes, one in which writers handle information they already possess, and another in which they discover the information they need.

13. Hairston, Maxine. "Different Products, Different Processes." *CCC* 37 (1986): 442–52.

Identifies and gives examples of the three kinds of composing, based on purpose, audience, and writer's information.

14. Hayes, John R., and Linda Flower. "Writing Research and the Writer." *American Psychologist* 41 (1986): 1106–13.

The fullest articulation of Flower and Hayes's theories to the date of publication, with full bibliography.

15. Heilker, Paul. "Public Products/Public Processes: Zoellner's Praxis and the Contemporary Composition Classroom." *Rhetoric Review* 10.2 (1992): 232–38.

Offers suggestions for incorporating talk-write pedagogy in the classroom.

16. Hume, Ann. "Research on the Composing Process." *Writing: Policies, Problems, and Possibilities.* Eds. Bruce Cronnell and Joan Michael. Los Alamitos, CA: Southwest Regional Laboratory of Educational Research and Development, 1982.

A comprehensive, detailed account of research on composing to about 1981.

17. Kantor, Kenneth. "Classroom Contexts and the Development of Writing Institutions: An Ethnographic Case Study." *RTE* 17 (1983): 72–94.

Case study of seven high-school students in a creative writing class, focusing on the revision stage of composing.

18. Lindemann, Erika. *A Rhetoric for Writing Teachers.* 2nd ed. NY: Oxford UP, 1987.

An overview of theories and research in the teaching of writing, with suggestions for classroom applications. A comprehensive and accessible summary for beginners and experts alike, with an extensive bibliography.

19. Lyon, Arabella. "Re-Presenting Communities: Teaching Turbulence." *Rhetoric Review* 10.2 (1992): 279–90.

Warns of the dangers in not exploring what we mean by "community" and "collaboration."

20. Moffett, James. *Teaching the Universe of Discourse.* Boston: Houghton, 1968.

A theory of discourse, drawing on students' cognitive development in producing increasingly more abstract texts. Emphasizes the relations between speaker and audience and speaker and subject.

21. ———, and Betty Jane Wagner. *Student-Centered Language Arts and Reading K–12.* 4th ed. Portsmouth, NH: Boynton-Cook/Heinemann, 1992.

A complete language arts text based on Moffett's discourse theory.

22. Murray, Donald M. *A Writer Teaches Writing.* 2nd ed. Boston: Houghton, 1985.

A book of advice for writers who are teachers, teachers who are writers, and nearly everyone else involved in composing. Sections on each of the stages of composing, with many teaching strategies and a full bibliography.

23. Odell, Lee, and Dixie Goswami, eds. *Writing in Nonacademic Settings.* NY: Guilford, 1985.

Fourteen essays on composing outside of the composition classroom.

24. Reither, James A. "Writing and Knowing: Toward Redefining the Writing Process." *CE* 47 (1985): 620–28.

Reminds us that the process (singular) is actually processes (plural), which are socially and culturally dependent.

25. Rohman, D. Gordon, and Albert O. Wlecke. *Pre-Writing: The Construction and Application of Models for Concept-Formation in Writing.* USOE Cooperative Research Project No. 2174. East Lansing: Michigan State University, 1964.

The writing process has three distinct stages: prewriting, writing, and revising. Prewriting has primacy; students can improve prewriting by keeping journals, writing meditations, and constructing analogies.

26. Scardamalia, Marlene, and Carl Bereiter. "Written Composition." *Handbook of Research on Teaching.* 3rd ed. Ed. Merlin C. Wittrock. NY: Macmillan, 1985.

A thorough survey of all areas of research on writing, including the composing process.

27. Sommers, Nancy. "Responding to Student Writing." *CCC* 33 (1982): 148–56.

Students confuse revision with correction because teacher comments usually focus on errors in editing. When teachers comment on matters of revision, students learn to pay more attention to this stage of composing.

28. ———. "Revision Strategies of Student Writers and Experienced Adult Writers." *CCC* 31 (1980): 378–88.

Suggests that major differences between students and experienced writers are the manner and amounts of their revisions; students make few revisions and focus on correctness, while adults are more willing to address global issues and to address the needs of their readers.

29. Warnock, John. "The Writing Process." *Research in Composition and Rhetoric.* Eds. Michael G. Moran and Ronald Lunsford. Westport, CT: Greenwood, 1984.

A review of recent research and theory of composing.

30. Zoellner, Robert. "Talk-Write: A Behavioral Pedagogy for Composition." *CE* 30 (1969): 267–320.

Monograph explaining and advocating this pedagogy, which has recently been "rediscovered" by the rhetorical community.

The History of Rhetoric: An Overview

William F. Woods

From its beginnings in Sicily around 450 B.C., rhetoric has been known as the art or "science" of persuasive discourse, the theory and practice of how to use available means of persuasion to affect the opinions of an audience. The earliest known treatise on rhetoric, by Corax of Syracuse, was a response to the citizens' need to speak well in litigations over land rights. A little more than a century later, Aristotle wrote his famous *Rhetoric* [item 15 in the Annotated Bibliography at the end of this essay] a work based on a systematic description of persuasive oratory as it was practiced in the law courts and the assembly of Athens. The key to Aristotle's approach to persuasion is *probability*. Logic can demonstrate a truth, but rhetoric can show that a position is worthy of belief— that it has a high probability of being true. Thus, while logical proofs are to be preferred in philosophical or scientific works, the persuasiveness of rhetoric is more effective in speaking or writing about practical affairs, and for a general audience.

Aristotle's *Rhetoric* assumes that there are three modes of appeal that can be used to reach an audience: the appeal to logic or reason (*logos*, in the Greek), the appeal to emotion (*pathos*), and the appeal to the moral or ethical sense (*ethos*). In themselves, these modes are only guidelines—ways of orienting the speaker to the task. However, each of the modes was also associated with certain kinds of discourse, as well as with the rhetorical devices proper to that sort of appeal. Perhaps the easiest way to give the flavor of Aristotle's rhetoric is to describe some of the devices he suggests for appealing to the mind, heart, and moral character of an audience.

As Aristotle saw it, the appeal to reason (*logos*) involved the use of certain basic concepts—fundamental, universally recognized formulas for thinking and expressing thought. Aristotle calls them the "common topics," because they are the commonplaces of thought. *Definition*, for example, is the classification of a subject, which in practice means identifying it by placing it in a class with other similar things (e.g., Man is an animal) and then further defining it by pointing out characteristics (*differentiae*) that distinguish it from the other things in that class (Man is a rational animal—"an animal that thinks"). The other topics that belong to the appeal to reason are as familiar and essential to us as definition. *Comparison* brings out the similarity, the difference, and the degree of difference between two subjects. *Relationship* refers to patterns such as cause and effect, antecedent and consequence, contraries, and contradictions. *Circumstance* refers to the process we go through in deciding whether something is or was possible or impossible, given the particular circumstances; here we are defining the subject in relation to its occasion, or context

WILLIAM F. WOODS is Associate Professor of English at Wichita State University, where he teaches medieval literature and the history of rhetoric. Some of his recently published articles are "The Reform Tradition in Nineteenth-Century Composition Teaching," *Written Communication 2* (October 1985): 377–90; "The Cultural Tradition of Nineteenth-Century "Traditional Grammar Teaching," *Rhetoric Society Quarterly 15* (nos. 1–2, 1985): 3–12; and "Emelye's Role in *The Knight's Tale*." *Studies in Philology* 88 (1991), 276–306.

These common topics were not originated by Aristotle, of course. He merely gave them names, grouped them, and showed how they function in persuasive discourse. In the history of rhetoric since Aristotle, however, the topics have been one of the most useful and enduring parts of classical rhetorical theory. In the Middle Ages and the Renaissance they were adapted to theories of logical proof. In the nineteenth and twentieth centuries they have been used mainly as patterns for the development and organization of paragraphs and essays. All of these uses are valid, for the topics are simply a formalized reflection of the ways in which we think, and so they enter into every intellectual task. Indeed, we need to keep in mind that the topics are both fundamental and versatile, hard to pigeonhole. They are handy for organizing one's thoughts, for shaping a paragraph, for arranging an essay—but they can also lend incisive clarity to efforts to revise a piece of writing; they can be a productive guide to the solving of a problem; and they can help writers to think about a subject in ways that will extend the material, unfolding its implications. That is why Aristotle also identified the topics as aids to *invention,* or the *discovery* of arguments for or against a position.

The second kind of appeal Aristotle talks about (*pathos*) is the appeal to the emotions—to the heart. Aristotle recognized that the most powerful appeals are those that harness the primal human emotions, our tendencies to feel protectiveness, anger, envy, pride, fear, desire. Aristotle and the rhetoricians who came after him devoted considerable thought to what we would call "audience psychology"—the types of emotions, and the types of people who experience them—but they also tried to identify the kinds of subjects that would evoke such an emotional response. What are the types of description, they asked, that powerfully involve an audience by helping them to place themselves within an imagined experience? What are the phrases and the words associated with deeply felt issues? And then there were the stylistic effects associated with emotional states. The periodic or suspended sentence, for instance, was thought to create tension and a feeling of building to climax. The "rhetorical" question had its place here, as did the use of exaggeration (hyperbole),

metaphor, and various other figures of speech. The study of style has always been closely connected with the appeal to the emotions. That is why the Sophists, professional orators who flourished about the second century A.D., were both praised and condemned for their panegyrics (elaborate eulogies and other ceremonial speeches) which appealed to the emotions but were not always calculated to inspire careful thought.

The third mode of appeal (*ethos*) is best described as a perceived relationship between the character of the speaker or writer, and the social and ethical beliefs of the audience. It is an appeal to ethical values, perhaps, but it also has much to do with the ability of the audience to *identify* with the speaker, to accept him or her as someone who speaks for *them.* This appeal often derives as much from the personal qualities of a speaker or writer as it does from the overt content of the discourse. "Is this a person like us, who shares our values, and whose opinion can be trusted?" These are the sorts of questions addressed by the ethical appeal, which has a great deal to do with the *tone* of a piece of writing, and therefore with its syntax and choice of words. Tone also depends on the purpose of the discourse (to explain, persuade, entertain, etc.), and on the level of style adopted by the writer or speaker. Classical rhetoricians after Aristotle liked to identify three levels of style: (1) the high, or grand style (appropriate for epics and for the sublime, high-flown passages of persuasive oratory); (2) the middle ("pleasing," ornate) style associated with literary works and with ceremonial oratory; and (3) the low or plain style associated with the language of instruction and everyday affairs. More recently, linguists have tended to identify levels of style by their social function. For instance, Martin Joos [33] identifies five levels of usage: frozen (genteel), formal, consultative, casual, and intimate.

It is worth noting that Aristotle's three modes of appeal—*logos, pathos,* and *ethos*—reflect a basic way in which western culture has conceived or "pictured" the mind ever since the days of Plato. We say *mind, body,* and *spirit,*—or *reason, memory, imagination*—as if thought and substance were somehow united by a perceptive consciousness: our bond with the world outside us and the source of our state of being. Indeed, there is

WILLIAM F. WOODS

a basic "threeness" that runs through classical discussions of art and psychology like a magic thread. For example, beginning, middle, and end stood for the parts of a narrative or dramatic plot (Aristotle again). Invention, arrangement (organization), and style were the three essential phases of composition as classical rhetoricians described it. That is, writers first *discover* and gather together their materials, then they *arrange* them, and finally they *express* them in language that is appropriate to the aim, audience, and circumstances of the discourse. Memory and the techniques of delivery were also included as parts of rhetoric, but they were not directly involved in what we in our industrial age call the "process" of writing. The actual teaching of rhetoric in classical times again took the form of a sequential, three-stage program: *precept,* the learning of principles; *practice,* under the supervision of a grammar or rhetoric teacher; and *imitation* of the style and structure of various model passages.

As oratory gave way to written rhetoric in the seventeenth and eighteenth centuries (a recurrent trend in the history of rhetoric), it became easier to characterize discourse by its literary form rather than by its appeal to an audience. Whereas ancient oratory had been divided into deliberative (persuasive), epideictic (ceremonial), and judicial (courtroom) oratory, the rhetorical spectrum by the 1700s had broadened to admit formal letters (epistles), history, argument, narration, description, persuasion, and poetry. Since spoken and written discourse were both represented, it was now customary to describe them as the art of "rhetoric and *belles lettres*" (borrowing a term from French literary criticism, which was then enjoying a period of authority). The theory of rhetoric was also changing. Rhetoricians had followed the empiricist philosophers (e.g., Locke) in assuming that language and thought reflected sense impressions, especially those received through sight. They further assumed that the forms of discourse must derive from the different patterns of language we use to record our perceptions, to form a "point of view," and to influence the opinions (views) of others. For example, we record our perceptions of things (thus, *descriptive* writing); we record our perceptions of events, or "things in action" (*narrative* writing); we interpret the pattern, or "logic" of relationships in the things and events perceived (*expository,* or explanatory writing); finally, we arrange our perceptions as proof, in support of our point of view (*argumentative* writing; "persuasion" generally meant spoken persuasive discourse). Authors of nineteenth-century textbooks on written rhetoric ("composition") found in these four terms, and in the kinds of writing they implied, a comprehensive schema for describing the teaching of writing.

These four "modes of discourse" [3] (which had little or nothing to do with Aristotle's three modes of appeal) were a typical feature of composition textbooks after 1850; they continued to shape teachers' approaches to English composition for at least the next hundred years. Rightly or wrongly, the four modes are now associated with the more conservative side of nineteenth-century composition teaching, which borrowed much from traditional methods of teaching English (and before that, Latin) grammar. There were other emphases, other theories at work in nineteenth-century composition teaching, but that period is remembered mainly for its drills, for the practice of having students memorize principles of grammar and style, for its increasing tendency to stress exposition (essay writing), and for giving first priority to the structuring of sentences, paragraphs, and essays. This was also a pedagogy associated with the rigorous methods and the sometimes endearing eccentricities of writing masters and textbooks writers like Alexander Bain, George Quackenbos, and A. S. (Adams Sherman) Hill.

But while the main thrust of nineteenth-century rhetoric and composition teaching was on style and structure, the *character* of the speaker or writer was beginning to receive a new emphasis. In a time when political, religious, and artistic individualism was much respected, the mental nature of the individual thinker, writer, and student became a serious subject of inquiry. The ultimate results of this spirit of romantic individualism, and the studies of child nature that accompanied it, can be seen today in the contemporary work of James Britton [29], a British educator specializing in research on student writing.

Britton's central insight was that written discourse can be described in terms of "function categories" (see

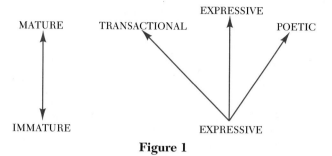

Figure 1

Figure 1) which represent what the writer is doing, in each case, in the act of writing. Writing is no longer seen as reflecting three aspects of the mind; rather, writing is assumed to represent three basic types of observed language behavior (which may, of course, reflect three types of mental activity).

In Britton's first function category, the *transactional,* students are participating in a problem, discussion, or other event: they are getting things done with words. The language relates closely to the needs of the audience and to the features of the task at hand. Language here is seen as a means to an end. In the second category, the *expressive,* the students express their responses to an outside situation in language that relates closely to their own points of view or inner experiences of the situation. Here the language is less a way of getting things done than it is a way of putting feelings into an intelligible form; thus, expressive discourse probably serves the writer's needs more than it does the needs of the audience or the demands of the task at hand. In the third category, the *poetic,* the writer is a spectator to the problem or situation at hand and uses language that relates closely to the overall concept, or "global context," of what is being done, created, or argued. Here the writer is more a disinterested analyst than a participator in an interactive task or someone trying to verbalize an inner experience.

The striking difference between Britton's system and the classical rhetorics is the centrality of the expressive, or personal, aspect of writing. Britton assumes that child language *begins* as expressive discourse and diversifies as the child grows older; the transactional and

poetic modes are gradually acquired, and the resources of the expressive mode are further developed. So while Aristotle's three modes of appeal were intended as ways of describing the impact of discourse on an audience, Britton's function categories are ways of identifying the kinds of discourse that emerge from three kinds of writing behavior. To put it another way, while Aristotle's modes are reader-oriented, Britton's categories are writer-oriented, since they describe discourse as the reflection of mental processes associated with certain adaptive social behaviors. Because of this emphasis on behavior, Britton's discussions are helpful to teachers trying to figure out "where students are coming from" in each of the various assignments that they write. Also, Britton's work may be a corrective influence on those who think of expressive discourse as a sloppy aberration from expository writing, or believe it should surface only in creative writing courses. Despite some real differences in theoretical orientation, however, Aristotle and Britton are not mutually exclusive. Teachers who have studied Aristotle's account of the appeals to the reason and the emotions will probably arrive at a better appreciation of Britton's transactional and poetic functions than those who come to Britton with no preparation in rhetoric.

In fact, even though social and historical conditions are vastly different now than they were in ancient Greece, Aristotle's *Rhetoric* continues to stand us in good stead, for the truth is that there have been no modern Aristotles, and no modern rhetoric has made the impact on rhetorical tradition that Aristotle and Cicero did. James Kinneavy [34] has come as close to that goal as anyone, perhaps, in his attempt to write a comprehensive modern theory of rhetoric, or "discourse," as he calls it, to allow for the enlarged role of writing in modern communication.

Kinneavy's achievement is to distinguish the basic kinds of discourse and describe the forms and characteristics that are essential to each of them. He derives four kinds of discourse from a theory of communication which he expresses by the familiar "communication triangle" (see Figure 2). The three points of the triangle refer to (1) the *writer,* (2) the *audience,* and (3) the *subject* of discourse, while the body of the triangle refers to

WILLIAM F. WOODS

Figure 2 (Adapted from Kinneavy)

(4) the *signal*, which is, in this case, the written language that conveys the message.

Each of these four terms is the point of origin for one of the four *aims*, the purposes for which we produce discourse: (1) Discourse that derives from the point of view or "inner experience" of the writer is *expressive* (as in Britton's function theory). (2) Discourse that is oriented more toward the audience's concerns, ideas, and feelings is called *persuasive* (as in Aristotle's theory of rhetoric). (3) Discourse that is meant to represent accurately a subject of investigation is called *reference* discourse—this aim includes the nonpersuasive aspects of most academic and scientific writing, as well as what we call *expository* prose. (4) Discourse that is self-referential or mimetic in purpose and that is meant to be used or enjoyed for its own sake is called *literary* discourse or literature (similar to Britton's *poetic* function category but not synonymous with it).

Unlike Britton, Kinneavy is not concerned mainly with the development of students' discourse toward maturity. His emphasis is on the description of the kinds of writing and on their use, rather than on the way they evolve in childhood or the ways they have evolved in history. We can generalize by calling Kinneavy's work a comprehensive, painstaking description of the ways prose writing is used or understood in the twentieth century. In this sense his work is reminiscent of Aristotle's systematic, analytical description of persuasive oratory in fourth-century Athens. A basic understanding of Kinneavy's four aims lends a perspective on written communication; moreover, it gives us a way of thinking about the entire profession of teaching writing. For example, it makes sense of the differences between the kinds of writing we find in personal experience papers and term papers. It also helps in defining the intellectual tasks we expect students to carry out when they write a particular assignment; for instance, a term paper is predominantly a piece of reference discourse and requires the skills of observation, distinction, comparison, and so forth. In general, teachers who know the four aims, and the features associated with them, can shape their students' writing with more confidence because they will have a better sense of the goals of each assignment. And for those who wish to backtrack Kinneavy's research and pursue their own investigations in one direction or another, full bibliographies are appended to each chapter of his book [34].

At the far end of our history lies rhetoric's growing edge, the gradual assimilation of modern theory and contemporary research into the body of the discipline. Slowly, the ideas of major theorists like I.A. Richards [38], Kenneth Burke [30], Chaim Perelman [37], and Stephen Toulmin [39], are entering our shared assumptions about written rhetoric, and research findings have begun to shape our teaching methods [VI]. But the central concerns, and thus the distinguishing traits of today's rhetoric have more to do with our students: a varied lot, they reflect, in their challenging array of needs and abilities, the fragmentation that characterizes not only our own profession, but academia at large and the arenas of national and international politics.

Responding to social changes beginning with the immigration and urbanization early in the century, rhetoric teaching has recurrently transformed itself, deepening its resources and broadening its scope to provide effective instruction for non-traditional students. The crisis-related efforts that produced Sterling A. Leonard's *English Composition as a Social Probem* (1917), for example, or William Labov's *The Study of Non-Standard English* (1970), or Mina Shaughnessy's *Errors and Expectations* (1977), have enabled significant pedagogical advances, and they remind us that "fragmentation" can also mean growth. The recent emphasis on writing across the curriculum, with its implied sensitivity to differences in discourse and audience, is a broader, organizational response to this century-long groundswell of pluralism, and the idea of "discourse communities" is our response at the level of theory.

What is a discourse community? It is a useful phrase, a good metaphor, because it gives form to our ambivalent thoughts about rhetoric's fractured audience. If doctors (or sociologists, literary critics, street people) share a specialized body of knowledge, a common jargon, and a rhetoric that specifies the kinds of arguments acceptable within that group, then they belong to a community of shared discourse features. These communities are, in effect, political entities which tend to overflow social, economic and geographical boundaries. They are "city states of language," and as such Aristotle would have understood them well, even though his rhetoric served a smaller, more unified world, and ours must speak to so many.

If there is a moral to be drawn from this lightning sketch of a few important works on rhetoric and composition, it is that a little knowledge is not a dangerous thing, but our only salvation. Not one of us has the time or dedication to absorb over two thousand years of rhetorical treatises, debates, and biases; even to desire such a thing is to miss the point badly. Our goal as teachers of writing is rather, by knowing something of the needs, ideas, and practices of former times, to understand more deeply and truly what we are engaged in doing and where we are tending. Neither Aristotle nor Kinneavy should be adopted as teachers' manuals. These two books, as well as the others that we have examined or that are listed in the bibliography, are parts of the history of our profession and should be sampled, experimented with, and pondered as we proceed with our own teaching, in our own times, in our own ways. To do so is to use history well; in so doing, we become rhetoricians—and enter history.

Annotated Bibliography of Suggested Readings

I. HISTORIES OF RHETORIC

1. Berlin, James. *Writing Instruction in Nineteenth-Century American Colleges.* Carbondale: Southern Illinois UP, 1984.

2. Bizzell, Patricia, and Bruce Herzberg, eds. *The Rhetorical Tradition: Readings from Classical Times to the Present.* Boston: St. Martin's, 1990.

   A superb anthology; the introductions and headnotes are in effect a substantial history of rhetoric.

3. Connors, Robert J. "The Rise and Fall of the Modes of Discourse." *CCC* 32 (1981): 444–55.

   A brief history of the growth and subsequent decline of the four "modes" of discourse (description, narration, exposition, and argumentation) in composition teaching.

4. Guthrie, Warren. "The Development of Rhetorical Theory in America, 1635-1850." *Speech Monographs* 13–16 (1946–49) and 18 (1951).

5. Halloran, Michael. "Rhetoric in the American College Curriculum: The Decline of Public Discourse." *Pre/Text* 3 (Fall 1982): 245–69.

6. Howell, Wilbur Samuel. *Eighteenth-Century British Logic and Rhetoric.* Princeton: Princeton UP, 1988.

7. ————. *Logic and Rhetoric in England, 1500–1700.* Princeton: Princeton UP, 1956.

   This classic study and its sequel catalog the changes rhetoric went through in response to the birth of empirical science and the resurgence of classical learning in the period between the early English Renaissance and the end of the seventeenth century.

8. Kennedy, George A. *Classical Rhetoric and Its Christian and Secular Tradition from Ancient to Modern Times.* Berkeley: California UP, 1980.

   A reliable overview of rhetoric in its cultural tradition, but weaker in the periods following the Middle Ages. For those interested in Greek, Roman, or early Christian rhetoric, Kennedy's specialized works in those areas are standard sources.

9. Kimball, Bruce. *Orators and Philosophers: A History of the Idea of Liberal Education*. New York: Teacher's College, Columbia University, 1986.

Examines the place of rhetoric in the development of the curriculum in England and America.

10. Murphy, James J. *Rhetoric in the Middle Ages*. Berkeley: California UP, 1974.

The best survey of medieval rhetoric now available.

11. Reid, Ronald F. "The Boyleston Professorship of Rhetoric at Harvard." *QJS* 45 (1959): 239–57.

Probably the best account of the nineteenth-century transition from spoken to written rhetoric.

12. Vickers, Brian. *Classical Rhetoric and English Poetry*. New York: St. Martin's, 1970.

13. ———. *In Defense of Rhetoric*. New York: Oxford UP, 1988.

Excellent chapters on various periods in the history of rhetoric.

14. Woods, William F. "Nineteenth-Century Psychology and the Teaching of Writing." *CCC* 36 (1985): 20–41.

Describes the three major theories of nineteenth century psychology which parallel, and therefore illuminate, similar developments in the teaching of writing.

II. CLASSICAL AND MEDIEVAL THEORIES OF RHETORIC

15. Aristotle. *Rhetoric and Poetics*. Trans. Rhys Carpenter and Ingram Bywater. New York: Modern Library, 1984.

This edition has the added benefit of a new preface by Edward P. J. Corbett, who edited the volume and contributed some useful bibliographies and notes to the text.

16. Augustine of Hippo. *De Doctrina Christiana*, trans. D. W. Robertson, Jr. Indianapolis: Bobbs Merrill, 1958.

Books I-III of this treatise are a guide to the reading and interpretation of the scriptures. Book IV (on preaching) is probably the most important statement of rhetorical theory in the Middle Ages.

17. Cicero. *De Oratore*. Trans. E. W. Sutton and H. Rackham. 2 vols. Loeb Classical Library. Cambridge, MA: Harvard UP, 1942.

The comprehensive treatise that represents Cicero's mature rhetorical theory.

18. Corbett, Edward J. P. *Classical Rhetoric for the Modern Student*. 2nd ed. New York: Oxford UP, 1971.

The best of the modern textbooks that make classical rhetorical theory and pedagogy available to teachers and students of English composition.

19. Quintilian. *Institutio Oratoria*. Trans. H. E. Butler. 4 vols. Loeb Classical Library. New York: Putnam's, 1921–22. See also J. J. Murphy's edition of Books 1, 2 and 10: *Quintilian on the Art of Speaking and Writing*. Carbondale: Southern Illinois UP, 1987.

Quintilian was a teacher of rhetoric in Rome, under the Empire. His "Institute" of rhetoric is a thoroughgoing description of the art as it was practiced and taught during his times.

20. Anon. *Rhetorica Ad Herennium*. Trans. Harry Caplan. 2 vols. Loeb Classical Library. Cambridge, MA: Harvard UP, 1954.

This relatively brief manual, and Cicero's early work *De Inventione (On Rhetorical Invention)*, were the classical treatises which most influenced medieval rhetoric.

III. RENAISSANCE AND NEOCLASSICAL THEORIES OF RHETORIC

21. Erasmus, Desiderius. *On Copia of Words and Ideas (De Utraque Verborem ac Rerum Copia)*. Trans. Donald B. King and H. David Rix. Milwaukee: Marquette UP, 1963.

A much imitated treatise on the art of writing an "amplified," or richly developed style, which reflects a major emphasis in Renaissance rhetoric.

22. Fenelon. *Fenelon's Dialogues on Eloquence.* Trans. W. S. Howell. Princeton: Princeton UP, 1951.

   "The greatest work on classical rhetoric written in French and the finest statement of the philosophical strand of the tradition since antiquity" (Kennedy).

23. Blair, Hugh. *Lectures on Rhetoric and Belles Lettres.* Ed. Harold F. Harding. 2 vols. 1783; Carbondale: Southern Illinois UP, 1965.

24. Campbell, George. *The Philosophy of Rhetoric.* Ed. Lloyd F. Bitzer. 1776; Carbondale: Southern Illinois UP, 1963.

25. Whately, Richard. *Elements of Rhetoric.* Ed. Douglas Ehninger. 1828; Carbondale: Southern Illinois UP, 1963.

   Blair, Campbell, and Whately—sometimes called the "Scottish rhetoricians"—reflect the influence of empirical philosophy (e.g., Hume, Locke) on rhetorical theory; they also foreshadow the nineteenth-century shift in emphasis from spoken to written rhetoric (or "composition").

IV. NINETEENTH-CENTURY THEORIES OF RHETORIC

26. Adams, John Quincey. *Lectures on Rhetoric and Oratory, Delivered to the Classes of Senior and Junior Sophisters in Harvard University.* 2 vols. 1810; New York: Russell and Russell, 1962.

27. Channing, Edward T. *Lectures Read to the Seniors at Harvard College.* 1856; Carbondale: Southern Illinois UP, 1968.

28. DeQuincey, Thomas. *Essays on Rhetoric.* Ed. Frederick Burwick. Carbondale: Southern Illinois UP, 1967.

V. MODERN THEORIES OF DISCOURSE

29. Britton, James, et al. *The Development of Writing Abilities* (11–18). London: Macmillan Education, 1975.

   Considered one of the best studies of how writing skills develop in young students. Britton offers a theory of composition based on extensive surveys of children's writing.

30. Burke, Kenneth. *A Grammar of Motives.* 1945; Berkeley: UP, 1969.

31. Gibson, Walker. *Tough, Sweet, and Stuffy: An Essay on Modern American Prose Styles.* Bloomington: Indiana UP, 1966.

   A readable yet relatively sophisticated attempt to characterize prose styles by classifying their choice of words, syntax, and other features.

32. Hirsch, E. D., Jr. *The Philosophy of Composition.* Chicago: Chicago UP, 1977.

   Known as a conservative approach to the theory of composition, Hirsch's book was nevertheless based on a careful study of discourse production, and it deserves a close reading.

33. Joos, Martin. *The Five Clocks.* Bloomington: Indiana UP, 1962.

   A modern classification of the levels of style by reference to their use in a social context.

34. Kinneavy, James. *A Theory of Discourse.* 1971. New York: Norton, 1980.

   Classifies the kinds of discourse according to purpose and describes the features associated with each of these purposes, or "aims." Grounded in the scholarship of linguistics, literature, communications, and philosophy, Kinneavy's is perhaps the reigning modern theory of discourse.

35. Moffett, James. *Teaching the Universe of Discourse.* Boston: Houghton, 1956.

   Helpful in understanding the neo-progressive or student-centered attitudes toward teaching writing that dominated the Dartmouth Conference (1966) and later produced the "open classroom."

36. Ong, Walter J. "The Writer's Audience Is Always a Fiction." *PMLA* 90 (1975): 9–21.

   In this milestone essay, Ong argues that writers project their own sense of an audience—an assumption that parallels current readerresponse theory.

37. Perelman, Chaim and L. Olbrechts-Tyteca. *The New Rhetoric: A Treatise on Argumentation.* Notre Dame: University of Notre Dame Press, 1969.

38. Richards, I. A. *The Philosophy of Rhetoric.* New York: Oxford, 1936.

39. Toulmin, Stephen E. *The Uses of Argument.* Cambridge: Cambridge UP, 1958.

VI. REFERENCE WORKS

40. Horner, Winifred, et al. *Historical Rhetoric: An Annotated Bibliography of Selected Sources in English.* Boston: Hall, 1980.

41. ———. *The Present State of Scholarship in Historical and Contemporary Rhetoric.* Columbia: University of Missouri Press, 1983.

42. Houlette, Forest. *Nineteenth-Century Rhetoric: An Enumerative Bibliography.* New York: Garland, 1989.

    Lists books and articles about rhetoric, composition, grammar, and the teaching of English which were published between 1800 and 1920.

43. Moran, Michael G. and Ronald F. Lunsford, eds. *Research in Composition and Rhetoric: A Bibliographical Sourcebook.* Westport, CT: Greenwood, 1984.

    A good supplement to Tate, *Teaching Composition.*

44. Mosenthal, Peter, et al., ed. *Research on Writing: Principles and Methods.* New York: Longman, 1983.

    Good discussions of empirical research and its basis in theory.

45. Tate, Gary, ed. *Teaching Composition: Twelve Bibliographical Essays.* Rev. and enlarged ed. Fort Worth: Texas Christian UP, 1987.

    Comprehensive overview of research in major areas related to rhetoric and composition.

Writing Across the Curriculum: An Overview

Barbara E. Walvoord

Halfway through a three-day workshop on writing across the curriculum that I was leading, a college chemistry instructor suddenly exclaimed, "This is really a workshop about thinking!" The "writing" in writing across the curriculum refers to the entire process of planning, gathering information, shaping, drafting, and revising.

BARBARA E. WALVOORD is Professor of English and Director of Writing Across the Curriculum at the University of Cincinnati. She was co-founder and co-director of the Maryland Writing Project and the Baltimore Consortium for Writing Across the Curriculum. She was instrumental in founding and directing two institutional writing-across-the-curriculum programs—at Central College in Pella, Iowa, during the 1970s and at Loyola College in Maryland during the 1980s. She conducts workshops on writing across the curriculum for interdisciplinary faculty groups at colleges and community colleges. Her guide for teachers, *Helping Students Write Well,* now in its second edition, is published by the Modern Language Association. In addition, she has authored two textbooks as well as a number of articles on writing. Her book *Thinking and Writing in College,* coauthored with Lucille McCarthy and others (Urbana: NCTE, 1991), reports the results of a seven-year study of students' thinking and writing processes in college classes in four disciplines.

WHY USE WRITING IN THE DISCIPLINES?

Why and how should instructors in the disciplines integrate this "writing" into their courses? One explanation lies in theories about the close relationship between thought and language. We experience this bond when we find ourselves thinking and discovering *as* we write. Philosopher Susanne Langer proposes that sense data are translated into symbols, which themselves are our ideas [item 11 in the Annotated Bibliography at the end of this essay]. In order to think and learn, we manipulate symbols by talking to ourselves in what psychologist Lev Vygotsky calls "inner speech"—the mediator between thought and language [22, p. 149]. "Thought is born through words," he says [22, p. 153].

A body of research in psychology [summarized in Walvoord, 23, pp. 35] indicates that when people verbalize an idea, they can remember it longer, understand it more thoroughly, and manipulate it in more sophisticated ways. Writing is one of the most effective modes for learning. "When I think back on my own student days, I realize I learned and retained more when I wrote" recalls Laurence Shute [19], an instructor at California Polytechnic Institute. "I'm going to give my students the same opportunity." He describes how, after a workshop on writing across the curriculum, he is "now rethinking every course I offer from the perspective of how to assign some kind of writing in each class." Because writing and thinking develop in complex ways across a student's years of schooling, every instructor needs to support that development.

Another reason for integrating writing across the disciplines is that a biologist and a literature teacher think,

BARBARA E. WALVOORD

write, explore, use evidence, and pose questions in different ways. Walvoord and McCarthy [24] demonstrate how differently questions of evaluation and problem-solving are handled in classrooms in biology, history, psychology, and business. Faigley and Hansen [4] show how differently an English instructor and a sociology instructor may react to a student's writing in sociology. Bartholomae [1] and Bizzell [3] have described some characteristics of writing and thinking common to the academic community as a whole and have explored how different these modes are from students' customary ways of thinking and writing outside the academy.

Elaine Maimon [12] characterizes students as "strangers" to the academic conversation. She recalls her own experience as a "stranger" when she was a new faculty member at a small college, joining a group of her new colleagues at lunch the first day, and understanding little of their talk, filled as it was with references to people, events, and ongoing debates unknown to her. As she gradually became part of the conversation of those lunchtime tables, so we, as college instructors, seek to help our students become participants in the conversations by which our disciplines advance and transmit knowledge. A discipline, as Bazerman [2] has noted, is heavily dependent upon written conversation. Each instructor, by helping students develop their ability to use language within a discipline, can contribute to students' ability to join the conversation of the discipline, and, more broadly, of educated people.

For further explication of the theories that undergird writing across the curriculum, see Fulwiler [5, 6] and Parker and Goodkin [16].

WHAT MIGHT FACULTY IN THE DISCIPLINES DO?

The following discussion of how faculty in the disciplines might implement writing across the curriculum relies on the example of a history instructor, John R. Breihan of Loyola College in Maryland, and a biology instructor, Virginia Johnson Anderson of Towson State University in Maryland. I have worked closely with both of them over the past nine years and have coauthored with them chapters in a book on how students write and think in the disciplines [24].

In any discipline, planning a college course that effectively integrates writing and thinking begins with clarification of course goals. For example, the biology instructor wanted her students to master a body of information and to be able to use the scientific method. The history instructor's goal was to help his students understand and write historical arguments.

The next step in course planning is to examine whether present practices are meeting the course goals. The biologist, who lectured to classes of more than 100 students, had been testing content by short-answer tests that often called for comparison/contrast, definition, or the explanation of a process. Tests sometimes showed her, too late, where students had not mastered lecture or laboratory material. Also, students were not skilled at handling comparison/contrast or shaping definitions and explanations in the ways that she wanted. She wondered whether, even in such a large class, there were ways to use writing to facilitate learning rather than just testing it.

The historian had been assigning essay tests, a term paper, and quizzes, but was very unhappy with the quality of student thinking and writing. He realized that he himself wrote arguments about material he knew well, he redrafted and revised many times, and he sought responses to drafts from colleagues. His essay tests, in contrast, were eliciting hasty, loosely connected "fact dumping" from students, and students' term papers were often thinly veiled paraphrases of library sources. Quizzes encouraged students to concentrate on the individual facts of their readings rather than on the arguments and lines of inquiry. At the end of the semester, he found himself writing, often in despair or frustration, red-ink comments on students' papers, telling them what they had done wrong and justifying the grades he was giving them. But his comments, he suspected, were neither carefully read nor fully used by his students. His traditional writing assignments, he concluded, neither were based on his own experience as a writer, nor were furthering his course goals as effectively as he wished.

To discover how they might better help students to learn, the biologist and the historian next took two steps: they examined their students and they explored what other teachers were doing. For example, the biologist recognized that students were passive (sometimes sound asleep) in lecture, and that in lab they went through the instructions cookbook style, sometimes without knowing the broader implications of what they were doing. The historian carefully examined his students' writing to identify specific competencies that his students needed for argument but did not always possess when they entered his class. He saw, for example, that they did not always know how to identify, in their reading, material that could be used as pros and cons for an argument, or how to categorize primary source material into factors such as social, economic, and religious, or how to defend a position on a debatable historical issue. As one of his history students said, "In high school we took the answers out of the book. I am not accustomed to writing arguments" [Walvoord and McCarthy, 24, p. 102].

The instructors also explored the options other teachers had used to integrate writing and learning in their courses. Such options are discussed, for example, in Fulwiler [5], Fulwiler and Young [7], Griffin [8], Stanford et al. [20], Thaiss [21], and Walvoord [23]. Other suggestions about using writing in disciplines outside English appear in journals, conference presentations, and documents that can be accessed through the computerized data base ERIC, using the search terms listed as item 26 in the bibliography at the end of this essay. A review of the literature on teaching strategies shows that instructors are:

- Using a wide variety of types of writing rather than relying only on essay tests and term papers.

- Using not just formal polished writing, but also informal writing such as journals, dialogues, responses to readings, and exploratory essays to help their students apply, challenge, and muse about what they read and learn.

- Varying their responses to student writing according to the type of writing, the goal, and the instructor's available time. For example, the instructor will respond to journals differently than to a formal, polished research paper.

- Guiding the writing process: helping students to select topics, generate ideas, and plan, shape, and

revise their writings, rather than merely giving the assignment and then collecting the finished product, with little attention to students' writing and thinking processes.

This last teaching approach is based on a body of literature that shows major differences between the writing processes of experienced writers and the processes of novice writers. The research is summarized in Hayes and Flower [9]. In brief, experienced writers appear to draw upon a broader base of knowledge, generate more comprehensive plans and goals for the writing task, and plan and revise with greater attention to the structure and purpose of the entire paper rather than merely to local issues.

Most writing-across-the-curriculum programs in colleges and universities across the country have begun with workshops for faculty to explore the theories and options we have just discussed. One description of such a workshop appears in Raimes [17]. Others, including descriptions of the larger programs of which workshops are a part, appear in McLeod [14] and Fulwiler and Young [7]. McLeod and Soven's 1992 collection [15] discusses many aspects of starting and nurturing a WAC program. David Russell [18] places the movement in historical perspective. More can be located through ERIC, using the search terms listed as item 25 in the bibliography at the end of this essay.

Building on such a workshop and also on their careful observation of their students, the biologist and historian revised their courses to integrate writing more effectively than before, but not to bury themselves under an insupportable avalanche of student papers which they had to "correct." To do this, they used four strategies: (1) they substituted a more effective type of writing assignment for a less effective one, (2) they shifted their own time from a less effective activity to a more effective one, (3) they sometimes moved a former in-class activity into out-of-class time so as to make more time for in-class writing or writing-based activities, and (4) they varied their responses to student writing depending on its purpose.

For example, the historian abandoned the essay tests and the long, final term paper in favor of three short but carefully crafted historical essays. Now his students were able to shape and reshape their arguments in the same way that he and other historians did. To help them further, the historian shifted his time investment from the end of the writing process to the middle—that is, instead of spending most of his time writing extensive comments on finished writings where students, faced with an unchangeable grade, were not motivated to read and apply his suggestions, he shifted his time to respond to students' *drafts*. When the final papers came in, he made much shorter and more general comments, trying to give students the one or two broad pieces of advice they could carry with them into the next paper or the next course. On the basis of his comments to their drafts, students were often able to see where their arguments were weak and then to apply their new understanding immediately by revising their arguments. The instructor was gratified by the improvement in his students' ability to shape historical arguments, and now, eleven years later, he is still doing draft response, despite the time it takes, because he shifted his time to make his load manageable.

The historian also instituted a series of informal writings, done outside of class, all designed to help students master the skills necessary to the historical arguments. For example, for one writing, students were asked to discuss, in a paragraph, how the material from that day's reading could be used as evidence in an argument over whether Louis XIV was a "good" king. On another day, students had to list the "economic," "social," "political," and "religious" factors from a series of first-hand accounts of seventeenth-century riots. The instructor was teaching students to read for arguments, not just for disconnected facts or mere summary, and he was teaching them to categorize data as historians do. The results of these exercises began to show in the essays. Because these short writings fed into the essays and because their primary purpose was to help students with reading and thinking, the instructor did not mark the writings extensively for grammar and punctuation, nor did he even try to comment on every point of content and structure. Rather, he read the short writings very quickly and concentrated on making one or two suggestions. For each short writing that met a minimum standard, the student accumulated points toward the final course grade. Further discussion of this historian (John R. Breihan) and his methods appears in Walvoord [23], Walvoord and McCarthy [24], and in Mallonee and Breihan [13].

Other instructors may use informal writings in different ways. The historian arranged for all writing to be completed by students outside of class; however, the biologist used class time during her lectures for writing, because she felt it was better to help students become active learners than to "cover" more material they would not learn. She would stop the lecture and ask students to write for five minutes on questions such as "Summarize the most important ideas of last Friday's lecture" or "Compare the phylum we've covered today to the phylum we covered last time." To help her students understand the implications of their lab work, she asked them, before they began the lab, to write, for example, "Why are we using E coli in the lab today?" Sometimes she asked students to share their writings with a peer in the next seat, or used them to encourage questions. Students kept all these short writings in their own folders, and at the end of the semester each student would choose three of his or her best short writings, polish them, and turn them in for a grade.

WHAT MIGHT ENGLISH FACULTY DO?

The role of the writing teacher in writing across the curriculum may encompass three areas: (1) articulation of the freshman composition course with other courses students take, (2) exemplification of strategies for integrating writing and learning, and (3) coordination of campus writing-across-the-curriculum activities.

Chapters 36-40 on "Writing Across the Curriculum" in the *Simon & Schuster Handbook for Writers*, Fourth Edition attempt to prepare composition students to understand the kinds of thinking and writing they will meet in other disciplines. In some schools, teachers of composition and teachers in the disciplines have agreed on basic terms or texts that will be required in the composition courses and used later by other teachers as well. Some instructors ask students to analyze the characteristics of writing in various disciplines or professions.

Instructors who teach writing often also teach literature. The literature class can be a model for the effective integration of writing and learning.

On most campuses it is the writing instructors who initiate and coordinate writing-across-the-curriculum programs. However, instructors in other disciplines must quickly become spokespeople and leaders in the effort, and the writing instructors must coordinate rather than dominate the program.

The task of integrating writing and learning within courses across the disciplines, including composition, is complex and difficult. Some of our best attempts so far, however, have come when instructors in composition and other disciplines identify their goals, examine their students' needs and their own practices, and then institute teaching strategies that seem best calculated to help students learn to participate in the ongoing conversation of the discipline and of the academy.

Annotated Bibliography of Suggested Readings

1. Bartholomae, David. "Inventing the University." *When a Writer Can't Write: Studies in Writer's Block and Other Composing-Process Problems.* Ed. Mike Rose. New York: Guilford, 1985.

   Characterizes various levels of students' ability to "invent" the university—that is, to adopt the specialized language and persona of someone who is a member of the discipline's community.

2. Bazerman, Charles. "What Written Knowledge Does: Three Examples of Academic Discourse." *Philosophy of the Social Sciences* 11 (1981): 361–87.

   Points out that academic disciplines are primarily bound by their exchange of written communication, and analyzes the features of that writing.

3. Bizzell, Patricia L. "What Happens When Basic Writers Come to College?" *College Composition and Communication* 337 (1986): 294–301.

   "Basic writers" (i.e., those least well prepared for college) face a conflict of world view, which may force them to give up old world views.

4. Faigley, Lester, and Kristin Hansen. "Learning to Write in the Social Sciences." *College Composition and Communication* 36 (1985): 140–49.

   Explores the learning and writing process of students in college social science classes and shows the differing reactions of social science and English teachers to the same piece of student writing.

5. Fulwiler, Toby. *Teaching with Writing.* Portsmouth, NH: Boynton, 1987.

   A guide for teachers in all disciplines who want to integrate writing with learning. Includes theoretical background on the interconnection of writing and learning, as well as practical suggestions for activities such as using journals or helping students revise.

6. ———. "Writing as an Act of Cognition." *Teaching Writing in All Disciplines.* Ed. C. Williams Griffin. San Francisco: Jossey, 1982.

   Explains how students learn through writing, particularly relying on James Britton. Discusses implications for classroom teachers in all disciplines.

7. Fulwiler, Toby, and Art Young, eds. *Writing Across the Curriculum: Programs, Practices, and Problems.* Portsmouth, NH: Boynton.

   Describes a number of outstanding writing-across-the-curriculum programs across the country.

8. Griffin, C. Williams, ed. *Teaching Writing in All Disciplines.* San Francisco: Jossey, 1981.

   A collection of essays about the practical and theoretical issues in writing across the curriculum.

9. Hayes, John R., and Linda S. Flower. "Writing Research and the Writer." *American Psychologist* 41 (1986): 1106–13.

   Summarizes research on the organization of cognitive processes underlying the act of writing, specifically the processes of planning, sentence generating, and revismg.

10. Kolln, Martha. "Closing the Books on Alchemy." *College Composition and Communication* 32 (1981): 139–51.

Explores the often misinterpreted research results on students' errors in punctuation and usage. Concludes that instruction in "grammar" should be integrated with writing experiences for students.

11. Langer, Susanne. *Philosophy in a New Key.* 3rd ed. Cambridge, MA: Harvard UP, 1957.

Describes human ability to perform "symbolic transformation" as the key to both scientific and humanistic problems.

12. Maimon, Elaine P. "Talking to Strangers." *College Composition and Communication* 30 (1979): 364–69.

Instructors are guides who help their students become part of the conversation of the academy. Explores implications of this concept for classroom teachers in all disciplines.

13. Mallonee, Barbara, and John R. Breihan. "Responding to Students' Drafts: Interdisciplinary Consensus." *College Composition and Communication* 36 (1985): 213–31.

Reports the team teaching experience of a history instructor and a writing instructor, exploring the points of difference with which they struggled and the areas of consensus they believe appropriate for teachers of writing and other disciplines.

14. McLeod, Susan, ed. *Strengthening Programs for Writing Across the Curriculum.* San Francisco: Jossey, 1988.

A collection of essays about supporting established writing-across-the-curriculum programs. Discusses issues such as developing programs beyond the initial workshops, finding continuing funding, assessing the program, and developing research projects.

15. McLeod, Susan, and Margot Soven, eds. *Writing Across the Curriculum: A Guide to Developing Programs.* Newbury Park, CA: Sage.

16. Parker, Robert, and Vera Goodkin. *The Consequences of Writing: Enhancing Learning in the Disciplines.* Upper Montclair, NJ: Boynton, 1987.

Describes the origins of the writing-across-the-curriculum movement and its theoretical background. Shows how writing is used in five courses in different disciplines.

17. Raimes, Ann. "Writing and Learning Across the Curriculum: The Experience of a Faculty Seminar." *College English* 41 (1980): 797–801.

Describes a series of writing-across-the-curriculum seminars held during the academic year at Hunter College.

18. Russell, David. *Writing in the Academic Disciplines, 1870–1990: A Curricular History.* Carbondale, IL and Edwardsville, IL: Southern Illinois UP, 1991.

19. Shute, Laurence. "Getting Them to Write." Letter to the Editor. *New York Times,* 5 Nov. 1988: 26.

A letter to the editor from a faculty member at California State Polytechnic University, urging teachers in the disciplines to integrate writing into their classrooms.

20. Stanford, Gene, and the Committee on Classroom Practices. *How to Handle the Paper Load.* Classroom Practices in Teaching English, 1979–1980. Urbana: National Council of Teachers of English, 1979.

Practical suggestions for teachers at all levels and in all disciplines, about how to use writing for learning.

21. Thaiss, Christopher, ed. *Writing to Learn: Essays and Reflections on Writing Across the Curriculum.* Dubuque: Kendall, 1983.

Essays about the writing-across-the-curriculum experiences and teaching strategies of faculty from a variety of disciplines at George Mason University.

22. Vygotsky, Lev S. *Thought and Language.* Cambridge, MA: MIT Press, 1962.

Shows how children and adults use language as a mediator between humans and the world of physical stimulation so that humans can react in terms of their own symbolic conception of reality.

23. Walvoord, Barbara E. Fassler. *Helping Students Write Well: A Guide for Teachers in All Disciplines.* 2nd ed. New York: MLA, 1986.

Guides college teachers in all disciplines through the process of planning a course that integrates writing and learning, guiding students' writing processes, and responding to student writers.

24. Walvoord, Barbara E., and Lucille McCarthy, with contributions by Virginia Johnson Anderson, John

R. Breihan, Susan Miller Robison, and A. Kimbrough Sherman. *Thinking and Writing in College.* Urbana: National Council of Teachers of English, 1991.

The results of a seven-year naturalistic study of students' thinking and writing processes as they fulfilled their normal assignments in college classes in four disciplines.

25. *ERIC descriptors:* For articles on the content and structure of writing across-the-curriculum workshops: "Higher-Education, " "Writing-Across-the-Curriculum," "Workshops," and inclusive dates.

26. *ERIC descriptors:* For articles on using writing in a particular discipline: "Higher-Education," "Writing Instruction," the name of the discipline, and inclusive dates.

Essay Testing: An Overview

Emily R. Gordon

The pressure on composition programs to "measure up" continues to increase. Our colleagues in colleges and universities complain about students' inability to write intelligibly, and even we composition instructors occasionally question the standards being applied in some writing classes. The pressure from the larger community is even more intense: parents, facing increasing tuition bills, demand that their children obtain salable skills; periodic tax revolts call into question the success of open admissions and compensatory programs, while demand increases in class size; personnel officers throughout industry complain that college graduates lack the writing skills needed for even entry-level positions. In response to all these pressures, more and more colleges have turned to uniform examinations to generate statistics that will support existing programs or argue for desired programs. These schools also increasingly are using such tests to determine student placement and to assess achievement against criteria for graduation.

Sometimes administrators see short-answer, objective tests as the most efficient way of making placement and graduation determinations. Yet, because essay tests are an important indicator of proficiency in composition, experts urge that essay tests be administered in place of, or in concert with, objective tests whenever possible.

This discussion first addresses the philosophical and pedagogical rationale for essay testing, then presents a plan for administering the examination, and finally explains the two most commonly used scoring procedures.

EMILY R. GORDON is Adjunct Instructor of English at Hofstra University, where she teaches composition and business communication. She is co-author of the *Simon & Schuster Workbook for Writers* (with Lynn Quitman Troyka) and author of the *Diagnostic and Competency Tests to Accompany the Simon & Schuster Handbook for Writers*, and she is a member of the editorial board of the *Journal of Basic Writing*. She has served as a reader for the Educational Testing Service, for Queensborough Community College of the City University of New York, and for Hofstra University; she also acts as Chief Reader and consultant to private institutions implementing holistically scored essay tests.

USES OF AN ESSAY TEST

Perhaps one of the most obvious characteristics of essay testing is that it is time-consuming. However, when essay testing is compared with objective testing, it becomes obvious that the time is well spent. Objective testing is simple to administer and grade and, when properly normed, it is highly predictive of students' composition skills. (For those who wish to complement essay tests with objective tests, Prentice Hall offers *Diagnostic and Competency Tests to Accompany the Simon & Schuster Handbook for Writers* [item 6 in the Annotated Bibliography at the end of this essay], a series of matching test forms useful for pre- and post-testing.)

Objective testing is only an indirect measure. It tests students' ability to manipulate the language of others rather than the ability to compose, a process that requires attention to multiple, overlapping concerns of audience, purpose, message, organization, grammar, diction, and mechanics.

Certainly, essay testing presents a few difficulties. Departmental consensus must be reached regarding the reason for testing, the skills to be evaluated, the test's wording, and scoring standards. Costly clerical and administrative support is essential to the reproduction of examinations, scheduling of testing and scoring facilities, notification of students, and recording and interpretation of scores.

Is this investment of time, energy, and resources worthwhile? The experts think so. According to Marie Jean Lederman [10], past University Dean for Academic Affairs of the City University of New York, essay tests serve as rites of passage to the world in which our students will eventually function: "drawing material together into a coherent written whole is vital to membership in a group of educated adults" (p. 45).

Essay testing also has other, more immediate, benefits. Preparing the prompt and scoring guidelines brings an English department together. Faculty share in the process of determining the purpose of the examination and deciding what constitutes acceptable and unacceptable writing for a particular situation. Participation in scoring contributes to a sense of unity among instructors and gives them a rare opportunity to share their responses and their underlying philosophy, a discussion that does not end with the last test paper.

Additional benefits of essay testing appear in the classroom. Where objective tests reign, institutions teach objective-test-taking. Conversely, where essay tests are given, instructors teach essay-test-taking strategies: brainstorming, outlining, thesis statements and topic sentences, relevant detail, supporting anecdotes and examples, editing, and proofreading. Finally, when students are required to take essay tests, they (and their parents and the community) realize that writing is important.

The benefits of giving essay tests may be summarized as follows:

- Instructors of English focus on the essay rather than on isolated grammatical errors.
- By sharing a uniform set of standards, instructors are less likely to use idiosyncratic standards in their own classrooms.
- More attention is placed on the teaching of writing as a process. Editing and proofreading skills are placed in perspective, as final steps rather than as ends in themselves.
- Faculty and administrators unite in the pursuit of a common goal.
- Assessment results can be used to revise curricula.
- Faculty in other disciplines see that writing is being stressed and so may be more willing to incorporate it into their own courses.
- Students take writing more seriously, realizing it can and will be evaluated.

ESSAY TEST TOPICS

Selecting a test topic (a prompt) depends upon two factors: the purpose of the examination and the amount of time available for testing. The two most commonly used time limits are 20 minutes and 50 minutes. Untimed essays also are a possibility, but the procedure is usually too cumbersome when large numbers of students are involved.

Purposes for testing can be divided into two broad categories: placement within a sequence of courses (including exemption from a required course) and exit from a program (for example, a departmental final for Freshman Composition or a graduation requirement). An exit examination seeks to ascertain whether certain minimum standards have been met. In this situation, a 20-minute test can provide enough information for readers to distinguish competent from incompetent writing.

A placement examination, in contrast, is given to a much more heterogeneous population. Far subtler distinctions must be made. It is not uncommon for one examination to be used to place students in one of as many as seven courses within a sequence. When such fine distinctions are being made, a 50-minute test is a necessity.

Students need to be prepared for whatever time limit has been set, by being given practice essays in class. If this is not possible, letters sent to students notifying them that they will be writing an essay test should specify the time limit.

The Qualities of a Good Topic

What makes a good essay topic? The Educational Testing Service offers some solid advice in their pamphlet for new readers of the English Composition Test [2]:

> [A good essay topic] must be self-explanatory; it must be defined and limited. It must be a topic that every student . . . can be expected to have some information about. It must be a topic so stimulating that every candidate will have something to say immediately. It must be a topic that young and inexperienced candidates can write about intelligently. (1)

Research by Gordon Brossell has done much to clarify what makes an effective topic. Brossell [1] shows how an overly elaborate prompt inhibits composition. Teachers have known for years that students need prompts that guide their thinking, that one-word prompts ("excellence" or "freedom") elicit fuzzy essays. In an effort to stimulate thought, some test-makers go too far in the other direction and offer students elaborate scenarios. The results are startlingly poor, with many students doing little more than parroting the prompts. Brossell's work shows that prompts of a few sentences work better than longer ones; students receive enough information to stimulate thought, but not so much as to intimidate them.

More recently, Brossell has joined with James Hoetker to make specific suggestions for generating useful topics [9]. In 1983 Hoetker and Brossell agreed to write a set of topics for Florida's College-Level Academic Skills Test (CLAST). Working with the underlying assumption that "wording and content of a topic may affect what and how well a student writes" (p. 328), they wrote short, simple topics, all having the same form. Their goal was to eliminate any factors that might misdirect students. To compensate for the varying intellectual backgrounds of students, Hoetker and Brossell engineered topics that let students write about the subjects they knew best. The resulting formula is modeled on the parts of the traditional definition: a category, a linking verb, a class specification, and differentiating criteria. The student is given the class specification and differentiating criteria. He or she then must supply an example of that category. By changing the class specification or the criteria, testers can produce similar topics.

> "A book/that many students read/that may affect them harmfully."

> "A book/that many students read/that may affect them beneficially."

> "A course/that many students take/that may affect them in important ways."

Topics such as these have produced positive results. Essays tend to have strong thesis statements rather than the rambling openings typical of essays written in response to earlier CLAST topics.

Despite the burgeoning interest in essay assessment over the last twenty years, the sharing of findings has been a haphazard affair. Leo Ruth and Sandra Murphy [11] have gone a long way toward correcting this situation. Drawing upon the work of ten leading practitioners ("'exemplars' of wise practice"), formal research in diverse areas (psychometrics, writing topics, and discourse theory), and their own experiences with the Bay Area Writing Project (1980–82), Ruth and Murphy suggest guidelines for designing topics for writing assessment. The scope of this review is impressive, and its tone is even-handed. The various studies are not always in agreement about the best way to reduce misinterpretation of text; test writers, students, and test readers do not all interpret directions and prompts in the same way, nor do student-writers and teacher-readers see the same essay in the same way. Ruth and Murphy point future research in the direction of reducing these "misfirings." Their book is presented not as the endpoint of research, but as a compilation of findings to date. They call emphatically for further exploration of the best way to create assessment situations in which writers can produce their best work.

Suggested Topics

You might want to create topics using the Hoetker/Brossell model above, or you may wish to use topics of the types illustrated below.

1. The following prompts guide students toward informative writing without imposing particular structures. Students are thus able to demonstrate their ability to organize an essay by choosing appropriate rhetorical strategies.

- Describe a visit to the dentist. Use specific details and anecdotes to convince the reader that your dental visits are as pleasant or unpleasant as you believe they are.

- What is your favorite color? Explain what this color represents that makes it special for you. Use specifics, such as details and anecdotes, to support your generalizations.

- Describe a formal social gathering that you have attended, such as a wedding or funeral. Compare the appearance and behavior of people on such an occasion with the way they usually look and behave.

- What career do you plan to pursue? Explain the reasons why you chose this field and tell what you hope to accomplish.

- Pick something you know how to do well, and teach someone how to do it. Be sure to include all the necessary steps and define any unusual terms.

2. Persuasive essays can be given focus if students are asked to agree or disagree with a brief statement. Often writers adapt this part of the prompt into a clear thesis statement. Background, such as that given here, stimulates thinking and suggests sources of evidence.

Follow each of the suggested prompts below with these directions: *Agree or disagree with this statement. Support your position with evidence based on your own experience, observation of others, and reading.*

- Overall, Americans feel the elderly are useless. We tear our older people away from their friends and send them off to live in nursing homes. Television and movies routinely portray the elderly as helpless, easily confused, and having little interest in life.
  In the United States, we have mistaken ideas about older people. [Insert above directions here.]

- Anyone who has ever tried to drive through the center of a large city must realize that something is wrong. Too many cars enter the central business districts, creating massive traffic jams that prevent emergency vehicles from passing, pollute the air, and waste gasoline.
  Private cars should be banned in the center of large cities. [Insert above directions here.]

- People have been arguing for years about whether boys and girls who return from school to an empty house are at a disadvantage. Some studies indicate that because these latchkey children do not have the supervision of an adult during the afternoon, they spend too much time alone watching television or getting into trouble. Other studies show, however, that latchkey children grow up to be responsible, self-confident adults.
  Children who return from school to a home wiithout supervision suffer. [Insert above directions here.]

- In recent years, students from the United States have scored lower than students from Europe and Asia on tests of basic academic skills and reasoning ability. Seeking an explanation, some people have suggested that American schools are too easy. They say students are not made to think through problems nor are they given enough homework to help them practice new skills.
  American high schools are too easy. [Insert above directions here.]

- The world seems to get noisier every day. Garbage trucks and the people who pick up the trash make a terrible noise. The sound of machinery coming from construction sites can make it impossible to concentrate. Also some people play their stereos at top volume in the middle of the night.

Local governments should enact laws to control noise pollution. [Insert above directions here.]

3. Some prompts enable students to choose whether they wish to inform or persuade their readers. With these prompts, students must make their own decisions about purpose, audience, and organization.

Follow each of the suggested prompts below with these directions: *Relate this statement to your personal experiences and your observation of others. You may also want to draw on your reading in your response.*

- Worries can be very distracting.

- Every person is a mirror of his or her parents.

- The only thing permanent in life is change.

- The person who speaks in anger will probably regret it.

- Every right brings with it an equal obligation.

4. More experienced writers can be asked to respond to brief quotations. However, the literary cadence of even the shortest quotations makes such prompts challenging. Again, students need to make independent decisions about audience, purpose, and organization.

Follow each of the suggested prompts below with these directions: *Relate this statement to your personal experiences and your observation of others. You may also want to draw on your reading in your response.*

- We must make the best of those ills which cannot be avoided. —ALEXANDER HAMILTON

- In a dream you are never eighty.
  —ANNE SEXTON

- Common sense is the knack of seeing things as they are, and doing things as they ought to be done. —JOSH BILLINGS

- Understanding is a two-way street.
  —ELEANOR ROOSEVELT

- Difficulties strengthen the mind, as labor does the body. —SENECA

ADMINISTERING AN ESSAY TEST

Administration of an essay test may be seen as having five stages: organization, on-site preparation, proctoring, scoring, and reporting. The first three stages are discussed below; scoring procedures are discussed in the next section. Reporting methods depend upon the facilities available at each institution; however, students should receive prompt written notice of their test scores, along with an explanation of what further steps they should take.

Organizing an Essay Test

Before the actual test day, certain essential preparations must be made.

1. After the department or a committee has decided what skills are being tested, a suitable topic must be chosen and directions written.

2. The examination must be reproduced and stored in a secure area.

3. The day (or days) for administering the test must be chosen and announced.

4. Unless the test will be administered during regular classes, a test location must be selected.

5. Time for scoring must be scheduled, and a location must be reserved.

6. Supplies must be ordered: blue books, pencils, perhaps microphones.

7. If any students who will take the test are not currently in English classes, letters must be written and mailed to their homes, telling them of the nature, time, place, and *significance* of the examination.

8. Student aides must be hired to help with paperwork and distribution and collection of materials.

On-Site Preparation for an Essay Test

If the test is to be given in individual English classes, someone must see that each teacher receives sufficient question sheets, blue books, and pencils a day in advance. Scrap paper is not necessary, since question sheets or the back of the blue book may be used.

If the test is to be given outside regular classes, each proctor should pick up supplies an hour before the test is scheduled to begin. This will give the proctor time to prepare the test room and greet early arrivals.

Since posting the time distracts some students seriously, try to have a working clock in each room, if possible. If no clock is available, then posting the time at 10- or 15-minute intervals is essential.

Proctoring an Essay Test

Proctors should not spend all their time at the desk reading, but neither should they be constantly pacing. The recommended procedure is to stay in the front of the room making occasional supportive eye contact with students.

To ensure uniform administration of the examination, the test committee should prepare a script—or at least a detailed set of directions—for all proctors. In this way, students are guaranteed a fair policy on such matters as time limit and use of dictionaries, and no students will receive more guidance than others.

SCORING AN ESSAY TEST

The two most widely used procedures for assessing essay examinations are holistic and analytical scoring. Studies indicate that holistic scoring is more efficient and reliable than analytical, but both systems are discussed here so that departments may select the one most in keeping with their needs.

Holistic Scoring

The underlying assumptions of holistic scoring are well stated in the Educational Testing Service pamphlet on scoring the English Composition Test [2]:

> The basic assumptions of holistic scoring are that each of the factors involved in writing skill is related to all the others and that no one factor can be separated from the others. Readers must judge each essay as a whole; they must read each paper for the impression its totality makes. A misspelled word, a comma splice, a sentence fragment, a misplaced modifier should carry no great weight in scoring an otherwise well-written paper. The candidate is entitled to make some mistakes: he or she is writing hurriedly in a tense situation. (2)

Holistic scoring has several advantages. First, by considering each essay as a whole, readers are encouraged to focus on writing as a process leading to a unified product, rather than as a series of minimally connected errors. Second, training enables readers to discover their implicit priorities and the rationales behind them. Third, because readers see a wider range of writing skill than is found in any single course, their perspective is enlarged and therefore their ability to grade their own students fairly increases. Fourth, having two readers per paper reduces the chances of any idiosyncratic judgments and increases reliability in assessment.

Admittedly, holistic scoring also has a few disadvantages. First, scoring sessions take time, especially when training is properly conducted. Second, scoring sessions can be expensive. Release time or stipends need to be provided to participating faculty, and additional clerical help must be hired and trained. Someone at the institution must have extensive experience with holistic scoring in order to organize a reading and conduct training. If no such person is available, a consultant must be hired to act as chief reader and to train an on-campus successor. Finally, holistic scoring neither diagnoses specific weaknesses nor prescribes appropriate action.

However, despite these drawbacks, holistic scoring is preferred by most experts in the field. A brief overview of holistic scoring follows; anyone interested in a more thorough presentation is referred to Edward M. White's *Teaching and Assessing Writing* [13].

A great deal of work occurs behind the scenes before the reading begins. The chief reader, assistant chief reader(s), and table leaders read a large sampling of the essays. From these, they select papers representing various levels of skill, and they assign scores that, in their experienced judgment, reflect the quality of these essays *in relation to the other essays written in response to this particular prompt.* These essays, reflecting the entire range of scores, will be used to train the readers.

The scoring procedures are designed to promote uniform standards. The session begins with the chief

EMILY R. GORDON

reader presenting the topic to the readers and explaining the purpose behind that topic. He or she then discusses key aspects of evaluating the papers, such as the amount of emphasis to be placed on surface features and what constitutes an off-topic response.

The chief reader next explains the process of scoring: Two readers independently grade each essay, and their scores are either recorded in code or covered with removable tape, so that the second reader is not influenced by the first. After a paper has been read twice, clerks decode the scores. If the scores match or are within one point of each other, they are totaled to give the paper's final score. If scores are more than one point apart, a third, highly experienced, reader independently scores the essay, and the two most closely matching scores are added together.

Then the chief reader explains the scoring scale. The number of scores on a scale vary depending upon the purpose of the examination. Common scoring systems include a four-point scale (recommended for uncomplicated situations, such as exiting a course or program) and a six-point scale (useful for making the finer discriminations needed to place students within a course sequence). Sample four- and six-point scales are given in Appendices A and B. Studies indicate that even-numbered scales are preferable, because tired readers are likely to fall toward a neutral middle score, if one is available, rather than making the sometimes difficult distinction between passing and failing essays. Whatever the number of scoring options on a scale, 1 represents the lowest score and the highest number represents the top score. The following discussion assumes a six-point scale.

Readers, initially working with the sample essays selected by the chief reader and his or her associates, are urged to decide on scores using a two-stage process. First, they must decide if an essay is above average (4 to 6) or below average (1 to 3). The second step is to decide if a passing paper is just above average (4), clearly above average (5), or well above average (6), and if a failing paper is just below average (3), clearly below average (2), or well below average (1).

Since no score exists to label a paper as exactly average, each reader must decide if such a piece is ever-so-slightly above or below average. In fact, one reader may give a score of 3 and another a 4. Some scoring systems treat this split grade as a pass; others treat it as a disagreement and refer the paper to a third reader. Each institution needs to agree on a policy for such scores.

During training, participants read and score up to twenty sample essays. Scores are tabulated, and in cases where readers disagree among themselves or with the scores given by the chief reader and his or her assistants, discussions are held to clarify criteria. Sample essays are read until readers have absorbed appropriate standards and are scoring consistently and accurately. Only then does actual reading of "live" essays begin.

To ensure that standards remain consistent, the reading is interrupted periodically for ongoing training. Even highly experienced readers need to participate in these sessions because they, as much as any beginner, tend to score more harshly when tired. As before, sample essays are read, scored, and discussed in an effort to maintain consensus. As a safeguard between training sessions, table leaders randomly select for review several of each reader's scored essays. If the two rate an essay differently, they discuss the reasons behind the scores. The table leader does not force a reader to change a score, but instead seeks to clarify how that score was determined and whether appropriate criteria are being applied.

The reading continues until all papers have been read twice (or three times, if necessary). Compilation of scores and reporting are left to clerical support personnel.

Analytical Scoring

The assumption behind analytical scoring is that the evaluation of discrete writing skills can be used to rate a whole piece of writing and simultaneously provide a prescription for further work.

Analytical scoring has a few advantages. First, the scoring of a limited number of preselected criteria makes reader training minimal. Second, students and teachers receive specific diagnoses; as a result, student objections to placement decisions are easily handled and teachers know immediately in what areas their students need work. Third, papers are read just once, reducing the clerical workload.

However, the disadvantages of analytical scoring are significant. First, measuring separate skills is incompatible with the philosophy that writing is a process leading to a single, complex product. Second, counting errors encourages readers (teachers who will carry the lesson of the reading back to their students) to focus on weaknesses rather than strengths. Finally, although each essay is read only once, that reading can take far longer than two readings done holistically.

If your department feels, nevertheless, that analytical scoring best suits its needs, two key decisions need to be made. First, decide what categories will be scored. Limit the number of characteristics to be rated, or readers will have to spend far too much time on each essay. Second, since points are awarded for high, middle, and low skill in each area, define what merits a high, middle, or low score. For some qualities, counting the number of errors will do. However, some important features of essay writing (among them, ideas, organization, and tone) do not easily lend themselves to quantification.

Anyone desiring more information about analytical scoring should see Paul B. Diederich's *Measuring Growth in English* [4], which features an analytical scale and an explanation of the criteria for high, middle, and low scores in each of eight areas.

APPENDIX A

A Four-Point Scale

4 This essay is *among the best* written on the topic. It is organized around a clear thesis that is relevant to the prompt. The essay contains numerous appropriate details and examples in support of generalizations. Paragraphs follow a logical order and exhibit unity and coherence. Sentences are grammatically correct and demonstrate the writer's mastery of subordination and coordination. Diction is lively, showing the writer's understanding of levels of diction, denotation and connotation, and metaphor. Errors in punctuation, mechanics, and usage are rare.

3 This essay is a *slightly better-than-average response* to the prompt. A thesis clearly states the author's purpose, although some sentences may not relate to that purpose. The essay contains appropriate details and examples in support of generalizations. Paragraphs generally follow a logical order; they exhibit unity and coherence most of the time. Sentences are usually grammatically correct and reflect some grasp of subordination and coordination. Diction is adequate, but not especially lively. Some errors in punctuation, mechanics, and usage occur, but they do not seriously interfere with meaning.

2 This essay is a *somewhat below-average response* to the prompt. It may lack a thesis statement altogether; if one is present, little is done to provide support. The essay contains some details and examples, but they may not be relevant to the generalizations which they follow. Paragraphs may relate to the thesis, but they are usually underdeveloped, vague, or lacking in unity and coherence. Sentences may be ungrammatical, illogical, or unsophisticated; they show little understanding of subordination or coordination. Diction is lackluster and sometimes inappropriate. Errors in punctuation, mechanics, and usage sometimes interfere with meaning.

1 This essay is a *well-below-average response* to the prompt. It may lack a thesis; if one is present, it is very weak. Details and examples are lacking or inappropriate. Most generalizations are completely unsupported or supported with other, often redundant, generalizations. Paragraphs are undeveloped and incoherent, and they have little connection to any thesis or to one another. Sentences may be illogical or badly constructed; most consist of simple subject-verb-object combinations, with little or no use of subordination and coordination. Diction is immature and often non-idiomatic. Errors in punctuation, mechanics, and usage seriously interfere with meaning.

APPENDIX B

A Six-Point Scale

6 This essay is *among the very best* written on the topic. It contains a clear thesis and is well organized throughout. Generalizations are supported with relevant details and explanations. Sentences demonstrate a mastery of basic grammar, as well as subordination, coordination, and parallel structure. Diction is highly appropriate. Punctuation, mechanics, and usage are almost always correct.

5 This essay is *clearly an upper-half response* to the topic. It contains a thesis and is generally well organized, including transitions between and within most paragraphs. Most generalizations are supported with appropriate details and examples. Sentence structure is generally correct, indicating some control of subordination, coordination, and parallel structure, although some errors may occur in especially complicated sentences. Diction is appropriate. Punctuation, mechanics, and usage are usually correct; whatever errors do occur are not particularly confusing to the reader.

4 This essay is a *slightly above-average response* to the topic. It contains a thesis and is fairly well organized, although digressions or omissions may occur. An attempt is made to support generalizations with appropriate details and examples. While sentence structure is correct enough to be clear, it is often unsophisticated, with little use of subordination, coordination, or parallel structure. Diction is usually appropriate, but some slang and regionalism may be present and vocabulary may be limited. Agreement, tense, and possession are usually, although perhaps not always, correct. Punctuation

shows an understanding of sentence boundaries, but other punctuation may sometimes be nonstandard. Spelling, including homonyms, is generally correct.

3 This essay is a *slightly below-average response* to the topic. Although the connection to the prompt is apparent, the thesis is either missing or vague. Most, but not all, paragraphs are underdeveloped and lacking in unity and coherence. Transitions within and between paragraphs are also missing. Sentence structure is monotonous and unsophisticated; few errors may occur because sentences are kept very simple, or there may be frequent errors in sentence punctuation. Diction is often inappropriately informal, and vocabulary is often inexact. Indirect and direct discourse are confused. Common words are sometimes misspelled.

2 This essay is *clearly a lower-half response* to the topic. Some attempt has been made to discuss the prompt, but ideas generally remain undeveloped. Supporting details and examples are rare; repetition and irrelevancies are common. Paragraph development is minimal. Sentence structure is elementary and often unclear. Diction is highly informal, more appropriate to conversation than to academic writing. Sound-alike words are frequently confused, and vocabulary is juvenile. Errors in punctuation, mechanics, and usage are common.

1 This essay is *among the weakest written* on the topic. It has no thesis or pattern of organization, and its connection to the prompt may not be apparent. Errors in grammar, punctuation, mechanics, usage, and spelling are so frequent as to seriously distract the reader. This grade is also given to any essay that is too brief to judge.

Annotated Bibliography of Suggested Readings

1. Brossell, Gordon. "Rhetorical Specification in Essay Examination Topics." *College English* 45 (1983): 165–73.

   Based upon experimental evidence, Brossell calls into question the assumed superiority of essay test prompts that provide detailed scenarios and that specify fictional speakers, purposes, and audiences. His findings suggest that the prompts most likely to elicit good impromptu responses are those that make only a brief statement about a subject before asking for a personal response.

2. Conlan, Gertrude. *How the Essay in the College Board English Composition Test Is Scored: An Introduction to the Reading for Readers.* Princeton: Educational Testing Service, 1985.

   This pamphlet is given to new readers of the English Composition Test, the essay portion of the College Board's English Achievement Test. The discussion, outlining how holistic scoring procedures operate for this particular test, is noteworthy for its emphasis on the respect due student writers.

3. Cooper, Charles R., and Lee Odell, eds. *Evaluating Writing: Describing, Measuring, Judging.* Urbana: National Council of Teachers of English, 1977.

   The editors present six essays, each discussing a different method of assessing writing. See especially "Holistic Evaluation of Writing" by Charles R. Cooper and "Primary Trait Scoring" by Richard Lloyd-Jones.

4. Diederich, Paul B. *Measuring Growth in English.* Urbana: National Council of Teachers of English, 1974.

   Diederich suggests ways of improving the reliability of essay scoring and argues that a properly graded final essay examination (supported by a short-answer test) can accurately assess each student's writing ability.

5. Fishman, Judith. "Do You Agree or Disagree: The Epistemology of the CUNY Writing Assessment Test." *WPA: Writing Program Administration* 8 (1984): 17–25.

   Fishman takes issue with the agree/disagree format of the much imitated Writing Assessment Test of the City University of New York, saying that it does not elicit each student's best writing. This critique is responded to by Greenberg [7] and by Troyka [12].

6. Gordon, Emily R. *Diagnostic and Competency Tests to Accompany the Simon & Schuster Handbook for Writers.* 2nd ed. Englewood Cliffs, NJ: Prentice Hall, 1990.

   This testing package offers two matching forms of diagnostic tests for use on IBM and Apple II computers (Form CX and Form CY); two different matching forms of printed diagnostic tests (Form A and Form B); and two matching forms of printed competency tests (Form AA and Form BB), along with guidelines for administration and scoring.

7. Greenberg, Karen L. "Writing Assessment Test Design: Response to Two *WPA* Essays." *WPA: Writing Program Administration* 9 (1985): 31–40.

   Greenberg responds to Fishman's charges (see item 5 above), noting that a competence test need not measure each student's best work, but must evoke thoughtful essays from members of a heterogeneous population while remaining valid and reliable.

8. Greenberg, Karen L., Harvey S. Wiener, and Richard A. Donovan, eds. *Writing Assessment: Issues and Strategies.* New York: Longman, 1986

   Three leading founders of the National Testing Network in Writing have gathered essays by major figures in writing assessment. The volume presents an overview of the issues facing the testing community, and several of the essays indicate fruitful directions for additional work.

9. Hoetker, James, and Gordon Brossell. "A Procedure for Writing Content-Fair Essay Examination Topics for Large-Scale Writing Assessment." *College Composition and Communication* 37 (1986): 328–35.

   Based on their work for Florida's College-Level Academic Skills Test, Hoetker and Brossell suggest that essay prompts based on the structure of formal definition reduce the chances of student misinterpretation and help students focus on subjects about which they are knowledgeable.

10. Lederman, Marie Jean. "Why Test?" *Journal of Basic Writing* 7 (1988): 38–46; rpt. Greenberg, Wiener, and Donovan [see item 8 above].

    Lederman places testing in a historical perspective in order to demonstrate that testing is a rite of passage. Hence the values and essential skills of a society must be determined and acknowledged by those developing tests.

11. Ruth, Leo, and Sandra Murphy. *Designing Writing Tasks for the Assessment of Writing*. Norwood: Ablex, 1988.

    Ruth and Murphy analyze a large body of studies conducted on variables in writing-topic design and on the potential for misinterpretation of topics and directions among test writers, students, and readers.

12. Troyka, Lynn Quitman. "The Phenomenon of Impact: The CUNY Writing Assessment Test." *WPA: Writing Program Administration* 8 (1984): 27–35.

    Writing in response to Fishman's attack on the CUNY WAT (see item 5 above), Troyka recounts the successes of the examination and provides guidelines for the development of unbiased assessment topics.

13. White, Edward M. *Teaching and Assessing Writing*. San Francisco: Jossey, 1986.

    White draws together previously hard-to-find information as he makes a case for schools using essay tests to evaluate writing ability. He shows how such tests can be fair, reliable, and economical and how they foster a variety of changes beneficial to students and teachers.

Teaching Composition to Speakers of Other Languages: An Overview

Joy Reid

Even experienced teachers of composition whose students are native English speakers may experience discomfort and puzzlement when they find non-native speakers of English (ESL students)* in their classes. New or inexperienced composition teachers of native English speakers may face those same feelings as they first begin to teach; however, they usually have the advantage that, at the very least, *they* have been the kinds of students they are teaching. Past experience as native English-speaking students, if not as teachers, prepares them to understand both the expectations of their students and the clues—verbal and nonverbal— that native English speakers (NESs) offer in the classroom: heads nodding, notetaking, raised eyebrows, shifting in seats, interruptions, and the like. When new teachers, experienced with NESs or not, encounter

ESL students, however, they may have only limited knowledge about and experience with diverse cultures.† The expected protocols for question-asking, teacher-student exchanges, and group work that seem so "normal" in a class of NESs may be foreign to ESL students.

Initially, the experience of teaching composition to ESL students may parallel the "blind-random" setting on an exercise "step" machine: at this setting, the rhythm of the stepping slows and speeds up automatically and randomly, and so the stepper is "blind": he or she does not control when the rhythm will change or in what direction. Almost certainly the inexperienced teacher of ESL students encounters periods of "randomness," of surprising incidents, time frames and rhythms; furthermore, because of the cultural differences between the teacher and the students, and among the students themselves, the randomness is frequently not preceded by any clues—it occurs "blindly." The results: frustration and misperceptions for both teachers and students. This essay discusses several major areas in which the needs of ESL students differ from those of NESs; it provides information from experienced ESL composition teachers concerning the identification of typical problems—and suggests solutions— in the NES/ESL composition class.

JOY REID teaches in the English Department and coordinates the ESL support program at the University of Wyoming. She has published ESL composition textbooks as well as articles on discourse analysis, computers and composition, learning styles, the writing-reading connection, and the change process. Her recent book is *Teaching ESL Writing* (Regents/ Prentice-Hall, 1993).

*To avoid confusion between native English speakers (NESs) and non-native speakers of English (NNSs), students for whom English is not a first language are called English as a Second Language (ESL) students in this essay, although of course English may be their third or fourth language.

†Richard Samovar and Larry Porter (1991) describe culture as the overall system of perceptions and beliefs, values and patterns of thought that direct and constrain a social group, from the way the group uses space to the meaning of widened eyes, and from the way members of the group approach relationships to the ways they view the world. Language—verbal, nonverbal, and written communication— is an integral part of culture.

JOY REID

INTERNATIONAL VS. RESIDENT ESL STUDENTS

In much the same way that NESs differ in background knowledge, motivation, and perspective, it is important to realize that ESL students are not a homogeneous group. Aside from the clear diversity in language and cultural backgrounds, ESL students in U.S. colleges and universities can also be described in terms of the scenarios in which they acquired their second language. Specifically, most of the "international" (or "visa") students, those students who travel to the U.S. from their homelands to attend post-secondary institutions, differ from ESL students who have grown up in the U.S., who have graduated from U.S. high schools, and/or who may be U.S. residents/citizens .

Students who have studied English outside the U.S., English as a foreign language (EFL), and who have entered post-secondary institutions in the U.S. following several years of EFL study in their native countries, have, for the most part, acquired English *visually;* they have learned about the structures of the language, but their practice in producing English has been limited to the classroom. Furthermore, as Ilona Leki [item 13 in the Annotated Bibliography below] points out, not many educational systems appear to teach rhetorical patterns directly in the school setting; in most countries outside the U.S. there are virtually no courses in writing. Therefore, many international students have underdeveloped rhetorical skills. Moreover, because cultures evolve writing styles appropriate to their own histories and the needs of their societies, many international students have assumptions about the presentation of written ideas that are appropriate for their native discourse communities (that is, the expectations and needs of audiences in their native cultures). These assumptions may be inappropriate for U.S. academic discourse communities.

In contrast, U.S. residents (that is, ESL students who have lived and attended secondary schools in the U.S.) have acquired much of their English through their *ears.* Although they may have had ESL classes alongside their regular public school work, their English has been learned mainly through immersion in the language. In some cases, the same may be true in their first lan-guage: although they speak that language fluently, they may not read or write it fluently. As a result of this aural basis, their spoken language may be fluent and comprehensible, and their writing may appear fluent. However, because these students have limited knowledge of the structures of English, their writing may appear more or less phonetic with little demonstration of the structures (e.g., correct use of verb tenses, prepositions, word forms) of the language. This single difference between international and resident ESL students bears directly on the strengths and weaknesses these students bring to their writing classes, and significantly affects the ways teachers can approach writing processes with the ESL students in each group.

CROSS-CULTURAL AND INTERCULTURAL COMMUNICATION

At the same time composition teachers are struggling to accommodate ESL student needs, their ESL students may also be struggling to adjust their perceptions to a "foreign" classroom environment; that is, "blind-random" occurs on both sides of the desk. Even ESL students who have attended U.S. public schools and have lived in the U.S. most of their lives carry many of their first-culture values, needs, and expectations into their second-language classrooms. Collections of essays about cross-cultural issues, edited by Patricia Byrd [1] and Joyce Valdes [17], have shown that cultural differences between (and among) ESL students and their teachers may include differences across cultures of how students view teachers and in student attitudes toward teaching and learning. The degree of authority invested in and expected from the teacher, as well as the degree to which the teacher directs and dominates class activities, depends to a large extent on culture. For example, many Asian cultures, both in North America and in Asia, have a tradition of deference: questioning a person in authority—a parent, a teacher—is disrespectful, and passive learning is the key to success. In a U.S. college composition class, however, such behavior may be seen as inappropriately silent and non-participatory. In contrast, the strong cooperative values and high level of social responsibility of many Latin societies, in both

North and South America, make the highly individualized and competitive values of many U.S. students seem unpleasantly aggressive. For the newly arrived international student, the adjustment may be even more jarring: a class in the U.S. must look like a structureless, anarchical situation for learning. In the U.S., composition students are expected to take an active part in the learning process, asking questions, challenging each other and their teachers, working (often loudly) in groups. Consequently, many ESL students must learn a variety of different assumptions about both learning and teaching. In fact, a truly multicultural class can result in substantial classroom imbalance in perspectives and even cross-cultural tensions as students and teachers struggle to find appropriate behaviors and interactions.

Contrastive Rhetoric

Robert Kaplan first defined contrastive rhetoric [9] when he sought to discover whether organizational patterns of written material vary from culture to culture. In his investigation of 600 student expository paragraphs, written in English by native speakers of many non-English language backgrounds, Kaplan used philosophical, psychological, anthropological, and linguistic insights to describe the differences between the essentially linear English paragraph, which does not tolerate digression or repetition, and paragraphs that he classified generally as Semitic, Oriental, Romance, and Russian. He represented the differences graphically; at the same time he cautioned that "much more detailed and more accurate descriptions are required before any meaningful contrastive system can be elaborated" (p. 12).

Since the appearance of Kaplan's article, the notion of contrastive rhetoric, along with the issues surrounding the transfer of rhetorical patterns in second language writing, has grown into an area of study. Research reported by proponents of this theory, published in collections edited by Kaplan [10] and by Ulla Connor and Robert Kaplan [4] demonstrate that the style in which each culture organizes and presents written material reflects the preferences of that particular culture. As a result, ESL writers often intuitively

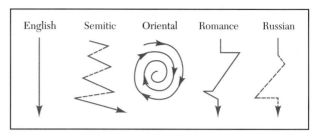

Kaplan's Contrastive Rhetoric Diagram

employ a rhetoric and sequence of thought that violate the expectations of the native reader; when they write for readers in another culture, they often have problems with the identifying audience expectations and communicating with different discourse communities.

Even *within* a language, there appear to be different rhetorical rules and conventions that govern different categories of texts. Leki [14] indicates that in U.S. academic classes, discipline-specific writing conventions differ in such diverse areas as length of sentences, choice of vocabulary, acceptability of using first person, extent of using passive voice, degree to which writers are permitted to interpret, and amount of metaphorical language accepted. According to William Grabe and Robert Kaplan [6], the ESL writer is also likely to have a different notion of what constitutes evidence, of the order in which evidence should best be presented, and of the amount of evidence needed in order to explain something to/or persuade the reader. Consequently, ESL students can face misunderstanding and even failure in their academic written work because they are often unaware of the content expectations and of the rhetorical problems in their prose.

While such differences between ESL and NES writers may affect communication in a U.S. academic discourse community, they should not be stigmatized as deficiencies. As Alan Purves and his colleagues note, differences among rhetorical patterns do not represent differences in cognitive ability but rather differences in cognitive style [14]. After all, arrangement and presentation of ideas as well as style, can all be defined, practiced, and valued in many ways. However, ESL writers (like NESs) must acquire the appropriate background knowledge necessary to identify and fulfill the expectations of the U.S. academic audience; knowledge about appropriate language use, content, and genre can empower ESL students.

Recent articles on cognition and the theory of expertise indicate that the problems students encounter as a result of their contrastive rhetorics may be partially solved by strategy training. Such research, for example, suggests that novice NES writers who attempt to perform in areas of knowledge in which they have little or no specific background rely on general strategies, particularly a dependence on "what the teacher wants." These students need—and often demand—that the teacher be more and more specific about form, content, and language that the student can imitate. Then, as students begin to develop more specific writing strategies (as they become more experienced writers), they gain more knowledge of and practice in such specific writing strategies as reading and analyzing academic assignments, generating ideas, getting started, overcoming writer's block, revising, determining audiences, writing for a purpose, and so forth.

While many NES writers are inexperienced with the specific strategies used by experienced NESs in academic discourse communities, many ESL students are unaware even of the general strategies of English writing. And there is no reason to assume that ESL writers will acquire the conventions of English without assistance. For ESL students, then, the composition course is much more than a skills course; it is also a *content* course in which they need to learn about audience and purpose, levels of content specificity, and academic formats, perhaps for the first time. The students need to know that writing involves not only linguistic processes but social and cognitive processes as well: when it is appropriate to write, what is appropriate to write for an identified audience in a specific situation, and how to organize ideas appropriately for that audience and purpose. In addition, ESL students (and less experienced NES writers as well) need to learn repertoires of strategies to generate ideas, draft pieces of writing, and encounter feedback from peers and teachers. To assist their ESL students toward these goals, composition teachers may well need to be more didactic; certainly they must become cultural informants for their students, by *researching* U.S. academic writing assignments and the discourse communities that design, assign, and evaluate those assignments. They can gather that information, identify the rules of use of that discourse community, and provide opportunities for students to identify, understand, practice and fulfill the expectations of the U.S. academic discourse communities they will enter.

Schema Theory

Successful communication rests on background knowledge and experience that is shared by writers and readers; the prior knowledge of student writers necessarily influences what, and how, they write. Patricia Carrell's research [2] with ESL readers and writers defines this previously acquired background knowledge as *schema*. If we think of the brain as a computer, ideas and words are "input" into "files" (or databases), which are in turn modified by that new information; these files are analogous to our background knowledge structures called schemata. Carrell found it useful to distinguish three forms of schema: linguistic (language knowledge), content (topic knowledge), and formal schemata (knowledge of the rhetorical structures of different types of texts). First, because the effectiveness of written communication and reader interpretation depends on the successful interaction between writer and reader, language knowledge—linguistic schema—plays an integral part in ESL writing. Second, the background of the writer in the subject of the text—content schema—determines, in part, the comprehension. Finally, formal or rhetorical schema includes knowledge that Connor [3] describes as such structural text elements as the relationships among items of information, the subordination and coordination of this information, paragraph structures, and cohesion devices. Carrell's research indicated that when language *and* form *and* content are familiar and expected, writing is relatively easy, but when one or the other (or all) are unfamiliar, efficiency, effectiveness, and success for the writer can be problematic.

Since ESL writers organize and present material in ways that are different from NESs, Carrell indicates that, by providing necessary cultural information about the rhetorical organization of U.S. academic expository text and audience expectations of such text, teachers will help their ESL students' writing to be more effective. In other words, teachers must help their ESL writing students to acquire appropriate schemata. In order to do so, teachers need (a) to become informed about appropriate U.S. academic discourse patterns; (b) to inform their ESL writing students about discourse differences and audience expectations; and (c) to provide practice and experience with the new schema.

ACCURACY AND FLUENCY

Teachers of ESL writers will almost certainly face student essays with linguistic and rhetorical problems that are related to (a) the first languages of the students and/or (b) "developmental" problems that are the result of limitations in students' previous education. It is unfortunate that the language errors of ESL student writers rarely approximate those of NESs either in number or in kind, and that their visibility immediately triggers negative responses in readers. While an error that interferes with clear communication is unacceptable in both NES and ESL writing, an understanding of the logical bases for second language error in writing may mediate the visceral reaction that excludes other components of the student writing.

The question of error and the dichotomy between fluency and accuracy have existed in language teaching for decades: should the language teacher concentrate on one or the other? Traditionally, accuracy has been defined as the focus on discrete elements of the rules of language, while fluency has been defined as the focus on the communication of ideas without consideration of discrete language elements. This is probably a false dichotomy. A focus on fluency does not necessarily exclude consideration of the systematic properties of language; after all, it is not possible to communicate successfully without some knowledge and monitoring of the language of the message. Similarly, a focus on accuracy demands concentration on discrete points of language, but does not necessarily curb creativity and self-expression, ignore cognitive processes, or overlook personality traits of the learner.

At the basis of the accuracy-fluency controversy is the question of error. Once thought to be deviant behavior, error—in both first and second language acquisition—is now seen as a natural phenomenon. Of course, errors in written language can be due to inattention, memory lapse, or indifference. Moreover, in an in-class writing situation, NESs as well as ESL students will make hasty "performance errors." However, as Barbara Kroll [11] points out, ESL errors are generally neither random nor sporadic nor deviant; instead, they are systematic, regular, and rule-governed, the result of intelligence, not stupidity. Errors come from a conscious or unconscious attempt by students to use what they have learned.

ESL language errors are influenced by three factors: native language transfer, overgeneralization, and difficulty level. First, when second language students encounter a language form, they often infer rules from previous knowledge of their first language; they "transfer" that knowledge into a hypothesis about the second language. For that reason, students from the same language background may well make some of the same types of errors, though their hypotheses (and therefore the resulting language) may not be exactly the same. For example, native speakers of Spanish may use adjectives that have both gender and number and that follow, rather than precede, the verb (e.g., the flowers *reds*) because these rules apply in Spanish. Such first-language transfer occurs not only with grammatical structures but also with first-language writing skills and strategies as well; ESL writers often transfer both good and weak writing skills from their first language into English, and many ESL students who have not developed good strategies for writing in their first language will not have appropriate strategies to transfer to their second language.

Overgeneralization of rules is a somewhat different reason for error: ESL students may hypothesize, consciously or subconsciously, about a language form by extending the use of a rule they have learned in the second language. For instance, if the rule says that third-person singular verbs must take an "s" (i.e., "he runs"), ESL students may "overgeneralize" the rule to include second-person singular verbs (i.e., "you runs"). The hypothesis is incorrect, but it is a systematic application of a rule. In each of these cases, students who can identify or "monitor" for language errors can learn to reformulate new hypotheses and adopt new learning strategies to correct the errors.

Finally, if a language rule is particularly complex or difficult, students may make errors as they attempt to construct the language form, or they may avoid the form altogether. Level of difficulty is a complicated concept, for it is in part dependent on both first language differences and prior student experience. For example, while English is a subject-verb-object (SVO) language, Korean is a subject-object-verb (SOV) language, and word order is relatively free. A sentence in English, translated into Korean and then retranslated, word for word, into English, shows the differences:

English: Even though I told John not to take the Chemistry class, he took it.
Korean: Even though I John Chemistry class not to take told John it took.

In addition to word order, many Asian languages are "tonal": That is, they have few or no inflections (such as verb tense and plural markers). Chinese, for instance, is a language that has no verb tenses and no articles; learning the complex rules for verb tense is an enormous task, and implementing those rules expands the task geometrically. Many of the rules for article use in English are at best eccentric; correct use of articles for an ESL student whose native language does not have articles is extremely difficult. For instance, try formulating the rules needed for the following examples and consider the consequent decisions Asian ESL students must make:

> She considered him (a) genius.
> (X) (The) number seven is lucky.
> (The) only girl at (the) party was Nanan.
> (A/The) funny picture on (a/the) page

> and

going to (a/the) church	vs.	going to (X) church
going to (a/the) store	vs.	going (X) (X) home
going on (a/the) journey	vs.	going to (X) work

For Arabic speakers, relative clauses are easier to use than auxiliary verbs in English because relative clauses in Arabic parallel use in English (though in Arabic, the relative clause requires the use of a personal pronoun, resulting in such structures as "The man who likes coffee *he* . . ."). In contrast, there are no auxiliary verbs in Arabic, so a structure like "She *taking* a class" is a common error. In short, ESL students are similar to other students of languages: native-like accuracy in non-native language writing is a life-long struggle, so both students and their teachers must expect language errors in student writing.

Error is an integral part of the learning process during a child's first language acquisition; however, quick intervention (say, by the mother of the young child) and direct or indirect correction, as well as continued exposure to correct language, allows the child to reformulate language hypotheses. Consider, however, the child raised in a relatively standard American English atmosphere who, as an adult, learns that she uses one English structure incorrectly: lay/ lie. Having habituated that error for her first twenty-five years, she spends the next twenty-five "monitoring" for that error, thinking about the rules governing lay/lie before she uses those words, "unlearning," relearning, practicing, and, more often than not, avoiding that structure. Such habituated or "fossilized" behavior, whether a single grammatical structure or an inappropriate oral response, are for the person making the error easy to identify but difficult to monitor, and that behavior is nearly impossible to change permanently, at least in a short period of time. For the ESL student with not one but rather dozens of habituated language errors, writing flawless English prose is at best an overwhelming prospect.

In light of these facts, teachers should see most ESL errors as a normal, natural, and necessary part of the learning process. Teachers of ESL students who are interested in their students' errors may fruitfully investigate contrastive analysis studies that examine features of a native language (e.g., English) that contrast with features of another language (e.g., Spanish, Japanese) to determine what areas of second language learning are most likely to cause difficulty for their students. In such an investigation, teachers may well discover that the students themselves are the best sources of contrastive analysis information and, importantly, that asking students to analyze (and perhaps to log) their errors may prove beneficial to their learning processes. Another interesting area for examination is "error gravity" studies, in which researchers investigate the "irritation" or "acceptance" levels of NESs—usually university non-ESL faculty—to specific second language errors. That is, the studies focus on what second language errors interfere most with NES comprehension in order to help teachers and students prioritize language errors and edit more successfully. For example, Roberta Vann and her colleagues [18] investigated the responses of 164 faculty members to twelve typical ESL errors. They found that most respondents did not judge all errors as equally severe; incorrect word order (as in the direct translation of the Korean sentence above) was considered the most serious, and spelling errors the least severe.

Kroll [11] demonstrates that ESL writing proficiency can be broadly divided into *plus-syntax* and *minus-syntax*, *plus-rhetoric* and *minus-rhetoric:* "one paper can provide insightful commentary on a substantive topic while replete with problems in spelling and punctuation [+rhetoric and –syntax]. Another paper can exhibit a wide range of sentence structures, flawless syntax, adherence to mechanics, yet lack development and support of its central thesis [–rhetoric and + syntax]" (p. 40). Still another paper may be hard to read because it contains both second language errors and a lack of coherence [–rhetoric and –syntax]. In terms of the two broad categories of ESL students described in this essay, typical international student writing will demonstrate limited coherence, and particularly a limited knowledge of academic forms and audience expectations [–rhetoric]. In contrast, typical resident student writing will often demonstrate [–syntax]; that is, the writing will be fluent but contain many language errors.

EVALUATION

Given the problems any second language learner can have with accuracy in writing, the problem of evaluation facing the composition teacher with ESL students is substantial. For the NES teacher, ESL language errors are even more visible (and so, perhaps, irritating) than common NES errors; looking beyond the errors to rhetorical and contextual successes or problems may therefore be difficult. "Lowering standards" or asking less of ESL student writing is not a viable solution, yet language errors must be seen in perspective: ESL students may have adequate knowledge of correct usage but find it difficult to produce accurate prose consistently. There is more, much more, to successful written communication than the use of articles. Therefore, as teachers develop criteria for evaluation by which the student writers will be judged, those criteria should be carefully developed, realistically grounded in the discourse communities the students will face outside the classroom, and explicitly articulated. The composition teacher might consider giving a separate grade for language, or even giving several grades for each paper in areas of focus for that paper: coherence, use of detail, audience awareness, etc. Such a grading scheme would allow students to identify more easily their writing strengths and weaknesses.

Liz Hamp-Lyons [8] notes that evaluation works best and is most fair to learners when it takes into account who the learner is, the situation in which the writer produces writing, and the overall context in which educational success is to be measured for the student writer. The objectives of correction, response, and evaluation are long-term improvement and cognitive change; sending students back into the writing process in order to work again (and again) with their writing is often more successful for the students than memorizing grammar rules. Moreover, students learn to do best what teachers can demonstrate. Researchers Ann Fathman and Elizabeth Whalley [5] found that teacher response/intervention during the writing process and teacher correction of error has impact when the feedback is clear. In other words, the response/correction must adequately describe the problem and then suggest methods of correction. Research has repeatedly shown that working with student errors in the context of their writing is more beneficial than studying discrete grammar points out of context. Teachers must also help ESL students monitor for error and to edit their almost-completed work for specific language problems.

Just as important, students must have the appropriate schema to be able to learn. Marking errors that students do not identify as errors is ineffectual; asking students to "organize" when they think they already have is at best confusing for the students. Instead, early intervention and explanation modes can assist students to identify and solve language problems before evaluation occurs. For example, teachers might begin by marking, but not correcting, language errors, then asking students to (a) distinguish between errors they immediately recognize (and can therefore monitor) and (b) those errors they do not recognize (and so need intervention and explanation). Identifying and then prioritizing language errors can make monitoring for error easier for ESL students. Next, careful planning of peer review and response groups can help ESL students to identify language problems and solutions; however, peer activities must allow ESL students to give as well as receive assistance. Conferencing, individually or in small groups, is another intervention technique that can prove useful for ESL students. Lynn Goldstein and Susan Conrad [7] discuss the problems and the benefits of conferencing with ESL students about specific language and rhetorical problems during the drafting process; they agree that successful conferencing can strengthen writing skills and develop the independent decision making so vital in successful writing. In addition, the students must have the strategies to deal with peer and teacher feedback and to correct their errors, the time to digest and then to practice corrections. In short, feedback without followup (in the form of discussion, practice, graded revisions) will be less than effective. Finally, as Robin Scarcella and Rebecca Oxford point out [16], strategy training in the processes of composing, drafting, and editing will facilitate student learning; knowledge of resources other than the teacher (e.g., reference books and textbooks, peers, the campus writing center, peer editors) will enable students to seek help outside of class even after the class has ended.

CONCLUSION

Identifying and studying the differences in communication styles and strategies between cultures is worthwhile, even necessary, for both ESL students and their teachers. The more understanding that exists, the better prepared teachers will be to communicate effectively with their students; the more students understand about those differences, the more easily they will fulfill their own and other people's expectations. In an ESL class, the differences in cultural knowledge can be dramatic; students without appropriate linguistic, content, and/or formal schemata encounter difficulty communicating effectively. However, acquiring relevant cultural schemata can facilitate the learning process by enabling students to learn the social processes and the rhetorical conventions for written communication with academic discourse communities.

How teachers focus on ESL students in their classrooms depends, at least in part, on their goals for all students, on how and for whom they want to empower those students. If, as Robert Land and Catherine Whitley [12] suggest, the objective of a composition class is "to acquire enough facility with Standard Written English (SWE) to succeed in school and in the workplace" (284), an effective pedagogy would include teaching composition not only as a skills course but also as a content course. Grabe and Kaplan [6] have indicated that, for ESL students, the content of a composition course must include such areas as composing strategies, coherence systems and mechanisms, language features, rhetorical patterns, audience characteristics and expectations, and genre conventions.

Annotated Bibliography of Suggested Readings

1. Byrd, P., ed. *Teaching Across Cultures in the University ESL Program.* Washington, D.C.: NAFSA, 1986.

   An excellent collection of articles that provides background discussions of relevant issues in cross-cultural communication, useful descriptions of cultural programs developed at several institutions, and explanations of materials and methods developed by individual teachers for use in cross-cultural classrooms.

2. Carrell, P. L. "Text as Interaction: Some Implications of Text Analysis and Reading Research for ESL Composition." *Writing Across Languages: Analysis of L2 Text.* Eds. U. Connor and R. B. Kaplan. Reading, MA: Addison-Wesley, 1987. 47–56.

3. Connor, U. "Introduction." *Coherence in Writing.* Eds. Ulla Connor and Ann Johns. Alexandria, VA: TESOL, 1990. 1--5.

4. Connor, U., and R. Kaplan, eds. *Writing Across Languages: Analysis of L2 Text.* Reading, MA: Addison-Wesley, 1987.

   This collection of articles describes the concept of contrastive rhetoric, discusses empirical research in the contrastive rhetoric of many languages with English, and suggests applications of such research in the teaching of ESL writing. The book is an excellent sourcebook for information concerning contrastive rhetoric.

5. Fathman, A., and E. Whalley, "Teacher Response to Student Writing: Focus on Form vs. Content." *Second Language Writing: Research Insights for the Classroom.* Ed. Barbara Kroll. New York: Cambridge UP, 1990. 178–90.

6. Grabe, W., and R. Kaplan, "Writing in a Second Language: Contrastive Rhetoric." *Richness in Writing: Empowering ESL Students.* Eds. D. Johnson and D. Roen. New York: Longman, 1989. 263–83.

7. Goldstein, L. M., and S. M. Conrad, "Student Input and Negotiation of Meaning in ESL Writing Conferences." *TESOL Quarterly* 24(3) (1990): 441–60.

8. Hamp-Lyons, L. *Assessing ESL Writing in Academic Contexts.* Norwood, NJ: Ablex, 1992.

   This collection of articles written by the growing number of researchers in ESL testing focuses on the testing of ESL writing. It follows a clear, carefully written explanation of the issues in this research area; the assessment issues discussed range from validity questions concerning commercial writing tests to practical questions concerning classroom testing. Other issues discussed include cross-cultural assessment, academic literacy, criteria and scoring models, needs assessment, and models of feedback.

9. Kaplan, R. B. "Cultural Thought Patterns in Intercultural Education." *Language Learning* 16 (1966): 1–20.

10. Kaplan, Robert B., ed. *Annual Review of Applied Linguistics:* 1982. Rowley, MA: Newbury House Publishers, 1983.

    The third volume of the series is directed toward studies related to written text, more specifically to contrastive rhetoric articles that study the rhetorical differences between English and such languages as German, Hindi, Korean, Mandarin, and Marathi. Kaplan introduces the collection and provides an integrative essay in conclusion.

11. Kroll, Barbara, ed. *Second Language Writing: Research Insights for the Classroom.* New York: Cambridge UP, 1990.

    This seminal collection of thirteen articles is addressed to teachers-in-training and to experienced teachers in the field of ESL teaching as well. It is divided into two sections: the first presents "the current state of thinking on what the teaching of writing to non-native speakers entails" (p. 3); the second section presents a "variety of specific studies, each focused on a different aspect of writing and/or the writing classroom" (pp.3–4).

12. Land, R., and C. Whitley. "Evaluating Second Language Essays in Regular Composition Classes: Toward a Pluralistic Society." *Richness in Writing: Empowering ESL Students.* D. Johnson and D. Roen, eds. New York: Longman, 1989. 284–93.

13. Leki, I. *Understanding ESL Writers: A Guide for Teachers.* New York: St. Martin's Press, 1992.

Written particularly for NES teachers of NES freshman English classes in which there are non-native speakers of English, the focus of this book is on immigrant students rather than international students: that is, students who may have had limited study of the English language, either in their native country or in the U.S., but whose oral (and listening) skills may be highly developed, the result of immersion in U.S. schools and culture. Their problems with reading and writing, and the problems faced by their teachers, are discussed in clear and cogent detail, with practical suggestions offered that are based on second language acquisition research and composition theory.

14. Purves, Alan, ed. *Writing Across Languages and Cultures: Issues in Contrastive Rhetoric.* Newbury Park, CA: Sage Press, 1988.

The collection of research articles from scholars of several countries address the issue of cultural expectations in the assessment of writing by non-native speakers of a language. How these writers deviate from the norms of the foreign culture in the kinds of material they choose, the style, and the organization of their prose is examined by the researchers.

15. Samovar, L., and R. Porter, eds. *Intercultural Communication: A Reader,* 6th ed. Belmont, CA: Wadsworth, 1991.

This book contains interesting and informative articles by a large number of international educators in the field of cross-cultural communication. Each chapter examines current issues in the field, ranging from the sociocultural necessity of effective communication to cultural-specific essays, from the impact of Confucianism in East Asia to Arabic concepts of effective persuasion, to the cultural patterns of the Masai.

16. Scarcella, R., and R. Oxford. *The Tapestry of Learning: The Individual in the Communicative Classroom.* Boston: Heinle and Heinle, 1992.

The authors present their approach to teaching, which is analogous to the weaving of many strands into a tapestry. The foundation of this approach defines the role of the teacher as information-gatherer, decision maker, motivator, facilitator of group dynamics, provider of language input, counselor and friend, provider of feedback, and promoter of a multicultural perspective. The book offers the theoretical bases for the approach and sequenced activities for the language classroom.

17. Valdes, Joyce M., ed. *Culture Bound: Bridging the Cultural Gap in Language Teaching.* Cambridge: Cambridge UP, 1986.

This collection of articles brings together representative theoretical and practical material in the field of cross-cultural communication. Part I contains articles focusing on language, thought, and culture as they affect language learning. Part II presents cultural phases of particular groups and practical applications of intercultural communication theory.

18. Vann, R., Meyer, D. E., and F. D. Lorenz. "Error Gravity: A Study of Faculty Opinion of ESL Errors." *TESOL Quarterly* 18(3) (1984): 427–40.

FOURTH EDITION

SIMON & SCHUSTER HANDBOOK

for WRITERS

Lynn Quitman Troyka

Prentice Hall
Upper Saddle River, New Jersey 07458

Library of Congress Cataloging-in-Publication Data

Troyka, Lynn Quitman,
  Simon and Schuster handbook for writers/Lynn Quitman Troyka
    p.   cm.
  Includes indexes
  ISBN 0–13–204215–0
  1. English language—Rhetoric—Handbooks, manuals, etc.
  2. English language—Grammar—Handbooks, manuals, etc.   I. Title.
PE1408.T696   1996
808'.042—dc20

95-35914
CIP

For David,
who makes it all great fun

President, Humanities and Social Sciences: J. Philip Miller
Development Editor: Joyce Perkins
Assistant Development Editor: Kara Hado
Production Editor: Andrew Roney
Executive Editor: Alison Reeves
Creative Design Director: Leslie Osher
Interior Design and Page Layout: Susan Walrath
Cover Design: Susan Walrath and Leslie Osher
Supervisor of Production Services: Lori Kane
Prepress and Manufacturing Buyer: Mary Ann Gloriande

Copyright © 1996, 1993, 1990, 1987 by Lynn Quitman Troyka
Simon & Schuster, A Viacom Company
Upper Saddle River, New Jersey 07458

Printed in the United States of America

10 9 8 7 6 5 4 3 2 1

ISBN 0-13-204215-0

Prentice-Hall International (UK) Limited, *London*
Prentice-Hall of Australia Pty. Limited, *Sydney*
Prentice-Hall Canada Inc., *Toronto*
Prentice-Hall Hispanoamericana, S.A., *Mexico*
Prentice-Hall of India Private Limited, *New Delhi*
Prentice-Hall of Japan, Inc., *Tokyo*
Simon & Schuster Asia Pte. Ltd., *Singapore*
Editora Prentice-Hall do Brasil, Ltda., *Rio de Janeiro*

Contents

PART II: UNDERSTANDING GRAMMAR   169

7 Parts of Speech and Structures of the Sentence   170

PARTS OF SPEECH   170

STRUCTURES OF THE SENTENCE   179

8 Verbs   195

VERB FORMS   198

PART IV: WRITING EFFECTIVE SENTENCES 329

PART VII: WRITING RESEARCH   517

31 Avoiding Plagiarism and Using Sources for Quoting, Paraphrasing, and Summarizing   518

32 The Processes of Research Writing   537

Preface

TO INSTRUCTORS

As evolving writers, students merit clarity, unwavering support, and respect. In that spirit, I offer the pages of the fourth edition of the *Simon & Schuster Handbook for Writers*. I believe that students are empowered, not intimidated, by knowledge. Information about writing processes and products provides students access to critical habits of mind that dramatically increase their chances to fulfill their academic, business, and personal potentials. I therefore have conceptualized the *Simon & Schuster Handbook for Writers*, Fourth Edition, to serve multiple roles in the intellectual lives of students: classroom text, source for students' self-instruction, and comprehensive reference volume for college and afterward.

As in the previous editions, I draw on many conversations—in person and on paper—with instructors and with students at dozens of colleges about what works best in a writer's handbook. I rely also on respected traditional and contemporary rhetorical theory, composition research, language studies, learning theory, and modern practice in the teaching of writing.

This fourth edition of the *Simon & Schuster Handbook for Writers* retains the innovations that have always set this *Handbook* apart, and it adds significant new features.

- It starts with six chapters about the whole essay, thus establishing contexts for writing.

- It sets the scene with a short first chapter about purposes, audiences, and tone. **New for this edition,** using sources for writing is introduced early and connected explicitly to detailed discussions of source-based writing in later chapters.

- It explains that the writing process is rarely linear and always varies with the writer, the topic, and the writing situation.

- It illustrates the variety of writing processes and purposes with four complete student essays. **New for this edition,** the essay with an informative purpose has a new topic: women pumping iron; its three drafts evolve from planning through a final draft, with the student's and the instructor's comments on interim drafts. **Also new for this**

edition is a student's critical response essay based on her reaction to, and synthesis of, an outside source.

■ **New for this edition,** the *Handbook* presents a greatly revised Chapter 5, Critical Thinking, Reading, and Writing. This chapter offers a sequence for critical thinking; differentiation of the separate processes of summary and synthesis; concrete advice on reading systematically and closely; and specific guidance on writing critically in response to a source (illustrated by the student's response essay mentioned above).

■ It devotes an entire chapter to writing argument, with two student essays, each taking a different position on the same topic. **New for this edition,** the Toulmin model for argument is introduced, with its explanations linked to one of the chapter's student essays.

■ It covers all topics of grammar, style, language, punctuation, and mechanics, with explanations and examples to facilitate visual as well as verbal learning. Focus on Revising sections apply concepts of revision to matters of grammar, punctuation, and style.

■ **New for this edition,** research writing is reconceived as three processes: conducting research, understanding the results of that research, and writing a paper based on that understanding. Thus, critical thinking and reading are explicitly integrated into the research process.

■ **New for this edition,** the *Handbook* gives greater attention to the roles of synthesis and critical assessment in the context of using sources. Also **new for this edition,** its research writing coverage includes accessing electronic sources and presents a "layering strategy" to help even first-time researchers pursue productive research and locate worthwhile sources. Two complete student research papers—one in MLA style and one in APA style—are accompanied by narratives of the students' processes. With the MLA-style research paper, Commentary featuring Process Notes illuminates the student writer's decision-making and composing processes.

■ **New for this edition,** the *Handbook* presents comprehensive coverage of four major documentation styles: MLA, APA, Chicago Manual, and CBE. The pages for each style are edged in a different color for instant access. Also, for each style a detailed chart lays out format requirements and other conventions.

■ It includes five chapters on writing across the curriculum. Writing about literature is illustrated with three complete student essays, one each on fiction, drama, and poetry. The last is a literary research paper analyzing two sonnets by Jamaican-born poet Claude McKay.

■ It addresses the concerns of students for whom English is a second language, offering ESL Notes throughout the text to augment six separate chapters on matters deserving longer discussion. **New for this edition** are additional ESL notes, more information in some ESL chapters, and a list for locating ESL Notes.

In writing this new edition of the *Simon & Schuster Handbook for Writers,* I continued to strive to be inclusive of all people. Role stereotyping and sexist language are avoided; *man* is not used generically for the human race; male and female writers are represented equally in examples; and many ethnic groups are represented in the mix of student and professional writing examples. Also, my pedagogic innovations from prior editions, and some new features, help deliver information to students efficiently and clearly.

■ **New for this edition,** an access bar runs down the outside edge of each page. In that bar, modeled on a software toolbar, are all chapter numbers, section codes, chart titles, and signals for ESL Notes (ESL) and Computer Tips and Alerts (!).

■ The ❖ ALERT ❖ system makes students aware of small matters in larger contexts. For example, a brief Punctuation Alert in an explanation of coordination puts into context a particular function of a comma. Full chapters on topics distilled in Alerts complete this dual-entry system, which helps students handle the interplay of variables during writing.

■ **New for this edition,** terms shown in SMALL CAPITAL LETTERS throughout the text are defined in the Terms Glossary. This identification feature allows students to concentrate on the material at hand, with the assurance that they can easily locate a definition they might need; students no longer need feel frustrated by what might seem a pileup of unfamiliar words that explain some aspect of writing or language.

■ Inside the back cover, a guide on how to use the *Handbook* leads students through four steps for locating information; it also visually displays *Handbook* page elements.

■ Response symbols, at the back of the *Handbook*, include notations to acknowledge and praise good student writing as well as to coexist with traditional correction symbols.

As a college student, I never encountered a handbook for writers. Questions about writing nagged at me, so I took to handbooks instantly when I discovered them in graduate school. I'd browse through them, sometimes to locate specific information and sometimes simply to root around and make discoveries. I could not have imagined then that I might some day set my hand to composing such a book. Now that I have completed this fourth edition of the *Simon & Schuster Handbook for Writers*, I am amazed that I ever had the audacity to start the first edition. This history proves, it seems to me, that anyone can write as long as she or he begins; that a handbook can be an evolving text as long as colleagues and students graciously join in the conversations its pages seek to invite; and that students, empowered by knowledge, can write effectively, even joyfully.

TO STUDENTS

You, along with each student I have ever taught in my writing classes, were in my mind's eye as I wrote this fourth edition of the *Simon & Schuster Handbook for Writers*. My goal is to serve you with uncomplicated, yet complete, explanations; contexts for you to enjoy (sometimes even smile at) in the examples and exercises; and a format that gives you quick, easy access to all the information you might want to help you write effectively. If I have succeeded, you will want to keep my handbook as a reference source throughout your college years and afterward.

Given the variety of information that the *Handbook* includes, where might you begin? Few people read it straight through from beginning to end. They browse. I suggest that you become familiar with the contents by scanning the Overview of Contents on the inside front cover, or the more complete Contents list before this Preface, or the detailed Index. When you spot the topic you want, you can turn to it immediately.

You might also want to read the section of this Preface addressed to your instructor. Note especially the explanation of my use of small capital letters: all words in small capital letters—WHICH LOOK LIKE THIS—are defined in the *Handbook*'s Terms Glossary. Whenever you encounter an unfamiliar term printed in small capital letters, rest assured that you can locate its meaning quickly.

The course for which you have bought this book can greatly influence your future. Writing is a skill you need for whatever career path you pursue. The ability to write and communicate clearly is crucial in the modern workplace and in life. I hope my handbook proves to be a trusted companion and friendly resource for many years. Hold onto it throughout your college career and beyond so that you can always look up whatever information you might need as a writer. Keep it close at hand in your permanent library, along with a dictionary and other reference books. As you use it, please feel welcome to write me with reactions, suggestions, and questions. Here's the address: Lynn Quitman Troyka, c/o English Composition Editor, Prentice Hall, 1 Lake Street, Upper Saddle River, NJ 07458. I promise to answer.

ACKNOWLEDGMENTS

Behind the pages of the fourth edition reside many voices—of students, colleagues, friends, and family. I treasure each and thank all.

Most substantively, Jo Ellen Coppersmith, Utah Valley State College, has added centrally to the rigor of concept and practice concerning research writing and critical thinking. Victoria Nelson contributed importantly with drafts of new exercise content and streamlining of some chapters. Barbara Gaffney lent her considerable expertise to an analysis of my treatment of English as a Second Language (ESL). Judith A. Stanford, Rivier College, oversaw the fourth edition of the *Annotated Instructor's Edition* with her special brand of grace and interest in students. Other colleagues whose valued contributions are reflected in the fourth edition include Jay Don Coppersmith, National Training Specialist in Technology and Research, Jostens Learning Corporation, advisor on documentation updates; Michael J. Freeman, Director of the Utah Valley State College Library, advisor on library use in this age of electronic information; Warren Herendeen, Mercy College, advisor on ESL; Scott Leonard, Youngstown State University, advisor on drafting and revision; Darlene Malaska, Youngstown Christian University, advisor on the critical response essay; Mary Ruetten, University of New Orleans, advisor on ESL; and Matilda Delgado Saenz, Northlake College, advisor on the Toulmin model for argument. To these major advisors to the prior edition, I renew my gratitude: Duncan Carter, Portland State University; Ann B. Dobie, University of Southwestern Louisiana; Emily R. Gordon, Queensborough Community College; Dorothy V. Lindman, Brookhaven College; Alice Maclin, DeKalb College; and Patricia Morgan, Louisiana State University.

Among my greatest pleasures in acknowledging others is to thank the many students who generously have given me permission to show their writing as exemplary models in the fourth edition. I appreciate also the opportunities I have had to meet with hundreds of students across the United States to hear their ideas for new editions of my handbooks, and I warmly thank all students who have written me letters in which they gracefully shared with me their reactions to and suggestions for my handbooks.

Many other faculty helped shape my decisions for the fourth edition. I am particularly grateful to members of the "Regional Advisory Board for Prentice Hall and Lynn Troyka" who set aside precious days in their busy lives to discuss key issues with me. In the Southeast, they are Peggy Jolly, University of Alabama at Birmingham; Stephen Prewitt, David Lipscomb University; Mary Anne Reiss, Elizabethtown Community College; Michael Thro, Tidewater Community College at

Virginia Beach; and Sally Young, University of Tennessee at Chattanooga. In the Southwest, they are Jon Bentley, Albuquerque Technical-Vocational Institute; Kathryn Fitzgerald, University of Utah; Maggy Smith, University of Texas at El Paso; Martha Smith, Brookhaven College; Donnie Yeilding, Central Texas College. I thank also those colleagues who have made specific suggestions in formal reviews as well as letters, e-mail, and relayed messages. They include Susan Ahrens, Valencia Community College; Virginia Anderson, University of Texas at Austin; Christopher Baker, Armstrong State College; Judy L. Burke, Macomb Community College; Jolayne Call, Utah Valley State College; James A. Coleman, Three Rivers Community & Technical College; Paula Gillespie, Marquette University; Jane Hikel, Central Connecticut State University; Sheila McGrory-Klyza, University of Vermont; Patricia McKeague, Moraine Valley Community College; Stuart Morton, Macomb Community College; Marcia Peabody, Mira Costa College; Blue Perry, Valenica Community College; and Don Tighe, Valencia Community College. Special thanks go to Michael Hassett for careful, thorough work, while he was a graduate student, on the writing of student research papers.

Over the course of my writing the prior edition of the *Handbook*, the reviews of many colleagues helped me draft and revise. I renew my thanks to all of them, including Nancy Westrich Baker, Southeast Missouri State University; Norman Bosley, Ocean Community College; Phyllis Brown, Santa Clara University; Robert S. Caim, West Virginia University at Parkersburg; Joe R. Christopher, Tarleton State University; Thomas Copeland, Youngstown State University; Joanne Ferreira, State University of New York at New Paltz and Fordham University; Michael Goodman, Fairleigh Dickinson University; Mary Multer Greene, Tidewater Community College at Virginia Beach; John L. Hare, Montgomery College; Lory Hawkes, DeVry Institute of Technology, Irving; Janet H. Hobbs, Wake Technical Community College; Frank Hubbard, Marquette University; Rebecca Innocent, Southern Methodist University; Ursula Irwin, Mt. Hood Community College; Denise Jackson, Southeast Missouri State University; Margo K. Jang, Northern Kentucky University; Myra Jones, Manatee Community College; Judith C. Kohl, Dutchess Community College; James C. McDonald, University of Southwestern Louisiana; Susan J. Miller, Santa Fe Community College; Jon F. Patton, University of Toledo; Pamela T. Pittman, University of Central Oklahoma; Kirk Rasmussen, Utah Valley State College; Edward J. Reilly, St. Joseph's College; Peter Burton Ross, University of the District of Columbia; Eileen Schwartz, Purdue University at Calumet; Lisa Sebti, Central Texas College; John S. Shea, Loyola University at Chicago; Tony Silva, Purdue University; Bill M. Stiffler, Harford Community College; Jack Summers, Central

Piedmont Community College; Vivian A. Thomlinson, Cameron University; Carolyn West, Daytona Beach Community College; and Roseanna B. Whitlow, Southeast Missouri State University.

The staff at Prentice Hall/Simon & Schuster continues to facilitate my writing with their extraordinary energy and talent. Central credit goes to Joyce F. Perkins, Senior Development Editor for English, whose voice joins and enhances mine on many pages. She is the dean of English development editors in college publishing today, and as all who have worked with her attest, to collaborate with her is a huge honor. Alison Reeves, Executive Editor for English, a woman of uncommon dedication and ethics, participated vigorously and wisely. Kara Hado, Assistant Development Editor for English, a gifted newcomer to our team, contributed much with unfailing skill. Andrew Roney, Senior Project Manager, shepherded this complex, multifaceted undertaking with gentle humor, a firm hand, and solid professionalism. Hilda Tauber, who will always be part of Prentice Hall for me, shared her keen eye and mind. Gina Sluss, Executive Marketing Manager for Humanities, informally but crucially part of our editorial team, clarified patiently and inspired frequently. Other people in indispensable roles included J. Phillip Miller, President, Humanities and Social Sciences; D. Anthony English, Editor in Chief for English; Carol Carter, Director of Student Programs; Leslie Osher, Creative Director; Susan Walrath, Designer; Lori Kane, Supervisor of Production Services; Mary Ann Gloriande, Manufacturing Buyer; Bud Therien, Publisher for Art and Music; Kane Tung, Editorial Assistant; and Jennifer Weinberg, Marketing Assistant.

Closer to home are many people who give delightful texture to my life. Ida Morea, my assistant, helps in ways both large and small with her warmth and excellence. Dear friends and family whose understanding and love grace my life include Susan Bartlestone; Kristen Black, with Dan, Lindsey, and Ryan Black; Rita and Hy Cohen; Ruth Davis; Elaine Gilden Dushoff, my cousin; Elliott Goldhush; Warren Herendeen; Kate Morgan Jackson; Edith Klausner, my sister; Myra Kogen; Jo Ann Lavery; Lisa Lavery; Marie Jean Lederman; Marilyn Maiz; Jerrold Nudelman; Belle and Sidney Quitman, my parents; Betty Renshaw; Magdalena Rogalskaja; Shirley and Don Sterns; Marilyn and Ernest Sternglass; Elsie Tischler; Muriel Wolfe; and Gideon and Tzila Zwas. Most of all, I thank my husband, David Troyka, my anchor, sweetheart, and best friend.

Lynn Quitman Troyka

SUPPLEMENTARY MATERIALS

As in other editions, the supplementary materials for the fourth edition of the *Simon & Schuster Handbook for Writers* assist teachers and students alike to use the text easily and to enhance the learning experience. The following list suggests the range of supplements available with this edition.

Print Supplements for Instructors

- *Annotated Instructor's Edition*, Fourth Edition, by Lynn Quitman Troyka with Judith Stanford, Ann Dobie, and Emily R. Gordon
- *Strategies & Resources for Teaching Writing* by Linda Julian with Patricia Kelvin and Scott A. Leonard, Laurel Black, Cynthia L. Myers, and Edgar V. Roberts
- *Teaching Writing Across the Curriculum* by Ann O. Gebhard
- *Computers and Writing* by Dawn Rodrigues
- *Teaching Writing* by Phyllis Hastings
- *Answer Key to the Simon & Schuster Workbook for Writers*
- Diagnostic Tests
- Response Symbols Chart

Print Supplements for Students

- *Simon & Schuster Workbook for Writers*, Fourth Edition, by Lynn Quitman Troyka
- *Simon & Schuster Guide to Research and Documentation*
- Prentice Hall/New York Times Contemporary View Program: *Writing*
- *Rough Drafts* by Kathleen Shine Cain
- *Model Research Papers*, Second Edition, by Janette S. Lewis
- *The Research Organizer* by Sue D. Hopke
- *Supplementary Essays for Writers*
- *Preparing for the TASP* by Matilda Delgado Saenz
- *Preparing for the CLAST* by Sybil Patterson
- *Webster's Dictionary* offers

Software Supplements

- On-Line Handbook
- Blue Pencil interactive editing program by Bob Bator
- Bibliotec bibliography generator

Audio-Visual Supplements

■ *Prentice Hall/Simon & Schuster Transparencies for Writers* by Duncan Carter

■ *Profiles of a Writer* Video Series

■ Prentice Hall Critical Thinking Skills audiocassette

For more information, contact your Prentice Hall representative or write to: Marketing Manager for English Composition, Prentice Hall, 1 Lake Street, Upper Saddle River, NJ 07458.

Prentice Hall and The New York Times proudly cosponsor A Contemporary View, a program designed to enhance student access in the classroom to relevant current information. Through this program, a collection of timely articles from *The New York Times*, one of the world's most distinguished newspapers, supplements the core subject matter of a course. These articles demonstrate the vital, ongoing connection between what is learned in the classroom and what is happening in the world around us. In newspaper format, with a range of articles and opinion pieces on topics of interest to today's students, *A Contemporary View: Writing* not only demonstrates purposeful writing but can serve to initiate it as well.

CREDITS

We gratefully acknowledge permission to reprint from the following sources:

CLARA BENNETT: Excerpt from a letter to the editor of *Newsday* by Clara Bennett, President of the Board of Trustees, Nassau County Library System. Reprinted with the kind permission of Clara Bennett.

HOUGHTON MIFFLIN COMPANY: "Sports Only Exercise Our Eyes" from *The Best of Sydney J. Harris*, pp. 111-112. Copyright © 1975 by Sydney J. Harris. Reprinted by permission of Houghton Mifflin Company. All rights reserved.

THE NEW YORK TIMES COMPANY

"The Emasculation of Sports," by Robert J. Lipsyte, *The New York Times Sunday Magazine*, May 2, 1995. Copyright © 1995 by The New York Times Company. Reprinted by permission.

Excerpt from "Personal Computers" by Erik Sanberg, *The New York Times*, June 18, 1985. Copyright © 1985 by The New York Times Company. Reprinted by permission.

Excerpt from "What Brand of Laughter Do You Use?" by Roger Rosenblatt, *The New York Times*, November 17, 1991. Copyright © by 1991 by The New York Times Company. Reprinted by permission.

Excerpt from "Safe Lifting Techniques" by John Warde, *The New York Times*, March 11, 1990. Copyright © 1990 by The New York Times Company. Reprinted by permission.

Excerpt from "Older than Forks, Safer than Knives" by Dena Kleinman, *The New York Times*, January 17, 1990. Copyright © 1990 by The New York Times Company. Reprinted by permission.

Excerpt from "A Hoarder's Life: Filling the Cache—and Finding It!" by Jane E. Brody, *The New York Times*, November 19, 1991. Copyright © 1991 by The New York Times Company. Reprinted by permission.

Excerpt from "Researchers Trace Empathy's Roots to Infancy" by Daniel Goleman, *The New York Times*, March 28, 1989. Copyright © 1989 by The New York Times Company. Reprinted by permission.

NEWSDAY

Excerpt from "Fighting Racism with Inclusion" by Randolph H. Manning in *Newsday*, 7 October 1990. Copyright © 1990 by Newsday. Reprinted by permission.

Excerpt from "Depth of Field" by Susan Howard in *Newsday*, 1 January 1991. Copyright © 1991 by Newsday. Reprinted by permission.

Excerpt from "If Lightning Strikes" by Gerald Secor Couzens in *Newsday*, 13 August 1988. Copyright © 1988 by Newsday. Reprinted by permission.

Excerpt from "A Slice of History" by Lisa Pratt from *The Newsday Magazine*, 29 April 1990. Copyright © 1990 by Newsday. Reprinted by permission.

OXFORD UNIVERSITY PRESS: Entry for *celebrate* excerpted from the *Oxford English Dictionary* (new edition, 1989). Reprinted by permission of Oxford University Press.

RANDOM HOUSE INC. and FABER & FABER: W. H. Auden, "Prologue: The Birth of Architecture." *Collected Poems* edited by Edward Mendelson. Copyright 1965 by W. H. Auden. Reprinted by permission of Random House and Faber & Faber.

READER'S DIGEST: Excerpt from "That Astounding Creature—Nature" by Jean George in *Reader's Digest*, January 1984. Copyright © 1984 by Reader's Digest Association and reprinted by permission.

SIMON & SCHUSTER, INC.: The entry for *celebrate* is from *Webster's New World Dictionary*, Third College Edition, Victoria Newfield, Editor in Chief. © 1994, 1991, 1988 by Simon & Schuster, Inc. Reprinted by permission of the publisher.

UNIVERSITY OF OKLAHOMA PRESS: Excerpt from "What Is Poverty?" by Jo Goodwin Parker in *America's Other Children* by George Henderson. Copyright © 1971. Published by the University of Oklahoma Press and reprinted with their permission.

Two poems by Claude McKay, "In Bondage" and "The White City," used by permission of The Archives of Claude McKay.

We also acknowledge the following writers, whose material supplied information used in various exercises.

Exercise 8-8 draws on information in "1 Part Earnestness, 1 Blast of Laughter" by James R. Oestreich, *The New York Times*, 21 Sep. 1994, C1, C6.

Exercise 8-11 draws on information in "Fantasy Coffins of Ghana" by Carol Beckwith with Angela Fisher, *National Geographic*, vol. 86, no. 3, Sep. 1994, 120-30.

Exercise 10-2 draws on information in "What Is Love?" by Paul Gray, *Time*, 15 Feb. 1993, pp. 47-51.

Exercise 11-2 draws on information in "Using Self-Esteem to Fix Society's Ills" by Lena Williams, *The New York Times*, 28 April 1990, C1+.

Exercise 11-4 draws on information in "Greetings! Have You Ever Sent a Louie?" by Ron Alexander, *The New York Times*, 20 May 1990, 48.

Exercise 11-5 draws on information in "Star Quality" by Perry W. Buffington, Ph.D., *Sky*, September 1990, pp. 101-4.

Exercise 12-1 draws on information in "TV, Seriously" by Larry Hartsfield, *Sky*, September 1990, pp. 84+.

About the Author

Lynn Quitman Troyka earned her Ph.D. at New York University and has taught for many years at the City University of New York (CUNY), including Queensborough Community College, the Center for Advanced Studies in Education at the Graduate School, and the graduate program in Language and Literacy at City College.

Dr. Troyka is an author in composition/rhetoric for the *Encyclopedia of Rhetoric*, 1994. Former editor of the *Journal of Basic Writing*, she has published in journals such as *College Composition and Communication*, *College English*, and *Writing Program Administration* and in books from Southern Illinois Press, Random House, and Heineman/Boynton/Cook.

Dr. Troyka is the author of the *Simon & Schuster Quick Access Reference for Writers*, Prentice Hall, 1995; the *Simon & Schuster Concise Handbook*, Prentice Hall, 1992; and *Structured Reading, Fourth Edition*, Prentice Hall, 1995. She is co-author (with John Gerber, Richard Lloyd-Jones, et al.) of *A Checklist and Guide for Reviewing Departments of English*, ADE of the Modern Language Association, 1985; and of *Steps in Composition, Sixth Edition* (with Jerrold Nudelman), Prentice Hall, 1994.

Dr. Troyka has conducted seminars at numerous colleges and universities and at national and international meetings. She is a past chair of the Conference on College Composition and Communication (CCCC), of the College Section of the National Council of Teachers of English (NCTE), and of the Writing Division of the Modern Language Association. Named Rhetorician of the Year in 1993, she was given the 1995 Picket Service Award by CCCC and the NCTE Two-Year College Association. She currently serves as Chair of the Task Force on the Future of CCCC.

"All this information," says Dr. Troyka, "tells what I've done, not who I am. I am a teacher. Teaching is my life's work, and I love it."

Writing An Essay

When you write an essay, you engage in a process. The parts of that process vary with the writer and the demands of the subject. Part One explains all aspects of the act of writing, and of thinking and reading in relation to writing, so that you can evolve your personal style of composing and thereby become an effective writer.

1 *Thinking about Purposes and Audiences*

REFERENCES TO SUPPLEMENTS

For more on the fact that cultural context can strongly affect the way some ESL students approach purpose and audience, see C. Myers, "ESL Writers in the Composition Class," in L. Julian, et al., *Strategies and Resources for Teaching Writing with the Simon & Schuster Handbook for Writers.*

For a discussion of realistic goals in writing courses, and using the handbook as a text, see L. Julian, "Strategies for Teaching Writing," ch. II, in L. Julian, et al., *Strategies and Resources for Teaching Writing with the Simon & Schuster Handbook for Writers.*

For various syllabi emphasizing the whole essay, paragraph development, language, or research, see L. Julian, "Strategies for Teaching Writing," ch. III, in L. Julian, et al., *Strategies and Resources for Teaching Writing with the Simon & Schuster Handbook for Writers.*

QUOTATION ABOUT WRITING

I shall live badly if I do not write, and I shall write badly if I do not live.

—Françoise Sagan

Why write? In this age of telephones and tape recorders, television and film, computers and communication satellites, why should you bother with writing? The answer has overlapping parts, starting with the inner life of a writer and moving outward.

Writing is a way of thinking and learning. Writing gives you unique opportunities to explore ideas and understand information. By writing, you come to know subjects well and make them your own. Even thirty years later, many people can recall details about the topics and content of essays they wrote in college, but far fewer people can recall specifics of a classroom lecture or a textbook chapter. Writing helps you learn and gain authority over knowledge. As you share what you learn, you also teach. When you write for a reader, you play the role of a teacher, someone who knows the material sufficiently well to organize and present it clearly.

Writing is a way of discovering. The act of writing allows you to make unexpected connections among ideas and language. As you write, thoughts emerge and interconnect in ways unavailable until the physical act of writing begins. An authority on writing, James Britton, describes discovery in writing as "shaping at the point of utterance." Similarly, well-known writer E. M. Forster talked about discovery during writing by asking, "How can I know what I mean until I've seen what I said?" You can expect many surprises of insight that come only when you write and rewrite, each time trying to get closer to what you want to say.

Writing creates reading. Writing is a powerful means of communication. It creates a permanent, visible record of your ideas for others to read and ponder. Reading informs and shapes human thought. In an open society, everyone is free to write and thereby to create reading for other people. For that freedom to be exercised, however, the ability to

2

write cannot be concentrated in a few people. All of us need access to the power of the written word. Writing ability is needed by educated people. In college, you must write many different types of assignments. In the workplace, most jobs, even in today's technological society, require writing skill for preparing documents ranging from letters to formal reports. Throughout your life, your writing reveals your ability to think clearly and to use language effectively.

Understanding the elements of writing   **1a**

Writing can be explained by its four elements: *Writing is a way of communicating a message to a reader for a purpose.* Each word in this definition carries important meaning. **Communicating** in writing means sending a message that has a destination. The **message** of the writing is its content, which originates in your motivation as a writer to engage in one or more of these activities: *observing, remembering, reporting, explaining, exploring, interpreting, speculating, evaluating,* and *reflecting.* The **reader,** usually called the audience, is explained in section 1c. **Purposes** for writing are discussed in section 1b.

Understanding purposes for writing   **1b**

Writing is often defined by its **purpose.** Writing purposes have to do with goals, sometimes referred to as *aims of writing* or *writing intentions.* Thinking about purposes for writing means thinking about the motivating forces that move people to write. As a student, you might assume that your only purpose for writing is to fulfill a class assignment. More is involved, however. As a writer in college, you are challenged to shape the content of your material and the style of your writing to suit your writing purpose. The overarching categories for the major purposes for writing are shown in Chart 1.

The purposes of writing *to express yourself* (see 1b-1) and *to create a literary work* contribute importantly to human thought and culture . This handbook concentrates on the two purposes most prominent and practical in your academic life: *to inform a reader* (see 1b-2) and *to persuade a reader* (see 1b-3). As a writer, you have many choices of writing strategies for presenting your message with clarity and impact. These strategies include *narrating, describing, illustrating, defining, analyzing and classifying, comparing and contrasting, drawing an anaogy, considering cause and effect,* and others; see Chapter 4, especially section 4f.

BACKGROUND

Linda Flower assesses the role of purpose in *The Construction of Purpose in Writing and Reading* (Pittsburgh: Center for the Study of Writing, 1988), concluding that it is constructive, cognitive, and rhetorical. It deserves attention because it can provide meaning and coherence in a piece of writing.

BACKGROUND

Writing is sometimes classified according to four modes of discourse: *narration, description, exposition,* and *argumentation.* These modes describe the *what* of writing. They describe characteristics that written products seem to feature, although much overlap exists. A writer can narrate an incident in the service of arguing an opinion; a writer can describe a scene in the service of offering information.

This handbook starts with the *why* of writing. Thus it begins with *purposes* for writing. Purposes are familiar territory for instructors used to modes, because two of the modes are purposes: people write for the purpose of informing (expositing) and for the purpose of persuading (arguing). Purposes are based on the notion that people write for a reason; most college writing is done either to inform or to persuade. Research shows that few writers sit down and say to themselves, "I am going to write a comparison and contrast essay"; instead they say to themselves, "I want to give my readers some information" or "I want to convince my readers to change their minds." In the service of those purposes, writers compare and contrast, narrate, describe, draw analogy, and so forth.

Narration and description are discussed fully in Chapter 4, "Writing Paragraphs," along with many other writing strategies for idea development, including process, definition, comparison and contrast, cause-and-effect relationship, and analogy.

1b
cont.

PURPOSES FOR
WRITING

1b-1

1b-2

PURPOSES FOR WRITING* | 1

■ to express yourself
■ to inform a reader
■ to persuade a reader
■ to create a literary work

*Adapted from ideas that James L. Kinneavy, a modern rhetorician, discusses in *A Theory of Discourse.* 1971; New York: Norton, 1980.

Writing to express yourself

Expressive writing is usually the private recording of your thoughts and feelings. (When expressive writing is intended for more public exposure, it is more like literary writing.) Consider this personal journal entry written by one of the students whose essay appears in Chapter 6; even though it is his private writing, it is published here with his permission.

> When we lived in Maine, the fall and winter holidays were my touchstones—the calendar moved along in comforting sequence. I wrapped the snow and foods and celebrations around me like a soft blanket. I burrowed in. Now that we live in New Mexico, I don't need that blanket. But I surely do miss it.
>
> —DANIEL CASEY, student

Writing to inform a reader

Informative writing seeks to give information and, frequently, to explain it. This writing is known also as **expository writing** because it expounds on, or sets forth, ideas and facts. *Informative writing focuses mainly on the subject being discussed.*

Informative writing includes reports of observations, ideas, scientific data, facts, and statistics. It can be found in textbooks, encyclopedias, technical and business reports, nonfiction, newspapers, and magazines.

When you write to inform, you are expected to offer information with a minimum of bias. You aim to educate, not persuade. Like all effective teachers, you need to present the information completely, clearly, and accurately. The material should be verifiable by additional reading, talking with others, or personal experience. For example, consider this passage that aims to inform the reader:

In 1914 in what is now Addo Park in South Africa, a hunter by the name of Pretorius was asked to exterminate a herd of 140 elephants. He killed all but 20, and those survivors became so cunning at evading him that he was forced to abandon the hunt. The area became a preserve in 1930, and the elephants have been protected ever since. Nevertheless, elephants now four generations removed from those Pretorius hunted remain shy and strangely nocturnal. Young elephants evidently learn from the adults' trumpeting alarm calls to avoid humans.

—CAROL GRANT GOULD, "Out of the Mouths of Beasts"

This passage is successful because it *communicates* (transmits) a *message* (about young elephants learning to avoid humans) to a *reader* (a person who might become or already is interested in the subject) for a *purpose* (to inform). In this passage, the writer's last sentence states the main idea. The other sentences offer support for the main idea.

CHECKLIST FOR INFORMATIVE WRITING   2

- Is its major focus the subject being discussed?
- Is its primary purpose to inform rather than persuade?
- Is its information complete and accurate?
- Can its information be verified?
- Is its information arranged for clarity?

Writing to persuade a reader

1b-3

Persuasive writing seeks to convince the reader about a matter of opinion. This writing is sometimes called **argumentative** because it argues a position. (Because the techniques of written argument can be especially demanding on a writer, this handbook devotes all of Chapter 6 to them.)

Persuasive writing focuses mainly on the reader, whom the writer wants to influence. When you write to persuade, you deal with the debatable, that which has other sides to it. Persuasive writing seeks to change the reader's mind or at least to bring the reader's point of view closer to the writer's. Even the writer who feels sure that the reader's position on the subject will never change is expected to argue as convincingly as possible.

To be persuasive, you cannot merely state an opinion. Your reader expects you to offer convincing support for your point of view. Such

---

BACKGROUND

A *Theory of Discourse* by James L. Kinneavy explores the fundamental purposes for which people use language. Kinneavy explains the centrality of the concept of *purpose* in writing:

> Purpose in discourse is all important. The aim of a discourse determines everything else in the process of discourse. "What" is talked about, the oral or written medium which is chosen, the words and grammatical patterns used—all of these are largely determined by the purpose of the discourse (48).

Kinneavy is enthusiastic about the potential for composition as a field of scholarship:

> It is the thesis of this work that the field of composition—or discourse as it will presently be termed—is a rich and fertile discipline with a worthy past which should be consulted before being consigned to oblivion, an exciting present, and a future that seems as limitless as either linguistics or literature (2).

Kinneavy's theories, and those of similar bent that focus on purposes for writing, are widely accepted today among scholars and teachers. Other modern influential theorists who concentrate on writers' purposes include the highly respected James Britton, who classifies purposes as *poetic, expressive,* and *transactional.*

In "On Intention in Student Texts" (*Encountering Student Texts: Interpretive Issues in Reading Student Writing,* ed. Bruce Lawson, Susan Sterr Ryan, and W. Ross Winterowd [NCTE, 1989]), Sharon Crowley discusses problems that can result from expecting writers always to have a clear purpose in mind before writing. Writers often discover their purpose as they write, and their purpose may change from draft to draft.

CHECKLIST FOR PERSUASIVE WRITING

TEACHING TIP

In "Reading Intention" (*Encountering Student Texts: Interpretive Issues in Reading Student Writing*, ed. Bruce Lawson, Susan Sterr Ryan, and W. Ross Winterowd [NCTE, 1989]), Norm Katz suggests that, for every rough draft and revision that a teacher or peer group will read, a student hand in "a letter that explains what the student is trying to do and how he or she is trying to do it" (111). The letter should explain the purpose not only for the entire paper but also behind each part of the paper and behind the changes made in a revision. These letters, Katz writes, "help readers distinguish goals from written results: they help students monitor what they have written, and they help the teacher understand what students have attempted" (119).

QUOTATION ABOUT WRITING

I started writing because of a terrible feeling of powerlessness: I felt I was drifting and obscure, and I rebelled against that. I didn't see what I could do to change my condition. I wanted to control rather than be controlled, to ordain rather than be ordained, and to relegate rather than be relegated.

—Anita Brookner

TEACHING TIP: COLLABORATION

Discourage groups from writing about volatile, irresolvable subjects. Collaboration works when students can share and develop concepts and ideas. Positions set in stone are rarely amenable to any kind of modification and an inability to negotiate a position on an issue will likely make negotiation of writing processes impossible as well.

1b-3 cont.

support often relies upon information that explains and defends a point of view. Persuasive writing, therefore, often calls for informative writing (see 1b-2) to provide the evidence that lends strength to an argument. Examples of persuasive writing include editorials, letters to the editor, reviews, sermons, business or research proposals, opinion essays in magazines, and books that argue a point of view. For example, consider this passage that aims to persuade the reader:

> The search for some biological basis for math ability or disability is fraught with logical and experimental difficulties. Since not all math underachievers are women, and not all women are mathematics-avoidant, poor performance in math is unlikely to be due to some genetic or hormonal difference between the sexes. Moreover, no amount of research so far has unearthed a "mathematical competency" in some tangible, measurable substance in the body. Since "masculinity" cannot be injected into women to test whether or not it improves their mathematics, the theories that attribute such ability to genes or hormones must depend for their proof on circumstantial evidence. So long as about 7 percent of the PhD's in mathematics are earned by women, we have to conclude either that these women have genes, hormones, and brain organization different from those of the rest of us, or that certain positive experiences in their lives have largely undone the negative fact that they are female, or both.
>
> —SHEILA TOBIAS, *Overcoming Math Anxiety*

This passage is successful because it sends a *message* (about math ability and disability) to a *reader* (a person who might become or already is interested in the subject) for a *purpose* (to persuade a reader that math ability or disability is not related to gender). The writer's first sentence summarizes the point of view that she argues in the rest of the paragraph. The other sentences support the writer's assertion.

CHECKLIST FOR PERSUASIVE WRITING   3

- ■ Is its major focus the reader?
- ■ Is its primary purpose to convince rather than inform?
- ■ Does it offer information or reasons to support its point of view?
- ■ Is its point of view based on sound reasoning and logic?
- ■ Are the points of its argument arranged for clarity?
- ■ Does it evoke an intended reaction from the reader?

EXERCISE 1-1

For each paragraph, decide if the dominant purpose is *informative* or *persuasive*. Then, answer the questions in Chart 2 or Chart 3 in relation to the paragraph, and explain your answers.

A.   Over a period of several days we map and describe nine new ruins. The process is somewhat mechanical, but we each take pleasure in the simple tasks. As the Anasazi had a complicated culture, so have we. We are takers of notes, measurers of stone, examiners of fragments in the dust. We search for order in chaos wherever we go. We worry over what is lost. In our best moments we remember to ask ourselves what it is we are doing, whom we are benefiting by these acts. One of the great dreams of man must be to find some place between the extremes of nature and civilization where it is possible to live without regret.

—BARRY LOPEZ, "Searching for Ancestors"

B.   We know very little about pain, and what we don't know makes it hurt all the more. Indeed, no form of illiteracy in the United States is so widespread or costly as ignorance about pain—what it is, what causes it, and how to deal with it without panic. Almost everyone can rattle off the names of at least a dozen drugs that can deaden pain from every conceivable cause—all the way from headaches to hemorrhoids. There is far less knowledge about the fact that about ninety percent of pain is self-limiting, that it is not always an indication of poor health, and that, most frequently, it is the result of tension, stress, idleness, boredom, frustration, suppressed rage, insufficient sleep, overeating, poorly balanced diet, smoking, excessive drinking, inadequate exercise, stale air, or any of the other abuses encountered by the human body in modern society.

—NORMAN COUSINS, *Anatomy of an Illness*

C.   Efforts to involve the father in the birth process, to enhance his sense of paternity and empowerment as he adjusts to his new role, should be increased. Having the father involved in labor and delivery can significantly increase his sense of himself as a person who is important to his child and to his mate. Several investigators have shown that increased participation of fathers in the care of their babies, increased sensitivity to their baby's cues at one month, and significantly increased support of their wives can result from the rather simple maneuver of sharing the newborn baby's behavior with the new father at three days, using the Neonatal Behavioral Assessment Scale (NBAS). In light of these apparent gains, we would do well to consider a period of paid paternity leave, which might

TEACHING TIP: COLLABORATION

Starting a course with a collaborative component

The concept underlying collaboration is that the whole is greater than the sum of its parts. Providing opportunities for students to work together allows them to see other points of view, to capitalize on each other's strengths, to develop concepts more extensively than they could do on their own, and to learn from each other. When you assign groups, allow students a little time to introduce themselves and get to know one another. Personalizing learning can be an important part of collaboration.

Collaborative groups work best when they comprise two or three students whose schedules allow them to work together outside class, if practical. When groups meet in class only, students can work toward the group's goals by completing individual responsibilities outside class and then merging their work during classtime. Collaborative papers, like single-authored texts, go through a series of drafts. But, unlike single-authored texts, collaborative papers will actively integrate concepts of audience, tone, planning and purpose into the writing process because at every step students must articulate to one another what they think the paper needs and why. [See also, chart 146 in Chapter 36 for detailed instructions to students.]

ANSWERS: EXERCISE 1–2

A. Answers will vary. Samples have to come from a single issue of a newspaper. Editorials, essays, letters to the editor, and reviews can serve as examples of writing with the dominant purpose of being persuasive. News reports can serve as examples of informative writing.

B. Answers will vary, as for above.

serve both symbolically and in reality as a means of stamping the father's role as critical to his family. Ensuring the father's active participation is likely to enhance his image of himself as a nurturing person and to assist him toward a more mature adjustment in his life as a whole.

—T. BERRY BRAZELTON, "Issues for Working Parents"

D.   During the past generation, the amount of time devoted to historical studies in American public schools has steadily decreased. About twenty-five years ago, most public high-school youths studied one year of world history and one of American history, but today, most study only one year of ours. In contrast, the state schools of many other Western nations require the subject to be studied almost every year. In France, for example, all students, not just the college-bound, follow a carefully sequenced program of history, civics and geography every year from the seventh grade through the twelfth grade.

—DIANE RAVITCH, "Decline and Fall of Teaching History"

E.   After proposing marriage to a neighbor girl, my grandfather used this hammer to build a house for his bride on a stretch of river bottom in northern Mississippi. The lumber for the place, like the hickory for the handle, was cut on his own land. By the day of the wedding he had not quite finished the house, and so right after the ceremony he took his wife home and put her to work. My grandmother had worn her Sunday dress for the wedding, with a fringe of lace tacked on around the hem in honor of the occasion. She removed this lace and folded it away before going out to help my grandfather nail siding on the house. "There she was in her good dress," he told me some fifty-odd years after that wedding day, "holding up them long pieces of clapboard while I hammered, and together we got the place covered up before dark." As the family grew to four, six, eight, and eventually thirteen, my grandfather used this hammer to enlarge his house room by room, like a chambered nautilus expanding its shell.

—SCOTT RUSSELL SANDERS, "The Inheritance of Tools"

EXERCISE 1-2

In one issue of a newspaper or a magazine, find an informative article and a persuasive article. Consulting section 1b, explain why you identify them as you do. Next, for each article, go back to Chart 2 or Chart 3, whichever is appropriate for the purpose you have identified, and answer the questions. Explain each answer.

EXERCISE 1-3

Consulting section 1b, assume that you have to write on each of these topics twice, once to inform and once to persuade your reader. Be prepared to discuss how your two treatments of each topic would differ.

1. diets
2. Canada
3. garbage
4. sense of humor
5. rap music
6. VCRs
7. drunk driving (DWI)
8. farming
9. tourists
10. good manners

Understanding audiences for writing   1c

Good writing is often judged by its ability to reach its intended **audience.** To be effective, informative and persuasive writing (see 1b) need to be geared to the fact that someone is "out there" to receive the communication. If you write without considering your reader, you risk communicating only with yourself.

As a writer for one or more readers, you need to consider who your audience is, especially concerning background. For example, in writing meant to persuade people to vote for a particular candidate, if you imply disrespect for people who stay home and raise children, you risk losing votes of many homemakers and their spouses. Or, if you want to persuade lawmakers that homemakers should be allowed to draw from the Social Security system, you would need to address some of the lawmakers' practical concerns, such as the impact of your proposal on the federal budget.

Also, as you write, you need to think about what you can assume an audience already knows. For example, a sales report filled with technical language assumes that its readers know the specialized vocabulary. The general reading public would have trouble understanding such a report. But if the material were rewritten without technical terms, general readers could understand it.

If you know or can reasonably assume even a few of the characteristics listed in Chart 4, your chances of reaching your audience improve. The more explicit your information about your audience, the better able you are to reach it. If you can only guess at the details, Chart 4 can help you get started.

ANSWERS: EXERCISE 1–3

For each topic the student should write one paragraph (or more, according to how you have assigned the exercise) with an informative purpose and one paragraph with a persuasive purpose. The student should also be prepared to discuss (orally or in writing, according to your assignment) the differences in the two treatments of the same topic.

REFERENCES TO SUPPLEMENTS

For this topic in the CLAST writing competency test, refer students to ch. 2, section A2 of *Preparing for the CLAST* by S. Patterson.

This topic is included in the TASP writing competency test. Refer students to *Preparing for the TASP* by M. Saenz.

For revising for audience awareness, refer students to *Rough Drafts* by K. S. Cain, Part II, Exercise 3.

See transparency 2–2 for classroom activities for a process approach to planning in the *Prentice Hall/Simon & Schuster Transparencies for Writers* by D. Carter.

TEACHING TIP

To help students understand the importance of audience, you may want to ask them to collect articles from various magazines and newspapers that are addressed to different types of readers. Giving them a list of publications popular with varied groups of people will ensure effective contrasts in the articles they find. (Consulting the *Writer's Digest* can be helpful in composing such a list, because it provides a brief description of the audience for numerous magazines.)

TEACHING TIP: COLLABORATION

While students understand the concept of audience in a general way, in their group they find that writing for others can be intimidating. The following collaborative exercise can help students overcome this anxiety and simultaneously explore the concrete characteristics of an audience.

Assign students to work in groups of three to four. Ask the class to envision a group of people who are time-travelers from an earlier era. They now take refuge in a modern American city. Even after being shown how to operate the lights and faucets in their apartments, these people remain innocent of technologies we take for granted. For example, they have no idea how to use modern appliances and so they wash their clothes by soaking them in the sink and then pounding them with heavy objects.

Ask each group to craft a set of instructions that would tell the time-travelers how to wash and dry their clothes using a modern washer and dryer. Students will have to bear in mind that they cannot take what they would consider "common knowledge" for granted. Even simple commands like "open the lid" or "check the lint filter" will require careful explanation—perhaps even illustration.

Because this exercise requires so much focus on audience, it encourages students to *articulate and practice* what they know about the needs of readers. By your visiting each of the groups as they work, you can gather a few representative comments demonstrating what your students already know about audience to share with the entire class when it comes time to discuss the activity.

CHECKLIST OF BASIC AUDIENCE CHARACTERISTICS   4

WHO ARE THEY?

- age, gender
- ethnic backgrounds, political philosophies, religious beliefs
- roles (student, parent, voter, wage earner, property owner, veteran, other)
- interests, hobbies

WHAT DO THEY KNOW?

- level of education
- amount of general or specialized knowledge about the topic
- preconceptions brought to the material

1c-1

Understanding the general reading public

The **general reading public** is composed of educated, experienced readers, people who regularly read newspapers, magazines, and books. These readers often have some general information about the subject you are dealing with, but they enjoy learning something new or seeing something from a different perspective. The general reading public expects material to be clear and to be free of advanced technical information.

1c-2

Understanding your instructor as a reader

When you write for a class assignment, your audience will almost certainly be your **instructor.** Sometimes, especially when you are planning or revising your work, your instructor might want other students in your class to collaborate as an audience. In most cases, however, your final audience remains your instructor.

Your instructor is a member of the general reading public and also someone who recognizes that you are an apprentice. Your instructor knows that few students are experienced writers or complete experts on their subjects. Still, your instructor always expects your writing to reflect that you took time to learn the material thoroughly and to write about it well. In part, therefore, an instructor is a *judge,* someone to whom you must demonstrate that you are doing your best. Instructors are very experienced readers who can quickly recognize a minimal effort or a negative attitude (as when a paper carries a tone that suggests "Tell me what you want and I'll give it to you").

Think of your instructor as a representative reader typical of the audience you want to reach. *Inexperienced writers sometimes wrongly assume that instructors will fill in mentally what is missing on the page.* Instructors expect what they read to include everything that the writer wants to say or imply. Do not leave out material. Even if you write immediately after your instructor has heard you give an oral report on the same subject, write as if no one is aware of what you know.

Your instructor is also an *academic*, a member of a group whose professional life centers on intellectual endeavors. You must, therefore, write within the constraints of academic writing. For example, if you are told to write on a topic of your choice, you definitely do not have total freedom to choose. Your topic must have some intrinsic intellectual interest. For example, an essay should not merely give directions on how to cut a wedding cake or use an eraser.

Understanding specialists as readers

1c-3

Specialists are members of the general reading public who have expert knowledge on specific subjects. In writing for specialists, you are expected to know the specialty and also to realize that your readers have advanced expertise.

Specialized readers often share not only knowledge but also assumptions, interests, and beliefs. For example, they may be members of a club that concentrates on a hobby, such as amateur astronomy or orchid raising. They may have similar backgrounds, such as having emigrated from another country or having worked at a similar job. They may have similar views on matters related to religion and politics. When you write for readers who share specialized knowledge, you have to balance the necessity to be thorough with the demand not to go into too much detail about technical terms and special references.

Understanding the effect of tone

1d

The **tone** of your writing is established by *what you say* and *how you say it*. Tone underlies much of written communication. This section gives a brief overview of tone, with references to longer discussions that you can consult elsewhere in this handbook.

The tone in your writing needs to be shaped to your purpose for writing (see 1b) and awareness of your audience (see 1c). Your tone reveals your attitude both toward the material about which you are writing and toward anyone you expect to read your writing. For example, if your tone implies that you feel superior to your readers, your material

To start a course in composition, you might ask students to think of personal experiences that support the three claims about writing that open this chapter. To get things started, you might talk about a few of your own experiences that support the claims. Do you recall a college paper you wrote? What do you remember about its contents and the experience of writing it? Have you found that writing about something makes you better able to teach it? Have you ever discovered what you wanted to say—or a connection among the ideas you already had in mind—as the words were formed "at the point of utterance"?

To encourage students to share their experiences, you might ask them first to jot down some notes and then participate in a discussion. If the group is large, you might divide it into small groups and give each group specific directions (written are more effective than oral) about what to discuss. The directions can have students discuss in turn each question listed in the paragraph above. You can appoint one person to serve as informal chair and another as secretary of the group. After a suitable amount of time, you might ask each group to report to the whole class.

1d
cont.

will be condescending and distasteful. Similarly, if your tone hints that you are uninformed or unsure, your readers will quickly lose confidence in what you are saying.

In academic writing, you want to convey a reasonable tone, both in the content of your material and in your choice of words. For example, readers might think a writer unreasonable who distorts information or tries to manipulate emotions unfairly by using slanted language (see 21a-4). Choose evenhanded or neutral words (*the politician being investigated for taking bribes*) rather than biased ones (*the corrupt, deceitful politician*). Also, readers can infer from sexist language (see 21b) that a writer is insensitive to gender issues in word choice. Choose gender-neutral terms and language that represents both men and women fairly (*police officer*, not *policeman; doctors and their spouses*, not *doctors and their wives*) rather than sexist language. Similarly, pretentious language (see 21e-1) reflects negatively on a writer because it can obscure the message. Choose straightforward rather than overblown words (*concert*, not *orchestral event*).

As important, when you move from writing privately for yourself to writing for an audience, the level of formality (see 21a-1) in your writing should reflect your goal. Although readers enjoy lively language, they can be jarred by an overly informal tone in a serious discussion. Readers of academic writing expect to be treated respectfully. A medium level of formality is most effective. For example, in a newspaper report about the results of an election, you would not refer to the loser or winner as *guy* or *gal*, no matter how relaxed the candidate appears.

EXERCISE 1-4

Each of these passages was written for a general reading audience. Consulting sections 1c and 1d, read each paragraph and decide (1) if its tone is appropriate for academic writing and (2) if the choice of words assumes knowledge that only a specialist would have.

A.   Pernicious anemia, a uniformly fatal disease, was spectacularly reversed by liver extract (much later found to be due to the presence of vitamin B_{12} in the extracts). Diabetes mellitus could be treated—at least to the extent of reducing the elevated blood sugar and correcting the acidosis that otherwise led to diabetic coma and death—by the insulin preparation isolated by Banting and Best. Pellagra, a common cause of death among the impoverished rural populations in the South, had become curable with Goldberger's discovery of the vitamin B complex and the subsequent identification of nicotinic acid. Diphtheria could be prevented by immunization against the toxin of diphtheria bacilli and, when it occurred, treated more or less effectively with diphtheria antitoxin.

—LEWIS THOMAS, "1933 Medicine"

B.   Forty-five minutes south of the capital city by train, in the small suburb of Myorenji, near Yokohama, 13-year-old Naoko Masuo returns from school, slips quietly into her family's two-story house and settles into her homework. She is wearing a plaid skirt and blue blazer, the uniform of the Shoe-ei Girls School, where she is a seventh-grader. "I made it," her smile seems to say. For three years, when she was in fourth through sixth grades in public school, Naoko's schedule was high-pressure: she would rush home from school, study for a short time and then leave again to attend *juku*, or cram school, three hours a day three times a week. Her goal was to enter a good private school, and the exam would be tough.

—CAROL SIMONS, "Kyoiku Mamas"

C.   Without mucus, a slug would quickly be invaded by a host of microbial denizens and die. It would also be immobile, for slugs require mucus underfoot on which to crawl. Secreted from the pedal gland, located just beneath the head, the mucus flows down to the slug's single muscular foot. Like a miniature asphalt machine, the slug first lays its road and then, with wavelike motions of its foot, moves over it. As the mucus "road" dries, it becomes a silvery map of a slug's travels.

—SCOTT MCCREDIE, "They're Still Slimy, But Naked Snails Are Finding New Friends"

D.   The consumer of electricity usually accepts the fact that power outages frequently occur during wind and thunderstorms. However, when outages occur during calm and dry weather, the consumer becomes upset and blames the power company. In reality, most non-weather-related outages occur either because of circumstances beyond the control of the power company or in order to insure the safety of its workers. Squirrels and other animals with the ability to reach the top of power poles cause outages by unknowingly completing a circuit between a hot wire and a ground wire, an act which can knock out power to many houses. Occasionally, rehabilitating old lines to decrease future outages forces the power company to kill the lines temporarily to insure safety. And, a power company that purchases its power from larger companies often loses power because of trouble on the other company's line.

—BURL CARRAWAY, student

E.   My husband and I constantly marvel at the fact that our two sons, born of the same parents and only two years apart in age, are such completely opposite human beings. The most obvious differences became apparent at their births. Our first born, Mark, was big and bold—his intense, already wise eyes, broad shoulders, huge and heavy hands, and powerful, chunky legs gave us the impression that he could have walked

ANSWERS: EXERCISE 1–4

A. (a) The tone is appropriate for academic writing.

   (b) The material assumes a specialized reader who would be familiar with words such as *diabetes mellitus*, *acidosis*, and *bacilli*.

B. (a) The tone is informal and may be inappropriate for academic writing in some courses.

   (b) The material does not assume a specialized reader.

C. (a) The tone is appropriate for academic writing.

   (b) The material assumes a specialized reader who would be familiar with words such as *microbial*, *mucus*, *pedal*, and *gland*.

D. (a) The tone is appropriate for academic writing.

   (b) The material assumes a small amount of specialized knowledge, though the gist of the message can be understood from the context. Specialized words include *outages*, *hot wire*, and *ground wire*.

E. (a) The tone is informal and may be inappropriate for academic writing in some courses.

   (b) The material does not assume a specialized reader.

TEACHING TIP

You might find that some students feel inhibited in their writing when they have to think about an audience for their writing. Studies show that some students misunderstand the concept of audience. They think it means that writers should act as if someone is constantly looking over their shoulders. Other students have trouble with the concept of audience because they think that they can never say something that would be unpopular with their audience. Some students might not want to admit these or other misunderstandings of the concept, so you might want to clear up the matter without asking anyone to give you their negative impressions. Once you start talking about the subject, you will often find that the students start chiming in to help you get at their concerns.

The concept of audience is meant to help writers get their message across. The concept is supposed to facilitate, not block. A writer is not expected to tell readers what they want to hear even if the writer disagrees with the readers. A writer is, however, expected to choose words the readers know and to use a tone suitable to the occasion. As writer Gary Provost says in "How to Make the Reader Like You," published in *Writer's Digest:*

> You need some sense of your reader's knowledge. If you're writing a report for oceanographers, mention the *dorsal carapace* and the *chelipeds* if you must, but if you're writing a brochure for visitors to a public aquarium, please write *shell* and *claws*. Remember that any time, you don't have your entire vocabulary to work with. You have only that portion of your vocabulary that you share with the readers (37–38).

out of the delivery room on his own. Our second son, Wayne, was delightfully different. Rather than have the football physique that Mark was born with, Wayne came into the world with a long, slim, wiry body more suited to running, jumping, and contorting. Wayne's eyes, rather than being intense like Mark's, were impish and innocent. When Mark was delivered, he cried only momentarily, then seemed to settle into a state of intense concentration, as if trying to absorb everything he could about the strange, new environment he found himself in. Conversely, Wayne screamed from the moment he first appeared until the nurse took him to the nursery. There was nothing helpless or pathetic about his cry either—he was damned angry!

—ROSEANNE LABONTE, student

Using sources for writing

You are your first **source** for writing. To write, you can always draw on the general fund of your prior knowledge—what you already know. Other sources for writing can be what you add to your prior knowledge by reading an article or book, watching television or movies, listening to lectures or speeches, or engaging in any other activity from which you can learn something. Writing based on your prior knowledge is something you have been doing ever since you started putting pencil to paper. Whatever ideas and details you include in your writing you have had to learn previously, with the possible exception of wholly personal writing about your own emotions experienced at the moment you are writing.

Some college writing assignments call for you to use only your prior knowledge. In those cases, do not consult sources for any kind of new information. (If you are not sure whether you can draw on outside sources for a specific assignment, ask your instructor before you use any.) To stimulate yourself to think of ideas and details you already know but perhaps have not thought about recently, use the techniques described in sections 2d through 2i.

For other writing assignments, you will consult sources—sometimes referred to as **outside sources**. The word *outside* means the knowledge is outside of what you already know. In such cases, you have some very important obligations. They are listed in Chart 5, which also refers you to more detailed discussions later in this handbook.

GUIDELINES FOR USING OUTSIDE SOURCES IN WRITING 5

- Evaluate sources critically, as explained in section 5h–2, Chart 34.

- Be sure to represent the material in each source accurately. For guidance in quoting, paraphrasing, or summarizing source material, see Chapter 31.

- Synthesize source material; do not merely report it. Make connections for your reader between the ideas and details in the source and your own ideas as stimulated by the source. For guidance in how to synthesize, as part of critical thinking, see sections 5b and 5f.

- Credit your source by naming it clearly and completely. Ask your instructor what method to use to give credit to the sources you use. Four widely used systems for communicating to a reader that you are giving credit to (documenting) sources are described in Chapter 33.

- Remember that using a source without informing readers of that use is plagiarism. For help in avoiding plagiarism, see Chapter 31.

BACKGROUND

Robert Brooke and John Hendricks, in *Audience Expectations and Teacher Demands* (Carbondale, IL: Southern Illinois UP, 1989), discuss two of the problems that students face in learning to write for different audiences in a composition course. One problem is that students know that, whatever audience the paper is purportedly written for, the teacher will be the one who reads and evaluates the essay. Another problem is that writing to an audience means establishing a relationship with that audience and creating an identity within a community. Students, especially in their first year in college, are often uncertain about their identities, trying to establish themselves in new communities—in college classes, dormitories, fraternities, sororities, majors, and professions. Often students are not sure whether they even belong in these communities. Writing to audiences, especially unfamiliar ones, as they try to understand the expectations of the teacher who will grade their papers is difficult, Brooke and Hendricks write, and students need support. The authors suggest that students need to feel "secure in their classroom positions," to feel a strong sense of membership or community in the class, and to feel secure about their relationship to the teacher before they can tackle difficult problems of audience (67). Early class discussions, group work, and journal writing can bring out class expectations and insecurities, clarify the support students can expect from the teacher and each other, and give students an opportunity to explore their identities in the unfamiliar world of college.

2 *Planning and Shaping*

REFERENCES TO SUPPLEMENTS

For teaching planning and shaping techniques in a computer classroom, see *Computers and Writing: Prentice Hall Resources for Composition* by D. Rodrigues.

For more about the fact that ESL students sometimes bring different assumptions about the planning and writing of an essay, see C. Myers, "ESL Writers in the Composition Class," in L. Julian, et al., *Strategies and Resources for Teaching Writing with the Simon & Schuster Handbook for Writers.*

For prewriting, refer students to *Rough Drafts* by K. S. Cain, Part I, Exercises 1–6.

For teaching the writing process with a collaborative approach, see P. Kelvin/S. Leonard, "Teaching Collaborative Writing," in L. Julian, et al., *Strategies and Resources for Teaching Writing with the Simon & Schuster Handbook for Writers.*

See transparencies 1–1 through 1–4a for useful classroom activities on the writing process in the *Prentice Hall/Simon & Schuster Transparencies for Writers* by D. Carter.

REFERENCE TO SUPPLEMENTS

For more on teaching the writing process, see *Teaching Writing: Prentice Hall Resources for Composition* by P. Hastings, ch. 5, "Interpreting the Writing Process."

2a

Understanding the writing process

Many people assume that a real writer can pick up a pen (or sit at a computer) and magically write a finished product, word by perfect word. Experienced writers know better. They know that **writing is a process,** a series of activities that start the moment they begin thinking about a subject and end when they complete a final draft. Experienced writers also know that good writing is rewriting. Their drafts are filled with additions, deletions, rearrangements, and rewordings.

Draft and Revision of Opening Paragraph in Chapter 2 by Lynn Troyka

For example, above you can see how the paragraph you just read was reworked into final form. Notice that two sentences were dropped, two sentences were combined, one sentence was added, and various words were dropped, changed, or added. Such activities are typical of writing.

Writing is an ongoing process of considering alternatives and making choices. The better you understand the writing process, the better you will write and the more you can enjoy writing. For the sake of explanation, the parts of the writing process are discussed separately in this chapter. In real life, the steps overlap, looping back and forth as each piece of writing evolves. Understanding writing as a multistage process allows you to work efficiently, concentrating on one activity at a time rather than trying to juggle all of the facets of a writing project simultaneously. Chart 6 summarizes the steps in the writing process.

THE WRITING PROCESS   6

- ■ **Planning** calls for you to gather ideas and think about a focus.
- ■ **Shaping** calls for you to consider ways to organize your material.
- ■ **Drafting** calls for you to write your ideas in sentences and paragraphs.
- ■ **Revising** calls for you to evaluate your draft and, based on your decisions, rewrite it by adding, cutting, replacing, moving—and often totally recasting material.
- ■ **Editing** calls for you to check the technical correctness of your grammar, spelling, punctuation, and mechanics.
- ■ **Proofreading** calls for you to read your final copy for typing errors or handwriting legibility.

Visualizing the Writing Process

If you are a writer who likes to visualize a process, see the diagram above. A straight line would not be adequate because it would exclude the recursive nature of writing. The arrows on the diagram imply move-

THE WRITING PROCESS

TEACHING TIP
The facsimile of my writing and revising at the opening of this chapter is completely authentic (though the handwriting is not mine because I tend to scrawl illegibly). I have included this draft to show students that most teachers and professional writers *evolve* a text rather than produce it in one swoop. When I do this in my writing classes, the students never fail to be surprised that their instructor's first draft could be so rough. You might also call attention to the clumsy opening sentences that I deleted and to other revisions that I made in my first draft.

You might also bring in a few examples of your own drafts. A paragraph or two can suffice. And if you use a word processor, as I do, plan ahead and keep those sentences you love to delete with the press of a key. I have found that a few students sometimes think that my rough drafts are better than their final drafts, but I try to emphasize that such a reaction misses the point. After all, I am not as much of an apprentice writer as the students are. And I am trying to better my writing from a base of where I am, not from a base that I started at back in college.

REFERENCE TO SUPPLEMENTS
This topic is included in the TASP writing competency test. Refer students to *Preparing for the TASP* by M. Saenz.

BACKGROUND
Over the past decade a number of theories about the process of writing have emerged. In *Discourse: A Critique and Synthesis of Major Theories* (New York: MLA, 1989), Timothy W. Crusius provides a helpful analysis of those put forward by James Kinneavy, James Moffett, James Britton, and Frank D'Angelo. Crusius pulls their views together in an attempt to find a unified view of the concept.

2a cont.

ment. Planning is not over when drafting begins, drafting is not necessarily over merely because the major activity shifts to revision, and editing sometimes inspires writers to see the need for additional revising—and perhaps some new planning.

As you work with the writing process, rest assured that there is no *one* way to write. When you start, allow yourself to move through each stage of the writing process and see what is involved. Then as you gain experience, begin to observe what works best for you. Once you have a general sense of the pattern of *your* writing process, you can adapt the process to suit each new situation that you encounter as a writer.

Most writers struggle some of the time with ideas that are difficult to express, sentences that will not take shape, and words that are not precise. Do not be impatient with yourself, and do not get discouraged. Writing takes time. The more you write, the easier it will be, but remember that experienced writers know that writing never happens magically.

An aside about the words used to discuss writing: Instructors refer to written products in different ways. Often the words are used interchangeably, but sometimes they have specific meanings for specific instructors. Listen closely and ask if you are unsure of what you hear. For example, the words *essay, theme,* and *composition* usually—but not always—refer to writing that runs from about 500 to 1,000 words. This handbook uses *essay.* The word *paper* can mean anything from a few paragraphs to a long and detailed report or a complex research project. This handbook uses *paper* to refer to longer writing projects, such as research papers, that draw on many outside sources.

2b

Adjusting for each writing situation

Writing begins with thinking about each **writing situation.** Your thinking involves answering the questions in Chart 7. Then you adjust your writing process (see 2a) to accommodate each particular writing situation.

ELEMENTS THAT INFLUENCE EACH WRITING SITUATION   7

- Topic: What will you be writing about in this situation?
- Purpose: What will be your writing purpose in this situation?
- Audience: Who will be your audience in this situation?
- Special requirements: How much time were you given, and what length should the paper be?

The **topic** underlies all aspects of the writing situation. If you must choose your own topic or narrow an assigned topic, keep in mind the constraints of academic writing (see 2c). If the topic is assigned, avoid going "off the topic." Whatever the topic, *you* are the starting place for your writing. Draw upon yourself as a source. Whatever you have seen, heard, read, and even dreamed contributes to your fund of ideas and knowledge. Keep in mind the need to marshal specific support for the points you make about your topic.

The **purpose** of your college writing is usually to inform or to persuade (see 1b). Effective writing reflects a clear sense of purpose. Some writing assignments include or clearly imply a statement of purpose. For example, your purpose is *informative* if you are writing about the dangers of smoking. Conversely, your purpose is *persuasive* if you are writing an argument against smoking. Other assignments do not stipulate the writing purpose, which means you must choose either an informative or persuasive purpose based on the topic, what you want to say about it (often referred to as the *focus*), and how you develop what you want to say.

Your **audience** (see 1c) for college writing is often primarily, though not exclusively, your instructor. Your instructor is both a member of the general reading public and an academic. Some writing assignments name a specialized audience, which means your readers have more technical knowledge than does the general reading public. You have to write to their level. Sometimes an assignment stipulates that the writing will be read by other students in the class. In such situations, students serve as surrogate instructors, so you are expected to write with the same tone and level of information as you would for your instructor alone.

Special requirements influence every writing situation. These include the time allotted for the assignment, the expected length of the writing, and other practical constraints. If an assignment is due in one week, you have to expect that your instructor wants writing that shows more than one day's work. If the paper is due overnight, it has to be written more hastily, though never carelessly. If reading or other research is required, you have to build time for it into your schedule.

Your assignment is a major resource for you as you write. Refer to it often. Ideally, your instructor writes the assignment on the board or distributes it on paper. Some instructors, however, only announce an assignment, in which case you are expected to write it down. Try to record every word spoken, always ask questions if you need clarifications, and write down the answers you get or any given in response to other students' questions.

To give you examples of the writing process in progress, this chapter shows you the work of two actual students—Carol Moreno and Daniel Casey—as they plan and shape their essays. Then in Chapter 3,

BACKGROUND

Lester Faigley classifies composing process theories into three categories— expressive, cognitive, and social—in "Competing Theories of Process: A Critique and a Proposal" (*College English* [October 1986]: 527–542). Expressive or neoromantic views, associated with Donald Stewart, Ken Macrorie, and Peter Elbow, emphasize writing with integrity, spontaneity, and originality. Cognitive theories, associated with Linda Flower, Janice Lauer, and Barry Kroll, have drawn on research on cognitive development by Jean Piaget and others, as well as on cybernetic theory, and describe composing as a recursive problem-solving activity. Social views of composing processes, a diverse group of theories influenced by poststructuralism, ethnography, the sociology of science, and Marxism, hold that writing "can be understood only from the perspective of a society rather than a single individual" (535) and explain the composing processes of writers in terms of their relationship to a community or culture. James Berlin, Patricia Bizzell, and David Bartholomae are among those advocating social theories. "Each view of process," Faigley writes, "has provided teachers with ways of resisting static methods of teaching writing" (537).

BACKGROUND

Donald Graves was the first to use the term *rehearsing* to describe the activities that precede a completed draft. In *Balance the Basics: Let Them Write* (Ford Foundation Papers on Research About Learning, 1978), he discusses the stage of the writing process in which the writer (mentally and on paper) prepares to write, without yet knowing what that writing will be. Drawing conclusions from his observations of children writing, Graves points out the importance of experimenting with meaning, form, and voices, an attitude of play that is important in making meaning. It allows the writer to make unexpected relationships from surprising inner voices.

ANSWERS: EXERCISE 2–1

1. The purpose is to inform. Because the assignment is for a biology class, the audience will likely be the instructor and perhaps other students in the class; these people are specialists. The assumption about an audience of specialists is further confirmed by the time limit of twenty minutes, which means that the student has to pack in many technical terms and processes in a short period of time. The special requirements include the twenty-minute time limit and, implied by the wording of the assignment, in-class writing.

2. The purpose is to persuade. The audience is the general reading public (such as the course instructor and students in the class). The special requirements include a 500- to 700-word limit and a due date of one week.

3. A student receiving this assignment has many decisions to make. The purpose can be either informative or persuasive, depending on the student's focus on the topic. The audience can be the general reading public or specialists, according to the student's judgment; if the political science course is advanced, chances are that the instructor expects the writing to be addressed to specialists. The only stated special requirement is a length of 1,000 words. The student should ask the instructor when the assignment is due and if the assignment calls for research. The student might also want to set a purpose and audience and check them with the instructor before proceeding, if time permits.

4. The purpose is to persuade. The audience is readers of the college's student newspaper; they could be considered specialists in that they share the experience of attending the same college, but they are not specialists in

➜

2b
cont.

Carol Moreno's essay is discussed as it evolves through three drafts (shown in section 3f). Daniel Casey's essay is developed in Chapter 6, and its final draft appears in section 6i. Here is the written statement of the assignment that each student received.

> *Carol Moreno was given this assignment:* Write an essay of 700 to 800 words in which you discuss a challenge you faced and tried to meet. Your writing purpose can be informative or persuasive. Expect to write three drafts. Your first draft (in rough form, showing your comments to yourself and changes you made) and your second (cleanly typed) draft are due in one week. I will read your second draft as an "essay in progress" and will make comments to help you toward a third, final draft. That third, final draft (cleanly typed) is due one week after I hand back your second draft with my comments.
>
> *Daniel Casey was given this assignment:* Write an essay of 500 to 700 words that argues about whether holidays have become too commercialized in the United States. Your final draft is due in one week. Bring your earlier drafts to class for possible discussion.

Moreno read her assignment with an eye toward analyzing the elements of her writing situation. The *topic* was a challenge she faced and tried to meet, a subject that Moreno realized she would have to narrow considerably (for her narrowing process, see 2c-2). For a writing *purpose*, Moreno tentatively chose an informative purpose, knowing that as she got further into her planning, she might change her mind. She saw that her instructor was to be her *audience* and that the *special requirements* of length and time were given in the assignment.

Casey read his assignment to analyze his writing situation. He saw immediately that most elements were stated. The *topic* was commercialization of holidays in the United States, and the *purpose* persuasive because students were expected to adopt and argue a position about the topic. The *audience* was the instructor, though Casey realized that the class might hear or see earlier drafts once the final draft was finished. The *special requirements* of length and time were given in the assignment.

EXERCISE 2-1

Consulting section 2b, for each assignment listed below, answer these questions: (a) Is its purpose to inform or to persuade? (b) Is the audience the general reading public or specialists? (c) What special requirements of length and time are stated or implied?

1. *English:* Write a 500- to 700-word essay arguing for or against doubling the size of your college's student body. This assignment is due in one week.

2. *Journalism:* Write a 300-word editorial for the student newspaper (to be published next week) praising or criticizing your college's policy on selling parking stickers to students and faculty. Draw on your personal experience, if any.

3. *Art:* You have twenty minutes in class to compare and contrast Greek and Roman styles of architecture.

4. *Chemistry:* Write a one-paragraph description of the process of hydration.

5. *Economics:* Write a 1,000-word essay on the broad impact of capitalism since 1989 on the former communist nations of Eastern Europe. Draw on your reading. This assignment is due in two weeks.

Choosing a topic for writing   2c

Choosing a topic calls for making sound decisions. Experienced writers know that the quality of their writing depends on how they handle a topic. Always think through a topic before you rush in and get too deeply involved to pull out within the time allotted.

Of course, some assignments leave no room for making choices about the topic. You may be given very specific instructions such as "Explain how oxygen is absorbed from the lungs," or you may be asked to describe the view from your classroom window. Your job with such assignments is to do precisely what is asked and not wander off the topic.

Selecting a topic on your own   2c-1

Some instructors ask students to choose their own topic. In such situations, do not assume that all subjects are suitable for college writing. Academic settings call for topics that can reflect your ability to think ideas through. For example, the old reliable essay about a summer vacation is probably not safe territory for a college essay if you have nothing extraordinary to report. Your essays need to dive into issues and concepts, and they should demonstrate that you can use specific, concrete details to support what you want to say.

When you choose a topic on your own, avoid topics so narrow that they give you little to say. For example, you would likely reach a dead end if you tried to write a 2,500-word essay about what your sleeping cat looks like.

ANSWERS: EXERCISE 2–1, *cont.*
technicalities concerning the functioning of college libraries. The special requirements include a 300-word limit, the need to draw on personal experience, and the need to interview a library staff member. The student should ask the instructor when the assignment is due.

5. The purpose is to inform. Because the assignment is only one paragraph and is for an art class, chances are high that the audience is the course instructor and perhaps other students in the class. An assumption of some specialized knowledge is appropriate (unless the instructor says to write the material for people totally unfamiliar with the topic). The special requirements include the one-paragraph limit and, perhaps implied by the wording of the assignment, in-class writing.

REFERENCES TO SUPPLEMENTS

For this topic in the CLAST writing competency test, refer students to ch. 2, section A5a of *Preparing for the CLAST* by S. Patterson.

This topic is included in the TASP writing competency test. Refer students to *Preparing for the TASP* by M. Saenz.

For more on selecting a topic, see *Teaching Writing: Prentice Hall Resources for Composition* by P. Hastings, ch. 5, "Stage One: Surveying Topics."

QUOTATION ABOUT WRITING

The best time for planning . . . is when you're doing the dishes.

—Agatha Christie

REFERENCES TO SUPPLEMENTS

For this topic in the CLAST writing competency test, refer students to ch. 2, section A3 of *Preparing for the CLAST* by S. Patterson.

TEACHING TIP: COLLABORATION

In both workplace and college settings, writers may team up to develop a single document. If you assign multi-author/single-document projects, remind students that in this writing situation, planning a collaboratively written document takes more time than planning a single-author document. Sharing each member's perspectives and synthesizing everyone's into a workable group project requires more time during the planning stage.

When two or three students write a paper together, they usually see the need to articulate the *how* and *why* of every dimension of the writing task from topic selection to word choice. This on-going discussion within collaborative groups about their writing encourages them to view effective writing as a process within each individual's conscious control.

TEACHING TIP

The concept of a "writing situation" might be new to many students. It is an inclusive term for the combination of topic, purpose, audience, and special requirements such as word or time limits. Each of these four variables influences every decision a writer makes. You might want to ask your students to memorize that short list of key variables: TOPAS (with the two letters "to" for "topic") can be an easy memory device for students. These variables are especially important in narrowing a topic, as demonstrated by the inclusion of "writing situation" in the examples for narrowing a topic.

2c-2

Narrowing an assigned topic

The real challenge in dealing with topics comes when you have a very broad subject. You have to *narrow the subject. Narrowing* means thinking of subdivisions of the subject, of different areas within the subject. Most very broad subjects can be broken down in hundreds of ways, but you need not think of all of them. When one seems possible, think it through at the start so that you can decide whether you can develop it well in writing. **What separates most good writing from bad is the writer's ability to move back and forth between general statements and specific details.**

For example, if the subject is marriage, you might narrow it to what makes marriages successful. But you cannot depend merely on generalizations such as "In successful marriages husbands and wives learn to accept each other's faults." You need to explain why accepting faults is important, and you need to give concrete illustrations of what you are talking about.

As you narrow a broad subject to obtain a writing topic, keep in mind the writing situation (see 2b) of each assignment. Think about what topics are possible and which of these you can handle well.

SUBJECT	*Music*
WRITING SITUATION	freshman composition class
	informative purpose
	instructor as audience
	500 words, one week
POSSIBLE TOPICS	the moods music creates
	classical music of the Renaissance
	country western music as big business
SUBJECT	*Cities*
WRITING SITUATION	sociology course
	persuasive purpose
	students and then instructor as audience
	500 to 700 words, one week
POSSIBLE TOPICS	comforts of city living
	discomforts of city living
	why city planning is important
SUBJECT	*Mythology*
WRITING SITUATION	humanities course
	informative purpose
	instructor, a specialist in mythology, as audience
	1,000 words, two weeks

POSSIBLE TOPICS   the purpose of myths

comparison of Navajo and Roman myths

explaining why seasons change

Carol Moreno narrowed the topic of her assignment (see page 20) because "a challenge you faced and tried to meet" was too vague and general. To stimulate her thinking, Moreno used some of the techniques for gathering ideas presented in the rest of this chapter. She used an entry from her journal (shown in 2e), freewriting (in 2f), and mapping (in 2i). As a result, Moreno decided to write about her need to build up her strength and stamina. Her essay is discussed in Chapter 3 as it evolves through three drafts, all of which are shown in section 3f.

Daniel Casey did not have to narrow his topic because it was stated in his assignment (see page 20): the commercialization of holidays in the United States. He did, however, have to choose a position to argue on the topic. What helped him the most were brainstorming (see his work in 2g), asking the "journalist's questions" (see his work in 2h), and using a subject tree (see his work in 2l). The development of Casey's essay is discussed in Chapter 6, and his final draft appears in section 6i.

EXERCISE 2-2

Consulting section 2c, for five of these general topics, think of three narrowed topics that would be suitable for a 500- to 700-word essay in a writing course. Assume that each essay is due in one week and that the audience is the general reading public, as represented by the course's instructor. List your three narrowed topics and explain briefly why each is suitable for the writing situation. Then repeat the exercise using an interesting topic not on this list.

1. clichés
2. television violence
3. music
4. ethnic identity
5. daydreaming
6. Valentine's Day
7. the Internet
8. self-improvement
9. cost of textbooks
10. humor

Gathering ideas for writing   2d

Techniques for gathering ideas, sometimes called *prewriting strategies* or *invention techniques,* can help you discover how much you know about a topic before you decide to write about it. Chart 8 on the next page lists various ways to gather ideas and refers to the sections in this handbook where you can find others.

BACKGROUND

In his article "To Be Read" (*English Journal* 57 [May 1968]: 686–692; rpt. *Rhetoric and Composition: A Sourcebook for Teachers and Writers,* ed. Richard L. Graves [Portsmouth, NH: Boynton/Cook, 1984]), Ken Macrorie discusses, among other issues, ways to help students arrive at a topic worth their effort. He begins by asking them for freewriting that strives to be honest (in contrast to phony), followed by discussion of strong passages that seem to speak the truth, a slowly developing focus on one subject, an effort to tighten the expression, and then an extension of the discussion to a full-length writing. By acting as editor instead of "grader" or "corrector," the teacher establishes a situation closer to that in which "real" writing takes place. Macrorie describes traditional "themes," papers assigned by teachers on topics that have no context, as papers that are "not meant to be *read,* but *corrected.*"

ANSWERS: EXERCISE 2–2

Answers will vary, but each topic should have an explanation of why it would be suitable for the writing situation described in the exercise.

REFERENCE TO SUPPLEMENTS

For more on the writing process, see *Teaching Writing: Prentice Hall Resources for Composition* by P. Hastings, ch. 5, "Stage Two: Inventing, Exploring, Observing, Collecting, Investigating."

BACKGROUND

Writers, both amateurs and professionals, tend to devise rituals that help them begin and carry out a piece of writing. Some of them are elaborate, some of them relatively simple. They are identifiable by the fact that they are repeated actions that seem to be irrelevant to the task at hand but that are in some way helpful to the writer looking for ideas and ways to express them. Some are silly, such as using the same coffee mug each time one writes, or illogical, such as sweeping the front walk before getting started, but the fact is that they are effective in helping a writer make the transition from some other activity to that of composition.

Writers who are in the process of devising writing rituals can make their individual habits more productive by being aware of which steps are helpful and which are not. They can begin by asking themselves questions about where, when, and with what they write. Where do they get the most work done? Does it afford them access to materials they need? Is it free from interruptions? Does it make them comfortable but not too relaxed? Can they see well? Do they have room to spread out notes and books? What time of day or night do they usually do their writing? Are they alert and energetic at that time? Does it give them a block of time in which to work? Do they use a typewriter? A legal pad? A word processor? A spiral notebook? What objects, environments, or activities that are not directly connected with writing provide a sense of well-being during the process? The answers will vary from one writer to another, but for best results the process should remain fairly constant with the individual.

Rituals are habits that provide structure—reassurance that the writer has done a task this way once before. With each repetition they become more comfortable, making the writer feel more competent, more at home with the act of writing.

WAYS TO GATHER IDEAS FOR WRITING   8

- Keeping an idea book (see 2e)
- Writing in a journal (see 2e)
- Freewriting (see 2f)
- Brainstorming (see 2g)
- Using the journalist's questions (see 2h)
- Mapping (see 2i)
- Reading (see 1e and Chapter 5)
- Incubating (see 2j)

Students sometimes worry that they have nothing to write about. Often, however, students know far more than they give themselves credit for. The challenge is to uncover what is there but seems not to be. As you use these various techniques for gathering ideas, find out which work best for *you* and *your* style of thinking.

No one technique of generating ideas always works for all topics. Experiment. If one method does not provide enough useful material, try another. Also, even if one strategy produces some good material, try another to turn up additional possibilities.

! ❖ COMPUTER TIPS: Using a computer, you can record your thoughts as they occur to you. Try freewriting (2f) or brainstorming (2g). Also, consider using invisible writing by dimming the screen so that you cannot see what you are writing. This helps you avoid the temptation to edit while you are getting your ideas down. After a while, brighten the screen to look at what you wrote.

As you use idea-gathering techniques, do not delete material. You never know what you might want later. A computer can save everything together for you and then retrieve it when you are ready to decide which material you might use and in what order. ❖

2e

Keeping an idea book and writing in a journal

Your ease with writing will grow as you develop the habits of mind that typify writers. Professional writers are always on the lookout for ideas to write about and for details to develop their ideas. They listen, watch, talk with people, and generally keep their minds open. Many writers always carry an **idea book**—a pocketsize notebook—to jot down ideas that spring to mind. Good ideas can melt away like snowflakes. Use an idea book throughout your college years, and watch your powers of observation increase.

Many writers, both amateur and professional, write in a **journal.** Keeping a journal gives you the chance to have a "conversation on paper" with yourself. Fifteen minutes a day can be enough—before going to bed, between classes, on a bus. *You* are your audience, so the content and tone can be as personal and informal as you wish.

Unlike a diary, a journal is not merely for listing what you did that day. A journal is for your thoughts. You can draw on your reading, your observations, your dreams. You can respond to quotations, react to movies or plays, or think through your opinions, beliefs, and tastes. Writing is a way of discovering, of allowing thoughts to emerge as the physical act of writing moves along.

Keeping a journal can help you in three ways. First, writing every day gives you the habit of productivity. The more you write, the more you get used to the feeling of words pouring out of you onto paper, the easier it will become for you to write in all situations. Second, a journal instills the habit of close observation and thinking. Third, a journal serves as an excellent source of ideas when you need to write in response to an assignment.

Here is an excerpt of a journal entry Carol Moreno had written before she got the assignment to write an essay about facing a challenge (see page 20). When reading through her journal for ideas for her essay, Moreno realized that she had faced the challenge of needing to develop more strength and stamina.

> September 30 I got to add 5 more reps today and it's only the sixth weight lifting class. I wasn't really surprised— I can tell I'm stronger. I wonder if I'm strong enough yet to lift Gran into the wheelchair alone. I was so scared last summer when I almost dropped her. Besides being terrified of hurting her, I thought that somehow the admissions committee would find out and tell me I was too weak to be accepted into nursing school. What if I hadn't noticed the weight lifting course for P.E. credit!?! Weight lifting is the best exercise I've ever done and I'm not getting beefy looking either.

Excerpt from Carol Moreno's Journal

TEACHING TIP: COLLABORATION

If you have assigned students a collaborative paper, you'll need to emphasize the importance of choosing a topic to which everyone in the group agrees. *Consensus* rather than *majority rule* is the key to successful collaboration. A student left out of the initial decision may feel no subsequent commitment to the group effort.

QUOTATION ABOUT WRITING

Writing is just having a sheet of paper, a pen and not a shadow of an idea of what you're going to say.

—Françoise Sagan

TEACHING TIP

Students may be surprised to learn that all writers find the blank sheet of paper (or empty computer screen) a source of anxiety. The experienced writer knows that the most effective way to move past that feeling is to write *something*, regardless of its value. Once the clean surface has words on it, other words follow more easily. Unrelated ideas, notes, questions, examples—all help to relieve the writer's discomfort with getting started. A good habit to cultivate is to jot down responses and reactions to writing tasks as soon as they are given.

QUOTATION ABOUT WRITING

Looking back, I imagine I was always writing. Twaddle it was too. But better far write twaddle or anything, anything, than nothing at all.

—Katherine Mansfield

REFERENCE TO SUPPLEMENTS

For prewriting and drafting techniques in a computer classroom, see *Computers and Writing: Prentice Hall Resources for Composition* by D. Rodrigues.

BACKGROUND

Much of what we know about the composing processes of students comes from the work of three researchers and their colleagues. James Britton in Britain's School Council Project *The Development of Writing Abilities, 11–18* (London: Macmillan Education, 1975) found that "writing is a deliberate act; one has to make up one's mind to do it." Once we decide to write, he points out, we begin the process by prewriting, which involves our trying to understand and solve a particular writing problem. Also fundamental to our current understanding of the writing process is the work of Janet Emig, reported in *The Composing Processes of Twelfth Graders* (NCTE Research Report No. 13 [Urbana: NCTE, 1971]). As the title suggests, she followed in detail the methods of high school seniors as they made their way through writing tasks. Finally, John R. Hayes and Linda S. Flower have provided a model for other researchers with their "thinking aloud" protocols, verbal descriptions of what writers report they think and do while they compose ("Identifying the Organization of Writing Processes" and "The Dynamics of Composing: Making Plans and Juggling Constraints," *Cognitive Processes in Writing*, ed. Lee W. Gregg and Erwin R. Steinberg [Hillsdale, N.J.: Lawrence Erlbaum Associates, 1980], pp. 3–50). Although the methods and terminology of these investigators vary, they arrive at fundamental agreement about the writing process.

2f Freewriting

Freewriting is writing nonstop about anything. It means writing down whatever comes into your mind without stopping to worry about whether the ideas are good or the spelling is correct. When you freewrite, do nothing to interrupt the flow. Do not censor any thoughts or flashes of insight. Do not go back and review. Do not cross out. Some days your freewriting might seem mindless, but other days it can reveal interesting ideas to you.

Freewriting helps get you used to the "feel" of pen moving across paper or of fingers in constant motion at a computer. Freewriting works best if you set a goal: perhaps writing for fifteen minutes or filling one or two pages. Keep going until you reach that goal, even if you have to write one word over and over until a new word comes to mind.

If you write on a computer, you can avoid the temptation to stop and criticize your writing by doing "invisible writing." Dim the screen so that you cannot see your writing. The computer will still be recording your ideas, but you will not be able to see them until you brighten the screen again. To create the same effect writing by hand, use a worn-out ballpoint pen and a piece of carbon paper between two sheets of paper.

Focused freewriting means starting with a set topic. You can focus your freewriting in any way—perhaps on a phrase from your journal or a quotation you like. Using the focus as a starting point, write until you meet the time or page limit you have set as a goal. Again, do not censor what you say. Keep moving forward.

Like journals, freewriting can be a source for ideas and details to write about. Carol Moreno wanted to explore the topic of her having

> Pumping iron—what the steroid jocks call it and exactly what I DO NOT want to be—a muscle cube. Great that Prof. Moore told us women's muscles don't bulk up much unless a weight lifting program is really intense—they just get longer. No bulk for me PLEASE. Just want upper body strength—oh and the aerobic stuff from swimming, which makes me feel great. Lift sweat swim, lift sweat swim, lift sweat swim.

Excerpt from Carol Moreno's Freewriting

learned to lift weights. She felt it had potential for her essay assignment (on page 20). On the bottom of the opposite page is an excerpt from her focused freewriting on "pumping iron."

EXERCISE 2-3

Consulting section 2f, freewrite for five minutes on one of these topics. Then think of an interesting topic not on this list, and freewrite on that topic.

1. pizza
2. procrastinating
3. a dream vacation
4. meeting deadlines
5. playing a sport
6. telling jokes
7. libraries
8. chocolate
9. falling in love
10. world peace

Brainstorming   2g

Brainstorming means listing all the ideas that come to mind associated with a topic. The ideas can be listed as words, phrases, or even random sentences. Let your mind range freely, generating quantities of ideas before eliminating some. You can brainstorm in one concentrated session or over several days, depending on how much time is available for the assignment. In courses that permit collaborative work, brainstorming in groups can work especially well because one person's ideas bounce off the next person's, and collectively more ideas get listed.

Brainstorming has two steps: First, you make a list, and then you try to find patterns in the list and ways to group the ideas into categories. Set aside any items that do not fit into groups. If an area interests you but its list is thin, brainstorm on that area alone. If you run out of ideas, ask yourself questions to stimulate your thinking. You might try exploratory questions about the topic, such as: What is it? What is it the same as? How is it different? Why or how does it happen? How is it done? What caused it or results from it? What does it look, smell, sound, feel, or taste like?

Daniel Casey's essay, discussed in Chapter 6, develops an argument concerning the benefits of the commercialization of holidays. For Casey's final draft, see section 6i. Realizing that his position was open to debate, Casey used the technique of brainstorming to help himself think through his opinion. On the next page is an excerpt from the ideas as they came to Casey at random. The items followed by an asterisk (*) are those Casey chose for the fourth paragraph—about the spirit of the holidays—of his essay, shown in section 6i.

BACKGROUND
In "Toward a Phenomenology of Freewriting" (*Journal of Basic Writing* 8 [Fall 1989]: 42–71), Peter Elbow discusses why freewriting is fundamental to his work. He explains that it helps him as a writer and as a teacher because it allows him to move "more easily and fully" into writing and thinking.

TEACHING TIP: COLLABORATION
Recent research on small group dynamics suggests that the quality and number of ideas generated by invention is enhanced by having group members first engage individually in such planning activities as mapping, clustering, and focused freewriting before coming together for group brainstorming. During group brainstorming, collaborative groups should elect a "scribe" to record all reactions and ideas that surface as the group discusses its approach to an assignment.

Sometimes the group will decide to narrow its focus to one of the ideas suggested during a brainstorming session. Before the group pursues its topic any further, you might repeat the individual-first, group-second planning process on the new, narrower idea.

QUOTATION ABOUT WRITING
Writing is no trouble: you just jot down ideas as they occur to you. The jotting is simplicity itself—it is the occurring which is difficult.

—Stephen Leacock

EXCERPT FROM DANIEL CASEY'S BRAINSTORMED LIST

people feel cheerful*
the economy is stimulated
people give to charities
strangers exchange friendly greetings*
everyone gives and gets gifts
children love visiting Santa (and the Easter Bunny)*
festive atmosphere in stores*
sending greeting cards helps friends stay in touch*
arouses positive sentimental feelings
stimulates good will

EXERCISE 2-4

Here is a brainstormed list for an assignment in a business class on ways to get the public to go see a new movie. Consulting section 2g, look over the list, and then group ideas. Some ideas may not fit into any group.

coming attractions	suspense
TV ads	book the movie was based on
provocative	locations
movie reviews	rating
how movie was made	adventure
sneak previews	newspaper ads
word of mouth	stars
director	dialogue
topical subject	excitement
special effects	photography
personal interviews	

EXERCISE 2-5

Consulting section 2g, brainstorm on a subject that interests you. First, make a list, and then group ideas within the list. If you cannot think of a subject, use one from Exercise 2-2 or Exercise 2-3.

TEACHING TIP

I've had great success asking students to write at least one journal entry a week that responds to (*not* summarizes) something that they have read. Students should include a photocopy of the article or pages from the book they've read. On the first day of class I show them a photocopy and sample entry as a model.

ANSWERS: EXERCISE 2–4

Class discussion will likely reveal disagreement about the main categories and the distribution of items. You can emphasize the role of the individual writer as decision maker. The list might be arranged in this way:

A. *Appeals of advertisement*: Celebrities (as salespeople), self-esteem (appeal to), sex appeal, suitability for readership, status symbols, level of sophistication
B. *Use of color*: black and white vs. color, stimulates senses
C. *Language*: amount of writing, connotations of words, intentional misuse of English, witty language, facts, slogans
D. *Layout*: size of advertisement, placement of objects, product identification, grabs readers' attention, focal point, clarity of design
Note. Imagination and *creativity* do not fit because they are part of all these and thus too general.

ANSWERS: EXERCISE 2–5

Answers to this exercise will vary. The writer should be able to explain the principle that underlies each grouping.

Using the journalist's questions

Journalist's questions ask *Who? What? When? Why? Where? How?* Asking these questions forces you to approach a topic from several different perspectives.

Daniel Casey used the journalist's questions to explore and expand his thinking about specific benefits of the commercialization of holidays in the United States. His answers to the questions helped him decide that he had enough details to write an effective essay (for his final draft, see section 6i).

WHO   Who specifically benefits from the commercial aspects of holidays?

WHAT   What specific benefits result from commercialization of holidays?

WHEN   When specifically do beneficial holidays fall?

WHY   Why specifically do some people object to the commercial aspects of holidays?

WHERE   Where specifically can evidence of benefits be seen or felt?

HOW   How do specific commercial aspects of holidays create benefits?

EXERCISE 2-6

Consulting section 2h, ask the journalist's questions about one of these subjects: day-care centers, watching soap operas, eating junk food, or shoplifting. Then think of an interesting topic not on this list, and ask the journalist's questions about that topic.

Mapping   2i

Mapping, also called *clustering* or *webbing*, similar to brainstorming (see 2g), is more visual and less linear. Many writers find that mapping frees them to think more creatively by associating ideas more easily.

To map, start with your topic circled in the middle of a sheet of unlined paper. Next, draw a line radiating out from the center and label it with the name of a major subdivision of your topic. Circle it and from that circle radiate out to more specific subdivisions. When you finish with one major subdivision of your subject, go back to the center and start again with another major division. As you go along, add anything that occurs to you for any section of the map. Continue the process until you run out of ideas. Mapping can also be used like a subject tree (see 2l) to lay out the logical relationships of ideas to each other. But many writers seem to prefer to use mapping for discovering ideas already known but not remembered, as Carol Moreno did. You use the techniques as they suit you best.

Individuals sometimes feel constrained to one answer when asking "Who?" "What?" "When?" "Where?" "Why?" and "How?" thus narrowing their focus too early during planning. But groups are more likely to come up with many *who*s, *what*s, *when*s, *where*s, and so forth. A group thinking about, for example, "paying college athletes" might see as affected groups (the *who*s)—the college athletes themselves, coaches, high school athletes, professional teams, families of student athletes, other students, college faculty, and alumni. An individual brainstorming on the same topic might well compose a shorter list. Clearly, two or more heads are better than one when generating ideas.

(When assigning collaborative projects, you may want to direct students' attention to chart 146 in Chapter 36b, "Guidelines for Collaborative Writing.")

ANSWERS: EXERCISE 2–6

Each student will come up with a different response, but each one should be encouraged to write as detailed an answer as possible. Here is a sample response for item 2, *watching soap operas:*

who?—housewives, college students of both sexes, an increasing number of males of all ages, unsupervised young children; *what?*—watching soap operas regularly; *where?*—everywhere from office lounges in companies to college dorm rooms and nursing homes; *how?*—some for whole afternoons, some for selective viewing of only one or two shows, some openly, some secretly; *why?*—to escape reality, perhaps, or possibly simply to relax regularly or to keep up with peers' interests.

Here is Carol Moreno's mapping for ideas to use in her essay about women lifting weights (for the three drafts of her essay, see section 3f). After Moreno finished mapping, she was satisfied that she had enough information to use in her essay.

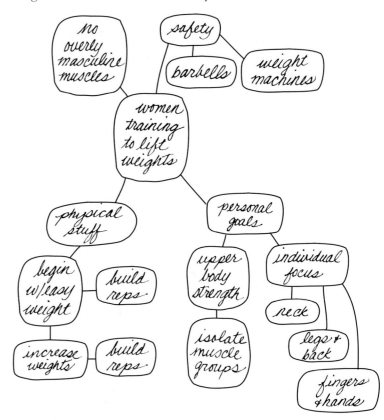

Carol Moreno's Mapping

EXERCISE 2-7

For a topic you have some information about, use mapping to chart what you know. Write the topic in the middle of a blank page, and work out from there.

Using incubation

When you allow your ideas to **incubate,** you give them time to grow and develop. Incubation works especially well when you need to solve a problem in your writing (for example, if material is too thin and needs expansion, if material covers too much and needs pruning, or if connections among your ideas are not clear for your reader). Time is a key element for successful incubation. Arrange your time to make sure that you will not be interrupted. You need time to think, to allow your mind to wander, and then to come back and focus on the writing. Sometimes incubating an idea overnight permits sleep to help you discover or clarify an idea.

One helpful strategy is to turn attention to something entirely different from your writing problem. Concentrate *very hard* on that entirely different matter so that your conscious mind is totally distracted from the writing problem. After a while, relax and guide your mind back to the writing problem you want to solve.

Another strategy is to allow your mind to relax and wander, without concentrating on anything special. Open your mind to random thoughts, but do not dwell on any one thought very long. After a while, guide your mind back to the writing problem you are trying to solve. When you come back to the writing problem, you might see solutions that did not occur to you before.

Shaping ideas   2k

Shaping activities are related to the idea that writing is often called *composing,* the putting together of ideas to create a *composition,* one of the synonyms for *essay.* To shape the ideas that you have gathered about your topic, you need to group them (see 2l) and sequence them (see 2m).

As you shape ideas, keep in mind that the form of an essay is related to the classical notion of a story's having a beginning, a middle, and an end. An academic essay always has an introduction, a body, and a conclusion. The length of each paragraph is in proportion to the overall length of the essay. Introductory and concluding paragraphs are generally shorter than body paragraphs, and no body paragraph should overpower the others by its length. (Types of paragraphs useful for academic writing are discussed in Chapter 4.)

Grouping ideas   2l

When you group ideas, you make connections and find patterns. To do this, put each batch of related ideas into its own group. As you create groups, use the concept of **levels of generality** to help you make decisions: One idea is more general than another if it falls into a larger, less specific category than the other. Remember that *generality* is a relative term. Each idea exists in the context of a whole relationship of ideas. An idea may be general in relationship to one set of ideas but specific in relation to another set. For example, "bank account" is more

21
cont.

general than "checking account." In turn, "checking account" is more general than "business checking account" or "regular checking account." And those terms are more general than "account 221222 at the EZ-Come-EZ-Go Bank."

To identify groups of ideas, review the material you accumulated while gathering ideas (see 2e through 2j). Look for general ideas. Then, group less general ideas under them. If your notes contain only general ideas, or only very specific details, return to techniques for gathering ideas to supply what you need. A standard tool for grouping ideas is to make a "subject tree" to see whether you have enough content to write about. A subject tree resembles a map (see 2i): It shows ideas and details in order from most general at the top to most specific at the bottom.

Daniel Casey used a subject tree while shaping his essay that takes the position that benefits result from the commercialization of holidays in the United States (for his final draft, see section 6i). He used the subject tree to lay out the ideas in his third paragraph according to their relative levels of generality. You can write out a subject tree for single paragraphs and for checking the interrelationships of the ideas in a whole essay. You use the techniques as they suit you best.

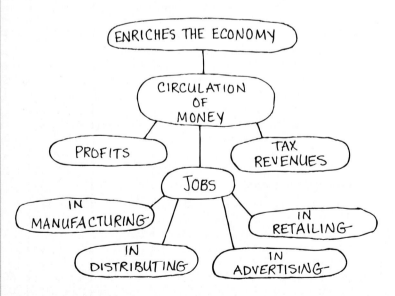

Daniel Casey's Subject Tree

plan **2**

Sequencing ideas for writing

2m

When you **sequence ideas** for writing, you decide what you want your readers to encounter first, second, and on until the last. When readers can follow your line of reasoning, they are more likely to understand the message that you want your material to deliver.

Within paragraphs, you can present ideas in any of the many ways explained in Chapter 4. Within an essay, the sequence in which you put those paragraphs reveals to your reader your evolving material. No one sequence or structure fits all college essays, but certain elements are usually present. For the major elements in essays with a persuasive purpose, see Chart 41 in section 6c. When you write essays with an informative purpose, be sure to include the elements in Chart 9. (The final draft of Carol Moreno's essay in 3f includes them.)

TYPICAL ELEMENTS IN AN ESSAY WITH AN INFORMATIVE PURPOSE   9

---

1. **Introductory paragraph:** leads into the topic of the essay, trying to capture the reader's interest. (For a discussion of introductory paragraphs, see 4g.)
2. **Thesis statement:** states the central message of the essay, accurately reflecting the essay's content. In an academic essay, the thesis statement usually appears at the end of the introductory paragraph. (For a discussion of thesis statements, see 2n.)
3. **Background information:** gives basic material, providing a context for the points being made in the essay. Depending on its complexity, this information appears in its own paragraph or is integrated into the introductory paragraph. (For an example of integrating background information into the introductory paragraph, see Daniel Casey's essay in 6i. For an example of a separate paragraph for background information, see Carol Moreno's essay in 3f.)
4. **Points of discussion:** support the essay's thesis, each consisting of a general statement backed up by specific details. This material forms the core of the essay, with each point occupying one or two paragraphs depending on the overall length of the essay. The general statements, seen as a group, comprise a "mini-outline" of the essay. The specific details bring the generalizations to life by using RENNS. (For a discussion of RENNS, see 4c.)
5. **Concluding paragraph:** ends the essay smoothly, not abruptly, flowing logically from the rest of the essay. (For a discussion of concluding paragraphs, see 4g.)

TYPICAL ELEMENTS IN AN ESSAY WITH AN INFORMATIVE PURPOSE

TEACHING TIP

Journal writing and freewriting are often unpopular with students at first, but on their end-of-the-semester evaluations of my classes, students consistently mention these activities as being among the most helpful in my course. Perhaps one of the reasons students resist at first is that they don't believe that journal writing and freewriting will not be corrected or graded. It is important, however, to respond to students' journals, although you should not feel obliged to read and respond to every entry of every journal. Responses should not be directive or critical but should create an informal dialogue with students that encourages them to discuss their ideas and experiences in greater depth and detail.

REFERENCE TO SUPPLEMENTS

For this topic in the CLAST writing competency test, refer students to ch. 2, section A5b of *Preparing for the CLAST* by S. Patterson.

REFERENCES TO SUPPLEMENTS

For this topic in the CLAST writing competency test, refer students to ch. 2, section A4 of *Preparing for the CLAST* by S. Patterson.

This topic is included in the TASP writing competency test. Refer students to *Preparing for the TASP* by M. Saenz.

For more on planning and shaping, see *Teaching Writing: Prentice Hall Resources for Composition* by P. Hastings, ch. 5, "Stage Three: Creating the Big Picture, Shaping, Planning, Goal-Setting, Formulating, Organizing."

See transparency 2–3 for useful classroom activities with a process approach to planning and shaping in the *Prentice Hall/Simon & Schuster Transparencies for Writers* by D. Carter.

BACKGROUND

On several occasions (e.g., "Understanding Composing," *CCC* 31 [December 1980]: 363–369), Sondra Perl has described the writing process as recursive, the several stages of planning, drafting, and revising occurring not in a straight, linear fashion, but doubling back on one another as the work takes shape. In the *New York University Education Quarterly* (1979), p. 18, she refers to the process as "retrospective structuring." "Composing," she writes, "does not occur in a straightforward, linear fashion. The process is one of accumulating discrete words or phrases down on the paper and then working from these bits to reflect upon, structure, and then further develop what one means to say." The reaching back and sensing forward have what she describes as "a clarifying effect," the written form serving, as it does, as a window on the intended meaning.

2n Shaping writing by drafting a thesis statement

A **thesis statement** is the central message of an essay. It is evidence that you have something definite to say about the topic. An effective thesis statement prepares your reader for the essence of what you discuss in an essay. As the writer, you want to compose a thesis statement with care so that it accurately reflects the content of your essay. If you find a mismatch between your thesis statement and the rest of your essay, revise to coordinate them better. The basic requirements for a thesis statement appear in Chart 10.

BASIC REQUIREMENTS FOR A THESIS STATEMENT   10

1. It states the essay's **subject**—the topic that you are discussing.

2. It reflects the essay's **purpose**—either to give your readers information or to persuade your readers to agree with you.

3. It includes a **focus**—your assertion that conveys your point of view.

4. It uses **specific language**—vague words are avoided.

5. It *may* briefly state the major subdivisions of the essay's topic.

Some instructors ask for more than the basic requirements. For example, you might be required to put your thesis statement at the end of your introductory paragraph. (For an example, see the final draft of Carol Moreno's essay in 3f.) Also, many instructors require that the thesis statement be contained in one sentence. Other instructors permit two sentences if the material to be covered warrants such length. All requirements, basic and additional, are designed to help you think in structured patterns that communicate clearly with readers. Be sure not to confuse a *title* (see 3c-2) with a thesis statement.

Until you have written one or more drafts, all parts of a thesis statement might not accurately reflect what you say in the essay. To begin, make an **assertion**—a sentence stating your topic and the point you want to make about it. The exact wording of this assertion probably will not appear in your final draft, but it serves as a focus for your thinking as you progress through a preliminary thesis statement toward a fully developed one.

To write her essay about women lifting weights, Carol Moreno used this progression from basic assertion to final thesis statement.

I think women can "pump iron" like men. [This assertion is a start.]

If she is trained well, any woman can "pump iron" well, just like a man. [This preliminary thesis is more developed because it mentions training, but the word *well* is used twice and is vague, and the word *any* is inaccurate.]

In spite of most people thinking only men can "pump iron," women can also do it successfully with the right training. [This draft is better because it is becoming more specific, but "most people thinking only men" is not an aspect of the topic Moreno intends to explore. Also, the concept of building strength, a major aspect of Moreno's final draft, is missing.]

With the right training, women can also "pump iron" successfully to build strength. [This is the final version of Moreno's thesis statement. *Also* is a transitional word connecting the thesis statement to the sentence that comes before it in Moreno's introductory paragraph.]

The final version fulfills the requirements for a thesis statement described in Chart 10.

Here are more examples of thesis statements, written for 500- to 700-word essays with an **informative purpose** (see section 1b-2). The ineffective versions resemble assertions or preliminary thesis statements. The effective versions are final thesis statements written by students after they had gathered and grouped ideas. The good versions fulfill the requirements in Chart 9.

TOPIC *classical music*

NO Classical music combines many different sounds.

YES Classical music can be played by groups of various sizes, ranging from chamber ensembles to full symphony orchestras.

TOPIC *malpractice suits*

NO There are many kinds of malpractice suits.

YES Most people are familiar with malpractice suits against physicians, but an increasing number of suits are being filed against lawyers, teachers, and even parents.

TOPIC *women artists*

NO The paintings of women are getting more attention.

YES During the past ten years the works of artists Mary Cassatt and Rosa Bonheur have finally gained widespread critical acclaim.

BACKGROUND

In his essay "Recent Developments in Rhetorical Invention" (*Teaching Composition: 12 Bibliographical Essays*, ed. Gary Tate [Fort Worth: Texas Christian UP, 1987], pp. 1–38), Richard Young classifies the theoretical bases for teaching invention into four main categories: classical invention, romantic invention, dramatism, and tagmemic invention. Classical invention refers to various systems based on the theories of ancient Greek and Roman rhetoricians such as Aristotle and Cicero. Romantic invention, associated with D. Gordon Rohman, tries to tap into the mysterious nonconscious and nonrational creative powers of the mind and often eschews formal methods of invention. Dramatistic invention is based on Kenneth Burke's pentad of agent, scene, act, agency, and purpose, first described in *A Grammar of Motives* (1945). Tagmemic invention is derived from Kenneth Pike's tagmemic linguistic theory, but it has its fullest realization in Richard Young, Alton Becker, and Kenneth Pike's *Rhetoric: Discovery and Change* (1950).

TEACHING TIP: COLLABORATION

Especially if their members have already engaged in individual prewriting activities, collaborative groups can benefit greatly from group mapping. If you can supply each group with large sheets of butcher paper, they can map out invention topics seated around a table. Or if your room has multiple chalkboards, supply your groups with enough chalk to map its ideas at one of the boards. When students map together, they can pool their resources for generating topic ideas and organizational strategies.

BACKGROUND

In "Writing as Process: How Writing Finds Its Own Meaning" (*Eight Approaches to Teaching Composition*, ed. Timothy Donovan and Ben McClelland [NCTE, 1980], pp. 3–20), Donald Murray discusses four forces that interact as the writer goes through the stages of rehearsing, drafting, and revising, moving in a recursive manner from exploration to clarification. They are the forces of collecting and connecting, writing and reading. Although writing may be ignited by any one of these forces in conjunction with any other, says Murray, once writing has begun, all of them begin to interact with each other. The writer is often unaware of this interaction, as innate curiosity leads naturally to the act of collecting information, which at some point calls for control and order that make the act of connecting necessary. Connections, in turn, make the writer see information in a new way, hence generating more collected data. The acts of writing and reading act in a similar fashion. The writer sets down what is heard mentally, then reads the product, checking it against what was heard, then rewrites it. Murray asserts that although each writing act is a complex, instantaneous interaction, the scale tips rapidly from one force to the other in response to the various needs of the writer dealing with rehearsing, drafting, or revising.

QUOTATION ABOUT WRITING

I like a room with a view, preferably a long view. I dislike looking out on gardens. I prefer looking at the sea, or ships, or anything which has a vista to it.
—Norman Mailer

BACKGROUND

Jeanette Harris explores the subject of invention in "Rethinking Invention" (*Freshman English News* 17 [Fall 1988]: 13–16). She calls for teachers to encourage students to include introspection and exploration of subjects in their heuristics.

For a persuasive purpose, Daniel Casey wrote this thesis statement for his essay about the commercialization of holidays in section 6i:

> After all, commercial uses of holidays benefit the economy and lift people's spirits.

Casey's thesis statement reveals that the *topic* is commercialization of holidays, the *purpose* is to persuade, and the *focus* is the benefits of holidays' commercial uses. For a discussion about how Casey moved from assertion to this final version, see 6i.

Here are ineffective and effective thesis statements written for 500- to 700-word essays with a **persuasive purpose.** The ineffective versions resemble some types of preliminary thesis statements. The effective versions are final thesis statements written by students after they had gathered and grouped ideas. For example, the material here on city living is built on one of the "possible topics" evolved from narrowing the large subject of cities (see 2c-2). The good versions fulfill the requirements in Chart 10.

TOPIC *discomforts of city living*

NO The discomforts of living in a modern city are many.

YES Rising crime rates, increasingly overcrowded conditions, and growing expenses make living comfortably in a modern city difficult.

TOPIC *government loans for higher education*

NO The federal government has inadequate loan programs for people seeking higher education.

YES Congress should enact a law setting up an education loan account for each U.S. citizen for college or for retraining.

TOPIC *deceptive advertising*

NO Deceptive advertising can cause many problems for consumers.

YES Deceptive advertising can cost consumers not only money but also their health.

The *No* examples of thesis statements shown above suffer from being too broad. They are so general that they offer no focus, and readers cannot predict the essay's thrust.

Another type of ineffective thesis statement results from an overly narrow focus. In such cases, the thesis statement is closer in scope to a topic sentence that begins a paragraph.

NO	The classical composer Béla Bartók was Hungarian.
YES	Although best-known today as a composer, Béla Bartók was also an important ethnomusicologist who studied Hungarian folk music in his native country as well as at Columbia University in New York.
NO	Car thefts on Silver Avenue between First and Second Streets are intolerable.
YES	Neighbors have overcome language obstacles and differences in customs to combat increasing car thefts on Silver Avenue.

EXERCISE 2-8

Each of the following sets of sentences offers several versions of a thesis statement. Within each set, the thesis statements progress from weak to strong. The fourth thesis statement in each set is the best. Based on the Basic Requirements listed in Chart 10, identify the characteristics of the fourth thesis statement in each set. Then explain why the other choices in each set are weak. (The first set relates to the material in Exercise 2-4.)

A. 1. Advertising is complex.
    2. Magazine advertisements appeal to readers.
    3. Magazine advertisements must be creative.
    4. To appeal to readers, magazine advertisements must skillfully use language, color, and design.
B. 1. Tennis is excellent exercise.
    2. Playing tennis is fun.
    3. Tennis requires various skills.
    4. Playing tennis for fun and exercise requires agility, stamina, and strategy.
C. 1. *Hamlet* is a play about revenge.
    2. Hamlet must avenge his father's murder.
    3. Some characters in *Hamlet* want revenge.
    4. In *Hamlet*, Hamlet, Fortinbras, and Laertes all seek revenge.
D. 1. Maintaining friendships requires work.
    2. To have good friends, a person must learn how to be a good friend.
    3. To be a good friend, a person must value the meaning of friendship.
    4. Unless a person is sensitive to others and communicates with them honestly, that person will not be able to build strong friendships.
E. 1. Many people are uninterested in politics.
    2. Adults have become increasingly dissatisfied with the political process.

ANSWERS: EXERCISE 2–8

A. The fourth thesis statement succeeds because it states a main idea (about magazine advertisements' appeal to readers); it reflects a purpose (to persuade); it has a focus (that magazine advertisements must be skillfully done); and it briefly presents subdivisions (language, color, and design). The first and second thesis statements are too general, showing neither a purpose nor a focus. The third thesis statement shows a persuasive purpose but is still too general and has no focus ("must" is not explained).

B. The fourth thesis statement succeeds because it states a main idea (about playing tennis for fun and exercise); it reflects a purpose (to inform); it has a focus (what is required for playing tennis for fun and exercise); and it briefly presents subdivisions (agility, stamina, and strategy). The first statement is too general ("excellent" is a very broad term) and shows no purpose or focus. The second statement is also too vague ("fun" is a very broad term when used without a context) and shows no purpose or focus. The third statement reflects an informative purpose but lacks a focus ("various skills" is too vague).

C. The fourth statement succeeds because it states a main idea (characters in *Hamlet* seek revenge); it reflects a purpose (to inform); it has a focus (all three characters seek revenge); and it briefly states the major subdivisions (Hamlet, Fortinbras, and Laertes). The first statement is much too general, and though it suggests an informative intent, the statement lacks a focus. The second and third

→

statements reflect an informative purpose but lack a focus ("must" and "want" are vague words here).

D. The fourth statement succeeds because it states a main idea (strong friendships); it reflects a purpose (to persuade); it has a focus (what builds strong friendships); and it briefly states the major subdivisions (sensitivity and communication). The first statement uses vague language ("maintaining" and "work"), and it suggests neither a persuasive nor informative intent. The second statement reflects a persuasive purpose but depends on "good" used in a vague sense. The third statement reflects a persuasive purpose but "value" is too vague to provide a focus.

E. The fourth statement succeeds because it states a main idea (college students voting); it reflects a purpose (to inform); and it has a focus (how these students voted in state primaries and state elections this year compared with the last two years). The first statement relies on too much vague language ("many," "people," "uninterested") and it lacks a purpose or focus. The second statement suggests an informative purpose, but it relies on vague language ("dissatisfied" and "political process") and it lacks a focus. The third statement suggests an informative purpose but lacks a focus.

ANSWERS: EXERCISE 2–9

1. The thesis is good because it reflects the purpose (to persuade), states a main idea, and focuses specifically on logical subdivisions of the topic.

2. The thesis suggests that the concert review will do what such reviews should do: evaluate in an attempt to persuade a reader. The words "was pleasing," however, are too vague; they need to be revised to be more specific. A brief indication of subdivisions might help the thesis communicate its message. →

3. Fewer adults than ever vote in local elections.
4. Fewer college students participated in state primaries and voted in state elections this year than in either of the last two elections.

EXERCISE 2-9

Here are writing assignments, narrowed topics, and tentative thesis statements. Evaluate each thesis statement according to the Basic Requirements in Chart 10.

1. **Marketing assignment:** 700- to 800-word persuasive report on the college's cafeteria. *Audience:* the instructor and the cafeteria's manager. *Topic:* cafeteria conditions. *Thesis:* The college cafeteria could attract more students if it improved the quality of its food, its appearance, and the friendliness of its staff.
2. **Music assignment:** 300- to 500-word review of a performance. *Audience:* the instructor and other students in the class. *Topic:* the local symphony's final spring concert. *Thesis:* The "Basically Beethoven" program that ended the local symphony's spring season was pleasing.
3. **Chemistry assignment:** 800- to 1,000-word informative report about the ozone layer. *Audience:* the instructor and visiting students and instructors attending a seminar at the State College. *Topic:* recent research on the ozone layer. *Thesis:* The United States should increase efforts to slow the destruction of the ozone layer.
4. **Journalism assignment:** 200- to 300-word article about campus crime. *Audience:* the instructor, the student body, and the college administration. *Topic:* recent robberies. *Thesis:* During the fall term, campus robberies at State College equaled the number of robberies that took place in the prior five years combined.
5. **Business writing assignment:** 400- to 500-word persuasive report about the career-counseling services of State College. *Audience:* college seniors, career counselors, and the instructor. *Topic:* job placement for seniors. *Thesis:* State College's liberal arts graduates are hired mainly by business and industry.

2o   Knowing how to outline

Many writers find outlining a useful planning strategy. If you are working from an outline and make changes in organization as you write, be sure to revise your outline at the end if you are expected to submit it as part of an assignment. An outline helps pull together the results of gathering and ordering ideas and preparing a thesis statement. It also provides a visual guide and checklist. Some writers always use outlines;

others prefer not to. Writers who do like outlines use them at various points in the writing process: for example, before drafting, to arrange material; during drafting, to keep track of evolving material; or while revising, to check the logic of an early draft's organization. Especially for academic writing, outlines can clearly reveal flaws: missing information, undesirable repetitions, digressions from the thesis. Some instructors require outlines because they want students to practice planning the arrangement and organization of a piece of writing.

An **informal outline** does not have to follow all the formal conventions of outlining. An informal outline is particularly useful for planning when the order within main ideas is still evolving or when topics imply their own arrangement, such as spatial arrangement for describing a room. An informal outline can also be considered a *working plan,* a layout of the major parts of the material intended for an essay. Here is part of an informal outline that served as a working plan for Carol Moreno when she was writing her essay on weight-lifting for women. (For Moreno's techniques of gathering ideas for writing, see 2e, 2f, and 2i; for the three drafts of her essay, see 3f.) This excerpt includes the essay's thesis statement and fourth paragraph.

Sample Informal Outline

Thesis Statement: With the right training, women can also "pump iron" for increased strength and stamina.

    using weights
        safety is vital
        free weights
            don't bend at waist
            do align neck and back
            do look straight ahead
        weight machines—safety is easier

❖ COMPUTER TIP: You can informally outline an essay on a computer, especially after one draft. Read what you have written, and put a symbol near what seems most important. Then, look over the marked parts, and copy them to the bottom of your text so that you can see them grouped together. Shuffle them into several different orders. Does it matter which part comes first, second, and so on? Are the parts equally important, or do some seem subordinate to others? Try indenting the subordinate parts to make a rough outline. ❖

A **formal outline** follows conventions concerning content and format. The conventions are designed to display material so that relationships among ideas are clear and so that the content is orderly. A formal outline can be a *topic outline* or a *sentence outline.* Each item in a topic outline is a word or phrase; each item in a sentence outline is a complete sentence. Formal outlines never mix the two.

REFERENCE TO SUPPLEMENTS

See transparencies 2–4, 2–5, and 3–3 through 3–9a for useful classroom activities on outlining, drafting, and revising in the *Prentice Hall/Simon & Schuster Transparencies for Writers* by D. Carter.

TEACHING TIP

Students can practice making outlines by dealing with published essays. They will sometimes discover that an essay lacks a clearly defined order, or, on the other hand, they may find ideas in the work that they missed before dividing it into its major headings and subheadings. You should prepare students for this exercise by composing an outline of one or two short essays with the class, perhaps including one essay without a well-defined organization. You may find it helpful to use an overhead projector for displaying the essay or writing the outline. Students can then prepare a topic outline or a sentence outline on a different essay. You might ask them to compare their outlines to see if they each found the same emphases and order of development.

QUOTATION ABOUT WRITING

Prose is architecture, not interior decoration.

—Ernest Hemingway

TEACHING TIP

You may want to ask your students to test their thesis statements by exchanging them with one another. By asking the readers to answer questions about the thesis statements, the writers may discover weaknesses (and strengths) that were not apparent to them. Some questions they can ask are the following:

1. Is the main idea, the central point, clearly stated?

2. Is the purpose of the essay clear?

3. What is the purpose: to inform or persuade?

4. What is the focus of the essay?

5. Does the thesis statement identify the major subdivisions of the essay's topic?

6. Does it make the topic seem interesting?

7. Can this thesis be developed in the time available?

8. Can this thesis be developed in an essay of the length planned?

9. Is the thesis limited enough for development, but general enough to be worth the effort?

10. Is the thesis stated in specific terms? Does it avoid overly general, vague ones?

BACKGROUND

For those teachers who encounter difficulty in following the various invention theories proposed by Kenneth Burke and Ken Macrorie, as well as by Richard Young, Alton Becker, and Kenneth Pike, help is available in Peggy Parris's "Helping Snoopy through the Dark and Stormy Night: Heuristics for Creative Writing" (*Iowa English Bulletin* 33 [1984]: 26–30). She discusses how Burke's pentad, Young, Becker, and Pike's tagmemic matrix, and Macrorie's freewriting can be used to teach creative writing.

Many writers who use formal outlines find that a sentence outline brings them closer to drafting than a topic outline does. For example, a topic outline carries less information with the item "Gathering information" than does a sentence outline with the corresponding item "Gathering information is the first step to being well-prepared."

Use Chart 11 for a summary of the conventions of formal outlining.

CONVENTIONS OF FORMAL OUTLINES   11

FORMAL OUTLINE PATTERN

Thesis Statement:

I. First main idea

   A. First subdivision of the main idea

      1. First reason or example

      2. Second reason or example

         a. First supporting detail

         b. Second supporting detail

   B. Second subdivision of the main idea

II. Second main idea

FORMAL OUTLINE GUIDELINES

1. Numbers, letters, and indentations signal groupings and levels of importance.

2. Each level has more than one entry.

3. All subdivisions are at the same level of generality.

4. Headings do not overlap.

5. Entries are grammatically parallel (see Chapter 18).

6. Only the first word of each entry is capitalized. (All proper nouns are also capitalized, of course.)

7. Periods end each sentence in a *sentence outline* but not the items in a *topic outline*.

8. The introductory and concluding paragraphs are omitted, but the thesis statement is usually given above the outline itself (see examples at end of this chapter).

---

1. **Numbers, letters, and indentations.** All parts of a formal outline are systematically indented and numbered or lettered. Capital roman numerals (I, II, III) signal major subdivisions of the topic. Indented capital letters (A, B) signal the next level of generality.

Further indented arabic numbers (1, 2, 3) show the third level of generality. Indented lowercase letters (a, b) show the fourth level, if there is one. The principle here is that within each major subdivision, each succeeding level of the outline shows more specific detail than the one before it. If an outline entry is longer than one line, the second line is indented as far as the first word of the preceding line.

2. **More than one entry at each level.** At all points on an outline, there is no I without a II, no A without a B, and so on. Unless a category has at least two parts, it cannot be divided. If a category has only one subdivision, you need to either eliminate that subdivision or expand the material to at least two subdivisions.

NO
    A. Free weights
        1. Safe lifting technique
    B. Weight machines

YES
    A. Free weights
    B. Weight machines

YES
    A. Free weights
        1. Unsafe lifting techniques
        2. Safe lifting techniques
    B. Weight machines

3. **Levels of generality.** All subdivisions are at the same level of generality. A main idea cannot be paired with a supporting detail.

NO
    A. Free weights
        1. Safe lifting techniques
    B. Weight machines

YES
    A. Free weights
    B. Weight machines

4. **Overlap.** Headings do not overlap. What is covered in subdivision 1, for example, must be quite distinct from what is covered in subdivision 2.

NO
    A. Free weights
        1. Unsafe lifting techniques
        2. Not aligning head and neck

YES
    A. Free weights
        1. Unsafe lifting techniques
        2. Safe lifting techniques

TEACHING TIP

If your students have trouble organizing an outline, you might suggest that they write each item on a 3 x 5 index card. The ability to move the cards around, make piles, and easily eliminate items often facilitates students' work.

BACKGROUND

In the chapter on "Shaping Discourse" in *A Rhetoric for Writing Teachers*, 2nd ed. (New York: Oxford UP, 1987, pp. 158–170), Erika Lindemann warns teachers and students against making inflexible writing plans that cause them to force ideas into a prescribed form. In particular, she points out that slavishly following an outline can limit a writer's options. It can, for example, prevent a writer from discovering the material's organic unity or from making choices that might improve the piece. Rigid adherence to an outline, says Lindemann, can create an inadequate and incomplete understanding of the paper, since an outline may offer little help in determining proportions or deciding on rhetorical strategies. In addition, it may also divert a writer from considering audience and purpose.

TEACHING TIP

Computers are increasingly helpful in organizing material and preparing outlines. Several software programs are commercially available for use in creating short outlines that can be expanded into more complex ones. They encourage experimentation with ideas and arrangements because they are flexible. Outlines can be quickly and easily expanded by the addition of subheadings or tightened by the removal of subheadings from the screen, though the writer can keep them available for possible inclusion.

2o cont.

TEACHING TIP

The notion of *focus* in a thesis statement might be new to some students. A useful analogy can be that the topic is the subject but the focus is the predicate. Without predication, sentences make no assertion. As Josephine Miles said in her important monograph "Working Out Ideas: Predication and Other Uses of Language": "Sentence making is predication, and to predicate is to assert an idea, selecting and treating facts from a point of view." Predication says something about, asserts something about, answers a question about, takes a position about the topic. It may, for example, define the topic, describe it, evaluate it, compare it to something, explain its purpose, or identify its causes. The topic of this section of the *S & S Handbook for Writers* is "a thesis statement." The predicate of the opening sentence of the section makes an assertion about "a thesis statement" by defining what one is—it "is the central message of an essay." A different predicate—for example, that a thesis statement "helps the writer focus the essay"—would change the focus, purpose, and direction of this section.

TEACHING TIPS

Writers use outlines in a variety of ways. They turn to them, for example, at different stages of the composing process. Whereas some find it productive to move from mapping or freewriting directly into a listing of ideas in a particular order, using the outline to plan the drafting process, others use outlines to check the organization of a draft after it is written, testing to see if the paper has order and balance. Some writers find topic outlines helpful; some prefer a sentence outline. Each writer has to find the shaping strategies that prove to be most effective in his or her case.

5. **Parallelism.** All entries within a level are parallel. For example, all might start with the *-ing* forms of VERBS.* (For more about parallelism in outlines, see 18h).

| NO | A. Free weights |
| | B. Using weight machines |

| YES | A. Free weights |
| | B. Weight machines |

| YES | A. Using free weights |
| | B. Using weight machines |

6. **Capitalization and punctuation.** Except for PROPER NOUNS, only the first word of each entry is capitalized. In a sentence outline, end each sentence with a period. Do not punctuate the ends of entries in a topic outline.

7. **Introductory and concluding paragraphs.** The content of the introductory and concluding paragraphs is not part of a formal outline. The thesis statement comes before (above) the roman numeral I entry.

Here is a topic outline of the final draft of Carol Moreno's essay on weight lifting for women (3f). A sentence outline starts on the opposite page so that you can compare the two types of outlines.

TOPIC OUTLINE

Thesis Statement: With the right training, women can also "pump iron" successfully for increased strength and stamina.

I. Avoiding massive muscle development
   A. Role of women's biology
      1. Not much muscle-bulking hormone
      2. Muscles get longer, not bulkier
   B. Role of combining exercise types
      1. Anaerobic (weight lifting)
      2. Aerobic (swimming)
II. Using weights safely
   A. Free weights
      1. Unsafe lifting technique
      2. Safe lifting technique
         a. Head alignment
         b. Neck and back alignment
   B. Weight machines (built-in safeguards)

*You can find the definition of a word printed in small capital letters (such as VERBS) in the Glossary of Terms toward the end of this handbook.

42

III. Individualizing the program based on physical condition
  A. Role of resistance and reps
  B. Characteristics considered for personalizing the program
    1. Weight
    2. Age
    3. Physical condition

IV. Individualizing the program for other reasons
  A. Upper body strength
  B. Individual objectives
    1. Mine
    2. Car-crash victim's
    3. Physical therapist's

SENTENCE OUTLINE

Thesis Statement: With the right training, women can also "pump iron" successfully for increased strength and stamina.

I. The right training lets women who life weights avoid developing massive muscles.
  A. Women's biology plays a role.
    1. Women don't produce much of a specific muscle-bulking hormone.
    2. Women's muscles tend to grow longer rather than bulkier.
  B. Combining exercise types plays a role.
    1. Anaerobic exercise, like weight-lifting, builds muscle.
    2. Aerobic exercise, like swimming, builds endurance and stamina.

II. The right training shows women how to use weights safely to prevent injury.
  A. Free weights require special precautions.
    1. Bending at the waist and jerking a barbell up is unsafe.
    2. Squatting and using leg and back muscles to straighten up is safe.
      a. The head is held erect and faces forward.
      b. The neck and back are aligned and held straight.
  B. Weight machines make it easier to lift safely because they force proper body alignment.

III. The right training includes individualized programs based on a woman's physical condition.

43

TEACHING TIP: JOURNALS FOR ESL STUDENTS

An activity that both ESL students and native speakers enjoy is the Exchange Journal. ESL students exchange entries on cultural matters with native speakers in a different class. In the first entry, students introduce themselves to their partners, perhaps including information like age, sex, marital status, place of birth, college major, hobbies or interests. They then list some topics they are interested in learning about. In each subsequent weekly or biweekly entry, students explain an aspect of their culture: dating, courtship, family structure, food, school, manners, holidays, language, sports, entertainment, and so on. Entries are as long as students want to make them. Instructors do not necessarily read the journals, and certainly do not correct them, but they may require a report about the experience at the end of the term (and perhaps interim reports). The two instructors pass the journals back and forth to each other to distribute in classes; they should also arrange for the students to meet and interview each other near the end of the term, if possible. The assignment helps break down stereotypes and develops students' fluency in writing; indeed, some students write considerably better in journals than in compositions.

  Note: Using two journals—one from ESL student to native speaker and one from native speaker to ESL student—makes it more convenient for students to write their reports. Blue books may be used for easy portability; when a student fills one, he/she can staple another to the back of the previous one.

QUOTATION ABOUT WRITING

In any work that is truly creative, I believe, the writer cannot be omniscient in advance about the effects that he [or she] proposes to produce. The suspense of a novel is not only in the reader, but in the novelist, who is intensely curious about what will happen to the hero.

—Mary McCarthy

A. Progress comes from resistance and from repetitions tailored to individual capabilities.
B. Programs consider a woman's physical characteristics.
   1. Her weight is considered.
   2. Her age is considered.
   3. Her physical conditioning is considered.

IV. The right training includes individualized programs based on a woman's personal goals.
   A. Certain muscle groups are targeted to increase women's upper body strength.
   B. Other muscle groups are targeted based on individual objectives..
      1. I wanted to strengthen muscles needed for lifting patients.
      2. An accident victim wanted to strengthen her neck muscles.
      3. A physical therapist wanted to strengthen her fingers and hands.

ALTERNATE EXERCISE

Write thesis statements for persuasive papers on the following topics, making sure that they have the five characteristics of a good thesis statement listed in the Basic Requirements chart.

1. Topic: rock music
2. Topic: athletic scholarships
3. Topic: ethnic foods
4. Topic: a holiday ritual
5. Topic: mothers and daughters

ANSWER: EXERCISE 2–10

Answer may vary from the following:

I. Sources of noise pollution
   A. Large cities
      1. Traffic
      2. Construction work
      3. Airplanes
   B. Workplace
      1. Factory machines
      2. Outdoor construction machines
   C. Leisure-time activities
      1. Stereo headphones
      2. Film soundtracks
      3. Disco music
II. Problems from noise pollution
   A. Damages hearing
   B. Alters moods
   C. Limits learning ability
III. How to reduce noise pollution
   A. Pressure from community groups
   B. Traffic regulations
   C. Pressure on management by workers
   D. Earplugs
   E. Reasonable sound levels

EXERCISE 2-10

Here is a sentence outline. Consulting section 2o, revise it into a topic outline. Then decide which form you would prefer as a guide to writing, and explain your decision.

Thesis Statement: Common noise pollution, although it causes many problems in our society, can be reduced.

I. Noise pollution comes from many sources.
   A. Noise pollution occurs in many large cities.
      1. Traffic rumbles and screeches.
      2. Construction work blasts.
      3. Airplanes roar overhead.
   B. Noise pollution occurs in the workplace.
      1. Machines in factories boom.
      2. Machines used for outdoor construction thunder.
   C. Noise pollution occurs during leisure-time activities.
      1. Stereo headphones blare directly into eardrums.
      2. Film soundtracks bombard the ears.
      3. Music in discos assaults the ears.

plan 2

II. Noise pollution causes many problems.
   A. Excessive noise damages hearing.
   B. Excessive noise alters moods.
   C. Constant exposure to noise limits learning ability.

III. Reduction in noise pollution is possible.
   A. Pressure from community groups can support efforts to control excessive noise.
   B. Traffic regulations can help alleviate congestion and noise.
   C. Pressure from workers can force management to reduce noise.
   D. People can wear earplugs to avoid excessive noise.
   E. Reasonable sound levels for headphones, soundtracks, and discos can be required.

BACKGROUND

Maxine Hairston states in "Different Products, Different Processes: A Theory about Writing" (*College Composition and Communication* [December 1986]: 442–452) that experienced writers employ different composing processes for different types of writing. Experienced writers generally give little thought to composing "routine maintenance or message writing"—brief notes and memos, lists, thank-you letters, and other short, simple writing that keeps "organizations and personal relationships functioning" (443). In extended "self-limiting" writing such as summaries, most reports, and essay examinations, writers know most of what they want to say and accomplish before they begin. Writers work mainly on organization, style, stance, and tone as they draft and revise, often following "traditional formulas," but skilled writers usually are able to complete these writing tasks easily and quickly, unless the paper is for a particularly important or difficult audience (444). "Extended reflective writing" is usually the most time-consuming and difficult but often the most satisfying to write. In these writings, writers make sense of their lives and their world and discover most of what they want to say only as they write. This kind of writing requires writers to "take risks because they are working at the edge of their abilities, operating in unfamiliar territory" (445). Writing courses, Hairston argues, should give students opportunities to practice self-limiting writing as well as reflective writing.

TEACHING TIP: COLLABORATION

Allow each group to develop its own drafting process. Some groups are happier if all members draft a separate section of the document that the group will merge together. Other groups prefer to have each member draft the entire document, with the group picking and choosing the best parts of each. If you have access to computers, you may also find that some groups prefer to huddle around a single computer and write the entire document together from the start.

3 Drafting and Revising

In the writing process, drafting and revising follow from planning and shaping, discussed in Chapter 2. **Drafting** means getting ideas onto paper in sentences and paragraphs. In everyday conversation, people usually use the word *writing* when they talk about the activities involved in drafting. In discussing the writing process, however, the word *drafting* is more descriptive. It conveys the idea that the final product of the writing process is the result of a number of versions, each successively closer to what the writer intends and to what will communicate clearly to readers. **Revising** means taking a draft from its preliminary to its final version by evaluating, adding, cutting, moving material, editing, and proofreading.

3a Getting started

If ever you have trouble getting started when the time arrives for drafting (or any other part of the writing process), you are not alone. When experienced writers get stalled, they recognize what is happening and deal with it. If you run into a writing block, it may be the result of one of these common myths about writing.

MYTH Writers are born, not made.

TRUTH Everyone can write. Writers do not expect to "get it right" the first time. Being a good writer means being a patient rewriter.

MYTH Writers have to be "in the mood" to write.

TRUTH If writers always waited for "the mood" to descend, few would write at all. After all, news reporters and other professional writers often have to meet deadlines.

REFERENCES TO SUPPLEMENTS

For teaching drafting and revising in a computer classroom, see *Computers and Writing: Prentice Hall Resources for Composition* by D. Rodrigues.

For this topic in the CLAST writing competency test, refer students to ch. 2, section B6 of *Preparing for the CLAST* by S. Patterson.

For teaching revision with a peer critiquing approach, see P. Kelvin/S. Leonard, "Teaching Collaborative Writing," in L. Julian, et al., *Strategies and Resources for Teaching Writing with the Simon & Schuster Handbook for Writers*.

REFERENCE TO SUPPLEMENTS

For more information on helping students write good first drafts, see *Teaching Writing: Prentice Hall Resources for Composition* by P. Hastings, ch. 5, "Stage Four: Writing the Draft."

QUOTATION ABOUT WRITING

Writing is a deliberate act; one has to make up one's mind to do it.

—James Britton

MYTH   Writers have to know how to spell every word and to recite the rules of grammar perfectly.

TRUTH   Writers do not let spelling and grammar block them. They write and then check themselves. A good speller is someone who does not ignore the quiet inner voice that urges checking a dictionary. Similarly, writers use a handbook to check grammar rules.

MYTH   Writers do not have to revise.

TRUTH   Writers expect to revise. Once words are on paper, writers can see what readers see. This "re-vision" helps writers revise so that their writing delivers its intended message.

MYTH   Writing can be done at the last minute.

TRUTH   Drafting and revising take time. Ideas do not leap onto paper in final, polished form.

Once you realize the truths behind myths about writing, you can try the time-proven ways that experienced writers get started when they are blocked. As you use these strategies, suspend judgment; do not criticize yourself when trying to get underway. The time for evaluation comes during revision, but revising too soon can stall some writers. While the writing is most certainly not a final draft, having something on paper is a comfort—and can serve as a springboard to drafting.

WAYS TO OVERCOME WRITER'S BLOCK   12

- **Avoid staring at a blank page.** Relax and move your hand across the page or keyboard. Write words, scribble, or draw while you think about your topic. The movement of filling the paper can help stimulate your mind to turn to actual drafting.

- **Visualize yourself writing.** Many professional writers say that they write more easily if they first picture themselves doing it. Before getting up in the morning, or waiting for a bus, or walking to classes, summon a full visual image of yourself in the place where you usually write, with the materials you need, busy at work.

- **Picture an image or a scene, or imagine a sound that relates to your topic.** Start writing by describing what you see or hear.

- **Write about your topic in a letter to a friend.** Relax and chat on paper to someone you feel comfortable with.

➡

WAYS TO OVERCOME WRITER'S BLOCK

TEACHING TIP

Getting started seems hardest for writers at the point when they have to move from planning and shaping to actual writing. Dealing with writer's block is no small matter for writers, instructors of writing, and students. You might take some class time to discuss myths about writing. I am interested in gathering more myths. If you or your students know any, please send me the MYTH/TRUTH information for publication—with a byline—in the next edition of this *Annotated Instructor's Edition.* Send the material to me c/o English Editor, Prentice Hall, Englewood Cliffs, NJ 07632. (In case of duplicates, we will use the first to arrive.)

TEACHING TIP

Students may be skeptical of the value of picturing themselves working. Share with them these examples of successful people who use visualization: John Ueless, a champion pole-vaulter, used visualization before each meet. He would see himself winning by clearing the bar at a particular height. In his mind, he rehearsed every movement, as well as seeing the crowd and even smelling the grass when pole-vaulting out of doors.

Jack Nicklaus says that visualization gives him a "winning feeling": "This gives me a line to the cup just as clearly as if it's been tattooed on my brain. With that feeling, all I have to do is swing the club and let nature take its course."

You might want to give students time to visualize in class prior to writing. Tell them to close their eyes and sit comfortably. Tell them to imagine themselves reading a question and realizing they know how they want to respond. Tell them to imagine themselves making a list of notes, rearranging their material, or writing. At each stage, remind them to

➡

TEACHING TIP, cont.

imagine themselves feeling confident and successful. Then have them write. Later, discuss how they felt when writing this time in contrast to their past experiences. This technique often does little for people at first, so try to give your students frequent opportunities to employ visualization techniques.

BACKGROUND

In an article published in *U.S. News & World Report* (November 9, 1987, p. 106), Erica E. Goode cites tips for people who tend to procrastinate. They include the following helpful suggestions.

1. Break your work into small, clearly defined steps. Instead of vowing vaguely to "catch up on paperwork," resolve to spend one hour sorting out the papers on your desk.

2. Reward yourself for progress toward your goal. Ice cream is nice, as is a walk in the park.

3. The hardest step to take is the first, so pick something easy. A task that can be polished off in fifteen minutes is a good one for a starter.

4. Set a series of small but realistic deadlines rather than a final date.

5. Enlist support. Other people may be able to tell you if you're setting up expectations that are impossible to meet.

QUOTATION ABOUT WRITING

To write is to write is to write is to write is to write is to write is to write.
—Gertrude Stein

REFERENCE TO SUPPLEMENTS

See transparency 3–1 for drafting techniques in the *Prentice Hall/Simon & Schuster Transparencies for Writers* by D. Carter.

WAYS TO OVERCOME WRITER'S BLOCK (continued) 12

- ■ **Try writing your material as if you were someone else.** Once you take on a role, you might feel less inhibited about writing.
- ■ **Start in the middle.** Begin with a body paragraph. Write from the center of your essay out, instead of from beginning to end.
- ■ **Use "focused freewriting"** (see 2f).
- ■ **Switch your method of writing.** If you usually typewrite or use a computer, try writing by hand. If you usually use a pen, switch to a pencil. When you write by hand, try to treat yourself to good quality paper. The pleasure of writing on smooth, strong paper helps many experienced writers want to keep going.

As you write, seek out places and times of the day that encourage you to write. You might write best in a quiet corner of the library; at 4:30 a.m. at the kitchen table before anyone else is awake; or outside when people are walking by. Most experienced writers find that they concentrate best when they are alone, working without the risk of interruption. But occasionally background noise—in a crowded cafeteria, for example—might be comforting. Be sure, however, not to mislead yourself: You will not write well or efficiently while you are talking to other people, stopping now and then to jot down a sentence or two. Also, do not mistake delaying tactics for preparation: You do need pencil and paper (or their equivalent) to write, but you do not need fifteen perfectly sharpened pencils sitting in a neat row.

❖ COMPUTER TIP: Some people write with a pen, some at a typewriter, and others at a computer. If you do not have a computer at your disposal, the usual methods of writing will continue to serve you well. As much as possible, tailor your use of a computer to your personal needs. Some experienced writers prefer to use a computer only for preparing the final copy. Others like to plan and shape by hand and to write all drafts on a computer. Still other writers feel more comfortable writing out drafts by hand and then revising with a computer. Yet others like to use a computer throughout the writing process. See what works best for you in each writing situation. ❖

3b   ## Knowing how to draft

Once you have your ideas planned and shaped for an essay, you are ready to **compose** them on paper. When you compose, you put together sentences and paragraphs into a unified whole. A first draft is a preliminary draft. Its purpose is to get your ideas onto paper, not to refine grammar and style (they come later, during revising). First drafts are not meant to be perfect; they are meant to give you something to revise. According to your personal preferences and each writing situation, you can use any of these ways (or your own ways) of writing a first draft.

♣ COMPUTER TIP: Make it a rule to save or back up your work every two pages or every ten to fifteen minutes. Also, some writers print out regularly. Printout, also called hard copy, gives you a record of your work, even if your disk develops problems. ♣

1. **Put aside all your notes from planning and shaping.** Write a "discovery draft." As you write, be open to discovering ideas and making connections that spring to mind during the physical act of writing. When you finish a discovery draft, you can decide to use it either as a first draft or as part of your notes when you write a structured first draft.

2. **Keep your notes from planning and shaping in front of you and use them as you write.** Write a structured first draft by arranging your notes in a preliminary sequence and working through them. Draft either the entire essay or blocks of a few paragraphs at one time.

3. **Use a combination of approaches.** When you know the shape of your material, write according to that structure. When you feel "stuck" about what to say next, switch to writing as you would for a discovery draft.

The direction of drafting is forward: *Keep pressing ahead.* If you are worried about the spelling of a word or a point in grammar, underline the material to check it later—and keep moving ahead. If you cannot think of an exact word, write an easy synonym and circle it to change later—and move on. If you are worried about your sentence style or the order in which you present the supporting details within a paragraph, write *Style?* or *Order?* in the margin and return to it later to revise—and press forward. If you begin to run dry, reread what you have written—but only to propel yourself to further writing, not to distract you into rewriting.

♣ COMPUTER TIP: Try to write a whole draft at one session, second-guessing and rewriting as little as possible. If you have questions, or think you may want to elaborate on something but cannot think how at the moment, insert a symbol that will alert you to "talk to yourself" later. When you finish the draft and begin revising, your symbols can help you focus on areas that need reworking. ♣

TEACHING TIP

Your students may find it helpful to keep a writing log. At the top of each piece of writing they can note where, when, and how they are working. The more detailed the notations, the more they will help students to draw conclusions about the manner in which their best writing takes place. After making a number of such notations, the students can write a paragraph evaluating the approaches used, trying to assess their effectiveness.

TEACHING TIP: COLLABORATION

One of the greatest benefits of assigning student groups to write a paper together is the degree to which students must explain specifically to one another what features of a draft require changes and why. Rather than settling for the typical "this doesn't sound right" comment, students in groups may be encouraged to develop a working vocabulary for changing their drafts and enunciate the reasons for doing so. To develop this vocabulary, you might ask your groups to divide up the revision checklists, with each group member responsible for answering the questions about the group's essay or about the members' individual essays.

BACKGROUND

Janet Emig suggests that the reason many experienced writers prefer to write in longhand is that it gives them more time to think. The slower pace of handwriting, as opposed to the typewriter (or word processor), allows ideas to develop and surface ("Hand, Eye, Brain: Some 'Basics' in the Writing Process," *Research on Composing: Points of Departure*, ed. Charles Cooper and Lee Odell [Urbana: NCTE, 1978]; 61).

BACKGROUND

Diana Hacker and Betty Renshaw (*Writing with a Voice* [Boston: Little, Brown, 1985], p. 26) have compiled a list of reasons students are reluctant to revise their writing. They include the following:

1. I wait until the last minute, so there's no time to rewrite.

2. My first draft is the best I can do. I can't improve it.

3. I don't know whether my first draft is any good or not, so how can I improve it?

4. I don't know where to begin, and I wouldn't know when to stop.

5. Well, frankly, I'm lazy.

6. When I tinker with my sentences, they just turn out worse.

7. I don't really care about what I'm writing, so I just want to get it over with.

8. Rewriting is too messy. I like to work with clean-looking pages.

9. I'm such a bad writer I hate to read my own writing.

10. Rewriting is my instructor's responsibility.

REFERENCES TO SUPPLEMENTS

For revising for tone and organization, refer students to *Rough Drafts* by K. S. Cain, Part II, Exercises 1 & 2.

For more on helping students understand revision, see *Teaching Writing*:

→

3b
cont.

As you draft, use the essay's thesis statement (see 2m) as your springboard. A thesis statement has great organizing power, for it controls and limits what the essay will cover. Also, use your thesis statement as a connecting thread that unifies the essay.

Unity is important for communicating clearly to an audience. You achieve unity when all parts of the essay relate to the thesis statement and to each other. An essay is unified when it meets two criteria: (1) the thesis statement clearly ties into all topic sentences: see 4b; and (2) the support for each topic sentence—the paragraph development—contains examples, reasons, facts, and details directly related to the topic and, in turn, to the thesis statement: see 4c.

Coherence is also important to communicate clearly to an audience. An essay is coherent when it supplies guideposts that communicate the relations among ideas. Coherence is achieved with transitional expressions, pronouns, repetition, and parallel structures. These techniques operate within paragraphs and to connect paragraphs (see 4d).

When you write, plan your practical arrangements. For example, try to work in a place where you are comfortable and will not be disturbed. If someone comes along and interrupts, you might lose a train of thought or an idea that has flashed into your mind. Also, keep enough paper at hand so that you use only one side of each sheet of paper. Later you will need to spread your full draft in front of you so that you can physically see how the parts relate to one another. As you write, leave large margins and plenty of room between lines so that you have space to enter changes later on.

To give you examples of the writing process used by college students, this chapter discusses the drafting and revising of two students—Carol Moreno and Daniel Casey, each of whom wrote in response to the assignments shown on page 20. You can see three complete drafts of Moreno's essay in this chapter (section 3f). Also, you can see the final draft of Daniel Casey's essay in section 6i. For examples of Moreno's and Casey's uses of the techniques of planning and shaping before they began drafting, see sections 2b through 2n.

3c

Knowing how to revise

To **revise** you must evaluate. You assess your first (or subsequent) draft and decide where improvements are needed. Then you make the improvements and evaluate each on its own as well as in the context of the surrounding material. The revision process continues until you are satisfied that the essay is the best that you can make it in the time available. Keep in mind that academic writing, especially through the vehicle of revision, is an engaging intellectual endeavor that encourages students to stretch to the maximum.

REFERENCES TO SUPPLEMENTS, cont.

Prentice Hall Resources for Composition by P. Hastings, ch. 5, "Stage Six: Revision."

See transparencies 3–2 and 3–2a for revising for purpose and structure in the *Prentice Hall/Simon & Schuster Transparencies for Writers* by D. Carter.

To revise successfully you need first to *expect to revise.* Some people think that anyone who revises is not a good writer. Only the opposite is true. Writing is largely revising. Experienced writers know that the final draft of any writing project shows on paper only a fraction of the decisions made from draft to successive draft. Revision means "to see again," to look with fresh eyes. Good writers can truly *see* their drafts and rework them so that they evolve and improve.

To revise successfully you need also to distance yourself from each draft. You need to read your writing with objective eyes. A natural reaction of many writers is to want to hold onto their every word, especially if they had trouble getting started with a draft. If you ever have such feelings, resist them and work on distancing yourself from the material. Before revising, give yourself some time for that rosy glow of authorial pride to dim a bit. The classical writer Horace recommended waiting nine years. Given the hectic pace of modern life, you do not have that much time. But do try to wait a few hours before going back to look anew at your work.

If an objective perspective still eludes you, try reading your draft aloud; hearing the material can give you a fresh new sense of content and organization. Another useful method is to read the paragraphs in reverse order, starting with the conclusion; eventually, of course, you must read your essay from beginning to end, but to achieve distance you can temporarily depart from that sequence.

Knowing the steps and activities of revision

3c-1

Once you understand the attitudes that underlie the revision process, you are ready to move into actual revising.

To revise, you work to improve your draft at all levels: whole essay, paragraph, sentence, and word. A revised draft usually looks quite different from its preceding draft. To revise effectively you likely need to engage in all the activities in Chart 13 and Chart 14.

As you engage in each activity, keep in mind the whole picture. Changes affect more than the place revised. Check that your separate changes operate well in the context of the whole essay or a particular paragraph. As with drafting (see 3b), getting distance from your material allows you the chance to be more objective.

Revising is usually separate from editing (see 3d). Editing involves concentrating on important surface features such as correct spelling and punctuation. During revising, you pay attention to the meaning that you want your material to deliver effectively.

♣ COMPUTER TIP: Relieved of the sometimes tedious work of copying and recopying material, many writers feel more creative when they use a computer. Their ideas seem to flow more freely when each new thought does not lead to a recopying job. Nevertheless, do not let

BACKGROUND

In "Revision Strategies of Student Writers and Experienced Writers" (*CCC* 31 [December 1980]; 46–49) Nancy Sommers makes distinctions between revising and editing. The former, she points out, encompasses the entire composition and often takes several times to complete; the latter, which has the purpose of polishing the text, deals with grammatical and usage problems. During the process of revision, the writer not only focuses on stylistic concerns, but also continues to mold the text to its purpose and audience. Sommers points out that student writers, in contrast to experienced writers, are more likely to edit than to revise. They approach revising primarily as a matter of rewording: eliminating repetition, finding synonyms, deleting words. Less frequently do they deal with rearrangement or addition of material. Experienced writers, on the other hand, continue to search for the shape of their discussion as they revise, making changes primarily in sentences, by addition and deletion. Sommers suggests the appropriate uses of revision in a question she raised a year earlier in "The Need for Theory in Composition Research" (*CCC* 30 [February 1979]; 48). She asks: "Instead of thinking of revision as an activity at the end of the process, what if we thought of revision as a process of making a work congruent with what a writer intends—a process that occurs throughout the writing of a work?"

yourself be seduced by the wonders of a computer. It is only a machine. A neatly printed page might "look" like a final draft, even when it is a very rough draft. Resist the urge to think neatness means completion. ❖

STEPS FOR REVISING

MAJOUR ADCITIVIES DURING REVISION

STEPS FOR REVISING   13

1. Shift mentally from suspending judgment (during idea gathering and drafting) to making judgments.
2. Read your draft critically to evaluate it. Be guided by the questions on the Revision Checklists (Charts 16 and 17) in this chapter or by material supplied by your instructor.
3. Decide whether to write an entirely new draft or to revise the one you have. Do not be overly harsh. While some early drafts serve best as "discovery drafts" rather than first drafts, many early drafts provide sufficient raw material for the revision process to get underway.
4. Be systematic. Do not evaluate at random. You need to pay attention to many different elements of a draft, from overall organization to choice of words. Some writers prefer to consider all elements concurrently, but most writers work better when they concentrate on different elements sequentially during separate rounds of revision.

MAJOR ACTIVITIES DURING REVISION   14

- **Add.** Insert needed words, sentences, and paragraphs. If your additions require new content, return to idea-gathering techniques (see 2d through 2k).
- **Cut.** Get rid of whatever goes off the topic or repeats what has already been said.
- **Replace.** As needed, substitute new words, sentences, and paragraphs for what you have cut.
- **Move material around.** Change the sequence of paragraphs if the material is not presented in logical order (see 2e-2). Move sentences within paragraphs or to other paragraphs if any paragraph arrangement seems illogical (see 4c).

TEACHING TIP
Many students think that revisers are poor writers. Indeed, I have been scolded more than once by people who have seen me writing in waiting rooms, on the bus, or on a park bench. "Don't you know not to make a mess when you write?" The tone is always well meaning, as if the person is trying help me out of a deep difficulty I seem to be having. I have always been amazed at how forward strangers can get after watching me write while they supposedly stare straight ahead. Some people start to squirm, and the wise ones simply move away. But a few hardy folks want to let me know that I could suddenly become A WRITER if only I would stop crossing out and drawing arrows on my paper. For a while the confrontations inhibited me about writing outside my home, but I soon became so interested in the reactions that I got caught up in the "research" of the situations. (Try it sometime—a doctor's office or a barber or beauty shop are prime territory.) Students are always similarly surprised when they see how messy real writing can be.

Using the organizing power of your thesis statement and essay title during revision

As you revise, pay special attention to your essay's thesis statement and title. Both features can help you stay on the track. Also, they orient your reader to what to expect, which helps you communicate your message as clearly as possible.

If your **thesis statement** (see 2n, especially Chart 10) does not match what you say in your essay, you need to revise either the thesis statement or the essay—and sometimes both. A thesis statement must present the topic of the essay, the writer's particular focus on that topic, and the writer's purpose for writing the essay. The first draft of a thesis statement is often merely an estimate of what will be covered in the essay. Early in the revision process, check the accuracy of your estimate. Then use the thesis statement's controlling power to bring it and your essay in line with each other.

Each writer's experience with revising a thesis statement varies from essay to essay. Carol Moreno wrote a number of versions of her thesis statement before she started drafting. After writing her first draft, she checked the thesis statement and satisfied herself that it communicated what she wanted to say. But she decided to change parts of her essay to conform more closely to her thesis statement. (For an example of a thesis statement being revised for a research paper, from the first through the final draft, see 32r).

The **title** of an essay also plays an important organizing role during revision. An effective title sets you on your course and tells your reader what to expect. (Some writers like to start a first draft with a title at the top of the page to focus their thinking. As they revise drafts, they revise the title as needed.) An effective title might not come to mind until you have drafted, revised, and edited your essay, by which time your thinking about your topic has crystallized. Remember that a title is never the same as a thesis statement.

Titles can be *direct* or *indirect*. A *direct title* tells exactly what the essay will be about. A direct title contains key words under which the essay would be cataloged in a library or other database system. The title of Carol Moreno's essay shown in 3f (see page 67) is direct: "Women Can Pump Iron, Too." Similarly, the title of Daniel Casey's essay in section 6i is direct: "Commercialism at Holiday Time Benefits the Nation." Each title is specific and prepares the reader for the topic of the essay.

A *direct title* should not be too broad. An overly broad title implies that the writer has not thought through the essay's content. An unsatisfactory title for Moreno's essay would be "Pumping Iron." Conversely, a direct title should not be too narrow. Equally unsatisfactory would be a title that is overly long—for example, by listing the

PROCESS/PRODUCT DEBATE

Writers are judged in the outside world by their products, not their processes. Teaching students to view writing as process is extremely useful as an instructional technique and as a guide to what real writers do. But telling students that product does not matter is to mislead them about what they will face in other courses and in the workplace.

The call for balance has been made particularly well by one of the editors of the journal *Research in the Teaching of English* in the "Musings" column in May 1984, excerpted here.

Yet that separation has been replaced by another that is likely to be equally unproductive. In the enthusiasm provoked by a focus on process, we have sometimes lost sight of the enterprise in which the process is engaged. Though our best philosophers have always warned us against false dualisms, our best research has often defined itself in reaction to the limitations of previous work. Thus the initial enthusiasm for the study of process was conditioned by a rejection of the earlier preoccupation with product. The research that has followed has been extraordinarily productive, extending both our theoretical understanding and our practical approaches. Yet one characteristic of any new idea is that, in the course of exploring its implications most fully, we learn not only its strengths but also its limitations. The strengths of the process studies of the last decade have been many, and the weaknesses minor relative to the insights we have gained. But as happens with most paradigms, we seem now to be approaching a point where the limitations as well as the advantages of process-oriented research are beginning to be clear.

➜

3c–2
cont.

topics of most of the essay's body paragraphs: "Women Pump Iron for Their Physical and Personal Objectives."

An *indirect title* is also acceptable in some situations, according to the writer's taste and instructor's requirements. An indirect title hints at the essay's topic. It presents a puzzle that can be solved by reading the essay. This approach can be intriguing for the reader, but the writer has to make sure that the title is not too obscure. For example, for Carol Moreno's essay a satisfactory indirect title would be "The Meaning of Muscles," but an unsatisfactory, overly indirect title would be "Equal Play."

Whether direct or indirect, a title stands alone. For example, Carol Moreno (whose essay's good title is "Women Can Pump Iron, Too") would have been wrong had she written as her essay's first sentence: "They certainly can" or "I am proof of that." Chart 15 gives guidelines for titles.

GUIDELINES FOR ESSAY TITLES

GUIDELINES FOR ESSAY TITLES   15

■ Do not wait until the last minute to tack on a title. You might write a title before you start to draft or while you are revising, but always check as you review your essay, to make sure that the title clearly relates to the content of the evolving essay.

■ For a direct title, use key words relating to your topic, but do not reveal your entire essay.

■ For an indirect title, be sure that it hints accurately and that its meaning will be clear once a reader finishes your essay.

■ Do not use quotation marks or underlining with the title (*unless* your title includes another title; see section 30f).

■ Do not refer to your essay title with words like *it* or *this,* as if the title were part of the first sentence in the essay.

3c-3

Using revision checklists

Revision checklists can help you focus your attention as you evaluate your writing to revise it. Either use a checklist provided by your instructor, or compile your own based on the revision checklists in Chart 16 and Chart 17. The checklists here are comprehensive and detailed; do not let them overwhelm you. Feel free to adapt them to your writing assignments as well as to your personal weaknesses and strengths. Also, the checklists here move from the **larger elements** of the whole essay and paragraphs to the **smaller elements** of sentences and words. This progression for the sake of self-evaluation works well for many writers. (To see how Carol Moreno used these Revision Checklists, see 3f.)

❖ ESL NOTE: If English is not your first language, you may want to consult Part Nine to check your use of VERB-PREPOSITION combinations, ARTICLES, word order, VERBALS, and MODAL AUXILIARIES in addition to using the Revision Checklists. ❖

REVISION CHECKLIST: THE WHOLE ESSAY AND PARAGRAPHS 16

The answer to each question should be "yes." If it is not, you need to revise. The reference numbers in parentheses tell you what chapter or section of this handbook to consult.

1. Is your essay topic suitable and sufficiently narrow (2c)?

2. Does your thesis statement communicate your topic and focus (2n) and your purpose (1b)?

3. Does your essay reflect awareness of your audience (1c)?

4. Is your tone appropriate (1d)?

5. Is your essay logically organized (2m) and are your paragraphs logically arranged (4e)?

6. Have you cut material that goes off the topic?

7. Is your reasoning sound (5h—5j) and do you avoid logical fallacies (5k)?

8. Is your introduction related to the rest of your essay (4g)?

9. Does each body paragraph express its main idea in a topic sentence as needed (4c)? Are the main ideas clearly related to the thesis statement, and have you covered all that your thesis statement "promises" (2n)?

10. Are your body paragraphs sufficiently developed with concrete support for their main idea (4c)?

11. Have you used necessary transitions (4d-1, 4d-5)?

12. Do your paragraphs maintain coherence (4d)?

13. Does your conclusion provide a sense of completion (4g)?

14. Does your title reflect the content of the essay (3c-2)?

PROCESS/PRODUCT DEBATE, cont.

In particular, the separation of process and product is beginning to reemerge as the unnatural dualism that our past might suggest it would inevitably become. Indeed, when reading, writing, or spoken language processes are separated from the ends they serve, we lose the essence of the process itself. Process does not consist of isolated behaviors that operate willy-nilly, but of purposeful activities that lead toward some end for the person who has chosen to engage in them.

Everyone seems to agree that process is good. So do we. The issue we raise is whether any process can ever be looked at alone. This comes from our belief that just as top-down and bottom-up approaches are interactive, so too do all processing behaviors need to be looked at interactively, as they interrelate with their outcomes. For us, process only has meaning as it works toward some end. Examination of *only* the means keeps us from understanding the most interesting complications of the human mind as it works in different ways toward different destinations.

—Judith A. Langer

TEACHING TIP

Students may find it helpful to know that the strengths and weaknesses in a piece of writing are often easier for the writer to recognize if a "cooling off" period intervenes between the time of writing and the time of revision. If there is an opportunity to put the piece away for a day or so, the writer returns to it not as the composer, but as a reader, thus finding it easier to spot confusing passages or awkward statements. Since students are not famous for working far ahead of schedule, they should be encouraged to provide at least a few hours to distance themselves from the writing before trying to revise it. On the other hand, if too much time elapses between the draft and the rereading, a writer is likely to lose the sense of purpose and meaning that accompanied the original effort.

TEACHING TIP

At the other end of the spectrum from non-revisers are over-revisers. Some students are never satisfied with their work and so never hand it in. This phenomenon is a form of writer's block. Students who suffer from this sort of inhibition often need a little special treatment at first. For example, you might help such students by telling them that for the first few assignments you will consider their work to be "in progress," even the final version. You might also share with them these words of Eudora Welty when she was interviewed by *U.S. News & World Report*.

> I know I can never get it perfect. You just have to know when you've done it the best way. A friend of mine who is a writer said he kept thirteen drafts of a story and put them all in a drawer. Years later he went back, and it was number 7 that was the right one. That taught me a real, true lesson.

REVISION CHECKLIST: SENTENCES AND WORDS   17

The answer to each question should be "yes." If it is not, you need to revise. The reference numbers in parentheses tell you what chapter or section of this handbook to consult.

1. Have you eliminated sentence fragments (13)?
2. Have you eliminated comma splices and fused sentences (14)?
3. Have you eliminated confusing shifts (15a)?
4. Have you eliminated misplaced and dangling modifiers (15b and 15c)?
5. Have you eliminated mixed and incomplete sentences (15d and 15e)?
6. Are your sentences concise (16)?
7. Do your sentences show clear relationships among ideas (17)?
8. Do you use parallelism to help your sentences deliver their meaning gracefully, and do you avoid faulty parallelism (18)?
9. Does your writing reflect variety and emphasis (19)?
10. Have you used exact words (20b)?
11. Is your usage correct (Usage Glossary)?
12. Do your words reflect an appropriate level of formality (21a-1)?
13. Do you avoid sexist language (21b); slang and colloquial language (21a-3), slanted language (21a-4), clichés (21d), and artificial language (21e)?

!

❖ COMPUTER TIP: The computer makes rearranging relatively painless. You may make endless versions of your draft until you are satisfied with the order. Try reordering your body paragraphs, splitting or joining some existing paragraphs, and moving your last paragraph to the first position. You may be surprised. Save the most promising versions, and perhaps ask your peers to react to them. Do not, however, be tempted to rearrange endlessly. Set limits or you will never finish. ❖

Knowing how to use criticism

When criticism is constructive, you can learn a great deal about your writing through the eyes of others. Still, you have much company among writers if your initial reaction to criticism is defensive. Someone else's reactions to your writing can feel like an intrusion at first. Writing is a personal act, even when a writer is trying to communicate with a reader. The more you write, however, the more you will come to welcome constructive criticism.

The eyes of another person, someone who cares to help you improve, can give you an objective view of your material. Useful criticism helps you move your writing closer to what a reader needs to complete the act of communication. When working with comments, look at each one separately. First, make sure that you understand what the comment says. If you are unsure, ask. Next, be open-minded about the comment so that you do not miss good opportunities to improve. Finally, use the comments to revise according to what you think will improve your draft.

Knowing how to be a peer critic   3c-5

Being a **peer critic** means using structured procedures to react to and make suggestions about another student's writing. Peer critiquing is an interactive communication process. It involves reading and thinking together, asking and explaining, talking and listening. As a student writer, be sure that your instructor wants you to use peer critiquing before you do so. There can be a fine line between giving opinions and doing others' work for them.

When you are a peer critic, you are part of a respected tradition of colleagues helping colleagues. Professional writers often seek to improve their rough drafts by asking other writers for comments. When you give comments as a student writer, know that you are not expected to be an expert. What you do offer can be quite valuable: opinions from the point of view of a writer who understands what his or her peer is going through. Try always to base your comments on an understanding of the writing process and of the features that characterize effective writing. The more concrete and specific your comments, the more helpful. The comment "this is good" might seem pleasant, but it says little. What makes the writing good: ideas? patterns of organization? sentences? words?

When you receive comments from a peer critic, remain open-minded about what is said. Constructive criticism can help you read your writing in a fresh way that results in better revision. Encourage your peer to be honest. You, however, are the person who decides which comments to use, and which to ignore, when revising.

If your instructor distributes a list to guide peer discussion, follow it carefully. If you are expected to decide what to discuss with peers, you can use or adapt the revision checklists in this handbook section. Guidelines for being an effective peer critic are in Chart 18 on the next page.

TEACHING TIP: COLLABORATION

Collaborative groups, like individual writers, can lose sight of the way their writing reads to others. Try countering this tendency by having groups exchange papers for response. Not only will students benefit from having fresh sets of eyes read their work, they will develop a greater sense of writing for a "real" audience if they know that the people in other groups will be responding to their work.

If you are teaching more than one composition class, exchanging papers across classes is less likely to foster the "kid glove" attitudes with which some students appraise the work of their classmates.

REFERENCES TO SUPPLEMENTS

For more on peer critiquing, see L. Julian, "Strategies for Teaching Writing," ch. VI, in L. Julian, et al., *Strategies and Resources for Teaching Writing with the Simon & Schuster Handbook for Writers.*

For more on helping student peer critiquing skills, see *Teaching Writing: Prentice Hall Resources for Composition* by P. Hastings, ch. 5, "Stage Five: Evaluating, Reviewing, Sharing Drafts, Peer Critiques."

TEACHING TIP

Many of us have had the experience of reading what is supposedly a student's revision of an essay we have already read and responded to, only to find that most of our comments have been ignored; the revision turns out to be the original essay with a few spelling errors corrected. Sometimes students do not know how to respond fully to an instructor's comments.

One step in demystifying comments is to have the class collectively respond

→

TEACHING TIP, cont.

to the instructor's comments on Carol Moreno's second draft. Ask the students to read the instructor's comments on Carol Moreno's essay and decide what Moreno might do in response to each one. You might lead a discussion of the options for fixing each problem. As you come to each comment, allow sufficient time for students to think about and draft revisions or to look up the needed information in their *S & S Handbook for Writers*. Invite students to offer their revisions at each comment, and keep students alert to the many good alternatives that can emerge in response to the instructor's questions. You might also point out that responses are more likely to be identical to the coded comments of the instructor because most of them call for corrections of grammar or punctuation.

An alternative to the class discussion comment-by-comment is to assign the entire revision as a home or class exercise. Then students can discuss their thought-through answers and compare their results.

As much as possible, try to use copies of the material or overhead transparencies for the discussion of alternate complete third drafts. Students often cannot follow the discussion if too much relies on memory of various similar versions.

REFERENCE TO SUPPLEMENTS

For more on helping students use editing, see *Teaching Writing: Prentice Hall Resources for Composition* by P. Hastings, ch. 5, "Stage Seven: Editing."

GUIDELINES FOR BEING AN EFFECTIVE PEER CRITIC 18

- Think of the writing as "work in progress."

- Think of yourself in the role of a coach, not a judge.

- After reading your peer's writing, give a brief summary of what you have read. This provides a check to determine that what you understand is what the writer intended.

- Be sure to compliment. Being specific, point out what you think is well done.

- Be sure to offer honest, constructive suggestions for improvement. Being specific, point out what you think needs revision.

- As you work through the material, invite the writer to ask questions and say how you might be most helpful.

- When possible, write down your comments to give to your peer (or provide for your peer to take notes while you comment).

3d ## Knowing how to edit

When you **edit,** you are expected to check the technical correctness of your writing. You pay attention to surface features of your writing, such as grammar, spelling, and punctuation, and the correct use of capitals, numbers, italics, and abbreviations. Writers sometimes refer to editing as revising (see 3c). In this handbook, editing is discussed separately because editing focuses more on presentation than on meaning.

If you edit too soon in the writing process, you might distract yourself from checking to see if your material delivers its meaning effectively. You are ready to edit when you have a final draft that contains suitable content, organization, development, and sentence structure. Your job during editing is not to generate a new draft but to fine-tune the surface features of the draft you have. Once you have polished your work, you are ready to transcribe it into a final copy and proofread (see 3e) it.

Editing is crucial in writing. No matter how much attention you have paid to planning, shaping, drafting, and revising, you must edit carefully. Slapdash editing will distract your readers and, in writing for assignments, lower your grade.

Editing takes patience. Inexperienced writers sometimes rush editing, especially if they have revised well and feel that they have prepared a good essay. When you edit, resist any impulse to hurry. Matters of grammar and punctuation take concentration—and frequently the time to check yourself by looking up rules and conventions in this handbook. As you edit, be systematic. Use a checklist supplied by your instructor or one that you compile from the editing checklist in Chart 19.

EDITING CHECKLIST   19

The answer to each question should be "yes." If it is not, you need to edit. The reference numbers in parentheses tell you what chapter of this handbook to consult.

1. Is your grammar correct (7 to 15)?
2. Is your spelling correct, and are your hyphens correct (22)?
3. Have you correctly used commas (24)?
4. Have you correctly used all other punctuation (25 through 29)?
5. Have you correctly used capital letters, italics, abbreviations, and numbers (30)?

EDITING CHECKLIST

Knowing how to proofread   3e

When you **proofread,** you check a final version carefully before handing it in. To make sure that your work is an accurate and clean transcription of your final draft, proofread after you REVISE and EDIT. If you try to proofread while you edit, one process might distract from the other.

Proofreading involves a careful, line-by-line reading of your writing. You may want to proofread with a ruler so that you can focus on one line at a time. Starting at the end also helps you avoid becoming distracted by the content of your paper. Another effective proofreading technique is to read your final draft aloud, to yourself or to a friend. This can help you hear and see errors that have slipped past your notice.

❖ COMPUTER TIP: You can use the screen to help you proofread and edit. Highlight a five- or six-line section, and read each section slowly and carefully. This strategy allows you to work in small segments, which reduces the tendency to read too quickly and ignore errors.

You might try making your own "spell-and-style checker" by keeping a file of the mistakes that you have made in the past. For example, if the difference between *its* and *it's* always escapes you or if you know that you tend to misuse the colon, call up your mistake file, and search your draft for those items. ❖

!

BACKGROUND

Many instructors are strongly attracted to the use of peer revision and editing groups, since they provide immediate feedback from an audience other than the teacher, plus the increased opportunity for one-on-one consultations between teacher and student. Some even build entire courses around the workshop model. A concise statement of how to use the classroom as a writing workshop appears in Chapter 12 of Erika Lindemann's *A Rhetoric for Writing Teachers*, 2nd ed. (New York: Oxford UP, 1987), pp. 184–186. Her suggestions include the following guidelines for teachers:

1. Use groups of no more than three students. Let students work with whomever they choose, as long as they do the work.

2. Assign specific work and define it concretely. Begin with brief tasks of 10 to 20 minutes, expanding the work period to a maximum of 30 or 35 minutes as students become comfortable working with each other.

3. Suggest specific questions, especially in the beginning, that writers and readers can ask each other. The session should begin with a writer's explanation of some strategy in the paper. Readers should begin by noting strengths of the writing. When readers or writers identify a problem, they should explain why it is a problem and suggest a solution.

4. Stay involved with what is going on, but avoid taking control. Initially make sure that each group is underway, then listen, from a distance, to each group, intervening only when one is not making progress. Refrain from giving "the answer" to groups that ask for help. Instead, pose questions that will help them discover a solution to their problems.

➜

BACKGROUND, *cont.*

The result, according to Lindemann, is a classroom that realizes the primary objective of a writing course: "students and teachers writing and discussing each other's work."

BACKGROUND

In "Revision with a Computer: Seven Strategies" (*The English Record* 39 [1988]: 18–21), James Strickland outlines revision techniques that can be taught to writers who have used word processing to enter text into a text file. He suggests the following helpful strategies. (They can be used in conjunction with Appendix A in this handbook.)

1. Students create cumulative sentences through the addition of noun phrases, verb phrases, and absolutes, as suggested by Christensen's generative rhetoric, which adds right-branch modifiers to sentences, elaborates on the basic premise, explains a term, or completes a thought. Students can return at any point in the text to add information, which may generate more ideas. Strickland comments that word processing "encourages cumulative sentence revision because it moves the text over to make room for the new modifiers, and with 'word-wrap' and 'paragraph reformatting' features, it adjusts everything so that the text looks untouched."

2. To check the coherence of a text, students select the MVS, the "most valuable sentence" of each paragraph. Working with a renamed copy of their text file to protect the original, they delete all but the MVS from each paragraph, producing a compressed version of the writing. As Strickland points out, it is "a map of the forward motion of the essay, a top-level view of its structure."

➔

3e
cont.

In proofreading, look for letters or words inadvertently left out. If you handwrite your material, be legible. If you type, neatly correct any typing errors. If a page has numerous errors, retype the page. Do not expect your instructor to make allowances for crude typing; if you cannot type well, arrange to have your paper typed properly. No matter how hard you have worked on other parts of the writing process, if your final copy is inaccurate or messy, you will not reach your audience successfully.

! ❖ COMPUTER TIP: Get to know any special tools for writers that are included in the software programs for your computer. For example:

■ *Spell-check programs* call attention to words that do not match their dictionaries. The programs are a big help for spotting typos, but they have limits. Suppose you intended to type "west" but instead typed "rest." Because "rest" appears as a correctly spelled word in the program's dictionary, the program will not call "west" to your attention. Always read your work carefully yourself.

■ *Thesaurus programs* are no different from printed thesauruses. You must evaluate each suggested substitution for sense within the context of what you are writing.

■ *Style-check programs* examine your file against grammar, usage, and punctuation rules, alerting you to writing in your paper that differs from a program's standards. Fixing what the program finds is still your job. Use style-check programs with caution. For example, if you are told some of your sentences are in the passive voice, change them to active voice only if you think the change is needed (see 8m and 8n).

■ *Tutorials* like **Blue Pencil**, available with this handbook, offer you exercises to work on at your own pace. **Blue Pencil** closely resembles the editing process. It scores your answers and explains what is wrong with and how to fix any incorrect ones. It also refers you to the appropriate section in this handbook. ❖

3f ## Case study: A student writing an essay

This section is a case study of a student, Carol Moreno, going through the process of writing an essay. As you examine her three drafts, refer back to her writing assignment on page 20. In addition, look at the discussion of how she mapped her ideas (see 2i) and wrote her thesis statement (see 2n). See 2o for sample outlines.

Writing and revising a first draft

Carol Moreno wrote about a challenge she faced and met. As a result of using planning techniques (see 2e, 2f, and 2i), she chose the topic of weight lifting for women who want to build up their strength. She decided that her writing purpose would be *to inform* (see 1b-2). She then wrote the first draft, expecting to revise it later.

As Moreno revised her first draft, she worked systematically through the larger elements of the whole essay and paragraphs, and then she turned to her sentences and words. As she did this, she referred to the Revision Checklists in Chart 16 and Chart 17. Here is Moreno's first draft, along with her notes to herself about revisions she wanted to make when she wrote her second draft.

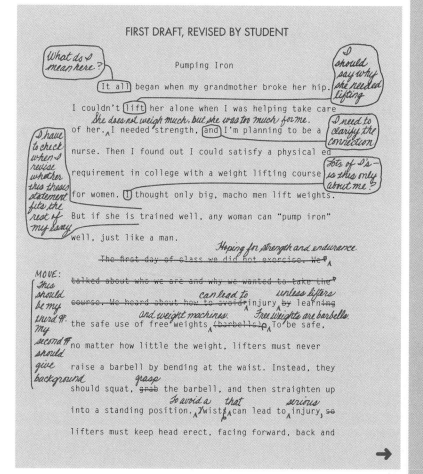

FIRST DRAFT, REVISED BY STUDENT

Pumping Iron

What do I mean here?

It all began when my grandmother broke her hip. I couldn't lift her alone when I was helping take care of her. *She does not weigh much, but she was too much for me.* I needed strength, and I'm planning to be a nurse. Then I found out I could satisfy a physical ed requirement in college with a weight lifting course for women. I thought only big, macho men lift weights. But if she is trained well, any woman can "pump iron" well, just like a man. *Hoping for strength and endurance.*

I should say why she needed lifting

I need to clarify the connection

Lots of I's — is this only about me?

I have to check when I revise whether this thesis statement fits the rest of my essay

Hoping for strength and endurance.

~~The first day of class we did not exercise. We~~ MOVE: ~~talked about who we are and why we wanted to take the~~ *can lead to* ~~course. We heard about how to avoid~~ injury *unless lifters* ~~by~~ learning *and weight machines.* *Free weights are barbells.* the safe use of free weights ~~(barbells)~~. To be safe, no matter how little the weight, lifters must never raise a barbell by bending at the waist. Instead, they should squat, *grasp* ~~grab~~ the barbell, and then straighten up into a standing position. *To avoid a* Twist *that* can lead to *serious* injury, ~~so~~ lifters must keep head erect, facing forward, back and

This should be my third ¶. My second ¶ should give background

→

61

BACKGROUND, cont.

7. The final strategy is a computer conversation, which Strickland calls collaborative revision. Writers respond to each other's writing by way of on-line conversations: a new version of writers talking to each other about their work.

The value of revision with a computer, says Strickland, is that students see their work as a fluid text that can be easily added to, subtracted from, rearranged, and manipulated.

BACKGROUND

Lenny Emmanuel suggests that teachers should help students learn how to revise "with a thorough knowledge of grammatical and rhetorical skills" (*Journal of Teaching Writing* 3 [Fall 1984]: 269–284).

QUOTATION ABOUT WRITING

There is always a point in the writing of a piece when I sit in a room literally papered with false starts and cannot put one word after another and imagine that I have suffered a small stroke, leaving me apparently undamaged but actually aphasic.

—Joan Didion

QUOTATION ABOUT WRITING

Let your literary compositions be kept from the public eye for nine years at least.

—Horace

[Handwritten note: I need to go into more detail here] neck aligned. Lifters use weight machines sitting down, which is a big advantage of the Nautilus and Universal. *[Handwritten note: I have to bring in more than myself to say who we are]*

[Handwritten note: move up to be #2 (background)] I was ~~relieved~~ *happy* that I won't develop overly masculine muscle mass. We learned that we can rely on women's biology. Our bodies produce only very small amounts of the hormones that enlarge muscles in men. *[Handwritten note: I need to tie these together check 4d]* ~~Normally,~~ *With normal training,* women's muscles grow longer rather than bulkier.

Weight lifting is a form of anareobic *[sp]* exercise. It does not make people breathe harder or their hearts *[sp]* beat faster. Arobic exercise like *running, walking, and* swimming build endurance, so I took up swimming. *[Handwritten note: Am I too informal here?]* *[Handwritten note: My topic sentence needs work]*

After safety comes our needs for physical strength. A well-planned, progressive weight training program. ~~You~~ *It* begin with whatever weight *a person* ~~you~~ can lift comfortably and ~~then~~ gradually add *to the base weight as one gets stronger.* What builds muscle strength is the number of "reps", *the lifter does,* ~~we do~~ not necessarily an increase in the amount of ~~added~~ *resistance from adding* weight. In my class, we ranged from 18 to 43, scrawny to *pudgy* ~~fat,~~ and *couch potato* ~~lazy~~ to superstar, and we each developed a program that was OK for us. *[Handwritten note: I'm not trying here]* *[Handwritten note: OK]* Some women didn't listen to our instructor who urged us not to ~~do~~ *try* more reps or weight than our programs called for, even if *our first workouts* it seemed too easy. This turned out to be good *[Handwritten note: Start sentence here? Not sure]* advice because those of us who didn't listen woke up *the next morning* feeling as though our bodies had been twisted by evil forces.

In addition to fitting to ~~After meeting~~ her physical capabilities, a weight lifter needs to design her personal goals.

Most students in my group wanted to improve their *(I need specific examples of students)* upper body strength. (Each) student learned to use specific exercises to isolate certain muscle groups, for example we might work on our arms and (abdomen) *(sf?)* one day and our shoulders and chest the next day. ~~My~~ goal is nursing, which I want to pursue. I ~~want~~ to help others, but I'm also very interested in the science I'll learn. I hear there is a lot of memorization, which I'm pretty good at. I also will have "clinical" assignments to give us hands ~~on~~ ~~experience in hospitals.~~ *(I'm off the topic)* Because I had had such trouble lifting my grandmother, I added exercises to strengthen my legs and back. Another student added neck strengthening exercises. Someone else added finger and hand exercises.

At the end of the course, we had to evaluate our progress. When I started, I could lift 10 pounds, *over my head for 3 reps.* ~~but~~ By the end, I could lift 10 pounds *over my head* for 20 reps and 18 pounds for 3 reps. I am so proud of my *(I forget to talk about my swimming)* accomplishments that I *still* work out three or four times *(I need a stronger ending)* a week. I am proof that any woman can become stronger and have more stamina.

Revising a second draft

    After Carol Moreno finished writing and entering notes to herself on her first draft (see 3f-1), she revised her work into a second draft and typed a clean copy to give to her instructor. As stated in the assignment (see page 20), Moreno's instructor considered the second draft an "essay in progress," so that all comments by the instructor were aimed at helping Moreno write an effective third, final draft.

    Here is Moreno's second draft with two types of comments from the instructor: **questions** to stimulate Moreno to clarify and expand on ideas in the draft and section **codes**—the number-letter combinations—for Moreno to consult in this handbook.

3f-2

3f–2
cont.

TEACHING TIP

Certainly, all of us sometimes feel that we are drowning in student writing. The battle rages constantly: Do I spend twenty minutes on each short essay or do I spend five minutes and get to respond to more of what my students write?

Given the few minutes that we have for each essay, decisions about what and how to write are important. Codes (abbreviations such *sp* and *agr*; references to the text, such as 15*a*) are a clear, fast way to refer to unambiguous matters in grammar, punctuation, and mechanics. Make sure students know what the symbols mean: you might review the symbols you ordinarily use as part of the follow-up to their receiving their first piece of writing back from you. Along with citing errors, many symbols send a secondary message: "This matter is important but relatively uninspiring. Fix it quickly (and learn the information) and move on to the more interesting aspects of your essay."

Many issues of substance are difficult to discuss exclusively by code. Besides, students like to feel that a real human being is reading their work—and real people ask questions when they are puzzled. Therefore, whenever possible, phrase your reactions as questions. Instead of writing *"unclear,"* ask "How does this relate to your thesis?" If you do not have time to write many questions, try to get at least one in per paper. Psychologically, people can't help but answer questions—at least in their own minds. So, to ask a question is to guarantee an answer. And with the answer in mind a student can revise.

Whenever time permits, a good description deserves more than "nice" scribbled in the margin; you might say "You really made me see the lake at sun-

➡

SECOND DRAFT WITH INSTRUCTOR'S COMMENTS

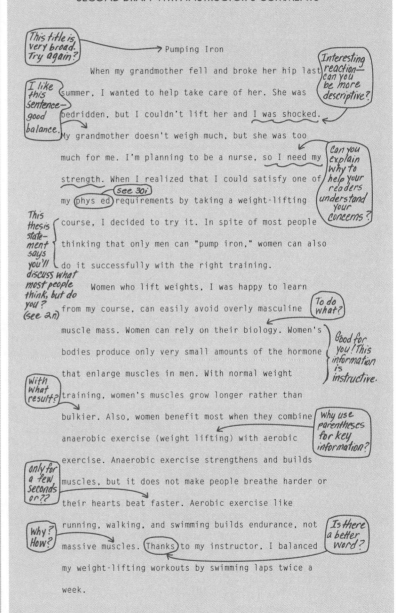

Hoping for strength and endurance can lead to

Can hope lead to injury?

injury unless lifters learn the safe use of free

I can't "see" these.

weights and weight machines. Free weights are

barbells. To be safe, no matter how little the weight,

This image seems incomplete. Help?!

lifters must never raise a barbell by bending at the

waist. Instead, they should squat, and then straighten

see 15d-1

up into a standing position. To avoid a twist can lead

to a serious injury, lifters must do this: head erect

Read this aloud to hear that the action to do is missing.

and facing forward back and neck aligned. The big

see 19B

advantage of weight machines is that lifters must use

them sitting down, so machines like the Nautilus and

Universal pretty much force lifters to sit straight,

which really does reduce the chance of injury.

Do you want to use one word so much?

Once a weight lifter understands how to lift

safely, she needs to meet her personal needs. No one

needs to be strong to get started. A well-planned

See 13a

progressive weight training program It begins with

whatever weight a person can lift comfortably and

gradually adds to the base weight as she gets

stronger. What builds strength is the number of "reps"

the lifter does, not necessarily an increase in the

meaning?

amount of resistance from adding weight. Our

instructor helped the women in our class, who ranged

These adjectives are fun.

from 18 to 43, scrawny to pudgy, couch potato to

superstar, to develop a program that suited us. Our

instructor urged us not to try more reps or weight

than our programs called for, even if our first

→

TEACHING TIP, cont.

down." If a student tells you about a cooking disaster, you might say "You had me laughing in sympathy. The same thing happened to me." Such comments validate students' experiences and also demonstrate compassionate reading.

In many cases, reaction comments are most useful in the final response to an essay. Many students turn to the end of their essays before reading marginal comments. After the grade, this is the part of our response that is most crucial to students. The final comment is our total impression, while the margins represent a kind of running commentary. To be useful, a closing comment needs to clarify our response, not duplicate the grade: a student whose grade has jumped from *D* to *B* knows his or her work is "better," so try to be specific.

A useful end comment consists of at least several sentences. A serviceable pattern consists of a personal response, a sentence about the content and organization of the piece (positive as well as negative observations—see the end comment to Foster), and, where pertinent, a few sentences about a recurring mechanical or grammatical issue (e.g., "Try to hear and pronounce the ends of words. You frequently omit -*s* and -*ed* endings, resulting in tense and number errors that can confuse a reader").

TEACHING TIP

Revising is a process just as composing is a process. Students may find it helpful to examine the steps they go through when revising, editing, and proofreading. Here are some questions they can use to look carefully at how they approach these final stages of writing a paper.

→

TEACHING TIP, cont.

1. How did you make the mental shift from suspending judgment to making judgment?

2. Did you use the questions in the Revision Checklist in this chapter or material supplied by your instructor?

3. How did you decide whether to write an entirely new draft or to revise the one you had?

4. If you had readers other than the teacher, how did you use their suggestions? Did you use all of them? None of them?

5. Did you reconsider your original purpose and audience?

6. Did you need to make any changes in your introduction or conclusion because of other changes in your text?

7. Was your original title still appropriate?

8. Did you consider different elements of your writing during separate rounds of revision?

9. How much new material did you add? In how many places did you add new words, sentences, or paragraphs?

10. How much material did you delete? In how many places did you cut out words, sentences, or paragraphs?

11. How many changes in the sequence of paragraphs did you make?

12. Did you use a checklist, either the one in this chapter, your own, or one supplied by your instructor, to examine your writing for grammar, spelling, punctuation, or capitalization problems?

13. Did you edit your paper in a single reading or look for possible errors in a series of readings?

14. Did you read your paper aloud to find errors? Did you start at the end? Did you read it line by line?

15. Did you reconsider the format of your paper?

workouts seemed too easy. This turned out to be good advice because those of us who did not listen woke up the next morning feeling as though our bodies had been twisted by evil forces.

Fun again. Your voice (personality) comes through.

In addition to fitting a program to her physical capabilities, a weight lifter needs to design her personal goals. Most students in my group wanted to improve their upper body strength, so we focused on exercises to strengthen our arms, shoulders, abdomens, and chests. Each student learned to use specific exercises to isolate certain muscle groups for example we might work on our arms and abdomen one day and our shoulders and chest the next day. Because I had had such trouble lifting my grandmother, I added exercises to strengthen my legs and back. Another student added neck strengthening exercises. Someone else, planning to be a physical therapist, added finger and hand-strengthening exercises.

Does one design a goal?

good details

Why important?

see 14a and 14e

see 24b-1

Excellent examples Carol!

Why did she choose this?

At the end of the course, we had to evaluate our progress. When I started, I could lift 10 pounds over my head for 3 reps. By the end, I could lift 10 pounds over my head for 20 reps and 18 pounds for 3 reps. Also I could swim for 20 sustained minutes instead of the 10 at first. I am so proud of my accomplishments that I still work out three or four times a week. I am proof that any woman can benefit from "pumping iron." Not only will she become stronger and have more stamina, she will also feel very good.

How long was it?

Can you communicate your enthusiasm to your reader more effectively?

see 24b-3

Isn't this a bit flat?

Dear Carol,
You have truly earned the right to feel proud of yourself. You've also inspired me to consider weight training myself!
As you revise for your final draft, I'd urge you to get more <u>voice</u> (your personality) into the essay. To do this, you don't have to become too informal; instead, find how you <u>felt</u> about what you were doing and try to put that into words. Also, think about my questions and the codes that refer you to sections of the Troyka handbook. I will enjoy reading your final draft, I'm sure.

K.N.

Revising, editing, and proofreading a final draft 3f-3

Moreno revised her essay in a third, final draft by working with the instructor's comments. Moreno started with the larger elements of the essay by thinking about the instructor's questions and suggestions. Next, Moreno used the codes—the number-letter combinations—that referred her to specific sections in this handbook concerning matters of word choice, style, grammar, and punctuation. She also referred to the Revision Checklists, Charts 16 and 17. Before typing a clean copy of her third, final draft, Moreno edited her writing by referring to the Editing Checklist in Chart 19. Here is the third, final draft of Moreno's essay. The labels in the margins are guideposts for you only in this handbook; do not use them on your final drafts.

THIRD, FINAL DRAFT BY STUDENT

title
                    Women Can Pump Iron, Too

introduction
        When my grandmother fell and broke her hip last

    summer, I wanted to help take care of her. Because she

    was bedridden, she needed to be lifted at times, but I

    was shocked to discover that I could not lift her

    without my mother's or brother's help. My grandmother

→

TEACHING TIP

A personal editing checklist, a list of problems that recur from one piece of writing to the next, can help any writer spot potential trouble spots. You may want to suggest that students go through returned papers, listing each marked error and grouping those that are similar, such as spelling errors, subject-verb agreement errors, and comma splices. After becoming aware of the kinds of problems that are most likely to occur, the writer can devise ways of checking new manuscripts to make sure they are not present. For example, if the *s* is left off most third-person singular verbs, the writer should go through a new paper checking each such construction for agreement.

BACKGROUND

In "The Apple in the Center" (*Writing Lab Newsletter* 9 [November 1984]: 9–10), Beatrice Jacobson assesses the impact of computers on the writing process, concluding that they make all of its stages easier and faster. She points out that computers make students want to write more. Students also gain a sense of professionalism when writing on computers.

In her study of student writers using computers, Wendy Colby Boserra found that students spent more time and energy revising and editing their work when using word processors, but that they did not significantly increase their prewriting ("Effects of Word Processors upon the Writing Processes of Basic Writers," *Dissertation Abstracts International* 48 [July 1987]: 34A).

QUOTATION ABOUT WRITING

When you say something, make sure you have said it. The chances of your having said it are only fair.

—E. B. White

3f-3
cont.

does not weigh much, but she was too much for me. My pride was hurt, and even more important, I began to worry about my plans to be a nurse specializing in care of elderly people. What if I were too weak to help my patients get around? When I realized that I could satisfy one of my Physical Education requirements by taking a weight-lifting course for women, I decided to try it. Many people picture only big, macho men wanting **[thesis statement]** to lift weights, but times have changed. With the right training, women can also "pump iron" successfully to build strength.

[background information]   Women who lift weights, I was happy to learn from my course, can easily avoid developing overly masculine muscle mass. Women can rely on their biology to protect them. Women's bodies produce only very small amounts of the hormones that enlarge muscles in men. With normal weight training, women's muscles grow longer rather than bulkier. The result is smoother, firmer muscles, not massive bulges. Also, women benefit most when they combine weight lifting, which is a form of anaerobic exercise, with aerobic exercise. Anaerobic exercise strengthens and builds muscles, but it does not make people breathe harder or their hearts beat faster for sustained periods. In contrast, aerobic exercise like running, walking, and swimming builds endurance, but not massive muscles, because they force a person to take in more oxygen, which increases lung capacity, improves circulatory health, and tones the entire body. Encouraged by my instructor, I balanced my weight-lifting workouts by swimming laps twice a week.

support: first aspect of training

Striving for strength can end in injury unless weight lifters learn the safe use of free weights and weight machines. Free weights are barbells, the metal bars that round metal weights can be attached to at each end. To be safe, no matter how little the weight, lifters must never raise a barbell by bending at the waist, grabbing the barbell, and then straightening up. Instead, they should squat, grasp the barbell, and then use their leg muscles to straighten into a standing position. To avoid a twist that can lead to serious injury, lifters must use this posture: head erect and facing forward, back and neck aligned. The big advantage of weight machines, which use weighted handles and bars hooked to wires and pulleys, is that lifters must use them sitting down. Therefore, machines like the Nautilus and Universal actually force lifters to keep their bodies properly aligned, which drastically reduces the chance of injury.

support: second aspect of training

Once a weight lifter understands how to lift safely, she needs a weight-lifting regimen personalized to her specific physical needs. Because benefits come from "resistance," which is the stress that lifting any

➡

BACKGROUND

Defining themselves and assuming the roles of a college writer are often difficult challenges for students, according to David Bartholomae in "Inventing the University" (*Perspective on Literacy*, ed. Eugene R. Kintgen, Barry M. Kroll, and Mike Rose [Carbondale, IL: Southern Illinois UP, 1988]). Bartholomae believes that "all writers, in order to write, must imagine for themselves the privilege of being 'insiders'—that is, of being both inside an established and powerful discourse, and of being granted a special right to speak" (277). But students are seldom able to write as insiders or authorities for they lack knowledge not only of the subject matter, but also of the vocabulary, audience, and genres of college writing. Students, then, "have to assume privilege without having any" (278). This problem is compounded by the fact that many high school and college assignments—exams, reports, and summaries—ask students to write "outside the working discourse of the academic community, where they are expected to admire and report on what we do, rather than inside that discourse, where they can do its work and participate in a common enterprise" (278).

amount of weight puts on a muscle, no one has to be strong to get started. A well-planned, progressive weight-training program begins with whatever weight a person can lift comfortably and gradually adds to the base weight as she gets stronger. What builds muscle strength is the number of repetitions, or "reps," the lifter does, not necessarily an increase in the amount of resistance from adding weight. Our instructor helped the women in the class, who ranged from 18 to 43, scrawny to pudgy, and couch potato to superstar, develop a program that was right for our individual weights, ages, and overall level of conditioning. Everyone's program differed in how much weight to start out with and how many reps to do for each exercise. Our instructor urged us not to try more weight or reps than our programs called for, even if our first workouts seemed too easy. This turned out to be good advice because those of us who did not listen woke up the next day feeling as though our bodies had been twisted by evil forces.

support: third aspect of training

In addition to fitting a program to her physical capabilities, a weight lifter needs to design an individual routine to fit her personal goals. Most students in my group wanted to improved their upper body strength, so we focused on exercises to strengthen arms, shoulders, abdomens, and chests. Each student learned to use specific exercises to isolate certain muscle groups. Because muscles strengthen and grow when they are rested after a workout, our instructor taught us to work alternate muscle groups on different days. For example, a woman might work on her arms and abdomen one day and then her shoulders and chest the next day. Because I had had such trouble lifting my grandmother, I added exercises to strengthen my legs and back. Another student, who had hurt her neck in a car crash, added neck-strengthening exercises. Someone else, planning to be a physical therapist, added finger- and hand-strengthening exercises.

conclusion: outcome with call to action

At the end of our 10 weeks of weight training, we had to evaluate our progress. Was I impressed! I felt ready to lift the world. When I started, I could lift only 10 pounds over my head for 3 reps. By the end of the course, I could lift 10 pounds over my head for 20 reps, and I could lift 18 pounds for 3 reps. Also, I could swim laps for 20 sustained minutes instead of the 10 I had barely managed at first. I am so proud of my weight-training accomplishments that I still work out three or four times a week. I am proof that any woman can benefit from "pumping iron." Not only will she become stronger and have more stamina, she will also feel energetic and confident. After all, there is nothing to lose--except maybe some flab.

4 Rhetorical Strategies in Paragraphs

REFERENCE TO SUPPLEMENTS

This topic is included in the TASP writing competency test. Refer students to *Preparing for the TASP* by M. Saenz.

TEACHING TIP

Essay paragraphing differs considerably from newspaper-article paragraphing. Anyone can see at a glance that newspapers frequently have paragraphs of only a sentence or two. Such short paragraphs are rare in essays, except perhaps as transitions. The reason for the difference in the look of essays and articles is the rationale behind each. Essays attempt to present material in a simultaneously logical and dramatic way. They begin with a hook to grab the reader's interest, and then usually proceed from point to point until the end (of the narrative or of the list of causes, etc.) is reached. Rarely is the first paragraph used to reveal key information. Essays are written on the assumption that they will be read from beginning to end.

In contrast, newspaper articles (not to be confused with essays in newspapers) use few such dramatic devices for suspense purposes. Usually, the only hook is

➡

Rhetorical strategies in writing are techniques for presenting ideas so that a writer's intended message is delivered with clarity and impact. The rhetorical strategies available to you as a writer are sufficiently varied to give you many choices of ways to make your writing effective. As you can see from the explanations and examples in this chapter, all rhetorical strategies reflect the typical patterns of thought that humans use quite naturally. As you try out these strategies, especially as they keep you aware of sequencing and arranging sentences, you can apply them to composing your paragraphs, and, in some situations, whole essays.

4a Understanding paragraphs

A **paragraph** is a group of sentences that work in concert to develop a unit of thought. Paragraphing permits you to subdivide material into manageable parts and, at the same time, to arrange those parts into a unified whole that effectively communicates its message.

Paragraphing is signaled by indentation. The first line is indented five spaces in a typewritten paper and one inch in a handwritten paper. (Business letters are sometimes typed in "block format," with paragraphs separated by a double space but no paragraph indentations. Generally block format is not appropriate for essays.)

The purpose of a paragraph helps to determine its structure. In college, the most common purposes for academic writing are to inform and to persuade (see 1b). Some paragraphs introduce, conclude, or provide transitions. Most paragraphs, however, are **topical paragraphs**, also called *developmental paragraphs* or *body paragraphs*. They consist of a statement of a main idea, and specific, logical support for that main idea. Consider paragraph 1, a topical paragraph that seeks to inform. (To help discussion and reference in this chapter, a red number appears at the left side of each sample paragraph.)

> The cockroach lore that has been daunting us for years is most-ly true. Roaches can live for twenty days without food, fourteen days without water; they can flatten their bodies and crawl through a crack thinner than a dime; they can eat huge doses of carcinogens and still die of old age. They can even survive "as much radiation as an oak tree can," says William Bell, the University of Kansas entomologist whose cockroaches appeared in the movie *The Day After.* They'll eat almost anything—regular food, leather, glue, hair, paper, even the starch in book bindings. (The New York Public Library has quite a cockroach problem.) They sense the slightest breeze, and they can react and start running in .05 seconds; they can also remain motion-less for days. And if all this isn't creepy enough, they can fly too.
>
> —JANE GOLDMAN, "What's Bugging You"

Goldman states her main idea in the first sentence. She then gives concrete examples supporting her claim that there is much truth to the lore about cockroaches. This paragraph relates to the thesis of the whole essay: "Roaches cannot be banished from the world, but they can be controlled in people's homes and apartments."

Consider this topical paragraph that seeks to persuade. It, too, consists of a main idea and support.

> The public library is the best, most democratic, most economi-cal mechanism ever devised to provide access to information and enlightenment on issues that range from the intensely personal to those that are global in nature. Individuals of all ages and from all walks of life, community groups, agencies, businesses, unions, and government institutions of every kind increasingly turn to the public library for assistance. It is the only library that is available to everyone in the community. Typically, it receives half of 1 percent of the gov-ernment's budget yet serves 30 to 50 percent of the people. No other community service is more cost effective.
>
> —CLARA BENNETT, President of the Board of Trustees,
> Nassau County Library System

Bennett states her main idea in the first two sentences. The sec-ond sentence narrows the focus of the first and sets the stage for the supporting statements that follow.

Goldman's and Bennett's paragraphs demonstrate the three major characteristics of an effective paragraph.(See Chart 20 on the next page).

Understanding paragraph structure can help you at various points during your writing process. Before DRAFTING, you might decide to sub-

TEACHING TIP, cont.

personal opinion. They may also notice the lack of a thesis statement and of a conclusion in the newspaper article and the presence of both in the essay.

You might also ask students how satisfied they would be if they were given only the first paragraph of the newspaper article and of the essay. The article's introduction will probably be far more satisfying in terms of information, less satisfying in terms of graceful presentation, background, pacing, and the like.

Another way to underscore the difference between the genres is to give students (or assign them to find) a meaty newspaper article—the kind that runs for two pages, usually about a scandal or a major crime. Have them rewrite the article as an essay. Before the students write, you might discuss with them the kinds of changes they anticipate making.

REFERENCES TO SUPPLEMENTS

For this topic in the CLAST writing competency test, refer students to ch. 2, section A5c of *Preparing for the CLAST* by S. Patterson.

See transparency 4–1 for revising for paragraph unity in the *Prentice Hall/Simon & Schuster Transparencies for Writers* by D. Carter.

BACKGROUND

u-ni-ty (yoó n tē) n. *pl* -ties (1) The state, property, or product of being united physically, socially, or morally; oneness; opposed to *division*, *plurality*.
—*Britannica World Language Dictionary*
Edition of Funk and Wagnalls Standard, p. 1373.

4a cont. divide your material into paragraphs and to develop each in an effective way. If you prefer to plan less at first and instead write a "discovery" or a rough draft that gets all your ideas down on paper, you can later sort out your material and arrange it into manageable paragraphs. When revising (see 3c), you might find that a particular paragraph is weak because it does not clearly state its main idea or it does not develop that idea well. Also, you might notice that although each paragraph is well structured on its own, the paragraphs do not work together very well. This chapter offers you paragraphing options to consider as you plan, draft, and revise your writing.

MAJOR CHARACTERISTICS OF AN EFFECTIVE PARAGRAPH   20

- **Unity:** clear, logical relationship between the main idea of a paragraph (see 4b) and supporting evidence for that main idea (see 4c).

- **Coherence:** smooth progression from one sentence to the next within a paragraph (see 4d).

- **Development:** arrange a paragraph (see 4e), and specific, concrete support for the main idea of the paragraph (see 4f).

4b ## Writing unified paragraphs

A paragraph is **unified** when all its sentences clarify or help support the main idea. Unity is lost if a paragraph goes off the topic by including sentences unrelated to the main idea. Here is a paragraph about databases, which lacks unity because two deliberately added sentences go off the topic.

NO   We have all used physical databases since our grammar school days. Grammar school is known today as grade school or elementary school. Our class yearbooks, the telephone book, the shoebox full of receipts documenting our deductions for the IRS—these are all databases in one form or another, for a database is nothing more than an assemblage of information organized to allow the retrieval of that information in certain ways. Anyone who is well organized has a better chance of succeeding in college or in the business world.

In the preceding paragraph, the second and last sentences wander away from the topic of databases. As a result, unity is lost. A reader quickly loses patience with material that rambles and therefore fails to communicate a clear message. Paragraph 3 is the original version. It is unified because all its sentences, including the ones adding interesting details, relate to the subject of databases.

YES

3

We have all used physical databases since our grammar school days. Our class yearbooks, the telephone book, the shoebox full of receipts documenting our deductions for the IRS—these are all databases in one form or another, for a database is nothing more than an assemblage of information in certain ways. A telephone book, for example, assuming that you have the right one for the right city, will enable you to find the telephone number for, say, Alan Smith. Coincidentally it will also give you his address, provided there is only one Alan Smith listed. Where there are several Alan Smiths, you would have to know the address, or at least part of it, to find the number of the particular Alan Smith you had in mind. Even without the address, however, you would still save considerable time by the telephone database. The book might list 50,000 names but only 12 Alan Smiths, so at the outset you could eliminate 49,988 telephone calls when trying to contact the elusive Mr. Smith.

—Erik Sanberg-Diment, "Personal Computers"

The sentence that contains the main idea of a paragraph, called the **topic sentence**, shapes and controls the content of the rest of the paragraph.

Some paragraphs use two sentences to present a main idea. In such cases, the topic sentence is followed by a **limiting** or **clarifying sentence,** which serves to narrow the paragraph's focus. In paragraph 3, the second sentence is its topic sentence, and the third sentence is its limiting sentence. The rest of the sentences support the main idea.

Professional essay writers do not always use topic sentences, because these writers have the skill to carry the reader along without explicit signposts. Student writers are often advised to use topic sentences so that their essays will be clearly organized and their paragraphs will not stray from the controlling power of each main idea.

Topic sentence at the beginning of a paragraph

Most informative and persuasive paragraphs place the topic sentence (shown in italics) first so that a reader knows immediately what to expect.

4

To travel the streets of Los Angeles is to glimpse America's ethnic future. At the bustling playground at McDonald's in Koreatown, a dozen shades of kids squirt down the slides and burrow through tunnels and race down the catwalks, not much minding that

BACKGROUND

In *Errors and Expectations* (New York: Oxford UP, 1977), Mina Shaughnessy points out that just as novice writers must learn the structure of sentences and words by viewing them in unfamiliar, more abstract ways, they must similarly develop a new way of thinking if they are to learn paragraph and essay structure. She names two types of instruction that have merit: practice in "seeing" structure in a wide range of written materials, and practice in recognizing thought patterns that frequently appear in conventional writing tasks for college.

BACKGROUND

Many of the conventions followed by contemporary writers did not exist in the ancient world. For example, words were not divided from each other until sometime in the seventh century A.D., and word division was not systematically practiced until the eleventh. Some marks of punctuation, such as the question mark and the exclamation mark, evolved during the Middle Ages. Paragraphs had been indicated since pre-Christian days, first by short horizontal strokes or wedge-shaped signs. Later they were noted in Latin manuscripts by a new line. At the same time, it became the practice to indicate the beginning of a new paragraph with enlarged letters, sometimes extending the length of the page. Such elaborate figures became the ancestors of our capital letters. The paragraph as it known today took shape late in the seventeenth century but was not systematically described until the nineteenth century, when Alexander Bain published his *English Composition and Rhetoric* (1866).

BACKGROUND

The use of topic sentences by published writers has been the subject of a great deal of research and study over the past two decades. Richard Braddock's "The Frequency and Placement of Topic Sentence in Expository Prose" (*Research in the Teaching of English* [1974]: 287–302; rpt. *The Writing Teacher's Sourcebook*, ed. Gary Tate and Edward P. J. Corbett, 2nd ed. [New York: Oxford UP, 1988]) reports the surprising information that in the 25 essays he examined, he found topic sentences in paragraphs only 13 percent of the time. Admitting that it is difficult to know exactly what a topic sentence is, he also points out that "percentages vary greatly among individual writers." Several years later, in 1979, William Irmscher reported in *Teaching Expository Writing* (New York: Holt, Rinehart and Winston, p. 98) that his graduate students found topic sentences in 40 to 50 percent of the paragraphs they analyzed, a significantly higher percentage than Braddock discovered. The percentages have varied in other studies, but most have found that under half of the paragraphs in published writing begin with topic sentences.

Braddock, however, ends his study with the opinion that "often the writing in the 25 essays would have been clearer and more comfortable to read if the paragraphs had presented more explicit topic sentences" (301). Frank J. D'Angelo agrees in "The Topic Sentence Revisited" (*College Composition and Communication* [December 1986]: 431–441), arguing that recent research shows that people are able to read faster and remember and comprehend more material when a paragraph begins with a sentence that states the main idea and indicates the organization of the paragraph that follows. D'Angelo believes that writers improve the readability of their papers by beginning many of their paragraphs (not all) with topic sentences.

no two of them speak the same language. Parents of grade-school children say they rarely know the color of their youngsters' best friends until they meet them; it never seems to occur to the children to say, since they have not yet been taught to care.

—NANCY GIBBS, "Shades of Difference"

Sometimes the main idea in the topic sentence starts a paragraph and is then restated at the end of the paragraph.

5   *Every dream is a portrait of the dreamer.* You may think of your dream as a mirror that reflects your inner character—the aspects of your personality of which you are not fully aware. Once we understand this, we can also see that every trait portrayed in our dreams has to exist in us, somewhere, regardless of whether we are aware of it or admit it. *Whatever characteristics the dream figures have, whatever behavior they engage in, is also true of the dreamer in some way.*

—ROBERT A. JOHNSON, *Inner Work*

Topic sentence at the end of a paragraph

Some informative and persuasive paragraphs reveal the supporting details before the main idea. The topic sentence, therefore, comes at the end of a paragraph. This approach is particularly effective for building suspense and for dramatic effect. This arrangement forces readers to move through all the details before encountering the organizing effect of a main idea.

Paragraphs 6 and 7 end with a topic sentence. In paragraph 6, the main idea is fairly easy to predict as the specific suggestions accumulate. In paragraph 7, the main idea is less predictable, and it is thus more satisfying for some readers but more challenging for others.

6   Burnout is a potential problem for any hard working and persevering student. A preliminary step for preventing student burnout is for students to work in moderation. Students can concentrate on school every day, provided that they do not overtax themselves. One method students can use is to avoid concentrating on a single project for an extended period of time. For example, if students have to read two books for a midterm history test, they should do other assignments at intervals so that the two books will not get boring. Another means to moderate a workload is to regulate how many extracurricular projects to take on. *When a workload is manageable, a student's immunity to burnout is strengthened.*

—BRADLEY HOWARD, student

Most people do not lose ten dollars or one hundred dollars when they trade cars. They lose many hundreds or even a thousand.

7 They buy used cars that will not provide them service through the first payment. They overbuy new cars and jeopardize their credit, only to find themselves "hung," unable even to sell their shiny new toys. *The car business is one of the last roundups in America, the great slaughterhouse of wheeling and dealing, where millions of people each year willingly submit to being taken.*

—REMAR SUTTON, *Don't Get Taken Every Time*

Topic sentence implied

Some paragraphs make a unified statement without the use of a topic sentence. Writers must construct such paragraphs carefully so that a reader can easily discern the main idea.

8 The Romans were entertained by puppets, as were the rulers of the Ottoman Empire with their favorite shadow puppet, Karaghoiz, teller of a thousand tales. In the Middle Ages, puppets were cast as devil and angel in religious mystery and morality plays until cast out entirely by the church. For centuries, there has been a rich puppetry heritage in India that matches that country's multilayered culture. The grace of Bali is reflected in its stylized, ceremonial rod and shadow puppets. The Bunraku puppets of Japan, unequaled for technique anywhere in the world, require a puppet master and two assistants to create one dramatic character on stage.

—DAN CODY, "Puppet Poetry"

Cody uses many examples to communicate the main idea that puppets have been popular in many cultures over time. A reader does not expect to puzzle over material, so implied topic sentences must be very clear, even though they are silent.

EXERCISE 4-1

Consulting sections 4a and 4b, identify all topic sentences, limiting sentences, and topic sentences repeated at the ends of paragraphs. If there is no topic sentence, compose an implied one.

9 A. A good college program should stress the development of high-level reading, writing, and mathematical skills and should provide you with a broad historical, social, and cultural perspective, no matter what subject you choose as your major. The program should teach you not only the most current knowledge in your field but also—just as important—prepare you to keep learning throughout your life. After all, you will probably change jobs, and possibly even careers, at least six times, and you'll have other responsibilities, too—perhaps as a spouse and as a parent and certainly as a member of a community whose bounds extend beyond the workplace.

—FRANK T. RHODES, "Let the Student Decide"

4b
cont.

QUOTATION ABOUT WRITING

There is no pleasure in the world like writing well and going fast. It's like nothing else. It's like a love affair, it goes on and on, and doesn't end in marriage. It's all courtship.

—Tennessee Williams

QUOTATION ABOUT WRITING

I just write, and things come to a crest, and that's how it is. My mind works in this way—it's sort of like a puzzle. I know where the pieces are, but I don't want to fit them for myself or for the reader. I just write.

—Jamaica Kincaid

QUOTATION ABOUT WRITING

When I sit down to write I feel extraordinarily at ease, and I move in an element which, it seems to me, I know extraordinarily well; I use tools that are familiar to me and they fit snugly in my hands.

—Natalia Ginzburg

B. The once majestic oak tree crashes to the ground amid the destructive flames, as its panic-stricken inhabitants attempt to flee the fiery tomb. Undergrowth that formerly flourished smolders in ashes. A family of deer darts furiously from one wall of flame to the other, without an emergency exit. On the outskirts of the inferno, fire fighters try desperately to stop the destruction. Somewhere at the source of this chaos lies a former campsite containing the cause of this destruction— an untended campfire. This scene is one of many which illustrate how human apathy and carelessness destroy nature.

—ANNE BRYSON, student

10

C. Rudeness is not a distinctive quality of our own time. People today would be shocked by how rudely our ancestors behaved. In the colonial period, a French traveler marveled that "Virginians do not use napkins, but they wear silk cravats, and instead of carrying white handkerchiefs they blow their noses either with their fingers or with a silk handkerchief that also serves as a cravat, a napkin, and so on." In the 19th century, up to about the 1830s, even very distinguished people routinely put their knives in their mouths. And when people went to the theater, they would not just applaud politely—they would chant, jeer, and shout. So, the notion that there has been a downhill slide in manners ever since time began is just not so.

—"Horizons," U.S. *News & World Report*

11

D. Peanuts contain no cholesterol and a lot of nutrition. A 3.5-ounce package of unsalted peanuts contains more than half of your daily protein requirement. But peanuts are far from a health food. That same 3.5-ounce package also contains 564 calories.

—LOUISE KLEIN, "Peanut Gallery"

12

E. There are at least two important reasons for the surplus of women in urban areas. First, cities are the best places for women to find jobs. Men account for 79 percent of the nation's farmers, 85 percent of miners, and 95 percent of loggers. But the service economy is urban and dominated by women. The second reason is the high death rate for young men in inner cities. The Bronx, for example, has only about 47 men for every 53 women in the target age group—the highest disparity of any county in New York State. Higher male mortality also explains the female skew in some rural counties, such as many of those that include Indian reservations.

—BRAD EDMONDSON AND BLAYNE CUTLER, "Where the Boys Are"

13

Supporting the main idea of a paragraph   4c

As a writer, when you know how to achieve effective **paragraph development,** your material is far more likely to deliver its message to your reader. Most successful topical paragraphs that seek to inform or persuade (see 1b) contain a generalization, which is communicated in the topic sentence of the paragraph (see 4b). But more is needed. In writing most topical paragraphs, you must be sure to *develop the paragraph.* Development is provided by specific, concrete details that support the generalization. Without development, a topical paragraph contains only the broad claim of the generalization. It goes around in circles because it merely repeats the generalization over and over. It therefore does little to inform or persuade the reader.

Here is a paragraph that is unsuccessful because it contains one generalization restated four times in different words. Compare it with paragraph 1, an example of a successful paragraph, early in this chapter.

> **NO**   The cockroach lore that has been daunting us for years is mostly true. Almost every tale we have heard about cockroaches is true. These tales have been disheartening people for generations. No one seems to believe that it is possible to control roaches.

This *No* paragraph is stalled. It goes nowhere. Such material does not hold the reader's interest because it neither informs nor persuades.

When you write a topical paragraph, remember that **what separates most good writing from bad is the writer's ability to move back and forth between generalizations and specific details.** A successful topical paragraph includes a generalization and specific, concrete supporting details.

Using detail is one of the keys to effective, successful development in topical paragraphs. Details bring generalizations to life by providing concrete, specific illustrations. "RENNS" is a memory device you can use to check whether you have included sufficient detail in a topical paragraph. Chart 21 on the next page explains RENNS.

A well-supported paragraph usually has only a selection of RENNS, so do not expect your paragraphs to have all categories in the list. Also, RENNS does not mean that the supporting details must occur in the order of the letters in RENNS. To see RENNS in action, read the many sample paragraphs in this chapter with an eye for the details. Also, consider paragraphs 14, 15, and 16 on the next two pages especially.

REFERENCE TO SUPPLEMENTS

For this topic in the CLAST writing competency test, refer students to ch. 2, section A5a of *Preparing for the CLAST* by S. Patterson.

QUOTATION ABOUT WRITING

I have two methods of working. One of them involves tapping the sources of creativity . . . . I might be anywhere when it comes and I could end up writing all over the floor or up the walls and not knowing what is going on. It is like having a fit . . . .

The second method is following a trail made by my words themselves—by sitting down and writing . . . writing anything, fast. The words include the vision. That rush—that vision or high or whatever it is—doesn't last very long. A lot of writing gets done in a very short time, but it's not very good writing. Often it turns out to be just a reminder about how something felt. It has to be reworked.

    —Maxine Hong Kingston

BACKGROUND

The concept of the paragraph as a self-contained or organic unit of language first appeared in *English Composition and Rhetoric* (1866), a textbook by Alexander Bain, professor of rhetoric at the University of Aberdeen in Scotland. Bain defined the paragraph as "a collection of sentences with unity of purpose" and declared unity, coherence, and emphasis to be the characteristics of an effective paragraph, a proclamation that has had a vast influence on textbooks ever since. He gave students seven guidelines for achieving these effects:

1. Distribution into sentences: The paragraph is composed of individual

➡

BACKGROUND, cont.

sentences, each with its own unity, working together to form the whole.

2. Explicit reference: The connection of each sentence to the ones preceding it must be clear.

3. Parallel construction: Consecutive sentences that carry the same meaning or idea should be formed alike.

4. Indication of the theme: The first sentence should indicate the scope of the paragraph.

5. Unity: Unity derives from a sustained purpose and admits no digressions or irrelevancies.

6. Consecutive arrangement: Related topics should be placed close together.

7. Marking of subordination: The principal and subordinate statements should have their relative importance clearly indicated, just as such elements in a sentence do.

Later textbooks influenced by Bain, notably Fred Newton Scott and Joseph Villiers Denney's *Paragraph-Writing* (1891), treated the paragraph as an "essay in miniature" and encouraged a meristic or parts-to-whole approach to teaching the essay, first teaching students how to write sentences and paragraphs and then teaching them to put these parts together to build essays.

QUOTATION ABOUT WRITING

"When *I* use a word," Humpty Dumpty said in a rather scornful tone, "it means just what I choose it to mean—neither more nor less."

"The question is," said Alice, "whether you *can* make words mean so many different things."

"The question is," said Humpty Dumpty, "which is to be master —that's all."

—Lewis Carroll

USING "RENNS" TO CHECK FOR SPECIFIC, CONCRETE DETAILS   21

- **R**easons
- **E**xamples
- **N**ames
- **N**umbers
- **S**enses (sight, sound, smell, taste, touch)

Here is a paragraph that has three of the five types of RENNS. Locate as many RENNS as you can before you read the analysis that follows the paragraph.

> 14   U.S. shores are also being inundated by waves of plastic debris. On the sands of the Texas Gulf Coast one day last September, volunteers collected 307 tons of litter, two-thirds of which was plastic, including 31,733 bags, 30,295 bottles, and 15,631 six-pack yokes. Plastic trash is being found far out to sea. On a four-day trip from Maryland to Florida that ranged 100 miles offshore, John Hardy, an Oregon State University marine biologist, spotted "Styrofoam and other plastic on the surface, most of the whole cruise."
>
> —"The Dirty Seas," *Time,* August 1, 1988

Paragraph 14 succeeds because it does more than merely repeat its topic sentence, which is its first sentence. It develops the topic sentence by offering concrete, specific illustrations to support the generalization that waves of plastic debris are inundating U.S. shores. It has Examples, including the kinds of litter found washed up on the beach and seen offshore. It has Names, such as Texas Gulf Coast; bags, bottles, six-pack yokes, which describe more specifically the general idea of 307 tons of litter; Maryland; Florida; John Hardy; Oregon State University; marine biologist; and Styrofoam. It has Numbers that describe the volume of litter collected (307 tons), the number of specific items (such as 31,733 bags and 30,295 plastic bottles), and the 100-mile distance from shore where John Hardy found floating plastic litter.

Here is a paragraph that has four of the five types of RENNS. Locate as many RENNS as you can before you read the analysis of RENNS that follows the paragraph.

> We live in a changed world from that of 1888, and we are a changed nation. Our founders knew an America with rising expectations, while we see a superpower riddled with self-doubt. Tropical rain forests were a mysterious challenge in 1888. The

challenge in 1988 is saving them from disappearance. Automobiles had just been invented, and airplanes were unknown. Would our founders be impressed by rush-hour traffic, a brown cloud over
15 Denver, or aerial gridlock at Chicago's O'Hare Airport? Could they have conceived of a Mexico City with 20 million people in an atmosphere so murky that the sun is obscured, so poisonous that school is sometimes delayed until late morning, when the air clears?

—GILBERT M. GROSVENOR, "Will We Mend Our Earth?"

Paragraph 15 succeeds because it does more than repeat its topic sentence, which is the first sentence. The paragraph develops its topic sentence with specific, concrete illustrations of the changed world that makes the United States a changed nation. It has Examples, including rain forests disappearing, automobiles and the rush-hour traffic they cause, airplanes and the aerial gridlock they cause, and air pollution that cars and planes cause. It has Names: America, Denver, Chicago's O'Hare Airport, and Mexico City. It has Numbers: the years 1888 and 1988, and 20 million people. And it elicits one of the five senses: the *sight* of a "brown cloud" over Denver and the *sight* of a murky atmosphere that obscures the sun.

Some well-developed paragraphs have a single extended example to support the topic sentence.

He was one of the greatest scientists the world has ever known, yet if I had to convey the essence of Albert Einstein in a single word, I would choose *simplicity*. Perhaps an anecdote will help. Once, caught in a downpour, he took off his hat and held it under his coat.
16 Asked why, he explained, with admirable logic, that the rain would damage the hat, but his hair would be none the worse for its wetting. This knack of going instinctively to the heart of the matter was the secret of his major scientific discoveries—this and his extraordinary feeling for beauty.

—BANESH HOFFMAN, "My Friend, Albert Einstein"

EXERCISE 4-2

Reread the paragraphs in Exercise 4-1 and identify the RENNS (consult 4c) in each paragraph.

EXERCISE 4-3

Using your own words to complete the thought, fill in the blanks with a word or phrase that is specific. Then choose one of the five as a topic sentence and write a well-developed paragraph. Use as many RENNS (consult 4c) as you need to give the topic sentence concrete, specific support.

1. The place where I feel most comfortable is _____.
2. _____ can cause major problems for students.

ANSWERS: EXERCISE 4–2

A (paragraph 9). Reasons include learning current knowledge, keeping you learning through life, having a job, being a spouse, a parent, and a member of the community. Examples include job, spouse, parent, and member of the community. Number named is six.

B (paragraph 10). Names include oak, deer, fire fighters. Senses are invoked by sound of crashing oak, sight of flames, "fiery tomb," smoldering in ashes, deer family darting furiously, and the smell (implied) of burning trees.

C (paragraph 11). Examples include colonial Virginians using their cravats as handkerchiefs and people putting their knives in their mouths. Names include the French traveler, distinguished people, people in the theater. Numbers include the dates 1830 and the 19th century. Senses include the noise—chants, jeers, and shouts—made by the audience in the theater.

D (paragraph 12). Reasons include the fact that a package of peanuts provides half the daily protein requirement. Names include peanuts, package, and protein. Numbers include the 3.5-ounce package, 564 calories.

E (paragraph 13). Reasons include cities are the best places for women to find jobs, and the death rate is higher for young men in cities. Example named is the Bronx. Names used are the Bronx, New York State. Numbers include 79 percent, 85 percent, 95 percent, and 47 men for every 53 women.

ANSWERS: EXERCISE 4–3

Obviously answers will vary considerably, but the main goal is to help students distinguish between generalities and good detail. Perhaps having each student share with the class what he or she considers the best detail in his or her paragraph would help make this point.

4c
cont.

3. Budgeting time is a skill I _____.
4. The greatest U.S. asset is _____.
5. Getting a good job depends largely on _____.

REFERENCES TO SUPPLEMENTS

For this topic in the CLAST writing competency test, refer students to ch. 2, section A5d of *Preparing for the CLAST* by S. Patterson.

For revising for coherence, refer students to *Rough Drafts* by K. S. Cain, Part II, Exercise 4.

See transparency 4–2 for revising for coherence in the *Prentice Hall/Simon & Schuster Transparencies for Writers* by D. Carter.

BACKGROUND

According to Aristotle's *Rhetoric*, the conclusion of an argument can have as many as four functions. It should create a favorable impression toward the speaker and an unfavorable impression toward the speaker's opponents. It should emphasize the points of the speaker while minimizing the points of the opposition. It should appeal strongly to the audience's emotions. And it should summarize the chief points of the argument.

4d

TECHNIQUES OF COHERENCE

Writing coherent paragraphs

A paragraph is **coherent** when its sentences are related to each other, not only in content but also in grammatical structures and choice of words. To achieve coherence in your writing, write each sentence of a paragraph so that it flows sensibly from the one before. A coherent paragraph gives a reader a sense of continuity. Note in paragraphs 17 through 20 that each sentence continues from the previous sentence, by use of the techniques of coherence listed in Chart 22. As you draft and revise, monitor continuity in your paragraphs.

TECHNIQUES OF COHERENCE　　　　　　　　　　22

- Use **transitional expressions** effectively (4d-1)
- Use **pronouns** effectively (4d-2)
- Use **deliberate repetition** effectively (4d-3)
- Use **parallel structures** effectively (4d-4)

4d-1

Using transitional expressions

Transitional expressions are words and phrases that signal connections among ideas. By signaling how ideas relate to each other, you achieve coherence in your writing. Commonly used transitional expressions are listed in Chart 23. When you use them, be sure to vary your choices within each list to achieve variety in your writing.

! ❖ COMMA ALERT: Transitional expressions are usually set off with commas; see 24b-3. Here are some illustrations:

CONTINUITY BY ADDITION

Woodpeckers use their beaks to find food and to chisel out nests. **In addition,** they claim their territory and signal their desire to mate by drumming their beaks on trees.

CONTINUITY BY CONTRAST

Most birds communicate by singing. Woodpeckers, **however,** communicate by the duration and rhythm of the drumming of their beaks.

CONTINUITY BY RESULT

Woodpeckers communicate by drumming their beaks on dry branches or tree trunks. **As a result,** they can communicate across greater distances than songbirds can. ❖

COMMON TRANSITIONAL EXPRESSIONS AND THE RELATIONSHIPS THEY SIGNAL

23

RELATIONSHIP	WORDS
ADDITION	also, in addition, too, moreover, and, besides, furthermore, equally important, then, finally,
EXAMPLE	for example, for instance, thus, as an illustration, namely, specifically,
CONTRAST	but, yet, however, on the other hand, nevertheless, nonetheless, conversely, in contrast, still, at the same time,
COMPARISON	similarly, likewise, in the same way,
CONCESSION	of course, to be sure, certainly, granted,
RESULT	therefore, thus, as a result, so, accordingly,
SUMMARY	hence, in short, in brief, in summary, in conclusion, finally,
TIME SEQUENCE	first, second, third, next, then, finally, afterwards, before, soon, later, meanwhile, subsequently, immediately, eventually, currently,
PLACE	in the front, in the foreground, in the back, in the background, at the side, adjacent, nearby, in the distance, here, there,

Consider how the transitional expressions (shown in boldface) help to make this paragraph coherent.

17 **In addition to** causing viewers to lose touch with society, television has had negative effects on viewers' imagination. Before the days of television, people were entertained by exciting radio shows such as *Superman, Batman,* and "War of the Worlds." Of course, the listener was required to pay careful attention to the story if all details were to be comprehended. **Better yet,** while listening to the stories, listeners would form their own images of the actions taking place.

EXTRA EXERCISE A

Mark all of the transitional expressions used in the following paragraph.

Edith Newbold Jones was the descendant of wealthy, socially prominent New York families. As a result, she made her formal debut before she married Edward Wharton of Boston in 1885. Soon after her marriage she began writing as a therapeutic measure. She also used her writing as a means of occupying her free time when her husband was suffering from a mental illness. Naturally, much of her writing was concerned with the closed, wealthy New York society which she had known as a child. In the 1890's, as a result of her "hobby," she published her first short stories in *Scribner's* magazine, leading, subsequently, to her recognition as one of America's best popular writers. For example, in 1924 she became the first woman ever to receive an honorary degree from Yale University. Equally important, she was awarded the Pulitzer Prize in 1921 for *The Age of Innocence*, a novel about the unbreakable moral code of Victorian society. Her most famous work, however, is *Ethan Frome*, a tragic love story. Although she continued to write about American subjects and characters, she spent much of her later life in France, where she had a home. She died there in 1937.

4d–1
cont.

EXTRA EXERCISE B

Rewrite the following paragraph using transitional words and phrases to make it more coherent. Combine and rearrange the sentences where necessary.

Americans are beginning to recognize the importance of regular exercise. Jogging gives the heart a good workout. It can damage the runner's ankles and calves. Jogging by itself does little to exercise the upper body. Some people prefer to walk. Bicycling is popular. In a pleasant setting it provides visual pleasures as well as a way to burn up calories. Some people ride a stationary bicycle at home. They can watch television while they rotate the pedals. Swimming involves the upper body as well as the legs. It allows a person to exert as much energy as possible without straining muscles. On a hot summer day swimming seems more like fun than exercise.

QUOTATION ABOUT WRITING

I don't know why I am so helplessly led to condensation in both my fiction and my essays. Some people find it hard to follow my meaning because I don't spell it out, not entirely. My writing is simple but I like to be sort of emphatic and let it go. I remember when I was writing exams in school I'd be the first one finished. All these people writing away. As I look back on it I think I didn't want to tell the teacher what he already knew, but to try to get at things from an angle—nothing very grand, just a little twist.

—Elizabeth Hardwick,
Writers at Work

When the broadcaster would give brief descriptions of the Martian space ships invading earth, **for example,** every member of the audience would imagine a different space ship. **In contrast,** television's version of "War of the Worlds" will not stir the imagination at all, **for** everyone can clearly see the actions taking place. All viewers see the same space ship with the same features. Each aspect is clearly defined, and **therefore,** no one will imagine anything different from what is seen. **Thus,** television cannot be considered an effective tool for stimulating the imagination.

—Tom Paradis, "A Child's Other World"

4d-2

Using pronouns

When you use PRONOUNS that clearly refer to NOUNS or other pronouns (see Chapter 10), you help your reader follow the bridges you build from one sentence to the next. Consider how the pronouns, shown in boldface, help make the following paragraph coherent.

The funniest people I know are often unaware of just how ticked off **they** are about things until **they** start to kid around about them. Nature did not build **these** people to sputter or preach; instead, in response to the world's irritations, **they** create little plays in their minds—parodies, cartoons, fantasies. When **they** see how funny **their** creations are, **they** also understand how really sore **they** were at **their** sources. **Their** anger is a revelation, one that works backward in the minds of an audience: the audience starts out laughing and winds up fuming.

—Roger Rosenblatt, "What Brand of Laughter Do You Use?"

4d-3

Using deliberate, selective repetition

You can achieve coherence by repeating key words in a paragraph. A key word is usually one related to the main idea in the topic sentence or to a major detail in one of the supporting sentences. Repeating a key word now and then helps your reader follow your material. This technique must be used sparingly, however, because you risk being monotonous. The shorter a paragraph, the less likely that repeated words will be effective.

Consider how the careful reuse of key words (shown in boldface) helps make this paragraph coherent.

Anthropologist Elena Padilla, author of *Up from Puerto Rico,* describing Puerto Rican **life** in a poor and squalid district of New York, tells **how** much people know about each other—**who** is to be trusted and **who** not, **who** is defiant of the law and **who** upholds it, **who** is competent and well informed and **who** is inept and ignorant—and **how** these things are known from the **public life** of the sidewalk and its associated enterprises. These are matters of **public** character. But she also tells **how** select are those permitted to drop into the kitchen for a cup of coffee, **how** strong are the ties, and **how** limited the number of a person's genuine confidants, those **who** share in a person's **private life** and **private affairs.** She tells **how** it is not considered **dignified** for everyone to know one's **affairs.** Nor is it considered **dignified** to snoop on others beyond the face presented in **public.** It does violence to a person's **privacy** and rights. In this, the people she describes are essentially the same as the people of the mixed, Americanized city street on which I **live,** and essentially the same as the people **who live** in high-income apartments or fine town houses, too.

—JANE JACOBS, *The Economy of Cities*

Using parallel structures

Parallel structures can help you achieve coherence in a paragraph. **Parallelism** is created when grammatically equivalent forms are used several times. The repeated tempos and sounds of parallel structures reinforce connections among ideas and create a dramatic effect. Be aware, however, that a thin line exists between effective parallelism (see Chapter 18) and lack of conciseness (see Chapter 16).

In paragraph 20, the authors use many parallel structures (shown in boldface) including a parallel series of words: *the sacred, the secular, the scientific.* They also use parallel PHRASES: *sometimes smiled at, sometimes frowned upon.* They end the paragraph with a group of six parallel CLAUSES, starting with *banish danger with a gesture.*

Superstitions are **sometimes smiled at** and **sometimes frowned upon** as observances characteristic of the old-fashioned, the unenlightened, children, peasants, servants, immigrants, foreigners or backwoods people. Nevertheless, they give all of us ways of moving back and forth among the different worlds in which we live— **the sacred, the secular,** and **the scientific.** They allow us to keep a private world also, where, smiling a little, we can **banish danger with a gesture** and **summon luck with a rhyme, make the sun shine in spite of storm clouds, force the stranger to do our bidding, keep an enemy at bay,** and **straighten the paths of those we love.**

—MARGARET MEAD AND RHODA METRAUX, "New Superstitions for Old"

Showing relationships among paragraphs

Paragraphs in an essay do not stand in isolation. You can use the techniques of coherence discussed in this chapter to communicate

---

4d-4

4d-5

QUOTATION ABOUT WRITING

You must once and for all give up being worried about successes and failures. Don't let that concern you. It's your duty to go on working steadily day by day, quite steadily, to be prepared for mistakes, which are inevitable, and for failures.

—Anton Chekhov

QUOTATION ABOUT WRITING

I don't wait for moods. You accomplish nothing if you do that. Your mind must know it has got to get down to work.

—Pearl Buck

relationships among paragraphs in an essay. Transitional expressions, pronouns, deliberate repetition, and parallel structures can all help you link ideas from paragraph to paragraph throughout an essay.

One excellent way to connect paragraphs is to start a new paragraph with a reference to the previous paragraph. Passage 21 uses this technique. Also, the student essays and research papers throughout this handbook make the connections among paragraphs that help to maintain coherence in longer pieces of writing.

Passage 21 shows two full paragraphs and the start of a third paragraph from an essay on health-care costs in the journal *Science*. Repeated words connecting these paragraphs include *commission, commissioners, list,* and *Oregon.* The "It sounds great" sentence tightly links the first and second paragraphs: A reader does not know what "sounds great" without the information in the first paragraph about cost-benefit ratios. In a similar way, the opening sentence of the third paragraph, "While commission members dismiss the first draft's failure . . . ," creates another strong link to the second and first paragraphs. From these two paragraphs a reader can understand the reference to "first draft's failure."

21

Oregon's commission thought it had the solution. And so did all the newspapers, magazines, and television stations that covered the commission's announcement last May. A means had been found, the stories went, to assign a cost-benefit rating to nearly 2,000 medical procedures. The basis of the list was a mathematical formula. All that had to be done was to feed piles of data into a computer, and the machine would respond with a list of procedures, carefully ordered according to their cost-benefit ratios.

It sounds great. But the list the computer actually spit out last May left the 11 commissioners reeling. Take thumb-sucking and acute headaches: treatments for these problems ranked higher than those for cystic fibrosis and AIDS. Immunizations for childhood diseases did not appear. Deeply embarrassed, the commissioners hastily withdrew the list, and three months later Oregon appears to be no closer to a second version. The current prognosis: a revised list is not expected until some time in the fall.

While commission members dismiss the first draft's failure as unimportant, it does indicate the complexity of the problem they face. [The paragraph continues, discussing specific details of the problem's complexity.]

—Virginia Morell, "Oregon Puts Bold Health Plan on Ice"

EXERCISE 4-4

Consulting section 4d, identify the techniques of coherence—words of transition, pronouns, deliberate repetition, and parallel structures—in each paragraph.

A.   Kathy sat with her legs dangling over the edge of the side of the hood. The band of her earphones held back strands of straight copper hair which had come loose from two thick braids that hung down her back. She swayed with the music that only she could hear. Her shoulders raised, making circles in the warm air. Her arms reached out to her side; her opened hands reached for the air; her closed hands brought the air back to her. Her arms reached over her head; her opened hands reached for a cloud; her closed hands brought the cloud back to her. Her head moved from side to side; her eyes opened and closed to the tempo of the tunes. Kathy was motion.

22

—CLAIRE BURKE, student

B.   Newton's law may have wider application than just the physical world. In the social world, racism, once set into motion, will remain in motion unless acted upon by an outside force. The collective "we" must be the outside force. We must fight racism through education. We must make sure every school has the resources to do its job. We must present to our children a culturally diverse curriculum that reflects our pluralistic society. This can help students understand that prejudice is learned through contact with prejudiced people, rather than with the people toward whom the prejudice is directed.

23

—RANDOLPH H. MANNING, "Fighting Racism with Inclusion"

C.   Elephant shrews come into the world nose first, and "nose first" they go through the rest of their nervous lives. Ever alert for danger, these tiny mammals depend on their noses as we do our eyes, mapping their twilight world primarily by scent. Their long, flexible noses twitch constantly, probing, sniffing, and exploring every detail of their brushy, dry habitat.

24

—SUSAN LUMPKIN, "The Elephant Shrew—By a Nose!"

D.   The snow geese are first, rising off the ponds to breakfast in the sorghum fields up the river. Twenty thousand of them, perhaps more, great white birds with black wing tips rising out of the darkness into the rosy reflected light of dawn. They make a sweeping turn, a cloud of wings rising above the cottonwoods. But *cloud* is the wrong word. They do not form a disorderly blackbird rabble but a kaleidoscope of goose formations, always shifting, but always orderly. The light catches them—white against the tan velvet of the hills. Then they are overhead, line after line, layer above layer of formations, and the sky is filled with the clamor of an infinity of geese.

25

—TONY HILLERMAN, *Hillerman Country*

E.   A full-grown brown bear can weigh more than 1,000 pounds, stand 12 feet tall on its hind legs and outrun a horse for short distances. Technically, brown bears are the same species as the grizzly bear—the one known as *Ursus arctos*. There are some differences, however. Brown

26

ANSWERS: EXERCISE 4–4

A (paragraph 22). *Pronouns*: her, she. *Deliberate repetition*: Kathy, arms, hands opened, closed. *Parallel structures*: Many parallel clauses, starting with "Her shoulders raised"; open hands reaching out and closed hands bringing back.

B (paragraph 23). *Pronouns*: we, this. *Deliberate repetition*: we. *Parallel structures*: Once set in motion, must remain in motion; we must.

C (paragraph 24). *Pronouns*: they, their, we, our. *Deliberate repetition*: nose first. *Parallel structures*: come nose first, go first; probing, sniffing, exploring.

D (paragraph 25). *Pronouns*: them, they. *Transitional expressions*: first, but, then. *Deliberate repetition*: cloud, always, line, layer. *Parallel structures*: always shifting but always orderly, line after line, layer above layer.

E (paragraph 26). *Transitional expressions*: however, also. *Deliberate repetition*: brown bear, grizzlies. *Parallel structures*: Brownies tend to be, grizzlies tend to be.

ANSWERS: EXERCISE 4–5

Students are likely to find more examples than the answers given here.

A (paragraph 9). *Transitional expressions*: after all, too. *Pronoun*: you. *Parallel structure*: historical, social, cultural; as a parent, as a member of the community.

B (paragraph 10). *Deliberate repetition*: destructive, destruction, destroy. *Parallel structure*: crashes, smolders, darts, lies.

C (paragraph 11). *Pronouns*: our, they. *Transitional expressions*: and, so. *Deliberate repetition*: people.

D (paragraph 12). *Transitional expressions*: but, that same. *Deliberate repetition*: peanuts, contains.

E (paragraph 13). *Transitional expressions*: first, but, second, for example. *Deliberate repetition*: men, women.

ANSWERS: EXERCISE 4–6

Each paragraph will obviously differ in content, but this exercise should help students see that they need to support general statements with graphic details (developed through RENNS) that are smoothly linked by the techniques of coherence discussed in 4b: transitional expressions, pronouns, repetition, and parallelism.

REFERENCES TO SUPPLEMENTS

For this topic in the CLAST writing competency test, refer students to ch. 2, section A5b of *Preparing for the CLAST* by S. Patterson.

See transparency 4–2 and 4–3 for revising for coherence in the *Prentice Hall/Simon & Schuster Transparencies for Writers* by D. Carter.

bears occupy the coastal rim of southern Alaska and parts of the Yukon and British Columbia. Grizzlies are found farther inland, for the most part; their range also includes much of western Canada and some of Montana, Idaho, and Wyoming. Brownies tend to be larger; grizzlies tend to have a more dish-shaped face and a more pronounced hump. The main difference, however, is that brown bears have access to migrating salmon and grizzlies don't.

—BOYD NORTON, "It's a Good Thing McNeil's Big Bears Get Plenty to Eat"

EXERCISE 4-5

Reread the paragraphs in Exercise 4-1, and then, consulting section 4d, identify all techniques of coherence—words of transition, pronouns, deliberate repetition, and parallel structures.

EXERCISE 4-6

Consulting sections 4c and 4d, develop three of the following topic sentences into paragraphs that are unified with RENNS and techniques of coherence. After you finish, list the RENNS and the techniques of coherence you have built into each paragraph.

1. Newspaper comic strips reflect many current problems.
2. What constitutes garbage in the United States says a great deal about American culture.
3. Children are taught to compete at too early an age.
4. Learning to do laundry can be perilous to one's clothes.
5. College athletics is big business.

4e Arranging a paragraph

Arranging a paragraph means putting its sentences into an order logical for communicating the message of the paragraph clearly and effectively. This section shows you the most common choices for arrangements of topical paragraphs. Choices include sequencing according to time and to location; moving from general to specific, from specific to general, and from least to most important; and progressing from problem to solution.

As you write, you might prefer to postpone your final decisions about the arrangement of your paragraphs until after you have written a first draft. As you revise, you can experiment to see how your sentences can be arranged for greatest impact.

According to time

A paragraph arranged according to time is put into a chronological sequence. It tells what happened or what is happening during a period of time.

27

> Other visitors include schools of dolphin swimming with synchronized precision and the occasional humpback whale. Before 1950, these 14-meter marine mammals were a common sight in the waters of the Great Barrier Reef as they passed on their annual migration between Antarctic waters and the tropics, where their calves were born. Then in the 1950s whaling stations were set up on the New South Wales and Queensland coasts, and together with the long-established Antarctic hunts by the Soviet Union and America, whales were slaughtered in the thousands. By the time the whaling stations on the eastern Australian coast closed in the early 1960s, it was estimated that only two hundred remained in these waters. Today, their numbers are slowly increasing, but sightings are still rare.
>
> —ALLAN MOULT, "Volcanic Peaks, Tropical Rainforest, and Mangrove Swamps"

According to location

A paragraph arranged according to location is put into a *spatial sequence*. It gives specific U.S. geographical areas and the most common natural disasters they can experience. The list moves across the United States from the West Coast to the Atlantic Ocean off the East Coast.

28

> In the United States, most natural disasters are confined to specific geographical areas. For example, the West Coast can be hit by damaging earthquakes at any time. Most Southern and Midwestern states can be swept by devastating tornadoes, especially in the spring, summer, and early fall. The Gulf of Mexico and the Atlantic Ocean can experience violent hurricanes in late summer and fall. These different natural disasters, and others as dangerous, teach people one common lesson—advance preparation can mean survival.
>
> —DAWN SEAFORD, student

From general to specific

An arrangement of sentences from the general to the specific is the most common organization for a paragraph. Seen in many of the examples earlier in this chapter, a general-to-specific arrangement begins with a topic sentence (and perhaps is followed by a limiting or clarifying sentence) and ends with specific details.

BACKGROUND, cont.

describe or exemplify the topic at a still lower level of generality.

The problem–solution or PS pattern states a problem or effect in the opening **P** slot, sometimes in question form, and follows by stating the solution or cause in the **S** slot. If the explanation of the solution or cause is extended, it may follow the TRI pattern. Becker illustrates both the TRI and PS patterns with a paragraph from Frank Gibney's *Five Gentlemen of Japan*:

(**P**) How obsolete is Hearn's judgment? (**S1**) (**T**) On the surface the five gentlemen of Japan do not themselves seem to be throttled by this rigid society of their ancestors. (**R**) Their world is in fact far looser in its demands upon them than it once was. (**I**) Industrialization and the influence of the West have progressively softened the texture of the web. Defeat in war badly strained it. A military occupation, committed to producing a democratic Japan, pulled and tore at it. (**S2**) (**T**) But it has not disappeared. (**R**) It is still the invisible adhesive that seals the nationhood of the Japanese. (**I**) Shimizu, Sanada, Yamazaki, Kisfi and Hirohito were all born within its bonds. Despite their individual work, surroundings and opinions, they have lived most of their lives as cogs geared into a group society. Literally as well as figuratively speaking, none of them has a lock on his house door.

29   Unwanted music is privacy's constant enemy. There is hardly an American restaurant, store, railroad station or bus terminal that doesn't gurgle with melody from morning to night, nor is it possible any longer to flee by boarding the train or bus itself, or even by taking a walk in the park. Transistor radios have changed all that. Men, women and children carry them everywhere, hugging them with the desperate attachment that a baby has for its blanket, fearful that they might have to generate an idea of their own or contemplate a blade of grass. Thoughtless themselves, they have no thought for the sufferers within earshot of their portentous news broadcasts and raucous jazz. It is hardly surprising that RCA announced a plan that would pipe canned music and pharmaceutical commercials to 25,000 doctors' offices in eighteen big cities—one place where a decent quietude might be expected. This raises a whole new criterion for choosing a family physician. Better to have a second-rate healer content with the sounds of his stethoscope than an eminent specialist poking to the rhythms of Gershwin.

—WILLIAM ZINSSER, *The Haircurl Papers*

From specific to general

A less common arrangement moves from the specific to the general. Like paragraphs 6 and 7 earlier in this chapter, a paragraph with such an arrangement ends with a topic sentence and begins with the details that support the topic sentence.

30   Replacing the spark plugs probably ranks number one on the troubleshooting list of most home auto mechanics. Too often this effort produces little or no improvement, as the problem lies elsewhere. Within the ignition system the plug wires, distributor unit, coil, and ignition control unit play just as vital a role as the spark plugs. However, performance problems are by no means limited to the ignition system. The fuel system and emissions control system also help determine engine performance, and each of these systems contains several components which equal the spark plug in importance. The do-it-yourself mechanic who wants to provide basic care for a car should be able to do more than change the spark plugs.

—DANNY WITT, student

From least to most important

A sentence arrangement that moves from the least to the most important is known as *climactic order* because it saves the climax for the end. This arrangement can be effective in holding the reader's interest because the best part comes at the end. In informative and persuasive writing, this type of arrangement usually calls for the topic sentence at the beginning of the paragraph, although sometimes the topic sentence works well at the end. Here is a climactic paragraph that begins with a topic sentence.

> But probably the most dumbfounding of nature's extraordinary creations is the horned toad of our Southwest. A herpetologist once invited me to observe one of these lizards right after it had molted. In a sand-filled glass cage I saw a large male. Beside him lay his old skin. The herpetologist began to annoy the beast with mock attacks, and the old man of the desert with his vulnerable new suit became frightened. Suddenly his eyeballs reddened. A final fast lunge from my friend at the beast and I froze in astonishment—a fine spray of blood shot from the lizard's eye, like fire from a dragon! The beast struck back with a weapon so shocking that it terrifies even the fiercest enemy.
>
> JEAN GEORGE, "That Astonishing Creature—Nature"

31

From problem to solution

An effective arrangement can be to present a problem and move quickly to a suggested solution. The topic sentence presents the problem, and the next sentence—the limiting or clarifying sentence—presents the main idea of the solution. The rest of the sentences give the specifics of the solution.

> When I first met them, Sara and Michael were a two-career couple with a home of their own, and a large boat bought with a large loan. What interested them in a concept called voluntary simplicity was the birth of their daughter and a powerful desire to raise her themselves. Neither one of them, it turned out, was willing to restrict what they considered their "real life" into the brief time before work and the tired hours afterward. "A lot of people think that as they have children and things get more expensive, the only answer is to work harder in order to earn more money. It's not the only answer," insists Michael. The couple's decision was to trade two full-time careers for two half-time careers, and to curtail consumption. They decided to spend their money only on things that contributed to their major goal, the construction of a world where family and friendship, work and play, were all of a piece, a world, moreover, which did not make wasteful use of the earth's resources.
>
> —LINDA WELTNER, "Stripping Down to Bare Happiness"

32

EXERCISE 4-7

For each paragraph, arrange the sentences into a logical sequence. Begin by locating the topic sentence and placing it at the beginning of the paragraph. As you work, consult sections 4b and 4e.

BACKGROUND

Richard M. Coe, in *Process, Form, and Substance: A Rhetoric for Advanced Writers*, 2nd ed. (Englewood Cliffs, NJ: Prentice Hall, 1990), groups patterns of development into report and explanatory patterns and into analytic and progressive patterns. Description and narration are report patterns that depend on observation and "compose our perceptions" (261). Explanatory patterns (comparison/contrast, classification and division, definition, analogy, process analysis, causal explanation, and logical progression), on the other hand, are "abstracted" from description and narration to explain and make distinctions (301). Analytic patterns (description, comparison/contrast, classification and division, definition, and analogy) report and explain in static and spatial terms. Progressive patterns (narration, process, cause and effect, and logical progression), in contrast, are organized by time, and report and explain process and change.

ANSWERS: EXERCISE 4–7

Answers to this exercise may vary; alternate versions that can be defended are acceptable.

➜

ANSWERS: EXERCISE 4–7, cont.

A. In the original paragraph, the sentences appeared in this order: 3, 2, 4, 1.

B. In the original paragraph, the sentences appeared in this order: 3, 7, 6, 1, 5, 2, 4.

C. In the original paragraph, the sentences appeared in this order 4, 3, 1, 2.

PARAGRAPH A

1. Remember, many people who worry about offending others wind up living according to other people's priorities.
2. Learn to decline, tactfully but firmly, every request that does not contribute to your goals.
3. Of all the time-saving techniques ever developed, perhaps the most effective is the frequent use of the word *no*.
4. If you point out that your motivation is not to get out of work but to save your time to do a better job on the really important things, you'll have a good chance of avoiding unproductive tasks.

—EDWIN BLISS, "Getting Things Done: The ABC's of Time Management"

PARAGRAPH B

1. After a busy day, lens wearers often do not feel like taking time out to clean and disinfect their lenses, and many wearers skip the chore.
2. When buying a pair of glasses, a person deals with just the expense of the glasses themselves.
3. Although contact lenses make the wearer more attractive, glasses are easier and less expensive to care for.
4. However, in addition to the cost of the lenses themselves, contact lens wearers must shoulder the extra expense of cleaning supplies.
5. This inattention creates a danger of infection.
6. In contrast, contact lenses require daily cleaning and weekly enzyming that inconvenience lens wearers.
7. Glasses can be cleaned quickly with water and tissue at the wearer's convenience.

—HEATHER MARTIN, student

PARAGRAPH C

1. The researchers found that the participation of women in sport was a significant indicator of the health and living standards of a country.
2. Today, gradually, women have begun to enter sport with more social acceptance and individual pride.
3. In 1952, researchers from the Finnish Institute of Occupational Health who conducted an intensive study of the athletes participating in the Olympics in Helsinki predicted that "women are able to shake off civil disabilities which millennia of prejudice and ignorance have imposed upon them."
4. Myths die hard, but they do die.

—MARIE HART, "Sport: Women Sit in the Back of the Bus"

EXERCISE 4-8

Consulting sections 4b and 4e, first identify all topic sentences. Then identify the arrangement or arrangements that organize the sentences in each paragraph. Choose from time, location, general to specific, specific to general, least to most important, and problem to solution.

A. A combination of cries from exotic animals and laughter and gasps from children fills the air along with the aroma of popcorn and peanuts. A hungry lion bellows for dinner, his roar breaking through the confusing chatter of other animals. Birds of all kinds chirp endlessly at curious children. Monkeys swing from limb to limb performing gymnastics for
33 gawking onlookers. A comedy routine by orangutans employing old shoes and garments incites squeals of amusement. Reptiles sleep peacefully behind glass windows, yet they send shivers down the spines of those who remember the quick death many of these reptiles can induce. The sights and sounds and smells of the zoo inform and entertain children of all ages.

—DEBORAH HARRIS, student

B. No one even agrees anymore on what "old" is. Not long ago, 30 was middle-aged and 60 was old. Now, more and more people are living into their 70s, 80s and beyond—and many of them are living
34 well, without any incapacitating mental or physical decline. Today, old age is defined not simply by chronological years, but by degree of health and well being.

—CAROL TAVRIS, "Old Age Is Not What It Used to Be"

C. Surprisingly, the very first Chinese to set foot on United States soil were not adventurers or laborers in search of gold but students in search of knowledge. In 1847, a year before the glitter of that metallic substance caught the eye of John Marshall on the south bank of the American River, an American missionary, the Reverend S. R. Brown, had
35 brought with him three Chinese boys to the United States to study at the Monson Academy in Massachusetts. One of them was Yung Wing, who later graduated from Yale and who attained high office in the Chinese government. He was successful in persuading the Emperor to send other students to the United States for specialized training and education, almost all of whom eventually rendered distinguished service to their country, then emerging from her self-isolation.

—BETTY LEE SUNG, *Mountain of Gold: The Story of the Chinese in America*

ANSWERS: EXERCISE 4–8

Students will likely see more than one arrangement in some of these paragraphs. *Note*: You might also ask students to analyze these paragraphs in light of what was previously discussed in this chapter: topic sentence, words in topic sentences that create focus and control (4a), development with RENNS (4c), and techniques of coherence (4d).

A (paragraph 33). Topic sentence last; specific to general

B (paragraph 34). Topic sentence last; problem to solution (and perhaps time)

C (paragraph 35). Topic sentence first; general to specific; (and perhaps least to most important)

D (paragraph 36). Topic sentence first; least to most important

E (paragraph 37). Topic sentence first and repeated last; time (and perhaps general to specific)

BACKGROUND

In *A Conceptual Theory of Rhetoric* (Boston: Little, Brown, 1975) Frank D'Angelo points out that the act of thinking involves relating objects and events to each other and to one's own past experiences. In other words, by thinking, we organize perceptions into patterns that are ultimately expressed in paragraphs. The process inevitably causes the categories to which we assign paragraphs to overlap. D'Angelo explains:

Description, for example, is related to definition. Describing something provides a means of analyzing and identifying it. Defining is a kind of abstract description. Definition, division into parts, and classification share fundamental relationships: to define is to limit or set boundaries to a thing by sep-

➡

BACKGROUND, cont.

arating it from other things (division); to define is to put the thing to be defined into a class (classification); to classify is to divide into categories, so classification and division are related categories. Exemplification is related to definition (giving examples is one way of defining), to division in parts (examples are parts of wholes), and to classification (each example is a member of a group or class of persons and things) (p. 44).

EXTRA EXERCISE C

Write a paragraph defining one of the terms listed below. You may find it helpful to begin by determining the class (genus) of the term and the characteristics that distinguish it from other members of the class. Means for developing paragraphs that have been discussed earlier in this chapter, such as examples and illustrations, can be used to develop the definition. In a paragraph of definition, synonyms, etymological information, and contrasting examples are also helpful.

1. chemistry
2. extrasensory perception
3. movies
4. weather
5. physical fitness

ANSWERS: EXERCISE 4–9

Answers will vary according to how each student conceives of each subject. Comparisons of the methods of arrangement can reveal the multiplicity of available choices.

D.   Lately, bee researchers have been distracted by a new challenge from abroad. It is, of course, the so-called "killer bee" that was imported into Brazil from Africa in the mid-1950s and has been heading our way ever since. The Africanized bee looks like the Italian bee but is more defensive and more inclined to attack in force. It consumes much of the honey that it produces, leaving relatively little for anyone who attempts to work with it. It travels fast, competes with local bees and, worse, mates with them. It has ruined the honey industry in Venezuela and now the big question is: Will the same thing happen here?

—JIM DOHERTY, "The Hobby That Challenges You to Think Like a Bee"

E.   When children begin to play with other children and when they finally go to school, their names take on a public dimension. The child with a "funny" name is usually in for trouble, but most kids are proud of their names and want to write them on their books and pads and homework. There was a time when older children carved their names or initials on trees. Now that there are so many people and so few trees, the spray can has taken over from the jackknife, but the impulse to put one's identifying mark where all the world can see it is as strong as ever. The popularity of commercially produced name-on objects of every kind, from tee-shirts to miniature license plates, also attests to the importance youngsters (and a lot of grown-ups too) place on claiming and proclaiming their names.

—CASEY MILLER AND KATE SWIFT, "Women and Names"

EXERCISE 4-9

Often more than one arrangement can be effective for discussing a subject. Think through the topics listed here and consider what arrangement (one or more) might be effective for discussing the subject. Consulting section 4e, choose from general to specific, specific to general, least to most important, problem to solution, location, and time. Be ready to explain your choices. As long as you can give a convincing rationale, you will be correct.

1. ways to make friends
2. automobile accidents
3. how to combine work and college
4. role of the U.S. Supreme Court
5. what parents of teenagers can learn from William Shakespeare's play *Romeo and Juliet*
6. the role of computers at home
7. traveling by bus

8. how to survive an earthquake
9. the problems with junk food
10. music favorites today

Knowing patterns for paragraphs   **4f**

Patterns for paragraph development in informative and persuasive writing (see 1b) have evolved as writers have sought methods to express their ideas most effectively. When you know a variety of patterns for paragraph development, you have more choices when you are seeking ways to help your paragraphs deliver their meanings most effectively.

For the purpose of illustration, the patterns in this section are discussed separately. In essay writing, however, paragraph patterns often overlap. For example, narrative writing often contains descriptions; explanations of processes often include comparisons and contrasts; and so on. As you write paragraphs of various patterns, you will likely find that many patterns share characteristics. Your goal is to use paragraph patterns in the service of communicating meaning, not for their own sakes.

COMMON PATTERNS FOR PARAGRAPH DEVELOPMENT   24

- narration
- description
- process
- example
- definition

- analysis and classification
- comparison and contrast
- analogy
- cause-and-effect analysis

Using narration   **4f-1**

Narrative writing tells about what is happening or what has happened. In informative and persuasive writing, narration is usually written in chronological sequence. Narrative paragraphs that illustrate other aspects of informative and persuasive writing include paragraphs 16, 21, 31, and 54. Another example of a narrative paragraph is on the next page. Its main idea appears in the next-to-last sentence, when Gordon Parks explains what kind of "weapon" cameras have been for him.

REFERENCES TO SUPPLEMENTS

For this topic in the CLAST writing competency test, refer students to ch. 2, section A5b of *Preparing for the CLAST* by S. Patterson.

See transparencies 4–4 through 4–8a for revising for development in the *Prentice Hall/Simon & Schuster Transparencies for Writers* by D. Carter.

EXTRA EXERCISE D

The sentences in the following paragraph of definition have been jumbled. Indicate which is the topic sentence, then record the order of the remaining sentences by numbering them.

_____**1**. It is the sum total of substantive things called economic goods.

_____**2**. In other words, wealth is a stock, while income is a flow of economic goods.

_____**3**. The wealth of a nation is the stock of economic goods owned by its inhabitants as individuals or as members of the national group.

_____**4**. Most economists use the term "economic goods" to refer to those sources of satisfaction which are scarce enough to be able to command a price.

_____**5**. Wealth differs from income because it is the sum of the goods owned at a particular time as opposed to the goods consumed during a specific period.

ANSWERS: EXTRA EXERCISE D

The order of sentences in the paragraph of definition above should be 3, 1, 4, 5, 2.

COMMON PATTERNS FOR PARAGRAPH DEVELOPMENT

4f–1
cont.

4f-2

4f-3

TEACHING TIP: COLLABORATION

With full class participation, establish a shared text by having students retell a traditional children's story (e.g. *Jack in the Beanstalk, Little Red Riding Hood*, and so forth). Divide the class into groups, assigning each group one pattern for developing a paragraph. Ask each group to choose any element in the story and write a paragraph according to the assigned pattern of development. One group might write a detailed *description* of the hen that lays golden eggs. Another might explain the *process* by which Jack climbs the beanstalk. Another might analyze the root cause of Jack and his mother's poverty. Have one member of each group read its paragraph aloud, providing you and the class an opportunity for comment and response. Such entertaining activities can also make the writing process seem less onerous to resistant students.

QUOTATION ABOUT WRITING

Like narration, process suggests ongoing movement and continuous action. The emphasis in a process theme, however, is on the *how*, rather than on the *what*.
—Frank D'Angelo

Gordon Parks speculates that he might have spent his life as a waiter on the North Coast Limited train if he hadn't strolled into one particular movie house during a stopover in Chicago. It was shortly before World War II began, and on the screen was a hair-raising newsreel of Japanese planes attacking a gunboat. When it was over the cameraman came out on stage and the audience cheered. From that moment on Parks was determined to become a photographer. During his next stopover, in Seattle, he went into a pawnshop and purchased his first camera for $7.50. With that small sum, Parks later proclaimed, "I had bought what was to become my weapon against poverty and racism." Eleven years later, he became the first black photographer at *Life Magazine*.

—Susan Howard, "Depth of Field"

Using description

Descriptive writing appeals to a reader's senses—sight, sound, smell, taste, and touch. Descriptive writing permits you to share your sensual impressions of a person, a place, or an object. Descriptive paragraphs that illustrate other aspects of informative and persuasive writing include paragraphs 1, 14, 18, 19, and 28. Here is another example of a descriptive paragraph.

Walking to the ranch house from the shed, we saw the Northern Lights. They looked like talcum powder fallen from a woman's face. Rouge and blue eyeshadow streaked the spires of a white light which exploded, then pulsated, shaking the colors down like lives—until they faded from sight.

—Gretel Ehrlich," Other Lives"

Using process

Process is a term used for writing that describes a sequence of actions by which something is done or made. Usually a process description is developed in chronological order. For an example, see paragraph 40. To be effective, process writing must include all steps. The amount of detail depends on whether you want to instruct the reader about how to do something or you want to offer a general overview of the process. Here is a process description written to give the reader a general picture. A process description giving directions appears in paragraph 41.

Making chocolate is not as simple as grinding a bag of beans. The machinery in a chocolate factory towers over you, rumbling and whirring. A huge cleaner first blows the beans away from their

38

39

accompanying debris—sticks and stones, coins and even bullets can fall among cocoa beans being bagged. Then they go into another machine for roasting. Next comes separation in a winnower, shells sliding out one side, beans falling from the other. Grinding follows, resulting in chocolate liquor. Fermentation, roasting, and "conching" all influence the flavor of chocolate. Chocolate is "conched"—rolled over and over against itself like pebbles in the sea—in enormous circular machines named conches for the shells they once resembled. Climbing a flight of steps to peer into this huge, slow-moving glacier, I was expecting something like molten mud but found myself forced to conclude it resembled nothing so much as chocolate.

40

—RUTH MEHRTENS GALVIN, "Sybaritic to Some, Sinful to Others"

Here is a process description that gives the reader specific, step-by-step instructions.

Carrying loads of equal weight like paint cans and toolboxes is easier if you carry one in each hand. Keep your shoulders back and down so that the weight is balanced on each side of your body, not suspended in front. With this method, you will be able to lift heavier loads and also to walk and stand erect. Your back will not be strained by being pulled to one side.

41

—JOHN WARDE, "Safe Lifting Techniques"

Using examples

4f-4

A paragraph developed by example uses illustrations to provide evidence in support of the main idea. Examples are highly effective for developing topical paragraphs. They supply a reader with concrete, specific information. Many of the sample paragraphs in this chapter are developed with examples, among them paragraphs 1, 3, 5, 6, 14, and 29. Here is another paragraph with examples used to develop the topic sentence.

One major value of rain forests is biomedical. The plants and animals of rain forests are the source of many compounds used in today's medicines. A drug that helps treat Parkinson's disease is manufactured from a plant that grows only in South American rain forests. Some plants and insects found in rain forests contain rare chemicals that relieve certain mental disorders. Discoveries, however, have only begun. Scientists say that rain forests contain over a thousand plants that have great anticancer potential. To destroy life forms in these forests is to deprive the human race of further medical advances.

42

—GARY LEE HOUSEMAN, student

EXTRA EXERCISE E

To practice the principles of classification, arrange the following terms into three groups based on their similarities. Give each group a heading.

1. violin
2. helmet
3. bulb
4. conductor
5. perennial
6. referee
7. concerto
8. Joe Montana
9. blossom
10. baton
11. Mozart
12. quarterback
13. leaves and stems
14. spectators
15. nursery

ANSWERS: EXTRA EXERCISE E

Symphony Orchestra
violin
conductor
concerto
baton
Mozart

Football
helmet
referee
Joe Montana
quarterback
spectators

Flowers
bulb
perennial
blossom
leaves and stems
nursery

→

4f-5

Using definition

A paragraph of definition develops a topic by explaining the meaning of a word or a concept. A paragraph of definition is an *extended definition*—it is more extensive than a dictionary denotation (although the paragraph may include a dictionary definition). An effective paragraph of definition does not use abstractions to explain abstractions. Here is a paragraph that offers an extended definition of tolerance.

> 43 The Latin root of the word "tolerance" refers to things that can be borne, endured, are supportable. The intrinsic meaning of "tolerance" is the capacity to sustain and endure, as of hardship. From this comes the inferential meaning of patience with the opinions and practices of those who differ. It is interesting that the word is used in connection with the coining of money and with machinery, to indicate the margin within which coins may deviate from the fixed standard, or dimensions or parts of machine from the norm.
>
> —DOROTHY THOMPSON, "Concerning Tolerance"

4f-6

Using analysis and classification

Analysis (sometimes called *division*) divides things up. Classification groups things together. A paragraph developed by analysis divides one subject into its component parts. Paragraphs of analysis written in this pattern usually start by identifying the one subject and continue by explaining that subject's distinct parts. For example, here is a paragraph that identifies a new type of zoo design and then analyzes changes in our world that have brought about that design.

> 44 The current revolution in zoo design—the landscape revolution—is driven by three kinds of change that have occurred during this century. First are great leaps in animal ecology, veterinary medicine, landscape design, and exhibit technology, making possible unprecedented realism in zoo exhibits. Second, and perhaps most important, is the progressive disappearance of wilderness—the very subject of zoos—from the earth. Third is knowledge derived from market research and from environmental psychology, making possible a sophisticated focus on the zoo-goer.
>
> —MELISSA GREENE, "No Rms, Jungle Vu"

A paragraph developed by classification groups information according to some scheme. The separate groups must be *from the same class*—they must have some underlying characteristics in common. For example, different types of building violations can be classified into two large, general groups—inside violations and outside violations. Here is a paragraph that discusses many violations grouped in these two main categories.

45

A public health student, Marian Glaser, did a detailed analysis of 180 cases of building code violation. Each case represented a single building, almost all of which were multiple-unit dwellings. In these 180 buildings, there were an incredible total of 1,244 different recorded violations—about seven per building. What did the violations consist of? First of all, over one-third of the violations were exterior defects: broken doors and stairways, holes in the walls, sagging roofs, broken chimneys, damaged porches, and so on. Another one-third were interior violations that could scarcely be attributed to the most ingeniously destructive rural southern migrant in America. There were, for example, a total of 160 instances of defective wiring or other electrical hazards, a very common cause of the excessive number of fires and needless tragic deaths in the slums. There were 125 instances of inadequate, defective, or inoperable plumbing or heating. There were 34 instances of serious infestation by rats and roaches.

—WILLIAM RYAN, "Blaming the Victim"

Using comparison and contrast

Comparison deals with similarities, while contrast deals with differences. Paragraphs using comparison and contrast can be structured in two ways. A *point-by-point structure* allows you to move back and forth between the two items being compared. A *block structure* allows you to discuss one item completely before discussing the other.

PATTERNS FOR COMPARISON AND CONTRAST 25

POINT-BY-POINT STRUCTURE

Student body: college *A*, college *B*
Curriculum: college *A*, college *B*
Location: college *A*, college *B*

BLOCK STRUCTURE

College A: student body, curriculum, location
College B: student body, curriculum, location

Here is a paragraph structured point-by-point for comparison and contrast.

In the business environment, tone is especially important. Business writing is not literary writing. Literary artists use unique styles to "express" themselves to a general audience. Business people

BACKGROUND

Many of the patterns of development for informative and persuasive paragraphs were first developed by Fred Newton Scott and Joseph Villiers Denney in their influential 1891 textbook, *Paragraph-Writing*. Scott and Denney's textbook was the first devoted entirely to teaching the paragraph, and instructed students in such now-familiar patterns as definition, comparison, contrast, example, and cause and effect.

As Frank D'Angelo points out in "Topoi and Form in Composition" (*The Territory of Language: Linguistics, Stylistics, and the Teaching of Composition*, ed. Donald A. McQuade [Carbondale: Southern Illinois UP, 1986]), this list of patterns appeared earlier in classical rhetoric as *topoi* or lines of reasoning for invention that speakers and writers used to generate ideas about a subject. Comparison and contrast, cause and effect, definition, and the other patterns, D'Angelo concludes, are methods for both discovering and organizing ideas.

EXTRA EXERCISE F

To practice the skills of comparing and contrasting, make a list of the most important aspects of the following pairs of words. Using that information, write a topic sentence about their relative value or about their similarities and differences.

1. Baseball and football
2. Halloween and the Fourth of July
3. Small towns and cities
4. Apartments and houses
5. Books and television

ANSWERS: EXTRA EXERCISE F

Answers to this exercise will vary, but in each case the information listed should lead to a topic sentence.

ALTERNATE EXAMPLE: ANALOGY

Consider the analogies developed by George Herbert in this short poem.

The Coming of Good Luck
So Good Luck came, and on my roof
   did light,
Like noiseless snow, or as the dew of
   night:
Not all at once, but gently, as the trees
Are, by the sun beams, tickled by
   degrees.

QUOTATION ABOUT WRITING

Philosophers sometimes talk about cause–effect thinking as "the billiard ball model of the universe." In cause–effect reasoning, events are explained in much the same way as a motion on the billiard table. . . . One billiard ball ("the cause") strikes another, which moves ("the effect"). But if the second ball also strikes something, it becomes a cause and the reaction of that something becomes an effect.

—Richard M. Coe

4f–7
cont.

46   write to particular persons in particular situations, not so much to express themselves as to accomplish particular purposes, "to get a job done." If a reader does not like a novelist's tone, nothing much can happen to the writer short of failing to sell some books. In the business situation, however, an offensive style may not only prevent a sale but may also turn away a customer, work against a promotion, or even cost you a job.

—JOHN S. FIELDEN, "What Do You Mean, You Don't Like My Style!"

Here is a block-form comparison of games and business.

47   Games are of limited duration, take place on or in fixed and finite sites and are governed by openly promulgated rules that are enforced on the spot by neutral professionals. Moreover, they are performed by relatively evenly matched teams that are counseled and led through every move by seasoned hands. Scores are kept, and at the end of the game, a winner is declared. Business is usually a little different. In fact, if there is anyone out there who can say that the business is of limited duration, takes place on a fixed site, is governed by openly promulgated rules that are enforced on the spot by neutral professionals, competes only on relatively even terms, and performs in a way that can be measured in runs or points, then that person is either extraordinarily lucky or seriously deluded.

—WARREN BENNIS, "Time to Hang Up the Old Sports Clichés"

4f-8

Using analogy

Analogy is a type of comparison. It compares objects or ideas from different classes—things not normally associated. For example, a fatal disease has certain points in common with war. Analogy is particularly effective when you want to explain the unfamiliar in terms of the familiar. Often a paragraph developed with analogy starts with a simile or metaphor (see 21c) to introduce the comparison. Here is a paragraph developed by analogy that starts with a simile and then explains the effect of casual speech by comparing it to casual dress.

48   Casual dress, like casual speech, tends to be loose, relaxed and colorful. It often contains what might be called "slang words": blue jeans, sneakers, baseball caps, aprons, flowered cotton housedresses, and the like. These garments could not be worn on a formal occasion without causing disapproval, but in ordinary circumstances they pass without remark. "Vulgar words" in dress, on the other hand, give emphasis and get immediate attention in almost any circumstances, just as they do in speech. Only the skillful can employ them without some loss of face, and even then they must be used in the right way. A torn, unbuttoned shirt, or wildly uncombed hair can signify strong emotions: passion, grief, rage, despair. They are most effective if

people already think of you as being neatly dressed, just as the curses of well-spoken persons count for more than those of the customarily foul-mouthed.

—ALISON LURIE, *The Language of Clothes*

Using cause-and-effect analysis

4f-9

Cause-and-effect analysis involves examining outcomes and the reasons for those outcomes. Causes lead to an event or an effect, and effects result from causes. (Section 5i describes making reasonable connections between causes and effects.) Here is a paragraph developed through a discussion of how television (the cause) becomes indispensable (the effect) to parents of young children.

49 Because television is so wonderfully available as child amuser and child defuser, capable of rendering a volatile three-year-old harmless at the flick of a switch, parents grow to depend upon it in the course of their daily lives. And as they continue to utilize television day after day, its importance in their children's lives increases. From a simple source of entertainment provided by parents when they need a break from child care, television gradually changes into a powerful and disruptive presence in family life. But despite their increasing resentment of television's intrusions into their family life, and despite their considerable guilt at not being able to control their children's viewing, parents do not take steps to extricate themselves from television's domination. They can no longer cope without it.

—MARIE WINN, *The Plug-In Drug*

EXERCISE 4-10

Consulting section 4f, identify the pattern or patterns each paragraph illustrates. Choose from narration, description, process, example, definition, analysis, classification, comparison and contrast, analogy, and cause and effect.

A. What was South Vietnam still seems like a different country from the North—more commercial, more casual, seemingly less wrapped up in political correctness. The main market in Hanoi had little to offer except local vegetables, a few plastic tools, and the incongruously colonial-looking green pith helmets that most northern men wear.

50 (Hanoi's market also featured several tubs of live bullfrogs while we were there. Two market ladies chatted with each other while lopping the frogs' legs off with strokes of their cleavers.) In Saigon, there are rows of "shop-houses," the tan-colored buildings with red-tile roofs and open storefronts that are found throughout Southeast Asia, and stores selling paintings, lacquerware, and a few cheap imported calculators and

4f–9
cont.

B (paragraph 51). *Examples*: upholstery, Renaissance dining room, figured silk hangings over stained-glass doors, velvet curtains, black pear wood. *Names*: Renaissance dining room, Papa's study, black pear wood. *Senses*: sight of red and black, sight of "dusty glooms," darkness, watching, touching.

C (paragraph 52). *Reasons*: felting causes wool to shrink, wool fibers stick together and cannot be pulled apart. *Names*: wool, fiber, yarn, fabric, garment. *Senses*: curly, rough surfaces

D (paragraph 53). *Reasons*: not even grained, not apt to split, take polish well. *Examples*: fruitwoods, cherry, apple, pear, orange, oak, mahogany, walnut, birch, holly, maple. *Senses*: white of holly, almost black of walnut.

E (paragraph 54). *Names*: Liverpool public library, middle-aged white women, old car, faded housedress, shapeless cardigan sweater. *Numbers*: forty-five, five.

F (paragraph 55). *Reasons*: chopsticks are like the stick shift because they enhance and give ceremony to the act of eating, force the eater to focus on the act. *Names*: chopsticks, stick shift. *Senses*: tactile.

G (paragraph 56). *Reasons*: animals hoard because food is not available to them all year around. *Examples*: beavers, honeybees, desert rodents, burying beetles, etc. *Names*: ants, wolves, creatures, goodies, MacGregor's bowerbird, etc.

3. Techniques of coherence. In this order, if they appear: transitional expressions (*te*), pronouns (*p*), deliberate repetition (*dr*), and parallel structures (*ps*).

➡

digital watches. In Hanoi, there are virtually no private cars—the streets look the way China's must have looked fifteen or twenty years ago, dense with bicycle traffic but very quiet. In Saigon, there are lots of motorcycles and a few private cars, including original Mustangs and other veteran American models. Still, no place in Vietnam has anything like the bustle of a typical Southeast Asian trading center.

—JAMES FALLOWS, "No Hard Feelings?"

B.

51   I retain only one confused impression from my earliest years: it is all red, and black, and warm. Our apartment was red: the upholstery was of red moquette, the Renaissance dining-room was red, the figured silk hangings over the stained-glass doors were red, and the velvet curtains in Papa's study were red too. The furniture in this awful sanctum was made of black pear wood; I used to creep into the knee-hole under the desk and envelop myself in its dusty glooms; it was dark and warm, and the red of the carpet rejoiced my eyes. That is how I seem to have passed the early days of infancy. Safely ensconced, I watched, I touched, I took stock of the world.

—SIMONE DE BEAUVOIR, *Memoirs of a Dutiful Daughter*

C.

52   In the case of wool, very hot water can actually cause some structural changes within the fiber, but the resulting shrinkage is minor. The fundamental cause of shrinkage in wool is felting, in which the fibers scrunch together in a tighter bunch, and the yarn, fabric, and garment follow suit. Wool fibers are curly and rough-surfaced, and when squished together under the lubricating influence of water, the fibers wind around each other, like two springs interlocking. Because of their rough surfaces, they stick together and cannot be pulled apart.

—JAMES GORMAN, "Gadgets"

D.

53   Hard, in terms of wood, really means harder to cut, but most hardwoods are also fine and even-grained. They are not apt to split, and they take polish well. For these reasons, they are generally better for small wood carving than the softwoods; most sculptors prefer to use hardwoods for large pieces, too. All the fruitwoods, like cherry, apple, pear, and orange, are hard, and so are oak, mahogany, walnut, birch, holly, and maple. Hardwoods range in color from the almost white of holly to the almost black of walnut. Oak and mahogany are the most open-grained, and therefore more apt to split. They are probably less good for small carvings than the other kinds.

—FLORENCE H. PETTIT, *How to Make Whirligigs and Whimmy Doodles*

E.

After our lunch, we drove to the Liverpool public library, where I was scheduled to read. By then, we were forty-five minutes late, and on arrival we saw five middle-aged white women heading away toward an old car across the street. When they recognized me, the women

54 came over and apologized: They were really sorry, they said, but they had to leave or they'd get in trouble on the job. I looked at them. Every one of them was wearing an inexpensive, faded housedress and, over that, a cheap and shapeless cardigan sweater. I felt honored by their open-mindedness in having wanted to come and listen to my poetry. I thought and I said that it was I who should apologize: I was late. It was I who felt, moreover, unprepared: What in my work, to date, deserves the open-minded attention of blue-collar white women terrified by the prospect of overstaying a union-guaranteed hour for lunch?

—JUNE JORDAN, "Waiting for a Taxi"

F.
55 In many ways, chopsticks are the culinary equivalent of the stick shift. They enhance the act of eating and make it more participatory, tactile, not to mention fun. They give a certain ceremony to consumption and force the calorie-conscious diner to focus on the ritual of gustation, and therefore on the amount of food being shoveled into the mouth at any time.

—DENA KLEIMAN, "Older than Forks, Safer than Knives"

G.
56 Lacking access to a year-round supermarket, the many species— from ants to wolves—that in the course of evolution have learned the advantages of hoarding must devote a lot of energy and ingenuity to protecting their stashes from marauders. Creatures like beavers and honeybees, for example, hoard food to get them through cold winters. Others, like desert rodents that face food scarcities throughout the year, must take advantage of the short-lived harvests that follow occasional rains. For animals like burying beetles that dine on mice hundreds of times their size, a habit of biting off more than they can chew at the moment forces them to store their leftovers. Still others, like the male MacGregor's bowerbird, stockpile goodies during mating season so they can concentrate on wooing females and defending their arena de l'amour.

JANE BRODY, "A Hoarder's Life: Filling the Cache—And Finding It"

EXERCISE 4-11

Consulting section 4f, write a paragraph for three of the following topics.

1. a classification of drivers
2. a personal definition of political freedom
3. a narrative of your first experience as an authority figure
4. a cause-and-effect analysis of the increase in crime in the United States
5. an analogy about learning to use a college library

ANSWERS: EXERCISE 4–13, cont.

A (paragraph 50). *te*: still; *dr*: Hanoi, Saigon; *ps*: In Saigon there are/in Hanoi, there are.

B (paragraph 51). *p*: I; *dr*: red, black; *ps*: red, and black, and warm / I watched, I touched, I took stock.

C (paragraph 52). *te*: but; *p*: their, they.

D (paragraph 53). *te*: too, there-fore; *p*: they, other kinds; *dr*: hard-woods, apt; *ps*: all verbs in simple present, they are.

E (paragraph 54). *te*: by then, moreover. *p*: our, I, we, they, them, their, it. *ps*: I thought and I said.

F (paragraph 55). *te*: not to men-tion, therefore. *p*: they, it. *dr*: they.

G (paragraph 56). *te*: for example, still, so. *p*: their, they. *dr*: others. *ps*: creatures / others / still others.

4. **Paragraph arrangement**

A (paragraph 50). general to spe-cific

B (paragraph 51). least to most im-portant

C (paragraph 52). general to spe-cific

D (paragraph 53). general to spe-cific

E (paragraph 54). time, least to most important

F (paragraph 55). general to spe-cific

G (paragraph 56). general to spe-cific

ANSWERS: EXERCISE 4–11

Each student's paragraph will differ, but they all should have in common a clear use of RENNS and techniques of coher-ence.

BACKGROUND

"The most important sentence in any article is the first one," according to William Zinsser in *On Writing Well*, 4th ed. (Perennial Press, 1990). "If it doesn't induce the reader to proceed to the second sentence, your article is dead." Zinsser sees the introduction or lead of an article as "a progression of sentences, each tugging the reader forward" until the reader is "safely hooked." He explains that while no rule can determine how long or short a lead must be, a writer should remember that readers are "fidgety" people who want to know right away "what's in it" for them when they pick up an article to read.

QUOTATION ABOUT WRITING

Etymologically, *introduction* means "a leading into." The Greek and Latin rhetorical terms for this part carried the same suggestion. The Greek term *proemium* meant "before the song"; the Latin term *exordium* meant "beginning a web"—by mounting a woof or laying a warp. The basic function then of the introduction is to lead the audience into the discourse. Instinctively we feel that an abrupt, immediate entry into the body of our discourse would unsettle and confuse the audience. We sense that in most instances an audience must, as it were, be "eased into" the subject of the discourse.

—Edward P. J. Corbett,
*Classical Rhetoric
for the Modern Student*

TEACHING TIP

To make students more aware of the wide variety of introductory strategies available to them, you may find it helpful to ask them to bring to class articles from the campus and city newspapers. Discussion can center on identifying the device, the type of introduction, and the appropriateness of both for the subject, audience, and purposes of the writer.

4g   # Writing introductory, transitional, and concluding paragraphs

Introductory, transitional, and concluding paragraphs are generally shorter than the topical paragraphs with which they appear.

Introductory paragraphs

In informative and persuasive writing, an introductory paragraph sets the stage and prepares a reader for what lies ahead. Introductions provide a bridge from the reader's mind to yours. In so doing, it needs to arouse the reader's interest in your subject. An introduction must clearly relate to the rest of your essay. If it points in one direction and your essay goes off in another, your reader will be confused, even annoyed, and will likely stop reading.

For college writing, many instructors require that an introductory paragraph include a statement of the thesis of the essay, so that the central idea of the essay is clearly available early on. Many instructors want students to demonstrate from the start that all parts of any essay are related. Professional writers do not necessarily include a thesis statement in their introductory paragraphs; with experience comes skill at maintaining a line of thought without overtly stating a central idea. Student writers, however, often need to practice explicitly and demonstrate openly external clues to essay organization. As you write successive drafts of an essay, expect to revise your introduction, in whole or part, so that it works well in concert with your other paragraphs.

When instructors require a thesis statement, they often want it to be in the last sentence or two of the introductory paragraph. Here is an example of an introductory paragraph with a thesis statement (shown in italics).

> Most sprinters live in a narrow corridor of space and time. Life rushes at them quickly, and success and failure are measured by frustrating, tiny increments. Florence Griffith Joyner paints her running world in bold, colorful strokes. *For her, there's a lot of romance to running fast.*
>
> —Craig A. Masback, "Siren of Speed"

You can see additional examples of introductory paragraphs with a thesis statement in the last sentence in the student essays in sections 3f and 6i.

An introductory paragraph often includes one or more **introductory devices** that serve to stimulate a reader's interest in the subject of the essay. Usually the introductory device precedes the thesis statement. As you write your introductory paragraphs, keep in mind the guidelines in Chart 26.

INTRODUCTORY PARAGRAPHS 26

DEVICES TO TRY

■ Providing relevant background information

■ Relating a brief, interesting story or anecdote

■ Giving a pertinent statistic or statistics

■ Asking a provocative question or questions

■ Using an appropriate quotation

■ Making an analogy

■ Defining a term used throughout the essay

■ Identifying the situation

STRATEGIES TO AVOID

■ Obvious statements that refer to what the essay is about or will accomplish, such as "I am going to discuss the causes of falling oil prices."

■ Apologies, such as "I am not sure this is right, but this is my opinion."

■ Overworked expressions such as "Haste really does make waste, as I recently discovered" or "Love is grand."

Here is an introduction that uses two anecdotes before its thesis statement (shown in italics).

On seeing another child fall and hurt himself, Hope, just nine months old, stared, tears welling up in her eyes, and crawled to her mother to be comforted—as though she had been hurt, not her friend. When 15-month-old Michael saw his friend Paul crying, Michael fetched his own teddy bear and offered it to Paul; when that didn't stop Paul's tears, Michael brought Paul's security blanket from another room. *Such small acts of sympathy and caring, observed in scientific studies, are leading researchers to trace the roots of empathy—the ability to share another's emotions—to infancy, contradicting a longstanding assumption that infants and toddlers were incapable of these feelings.*

58

—DANIEL GOLEMAN, "Researchers Trace Empathy's Roots to Infancy"

BACKGROUND

"Write leads, not introductions," teacher and journalist Donald M. Murray advises in *Learning by Teaching* (Portsmouth, NH: Boynton/Cook, 1982, p. 109). "The introduction tells the reader what you intend to say. The lead draws the reader right into the subject. The introduction gets between the reader and the subject; the lead is the subject evolving." Murray points out that people reading a newspaper, magazine, or journal often decide whether to read an article after just five seconds of reading. "Clearly the writer must realize that he or she has ten lines or less in which to capture and hold the reader.

"The discipline of the lead, however, is not only a service to the reader, it is an opportunity for the writer. As the title helps the writer focus on the subject, so does the lead. The lead eliminates much of what might intrude upon the subject. It focuses, it establishes the dimensions of the piece. It often identifies the audience, and it sets the voice." Murray says that he frequently composes fifty leads or first paragraphs before continuing a draft.

TEACHING TIP: ESL STUDENTS' INTRODUCTIONS

Some ESL students, particularly those from Asian countries, may attempt to weave every fact included in the body of the paper into their introductions. Unfortunately, this "tapestry" technique usually strikes native speakers as repetitive, even though it demonstrates considerable skill. Instructors might explain that introductions in English are less complete and more subtle.

QUOTATION ABOUT WRITING

One of the most difficult things is the first paragraph. I have spent many months on a first paragraph, and once I get it, the rest just comes out very easily.

—Gabriel Garcia Márquez

BACKGROUND

The theory that paragraph structures often resemble sentence structures was presented by Francis Christensen in "A Generative Rhetoric of the Paragraph" (*Notes Toward a New Rhetoric* [New York: Harper & Row, 1967]). He points out that the topic sentence is parallel to the base clause of a sentence, and the supporting sentences are parallel to the added sentence modifiers. Given such a structure, the paragraph, like the sentence, develops with *addition* that has *direction of modification* or *direction of movement*. When sentences are added to develop a topic, they are usually at a lower *level of generality*, and the more sentences the writer adds, the denser the *texture*. To use this structural analysis of the paragraph to generate paragraphs, Christensen proposes nine principles that can be applied and taught. Your students should not regard these principles as laws but as rules of thumb that can help them generate certain kinds of paragraphs but cannot be applied to all writing situations.

1. The paragraph may be defined as a sequence of sentences that are related by coordination and subordination.

2. The most general sentence of the sequence is often the topic sentence, the sentence on which the others depend.

3. The topic sentence is typically the first sentence of the sequence. Topics may be established explicitly or may be only suggested.

4. Simple sequences are of two sorts—coordinate and subordinate. In a coordinate sequence, repetition of structure—parallelism—is necessary; in a subordinate sequence, repetition must be avoided, each added sentence taking a different form.

➔

4g
cont.

The key to the effectiveness of an introductory device is how well it relates to the essay's thesis and to the material in the topical paragraphs. An introductory device must be well integrated into the paragraph, not mechanically slotted in for its own sake. Note how smoothly the message of the quotation in the following introduction becomes a dramatic contrast that leads into the thesis statement (shown in italics).

> 59   "Alone one is never lonely," says May Sarton in her essay "The Rewards of Living a Solitary Life." Most people, however, do not share Sarton's opinion: They are terrified of living alone. They are used to living with others—children with parents, roommates with roommates, friends with friends, husbands with wives. When the statistics catch up with them, therefore, they are rarely prepared. *Chances are high that most adult men and women will need to know how to live alone, briefly or longer, at some time in their lives.*
>
> —Tara Foster, student

In the following paragraph, the author uses a question and some dramatic description to arouse interest and to set the stage for his thesis statement (shown in italics).

> 60   What should you do? You are out riding your bike, playing golf, or in the middle of a long run when you look up and suddenly see a jagged streak of light shoot across the sky, followed by a deafening clap of thunder. *Unfortunately, most outdoor exercisers do not know whether to stay put or make a dash for shelter when a thunderstorm approaches, and sometimes the consequences are tragic.*
>
> —Gerald Secor Couzens, "If Lightning Strikes"

In the following paragraph, statistics and numbers help the author lead into his thesis statement (shown in italics).

> 61   In a Milwaukee suburb, a teenage gang awarded points to members for vandalizing streetlights and lawns. A 16-year-old in Santa Clara County, California, took 12 classmates to look at the body of his ex-girlfriend. None of them told police. Later, the boy was charged with her murder. In Chicago's affluent North Shore suburbs, more than 40 teenagers have taken their own lives in the past two years. *These episodes point up what many social scientists regard as one of the most significant—and disturbing—trends of recent years: A new generation of American teenagers is deeply troubled, unable to cope with the pressures of growing up in what they perceive as a world that is hostile or indifferent to them.*
>
> —Stanley N. Wellborn, *Troubled Teenagers*

Transitional paragraphs

A transitional paragraph usually consists of one or two sentences that help you move from a few pages on one subtopic to the next large group of paragraphs on a second subtopic. Transitional paragraphs are uncommon in short essays. In longer papers written for college, transitional paragraphs sometimes recapitulate the thesis in the context of what was just discussed and what will follow.

Here is a two-sentence transitional paragraph written as a bridge between a lengthy discussion of people's gestures and the coming long discussion of people's eating habits.

> 62   Like gestures, eating habits are personality indicators, and even food preferences and attitudes toward food reveal the inner self. Food plays an important role in the lives of most people beyond its obvious one as a necessity.
>
> —JEAN ROSENBAUM, M.D., *Is Your Volkswagen a Sex Symbol?*

Concluding paragraphs

A concluding paragraph serves to bring your discussion to an end that logically follows from your thesis and its discussion. A conclusion that is merely tacked onto an essay does not give the reader a sense of completion. An ending that flows gracefully and sensibly from what has come before it reinforces the writer's ideas and enhances an essay. A concluding paragraph often includes one or more **concluding devices.** As you write your concluding paragraphs, keep in mind the guidelines listed in Chart 27.

CONCLUDING PARAGRAPHS   27

DEVICES TO TRY

- Using any device appropriate for introductory paragraphs—(see Chart 26)—but avoid using the same one in both the introduction and conclusion.

- Summarizing the main points of the essay—but avoid a summary if the essay is less than three pages long.

- Asking for awareness, action, or a similar resolution from readers.

- Looking ahead to the future.

CONCLUDING PARAGRAPHS

BACKGROUND, cont.

5. The two sorts of sequence combine to produce the commonest sort—the mixed sequence. The opportunity to generate the paragraph lies here with the addition of subordinate sentences to clarify and of coordinate sentences to emphasize or to enumerate.

6. Some paragraphs have no topic sentence; in these cases the topic can usually be inferred from the preceding paragraph, where it may be implied or placed.

7. Some paragraphs have sentences at the beginning or at the end that do not belong to the sequence. They furnish a transition either to the new paragraph (at the beginning) or from the current paragraph (at the end), or they may provide a conclusion or coda at the end.

8. Some paragraphing is illogical.

9. Punctuation should be by the paragraph, not by the sentence. Paragraph punctuation involves choosing whether to make compound sentences or not.

BACKGROUND

"The perfect ending should take the reader slightly by surprise and yet seem exactly right," writes William Zinsser in *On Writing Well*, 4th ed. (Perennial Press, 1990). A good ending "is like the curtain line in a theatrical comedy. We are in the middle of a scene (we think) when suddenly one of the actors says something funny, or outrageous, or epigrammatic, and the lights go out. We are momentarily startled to find the scene over, and then delighted by the aptness of how it ended. What delights us, subconsciously, is the playwright's perfect control."

QUOTATION ABOUT WRITING

You must *write*, not just think you're going to. . . . And you must widen your vocabulary, enjoy words. You just read widely, not in order to copy, but to find your own voice. It's a matter of going through life with all one's senses alive, to be responsive to experience, to other people.

—P. D. James

QUOTATION ABOUT WRITING

Sometimes you get a line, a phrase, sometimes you're crying, or it's the curve of a chair that hurts you and you don't know why, or sometimes you just want to write a poem, and you don't know what it's about. I will fool around on the typewriter. It might take me ten pages of nothing, of terrible writing, and then I'll get a line, and I'll think, "That's what I mean!" What you're doing is hunting for what you mean, what you're trying to say. You don't know when you start.

—Anne Sexton

QUOTATION ABOUT WRITING

The first four months of writing the book, my mental image is scratching with my hands through granite. My other image is pushing a train up the mountain, and it's icy, and I'm in bare feet.

—Mary Higgins Clark

CONCLUDING PARAGRAPHS (continued)　　27

STRATEGIES TO AVOID

■ Introducing new ideas or facts that belong in the body of the essay.

■ Rewording your introduction.

■ Announcing what you have done, as in "In this paper, I have explained the drop in oil prices."

■ Making absolute claims, as in "I have proved that oil prices do not affect gasoline prices."

■ Apologizing, as in "Even though I am not an expert, I feel my position is correct" or "I may not have convinced you, but there is good evidence for my position."

Here is a concluding paragraph that summarizes an essay that discusses pizza, including the many versions of pizzalike foods enjoyed by various cultures throughout time.

63　　For a food that is traced to Neolithic beginnings, like Mexico's tortillas, Armenia's lahmejoun, Scottish oatcakes, and even matzohs, pizza has remained fresh and vibrant. Whether it is galettes, the latest thin-crusted invasion from France with bacon and onion toppings, or a plain slice of a cheese pie, the varieties of pizza are clearly limited only by one's imagination.

—LISA PRATT, "A Slice of History"

The essay for which the following conclusion was written is a condemnation of racism as demonstrated by the existence of urban ghettos. This concluding paragraph reinforces the message of the essay by calling for awareness and, by extension, action.

64　　It is a terrible, an inexorable, law that one cannot deny the humanity of another without diminishing one's own: in the face of one's victim, one sees oneself. Walk through Harlem and see what we, this nation, have become.

—JAMES BALDWIN, "Fifth Avenue, Uptown: A Letter from Harlem"

The following conclusion ends an essay that discusses the risks of genetic engineering. The author points to the future and calls for action.

> I am not advocating that we stop the development of the new biology. I believe that we can achieve wonderful and important results with it. But we do need to ensure that its application is both peaceful and safe. We have to learn from the history of nuclear physics and organic chemistry. Indeed, I believe we have no real choice. We cannot afford to develop the new biological technologies without controlling them.
>
> —SUSAN WRIGHT, "Genetic Engineering: The Risks"

65

EXERCISE 4-12

Consulting section 4g, write an introduction and conclusion for each essay informally outlined below. To gain additional experience, write an alternate introductory and concluding paragraph for one of the essays.

A. Reading for fun
   Thesis: People read many kinds of books for pleasure.
   Topical paragraph 1: murder mysteries and thrillers
   Topical paragraph 2: romances and westerns
   Topical paragraph 3: science fiction

B. Computer games
   Thesis: Interactive video games require players to exercise their skills of dexterity, intelligence, and imagination.
   Topical paragraph 1: manual dexterity
   Topical paragraph 2: intelligence
   Topical paragraph 3: imagination

C. Using credit cards
   Thesis: Although credit cards can help people manage their finances wisely, they can also offer too much temptation.
   Topical paragraph 1: convenience and safety
   Topical paragraph 2: tracking purchases
   Topical paragraph 3: overspending dangers

EXERCISE 4-13

Reread the paragraphs in Exercise 4-10 and do the following:

1. Consulting section 4b, identify all topic sentences, limiting sentences, and implied topic sentences.
2. Consulting section 4c, identify all RENNS.
3. Consulting section 4d, identify all techniques of coherence.
4. Consulting section 4e, identify paragraph arrangements.

QUOTATION ABOUT WRITING

If I didn't know the ending of a story, I wouldn't begin. I always write my last line, my last paragraph, my last page first.
—Katherine Anne Porter

TEACHING TIP: EXERCISE 4–12

One way to help students succeed with this exercise is to talk them through these imaginary essays before they think about the beginnings and endings. A class discussion about what details might support the topics of each paragraph will strengthen students' understanding of the importance of evidence. At the same time, it will give students a fuller concept of the essay on which to base their introductory and concluding paragraphs. When the students write the introductions and conclusions, alert them to the lists of useful devices and of "what to avoid," explained in section 4e.

ANSWERS: EXERCISE 4–13

Exercise 4–13 refers students to the paragraphs in Exercise 4–10. Answers to Exercise 4–13 are on pages 101–103, at Exercise 4–10.

5 *Critical Thinking, Reading, and Writing*

REFERENCES TO SUPPLEMENTS

For teaching reading and critical thinking skills in a computer classroom, see *Computers and Writing: Prentice Hall Resources for Composition* by D. Rodrigues.

For teaching critical analysis using a collaborative classroom approach, see P. Kelvin/S. Leonard, "Teaching Collaborative Writing," in L. Julian, et al., *Strategies and Resources for Teaching Writing with the Simon & Schuster Handbook for Writers.*

For more on teaching students to read effectively, see *Teaching Writing: Prentice Hall Resources for Composition* by P. Hastings, ch. 4, "Activating the Reading Process."

BACKGROUND

Robert J. Tierney and P. David Pearson write that it is important to understand reading and writing "as essentially similar processes of meaning construction," active and recursive processes of composing ("Toward a Composing Model of Reading," *Language Arts* [1983]: 568–580; rpt. *Perspectives on Literacy*, ed. Eugene R. Kintgen, Barry M. Kroll, and Mike Rose [Carbondale, IL: Southern Illinois UP, 1988]). Like writers, readers

➡

This chapter shows you how to participate actively in the ongoing exchanges of ideas and opinions that you encounter in college and beyond. To participate, you need to understand **critical thinking** as a concept (see 5a) and as an activity (see 5b); **critical reading** as a concept (see 5c) and as an activity (see 5d through 5f); **writing critically** (see 5g); and **reasoning critically** (see 5h through 5k).

5a Understanding critical thinking

Thinking is not something you choose to do, any more than a fish "chooses" to live in water. To be human *is* to think. But while thinking may come naturally, awareness of *how* you think does not. Thinking about thinking is the key to **critical thinking.** When you think critically, you take control of your conscious thought processes. Without such control, you risk being controlled by the ideas of others. Indeed, critical thinking is at the heart of a liberal (from the Latin word for *free*) education.

The word *critical* here has a neutral meaning. It does not mean taking a negative view or finding fault, as when someone criticizes another person for doing something wrong. The essence of critical thinking is thinking beyond the obvious—beyond the flash of visual images on a television screen, the alluring promises of glossy advertisements, the evasive statements by some people in the news, the half-truths of some propaganda, the manipulations of slanted language and faulty reasoning.

Critical thinking is an attitude as much as an activity. If you face life with curiosity and a desire to dig beneath the surface, you are a critical thinker. If you do not believe everything you read or hear, you are a critical thinker. If you find pleasure in contemplating the puzzle of conflicting ideologies, theories, personalities, and facts, you are a critical thinker.

Activities of the mind and higher-order reasoning—the core of a college education—are processes of contemplation and deliberation. These processes take time. They contrast with the glorification of speed in today's culture: fast foods, instant mixes, self-developing film, short-spurt images in movies and videos. If you are among the people who assume that speed is a measure of intelligence, consider this true anecdote about Albert Einstein. The first time that Banesh Hoffman, a scientist, was expected to talk about his work to Albert Einstein, Hoffman was speechless and overawed. Einstein instantly put Hoffman at ease when he said: "Please go slowly. I don't understand things quickly."

Engaging in critical thinking   5b

Critical thinking is a process that progresses from becoming fully aware of something, to reflecting on it, to reacting to it. You use this sequence often in your life, even if you have never called the process "critical thinking." You engage in it when you meet someone new and decide whether you like the person; when you read a book and form an opinion of it; when you learn a new job and then evaluate the job itself as well as your ability to do the work.

Applied in academic settings, the general process of critical thinking is described in Chart 28. That process holds not only for thinking critically but also for reading critically (see 5c and 5e) and writing critically (see 5g).

STEPS IN THE CRITICAL THINKING PROCESS   28

1. **Analyze:** Consider the whole and then break it into its component parts so that you can examine them separately. By seeing them as distinct units, you can come to understand how they interrelate.

2. **Summarize:** Extract and restate the material's main message or central point at the literal level (see 5d-1). (For a discussion of the differences between summary and synthesis, see 5f; for guidelines on writing a summary, see 31e.)

3. **Interpret:** Read "between the lines" to make inferences (see 5d-2) about the unstated assumptions implied by the material. Also, evaluate the material for its underlying currents as conveyed by tone, slant, and clarity of distinctions between fact and opinion (see 5d-3); by the quality of evidence (see 5h); and by the rigor of its reasoning (see 5i through 5j) and logic (see 5k).

➡

BACKGROUND, cont.

plan by determining their purposes for reading a text, assessing what they know about the topic, focusing their goals and topics, and questioning themselves. Each reader's goals and knowledge influence how he or she reads and understands the text. Like writers, when they begin readers approach the text with particular goals and review what they know about a subject and then discover, revise, and delete goals and call up other knowledge as they read.

Like writers, readers draft, at first trying to discover a lead or hypothesis that will help them make sense of the rest of the text, refining and developing that lead as they read, making connections and filling in gaps in the text with their own inferences and knowledge, and trying to fit all the pieces of the text together into a coherent whole. Readers and writers also both engage in aligning. Readers take a stance (passive, critical, sympathetic, challenging) in relation to the author to better enable them to construct meaning from the text, just as writers take a stance toward their audiences.

Readers and writers both need to revise. Readers need to reflect on and evaluate the meanings they have constructed from the text, rereading the text and questioning and revising their interpretations. Finally, readers and writers need to monitor themselves as they compose, distancing themselves from the meaning they compose and examining their composing activities. Readers and writers should both be in dialogue with their "other self," to determine how well they are accomplishing their purposes.

QUOTATION ABOUT THINKING

Cogito, ergo sum. (I think, therefore I am.)

—René Descartes, *Principles of Philosophy*

5b
cont.

STEPS IN THE CRITICAL THINKING PROCESS (continued)

QUOTATION ABOUT THINKING

Man is but a reed, the weakest in nature, but he is a thinking reed.

—Blaise Pascal,
Pensées, VI

QUOTATION ABOUT TEACHING

Our first task, it seems to me, is to offer our students assisted invitations to discover the naming and articulating powers of language, to see how language provides the means of making meaning.

—Ann E. Berthoff

QUOTATION ABOUT WRITING

If any man wishes to write in a clear style, let him first be clear in his thoughts.

—Goethe

QUOTATION ABOUT WRITING

Good writing uses every technique and tool available in order to make its effect.

—Gloria Anzaldua

BACKGROUND

According to Larry Mikulecky of Indiana University, the level of the literacy skills needed for a person to function in American society is rising. Surveying 107 workers in this country, he discovered that 99 did "some reading" on the job. The average time spent reading was 113 minutes per day. He also notes that the readability level of news articles has risen since the end of World War II from about a sixth-grade level to an eleventh-grade level today (E. B. Fiske, *New York Times*, September 8, 1983, p. 1).

5b cont.

STEPS IN THE CRITICAL THINKING PROCESS (continued)   28

4. **Synthesize:** Pull together what you have summarized, analyzed, and interpreted to connect it to what you already know (your prior knowledge) or what you are currently learning. Find links that help you grasp the new material to create a new whole, one that reflects your ability to see and explain relationships among ideas (see also 5f).

5. **Assess critically:** Judge the quality of the material on its own and as it holds up in your synthesis of it with related material.

As with the writing process (see 2a), the steps of the critical thinking process are not rigidly in place. Each element is described separately in this handbook to help you understand its operation, but in reality the elements are intertwined. Expect, therefore, to sometimes combine steps, reverse their order, and return to parts of the process needed anew. Synthesis and assessment, in particular, tend to operate concurrently. Still, stay aware that they are two different mental activities: synthesis is making connections, and assessment is making judgments.

! ❖ ALERT: Summary (step 2 in Chart 28) and synthesis (step 4) are two different processes. Be careful not to think that your summary is a synthesis. For fuller discussion of the differences, see 5f. ❖

5c

Understanding the reading process

If you understand **the reading process,** you can effectively come to "know," to compose meaning. Reading is not a passive activity. It involves more than looking at words. Reading is an active process—a dynamic, meaning-making encounter involving the interaction of the page, eye, and brain. When you read, your mind actively makes connections among what you already know, what you are currently learning, and what is new to you. By this process you comprehend and absorb new material.

Reading calls for **making predictions.** As you read, your mind is always involved in guessing what is coming next. Once it discovers what comes next, it either confirms or revises its prediction and moves on. For example, if you encountered a chapter title "The Heartbeat," your predictions could range from romance to how the heart pumps blood. As you read on, you would confirm or revise your prediction according to what you found—you would be in the realm of romance if you encountered a paragraph about lovers and roses, and you would be in the realm of biology if you encountered material that included diagrams of the physiology of the heart.

Predicting during reading happens at split-second speed without the reader's being aware of it. Without predictions, the mind would have to consider infinite possibilities for assimilating every new piece of information; with predictions, the mind can narrow its expectations to reasonable proportions.

Deciding on your **purpose for reading** before you begin can help your prediction process. Purposes for reading vary. Most reading in college is for the purpose of learning new information, appreciating literary works, or reviewing notes on classes or readings. These types of reading involve much *rereading;* one encounter with the material rarely suffices. According to the late Vladimir Nabokov, a respected novelist and teacher, "Curiously enough, one cannot *read* a book: one can only *reread* it. A good reader, a major reader, an active and creative reader, is a rereader."

Your purpose in reading determines the speed at which you can expect to read. When you are hunting for a particular fact in an almanac, you can skim the material until you come to what you want. When you read about a subject you know well, your mind is already familiar with the material, so you can move somewhat rapidly, slowing down when you come to new material. When you are unfamiliar with the subject, your mind needs time to absorb the new material, so you have to proceed slowly.

Engaging in the reading process

5d

During the reading process, full meaning emerges on the three levels described in Chart 29. Be careful as a reader not to stop at the literal level. Only when you go to the next two levels is complete understanding possible.

STEPS IN THE READING PROCESS	29

1. **Read for literal meaning:** Read "on" the lines to see what is stated (see 5d-1).
2. **Read to make inferences:** Read "between" the lines to see what is not stated but implied (see 5d-2).
3. **Read to evaluate:** Read "beyond" the lines to assess the soundness of the writer's reasoning, the accuracy of the writer's choice of words, and the fairness of the writer's treatment of the reader (see 5d-3).

STEPS IN THE READING PROCESS

BACKGROUND

In *Illiterate America* (1985) Jonathan Kozol cites figures from a 1979 Ford Foundation study that places the number of illiterate Americans at about 60 million. Supporting those assertions are United Nations statistics that rank the United States forty-ninth in literacy among 158 U.N. countries.

BACKGROUND

In a 1982 study of high school students (*Learning from Expository Text: The Interaction of Text Structure with Reader Characteristics*, National Institute of Education), Diane Schallert and Robert J. Tierney discovered that most students believe that the mark of a competent reader is the ability to read a text once quickly and remember much of what was read. As a result, students seldom saw a need to reread a text, to reflect on what they had read, or to question their interpretations and, in fact, often viewed these practices as inefficient. In order to learn critical reading practices, students need support and encouragement from teachers, just as they do to learn and use planning and revising strategies when they write.

QUOTATION ABOUT READING

When I am not walking, I am reading; I cannot sit and think. Books think for me.
—Charles Lamb,
Last Essay of Elia

BACKGROUND

In *The Elements of Critical Reading* (New York: Macmillan, 1991, pp. 13–27), John Peters explains several useful elementary reading habits.

1. Examine organizational features. "When you first encounter a text of any kind, you should pause to examine its outward features. Depending on the kind of text, those may include cover, title page, table of contents, chapter or section divisions, glossary, notes, bibliography, and other accessories" (13). They will provide a useful first impression of the text.

2. Know when the text was written.

3. Determine apparent aims. "Spot reading" selected passages (also known as "pre-reading" and "x-raying") "allows you to inspect parts which can give you an idea of the text's aims and audience level" (15). Generally, begin with the preface or the opening paragraphs and, with nonfiction texts, then skip to the conclusion because it often summarizes the main points and purposes of the text. You should also drift a little back and forth through the center of the text, "eyeing those spots where expository writing often focuses its aims" (15–16), such as the first and last paragraphs of a section, the first sentence of each body paragraph, and any visual aids and illustrations.

4. Adapt to the genre. "From nonfiction you should usually expect an orderly discussion such as you might hear at a lecture or business meeting. In general, your relation to nonfiction is that of a student, colleague, or general reader who wants information upon which to base opinions, decisions, or future activity related to the subject— but it's a good idea to be slightly skeptical, aware that a text may have misinformation or raise more questions than it answers" (16–17).

➡

5d-1   ## Reading for literal meaning

Reading for literal meaning, sometimes called *reading "on" the line,* calls for you to understand what is said. It does not include impressions or opinions about the material. Depending on whether you are reading a text written for an informative, persuasive, or expressive purpose (see Chapter 1), the literal level has to do with (1) the key facts, the line of reasoning in an argument, or the central details of plot and character; and (2) the minor details that lend texture to the picture.

Whenever you encounter a complex writing style, take time to "unpack" the sentences. Try to break them down into shorter units or reword them into a simpler style. Do not assume that all writing is clear merely because it is in print. Authors write with a rich variety of styles, and not all are equally accessible on a first reading.

When you find a concept that you need to think through, take the time to come to know the new idea. Although no student has unlimited time for reading and thinking, rushing through material to "cover" it rather than understand it costs more time in the long run.

Chart 30 offers suggestions that can help you comprehend most efficiently what you are reading.

WAYS TO HELP YOUR READING COMPREHENSION   30

- When reading about an unfamiliar subject, associate the new material with what you already know. If necessary, build your store of prior knowledge by reading easier material on the subject in other sources. Then, return to the more difficult material; your way will be eased by having established a knowledge base.

- If your mind wanders, comprehension can elude you because your mind is occupied with extraneous material. Be fiercely determined to concentrate, and resist the appeal of other thoughts. Do whatever it takes: Arrange for silence or music, for being alone or in a crowded library's reading room, for reading at your best time of day (some people concentrate better in the morning, others in the evening).

- Unless you have allotted sufficient time to work with new material, you cannot comprehend it. College students can be pulled in many different directions, so be sure to discipline yourself to balance classes, working, socializing, and participating in family activities with the unavoidable, time-consuming, yet totally engaging demands of reading, learning, and studying. Nothing prevents your success as much as lack of time.

➡

WAYS TO HELP YOUR READING COMPREHENSION (continued)   30

■ If you are unfamiliar with any key terms in your reading, you cannot fully understand the material. Take time to list them and their meanings. Try to figure meanings out by using context clues (see 20c-2). Also, many textbooks have a list of important terms and their definitions (often called a "glossary") at the end of each chapter or at the back of the book (as in this handbook). Also, always have a good dictionary at hand (see 20a). As you accumulate new words, keep your list taped inside your book so that you can consult the information easily.

Reading to make inferences

Reading to make inferences, sometimes called *reading "between" the lines,* means understanding what is implied but not stated. Often you have to infer information, or background, or the author's purpose. Consider this passage:

> How to tell the difference between modern art and junk puzzles many people although few are willing to admit it. The owner of an art gallery in Chicago had a prospective buyer for two sculptures made of discarded metal and put them outside his warehouse to clean them up. Unfortunately, some junk dealers, who apparently didn't recognize abstract expressionism when they saw it, hauled the two 300-pound pieces away.
>
> —ORA GYGI, "Things Are Seldom What They Seem"

The literal meaning is that many people cannot tell the difference between art and junk. A summary of the passage is that two abstract metal sculptures were carted away as junk when an art dealer left them outside a warehouse to clean them.

Now read the material inferentially. You can begin with the unexplained statement "few are willing to admit" they do not know the difference between art and junk. Reading between the lines, you realize that people feel embarrassed *not* to know; they feel uneducated, or without good taste, or perhaps left out.

With this inference in mind, you can move to the last two sentences, in which the author offers not only the literal irony (see 21c) of the art's being carted away as junk, but also the implied irony that the people who carted it away are not among those who might feel embarrassed. This implied irony suggests that the people either do not care if they know the difference between art and junk (after all, they assumed

BACKGROUND, cont.

5. Listen to the language. Reading only for the message of the text, ignoring its emotions, tone, and rhythms, can cause a reader to miss much of what the text offers as well as much of the pleasure in reading.

6. Become aware of contrasts. "It is said that there are two sides to everything. As a reader you should become aware of the contrasts within a text. The inner structure is bound to reveal a play of opposites that close reading uncovers" (21).

7. Get to the heart of the matter. "For some readers, the heart of a text may be a passage or series of passages that seem to tie everything together and coordinate the flow of ideas throughout the entire work" (23). "The 'heart' can also be viewed as a sort of overall personality that characterizes the text. . . . But on the best occasions and as a result of our patient attentiveness, the heart of a text may reveal itself in the fullness of its meaning, both logical and emotional, and make us feel that we truly *know* what we've read" (25).

8. Sense what may be missing. "Of the many responses that reading can inspire, a few may be strong while plenty of others remain inactive. The intensity of your feelings is important, but so is the absence of those emotions which a text might have brought you but did not. . . . Knowing what a text means to you depends on your sense of what is present or missing in the relationship you've just concluded" (26).

5d-2
cont.

TEACHING TIP: COLLABORATION

Choose a single subject about which your students are likely to have some knowledge (e.g., their first experiences at college). Assign to each group an audience to which they will write a letter describing the situation: a parent, grandparent, good friend, sibling, a former teacher, their former high school principal. To get them to think about the different language choices they must use to make a favorable impression on different audiences, it is often very effective to assign groups a comparatively informal, friendly audience first. After they have finished writing to a friend or sibling, have them describe the same event to someone with whom they have a bit more formal, yet still friendly, relationship—a grandparent, a member of the clergy, a favorite high school teacher. Even without being coached, students will notice the difference that audience makes to word choice, information selection, and tone.

it was junk and went on their way) or they "apparently" (a good word for inference making) want to give the impression that they do not know the difference. Thus, it is the art dealer who ends up being embarrassed, for it is he who created the problem by leaving the sculptures outdoors unattended.

The process of inferring adds texture and invaluable background to facilitate your interpretation of a passage. As you read to make inferences, consult Chart 31.

CHECKLIST FOR MAKING INFERENCES DURING READING 31

1. What is being said beyond the literal level?

2. What is implied rather than stated?

3. What words need to be read for their implied meanings (connotations) as well as for their stated meanings (denotations)? (For more about word meanings, see 20b-1.)

4. What information does the author expect me to have before I start to read the material?

5. What information does the author expect me to have about his or her background, philosophy, and the like?

6. What does the author seem to assume are my biases?

7. What do I need to be aware of concerning author bias?

5d-3

Reading to evaluate

Evaluative reading, sometimes called *reading "beyond" the lines*, calls for many skills, including recognizing the impact of the author's tone, detecting prejudice, and differentiating fact from opinion.

Recognizing whether an author's tone is appropriate

Tone is communicated by all aspects of a piece of writing, from the writer's choice of words to the content of the message (see 1d). An author's tone should be appropriate to the author's PURPOSE and AUDIENCE. For example, most academic writing should not use language that is either informal or overly stiff and formal (see 21a-1).

Most authors use a serious tone, but sometimes they use humor to get their point across; if you read such material exclusively for its literal meaning, you will miss the point. Here is a passage from an argument against the destruction of buildings that house small, friendly neighborhood stores and their replacement by large, impersonal buildings.

Every time an old building is torn down in this country, and a new building goes up, the ground floor becomes a bank. The reason for this is that banks are the only ones who can afford the rent for the ground floor of the new buildings going up. . . . Most people don't think there is anything wrong with this, and they accept it as part of the American free-enterprise system. But there is a small group of people in this country who are fighting for Bank Birth Control.

—ART BUCHWALD, "Birth Control for Banks"

Buchwald clearly respects his readers, for he expects that they will realize that (1) although he is talking only of banks, the banks stand for many aspects of urban renewal; (2) the first sentence is an exaggeration intended to elicit a smile—Buchwald is being slightly ridiculous to get across his point; and (3) the group "Bank Birth Control" does not exist—it is Buchwald's creation to advance his argument.

Most readers are wary of a highly emotional tone whose purpose is not to give information but to incite the reader.

NO Urban renewal must be stopped! Urban redevelopment is ruining this country. Money-hungry capitalists are robbing treasures from law-abiding citizens! Corrupt politicians are murderers, caring nothing about people being thrown out of their homes into the streets.

Writers of such material do not respect their readers, for such writers assume that readers do not recognize screaming in print when they see it. Discerning readers instantly know the tone here is emotional and unreasonable. The exaggerations (robbing treasures, politicians as murderers) hint at the truth of some cases, but they are generalizations too extreme to be taken seriously.

On the other hand, if a writer's tone sounds reasonable and moderate, readers are more likely to pay attention.

YES Urban renewal is revitalizing our cities, but it has caused some serious problems. While investors are trying to replace slums with decent housing, they must also remember that they are displacing people who do not want to leave their familiar neighborhoods. Surely a cooperative effort between government and the private sector can lead to creative solutions.

Detecting prejudice

In writing, **prejudice** is revealed in negative opinions based on beliefs rather than on facts or evidence. Negative opinions might be expressed in positive language, but the underlying assumptions are negative.

BACKGROUND

In *Society and Solitude*, Emerson suggests three practical rules for reading.

1. Never read any book that is not a year old.

2. Never read any but the famed books.

3. Never read any but what you like.

TEACHING TIP

Your students may enjoy analyzing the tone of the following two passages. How can they be compared and contrasted?

A. I can't eat or drink anything. I can't go anywhere. I have become a victim of the consumer reporter. Ever since Ralph Nader and his pals started investigating, I have gradually become an anorexia nervosa hermit. My friends warn me that I've been taking the news too seriously. But if you read the paper and watch television every night, you begin to get the feeling that if the mugger doesn't kill you—BOTULISM will!

—Joanna Wolper,
"A Victim of the
Consumer Crusaders"

B. Too much of anything—too much music, entertainment, happy snacks, or time spent with one's friends, creates a kind of impotence of living by which one can no longer hear, or taste, or see, or love, or remember. Life is short and precious, and appetite is one of its guardians, and loss of appetite is a sort of death. So if we are to enjoy this short life we should respect the divinity of appetite, and keep it eager and not too much blunted.

It is a long time now since I knew that acute moment of bliss that comes from putting parched lips to a cup of cold water. The springs are still there to be enjoyed—all one needs is the original thirst.

—Laurie Lee,
"Appetite,"
from *I Can't Stay Long*

EXTRA EXERCISE A

Determine which of the following sentences state facts and which state opinions.

1. Nuclear fusion releases energy.
2. Nuclear fusion is a possible solution of our energy problems.
3. Solar energy has attracted a great deal of public attention over the past decade.
4. Many people hope that it will produce a clean, nonpolluting means of heating our homes and offices.
5. Oil and gas production in the United States has been falling for over a decade.
6. The petroleum industry is shrinking yearly.
7. In the interest of national security, the petroleum industry should be encouraged by government legislation.
8. The early pioneers generated energy from the wind on the frontier.
9. Such nonpolluting means of creating energy should replace those produced by fossil fuels immediately.
10. Because natural gas, methane, is a clean fuel, the government should encourage its use.

ANSWERS: EXTRA EXERCISE A

1. fact
2. opinion
3. fact
4. fact
5. fact
6. fact
7. opinion
8. fact
9. opinion
10. opinion

5d-3
cont.

Prejudicial statements are like these: *Poor people like living in crowded conditions because they are used to the surroundings; Women are not aggressive enough to succeed in business; Men make good soldiers because they enjoy killing.* Often writers imply their prejudices rather than state them outright. Detecting underlying negative opinions that distort information is important because discerning readers must call into question any argument that rests upon a weak foundation. (See also Hasty Generalization in 5k.)

Differentiating fact from opinion

Facts are statements that can be verified. A person may use experiment, research, and/or observation to verify facts. *Opinions* are statements of personal beliefs. Because they contain ideas that cannot be verified, opinions are open to debate.

An author sometimes intentionally blurs the difference between fact and opinion. A discerning reader must be able to tell the difference. Sometimes that difference is quite obvious. Consider these statements:

A. A woman can never make a good mathematician.
B. Although fear of math is not purely a female phenomenon, girls tend to drop out of math sooner than boys, and adult women experience an aversion to math and math-related activity that is akin to anxiety.

Because of the word *never,* statement A is clearly an opinion. Statement B seems to be factual. Knowing who made these statements can sometimes help a reader distinguish between fact and opinion. Statement A is by a male Soviet mathematician living in Russia, as reported by David K. Shipler, a well-respected veteran reporter on Russian affairs for *The New York Times.* Statement B is in a book called *Overcoming Math Anxiety* by Sheila Tobias, a university professor who has undertaken research studies to find out why many people dislike math. Tobias's research may confirm statement B as fact.

One aid in differentiating between fact and opinion is to *think beyond the obvious.* For example, is "Strenuous exercise is good for your health" a fact? Although the statement has the ring of truth, it is not a fact. People with severe arthritis or heart trouble could be harmed by some forms of exercise. Also, what does "strenuous" mean—a dozen pushups, jogging, aerobics, or playing tennis?

A second aid in differentiating between fact and opinion is to *remember that facts sometimes masquerade as opinions, and opinions sometimes try to pass for facts.* Evaluative reading demands concentration and a willingness to deal with matters that are relative and sometimes ambiguous. For example, in an essay for or against capital punishment, you would likely evaluate the argument differently if you knew that the author is currently on death row, or a disinterested party with a philosophy to discuss.

At times, however, the stance of the author is less clear. Consider these statements:

C. Common warts usually occur on the hands, especially on the backs of the fingers, but they may occur on any part of the skin. These dry, elevated lesions have numerous projections on the surface.

D. Warts are wonderful structures. They can appear overnight on any part of the skin, like mushrooms on a damp lawn, full grown and splendid in the complexity of their architecture.

Both statements are about warts. Judging only from the words—often all the evidence available—and without knowing who the authors are, we might say that *C* is fact and *D* is opinion.

If you have information about the authors, your judgments can be more subtle and therefore more reliable. Statement *C* is from a respected medical encyclopedia; thus it can be confirmed as fact. Statement *D* is by the late Lewis Thomas, who was a distinguished physician, hospital administrator, researcher, and writer, as well as a winner of the National Book Award for his popular essays revealing the intricacies of biology to laypeople. Given this information about Thomas, you would be justified in judging statement *D* to be factual—facts brought to life by drawing on metaphor (see 21c) to illustrate them in a new way and explain them inventively.

EXERCISE 5-1

Consulting section 5d, decide if each statement is a fact or an opinion. When the author and source are provided, explain how that information influences your judgment.

1. "The life of people on earth is better now than it has ever been—certainly much better than it was 500 years ago." (Peggy Noonan, "Why Are We so Unhappy when We Have It so Good?")
2. Every three minutes a woman in the United States learns she has breast cancer.
3. "Every journey into the past is complicated by delusions, false memories, false namings of real events." (Adrienne Rich, poet, *Of Woman Born*)
4. "A mind is a terrible thing to waste." (Slogan, United Negro College Fund fund-raising campaign)
5. "History is the branch of knowledge that deals systematically with the past." (*Webster's New World Dictionary*, Third College Edition)
6. "In 1927, F. E. Tylcote, an English physician, reported in the medical journal *Lancet* that in almost every case of lung cancer he had seen or

We always read for some purpose—unless some sad, bad, mad schoolteacher has got hold of us. There is no such thing as merely reading words; always through the words we are trafficking or trying to traffic with things—things gone by, present, to come or eternal.
—I. A. Richards, "How to Read a Page"

QUOTATION ABOUT READING
There is no frigate like a book
  To take us lands away,
Nor any coursers like a page
  Of prancing poetry.
—Emily Dickinson, *Poems*

QUOTATION ABOUT READING
The best effect of any book is that it excites the reader to self-activity.
—Thomas Carlyle

ANSWERS: EXERCISE 5–1
1. opinion
2. fact
3. opinion
4. fact
5. fact (It's a dictionary definition.)
6. fact
7. fact
8. opinion
9. opinion
10. fact

ANSWERS: EXERCISE 5–2

Answers may vary somewhat, but here is a fairly complete list of possibilities:

A. Literal information

1. It is the first of February.
2. "Everyone" (see implied information, below) is talking about starlings.
3. Starlings came to this country on a passenger liner from Europe.
4. "This country" is the United States. (Central Park and New York are mentioned.)
5. One hundred starlings were deliberately released in Central Park.
6. From these 100 are descended the countless millions of starlings today.
7. Edwin Way Teale said, "Their . . . Shakespeare."
8. Eugene Schieffelin was a wealthy New York drug manufacturer.
9. Schieffelin's hobby was introducing into America all the

➡

known about, the patient smoked." (William Ecenbarger, "The Strange History of Tobacco.")

7. The earth's temperature is gradually rising.
8. "You can, Honest Abe notwithstanding, fool most of the people all of the time. (Stephen Jay Gould, "The Creation Myths of Cooperstown")
9. "You change laws by changing lawmakers." (Sissy Farenthold, political activist, interview reported in *The Bakersfield Californian*)
10. "But since it opened to the public in 1982, Elvis's place in suburban Whitehaven, a 30-minute drive from downtown Memphis, has attracted more than 3 million visitors. That figure makes it one of the top house attractions in the U.S. This year alone, some 640,000 people will visit Graceland, and in the process they will spend more than $10 million on tickets, food, and souvenirs." (J. D. Reed, "The Mansion Music Made," *Time*)

EXERCISE 5-2

Consulting section 5d, after you read this passage, (1) list all literal information, (2) list all implied information, and (3) list the opinions stated.

EXAMPLE   The study found many complaints against the lawyers were not investigated, seemingly out of a "desire to avoid difficult cases."

—NORMAN F. DACEY

Literal information: Few complaints against lawyers are investigated.

Implied information: The words "difficult cases" imply a coverup: Lawyers, or others in power, hesitate to criticize lawyers for fear of being sued, or for fear of a public outcry if the truth about abuses and errors were revealed.

Opinions: None—all is factual because it refers to, and contains a quote from, a study.

A.   It is the first of February, and everyone is talking about starlings. Starlings came to this country on a passenger liner from Europe. One hundred of them were deliberately released in Central Park, and from those hundred descended all of our countless millions of starlings today. According to Edwin Way Teale, "Their coming was the result of one man's fancy. That man was Eugene Schieffelin, a wealthy New York drug manufacturer. His curious hobby was the introduction into America of all the birds mentioned in William Shakespeare." The birds adapted to their new country splendidly.

—ANNIE DILLARD, *Pilgrim at Tinker Creek*

B.   The kind of constitution and government Gandhi envisaged for an independent India was spelled out at the forty-fifth convention of the All-India Congress, which began at Karachi on March 27, 1931. It was a party political convention the like of which I had not seen before—nor seen since—with its ringing revolutionary proclamations acclaimed by some 350 leaders, men and women, just out of jail, squatting in the heat under a tent in a semicircle at Gandhi's feet, all of them, like Gandhi, spinning away like children playing with toys as they talked. They made up the so-called Subjects Committee, selected from the five thousand delegates to do the real work of the convention, though in reality, it was Gandhi alone who dominated the proceedings, writing most of the resolutions and moving their adoption with his customary eloquence and surprising firmness.

—WILLIAM L. SHIRER, *Gandhi: A Memoir*

Engaging in critical reading **5e**

The concept of **critical reading** parallels that of critical thinking (see 5a and 5b). To read critically is to think about what you are reading while you are reading it. Do not let words merely drift by as your eyes scan the pages. Remain conscious of how the reading process operates, especially the roles of *prior knowledge* and *prediction* (see 5c); and get to know the material on all three levels of meaning—*the literal, the inferential,* and *the evaluative* (see 5d).

To help yourself along, use very specific approaches such as reading systematically (see 5e-1) and reading actively and closely (see 5e-2). As you use them, adapt them to your personal style of getting the most out of your reading.

Reading systematically **5e-1**

To **read systematically** is to use a structured plan for delving into the material. Your goal is to come to know and truly understand the material and—equally important—to be able to discuss it and even write about it. Guidelines for reading systematically start below and continue on the next page.

1. **Preview:** Before you start reading, look ahead. Glance over the pages you intend to read so that your mind can start making predictions (see 5c). Looking ahead "prepares" your mind for the material. As you look over the pages, ask yourself questions that the material stimulates. Do not expect to answer all the questions at this point; their purpose is to focus your thoughts.

---

birds mentioned in Shakespeare.

10. The starlings adapted to their new country.

A. Implied information

1. "Everyone" is used for effect; the author does not mean each and every person.

2. By saying that the birds came "on a passenger liner" (rather than, for example, "in the cargo hold of a ship") the author begins to alert the reader to expect the unexpected (in this case, that someone wanted to introduce to America all the birds in Shakespeare).

3. Central Park is in New York City. (This is information the author assumes the reader has.)

4. "One man's fancy" are words that suggest that the man had somewhat unusual tastes.

5. The drugs that Schieffelin manufactured were legitimate, not illegal.

6. See item 2 in "Opinions" below.

A. Opinions

1. (In Teale's opinion) Schieffelin's hobby was somewhat strange ("curious").

2. (In Dillard's opinion) the starlings adapted too well ("splendidly"); here Dillard assumes that the reader knows that flocks of starlings can be a nuisance and even a danger (e.g., getting into airplane engines).

B. Literal information

1. Gandhi envisaged a constitution and government for an independent India.

2. The constitution was spelled out at the forty-fifth convention of the All-India Congress.

3. The Congress began at Karachi on March 27, 1931.

4. The Congress was a political convention.

5. The Congress was attended by some 350 leaders.

6. The leaders were both men and women.

7. The leaders were just out of jail.

8. The leaders squatted in the heat under a tent in a semicircle at Gandhi's feet.

9. They all worked at spinning wheels.

10. They made up the so-called Subjects Committee, which was selected from the 5,000 delegates.

11. Gandhi wrote most of the resolutions and moved their adoption.

B. Implied information

1. India was not independent before March 27, 1931.

2. Even though the Congress had met 45 times, India was still not independent.

3. The Congress took more than one day—it only "began" on March 27, 1931.

4. Most of the leaders likely were revolutionaries who had been political prisoners—because all were "just out of jail."

5. The leaders were very dedicated—they were willing to squat in the heat under a tent.

➡

■ To preview a textbook, first survey the whole book by reading chapter titles for an overview (book titles can be misleading). Next, survey the chapter you are assigned by reading all headings large and small; boldface words (in darker print); and all visuals and their captions, including photographs, drawings, tables, figures, and charts. If a glossary is at the end of the chapter, scan it for words you do and do not know.

■ To preview material that has few or no headings, read and ask questions of the book and (if any) chapter titles; of the author's name and any introductory notes about the author, such as those that precede the essays in many books of collected essays; and of pivotal paragraphs, such as the first few paragraphs and (unless you are reading for suspense) the last pages or paragraphs. If a preface or introduction begins a book, skim it.

2. **Read:** Read the material actively and closely as explained in 5e-2. Seek the full meaning at all levels explained in 5d. Most of all, expect to reread. College-level material can rarely be fully understood and absorbed in one reading. Budget your time so that you can make many passes through the material.

3. **Review:** Go back to the spots you looked at when you previewed the material. Look, too, at other pivotal places that you discovered. Ask yourself the same sort of questions, this time answering them as fully as possible. If you cannot, reread for the answers. For best success, review in *chunks*—small sections that you can capture comfortably. Do not try to cover too much at once.

■ To stimulate your concentration during reading, keep in mind that you intend to review. This awareness will help you to stay alert. Also, the next day, and again about a week later, repeat your review—always adding new material that you have learned since the previous review. As much as time permits, re-review at intervals during a course. The more reinforcement, the better.

■ Collaborative learning can help you reinforce what you learn from reading. Ask a friend or classmate who knows the material to discuss it with you, even test you. Conversely, offer to teach the material to someone; you will quickly discover whether or not you have mastered it well enough to communicate it.

The steps for reading systematically closely parallel those in the **writing process** (see Chapters 2 and 3). Like *planning* in writing, *pre-*

viewing gets you ready and keeps you from plunging ahead inefficiently. Like *drafting* in writing, *reading* means moving through the material so that you come to "know" it and gain authority over it. Like *revising* in writing, *reviewing* involves going back over the material to clarify, fine-tune, and make it thoroughly your own.

Reading actively and closely

The secret to **reading actively and closely** is to annotate as you read. *Annotating* means writing notes to yourself in a book's margins, underlining or highlighting key passages, and using asterisks and other codes to alert you to special material. A well-annotated book is usually a well-read book.

Most readers annotate only after they have previewed the material and read it once, as explained in 5e-1. You might find, however, that you like to have a pencil in your hand from the moment you start to read. Experiment to find what works best for you.

Active reading calls for making annotations that relate to the content and meaning of the material. Restate major points "in a nutshell" in the margin. When you review, they will stand out. If you underline or highlight, be sure to jot in the margin key words or phrases that will jog your memory when you need to recall what is important. Extract meaning on the literal, inferential, and evaluative levels (see 5d.) The excerpt on page 124 shows active-reading annotations in blue ink.

Close reading calls for making annotations that record the connections you make between the material and your prior knowledge and experience. Close reading can also elicit questions and opinions about the material. This is your chance to think on paper. It opens a conversation between you and the author. If this is a relatively new practice for you, do not lose your nerve or get discouraged. Let your mind range across ideas that you associate with what you are reading. Consider yourself a partner in the making of meaning, a full participant in the exchange of ideas, opinions, and experiences that typify a college education. The excerpt on page 124 shows close-reading annotations in red ink.

If you feel unable to write in a book—even though the practice of annotating texts dates back to the Middle Ages—try keeping a "double-entry notebook." On one side of each sheet of paper write "close reading" notes on the content; on the other side, enter "active reading" notes detailing the connections you make. Be sure to include information that identifies the passages referred to so that you can easily relocate them. On page 125 is a short example from a double-entry notebook (the symbol ¶ stands for "paragraph.").

TEACHING TIP: COLLABORATION

Many first-year college students have difficulty understanding that their own perspectives are not shared by their peers. Ask groups of students to go to a place where they can sit for at least 15 minutes without talking to each other. Have students record in as much detail as possible what they perceive with their five senses. When they return to class, have them pool their primary evidence and compare their individual experiences to write a group description of the place. Students are usually surprised to find how differently they have recorded the same situation.

QUOTATION ABOUT WRITING AND READING

Read, read. read. Read everything— trash, classics, good and bad, and see how they do it. Just like a carpenter who works as an apprentice and studies the master. Read! You'll absorb it. Then write. If it is good, you'll find out. If it's not, throw it out the window.

—William Faulkner

ANSWERS: EXERCISE 5–3

Answers will vary.

QUOTATION ABOUT READING AND WRITING

For me, philosophically, existentially, the fundamental task of human beings should be reading the world, writing the world; reading the words, writing the words. If we did that consciously, with a critical consciousness, of course we would be active, willing, choosing subjects of history. Then we could speak freely about our presence in the world.

—Paulo Freire

> *Doesn't matter who wins, but tactics and prowess can be admired.*

Although I like to play, and sometimes like to watch, I cannot see what possible difference it makes which team beats which. The tactics are sometimes interesting, and certainly the prowess of the players deserves applause— but most men seem to use commercial sports as a kind of narcotic, shutting out reality, rather than heightening it.

> *Sports talk is boring.*

> *When my son and husband watch together, the rapport is very real.*

There is nothing more boring, in my view, than a prolonged discussion by laymen of yesterday's game. These dreary conversations are a form of social alcoholism, enabling them to achieve a dubious rapport without ever once having to come to grips with a subject worthy of a grown man's concern.

> *Other examples include soap operas and sitcoms.*

It is easy to see the opiate quality of sports in our society when tens of millions of men will spend a splendid Saturday or Sunday fall afternoon sitting stupefied in front of the TV, watching a "big game," when they might be out exercising their own flaccid muscles and stimulating their lethargic corpuscles.

> *Instead of watching men should exercise.*

Annotations of excerpt from essay shown in Exercise 5-3 [blue for content (active reading) and red for synthesis (close reading)].

EXERCISE 5-3

Below and on the next two pages is the complete, brief essay from which the excerpt in the example above was taken. The essay was first published as an informal opinion in a newspaper column. Annotate the entire essay, with notes about content in blue and your notes synthesizing the material in red.

Sports Only Exercise Our Eyes
Sydney J. Harris

Before I proceed a line further, let me make it clear that I enjoy physical exercise and sport as much as any man. I like to bat a baseball, dribble a basketball, kick a soccer ball and, most of all, swat a tennis ball. A man who scorned physical activity would hardly build a tennis court on his summer-house grounds, or use it every day.

S. Harris essay. "Sports Only"

content	connections I make
#1 H. likes sports and exercise. He even built a tennis court for his summer home.	H. isn't "everyman". It takes big bucks to build one's own tennis court.
#2 H. thinks the average American male is obsessed with sports.	That "average" (if there is such a thing) male sounds a lot like my husband.
#3 Athletics/Sports are one strand, not the web, of society.	It's worth thinking why sports have such a major hold on men. And why not women, on "average"? (This might be a topic for a a paper someday.)

Double-entry notebook excerpt, based on first three paragraphs of the essay in Exercise 5-3 [left side for content (active reading) and right side for synthesis (close reading)].

Having made this obeisance, let me now confess that I am puzzled and upset—and have been for many years—by the almost obsessive interest in sports taken by the average American male.

Athletics is one strand in life, and even the ancient Greek philosophers recognized its importance. But it is by no means the whole web, as it seems to be in our society. If American men are not talking business, they are talking sports, or they are not talking at all.

This strikes me as an enormously adolescent, not to say retarded, attitude on the part of presumed adults. Especially when most of the passion and enthusiasm center around professional teams which bear no

5e-2
cont.

QUOTATION ABOUT WRITING

To write fiction, one needs a whole series of inspirations about people in an actual environment, and then a whole lot of hard work on the basis of those inspirations.

—Aldous Huxley

QUOTATION ABOUT READING

A reflection on having once read 800 pages of *War and Peace* in one day:

It took me a long time to forget the way I read that book. For a long time it seemed to me I had betrayed reading itself. Coming back to it now, I still find it disturbing. Something had been sacrificed in my quick dash through the book—another reading altogether. I had limited myself to the story at the expense of a deep, receptive, non-narrative reading of Tolstoy's writing itself. It was as though I had realized that day, once and for all, that a book consists of two layers: on top, the readable layer I had read that day on the train, and underneath, a layer that was inaccessible. You only sense its existence in a moment of distraction from the literal reading, the way you see childhood through a child. It would take forever to tell what you see, and it would be pointless.

—Marguerite Duras,
"On Tolstoy,
Racine, and Reading by the
Light of the Book"

indigenous relation to the city they play for, and consist of mercenaries who will wear any town's insignia if the price is right.

Although I like to play, and sometimes like to watch, I cannot see what possible difference it makes which team beats which. The tactics are sometimes interesting, and certainly the prowess of the players deserves applause—but most men seem to use commercial sports as a kind of narcotic, shutting out reality, rather than heightening it.

There is nothing more boring, in my view, than a prolonged discussion by laymen of yesterday's game. These dreary conversations are a form of social alcoholism, enabling them to achieve a dubious rapport without ever once having to come to grips with a subject worthy of a grown man's concern.

It is easy to see the opiate quality of sports in our society when tens of millions of men will spend a splendid Saturday or Sunday fall afternoon sitting stupefied in front of the TV, watching a "big game," when they might be out exercising their own flaccid muscles and stimulating their lethargic corpuscles.

Ironically, our obsession with professional athletics not only makes us mentally limited and conversationally dull, it also keeps us physically inert—thus violating the very reason men began engaging in athletic competitions. It is tempting to call this national malaise of "spectatoritis" childish—except that children have more sense, and would rather run out and play themselves.

5f Distinguishing between summary and synthesis

A crucial distinction in critical thinking, critical reading, and critical writing resides in the **differences between summary and synthesis.**

Summary comes before synthesis (see Chart 28 in 5b). To summarize is to extract the main message or central point of a passage.

A summary does not include supporting evidence or details. It is the gist, the hub, the seed of what the author is saying; it is not your reaction to it.

You summarize informally in a conversation and more formally in a speech. When you write a summary, use the guidelines in Chart 132 in section 31e. They apply generally to the kind of summarizing you do in content annotations (see 5e-2), in writing an essay that draws on only one source (see 5g), and in a research paper based on multiple sources (see Chapters 31, 34, and 35).

Synthesis comes after analysis, summary, and interpretation (see Chart 28 in 5b). To synthesize is to weave together ideas from more than one source; to connect ideas from one or more sources to what you already know from your having read, listened, and experienced life; to create a new whole that is your own as a result of your thinking about diverse yet related ideas. Unsynthesized ideas and information are like separate spools of thread, neatly lined up, possibly coordinated, but not integrated. Synthesized ideas and information become threads woven into a tapestry that creates a new whole. Synthesis is the evidence of your ability to tie ideas together in the tapestry of what you learn and know and experience.

Many techniques can help that thinking along. When you synthesize unconsciously, your mind connects ideas by thought processes mirrored in the rhetorical strategies discussed in section 4f. To synthesize, consciously apply these strategies. For example, compare ideas in sources; contrast ideas in sources; create definitions that combine and extend definitions in individual sources; apply examples or descriptions from one source to illustrate ideas in another; find causes and/or effects described in one source that explain another.

❖ ALERT: "Synthesis by summary"—a mere listing of who said what about a topic—is not true synthesis. It does not create new connections among ideas. ❖

Here is an example of synthesis connecting the essay in Exercise 5-3 to the excerpt below by Robert Lipsyte. (Lipsyte, a sports columnist for the *New York Times,* who published his long essay in the spring of 1995 at the end of a nine-month-long U.S. baseball strike, asserts that sports have become too commercialized and no longer inspire loyalty, teach good sportsmanship, or provide young people with admirable role models.)

> Baseball has done us a favor. It's about time we understood that staged competitive sports events—and baseball can stand for all the games—are no longer the testing ground of our country's manhood and the theater of its once seemingly limitless energy and power.
>
> As a mirror of our culture, sports now show us spoiled fools as role models, cities and colleges held hostage and games that exist only to hawk products. ➔

QUOTATION ABOUT WRITING

Writers love quotations. . . . We consider a well-placed quotation, whether it be Shakespeare, Twain or Groucho Marx, to be one of the signs of an erudite and educated person. It lends weight to one's own opinions by somehow invoking greater—or at least more well known—authority.

—James Charlton

QUOTATION ABOUT READING

The one thing I regret is that I will never have time to read all the books I want to read.

—Françoise Sagan

QUOTATION ABOUT READING

No man understands a deep book until he has seen and lived at least part of its contents.

—Ezra Pound

QUOTATION ABOUT WRITING AND READING

The main suggestion from me is *read.* It is impossible for a writer to be able to write honestly and eloquently without having at one time or another acquainted himself with such writers as Sir Thomas Browne.

—William Styron

The pathetic posturing of in-your-face macho has replaced a once self-confident masculinity.

— ROBERT LIPSYTE, "The Emasculation of Sports"

SYNTHESIS BY COMPARISON AND CONTRAST

Both Harris and Lipsyte criticize professional sports, but their reasons differ. In part, Harris thinks that people who passively watch sports on TV and rarely exercise are destroying their physical health. Lipsyte sees something less obvious, put potentially more sinister: the destruction of traditional values in sports. No longer are athletes heroes who inspire; they are puppets of sports as "big business."

SYNTHESIS BY DEFINITION

The omission of women from each writer's discussion seems a very loud silence. Considered together, these essays define sports as a male preoccupation and undertaking. Harris condemns only men for their inability to think and talk beyond sports and business, an insulting and exaggerated description made even less valid by the absence of women. Lipsyte, even in the 1995 atmosphere of women excelling in many team and individual sports, claims that we have lost a "once self-confident masculinity." An extended definition would include women, even though they might prefer to avoid the negative portraits of Harris and Lipsyte.

A synthesis belongs to the person who made the connections; someone else might make entirely different connections. Still, any synthesis needs to be sensibly reasoned and informed by an individual intelligence.

Try these techniques for stimulating your mind to recall prior knowledge and work toward creating a synthesis. (The critical response essay by a student, Anna Lozanov, in 5g, is an excellent example of making connections between reading and one's personal experience.)

■ Use the technique of mapping (see 2i) to lay out and discover relationships between elements in the material and between the material and other ideas that come to mind.

■ Use your powers of play. Mentally toss ideas around, even if you make connections that seem outrageous. Try opposites (for example, read about athletes and think about the most unathletic person you know). Try turning an idea upside down (for example, read about the value of being a good sport and list the benefits of being a bad sport). Try visualizing what you are reading about, and then tinker with the mental picture (for example, picture two people playing tennis and substitute dogs playing frisbee or seals playing ping pong). The possibilities are endless—make word associations, think up song lyrics, draft a TV advertisement. The goal is always to jump-start your thinking so that you see ideas in new ways.

■ Discuss your reading with someone else. Summarize its content and elicit the other person's opinion or ideas. Deliberately debate that opinion or challenge those ideas. Discussions and debates can get your mind moving.

EXERCISE 5-4

Here is an excerpt from an essay by Robert Lipsyte. (Another excerpt from this essay is shown on pages 127–28.) The words in brackets are added in this exercise to supply background information some readers might need.

> We have come to see that [basketball star Michael] Jordan, [football star] Troy Aikman, and [baseball star] Ken Griffey have nothing to offer us beyond the gorgeous, breathtaking mechanics of what they do. And it's not enough, now that there is no longer a dependable emotional return beyond the sensation of the moment itself. The changes in sports— the moving of franchises, free agency— have made it impossible to count on a player, a team, an entire league still being around for next year's comeback. The connection between player and fan has been irrevocably destabilized, for love and loyalty demand a future. Along the way, those many virtues of self-discipline, responsibility, altruism and dedication seem to have been deleted from the athletic contract with America.
>
> —ROBERT LIPSYTE, "The Emasculation of Sports"

Consulting sections 5e-2 and 5f, do this:

1. Summarize the excerpt here.
2. Annotate it for its content and for the connections you make to its content.
3. Draft a synthesis connecting this excerpt and the essay by Sydney J. Harris reprinted in Exercise 5-3.

Writing a critical response   5g

A **critical response** essay has two missions: to summarize a source's central point or main idea; second, to respond to the source's main idea with your reactions based on your synthesis (see 5b and 5f).

A well-written critical response accomplishes these two missions with grace and style. That is, it does not say "My summary is . . ." and "Now, here's what I think. . . ." Your goal is to write a well-integrated essay. Its length and whether you respond to a single passage or to an entire work vary with the assignment. Chart 32 gives general guidelines for writing a critical response.

ANSWERS: EXERCISE 5–4
Answers will vary.

QUOTATION ABOUT WRITING
I've always disliked words like *inspiration*. Writing is probably like a scientist thinking about some scientific problem, or an engineer about an engineering problem.

—Doris Lessing

QUOTATION ABOUT READING

Texts are lazy machineries that ask someone to do part of their job.

—Umberto Eco

QUOTATION ABOUT READING

Like writing, reading requires the creation of meaning, this time in collaboration with an author. Like writing, reading becomes meaningful only when it involves the particular response of an individual—one's own ways of perceiving reality through the prism of written language.

—Nancie Atwell,
In the Middle

QUOTATION ABOUT WRITING

Thinking is the activity I love best, and writing to me is simply thinking through my fingers. I can write up to 18 hours a day. Typing 90 words a minute, I've done better than 50 pages a day. Nothing interferes with my concentration. You could put on an orgy in my office and I wouldn't look up—well, maybe once.

—Isaac Asimov

GUIDELINES FOR WRITING A CRITICAL RESPONSE 32

- Write a summary of the main idea or central point of what you are responding to (whether you are responding to part or all of a source).
- Write a smooth transition between that summary and your response. Although a statement bridging the two parts of a critical response paper need not observe all the formal requirements of a thesis statement (see 2n), it should at least subtly signal the beginning of your response.
- Respond to the source, basing your reaction on the influences of your own experience, your prior knowledge, and your opinions.
- Fulfill all documentation requirements. See Chapter 33 for coverage of four widely used documentation systems (MLA, APA, CM, and CBE), and ask your instructor which to use.

Here is a critical response essay written by Anna Lozanov, a student at a state university. The assignment was to read and respond to the brief essay "Sports Only Exercise Our Eyes" by Sydney J. Harris shown in Exercise 5-3. Lozanov's bridge statement comes at the beginning of the third paragraph: "Just this weekend, however, I had an occasion to reconsider the value of sports." The Work Cited at the end of the essay uses MLA documentation style (see 33c) to identify the source. The numbers in parentheses in the essay indicate the pages in the cited work where the quoted words can be found.

```
              Critical Response by Anna Lozanov
     to "Sports Only Exercise Our Eyes" by Sydney J. Harris
          Except for a brief period in high school when I was
     wild about a certain basketball player, I never gave
     sports much thought. I went to games because my friends
     went, not because I cared about football or baseball or
     track. I certainly never expected to defend sports, and
     when I first read Sydney Harris's essay "Sports Only
     Exercise Our Eyes," I thoroughly agreed with him. Like
     Harris, I believed that men who live and breathe sports
     are "mentally limited and conversationally dull" (111).
```

For the entire thirteen years of my marriage, I have complained about the amount of time my husband, John, spends watching televised sports. Of course, I've tried to get him to take an interest in something else. There was the time as a newlywed when I flamboyantly interrupted the sixth game of the World Series--wearing only a transparent nightie. Then, in 1978, I had the further audacity to go into labor with our first child--right in the middle of the Super Bowl. Even the child tried to help me cure my husband of what Harris calls an "obsession" (111). Some months after the fateful Super Bowl, the kid thoroughly soaked his father, who was concentrating so intently on the Tigers' struggle for the American League pennant that he didn't even notice! Only a commercial brought the dazed sports fan back into the living room from Tiger Stadium.

Just this weekend, however, I had an occasion to reconsider the value of sports. Having just read the Harris essay, I found myself paying closer attention to my husband and sons' Saturday afternoon television routine. I was surprised to discover that they didn't just "vegetate" in front of the TV; during the course of the afternoon, they actually discussed ethics, priorities, commitments, and the consequences of abusing one's body. When one of the commentators raised issues like point shaving and using steroids, John and the kids talked about cheating and using drugs. When another commentator brought up the issue of skipping one's senior year to go straight to the pros, John explained the importance of a college education and discussed the short career of most professional football players.

Then, I started to think about all the times I've gone to the basement and found my husband and sons performing exercise routines as they watched a game on TV. Even our seven year old, who loathes exercise, pedals vigorously on the exercise bike while the others do sit-ups and curls. Believe it or not, there are times when they're all exercising more than just their eyes.

➜

QUOTATION ABOUT READING

Do not dictate to your author; try to become him. Be his fellow-worker and accomplice. If you hang back, and reserve and criticize at first, you are preventing yourself from getting the fullest possible value from what you read. But if you open your mind as widely as possible, then signs and hints of almost imperceptible fineness, from the twist and turn of the first sentences, will bring you in the presence of a human being unlike any other. Steep yourself in this, acquaint yourself with this, and soon you will find that your author is giving you, or attempting to give you, something far more definite.

—Virginia Woolf,
"How Should One Read a Book?"

5g
cont.

> I still agree with Harris that many people spend
> too much time watching televised sports, but after this
> weekend, I certainly can't say that all of that time is
> wasted--at least not at my house. Anything that can turn
> my couch potatoes into thinking, talking, active human
> beings can't be all bad. Next weekend, instead of putting
> on a nightie, I think I'll join my family on the couch.
>
> Work Cited
> Harris, Sydney J. "Sports Only Exercise Our Eyes." The
>   Best of Sydney J. Harris. Boston: Houghton, 1975.
>   111-12.

REFERENCE TO SUPPLEMENTS

The Prentice Hall Critical Thinking Audio Tape, section 1c, question 5, provides additional guidelines on using evidence.

5h ## Assessing evidence critically

The cornerstone of all reasoning is evidence. As a reader, you expect writers to provide solid evidence for any claim made or conclusion reached. As a writer, you want to use evidence well to support your claims or conclusions. Evidence consists of facts, statistical information, examples, and opinions of experts.

5h-1 ### Evaluating evidence

Chart 33 lists guidelines for evaluating evidence that you read and for deciding what evidence to include in your writing. Each guideline is discussed after the chart.

GUIDELINES FOR EVALUATING EVIDENCE	33
■ Is the evidence sufficient?	
■ Is the evidence representative?	
■ Is the evidence relevant?	
■ Is the evidence accurate, whether from primary or secondary sources?	
■ Are the claims qualified fairly, based on the evidence?	

GUIDELINES FOR EVALUATING EVIDENCE

■ **Is the evidence sufficient?** A general rule for both readers and writers is the more evidence, the better. As a reader, you usually have more confidence in the results of a survey that draws on a hundred respondents rather than ten. As a writer, you may convince your reader that violence is a serious problem in high schools on the basis of two specific examples, but you will be more convincing if you can give five examples—or, better still, statistics for a school district, a city, or a nation.

■ **Is the evidence representative?** As a reader, assess objectivity and fairness; do not assume them because words are in print. Do not trust a claim or conclusion about the group based on only a few members rather than on a truly representative or typical sample. A pollster surveying national political views would not get representative evidence by asking questions of the first 1,500 people to walk by a street corner in Austin, Texas, because that group would not truly represent the various regional, racial, political, and ethnic makeup of the U.S. electorate. As a writer, make sure the evidence you offer represents your claim fairly; do not base your point on exceptions.

■ **Is the evidence relevant?** Determining relevance can demand subtle thinking. Suppose you read evidence that one hundred students who had watched television for more than two hours a day throughout high school earned significantly lower scores on a college entrance exam than one hundred students who had not. Would you conclude that students who watch less television perform better on college entrance exams? Perhaps, but closer examination of the evidence might reveal other differences between the two groups—differences in geographical region, family background, socioeconomic group, quality of schools attended. Therefore, the evidence would not be relevant to that conclusion about TV watching and college entrance exams.

■ **Is the evidence accurate?** Without accuracy, evidence is useless. Evidence must come from reliable sources, whether they are *primary sources* or *secondary sources* (see 5h-2). Equally important, reliable evidence must be carefully presented so that it does not misrepresent or distort information.

■ **Is the evidence qualified?** Evidence rarely justifies claims that use words such as *all, certainly, always,* or *never.* Conclusions are more reasonable when qualified with words such as *some, many, a few, probably, possibly, perhaps, may, usually,* and *often.* Remember that today's "facts" may be revised as time passes, information changes, and knowledge grows.

5h-2

Understanding differences between primary and secondary sources as evidence

Primary sources present first-hand evidence based on your own or someone else's original work or direct observation. First-hand evidence has the greatest impact on a reader. Consider this eyewitness account:

> Poverty is dirt. . . . Let me explain about housekeeping with no money. For breakfast I give my children grits with no oleo or cornbread without eggs and oleo. This does not use up many dishes. What dishes there are, I wash in cold water and with no soap. Even the cheapest soap has to be saved for the baby's diapers. Look at my hands, so cracked and red. Once I saved for two months to buy a jar of Vaseline for my hands and the baby's diaper rash. When I had saved enough, I went to buy it and the price had gone up two cents. The baby and I suffered on. I have to decide every day if I can bear to put my cracked sore hands into the cold water and strong soap. But you ask, why not hot water? Fuel costs money. If you have a wood fire it costs money. If you burn electricity, it costs money. Hot water is a luxury. I do not have luxuries. . . .
>
> —Jo Goodwin Parker, in *America's Other Children*

As a reader and as a writer, remember that not all eyewitness accounts are equally reliable. What is it about Parker's account that makes you trust what she says? She is specific. She is also authoritative. It is doubtful that anyone would have invented the story about being two cents short of the price of a jar of Vaseline. As a writer of personal observations, you need to be as specific as possible—to prove that you truly saw what you say you saw. Use language that appeals to all five senses: describe sights, sounds, and experiences that could have been seen, heard, or experienced only by someone who was there. Show your readers *your* cracked, red hands.

As evidence, primary sources that meet the guidelines in Chart 33 can provide invaluable reports of observations. Few will ever see the surface of the moon or the top of Mt. Everest. People rely, therefore, upon the first-hand reports of the astronauts and mountain climbers who have been there. Indeed, much of history depends heavily on letters, diaries, and journals—the reports of eyewitnesses who saw events unfold.

Surveys, polls, and experiments are some of the means by which people extend their powers of observation beyond what can be "seen" in the everyday sense of the word. Jo Parker could look at her hands. Who can see, however, the attitude of the American public toward marriage, toward a presidential candidate, toward inflation? For evidence on such matters, polls or surveys are necessary. They constitute primary evidence and must be carefully controlled—through weighing, measuring, or quantifying information that would otherwise not be available.

Secondary sources report, describe, comment on, or analyze the experiences or the work of others. As evidence, a secondary source is at least once removed from the primary source. It reports *about* the original work, the direct observation, or the first-hand experience. Still, such evidence can have great value and enormous impact. Consider this second-hand, reported observation.

> The immediate causes of death from nuclear attack are the blast wave, which can flatten heavily reinforced buildings many kilometers away, the firestorm, the gamma rays and the neutrons, which effectively fry the insides of passersby. A school girl who survived the American nuclear attack on Hiroshima, the event that ended the Second World War, wrote this first-hand account:
>
>> Through a darkness like the bottom of hell, I could hear the voices of the other students calling for their mothers. And at the base of the bridge, inside a big cistern that had been dug out there, was a mother weeping, holding above her head a naked baby that was burned bright red all over its body. . . . But every single person who passed was wounded, all of them, and there was no one, there was no one to turn to for help. And the singed hair on the heads of the people was frizzled and whitish and covered with dust. They did not appear to be human, not creatures of this world.
>
> —CARL SAGAN, *Cosmos*

As with Parker's eyewitness account, the strength or value of a second-hand account hinges on the reliability of the reporter. That reliability is a function of how specific, accurate, and authoritative the observations are. Here the standard maxim "consider the source" becomes crucial. An expert's reputation must stem from some special experience (as the parents of many children could be "experts" on child reading) or training (as an accountant could be an expert on taxes). Because the author of the example paragraph, Carl Sagan, is a respected scientist, scholar, and writer, his report of the schoolgirl's eyewitness account is likely to be reliable, authoritative, worthwhile secondary evidence.

Sagan is a secondary source because although readers can feel quite confident that Sagan is fully and fairly representing what the schoolgirl said, no one can be sure of that without seeing her original account. If you were to use Sagan's version of her account as evidence, it would be third-hand evidence: one person (you) further removed from another (Sagan) and yet further from the original source (the schoolgirl). In college, you must often depend on secondary sources (for example, most textbooks), but sometimes you are expected to use primary sources (for example, a published diary, scientists' journal articles

---

QUOTATION ABOUT READING

It is absurd to have a hard-and-fast rule about what one should read and what one shouldn't. More than half of modern culture depends on what one shouldn't read.

—Oscar Wilde

QUOTATION ABOUT WRITING

There is only one trait that marks the writer. He is always watching. It's a kind of trick of the mind and he is born with it.

—Morley Callaghan

QUOTATION ABOUT WRITING

We have read your manuscript with boundless delight. If we were to publish your paper, it would be impossible for us to publish any work of lower standard. And as it is unthinkable that in the next thousand years we shall see its equal, we are, to our regret, compelled to return your divine composition, and to beg you a thousand times to overlook our short sight and timidity.

—Rejection slip from a Chinese economic journal, quoted in the *Financial Times*

reporting their research, works of literature). Chart 34 gives guidelines for evaluating a secondary source.

✤ ALERT: You can use the guidelines in Chart 34 to evaluate electronic sources as well as conventional print sources. Be skeptical about any electronically accessed source that cannot be verified according to these guidelines. ✤

GUIDELINES FOR EVALUATING A SECONDARY SOURCE 34

- **Is the source authoritative?** Was it written by an expert or a person whom you can expect to write credibly on the subject?

- **Is the source reliable?** Does the material appear in a reputable publication—in a book published by an established publisher or in a respected journal or magazine?

- **Is the source well known?** Is the source cited elsewhere as you read about the subject? (If so, the authority of the source is probably widely accepted.)

- **Is the information well supported?** Is the source *based on* primary evidence? If secondary evidence, is it authoritative and reliable?

- **Is the tone balanced?** Is the language relatively objective (therefore more likely reliable) or slanted (probably not reliable)?

- **Is the source current?** Is the material current (therefore more likely reliable), or has later authoritative and reliable research made it outdated? ("Old" is not necessarily unreliable. In many fields, classic works of research remain authoritative for decades or even centuries.)

EXERCISE 5-5

Consulting section 5h, decide the following: (a) Would each passage constitute primary or secondary evidence? (b) Is the evidence acceptable? Why or why not?

1.   I went one morning to a place along the banks of the Madeira River where the railroad ran, alongside rapids impassable to river traffic, and I searched for any marks it may have left on the land. But there was nothing except a clearing where swarms of insects hovered over the dead black hen and other items spread out on a red cloth as an offering to the gods of macumba, or black magic. This strain of African origins in Brazil's ethnic character is strong in the Northwest Region.

—WILLIAM S. ELLIS, "Brazil's Imperiled Rain Forest"

ANSWERS: EXERCISE 5–5

1. *Primary evidence:* The author is describing his own experiences in a first-person narrative. It can be assumed to be reliable since a reliable journal, *National Geographic*, published the account.

➜

2.   Most climatologists believe that the world will eventually slip back into an ice age in 10,000 to 20,000 years. The Earth has been unusually cold for the last two to three million years, and we are just lucky to be living during one of the warm spells. But the concern of most weather watchers looking at the next century is with fire rather than ice. By burning fossil fuels and chopping down forests, humans have measurably increased the amount of carbon dioxide in the atmosphere. From somewhere around 300 parts per million at the turn of the century, this level has risen to 340 parts per million today. If the use of fossil fuels continues to increase, carbon dioxide could reach 600 parts per million during the next century.

—STEVE OLSON, "Computing Climate"

3.   Marriages on the frontier were often made before a girl was half through her adolescent years, and some diaries record a casualness in the manner in which such decisions were reached. Mrs. John Kirkwood recounts.

> The night before Christmas, John Kirkwood . . . the path finder, stayed at our house over night. I had met him before and when he heard the discussion about my brother Jasper's wedding, he suggested that he and I also get married. I was nearly fifteen years old and I thought it was high time that I got married so I consented.

—LILLIAN SCHLISSEL, Women's Diaries of the Westward Journey

Assessing cause and effect critically   5i

Cause and effect is a mode of thinking that seeks to establish some relationship, or link, between two or more specific pieces of evidence. Regardless of whether you begin with a cause or an effect, you are working with this basic pattern:

BASIC PATTERN FOR CAUSE AND EFFECT

Cause A ⟶ produces ⟶ effect B

You may seek to understand the effects of a known cause (for example, studying two more hours each night):

More studying ⟶ produces ⟶ ?

Or you may attempt to determine the cause or causes of a known effect (for example, recurrent headaches):

? ⟶ produces ⟶ recurrent headaches

---

2. *Secondary evidence:* The assertions in this paragraph are carefully qualified and seem well substantiated by evidence. The material was published in a reliable science magazine.

3. *Both secondary and primary evidence:* The opening paragraph presents secondary evidence, but the quoted material that follows this paragraph serves to make Schlissel's observations reliable. The second paragraph presents primary evidence—a first-hand account from a diary by Mrs. John Kirkwood.

TEACHING TIP

You may want to ask your students to think about their own experiences, analyzing them for their causes and effects. You might ask your students to diagram these causes and effects and to write some of these diagrams on the board for discussion. The questions that follow can help to stimulate students' thinking.

1. How did you get your first job?

2. What did you learn from that job?

3. Whose advice is particularly important to you?

4. How do you reach a decision?

5. What difference do you expect college to make in your life?

6. Why do you have a particular way of doing something?

7. How do you make friends?

8. Who is the most important person in your life? Why?

9. When did you learn to drive a car?

10. What will you be doing in ten years?

EXTRA EXERCISE B

Supply answers for the blanks in the sentences that follow, checking each choice by the guidelines for evaluating cause and effect to be sure that it is accurate.

1. Frequently eating food with high sodium content can cause _____.

2. _____ can lead to a traffic violation.

3. Regular exercise produces _____.

4. _____ is a leading cause of _____.

5. Because she _____, she is expected to be named Gourmet of the Year.

6. Her mother refuses to intervene so that _____.

7. If you don't quit _____, you are likely to end up in a lawsuit.

8. She decided to stay in college when she learned that _____.

9. Additional funding for preschool education is needed in order to _____.

10. _____ has resulted in increased numbers of homeless people in our major cities.

ANSWERS: EXTRA EXERCISE B

Answers will vary, but here are possible responses:

1. high blood pressure
2. Ignoring a stop sign
3. better health
4. Inattention in class, low grades
5. led a revolt against the school cafeteria
6. the daughter will become more independent
7. telling lies about your neighbor
8. employers in her profession usually hire people with college degrees
9. prepare all children adequately for school
10. Slashing the budget for public housing

If you want to use reasoning based on a relationship of cause and effect, evaluate the connections carefully. As you evaluate cause-and-effect relationships, keep in mind the guidelines in Chart 35. Each guideline is discussed after the chart.

GUIDELINES FOR ASSESSING CAUSE AND EFFECT	35

- Is there a clear relationship between events?
- If the events recur, are they always in the same sequence?
- Are there multiple causes and/or effects?

- **Is there a clear relationship between events?** When you read or write about causes and effects, carefully think through the reasoning. Related causes and effects happen in sequence: A cause exists or occurs before an effect. *First* the wind blows; *then* a door slams; *then* a pane of glass in the door breaks. But just because the order of events implies a cause-and-effect relationship, that relationship does not necessarily exist. Perhaps someone slammed the door shut. Perhaps someone threw a baseball through the glass pane. A cause-and-effect relationship must be linked by more than chronological sequence. The fact that *B* happens after *A* does not prove that *A* causes *B*.

- **Is there a pattern of repetition?** To establish that *A* causes *B*, there must be proof that every time *A* is present, *B* occurs—or that *B* never occurs unless *A* is present. The need for a pattern of repetition explains why the Food and Drug Administration performs thousands of tests before declaring a new food or medicine safe for human consumption.

- **Are there multiple causes and/or effects?** Avoid oversimplification. The basic pattern of cause and effect—single cause, single effect (*A* causes *B*)—rarely represents the full picture.

$$\left.\begin{array}{l} \text{Cause 1} \\ \text{Cause 2} \\ \text{Cause 3} \end{array}\right\} \longrightarrow \text{produce} \longrightarrow \text{effect } B$$

It was oversimplification when some people assumed that high schools were the only cause of a quite dramatic nationwide decline in SAT scores between 1964 and 1984. Not only was that unfair to high schools, it also ignored a variety of other causes, possibly including television viewing habits, family life, level of textbooks, and so on. Similarly, one cause can produce multiple effects:

Oversimplification of effects usually involves focusing on one effect and ignoring others. For example, advertisements about a liquid diet drink focus on its most appealing effect: rapid weight loss. But they ignore other less desirable effects such as loss of nutrients and vulnerability to rapidly regaining the weight.

Assessing reasoning processes critically   5j

To think critically, you need to understand reasoning processes so that you can recognize and evaluate them in your reading and use them correctly in your writing. **Induction** and **deduction** are reasoning processes. They are natural thought patterns that people use every day to think through ideas and make decisions. The differences between the two processes are summarized in Chart 36.

COMPARISON OF INDUCTIVE AND DEDUCTIVE REASONING		36
	INDUCTIVE REASONING	**DEDUCTIVE REASONING**
ARGUMENT BEGINS	with specific evidence	with a general claim
ARGUMENT CONCLUDES	with a general claim	with a specific statement
CONCLUSION IS	reliable or unreliable	true or false
REASONING IS USED	to discover something new	to apply what is known

COMPARISON OF INDUCTIVE AND DEDUCTIVE REASONING

5j-1

TEACHING TIP

Using analogy is a way to think inductively. An analogy compares two dissimilar objects, ideas, or experiences by focusing on what they have in common. For example, some people make an analogy between the role of a teacher and that of a coach. Like coaches, teachers train people in fundamentals through repetition and practice, recommend changes in technique, and try to inspire excellence. However, despite points of similarity, two dissimilar items remain dissimilar.

First, coaches work primarily with the body rather than the mind, developing physical rather than mental skills. Second, team coaches praise the team player while good teachers reward independence and originality. Thus the analogy between teachers and coaches breaks down at some point.

In the absence of other evidence, an analogy will not *prove* anything. Nevertheless, although an analogy can always be shown as flawed under close scrutiny, it can still help explain a point and thus help persuade an audience.

Recognizing and using inductive reasoning

Induction is the process of arriving at general principles from particular facts or instances, as summarized in Chart 37. Suppose that you go to the Registry of Motor Vehicles to renew your driver's license, and you have to stand in line for two hours until you get the document. Then a few months later, when you return to the Registry for new license plates, a clerk gives you the wrong advice, and you have to stand in two different lines for three hours. Another time you go there in response to a letter asking for information, and you discover that you should have brought your car registration form, although the letter failed to mention that fact. You conclude that the Registry is inefficient and seems not to care about the convenience of its patrons. You have arrived at this conclusion by means of induction.

SUMMARY OF INDUCTIVE REASONING   37

1. **Inductive reasoning moves from the specific to the general.**
   It begins with the evidence of specific facts, observations, or experiences and moves to a general conclusion.
2. Inductive conclusions are considered *reliable* or *unreliable*, not true or false. An inductive conclusion indicates probability, the degree to which the conclusion is likely to be true. Frustrating though it may be for those who seek certainty, inductive thinking is, of necessity, based only on a sampling of the facts.
3. An inductive conclusion is held to be reliable or unreliable in relation to the quantity and quality of the evidence (see 5h) supporting it.
4. Induction leads to new "truths." Induction can support statements about the unknown on the basis of what is known.

5j-2

Recognizing and using deductive reasoning

Deduction is the process of reasoning from general claims to a specific instance. If several unproductive visits to the Registry of Motor Vehicles have convinced you that the Registry cares little about the convenience of its patrons (as the experiences described in 5j-1 suggest), you will not be happy the next time you must return. Your reasoning might go something like this:

The Registry wastes people's time.
I have to go to the Registry tomorrow.
Therefore, tomorrow my time will be wasted.

SUMMARY OF INDUCTIVE REASONING

You reached the conclusion—"therefore, tomorrow my time will be wasted"—by means of deduction.

Deductive arguments have three parts: two **premises** and a **conclusion**. This three-part structure is known as a **syllogism.** The first premise of a deductive argument may be a fact or an assumption. The second premise may also be a fact or an assumption.

Whether or not an argument is **valid** has to do with the argument's form or structure. Here the word *valid* is not the general term people use in conversation to mean "acceptable" or "well grounded." In the context of reading and writing logical arguments, the word *valid* has a very specific meaning. A deductive argument is *valid* when the conclusion logically follows from the premises. The following argument is valid.

VALID

PREMISE 1	When it snows, the streets get wet. [fact]
PREMISE 2	It is snowing. [fact]
CONCLUSION	Therefore, the streets are getting wet.

The following argument is invalid.

INVALID

PREMISE 1	When it snows, the streets get wet. [fact]
PREMISE 2	The streets are getting wet. [fact]
CONCLUSION	Therefore, it is snowing.

The invalid argument has acceptable premises because the premises are facts. The argument's conclusion, however, is wrong. It ignores other reasons for why the streets may be wet. The street could be wet from rain, from street-cleaning trucks that spray water, or from people using hoses to cool off the pavement or to wash their cars. Because the conclusion does not follow logically from the premises, the argument is invalid.

The following argument is also invalid. The conclusion does not follow from the premises (the car may not start for many reasons other than a dead battery).

INVALID

PREMISE 1	When the battery is dead, a car will not start. [fact]
PREMISE 2	My car will not start. [fact]
CONCLUSION	My battery is dead.

When a premise is an assumption, the premise must be able to be defended with evidence. The next argument about the unemployment

ALTERNATE EXAMPLES
Invalid:
Some circular things are bubbles.
Some human heads are circular things.
Some human heads are bubbles.
Valid:
All mammals are animals.
All whales are mammals.
Therefore, all whales are animals.

QUOTATION ABOUT READING
Reading is to the mind what exercise is to the body.
—Joseph Addison and Richard Steele

5j–2
cont.

rate and recession is valid. Its conclusion follows logically from the premises. An argument's validity, however, is independent of its truth. Is premise 1 true? Different economists will offer different opinions. *Only if both premises are true is an argument true.* This argument may be true or false depending on whether the first premise is true or false. The writer must support the claim that is the first premise.

	VALID (AND POSSIBLY TRUE)
PREMISE 1	When the unemployment rate rises, an economic recession occurs. [assumption: the writer must present evidence in support of this statement]
PREMISE 2	The unemployment rate has risen. [fact]
CONCLUSION	An economic recession will occur.

The following argument is valid. Its conclusion follows from its premises. Is the argument, however, true? Because the argument contains an assumption in its first premise, the argument can be true only if the premise is proved true. Such proof is not possible. Therefore, although the argument is valid, it is not true.

	VALID (BUT NOT TRUE)
PREMISE 1	If you buy a Supermacho 357 sports car, you will achieve instant popularity. [assumption]
PREMISE 2	Kim just bought a Supermacho 357 sports car. [fact]
CONCLUSION	Kim will achieve instant popularity.

In any deductive argument, beware of premises that are implied but not stated—called **unstated assumptions.** Remember that an argument can be logically valid even though it is based on wrong assumptions. The response to such an argument is to attack the assumptions, not the conclusion. Often the assumptions are wrong. For example, suppose a corporation argued that it should not be required to install pollution control devices because the cost would cut into its profits. This argument rests on the unstated assumption that no corporation should do something that would lower its profits. That assumption is wrong, and so is the argument. But it can be shown to be wrong only when the assumptions are challenged. Similarly, if someone says that certain information has to be correct because it was printed in a newspaper, the person's deductive reasoning is flawed. Here the unstated assumption is that everything in a newspaper is correct—which is not true. Whenever there is an unstated assumption, supply it and then check to make sure it is true. Deductive reasoning is summarized in Chart 38.

SUMMARY OF DEDUCTIVE REASONING   38

1. **Deductive reasoning moves from the general to the specific.**
   The three-part structure that makes up a deductive argument includes two premises and a conclusion drawn from them.
2. A deductive argument is valid if the conclusion logically follows from the premises.
3. A deductive conclusion may be judged true or false. If both premises are true, the conclusion is true. If the argument contains an assumption, the writer must prove the truth of the assumption to establish the truth of the argument.
4. Deductive reasoning applies what the writer already knows. Though it does not yield anything new, it builds stronger arguments than does inductive reasoning because it offers the certainty of a conclusion's being true or false.

EXERCISE 5-6

Consulting section 5j-2, ignore for the moment whether the premises seem to you to be true, but determine if each conclusion is valid. Explain your answer.

1. Faddish clothes are expensive.
   This shirt is expensive.
   This shirt must be part of a fad.
2. When a storm is threatening, small-craft warnings are issued.
   A storm is threatening.
   Small-craft warnings will be issued.
3. The Pulitzer Prize is awarded to outstanding literary works.
   The Great Gatsby never won a Pulitzer Prize.
   The Great Gatsby is not an outstanding literary work.
4. All states send representatives to the United States Congress.
   Puerto Rico sends a representative to the United States Congress.
   Puerto Rico is a state.
5. All risks are frightening.
   Changing to a new job is a risk.
   The change to a new job is frightening.
6. Before an occupancy permit can be issued, a new home must be inspected.
   Our new home has been issued an occupancy permit.
   Our new home has been inspected.

ANSWERS: EXERCISE 5–6

1. Invalid. The shirt's being expensive does not mean that it shares other characteristics of faddish clothing.

2. Valid. The conclusion follows logically from the premises.

3. Invalid. Some outstanding literary works have not received a Pulitzer Prize.

4. Invalid. All states do send representatives, but that does not mean that all representatives come from a state.

5. Valid. The argument is valid, although some people may not agree that all risks are frightening.

6. Valid. The conclusion flows logically from the premises.

ANSWERS: EXERCISE 5-6, cont.

7. Invalid. The premises do not contain the conclusion. It is impossible to know whether this magazine is part of "most."

8. Invalid. The qualifying word "usually" in the first premise leaves open the possibility that there are science fiction novels that are not violent.

9. Valid. The conclusion is contained in the premises.

10. Invalid. The first premise does not stipulate that all great college basketball teams come from the Midwest (and Georgetown is among universities not in the Midwest that produce great basketball teams).

EXTRA EXERCISE C

Each analogy here can be defended. Like all analogies, each can also be attacked. First, defend each one—give one or more arguments to show that the two parts of the analogy are similar and are relevant to the claim being made. Second, attack each one by pointing out how they are not similar. Finally, offer other types of evidence that would help make the claim ultimately more convincing.

1. Like warfare, the aim of football is to destroy.

2. Don't bother to take your books home over vacation. Vacation is like a "study date"—no studying ever takes place.

3. Taking care of a group of young children is like trying to string beads without a knot on the end of the string.

4. The atom is like a small solar system, with its own "sun" and its own satellites.

5j–2 cont.

7. Most weekly news magazines give only superficial coverage of world affairs.

This is a weekly news magazine.

This will give only superficial coverage of world affairs.

8. Science fiction novels are usually violent.

This is a science fiction novel.

This novel is obviously violent.

9. All veterans are entitled to education benefits.

Elaine is a veteran.

Elaine is entitled to education benefits.

10. Midwestern universities produce great college basketball teams.

Georgetown has a great college basketball team.

Georgetown is a midwestern university.

5k   Recognizing and avoiding logical fallacies

Logical fallacies are flaws in reasoning that lead to illogical statements. They tend to occur most often when ideas are being argued, although they can be found in all types of writing. Most logical fallacies masquerade as reasonable statements, but they are in fact attempts to manipulate readers by reaching their emotions instead of their intellects, their hearts rather than their heads. Most logical fallacies are known by labels; each indicates a way that thinking has gone wrong during the reasoning process.

Hasty generalization

A **hasty generalization** occurs when someone generalizes from inadequate evidence. If the statement "My hometown is the best place in the state to live" is supported with only two examples of why it is pleasant, the generalization is hasty. **Stereotyping** is a type of hasty generalization that occurs when someone makes prejudiced, sweeping claims about all of the members of a particular religious, ethnic, racial, or political group: "Everyone from country X is dishonest." **Sexism** occurs when someone discriminates against people on the basis of sex. (See 11q and 21b for advice on how to avoid sexist language, a form of sexism, in your writing.) One often-heard combination of stereotyping and sexism occurs when a car driven by a woman has hit a car driven by a man, and the man says, "That's just like a woman."

False analogy

A **false analogy** is a comparison in which the differences outweigh the similarities, or the similarities are irrelevant to the claim the analogy is intended to support. "Old Joe Smith would never make a good President because an old dog cannot learn new tricks." Homespun analogies like this often seem to have an air of wisdom about them, but just as often they fall apart when examined closely. Learning the role of the President is hardly comparable to a dog's learning new tricks.

Begging the question

An argument that **begs the question** states a claim, but the support is based on the claim, so the reasoning is circular. Sometimes, the support simply restates the claim: "Wrestling is a dangerous sport because it is unsafe." "Unsafe" conveys the same idea as "dangerous"; it does not provide evidence to support the claim that wrestling is dangerous. Another question-begging argument offers a second statement as support, but the support for the second statement is the argument in the first statement: "Wrestling is a dangerous sport because wrestlers get injured. Anyone as big and strong as a wrestler would not get injured if the sport were safe." Begging the question also occurs in statements such as "Wrestlers love danger." There is an unstated assumption that wrestling is dangerous as well as an assumption that no proof is called for because the audience shares the opinion that wrestling is dangerous.

Irrelevant argument

An **irrelevant argument** is called *non sequitur* in Latin, which translates as "it does not follow." This flaw occurs when a conclusion does not follow from the premises: "Jane Jones is a forceful speaker, so she will make a good mayor." It does not follow that someone's ability to be a forceful speaker means that person would be a good mayor.

False cause

The fallacy of **false cause** is called *post hoc, ergo propter hoc* in Latin—which means "after this, therefore because of this." This fallacy results when someone assumes that because two events are related in time, the first one causes the second one. This cause-and-effect fallacy is very common. "A new weather satellite was launched last week, and it has been raining ever since" implies—illogically—that the rain (the second event) is a result of the satellite launch (the first event).

Self-contradiction

Self-contradiction occurs when two premises are used that cannot simultaneously be true: "Only when nuclear weapons have finally destroyed us will we be convinced of the need to control them." This statement is self-contradictory in that no one would be around to be convinced if everyone had been destroyed.

ANSWERS: EXTRA EXERCISE C

Answers will vary. Answers here are intended to be suggestive.

1. *Pro:* Both involve uniformed "teams" inflicting injury upon each other in pursuit of territorial gain. *Con:* Football is played according to rules, with clear time limits, for entertainment. *To revise:* Add statistics on actual injuries inflicted upon high school, college, and professional football players, as well as evidence of asocial attitudes (if any) developed by players.

2. *Pro:* In both cases, serious intentions readily give way to the pursuit of pleasure. *Con:* A study date ostensibly has a serious purpose whereas vacation, by definition, is unstructured free time. *To revise:* Add eyewitness accounts or reported observations about how time was spent on actual study dates, actual vacations.

3. *Pro:* Both are nearly impossible to control. The moment you get one "on the string," the others fall off. *Con:* Beads are much easier to control. *To revise:* Provide eyewitness accounts of babysitting experiences.

4. *Pro:* Both have large centers with smaller objects orbiting them. *Con:* The sun is chemically more complex than the nuclei of atoms; planets orbit the sun because of gravity rather than electrical charge. *To revise:* Other than listing additional similarities, the analogy cannot be made stronger—the properties of the solar system and of the atom are what they are.

TEACHING TIP

Many students enjoy finding and correcting logical fallacies in newspaper editorials and opinion columns, as well as in the work of their peers. You might distribute copies of works containing fallacies, as a spur to class discussion or for revision. A less adept class might benefit from a preliminary lesson based on a list of logical fallacies you can cull from assorted sources (newspapers, political literature, advertisements, student papers, etc.); tell the students all the passages are illogical and have them explain why, as a prelude to revision (oral or written, as time allows).

Your analytically minded students may be interested in additional logical fallacies:

A *question-begging phrase* (sometimes called *alleged certainty*) presents something as certain that is open to debate: "Everyone knows" and "It is obvious that" are typical phrases that beg the question. This statement is flawed: "It is common knowledge that jobs in Texas pay more than do jobs in Idaho"; this statement is logical: "A recent government survey revealed that, on the average, workers in the oil fields of Texas are paid more than are loggers in the timber industries of Idaho." *To correct*: Drop the phrase and substitute evidence that supports your claim.

A *complex question* (also known as a *loaded question*) contains one or more unproven assumptions: "Are you still spending time with known drug addicts?" Notice what happens when you try to answer such a question. If you say "yes," you are guilty. If you say "no," you are still guilty, because you are admitting that you used to spend time with drug addicts. *To correct*: Split the question into its parts ("Are you still spending time with those people?" "Are those people drug addicts?") and deal with each separately.

➜

Red herring

A **red herring,** sometimes referred to as **ignoring the question,** sidetracks an issue by bringing up a totally unrelated issue: "Why worry about pandas becoming extinct when we should be concerned about the plight of the homeless?" Someone who introduces an irrelevant issue hopes to distract the audience as a red herring might distract bloodhounds from a scent.

Argument to the person

An **argument to the person,** also known as **ad hominem,** attacks a person's appearance, personal habits, or character instead of dealing with the merits of the individual's arguments, ideas, or opinions. "We could take her position in favor of jailing child abusers seriously if she were not so nasty to the children who live next door to her" is one type of ad hominem attack. It seems so reasonable to belittle suggestions about dealing with child abusers from someone who may (or may not) be nasty to the children next door. In truth, however, the suggestions, not the person who makes them, must be dealt with. The person who argues is not the argument.

Guilt by Association

Guilt by association is a kind of ad hominem attack implying that an individual's arguments, ideas, or opinions lack merit because of that person's activities, interests, or associates. The claim that because Jack belongs to the International Hill Climbers Association, which declared bankruptcy last month, he is unfit to be mayor uses guilt by association.

Bandwagon

Bandwagon, also known as **going along with the crowd** or **ad populum,** implies that something is right because everyone is doing it, that truth is determined by majority vote: "Smoking is not bad for people because millions of people smoke."

False or irrelevant authority

Using **false or irrelevant authority,** sometimes called **ad verecundiam,** means citing the opinion of an "expert" who has no claim to expertise about the subject at hand. This fallacy attempts to transfer prestige from one area to another. Many television commercials rely on this tactic—a famous tennis player praising a brand of motor oil or a popular movie star lauding a brand of cheese.

Card-stacking

Card-stacking, also known as **special pleading,** ignores evidence on the other side of a question. From all the available facts, the person arguing selects only those that will build the best (or worst) possible case. Many television commercials use this strategy. When three slim, happy consumers rave about a new diet plan, they do not mention that (a) the plan does not work for everyone and that (b) other plans work better for some people. The makers of the commercial select evidence that helps their cause and ignore any that does not.

The either-or fallacy

The **either-or fallacy,** also known as **false dilemma,** offers only two alternatives when more exist. Such fallacies often touch on emotional issues and can therefore seem accurate at first. When people reflect, however, they quickly come to realize that more alternatives are available. Here is a typical example of an either-or fallacy: "Either go to college or forget about getting a job." This statement implies that a college education is a prerequisite for all jobs, which is not true.

Taking something out of context

Taking something out of context separates an idea or fact from the material surrounding it, thus distorting it for special purposes. Suppose a critic writes about a movie saying, "The plot was predictable and boring but the music was sparkling." Then an advertisement for the movie says, "Critic calls this movie 'sparkling.'" The critic's words have been taken out of context—and distorted.

Appeal to ignorance

Appeal to ignorance assumes that an argument is valid simply because it has not been shown to be false. Conversely, something is not false simply because it has not been shown to be true. Appeals to ignorance can be very persuasive because they prey on people's superstitions or lack of knowledge. Here is a typical example of such flawed reasoning: "Since no one has proven that depression does not cause cancer, we can assume that it does." The absence of opposing evidence proves nothing.

Ambiguity and equivocation

Ambiguity and **equivocation** describe expressions that are not clear because they have more than one meaning. An ambiguous expression may be taken either way by the reader. A statement such as "They were entertaining guests" is ambiguous. Were the guests amusing to be with or were people giving hospitality to guests? An equivocal expression, by contrast, is one used in two or more ways within a single argument. If someone argued that the President played a role in arms control negotiations and then, two sentences later, said that the President was playing a role when he called himself "the education President," the person would be equivocating.

TEACHING TIP, cont.

Appeal to fear uses scare tactics instead of legitimate evidence. Such an argument implies danger: "Anyone who stages a protest against the government is a communist, so we must outlaw all protests."

Appeal to the people (also known as *ad populum*) draws on whatever the people hold dear—for example, country, religion, or family. This approach tries to sway people by using a favorable label instead of providing reasons: "A vote for Joe Smith is a vote for the flag."

Name-calling attaches an unpleasant label to something or someone. Consider how a label can stop people from thinking: "Jane Jones was once an alcoholic, so she cannot possibly say anything of value about politics."

Appeal to pity attempts to arouse sympathy: "He embezzled $1,500 of company money, but after all, his wife recently died and his child needs surgery."

The *genetic fallacy*, a special form of *hasty generalization*, predicts something about a person based on that person's origins: "Joe Smith is from New York City, so he knows how to deal with street crime." Often this fallacy involves a person's religion, sex, race, or economic status.

SUMMARY OF LOGICAL FALLACIES

- **Hasty generalization:** generalizing from inadequate evidence. Stereotyping is hasty generalization using prejudiced claims about a group of people.

- **False analogy:** using a comparison in which the differences outweigh the similarities, or in which the similarities are irrelevant to the claim the analogy is intended to support

- **Begging the question:** a kind of circular reasoning that offers as proof of an argument a version of the argument itself or uses a (presumably) shared assumption to stand for proof

- **Irrelevant argument:** reaching a conclusion that does not follow from the premises

- **False cause:** assuming that because two events are related in time, the first caused the second

- **Self-contradiction:** using two premises that cannot both be true

- **Red herring:** sidetracking the issue by raising a second, unrelated issue

- **Argument to the person:** attacking the person making the argument rather than the argument itself

- **Guilt by association:** attacking a person's ideas because of that person's interests or associates

- **Bandwagon:** implying that something is right or is permissible because "everyone" does it

- **False or irrelevant authority:** citing the opinion of a person who has no expertise about the subject

- **Card-stacking:** ignoring evidence on the other side of a question

- **The either-or fallacy:** offering only two alternatives when more exist

- **Taking something out of context:** distorting an idea or fact by separating it from the material surrounding it

- **Appeal to ignorance:** assuming that an argument is valid simply because there is no evidence on the other side of the issue

- **Ambiguity and equivocation:** using expressions that are not clear because they have more than one meaning

EXERCISE 5-7

Consulting section 5k, identify and explain the fallacy in each item. If the item does not contain a logical flaw, circle its number.

EXAMPLE   Seat belts are the only hope for reducing the death rate from automobile accidents. [This is an *either-or fallacy* because it assumes that nothing but seat belts can reduce the number of fatalities from car accidents.]

1. Joanna Hayes should write a book about the Central Intelligence Agency (CIA). She has starred in three films that show the inner workings of the CIA.

2. It is ridiculous to have spent thousands of dollars to rescue those two whales from being trapped in the Arctic ice. Why, look at all of the people trapped in jobs that they don't like.

3. Every time my roommate has a math test, she becomes extremely nervous. Clearly, she is not good at math.

4. Plagiarism is deceitful because it is dishonest.

5. The local political coalition to protect the environment would get my support and that of many other people if its leaders did not drive cars that get poor gasoline mileage.

6. UFOs must exist because no reputable studies have proven conclusively that they do not.

7. Water fluoridation affects the brain. Citywide, students' test scores began to drop five months after fluoridation began.

8. Learning to manage a corporation is exactly like learning to ride a bicycle: Once you learn the skills, you never forget how, and you never fall.

9. Medicare is free; the government pays for it from taxes.

10. Reading good literature is the one way to appreciate culture.

ANSWERS: EXERCISE 5–7

1. *False authority.* A movie star is not an authority on the CIA.

2. *Red herring.* The social issue is introduced to divert attention from the real issue—whether or not money should have been spent to rescue the whales.

3. *Irrelevant argument,* or *non sequitur.* A person can be nervous about something and still be very good at it.

4. *Begging the question* or *circular argument.* "Dishonest" is merely a slightly different term for "deceitful."

5. *Argument to the person,* or *ad hominem.* These people are being attacked for materialism, but they are perhaps excellent environmentalists, whose cars and shoes are irrelevant to their environmental stance.

6. *Appeal to ignorance.* Just because no evidence exists for one side of the argument does not mean that the other side of the argument is valid.

7. *False cause,* or *post hoc ergo propter hoc.* The sequence of events does not prove any connection between them.

8. *False analogy.* Analogies are dangerous in argument because they equate things that are not the same. Riding a bicycle is much different from learning to run a company, and although the skills for riding a bicycle remain the same, those of running a company may change with the economy and other pressures so that one could "fall" if he or she did not adopt those skills.

9. *Self-contradiction.* Medicare cannot be free if it is paid for.

10. *Either-or.* Reading good literature is not the only way to appreciate culture.

6 Writing Argument

REFERENCE TO SUPPLEMENTS

For more on the fact that ESL students sometimes need help adapting to argumentation style in the U.S. classroom, see C. Myers, "ESL Writers in the Composition Class," in L. Julian, et al., *Strategies and Resources for Teaching Writing with the Simon & Schuster Handbook for Writers*.

QUOTATION ABOUT WRITING

Rhetoric may be defined as the faculty of observing in any given case the available means of persuasion.

—Aristotle

QUOTATION ABOUT WRITING

The art of writing has for backbone some fierce attachment to an idea.

—Virginia Woolf

BACKGROUND

Available from ERIC is Karen Quinn and Ann Matsuhashi's article "Stalking Ideas: The Generation and Elaboration of Arguments," in which they report on specific college students who used reading to generate argumentative writing (ERIC ED 257 043).

When writing **argument** for your college courses, you seek to convince a reader to agree with you concerning a topic open to debate. A written argument states and supports one position about the debatable topic. Support for that position depends on evidence, reasons, and examples chosen for their direct relation to the point being argued. One section of the written argument might present and attempt to refute other positions on the topic, but the central thrust of the essay is to argue for one point of view.

Taking and defending a position in a written argument is an engaging intellectual process, especially when it involves a topic of substance about which universal agreement is unlikely. The ability to think critically (see Chart 28 in section 5b) is challenged by the activity of examining all sides of a topic, choosing one side to defend, and marshaling convincing support for that one side.

If you are among the people who find any type of arguing distasteful, you are not alone. But rest assured that written argument differs drastically from everyday, informal arguing. Informal arguing sometimes originates in anger and might involve bursts of temper or unpleasant emotional confrontations. Written argument, in contrast, can always be a constructive activity. When you write an argument, you can disagree without being disagreeable. An effective written argument sets forth its position calmly, respectfully, and logically. Any passion that underlies a writer's position is evident not from angry words but from the force of a balanced, well-developed, clearly written discussion.

The ability to argue reasonably and effectively is an important skill that people need not only in college but throughout their lives—in family relationships, with friends, and in the business world. People engage in debates (perhaps more often in speaking than in writing) that call for an exchange of solidly supported views. Once you become adept at the techniques of written argument, you can use them equally effectively for oral argument.

Much of the material in the earlier chapters of this handbook can help you compose a written argument. A list of useful sections is given in Chart 40. This chapter concentrates on the special demands of writing argument. The writing of two student essays is discussed in this chapter, and the final draft of each essay appears in section 6i.

MATERIAL FROM EARLIER CHAPTERS IN THIS HANDBOOK   40
TO USE WHEN WRITING AN ARGUMENT

- Checklist for persuasive writing (1b-3)
- Audiences for writing (1c)
- Establishing a suitable tone (1d)
- Choosing a topic (2c)
- The writing process: planning and shaping (Chapter 2)
- The writing process: drafting and revising (Chapter 3)
- Writing paragraphs (Chapter 4)
- Thinking, reading, and writing critically (Chapter 5)
- Using evidence to think critically (5h)
- Analyzing cause and effect (5i)
- Using inductive and deductive reasoning (5j)
- Avoiding logical fallacies (5k)

The terms *persuasive writing* and *argumentative writing* often are used interchangeably. When a distinction is made between them, persuasive writing is the broader term. It includes advertisements, letters to editors, emotional pleas in speeches or writing, and formal written arguments. The focus of this chapter is formal written argument as usually assigned in college courses.

Choosing a topic for a written argument   6a

When you choose a topic for written argument, be sure that it is open to debate. Be careful not to confuse matters of information with matters of debate. Facts are matters of information, not debate. An essay becomes an argument when it takes a position concerning the fact or other piece of information.

MATERIAL FROM EARLIER CHAPTERS IN THIS HANDBOOK TO USE WHEN WRITING AN ARGUMENT

BACKGROUND
Chapter Two of this book, Planning and Shaping, lists four aspects of writing situations that affect the decisions that the writer makes. They are (1) the topic, (2) the purpose, (3) the audience that will read or hear it, and (4) the special requirements that influence every writing situation, such as deadlines and length. For explanations of each aspect, see Section 2b.

BACKGROUND
Although rhetoric, as defined by Aristotle, appears in the speeches and debates of the epics and plays of ancient Greece, its principles were not systematically formulated until the fifth century B.C. Corax of Syracuse, recognizing the need for a system by which citizens of Sicily could argue in the courts to recover property that they had lost during the reign of Thrasybulus, began to set down the principles of argumentation. Lacking documents to prove their claims, ordinary citizens had to argue their cases by relying on inferential reasoning and probability. Tisias, the student of Corax, extended the study of rhetoric from the courtroom and wrote speeches for other people to deliver. Others who quickly followed to develop the art of rhetoric, or persuasion, include Gorgias of Leotini (*fl.* 420 B.C.), known principally for his ornate style characterized by extensive use of figures of speech, and Isocrates (436–338 B.C.), one of the leading Athenian teachers of rhetoric and an author of influential books on rhetorical theory.

BACKGROUND
In a paper given at the Wyoming Conference on Freshman and Sophomore English in 1983, Mary C. Fenton explored four models for teaching argumentative discourse. Her synthesis of the models is explained in "Teaching Persuasion: A Positive Approach," found in ERIC ED 233 396.

EXTRA EXERCISE A

Which of the following topics are concerned with fact and which state a position open to debate?

1. The term *journalism* refers to the business of publishing a regularly recurring text.

2. Television news programs are more influential than they should be.

3. Journalists in the United States operate under the protection of the First Amendment to the Constitution.

4. Most reporters are biased in their descriptions of political figures.

5. The government should not let journalists have access to information dealing with national security.

6. Journalism involves both reporting the news and forming public opinion.

7. Reporters should verify a controversial story with two sources before running it.

8. Weekly newspapers are becoming increasingly popular in large cities.

9. Cartoons furnish one of the more entertaining features of newspapers.

10. Television commentators should not give their own opinions about political and social matters.

ANSWERS: EXTRA EXERCISE A

1. fact
2. opinion
3. fact
4. opinion
5. opinion
6. fact
7. opinion
8. fact
9. opinion
10. opinion

FACT	Students at Deitmer College **are required** to take physical education.
POSITION OPEN TO DEBATE	Students at Deitmer College **should not be required** to take physical education.
OPPOSITE POSITION OPEN TO DEBATE	Students at Deitmer College **should be required** to take physical education.

A written argument could take one of these opposing positions and defend it. The essay could not argue for two or more sides, though it might mention other points of view and attempt to refute them.

When you are assigned a written argument, be sure to read and think through the assignment carefully. Instructors construct assignments for written argument in a number of ways. You might be given both the topic and the position to take on that topic. In such cases, you are expected to fulfill the assignment whether or not you agree personally with the given point of view. You are judged on your ability to marshal a defense of the assigned position and to reason logically about it. Another type of assignment is unstructured, requiring you to choose the debatable topic and the position to defend. In such cases, the topic that you choose should be **suitable for college writing** (see 2c-1), not trivial (for example, *not* the best way to chew gum). The topic should be **narrowed sufficiently** (see 2c-2) to fit the writing situation. You are judged on your ability to think of a debatable topic of substance, to narrow the topic so that your essay can include general statements and specific details, to choose a defensible position about that topic, and to present and support your position convincingly. If you cannot decide what position you agree with personally because all sides of a debatable topic have merit, do not get blocked. You need not make a lifetime commitment to your position. Rather, concentrate on the merits of one position, and present that position as effectively as possible.

The two sample essays at the end of this chapter were written in response to the assignment shown in the box below. This assignment states the topic but asks students to take a position about it.

> *Lindsey Black and Daniel Casey were given this assignment:* Write an essay of 500 to 700 words that argues about whether holidays have become too commercialized in the United States. Your final draft is due in one week. Bring your earlier drafts to class for possible sharing and discussion.

Black and Casey analyzed the four aspects of the **writing situation** (see 2b) reflected in the assignment. The essay *topic* is stated (whether holidays have become too commercialized in the United States). The essay's *purpose* is persuasive, but students are free to choose the position to argue for (the student can choose to argue that the holidays have become too commercialized *or* that they have not become too commercialized). The *audience* for the essay is not specified and is therefore assumed to be the instructor and, perhaps, other members of the class. The *special requirements* include the essay's length (between 500 and 700 words) and the time for getting the essay into final draft (one week).

Developing an assertion and a thesis statement for written argument

6b

An **assertion** is a statement that gives a position about a debatable topic and that can be supported by evidence, reasons, and examples (including facts, statistics, names, experiences, and experts). The thinking process that moves you from a topic to a defensible position calls, first, for you to make an assertion about the topic. The exact wording of the assertion often does not find its way into the essay, but the assertion serves as a focus for your thinking and your writing.

TOPIC	*The commercialization of holidays.*
ASSERTION	Holidays have become too commercialized.
ASSERTION	Holidays have not become too commercialized.

Before you decide on an assertion—the position that you want to argue—you need to explore the topic. Do not rush into deciding on your assertion. Try to wait until you have as full a picture as possible. Consider all sides. Remember that **what mainly separates most good writing from bad is the writer's ability to move back and forth between general statements and specific details.** Try to avoid a position that limits you to *only* general statements or to *only* specific details. In deciding on your assertion, apply the memory device of RENNS (see 4c) to see whether you can marshal sufficient details to support your generalizations.

Even if you know immediately what assertion you want to argue for, do not stop there. The more you think through all sides of the topic, the broader will be the perspective that you bring to your writing. Also, as you think through your position and consider alternative points of view, be open to changing your mind and taking an opposite position. Before too long, however, do settle on a position; switching positions at the last minute lessens your chances of writing an effective essay.

BACKGROUND, cont'd.

an effective way to present it. They include the topics of definition (including genus and division), comparison (similarity, difference, and degree), relationship (cause and effect, antecedent and consequence, contraries, and contradictions), circumstance (the possible and impossible, past and future fact), and testimony (authority, testimonial, statistics, maxims, law, and examples). They remain the basis for many arguments of a general nature presented today. Particular kinds of argument were (and are) drawn from special topics devised to suit the type of discourse chosen by the writer. For example, the writer, or speaker, engaged in judicial discourse is concerned with justice and injustice, making it necessary to establish whether something happened (evidence), what it is (definition), and what kind of thing it is (cause and effect).

EXTRA EXERCISE B

Practice devising assertions and thesis statements by working with some of the following topics.

1. Safety on interstate highways

2. The importance of knowing a second language

3. U.S. Savings Bonds as investments

4. The use of television with commercials in elementary school classrooms

5. Diminishing access to clean water

6. The future of motion pictures

7. Violence on television

8. The need for greater airport security

9. Computer literacy as a requirement for high school graduation

10. Sex education in public schools

To stimulate your thinking about the topic and your assertion about it, use the techniques for gathering ideas explained and illustrated in sections 2e through 2k. Jot down your thoughts as they develop. Do not lose the unique opportunity that the act of writing gives you to discover new ideas and fresh insights. Writers of effective arguments often list for themselves the various points that come to mind, using two columns to represent visually two contrasting points of view. (Head the columns with labels that emphasize contrast: for example, *agree* and *disagree* or *for* and *against*.) The lists can then supply ideas during drafting and revising.

Whenever possible, use outside resources for developing an assertion. These include talking with other people and conducting research. Getting points of view from other people helps you explore a debatable topic. As you talk with people, interview them rather than argue with them. Your goal is to come to know opposing points of view, so resist any temptation to "win" a verbal argument; people sometimes hesitate to offer their ideas fully and openly when their listener is hostile. If your assignment permits you to use the library, do so. Written argument can be particularly enhanced when your position is supported with facts and reference to experts. (See 1e, 5h, and Chapters 31–35.)

Next, using your assertion as a base, compose a thesis statement (see 2n) to use in the essay. It states the position that you present and support in the essay. To write his essay about holiday commercialism shown in 6i, Daniel Casey used this progression from basic assertion to final thesis statement.

> I think holiday commercialism is a good thing. [This assertion is a start.]

> All commercial uses of holidays are very good for our economy and people's spirits. [This preliminary thesis is more developed because it gives reason—economic and emotional benefits—but the word *all* is misleading and the vocabulary level of *very good* needs work.]

> In spite of what some people think, commercial uses of holidays benefit the nation's economy and people's spirits. [This draft is better, but "what some people think" was not an aspect of the topic Casey intended to explore. Also, *benefit spirits* needs revision.]

> Such commercial uses of holidays benefit the nation's economy and lift people's spirits. [This is the final version of Casey's thesis statement; *Such* is a transitional word connecting the thesis statement to sentences in the introductory paragraph that describe several holiday activities.]

The final version meets the requirements listed in Chart 10 in section 2n.

EXERCISE 6-1

Develop an assertion and a thesis statement for a written argument on each of the following topics. You may choose any defensible position.

EXAMPLE   **Topic:** *Book censorship in high school*
            Assertion: *Books should not be censored in high school.*
            Thesis statement: *When books are taken off high school library shelves and are dropped from high school curricula, students are denied exposure to an open exchange of ideas.*

1. television
2. prisons
3. drugs and athletics
4. diets for weight loss
5. grades

Considering the audience for written argument   6c

The purpose of written argument is to convince a reader—the audience—about a matter of opinion. Key factors in considering audience are discussed in 1c. When you write argument, consider one additional factor about audience: the degree of agreement expected from the reader.

When a topic is emotionally charged, chances are high that any position being argued will elicit either strong agreement or strong disagreement. For example, topics such as abortion, capital punishment, and gun control arouse very strong emotions in many people. Such topics are emotionally loaded because they touch on matters of personal beliefs, including religion and individual rights. A topic such as the commercialization of holidays (see the two essays in section 6i) is somewhat less emotionally loaded. Even less emotionally loaded, yet still open to debate, are topics such as whether everyone needs a college education or whether Computer X is better than Computer Y.

The degree to which a reader might be friendly or hostile can influence what strategies you use to try to convince that reader. For example, when you anticipate that many readers will not agree with you, consider using techniques of **Rogerian argument.** Rogerian argument has been adapted from the principles of communication developed by psychologist Carl Rogers. Communication, according to Rogers, is eased when people find common ground in their points of view. The common ground in a debate over capital punishment might be that both sides find crime to be a growing problem today. Once both sides agree

---

ANSWERS: EXERCISE 6–1
Assertions and thesis statements will vary for this exercise.

QUOTATION ABOUT WRITING
Real communication occurs . . . when we listen with understanding. What does this mean? It means to see the expressed idea and attitude from the other person's point of view, to sense how it feels to him, to achieve his frame of reference in regard to the thing he is talking about.
           —Carl Rogers

BACKGROUND
The theories of Carl Rogers have had important consequences for the teaching of argumentative writing. If Rogerian argument is of interest to you, you will want to read an article by Nathaniel Teich (*Journal of Advanced Composition* 7 [1987]: 52–61). In it he argues against the existence of Rogerian rhetoric. However, he goes on to suggest that Rogerian principles can supplement the teaching of policy arguments.

BACKGROUND
The ideal format of a Rogerian argument, according to Richard Coe (*Form and Substance*, John Wiley and Sons, 1981, pp. 342–343) follows this pattern:
     Introduction. State the subject as a problem rather than as an issue to interest your audience in reading about something with which they disagree.
     Fair statement of the opposing position. In this section the writer states the reader's position in a manner that seems fair and accurate to the reader.
     Statement of contexts in which that position may be valid. Here the writer is trying to show readers that he or she understands their position by asserting that it is valid in some contexts.

→

BACKGROUND, *cont'd.*

Fair statement of the writer's position. The goal of this section is to get readers to understand the writer's position as fairly and thoroughly as the writer has understood theirs.

Statement of contexts in which the writer's position is valid. The writer tries to get readers to look at the problem from new perspectives and in new contexts.

Statement of how readers would benefit by adopting at least some elements of the writer's position. The writer appeals to readers' self-interest. In this section the writer's position turns from a threat to a promise.

BACKGROUND

Classical persuasion consisted of six parts that represented six basic functions. Although the writer or orator was granted some flexibility in how and in what order the parts were presented, they provided effective guidelines for presenting an argument. Often used today, the six parts of an argument, according to the classical precept, are:

1. *Exordium*, meaning "beginning a web." As an introduction, the purpose of the exordium is to attract the attention of the audience, indicate the subject, and favorably dispose the audience to what will follow.

2. *Narratio.* In this section, now usually referred to as "statement of fact," the issue is defined by stating pertinent facts about the subject. It is, therefore, basically expository.

3. *Partitio.* If the thesis has not yet been identified, it will be presented here, along with an indication of how the rest of the argument will be organized. The purpose of partition is to prepare the reader or listener for what will follow.

➡

about the problem, they might have more tolerance for the divergence of opinion concerning whether capital punishment is a deterrent to crime.

Using the classical pattern for written argument

No one structure fits all written argument. For college courses, most written arguments include certain elements. Lindsey Black's essay in section 6i uses a structure based on the **classical pattern of argument** developed by the ancient Greeks and Romans and still highly respected today. Daniel Casey's essay in section 6i uses a modified form of that structure. Chart 41 will help you recognize the elements in a written argument.

ELEMENTS IN THE CLASSICAL PATTERN FOR WRITTEN ARGUMENT

ELEMENTS IN THE CLASSICAL PATTERN FOR WRITTEN ARGUMENT

ELEMENTS IN THE CLASSICAL PATTERN FOR WRITTEN ARGUMENT   41

1. **Introductory paragraph:** sets the context for the position that is argued in the essay. (For a discussion of introductory paragraphs, see 4g.)

2. **Thesis statement:** states the position being argued. In a short essay, the thesis statement often appears at the end of the introductory paragraph. (For a discussion of thesis statements, see 2m.)

3. **Background information:** gives the reader basic information needed for understanding the position being argued. This information can be part of the introductory paragraph (as in Daniel Casey's essay in section 6i) or can appear in its own paragraph (as in Lindsey Black's essay in section 6i).

4. **Reasons or evidence:** supports the position being argued. This material is the core of the essay. If the support consists of evidence, consult the discussion in 5h. Also, be sure that your reasoning is logical (see 5k). Each type of evidence or reason usually consists of a general statement backed up with specific details or examples. Depending on the length of the essay, one or two paragraphs are devoted to each reason or type of evidence.

➡

ELEMENTS IN THE CLASSICAL PATTERN FOR 41
WRITTEN ARGUMENT (continued)

The best sequence for presenting the complete set of reasons and types of evidence depends on the impact you want to achieve. Moving from evidence most familiar to the reader to evidence least familiar helps the reader move from the known to the unknown. This order might catch the reader's interest early on. Moving from evidence least important to evidence most important might build the reader's suspense. (For more about various types of paragraph arrangement, see 4e.)

5. **Anticipation of likely objections and responses to them:** mentions positions opposed to the one being argued and rebuts them briefly. In classical argument, this "refutation" appears in its own paragraph, immediately before the concluding paragraph (as in Lindsey Black's essay). An alternative placement is immediately after the introductory paragraph, as a bridge to the rest of the essay; in such arrangements the essay's thesis statement falls either at the end of the introductory paragraph or at the end of the "refutation" paragraph (as in Daniel Casey's essay in section 6i). In still another arrangement, each paragraph that presents a type of evidence or reason (item 4 on this list) also mentions and responds to the opposing position.

6. **Concluding paragraph:** brings the essay to an end that flows logically and gracefully from the rest of the essay. It does not cut off the reader abruptly. (For a discussion of concluding paragraphs, see 4g.)

ELEMENTS IN THE CLASSICAL PATTERN FOR WRITTEN ARGUMENT (continued)

Using the Toulmin model for argument 6e

The **Toulmin model** for argument has recently gained popularity among teachers and students because it clarifies the major elements in an effective argument. The terms used in the Toulmin model may seem unfamiliar, even intimidating, at first. But worry not. The concepts that the terms describe are ones you have encountered before. What is new is placing those concepts into the vocabulary and structure of the Toulmin model.

The essential elements of the Toulmin model are presented in Chart 42 on the next page.

BACKGROUND, cont'd.

4. *Confirmatio.* Arguments to support the thesis, forming the bulk of the piece, are developed at this point. The question of the order of presentation of arguments is critical to the effectiveness of the confirmation.

5. *Refutatio.* Opposing arguments are considered and rendered ineffective in the refutation section. To ignore them is to risk letting them appear to be more attractive than one's own thesis. The refutation may be placed at various points in the piece, depending on where it will be most effective.

6. *Peroratio.* While the classical rhetoricians used a number of different terms to indicate the conclusion of a piece, it usually furnished a summary of proofs and refutations, a restatement of the major points, and a recreation of emotional and ethical appeals.

BACKGROUND

In "Using Toulmin's Model of Argumentation" (*Journal of Teaching Writing* 6 [Spring 1987]: 81–92) Joan Karback reviews the structure of warrants, grounds, and claims. She finds Toulmin's model to be an effective one because it is flexible, it has value as a heuristic, and it focuses on audience.

ELEMENTS IN THE TOULMIN MODEL OF ARGUMENT   42

TOULMIN'S TERM	MORE FAMILIAR TERMS
the claim	the main point or central message, usually disclosed in the thesis statement
the support	data or other evidence, from broad reasons to specific details
the warrant	underlying assumptions, usually not stated but clearly implied; readers infer assumptions

The elements in Chart 42 can be identified in Daniel Casey's written argument shown in 6i:

■ **Casey's claim:** Commercial uses of holidays benefit the nation's economy and lift people's spirits.

■ **Casey's support:** (1) Economic prosperity creates circulation of money which in turn creates jobs. (2) Holidays are festive times that cheer people up with decorations, costumes, gift-giving, and a friendly atmosphere. (3) Successful businesses improve everyone's quality of life by sponsoring charitable causes, parades, firework displays, and cultural events.

■ **Casey's warrants:** (1) Benefiting the nation's economy is an important objective from which everyone gains. (2) Even the spiritual aspects of the holidays are not paramount.

The concept of a warrant may seem difficult to understand. It can help to think of warrants as related to the concept of reading to make inferences, a key part of reading critically (see 5d). Like inferences, which are implications you must find "between the lines," warrants are implied assumptions you must infer from the stated argument.

To help you figure out the warrant that underlies an argument you are writing or reading, try placing it into one of Toulmin's three broad categories for warrants: (1) A warrant based on **authority** rests on respect for the credibility and trustworthiness of the person; (2) a warrant based on **substance** rests on the reliability of factual evidence; (3) a warrant based on **motivation** rests on the values and beliefs of the audience and the writer. Daniel Casey's second warrant, listed above, is a motivational warrant because it is not based on authority or factual evidence—it is based on the writer's valuing of economic prosperity over spiritual considerations.

The concepts in the Toulmin model can help you read arguments with a critical eye. The concepts are equally useful for you as a writer. As you draft and revise your written argument, evaluate what you are saying by checking whether you can analyze it for the elements in the Toulmin model. If you can't, your argument needs work.

Defining terms in written argument   **6f**

When you **define terms,** you explain what you mean by key words that you use. Words are key words when they are central to the message that you want to communicate. The meaning of some key words is readily evident. Key words open to interpretation, however, should be made specific enough to be clear.

NO   Commercialism at holiday time is **bad.**

YES   Commercialism at holiday time is **ruining the spirit of the holidays.**

YES   Commercialism at holiday time **tempts too many people to spend more money than they can afford.**

Some key words might vary with the context of a discussion and should be explained in an essay. Abstract words such as *love, freedom,* and *democracy* have to be explained because they have different meanings in different contexts. In his paper (see 6i), Daniel Casey uses *economy,* a word with many meanings, in the topic sentence of the third paragraph of his essay. He explains *economy* as the *ongoing circulation of money,* and he uses the rest of the paragraph to explain how that circulation operates. In this way, Casey makes clear that he is not referring to any of the other meanings of *economy:* the management of finances, the avoidance of waste, or the efficient use of resources.

Other key terms might be unfamiliar to the reader even though they are known words. For example, Casey opens his essay with the words *signs of commercialism.* Although each word by itself is familiar, the term is not. Casey therefore gives examples to illustrate the concept. In so doing, he creates an effective introduction to his essay by bringing the reader to a quick understanding of his topic.

Many students ask whether they should use actual dictionary definitions in an essay. Looking words up in a dictionary to understand precise meanings is a very important activity for writers. Quoting a dictionary definition, however, is not always wise. Dictionary definitions tend to be overused in student writing, and they are often seen as the "easy way out." Using an **extended definition** is usually a more effective approach, which is what Casey did for *economy* in the third paragraph of his essay. (For another example of extended definition, of *tolerance,*

EXTRA EXERCISE C
Rewrite the following paragraph, improving its persuasiveness by defining key words that may be vague to the reader.

Some Americans react strongly to actions that show disrespect for our flag. They revere it as a symbol of the values for which the United States is known around the world. They are quick to rise up against those who would use their freedom to desecrate Old Glory, calling them traitors to the Constitution and all it upholds: our rights and our democratic form of government. Calling for a Constitutional amendment, they even want to restrict our freedoms by making it illegal to misuse the flag. Wouldn't such an amendment show disrespect for the freedom the flag represents?

A SAMPLE REWRITE FOR EXTRA EXERCISE C
Some Americans react strongly to acts that they construe to be insulting to our flag. Television news footage showing the flag being burned or torn apart makes them violently angry because they revere it as a symbol of the freedom and liberty for which this country is known around the world. They are quick to rise up against fellow citizens who use their freedom to desecrate Old Glory, calling them traitors to the Constitution and its guarantees of legislative representation and civil rights, such as the right of free speech. Calling for a Constitutional amendment, they even want to restrict citizens' freedoms by making it illegal to misuse the flag. But what constitutes misuse: wearing it? letting it fly outside on a rainy day? displaying it on a banquet table? A more important question is: Wouldn't such an amendment show disrespect for the freedom the flag represents?

6f cont. see paragraph 43 in 4f-5.) If you do use a dictionary definition in your writing, be sure to work it into your material gracefully. Do not simply tack it on abruptly to what you are saying. In general, do not rely on it for your opening sentence. Also, be aware that references to a dictionary must be complete. Do not simply refer to "Webster's," which is far too general. Each dictionary has its own name, such as *Webster's New World Dictionary*.

6g ## Reasoning effectively in written argument

When you reason effectively, you increase your chances of convincing your reader to agree with you. In many instances, of course, you cannot expect actually to change your reader's mind. The basis for a debatable position is often personal opinion or belief, neither of which can be expected to change as the result of one written argument. Nevertheless, you still have an important goal: to convince your reader that your point of view has merit. People often "agree to disagree," in the best spirit of intellectual exchange. Round-table discussions among various experts heard on National Public Radio (NPR) or television's Public Broadcast System (PBS) are conducted in such a spirit.

The opposite positions taken by Lindsey Black and Daniel Casey (see 6i) concerning commercialism at holiday time stem from their personal beliefs and perceptions of the world. Black feels that commercialism is ruining the holidays. Casey recognizes the existence of commercialism, but he sees it as beneficial. The chance of either person convincing the other is slight. What can happen, however, is that each person can respect the quality of the other's argument.

An argument of good quality relies on three types of appeals to reason: the logical, the emotional, and the ethical. Chart 43 gives a summary of how to use the three appeals.

GUIDELINES FOR REASONING EFFECTIVELY IN WRITTEN ARGUMENT

GUIDELINES FOR REASONING EFFECTIVELY IN WRITTEN ARGUMENT   43

- ■ **Be logical:** Use sound reasoning.

- ■ **Enlist the emotions of the reader:** Enlist the values and beliefs of the reader, usually by arousing "the better self" of the reader.

- ■ **Establish credibility:** Show that you as the writer can be relied upon as a knowledgeable person with good sense.

The most widely used appeal in written argument is the **logical appeal,** called *logos* by the ancient Greeks. Logical reasoning is sound reasoning. This type of reasoning is important in all thinking and writing. Chapter 5 of this handbook, therefore, is a close companion to this chapter. Logical reasoning calls for using evidence well, as explained in 5h. Logical reasoning also means analyzing cause and effect correctly, as explained in 5i. A sound argument uses patterns of inductive reasoning and deductive reasoning, as explained in 5j. A sound argument also clearly distinguishes between fact and opinion, as explained in 5d-3. Finally, sound reasoning means avoiding logical fallacies, as explained in 5k.

Written argument for college courses relies heavily on logic. Both Lindsey Black and Daniel Casey (see 6i) used logical reasoning throughout their essays. While the reader might not agree with the reasons or types of evidence presented, the reader can respect the logic of their arguments.

The **emotional appeal,** called *pathos* by the ancient Greeks, can be effective when used in conjunction with logical appeals. The word *emotional* has a specific meaning in this context. It means arousing and enlisting the emotions of the reader. Often it arouses the "better self" of the reader by eliciting sympathy, civic pride, and other feelings based on values and beliefs. Effective emotional appeals use description and examples to stir emotions, but they leave the actual stirring to the reader. Restraint is more effective than excessive sentimentality.

Both Casey and Black (see 6i) use emotional appeals in their essays, but always in conjunction with a logical presentation of material. Casey appeals to the emotions when in his fifth paragraph he mentions stores giving toys to children in hospitals. But he does not overdo it. He does not say that anyone who disagrees with him hates children and feels no pity for their suffering from dreadful illnesses that ravage their tiny bodies. If he had indulged in such excesses, the reader would resent being manipulated and therefore would probably reject his argument. Black appeals to the emotions when she writes in her second paragraph about the origins of the holiday spirit. With restraint, she mentions the meaning of each holiday. She does not attempt to tell the reader how to feel; she simply points out facts that support the logic of her argument and that might also stir the reader's pride in country and heritage.

The **ethical appeal,** called *ethos* by the ancient Greeks, means establishing the ethics and credibility of the writer. Credibility is gained if the writer uses correct facts, undistorted evidence, and accurate interpretations of events. Readers do not trust a writer who states opinions as fact or who makes a claim that cannot possibly be supported. The statement "A child who does not get gifts for Christmas suffers a trauma from which recovery is impossible" is an opinion as well as an exaggera-

ALTERNATE EXAMPLES, *cont'd.*

Emotional Appeal

A child's world is fresh and new and beautiful, full of wonder and excitement. It is our misfortune that for most of us that clear-eyed vision, that true instinct for what is beautiful and awe-inspiring, is dimmed and even lost before we reach adulthood. If I had influence with the good fairy who is supposed to preside over the christening of all children I should ask that her gift to each child in the world be a sense of wonder so indestructible that it would last throughout life, as an unfailing antidote against the boredom and disenchantments of later years, the sterile preoccupation with things that are artificial, the alienation from the sources of our strength.

I sincerely believe that . . . it is not half so important to *know* as to *feel*. If facts are the seeds that later produce knowledge and wisdom, then the emotions and the impressions of the senses are the fertile soil in which the seeds must grow. The years of early childhood are the time to prepare the soil. Once the emotions have been aroused—a sense of the beautiful, the excitement of the new and the unknown, a feeling of sympathy, pity, admiration or love—then we wish for knowledge about the object of our emotional response.

—Rachel Carson,
The Sense of Wonder

Ethical Appeal

Our tragedy today is a general and universal physical fear so long sustained by now that we can even bear it. There are no longer problems of the spirit. There is only the question: When will I be blown up? Because of this, the young man or woman writing today has forgotten the problems of the human heart in conflict with itself which alone can make good writing because only this is worth writing about, worth the agony and the sweat.

➔

tion. It has no place in written argument. Ethical appeals cannot take the place of logical appeals, but the two types of appeals work well together. One effective way to make an ethical appeal is to draw on personal experience. (Some college instructors do not want students to write in the first person, so ask your instructor before you use it.) If you use personal experience, always be sure that it relates directly to a generalization that you are supporting. Also, be aware that a personal experience can say as much about the writer as about the experience. For example, if Casey had been a volunteer at a hospital when gifts from a local business were distributed, the story of the experience not only would have supported his claim in his fifth paragraph, but also would have illustrated his good character.

6h Establishing a reasonable tone in written argument

To be reasonable, you have to be fair. By anticipating opposing positions and responding to them (see 6c), you have a particularly good chance to show that you are fair. When you alert your reader to other ways of thinking about the issue, you demonstrate that you have not ignored other positions. Doing this implies respect for the other side, which in turn makes the tone (see 1d) of the essay more reasonable.

To achieve a reasonable tone, choose your words carefully. Avoid words that exaggerate. Use figurative language, such as similes and metaphors (see 21c), to enhance your point rather than distort it. No matter how strongly you disagree with opposing arguments, never insult the other side. Name-calling is impolite, shows poor self-control, and demonstrates poor judgment. The more emotionally loaded a topic (for example, abortion, capital punishment, and gun control), the more might be the temptation to use angry words. Words such as *stupid* or *pigheaded,* however, say more about the writer than about the issue.

Artificial language (see 21e) also ruins a reasonable tone. The *Yes* example that follows is used by Daniel Casey as the first sentence in his essay in section 6i. Compare its impact with what would happen if Casey had used the *No* example.

NO Emblems of commercial enterprise are ubiquitously visible as the populace prepares for the celebration of festivals and commemorations throughout the venerable United States of America.

YES Signs of commercialism at holiday time are easy to see in the United States.

Writing and revising a written argument   6i

Lindsey Black chose the position that holidays have become too commercialized. Daniel Casey, on the other hand, chose the position that the commercialization of holidays has advantages. The final draft of each essay appears at the end of this chapter. The labels identify the structural elements of written argument discussed in 6d.

In an early draft of her essay, Black wrote an introduction that included the background information on the holidays, now in her second paragraph. When she revised, she moved the information to a separate paragraph because she saw that the introductory paragraph was too long and the thesis statement was being overshadowed. Also, she felt that a separate paragraph giving background information had the additional advantage of giving her enough space to use an emotional appeal (see 6g). An early draft of Black's third paragraph consisted only of the topic sentence and the last three sentences of the final draft. When she revised, Black saw that she needed more examples to support the generalization in her topic sentence. She added the material about greeting cards and about time and stress.

Daniel Casey wrote a discovery draft (see 3b) to explore further the ideas that he evolved while planning his essay (for his brainstorming, see section 2g; for his use of the journalist's questions, see section 2h; for the sequencing of his ideas, see section 2l-2). As he wrote his draft, he discovered, for example, that he needed to define the term *signs of commercialism* by giving specific examples. He also found that he had two reasons he could develop in support of his thesis: an enriched economy and an enhanced spirit. He wanted a third reason, so he interviewed some friends who worked in a shopping mall, and they mentioned what some of the stores do for the community at holiday time. The second paragraph of Casey's essay was the next-to-last paragraph in an early draft. He moved it when he revised because he decided that it built an effective bridge to his thesis statement.

As both Black and Casey revised, they consulted the Revision Checklists in 3c to remind them of general principles of writing, and they looked over the checklist in Chart 44.

REVISION CHECKLIST FOR WRITTEN ARGUMENT   44

1. Does the thesis statement concern a debatable topic (see 6b)?
2. Is the material structured well for a written argument (see 6d)?
3. Do the reasons or evidence support the thesis statement? Are the generalizations supported by specific details? (See 6d.) ➜

REFERENCE TO SUPPLEMENTS

For revising for support, refer students to *Rough Drafts* by K. S. Cain, Part II, Exercise 5.

QUOTATION ABOUT WRITING

I work four hours a day and then usually early in the evening I read over what I've written during the day and I do a lot of changing and shifting around. See, I write in longhand and I do two versions of whatever I'm doing. I write first on yellow paper and then I write on white paper and then when I finally have it more or less settled the way I want, then I type it. When I'm typing it, that's when I do my final rewrite. I almost never change a word after that.

—Truman Capote

EXTRA EXERCISE D

Analyze the following paragraphs to discover the dominant appeal of each.

1. We observe today not a victory of party but a celebration of freedom—symbolizing an end as well as a beginning—signifying renewal as well as change. For I have sworn before you and Almighty God the same solemn oath our forebears prescribed nearly a century and three quarters ago.

The world is very different now. For man holds in his mortal hands the power to abolish all forms of human poverty and all forms of human life. And yet the same revolutionary beliefs for which our forebears fought are still at issue around the globe—the belief that the rights of man come not from the generosity of the state but from the hand of God.

We dare not forget today that we are the heirs of that first revolution. Let the word go forth from this time ➜

EXTRA EXERCISE D, cont'd.

and place, to friend and foe alike, that the torch has been passed to a new generation of Americans—born in this century, tempered by war; disciplined by a hard and bitter peace, proud of our ancient heritage—and unwilling to witness or permit the slow undoing of those human rights to which this nation has always been committed, and to which we are committed today at home and around the world.

—John F. Kennedy, "Inaugural Address"

2. Harlem got its first private project, Riverton—which is now, naturally, a slum—about twelve years ago because at that time Negroes were not allowed to live in Stuyvesant Town. Harlem watched Riverton go up, therefore, in the most violent bitterness of spirit, and hated it long before the builders arrived. They began hating it at about the time people began moving out of their condemned houses to make room for this additional proof of how thoroughly the white world despised them. And they had scarcely moved in, naturally, before they began smashing windows, defacing walls, urinating in the elevators, and fornicating in the playgrounds. Liberals, both white and black, were appalled at the spectacle. I was appalled by the liberal innocence— or cynicism, which comes out in practice as much the same thing. Other people were delighted to be able to point to proof positive that nothing could be done to better the lot of the colored people. They were, and are, right in one respect: that nothing can be done as long as they are treated like colored people. The people in Harlem know they are living there because white people do not think they are good enough to live anywhere else. No ➜

4. Are opposing positions mentioned and responded to (see 6d)?
5. Are terms defined (see 6f)?
6. Are the appeals to reason used correctly and well (see 6g)?
7. Is the tone reasonable (see 6h)?

EXERCISE 6-2

Choose a topic below, and write an essay that argues for a debatable position about the topic. Apply all the principles you have learned in this chapter.

1. animal experimentation
2. nuclear power
3. value of the space program
4. celebrity endorsements
5. day-care centers
6. surrogate mothers
7. gun control
8. school prayer
9. optimism
10. highway speed limits

Lindsey Black
Professor Gregory
English 101
April 10, 19XX

Commercialism Is Ruining the Holidays

introduction:
identification of
the situation

     Holidays should be special occasions that have religious, historical, and cultural significance. Increasingly, however, holidays in the United States are turning into little more than business opportunities. From coast to coast, the jingles and beeps of cash registers drown out the traditional

thesis statement

sounds of holiday observance. The spirit of the holidays is being destroyed by commercialism.

background:
origins and
significance

     The origins of the holiday spirit are varied in the United States. Thanksgiving reminds Americans to be grateful for their blessings, and the Fourth of July stimulates pride in the founding of the nation. Labor

Day is a tribute to workers. Memorial Day honors soldiers who died in defense of the country, and Veterans Day honors all veterans of the armed forces. Christmas and Easter have great religious significance to Christians. Holidays used to be occasions for people to come together and celebrate their heritages. Today, however, the overriding message of the holidays is "spend money."

evidence: one type

The most visible evidence that commercialism now dominates holidays is the unfortunate emphasis on spending money in preparation for religious holidays. For example, buying and mailing Christmas cards has become standard practice for individuals, families, and industry. How many people can ignore the social and the business pressures to mail cards? The commitment of money and time for this activity is not small. The gift situation is equally stressful. Although exchanging gifts on Christmas or Hanukah was always part of the celebration, the thought behind the present used to be the point. Today, however, advertising--particularly on television--sets a high standard of expectations. Can home-baked cookies compare to a microwave oven? Can hand-drawn, handwritten cards be as impressive as elaborate greeting cards that play music?

evidence: another type

Other evidence that commercialism is ruining holidays is the emphasis on shopping for bargains rather than on activities related to cultural history. Huge sales held before holidays, and often on the holiday itself, are advertised heavily in newspapers, on television, and on radio. Veterans Day has become the day to buy fall and winter clothing at reduced prices, and Memorial Day means specially lowered prices on products for the coming summer. Parades and ceremonies on Labor Day honoring the workers of America get less attention than back-to-school sales. The image of the family gathering on Thanksgiving Day is being

→

---

amount of "improvement" can sweeten this fact. Whatever money is now being earmarked to improve this, or any other ghetto, might as well be burnt. A ghetto can be improved in one way only: out of existence.

—James Baldwin,
"Fifth Avenue Uptown:
A Letter from Harlem"

ANALYSIS OF APPEALS IN EXTRA EXERCISE D

1. In his Inaugural Address, John F. Kennedy makes extensive use of ethical appeal. By referring to the "solemn oath" he had just taken before God and the American people, he calls attention to his commitment to work for that which is good and right. When, in reference to the complexity of the modern world, he again invokes the name of God as the source of "the rights of man," he underscores the high moral calling of his office. In the final paragraph, he appeals to the ethical sense of the audience by exhorting citizens to join him in the struggle to make a better world. By using the pronoun *we*, he re-pledges himself to work with all Americans for the spread and preservation of those beliefs on which this country was founded.

2. James Baldwin's comments about Riverton seethe with anger, bitterness, and even hatred. The strong emotions that the reader hears and feels emanate not only from words such as "violent bitterness of spirit," "hated it," "hating it," and "despised them," but from the images of destruction that he provides: "smashing windows, defacing walls, urinating in the elevators, and fornicating in the playgrounds." Any positive term that Baldwin uses, such as "improvement," he puts in quotation marks, suggesting its unreality.

QUOTATION ABOUT WRITING

You must now draw up a timetable and stick to it. When you'll write and what rate you'll write at are a matter of individual capacity and circumstance, but I suggest that three two-hourly sessions a week are quite enough. It is essential that you record the number of words written each session. This has a valuable psychological effect. Whether you're pleased with what you've written or not, you have before you the proof that you're achieving something, that you actually are working.

—John Braine

QUOTATION ABOUT WRITING

Technique alone is never enough. You have to have passion. Technique alone is just an embroidered potholder.

—Raymond Chandler

replaced with the image of the family shopping the day after Thanksgiving, when stores are more crowded than any other day except the day before Christmas.

major likely objections and responses to them

In spite of all this, not all people are troubled by the spirit of commercialism on holidays. Many people enjoy the festivity of exchanging cards and gifts. Some people feel that the chance to buy at sales helps them stay within their budgets and therefore enjoy life more. What these people do not realize is that the festive spirit of giving can quickly turn sour when large amounts of money are suddenly not available for necessities. Also, these people do not realize that holiday sales tend to lure shoppers into spending more money than they had planned, often for things that they did not think they needed until they saw them "on sale."

conclusion: call for awareness

Holiday celebrations in the United States today have more to do with the wallet than the spirit. Some people refuse to participate in the frenzy of a commercial interpretation of holidays, of course. But for too many people, holidays are becoming stressful rather than joyful, and upsetting rather than uplifting.

Daniel Casey

Professor Gregory

English 101

April 10, 19XX

Commercialism at Holiday Time Benefits the Nation

introduction: gives background

Signs of commercialism at holiday time are easy to see in the United States. Christmas decorations begin their call to consumers in October. Memorial Day and Labor Day remind shoppers to prepare for the seasonal change in clothing fashions. Halloween and Easter mean children can make toll calls to the Great Pumpkin or the Easter Bunny.

presentation and refutation of opposite view

Some people disapprove of these commercial uses of holidays in the United States. These people feel that the meaning of a holiday gets lost when television is blaring news of the latest holiday sale or expensive gift item. Many people also feel that the proliferation of gifts and greeting cards creates stressful pressure on budgets and ruins any pleasure derived from giving and receiving. No one, however, has to forget the meaning of a holiday simply because commerce is involved. In fact, commercialism can increase people's **thesis statement** enjoyment of the holidays. After all, commercial uses of holidays benefit the nation's economy and lift people's spirits.

reason: one effect Commerce at holiday time in the United States enriches the economy. Prosperity in the United States is based on the ongoing circulation of money, which holidays encourage. When people spend money on gifts and holiday products, jobs are created. The jobs are in many sectors of the economy: manufacturing, distribution, advertising, and retailing. Jobs help people support their families. Profits help business and industry grow. Salaries and profits bring about tax revenues that support schools, police, hospitals, and other government services.

reason: second effect In addition to economic benefits, commercial activity enhances the spirit of holidays. Most people feel more cheerful at holiday time. Everyone takes part in one big party. Advertising related to holidays, along with stores filled with holiday products, creates an atmosphere of festivity across the nation. Being able to say "Happy Thanksgiving" or "Merry Christmas" to strangers while shopping breaks down barriers and helps everyone feel part of one big family. The festivity on the streets, in malls, and in stores is infectious. Giving and getting gifts and greeting cards helps people stay in touch with each other and express their feelings. Children look forward all year to

➔

BACKGROUND
Because of the increasing use of peer reader-response groups in writing classrooms, there is a growing interest in how they can be used to teach argumentative writing more effectively. In "Developing a Position Statement in the Collaborative Classroom" (*Exercise Exchange* 34 [Spring 1989]: 3–5), Peg Peoples suggests an answer. She describes a group activity that she has found to be helpful in getting students to see both sides of an issue.

QUOTATION ABOUT WRITING
. . . In order to persuade, there are two things which must be carefully studied by the orator. The first is to excite some desire or passion in the hearers; the second is to satisfy their judgment that there is a connection between the action to which he would persuade them and the gratification of the desire or passion he excites.
—George Campbell

wearing a store-bought costume for Halloween, sitting on Santa's lap in a department store, and talking to the Easter Bunny at the local shopping mall.

reason: third effect

The holiday activities that help businesses prosper also inspire many businesses to improve everyone's quality of life. Many companies, for example, organize collections of clothing and preparation of hot meals for needy people at holiday time. Toy stores often give away toys for Christmas and Hanukah to children in hospitals and in caretaking homes. Macy's department store annually delights people of all ages with its Thanksgiving Day Parade in New York City. The entire nation is invited to enjoy the parade in person or on television. In small towns and large cities, many businesses sponsor fireworks, mounted and displayed safely by professionals, to celebrate the Fourth of July. Good will and good business go together to everyone's benefit at holiday time.

conclusion: summary of main points

The United States is a nation blessed with economic strength and resourceful people. While commercialism can detract from the true meaning of a holiday, it does not have to. People can discipline themselves to balance the spiritual with the commercial. Americans recognize that the advantages of a stimulated economy and a collective festive spirit are worth the effort of such self-discipline.

Understanding Grammar

When you understand grammar, you have one tool to help you think about and discuss the ways that your sentences deliver their meaning to your readers. Part Two describes the elements of language and explains the standard rules for using those elements. As you use Chapters 7 through 12, remember that grammar is only a tool. Other parts of this handbook offer you additional perspectives on writing and the choices that writers can make.

7 *Parts of Speech and Structures of the Sentence*

REFERENCES TO SUPPLEMENTS
This topic is included in the TASP writing competency test. You can refer students to *Preparing for the TASP* by M. Saenz.

See transparency 7–8 on agreement with collective nouns in the *Prentice Hall/Simon & Schuster Transparencies for Writers* by D. Carter.

TEACHING TIP: ESL
ESL students may have questions about the difference in usage between indefinite *a/an* and definite *the*. In sentence 3 in Exercise 7–1, the article *a* is used

�➔

PARTS OF SPEECH

Knowing **parts of speech** gives you a basic vocabulary for identifying words and understanding how language works. Sections 7a through 7i explain the **noun, pronoun, verb, adjective, adverb, preposition, conjunction,** and **interjection**. As you use this material, be aware that no part of speech exists in a vacuum. To identify a word's part of speech correctly, see how the word functions in the sentence you are analyzing. Often, the same word functions differently in different sentences.

> We ate **fish**. [*Fish* is a noun. It names a thing.]
> We **fish** on weekends. [*Fish* is a verb. It names an action.]

7a   **Recognizing nouns**

A **noun** names a person, place, thing, or idea: student, college, textbook, education. For a list of types of nouns, see Chart 45. Nouns function as SUBJECTS,* OBJECTS, and COMPLEMENTS.

!   ❖ ALERT: Words that often appear with nouns tell how much or many, whose, which one, and similar information. These words include **articles** (*a, an, the*) and other **determiners** or **limiting adjectives**. For more about these words, see 7e and Chapter 42ESL.❖

ESL   ❖ ESL NOTE: Sometimes a suffix (a word ending) can help you identify the part of speech. Usually, words with these suffixes are nouns: *-ness, -ence, -ance, -ty,* and *-ment.* For more on suffixes, see 20c-1 and 22d.❖

---

*You can find the definition of a word printed in small capital letters (such as SUBJECT) in the Glossary of Terms toward the back of this handbook.

NOUNS		45
PROPER	names specific people, places, or things (first letter is always capitalized)	*John Lennon, Paris, Buick*
COMMON	names general groups, places, people, or things	*singer, city, automobile*
CONCRETE	names things experienced through the senses: sight, hearing, taste, smell, and touch	*landscape, pizza, thunder*
ABSTRACT	names things *not* knowable through the senses	*freedom, shyness*
COLLECTIVE	names groups	*family, team*
NONCOUNT OR MASS	names "uncountable" things	*water, time*
COUNT	names countable items	*lake, minute*

Recognizing pronouns

7b

A **pronoun** takes the place of a NOUN. The word (or words) a pronoun replaces is called its **antecedent**. Some pronouns have three different forms, known as **cases**: subjective case, objective case, and possessive case. For more details about pronoun case, see Chapter 9. For types of pronouns, see Chart 46 on the next page.

> **David** is an accountant. [noun]
>
> **He** is an accountant. [pronoun]
>
> The finance committee needs to consult **him**. [The pronoun *him* refers to its antecedent, *David*.]

EXERCISE 7-1

Consulting sections 7a and 7b, underline and label all nouns (N) and pronouns (P). Circle all articles.

$$\overset{\text{N}}{\underline{\text{EXAMPLE}}}\quad \underline{\text{Treadmills}} \text{ can be } \textcircled{a}\, \overset{\text{N}}{\underline{\text{way}}} \text{ to } \overset{\text{N}}{\underline{\text{fitness}}} \text{ and } \overset{\text{N}}{\underline{\text{rehabilitation}}}.$$

1. Not only humans use them.
2. Scientists conduct experiments by placing lobsters on treadmills.
3. Scientists can study a lobster when it is fitted with a small mask.
4. The lobster may reach speeds up to a kilometer an hour.
5. Through the mask, researchers can monitor the heartbeat of the crustacean that they are studying.

TEACHING TIP: ESL, cont.

because the nouns *lobster* and *mask* are mentioned for the first time. (The "first mention" rule applies only to singular countable nouns, not to plurals like *humans, scientists, experiments, treadmills.*) In 4, *a* and *an* mean "one," reflecting their historical origin; the indefinite articles developed from the Anglo-Saxon word for *one*.

The refers to a noun that is definite, often because it has already been mentioned ("the lobster," "the mask," "the crustacean," which is a synonym for *lobster*) and/or because the context makes it specific, usually with a phrase ("of the crustacean") or clause ("that they are studying") following the noun.

REFERENCES TO SUPPLEMENTS

This topic is included in the TASP writing competency test. Refer students to *Preparing for the TASP* by M. Saenz.

See transparency 7–7 on agreement with indefinite pronouns in the *Prentice Hall/Simon & Schuster Transparencies for Writers* by D. Carter.

ANSWERS: EXERCISE 7–1

1. Not only humans[N] use them.[P]
2. Scientists[N] conduct experiments[N] by placing lobsters[N] on treadmills.[N]
3. Scientists[N] can study (a) lobster[N] when it[P] is fitted with (a) small mask.[N]
4. The lobster[N] may reach speeds[N] up to (a) kilometer[N] an hour.[N]
5. Through (the) mask,[N] researchers[N] can monitor (the) heartbeat[N] of (the) crustacean[N] that[P] they[P] are studying.

7b
cont.

PRONOUNS

BACKGROUND

Grammar is one of the oldest fields of study in Western education. Greek and Roman boys were enrolled in grammar schools to study language and literature in preparation for the study of rhetoric in their adolescence. The *praelectio* was the central exercise of these schools. After reading a model of good or bad writing, the teacher dissected it meticulously and systematically, one word and sometimes one syllable at a time. The *praelectio* identified parts of speech, inflections, gender, meter, figures of speech, and other grammatical and stylistic concerns in the model; provided background about the work; discussed its meaning; noted errors and ineffective passages; and praised eloquent passages. As students advanced, they analyzed the works themselves, answering the teacher's questions. Each student's composition was also subject to the same microanalysis.

QUOTATION ABOUT WRITING

Like everything metaphysical the harmony between thought and reality is to be found in the grammar of the language.
—Wittgenstein,
Zette

PRONOUNS   46

PERSONAL *I, you, they, her, its, ours,* and others	refers to people or things	**I** saw **her** take a book to **them**.
RELATIVE *who, which, that*	introduces certain NOUN CLAUSES and ADJECTIVE CLAUSES	The book **that** I lost was valuable.
INTERROGATIVE *who, whose, what, which,* and others	introduces a question	**Who** called?
DEMONSTRATIVE *this, these, that, those*	points out the ANTECEDENT	Whose books are **these**?
REFLEXIVE; INTENSIVE *myself, themselves,* and other *-self* or *-selves* words	reflects back to the antecedent; intensifies the antecedent	They claim to support **themselves**. I **myself** doubt it.
RECIPROCAL *each other, one another*	refers to individual parts of a plural antecedent	We respect **each other**.
INDEFINITE *all, anyone, each,* and others	refers to nonspecific persons or things	**Everyone** is welcome here.

TEACHING TIP

Using the most appropriate verb can make the difference between writing a vague sentence and a meaningful one. You might stimulate a lively discussion if you ask students to explain the differences in meanings (and to compose a sentence for each meaning) of these verbs that deal with the same subjects.

- stride   march   glide   strut
- gobble   nibble   devour   eat
- giggle   guffaw   chuckle   snicker

7c   ## Recognizing verbs

Main verbs express action, occurrence, or state of being.

I **dance**. [action]
The audience **became** silent. [occurrence]
Your dancing **was** excellent. [state of being]

!   ✦ ALERT: If you are not sure whether a word is a verb, try putting the word into a different TENSE. If the sentence still makes sense, the word is a verb. (For an explanation of verb tense, see 8g.)

    NO   He is a **changed** man. He is a **will change** man. [The sentence does not make sense when the verb *will change* is substituted, so *changed* is not functioning as a verb.]

YES   The store **changed** owners. The store **will change** owners. [Because the sentence still makes sense when the verb *will change* is substituted, *changed* is functioning as a verb.] ✤

For a detailed discussion of all verb types and the information that they convey, see Chapter 8.

EXERCISE 7-2

Consulting section 7c, underline all verbs.

EXAMPLE   A famous holiday poem <u>was published</u> only because of a good-hearted thief.

1. Clement C. Moore wrote the poem for his three daughters.
2. Moore intended it as a private gift, not for publication.
3. He called the poem "An Account of a Visit from St. Nicholas."
4. Mysteriously and fortunately, the poem was mailed to a newspaper editor.
5. Today, we know that poem as "The Night Before Christmas."

Recognizing verbals   **7d**

Verbals are verb parts functioning as NOUNS, ADJECTIVES, or ADVERBS. For types of verbals, see Chart 47.

✤ **ESL NOTE:** For information about using gerunds and infinitives as objects, see Chapter 45ESL.✤   **ESL**

VERBALS AND THEIR FUNCTIONS   47

INFINITIVE *to* + SIMPLE FORM of VERB	1. NOUN 2. ADJECTIVE or ADVERB	**To eat** now is inconvenient. Still, we have far **to go.**
GERUND *-ing* form of verb	NOUN	**Eating** in turnpike restaurants can be an adventure.
PAST PARTICIPLE *-ed* form of REGULAR VERB or equivalent IN IRREGULAR VERB	ADJECTIVE	**Boiled, filtered** water is usually safe to drink.
PRESENT PARTICIPLE *-ing* form of verb	1. ADJECTIVE 2. NOUN	**Hiking** gear is expensive. **Hiking** is healthy.

(side margin: VERBALS AND THEIR FUNCTIONS)

ANSWERS: EXERCISE 7–2

1. Clement C. Moore <u>wrote</u> the poem for his three daughters.

2. Moore <u>intended</u> it as a private gift, not for publication.

3. He <u>called</u> the poem "An Account of a Visit from St. Nicholas."

4. Mysteriously and fortunately, the poem <u>was mailed</u> to a newspaper editor.

5. Today we <u>know</u> that poem as "The Night Before Christmas."

TEACHING TIP: ESL

An inductive way to help students discover and thus remember the differences among *-ing* forms is to have them circle the forms in a piece of writing and discuss which type is used: participles (adjectives), gerunds (nouns), or parts of verb phrases. For example, they could exchange papers with other students, then analyze and discuss all the *-ing* forms.

TEACHING TIP

To give students a sense of the range of uses for *-ing* words, you might hand out a list of *-ing* words and ask your students to use each word in three different sentences: in one as a noun, in another as an adjective, and in a third as part of a verb phrase. Then you can collect the sentences and select 25 to 30 to reproduce and distribute. As an exercise or quiz, you can ask the students to identify each *-ing* word as a noun, an adjective, or part of a verb phrase. Often the author of a sentence is eager for others to get the identification correct and is therefore quite willing to explain the answer.

REFERENCES TO SUPPLEMENTS

For this topic in the CLAST writing competency test, refer students to ch. 1, section B4e of *Preparing for the CLAST* by S. Patterson.

This topic is included in the TASP writing competency test. Refer students to *Preparing for the TASP* by M. Saenz.

TEACHING TIP

The following passage from "The Mark on the Wall" by Virginia Woolf provides important sensory details through the use of well-chosen adjectives. To heighten student awareness of strong adjectives, you may want to read the excerpt aloud, asking students afterwards how many of those details they can recall.

Perhaps it was the middle of January in the present year that I first looked up and saw the mark on the wall. In order to fix a date it is necessary to remember what one saw. So now I think of the fire; the steady film of yellow light upon the page of my book; the three chrysanthemums in the round glass bowl on the mantelpiece. Yes, it must have been the wintertime, and we had just finished our tea, for I remember that I was smoking a cigarette when I looked up and saw the mark on the wall for the first time. I looked up through the smoke of my cigarette and my eye lodged for a moment upon the burning coals, and that old fancy of the crimson flag flapping from the castle tower came into my mind, and I thought of the cavalcade of red knights riding up the side of the black rock. Rather to my relief the sight of the mark interrupted the fancy, for it is an old fancy, an automatic fancy, made as a child perhaps. The mark was a small round mark, black upon the white wall, about six or seven inches above the mantelpiece.

7e   Recognizing adjectives

Adjectives modify—that is, they describe or limit—NOUNS, PRONOUNS, and word groups that function as nouns. For a detailed discussion of adjectives, see Chapter 12.

I saw a **green** tree. [*Green* modifies the noun *tree.*]
It was **leafy**. [*Leafy* modifies the pronoun *it.*]
The flowering trees were **beautiful**. [*Beautiful* modifies the noun phrase *the flowering trees.*]

Descriptive adjectives, like *leafy* and *green*, can show levels of intensity: *green, greener, greenest; leafy, more leafy, most leafy.* **Proper adjectives** are formed from PROPER NOUNS: *American, Victorian.*

❖ ESL NOTE: Usually, words with these suffixes are adjectives: *-ful, -ish, -less,* and *-like.* For more about suffixes, see 20c-1 and 22d.❖

Determiners are sometimes called **limiting adjectives**. They "limit" nouns by conveying information such as whether a noun is general (*a tree*) or specific (*the tree*). They also tell which one (*this tree*), how many (*twelve trees*), whose (*our tree*), and similar information.

DETERMINERS (LIMITING ADJECTIVES)	48
ARTICLES *a, an, the*	**A** reporter working on **an** assignment is using **the** telephone.
DEMONSTRATIVE *this, these, that, those*	**Those** students rent **that** house.
INDEFINITE *any, each, few, other, some,* and others	**Few** films today have complex plots.
INTERROGATIVE *what, which, whose*	**What** answer did you give?
NUMERICAL *one, first, two, second,* and others	The **fifth** question was tricky.
POSSESSIVE *my, your, their,* and others	**My** violin is older than **your** cello.
RELATIVE *what, which, whose, whatever,* and others	We do not know **which** road to take.

ESL

DETERMINERS (LIMITING ADJECTIVES)

The determiners *a, an,* and *the* are also called **articles**. *The* is a **definite article**. Before a noun, *the* conveys that the noun refers to a specific item (*the plan*). *A* and *an* are **indefinite articles**. They convey that a noun refers to an item in a nonspecific or general way (*a plan*). When you choose between *a* and *an,* remember to use *a* when the word following it starts with a consonant sound: *a carrot, a broken egg, a hip*; use *an* when the word following it starts with a vowel sound: *an egg, an old carrot, an honor*. For more on articles, see Chapter 42ESL. Chart 48 lists determiners. Some words in the chart also function as pronouns. To identify a word's part of speech, see how it functions in a sentence.

> **That** car belongs to Harold. [*that* = demonstrative adjective]
>
> **That** is Harold's car. [*that* = demonstrative pronoun]

Recognizing adverbs   7f

An **adverb** modifies—that is, describes or limits—VERBS, ADJECTIVES, other adverbs, and entire sentences. For a detailed discussion of adverbs, see Chapter 12.

> Chefs plan meals **carefully**. [*Carefully* modifies the verb *plan*.]
>
> Vegetables provide **very** important vitamins. [*Very* modifies the adjective *important*.]
>
> Those potato chips are **too** heavily salted. [*Too* modifies the adverb *heavily*.]
>
> **Fortunately**, people are learning that salt can be harmful. [*Fortunately* modifies the entire sentence.]

Many adverbs are easy to recognize because they are formed by adding *-ly* to adjectives: *sadly, loudly, normally*. Some adjectives, however, end in *-ly*: *brotherly, lovely*. Also, many adverbs do not end in *-ly*: *very, much, always, not, yesterday, so,* and *well* are a few that do not.

Descriptive adverbs can show levels of intensity, usually by adding *more* (or *less*) and *most* (or *least*): *more happily, least clearly*.

Conjunctive adverbs modify by creating logical connections in meaning, as shown in Chart 49 on the next page. Conjunctive adverbs can appear in the first position of a sentence, in the middle of a sentence, or in the last position of a sentence.

> **Therefore**, we consider Isaac Newton an important scientist.
>
> We consider Isaac Newton, **therefore**, an important scientist.
>
> We consider Isaac Newton an important scientist, **therefore**.

Relative adverbs are words such as *where* and *when* used to introduce ADJECTIVE CLAUSES; see 7o-2.

QUOTATION ABOUT WRITING

The Middle Ages envisioned the goddess of grammar, Grammatica, as an old woman. In one later incarnation, she is depicted as severe, with a scalpel and a large pair of pincers. Her right hand, which is by her side, grasps a bird by its neck, its mouth open as if in a gasp or a squawk. All this was emblematic, meant as a memory aid for the budding grammarian. But, Lord, how fitting the choices of emblem were—the living thing being strangled, beak open but silent, muted by the goddess Grammatica. And the scalpel, the pincers, are reminders to the teacher to be vigilant for error, to cut it out with the coldest tool.

—Mike Rose

ANSWERS: EXERCISE 7–3

Some students may also underline *a, an,* and *the* as limiting adjectives.

   1. determined (adj); successfully (adv); three (adj); very (adv); old (adj)
   2. Eventually (adv); civic (adj); closely (adv); local (adj); only (adv); native (adj); open (adj)
   3. second (adj); carefully (adv); recycling (adj); his (adj); widely (adv); unusual (adj)
   4. New (adj); gratefully (adv); this (adj); where (adv); discarded (adj); glass (adj); aluminum (adj); mandatory (adj)
   5. third (adj); so (adv); passionately (adv) beautiful (adj); tall (adj); her (adj); Texas (adj); those (adj); grassy (adj); popular (adj)

QUOTATION ABOUT WRITING

Grammarians are not necessarily writers, but writers must always be grammarians, whether they are conscious of what they are doing or not.

—William F. Irmscher,
Teaching Expository Writing

7f **cont.**

CONJUNCTIVE ADVERBS AND THE RELATIONSHIPS THEY EXPRESS   49

RELATIONSHIP	WORDS
ADDITION	*also, furthermore, moreover, besides,*
CONTRAST	*however, still, nevertheless, conversely, nonetheless, instead, otherwise,*
COMPARISON	*similarly, likewise,*
RESULT OR SUMMARY	*therefore, thus, consequently, accordingly, hence, then,*
TIME	*next, then, meanwhile, finally, subsequently,*
EMPHASIS	*indeed, certainly,*

EXERCISE 7-3

Consulting sections 7d, 7e, and 7f, underline and label all adjectives (ADJ) and adverbs (ADV).

EXAMPLE
                    ADJ   **ADJ**
         Do you believe the <u>common</u> claim that <u>one</u> person

    ADV   **ADJ**
    can <u>really</u> make a <u>big</u> difference?

1. A determined woman in Atlanta fought successfully to save three very old oaks from being cut down.
2. Eventually, she founded a civic group, which works closely with local businesspeople, to plant only native trees in the open places in Atlanta.
3. A second individual carefully mapped the recycling sites in his town and then widely distributed the unusual map.
4. New residents gratefully consult this map to learn where to take discarded newspapers, glass bottles, and aluminum cans for mandatory recycling.
5. A third person spoke so passionately about the beautiful tall grass of her Texas homeland that the city turned those grassy plains into a popular park.

7g # Recognizing prepositions

    Prepositions include common words such as *in, under, by, after, to, on, over,* and *since*. Prepositions function with other words in **prepo-**

sitional phrases. Prepositional phrases often set out relationships in time or space: *in April, under the orange umbrella.*

> **In the fall**, we will hear a concert **by our favorite tenor**.
> **After the concert**, he will fly **to Paris**.

Some words that function as prepositions also function as other parts of speech. To check whether a word is a preposition, see how it functions in its sentence.

> The mountain climbers have not radioed in **since** yesterday. [preposition]
> **Since** they have left the base camp, the mountain climbers can communicate with us only by radio. [subordinating conjunction: see 7h]
> At first I was not worried, but I have **since** changed my mind. [adverb: see 7f]

♣ ESL NOTE: For a list of prepositions and the idioms they involve, see Chapter 44ESL.♣

ESL

Recognizing conjunctions

7h

A **conjunction** connects words, PHRASES, or CLAUSES. **Coordinating conjunctions,** listed in Chart 50, join two or more grammatically equivalent structures.

> We hike **and** camp every summer. [*And* joins two words.]
> I love the outdoors, **but** my family does not. [*But* joins two sentences.]

COORDINATING CONJUNCTIONS AND THE RELATIONSHIPS THEY EXPRESS		50
RELATIONSHIP	WORDS	
ADDITION	*and*	
CONTRAST	*but, yet*	
RESULT OR EFFECT	*so*	
REASON OR CAUSE	*for*	
CHOICE	*or*	
NEGATIVE CHOICE	*nor*	

COORDINATING CONJUNCTIONS AND THE RELATIONSHIPS THEY EXPRESS

A HUMOROUS NOTE

Misplaced prepositions and prepositional phrases can sometimes turn the serious into the comical, as Richard Lederer demonstrates in sentences he has collected from various publications.

- The patient was referred to a psychiatrist with a severe emotional problem.
- The judge sentenced the killer to die in the electric chair for the second time.
- Two cars were reported stolen by the Groveton police yesterday.
- Please take time to look over the brochure that is enclosed with your family.
- Berra had driven over with his wife, Carmen, from their home in a Mercedes for the softball game.

> —From Richard Lederer,
> *Anguished English*
> (Wyrick and Company, 1987).

TEACHING TIP

To help students become aware of what conjunctions do, you might want to distribute the following passage from "Salvation" by Langston Hughes. Omit all conjunctions and ask students to supply them. When the passage is complete, ask students to discuss the function and the effect of each word they supplied. Then distribute the original, complete passage.

> I was saved from sin *when* I was going on thirteen. *But* not really saved. It happened like this. There was a big revival at my Auntie Reed's church. Every night for weeks there had been much preaching, singing, praying *and* shouting, *and* some very hardened sinners had been brought to Christ, *and* the membership of the church had grown ➔

TEACHING TIP, cont.

by leaps *and* bounds. Then just *before* the revival ended, they held a special meeting for children, "to bring the young lambs to the fold." My aunt spoke of it for days ahead. That night I was escorted to the front *and* placed on the mourners' bench with the other young sinners, who had not yet been brought to Jesus . . . Then I was left all alone on the mourners' bench. My aunt came *and* knelt at my knees *and* cried, *while* prayers *and* songs swirled all around me in the little church. The whole congregation prayed for me alone, in a mighty wail of moans *and* vices. *And* I kept waiting serenely for Jesus, waiting, waiting—*but* he didn't come. I wanted to see him, *but* nothing happened to me. Nothing! I wanted something to happen to me, *but* nothing happened.

TEACHING TIP

In the chapter on "Common Errors" in *Errors and Expectations* (New York: Oxford UP, 1977, pp. 90–159), Mina Shaughnessy recommends approaching the study of grammar inductively by encouraging students not only to have the right answers but to know why they do what they do. "Grammar," she states, "is more a way of thinking, a style of inquiry, than a way of being right." Students who have been introduced to key concepts in grammar have a frame within which to recognize, analyze, and address their own problems. They can develop their editorial skills by looking closely at their own work to mine those concepts. They can practice and improve them by carrying out appropriate exercises and drills.

Correlative conjunctions function in pairs to join equivalent grammatical structures. They include *both . . . and, either . . . or, neither . . . nor, not only . . . but (also), whether . . . or,* and *not . . . so much as.*

Both English **and** Spanish are spoken in many homes in the United States.

Not only students **but also** business people should study a second language.

Subordinating conjunctions introduce DEPENDENT CLAUSES, which are structures that are grammatically less important than those in an INDEPENDENT CLAUSE within the same sentence. Subordinating conjunctions are listed in Chart 51.

Many people were happy **after** they heard the news.
Because it snowed, school was canceled.

SUBORDINATING CONJUNCTIONS AND THE RELATIONSHIPS THEY EXPRESS	51

RELATIONSHIP	WORDS
TIME	*after, before, once, since, until, when, whenever, while*
REASON OR CAUSE	*as, because, since*
RESULT OR EFFECT	*in order that, so, so that, that*
CONDITION	*if, even if, provided that, unless*
CONTRAST	*although, even though, though, whereas*
LOCATION	*where, wherever*
CHOICE	*rather than, than, whether*

Recognizing interjections

An **interjection** is a word or expression that conveys surprise or another strong emotion. Alone, an interjection is usually punctuated with an exclamation point (!). As part of a sentence, an interjection is set off by a comma (or commas). In academic writing, use interjections sparingly, if at all.

Hooray! I got the promotion.
Oh, they are late.

EXERCISE 7-4

Consulting sections 7a through 7i, identify the part of speech of each numbered and underlined word. Choose from noun, pronoun, verb, adjective, adverb, preposition, coordinating conjunction, correlative conjunction, and subordinating conjunction.

                 1   **2**   **3**
Some <u>people</u> have had <u>tantalizing</u> clues to the possibility of life <u>after</u>

                4
death. Near-death experiences <u>have</u> been reported by more than eight million

     5   **6**   **7**
people <u>in</u> many cultures. Today, researchers <u>are</u> studying these <u>strange</u>

                        8
experiences. Some people report that their thought <u>processes</u> were

  9   **10**   **11**   **12**
<u>extraordinarily</u> fast and clear. <u>Others</u> describe <u>intense</u> feelings of peace <u>and</u>

13   **14**   **15**   **16**   **17**
<u>joy</u>, accompanied <u>by</u> brilliant light. Still others <u>mention</u> <u>enhanced</u> vision <u>or</u>

       18   **19**
hearing. <u>Furthermore</u>, they seemed to be watching <u>themselves</u> from a

  20   **21**   **22**   **23**
<u>distance</u>. Researchers <u>believe</u> <u>that</u> these experiences are <u>both</u> too numerous

23   **24**   **25**
<u>and</u> <u>too</u> <u>similar</u> to ignore.

STRUCTURES OF THE SENTENCE

When you know how sentences are formed, you have one tool for understanding the art of writing.

Defining the sentence   **7j**

The sentence has several definitions, each of which views it from a different perspective. On its most mechanical level, a sentence starts with a capital letter and finishes with a period, question mark, or exclamation point. A sentence can be defined according to its purpose. **Declarative sentences** make a statement: *Sky diving is dangerous.* **Interrogative sentences** ask a question: *Is sky diving dangerous?* **Imperative sentences** give a command: *Be careful when you skydive.* **Exclamatory sentences** begin with *What* or *How* and express strong

---

ANSWERS AND COVERAGE: EXERCISE 7–4

Instructors can require students to identify the part of speech of any word in this paragraph, in addition to those with superscript numbers.

  1. noun [7a]
  2. adjective [7e]
  3. preposition [7g]
  4. verb [7c]
  5. preposition [7c]
  6. verb [7c]
  7. adjective [7e]
  8. verbal [7d]
  9. adverb [7f]
10. noun [7a]
11. adjective [7e]
12. coordinating conj. [7h]
13. noun [7a]
14. preposition [7g]
15. verb [7c]
16. adjective [7e]
17. coordinating conj. [7h]
18. conjunctive adverb [7f]
19. pronoun [7b]
20. noun [7a]
21. verb [7c]
22. subordinating conj. [7h]
23. correlative conjs. [7h]
24. adverb [7f]
25. adjective [7e]

REFERENCE TO SUPPLEMENT

This topic is included in the TASP writing competency test. Refer students to *Preparing for the TASP* by M. Saenz.

QUOTATION ABOUT WRITING

When it comes to language, nothing is more satisfying than to write a good sentence.

—Barbara Tuchman

7j cont. feeling: *How I love sky diving!* Grammatically, a sentence contains an **independent clause** (a group of words that can stand alone as an independent unit): *Sky diving is dangerous.* Sometimes a sentence is described as a "complete thought," but the concept of "complete" is too subjective to be reliable.

An infinite variety of sentences can be composed, but all sentences share a common foundation. Sections 7k through 7p present the basic structures of sentences.

7k Recognizing subjects and predicates

A sentence consists of two basic parts: a **subject** and a **predicate**.

SENTENCE PATTERNS: GROUP I

52

■ COMPLETE SUBJECT + COMPLETE PREDICATE
The red telephone   rang loudly.
↑ SIMPLE SUBJECT   ↑ SIMPLE PREDICATE (VERB)

■ COMPLETE SUBJECT + COMPLETE PREDICATE
The telephone and the doorbell   rang loudly.
↑   ↑ COMPOUND SUBJECT

■ COMPLETE SUBJECT + COMPLETE PREDICATE
The red telephone   rang and startled everyone in the room.
↑   ↑ COMPOUND PREDICATE

The **simple subject** is the word or group of words that acts, is described, or is acted upon.

The **telephone** rang. [Simple subject, *telephone*, acts.]
The **telephone** is red. [Simple subject, *telephone*, is described.]
The **telephone** was being connected. [Simple subject, *telephone*, is acted upon.]

The **complete subject** is the simple subject and its modifiers (all the words that describe or limit it): *The red telephone* rang.

A **compound subject** consists of two or more NOUNS or PRONOUNS and their modifiers: *The telephone and the doorbell* rang.

The **predicate** is the part of the sentence that contains the VERB. The predicate tells what the subject is doing or experiencing or what is being done to the subject.

The telephone **rang**. [*Rang* tells what the subject, *telephone*, did.]

The telephone **is** red. [*Is* tells what the subject, *telephone*, experiences.]

The telephone **was being connected**. [*Was being connected* tells what was being done to the subject, *telephone*.]

A **simple predicate** contains only the verb: *The lawyer* **listened**. A **complete predicate** contains the verb and its modifiers: *The lawyer* **listened carefully**. A **compound predicate** contains two or more verbs: *The lawyer* **listened and :vaited**.

❖ ALERT: In sentences that make a statement, the subject usually comes before the predicate. (One exception is INVERTED SENTENCES; see 19f.) In sentences that ask a question, part of the predicate usually comes before the subject. For more about word order, see Chapter 43ESL.❖ **!**

❖ ESL NOTE: Avoid repeating a subject with a personal pronoun in the same clause. **ESL**

NO	My grandfather, **he** lived to be eighty seven.
YES	My grandfather lived to be eighty seven.
NO	Winter storms that bring ice, sleet, and snow **they** can cause traffic problems.
YES	Winter storms that bring ice, sleet, and snow can cause traffic problems.❖

EXERCISE 7-5

Consulting section 7k, separate the complete subject from the complete predicate with a slash.

EXAMPLE One of the most devastating natural disasters of recorded history / began on April 5, 1815.

1. Mount Tambora, located in present-day Indonesia, erupted.
2. The eruption exploded the top 4,000 feet of the mountain.
3. The blast was heard over 900 miles away.

QUOTATION ABOUT WRITING

In a significant way, a predicate is more intensely a word than a subject of a sentence is. . . . A word is an event, it is a happening.

—Walter J. Ong

QUOTATION ABOUT WRITING

Just as verbs and actions go together, so do subjects and characters. There are different kinds of characters. Usually—but not always—the most important characters are the agents of actions, the source of action or the condition that the writer is describing.

—Joseph M. Williams,
Style: Ten Lessons in Clarity and Grace

QUOTATION ABOUT WRITING

I work on each sentence until I'm satisfied with it and go on. I may rewrite one sentence nineteen times, and the next sentence eight times, and the next sentence three times. When I'm lucky, one sentence just once.

—Larry L. King

ANSWERS: EXERCISE 7–5

1. Mount Tambora, in present-day Indonesia, / erupted.
2. The eruption / exploded the top 4,000 feet of the mountain.
3. The blast / was heard over 900 miles away.

➜

ANSWERS: EXERCISE 7–5, cont.

4. A thick cloud of volcanic ash / circled the globe and reached North America the following summer.

5. The sun / could not penetrate the cloud throughout the entire summer.

7k
cont.

4. A thick cloud of volcanic ash circled the globe and reached North America the following summer.

5. The sun could not penetrate the cloud throughout the entire summer.

7l

Recognizing direct and indirect objects

Direct objects and **indirect objects** occur in the PREDICATE of a sentence.

A **direct object** receives the action—it completes the meaning—of a TRANSITIVE VERB. To find a direct object, make up a *whom?* or *what?* question about the verb.

An **indirect object** answers a *to whom? for whom? to what?* or *for what?* question about the verb. Chart 53 shows the relationships of direct and indirect objects in sentences.

SENTENCE PATTERNS: GROUP II		53

■ COMPLETE SUBJECT   +   COMPLETE PREDICATE

The caller   offered   money.
    ↑   ↑
    VERB DIRECT OBJECT

■ COMPLETE SUBJECT   +   COMPLETE PREDICATE

The caller   offered the lawyer money.
  ↑   ↑   ↑
VERB INDIRECT DIRECT
    OBJECT OBJECT

■ COMPLETE SUBJECT   +   COMPLETE PREDICATE

The caller   offered money to the lawyer.
  ↑   ↑   ↑
VERB DIRECT INDIRECT
    OBJECT OBJECT

❖ ESL NOTES: (1) In sentences with indirect objects that follow the word *to* or *for*, always put the direct object before the indirect object.

NO	Will you please give **to John** this letter?
YES	Will you please give this letter **to John**?

(2) When a pronoun is used as an indirect object, always use *to* or *for* before the pronoun.

NO	Please explain me the rule.
YES	Please explain the rule to me.❖

EXERCISE 7-6

Consulting section 71, draw a single line under all direct objects and a double line under all indirect objects.

EXAMPLE   Television-watching guarantees injury to people by the thousands every year, a British survey claims.

1. Gory scenes on television give some people such a severe fright that they faint.
2. Others are injured when they try ironing or perhaps painting while they give the television screen their full attention.
3. Last month, the survey reports, one person threw a glass at the screen and sprained his wrist.
4. Another person gave her knee a bad twist while dancing along with a music video.
5. Also, an enthusiastic sports fan jumped for joy and banged his head on a chandelier.

Recognizing complements, modifiers, and appositives

Recognizing complements

A **complement** occurs in the PREDICATE of a sentence. It renames or describes a SUBJECT or an OBJECT.

A **subject complement** is a NOUN, PRONOUN, or ADJECTIVE that follows a LINKING VERB (for an explanation of linking verbs, see 8a, especially Chart 58). Some systems of grammar use the term **predicate nominative** for a noun used as a subject complement and the term **predicate adjective** for an adjective used as a subject complement.

7m

7m-1

QUOTATION ABOUT WRITING

Language, like the body, is so comfortable and familiar that we hardly notice its presence or complexity. Yet once examined closely, the accomplishment of any ordinary speaker is rather astonishing. He can produce and understand an indefinite number of new sentences—sentences he has never encountered previously.

—Richard Ohmann,
"Grammar and Meaning"

ANSWERS: EXERCISE 7–6

1. Gory scenes on television give some people such a severe fright that they faint.

2. Others are injured when they try ironing or perhaps painting while they give the television screen their full attention.

3. Last month, the survey reports, one person threw a glass at the screen and sprained his wrist.

4. Another person gave her knee a bad twist while dancing along with a music video.

5. Also, an enthusiastic sports fan jumped for joy and banged his head on a chandelier.

QUOTATION ABOUT WRITING

If you want to write, and I hope you do, the sentence is your point of departure. Part of the art of creating a sentence is knowing the substance and elements of which it is composed. We all know, or let us assume, that sentences are made of words. But words come in various guises, whatever they are intended to hide or reveal, and so we must begin with them—seeing just what they think they are, as grammarians have defined them, and bringing them together into the realm of sense.

—Karen Elizabeth Gordon,
The Transitive Vampire

QUOTATION ABOUT WRITING

People who don't understand linguistic principles generally confuse the terms *grammar* and *usage.* . . . *Grammar* has several meanings. First, it denotes that intuitive knowledge of language human beings gain by about age five. In this sense, *grammar 1* means "a capacity for language," a native ability to create and comprehend English utterances. The term also refers to various formal systems (*grammar 2*) scholars developed to explain our capacity for language. Traditional grammar, for example, represents an accumulation of terms, rules, and methods for analyzing what we do when we use language. *Grammar 2*, the field of study, generates theories about *grammar 1*, an unconscious process or behavior. *Usage*, on the other hand, refers to linguistic etiquette, to socially sanctioned styles of language appropriate to given situations and audiences.

—Erika Lindemann,
A Rhetoric for Writing Teachers, 2nd ed.

ANSWERS: EXERCISE 7–7

1. hominy [object complement]
2. whole dried corn kernels [subject complement]
3. inexpensive but time-consuming [subject complement]
4. breakfast treat [object complement]
5. delicious [subject complement]

REFERENCE TO SUPPLEMENTS

See transparency 7–10 on problems with modifiers in the *Prentice Hall/Simon & Schuster Transparencies for Writers* by D. Carter.

7m-1
cont.

An **object complement** is a noun or an adjective that follows a DIRECT OBJECT (see section 7l) and either describes or renames it. Chart 54 shows the relationships of subject complements and object complements in sentences.

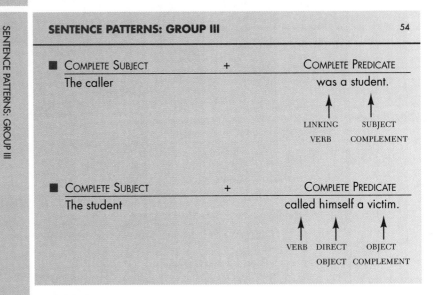

SENTENCE PATTERNS: GROUP III   54

EXERCISE 7-7

Consulting section 7m-1, underline all complements and identify each as a subject complement (SUB) or an object complement (OB).

EXAMPLE   The Native American Shawnee of Tennessee called

                              OB
      their principal food <u>rockahominie</u>.

1. Many people know this food as hominy.
2. Hominy is whole dried corn kernels cooked until the skins come off.
3. The process of turning dried corn into hominy is inexpensive but time-consuming.
4. In the southern United States, many consider hominy a breakfast treat.
5. Patties of hominy grits, which are ground kernels rather than whole ones, taste delicious fried.

Recognizing modifiers

7m-2

A **modifier** is a word or group of words that functions as an ADJECTIVE or ADVERB. Modifiers can appear in the SUBJECT or the PREDICATE of a sentence.

The **large red** telephone rang. [Adjectives *large* and *red* modify the noun *telephone*.]

The lawyer answered **quickly.** [The adverb *quickly* modifies the verb *answered*.]

The person **on the telephone** was **extremely** upset. [The PREPOSITIONAL PHRASE *on the telephone* modifies the noun *person*; the adverb *extremely* modifies the adjective *upset*.]

Therefore, the lawyer spoke gently. [The ADVERB *therefore* modifies the INDEPENDENT CLAUSE *the lawyer spoke gently*.]

Because the lawyer's voice was calm, the caller felt reassured. [The ADVERB CLAUSE *because the lawyer's voice was calm* modifies the independent clause *the caller felt reassured*.]

Recognizing appositives   7m-3

An **appositive** is a word or group of words that renames the NOUN or PRONOUN preceding it.

The student's story, **a tale of broken promises**, was complicated. [*A tale of broken promises* is an appositive that renames the noun *story*.]

The lawyer consulted an expert, **her law professor.** [*Her law professor* is an appositive that renames the noun *expert*.]

The student, **Joe Jones**, asked to speak to his lawyer. [*Joe Jones* is an appositive that renames the noun *student*.]

❖ PUNCTUATION ALERT: When an appositive is not essential for identifying the noun or pronoun it renames (that is, when an appositive is nonrestrictive), use a comma or commas to set it off from whatever it renames and any words following it (see 24e-2).❖

Recognizing phrases   7n

A **phrase** is a group of related words that does not contain both a SUBJECT and a PREDICATE. A phrase cannot stand alone as an independent unit. Phrases function as parts of speech. A **noun phrase** functions as a NOUN in a sentence.

The modern population census dates back to the **seventeenth century.**

A **verb phrase** functions as a VERB in a sentence.

Two military censuses **are mentioned** in the Bible.

The Romans **had been conducting** censuses every five years to establish tax liabilities.

TEACHING TIP

You might help students expand short, choppy sentences by asking them to add modifiers that describe and tell *where*, *when*, and *how*. For example: Sigmund Freud was a doctor. Sigmund Freud was a Viennese doctor who influenced twentieth-century thinking about nervous diseases.

BACKGROUND

For an early, landmark work on expanding sentences by adding and directing modifiers, see Francis Christensen's "A Generative Rhetoric of the Sentence," in *Notes Toward a New Rhetoric*, 2nd ed., ed. Bonniejean Christensen (New York: Harper & Row, 1978, pp. 23–44). Christensen maintains that instructional time is most effectively spent in dealing with the cumulative sentence. This type of sentence presents the main clause first, then adds details that "move backward . . . to modify the statement of the main clause or more often to explicate or exemplify it, so that the sentence has a flowing and ebbing movement, advancing to a new position and then pausing to consolidate it, leaping and lingering as the popular ballad does." The additions are usually at a lower level of generality, going back over the main point in a more concrete and specific manner.

REFERENCE TO SUPPLEMENTS

This topic is included in the TASP writing competency test. Refer students to *Preparing for the TASP* by M. Saenz.

A HUMOROUS NOTE

Dangling participial phrases can produce some unintended meanings, such as these:

- Plunging 1,000 feet into the gorge, we saw Yosemite Falls.
- He rode his horse across Highway 12 and up and down the sidewalk in front of the saloon a good half hour before deputies arrived, shouting obscenities and being obnoxious.
- Locked in a vault for 50 years, the owner of the jewels has decided to sell them.

—Richard Lederer,
Anguished English
(Wyrick and Company, 1987)

TEACHING TIP

Because students sometimes feel that phrases are peculiar constructions of grammar books, you might find it useful to reproduce and distribute copies of a newspaper article on a popular subject. Ask students to identify noun phrases, verb phrases, and prepositional phrases. Students will be amazed at how often phrases appear in "real" writing. Class discussion might next cover the functions of the noun phrases and prepositional phrases (subject, object, complement, adjective, adverb).

ANSWERS AND COVERAGE: EXERCISE 7–8, page 187

Answers will vary. Here is one set of possibilities.

1. Juliette Low lived in England for a time *and learned* [verb phrase] about Boy Scouting from its founder, Sir Robert Baden-Powell.

2. His sister Agnes Baden-Powell had started a similar organization, *called Girl Guides* [verbal (participial) phrase], for girls.

➜

7n
cont.

A **prepositional phrase** always starts with a PREPOSITION and functions as a MODIFIER.

After the collapse of Rome, censuses were discontinued **until modern times**. [*After the collapse, of Rome,* and *until modern times* are all prepositional phrases.]

William the Conqueror conducted a census **of landowners in newly conquered England in 1086**. [three prepositional phrases in a row beginning with *of, in, in*]

An **absolute phrase** usually contains a noun or PRONOUN and a PARTICIPLE. It modifies the entire sentence to which it is attached.

Censuses being the fashion, Quebec and Nova Scotia took sixteen counts between 1665 and 1754.

Eighteenth-century Sweden and Denmark had complete records of their populations, **each adult and child having been accounted for.**

A **verbal phrase** is a word group that contains a verbal. Verbals are INFINITIVES, PRESENT PARTICIPLES, and PAST PARTICIPLES. **Infinitive phrases** function as nouns or modifiers. (An infinitive is the SIMPLE FORM of a verb, usually preceded by the word *to*; see 8b.) **Participial phrases** function as ADJECTIVES. Participial phrases can be formed from a verb's present participle (its *-ing* form) and from its past participle (the *-ed* form of a regular verb or the irregular form; see 8d).

In 1624, Virginia began **to count its citizens** in a census. [infinitive phrase = direct object]

Going from door to door, census takers interview millions of people. [participial phrase = adjective modifying *census takers*]

Amazed by some people's answers, the census takers always listen carefully. [participial phrase = adjective modifying *census takers*]

Gerund phrases function as nouns. Telling the difference between a gerund phrase and a participial phrase using a present participle can be tricky because both use the *-ing* verb form. The key is to determine how the verbal phrase is functioning: a gerund phrase functions only as a noun, and a participial phrase functions only as a modifier.

Including each person in the census was important. [gerund phrase = noun used as the subject]

Including each person in the census, Abby spent many hours on the crowded city block. [participial phrase = modifier used as adjective describing *Abby*]

EXERCISE 7-8

Consulting section 7n, combine each set of sentences into a single sentence, converting one sentence in each set into a phrase. Choose from among noun phrases, verb phrases, prepositional phrases, participial phrases, and gerund phrases. You can omit, add, or change words. Most sets can be combined in several equally correct ways, but be sure to check that your combined sentence makes sense.

EXAMPLE   Juliette Gordon Low is the founder of Girl Scouting in the United States. She was born in Savannah, Georgia, in 1860.

Juliette Gordon Low, the founder of Girl Scouting in the United States, was born in Savannah, Georgia, in 1860. (noun phrase)

1. Juliette Low lived in England for a time. There she learned about Boy Scouting from its founder, Sir Robert Baden-Powell.
2. His sister Agnes Baden-Powell had started a similar organization for girls. It was called Girl Guides.
3. Low returned to Savannah in 1912. She started the first U.S. Girl Scout troop there.
4. "Scout" was more suitable to the adventuresome U.S. spirit than "Guide." Thus Low called her organization "Girl Scouts."
5. The girls hiked and camped and rode horses and climbed trees. These activities were not considered suitable for young ladies.
6. Low refused to let anyone tell her that girls were not capable of vigorous activities. She recruited volunteers and raised money so that the girls could have challenging experiences.
7. Low had become partially deaf as a young woman. This fact was unknown to most of her friends.
8. Low made her hearing loss an asset. She asked for help for the girls, but she never heard a refusal.
9. Most people found it impossible to turn her away. Her persistence was a significant factor in the early success of Girl Scouting.
10. Today, Girl Scouts of the U.S.A. serves girls in more than three hundred councils. It has members in the United States, the Virgin Islands, Guam, and Puerto Rico.

ANSWERS AND COVERAGE: EXERCISE 7–8, cont.

3. Low returned to Savannah in 1912 *to start the first U.S. Girl Scout troop there* [infinitive phrase].

4. *"Scout" being more suitable to the adventuresome U.S. spirit than "Guide"* [absolute phrase], Low called her organization "Girl Scouts."

5. *The girls' hiking, camping, riding horses, and climbing trees* [noun phrase using gerunds] were activities not considered suitable for young ladies.

6. *Refusing to let anyone tell her that girls were not capable of vigorous activities* [verbal (participial) phrase], Low recruited volunteers and raised money so that the girls could have challenging experiences.

7. *A fact unknown to most of her friends* [noun phrase] was that Low had become partially deaf as a young woman.

8. Low made her hearing loss an asset *by asking for help* [prepositional phrase] for the girls but never hearing a refusal [for parallelism with *asking*, the second independent clause has been changed to a gerund phrase].

9. Most people found it impossible to turn her away, *her persistence being a significant factor in the early success of Girl Scouting* [absolute phrase].

10. *With members in the United States, the Virgin Islands, Guam, and Puerto Rico* [prepositional phrase], today Girl Scouts of the U.S.A. serves girls in more than three hundred councils.

Recognizing clauses   **7o**

A **clause** is a group of words that contains a SUBJECT and a PREDICATE. Clauses are divided into two categories: **independent clauses** (also known as **main clauses**) and **dependent clauses** (also known as **subordinate clauses**).

REFERENCE TO SUPPLEMENTS

This topic is included in the TASP writing competency test. Refer students to *Preparing for the TASP* by M. Saenz.

TEACHING TIP

To determine whether a clause is independent or dependent, Robert DeBeaugrande asks students to make up a "yes/no" question about the clause's statement ("Forward to the Basics: Getting Down to Grammar" [*College Composition and Communication* 35 (1984): 362–367]). "Only an independent clause will yield a sensible 'yes/no' question."

> The knave stole the tarts.
> Did the knave steal the tarts? (a sensible question)
> Because he was very hungry.
> Because was he very hungry? (not a sensible question)

QUOTATION ABOUT WRITING

A *dependent clause* is like a dependent child: incapable of standing on its own but able to cause a lot of trouble.
> —William Safire,
> "About Language"

A HUMOROUS NOTE

Each year the number of children coming to the mall to see Santa Claus grew larger, so the store owners decided to hire additional Santas and stationed them around the mall. The most experienced Santa was in charge. He referred to the trainees as his "Subordinate Clauses."

7o-1

Recognizing independent clauses

An **independent clause** contains a SUBJECT and a PREDICATE. It can stand alone as a sentence because it is an independent grammatical unit (see 7j). Chart 55 shows the basic pattern.

SENTENCE PATTERNS: GROUP IV		55
THE SENTENCE		
INDEPENDENT CLAUSE		
■ COMPLETE SUBJECT	+	COMPLETE PREDICATE
The telephone		rang.

7o-2

Recognizing dependent clauses

A **dependent clause** contains a subject and a predicate but cannot stand alone as a sentence. A dependent clause must be joined to an INDEPENDENT CLAUSE (see 7o-1).

Some dependent clauses start with subordinating conjunctions such as *although, because, when, until*. A subordinating conjunction expresses a relationship between the meaning in the dependent clause and the meaning in the independent clause (see Chart 51). Clauses that start with subordinating conjunctions function as ADVERBS and so are called **adverb clauses** (or sometimes **subordinate clauses**).

Adverb clauses usually answer some question about the independent clause: *how? why? when? under what circumstances?* Adverb clauses modify VERBS, ADJECTIVES, other adverbs, and entire independent clauses.

! ✤ PUNCTUATION ALERT: When an adverb clause comes before its independent clause, the clauses are usually separated by a comma (see 24b-1).

> **If the bond issue passes**, the city will install sewers. [The adverb clause modifies the verb *install*; *install* explains "under what circumstances."]
> They are drawing up plans **as quickly as they can**. [The adverb clause modifies the verb *drawing up*; it explains "how."]
> The homeowners feel happier **because they know the flooding will soon be better controlled**. [The adverb clause modifies the entire independent clause; it explains "why."] ✤

Adjective clauses (also called *relative clauses*) start with RELATIVE PRONOUNS, the most common of which are *who, which*, and *that*, or relative adverbs such as *when* or *where*. An adjective clause modifies the NOUN or PRONOUN that it follows.

The car **that Jack bought** is practical. [The adjective clause describes the noun *car*; *that* refers to *car*.]

The day **when I can buy my own car** is getting closer. [The adjective clause modifies the noun *day*; *when* refers to *day*.]

Chart 56 shows common sentence patterns for adverb and adjective clauses.

SENTENCE PATTERNS: GROUP V 56

■ DEPENDENT (ADVERB) CLAUSE + INDEPENDENT CLAUSE

Although the hour was quite late, the telephone rang.

SUBORDINATING CONJUNCTION / COMPLETE SUBJECT / COMPLETE PREDICATE / COMPLETE SUBJECT / COMPLETE PREDICATE

■ FIRST PART OF INDEPENDENT CLAUSE + DEPENDENT (ADJECTIVE) CLAUSE + SECOND PART OF INDEPENDENT CLAUSE

The red telephone, **which** belonged to Ms. Smythe, rang loudly.

COMPLETE SUBJECT / RELATIVE PRONOUN / COMPLETE PREDICATE

When you write adjective clauses, use *who, whom, whoever, whomever*, and *whose* when the ANTECEDENT is a person or an animal with a name.

The Smythes, **who collect cars**, are wealthy.

Their dog Bowser, **who is quite large**, is spoiled.

When you write adjective clauses, use *which* or *that* if the antecedent is a thing or an animal. Either *which* or *that* begins RESTRICTIVE adjective clauses, and *which* begins NONRESTRICTIVE ones.

SENTENCE PATTERNS: GROUP V

TEACHING TIP

To improve students' recognition of adjective and adverb clauses, as well as to increase their powers of concentration, you may want to read aloud the following passage from Katherine Anne Porter's "Memories of the Old South." Ask students to note every use of an adverb or adjective clause by listening for key words such as relative pronouns and subordinating conjunctions. After you read the passage, you may want to distribute and discuss it.

In my grandmother's day, in Texas, everybody seemed to remember that man *who* had a way of showing up with a dozen grains of real coffee in his hand, *which* he exchanged for a month's supply of corn meal. My grandmother parched a mixture of sweet potato and dried corn *until* it was black, ground it up and boiled it, *because* her family couldn't get over its yearning for a dark hot drink in the mornings, but she would never allow them to call it coffee. It was known as That Brew. . . . The woman *who* made That Brew and the soldier *who* ate the bacon rind had been bride and groom in a Kentucky wedding somewhere around 1850. Only a few years ago a cousin of mine showed me a letter from a lady then rising ninety-five *who* remembered that wedding *as if* it had been only yesterday.

TEACHING TIP

Combining sentences by using modifiers and appositives can not only reduce repetition but also create more graceful statements. Students are sometimes surprised by what they produce when they are asked to combine several choppy sentences into a single effective one.

TEACHING TIP

Imitation can be an effective means of expanding students' sentence-writing strategies. You can provide some samples, asking students to write a sentence on another topic, following the pattern of clauses and phrases in the model. Here are some varied possibilities for imitation, though you may want to choose your own.

- The sea, which looks so near and so tempting, is often difficult to reach.
  —Henry Miller,
  "The Big Sur"

- Hearing the rising tide, I think how it is pressing also against other shores I know—rising on a southern beach where there is no fog, but a moon edging all the waves with silver and touching the wet sands with lambent sheen, and on a still more distant shore sending its streaming currents against the moonlit pinnacles and the dark caves of the coral rock.
  —Rachel Carson,
  "The Enduring Sea"

ANSWERS: EXERCISE 7–9

1. *Although Sao Miguel's Furnas volcano erupted thousands of years ago* (ADV), the collapsed mountain top formed a lake bed *that is still hot* (ADJ).

2. The ground around Lake Furnas acts as a natural oven *because its temperature is more than 200 degrees Fahrenheit* (ADV).

3. To prepare the famous stew, *which is called* cozido (ADJ), cooks assemble chicken, beef, sausage, and vegetables in a pan.

4. *After the pan is tied in a cloth bag* (ADV), it is buried in the hole.

5. The *cozido* simmers for about six hours, a cooking time *that brings it to tasty perfection* (ADJ).

7o-2 cont.

❖ PUNCTUATION ALERT: When an adjective clause is nonrestrictive, use commas to separate it from the independent clause. (A restrictive clause is essential to limit meaning; a nonrestrictive clause is nonessential; see 24e.)

> The car **that I want to buy** has a cassette player.
>
> The car **which I want to buy** has a cassette player. [The adjective clause is restrictive, and so either *that* or *which* may be used.]
>
> My current car, **which I bought used**, needs major repairs. [The adjective clause is nonrestrictive, so it begins with *which* and is set off with commas.] ❖

Sometimes, *that* can be omitted from a sentence. For purposes of grammatical analysis, however, the omitted *that* is considered to be implied and therefore present.

> The car [that] I buy will have to get good mileage.

❖ ALERT: Omitting the word *that* can make a sentence harder to understand. Be sure to use *that* when it makes your writing clearer.

> **NO** I know Dale Smythe, who won a car in a raffle, is selling it.
>
> **YES** I know **that** Dale Smythe, who won a car in a raffle, is selling it. ❖

EXERCISE 7-9

Consulting section 7o-2, underline the dependent clauses. Write ADJ at the end of adjective clauses and ADV at the end of adverb clauses.

> ADV
> EXAMPLE   When cooks on São Miguel island in the Azores decide to
> prepare their favorite stew, they dig a hole on the shores
> of Lake Furnas.

1. Although Sao Miguel's Furnas volcano erupted thousands of years ago, the collapsed mountaintop formed a lake bed that is still hot.

2. The ground around Lake Furnas acts as a natural oven because its temperature is more than 200 degrees Fahrenheit.

3. To prepare the famous stew, which is called *cozido*, cooks assemble chicken, beef, sausage, and vegetables in a pan.

4. After the pan is tied in a cloth bag, it is buried in the hole.

5. The *cozido* simmers for about six hours, a cooking time that brings it to tasty perfection.

Noun clauses often begin with many of the same words as adjective clauses: *that, who, which,* and their derivatives, as well as *when,* *where, whether, why*, or *how*. Noun clauses, however, do not modify; they replace nouns.

> **Promises** are not always dependable. [noun]
>
> **What politicians promise** is not always dependable. [noun clause]
>
> The electorate often cannot figure out the **truth**. [noun]
>
> The electorate often cannot know **that the truth is being manipulated**.[noun clause]

Because they start with similar words, noun clauses and adjective clauses are sometimes confused with each other. A noun clause *is* a subject, object, or complement. An adjective clause *modifies* a subject, object, or complement. The word starting an adjective clause has an antecedent in the sentence. The word starting a noun clause does not.

> Politicians understand **whom they must please**. [Noun clause is an object; *whom* does not need an antecedent here.]
>
> Politicians **who make promises** sometimes fail to keep them. [Adjective clause modifies *politicians*, which is the antecedent of *who*.]

❖ ESL NOTE: Noun clauses in indirect questions are phrased as statements, not questions: *Kara asked why we needed the purple dye.* Avoid such sentences as *Kara asked why did* [or *do*] *we need the purple dye?* Tense, pronoun, and other changes may be necessary when a direct question is rephrased as an indirect question; see 15a-4.❖

Elliptical clauses are grammatically incomplete for the deliberate purpose of concise prose (see Chapter 16). The term *elliptical* comes from the word *ellipsis*, meaning "omission." An elliptical clause delivers its meaning only if the context makes clear what the missing elements are. Common omissions are *that* or *which* in adjective clauses, *that* in some noun clauses, subject and verb in adverb clauses, and the second half of comparisons.

> Engineering is one of the majors **[that] she considered**. [relative pronoun omitted from adjective clause]
>
> She decided **[that] she would prefer to major in management**. [relative pronoun omitted from noun clause]
>
> **After [he takes] a refresher course**, he will be eligible for a raise. [subject and verb omitted from adverb clause]
>
> Broiled fish tastes better **than boiled fish [tastes]**. [second half of the comparison omitted]

Sometimes an omission, although grammatically acceptable, interferes with the ability of a sentence to deliver its meaning, so omit nothing that helps clarity.

ESL

BACKGROUND

Marilyn Sternglass, in "Sentence-Combining and the Reading of Sentences" (*College Composition and Communication* 31 [1980], 325–328), maintains that sentence combining shows students how to cluster groups of words into phrases and clauses. This activity improves students' ability to recognize word groups as meaning-bearing units. She finds strong justification for including sentence-combining activities in writing classes, not only for their positive effect on writing skills, but also because they improve a student's ability to read sentences.

TEACHING TIP

Elliptical clauses: To enhance students' appreciation of their options, you might ask them whether they prefer the elliptical or full forms of the text's sentences—and why. Here are alternate examples to use also.

- Living in Spain was one of the best experiences [that] Carol had during college. When [she was] living with a family in Spain, Carol started to feel like a native. Air travel is faster than sea [travel].

- James Naismith, [who was] a Presbyterian minister, believed that through athletics he could teach lessons in Christian ideals. After [he had graduated from] divinity school, Naismith enrolled in the School for Christian Workers, [which] later [became] known as the International YMCA Training School. Naismith, [who was] a young man full of ideas, was given the job of devising a game that had less running and tackling than other ball games [had]. Limited indoor space and the hard surface of a wooden floor were two of the biggest problems [that] he faced. The game [that] he devised is known today as basketball.

1. Most U.S. military personnel who overheard the unintelligible messages thought that they were some strange Japanese code. (One elliptical possibility is *Most U.S. military personnel who overheard the unintelligible messages thought them some strange Japanese code*, with *thought them* replacing *thought that they were*.)

2. When the Japanese were listening in, they could not understand the messages either. (One elliptical possibility is *The Japanese listening in could not understand the messages either.*)

3. A few members of the U.S. forces, Navajo speakers, understood what the messages said. (The elliptical phrase *Navajo speakers* omits *who were*.)

4. The overheard messages were in a code based on the Navajo language.

5. After Navajo Marines were specially recruited for this assignment, only they sent and received these messages. (One elliptical version is *Only Navajo Marines specially recruited for this assignment sent and received these messages.*)

6. Since the messages conveyed meaning by tone of voice as well as vocabulary, decoding techniques using only written words could not break the code.

7. If any Navajos were living in Japan, they never explained the mystery of the messages.

8. Because Navajo is an extraordinarily complex language, the Japanese were never able to break the code.

9. The Navajo code talkers conveyed important messages that affected the key battles of Saipan, Guadalcanal, and Iwo Jima.

10. Even though the Navajo were asked to avoid publicity after the war in case the code was needed again, ultimately, their achievement was widely recognized.

7o-2
cont.

EXERCISE 7-10

Consulting section 7o, use some of the subordinating conjunctions and relative pronouns from this list to combine each of the following pairs of sentences. Some pairs may be combined in a variety of ways. Create at least one elliptical construction. Subordinators may be used more than once, but try to use as many different ones as possible.

EXAMPLE   The Pacific fighting was reaching its peak during World War II. U.S. and Japanese forces began to pick up strange radio messages.

As the Pacific fighting was reaching its peak during World War II, U.S. and Japanese forces began to pick up strange radio messages.

who	that	although	because	if	when
which	after	as	even though	since	unless

1. Most U.S. military personnel thought that the unintelligible messages were some strange Japanese code. The U.S. military personnel overheard the messages.

2. The Japanese were listening in. They could not understand the messages either.

3. A few members of the U.S. forces understood what the messages said. Those members of the U.S. forces were Navajo speakers.

4. The overheard messages were in a code. This code was based on the Navajo language.

5. Only Navajo Marines sent and received these messages. The Navajo Marines were specially recruited for this assignment.

6. The messages conveyed meaning by tone of voice as well as vocabulary. Decoding techniques using only written words could not break the code.

7. Were any Navajos living in Japan? The mystery of the messages was never explained.

8. Navajo is an extraordinarily complex language. The Japanese were never able to break the code.

9. The Navajo code talkers conveyed important messages. The messages affected the key battles of Saipan, Guadalcanal, and Iwo Jima.

10. The Navajo were asked to avoid publicity after the war in case the code was needed again. Ultimately, their achievement was widely recognized.

7p

Recognizing sentence types

Sentences can be **simple, compound, complex,** and **compound-complex.**

A **simple sentence** is composed of a single INDEPENDENT CLAUSE with no DEPENDENT CLAUSES.

Charlie Chaplin was born in London on April 16, 1889.

A mime, he became famous for his character the Little Tramp.

A **compound sentence** is composed of two or more independent clauses. These clauses may be connected by a coordinating conjunction (*and, but, for, or, nor, yet,* or *so*) or by a semicolon alone or with a conjunctive adverb.

❖ PUNCTUATION ALERT: Use a comma before a coordinating conjunction connecting two independent clauses (see 24a).

His father died early, **and** his mother spent time in mental hospitals.

Many people enjoy Chaplin films; others do not.

Many people enjoy Chaplin films; **however,** others do not.❖

A **complex sentence** is composed of one independent clause and one or more dependent clauses.

❖ PUNCTUATION ALERT: When a dependent clause comes before its independent clause, the clauses are usually separated by a comma (see 24b-1).

When times were bad, Chaplin lived in the streets. [dependent clause starting *When*; independent clause starting *Chaplin*]

When Chaplin was performing with a troupe that was touring the United States, he was hired by Mack Sennett, **who owned the Keystone Comedies**. [dependent clause starting *When*; dependent clause starting *that*; independent clause starting *he*; dependent clause starting *who*] ♣

A **compound-complex sentence** joins a compound sentence and a complex sentence. It contains two or more independent clauses and one or more dependent clauses.

Chaplin's comedies were immediately successful, **and** his salaries were huge **because of the enormous popularity of his tramp character, who was famous for his tiny mustache, baggy trousers, big shoes, and trick derby**. [independent clause starting *Chaplin's*; independent clause starting *his salaries*; dependent clause starting *because*; dependent clause starting *who*]

Once studios could no longer afford him, Chaplin co-founded United Artists, **and** then he was able to produce and distribute his own films. [dependent clause starting *Once*; independent clause starting *Chaplin*; independent clause starting *then he was able*]

ANSWERS: EXERCISE 7–11

1. simple
2. compound
3. complex
4. compound-complex
5. complex
6. simple
7. compound
8. compound
9. complex
10. compound-complex

TEACHING TIP

Edward Corbett, in *Classical Rhetoric for the Modern Student*, 2nd ed. (New York: Oxford UP, 1971), suggests having students analyze their own writing by counting the number of words in the sentences of a paper they have written, then identifying the longest sentence (in number of words), the shortest sentence, and the average sentence. The student can go on to compute the number of sentences and the percentage of sentences that contain more than ten words over the average and five below the average. The whole can be compared with a passage from an essay by a professional writer.

QUOTATION ABOUT WRITING

A story can be wrecked by a faulty rhythm in a sentence—especially if it occurs toward the end—or a mistake in paragraphing, even punctuation.
—Truman Capote

7p
cont.

EXERCISE 7-11

Consulting section 7p, identify each sentence as simple, compound, complex, or compound-complex.

EXAMPLE   The restoration of Ellis Island was started in 1983 and completed in 1990. (simple)

1. Immigrants from many nations have come to the United States through New York City for hundreds of years.
2. The Federal government took control over immigration from New York State in 1891, and Ellis Island was designated as a federal immigration center in 1892.
3. Although it was built to accommodate half a million immigrants a year, Ellis Island saw the arrival of almost double that number in 1907.
4. On the average, 80 percent of the immigrants passed inspection each day, while 20 percent were detained to be checked for disease or the ability to support themselves, but only 2 percent of the Ellis Island immigrants were ever refused admission.
5. Because the two World Wars and more restrictive immigration laws dramatically reduced the number of immigrants to the United States, Ellis Island eventually became much quieter.
6. Concern about security risks during World War II led officials to confine illegal aliens in detention centers.
7. Ellis Island was designated a detention center for illegal aliens during World War II; it also served as a training center for the U.S. Coast Guard.
8. Immigration slowed to a trickle after World War II, and the aging facility was no longer needed.
9. Ellis Island, which was officially closed in 1954, was left with forty-two structures decaying under the effects of time, weather, and vandalism.
10. Ellis Island was targeted for restoration in the 1980s, and today the Ellis Island Immigration Museum honors all immigrants who entered the United States through any point.

8 Verbs

Understanding verbs

Verbs convey information about what is happening, what has happened, and what will happen. In English, a verb tells of an action, an occurrence, or a state of being.

> Many people **overeat** on Thanksgiving. [action]
> Mother's Day **fell** early this year. [occurrence]
> Memorial Day **is** tomorrow. [state of being]

To understand more about the information verbs convey and the various types of verbs, see Chart 57.

OVERVIEW OF VERBS   57

INFORMATION VERBS CONVEY

PERSON	Who or what acts or experiences an action—*first person* (the one speaking), *second person* (the one being spoken to), or *third person* (the person or thing being spoken about).
NUMBER	How many SUBJECTS act or experience an action—*singular* (one) or *plural* (more than one).
TENSE	When an action occurs—*past, present,* or *future*; see 8g-8k.
MOOD	What attitude is expressed toward the action—*indicative, imperative,* or *subjunctive*; see 8l-8m.
VOICE	Whether the subject acts or is acted upon—*active voice* or *passive voice*; see 8n-8o.

➡

OVERVIEW OF VERBS

REFERENCES TO SUPPLEMENTS
For this topic in the CLAST writing competency test, refer students to ch. 1, section B4a of *Preparing for the CLAST* by S. Patterson.

For editing for correct use of verbs, refer students to *Rough Drafts* by K. S. Cain, Part IV, Exercise 8.

TEACHING TIP
Some students may feel overwhelmed by verb tenses—which they may perceive to be infinite in number—with the result that they refuse to face the fearsome verb and thus pick a form at random (or so it seems to us). It may be helpful to show them the basic distinction between tense and aspect.

Time can be divided into past, present, and future. *Tense* refers to the reflection of one of these times in a verb. Therefore, there are three basic tenses: past, present, future. *Aspect* says something about the way the action is experienced. The progressive aspect (*to be* + *ing*) shows an action still in progress and the perfect aspect (*has, have,* or *had* + past participle) shows a completed action or one being continued into the present from a specific point in the past. *Mood,* which describes conditions such as certainty, necessity, and possibility, is a separate issue, and so is *voice*. A verb can show all four qualities, but you might want to focus on the interplay of tense and aspect first.

WORD HISTORY

Verb shares the same Latin root as *word—verbum*, meaning word. *Verbum* is related to the Greek verb *eirein*, to say or to speak.

TEACHING TIP

Some of your students may speak a nonstandard English dialect. Black English is perhaps the most discussed of these, but nonblack rural and inner-city students and students (of any color) from former British colonies and U.S. protectorates may also speak nonstandard dialects.

Two-dialect students can pick up changes in vocabulary comparatively easily. Their verbs, however, might need to be monitored with care. You might consider reviewing the following chart with such students:

NONSTANDARD ENGLISH	STANDARD ENGLISH
Present Tense	
I	I
you ⎫	you ⎫
we ⎬ *loves*	we ⎬ *love*
they ⎭	they ⎭
he, she, it *love*	he, she, it *loves*
Past Tense	
I	I
you ⎫	you ⎫
we ⎬ *love*	we ⎬ *loved*
they ⎭	they ⎭
he, she, it *love*	he, she, it *loved*

OVERVIEW OF VERBS (continued)   57

TYPES OF VERBS

MAIN VERB	A verb expressing action, occurrence, or state of being.
	She **talked** to the group.
LINKING VERB	A main verb that conveys a state of being (*is*), relates to the senses (*taste*), or indicates a condition (*grow*) and that joins a subject to a word or words that rename or describe it. (More about linking verbs follows this chart.)
	She **was** happy about speaking.
AUXILIARY VERB	A verb that combines with a main verb to convey information about tense, mood, or voice.
	She **has** talked to them before.
	MODAL AUXILIARY VERBS include *can, could, may, might, should, would, must,* and others that add shades of meaning such as ability or possibility to verbs (see 8e and Chapter 46ESL).
	She **might** talk to them again.
TRANSITIVE VERB	A verb that must be followed by a DIRECT OBJECT— a NOUN or PRONOUN that completes the verb's message (see 8f).
	She **spoke French** to them.
INTRANSITIVE VERB	A verb that does not have a direct object completing its message (see 8f).
	She **talked** slowly.

Linking verbs are main verbs that indicate a state of being or a condition. They link a subject with a **subject complement**—a word (or words) that renames or describes the subject.

Some systems of grammar use the term **predicate nominative** for a subject complement that is a NOUN or PRONOUN renaming the subject and the term **predicate adjective** for a subject complement that is an ADJECTIVE describing the subject.

Some people consider a linking verb as an equal sign between a subject and its complement. Chart 58 presents an overview of linking verbs.

LINKING VERBS   58

- Linking verbs may be forms of the verb *to be* (*am, is, was, were*; see 8e for a complete list).

George Washington   **was**   president.
SUBJECT   LINKING VERB   COMPLEMENT (PREDICATE NOMINATIVE: RENAMES SUBJECT)

- Linking verbs may deal with the senses (*look, smell, taste, sound,* and *feel*).

George Washington   **sounded**   confident.
SUBJECT   LINKING VERB   COMPLEMENT (PREDICATE ADJECTIVE: DESCRIBES SUBJECT)

- Certain other verbs that convey a sense of existing or becoming— *appear, seem, become, get, grow, turn, remain, stay,* and *prove,* for example—can be linking verbs.

George Washington   **grew**   old.
SUBJECT   LINKING VERB   COMPLEMENT (PREDICATE ADJECTIVE: DESCRIBES SUBJECT)

- To test whether a verb other than a form of *to be* is functioning as a linking verb, substitute *was* (for a singular subject) or *were* (for a plural subject) for the original verb. If the sentence makes sense, the original verb is functioning as a linking verb.

NO   George Washington **grew** a beard → George Washington **was** a beard. [*Grew* is not functioning as a linking verb.]

YES   George Washington **grew** old → George Washington **was** old. [*Grew* is functioning as a linking verb.]

TEACHING TIP

Although *to be* is always a linking verb, other verbs may or may not be, depending upon how they are used in a given sentence. When in doubt, try substituting a form of *to be:* If the sentence makes sense, it contains a linking verb; if it no longer makes sense, it does not contain a linking verb.

> He *seems* ill./He *is* ill. [The *to be* verb makes sense, so *seems* is a linking verb.]

> Daisies *grow* in the park./Daisies *are* in the park. [The *to be* verb makes sense, so *grow* is a linking verb.]

> Joyce *grows* orchids./Joyce *is* orchids. [The *to be* verb does not make sense, so *grows* is not a linking verb.]

QUOTATION ABOUT WRITING

Writers have two main problems. One is writer's block, when the words won't come at all, and the other is "logorrhea," when the words come so fast that they can hardly get to the wastebasket in time.
—Cecilia Bartholomew

VERB FORMS

WORD HISTORY

Infinitive comes from the Latin *infinitivus*, meaning *unlimited* or *indefinite*. This is appropriate, since the infinitive shows no person or number. Coming from the same Latin verb, *finire (to limit),* the term *finite verb* refers to a verb that is limited by person and number. In contrast, a *nonfinite verb* (also known as a *verbal*) is not limited in these ways.

TEACHING TIP

Leaving the *-s* off verbs is a common error, even among students who can quote the rule for its use. Many of these students speak or have studied second languages that have much more complex systems of verb endings. A discussion of the English *-s* in the context of other languages the students know may reduce the number of carelessly omitted *-s*'s. You can let students know, jokingly, that anyone who accurately writes and speaks French, Spanish, or Italian and still doesn't bother to keep track of "one little *s*" is too strange to be believed.

Here is a comparison of the verb *speak* (present tense) in four languages, with endings shown in boldface. When no pronouns are given, the pronoun is communicated by the verb's ending.

ENGLISH

Singular	*Plural*
I speak	we speak
you speak	you speak
he, she, it speaks	they speak

SPANISH

habl**o**	habl**amos**
habl**as**	habl**áis**
habl**a**	habl**an**

8b **Recognizing the forms of main verbs**

A **main verb** names an action (*people **dance***), an occurrence (*Mother's Day **fell** early this year*), or a state of being (*Memorial Day **is** tomorrow*). Every main verb has five forms.

- The **simple form** conveys an action, occurrence, or state of being taking place in the present (*I **laugh***) or, with an AUXILIARY VERB, in the future (*I **will laugh***).
- The **past-tense form** is the basis for conveying an action, occurrence, or state completed in the past (*I **laughed***). REGULAR VERBS add *-ed* or *-d* to the simple form. IRREGULAR VERBS vary; see Chart 59.
- The **past-participle form** in regular verbs uses the same form as the past tense. Irregular verbs vary; see Chart 59. To function as a verb, a past participle must combine with a SUBJECT and one or more auxiliary verbs: *I **have laughed***. Otherwise, past participles function as ADJECTIVES: ***crumbled** cookies*.
- The **present participle form** adds *-ing* to the simple form (*laugh**ing***). To function as a verb, a present participle combines with a subject and one or more auxiliary verbs (*I **was laughing***). Otherwise, present participles function as adjectives (*my **laughing** friends*) or as NOUNS (***laughing** is healthy*).
- The **infinitive** uses the simple form, usually but not always following *to* (*I started **to laugh***). The infinitive functions as a noun or an adjective, not a verb.

ESL ❖ ESL NOTE: When they function as parts of speech other than verbs, verb forms are called VERBALS (see 7d). Present participles functioning as nouns are called GERUNDS. For information about using gerunds and infinitives as objects after certain verbs, see Chapter 45ESL.❖

8c **Using the -s form of verbs**

The *-s* form of a verb occurs in the third-person singular in the PRESENT TENSE. The *-s* ending is added to a verb's simple form *smell, smells: The bread **smells** delicious.*

The verbs *be* and *have* are irregular verbs. For the third-person singular, present tense, *be* uses **is** and *have* uses **has.**

The cheesecake **is** popular.
The eclair **has** chocolate on top.

Even if you tend to drop the *-s* or *-es* ending when you speak, do not forget to use it when you write. Proofread carefully for the correct use of the *-s* form. (For the *-s* form of verbs in subject-verb agreement, see 11b.)

❖ USAGE ALERT: Academic writing requires standard, not dialectal, third-person singular forms in the present tense: for example, **he is** (not *he be*) *hungry*; and *the **bakery has*** (not *the bakery have*) *fresh bread.*❖

EXERCISE 8-1

Consulting sections 8b and 8c, rewrite each sentence, changing the subject to the word given in parentheses. Change the form of the italicized verb to match this new subject. Keep all sentences in the present tense.

EXAMPLE   Often in literature, a colorful figure *suggests* particular feelings or special characteristics. (colorful figures)

Often in literature, *colorful figures suggest* particular feelings or special characteristics.

1. A green figure *appears* in ancient folklore. (Green figures)
2. These characters *represent* nature, fertility, and growing things. (This character)
3. This fertility symbol *takes* part in dances and other celebrations of spring's return. (These fertility symbols)
4. In many cultures, any signs of spring *trigger* festivals that *emphasize* the color green. (any sign of spring) (a festival)
5. Today, a person who *has* a talent for gardening *is* said to have a green thumb, and green giants *adorn* one company's cans of vegetables. (people who) (a green giant)

Using regular and irregular verbs   8d

A **regular verb** forms its past tense and past participle by adding *-ed* or *-d* to the simple form. Most verbs in English are regular. Some English verbs are **irregular**. They form the past tense and past participle in various ways. For a list of the most common irregular verbs, see Chart 59.

❖ SPELLING ALERT: For information about when to change a *y* to an *i* when adding the *-ed* ending, see 22c. For information about when to double a final consonant before the *-ed* ending, see 22c.❖

199

ANSWERS: EXERCISE 8–1

1. Green figures appear
2. This character represents
3. These fertility symbols take
4. any sign of spring triggers; a festival that emphasizes
5. people who have . . . are said; a green giant adorns

REFERENCE TO SUPPLEMENTS

This topic is included in the TASP writing competency test. Refer students to *Preparing for the TASP* by M. Saenz.

8d
cont.

Speakers sometimes skip over the -ed sound, hitting the sound lightly or not at all. Even if you are not used to hearing or pronouncing this sound, do not forget to add it when you write. Proofread carefully for -ed endings.

NO The cake was **suppose** to be tasty.

YES The cake was **supposed** to be tasty.

About two hundred verbs in English are **irregular**. Unfortunately, a verb's simple form does not provide a clue about whether the verb is irregular or regular. Irregular verbs do not consistently add -ed or -d to form the past tense and past participle. Some irregular verbs change an internal vowel to make past tense and past participle: *sing, sang, sung.* Some change an internal vowel and add an ending other than -ed or -d; *grow, grew, grown.* Some use the simple form throughout: *cost, cost, cost.*

Although you can always look up the principal parts of any verb, memorizing any you do not know is much more efficient in the long run. The most frequently used irregular verbs are listed in Chart 59.

COMMON IRREGULAR VERBS 59

SIMPLE FORM	PAST TENSE	PAST PARTICIPLE
arise	arose	arisen
awake	awoke *or* awaked	awaked *or* awoken
be (is, am, are)	was, were	been
bear	bore	borne *or* born
beat	beat	beaten
become	became	become
begin	began	begun
bend	bent	bent
bet	bet	bet
bid ("to offer")	bid	bid
bid ("to command")	bade	bidden
bind	bound	bound
bite	bit	bitten *or* bit
blow	blew	blown
break	broke	broken
bring	brought	brought
build	built	built

COMMON IRREGULAR VERBS (continued)   59

SIMPLE FORM	PAST TENSE	PAST PARTICIPLE
burst	burst	burst
buy	bought	bought
cast	cast	cast
catch	caught	caught
choose	chose	chosen
cling	clung	clung
come	came	come
cost	cost	cost
creep	crept	crept
cut	cut	cut
deal	dealt	dealt
dig	dug	dug
dive	dived *or* dove	dived
do	did	done
draw	drew	drawn
drink	drank	drunk
drive	drove	driven
eat	ate	eaten
fall	fell	fallen
feed	fed	fed
feel	felt	felt
fight	fought	fought
find	found	found
flee	fled	fled
fling	flung	flung
fly	flew	flown
forbid	forbade *or* forbad	forbidden
forget	forgot	forgotten *or* forgot
forgive	forgave	forgiven
forsake	forsook	forsaken
freeze	froze	frozen
get	got	got *or* gotten
give	gave	given

➡

EXTRA EXERCISE A

For practice identifying verbs and forming past-tense verbs, rewrite the following paragraph from Gretel Ehrlich's essay "Spring," changing the present-tense verbs to past tense. (Answers are in italics.)

Recuperation is *(was)* like spring: dormancy and vitality collide *(collided)*. In any year I'm *(I was)* like a bear, a partial hibernator. During January thaws I stick *(stuck)* my nose out and peruse *(perused)* the frozen desolation as if reading a book whose language I don't *(didn't)* know. In March I'm *(I was)* ramshackle, weak in the knees, giddy, dazzled by broken-backed clouds, the passing of Halley's comet, the on-and-off strobe of sun. Like a sheepherder I X *(Xed)* out each calendar day as if time were *(no change, subjunctive voice)* a forest through which I could clear-cut *(no change, subjunctive voice)* a way to the future. My physicist friend straightens *(straightened)* me out on this point too. The notion of "time passing," like a train through a landscape, is *(was)* an illusion, he says *(said.)* I hold *(held)* the Big Ben clock taken from a dead sheepherder's wagon and look *(looked)* at it. The clock measures *(measured)* intervals of time, not the speed of time, and the calendar is *(was)* a scaffolding we hang *(hung)* as if time were *(no change, subjunctive voice)* rushing water we could harness *(no change, subjunctive voice.)* Time-bound, I hinge *(hinged)* myself to a linear bias—cause and effect all laid out in a neat row—and in this we learn *(learned)* two things: blame and shame.

QUOTATION ABOUT WRITING

Grammar is the prism through which all writing is refracted.

—Patricia Robertson

QUOTATION ABOUT WRITING

True ease in writing comes from art, not chance,

As those move easiest who have learned to dance.

'Tis not enough no harshness gives offense,

The sound must seem an echo to the sense.

—Alexander Pope

QUOTATION ABOUT WRITING

Grammar is a piano I play by ear. All I know about grammar is its power.

—Joan Didion

A HUMOROUS NOTE

The English major was working for the summer as morning shift manager at a fast-food restaurant. One day her least reliable worker was missing again. She called over a friend of the boy and asked, "Where's Bill?"

"He decided to lay on the beach," replied the friend.

Not wishing to embarrass the worker but unable to overcome the urge to correct him the manager whispered, "Lie."

"All right," he said with a shrug, "Bill had to take his cat to the vet for an emergency appendectomy."

COMMON IRREGULAR VERBS (continued) 59

SIMPLE FORM	PAST TENSE	PAST PARTICIPLE
go	went	gone
grow	grew	grown
hang ("to suspend")*	hung	hung
have	had	had
hear	heard	heard
hide	hid	hidden
hit	hit	hit
hurt	hurt	hurt
keep	kept	kept
know	knew	known
lay	laid	laid
lead	led	led
leave	left	left
lend	lent	lent
let	let	let
lie	lay	lain
light	lighted *or* lit	lighted *or* lit
lose	lost	lost
make	made	made
mean	meant	meant
pay	paid	paid
prove	proved	proved *or* proven
quit	quit	quit
read	read	read
rid	rid	rid
ride	rode	ridden
ring	rang	rung
rise	rose	risen
run	ran	run
say	said	said
see	saw	seen
seek	sought	sought

*When it means "to execute by hanging," *hang* is a regular verb: *In wartime, some armies routinely **hanged** deserters.*

COMMON IRREGULAR VERBS (continued)

SIMPLE FORM	PAST TENSE	PAST PARTICIPLE
send	sent	sent
set	set	set
shake	shook	shaken
shine ("to glow")*	shone	shone
shoot	shot	shot
show	showed	shown *or* showed
shrink	shrank	shrunk
sing	sang	sung
sink	sank *or* sunk	sunk
sit	sat	sat
slay	slew	slain
sleep	slept	slept
sling	slung	slung
speak	spoke	spoken
spend	spent	spent
spin	spun	spun
spring	sprang *or* sprung	sprung
stand	stood	stood
steal	stole	stolen
sting	stung	stung
stink	stank *or* stunk	stunk
stride	strode	stridden
strike	struck	struck
strive	strove	striven
swear	swore	sworn
sweep	swept	swept
swim	swam	swum
swing	swung	swung
take	took	taken
teach	taught	taught
tear	tore	torn
tell	told	told

*When it means "to polish," *shine* is a regular verb: *We **shined** our shoes.*

➡

QUOTATION ABOUT WRITING

You don't know what it is to stay a whole day with your head in your hands trying to squeeze your unfortunate brain so as to find a word. Ah! I know the agonies of style.

—Gustave Flaubert,
writing to George Sand

QUOTATION ABOUT WRITING

Nice writing isn't enough. It isn't enough to have smooth and pretty language. You have to surprise the reader frequently, you can't just be nice all the time. Provoke the reader. Astonish the reader. Writing that has no surprises is as bland as oatmeal. Surprise the reader with the unexpected verb or adjective. Use one startling adjective per page.

—Anne Bernays

8d
cont.

COMMON IRREGULAR VERBS
(continued)

QUOTATION ABOUT WRITING

Erasure is quite as important a function of the pen as actual writing. . . . For we have to condemn what had previously satisfied us and discover what had escaped our notice.

—Quintilian

WORD HISTORY

The word *conjugation* has been used since the early sixteenth century to refer to all the forms of a particular verb. *Conjugation* and *conjugate* both come from the Latin *conjugāre*, basically meaning *to join together*. In Latin, a list of the forms of a verb was called a *conjugatio*, and *conjugata verba* (literally *joined words*) referred to words that were etymologically related.

ANSWERS: EXERCISE 8–2

1. contained
2. believed; occurred
3. feared; contributed
4. pointed; released; acted
5. absorbed; warmed

ANSWERS: EXERCISE 8–3

1. rose; saw; crept
2. sprang; caught; ate
3. stole; stood

➜

COMMON IRREGULAR VERBS (continued)

59

SIMPLE FORM	PAST TENSE	PAST PARTICIPLE
think	thought	thought
throw	threw	thrown
understand	understood	understood
wake	woke *or* waked	waked *or* woken
wear	wore	worn
wring	wrung	wrung
write	wrote	written

EXERCISE 8-2

Consulting section 8d, in each blank write the correct past-tense form of the regular verb (simple form) in parentheses.

EXAMPLE   Rising annual temperatures over the last ten years (cause) **caused** many scientists to predict climate changes.

(1) The 1980s (contain) _____ six of the warmest years ever recorded. (2) Some scientists (believe) _____ that rises and falls in annual temperatures (occur) _____ naturally over time. (3) Others (fear) _____ that human behavior (contribute) _____ to a warming climate. (4) They (point) _____ out that fossil fuels (release) _____ gases that (act) _____ like a layer of insulation around the earth. (5) This layer (absorb) _____ heat and (warm) _____ the earth's atmosphere.

EXERCISE 8-3

Consulting section 8d, in each blank write the correct past–tense form of the irregular verb for which the simple form is given in parentheses. Use the list of irregular verbs in Chart 59.

EXAMPLE   In a small hole at the top of a tall saguaro cactus, two elf owls (sit) **sat** watching the desert.

(1) As the sun (rise) _____ , the elf owls (see) _____ a roadrunner stalking a kingsnake as it (creep) _____ toward their nest. (2) The roadrunner (spring) _____ on the snake, (catch) _____ it by the head, and then (eat) _____ it slowly. (3) At night, the coyotes, foxes, skunks, and rabbits of the desert (steal) _____ to the waterhole at the foot of the saguaro and (stand) _____ there drinking thirstily. (4) A shaggy mountain

sheep, with huge corkscrew horns, (bend) _____ its head and (drink) _____ at the pool. (5) When a mountain lion (draw) _____ near, the terrified sheep (freeze) _____ and then (flee) _____ . (6) The mountain lion (lay) _____ down its catch, (swim) _____ in the waterhole, and then (lie) _____ in the sand to eat the rabbit it had caught. (7) As the night (wear) _____ on, the female elf owl (grow) _____ tired of tending her eggs, so she (leave) _____ the nest in the saguaro and (fly) _____ off. (8) When the male elf owl (see) _____ her leave, he (come) _____ to the nest and (sit) _____ on the eggs for the female while she (take) _____ a break and (do) _____ the hunting. (9) While hunting, the female (find) _____ a wood spider, (catch) _____ it, (bring) _____ it to the nest, and (feed) _____ it to her mate. (10) In time, the waterhole (shrink) _____ to a puddle, and the desert animals, (lead) _____ by the elf owls, desperately (seek) _____ new sources of water. (11) The drought (break) _____ in late July, when storm clouds (burst) _____ overhead, rain (fall) _____ in torrents, and flash floods (sweep) _____ through, restoring the desert to life.

Using auxiliary verbs   8e

Auxiliary verbs, also called **helping verbs**, combine with MAIN VERBS to make VERB PHRASES.

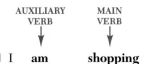

■ I   **am**   **shopping**   for new shoes.

VERB PHRASE

■ Clothing prices   **have**   **soared**   recently.

VERB PHRASE

■ Leather shoes   **might**   **cost**   hundreds of dollars.

VERB PHRASE

WORD HISTORY

An *auxiliary verb* is also called a *helping verb*, and, not surprisingly, *auxiliary* comes from *auxiliarius*, a Latin word for *help*. Linking verbs were, until recently, often called *copulative verbs*. This usage dates back to the seventeenth century and comes from the Latin *copulativus*, meaning *connective*.

EXTRA EXERCISE B

Identify all modal auxiliaries in the following passage. (Answers are in italics.)

Most professionals in the field of medicine agree that the public *ought to* be better informed about recent developments in medical science. One of the tools that patients frequently experience but *may* know little about is the X-ray. Its discoverer, Professor Wilhelm Roentgen, thought he *might* have a powerful new means of examining the body when, in 1895, he saw the glimmer of a fluorescent screen. His discovery meant that medical professionals *could* peer into the innermost recesses of the body without surgery. For example, Dr. William B. Cannon realized that fluoroscopy *could* be used to examine the alimentary canal or digestive system. Today X-ray means that doctors *can* carry diagnostic methods to previously inaccessible areas of the human body by painless techniques. A list of all of the diagnostic uses of X-ray films *would* be too lengthy to include here, but it is safe to say that they *can* be used on all parts of the body. Of course, because improper use of X-rays *may* be harmful, technologists *should* have adequate training. They *must* complete a rigorous course of study before being allowed to operate X-ray machines.

8e cont.

Auxiliary verbs deserve special attention because they occur very frequently in English. Also, the forms of the three most common auxiliaries—*be, do,* and *have*—vary more than usual; see Charts 60 and 61.

THE FORMS OF THE VERB *BE*			60

SIMPLE FORM	be	**-S FORM**	is
PAST TENSE	was, were	**PRESENT PARTICIPLE**	being
PAST PARTICIPLE	been		

PERSON	PRESENT TENSE	PAST TENSE
I	am	was
you (singular)	are	were
he, she, it	is	was
we	are	were
you (plural)	are	were
they	are	were

! ❖ ALERT: The verb *be*, along with its various forms, can also function as a *linking verb* (see Chart 58). In joining a SUBJECT to a SUBJECT COMPLEMENT, it acts as a MAIN VERB rather than an auxiliary verb. Academic writing requires standard forms and uses of the verb *be* as a main verb and as an auxiliary verb.

> The gym **is** [not *be*] a busy place. [*Gym* is the subject; *is* is the linking verb, which acts as a main verb; *busy place* is the subject complement.]

> The gym **is** [not *be*] filling with spectators. [*Gym* is the subject; *is* is the auxiliary verb and *filling* is the main verb; together *is filling* is a verb phrase.] ❖

THE FORMS OF THE VERBS *DO* AND *HAVE*				61

SIMPLE FORM	do		SIMPLE FORM	have
PAST TENSE	did		PAST TENSE	had
PAST PARTICIPLE	done		PAST PARTICIPLE	had
-S FORM	does		-S FORM	has
PRESENT PARTICIPLE	doing		PRESENT PARTICIPLE	having

ESL ❖ ESL NOTE: When an auxiliary verb is used with a main verb, the auxiliary may change form to agree with a third-person singular subject, but the main verb does not change.

NO   **Does** the library **closes** at 6:00?

YES   **Does** the library **close** at 6:00? ❖

The verbs *can, could, may, might, must, shall, should, will, would,* and others are **modal auxiliary verbs**. Modal auxiliaries work with main verbs in verb phrases to communicate a meaning of ability, permission, obligation, advisability, necessity, or possibility.

Exercise **can lengthen** lives. [possibility]

The exercise **must occur** regularly. [necessity, obligation]

People **should protect** their bodies. [advisability]

May I **exercise?** [permission]

She **can jog** for five miles. [ability]

❖ ESL NOTE: For more about modal auxiliary verbs and the meanings they communicate, see Chapter 46ESL.❖   ESL

EXERCISE 8-4

Consulting section 8e, use auxiliary verbs from the list below to fill in the blanks. Use each auxiliary verb only once.

~~might~~   can   was   will   have   would

EXAMPLE   A shy person or one who is nervous about making conversation just **might** find help at Ireland's Blarney Castle.

(1) The block of limestone known as the Blarney Stone _____ set in a tower in 1446 at Blarney Castle. (2) According to legend, when the king of the castle saved an old woman from drowning, she promised the king that if he kissed the stone, he _____ be able to speak sweetly and convincingly. (3) Since then, Irish people claim that anyone who kisses the Blarney Stone _____ receive the gift of eloquence. (4) Today, a person who _____ speak witty words of flattery is said to have "the gift of blarney." (5) Tourists who _____ heard the legend travel to the castle near Cork, Ireland, hoping that the Blarney Stone will work its magic on their words.

BACKGROUND

In late antiquity and the Middle Ages, grammar, rhetoric, and logic were organized into the *trivium*, the three language arts of education. The trivium and *quadrivium* (geometry, arithmetic, astronomy, and music) together formed the Seven Liberal Arts. Grammar meant the study of Latin until the eighteenth and nineteenth centuries, when English and other vernacular languages began to displace Latin as the language of education.

ANSWERS: EXERCISE 8–4

Note: The following answers create the only possible set. Although both *can* and *will* would be correct in item 3, only *can* is correct in item 4. (Used in item 4, *will* creates a tense-sequence error.)

1. was
2. would
3. will
4. can
5. have

ANSWERS AND COVERAGE: EXERCISE 8–5

This exercise has many possible sets of answers. Only item 4 is invariable and only by default. Its answer must be *do* because *do* cannot be used in any other item. Here is one set of answers.

1. will [*should* is acceptable, suggesting speculation; *will* is more definite]

2. must [*should* is acceptable, suggesting possibility; *can* is acceptable but less appropriate than *must* or *should*]

3. should [*will* is acceptable, suggesting certainty; *should* is acceptable, suggesting possibility; although both *can* and *must* are grammatically acceptable, they suggest a fervent stance that is less appropriate in tone than the other choices]

4. do [only item where *do* is correct]

5. can [*should* is acceptable, suggesting possibility; although *must* is grammatically correct, its suggestions of either demand or resignation are inappropriate in tone; *will* is grammatically correct but the singular subject is logically inappropriate for a predictive general statement—compare *Salespeople will expect . . .*]

EXTRA EXERCISE C

Circle all transitive verbs and underline all intransitive verbs in the following paragraph.

1. Yellowstone National Park is the oldest and largest park in the national system.

2. It lies in the northwestern corner of Wyoming, slightly overlapping the boundaries of Montana on the north and Idaho on the west and south.

➡

EXERCISE 8-5

Consulting section 8e, use each of the auxiliary verbs listed below to fill in the blanks. For some sentences, more than one correct answer is possible, but use each auxiliary verb only once.

must   should   will   can   ~~are~~   do

EXAMPLE   After years of being ignored by car dealers, women **are** finally being recognized as intelligent customers.

(1) In the next few years, women _____ buy about half the cars sold in the United States. (2) To be effective, car salespeople _____ pay attention to the woman buyer. (3) The old ideas that women are interested only in style and color _____ change. (4) Salespeople now realize that women _____ understand technical information about a car's performance. (5) A salesperson _____ expect both men and women buyers to evaluate factors like dependability, value, safety, and comfort.

Using intransitive and transitive verbs

A verb is **intransitive** when an OBJECT is not required to complete its meaning: *I sing loudly*. A verb is **transitive** when an object is necessary to complete its meaning: *I need a guitar*. Some verbs are transitive only (for example, *need, have, like, owe, remember*). Many verbs have both transitive and intransitive meanings. Other verbs are intransitive only. Dictionaries usually label verbs as transitive (vt) or intransitive (vi). Chart 62 shows how transitive and intransitive verbs function.

COMPARISON OF INTRANSITIVE AND TRANSITIVE VERBS   62

INTRANSITIVE (OBJECT NOT NEEDED)

They **sat** together quietly. [*Together* and *quietly* are not DIRECT OBJECTS; they are MODIFIERS.]

The cat **sees** in the dark. [*In the dark* is not a direct object; it is a modifier.]

I can **hear** well. [*Well* is not a direct object; it is a modifier.]

TRANSITIVE (OBJECT NEEDED)

They **sent** a birthday card to me. [*a birthday card* = direct object]

The cat **sees** the dog [*dog* = direct object]

I can **hear** you. [*you* = direct object]

The verbs *lie* and *lay* are particularly confusing. *Lie* is intransitive (it cannot be followed by an object). *Lay* is transitive (it must be followed by an object). Some of their forms, however, are similar. Get to know these forms so that you can use them with ease.

	LIE	LAY
SIMPLE FORM	lie	lay
PAST TENSE	lay	laid
PAST PARTICIPLE	lain	laid
-S FORM	lies	lays
PRESENT PARTICIPLE	lying	laying

To *lie* means "to recline, to place oneself down, or to remain"; to *lay* means "to place something down." Note from the examples that the word *lay* is both the past tense of *lie* and the present-tense simple form of *lay*.

INTRANSITIVE

PRESENT TENSE	The hikers **lie** down to rest.
PAST TENSE	The hikers **lay** down to rest.

TRANSITIVE

PRESENT TENSE	The hikers **lay** their backpacks on a rock. [*Backpacks* is an object.]
PAST TENSE	The hikers **laid** their backpacks on a rock. [*Backpacks* is an object.]

EXERCISE 8-6

Consulting section 8f, in each blank write the correct word from each pair in parentheses.

EXAMPLE   Memory of last year's outdoor camping trip (lies, lays) **lies** heavy on my mind.

(1) Planning on two days and a night in the woods, we left early and were soon (lying, laying) _____ our supplies in the shade of an old oak tree. (2) We were sure the supplies could safely (lay, lie) _____ in that spot all afternoon. (3) When the sun rose higher in the sky, the shade moved so that each bundle of food (lay, laid) _____ in the sun for hours. (4) As the spot where our gear was (laying, lying) _____ heated up, our food overheated and spoiled. (5) While we (lay, laid) _____ hungry in our tent that night, we vowed not to go camping again.

EXTRA EXERCISE C, cont.

3. The planners originally designed the park to run 62 miles east–west and 54 miles north–south.

4. Yellowstone has several lofty plateaus, and the Continental Divide crosses it.

5. The Yellowstone River flows north into Yellowstone Lake, then through its canyon across Montana to join the Missouri.

6. The most famous sights in Yellowstone Park are the geysers.

7. The park has more than 3,000 springs, pools, and geysers.

8. Old Faithful is the most famous of the geysers, but in the same basin with it are a number of other impressive water jets.

9. Wildlife in the park, which includes bear, deer, elk, antelope, and mountain sheep, is protected.

ANSWERS: EXTRA EXERCISE C

1. is (intransitive)

2. lies (intransitive)

3. designed (transitive)

4. has (transitive); crosses (transitive)

5. flows (intransitive)

6. are (intransitive)

7. has (transitive)

8. is (intransitive); are (intransitive)

9. includes (transitive); is (intransitive)

ANSWERS AND COVERAGE: EXERCISE 8–6

1. laying [3rd person plural past progressive of *lay*]

2. lie [simple form of *lie* with modal auxiliary verb *could*]

3. lay [3rd person singular past tense of *lie*]

4. lying [3rd person singular past progressive of *lie*]

5. lay [3rd person plural past tense of *lie*]

VERB TENSE

8g Understanding verb tense

Verbs use **tense** to express time. They do this by changing form. English has six verb tenses, divided into simple and perfect groups. The three **simple tenses** divide time into present, past, and future. The **present tense** describes what happens regularly, what takes place in the present, and what is consistently or generally true: *Rick **wants** to speak Spanish fluently*. The **past tense** tells of an action completed or a condition ended: *Rick **wanted** to improve rapidly*. The **future tense** indicates action yet to be taken or a condition not yet experienced: *Rick **will want** to progress even further next year*.

The three **perfect tenses** also divide time into present, past, and future. They show more complex time relationships than do the simple tenses, as explained in 8i.

The three simple tenses and the three perfect tenses also have **progressive forms**. These forms show an ongoing or a continuing dimension to whatever the verb describes, as explained in 8j. Chart 63 summarizes verb tenses and progressive forms.

SUMMARY OF TENSES—INCLUDING PROGRESSIVE FORMS 63

	REGULAR VERB	IRREGULAR VERB	PROGRESSIVE FORM
SIMPLE TENSES			
PRESENT	I talk	I eat	I am talking; I am eating
PAST	I talked	I ate	I was talking; I was eating
FUTURE	I will talk	I will eat	I will be talking; I will be eating
PERFECT TENSES			
PRESENT PERFECT	I have talked	I have eaten	I have been talking; I have been eating
PAST PERFECT	I had talked	I had eaten	I had been talking; I had been eating
FUTURE PERFECT	I will have talked	I will have eaten	I will have been talking; I will have been eating

REFERENCES TO SUPPLEMENTS

This topic is included in the TASP writing competency test. Refer students to *Preparing for the TASP* by M. Saenz.

See transparency 7–5 on shifts of verb tense in the *Prentice Hall/Simon & Schuster Transparencies for Writers* by D. Carter.

BACKGROUND

Old English, ancestor of our language as we know it today, used only two tenses, present and past. All other information, such as number, person, mood, and voice, was indicated by inflectional endings. All that remains of the personal endings is the *-es* or *-s* of the third person singular, which comes from the Middle English and Early Modern English *-eth* used by Chaucer, translators of the King James Bible, and Shakespeare. English verbs, like all their Germanic cognates, are distinguished by their division into weak and strong classes. In Old English the strong classes indicated tense by changing the medial vowels; the weak ones did so by their endings. After the Norman Invasion, when French and Latin became the languages of power (the court and the church), many strong English verbs became weak, adopting the *-ed* ending to indicate tense changes. New verbs admitted to the language were all placed in the weak category. Today the mixture of strong and weak forms makes it necessary for English speakers to memorize the principal parts of irregular verbs.

❖ ESL NOTE: Chart 63 shows that most verb tenses are formed by combining one or more AUXILIARY VERBS with the SIMPLE FORM, the PRESENT PARTICIPLE, or the PAST PARTICIPLE of a MAIN VERB. Auxiliary verbs are necessary in the formation of most tenses, so be sure not to omit them.

NO   I **talking** to you.

YES   I **am talking** to you.❖

Using the simple present tense   8h

The **simple present tense** uses the simple form of the verb (see 8-b). It describes what happens regularly, what takes place in the present, and what is generally or consistently true. Also, it can convey a future occurrence with verbs like *start, stop, begin, end, arrive,* and *depart.*

> Calculus class **meets** every morning. [regularly occurring action]
> Mastering calculus **takes** time. [general truth]
> The course **ends** in eight weeks. [future event with end]

❖ VERB ALERT FOR WRITING ABOUT LITERATURE: Use the present tense to describe or discuss action in a work of literature, no matter how old the work; see 37b-2.

> In Shakespeare's *Romeo and Juliet*, Juliet's father **wants** her to marry Paris, but Juliet **loves** Romeo.❖

For action prior to or after the action you are describing or discussing, use the correct sequence of tenses as explained in 8k.

Forming and using the perfect tenses   8i

The **perfect tenses** generally describe actions or occurrences completed, or to be completed, before a more recent point in time. They use the PAST PARTICIPLE (see 8b) together with AUXILIARY VERBS to form VERB PHRASES. For the present perfect, use *has* for THIRD-PERSON SINGULAR SUBJECTS and *have* for all other subjects, along with the past participle.

PRESENT PERFECT	Our government **has offered** to help. [action completed but condition still in effect]
PRESENT PERFECT	The drought **has created** terrible hardship. [condition completed and still prevailing]
PRESENT PERFECT	We **have** always **believed** in freedom of speech. [condition true once and still true] ➜

TEACHING TIP: ESL
The term "present" can be misleading, since the simple present tense does not describe the present moment; it is "timeless" (The sun *rises* in the east and *sets* in the west) or general (*Democracy* means "rule by the people"), while the present progressive expresses "now." Compare the following: I *work* in an office. I *am working* on a report [now].

EXTRA EXERCISE D
Identify the tenses of the verbs in the following sentences.

1. My neighbor walks to work every morning.

2. Thomas is studying for his chemistry examination.

3. I will take my lunch with me to the park.

4. The secretary has been typing the manuscript for days.

5. Her mother will be speaking with the supervisor in the morning.

6. Ms. Conrad had been planning to change jobs when her company was sold.

7. I closed my bank account yesterday.

8. We will have discussed the topic by the time you get to the meeting.

9. The program has generated a great deal of interest.

10. The babies in the nursery were crying when I went in.

ANSWERS: EXTRA EXERCISE D

1. present
2. present progressive
3. future
4. present perfect progressive
5. future progressive
6. past perfect progressive; past
7. past
8. future perfect; present
9. present perfect
10. past progressive

EXTRA EXERCISE E

Supply the progressive form of an appropriate verb in the blanks in the following sentences. (Answers will vary.)

1. Don't bother me now; I am _____.

2. My brother is _____ to apply for a job in France.

3. The committee is _____ at 5 P.M.

4. The professor was _____ on the topic of the European Common Market.

5. The doctor was _____ in the hospital.

6. My dog was _____ in the yard.

7. I can't go swimming because I am _____.

8. The garden is _____ more beautifully every day.

9. Whose car is _____ in the driveway?

10. The telephone has been _____ all day.

8i
cont.

For the past perfect, use *had* with the past participle. For the future perfect, use *will have* with the past participle.

PAST PERFECT	As soon as the tornado **had passed**, the heavy rain started. [Both events occurred in the past; the earlier event, the tornado's passing, was completed before the later event, the rain's starting, took place, so the earlier event uses *had*.]
FUTURE PERFECT	Our chickens' egg production **will have reached** 500 per day by next year. [The event will be complete before a specified or predictable time.]

8j **Forming and using progressive forms**

Progressive forms show an ongoing action or condition. They also express habitual or recurring actions or conditions. They use the PRESENT PARTICIPLE (the *-ing* form) of the verb together with the appropriate form of the verb *be* as an AUXILIARY VERB. (See Chart 63.)

For the present progressive, use the form of *be* that fits with the subject in PERSON and NUMBER, plus the present participle: *I am thinking*, *you are* thinking, *she is* thinking. For the past progressive, use *was* or *were* to fit with the subject in person and number, plus the present participle: *I was thinking*, *you were thinking*, *she was thinking*. For the present perfect progressive, use *have been* or *has been* to fit with the subject. In all other progressive tenses, the auxiliary verbs do not change form to show person and number.

PRESENT PROGRESSIVE	The smog **is stinging** everyone's eyes. [event taking place now]
PAST PROGRESSIVE	Eye drops **were selling** well last week. [event ongoing in the past within stated limits]
FUTURE PROGRESSIVE	We **will be ordering** more eye drops than usual this month. [recurring event that will take place in the future]
PRESENT PERFECT PROGRESSIVE	Scientists **have been warning** us about air pollution for years. [recurring event that took place in the past and may still take place]
PAST PERFECT PROGRESSIVE	We **had been ordering** three cases of eye drops a month until the smog worsened. [recurring past event that has now ended]
FUTURE PERFECT PROGRESSIVE	In May, we **will have owned** this pharmacy for five years. [ongoing condition to be completed at a specific time in the future]

EXERCISE 8-7

Consulting sections 8g through 8j, select the verb in parentheses that best suits the meaning. If more than one answer is possible, be prepared to explain the differences in meaning between the choices.

EXAMPLE   Before 1960, astronomers (have not spotted, had not spotted) stars that send out both light and sound waves.

         Before 1960, astronomers *had not spotted* stars that send out both light and sound waves.

1. In 1960, two astronomers at Mount Palomar Observatory (had discovered, discovered) a starlike object at the edge of the universe.

2. The astronomers were astounded to discover that this object (emits, was emitting) as much light as 1,000 galaxies.

3. Today, we (use, are using) the name *quasar,* which (stands for, stood for) *quasistellar. Quasistellar* (meant, means) "starlike object."

4. Up to now, more than 300 quasars (had been found, have been found) in space.

5. Although astronomers today generally (had agreed, agree) that quasars are powerful, fast-moving energy sources, they (will contradict, contradict) each other's theories about the origin of quasars.

6. One group currently (has been believing, believes) that quasars (consisted, consist) of giant, swirling masses of gas.

7. These astronomers (say, said) that the gas (collapsed, is collapsing) on itself all the time, so that quasars (had generated, are generating) and releasing tremendous energy.

8. Other scientists (were asserting, assert) that quasars (develop, have been developing) from explosions of matter and antimatter, just as science fiction writers (predict, have been predicting) for many years.

9. When scientists (had conducted, conduct) experiments that (brought, bring) matter and antimatter together, an explosion (will occur, occurs).

10. Until we (understand, understood) more about the birth and death of galaxies, we probably (will not discover, have not discovered) the real story behind quasars.

Using accurate tense sequence   8k

     When you want your sentences to deliver messages about actions, occurrences, or states that occur over time, you must depend on verb tenses in sequences. These sequences often include more than one verb. Using **accurate tense sequences** —that is, showing time relationships correctly—is important for clear communication (see Chart 64).

ANSWERS AND COVERAGE: EXERCISE 8–7

1. discovered [past tense for completed action; 8g]

2. was emitting [past progressive for a continuing past action in the past concurrent with the time of *were astounded;* 8j]

3. use [simple present for regularly recurring action]; stands for, means [simple present for general truth; 8h]

4. have found [present perfect for action completed and condition still prevailing; 8i]

5. agree [simple present for general truth]; contradict [simple present for recurring action; 8h]

6. believes [simple present for current action]; consist [simple present for general truth; 8h]

7. say; generates; release [simple present for regularly recurring actions; 8h]

8. assert; develop [simple present for regularly recurring actions; 8h]; have predicted [present perfect for action completed but condition still in effect; 8i]

9. conduct; bring; occurs [simple present for regularly occurring general truths; 8h]

10. understand [simple present for general truth; 8h]; will not discover [simple future for condition not yet experienced; 8g]

TEACHING TIP

In *Teaching One-to-One: The Writing Conference* (NCTE, 1986), Muriel Harris suggests that teachers help students with tense shift problems by taking a passage and asking students to identify the tense of every sentence. After several sentences most students recognize problems in the tense sequence.

EXTRA EXERCISE F

Circle the verbs in the following sentences, then name their tenses and explain what meaning is expressed by them.

1. Dolphins, porpoises, and whales belong to the order Cetacea, which are not fish, but mammals.

2. They give birth to their young, nourish them with milk, and have warm blood.

3. Once whales probably lived on the land and walked on four legs, but now they are completely aquatic.

4. Once they had left the land and moved to the water, their body structure changed radically.

5. Because they are land mammals that have become adapted to an aquatic existence, if water enters their lungs, they will die.

6. Consequently, when a whale is diving beneath the surface, it literally holds its breath by closing its nostrils.

7. Whales dive for different periods of time to various depths.

8. The humpback whale has been known to remain submerged for twenty minutes and the blue whale for fifty, though both could probably remain longer if necessary.

9. For years scientists have been researching the depths to which the various types of whale can dive.

10. The sperm whale has been known to dive to a depth of over 3,000 feet, subjecting it to a pressure of around 1,400 pounds per square inch.

8k
cont.

SUMMARY OF SEQUENCE OF TENSES 64

WHEN INDEPENDENT-CLAUSE VERB IS IN THE SIMPLE PRESENT TENSE, FOR THE DEPENDENT-CLAUSE VERB:

- Use the PRESENT TENSE to show same-time action.
  The director **says** that the movie **is** a tribute to Chaplin.
  I **avoid** shellfish because I **am** allergic to it.
- Use the PAST TENSE to show earlier action.
  I **am** sure that I **deposited** the check.
- Use the PRESENT PERFECT TENSE to show (1) a period of time extending from some point in the past to the present—often accompanied by for or since—or (2) an indefinite past time.
  They **say** that they **have lived** in Canada since 1979.
  I **believe** that I **have seen** that movie before.
- Use the FUTURE TENSE for action to come.
  The book **is** open because I **will be reading** it later.

WHEN INDEPENDENT-CLAUSE VERB IS IN THE PAST TENSE, FOR THE DEPENDENT-CLAUSE VERB:

- Use the PAST PERFECT TENSE to show earlier action.
  The sprinter **knew** that she **had broken** the record.
- Use the present tense to state a general truth.
  Christopher Columbus discovered that the world **is** round.

WHEN INDEPENDENT-CLAUSE VERB IS IN THE PRESENT PERFECT OR PAST PERFECT TENSE, FOR THE DEPENDENT-CLAUSE VERB:

- Use the past tense.
  The agar plate **has become** moldy since I **poured** it last week.
  Sugar prices **had** already **declined** when artificial sweeteners first **appeared**.

WHEN THE INDEPENDENT-CLAUSE VERB IS IN THE FUTURE TENSE, FOR THE DEPENDENT-CLAUSE VERB:

- Use the present tense to show action happening at the same time.
  You **will be** rich if you **win** the prize.
- Use the past tense to show earlier action.
  You **will** surely **win** the prize if you **remembered** to mail the entry form.
- Use the present perfect tense to show future action earlier than the action of the independent-clause verb.
  The river **will flood** again next year unless we **have built** a better dam by then.

SUMMARY OF SEQUENCE OF TENSES (continued)   64

WHEN THE INDEPENDENT-CLAUSE VERB IS IN THE FUTURE PERFECT TENSE, FOR THE DEPENDENT-CLAUSE VERB:

■ Use either the present tense or the present perfect tense.

> Dr. Chang **will have delivered** 5,000 babies by the time she **retires**.

> Dr. Chang **will have delivered** 5,000 babies by the time she **has retired**.

❖ ALERT: When an independent-clause verb is in the future tense, do not use a future-tense verb in the dependent clause.

NO   The river **will flood** again next year unless we **will build** a better dam.

YES   The river **will flood** again next year unless we build a better dam. [Dependent-clause verb *build* is in the present tense.]

YES   The river **will flood** again next year unless we **have built** a better dam by then. [Dependent-clause verb *have built* is in the present perfect tense.] ❖

Tense sequences that include INFINITIVES or PARTICIPLES must be correct. The **present infinitive** can name or describe an activity or occurrence coming either at the same time or after the time expressed in the MAIN VERB.

> I **hope to buy** a used car. [*To buy* comes at a future time. *Hope* is the main verb, and its action is now.]

> I **hoped to buy** a used car. [*Hoped* is the main verb, and its action is over.]

> I **had hoped to buy** a used car. [*Had hoped* is the main verb, and its action is over.]

The **present participle** (a verb's -*ing* form) can describe action happening at the same time.

> **Driving** his new car, the man **smiled**. [The driving and the smiling happened at the same time.]

ANSWERS: EXTRA EXERCISE F

1. belong [present tense, expresses a general truth]; are [present tense, expresses a general truth]

2. give [present tense, expresses a general truth]; nourish [present tense, expresses a general truth]; have [present tense, expresses a general truth]

3. lived [past tense, expresses past event]; walked [past tense, expresses past event]; are [present tense, expresses current fact]

4. had left [past perfect tense, expresses an act completed in the past before another one took place]; changed [past tense, expresses an act completed in the past]

5. are [present tense, expresses current truth]; have become adapted [present perfect tense, act begun and completed in the past but continuing into the present]; enters [present tense, expresses general truth]; will die [future tense, expresses future action]

6. is diving [present progressive tense, expresses an action taking place at the moment]; holds [present tense, expresses regularly occurring action]

7. dive [present tense, expresses habitual action]

8. has been known [present perfect tense, expresses action in the past which continues into the present]; could remain [present tense with modal auxiliary, expresses possible action]

9. have been researching [present perfect progressive, expresses action ongoing in the past and likely to continue in the future]; can dive [present tense with modal auxiliary, expresses possible action]

10. has been known [present perfect tense, expresses action in the past that continues into the present]

8k
cont.

To describe an action that occurs before the action in the MAIN VERB, use the PERFECT INFINITIVE (*to have gone, to have smiled*); the PAST PARTICIPLE; or the PRESENT PERFECT PARTICIPLE (*having gone, having smiled*).

> Candida **claimed to have written** fifty short stories in college. [First Candida wrote; then she claimed.]
>
> **Pleased** with the short story, Candida **mailed** it to several magazines. [First Candida was pleased; then she mailed.]
>
> **Having sold** one short story, Candida **invested** in a word processor. [First Candida sold a story; then she bought a word processor.]

EXERCISE 8-8

Consulting section 8k, select the verb form in parentheses that best suits the sequence of tenses. Be ready to explain your choices.

EXAMPLE   When he (is, was) seven years old, Yo Yo Ma, possibly the world's greatest living cellist (moves, moved) to the United States with his family.

                  When he *was* seven years old, Yo Yo Ma, possibly the world's greatest living cellist, *moved* to the United States with his family.

1. Yo Yo Ma, who (had been born, was born) in France to Chinese parents, (lived, lives) in Boston, Massachusetts, today and (toured, tours) as one of the world's greatest cellists.

2. By the time his next concert tour ends, Mr. Ma (will be, will have been) away from home more than half the year.

3. Mr. Ma's older sister, Dr. Yeou-Cheng Ma, was nearly the person with the concert career. She had been training to become a concert violinist until her brother's musical genius (began, had begun) to be noticed.

4. Even though Dr. Ma eventually (becomes, became) a physician, she still (had been playing, plays) the violin.

5. The family interest in music (continues, was continuing), for Mr. Ma's children (take, had taken) piano lessons.

6. Although most people today (knew, know) Mr. Ma as a brilliant cellist, he (was making, has made) films as well.

7. Last year, while he (had been traveling, was traveling) in the Kalahari desert, he (was filming, filmed) dances of southern Africa's Bush people.

8. Mr. Ma first (becomes, became) interested in the Kalahari people when he (had studied, studied) anthropology 20 years ago at Harvard University.

9. Living near Harvard University now, Mr. Ma has been known to point out to visitors the university library where, he claims, he (fell asleep, was falling asleep) in the stacks when he (had been, was) a student.

10. Indicating another building, Mr. Ma admits that in one of its classrooms he almost (failed, had failed) German.

ANSWERS AND COVERAGE: EXERCISE 8–8

1. was born [dependent clause past tense for completed action]; lives [independent clause present tense for happening now]; tours [present tense for regularly occurring action]

2. will have been [independent clause future perfect tense for action completed by a specified time]

3. began [dependent clause past tense]

4. became [dependent clause simple past for a completed action]; plays [independent clause simple present for regularly occurring action]

5. continues [independent clause simple present]; take [dependent clause simple present for same-time action]

6. know [dependent clause simple present for general truth]; has made [independent clause present perfect for action completed but condition still in effect]

7. was traveling [independent clause in simple past for action completed in the past]; filmed [dependent clause in past progressive for ongoing action completed in the past]

8. became; studied [independent and dependent clauses in simple past for actions completed in the past]

9. fell asleep . . . was [dependent clause simple past for completed past action]

10. failed [dependent clause simple past for completed past action]

EXERCISE 8-9

The verbs in each of the following sentences are in correct sequence. For each sentence, change the main verb as directed in the parentheses. Then, consulting section 8k, adjust dependent-clause verbs, infinitives, or participles if necessary to maintain correct verb sequence. Some sentences may have several correct answers.

EXAMPLE   When people exercise regularly, their physical fitness improves almost daily. (Change *exercise* to *exercised*.)
               When people *exercised* regularly, their physical fitness *improved* almost daily.

1. As research studies show, regular exercise boosts oxygen in the blood and increases physical endurance. (Change *show* to *showed*.)
2. Another effect of exercise was that it caused the body to produce substances linked to feelings of well-being. (Change *was* to *is*.)
3. Some people who exercise regularly for several months find that exercise makes them more creative because it helps them to think clearly and concentrate well. (Change *exercise* to *had exercised*.)
4. After several months, exercisers also had a better sense of their own capabilities and exhibited signs of greater self-esteem. (Change *had* to *will have*.)
5. Because effective exercise required that a person make and observe a consistent routine, regular exercisers became efficient time managers. (Change *required* to *requires*.)

ANSWERS: EXERCISE 8–9

1. As research studies *showed*, regular exercise *boosted* oxygen in the blood and *increased* physical endurance.

2. Another effect of exercise *is* that it *causes* the body to produce substances linked to feelings of well-being.

3. People who exercise regularly for several months sometimes find that exercise *can make* them more creative because it *helps* (or *can help*) them to think clearly and concentrate well.

4. After several months, exercisers also *will have* a better sense of their own capabilities and *will exhibit* signs of greater self-esteem.

5. Because effective exercise *requires* that a person make and observe a consistent routine, regular exercisers *become* efficient time managers.

MOOD

Understanding mood   8l

Mood refers to the ability of verbs to convey a writer's attitude toward a statement. The most common mood in English is the **indicative mood**. It is used for statements about real things, or highly likely ones, and for questions about fact.

INDICATIVE   The door to the tutoring center opened.
               She seemed to be looking for someone.
               Do you want to see a tutor?

The **imperative mood** expresses commands and direct requests. When the subject is omitted in an imperative sentence—and it often is—the subject is implied to be either *you* or the indefinite pronoun *anybody*, *somebody*, or *everybody*.

8l
cont.

❧ **PUNCTUATION ALERT:** A strong command is followed by an exclamation point; however, a mild command or a request is followed by a period (see 23a and 23e).

IMPERATIVE Please shut the door.

       Watch out, that hinge is broken! ❧

The **subjunctive mood** can express speculations and other unreal conditions, conjectures, wishes, recommendations, indirect requests, and demands. Subjunctive verb forms are used much less often in English than they once were. Still, they are common for expressing unreal conditions or conjectures in *if* CLAUSES and in such PHRASES as *far be it from me* and *come what may*.

SUBJUNCTIVE If I **were** you, I would ask for a tutor.

BACKGROUND

William Safire recently quoted Robert Burchfield, overseer of the new four-volume *Oxford English Dictionary*, on the supposed death of the subjunctive mood: "'This very useful verbal distinction is not at all tottering toward extinction.'" Safire adds:

> If it were not for the subjunctive, we would be less able to express desire, supposition, doubt; more important, we would find it hard to set up a situation contrary to fact—a shocker, something ridiculous—to see how we would deal with it.

Then he gives a complex but thought-provoking example:

> A law professor testified at a recent Congressional hearing that Senator John C. Danforth's product-liability bill "reads as though it were written by James Joyce." Obviously, the bill was not written by the long-dead author of the punctuation-disdaining novel "Ulysses," which meant that the witness's don't-you-believe-it subjunctive *were* was necessary; if the indicative, here-comes-a-fact *was* had been used, hordes of illiterate legislators would have been led to assume that James Joyce was a Danforth staffer.

8m

Using correct subjunctive forms

For the **present subjunctive**, always use the simple form of the verb (see 8b) for all PERSONS and NUMBERS.

The prosecutor asks that **she testify** [not *testifies*] again.

It is important that **they be** [not *are*] allowed to testify.

For the **past subjunctive**, use the same form as the simple past tense: *I wish that **I had** a car.* The one exception is for the past subjunctive of *be*: Use *were* for all persons and numbers.

I wish that **I were** [not *was*] leaving on vacation today.

They asked if **she were** [not *was*] leaving on vacation today.

8m-1

Using the subjunctive in *if, as if, as though,* and *unless* clauses

In dependent clauses introduced by *if* and sometimes by *unless,* the subjunctive is often used to describe speculations or conditions contrary to fact.

If **it were** [not *was*] to rain, attendance at the race would be disappointing. [speculation]

In an unless clause, the subjunctive signals that what the clause says is highly unlikely.

Unless **rain were** [not *was*] to create floods, the race will be held this Sunday. [Floods are highly unlikely.]

The runner looked as if **he were** [not *was*] winded.

218

❖ ALERT: Not every clause introduced by **if, unless, as if,** or **as though** requires the subjunctive. Use the subjunctive only when the dependent clause describes a speculation or condition contrary to fact.

INDICATIVE	If **she is** going to leave late, **I will** drive her to the race. [Her leaving late is highly likely.]
SUBJUNCTIVE	If **she were** going to leave late, **I would** drive her to the race. [Her leaving late is speculative.] ❖

Using the subjunctive in *that* clauses for wishes, indirect requests, recommendations, and demands

When *that* clauses describe wishes, requests, demands, or recommendations, the subjunctive can convey the message.

I wish that this **race were** [not *was*] over. [wish about something happening now]

He wishes that **he had seen** [not *saw*] the race. [wish about something that is past]

The judges are demanding that the **doctor examine** [not *examines*] the runners. [demand for something that would happen in the future]

❖ ALERT: Modal auxiliary verbs like *would, could, might,* and *should* can convey speculations and conditions contrary to fact: *If the **runner** were* [not *was*] *faster, **we would** see a better race.* When the independent clause expresses a conditional statement with a modal auxiliary, be sure to use the appropriate subjunctive form, not another modal auxiliary, in the dependent clause.

NO	If **I would have** trained for the race, **I might have** won.
YES	If **I had** trained for the race, **I might have** won. ❖

EXERCISE 8-10

Consulting sections 8l and 8m, fill in the blanks with the appropriate subjunctive form of the verb in parentheses.

EXAMPLE   Imagining the possibility of brain transplants requires that we (to be) **be** open minded, as it (to be) **were**.

(1) If almost any organ other than the brain (to be) _____ the candidate for a swap, we would probably give our consent. (2) If the

---

ALTERNATIVE EXAMPLES OF SUBJUNCTIVE MOOD

People find it interesting to speculate about how the future *could be* affected if a single aspect of our world *were* different today. For example, if the average yearly temperature *were* only a few degrees higher, the oceans *would* rise due to the melting of the polar icecaps. If serious worldwide droughts *were* to occur in several successive summers, the food supply *would* dwindle. Unless science *were* able to divert the swelling oceans or grow crops without the use of water, civilization as we know it *would be* radically changed. It is, consequently, important that mankind *recognize* the importance of environmental decisions. The world *should* not act as though the future *were* inevitably bad. If, in the early part of this century, the industrialized world *had considered* the effects of water and air pollution, our world *would* be a healthier one today.

TEACHING TIP: ESL

For ESL students. conditions and wishes are often difficult to master because they employ changes in verb forms that usually indicate *time* shifts to indicate hypothetical or unreal states. For example, the past form in a wish or *present* unreal condition (*I wish I had a car* or *If I **were** you. . . .*) refers to the present. Similarly, the past perfect form indicates past unreality (*I wish he had told me his problem*). Students can better understand these tricky structures when they can be seen and analyzed, preferably in essays the class is reading.

ANSWERS AND COVERAGE: EXERCISE 8–10

1. were [8m–1]

→

8m-2
cont.

brain (to be) _____ to hold whatever impulses form our personalities, few people would want to risk a transplant. (3) Many popular movies have asked that we (to suspend) _____ disbelief and imagine the consequences should a personality actually (to be) _____ transferred to another body. (4) In real life, however, the complexities of a successful brain transplant require that not-yet-developed surgical techniques (to be) _____ used. (5) For example, it would be essential that during the actual transplant each one of the 500 trillion nerve connections within the brain (to continue) _____ to function as though the brain (to be) _____ lying undisturbed in a living human body.

VOICE

8n   ## Understanding voice

Voice refers to a verb's ability to show whether a SUBJECT acts or receives the action named by the verb. English has two voices: active and passive. In the **active voice**, the subject performs the action.

> Most clams ***live*** in salt water. [The subject *clams* does the acting; clams *live*.]

> They ***burrow*** into the sandy bottoms of shallow waters. [The subject *they* does the acting; they *burrow*.]

In the **passive voice**, the subject is acted upon, and the person or thing doing the acting often appears as the OBJECT of the PREPOSITION *by*. Verbs in the passive voice add forms of *be* and *have*, as well as *will*, as auxiliaries to the PAST PARTICIPLE of the MAIN VERB.

> Clams **are considered** a delicacy by many people. [The subject *clams* is acted upon by *people*, the object of the preposition *by*.]

> They **are** also **admired** by crabs and starfish. [The subject *they* is acted upon by *crabs and starfish*, the objects of the preposition *by*.]

When you write, your decisions about AUDIENCE and PURPOSE should influence the voice that you choose for a sentence. Misusing voice usually creates problems of writing style rather than problems of incorrect grammar. For ways to identify and correct confusing SHIFTS in voice, see 15a-2.

ANSWERS AND COVERAGE: EXERCISE 8–10, cont.

2. were [8m–1]
3. suspend [8m–2]; be [8m–1]
4. be [8m–1]
5. continue [8m–1]; were [8m–2]

REFERENCE TO SUPPLEMENTS

For this topic in the CLAST writing competency test, refer students to ch. 2, section B3b of *Preparing for the CLAST* by S. Patterson.

TEACHING TIP

"To choose between the active and the passive," writes Joseph M. Williams, "we have to answer three questions: First, must our audience know who is performing the action? Second, are we maintaining a logically consistent string of subjects? And third, if the string of subjects is consistent, is it the right string of subjects?" (*Style: Ten Lessons in Clarity and Grace*, 3rd ed. [Chicago: Scott, Foresman, 1989], p. 24). Writers may choose the passive voice when they don't know the agent of the action, don't care, or want to keep that information confidential. Writers may also choose the voices of verbs "to create a sequence of sentences with subjects that the reader will feel are consistent, logically related," to avoid "constantly shifting from one unrelated subject to another" (p. 25).

Writing in the active voice, not the passive voice, except to convey special types of emphasis

8o

Because the active voice emphasizes the doer of an action, active constructions are more direct and dramatic. Active constructions often use fewer words than passive constructions and are therefore more concise (see 16a-2). Any sentence in the passive voice that expresses the doer of the action can easily be converted to the active voice.

PASSIVE   African tribal masks are often imitated by Western sculptors.

ACTIVE   Western sculptors often imitate African tribal masks.

The passive voice, however, does have some uses. If you learn what they are, you can use the passive to advantage.

Using the passive voice when the doer of the action is unknown or unimportant

8o-1

When no one knows who or what did something, the passive voice is useful.

The lock **was broken** sometime after four o'clock. [Who broke the lock is unknown.]

When the doer of an action is unimportant, writers often use the passive voice.

In 1899, the year I was born, **a peace conference was held** at The Hague. [The doers of the action—holders of the conference—are unimportant to White's point.]

—E. B. WHITE, "Unity"

Using the passive voice to focus attention on the action rather than on the doer of the action

8o-2

The passive voice emphasizes the action, while the active voice focuses on the doer of the action. In a passage about important contributions to the history of science, you might want to emphasize a doer by using the active voice.

ACTIVE   **Joseph Priestley discovered** oxygen in 1774.

EXTRA EXERCISE G

Identify the verbs in the following sentences, then decide if they are in the active or the passive voice.

1. Windsor Castle is an official residence of the monarchs of Great Britain.
2. In the year 1070 William the Conqueror built a fortress on the site it now occupies.
3. It was improved by succeeding rulers until the reign of Edward III (1327–1377).
4. Edward III demolished the old castle and built a new one.
5. Additions were made by later kings of England.
6. Sir Christopher Wren was asked by Charles II to design several important additions.
7. The state apartments are open to the public when the royal family is not in residence.
8. The state apartments include the grand staircase, state bedrooms, and reception rooms.
9. Many rulers were buried at Windsor Castle, including Henry VIII.

ANSWERS: EXTRA EXERCISE G

1. is, active voice
2. built, active voice; occupies, active voice
3. was improved, passive voice
4. demolished, active voice; built, active voice
5. were made, passive voice
6. was asked, passive voice
7. are, active voice; is, active voice
8. include, active voice
9. were buried, passive voice

ALTERNATE EXAMPLE: NECESSARY PASSIVE VOICE

In the days of Aristotle, air was believed to be one of four fundamental substances that could not be further subdivided into constituent components.

—Frederick K. Lutgens and Edward J. Tarbuck, *The Atmosphere*

ANSWERS AND COVERAGE: EXERCISE 8–11

Rewrites may vary somewhat from the possibilities shown here. Coverage is three passive to active sentences; two active to passive sentences.

1. *Passive, change to active*: A farmer chose a coffin in the shape of a green onion.

2. *Active, change to passive*: A hunter was buried by his family in a wooden coffin shaped like a leopard.

3. *Passive, change to active*: The friends and relatives of a dead chief carried his body through his fishing village in a large, pink, wooden replica of a fish.

4. *Active, change to passive*: About ten coffins a year can be turned out by woodcarver Paa Joe.

5. *Passive, change to active*: Museums have displayed a few of these fantasy coffins, although most of the coffins end up buried in the ground.

8o-2 cont.

But in a passage summarizing what is known about oxygen, you may want to make oxygen, rather than Priestley, the sentence subject. Doing so requires a passive-voice verb.

PASSIVE Oxygen **was discovered** in 1774 by Joseph Priestley.

PASSIVE The unsigned letter **was sent** before it **could be retrieved** from the mailroom. [Emphasis on events, not on the doers of the action.]

ACTIVE The postal clerk sent the unsigned letter before **I could retrieve** it from the mail room. [Emphasis is on the people rather than the actions.]

8o-3

Using active or passive voice in the social and natural sciences

Many writers in scientific disciplines (see Chapter 38) use the passive voice. Yet style manuals for scientific disciplines agree with the advice given in this section: Prefer the active voice. "Verbs are vigorous, direct communicators," point out the editors of the *Publication Manual of the American Psychological Association* (the APA). "Use the active rather than the passive voice. . . ."*

EXERCISE 8-11

Consulting sections 8n and 8o, determine first whether each of these sentences is in the active voice or the passive voice. Second, rewrite the sentence in the other voice. Then decide which voice best suits the meaning, and be ready to explain your choice.

EXAMPLE   In the West African country of Ghana, a few wood carvers are creating coffins that reflect their occupants' special interests. (*Active; change to passive.*)

In the West African country of Ghana, coffins that reflect their occupants' special interests *are being created* by a few wood carvers.

1. A coffin in the shape of a green onion was chosen by a farmer.
2. A hunter's family buried him in a wooden coffin shaped like a leopard.
3. A dead chief was carried through his fishing village by friends and relatives bearing his body in a large, pink, wooden replica of a fish.
4. Wood carver Paa Joe can turn out about ten coffins a year.
5. A few of these fantasy coffins have been displayed in museums, although most of them end up buried in the ground.

*American Psychological Association, *Publication Manual of the American Psychological Association*, 4th ed. (Washington: APA, 1994), 32.

Focus on Revising

REVISING YOUR WRITING

If you have trouble with your verbs when you write, including unnecessary use of the passive voice, go back to your writing and locate the problems. Using this chapter as a resource, revise your writing to correct these kinds of problems: *-s* endings (see 8c); *-ed* endings (see 8d); auxiliary verbs (see 8e); transitive and intransitive verbs, including *lie* and *lay* (see 8f); tenses (see 8g-8j); tense sequences (see 8k); the subjunctive mood (see 8l-8m); active versus passive voice (see 8n-8o).

CASE STUDY: REVISING TO ELIMINATE VERB ERRORS

In these case studies, you can observe a student writer revising. Then, you have the chance to revise other student writing on your own.

Observation

A student wrote the following draft for a course called Popular Culture. The assignment called for choosing one year in which important contributions were made to popular culture in the United States and then writing about it. While this paragraph is well organized and offers good examples to support its topic, the draft's effectiveness is diminished by the presence of errors in verb forms and verb tense, and by the unnecessary use of the passive.

Read through the draft. The verb errors are highlighted and explained. Before you look at the student's revision, revise the material yourself. Then compare what you and the student did.

unneeded passive voice: 8n

past perfect tense used; need simple past: 8i

subjunctive needed for *if* clause: 8m-1

A number of important contributions in the year 1925 likely will be agreed upon by anyone who has studied popular culture in the United States. The Charleston, a dance most often associate with the 1920s, had become popular in 1925. Along with the new dance comes a new fashion trend. If a woman of today was to find herself transported to 1925, she would be in style if she was to appear in a straight, long-

-ed missing: 8d

present tense used; need simple past: 8h

ANSWER: PARTICIPATION ESSAY, PAGE 225

This version revises the errors in verb forms and verb tense and the unnecessary use of the passive voice. Answers might vary slightly, especially in the revisions of the passives. Also, answers will vary if students have revised for content, organization, or style.

At election time, government leaders and the media always encourage citizens to exercise one of their most basic rights: the right to vote. How many young women today realize that until the Nineteenth Amendment to the United States Constitution was approved in 1920, women in the United States were denied the right to vote?

In the 1830s, almost a century before the Nineteenth Amendment was approved, Elizabeth Cady Stanton and other leading women waged the battle for women's rights. In 1848, the first women's rights convention took place in Seneca Falls, New York. Stanton rose to the occasion and produced what was called "A Declaration of Sentiments." Its inspiration lay in the Declaration of Independence, but it revealed one shortcoming in Thomas Jefferson's language. Instead of the words "all men are created equal," Stanton's document proclaimed that "all men and women are created equal."

Later, Stanton convinced California Senator Aaron Sargeant to propose a constitutional amendment that would give women the vote. He introduced it to the U.S. Congress in 1878. Forty years later the amendment was approved, but Stanton never saw the victory because she died eighteen years before the amendment became law. Her legacy lives and should be remembered by all women when the time comes to vote.

waisted dress with a hemline above the knee. This revealing look was found to be shocking by some people of that era. A less controversial development was the opening of Madison Square Garden in New York City. Boxing and other events now were able to be seen by thousands of people. While sports fans were enjoying the new facility, movie audiences laugh at Charlie Chaplin in his popular film *The Gold Rush*. Clearly, popular culture in the year 1925 had been thriving.

unneeded passive voice: 8o

-ed missing: 8d

past perfect progressive tense used; need simple past: 8j

Here is how the student revised the material to eliminate the verb errors. In revising from the unneeded passive voice to the active voice, the student had alternatives in word choice. Your revisions into the active voice might differ in wording from the student's.

Anyone who has studied popular culture in the United States likely will agree upon a number of important contributions in the year 1925. The Charleston, a dance most often associated with the 1920s, became popular in 1925. Along with the new dance came a new fashion trend. If a woman of today were to find herself transported to 1925, she would be in style if she were to appear in a straight, long-waisted dress with a hemline above the knee. Some people of that era found this revealing look shocking. A less controversial development was the opening of Madison Square Garden in New York City. Thousands of people could now see boxing and other events. While sports fans were enjoying this new facility, movie audiences laughed at Charlie Chaplin in his popular film *The Gold Rush*. Clearly, popular culture in the year 1925 was thriving.

Participation

A student wrote the following draft for a course called Introduction to Women's Studies. The assignment was to write a brief report about a significant contribution to society in the United States. The material is concise and logical, but the draft's effectiveness is diminished by errors in verb forms and verb tense and by the unnecessary use of the passive voice.

Read through the draft. Then revise it to eliminate the errors. Also, make any additional revisions you think would improve the content, organization, and style of the material.

At election time, government leaders and the media always encouraged citizens to exercise one of their most basic rights: the right to vote. How many young women today realize that until the Nineteenth Amendment to the United States Constitution was approve in 1920, women in the United States were deny the right to vote?

In the 1830s, almost a century before the Nineteenth Amendment was approved, the battle for women's rights was being waged by Elizabeth Cady Stanton and other leading women. In 1848, the first women's rights convention take place in Seneca Falls, New York. Stanton rises to the occasion and produced what was call "A Declaration of Sentiments." Its inspiration lays in the Declaration of Independence, but it revealed one shortcoming in Thomas Jefferson's language. Instead of the words "all men are created equal," Stanton's document proclaim that "all men and women are created equal."

Later, Stanton was working to convince California Senator Aaron Sargeant to propose a constitutional amendment that would give women the vote. It was introduced to the U.S. Congress by him in 1878. Forty years later the amendment was approved, but Stanton never seen the victory because she died eighteen years before the amendment became law. Her legacy lives and should be remembered by all women when the time come to vote.

COVERAGE: PARTICIPATION ESSAY

At election time, government leaders and the media always *encouraged* [8h: simple present needed] citizens to exercise one of their most basic rights: the right to vote. How many young women today realize that until the Nineteenth Amendment to the United States Constitution *was approve* [8d: -*ed* needed] in 1920, women in the United States were deny [8d: -[*i*] *ed* needed] the right to vote?

In the 1830s, almost a century before the Nineteenth Amendment was approved, *the battle for women's rights was being waged by Elizabeth Cady Stanton and other leading women.* [8o: unneeded passive voice] In 1848, the first women's rights convention *take* [8h: present tense used; need simple past of irregular verb] place in Seneca Falls, New York. Stanton *rises* [8f: present tense of intransitive verb used; simple past needed] to the occasion and produced what was *call* [8d: -*ed* needed] "A Declaration of Sentiments." Its inspiration *lays* [8f: -*s* form of transitive verb used; past tense of intransitive verb needed] in the Declaration of Independence, but it revealed one shortcoming in Thomas Jefferson's language. Instead of the words "all men are created equal," Stanton's document *proclaim* [8d: -*ed* needed] that "all men and women are created equal."

Later, Stanton *was working* [8j: past progressive form used; simple present needed] to convince California Senator Aaron Sargeant to propose a constitutional amendment that would give women the vote. *It was introduced to the U.S. Congress by him in 1878.* [8o: unneeded passive voice] Forty years later the amendment was approved, but Stanton never *seen* [8d: past participle of irregular verb used; simple past needed] the victory because she died eighteen years before the amendment became law. Her legacy lives and should be remembered by all women when the time *come* to vote. [8c: simple present used; -*s* form needed]

9 *Case of Nouns and Pronouns*

REFERENCES TO SUPPLEMENTS

For this topic in the CLAST writing competency test, refer students to ch. 1, section B4c of *Preparing for the CLAST* by S. Patterson.

This topic is included in the TASP writing competency test. Refer students to *Preparing for the TASP* by M. Saenz.

For editing for correct pronoun reference and case, refer students to *Rough Drafts* by K. S. Cain, Part IV, Exercise 9.

QUOTATION ABOUT WRITING

I am strongly in favor of intelligent, even fastidious revision, which is, or certainly should be, an art in itself.

—Joyce Carol Oates

QUOTATION ABOUT WRITING

I literally draw a train of linked boxes, beginning with the central event in the middle of the page, then building the Super Chief in both directions, backward to the start, forward to the end. The very mechanical process is excellent for helping you sort your material by weight, separating incident from chapter, etc.

—Edward Hannibal

9a Understanding case

Case refers to the different forms that NOUNS and PRONOUNS take to deliver information. Case communicates how the noun or pronoun relates to other words in a sentence.

Nouns "show" case only in the possessive, by the use of the apostrophe (see Chapter 27) or by an *of* construction. Pronouns have three cases: SUBJECTIVE CASE, OBJECTIVE CASE, and POSSESSIVE CASE.

Personal pronouns, the most common type of pronouns, have a full range of cases that show changes in **person** (first, second, and third person) and **number** (singular and plural). (See Chart 65.) For more about the concepts of person and number, see Chart 72 in section 11a.

CASES OF PERSONAL PRONOUNS

CASES OF PERSONAL PRONOUNS						65
	SUBJECTIVE		**OBJECTIVE**		**POSSESSIVE**	
PERSON	SING.	PLUR.	SING.	PLUR.	SINGULAR	PLURAL
FIRST	I	we	me	us	my/mine	our/ours
SECOND	you	you	you	you	your/yours	your/yours
THIRD	he she it	they	him her it	them	his her/hers its	their/theirs

A pronoun in the **subjective case** functions as a subject.

We were going to get married. [*We* is the subject.]

John and **I** wanted an inexpensive band to play at our wedding. [*I* is part of the compound subject *John and I.*]

He and I found an affordable one-person band. [*He and I* are compound subjects.]

A pronoun in the **objective case** functions as a DIRECT OBJECT, an INDIRECT OBJECT, or the OBJECT OF A PREPOSITION.

We saw **him** perform in a public park. [*Him* is the direct object.]

We showed **him** our budget. [*Him* is the indirect object.]

He wrote down what we wanted and shook hands with **us**. [*Us* is the object of the preposition *with.*]

A pronoun in the **possessive case** indicates possession or ownership. For a discussion of the possessive case before gerunds, see 9h.

The **musician's** contract was in the mail the next day. [*Musician's,* a noun in the possessive case, indicates ownership.]

The first signature on the contract was **mine**. [*Mine,* a pronoun in the possessive case, indicates ownership and refers to the noun *signature.*]

My fiance signed **his** name next to **mine**. [*His* and *mine,* pronouns in the possessive case, indicate ownership and refer to the noun *name.*]

❖ PUNCTUATION ALERT: Do not use an apostrophe for a personal pronoun in the possessive case (see 27b).❖

The pronouns *who* and *whoever* also change form for case changes, as explained in 9e.

!

Using the same cases for pronouns in compound constructions as in single constructions

9b

A compound construction contains more than one SUBJECT or OBJECT.

He saw the eclipse of the sun. [single subject]

He and I saw the eclipse of the sun. [compound subject]

That eclipse astonished **us**. [single object]

That eclipse astonished **him and me**. [compound object]

LANGUAGE FACTS

Many languages have noun and/or pronoun case systems. The smallest number of cases is two, as in the Masai language of East Africa. In contrast, Sanskrit has eight cases. Latin has six, Greek has five. The prize, however, goes to Finnish, with fifteen noun cases.

BACKGROUND ON LANGUAGE

The pronoun *you* indicates little more than that the second person is being used. Unlike the first- and third-person personal pronouns, it tells the reader nothing about gender or number. Until the thirteenth century, however, *th*-forms, such as *thee, thy,* and *thou,* indicated use of the singular, and *y*- forms, such as *ye, you,* and *your,* indicated the plural. Later, the *th*- forms came to suggest a close relationship between the speaker and listener, the *y*- forms to suggest a formal one. Today the pronouns *thou* and *thee* linger only among some religious sects.

TEACHING TIP

If you have students who know other languages, they may enjoy explaining the noun and pronoun case systems of those other tongues to the native English speakers in the class. Their examples will demonstrate that case is not nearly as important an aspect of English as it is of other languages.

TEACHING TIP

Just as English once distinguished between the personal and impersonal relationships in the second-person pronoun *you,* some modern languages continue to do so. French, for example, makes a distinction between *tu* and *vous;* Spanish does so between *tu* (singular) *vosotros* (plural) informally and *usted* (singular) *ustedes* (plural) formally. You might wish to have your bilingual students explain the difference in such forms.

TEACHING TIP

The "drop test" can be more effective if students are given both oral and written activities in which they are asked not only to select correct pronouns from prepared sentences but also to generate their own sentences using pronouns as parts of compounds.

QUOTATION ON LANGUAGE

Words are like leaves, and where they most abound, / Much fruit of sense beneath is rarely found.
—Alexander Pope

QUOTATION ON LANGUAGE

High thoughts must have high language.
—Aristophanes

BACKGROUND ON LANGUAGE

Joseph M. Williams explains in *Origins of the English Language* (New York: Free Press, 1975, 248–49) that changes in the second-person singular pronouns (subjective and objective cases) are rooted in the Roman Empire of the fourth century A.D. At that time there were two emperors, one in Rome and one in Constantinople. People speaking to either emperor were required to use the plural form of address. The practice of using the plural as a sign of respect slowly spread to France, where *tu* is the second-person singular pronoun and *vous* the plural. During the thirteenth century, in imitation of the *tu/vous* of the French nobles who occupied their country, the English began using *thee* (objective), *thou* (subjective), and *you* the same way. *You* became a mark of mutual respect in conversations among the elite and a sign of deference when a person spoke to a social superior. In contrast, *thee/thou* became a sign of intimacy among members of the same family or among those who believed in the same things.

9b
cont.

A compound construction has no effect on the choice of pronoun case. A compound subject uses the subjective case, and a compound object uses the objective case. Sometimes, however, people make the mistake of switching cases for compounds. If you are unsure which case to use, try the "drop test." Temporarily drop all words of the compound element except the pronoun in question, as explained in Chart 66.

TEST FOR COMPOUND SUBJECTS   66

~~Janet and~~ me

~~Janet and~~ I

learned about the moon.

After dropping **Janet and**, only **I learned about the moon** is correct; therefore, **Janet and I** is the right choice.

This "drop test" also works when a compound subject contains only pronouns: **She and I** [not **Her and me, She and me,** or **Her and I**] *learned about the moon.*

TEST FOR COMPOUND OBJECTS   67

The instructor told ~~Janet and~~ I

The instructor told ~~Janet and~~ me

about the moon's phases.

After dropping **Janet and**, only **The instructor told me** is correct; therefore, **Janet and me** is the right choice.

The "drop test" in Chart 67 works for compound objects. Also, this test works when a compound object contains only pronouns: *The instructor told **her and me*** [not ***she and I, her and I,*** or ***she and me***] *about the moon's phases.*

These principles apply to all sequences of pronouns (for example, the rules that govern *her and me* apply also to *me and her*). Also, when you write compound constructions that contain pronouns, do not mix pronouns in the subjective case with pronouns in the objective case: For example, do not use the combinations *him and I* (objective and subjective) or *she and me* (subjective and objective).

When pronouns in a PREPOSITIONAL PHRASE are compound, do not allow pronouns to slip into the wrong case. A prepositional phrase always has an OBJECT, so any pronouns that follow words such as *to*, *with*, *from*, and *for* must be in the objective case.

NO   The instructor gave an assignment **to Sam and I**. [*To* is a preposition; *I* is in the subjective case and cannot follow a preposition.]

YES   The instructor gave an assignment to **Sam and me**. [*To* is a preposition; *me* is in the objective case, so it is correct.]

NO   The instructor spoke **with he and I**. [*With* is a preposition; both *he* and *I* are in the subjective case and cannot follow a preposition.]

NO   The instructor spoke **with him and I**. [*With* is a preposition; *him* is in the objective case, so it is correct. *I* is in the subjective case and cannot follow a preposition.]

YES   The instructor spoke **with him and me**. [*With* is a preposition; *him* and *me* are both in the objective case, so this construction is correct.]

Between is a preposition that frequently leads people to pronoun error. A pronoun after *between*, like those after other prepositions, must always be in the objective case.

NO   The instructor divided the work between **Sam and I**. [*Between* is a preposition; *I* is in the subjective case and cannot follow a preposition.]

YES   The instructor divided the work **between Sam and me**. [*Between* is a preposition; *me* is in the objective case, so it is correct.]

When you are in doubt about pronoun case in prepositional phrases, use the "drop test" for compound objects in Chart 67.

BACKGROUND

In Standard American English, *you* is the form for both singular and plural. But, according to Richard Veit in *Discovering English Grammar* (Boston: Houghton Mifflin, 1986, p.47), for informal situations, some regional dialects employ other plural forms for second person such as *y'all*, *y'uns*, *yuz*, and *you guys*.

QUOTATION ON LANGUAGE

A writer lives in awe of words for they can be cruel or kind, and they can change their meanings right in front of you. They pick up flavors and odors like butter in a refrigerator.

—John Steinbeck

QUOTATION ON LANGUAGE

The difference between the right word and the almost right word is the difference between lightning and the lightning bug.

—Mark Twain

QUOTATION ABOUT WRITING

You can be a little ungrammatical if you come from the right part of the country.

—Robert Frost

QUOTATION ABOUT LANGUAGE

Our mother tongue is bettered or worsened by the way each generation uses it. Languages evolve like species. They can degenerate; just as oysters and barnacles have lost their head.

—F. S. Lucas, "What Is Style?"

9b
cont.

EXERCISE 9-1

Consulting section 9b, select the correct pronoun from each pair in parentheses and write it in the blank.

EXAMPLE   "Just between you and (I, me) **me**," said my workout partner, "I could stand to lose a few pounds."

I suggested that [1](us, we) _____ both consider going on a low-fat diet. Consulting a doctor first seemed like the right plan for Al and [2](I, me) _____ , and so I made appointments for [3](he and I, him and me) _____ with Mary Standish, my own physician. [4](We, Us) _____ both were seen the next evening. After examining us separately, Dr. Standish told Al and [5](I, me) _____ that between [6](he and I, him and me) _____ [7](we, us) _____ should lose 25 pounds. Dr. Standish gave a list of desirable and undesirable foods to [8](we, us) _____ two. Naturally, the desirable list seemed undesirable and the undesirable delicious, agreed Al and [9](I, me) _____ . Al had a different problem. Because the diet was now the same goal for both [10](he and I, him and me) _____ , he dreaded the competition between [11](we, us) _____ two. "Don't worry," I told Al. "It's not a matter of you versus [12](me, I) _____ because the big loser is the real winner!"

9c

Matching noun and pronoun cases in appositives

The case rules hold when pronouns are renamed by APPOSITIVES and when they are appositives themselves. The pronouns and nouns must be in the same case. To check, temporarily drop the noun to see whether subjective or objective pronouns read correctly.

We ~~tennis players~~
Us ~~tennis players~~
practice hard.

After dropping *tennis players*, only *we* is correct; therefore, *We practiced hard* is the right choice.

This test also works when the pronouns function as the appositive, coming after the noun: *The winners,* **she and I** [not *her* and *me*], *advanced to the finals.* Because they rename *winners*, which is the subject, the pronouns must be in the subjective case.

This test also works when the nouns and pronouns are in the objective case: *The coach tells* **us** [not *we*] *tennis players to practice hard. The crowd cheered the winners,* **her** *and* **me** [not *she and I*].

Avoiding the objective case after linking verbs

9d

A **linking verb** connects a SUBJECT to a word that renames it. Linking verbs indicate a state of being (*am, is, are, was, were,* etc.), relate to the senses (*look, smell, taste, sound, feel*), or indicate a condition (*appear, seem, become, grow, turn, remain,* and *prove*).

Because a pronoun coming after any linking verb renames the subject, the pronoun cannot be in the objective case.

> The contest winner was **I**. [*I* renames *the contest winner*, the subject, so the subjective case is correct.]

> The ones who will benefit are **they** and **I**. [*They* and *I* rename *the ones who will benefit*, the subject, so the subjective case is correct.]

> Who is there? It is **I**. [*I* renames *it*, the subject, so the subjective case is correct.]

Although in speech and informal writing, the objective case is sometimes substituted in the constructions shown in the last two examples above, always use the subjective case in academic writing.

EXERCISE 9-2

Consulting sections 9a through 9d, select the correct pronoun of each pair in parentheses and write it in the blank.

EXAMPLE   The two of you have suggested that (we, us) **we** roommates all have sausage and mushroom pizza for dinner tonight.

After much discussion, Kari and ¹(I, me) _____ have reached a decision. We thought carefully about what you and Saroya have asked Kari and ²(I, me) _____ to do, because it is ³(we, us) _____ who have to live with ⁴(you and she, you and her) _____ for the rest of the semester. Because Kari hates mushrooms and I hate sausage, this proposal has no appeal whatsoever for either ⁵(she, her) _____ or ⁶(I, me) _____ . We have now thought of a compromise that should satisfy you two as well as ⁷(we, us) _____ . Tell Saroya that tonight's pizza eaters can certainly be you and ⁸(she, her) _____ , but hamburgers are on the menu for Kari and ⁹(I, me) _____ .

BACKGROUND

In *Talkin and Testifyin: The Language of Black America* (Boston: Houghton Mifflin, 1977; rpt. Wayne State UP, 1986), Geneva Smitherman-Donaldson writes that the cases of personal pronouns in Black English are not as differentiated as in Standard English:

> Thus, for example, with the third person plural pronoun, *they*, the same form serves for subject, possessive, and so-called reflexive as in *The expressway bought they house* and *They should do it theyselves*. In the case of the third person singular pronoun, *he*, we will hear both *He gone* and *Him cool*, and in the reflexive, *He did it all by hisself*. At an earlier stage in the development of Black English, forms like *he book* (for *his book*) and *she house* (for *her house*) were prominent, but these have gradually disappeared. (29)

ANSWERS AND COVERAGE: EXERCISE 9–2

1. I [subjective case, 9a]
2. me [objective case, 9b]
3. we [subjective case, 9d]
4. you and her [objective case, 9b]
5. her [objective case, 9b]
6. me [objective case, 9b]
7. us [objective case, 9b]
8. she [subjective case, 9d]
9. me [objective case, 9b]

Circle the correct pronoun in each pair in parentheses.

1. Carl's resolution to study more is a result of (him, his) making poor grades last semester. [*his*]

2. The Dean almost required (he, him) to stay out a semester. [*him*]

3. His parents were angry about (him, his) partying too much. [*his*]

4. Not only as bright as his older brother, Carl was also as lazy as (he, him). [*he*]

5. He worked more diligently after his parents called (he, him) to see how he was doing. [*him*]

6. (Them, Their) calling was evidence that they cared about (he, him). [*Their, him*]

7. After that incident, (him, his) studying became more serious. [*his*]

QUOTATION ABOUT WRITING

For my money we should get rid of "whom" (and "whomever" and "whomsoever") completely, irrevocably, immediately. Whom and the like are show-off words, painstakingly crafted to let you know you are in the company of a superior being. But more often than not they get in the way—of meaning, of style, of the natural flow of language . . .

Whom is unnatural in everyday speech.

For whom are you looking? Well, well, whom have we here? It's not what you know but whom you know. I forgot whom I was going to see. All these constructions are right, but that is about all they have going for them.

Real English doesn't take this guff. It laughs off a stiff, labored sentence like "For whom are you looking?" and says instead, "Who're you looking for?" There is no confusion here about who is who.

—John Allemang,
"The Objectionable Pronoun,"
The Toronto Globe and Mail,
June 30, 1990

9e Using *who*, *whoever*, *whom*, and *whomever*

The pronouns *who* and *whoever* are in the subjective case. The pronouns *whom* and *whomever* are in the objective case. (See Chart 68.) They do not change form.

CASES OF RELATIVE AND INTERROGATIVE PRONOUNS

CASES OF RELATIVE AND INTERROGATIVE PRONOUNS			68
SUBJECTIVE	**OBJECTIVE**	**POSSESSIVE**	
who	whom	whose	
whoever	whomever	—	

9e-1 Using *who*, *whoever*, *whom*, and *whomever* in dependent clauses

Pronouns such as *who, whoever, whom,* and *whomever* start many DEPENDENT CLAUSES. To determine what pronoun case is correct in a dependent clause, find out whether the pronoun is functioning as a SUBJECT or an OBJECT in its own clause. Informal spoken English tends to blur distinctions between *who* and *whom,* so you might not want to rely entirely on what sounds right.

To check your use of *who* and *whom,* adapt the "drop test" introduced in section 9b. As Chart 69 shows, temporarily drop everything in the sentence up to the pronoun in question, and then make substitutions. Remember that *he, she, they, who,* and *whoever* are subjects, and *him, her, them, whom,* and *whomever* (the -*m* forms and *her*) are objects.

TEST FOR *WHO/WHOM* IN SUBJECTIVE CASE

TEST FOR *WHO/WHOM* IN SUBJECTIVE CASE		69
EXAMPLE	I wondered **(who, whom)** would vote.	
DROP	*I wondered*	
TEST	Temporarily substitute *he* and *him* (or *she* and *her*): "**He** would vote" or "**Him** would vote."	
ANSWER	**He.** Therefore, because *he* is subjective, *who,* which is also the subjective, is correct: "I wondered **who** would vote."	

The subjective case is used even if words such as *I think* or *he says* come between the subject and verb. Ignore these expressions to determine the correct pronoun: *She is the candidate who [I think] will get my vote.* The "drop test" in Chart 70 also works for *whoever:*

Voter registration drives attempt to enroll **whoever** is eligible to vote. ["**He** (not *him*) is eligible to vote" proves that the subjective case of **whoever** is needed.]

	TEST FOR *WHO/WHOM* IN OBJECTIVE CASE	70
EXAMPLE	Volunteers go to senior citizen centers hoping to enroll people **(who, whom)** others have ignored.	
DROP	Volunteers go to senior citizen centers hoping to enroll people.	
TEST	Try *they* and *them* at the end of the sentence: "Others have ignored **they**" or "Others have ignored **them**."	
ANSWER	**Them.** Therefore, because *them* is objective, *whom,* which is also objective, is correct: "Volunteers go to senior citizen centers hoping to enroll people **whom** others have ignored."	

The "drop test" in Chart 70 also works for *whomever:*

The senior citizens can vote for **whomever** they wish. ["The senior citizens can vote for **him** (not *he*)" proves that the objective case of **whomever** is needed.]

Using *who* and *whom* in questions

At the beginning of questions, use *who* if the question is about the SUBJECT and *whom* if the question is about the OBJECT. To determine case, recast the question into a statement, temporarily substituting *he* or *him* (or *she* or *her*).

Who watched the space shuttle lift off? ["**He** (not *Him*) watched the space shuttle lift off" uses the subjective case, so *Who* is correct.]

Ann admires **whom**? ["Ann admires **him** (not *he*)" uses the objective case, so *whom* is correct.]

Whom does Ann admire? ["Ann admires **him** (not *he*)" uses the objective case, so *whom* is correct.]

To **whom** does Ann speak about becoming an astronaut? ["Ann speaks to **them** (not *they*) about becoming an astronaut" uses the objective pronoun *them. Whom* is therefore correct.]

9e-2

TEACHING TIP

If your students have trouble choosing the appropriate relative pronoun in dependent clauses, they can do the drop test using these additional sentences.

SUBJECTIVE CASE

1. I enjoy playing volleyball with anyone (who, whom) has time to play. [*who*]

2. (Whoever, whomever) wins is obligated to buy lunch for the rest. [*Whoever*]

3. I wonder (who, whom) will show up for today's game. [*who*]

OBJECTIVE CASE

1. The volleyball players (who, whom) I met yesterday were too skillful for me. [*whom*]

2. I reserve the right to play with (whoever, whomever) I choose. [*whomever*]

3. The opponent (who, whom) I want is honest as well as skillful. [*whom*]

EXTRA EXERCISE C

From each group of pronouns in parentheses, select the correct word.

EXAMPLE

My softball teammates and (myself, me, I) are confident we will make the finals this year. [*I*]

1. I am so certain that I have already bought (me, myself) a new glove to celebrate. [*myself*]

2. Every practice session the coach tells the others and (me, myself) that we are getting better and better. [*me*]

3. The sponsor (himself, hisself), Big Al of Big Al's Used cars, even comes to games now. [*himself*]

4. The other women and (I, myself) are glad that our hard work has paid off. [*I*]

5. We had an exhibition game against our husbands, who tired (theirselves, themselves) out and lost by four runs. [*themselves*]

9e-2
cont.

EXERCISE 9-3

Consulting section 9e, select the correct pronoun of each pair in parentheses and write it in the blank.

EXAMPLE   Is there an age group of children (who, whom) **who** do not tell lies?

If the word *liar* means ¹(whoever, whomever) _____ makes false statements with the intent to deceive, then even three- and four-year-olds fit the definition. Studies show that young children will lie to ²(whoever, whomever) _____ they think might be angered by the truth. Because young children may not define lying the way adults do, ³(whoever, whomever) _____ the child considers to have given false information may be considered a liar. For example, a parent ⁴(who, whom) _____ changes plans because of bad weather may be accused of lying by a young child. To the child ⁵(who, whom) _____ the change affects, the original statements were false and therefore the person ⁶(who, whom) _____ made them is a liar.

QUOTATION ABOUT WRITING

For your born writer, nothing is so healing as the realization that he has come upon the right word.
—Catherine Drinker Bowen

TEACHING TIP

If your students have trouble choosing the appropriate pronoun after *than* or *as*, you might try expanding elliptical comparisons with them to verify the best choice. Here are a few practice sentences.

1. You are taller than (I, me). [*I*]
2. Your parents are taller than (me, mine). [*mine*]
3. My brother is as short as (I, me). [*I*]
4. Your sisters are as smart as (me, mine). [*mine*]

9f

Using the appropriate pronoun case after *than* or *as*

A sentence of comparison often can be clear even though some of the words following *than* or *as* are implied rather than directly stated. For example, *are* need not be expressed at the end of this sentence: *My two-month-old Saint Bernard is larger **than** most full-grown dogs [are].*

When a pronoun follows *than* or *as*, the pronoun case carries essential information about what is being said. For example, these two sentences convey two very different messages, simply because of the choice between the words *me* and *I* after *than*.

1.   My sister loved that dog more **than me.**
2.   My sister loved that dog more **than I.**

Because the pronoun *me* functions as a subject, sentence 1 means "My sister loved that dog more *than she loved me.*" On the other hand, sentence 2 means "My sister loved that dog more *than I loved it.*" To make sure that any sentence of comparison delivers its message clearly, either mentally fill in the words to check that you have chosen the correct pronoun case, or write in all words after *than* or *as*.

234

Using pronouns with infinitives

9g

An **infinitive** is the SIMPLE FORM of a verb usually, but not always, following *to: to laugh.* Objective-case pronouns serve as both SUBJECTS of infinitives and OBJECTS of infinitives.

> Our tennis coach expects **me to serve.** [The word *me* is the subject of the infinitive *to serve,* and so it is in the objective case.]

> Our tennis coach expects **him to beat me.** [The word *him* is the subject of the infinitive *to beat,* and *me* is the object of the infinitive; so both are in the objective case.]

Using pronouns with *-ing* words

9h

A **gerund** is a verb's *-ing* form functioning as a NOUN. (***Brisk walking*** *is excellent exercise.*) When a noun or pronoun precedes a gerund, the possessive case is called for. (***Kim's brisk walking*** *built up his stamina.* ***His brisk walking*** *built up his stamina.*) In contrast, a present participle—a form that also ends in *-ing*—functions as a modifier. It does not take the possessive case. (*Kim,* ***walking briskly,*** *caught up to me.*)

The possessive case, therefore, communicates important information. Consider these two sentences, which convey two different messages, entirely as a result of the possessive:

1. The detective noticed the **man staggering.**
2. The detective noticed the **man's staggering.**

Sentence 1 means that the detective noticed the man; sentence 2 means that the detective noticed the staggering. The same distinction applies to pronouns:

1. The detective noticed **him** staggering.
2. The detective noticed **his** staggering.

In conversation, such a distinction is often ignored, but readers of academic writing expect that information will be precise. Consider the difference in the following two examples:

GERUND (AS SUBJECT)	The **governor's calling for a tax increase** surprised her supporters.
PARTICIPLE (AS MODIFIER)	The governor, **calling for a tax increase,** surprised her supporters.

EXTRA EXERCISE D

From the pronouns in parentheses, select the correct one and circle it.

 1. My friend and (I, me) agreed long ago that we would someday take a romantic ocean cruise together.

 2. (We, Us) and a few friends would sail the legendary seas and dock at exotic ports.

 3. Together, (they, them) and (we, us) would shop in the mysterious bazaars of ancient cultures and eat the spicy foods of distant lands.

 4. Unfortunately, an unexpected misfortune was visited on (she, her) and (I, me).

 5. (She, her) and (I, me) both discovered that we had chicken pox on the day we were to leave.

 6. Instead of visiting romantic places, the romantic places visited (she, her) and (I, me).

 7. Our friend Tom gave (we, us) travel books with pictures of the many places we longed to see.

 8. They were the same books someone had given (he, him) when he missed his trip to Mexico.

 9. I guess (we, us) will have to give them to (whoever, whomever) can't make the next scheduled vacation trip.

ANSWERS TO EXTRA EXERCISE D

 1. I
 2. We
 3. they, we
 4. her, me
 5. She, I
 6. her, me
 7. us
 8. him
 9. we, whoever

ANSWERS AND COVERAGE: EXERCISE 9–4

1. he [subjective case in elliptical *as the careers that he and his friend Steve Jobs have had*; 9f]

2. their [possessive case before gerund; 9h]

3. them [objective case for object of infinitive *to get*; 9g]

4. they [subjective case as subject of elliptical clause *than they are*; 9f]

5. its [possessive case before gerund *creating*; 9h]

6. their [possessive case before gerund *leaving*; 9h]

7. them [objective case for object of infinitive *to interest*; 9g]

8. him [objective case for object of infinitive *to want*; 9g] [Note that in this sentence, *conceptualizing*, *designing*, and *engineering* are functioning as participial modifiers rather than as gerunds; see 9h.]

9. its [possessive case before gerund *repeating*; 9h]

EXERCISE 9-4

Consulting sections 9f, 9g, and 9h, select the correct pronoun of each pair in parentheses and write it in the blank.

EXAMPLE   When executives at the Hewlett Packard Company decided not to manufacture a personal computer brought to them by its designer, young Steve Wozniak, the rejection motivated (him, his) **his** founding the Apple Computer Company.

Few people in Steve Wozniak's world of personal computers have had careers as rewarding as ^{1}(he, him) _____ and his friend Steve Jobs. Their story begins with ^{2}(them, their) _____ selling a van and a calculator to get ^{3}(they, them) _____ enough cash to make a prototype computer. Many people with an idea like Wozniak and Jobs's are less willing than ^{4}(them, they) _____ to take risks. Apple's spectacular success as a company came from ^{5}(it, its) _____ creating computers easy for individuals to own and use. Because their idea made both Wozniak and Jobs multimillionaires before age thirty, the notion of ^{6}(them, their) _____ leaving the business world seemed to interest ^{7}(they, them) _____ . Wozniak went back to college but eventually returned to Apple, which continued to want ^{8}(his, him) _____ conceptualizing, designing, and engineering computers for them. Jobs started a new computer company, NExt, but ^{9}(it, its) _____ repeating Apple's success is still only a dream.

9i   Using *-self* pronouns

Reflexive pronouns reflect back on the SUBJECT or OBJECT: *The detective disguised **himself**. He relied on **himself** to solve the mystery.*

Do not use reflexive pronouns to substitute for PERSONAL PRONOUNS as subjects or objects: *The detective and **I** [not *myself*] had a long talk. He wanted my partner and **me** [not *myself*] to help him.*

Intensive pronouns provide emphasis by making another word more intense in meaning: *The detective felt that his career **itself** was at stake.*

! ❖ USAGE ALERT: Avoid nonstandard forms of reflexive and intensive pronouns. Use *himself*, never *hisself*; use *themselves*, never *theirself*, *theirselves*, *themself*, or *themselfs*.❖

10 *Pronoun Reference*

A PRONOUN always refers to a NOUN or another pronoun, which is called the pronoun's **antecedent**. The term **pronoun reference** refers to this pronoun-antecedent relationship. For writing to communicate a clear message, each pronoun must relate directly to an antecedent.

Consider these sentences and lines of poetry in which each pronoun has a clear referent.

Facts do not cease to exist just because **they** are ignored.
—ALDOUS HUXLEY

I have found that the best way to give advice to **children** is to find out what **they** want and then advise **them** to do it.
—HARRY S TRUMAN

I knew a woman, lovely in **her** bones,
When small birds sighed, **she** would sigh back at **them;**
—THEODORE ROETHKE, "I Knew a Woman"

Chart 71 is a guide to avoiding unclear presentation of the connections between pronouns and their antecedents.

HOW TO CORRECT FAULTY PRONOUN REFERENCE   71

- Make a pronoun refer clearly to a single nearby antecedent (see 10a).
- Place pronouns close to their antecedents (see 10b).
- Make a pronoun refer to a definite antecedent (see 10c).
- Do not overuse *it* (see 10d), and reserve *you* only for DIRECT ADDRESS (see 10e).
- Use *who, which,* and *that* correctly (see 10f).

Making a pronoun refer clearly to a single antecedent   10a

When pronoun reference is unclear, the meaning gets muddled. Be sure that each pronoun that you use refers clearly to a single, nearby antecedent. If you find that you need the same pronoun to refer to

10a cont. more than one antecedent, revise the passage by replacing some pronouns with nouns so that all the remaining pronouns clearly refer to a single antecedent.

NO In 1911, **Roald Amundsen** reached the South Pole just thirty-five days before **Robert F. Scott** arrived. **He** [who? Amundsen or Scott?] had told people that **he** was going to sail for the Arctic but then **he** turned south for the Antarctic. Then on the journey home, **he** [who? Amundsen or Scott?] and **his** party froze to death just a few miles from safety.

YES In 1911, **Roald Amundsen** discovered the South Pole just thirty-five days before **Robert F. Scott** arrived. **Amundsen** had told people that **he** was going to sail for the Arctic but then **he** turned south for the Antarctic. On the journey home, **Scott** and **his** party froze to death just a few miles from safety.

When you use more than one pronoun in a sentence, be sure that each has a clear antecedent.

Robert F. Scott used **horses** for **his** trip to the Pole, but **they** perished quickly because **they** were not suited for travel over ice and snow.

Said and *told*, when used with pronouns that refer to more than one person, are particularly likely to create confusion for readers. Quotation marks and slight rewording can clarify meaning.

NO Her mother told her she was going to visit Alaska.
YES Her mother told her, "You are going to visit Alaska."
YES Her mother told her, "I am going to visit Alaska."

10b Placing pronouns close to their antecedents for clarity

If too much material comes between a pronoun and its antecedent, even though they may be logically related, unclear pronoun reference results. Readers lose track of the meaning of a passage if they have to trace back too far to find the antecedent of a pronoun.

NO **Alfred Wegener**, a highly trained German meteorologist and professor of geophysics and meteorology at the University of Graz in Austria, was the first person to suggest that all the continents on earth were originally part of one large land mass. According to his theory, the supercontinent broke up long ago and the fragments drifted apart. **He** named this supercontinent Pangaea. [Although *he* can refer only to *Wegener*, too much material intervenes between the pronoun and its antecedent.]

YES   **Alfred Wegener,** a highly trained German meteorologist and professor of geophysics and meteorology at the University of Graz in Austria, was the first person to suggest that all the continents on earth were originally part of one large land mass. According to his theory, the supercontinent broke up long ago and the fragments drifted apart. **Wegener** named this supercontinent Pangaea.

At the beginning of a new paragraph within an essay, many writers avoid using a pronoun to refer to a name in a prior paragraph. They prefer to repeat the name instead, particularly when the prior paragraph is long or when the subject matter is complex. Your repeating the name can help your reader follow more easily the message that you want your material to deliver.

❖ **ESL NOTE:** Many languages omit a pronoun as a SUBJECT because the VERB delivers the needed information. English, however, requires the use of the pronoun as a subject.

NO   Political science is an important academic subject; **is** studied all over the world.

YES   Political science is an important academic subject; **it is** studied all over the world.❖

EXERCISE 10-1

Consulting sections 10a and 10b, revise so that each pronoun refers clearly to its antecedent. Either replace pronouns with nouns or restructure the material to clarify pronoun reference.

EXAMPLE   When Ludwig II became king of Bavaria in 1864, he was a passionate admirer of composer Richard Wagner. He had first heard one of his operas a few years earlier and had fallen in love with the exciting world of German legend that he portrayed.

Here is one acceptable revision: *When Ludwig II became king of Bavaria in 1864, he was a passionate admirer of composer Richard Wagner. Ludwig had first heard one of Wagner's operas a few years earlier and had fallen in love with the exciting world of German legend that Wagner portrayed.*

➜

ESL

TEACHING TIP

To help students become more aware of the connections between pronouns and their antecedents, you might want to use this excerpt from Jim Bouton's essay "A Few World Series Sinkers." You might ask students to draw connecting lines between each pair. (The pronouns are italicized here.) Do they find any misleading or vague references?

Another thing to watch during one of the little delays *that* make up such a big part of the [baseball] game is *what* the pitcher is up to. *I* don't mean when *he's* looking in to get the sign, winding up, throwing the ball. *I* mean during the time *he* steps off the mound and seems to be looking out at *his* outfielders or into the stands at girls. What *he's* really doing is rubbing up the ball and under the latest rules *he* has to walk off the mound to do so.

This gives him some marvelous opportunities. *He* can, for one thing, stick a finger between *his* belt and trousers and come up with a gob of previously concealed vaseline. *This* while *he* has *his* back to the plate umpire. And what good is vaseline? Well, *it's* slippery like spit. *This* means *you* can throw the ball exactly as hard as *you* would a fastball and have *it* come off *your* hand behaving like a curve. *This* is very confusing for the hitter.

ANSWERS: EXERCISE 10–1

Answers may vary somewhat. Some students may think that some of the pronouns replaced here with nouns are acceptable, but clarity is the issue—avoiding intervening information that distracts the reader, ambiguous references, and so on. One possible answer is shown on page 240.

➜

ANSWERS: EXERCISE 10–1, cont.

At the time Ludwig was crowned king, Wagner had gone into hiding to escape his many creditors. Ludwig sent his secretary to find Wagner and offer him the protection that only a royal patron could provide. The secretary delivered this message, telling Wagner to go at once to the royal court at Munich, where all his debts would be paid; moreover, Ludwig would provide him with everything he needed so that he could continue his composing free of material cares.

Thus began an intense friendship. Wagner enjoyed Ludwig's company, playing hard with him but also working hard. He spent Ludwig's money freely—too freely, many Bavarians believed. When he began to try to influence Bavarian politics, the people became restless.

Finally, Ludwig's advisors told him to choose between this friendship and his royal obligations. Regretfully, he chose to honor his responsibilities as king and told Wagner to leave the court. Ludwig's devotion continued, however, until Wagner's death. Ludwig himself met a bizarre end. Declared insane and forced to give up the monarchy, he was found drowned. The mystery of his death—murder, suicide, accident—was never solved.

10b
cont.

At the time he was crowned king, Wagner had gone into hiding to escape his many creditors. He sent his secretary to find him and offer him the protection that only a royal patron could provide. The secretary delivered this message, telling him to go at once to the royal court at Munich, where all his debts would be paid. Moreover, he would provide him with everything he needed so that he could continue his composing free of material cares.

Thus began an intense friendship. Wagner enjoyed Ludwig's company, playing hard with him but also working hard. He spent his money freely—too freely, many Bavarians believed. When he began to try to influence Bavarian politics, the people became restless.

Finally, his advisors told him to choose between this friendship and his royal obligations. Regretfully, he chose to honor his responsibilities as king and told him to leave the court. His devotion to him continued, however, until his death. He himself met a bizarre end. Declared insane and forced to give up the monarchy, he was found drowned. The mystery of his death—murder, suicide, accident—was never solved.

10c Making a pronoun refer to a definite antecedent

10c-1 Not using a pronoun to refer to a noun's possessive form

A noun's possessive form cannot be the ANTECEDENT to a pronoun, unless the pronoun is also in the possessive case.

NO The **geologist's** discovery brought **him** fame. [The pronoun *him* is not possessive and therefore cannot refer to the possessive *geologist's*.]

YES The **geologist** became famous because of **his** discovery.

YES The **geologist's** discovery was **his** alone.

10c-2 Not using a pronoun to refer to an adjective

An ADJECTIVE cannot be an antecedent. A pronoun, therefore, cannot refer to an adjective.

NO   Avery likes to study **geological** records. **That** will be her major. [*That* cannot refer to the adjective *geological*.]

YES   Avery likes to study **geological** records. **Geology** will be her major.

Making *it*, *that*, *this*, and *which* refer to only one antecedent

10c-3

When you use *it*, *that*, *this*, and *which*, check to see that the referent of these pronouns can be determined easily by your readers.

NO   Comets usually fly by the earth at 100,000 m.p.h., whereas asteroids sometimes collide with the earth. **This** interests scientists. [Does *this* refer to the speed of the comets, comets flying by the earth, or asteroids colliding with the earth?]

YES   Comets usually fly by the earth at 100,000 m.p.h., whereas asteroids sometimes collide with the earth. **This difference** interests scientists. [Adding a noun after *this* or *that* is an effective way to make your meaning clear.]

NO   A fireball, caused by the impact of either a comet or an asteroid, rose twelve miles somewhere above central Siberia in 1908, but **it** is still unknown. [Does *it* refer to the cause of the fireball or its size and location?]

YES   A fireball, caused by the impact of either a comet or an asteroid, rose twelve miles above central Siberia in 1908, but **the source of the explosion** is still unknown.

NO   I told my friends that I was going to major in geology, **which** annoyed my parents. [What does *which* refer to?]

YES   My parents were annoyed **because I discussed my major with my friends.**

YES   My parents were annoyed **because I chose to major in geology.**

Using *they* and *it* precisely

10c-4

The expression *they say* cannot take the place of stating precisely who is doing the saying. Your reader is entitled to more than a *they* to provide authority for a statement.

NO   **They** say that earthquakes are becoming more frequent.

YES   **Seismologists** say that earthquakes are becoming more frequent.

BACKGROUND

Pronoun reference errors can have several causes. Sometimes the errors occur when students try to improve a sentence in revision without paying attention to how the changes affect the relationship between a pronoun and its referent. Sometimes, as Mina Shaughnessy writes in *Errors and Expectations* (New York: Oxford UP, 1977, p. 114), errors in pronoun reference and agreement are signs of problems a student has with perception, with keeping track of what he or she has written in previous sentences and clauses. Shaughnessy also points out that the impersonal conventions of much academic writing compared to other kinds of writing also make pronoun reference errors more likely. Analytical style often "pushes writers out of reportage (description and narration), where experience grounds their generalizations, into vaguer statements about a *person* or *they* or *one*, which are more difficult to control, or even care about."

TEACHING TIP

In *Teaching One-to-One: The Writing Conference* (NCTE, 1986), Muriel Harris describes several methods for helping students with pronoun reference problems in their papers. (1) Have students circle each pronoun and draw a line to the antecedent. (2) Ask the student to clarify the meaning of a pronoun that has a vague antecedent. (3) React as a reader to confusing pronouns by pointing out the different possible meanings that the pronoun could have. "After a few rounds of this," Harris writes, "most students eventually begin to anticipate reader problems with their pronouns" (132).

10c-4 cont.

In speech, common statements are *It said on the radio* or *In Washington they say*. Because such expressions are inexact and wordy, they should be avoided in academic writing: ***The newspaper reports*** [not *It said in the newspaper*] *that minor earthquakes occur almost daily in California.*

10c-5

Not using a pronoun in the first sentence of a work to refer to the work's title

When referring to a title, repeat or reword whatever part of the title you want to use.

TITLE   Geophysics as a Major

FIRST SENTENCE

NO   This subject unites the sciences of physics, biology, and ancient life.

YES   Geophysics unites the sciences of physics, biology, and ancient life.

10d

Not overusing *it*

It has three different uses in English.

1. *It* is a personal pronoun: *Doug wants to visit the 18-inch Schmidt telescope, but **it** is on Mount Palomar.*

2. *It* is an expletive, a word that postpones the subject: ***It** is interesting to observe the stars.*

3. *It* is part of idiomatic expressions of weather, time, or distance: ***It** is sunny. **It** is midnight. **It** is not far to the hotel.*

All of these uses are acceptable, but combining them in the same sentence can create confusion.

NO   Because our car was overheating, **it** came as no surprise that **it** broke down just as **it** began to rain. [*It* is overused here even though all three uses—2, 1, and 3 above, respectively—are acceptable.]

YES   **It** came as no surprise that our overheating car broke down just as the rain began to fall.

See section 16a-1 for advice about revising wordy sentences that use expletive structures, and see section 11f for advice about using singular verbs with *it* expletives.

242

❖ ESL NOTE: Be careful not to omit *it* from an expletive (also called a *subject filler*).

NO   **Is** a lovely day.

YES   **It is** a lovely day.❖

Using *you* only for direct address   **10e**

In academic writing, *you* is not a suitable substitute for specific words that refer to people, situations, and occurrences. Exact language is always preferable. Also, *you* used for other than direct address tends to lead to wordiness. This handbook uses *you* to address you directly as the reader; it never uses *you* to refer to people in general.

NO   Uprisings in prison often occur when **you allow** overcrowded conditions to continue. [Are you, the reader of this handbook, allowing the conditions to continue?]

YES   Uprisings in prison often occur when **the authorities allow** overcrowded conditions to occur.

NO   In many states, **you have your prisons** with few rehabilitation programs. [Do you, the reader, have few programs? Also, are the prisons yours?]

YES   In many states, **prisons have** few rehabilitation programs.

NO   In Russia **you** usually have to stand in long lines to buy groceries. [Are you, the reader, planning to do your grocery shopping in Russia?]

YES   **Russian consumers** usually have to stand in long lines to buy groceries.

EXERCISE 10-2

Consulting sections 10a to 10e, revise each sentence so that all pronoun references are clear. If you consider a passage correct as written, circle its number.

EXAMPLE   In a research study, it says that romantic love is a chemical process.
A research study claims that romantic love is a chemical process.
[Revision avoids imprecise use of *it says*.]

1. Scientific evidence supports lovers' claims that they feel swept away.

2. When you fall in love, you are flooded with substances that your body manufactures.

BACKGROUND

The usefulness of pronouns is clearly demonstrated by W. Nelson Francis and Henry Kucera in their *Frequency Analysis of English Usage* (Boston: Houghton, Mifflin, 1982). After analyzing a substantial body of publications in Edited American English, Francis and Kucera determined the frequency with which specific words are used. They report that when compared with other words, the following pronouns were ranked as follows in frequency of usage.

Word	Rank
he	10
it	12
his	15
I	20
they	30
you	33
she	37
we	41
him	42

ANSWERS: EXERCISE 10–2

Answers will vary somewhat. Here is one set of possibilities.

1. Scientific evidence supports lovers who claim that they feel swept away. [10c-1; revision changes referent for *they* from the possessive case, *lovers'*, to *lovers*, a noun in the objective case.]

2. A person who falls in love is flooded with substances that the body manufactures. *Or:* When people fall in love, they are flooded with substances that their body manufactures. [10e; revision changes person from *you* not used for direct address to third person.]

→

3. Surprisingly, love owes its "natural high" to phenylethylamine (PEA), a chemical cousin of the amphetamines, as well as to emotion. [10c-4, 10d; revision eliminates overuse and imprecise use of *it* and *its*.]

4. As the body builds up a tolerance for PEA, more and more must be produced to create the euphoria of romantic love. [10c-3; revision eliminates two *its* with different referents.]

5. Although chocolate is high in PEA, gobbling it will not revive a wilting love affair. [10e; revision eliminates *your* not used for direct address.]

6. Infatuation based on PEA lasts no longer than four years. Most divorces take place after four years of marriage. [10c-3; revision eliminates imprecise use of *this*.]

7. Chemicals called endorphins are good news for romantics. Endorphins promote long-term intimate attachments. [10c-4; revision removes *they*, which seemed to refer to both *endorphins* and *romantics*.]

8. Endorphins' special effects on lovers allow these drugs to exert a soothing, not an exciting, influence. [10c-1; revision eliminates *they*, which referred to a possessive noun.]

9. Oxytocin is called the "cuddle chemical" because it seems to encourage mothers to nuzzle their babies. [10d; revision eliminates second *it*; excessive use of *it*.]

10. Romantic love also owes a debt to oxytocin, for this drug promotes similar feelings in adult lovers. [10c-3; revision removes imprecise uses of *this* and *it*.]

QUOTATION ABOUT WRITING
We are all apprentices in a craft where no one ever becomes a master.
— Ernest Hemingway

10e cont.

3. It is surprising that love owes its "natural high" to phenylethylamine (PEA), a chemical cousin of the amphetamines, as well as to emotion.
4. As the body builds up a tolerance for PEA, it is necessary to produce more and more of it to create the euphoria of romantic love.
5. Although chocolate is high in PEA, gobbling it will not revive your wilting love affair.
6. Infatuation based on PEA lasts no longer than four years. This is when most divorces take place.
7. Chemicals called endorphins are good news for romantics. They promote long-term intimate attachments.
8. Endorphins' special effects on lovers allow them to exert a soothing, not an exciting, influence.
9. Oxytocin is called the "cuddle chemical" because it seems that it encourages mothers to nuzzle their babies.
10. Romantic love also owes a debt to this, for it promotes similar feelings in adult lovers.

10f

Using *who*, *which*, and *that* correctly

Who refers to people or to animals with names or special talents.

Theodore Roosevelt, who served from 1901 to 1909 as the twenty-sixth President of the United States, inspired the creation of the stuffed animal known as the "teddy bear."

Lassie, who was known for her intelligence and courage, was actually played by a series of male collie dogs.

Which and *that* refer to animals, things, and sometimes anonymous or collective groups of people. Some writers use *which* both for restrictive clauses (clauses that add essential information to a sentence) and for nonrestrictive clauses (clauses that could be omitted from a sentence without changing the essential meaning). Other writers reserve *which* for nonrestrictive clauses and *that* for restrictive clauses. You can follow either practice as long as you are consistent in each piece of writing. For help in distinguishing between restrictive and nonrestrictive clauses, see 24e.

The zoos **that most delight children** display newborn animals as well as animals that can be touched safely. [*That* introduces information essential for understanding which zoos are being referred to.]

Zoos, **which delight most children,** have been attracting fewer visitors each year. [*Which* introduces information that could be dropped from the sentence without changing the essential message.]

Who can be used for restrictive and nonrestrictive clauses alike.

244

✤ COMMA ALERT: Set off nonrestrictive clauses with commas. Do not set off restrictive clauses with commas (see 24e).✤

EXERCISE 10-3

Consulting section 10f, fill in the blanks with *who, which,* or *that.*

EXAMPLE   Psychologists have found that most people **who** believe that the moon influences behavior actually believe that others, not they themselves, are affected by the moon.

1. Does the moon really affect human behavior? Ancient people believed the power _____ came from the moon was divine.

2. The word *lunatic,*_____ is derived from the Latin *luna,* suggests that people _____ are exposed to the moon become mad.

3. The moon, _____ has been credited by some researchers with influencing the stock market, is also thought by some experts to affect agricultural yields.

4. Some nurses _____ work in hospital delivery rooms claim it is the moon _____ stimulates labor pains to begin.

5. The moon may also affect certain groups of people, _____ include sleepwalkers and those _____ suffer from migraine headaches.

ANSWERS AND COVERAGE: EXERCISE 10–3

Note: Reserving *that* for restrictive clauses and *which* for nonrestrictive clauses when the relative pronoun's referent is a thing (rather than a person) is a useful distinction. Because it is an often-ignored distinction, item 1 and the second part of item 4 show both *that* and *which* as acceptable. (Nonrestrictive relative clauses that have inanimate or nonhuman referents use *which*.)

1. that [restrictive reference to *power,* a thing; *which* is also acceptable]

2. which [nonrestrictive reference to *word lunatic,* a thing]

3. which [nonrestrictive reference to *moon,* a thing]

4. who [reference to *nurses,* people; restrictive]; that [restrictive reference to *moon,* a thing; *which* is also acceptable]

5. which [nonrestrictive reference to *groups,* a thing]; who [restrictive reference to *those,* which refers to *people*]

11 *Agreement*

The concept of *agreement* in human affairs implies the aligning or matching of ideas. Grammatical agreement is also based on matching. Applying the rules governing grammatical agreement can be tricky, so almost everyone consults a handbook now and then to check one or another rule.

This chapter discusses agreement between subjects and verbs (see 11a through 11l) and between pronouns and antecedents (see 11m through 11r).

SUBJECT-VERB AGREEMENT

11a Understanding subject-verb agreement

Subject-verb agreement means that SUBJECTS and VERBS in clauses must "match" in form. To agree grammatically, subjects and verbs must match in number (singular or plural) and in person (first, second, or third person). The major concepts in grammatical agreement are explained in Chart 72.

The **firefly glows** with luminescent light. [*firefly* = singular subject in the third person; *glows* = singular verb in the third person]

Fireflies glow with luminescent light. [*fireflies* = plural subject in the third person; *glow* = plural verb in the third person]

This **insect is** nocturnal. [*insect* = singular subject in the third person; *is* = singular verb in the third person]

These **insects are** nocturnal. [*insects* = plural subject in the third person; *are* = plural verb in the third person]

MAJOR CONCEPTS IN GRAMMATICAL AGREEMENT 72

- **Number**, as a concept in grammar, refers to *singular* and *plural*.

- The **first person** is the speaker or writer. *I* (singular) and *we* (plural) are the only subjects that occur in the first person.

SINGULAR	**I** see a field of fireflies.
PLURAL	**We** see a field of fireflies.

- The **second person** is the person spoken or written to. *You* (for both singular and plural) is the only subject that occurs in the second person.

SINGULAR	**You** see a shower of sparks.
PLURAL	**You** see a shower of sparks.

- The **third person** is the person or thing being spoken or written of. Most rules for subject-verb agreement involve the third person.

SINGULAR	The **scientist sees** a cloud of cosmic dust.
PLURAL	The **scientists see** a cloud of cosmic dust.

Using the final -s or -es either for plural subjects or for singular verbs   11b

Subject-verb agreement often involves one letter: *s*. The basic pattern for agreement is shown in Chart 73. Keep in mind that the *-s* added to subjects and the *-s* added to verbs serve very different functions.

Most **plural subjects** are formed by adding an *-s* or *-es: lip* becomes *lips; princess* becomes *princesses*. Exceptions include most pronouns (*they, it*) and a few nouns that for singular and plural either do not change (*deer, deer*) or change internally (*mouse, mice; child, children*).

Singular verbs in the present tense of the third person are formed by adding *-s* or *-es* to the simple form of the verb: *laugh, laughs; kiss, kisses*. Even the exceptions—namely, the verbs *be* (*is*) and *have* (*has*)—end in *s*.

PATTERN FOR BASIC SUBJECT-VERB AGREEMENT

EXTRA EXERCISE A

Fill in the blank with the correct present-tense form of the verb in parentheses.

EXAMPLE

Psychologists often (to use) _____ projective tests to investigate clients' unconscious memories and drives. [*use*]

1. Psychologists sometimes (to present) _____ their clients with questions to which there are no correct answers.

2. The client then (to tell) _____ what he (to see) _____ , thus showing the psychologist some of his inner self.

3. The popular *Rorschach Psychodiagnostic Inkblot Test* (to require) _____ the client to examine ten cards containing symmetrical inkblots and say what he (to think) _____ each means.

4. Next, the client (to point) _____ out where in the blot he (to find) _____ each image or idea.

5. Several scoring systems (to exist) _____ to help psychologists interpret clients' responses.

ANSWERS: EXTRA EXERCISE A

1. present
2. tells; sees
3. requires; thinks
4. points; finds
5. exist

QUOTATION ABOUT WRITING

After college, I sat all day in a captain's chair up on 84th Street trying to write plays for live television. Each morning I would thread my bathrobe sash through the spokes of the chair and tie myself in.
—John McPhee

PATTERN FOR BASIC SUBJECT-VERB AGREEMENT   73

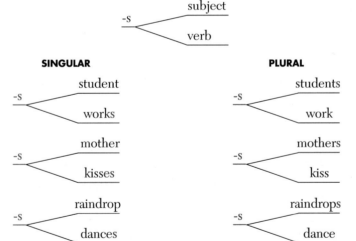

The **student disagrees** that **students watch** too much television.

Most part-time **jobs involve** ten or twenty hours a week.

Studying requires all remaining time.

Here is a memory device to help you visualize how, in most cases, the -*s* works in agreement. The -*s* (or -*es*) can take only one path at a time, going either to the top or to the bottom.

MODEL

-s   subject / verb

SINGULAR

-s   student / works

-s   mother / kisses

-s   raindrop / dances

PLURAL

-s   students / work

-s   mothers / kiss

-s   raindrops / dance

The principle of the memory device holds, even for the exceptions mentioned earlier in this section: **It** (singular pronoun) **is** *late; the* **mice** (plural with internal change) **are** *sleeping.*

✤ USAGE ALERT: Do not add -*s* to a main verb used with an auxiliary verb (a helping verb such as *be, do, can, might, must, would;* see 8e): *The coach* **can walk** (not *can walks*) *to campus.*✤

EXERCISE 11-1

Consulting sections 11a and 11b, use the subject and verb in each set to write two complete sentences—one with the subject as a singular and one with the subject as a plural. Keep all verbs in the present tense.

1. child
   laugh
2. theory
   state
3. match
   might light
4. committee
   vote

5. man
   smile
6. it
   change
7. bus
   speed
8. parade
   celebrate

For agreement, ignoring words between a subject and verb   **11c**

Words that separate the SUBJECT from the VERB do not affect what the verb should agree with. The pattern is shown in Chart 74. Such intervening material often appears as a PREPOSITIONAL PHRASE. Eliminate all prepositional phrases from consideration when you look for the subject of a clause.

NO   **Winners** of the state contest **goes** to the national finals.
        [*Winners* is the subject. The verb must agree with it; *of the state contest* is a prepositional phrase.]

YES   Winners of the state contest go to the national finals.

PATTERN WHEN WORDS SEPARATE A SUBJECT AND VERB   74

Answers will vary. Each set of sentences must use the subject once as a singular and once as a plural, and the verbs must agree accordingly.

EXTRA EXERCISE B
Fill in the blank with the correct present-tense form of the verb in parentheses.

EXAMPLE
In the eyes of many people, the Rorschach Inkblots (to be) _____ the psychologists' standard tool for getting at clients' hidden thoughts and feelings. [*are*]

1. Yet either the Holtzman Inkblot Technique or the Thematic Apperception Test (TAT) (to be) _____ given by psychologists who feel the Rorschach is unreliable.

2. Not only does the Holtzman series have more inkblots (45) than the Rorschach (10), but it also (to have) _____ a more standardized system of administration.

3. The TAT (to use) _____ a series of pictures showing people engaged in a wide range of activities.

4. Although the pictures show people in realistic situations, there (to be) _____ many possible acceptable answers.

5. It (to be) _____ the task of the person interpreting the picture to make up a story, deciding what has occurred and what the characters are thinking and feeling.

ANSWERS: EXTRA EXERCISE B
1. is
2. has
3. uses
4. are
5. is

Rewrite the following passages making the following changes: For "children" substitute "a child." For "adults" substitute "an adult." For "unicorns" substitute "a unicorn." For "books" substitute "a book." For "a dragon" substitute "dragons." For "they" substitute "he," "she," or "it," considering the antecedent. Make sure that the verbs agree with the new subjects.

So I believe that we should trust our children. Normal children do not confuse reality and fantasy—they confuse them much less often than we adults do (as a great fantasist pointed out in a story called "The Emperor's New Clothes"). Children know perfectly well that unicorns aren't real, but they also know that books about unicorns, if they are good books, are true books. All too often, that's more than Mummy and Daddy know; for, in denying . . . childhood, the adults have denied half their knowledge, and are left with the sad, sterile little fact: "Unicorns aren't real." And that fact is one that never got anybody anywhere (except in the story "The Unicorn in the Garden," by another great fantasist, in which it is shown that a devotion to the unreality of unicorns may get you straight into the loony bin). It is by such statements as, "Once upon a time there was a dragon," or "In a hole in the ground there lived a hobbit"—it is by such beautiful non-facts that we fantastic human beings may arrive, in our peculiar fashion, at the truth.

—Ursula K. Le Guin,
"Why Are Americans Afraid
of Dragons?"

➜

Be especially careful with a construction that starts *one of the*. This construction takes a singular verb to agree with the word *one*. Do not be distracted by the plural noun that comes after *of the*.

NO   **One** of the problems **are** broken equipment.
     One of the problem **is** broken equipment.

YES   **One** of the problems **is** broken equipment.

Similarly, to locate the subject of a sentence, eliminate any phrases that start with *including, together with, along with, accompanied by, in addition to, except,* and *as well as.* Be sure that the verb agrees with the subject, not with the intervening material.

NO   **The moon,** as well as Venus, **are** visible in the night sky.
     [*The moon* is the subject. The verb must agree with it. Ignore *as well as Venus.*]

YES   **The moon,** as well as Venus, **is** visible in the night sky.

NO   **The Big Dipper,** along with many other constellations, **are** easy to learn to find. [*The Big Dipper* is the subject. The verb must agree with it. Ignore *along with many other constellations.*]

YES   **The Big Dipper,** along with many other constellations, **is** easy to learn to find.

11d   **Using verbs with subjects connected with *and***

When two subjects are connected with *and*, they comprise a COMPOUND SUBJECT (see 7k) and require a plural verb. Chart 75 shows this pattern.

PATTERN WHEN TWO SUBJECTS ARE JOINED BY AND   75

The student and the instructor work long hours.

⬆   ⬆
COMPOUND   PLURAL
SUBJECT   VERB
(uses *and*)

The Cascade Diner *and* **the Wayside Diner** *have* [not *has*] fried catfish today. [two separate diners]

An exception occurs when *and* joins parts that combine to form a single thing or person.

My **best friend and neighbor** **makes** [not *make*] excellent chili. [The best friend is the same person as the neighbor. If two different people were involved, *makes* would become *make*.]

Macaroni and cheese **contains** [not *contain*] pasta, protein, and many calories.

each, every

The words *each* and *every* remain singular even when they MODI-FY a compound subject. Therefore, when *each* or *every* is used with a compound subject, the verb must be singular, not plural. (For information about verb agreement for *each* or *every* used alone, not as a modifi-er, see 11g.)

Each human hand and foot **makes** (not *make*) a distinctive print.

To identify lawbreakers, **every police chief, sheriff, and federal marshal depends** (not *depend*) on such prints.

✤ USAGE ALERT: Use either *each* or *every*, not both together, to single out something: ***Each*** (not *each and every*) *robber has been caught.*✤

Making the verb agree with the nearest subject

11e

| PATTERN WHEN SUBJECTS ARE JOINED BY *OR* | 76 |

~~Either the instructor or~~
~~Either the instructors or~~ the **student knows** the answer.

SINGULAR SINGULAR
SUBJECT VERB

~~Either the instructor or~~
~~Either the instructors or~~ the **students know** the answer.

PLURAL PLURAL
SUBJECT VERB

QUOTATION ABOUT WRITING

The author does not only write when he's at his desk, he writes all day long, when he is thinking, when he is reading, when he is experiencing; everything he sees and feels is significant to his purpose and, consciously or unconsciously, he is for-ever storing and making over his im-pressions.

—Somerset Maugham

QUOTATION ABOUT WRITING

You never have to change anything you got up in the middle of the night to write.

—Saul Bellow

TEACHING TIP

Robert DeBeaugrande in his article "Forward to the Basics: Getting Down to Grammar" (*College Composition and Communication* 35 [1984]: 358–367) suggests a simple technique to help students determine which verb must agree with the subject:

> Insert what I call a *denial word* into the statement, namely, "doesn't/don't," "didn't," or "won't." The agreeing verb of the original statement is the one now located *after* the denial word, e.g.:

A blackbird came to peck off her nose.
A blackbird *didn't come* to peck off her nose.
[agreeing verb F *came*, not *peck*]

> If you can't insert a "denial word," just try "-*n't*," and the agreeing verb is the one *before* this insertion:

The Knave of Hearts was taken to prison.
The Knave of Hearts *wasn't* taken to prison.
[agreeing verb F *was*, not *taken*]

11e
cont.

When subjects are joined with *or, nor, either . . . or, neither . . . nor,* or *not only . . . but (also),* make the verb agree with the subject closest to it. For subject-verb agreement, ignore everything before the final subject.

~~Not only the spider but also all other~~ **arachnids have** four pairs of legs.

~~Neither spiders nor~~ **flies tempt** my appetite.

~~Six clam fritters, four blue crabs, or one steamed~~ **lobster tempts** my appetite. [For less awkward wording, rearrange the items to place the plural subject next to the verb: *One steamed lobster, four blue crabs, or six clam fritters tempt my appetite.*]

11f   **Using verbs in inverted word order**

In English, the SUBJECT of a sentence normally precedes its VERB: *Astronomy is interesting.* Inverted word order means a change in that usual order. Most questions use inverted word order. Be sure to look after the verb, not before it, to check that the subject and verb agree.

Is astronomy interesting?

What **are** the **requirements** for the major?

Do John and Mary study astronomy?

If you occasionally choose to write a sentence in inverted word order to convey emphasis (see 19f), be sure to locate the subject and then make the verb agree with it.

Into deep space **shoot** probing **satellites.** [The plural verb *shoot* agrees with the inverted plural subject *satellites.*]

On the television screen **appears** an **image** of Saturn. [The singular verb *appears* agrees with the inverted singular subject *image.*]

Expletive constructions use inverted word order. With the use of *there* or *it,* they postpone the subject. Check ahead in such sentences to identify the subject, and then make sure that the verb agrees with the subject. For advice on being concise by eliminating some expletives, see 16a-1.

> **There are** nine **planets** in our solar system. [The verb *are* agrees with the subject *planets*.]
>
> **There is** probably no **life** on eight of them. [The verb *is* agrees with the subject *life*.]

It plus a singular form of the verb *be* can be an expletive construction as well: ***It is** astronomers who want new telescopes.*

EXERCISE 11-2

Consulting sections 11e and 11f, supply the correct present-tense form of the verb in parentheses.

EXAMPLE   One of the many new programs taking hold in U.S. school systems (to be) **is** the self-esteem movement.

1. Of course, there (to be) _____ some skeptics who doubt the self-esteem movement's claim to address widespread social problems.
2. California schoolteacher Jack Canfield and many of his colleagues (to believe) _____ that motivational training in self-esteem can help reduce drug abuse, teenage pregnancy, and welfare dependency.
3. In Canfield's seminars, either his team leaders or Canfield himself (to ask) _____ participants to make up events, act out their responses, and explain the outcomes.
4. From such role-playing techniques (to come) _____ awareness that actions have consequences.
5. There (to be) _____ also great security in being able to act out a risky situation in a safe environment.

Using verbs with indefinite pronouns   11g

Many **indefinite pronouns** refer to unknown persons, things, quantities, or ideas—thus the label "indefinite." In context in a sentence, even indefinite pronouns that do not have a specific ANTECEDENT can take on clear meaning. Most indefinite pronouns are singular and require a singular verb for agreement. Two indefinite pronouns, *both* and *many*, are always plural and require a plural verb. A few indefinite pronouns can be singular or plural. See Chart 77 for a list of indefinite pronouns and their numbers. (For advice on avoiding sexist language with indefinite pronouns, see 11q and 21b.)

BACKGROUND ON LANGUAGE, cont.

According to Martha Kolln of Pennsylvania State University, we shouldn't be too concerned about this usage. In "Everyone's Right to Their Own Language" (*College Composition and Communication* 37 [1986]: 100–102), she looks at the issue. Most handbooks treat this usage as, at best, informal, while some continue to label it an outright error. Yet, Kolln points out, studies of usage patterns indicate that *everybody* has been treated as a plural for over four hundred years and *everyone* for over two hundred, appearing this way in the works of Cardinal Newman, Shakespeare, and Swift. Despite this evidence (available since 1957), the rule stands—at least on the record.

Kolln argues for treating indefinite pronouns as we treat collective nouns. A collective noun such as *crowd* takes a singular verb but takes a plural pronoun when it clearly refers to more than one person. She gives as an example:

> At first *the crowd* was singing; then *they* began to laugh.

Kolln gives this example for indefinite pronouns:

> At first *everyone* in the room was singing; then *they* began to laugh.

In fact, a singular pronoun would be out of place in the second clause. She demonstrates that the same applies when the indefinite pronoun appears as the direct object or as the subject of a tag question.

Kolln ends by calling for the acceptance of the plural possessive pronoun (*their*) after collective indefinite pronouns:

> These dicta that designate all indefinite pronouns as singular have no basis either in actual usage or in the rules of

➡️

COMMON INDEFINITE PRONOUNS

77

ALWAYS PLURAL

both	many

ALWAYS SINGULAR

another	every	no one
anybody	everybody	nothing
anyone	everyone	one
anything	everything	somebody
each	neither	someone
either	nobody	something

SINGULAR OR PLURAL DEPENDING ON CONTEXT

all	more	none
any	most	some

SINGULAR INDEFINITE PRONOUNS

Everything about that intersection **is** dangerous.

But whenever **anyone says** anything, **nothing is** done.

Each of us **has** (not *have*) to shovel snow; **each is** (not *are*) expected to help.

Every snowstorm of the past two years **has** (not *have*) been severe. **Every** one of them **has** (not *have*) caused massive traffic jams.

SINGULAR OR PLURAL INDEFINITE PRONOUNS

Some of our streams **are** polluted. [*Some* refers to the plural *streams*, so the plural verb *are* is correct.]

Some pollution **is** reversible, but **all** pollution **is** a threat to the balance of nature. [*Some* and *all* refer to the singular *pollution*, so the singular verb *is* is correct in both cases.]

All that environmentalists ask **is** to give nature a chance. [*All* has the meaning here of "the entire thing" or "the only thing," so the singular verb *is* is correct.]

Winter has driven the birds south; **all have** left. [*All* refers to *birds,* so the plural verb *have* is correct.]

❖ USAGE ALERT: Do not mix singular and plural when indefinite pronouns function as ADJECTIVES, as in constructions such as *this kind, this type, these kinds,* and *these types. This* is singular, as are *kind* and *type; these* is plural, as are *kinds* and *types:* **This kind** of *weather* **makes** me *shiver.* **These kinds** of *sweaters* **keep** me *warm.*❖

Using verbs in context for collective nouns **11h**

A **collective noun** names a group of people or things: *family, group, audience, class, number, committee, team,* and the like. When the group acts as one unit, use a singular verb. When the members of the group act individually, thus creating more than one action, use a plural verb.

The senior class nervously **awaits** final exams. [*Class* is acting as a single unit, so the verb is singular.]

The senior class were fitted for their graduation robes today. [Each member was fitted individually, so because more than one fitting was involved, the verb is plural.]

The couple in blue **is** engaged. [*Couple* refers to a single unit, so the verb is singular.]

The couple say their vows tomorrow. [Each of the two people will take a separate action, so because more than one action is involved, the verb is plural.]

Making a linking verb agree with the subject—not the subject complement **11i**

Linking verbs indicate a state of being or a condition. They connect the subject to its **complement,** which is a word that renames or describes the subject. You can think of a linking verb as an equal sign between a subject and its complement, called the **subject complement.**

The car **looks** new. [*The car = new; the car* is the subject, *looks* is the linking verb, and *new* is the subject complement.]

BACKGROUND ON LANGUAGE, cont.

logic. Yet the current handbooks apply the same rule to all of the indefinite pronouns, whether they are collective or not, whether singular or not. (102)

Whether you agree or disagree with Kolln, the issue is certainly worth discussion.

BACKGROUND

Usage of masculine generic pronouns, "he or she," and the "singular *they*" (referring to a singular antecedent) has undergone considerable change in the last sixty years, according to Miriam Watkins Meyers in "Current Generic Pronoun Usage: An Empirical Study" (*American Speech* 65 [1990]: 228–237). A 1932 survey by Sterling A. Leonard reported that linguists "regarded *he or she* as established usage and singular *they* as established in some contexts." But a 1985 survey revealed that almost no American editors approved the singular *they* and only half preferred *he or she* to *he.* A 1982 study of college students found that 42 percent used *he,* 42 percent singular *they,* and only 7 percent *he or she.* Meyers's own study of writings by 392 adult college juniors and seniors, ranging from 22 to 64 in age, showed that "singular *they* is well established in the public writing of adult Americans" and that *he or she* is preferred increasingly to masculine generic pronouns. Women and younger adults are more likely to use alternatives to masculine generic pronouns than men and older adults.

11i
cont.

When you write a sentence that contains a subject complement, remember that the verb always agrees with the subject. For the purposes of agreement, ignore the subject complement.

NO **The worst part** of owning a car **are** the bills. [The subject is *the worst part,* with which the verb *are* does not agree; the subject complement is *the bills.*]

YES **The worst part** of owning a car **is** the bills. [The subject *the worst part* agrees with the verb *is*; the subject complement is *the bills.*]

When the wording of a sentence is revised so that the word or words that were the subject complement become the subject, the same rule applies: the verb always agrees with the subject. For the purposes of agreement, ignore the subject complement.

NO **Bills is** the worst part of owning a car.

YES **Bills are** the worst part of owning a car.

11j   Using verbs that agree with the antecedents of *who, which,* and *that*

The pronouns *who, which,* and *that* have the same form in singular and plural. Before deciding whether the VERB should be singular or plural, find the pronoun's ANTECEDENTS.

The scientist will share the income from her new patent with the graduate **students who work** with her. [*Who* refers to *students,* so the plural verb *work* is used.]

George Jones is **the student who works** in the science lab. [*Who* refers to *student,* so the singular verb *works* is used.]

Be especially careful when you use *one of the* or *the only one of the* in a sentence before *who, which,* or *that.* If the pronoun refers to *one,* use a singular verb. If the pronoun refers to what comes after *one of the,* use a plural verb.

Tracy is one of the students **who talk** in class. [*Who* refers to *students,* so *talk* is plural.]

Jim is one of the students **who talks** in class. [*Who* refers to *one,* so *talks* is singular.]

EXERCISE 11-3

Consulting sections 11g through 11j, supply the correct present-tense form of the verb in parentheses.

EXAMPLE   Everyone (to know) **knows** that a good laugh (to make) **makes** most people feel better.

1. Daily, a group of humor consultants (to work) _____ to introduce laughter into American businesses.

2. The humorists believe that the best introduction for a speech (to be) _____ jokes and humorous observations.

3. C. W. Metcalf has developed one of the programs that (to encourage) _____ people to laugh at their own problems.

4. A large number of personnel officers (to say) _____ they prefer to hire workers who (to have) _____ a sense of humor.

5. Sales representatives find that almost anyone (to listen) _____ more attentively to a person who (to make) _____ an amusing comment.

Using singular verbs with subjects that specify amounts and with singular subjects that are in plural form   **11k**

Subjects that refer to times, sums of money, distance, or measurement are considered singular and take singular verbs.

Two hours is not enough time to finish that project.

Three hundred dollars is what we must pay.

Three-quarters of an inch is needed for a perfect fit.

Two miles is a short sprint for some serious joggers.

Many words that end in *-s* or *-ics* are singular in meaning and so need singular verbs, despite their plural appearance. These words include *news, ethics,* and *measles.* They also include *economics, mathematics, physics,* and *statistics* when these words refer to courses of study. Also, the *United States of America* is singular (see also 41c).

The **news gets** better each day. [*News* is singular, so the singular verb *gets* is correct.]

Statistics is required of science majors. [*Statistics* is a course of study, so the singular verb *is* is correct.]

Statistics show that a teacher shortage is coming. [*Statistics* refers to separate pieces of information, so the plural verb *show* is correct.]

EXTRA EXERCISE E

Complete the following sentences by supplying an appropriate verb.

1. Physics _____ a demanding subject.

2. Do you think physics or economics _____ harder?

3. Sports _____ the popular favorite.

4. Three-quarters of an hour of exercise several times a week _____ enough to keep a person in reasonably good shape.

5. Statistics _____ that exercise of the body as well as the mind _____ important for good health.

ANSWERS: EXTRA EXERCISE E

1. is
2. is
3. is
4. is
5. show (indicate); is

11k **cont.**

Some NOUNS are singular in some contexts and plural in others. They include *politics* and *sports*. Such words agree with singular or plural verbs, depending on the meaning of the sentence.

> **Sports is** a good way to build physical stamina.

> Three **sports are** offered at the recreation center.

Some words require a plural verb even though they refer to one thing: *jeans, pants, scissors, clippers, tweezers, eyeglasses, thanks,* and *riches.* If, however, the word *pair* is used in conjunction with *jeans, pants, scissors, clippers, tweezers,* or *eyeglasses,* a singular verb is required to agree with *pair.*

> **My slacks need** pressing.

> **My pair of slacks needs** pressing.

Series and *means* have the same form in singular and plural, so the meaning determines whether the verb is singular or plural.

> **Six new television *series are*** beginning this week.

> **A *series* of disasters *is*** plaguing our production.

11l ## Using singular verbs for titles of written works, companies, and words as terms

Even when PLURAL and COMPOUND NOUNS occur in a title, the title itself indicates one work or entity. Therefore, titles of written works are singular and require singular verbs.

> ***Breathing Lessons*** by Anne Tyler **is** a prize-winning novel.

If a word that is plural is referred to as a term, it requires a singular verb.

> **We implies** that I am included.

> During the Vietnam War, ***protective reaction strikes* was** a euphemism used by the U.S. government to mean *bombing.*

EXERCISE 11-4

Consulting sections 11a through 11l, supply the correct form of the verb in parentheses.

EXAMPLE   Although it names awards as desirable as Oscars, the term Louies rarely (to gain) **gains** instant recognition.

1. One of the highlights of the greeting-card industry (to be) _____ its annual international meeting, at which Louies are awarded to the year's outstanding cards.

ANSWERS AND COVERAGE: EXERCISE 11–4

1. is [*one of the* construction; 11c]

→

2. Louis Prang, a nineteenth-century lithographer who has been called the father of the American greeting card, (to be) _____ the guiding spirit behind this award.

3. There (to be) _____ more than 900 greeting-card publishers in the United States, many of whom (to enter) _____ this competition each year.

4. Thirty (to be) _____ an astonishing number of categories for greeting cards, including graduation, get well, religious holidays, other holidays, and special effects.

5. The category special effects (to include) _____ cards with pop-up, musical, and even lighted messages, which flash out their greetings.

6. Moon and star designs (to seem) _____ to be the most popular format for romantic greeting cards.

7. Each birth announcement card from one publisher (to come) _____ with two envelopes, one pink and one blue.

8. Lacking an official category (to be) _____ cards that congratulate their recipient on gaining a scouting award, a driver's license, or U.S. citizenship.

9. The community of greeting-card companies (to believe) _____ that encouragement cards of this sort (to cover) _____ too many situations to be judged in a single category.

10. Of all the many greetings sent through the mail, the number-one bestseller (to remain) _____ Christmas cards.

PRONOUN-ANTECEDENT AGREEMENT

Understanding pronoun-antecedent agreement   11m

Pronoun-antecedent agreement means that pronouns (such as *it, they, their*; see 7b) must "match" in form with their **antecedents**— the NOUNS, NOUN PHRASES, or other pronouns to which they refer. To agree gramatically, pronouns must match in number (singular or plural) and in person (first, second, or third person); chart 78 shows these relationships. For explanations of major concepts in grammatical agreement, consult Chart 72 in section 11a.

Agreement between pronouns and antecedents must be clear so that readers are not distracted by having to figure out the intended meaning of a sentence. (For related material on subjects and verbs, see section 11a. Also, for advice about staying consistent in person and number, see section 15a-1.)

ANSWERS AND COVERAGE:
EXERCISE 11–4, cont.

2. **was** [singular subject; 11a]
3. **are** [words in inverted order; 11f]; **enter** [agrees with antecedent of *whom* (*publishers*); 11j]
4. **is** [singular verb with specific amount subject; 11k]
5. **includes** [singular subject in plural form; 11k]
6. **seem** [plural subject; 11b]
7. **comes** [singular verb with *each*; 11g]
8. **are** [inverted order; 11f]
9. **believes** [singular-context collective noun; 11h]; **cover** [ignoring intervening words; 11c]
10. **remains** [agreeing with subject *bestseller*, not subject complement *cards*; 11f]

EXTRA EXERCISE F

In writing groups students can work together to edit the inaccurate agreement of pronouns and antecedents in the following paragraph.

Plaids have been a favorite fabric design for many centuries. It consists of bars of color crossing each other at right angles. Scotland is the home of the plaid, where they are called a tartan, or, in song, story, and legend, *plaidies*. The tartan, which distinguish the clan of their wearers, is ancient, but their origin is unknown. In its earliest forms they were pieces of cloth about two yards broad and four yards long, which was drawn round the waist in folds that was tightly buckled with a belt. The lower part came down to the knees, and the upper part fell over the left shoulder so that they left the right arm free. Early in the eighteenth century, the "belted plaid" disappeared. They were replaced by the kilt. The particular pattern of tartans which distinguish each clan must have been fixed before 1645, probably before 1600. Later, in 1746, trying to end the clan system, the British Parliament prohibited the Scots from wearing tartans. The action against it was taken following the Battle of Culloden where Prince Charles Edward Stuart, grandson of James II, was defeated by the Duke of Cumberland. To be caught wearing them carried a penalty of six months' imprisonment. The kilt is worn today so that when the wearer is standing erect, their edges should reach the center of the kneecap. They should be made of a tartan associated with the name of the wearer. In the absence of a family claim to wear them, the Scots allow the wearing of the Royal Stuart tartan.

11m cont.

The **firefly** glows with luminescent light when **it** emerges from **its** nest at dusk. [The singular pronouns *it* and *its* match their singular antecedent *firefly*.]

Fireflies glow with luminescent light when **they** emerge from **their** nests at dusk. [The plural pronouns *they* and *their* match their plural antecedent *fireflies*.]

PATTERN FOR BASIC PRONOUN-ANTECEDENT AGREEMENT   78

Loud music has **its** harmful side effects.

THIRD-PERSON	THIRD-PERSON
SINGULAR	SINGULAR
ANTECEDENT	PRONOUN

The **musicians** damaged **their** hearing.

THIRD-PERSON	THIRD-PERSON
PLURAL	PLURAL
ANTECEDENT	PRONOUN

11n   ## Using pronouns with antecedents connected with *and*

When two or more antecedents are connected with *and*, they require a plural pronoun, even if the separate antecedents are singular. (For related material on subjects and verbs, see 11d.)

The Cascade Diner *and* the Wayside Diner closed for New Year's Eve to give **their** (not *its*) employees the night off. [separate diners]

An exception occurs when *and* joins singular nouns that combine to form a single thing or person.

My **best friend *and* neighbor** makes **his** (not *their*) excellent chili every Saturday. [The *best friend* is the same person as the *neighbor*. If two different people were involved, *his* would become *their*—and *makes* would become *make*.]

each, every

The words *each* and *every* are always singular. When *each* or *every* precedes antecedents joined by *and*, the pronoun must be singular. (For related material on subjects and verbs, see 11d. Also, for advice about pronoun agreement for *each* or *every* used alone, see 11p.)

Each human hand and foot leaves **its** (not *their*) distinctive print.

The same rule holds when the construction *one of the* follows *each* or *every*: **Each one of the robbers** left **his** (not *their*) *fingerprints at the scene.*

Making the pronoun agree with the nearest antecedent

11o

Antecedents joined by *or, nor,* or correlative conjunctions (such as *either . . . or, not only . . . but [also]*; for a list, see 7h) often mix singular and plural. For the purposes of agreement, ignore everything before the final antecedent. (For related material on subject-verb agreement, see 11e.) The pattern in Chart 79 illustrates this principle.

PATTERN WHEN ANTECEDENTS ARE JOINED BY *OR*   79

~~Either the loudspeakers or~~ **the microphone** needs **its** electric cord repaired.

SINGULAR ANTECEDENT   SINGULAR PRONOUN

~~Either the microphone or~~ **the loudspeakers** need **their** electric cords repaired.

PLURAL ANTECEDENT   PLURAL PRONOUN

Each night after the restaurant closes, either the resident mice or **the owner's cat** manages to get **itself** a good meal of leftovers.

Each night after the restaurant closes, either the owner's cat or **the resident mice** manage to get **themselves** a good meal of leftovers.

PATTERN WHEN ANTECEDENTS ARE JOINED BY OR

ANSWERS: EXTRA EXERCISE F

Plaids have been favorite fabric *designs* for many centuries. *They* consist of bars of color crossing each other at right angles. Scotland is the home of the plaid, where *it* is called a tartan, or, in song, story, and legend, a *plaidie*. The tartan, *which distinguishes* the clan of *its wearer*, is ancient, but *its* origin is unknown. In its earliest form, *it* was *a piece* of cloth about two yards broad and four yards long, which was drawn round the waist in folds that *were* tightly buckled with a belt. The lower part came down to the knees, and the upper part fell over the left shoulder so that *it* left the right arm free. Early in the eighteenth century, the "belted plaid" disappeared. *It* was replaced by the kilt. The particular pattern of *tartan which distinguishes* each clan must have been fixed before 1645, probably before 1600. Later, in 1746, trying to end the clan system, the British Parliament prohibited the Scots from wearing *the tartan*. The action against it was taken following the Battle of Culloden where Prince Charles Edward Stuart, grandson of James II, was defeated by the Duke of Cumberland. To be caught wearing *it* carried a penalty of six months' imprisonment. The kilt is worn today so that when the wearer is standing erect, *its* edges should reach the center of the kneecap. *It* should be made of a tartan associated with the name of the wearer. In the absence of a family claim to wear *one*, the Scots allow the wearing of the Royal Stuart tartan.

EXTRA EXERCISE G

Rewrite this paragraph so that pronoun-antecedent agreement in person and number is maintained. It may also be necessary to change verbs or other words.

Buying stock involves many steps. Once a stockbroker receives an order,

→

EXTRA EXERCISE G, cont.

they call their firm's telephone clerk, who is located near the edge of the trading area. The telephone clerk summons his firm's floor broker by flashing their code number on a large electronic board posted in the trading area. Seeing their number, the floor broker goes to the telephone clerk and picks up the buy order. You then go to the small area set aside for trading in that company's stock. An employee of the Stock Exchange keeps track of all bids to buy and sell that particular stock. The floor broker makes an offer. If they are accepted by the selling broker, the stock is his. If you have bid too low, he must make another bid before someone else gets the stock. Then a reporter enters the deal into the Exchange computer, and they become part of the official record in seconds. After all this, the floor broker returns to the telephone clerk, who reports the deal to the original stockbroker, who bills the client.

ANSWERS: EXTRA EXERCISE G

Buying stock involves many steps. Once a stockbroker receives an order, *he* calls *his* firm's telephone clerk, who is located near the edge of the trading area. The telephone clerk summons his firm's floor broker by flashing *his* code number on a large electronic board posted in the trading area. Seeing *his* number, the floor broker goes to the telephone clerk and picks up the buy order. *He* then goes to the small area set aside for trading in that company's stock. An employee of the Stock Exchange keeps track of all bids to buy and sell that particular stock. The floor broker makes an offer. If *it is* accepted by the selling broker, the stock is his. If *he has* bid too low, he must make another bid before someone else gets the stock. Then a reporter enters the deal into the Exchange computer, and *it* becomes part of the official record in seconds. After all this, the floor broker returns to the telephone clerk, who reports the deal to the original stockbroker, who bills the client.

11p | # Using pronouns with indefinite-pronoun antecedents

Many indefinite pronouns refer to unknown persons, things, quantities, or ideas—thus the label "indefinite." In context within a sentence, even indefinite pronouns that do not have a specific antecedent take on clear meaning. Most indefinite pronouns are singular. Two indefinite pronouns, *both* and *many*, are plural and thus function as plurals when they are antecedents. A few indefinite pronouns can be singular or plural, depending on the meaning of the sentence. (For a list of indefinite pronouns grouped by number, see Chart 77 in section 11g. For advice on avoiding sexist language with indefinite pronouns, see 11q and 21b.)

SINGULAR INDEFINITE PRONOUNS

Everyone taking this course hopes to get **his or her** [not *their*] college degree within a year.

Anybody wanting to wear a cap and gown at graduation must have **his or her** [not *their*] measurements taken.

Each student **is** [not *are*] hoping for a passing grade.

Each of the students handed in **his or her** [not *their*] final term paper.

Every student **needs** [not *need*] encouragement now and then.

Every student in my classes **is** [not *are*] studying hard.

SINGULAR OR PLURAL INDEFINITE PRONOUNS

When winter break arrives for students, **most** leave **their** dormitories for the comforts of home. [*Most* refers to students, so the plural pronoun *their* is correct.]

As for the luggage, **most** is already on **its** way to the airport. [*Most* refers to *luggage*, so the singular pronoun *its* is correct.]

None fear that **they** will fail. [The entire group does not expect to fail, so a plural pronoun is correct.]

None fears that **he or she** will fail. [No one individual expects to fail, so a singular pronoun is correct; note that *he or she* always functions as a singular pronoun (see Chart 80).]

Avoiding sexist pronoun use

In the past, grammatical convention specified using masculine pronouns to refer to indefinite pronouns: "*Everyone* open *his* book." Today, people are more conscious that the pronouns *he, his, him,* and *himself* exclude women, who comprise over half the population. Many experienced writers try to avoid using masculine pronouns to refer to the entire population. Chart 80 shows three ways to avoid using masculine pronouns when referring to males and females together. (For advice on how to avoid other types of sexist language, see 21b.)

WAYS TO AVOID USING ONLY THE MASCULINE PRONOUN TO REFER TO MALES AND FEMALES TOGETHER   80

Solution 1: Use a pair of pronouns—but try to avoid a pair more than once in a sentence or in many sentences in a row. When you use a *he or she* construction, remember that it acts as a singular pronoun.

> **Everyone** hopes that **he or she** wins the scholarship.
>
> With the explosion of information, a **doctor** usually has time to read in only **his or her** specialty.

Solution 2: Revise into the plural.

> **Many people** hope that **they** win the scholarship.
>
> With the explosion of information, few **doctors** have time to read outside **their** specialties.

Solution 3: Recast the sentence.

> Everyone hopes to win the scholarship.
>
> With the explosion of medical information, few specialists have time for general reading.

Using pronouns with collective-noun antecedents

A **collective noun** names a group of people or things, such as *family, group, audience, class, number, committee,* and *team.* When the group acts as one unit, use a singular pronoun to refer to it. When the members of the group act individually, thus creating more than one action, use a plural pronoun.

REFERENCE TO SUPPLEMENT

This topic is included in the TASP writing competency test. Refer students to *Preparing for the TASP* by M. Saenz.

QUOTATION ABOUT WRITING

They ask me if I were on a desert island and knew nobody would ever see what I wrote, would I go on writing. My answer is most emphatically yes, I would go on writing for company. Because I'm creating an imaginary—it's always imaginary—world in which I would like to live.
—William Burroughs

The audience was cheering as **it** stood to applaud the performers. [The *audience* was acting as one unit, so the singular pronoun *it* is correct.]

The audience put on **their** coats and walked out. [The members of the audience were acting as individuals, so all actions collect to become plural; therefore, the plural pronoun *their* is correct.]

The family is spending **its** vacation in Rockport, Maine. [All the family members went to one place together.]

The family are spending **their** vacations in Maine, Hawaii, and Rome. [Each family member went to a different place.]

EXERCISE 11-5

Consulting sections 11m through 11r, choose the proper pronoun to agree with its antecedent.

EXAMPLE   Many people wonder what gives certain leaders (his or her, their) **their** spark and magnetic personal appeal.

1. The cluster of personal traits that produces star quality is called *charisma*, a state that bestows special power on (its, their) _____ bearers.

2. Charisma is the quality that allows an individual to empower (himself, herself, himself or herself, themselves) _____ and others.

3. Power and authority alone do not guarantee charisma; to produce it, (it, they) _____ must be combined with passion and strong purpose.

4. A charismatic leader has the ability to draw other people into (his, her, his or her, their) _____ dream or vision.

5. (He, She, He or she, They) _____ inspires followers to believe that the leader's goals are the same as (his, her, his or her, their) _____ own.

6. Not all leaders who possess charisma enjoy having this ability to attract and influence (his, his or her, their) _____ followers.

7. Charismatic leaders are often creative, especially in (his, his or her, their) _____ capacity for solving problems in original ways.

8. Today, a number of major corporations offer (its, their) _____ employees charisma-training courses to enhance leadership qualities.

9. Usually, it is not the quiet, low-profile manager but rather the charismatic manager with strong leadership qualities who convinces others that (his, her, his or her, their) _____ best interests are served by the course of action (he, she, he or she, they) _____ is proposing.

10. Charisma trainers advise would-be leaders to start by bringing order to (his, her, his or her, their) _____ activities; in stressful times, anyone who appears to have some part of (his, her, his or her, their) _____ life under control makes others relax and perform (his, her, his or her, their) _____ responsibilities better.

ANSWERS AND COVERAGE: EXERCISE 11–5

1. *its* bearers [11m]
2. to empower *himself or herself* [11q]
3. *they* must [11n]
4. ... leader ... into *his or her* [11q]
5. *He or she* inspires [11q]; *their* [11m] dream
6. Not all leaders ... *their* [11m]
7. ... leaders ... *their* [11m]
8. ... a number of major corporations offer *their* own [11m]
9. others that *their* [11m]; *he or she* is proposing [11q]
10. order to *their* [11m]; *his or her* life [11q]; perform *their* [11m]

Focus on Revising

If you make errors in agreement when you write, go back to your writing and locate the errors. Using this chapter as a resource, revise your writing to correct the problems. Sections 11a through 11l discuss subject-verb agreement. Sections 11m through 11r discuss pronoun-antecedent agreement.

CASE STUDY: REVISING FOR AGREEMENT

In these case studies, you can observe a student writer revising. Then you have the chance to revise other student writing on your own.

OBSERVATION

A student wrote the following draft for a course in training as rehabilitation therapists. The assignment was to discuss the main idea of a film about handicapped athletes. The material offers a good summary of the film, but the draft's effectiveness is diminished by errors in subject-verb agreement and in pronoun-antecedent agreement.

Read through the draft. The errors are highlighted and explained. Before you look at the student's revision, revise the material yourself. Then compare what you and the student did.

Last week, students training as physical therapists saw a film about severely handicapped people participating actively in sports. The class know now that doing the impossible is becoming normal for many handicapped people.

General fitness and eagerness to compete is among the reasons that a handicapped person might want to develop their skill in sports. All that is needed is a minimum of mobility and the will to train very hard. Either artificial limbs—called *prostheses*—or a wheelchair allow many severely handicapped people to become athletes. Advances in

singular verb needed for this collective noun: 11h

singular pronoun needed: 11m

verb should be plural for subjects joined by *and*: 11d

the linking verb should agree with the subject: 11i

verb should agree with subject closer to it: 11e

→

COVERAGE: PARTICIPATION ESSAY, PAGE 267

Without kidney function, the body's ability to regulate fluids, blood pressure, red-cell production, protein levels, and blood chemistry *are* [11c: intervening words, singular verb needed] destroyed. If the kidneys no longer function, the standard prescription *are* [11i: linking verb, singular verb needed] dialysis treatments. Two or three times a week *are* [11k: amounts, singular verb needed] the norm for the treatments, which sometimes *continues* [11j: plural verb needed to agree with *treatments*] for months or even years. Dialysis, though, does not do everything that healthy kidneys *does* [11j: relative pronoun use here calls for plural verb].

Reregulating the amount of water in the blood and tissues *are* [11c: intervening words, singular verb needed] the best-known function of the kidney. Therefore, someone without functioning kidneys must be careful to keep *their* [11p: indefinite pronoun as antecedent, *his or her* needed] fluid intake within limits set by the doctor. Dialysis *help* [11a: singular subject calls for singular verb] to remove excess fluid. Reducing salt and controlling fluid intake also *helps* [11d: compound subject, plural verb needed]. Neither medical procedures nor diet *are* [11e: closest subject calls for singular verb] effective, however, without cooperation from the patient.

The whole family *are* [11h: collective noun calls for singular verb] affected, so it is important that the medical team *discuss* [11h: collective noun calls for singular verb] the functions of a healthy kidney with the patient and the family so that *he* [11n: compound antecedent calls for plural pronoun *they*] better understand the problems involved. Once the team makes *their* [11r: collective noun calls for singular pronoun *its*] treatment recommendations known, everyone can work together with greater patience and understanding.

design and material have led to better athletic equipment for the handicapped.

Barriers are broken daily. Rafting, rock climbing, and basketball have found enthusiasts among the handicapped. Marathon racing, along with skiing and cycling, also have great appeal. Many have tried their skill at these sports. One competitive event for the handicapped was the eighth Paralympic Games, which was held in Seoul, South Korea, the site of the 1988 Olympics.

Every disabled athlete needs to train somewhat differently to accommodate their particular handicap. One of today's most versatile athletes compete in a triathlon event by wearing one kind of prosthesis for cycling, another for running, and none for swimming.

verb should agree with subject, not with words between subject and verb: 11c

plural verb needed to agree with this use of which: 11j

singular pronoun needed: 11p

singular verb needed to agree with one: 11c

Here is how the student revised the paragraph to correct the agreement errors. In a few places, the student had alternatives for the revision, so your revision might not match this one exactly. Your revision should, however, deal with each error highlighted on the draft.

Last week, students training as physical therapists saw a film about severely handicapped people participating actively in sports. The class knows now that doing the impossible is becoming normal for many handicapped people.

General fitness and eagerness to compete are among the reasons that a handicapped person might want to develop his or her skill in sports. All that is needed are a minimum of mobility and the will to train very hard. Either artificial limbs—called *prostheses*—or a wheelchair allows many severely handicapped people to become athletes. Advances in design and material have led to better athletic equipment for the handicapped.

Barriers are broken daily. Rafting, rock climbing, and basketball have found enthusiasts among the handicapped. Marathon racing, along with skiing and cycling, also has great appeal. Many have tried their skill at these sports. One competitive event for the handicapped was the eighth Paralympic Games, which were held in Seoul, South Korea, the site of the 1988 Olympics.

Every disabled athlete needs to train somewhat differently to accommodate his or her particular handicap. One of today's most versatile athletes competes in a triathlon event by wearing one kind of prosthesis for cycling, another for running, and none for swimming.

Participation

A student wrote the following draft for a course called Introduction to Health Sciences. The assignment was to write about a function of the body. The material is concisely written and explains the material clearly, but the draft's effectiveness is diminished by pronoun-antecedent agreement errors and by subject-verb agreement errors.

Read through the draft. Then revise it to eliminate the errors. Also, make any additional revisions you think would improve the content, organization, and style of the material.

Without kidney function, the body's ability to regulate fluids, blood pressure, red-cell production, protein levels, and blood chemistry are destroyed. If the kidneys no longer function, the standard prescription are dialysis treatments. Two or three times a week are the norm for the treatments, which sometimes continues for months or even years. Dialysis, though, does not do everything that healthy kidneys does.

Regulating the amount of water in the blood and tissues are the best-known function of the kidney. Therefore, someone without functioning kidneys must be careful to keep their fluid intake within limits set by the doctor. Dialysis help to remove excess fluid. Reducing salt and controlling fluid intake also helps. Neither medical procedures nor diet are effective, however, without cooperation from the patient.

The whole family are affected, so it is important that the medical team discuss the functions of a healthy kidney with the patient and the family so that he better understand the problems involved. Once the team makes their treatment recommendations known, everyone can work together with greater patience and understanding.

ANSWER: PARTICIPATION ESSAY

This version revises the agreement errors. Answers will vary if students have revised for content, organization, or style.

Without kidney function, the body's ability to regulate fluids, blood pressure, red-cell production, protein levels, and blood chemistry is destroyed. If the kidneys no longer function, the standard prescription is dialysis treatments. Two or three times a week is the norm for the treatments, which sometimes continue for months or even years. Dialysis, though, does not do everything that healthy kidneys do.

Regulating the amount of water in the blood and tissues is the best-known function of the kidney. Therefore, someone without functioning kidneys must be careful to keep his or her fluid intake within limits set by the doctor. Dialysis helps to remove excess fluid. Reducing salt and controlling fluid intake also help. Neither medical procedures nor diet is effective, however, without cooperation from the patient.

The whole family is affected, so it is important that the medical team discusses the functions of a healthy kidney with the patient and the family so that they better understand the problems involved. Once the team makes its treatment recommendations known, everyone can work together with greater patience and understanding.

12 *Using Adjectives and Adverbs*

REFERENCES TO SUPPLEMENTS
For this topic in the CLAST writing competency test, refer students to ch. 1, section B4e of *Preparing for the CLAST* by S. Patterson.

This topic is included in the TASP writing competency test. Refer students to *Preparing for the TASP* by M. Saenz.

WORD DERIVATION
Adjective comes from the Latin *adjectus*, meaning *that is added*, and *adverb* comes from the Latin *adverbus*, meaning *to a word*. Both etymologies reflect the use of adjectives and adverbs as enhancers of other words' meanings.

QUOTATION ABOUT WRITING
The adjective is the enemy of the noun.
—Voltaire

QUOTATION ABOUT WRITING
What you say is found not in the noun but in what you add to qualify the noun. . . . The noun, the verb, and the main clause serve merely as the base on which meaning will rise. . . . The modifier is the essential part of any sentence.
—John Erskine, "The Craft of Writing"

QUOTATION ABOUT WRITING
I don't think in any language. I think in images. I don't believe that people think in languages.
—Vladimir Nabokov

12a **Distinguishing between adjectives and adverbs**

Both **adjectives** and **adverbs** are modifiers—words or groups of words that describe other words.

ADJECTIVE	The **brisk** *wind* blew. [Adjective *brisk* modifies noun *wind*.]
ADVERB	The wind *blew* **briskly**. [Adverb *briskly* modifies verb *blew*.]

The key to distinguishing between adjectives and adverbs is understanding that they modify different words or groups of words. As Chart 81 demonstrates, if you want to modify a NOUN or PRONOUN, use an adjective. If you want to modify a VERB, an adjective, or another adverb, use an adverb.

SUMMARY OF DIFFERENCES BETWEEN ADJECTIVES AND ADVERBS

SUMMARY OF DIFFERENCES BETWEEN ADJECTIVES AND ADVERBS 81

WHAT ADJECTIVES MODIFY	EXAMPLE
nouns	The **busy** *lawyer* took a **quick** *look* at the members of the jury.
pronouns	*She* felt **triumphant**, for *they* were **attentive.**

WHAT ADVERBS MODIFY	EXAMPLE
verbs	The lawyer *spoke* **quickly** and **well.**
adverbs	The lawyer spoke **very** *quickly.*
adjectives	The lawyer was **extremely** *busy.*
independent clauses	**Therefore,** the *lawyer* rested.

Inexperienced writers sometimes interchange adjectives and adverbs because of the *-ly* ending. Even though many adverbs do end in *-ly* (eat *swiftly*, eat *frequently*, eat *hungrily*), some do not (eat *fast*, eat *often*, eat *seldom*). To complicate matters further, some adjectives end in *-ly* (*lovely* flower, *friendly* dog). The *-ly* ending, therefore, is not a reliable way to identify adverbs.

EXERCISE 12-1

Consulting section 12a, first underline and label all adjectives (ADJ) and adverbs (ADV). Then draw an arrow from each adjective or adverb to the word or words it modifies.

| | ADJ | ADV | ADJ | | ADJ |

EXAMPLE   Are television shows really a suitable subject for scholarly inquiry?

1. A rapidly growing group of investigators now takes television programming seriously.
2. These investigators say that television dramatically influences everything in our lives from political campaigns to breakfast foods.
3. Most Americans usually spend many years learning to read and understand printed language but practically no time learning to understand the messages that television delivers.
4. Now college students can take newly created courses in television studies, in which they analyze the situation comedy as intensely as the classic novel.
5. Are there better ways to study the changes in families in the United States than studying *Father Knows Best, All in the Family,* and *Family Matters?*

Using adverbs—not adjectives—to modify verbs, adjectives, and other adverbs   12b

Do not use adjectives as adverbs. Always use adverbs to modify verbs, adjectives, and other adverbs.

NO   The candidate inspired us **great.** [Adjective *great* cannot modify verb *inspired*.]

YES   The candidate inspired us **greatly.** [Adverb *greatly* can modify verb *inspired*.]

ANSWERS: EXERCISE 12–1

                 ADV   ADJ
1. A rapidly growing group

   ADV   ADJ
   now takes television programming

   ADV
   seriously.

                 ADJ
2. These investigators

   ADV   ADJ
   dramatically influences . . . our lives

        ADJ
   from political campaigns

        ADJ
   to breakfast foods.

        ADJ   ADV
3. Most Americans usually spend

   ADJ   ADJ
   many years . . . printed language

   ADV   ADJ
   practically no time

ANSWERS: EXERCISE 12–1, cont.

ADV   ADJ
4. Now college students can take

ADV   ADJ
newly created courses

ADJ
in television studies,

ADJ
analyze the situation comedy

ADV   ADJ
intensely as the classic novel.

ADJ
5. better "texts"

ADV
closely studying

QUOTATION ABOUT WRITING

I don't like too many adjectives or adverbs—I say if a noun or a verb is worth describing, do it properly, take a sentence to do it.

—Fay Weldon

12b
cont.

NO   The candidate felt **unusual** energetic. [Adjective *unusual* cannot modify adjective *energetic*.]

YES   The candidate felt **unusually energetic.** [Adverb *unusually* can modify adjective *energetic*.]

NO   The candidate spoke **exceptional forcefully.** [Adjective *exceptional* cannot modify adverb *forcefully*.]

YES   The candidate spoke **exceptionally forcefully.** [Adverb *exceptionally* modifies adverb *forcefully*.]

12c   **Not using double negatives**

A **double negative** is a statement with two negative modifiers, the second of which repeats the message of the first. (This form, nonstandard today, was standard in the days of Chaucer and Shakespeare.) Negative modifiers include *no, never, not, none, nothing, hardly, scarcely,* and *barely.*

NO   The factory workers will **never** vote for **no** strike.

YES   The factory workers will **never** vote for **a** strike.

The words *not, no,* and *nothing* are particularly common in double negatives.

NO   The union members did **not** have **no** money in reserve.

YES   The union members did **not** have **any** money in reserve.

YES   The union members had **no** money in reserve.

If you use contractions, which many writers prefer to avoid in their academic writing, be especially careful not to use double negatives. When the word *not* is used in a contraction (such as *isn't, don't, didn't,* or *haven't*), the negative message carried by the contracted *not* applies to the entire statement. Do not let the *not* slip by your notice; do not add a second negative.

NO   He did**n't** hear **nothing.**

YES   He did**n't** hear **anything.**

NO   They have**n't** had **no** meetings.

YES   They have**n't** had **any** meetings.

Using adjectives—not adverbs—as complements after linking verbs

12d

Linking verbs indicate a state of being or a condition. They include *be (am, is, are, was, were);* verbs related to the senses, including *look, smell, taste, sound,* and *feel;* and verbs such as *appear, seem, become, grow, turn, remain,* and *prove.* Linking verbs connect the SUBJECT to a COMPLEMENT—a word that renames or describes the subject (see 7m-1). You can think of a linking verb as an equal sign between a subject and its complement.

The guests looked **happy.** [subject *guests* = adjective *happy*]

Problems can arise with verbs that function sometimes as linking verbs and sometimes as action verbs, depending on the structure of the sentence. As linking verbs, these verbs use adjectives in complements. As action verbs, these verbs use adverbs.

Zora **looks happy.** [*looks* = linking verb; *happy* = adjective]

Zora **looks happily** at the sunset. [*looks* = action verb; *happily* = adverb]

Bad—Badly

The words *bad* (adjective) and *badly* (adverb) are particularly prone to misuse with linking verbs such as *feel, grow, smell, sound, taste.* Only the adjective *bad* is correct when a verb is functioning as a linking verb. (When a verb functions as an action verb, *badly* is fine: *Zora **played** the piano **badly.***)

FOR DESCRIBING A FEELING

NO   The student felt **badly.**

YES   The student felt **bad.**

FOR DESCRIBING A SMELL

NO   The food smelled **badly.**

YES   The food smelled **bad.**

Good—Well

Well functions both as an adverb and as an adjective. As a MODIFIER, *good* is always an adjective: *He wore his **good** suit. Well* is an adjective referring to good health, but it is an adverb in all other contexts. ➜

271

REFERENCE TO SUPPLEMENTS

The topic in 12C is included in the TASP writing competency test. Refer students to *Preparing for the TASP* by M. Saenz.

BACKGRO\UND

Warnings about the overuse of adjectives and adverbs abound in books about good writing. William Zinsser, for instance, reiterates Thoreau's advice to "simplify, simplify." He recommends that the would-be writer use strong nouns and verbs that carry effective connotations instead of relying on strings of modifiers (*On Writing Well* [New York: Harper & Row, 1980]).

QUOTATION ABOUT WRITING

As to the adjective: when in doubt, strike it out.

—Mark Twain

QUOTATION ABOUT WRITING

In advertising there is a direct, inverse proportion between the number of adjectives and the number of facts.

—Paul Stevens

LANGUAGE HISTORY

Adverbs in Old English and Middle English were formed differently than they are today: to make an adverb, an *-e* was simply added to an adjective. The modern *-ly* ending for adverbs comes from an adjective ending, *-lice* (meaning *like*), which became softened to *-ly* and was somehow reinterpreted as an adverb signal. Some modern adjectives ending in *-ly* (such as *friendly* and *heavenly*) are descendants of those old *-lice* adjectives.

12d
cont.

You look **well** = You look to be in good health. [*well* = adjective]

You write **well** = You write skillfully. [*well* = adverb]

Except when *well* is an adjective referring to health, use *good* only as an adjective and *well* only as an adverb.

> **NO**   She sings **good**. [*sings* = action verb; adverb, not adjective, required; *good* is adjective]
>
> **YES** She sings **well**. [*well* = adverb]

EXERCISE 12-2

Consulting sections 12a, 12b, 12c, and 12d, choose the correct uses of negatives and of adjectives and adverbs.

EXAMPLE   If Halloween and horror stories are a (good, well) **good** indicator, most people never want (nothing, anything) **anything** to do with bats.

1. Myths have labeled bats as (aggressively, aggressive) _____ and short-tempered, but biologists who (frequent, frequently) _____ handle bats call them (extreme, extremely) _____ shy and (gently, gentle) _____ .

2. These researchers who feel (bad, badly) _____ about the bats' terrifying reputation report that bats don't (never, ever) _____ act like the fearsome creatures in legends.

3. Bats (actual, actually) _____ (greedily, greedy) _____ eat insects by the millions, a fact that might make some people begin to feel (well, good) _____ about bats.

4. Varying (wide, widely) _____ in size and weight, some bats have a (terrifyingly, terrifying) _____ six-foot wingspan, while others weigh less than a penny.

5. Many people think bats come in nothing but neutral colors like mouse gray or brown, but some bats are (bright, brightly) _____ red or yellow.

ANSWERS AND COVERAGE: EXERCISE 12–2

1. aggressive [12a, adj. modifies noun *bats*] frequently [12b, adv. modifies verb *handle*] extremely [adv. modifies adj. *shy*] gentle [12a, adj. modifies pronoun *them*]

2. bad [12d, adj. after linking verb *feel*] ever [12c, avoid double negative with *don't*]

3. actually, greedily [advs. modify verb *eat*] good [12d, adj. after linking verb *feel*]

4. widely [12b, adv. modifies adj. *varying*] terrifying [12a, adj. modifies noun *wingspan*]

5. bright [12d, adj. after linking verb *are*]

12e

Using correct comparative and superlative forms of adjectives and adverbs

When comparisons are made, descriptive adjectives and adverbs often carry the message. Adjectives and adverbs, therefore, have forms that communicate relative degrees of intensity.

Using correct forms of comparison for regular adjectives and adverbs

Most adjectives and adverbs show degrees of intensity by adding *-er* and *-est* endings or by combining with the words *more, less, least* (see Chart 82). A few adjectives and adverbs are irregular, as explained in 12e-2.

FORMS OF COMPARISON FOR REGULAR ADJECTIVES AND ADVERBS		82
FORM	**FUNCTION**	
■ Positive	Used when nothing is being compared	
■ Comparative	Used when two things are being compared, with *-er* ending or *more/less*	
■ Superlative	Used when three or more things are being compared, with *-est* ending or *most/least*	

POSITIVE	COMPARATIVE	SUPERLATIVE
green	greener	greenest
happy	happier	happiest
selfish	less selfish	least selfish
beautiful	more beautiful	most beautiful

Her tree is **green.**

Her tree is **greener** than his tree.

Her tree is the **greenest** tree on the block.

The choice of whether to use *-er, -est* or *more, most, less, least* depends largely on the number of syllables in the adjective or adverb.

■ With **one-syllable words,** the *-er* and *-est* endings are most common: *large, larger, largest* (adjective); *far, farther, farthest* (adverb).

■ With **three-syllable words,** *more, most, less, least* are used.

■ With **adverbs of two or more syllables,** *more, most, less, least* are used: *easily, more easily, most easily.*

■ With **adjectives of two syllables,** practice varies: some take the *-er, -est* endings; others combine with *more* and *most.*

LANGUAGE HISTORY

The rule banning double negatives in English is a relatively new one. Double, triple, and even quadruple negatives were acceptable in Old English and Middle English. They are also acceptable in many modern languages. In the eighteenth century, the first attempts were made to regularize English. It was then that the first English dictionaries and usage books were written. One of these was Robert Lowth's *Short Introduction to English Grammar*, in which he stated that "two Negatives in English destroy one another, or are equivalent to an affirmative." The new rich of the merchant class, eager to fit in by speaking and writing correctly, accepted Lowth's rule, and it became the standard despite the thousand-year history of acceptable double negatives in English.

BACKGROUND

In the chapter on vocabulary in *Errors and Expectations* (New York: Oxford UP, 1977), Mina Shaughnessy describes the use of modifiers by three groups of freshman writers. The few adverbs used by *basic* writers, she notes, usually come from the most overworked ones in the language, such as *too, very, quite,* and *hardly.* Similarly, basic writers modify their nouns and verbs with what she calls "the common adjectives": *a lot, many, good, easy, big, certain,* familiar words that slip into place without mental effort, thereby making it impossible for the writer to achieve the precision needed for complex consideration of the topic. *Intermediate* writers, moving closer to precise diction, use *-ly* adverbs and more specific adjectives. Although they are likely to use multiple adjectives, doing so does not usually increase the precision of the statement. *Advanced* freshman writers, working with more confidence, lean on adverbial conjunctions for paragraph cohesion—e.g., *furthermore, however, consequently*—and even include figurative language in an effort to be descriptive.

BACKGROUND

"Jokes play across grammar," writes Josephine Miles in "The Humor of Composition" (*Composition and Literature*: *Bridging the Gap*, ed. Winifred Bryan Horner [Chicago: U of Chicago P, 1983]), and many jokes play on the "subtle tricks" of modifiers. In the following story, Miles observes, "a lot of superlative adjectives are shifted to one simple comparative":

> James Thurber and a friend attended the opening of a play that proved to be a bore from beginning to end. As they left the theater, the friend said, "That was the dullest, dreariest, and shoddiest play I ever saw."
>
> This off his chest, he continued, "And what did you think of it?"
>
> "Well," said the humorist, "I didn't think it was that good."

The punchline, Miles writes, depends on "Thurber's use of a predicate, a verb, and an intensive adverb instead of the negative adverb" (34). She does not, however, recommend analyzing jokes in class. That seems just as well.

WORD HISTORIES

Common irregular adjectives (and adverbs) can be confusing to students because the comparative and superlative forms seem unconnected to the positive form. The realization that these irregularities are only accidents of history rather than the product of difficult rules can make them less intimidating.

For example, *good* comes from the Old English *god*, related to the German *gut*, both of which come from the Indo-European word meaning *to be suitable*. *Better* and *best* come from Old English *betera* and *betst* respectively, based on the Indo-European word meaning *good*.

Another example is *worse* and *worst*, which come from their Old English synonyms: *wiersa* and *wyrsta*. However, *bad* does not come from *yfel*, the Old English word for *bad* or *evil*, but from Old English *baeddel*, meaning *hermaphrodite*.

12e-1 cont.

One general rule covers two-syllable adjectives ending in -*y*: use the -*er*, -*est* endings after changing the -*y* to *i*: *pretty, prettier, prettiest*. For other two-syllable adjectives, form comparatives and superlatives intuitively, based on what you have heard or read for a particular adjective.

Be careful not to use a **double comparative** or **double superlative.** The words *more, most, less, least* cannot be used if the -*er* or -*est* ending has been used.

He was **younger** [not *more younger*] than his brother.

Her music was the **snappiest** [not *most snappiest*] on the radio.

People danced **more easily** [not *more easier*] to her music.

12e-2

Using correct forms of comparison for irregular adjectives and adverbs

A few comparative and superlative forms are irregular. They are listed in Chart 83. Memorize them so that they always spring easily to mind.

IRREGULAR COMPARATIVES AND SUPERLATIVES   83

POSITIVE [1]	COMPARATIVE [2]	SUPERLATIVE [3+]
good (adjective)	better	best
well (adjective and adverb)	better	best
bad (adjective)	worse	worst
badly (adverb)	worse	worst
many	more	most
much	more	most
some	more	most
little	less	least

The Perkinses saw a **good** movie.

The Perkinses saw a **better** movie than the Smiths did.

The Perkinses saw the **best** movie that they had ever seen.

The Millers had **little** trouble finding jobs.

The Millers had **less** trouble finding jobs than the Smiths did.

The Millers had **the least** trouble finding jobs of everyone.

❖ USAGE ALERT: Do not use *less* and *fewer* interchangeably. Use *less* with noncountable items or values that form one whole. Use *fewer* with numbers or anything that can be counted: *They consumed **fewer calories**; the sugar substitute had **less aftertaste**.* ❖

!

EXERCISE 12-3

Consulting section 12e, do two things: First, complete this chart. Next, write sentences that set a context for each word in the completed chart.

EXAMPLE   *little:* Towering redwoods dwarfed the little Douglas fir.

POSITIVE [1]	COMPARATIVE [2]	SUPERLATIVE [3+]
little		
	greedier	
		most complete
gladly		
		fewest
	thicker	
some		

Avoiding too many nouns as modifiers   **12f**

Sometimes nouns—words that name a person, place, thing, or idea—function as MODIFIERS of other nouns: *truck driver, train track, security system.* These very familiar terms create no problems. However, when nouns pile up in a sequence of modifiers, the reader has difficulty figuring out which nouns are being modified and which nouns are doing the modifying. As you revise such sentences, you can use any of several routes to clarify your material.

SENTENCE REWRITTEN

NO   I asked my advisor to write **two college recommendation** letters for me.

YES   I asked my advisor to write **letters of recommendation** to **two colleges** for me.

ONE NOUN CHANGED TO POSSESSIVE CASE AND ANOTHER TO ADJECITVE FORM

NO   Some students might take the **United States Navy examination** for **navy engineer training.**

YES   Some students might take the United States **Navy's examination** for **naval engineer training.**

➡

➡

12f
cont.

NOUN CHANGED TO PREPOSITIONAL PHRASE

NO   Our **student advisor training program** has won awards for excellence.

YES   Our training program **for student advisors** has won awards for excellence. [Notice that this change requires the plural *advisors*.]

EXERCISE 12-4

Consulting all sections of this chapter, select the better choice from each set of words in parentheses so that these sentences are suitable for academic writing.

EXAMPLE   Stunt work is a visual art that (frequent, frequently) **frequently** involves physical risk to the performer.

1. The first stunt performers were (most likely, likeliest) _____ the Roman gladiators, trained to entertain the crowds with their great skill in chariot driving and sword play.

2. Actors in the early silent movies sustained (many, more) _____ injuries during filming because they used no doubles for their stunts.

3. In a 1916 movie about the Civil War, no (fewer, less) _____ than sixty-seven extras suffered injuries during the filming of one scene.

4. Today, more than two hundred (high, highly) _____ trained stunt performers, ranging in age from ten to eighty-two, work (regular, regularly) _____ in Hollywood movies.

5. In a single year, stunt performer Harry Madsen was beaten, knifed, shot, set on fire, and thrown out a fourth-floor window. He was paid (good, well) _____ and had a (good, well) _____ time, too.

Writing Correct Sentences

When you write correct sentences, you increase your chances of communicating clearly with your readers. Part Three offers you practical advice about how to avoid the most common sentence errors that interfere with the delivery of meaning. As you use Chapters 13 through 15, keep in mind that correct sentences give you a foundation on which you can build an effective, graceful, and memorable writing style.

13 *Sentence Fragments*

REFERENCES TO SUPPLEMENTS

For this topic in the CLAST writing competency test, refer students to ch. 1, section B2d of *Preparing for the CLAST* by S. Patterson.

This topic is included in the TASP writing competency test. Refer students to *Preparing for the TASP* by M. Saenz.

For revising to eliminate sentence fragments, refer students to *Rough Drafts* by K. S. Cain, Part III, Exercise 1.

QUOTATION ABOUT WRITING

I am unlikely to trust a sentence that comes easily.

—William Gass

QUOTATION ABOUT WRITING

When it comes to language, nothing is more satisfying than to write a good sentence. . . . This does not just happen. It requires skill, hard work, a good ear, and continued practice, as much as it takes Heifetz to play the violin.

—Barbara Tuchman

A sentence fragment occurs when a portion of a sentence is punctuated as a complete sentence. This chapter shows you how to distinguish between sentence fragments and complete sentences.

FRAGMENT	The telephone with redial capacity. [no VERB*]
REVISED	The telephone has redial capacity.
FRAGMENT	Rang loudly for ten minutes. [no SUBJECT]
REVISED	The telephone rang loudly for ten minutes.
FRAGMENT	At midnight. [no verb or subject]
REVISED	The telephone rang at midnight.
FRAGMENT	**Because** the telephone rang loudly. [DEPENDENT CLAUSE with SUBORDINATING CONJUNCTION]
REVISED	Because the telephone rang loudly, the family was awakened in the middle of the night.
FRAGMENT	The telephone call **that** woke the family. [dependent clause with RELATIVE PRONOUN]
REVISED	The telephone call that woke the family was a wrong number.

Sentence fragments distract readers by intruding on the clarity of the message that you want your material to deliver.

NO	The lawyer was angry. When she returned from court. She found the key witness waiting in her office. [Was the lawyer angry when she returned from court or when she found the witness in her office?]
YES	The lawyer was angry when she returned from court. She found the key witness waiting in her office.
YES	The lawyer was angry. When she returned from court, she found the key witness waiting in her office.

*You can find the definition of a word printed in small capital letters (such as VERB) in the Glossary of Terms toward the back of this handbook.

Wait until the REVISING and EDITING stages of your writing process to check for sentence fragments. While you are DRAFTING, if you suspect a sentence fragment, quickly underline or highlight the material. Then, you can easily find and check it later.

Testing for sentence completeness   13a

If you write sentence fragments frequently, you need a system to check that your sentences are complete. Here is a test you can use.

TEST FOR SENTENCE COMPLETENESS   84

Question 1:   **Is there a VERB?** If no, there is a fragment. To revise, see 13c.

     NO Thousands of whales in the Arctic Ocean because of an early winter. [a fragment]

Question 2:   **Is there a SUBJECT?** If no, there is a fragment. To revise, see 13c.

     NO Raced to reach the whales. [a fragment]

Question 3:   **Does the word group include a SUBORDINATING WORD and lack an INDEPENDENT CLAUSE?** If yes, there is a fragment. To revise, see 13b.

     NO Because the ship intended to cut a path through the ice. [a fragment]

QUESTION 1: Is there a verb?

If there is no verb, you are looking at a sentence fragment. Verbs convey information about what is happening, what has happened, or what will happen. In testing for sentence completeness, find a verb that can change form to communicate a change in time.

     Yesterday, the telephone **rang.**
     Now the telephone **rings.**

VERBALS do not function as verbs. Verbals are GERUNDS (*-ing* forms as NOUNS), PRESENT PARTICIPLES (*-ing* forms as MODIFIERS), PAST PARTICIPLES (*-ed* and irregular past forms as modifiers), and INFINITIVES (*to* forms).

TEACHING TIP

You might find it useful to have students work in groups to identify and correct fragments found in paragraphs taken from their own writing or those that occur in the paragraph below. Each group can present to the class a revision of a paragraph, pointing out the merits of the new version. In the paragraph shown here, fragments are often signaled by the words *just, only, for example, also, mainly,* and *such as.*

REFERENCE TO SUPPLEMENTS

See transparency 7–1 on testing and revising for sentence completeness in the *Prentice Hall/Simon & Schuster Transparencies for Writers* by D. Carter.

TEACHING TIP

Students sometimes create fragments as they attempt to write longer or more complicated sentences and experiment with their style. Without a range of syntactic structures available to them, students may try to vary the rhythm of their sentences, suggest pauses for emphasis, and establish sentence variety with the placement of periods. Fragments often appear because students begin using dependent clauses, participial phrases, elliptical constructions, and absolute phrases in their writing before they have enough knowledge and control of these structures. Students often benefit when they learn new sentence patterns as they learn to avoid fragments. Students who use periods to suggest a long pause may benefit from instruction on the dash (Chapter 29). Students creating fragments from dependent clauses, absolute phrases, and participial phrases may benefit from studying coordination and subordination (Chapter 17), parallelism (Chapter 18), and techniques for achieving sentence variety and emphasis (Chapter 19).

13a cont.

TEACHING TIP, cont.

In their early history, the people of Asia followed the seasons through the valleys until they found no more land. Only the sea and sky and a sheet of ice stretching across the Bering Strait. They did not think about the past. Just the present. For example, making weapons. Such as tree limbs used for bows. Also knives made from sharpened stones. Just like their forefathers. Moving south, they eventually reached the Rio Grande. Mainly known today as the river that separates Mexico and the United States.

TEACHING TIP

To discuss fragments, you might ask students to bring in samples of public writing that contain fragments. Fruitful sources include advertisements, mail solicitations, and memos from companies where the students work. Collect, reproduce, and distribute a sampling of the passages. Ask students to identify all the fragments and to determine which, if any, are acceptable. Then have them revise the passages to eliminate the unacceptable fragments.

This lesson can be enlivened by the use of an overhead projector. Prepare transparencies of the original passages, and use a series of overlays to record and compare student revisions.

Students may ask why they must avoid unacceptable fragments when these errors can be found in published writing. You may want to discuss what impressions about the writers and their companies these errors create.

BACKGROUND

In a survey of 84 professionals representing 63 different occupations (Maxine Hairston, "Not All Errors Are Created Equal: Nonacademic Readers in the Profession Respond to Lapses in Usage," *College English* [1981]: 794–806), respondents ranked sentence fragments ➜

FRAGMENT	Yesterday, the students registering for classes.
REVISED	Yesterday, the students **were** registering for classes.
FRAGMENT	Now the students registering for classes.
REVISED	Now the students **are** registering for classes.
FRAGMENT	Told about an excellent teacher.
REVISED	**They had been** told about an excellent teacher.
FRAGMENT	Now the students to register for classes.
REVISED	Now the students **want** to register for classes.

QUESTION 2: *Is there a subject?*

If there is no subject, you are looking at a sentence fragment. To find a subject, ask the verb "who?" or "what?"

FRAGMENT	Studied hard for class. [Who studied? unknown]
REVISED	The students studied hard for class. [Who studied? students]
FRAGMENT	Contained some difficult questions. [What contained? unknown]
REVISED	The test contained some difficult questions. [What contained? the test]

Every sentence must have its own subject. A sentence fragment without a subject often occurs when the missing subject is the same as the subject in the preceding sentence.

NO	The students formed a study group to prepare for the midterm exam. **Decided** to study together for the rest of the course.
YES	The students formed a study group to prepare for the midterm exam. **They decided** to study together for the rest of the course.
YES	The students formed a study group to prepare for the midterm exam, **and they decided** to study together for the rest of the course.

Imperative statements—commands and some requests—are an exception. They are not sentence fragments. Imperative statements imply the word *you* as the subject.

Run! = (You) run!
Study hard. = (You) study hard.
Please return my books. = (You) please return my books.

QUESTION 3: Do the subject and verb start with a subordinating word and lack an independent clause to complete the thought?

If the answer to Question 3 is "yes," you are looking at a sentence fragment. Subordinating words begin **dependent clauses.** A dependent clause cannot stand alone as an independent unit; it must be joined to an independent clause to be part of a complete sentence.

One type of subordinating word is a **subordinating conjunction.** A subordinating conjunction comes at the beginning of a dependent clause. Here are frequently used subordinating conjunctions. (For a more complete list that also tells the relationship each word expresses, see Chart 51 in section 7h.)

after	because	since	when
although	before	unless	whenever
as	if	until	where

FRAGMENT	**Because** she returned my books.
REVISED	**Because** she returned my books, I can study.

FRAGMENT	**When** I study.
REVISED	I have to concentrate **when** I study.

❖ PUNCTUATION ALERT: When a dependent clause starting with a subordinating conjunction (an adverb clause), comes before an independent clause, a comma usually separates the clauses (see 24b-1). ❖

Another type of subordinating word is a **relative pronoun.** The most common relative pronouns are *who, which,* and *that.*

FRAGMENT	The test **that** we studied for.
REVISED	The test **that** we studied for was canceled.

FRAGMENT	The professor **who** taught the course.
REVISED	The professor **who** taught the course was ill.

Questions can begin with words such as *when, where, who,* and *which* without being sentence fragments: *When do you want to study? Where is the library? Who is your professor? Which class are you taking?*

Chart 85 summarizes information on correcting a sentence fragment once you have identified its grammatical structure.

!

BACKGROUND, *cont.*

among the most serious of errors, below only "status markers" such as nonstandard verbs ("brung"), double negatives, and beginning a sentence with an objective pronoun.

ALTERNATE EXAMPLE

If your students have trouble recognizing dependent clauses as fragments, you may want to give them practice. Ask them to locate the fragments in the following mixture of complete and incomplete sentences. You might also ask them to combine the sentences so that each one is complete, being careful to separate with a comma each opening dependent clause from the independent one that follows.

Many elderly people have pets as companions. Because the elderly are often lonely. Nevertheless, pets make demands on their energy. For example, if a cat is sick, and when a dog must be bathed. Unless the owner has the strength and funds to care for the pet's needs. Then the pet is better off with a younger owner. Since the pet deserves a good home too. Before getting a cat or dog, people should be certain that they can provide adequate care.

QUOTATION ABOUT WRITING

With sixty staring me in the face, I have developed inflammation of the sentence structure and a definite hardening of the paragraphs.

—James Thurber

QUOTATION ABOUT WRITING

Anyone who can improve a sentence of mine by the omission or placing of a comma is looked upon as my dearest friend.

—George Moore

HOW TO CORRECT SENTENCE FRAGMENTS 85

REVISION STRATEGY

- If the sentence fragment is a DEPENDENT CLAUSE, join it to an adjacent INDEPENDENT CLAUSE (see 13b).
- If the sentence fragment is a dependent clause, revise it into an independent clause (see 13b).
- If the sentence fragment is a PHRASE, join it to an adjacent independent clause (see 13c).
- If the sentence fragment is a phrase, revise it into an independent clause (see 13c).

ANSWERS AND COVERAGE: EXERCISE 13–1

Two pieces of information are given for each item: the reason for the sentence fragment and the number of the question in the "Test for Sentence Completeness" that explains what has caused each sentence fragment. (Exercise 13–3 asks students to correct the sentence fragments in this exercise.)

1. No verb (*unwrapping* is a verbal); question 1

2. Starts with the subordinating word *which*; questions 2 and 3

3. No subject; question 2

4. Complete sentence

5. Starts with a subordinating word and lacks independent clause to complete thought; question 3

6. No verb; question 1

7. No subject; question 2

8. Complete sentence

9. Starts with a subordinating word but lacks an independent clause to complete the thought; question 3

10. No subject; question 2

EXERCISE 13-1

Using the Test for Sentence Completeness in Chart 84, check each word group. If a word group is a sentence fragment, explain what makes it incomplete. If a word group is a complete sentence, circle its number.

EXAMPLE   In 1972, a mummy discovered in a Chinese tomb. [No verb; Question 1 in Chart 84]

1. Researchers unwrapping the mummy containing carefully preserved body of a woman in an ancient tomb.
2. Which had been wound in twenty layers of silk.
3. Turned out to be a Chinese aristocrat named Lady Dai.
4. She was embalmed in a bath of mercury salts.
5. When she died around 168 B.C.
6. Bamboo matting and five tons of charcoal.
7. Absorbed excess water in the tomb and kept the body dry.
8. The body of another Chinese princess had been buried in a magnificent jade suit.
9. Because jade was also believed to preserve bodies.
10. Had decayed, unlike Lady Dai's.

13b   Revising dependent clauses punctuated as sentences

A **dependent clause** contains both a SUBJECT and a VERB but also contains a SUBORDINATING WORD (see Question 3 in Chart 84). It cannot stand on its own as a sentence.

To correct a dependent clause punctuated as a sentence, you may choose to (1) join the dependent clause to an independent clause that comes directly before or after, or (2) drop the subordinating word. Whichever strategy you use, if necessary, add words to create an independent clause that makes sense.

FRAGMENT	Many people over twenty-five years of age are deciding to get college degrees. **Because they want the benefits of an advanced education.**
REVISED	Many people over twenty-five years of age are deciding to get college degrees because they want the benefits of an advanced education. [joined into one sentence]
REVISED	Many people over twenty-five years of age are deciding to get college degrees. They want the benefits of an advanced education. [SUBORDINATING CONJUNCTION dropped to create an independent clause]
FRAGMENT	College attracts many older students. **Who could not attend upon graduation from high school.**
REVISED	College attracts many older students who could not attend upon graduation from high school. [joined into one sentence]
REVISED	College attracts many older students. They could not attend upon graduation from high school. [relative pronoun dropped and *they* added to create an independent clause]

❖ USAGE ALERT: When trying to identify dependent clauses, be especially careful with words that indicate time—such as *after, before, since,* and *until.* In some sentences, they function as subordinating conjunctions, but in other sentences they function as ADVERBS and PREPOSITIONS. Do not automatically assume when you see these words that you are looking at a dependent clause.

Before, the class was never full. Now it is overfilled. [These are two complete sentences. In the first sentence, *before* is an adverb modifying the INDEPENDENT CLAUSE *the class was never full.*]

Before this semester, the class was never full. [This is a complete sentence. *Before* is the PREPOSITION in the PREPOSITIONAL PHRASE *before this semester.*]

Before the professor arrived. [This is a sentence fragment caused by a DEPENDENT CLAUSE being punctuated as a sentence. *Before* is a subordinating conjunction.]

Before the professor arrived, the room was empty. [This is a complete sentence. The dependent clause precedes an independent clause.] ❖

!

TEACHING TIP

In *Grammar and the Teaching of Writing: Limits and Possibilities* (NCTE, 1991), Rei R. Noguchi proposes that students can identify declarative sentences and fragments if they attempt to transform the construction into tag questions and yes-no questions. For example, "Doing math problems isn't one of Billy's favorite activities" can be transformed into the tag question "Doing math problems isn't one of Billy's favorite activities, is it?" and the yes-no question "Isn't doing math problems one of Billy's favorite activities?" With fragments such as "Enjoyed the baseball game on Saturday" or "Whatever you could do to help my sister," students will find it impossible to create such questions unless they add words to the fragment, revealing that the construction was an incomplete sentence. You might ask students to try this method with Exercise 13–1.

TEACHING TIP

Dictating a passage like the one below for students to copy and punctuate can be a helpful exercise for students in identifying sentence boundaries. Students can compare their versions and discuss any differences.

We have a nine-acre lake on our ranch and a warm spring that feeds it all winter. By mid-March the lake ice begins to melt where the spring feeds in, and every year the same pair of mallards come ahead of the others and wait. Though there is very little open water they seem content. They glide back and forth through a thin estuary, brushing watercress with their elegant folded wings, then tip end-up to eat and, after, clamber onto the lip of ice that retreats, hardens forward, and retreats again.

—Gretel Ehrlich

ANSWERS AND COVERAGE: EXERCISE 13–2

Answers will vary. Here is one set of possible responses.

1. Kwanzaa was created in 1966 by Maulana Karenga, an African-American teacher who wanted to teach people about their African heritage. [dependent (relative) clause attached to independent clause]

2. The word *Kwanzaa* comes from the Swahili phrase *ya kwanza*, which means "first." [dependent (relative) clause attached to independent clause]

3. Kwanzaa allows African Americans to honor the history of black people. [subordinating conjunction dropped from dependent (adverb) clause]

4. Correct complete sentence

5. Although Christmas and Hanukkah are religious holidays, Kwanzaa is a cultural holiday. [subordinating phrase linked to independent clause]

6. The festival, which lasts seven days, celebrates seven principles that are called the *nguzo saba* in Swahili. [dependent (relative) clause attached to independent clause]

7. The seven principles are unity, self-determination, collective responsibility, cooperative economics, purpose, creativity, and faith. [relative pronoun dropped from dependent (relative) clause]

8. Each evening during the seven days of Kwanzaa, observers light one of the candles in the *kinara*, which is a seven-cup candelabrum. [dependent (relative) clause attached to independent clause]

9. They discuss how the principle of the day affects their lives. [subordinating conjunction dropped from dependent clause]

10. Correct complete sentence

13b
cont.

EXERCISE 13-2

Consulting sections 13a and 13b, find and correct any sentence fragments. If a sentence is correct, circle its number.

EXAMPLE   Kwanzaa is an African-American holiday. That is observed from December 25 to January 1.

Kwanzaa is an African-American holiday that is observed from December 25 to January 1.

1. Kwanzaa was created in 1966 by Maulana Karenga, an African-American teacher. Who wanted to teach people about their African heritage.

2. The word *Kwanzaa* comes from the Swahili phrase *ya kwanza*. Which means "first."

3. Although Kwanzaa allows African Americans to honor the history of black people.

4. The holiday also gives other North Americans a chance to learn African traditions.

5. Although Christmas and Hanukkah are religious holidays. Kwanzaa is a cultural holiday.

6. The festival, which lasts seven days, celebrates seven principles. That are called the *nguzo saba* in Swahili.

7. The seven principles, which are unity, self-determination, collective responsibility, cooperative economics, purpose, creativity, and faith.

8. Each evening during the seven days of Kwanzaa, observers light one of the candles in the *kinara*. Which is a seven-cup candleholder.

9. When they discuss how the principle of the day affects their lives.

10. When family and friends gather on the final night, they celebrate the feast known as the *Karamu*.

13c   Revising phrases punctuated as sentences

A **phrase** is a group of words that lacks a SUBJECT, a VERB, or both. A phrase cannot stand on its own as a sentence. To revise a phrase punctuated as a sentence, you may choose to (1) rewrite it to become an INDEPENDENT CLAUSE, or (2) join it to an independent clause that comes directly before or after.

A phrase containing only a verbal (an INFINITIVE, a PAST PARTICIPLE, or a PRESENT PARTICIPLE) but no verb is a fragment, not a sentence.

284

frag 13

FRAGMENT   The mayor called a news conference last week. **To announce new programs for crime prevention and care for the homeless.** [*To announce* starts an infinitive phrase, not a sentence.]

REVISED   The mayor called a news conference last week to announce new programs for crime prevention and care for the homeless. [joined into one sentence]

REVISED   The mayor called a news conference last week. She wanted to announce new programs for crime prevention and care for the homeless. [rewritten]

FRAGMENT   **Introduced by her assistant.** The mayor began with an opening statement. [*Introduced* starts a participial phrase, not a sentence.]

REVISED   Introduced by her assistant, the mayor began with an opening statement. [joined into one sentence]

REVISED   The mayor was introduced by her assistant. She began with an opening statement. [rewritten]

FRAGMENT   **Hoping for strong public support.** She gave many examples of problems everywhere in the city. [*Hoping* starts a participle phrase, not a sentence.]

REVISED   Hoping for strong public support, she gave many examples of problems everywhere in the city. [joined into one sentence]

REVISED   She was hoping for strong public support. She gave many examples of problems everywhere in the city. [rewritten]

A **prepositional phrase** starts with a PREPOSITION. It is not a sentence.

FRAGMENT   Cigarette smoke made the conference room seem airless. **During the long news conference.** [*During* starts a prepositional phrase, not a sentence.]

REVISED   Cigarette smoke made the conference room seem airless during the long news conference. [joined into one sentence]

REVISED   Cigarette smoke made the conference room seem airless. It was hard to breathe during the long news conference. [rewritten]

TEACHING TIP

To demonstrate how phrases can be turned into complete sentences, you might ask two students to read the following dialogue aloud in class, and then to improvise each comment as a sentence.

A: When are you coming?
B: In a minute.
A: Really?
B: Really.
A: Hurry up!
B: O.K. O.K. Just a second. How about Mother?
A: Who?
B: Mother.
A: Sure. Ready hours ago.

An **appositive** is one or more words that renames a NOUN. It is not a sentence.

FRAGMENT	Most people respected the mayor. **A politician with fresh ideas and practical solutions.** [*A politician* starts an appositive, not a sentence.]
REVISED	Most people respected the mayor, a politician with fresh ideas and practical solutions. [joined into one sentence]
REVISED	Most people respected the mayor. She seemed to be a politician with fresh ideas and practical solutions. [rewritten]

A **compound predicate** contains two or more verbs. To be part of a complete sentence, a predicate must have a subject. When the second half of a compound predicate is punctuated as a separate sentence, it is not a sentence.

FRAGMENT	The reporters asked the mayor many questions about the details of her program. **And then discussed her answers among themselves.** [*And then discussed* is the start of a compound predicate, not a sentence.]
REVISED	The reporters asked the mayor many questions about the details of her program and then discussed her answers among themselves. [joined into one sentence]
REVISED	The reporters asked the mayor many questions about the details of her program. Then the reporters discussed her answers among themselves. [rewritten]

EXERCISE 13-3

Go back to Exercise 13-1 and revise any sentence fragments into complete sentences. In some cases, you may be able to combine two fragments into one complete sentence.

EXERCISE 13-4

Consulting sections 13a, 13b, and 13c, revise this paragraph to eliminate any sentence fragments. In some cases, you can combine word groups to create complete sentences; in other cases, you must supply missing elements to revise word groups. Some sentences may not require revision. In your final version, check not only the individual sentences but also the clarity of the whole paragraph.

**ANSWERS AND COVERAGE:
EXERCISE 13–3**

Answers will vary. Added or altered words are italicized. Here is one set of possibilities.

1. Researchers *unwrapped* [verbal changed to verb] the mummy containing the carefully preserved body of a woman in an ancient tomb.

2. *The body* [subordinating word *which* dropped, noun supplied] had been wound in twenty layers of silk.

3. *She* [pronoun supplied] turned out to be a Chinese aristocrat named Lady Dai.

4. *She* [subordinating conjunction *when* dropped] died around 168 B.C.

5. Correct complete sentence

6. and 7. combined to create correct complete sentence

8. Correct complete sentence

9. Jade was also believed to preserve bodies. [subordinating conjunction *because* dropped]

10. Her body [noun supplied] had decayed, unlike Lady Dai's.

(1) The technological accomplishments of the first Americans are overlooked by modern textbooks on the history of science. (2) And have often been underestimated. (3) One example being the great earthen mounds constructed by the Adena Mound Builders along the shores of the Mississippi River and its tributaries in the United States. (4) More than 100,000 of such temple, burial, and dwelling sites left today. (5) As reflected in the names of such modern U.S. towns as Moundville, Missouri; Mound City, South Dakota; Mound Bayou, Mississippi, and Mound Valley, Kansas. (6) In addition, as many as 30,000 people may have lived in Cahokia. An ancient urban complex of mounds and house sites. (7) Located on the eastern bank of the Mississippi across from the present city of St. Louis. (8) The average mound involving some 3 million hours of human labor. (9) To transport the same amount of earth as forty mile-long freight trains could carry. (10) All this earth moved without wheelbarrows. (11) Because the wheel was unknown to the early American cultures. (12) The great mound at Cahokia is not as high as the pyramid of Pharaoh Cheops in Egypt, but it is much larger at its base. (13) Representing a greater achievement than the Egyptian pyramid.

Recognizing intentional fragments   13d

Professional writers sometimes intentionally use fragments for emphasis and effect.

> But in the main I feel like a brown bag of miscellany propped against a wall. Pour out the contents, and there is discovered a jumble of small things priceless and worthless. **A first-water diamond, an empty spool, bits of broken glass, lengths of string, a key to a door long since crumbled away, a rusty knife-blade, old shoes saved for a road that never was and never will be, a nail bent under the weight of things too heavy for any nail, a dried flower or two still a little fragrant.**
>
> —ZORA NEALE HURSTON, *How It Feels to Be Colored Me*

The ability to judge the difference between an acceptable and unacceptable sentence fragment comes from much exposure to reading the work of skilled writers. Many instructors, therefore, often do not accept sentence fragments in student writing until a student can demonstrate the consistent ability to write well-constructed complete sentences.

ANSWERS: EXERCISE 13–4

Answers will vary. One possible is:

The technological accomplishments of the first Americans are overlooked by modern textbooks on the history of science and have often been underestimated. One example is the great earthen mounds constructed by the Adena Mound Builders along the shores of the Mississippi River and its tributaries in the United States. More than 100,000 of such temple, burial, and dwelling sites are left today, as reflected in the names of such modern towns as Moundville, Missouri; Mound City, South Dakota; Mound Bayou, Mississippi; and Mound Valley, Kansas. In addition, as many as 30,000 people may have lived in Cahokia, an ancient urban complex of mounds and house sites located on the eastern bank of the Mississippi across from the present city of St. Louis. The average mound involved some 3 million hours of human labor to transport the same amount of earth as forty mile-long freight trains could carry. All this earth was moved without wheelbarrows, because the wheel was unknown to the early American cultures. The great mound at Cahokia is not as high as the pyramid of Pharaoh Cheops in Egypt, but it is much larger at its base, representing a greater achievement than the Egyptian pyramid.

COVERAGE: EXERCISE 13–4

(1) correct complete sentence; (2) predicate with coordinating conjunction; (3) verbal phrase (present participle); (4) verbal phrase (past participle); (5) dependent clause with subordinating conjunction; (6) complete sentence; (7) prepositional phrase; (8) verbal phrase (present participle); (9) verbal phrase (infinitive); (10) predicate; (11) dependent clause with subordinating conjunction; (12) correct complete sentence; (13) verbal phrase (present participle)

ANSWERS: EXERCISE 13–5

Answers will vary. Here is one set of possibilities.

Some of the most magnificent Easter eggs in the world were created by Peter Carl Fabergé, a master Russian goldsmith. In 1884, Czar Alexander III wanted a special Easter gift for his wife, the Czarina. Although Fabergé's first Imperial Easter egg appeared to be an ordinary hen's egg, the outer shell, made of gold, had been enameled to the off-white color of a hen's egg. It [or The shell] opened to reveal a yolk, also of gold, which contained a tiny chicken, elaborately crafted of several shades of gold. Hidden inside the chicken was a surprise, [or :] an intricate jewelled model of the imperial crown, which opened to reveal a tiny ruby egg. Because the Czar was so delighted, he commissioned Fabergé to create a new egg each Easter and gave the goldsmith one other instruction. The czar told Fabergé to include a surprise in each egg, which, of course, Fabergé wisely did.

ANSWERS: EXERCISE 13–6

Answers will vary. Here is one set of possible answers.

Students looking for jobs need more than the "Help Wanted" section of a newspaper. One major tool is a carefully written résumé. A résumé should be written in a standard form (see Chapter 39) and proofread carefully to eliminate errors in spelling, punctuation, or grammar. For the content of the résumé students should analyze all types of experiences. A résumé can include not only paid jobs but also volunteer positions and extracurricular activities. Students have a better chance of getting a job if they have supervised other people, handled money, or taken on highly responsible tasks such as participating in political campaigns or chairing major committees at school. Many employers will consider student résumés, especially when the résumés include names of the students' supervisors.

13d
cont.

EXERCISE 13-5

Consulting sections 13a, 13b, and 13c, revise this paragraph to eliminate any sentence fragments. In some cases, you can combine word groups to create complete sentences; in other cases, you must supply missing elements to revise word groups. In your final version, check not only the individual sentences but also the clarity of the whole paragraph.

(1) Some of the most magnificent Easter eggs in the world. (2) Created by Peter Carl Fabergé. (3) A master Russian goldsmith. (4) In 1884, Czar Alexander III, wanting a special Easter gift for his wife, the Czarina. (5) Although Fabergé's first Imperial Easter Egg appeared to be an ordinary hen's egg. (6) The outer shell made of gold that had been enameled to the off-white color of a hen's egg. (7) Opening to reveal a yolk, also of gold, which contained a tiny chicken, elaborately crafted of several shades of gold. (8) Hidden inside the chicken was a surprise. (9) An intricate jeweled model of the imperial crown. (10) Which opened to reveal a tiny ruby egg. (11) Because the Czar was so delighted. (12) He commissioned Fabergé to create a new egg each Easter. (13) And gave the goldsmith one other instruction. (14) To include a surprise in each egg. (15) Which, of course, Fabergé wisely did.

EXERCISE 13-6

Consulting sections 13a, 13b, and 13c, revise this paragraph to eliminate any sentence fragments. In some cases, you can join word groups to create complete sentences; in other cases, you have to revise the word groups into complete sentences. In your final version, check not only the individual sentences but also the clarity of the whole paragraph.

(1) Students looking for jobs need more than the "Help Wanted" section of a newspaper. (2) One major tool, a carefully written résumé. (3) A résumé should be written in a standard form. (4) And proofread carefully to eliminate errors in spelling, punctuation, or grammar. (5) For the content of the résumé. (6) Students should analyze all types of experiences. (7) A résumé including not only paid jobs but also volunteer positions and extracurricular activities. (8) Students have a better chance of getting a job. (9) If they have supervised other people, handled money, or taken on highly responsible tasks. (10) Such as participating in political campaigns or chairing major committees at school. (11) Many employers will consider student résumés. (12) Especially when the résumés include names of the students' supervisors.

Focus on Revising

REVISING YOUR WRITING

If you write sentence fragments, go back to your writing and locate them. Then figure out why each is a sentence fragment by using the Test for Sentence Completeness in 13a. Next, revise each sentence fragment into a complete sentence, referring to 13a, 13b, and 13c.

CASE STUDIES: REVISING TO AVOID SENTENCE FRAGMENTS

In these case studies, you can observe a student writer revising. Then you have the chance to revise other student writing on your own.

Observation

A student wrote the following draft for a course called Introduction to the Novel. The assignment was to compose a paragraph about the childhood of a major novelist. This material is well organized as a narrative and tells an interesting story, but the draft's effectiveness is diminished by the presence of sentence fragments.

Read through the draft. The sentence fragments are highlighted. Before you look at the student's revision, revise the material yourself. Then compare what you and the student did.

dependent clause punctuated as a sentence: 13b

phrase—with -ing form of verb—punctuated as a sentence: 13c

phrase—with past participle of verb—punctuated as a sentence: 13c

The creative imagination of Victorian novelist Charlotte Brontë got an early start. When she was a child. Her father brought her brother, Branford, a set of wooden soldiers. Her father who was a clergyman and who wrote poetry and a novel as well as sermons. After he gave Branford the set. He told Charlotte and her sisters, Emily and Anne, each to pick one of the toy soldiers. And give it a name. Each sister then made up a history of her soldier. Soon creating tales of heroism. Inspired by the pleasure of telling stories. Charlotte, together with her brother, invented an

phrase—part of compound predicate—punctuated as a sentence: 13c

→

COVERAGE: PARTICIPATION ESSAY, page 291

In seventeenth-century England, from the death of Elizabeth I in 1603 to William of Orange's ascension to the throne in 1689 [13c: prepositional phrase punctuated as sentence]. The monarchy of England was the cause of unrest and uncertainty.

Queen Elizabeth I died single and childless in 1603. *Because she did not have a direct descendent* [13b: dependent clause punctuated as a sentence]. The throne passed to the Queen's cousin. *Who was crowned James I* [13b: dependent clauses punctuated as sentence]. Discord over the relative power of Parliament and the crown emerged under James I. *And erupted during the reign of James's son, Charles I* [13c; second half of compound predicate punctuated as sentence]. Incapable of resolving the conflicts, Charles I lost both the crown and his head to Oliver Cromwell's Puritan Revolution in 1649.

Holding fast to his anti-monarchy sentiments and refusing a crown [13c: participial phrase punctuated as sentence]. Oliver Cromwell did not establish a new line of English monarchs. Instead, he became Lord Protector of England. When Cromwell died, his son Richard lacked the charisma and political astuteness to hold on to power. As a result, the son of Charles I was recalled from France. *Where he had fled to live in safety.* [13b: dependent clause punctuated as sentence]. He was crowned Charles II in 1660. *And had very limited power, according to new laws passed by*

→

FOCUS ON REVISING

Parliament [13c: second half of compound predicate punctuated as sentence]. Charles II sired no legitimate heirs, so the succession passed to his brother, James. *An apparently able man with one serious political handicap in seventeenth-century England* [13c: phrase punctuated as sentence]. He was Catholic, at a time when England feared that the Pope was plotting to reclaim England and rule it from Rome. *When the second wife of James baptized her newborn son Catholic* [13b: dependent clause punctuated as sentence]. Unease over James's rule escalated rapidly. *To ensure the safety of his wife and new son* [13c: phrase punctuated as sentence]. James sent them to France and followed soon after James's Protestant daughter Mary took the throne. *With her husband William of Orange* [13c: phrase punctuated as sentence]. A Dutchman who was a staunch supporter of Protestantism [13b: dependent clause punctuated as sentence]. Their union was so popular with the English that William continued to rule after Mary's death in 1694. Thus, the century that saw much upheaval and instability in England ended in relative calm.

ANSWER: PARTICIPATION ESSAY

This version is revised to correct the sentence fragments. Because of the many options available for corrections, answers will vary somewhat. Also, answers will vary if students have revised for content, organization, or style.

In seventeenth-century England, from the death of Elizabeth I in 1603 to William of Orange's ascension to the throne in 1689, the monarchy in England was the cause of unrest and uncertainty.

➡

imaginary kingdom. With Angria as its name. Because she treasured her fantasies and wanted to remember them. Charlotte began to write them in notebooks. Wanting them to look like miniature editions of books. She printed in a tiny, almost microscopically small handwriting. Those notebooks stand as a reminder of how early in life Charlotte Brontë expressed her creativity.

dependent clause punctuated as a sentence: 13b

prepositional phrase punctuated as a sentence: 13c

phrase—using *-ing* form of verb—punctuated as a sentence: 13c

Here is how the student revised the paragraph to eliminate the sentence fragments. In many places, the student could correct the error in more than one way. Your revision, therefore, might not be exactly like this one, but it should not contain any sentence fragments.

The creative imagination of Victorian novelist Charlotte Brontë got an early start. When she was a child, her father brought her brother, Branford, a set of wooden soldiers. Her father was a clergyman who wrote poetry and a novel as well as sermons. After he gave Branford the set, he told Charlotte and her sisters, Emily and Anne, each to pick one of the toy soldiers and give it a name. Each sister then made up a history of her soldier, and each soon was creating tales of heroism. Inspired by the pleasure of telling stories, Charlotte, together with her brother, invented an imaginary kingdom with Angria as its name. Because she treasured her fantasies and wanted to remember them, Charlotte began to write them in notebooks. Wanting her notebooks to look like miniature editions of books, she printed in a tiny, almost microscopically small handwriting. Those notebooks stand as a reminder of how early in life Charlotte Brontë expressed her creativity.

Participation

A student wrote the following draft for a course called European History. The assignment was to discuss the political atmosphere of a European nation during the seventeenth century. This material is effectively organized for chronological presentation of information, and it uses specific details well. The draft's effectiveness, however, is diminished by the presence of sentence fragments.

Read through the draft. Then revise it to eliminate the sentence fragments. Also, make any additional revisions that you think would improve the content, organization, and style of the material.

In seventeenth-century England, from the death of Elizabeth I in 1603 to William of Orange's ascension to the throne in 1689. The monarchy of England was the cause of unrest and uncertainty.

Queen Elizabeth I died single and childless in 1603. Because she did not have a direct descendant. The throne passed to the Queen's cousin. Who was crowned James I. Discord over the relative power of Parliament and the crown emerged under James I. And erupted during the reign of James's son, Charles I. Incapable of resolving the conflicts, Charles I lost both the throne and his head to Oliver Cromwell's Puritan Revolution in 1649.

Holding fast to his anti-monarchy sentiments and refusing a crown. Oliver Cromwell did not establish a new line of English monarchs. Instead, he became Lord Protector of England. When Cromwell died, his son Richard lacked the charisma and political astuteness to hold on to power. As a result, the son of Charles I was recalled from France. Where he had fled to live in safety. He was crowned Charles II in 1660. And had very limited power, according to new laws passed by Parliament. Charles II sired no legitimate heirs, so the succession passed to his brother, James. An apparently able man with one serious political handicap in seventeenth-century England. He was Catholic, at a time when the English feared that the Pope was plotting to reclaim England and rule it from Rome. When the second wife of James baptized her newborn son Catholic. Unease over James's rule escalated rapidly. To ensure the safety of his wife and new son. James sent them to France and followed soon after. James's Protestant daughter Mary took the throne. With her husband William of Orange. A Dutchman who was a staunch supporter of Protestantism. Their union was so popular with the English that William continued to rule after Mary's death in 1694. Thus, the century that saw much upheaval and instability in England ended in relative calm.

ANSWER: PARTICIPATION ESSAY, cont.

Queen Elizabeth I died single and childless in 1603. Because she did not have a direct descendent, the throne passed to the Queen's cousin who was crowned James I. Discord over the relative power of Parliament and the crown emerged under James I and erupted during the reign of James's son, Charles I. Incapable of resolving the conflicts, Charles I lost both the crown and his head to Oliver Cromwell's Puritan Revolution in 1649.

Holding fast to his anti-monarchy sentiments and refusing a crown, Oliver Cromwell did not establish a new line of English monarchs. Instead, he became Lord Protector of England. When Cromwell died, his son Richard lacked the charisma and political astuteness to hold on to power. As a result, the son of Charles I was recalled from France, where he had fled to live in safety. He was crowned Charles II in 1660 and had very limited power, according to new laws passed by Parliament. Charles II sired no legitimate heirs, so the succession passed to his brother, James, an apparently able man with one serious political handicap in seventeenth-century England. He was Catholic, at a time when England feared that the Pope was plotting to reclaim England and rule it from Rome. When the second wife of James baptized her newborn son Catholic, unease over James's rule escalated rapidly. To ensure the safety of his wife and new son, James sent them to France and followed soon after. James's Protestant daughter Mary took the throne with her husband William of Orange, a Dutchman who was a staunch supporter of Protestantism. Their union was so popular with the English that William continued to rule after Mary's death in 1694. Thus, the century that saw much upheaval and instability in England ended in relative calm.

14 *Comma Splices and Fused Sentences*

REFERENCES TO SUPPLEMENTS
For this topic in the CLAST writing competency test, refer students to ch. 1, section B2d of *Preparing for the CLAST* by S. Patterson.

This topic is included in the TASP writing competency test. Refer students to *Preparing for the TASP* by M. Saenz.

For revising to eliminate comma splices and fused sentences, refer students to *Rough Drafts* by K. S. Cain, Part III, Exercise 6.

QUOTATION ABOUT WRITING
A writer is not someone who expresses his thoughts, his passion or his imagination in sentences but someone who thinks sentences. A Sentence-Thinker.
—Roland Barthes

QUOTATION ABOUT WRITING
Word-carpentry is like any other kind of carpentry: you must join your sentences smoothly.
—Anatole France

QUOTATION ABOUT WRITING
What's so hard about the first sentence is that you're stuck with it. Everything else is going to flow out of that sentence. And by the time you've laid down the first two sentences, your options are all gone.
—Joan Didion

A **comma splice** (or **comma fault**) is an error that occurs when a comma by itself joins INDEPENDENT CLAUSES. A comma is correct between two independent clauses only when it is followed by a coordinating conjunction (*and, but, for, or, nor, yet,* and *so*). The word *splice* means "to fasten ends together." The end of one independent clause and the beginning of another should not be fastened together with a comma alone.

COMMA SPLICE The iceberg broke off from the glacier, it drifted into the sea.

A **fused sentence** is an error that occurs when two independent clauses are not joined by a comma with a coordinating conjunction (*and, but, for, or nor, yet,* and *so*) or by other punctuation. The word *fused* means "united as if by melting together." Two independent clauses cannot be united as if melted together. A fused sentence is also known as a *run-on sentence* or a *run-together sentence*.

FUSED SENTENCE The iceberg broke off from the glacier it drifted into the sea.

Comma splices and fused sentences are two versions of the same problem: incorrect joining of independent clauses. Both comma splices and fused sentences distract readers from understanding the meaning you want your material to deliver.

If you tend to write comma splices and fused sentences, you might have trouble recognizing them, because they can seem to blend with surrounding sentences. Expect, therefore, to analyze your sentences individually. Wait until the REVISING and EDITING stages of your writing process to check for commas splices and fused sentences. While you are DRAFTING, if you suspect that you have made one of these errors, quickly underline or highlight the material and keep drafting. Then, you can easily find and check it later.

Chart 86 shows ways to find and correct these errors and refers to sections in this chapter for fuller explanations.

HOW TO FIND AND CORRECT COMMA SPLICES AND FUSED SENTENCES

86

FINDING COMMA SPLICES AND FUSED SENTENCES

■ Look for a PRONOUN starting the second independent clause.

NO   The physicist Marie Curie discovered radium**, she** won two Nobel prizes.

■ Look for a CONJUNCTIVE ADVERB (Chart 49 in 7f) or TRANSITIONAL EXPRESSION starting the second INDEPENDENT CLAUSE.

NO   Marie Curie and her husband, Pierre, worked together at first**, however,** he died at age 47.

■ Look for a second independent clause that explains, amplifies, contrasts with, or gives an example of information in the first independent clause.

NO   Radium can cause cancer **radium is used to cure cancer.**

FIXING COMMA SPLICES AND FUSED SENTENCES

■ Use a period (14b) or a semicolon (14e) between independent clauses.

YES   The physicist Marie Curie discovered radium**. She** won two Nobel Prizes.

■ Use a comma + COORDINATING CONJUNCTION between the clauses (14c).

YES   The physicist Marie Curie discovered radium, and she won two Nobel Prizes.

■ Use a semicolon + conjunctive adverb or transitional expression between the clauses (14e).

YES   Marie Curie and her husband, Pierre, worked together at first**; however,** he died at age 47.

■ Revise one independent clause into a DEPENDENT CLAUSE (14d).

YES   Radium, **which can cause cancer,** is also used to cure cancer.

Recognizing comma splices and fused sentences

14a

To recognize comma splices and fused sentences, you need to be able to recognize an independent clause, a clause which contains a

BACKGROUND

David Bartholomae ("Released into Language: Errors, Expectations, and the Legacy of Mina Shaughnessy," *The Territory of Language: Linguistics, Stylistics, and the Teaching of Composition*, ed. Donald A. McQuade [Carbondale, IL: Southern Illinois UP, 1986]) concludes that many student errors result from "idiosyncratic" hypotheses about language that students form as they try to learn academic prose and enter into "the language of others." They experiment with conventions and structures that they do not entirely understand or control and form transitional rules to make sense of this language that often only approximate the conventions governing standard English and academic writing. For an example, Bartholomae writes, "A student uses commas and periods in a manner that seems to have little to do with the structure of the sentence, but, perhaps, she is applying her version of some advice she once heard about long pauses and short pauses or about marking off 'complete thoughts'" (70). Bartholomae encourages teachers not just to mark errors but to interpret them to discover a student's underlying idiosyncratic rule.

QUOTATION ABOUT WRITING

It takes me six months to do a story. I think it out and then write it sentence by sentence—no first draft. I can't write five words but that I change seven.

—Dorothy Parker

REFERENCE TO SUPPLEMENTS

See transparency 7–2 on comma splices and fused sentences in the *Prentice Hall/Simon & Schuster Transparencies for Writers* by D. Carter.

14a
cont.

SUBJECT and PREDICATE. An independent clause can stand alone as a sentence because it is an independent grammatical unit.

SUBJECT	PREDICATE
The physicist Marie Curie	discovered radium in 1898.

If you tend to write comma splices, here is a useful technique for proofreading your work. Cover all the words on one side of the comma and see if the words remaining constitute an independent clause. If they do, cover that clause and uncover all the words on the other side of the comma. If the second side of the comma is also an independent clause, you have written a comma splice. Also, to help yourself avoid writing comma splices, become familiar with correct uses for commas, explained in Chapter 24.

Experienced writers sometimes use a comma to join very brief parallel independent clauses, especially if one independent clause is negative and the other is positive: *Mosquitos do not bite, they stab.* Many instructors consider this form an error in student writing; you will never be wrong if you use a semicolon or period.

14b

Using a period or semicolon to correct comma splices and fused sentences

You can use a period or semicolon to correct comma splices and fused sentences. For the sake of sentence variety and emphasis, however, do not always choose punctuation to correct this type of error. (Other methods are discussed in 14c and 14d.) Strings of too many short sentences rarely establish relationships and levels of importance among ideas.

A **period** can separate the independent clauses in a comma splice or fused sentence.

COMMA SPLICE	A shark is all cartilage, it does not have a bone in its body.
FUSED SENTENCE	A shark is all cartilage it does not have a bone in its body.
CORRECTED	A shark is all cartilage. It does not have a bone in its body.

A **semicolon** can separate the INDEPENDENT CLAUSES in a comma splice or fused sentence. Choose a semicolon only when the separate sentences are closely related in meaning. (See also 25a.)

COMMA SPLICE	Sharks can smell blood from a quarter mile away, they swim toward the source like a guided missile.

FUSED SENTENCE	Sharks can smell blood from a quarter mile away they swim toward the source like a guided missile.
CORRECTED	Sharks can smell blood from a quarter mile away; they swim toward the source like a guided missile.

Using coordinating conjunctions to correct comma splices and fused sentences

14c

When ideas in INDEPENDENT CLAUSES are closely related and grammatically equivalent, you can connect them with a COORDINATING CONJUNCTION (*and, but, or, nor, for, so,* and *yet*). If you are correcting a comma splice, keep the comma and insert a coordinating conjunction after it. If you are correcting a fused sentence, insert a comma followed by a coordinating conjunction.

✤ PUNCTUATION ALERT: Use a comma before a coordinating conjunction that links independent clauses (see 24a). ✤   **!**

✤ USAGE ALERT: When using a coordinating conjunction, be sure that it fits the meaning of the material. *And* signals addition, *but* and *yet* signal contrast, *for* and *so* signal cause, and *or* and *nor* signal alternatives. ✤   **!**

COMMA SPLICE	Every living creature gives off a weak electrical charge in the water, special pores on a shark's skin can detect these signals.
FUSED SENTENCE	Every living creature gives off a weak electrical charge in the water special pores on a shark's skin can detect these signals.
CORRECTED	Every living creature gives off a weak electrical field in the water, and special pores on a shark's skin can detect these signals.
COMMA SPLICE	The great white shark supposedly eats humans, however most white sharks spit them out after the first bite.
FUSED SENTENCE	The great white shark supposedly eats humans however most white sharks spit them out after the first bite.
CORRECTED	The great white shark supposedly eats humans, but most white sharks spit them out after the first bite.

295

BACKGROUND

In the second chapter of *Errors and Expectations*, entitled "Handwriting and Punctuation," (Oxford UP: Oxford, UK 1977), Mina Shaughnessy observes that the urge to string sentences together reflects a need on the part of the writer for other ways of making links between sentences. Comma splices, for example, reflect a writer's effort to control a sentence, to simplify it by breaking it up into smaller segments by the use of a comma as a conjunction. She argues that punctuation should not be studied apart from other aspects of writing; instead, it should be integrated with work in composition, for "the process whereby writers *mark* sentences is related to the process whereby they *make* them." She suggests that punctuation skills will improve as novice writers study first to recognize and create simple subject and predicate phrases; second, to embed sentences in sentences (using *who, which, that, when,* and *if*); third, to embed appositional forms; and fourth, to embed *-ing* phrases.

TEACHING TIPS

Students can use a simple test to determine whether a word is a conjunction or a conjunctive adverb. Conjunctive adverbs can be shifted from the beginning of a clause to another position in the middle of the clause; conjunctions, however, cannot be shifted.

Comma splices and fused sentences sometimes occur when students begin a sentence with "not only" but omit "but also" at the start of the second clause. Students should remember that "but" is functioning as a conjunction in this construction and that they need to separate the clauses with a period or semicolon when they omit "but."

ANSWERS AND COVERAGE: EXERCISE 14–1

The correction strategies will vary. Here is one set of possibilities:

1. Urban veterinarians report that summer in New York City can be hard on pets; however, [14c; comma splice corrected by using semicolon and comma] cats suffer less than other animals.

2. Many pets accidentally fall from open twenty-story windows. [14b; fused sentence corrected by using a period] Cats are the most common victims along with dogs, rabbits, iguanas, and turtles.

3. A research paper reports an amazing finding. [14b; comma splice caused by explanation corrected by using a period] Cats that fall five to nine stories suffer worse injuries than cats that fall much farther.

4. The average falling cat reaches maximum speed at five stories. [14c; fused sentence corrected by using a comma and a coordinating conjunction] Then after nine stories, the cat manages to get into a position that cushions the impact of landing.

5. A Manhattan cat has set a new record for surviving a high-rise fall. [14b; fused sentence corrected by using a period] It dropped forty-six stories from a midtown apartment balcony and landed unharmed in a café awning below.

REFERENCE TO SUPPLEMENTS

See transparency 7–3 on revising to avoid comma splices and fused sentences in the *Prentice Hall/Simon & Schuster Transparencies for Writers* by D. Carter.

14c
cont.

EXERCISE 14-1

Consulting sections 14a, 14b, and 14c, revise any comma splices or fused sentences by using a period, a semicolon, or a coordinating conjunction and comma.

EXAMPLE   In Los Angeles, animals contract skin cancer, in New York, they suffer from high-rise syndrome.

✓   *In Los Angeles, animals contract skin cancer; in New York, they suffer from high-rise syndrome.*

1. Urban veterinarians report that summer in New York City can be hard on pets, however cats suffer less than other animals.

2. Many pets fall accidentally out of open twenty-story windows cats are the most common victims along with dogs, rabbits, iguanas, and turtles.

3. A research paper reports an amazing finding, cats that fall five to nine stories are more seriously hurt than cats that fall much farther.

4. The average falling cat reaches maximum speed at five stories then after nine stories the cat manages to get into a position that cushions the impact of landing.

5. A Manhattan cat has set a new record for surviving a high-rise fall, it dropped forty-six stories from a midtown apartment balcony and landed unharmed on a café awning below.

14d

Revising an independent clause into a dependent clause to correct a comma splice or fused sentence

You can revise a comma splice or fused sentence by changing one of two INDEPENDENT CLAUSES into a DEPENDENT CLAUSE. This method is suitable when one idea can logically be subordinated to the other.

One way to create a dependent clause is to insert a subordinating conjunction (such as *because* and *although*; for a complete list, see Chart 51 in section 7h.) When using a subordinating conjunction, be sure that it fits the meaning of the material: for example, *as* and *because* signal reason, *although* signals contrast, *if* signals condition, and *when* signals time. This type of dependent clause is called an **adverb clause**.

! ❖ PUNCTUATION ALERTS: (1) If you put a period after a dependent clause that is not attached to an independent clause, you will create the error called a *sentence fragment*; see Chapter 13. (2) Generally, use a comma after an introductory dependent clause that starts with a subordinating conjunction; see 24b-1. ❖

COMMA SPLICE	Homer and Langley Collyer had packed their house from top to bottom with junk, police could not open the front door to investigate a missing-persons report on the brothers.
FUSED SENTENCE	Homer and Langley Collyer had packed their house from top to bottom with junk police could not open the front door to investigate a missing-persons report on the brothers.
CORRECTED	**Because Homer and Langley Collyer had packed their house from top to bottom with junk,** police could not open the front door to investigate a missing-persons report on the brothers.
COMMA SPLICE	Old newspapers, toys, car parts, and books filled every room to the ceiling, enough space remained for fourteen pianos.
FUSED SENTENCE	Old newspapers, toys, car parts, and books filled every room to the ceiling enough space remained for fourteen pianos.
CORRECTED	**Although old newspapers, toys, car parts, and books filled every room to the ceiling,** enough space remained for fourteen pianos.

Another way to create a dependent clause is to use a **relative pronoun** (*that, which, who*). This type of dependent clause is called an **adjective clause**.

♣ PUNCTUATION ALERT: To determine whether you need commas to set off an adjective clause, check whether it is NONRESTRICTIVE (nonessential) or RESTRICTIVE (essential), as explained in 24e. ♣

COMMA SPLICE	The Collyers had been crushed under a pile of newspapers, the newspapers had toppled onto the brothers.
FUSED SENTENCE	The Collyers had been crushed under a pile of newspapers the newspapers had toppled onto the brothers.
CORRECTED	The Collyers had been crushed under a pile of newspapers **that had toppled onto the brothers.**

!

ANSWERS AND COVERAGE: EXERCISE 14–2

(1) Correct complete sentence (2) The Internet connects thousands of on-line computer networks around the world, and [fused sentence caused by pronoun corrected by comma and coordinating conjunction *and*] it has created a new form of personal communication that requires new rules. (3) Correct complete sentence (4) Sometimes the faceless communication gives timid on-liners confidence to speak their minds. However, other times some users have less pleasant experiences. [comma splice corrected by a period] (5) A flame, for example, is an insulting message that is [fused sentence corrected by relative pronoun *that* to make final clause dependent] the on-line equivalent of a poison pen letter. (6) The quick response time of electronic mail encourages hasty people to react hastily, and [fused sentence corrected by adding coordinating conjunction *and*] instant anger can be thoughtlessly expressed. (7) Flamers cannot always be identified because [comma splice caused by explanation corrected by adding subordinating conjunction *because*] their real names are concealed by passwords. (8) Another prank is to impersonate another user by adopting his or her on-line name. As a result, [comma splice corrected by using a period] there is no way to identify the person sending a fake message. (9) Internet lurkers, who [fused sentence caused by pronoun corrected by adding relative pronoun *who*] read other people's messages in the public spaces but are too fearful of being flamed to send their own messages, are undesirable too.

QUOTATION ABOUT WRITING

Wearing down seven number two pencils is a good day's work.

—Ernest Hemingway

EXERCISE 14-2

Consulting sections 14a through 14d, revise any comma splices or fused sentences.

(1) Because millions of Americans are now cruising the information superhighway, traffic pileups and confrontations are more likely. (2) The Internet connects thousands of on-line computer networks around the world it has created a new form of personal communication that requires new rules. (3) Just as on a real highway, not all users of the information highway observe "netiquette," the rules governing on-line courtesy. (4) Sometimes the faceless communication gives timid on-liners confidence to speak their minds, however, at other times some users have less pleasant experiences. (5) A flame, for example, is an insulting message it is the on-line equivalent of a poison pen letter. (6) The quick response time of electronic mail encourages hasty people to react hastily instant anger can be thoughtlessly expressed. (7) Flamers cannot always be identified, their real names are concealed by passwords. (8) Another prank is to impersonate another user by adopting his or her on-line name, as a result, there is no way to identify the person sending a fake message. (9) Internet lurkers are undesirable too they read other people's messages in the public spaces but are too fearful of being flamed to send their own messages.

14e Using a semicolon or a period before a conjunctive adverb or other transitional expression between independent clauses

Conjunctive adverbs and other transitional expressions link ideas between sentences. When these words fall between sentences, a period or semicolon must immediately precede them.

Conjunctive adverbs include such words as *however, therefore, also, next, then, thus, furthermore,* and *nevertheless* (for a complete list, see Chart 49 in section 7f). Remember that these words are *not* coordinating conjunctions, which work in concert with commas to join independent clauses (see 14c).

! ❖ PUNCTUATION ALERT: A conjunctive adverb at the beginning of a sentence is usually followed by a comma (see 24b-3). ❖

COMMA SPLICE	Buying or leasing a car is a matter of individual preference, **however,** it is wise to consider several points before making a decision.
FUSED SENTENCE	Buying or leasing a car is a matter of individual preference **however,** it is wise to consider several points before making a decision.

CORRECTED	Buying or leasing a car is a matter of individual preference; **however,** it is wise to consider several points before making a decision.

Transitional expressions include *for example, for instance, in addition, in fact, of course,* and *on the other hand* (for a complete list, see Chart 23 in section 4d-1).

❖ PUNCTUATION ALERT: A transitional expression at the beginning of a sentence is usually followed by a comma (see 24b-3). ❖   **!**

COMMA SPLICE	Car leasing requires a smaller down payment, **for example,** in many cases you need only $1,000 or $2,000 and the first monthly payment.
FUSED SENTENCE	Car leasing requires a smaller down payment **for example,** in many cases you need only $1,000 or $2,000 and the first monthly payment.
CORRECTED	Car leasing requires a smaller down payment. **For example,** in many cases you need only $1,000 or $2,000 and the first monthly payment.

A conjunctive adverb or other transitional expression can appear in more than one location within an INDEPENDENT CLAUSE. In contrast, a coordinating conjunction (*and, but, or, nor, for, so,* and *yet*) can appear only between independent clauses that it joins.

Car leasing grows more popular every year. **However,** leasers have nothing to show for their money when the lease ends. [conjunctive adverb]

Car leasing grows more popular every year. Leasers, **however,** have nothing to show for their money when the lease ends. [conjunctive adverb]

Car leasing grows more popular every year. Leasers have nothing to show for their money, **however,** when the lease ends. [conjunctive adverb]

Car leasing grows more popular every year. Leasers have nothing to show for their money when the lease ends, **however**. [conjunctive adverb]

Car leasing grows more popular every year, **but** leasers have nothing to show for their money when the lease ends. [coordinating conjunction]

EXERCISE 14-3 ✓

Consulting section 14e, revise any comma splices or fused sentences caused by a conjunctive adverb or other transitional expression. If an item is correct, circle its number.

ANSWERS AND COVERAGE: EXERCISE 14–3

1. Lovecraft wrote vividly of monsters from beyond space and time; however, [fused sentence: conjunctive adverb] he insisted that he did not believe in the supernatural.

2. "The Shadow over Innsmouth" is Lovecraft's famous tale about the strange inhabitants of a New England port; specifically, [comma splice: transitional expression] they are part fish and part human.

3. Correct complete sentence

4. Many of Lovecraft's stories mention a sinister volume of secret lore called the *Necronomicon*; however, it [comma splice: conjunctive adverb] was entirely a product of his imagination.

5. No such book exists. [fused sentence: conjunctive adverb] Nevertheless, U.S. libraries still receive call slips for the *Necronomicon* filled out by gullible Lovecraft readers.

ANSWERS AND COVERAGE: EXERCISE 14–4

Answers will vary. Here is one set of revisions.

1. Ostriches are said to bury their heads in the sand so that their enemies will not notice them, but this, naturalists maintain, is a myth. [14c, fused sentence corrected with comma and coordinating conjunction]

2. A South African naturalist who examined eighty years of records from ostrich farms where over 200,000 of the birds were reared found that no one reported a single case of an ostrich burying its head, or even attempting to do so. [14d, comma splice corrected by creating dependent clause beginning with relative pronoun *who*]

3. Ostriches do listen intently for chirps, cries, and approaching footsteps with their heads near the ground;

➡

14e
cont.

EXAMPLE   The horror stories of the New England writer H. P. Lovecraft were little known during his lifetime however they gained a following of enthusiastic readers after his death in 1937.

The horror stories of the New England writer H. P. Lovecraft were little known during his lifetime. However, they gained a following of enthusiastic readers after his death in 1937.

1. Lovecraft wrote vividly of monsters from beyond space and time however, he insisted that he did not believe in the supernatural.

2. "The Shadow over Innsmouth" is Lovecraft's famous tale about the strange inhabitants of a New England port, specifically, they are part fish and part human.

3. Lovecraft wanted his invented historical backgrounds to sound factual so he often cited impressive-sounding reference works; of course, he simply made most of them up.

4. Many of Lovecraft's stories mention a volume of secret lore called the *Necronomicon,* however, it was entirely a product of his imagination.

5. No such book exists nevertheless U.S. libraries still receive call slips for the *Necronomicon* filled out by gullible Lovecraft readers.

EXERCISE 14-4

Consulting all sections in this chapter, revise all comma splices, using a different method of correction for each one. If an item is correct, circle its number.

EXAMPLE   People hold strong but erroneous beliefs about animal behavior, for example, it is commonly thought that ostriches bury their heads in the sand.

People hold strong but erroneous beliefs about animal behavior. For example, it is commonly thought that ostriches bury their heads in the sand.

1. Ostriches are said to bury their heads in the sand so that their enemies will not notice them this, naturalists maintain, is a myth.

2. A South African naturalist examined eighty years of records from ostrich farms where more than 200,000 of the birds were reared, he found that no one reported a single case of an ostrich burying its head.

3. Ostriches do listen intently for chirps, cries, and approaching footsteps with their heads near the ground, sometimes, they even lower their heads just to rest their neck muscles.

4. They also poke their heads into bushes because they are curious animals.

5. They never bury their heads in sand, they would probably suffocate if they did.

EXERCISE 14-5

Consulting all sections in this chapter, revise any fused sentences, using as many different methods explained in this chapter as you can.

(1) During the nineteenth century, a number of fearless women traveled long distances from their homes they visited places far more exotic than their native France or England. (2) Isabella Bird, for example, a British clergyman's daughter, began traveling and writing when she was in her forties she often wrote by the light of a portable oil lamp and with a gun in her pocket. (3) In 1896, she celebrated her sixty-fourth birthday that same year she crossed northwest China she hoped to reach Tibet. (4) While she was traveling, her guides collapsed with fever then her rice supply grew dangerously low. (5) Only when tribal warfare broke out, however, and the bridges were torn down did she turn around. (6) Like Isabella Bird, Flora Tristan, a native of France, proved her adventurous spirit she sailed from France to Peru, a trip that inspired her to write a book. (7) The book was published in 1838 however, its title, *Peregrinations of a Pariah,* meaning "travels of an outcast," suggests that not everyone admired its courageous author.

EXERCISE 14-6

Consulting all sections in this chapter, revise all comma splices or fused sentences, using as many different methods of correction as you can. If a sentence is correct, circle its number. After you have corrected the comma splices and fused sentences, check not only the correctness of the individual sentences but also the clarity of the entire paragraph.

(1) Archaeologists are studying modern Australia to learn how humans lived on this planet thousands of years ago many customs of the Stone Age are still practiced by some Australian Aborigines today. (2) French archaeologist and painter Michel Lorblanchet spent four years in Northern Australia studying painting techniques. (3) Lorblanchet watched the Aboriginal painters work, these artists create dramatic images by spitting red ocher paint on sandstone walls in caves. (4) The artists put a mixture of red ocher and water in their mouths, as a result saliva becomes the third ingredient, which gives the paint the right consistency so that it adheres to the wall. (5) To create the mixture, they chew for several minutes their lips and teeth turn brick-red.(6) Next, they place their left hands against the wall and spit rapidly around their hands. (7) The imprint of an artist's hand is unique indeed it acts as an identifying marker. (8) Spit-painting is spiritually significant it is an act that unites painter and painting. (9) Spit is the product of human breath, it is believed to imprint images of the artist's soul on the cave wall. (10) Similar hand prints were found in an 18,000-year-old cave painting in France therefore Lorblanchet believes they were painted the same way.

sometimes, they even lower their heads just to rest their neck muscles. [14b, fused sentence corrected with semicolon]

4. Correct complete sentence.

5. They never bury their heads in sand, and they would probably suffocate if they did. [14c, comma splice corrected with coordinating conjunction]

ANSWERS: EXERCISE 14–5

Answers will vary. Here is one possible revision.

(1) During the nineteenth century, a number of fearless women traveled long distances from their homes. They visited places far more exotic than their native France or England. (2) Isabella Bird, for example, a British clergyman's daughter, began traveling and writing when she was in her forties; she often wrote by the light of a portable oil lamp and with a gun in her pocket. (3) In 1896, she celebrated her sixty-fourth birthday, and that same year she crossed northwest China hoping to reach Tibet. (4) While she was traveling, her guides collapsed with fever. Then her rice supply grew dangerously low. (5) Only when tribal warfare broke out, however, and the bridges were torn down did she turn around. (6) Like Isabella Bird, Flora Tristan, a native of France, proved her adventurous spirit when she sailed from France to Peru, a trip that inspired her to write a book. (7) The book was published in 1838; however, its title, *Peregrinations of a Pariah*, meaning "travels of an outcast," suggests that not everyone admired its courageous author.

ANSWERS AND COVERAGE: EXERCISE 14–6

Answers will vary. One possible revision is shown on page 302. ➔

Focus on Revising

ANSWERS AND COVERAGE:
EXERCISE 14–6, page 301

(1) Archaeologists are studying modern Australia to learn how humans lived on this planet thousands of years ago because many customs of the Stone Age are still practiced by some Australian Aborigines today. [14d; fused sentence with second clause explaining first] (2) Correct complete sentence (3) Lorblanchet watched the Aboriginal painters work. These artists [14d; comma splice with second clause explaining first] create dramatic images by spitting red ocher paint on sandstone walls in caves. (4) The artists put a mixture of red ocher and water in their mouths; as a result [14e; comma splice with transitional expression] saliva becomes the third ingredient, which gives the paint the right consistency so that it adheres to the wall. (5) To create the mixture, they chew for several minutes, and [14c; fused sentence with second clause amplifying first] their lips and teeth turn brick-red. (6) Correct complete sentence (7) The imprint of an artist's hand is unique; indeed, [14e; fused sentence with transitional expression] it acts as an identifying marker. (8) Spit-painting is spiritually significant [14d; Fused sentence with pronoun beginning second clause]; it is an act that unites painter and painting. (9) Spit, which [14d; comma splice with pronoun] is the product of human breath, is believed to imprint images of the artist's soul on the cave wall. (10) Similar hand prints were found in an 18,000-year-old cave painting in France; therefore, [14c, fused sentence with conjunctive adverb] Lorblanchet believes they were painted the same way.

REVISING YOUR WRITING

If you write comma splices or fused sentences, go back to your writing and locate them. Then figure out why each is an error by using Chart 86 in section 14a on How to Find and Correct Comma Splices and Fused Sentences. Next, using the explanations in 14b through 14e, revise your writing to eliminate the errors.

CASE STUDIES: REVISING TO AVOID COMMA SPLICES AND FUSED SENTENCES

In these case studies, you can observe a student writer revising. Then you have the chance to revise other student writing on your own.

Observation

A student wrote the following draft for a course called Introduction to Criminal Justice. The assignment was to discuss a current controversy in trial law. This material is well organized and presents its information clearly and fully. However, the draft's effectiveness is diminished by comma splices and fused sentences.

Read through the draft. The errors are highlighted and explained. Before you look at the student's revision, revise the material yourself. Then compare what you and the student did.

comma splice with pronoun *it:* 14a

When fingerprinting was first introduced in the late nineteenth century, many judges hesitated to accept fingerprints as legal evidence. Recently, a similar controversy has arisen, it involves hypnosis. During this century, various state and federal courts have issued contradictory rulings on the admissibility of testimony obtained under hypnosis, however, in 1987 the United States Supreme Court ruled that such evidence is admissible. This ruling is a major new development, but the

comma splice with conjunctive adverb *however:* 14a

public should not look to hypnosis as a miracle technique, because testimony obtained under hypnosis is no more reliable than that obtained when witnesses search their memories.

    There is one major advantage of hypnosis it usually allows witnesses to recall incidents in far greater detail than they would otherwise. Hypnotized people will still recall what they think they saw or what they wished they had seen. In fact, it is possible for people to lie when hypnotized furthermore, a hypnotist can unintentionally lead witnesses to give certain responses.

    One thing is certain, lively legal debates lie ahead. Hypnotists are not licensed professionals, they can be circus entertainers or serious practitioners. It would be up to a jury to decide on the competence of a hypnotist most people who sit on juries have no idea of what standards to apply.

fused sentence with pronoun it: 14a

fused sentence with conjunctive adverb furthermore: 14a

fused sentence with explanation in second independent clause: 14a

comma splice with explanation in second independent clause: 14a

comma splice with pronoun they: 14a

Here is how the student revised the draft to correct comma splices and fused sentences. In many places, the student could correct the errors in more than one way. Your revision, therefore, might not be exactly like this one, but it should deal with each error highlighted on the draft.

    When fingerprinting was first introduced in the late nineteenth century, many judges hesitated to accept fingerprints as legal evidence. Recently, a similar controversy has arisen. It involves hypnosis. During this century, various state and federal courts have issued contradictory rulings on the admissibility of testimony obtained under hypnosis. However, in 1987 the United States Supreme Court ruled that such evidence is admissible. This ruling is a major new development, but the public should not look to hypnosis as a miracle technique, because testimony obtained under hypnosis is no more reliable than that obtained when witnesses search their memories.

→

FOCUS ON REVISING   FOCUS ON REVISING   FOCUS ON REVISING   FOCUS ON REVISING

COVERAGE: PARTICIPATION ESSAY, pages 304–305

As consumers, when we buy clothes, we often make choices on the basis of the *fabric of an article of clothing, therefore,* [14a; comma splice with conjunctive adverb] fashion designers always pay attention to matters of composition and design in fabrics.

    Fabric is composed of natural fibers, synthetic fibers, and blends of the two. Natural fibers include cotton, linen, and *wool, they* [14a; comma splice with pronoun] offer the advantages of durability and absorbency. Synthetic fibers include rayon, polyester, acrylic, or combinations of them and other synthetic *fibers they* [14a; fused sentence with pronoun] resist wrinkling and retain their color well. Fiber blends combine natural and synthetic fibers to create combinations such as cotton and polyester, which offer the advantages of each but have their own problems, such as retaining stains.

    The design of fabric is affected by the way *that the fabric is produced, for example,* [14a; comma splice with transitional expression] a fabric can be produced on a loom to create woven fabrics such as crepe and *denim, conversely,* [14a; fused sentence with transitional expression] a fabric can be produced on a knitting machine to create fabrics such as jersey and velour. Once the basic fabric is being produced, special patterns can be woven or knit into it, *for instance,* [14a; comma splice with transitional expression] diagonal patterns can be woven into cotton fabrics for a geometric effect, and vertical patterns can be woven into a cable-stitched fabric for a thicker look and feel. Various finishes can further alter a fabric's *appearance stone* [14a; fused sentence with example] washing gives denim a worn look, and brushing gives flannel a softer look. Puckers or wrinkles can be set into a *fabric, these* [14a; comma splice with pronoun] features characterize fabrics such as seersucker and crinkle gauze.

→

COVERAGE: PARTICIPATION ESSAY, cont.

These many options, and others, in fabrics permit fashion designers to satisfy the needs of many different types of *people, some* [14a; Fused sentence with example] consumers care more about being in style than building a long-lasting wardrobe, while others place high priority on ease of care or on comfortable fit.

ANSWER: PARTICIPATION ESSAY, pages 304–305

This version revises the common splices and fused sentences. Answers might vary because of the options in correcting the errors. Also, answers will vary if a student revised the content, organization, or style.

As consumers, when we buy clothes, we often make choices on the basis of the fabric of an article of clothing. Therefore, fashion designers always pay attention to matters of composition and design in fabrics.

Fabric is composed of natural fibers, synthetic fibers, and blends of the two. Natural fibers include cotton, linen, and wool. They offer the advantages of durability and absorbency. Synthetic fibers include rayon, polyester, acrylic, or combinations of them and other synthetic fibers; they resist wrinkling and retain their color well. Fiber blends combine natural and synthetic fibers to create combinations such as cotton and polyester, which offer the advantages of each but have their own problems, such as retaining stains.

The design of fabric is affected by the way that the fabric is produced. For example, a fabric can be produced on a loom to create woven fabrics such as crepe and denim; conversely, a fabric can be produced on a knitting machine to create fabrics such as jersey and velour. Once the basic fabric is being produced,

→

There is one major advantage of hypnosis; it usually allows witnesses to recall incidents in far greater detail than they would otherwise. Hypnotized people will still recall what they think they saw or what they wished they had seen. In fact, it is possible for people to lie when hypnotized; furthermore, a hypnotist can unintentionally lead witnesses to give certain responses.

One thing is certain. Lively legal debates lie ahead. Hypnotists are not licensed professionals. They can be circus entertainers or serious practitioners. It would be up to a jury to decide on the competence of a hypnotist, but most people who sit on juries have no idea of what standards to apply.

Participation

A student wrote the following draft for a course called Introduction to Fashion Design. The assignment was to describe characteristics of fabric. This material is well organized and uses specific examples well, but the draft's effectiveness is diminished by comma splices and fused sentences.

Read through the draft. Then revise it to eliminate the comma splices and fused sentences. Also, make any additional revisions that you think would improve the content, organization, and style of the material.

As consumers, when we buy clothes, we often make choices on the basis of the fabric of an article of clothing, therefore, fashion designers always pay attention to matters of composition and design in fabrics.

Fabric is composed of natural fibers, synthetic fibers, and blends of the two. Natural fibers include cotton, linen, and wool, they offer the advantages of durability and absorbency. Synthetic fibers include rayon, polyester, acrylic, or combinations of them and other synthetic fibers they resist wrinkling and retain their color well. Fiber blends combine natural and synthetic fibers to create combinations such as cotton and polyester, which offer the advantages of each but have their own problems, such as retaining stains.

The design of fabric is affected by the way that the fabric is produced, for example, a fabric can be produced on a loom to create woven fabrics such as crepe and denim, conversely, a fabric can be produced on a knitting machine to create fabrics such as jersey and velour. Once the basic fabric is being produced, special patterns can be woven or knit into it, for instance, diagonal patterns can be woven into cotton fabrics for a geometric effect, and vertical patterns can be woven into a cable-stitched fabric for a thicker look and feel. Various finishes can further alter a fabric's appearance stone washing, for example, gives denim a worn look, and brushing gives flannel a softer look. Puckers or wrinkles can be set into a fabric, these features characterize fabrics such as seersucker and crinkle gauze.

These many options, and others, in fabrics permit fashion designers to satisfy the needs of many different types of people, some consumers care more about being in style than building a long-lasting wardrobe, while others place a high priority on ease of care or on comfortable fit.

ANSWER: PARTICIPATION ESSAY, cont.

special patterns can be woven or knit into it. For instance, diagonal patterns can be woven into cotton fabrics for a geometric effect, and vertical patterns can be woven into a cable-stitched fabric for a thicker look and feel. Various finishes can further alter a fabric's appearance. Stone washing gives denim a worn look, and brushing gives flannel a softer look. Puckers or wrinkles can be set into a fabric; these features characterize fabrics such as seersucker and crinkle gauze.

These many options, and others, in fabrics permit fashion designers to satisfy the needs of many different types of people. Some consumers care more about being in style than building a long-lasting wardrobe, while others place a high priority on ease of care or on comfortable fit.

15 *Sentences that Send Unclear Messages*

A sentence can seem structurally correct at first glance, as if no grammatical principles of English had been violated, but can still have internal flaws that keep it from delivering a sensible message. Wait until the REVISING and EDITING stages of your writing process to check your sentences for the problems listed in Chart 87. While you are DRAFTING, if you suspect that you have made one of these errors, quickly underline or highlight the material and continue drafting. Then, you can easily find and check it later.

WAYS THAT SENTENCES SEND UNCLEAR MESSAGES	87
PROBLEM	**SEE SECTION**
■ Unnecessary shifts	
PERSON and NUMBER	15a-1
SUBJECT and VOICE	15a-2
TENSE and MOOD	15a-3
DIRECT DISCOURSE and INDIRECT DISCOURSE	15a-4
■ MISPLACED MODIFIERS	15b
■ DANGLING MODIFIERS	15c
■ Mixed sentences	
MIXED CONSTRUCTIONS	15d-1
FAULTY PREDICATION	15d-2
■ Incomplete sentences	15e

Many sentence flaws that send unclear messages can be hard to spot because of the way the human brain works. When writers know what they mean to say, they sometimes misread what is on the paper for what they intend. The mind unconsciously adjusts an error or fills in missing material. Readers, on the other hand, see only what is on the paper. For suggestions to help you see such flaws, see Chart 88.

NO   Heated for 30 seconds, you get bubbles on the surface of the mixture. [This sentence says *you* are heated for 30 seconds.]

YES   After the mixture is heated for 30 seconds, bubbles form on the surface.

NO   After you boil the mixture for two minutes, it is cooled in a test tube. [This sentence shifts unnecessarily from *you* to *it* and from the ACTIVE VOICE to the PASSIVE VOICE.]

YES   After the mixture is boiled for two minutes, it is cooled in a test tube.

YES   After boiling the mixture for two minutes, cool it in a test tube.

NO   The chemical reaction taking place rapidly creates a salt. [*Rapidly* could refer to the speed of the reaction or to the speed at which the salt is created; readers cannot know.]

YES   The chemical reaction takes place rapidly and creates a salt.

YES   The chemical reaction rapidly creates a salt.

PROOFREADING TO FIND SENTENCE FLAWS   88

- Finish your revision in enough time so that you can put it aside and go back to it with fresh eyes that can spot flaws more easily.

- Work backwards, from your last sentence to your first, so that you can see each sentence as a separate unit free of a context that might lure you to overlook flaws.

- Ask an experienced reader to check your writing for sentence flaws. If you make an error discussed in this chapter, you likely make that error repeatedly. Once you become aware of it, you will have made a major step toward eliminating that type of error.

- Proofread an extra time exclusively for any error that you tend to make more than any other.

Avoiding unnecessary shifts   15a

Shift is a term for an abrupt, unneeded change of PERSON, NUMBER, SUBJECT, VOICE, TENSE, MOOD, or kind of discourse (DIRECT or INDIRECT). Unnecessary shifts blur meaning. Readers expect to stay on

QUOTATION ABOUT WRITING

Everything that can be thought at all can be thought clearly. Everything that can be said can be said clearly.
—Ludwig Wittgenstein

REFERENCES TO SUPPLEMENTS

For this topic in the CLAST writing competency test, refer students to ch. 1, section B4b2 and to ch. 2, section B4d of *Preparing for the CLAST* by S. Patterson.

See transparency 7–6 for shifts in person or number in the *Prentice Hall/Simon & Schuster Transparencies for Writers* by D. Carter.

ALTERNATE EXAMPLE

To improve students' skills in recognizing person and number, you might ask them to read the following passage from Susan Allen Toth's "Cinematypes." Then ask students to work in groups to label the subject of each clause by person and number. (The subjects here appear in italics.)

When *Pete and I* [third, first, plural] go to the movies, *we* [first, plural] take turns driving so *no one* [third, singular] owes anyone else anything. *We* [first, plural] leave the car far from the theater so *we* [first, plural] don't have to pay for a parking space. If *it's* [third, singular] raining or snowing, *Pete* [third, singular] offers to let me off at the door, but *I* [first, singular] can tell *he'll* [third, singular] feel better if *I* [first, singular] go with him while *he* [third, singular] finds a spot, so *we* [first, plural] share the walk too. Inside the theater *Pete* [third, singular] will hold my hand when *I* [first, singular] get scared if *I* [first, singular] ask him. *He* [third, singular] puts my hand firmly on his knee and covers

➜

the track that you as the writer start them on. If you switch tracks, your readers become confused.

Staying consistent in person and number

Person in English consists of the *first person (I, we)*, words that designate the speaker or writer; *second person (you)*, words that designate the one being spoken or written to; and *third person (he, she, it, they)*, words that designate the person or thing spoken or written about. All COMMON NOUNS are third-person words. (For more about person, see Chart 72 in section 11a.)

NO   **They** enjoy feeling productive, but when a job is unsatisfying, **you** usually become depressed. [*They* shifts to *you*.]

YES   **They** enjoy feeling productive, but when a job is unsatisfying, **they** usually become depressed.

Number refers to *singular* (one) or *plural* (more than one). Do not start to write in one number and then shift for no reason to the other number. Such shifting gives your sentences an unstable quality, and your message becomes fuzzy.

NO   Because most **people** are living longer, an **employee** in the twenty-first century will retire later. [The *plural* people shifts to the singular *employee*.]

YES   Because most **people** are living longer, **employees** in the twenty-first century will retire later.

A common cause of inconsistency in person and number is shifts to *you* (second person) from *I* (first person) or from a noun (third person) such as *person, the public,* or *people*. In academic writing, reserve *you* for sentences that address the reader directly; use the third person for general statements.

NO   I enjoy reading forecasts of the future, but **you** wonder which will turn out to be correct. [*I*, which is first person, shifts to *you*, which is second person.]

YES   I enjoy reading forecasts of the future, but **I** wonder which will turn out to be correct.

NO   By the year 2000, **Americans** will pay twice today's price for a car, and **you** will get twice the gas mileage. [*Americans*, which is third person, shifts to *you*, which is second person.]

YES   By the year 2000, **Americans** will pay twice today's price for a car, and **they** will get twice the gas mileage.

Another common cause of inconsistency in number is a shift from singular to plural in the third person. A plural pronoun (for example, *they*) should not be used to refer to a singular noun (for example, *employee*) or a singular third-person pronoun (for example, *someone*). Use *he* or *she* (or *he or she,* which acts as a singular pronoun) or *it* to refer to a singular noun. When you use words such as *employee* or *someone* in a general sense, without any specific "employee" or "someone" in mind, you might think that a "he" or "she" is not involved. Still, you have to choose a singular pronoun. Another choice is to change to the plural *employees,* in which case the plural pronoun *they* would be correct. A third possibility is revising so that personal pronouns are unneeded.

NO	When an **employee** is treated with respect, **they** usually feel highly motivated.
YES	When an **employee** is treated with respect, **he** or **she** usually feels highly motivated.
YES	When **employees** are treated with respect, they usually feel highly motivated.
YES	**Employees** who are treated with respect usually feel highly motivated.
YES	An **employee** who is treated with respect usually feels highly motivated.

Try to avoid sexist language when you use indefinite pronouns (such as *someone* or *everyone;* for a complete list, see Chart 77 in 11g); see 11q and especially 21b for advice about nonsexist language.

✤ VERB ALERT: After you have revised person or number based on the advice here, check the verbs in the sentence to see whether any verb needs a change in number as well (see 8c). In the examples just shown, all Yes choices contain verb changes. ✤

EXERCISE 15-1

Consulting section 15a-1, eliminate shifts in person and number. Be alert to shifts between, as well as within, sentences. Some sentences may not need revision.

(1) According to some experts, snobbery is measured by your mental attitude, not the extent of your worldly goods. (2) Because a snob is unsure of his or her social position, snobs are driven by what others think of them. (3) You tend to be too dependent on buying status symbols to define your place in the world, and snobs look down on others. (4) The origin of this word can be traced to the British Isles. (5) When commoners were first allowed to enter England's Cambridge University in the 1700s, each student was required to identify their social position. (6) The commoner had to use the Latin words *sine nobilitate,* meaning "without nobility." (7) Eventually, the students shortened this phrase to "s.nob," and the word came to signify persons aspiring to a higher social level.

---

it completely with his own hand. His *knee* [third, singular] never twitches. After a while, when the scary *part* [third, singular] is past, *he* [third, singular] loosens his hand slightly and *I* [first, singular] know *that* [third, singular] is a signal to take mine away. *He* [third, singular] sits companionably close, letting his *jacket* [third, singular] just touch my sweater, but *he* [third, singular] does not infringe. *He* [third, singular] thinks *I* [first, singular] ought to know *he* [third, singular] is there if *I* [first, singular] need him.

ANSWERS AND COVERAGE: EXERCISE 15–1

Answers may vary somewhat because of the alternate ways to eliminate shifts in person and number.

(1) According to some experts, snobbery is measured by mental attitude, not extent of worldly goods [15a-1, reserve *you* for direct address]. (2) Because *they* are unsure of *their* social position, snobs are driven by what others think of them [15a-1, shift in number]. (3) *Snobs* tend to be too dependent on buying status symbols to define *their* place in the world, and *they* look down on others [15a-1, shift in person, shift in number]. (4) Correct sentence (5) When commoners were first admitted to Cambridge University in the 1700s, *all students* were required to identify *their* social position [15a-1, shift in number]. (6) The *commoners* had to use the Latin words *sine nobilitate,* meaning "without nobility" [15a-1, shift in number]. (7) Eventually, the students shortened this phrase to "s.nob," and the word came to signify *a person* aspiring to a higher social level [15a-1, shift in number, must agree with "s.nob."].

REFERENCE TO SUPPLEMENTS

For this topic in the CLAST writing competency test, refer students to ch. 2, section B3b of *Preparing for the CLAST* by S. Patterson.

WORD HISTORY

According to the *Oxford English Dictionary* (OED), the word *voice* comes from the Latin word *vox*, meaning *voice* or *sound*. The earliest recorded statement in English using *voice* as a grammatical term is from 1382 by Wyclif: "A participle of a present tens, either preterit, or actif vois, eithir passif."

REFERENCE TO SUPPLEMENTS

For this topic in the CLAST writing competency test, refer students to ch. 1, section B4f of *Preparing for the CLAST* by S. Patterson.

WORD HISTORY

According to the *Oxford English Dictionary* (OED), the term *mood* has been used since the sixteenth century to refer to verb forms that indicate commands or wishes. The earliest recorded use of the word in this way dates back to 1573, when a scholar named Golding asked a question that still concerns our students: "How shall men directly fynde the Coniugation, Nomber, Person, Tence and Moode of Verbes togither in their Kynde?"

When we speak of the *mood* of a verb, we are not discussing its emotional state. *Mood* when it refers to a mental state is related to Latin *mos*, meaning *custom*. In contrast, *mood* used to discuss verbs is an alteration of *mode*, which comes from the Latin *modus* meaning *measure*, *moderation*, or (most relevant here) *manner*. The earliest use of *mode* to refer to verbs dates back to 1520: "Sometyme of the infinytyve mode folowynge." Other early references make it clear that *mood/mode* was originally used for discussions of Greek and Latin rather than of English.

15a-2 Staying consistent in subject and voice

The **subject** of a sentence is the word or group of words that acts, is acted upon, or is described: **People** *laugh,* **people** *were entertained,* **people** *are nice.*

Some subject shifts are justified by the meaning of a passage: **People** *look forward to the future, but* **the future** *holds many secrets.*

A shift in subject is rarely justified when it is accompanied by a shift in **voice.** The voice of a sentence is either *active (People expect changes)* or *passive (Changes are expected).* (For information about active and passive voice, see 8n–8o.) Unnecessary shifts in subject and voice cause a sentence or a longer stretch of writing to drift out of focus.

NO   Most **people expect** major improvements in the future, but some **hardships are also anticipated.** [The subject shifts from *people* to *hardships,* and the voice shifts from active to passive.]

YES   Most **people expect** major improvements in the future, but **they also anticipate** some hardships.

YES   Most people expect major improvements in the future but also anticipate some hardships.

15a-3 Staying consistent in tense and mood

Tense refers to the ability of verbs to show time. Tense changes are required to describe time changes: *We will go to the movies after we finish dinner.* If a tense shift within or between sentences is illogical, clarity suffers. (For information about correct sequences of tenses, see section 8k.)

NO   The campaign in the United States to clean up the movies **began** in the 1920s as civic and religious groups **try** to ban sex and violence from the screen. [The tense shifts from the past *began* to the present *try.*]

YES   The campaign in the United States to clean up the movies **began** in the 1920s as civic and religious groups **tried** to ban sex and violence from the screen.

NO   Producers and distributors **created** a film Production Code in the 1930s. At first, violating its guidelines **carried** no penalty. Eventually, however, films that **fail** to get the board's Seal of Approval **do not receive** wide distribution. [This shift occurs between sentences: the past tense *created* and *carried* shift to the present tense *fail* and *do not receive.*]

YES   Producers and distributors **created** a film Production Code in the 1930s. At first, violating its guidelines **carried** no penalty. Eventually, however, films that **failed** to get the board's Seal of Approval **did not receive** wide distribution.

Mood refers to whether a sentence is a statement or question (*indicative mood*), a command or request (*imperative mood*), or a conditional or other-than-real statement (*subjunctive mood*); see section 8l. A shift between moods may blur the message of a passage.

> **NO** The Production Code included two guidelines about violence. **Do not show** the details of brutal killings, and **movies should not be** explicit about how to commit crimes. [The verbs shift from the imperative mood *do not show* to the indicative mood *movies should not be*.]
>
> **YES** The Production Code included two guidelines about violence: **Do not show** the details of brutal killings, and **do not show** explicitly how to commit crimes. [This revision uses the imperative mood for both guidelines.]
>
> **YES** The Production Code included two guidelines about violence. **Movies were not to show** the details of brutal killings or explicit ways to commit crimes.
>
> **NO** The Code writers worried that if a crime were to be accurately depicted in a movie, copycat crimes will follow. [The sentence shifts from the subjunctive mood *if a crime were to be depicted* to the indicative mood *copycat crimes will follow*.]
>
> **YES** The Code writers worried that if a crime were to be accurately depicted in a movie, copycat crimes would follow.

Avoiding unmarked shifts between indirect and direct discourse

15a-4

Indirect discourse reports speech or conversation and is not enclosed in quotation marks. **Direct discourse** repeats speech or conversation exactly and encloses the spoken words in quotation marks (see 24g). Sentences that merge indirect and direct discourse without quotation marks and without other necessary changes that mark words as either reported or quoted distort the intended message.

> **NO** A critic said that board members were acting as censors and **what you are doing is unconstitutional.** [The first clause is indirect discourse; the second clause shifts into unmarked direct discourse, garbling the message.]
>
> **YES** A critic said that board members were acting as censors and **that what they were doing was unconstitutional.** [This revision consistently uses indirect discourse.]
>
> **YES** A critic said that board members were acting as censors and added, **"What you are doing is unconstitutional."** [This revision uses indirect and direct discourse correctly, with quotation marks and other changes to distinguish reported words from spoken words.]

ALTERNATE EXAMPLE

To improve your students' skill in identifying subject and voice, you might ask them to work in groups to locate the subject and name the voice in each of the clauses in the following passage from Jack London's description of the San Francisco earthquake. (The subjects and verbs here appear in italics.)

The *earthquake* [subject] *shook* [active] down in San Francisco hundreds of thousands of dollars' worth of walls and chimneys. But the conflagration [subject] *that* [subject] *followed* [active] *burned* [active] up hundreds of millions of dollars' worth of property. *There* ["dummy" subject] *is* [active] no estimating within hundreds of millions the actual damage *that* [subject] *was wrought* [**passive**].

Not in history *has* a modern imperial *city* [subject] *been* so completely *destroyed* [**passive**]. *San Francisco* [subject] *is* [active] gone. *Nothing* [subject] *remains* [active] of it but memories and a fringe of dwelling houses on its outskirts. Its industrial *section* [subject] *is* [active] wiped out. Its social and residential *section* [subject] *is* [active] wiped out. The *factories* [subject] and *warehouses* [subject], the great *stores* [subject] and newspaper *buildings* [subject], the *hotels* [subject] and *palaces* [subject] of the nabobs, *all* [subject] *are* [active] gone. *There remains* [active] only the *fringe* [subject] of dwelling houses on the outskirts of *what* [subject] *was* [active] once San Francisco.

QUOTATION ABOUT WRITING

I'm a bit like a sponge. When I'm not writing I absorb life like water. When I write I squeeze the sponge a little—and out it comes, not water but ink.

—Georges Simenon

Changing a message from a direct-discourse version to an indirect-discourse version usually requires changes of VERB TENSE and other grammatical features. Simply removing the quotation marks is not enough.

NO	He asked **did we enjoy** the movie? [This version has the verb form needed for direct discourse, but the pronoun *we* is wrong and quotation punctuation is missing.]
YES	He asked **whether we enjoyed** the movie. [This version is entirely indirect discourse, and the verb has changed from *enjoy* to *enjoyed*.]
YES	He asked, **"Did you enjoy the movie?"** [This version is direct discourse. It repeats the original speech exactly, with correct quotation punctuation.]

EXERCISE 15-2

Consulting section 15a, revise these sentences to eliminate all incorrect shifts. Some sentences can be revised several ways.

EXAMPLE   During the Victorian era, all gentlemen worthy of the name are obliged to raise their hats to ladies.

During the Victorian era, all gentlemen worthy of the name *were* obliged to raise their hats to ladies.

1. The Victorian male's custom of tipping his hat had serious drawbacks, though; for instance, if you were carrying parcels you would have to set them down first.

2. In 1896, an inventor named James Boyle developed a self-tipping hat that solves the problem.

3. If a man nodded while wearing Boyle's invention, they activated a lifting mechanism concealed in the hat's crown.

4. Boyle claimed that since the novelty of the moving hat would attract attention, advertising also can be one of its uses.

5. He said that companies could place signs on the hats and you will be able to advertise any product innovatively and inexpensively.

EXERCISE 15-3

Consulting section 15a, revise this paragraph to eliminate incorrect shifts between, as well as within, sentences.

(1) The robots of today can perform many more tasks than its earlier counterpart. (2) Twenty years ago, a robot remained stationary and welded a car body or lifted heavy steel bars. (3) Today's robot, on the other hand, performs work that included cleaning offices, guarding a hotel room, and

---

Answers will vary. Here is one set of possibilities.

1. The Victorian male's custom of tipping his hat had serious drawbacks, though; for instance, if he was carrying parcels he would have to set them down first. [15a-1, shift in person]

2. In 1896, an inventor named James Boyle developed a self-tipping hat that solved the problem. [15a-3, shift in tense]

3. If a man nodded while wearing Boyle's invention, he activated a lifting mechanism concealed in the hat's crown. [15a-1, shift in number]

4. Boyle claimed that since the novelty of the moving hat would attract attention, it also could be used for advertising. [15a-2, shift in subject and voice]

5. He said that companies could place signs on the hats and that they would be able to advertise any product innovatively and inexpensively. [15a-4, indirect-direct discourse shift]

ANSWERS: EXERCISE 15-3

(1) The robots of today can perform many more tasks than their earlier counterparts. (2) Twenty years ago, robots remained stationary and welded car bodies or lifted heavy steel bars. (3) Today's robots, on the other hand, perform work that includes cleaning offices, guarding hotel rooms, and inspecting automobiles. (4) At California's Memorial Medical Center of Long Beach, a doctor has performed brain surgery using a robot arm that allows her [or him] to drill into a person's skull and reach the brain more accurately. (5) A robot recently joined the police force in Dallas, and it forced a suspect into surrendering. (6) When the robot broke a window, the suspect shouted, "Help!" and asked, "What is that?" (7) ➡

inspecting automobiles. (4) At California's Memorial Medical Center of Long Beach, a doctor has performed brain surgery using a robot arm that allows them to drill into a person's skull and reach your brain more accurately. (5) A robot recently joined the police force in Dallas, and a suspect was forced into surrendering by the robot. (6) When the robot broke a window, the suspect shouted "Help," and asked what is that? (7) Many people do not realize that service robots often prepare your fast food or sort the packages you brought to the post office. (8) In the near future, robots selling for about $20,000 will work without human assistance, and you will be able to buy a robot costing $50,000 that will do household chores.

Avoiding misplaced modifiers

15b

A **modifier** is a word, PHRASE, or CLAUSE that describes other words, phrases, or clauses. A **misplaced modifier** is a describer that is positioned incorrectly in a sentence, thus distorting meaning. As you write and revise, always check to see that your modifiers are placed as close as possible to what they describe so that your reader will attach the meaning where you intend it to be.

Avoiding ambiguous placements

15b-1

With **ambiguous placement,** a modifier is confusing to a reader because it can refer to two or more words in a sentence.

Limiting words (such as *only, not only, just, not just, almost, hardly, nearly, even, exactly, merely, scarcely, simply*) can change meaning according to where they are placed. When you use such words, position them precisely. Consider how different placements of *only* change the meaning of this sentence: *Professional coaches say that high salaries motivate players.*

Only professional coaches say that high salaries motivate players. [No one else says this.]

Professional coaches **only** say that high salaries motivate players. [The coaches probably do not mean what they say.]

Professional coaches say **only** that high salaries motivate players. [The coaches say nothing else.]

Professional coaches say that **only** high salaries motivate players. [Nothing except high salaries motivates players.]

Professional coaches say that high salaries **only** motivate players. [High salaries do nothing other than motivate players.]

Professional coaches say that high salaries motivate **only** players. [No others on the team, such as coaches and managers, are motivated by high salaries.]

TEACHING TIP, cont.

2. The man kissed the baby with a beard.

3. Walking down the street, the Eiffel Tower came into view.

4. The wildlife specialist said that most bears are dangerous on television.

5. Poison ivy is common in the forest which gives many people an itchy rash.

TEACHING TIP

Students frequently become aware of problem sentences when they hear their papers read aloud. Particularly with long sentences, students sometimes compose chunk by chunk and fail to notice how the sections are connected. Reading aloud forces students to read the entire sentence, and hearing themselves stumble may signal a poorly constructed sentence. At home, students can read their papers into a tape recorder and then play back the tape to identify problem sentences. In class, student groups can listen for sentences that need revision as students read their papers aloud. Because some students make verbal corrections in their problem sentences when they read aloud without noticing a problem on the page, it is often useful to ask students to exchange their papers with another student and listen to that student read their paper aloud.

TEACHING TIP

In *Revision: The Rhythm of Meaning* (Portsmouth, NH: Boynton/Cook, 1984), Marian M. Mohr suggests a sentence-revising exercise for small groups. Each student exchanges two problem sentences from his or her rough draft for two sentences by another student who has read the draft. Each student then suggests a couple of possible revisions for each sentence.

15b-1
cont.

Squinting modifiers are ambiguous because they can describe both what precedes and what follows them. Since a modifier cannot do double duty, the reader must make a choice and may make the one that the writer did not intend. For clarity, revise the sentence, making sure that the modifier is positioned where its meaning is precise.

NO   The football player being recruited **fervently** believed each successive offer would be better. [What was active, the recruitment or the player's belief?]

YES   The football player being recruited believed **fervently** that each successive offer would be better.

YES   The **fervently** recruited football player believed that each successive offer would be better.

15b-2

Avoiding awkward placements

Awkward placements are interruptions that seriously break the flow of a message and thereby distract your reader from understanding your material. A **split infinitive** is one type of awkward placement. An **infinitive** is a verb form that starts with *to: to convince, to create*. When material comes between the *to* and its verb, it can interrupt meaning.

NO   Orson Welles's radio drama "War of the Worlds" managed **to,** in October 1938, **convince** listeners that they were hearing an invasion by Martians.

YES   In October 1938, Orson Welles's radio drama "War of the Worlds" managed **to convince** listeners that they were hearing an invasion by Martians.

Often the intervening word that splits an infinitive is an adverb ending in *-ly*. Many such adverbs sound awkward unless they are placed either before or after the infinitive.

NO   People feared they would no longer be able to **happily** live in peace.

YES   People feared they would no longer be able to live **happily** in peace.

Nevertheless, sometimes an ADVERB seems awkward in any position except between *to* and the VERB. Many readers, therefore, are not distracted by SPLIT INFINITIVES like this one:

Welles wanted **to** realistically **portray** a Martian invasion for the radio audience.

If you think your readers prefer that infinitives never be split, you can usually revise the sentence to avoid the split:

Welles wanted his "Martian invasion" **to sound** realistic for the radio audience.

Interruptions of SUBJECTS and verbs, VERB PHRASES, and verbs and OBJECTS can disturb the smooth flow of a sentence.

NO The **announcer,** because the script, which Welles himself wrote, called for perfect imitations of emergency announcements, **opened** with a warning that included a description of the "invasion." [subject-verb interrupted]

YES Because the script, which Welles himself wrote, called for perfect imitations of emergency announcements, the **announcer opened** with a warning that included a description of the "invasion."

NO Police switchboards **were,** not surprisingly, **jammed** with frantic phone calls. [verb phrase interrupted]

YES Not surprisingly, police switchboards **were jammed** with frantic phone calls.

NO Many churches **held** for their frightened communities **"end of the world" prayer services.** [verb-direct object interrupted]

YES Many churches **held "end of the world" prayer services** for their frightened communities.

EXERCISE 15-4

Consulting section 15b, revise these sentences to correct any ambiguous, wrong, or awkward placements. If a sentence is correct, circle its number.

EXAMPLE   In 1876, a group of Mormon settlers from Utah founded a community in Ramah, New Mexico, a time of shifting populations in the Southwest.

In 1876, *a time of shifting populations in the Southwest,* a group of Mormon settlers from Utah founded a community in Ramah, New Mexico.

1. The Ramah people of the Navajo nation had for many centuries made this land their home.
2. The Mormons established shortly after they arrived a small cemetery on a knoll surrounded by farms and ranchland.
3. Only they were not the ones to make use of this graveyard.
4. The Navajo even though their beliefs and practices differed strikingly from the those of the Mormons began burying their own dead there, too.

315

ANSWERS AND COVERAGE: EXERCISE 15-4

Answers may vary somewhat. The final result must avoid all shifts.

1. *For many centuries,* the Ramah people of the Navajo nation had made this land their home [15b-2, interrupted verb phrase].

2. *Shortly after they arrived,* the Mormons established a small cemetery on a knoll surrounded by farms and ranchland [15b-2, awkward placement].

3. They were not the *only* ones to make use of this graveyard [15b-1, ambiguous placement].

4. *Even though their beliefs and practices differed strikingly from those of the Mormons,* the Navajo began burying their own dead there, too [15b-2, interruption of subject and verb].

5. Correct sentence

6. The Mormon graves, *grouped according to family relationships,* have headstones in a wide variety of folk art and commercially manufactured styles [15b-2, awkward placement (phrase modifies *graves,* not *headstones*].

7. *Painstakingly engraved* Mormon headstones display floral designs and representations of Mormon temples in Salt Lake City and elsewhere [15b-1, squinting modifier].

8. *In contrast,* the Navajo graves have simple metal markers and are not arranged by family relationship [15b-2, awkward placement].

9. *To speed the soul on its journey,* the Navajo bury valuable turquoise jewelry with their dead [15b-2, interruption of subject and verb].

10. *In all,* the little cemetery now contains about 71 Navajo graves and 209 Mormon graves [15b-2, awkward placement].

ANSWERS TO EXERCISE 15–5

1. (a) To become / an entertainment lawyer, / the student / studied / corporate and copyright law / intensively.

(b) The student / studied / corporate and copyright law / intensively / to become / an entertainment lawyer.

(c) To become / an entertainment lawyer, / the student / intensively / studied / corporate and copyright law.

2. (a) The matchmaker / happily / introduced the / wrestler / to the / muscular artist.

(b) The matchmaker / happily / introduced the / muscular artist / to the / wrestler.

(c) Happily, / the matchmaker / introduced the / wrestler / to the / muscular artist.

(d) Happily, / the matchmaker / introduced the / muscular artist / to the / wrestler.

(e) The matchmaker / introduced the / wrestler / to the / muscular artist / happily.

(f) The matchmaker / introduced the / muscular artist / to the / wrestler / happily.

3. (a) The computer hacker used / only / one simple password / to break into / the company files.

(b) Only / the computer hacker used / one simple password / to break into / the company files.

(c) To break into / the company files, / the computer hacker used / only / one simple password.

(d) To break into / the company files, / only / the computer hacker used / one simple password.

4. (a) Not just / pediatricians / know / that / children / need / love.

(b) Pediatricians / know / that / not just / children / need / love.

(c) Pediatricians / know / that / children / need / not just / love.

(d) Pediatricians / know / not just / that / children / need / love.

➔

15b-2 cont.

5. For over a century now the cemetery has continued to serve families of both cultures.

6. The Mormon graves have headstones in a wide variety of handmade and commercially manufactured styles, grouped according to family relationships.

7. Mormon headstones that were engraved painstakingly display floral designs and representations of Mormon temples in Salt Lake City and elsewhere.

8. The Navajo graves have simple metal markers in contrast and are not arranged by family relationship.

9. The Navajo to speed the soul on its journey bury valuable turquoise jewelry with their dead.

10. The little cemetery now contains about 71 Navajo graves in all and 209 Mormon graves.

EXERCISE 15-5

Consulting section 15b, combine each list of word groups to create all the possible logical sentences (each list offers more than one possibility). Insert commas as needed. Use a slash to indicate where each word or group of words ends. Explain differences in meaning, if any, among the alternatives you create.

EXAMPLE   runners
                than couch potatoes do
                have lower blood pressure
                for the most part

A. For the most part, / runners / have lower blood pressure / than couch potatoes do. /

B. Runners / have lower blood pressure, / for the most part, / than couch potatoes do. /

C. Runners, / for the most part, / have lower blood pressure / than couch potatoes do. /

D. Runners / have lower blood pressure / than couch potatoes do, / for the most part. /

1. studied
   an entertainment lawyer
   corporate and copyright law
   the student
   to become
   intensively

2. introduced the
   happily
   muscular artist
   the matchmaker
   to the
   wrestler

3. the computer hacker used
   broke into
   only
   one simple password
   the company files

4. need
   love
   that
   know
   pediatricians
   not just
   children

5. have more patience
   as a rule
   bus drivers
   than the average citizen

ANSWERS TO EXERCISE 15–5, cont.

5. **(a)** As a rule, / bus drivers / have more patience / than the average citizen.

(b) Bus drivers, / as a rule, / have more patience / than the average citizen.

(c) Bus drivers / have more patience, / as a rule, / than the average citizen.

(d) Bus drivers / have more patience / than the average citizen, / as rule.

Avoiding dangling modifiers   15c

A **dangling modifier** describes or limits a word or words that are not stated in a sentence. Because a reader will "attach" the information in the dangling modifier to a NOUN or PRONOUN that does appear in the sentence, the writer's intended meaning is lost.

Dangling modifiers can be hard for a writer to spot. Aware of the intended meaning, the writer unconsciously supplies the missing material, but the reader usually sees only the error and realizes that the meaning is flawed.

The first *No* example below says that the story's ending is doing the reading. The implied subject of the modifier is *we*, but nowhere is that subject stated—thus the modifier dangles. You can correct a dangling modifier by revising the sentence so that the intended SUBJECT is stated.

NO   **Reading Faulkner's short story "A Rose for Emily,"** the ending surprised us.

YES   **Having read Faulkner's short story "A Rose for Emily," we** were surprised by the ending.

YES   We read Faulkner's short story "A Rose for Emily" and were surprised by the ending.

NO   **When courting Emily, the townspeople** gossiped about her. [*The townspeople* were not courting Emily.]

YES   **When Emily was being courted by Homer Barron, the townspeople** gossiped about her.

Dangling modifiers are sometimes caused by unnecessary use of the PASSIVE VOICE (see 8n-8o).

REFERENCES TO SUPPLEMENTS

For this topic in the CLAST writing competency test, refer students to ch. 1, section B2a of *Preparing for the CLAST* by S. Patterson.

This topic is included in the TASP writing competency test. Refer your students to *Preparing for the TASP* by M. Saenz.

BACKGROUND

Cornelia and Bergen Evans conclude that frequently the only way to avoid a split infinitive and still write good English is to avoid the infinitive. However, with the increasing use of the infinitive, in place of the *-ing* form or clause that was previously preferred, avoiding the infinitive may lead to wordy paraphrases that are not good English (*A Dictionary of Contemporary American Usage* [New York: Random House, 1957]).

QUOTATION ABOUT WRITING

Writing is like exploring. . . . As an explorer makes maps of the country he has explored, so a writer's works are maps of the country he has explored.

—Lawrence Osgood

ANSWERS AND COVERAGE: EXERCISE 15–6

Answers may vary somewhat. Here is one set of possibilities.

1. To be successful, the student journalist must plan carefully. [dangling infinitive]

2. Being tense, an inexperienced journalist might begin on the wrong note. [dangling participle]

3. Until relaxed, the student journalist should mention only neutral topics. [unexpressed subject]

4. Correct

5. With a list of questions, the interviewer can make the process go more smoothly for everyone involved. [unexpressed subject]

6. A hostile interviewee sometimes answers factual questions incorrectly, although they are easy to answer. [unnecessary passive voice]

7. By being analytic and evaluative, an experienced journalist can learn a great deal from those mistakes. [dangling participle]

8. Knowing how to pace an interview, a journalist will more likely get honest answers to hard questions after he or she has caught the interviewee off guard. [unexpressed subject]

9. Correct

10. Essential information might be revealed when the journalist is leaving. [unexpressed subject]

QUOTATION ABOUT WRITING

Good writers are those who keep the language efficient. That is to say, keep it accurate, keep it clear.
— Ezra Pound

QUOTATION ABOUT WRITING

You write with ease to show your breeding, but easy writing's curst hard reading.
— Richard Brinsley Sheridan

15c
cont.

NO	**To earn money, china-painting lessons** were offered by Emily to wealthy young women. [*China-painting lessons cannot earn money.*]
YES	**To earn money, Emily** offered china-painting lessons to wealthy young women.

EXERCISE 15-6

Consulting section 15c, identify and correct any dangling modifiers in these sentences. If a sentence is correct, circle its number.

EXAMPLE   Assigned to interview an unfriendly person, the experience can be instructive to a student journalist.

                 Assigned to interview an unfriendly person, *a student journalist can find the experience instructive.*

1. To be successful, careful plans must be made by the student journalist.

2. Being tense, the interview might begin on the wrong note for an inexperienced journalist.

3. Until relaxed, questions should mention only neutral topics.

4. After the journalist is more at ease, the person being interviewed might also relax.

5. With a list of questions, the interview process goes more smoothly for everyone involved.

6. Although easy to answer, mistakes are sometimes made on factual questions by a hostile interviewee.

7. By being analytic and evaluative, those mistakes can reveal a great deal to an experienced journalist.

8. Knowing how to pace an interview, the hard questions are more likely to be answered honestly after the interviewee has been caught off guard.

9. Until an interview is complete, the seasoned journalist always remains alert.

10. Essential information might be revealed when leaving.

15d   ## Avoiding mixed sentences

    A **mixed sentence** consists of parts that do not make sense together because the writer has lost track of the beginning of a sentence while writing the end. Careful proofreading, including reading aloud, can help a writer avoid this error.

Revising mixed constructions

A **mixed construction** starts out taking one grammatical form and then changes, derailing the meaning of the sentence.

NO   Because television's first transmissions in the 1920s included news programs quickly became popular with the public. [The opening DEPENDENT CLAUSE starts off on one track, but the INDEPENDENT CLAUSE goes off in another direction. What does the writer want to emphasize—the first transmissions or the popularity of news programs?]

YES   Television's first transmissions in the 1920s included news programs, which quickly became popular with the public. [The idea of the first transmissions is emphasized.]

YES   Because television's first transmissions in the 1920s included news programs, television quickly became popular with the public. [The idea of the popularity of the news programs is now emphasized.]

NO   By doubling the time allotment for network news to thirty minutes increased the prestige of network news programs. [A PREPOSITIONAL PHRASE, such as *by doubling*, cannot be the subject of a sentence.]

YES   Doubling the time allotment for network news to thirty minutes increased the prestige of network news programs. [Dropping the preposition *by* clears up the problem.]

YES   By doubling the time allotment for network news to thirty minutes, the network executives increased the prestige of network news programs. [Inserting a logical subject, *the network executives*, clears up the problem; an independent clause is now preceded by a modifying prepositional phrase.]

The phrase *the fact that* is sometimes the cause of a mixed sentence.

NO   The fact that quiz show scandals in the 1950s prompted the networks to produce even more news shows.

YES   The fact is that quiz show scandals in the 1950s prompted the networks to produce even more news shows. [The added *is* clarifies the meaning.]

YES   Quiz show scandals in the 1950s prompted the networks to produce even more news shows. [Dropping *the fact that* clarifies the meaning.]

15d-1

ALTERNATE EXAMPLE

To improve your students' skill in identifying direct and indirect discourse, you might ask them to work in groups to identify the types of discourse found in the following passage from Russell Baker's "Country Living."

> In the country, I am told, the trick is to let the weather roam free through the house. [indirect] "You're spoofing me, aren't you?" [direct] I asked the real-estate man. He wasn't.
>
> In the country, he explained, you're supposed to wear long underwear all winter. [indirect] "It can get itchy if you don't have freezing wind coming between the logs," [direct] he said.
>
> In the summer, you're expected to hang flypaper in the kitchen. "If your logs are chinked tightly they'll keep out the varmints that give your flypaper a businesslike appearance," [direct] he explained.

ALTERNATE EXAMPLES

What is inconsistent in the following mixed constructions? You might want to ask students to work in groups to revise these four sentences so that the parts make sense together.

1. Because you want to visit the great art museums of the world is why you should go to the Louvre in Paris.

2. Paris, the capital of France, one of the great museums of the world is located there.

3. Tourists from all over the world, the Louvre draws them.

4. The collection is composed of art works from many cultures is what distinguishes the Louvre.

15d-2

Revising faulty predication

Faulty predication, sometimes called *illogical predication,* occurs when a SUBJECT and its PREDICATE do not make sense together.

NO   The **purpose** of television **was invented** to entertain people.

YES   The **purpose** of television was to entertain people.

YES   **Television was invented** to entertain people.

One key cause of illogical predication is a breakdown in the connection between a subject and its COMPLEMENT. (A subject complement can be a NOUN, a PRONOUN, a NOUN CLAUSE renaming a sentence subject, or an ADJECTIVE describing a sentence subject; see 7m-1.)

In the following *No* example, the subject complement *credible* could logically describe *Walter Cronkite,* but Walter Cronkite is not the subject. The subject is *characteristic,* so the meaning calls for a subject complement that renames some characteristic of Walter Cronkite as a newscaster: thus, *credibility* instead of *credible.*

NO   Walter Cronkite's outstanding **characteristic** as a newscaster **was credible.**

YES   Walter Cronkite's outstanding **characteristic** as a newscaster **was credibility.** [The noun *credibility* renames *characteristic.*]

YES   **Walter Cronkite was credible** as a newscaster. [The adjective *credible* describes the subject *Walter Cronkite.*]

Illogical predication is a problem in many constructions that include **is when** or **is where.** Avoid these phrases in academic writing.

NO   A disaster **is when** television news shows get some of their highest ratings.

YES   Television news shows get some of their highest ratings during a disaster.

Also, avoid *reason . . . is because* constructions. Use *reason . . . is that* instead. Remember that *because* means "for the reason that," so *reason . . . is because* literally means "reason . . . is for the reason that," which is repetitious.

NO   One **reason** television news captured national attention **is because** it covered the Vietnam War thoroughly.

YES   One **reason** television news captured national attention **is that** it covered the Vietnam War thoroughly.

YES   Television news captured national attention **because** it covered the Vietnam War thoroughly.

EXERCISE 15-7

Consulting section 15d, revise the mixed sentences below so that the beginning of each sentence fits logically with its end. If a sentence is correct, circle its number.

EXAMPLE   The main reason for the U.S. bomb shelter craze from 1950 to 1962 was because people believed that global nuclear war was about to take place.

The main reason for the U.S. bomb shelter craze from 1950 to 1962 was that people believed that global nuclear war was about to take place.

1. Because of the Cold War between the United States and Russia motivated some 200,000 American families to construct backyard bomb shelters stocked with canned food, bottled water, batteries, and board games.

2. The reason that a frenzy of bomb shelter building took place is because President John F. Kennedy warned people that they might need to make individual preparations against nuclear attack during the Berlin Wall crisis in 1961.

3. During periods of panic is always when a few enterprising souls make money, and shelter peddlers hurried to cash in on fears of imminent mass destruction.

4. In this era predating shopping malls, model bomb shelters were set up outside supermarkets, at county fairs, and in downtown department stores.

5. The purpose of a bomb shelter was built to protect people underground for at least ninety days until, presumably, the air was free of radioactivity.

6. By spending their two-week honeymoon in a bomb shelter won nationwide publicity for a Miami couple.

7. When the couple declared they had spent the entire two weeks playing cards, and suddenly the public lost interest.

8. One debate concerned whether a family safely locked in its bomb shelter could refuse to admit desperate neighbors is controversial.

9. In the late 1960s is when fear of the Cold War faded and bomb shelters were turned into wine cellars, mushroom gardens, or sites for teenage parties.

10. The fact that a solid steel "shelter for four" was dug up in Fort Wayne, Indiana, and now on exhibit at the Smithsonian National Museum of American History in Washington, D.C.

Avoiding incomplete sentences   15e

An **incomplete sentence** is missing words, PHRASES, or CLAUSES necessary for grammatical correctness or sensible meaning. Such omis-

---

ANSWERS AND COVERAGE: EXERCISE 15–7, cont.

during the Berlin Wall crisis in 1961. [15d-2, faulty predication with *reason is . . . because*]

3. A few enterprising souls always make money during periods of panic, and shelter peddlers swarmed to cash in on fears of imminent mass destruction. [15d-2, faulty predication with *is where*]

4. Correct sentence

5. The purpose of a bomb shelter was to protect people underground for at least ninety days until, presumably, the air was free of radioactivity. [15d-2, faulty predication]

6. Spending their two-week honeymoon in a bomb shelter won nationwide publicity for a Miami couple. [15d-1, mixed construction]

7. The couple declared they had spent the entire two weeks playing cards, and suddenly the public lost interest. [15d-1, mixed construction]

8. One debate concerned whether a family safely locked in its bomb shelter could refuse to admit desperate neighbors. [15d-2, faulty predication]

9. In the late 1960s, fear of the Cold War faded and bomb shelters were turned into wine cellars, mushroom gardens, or sites for teenage parties. [15d-2, faulty predication with *is when*]

10. A solid steel "shelter for four" was dug up in Fort Wayne, Indiana, and is now on exhibit at the Smithsonian National Museum of American History in Washington, D.C. [15d-1, mixed construction with *the fact that*]

REFERENCE TO SUPPLEMENTS

For this topic in the CLAST writing competency test, refer students to ch. 1, section B4g of *Preparing for the CLAST* by S. Patterson.

TEACHING TIP

Working in groups, your students might enjoy experimenting with the following passage from Colin Fletcher's *The Winds of Mara* to see how movement of the italicized modifiers will change the meaning. The groups can compare their completed versions to see how many different readings have been created from the same original one simply by the change of location of modifiers.

> The lions continued their *slow and lazy* passage, directly toward us. Once a lioness stopped and turned her head to look *briefly* at the zebras, then walked on. A trio of cubs began to romp and tumble; an adult cuffed them into order. The gap between us narrowed. Soon we could see *magnificently self-assured* expressions on *golden* faces; then rib cages showing *faintly, sculpturally*; then muscles rippling beneath *powerful* haunches. Eventually it seemed as if we could see each hair adjusting to the animal's *slow and lazy* movements.

BACKGROUND

Cornelia and Bergen Evans comment that speech, which is highly elliptical, would "scarcely be endurable otherwise." Ellipsis is also "indispensable to the writer or speaker who wants to be brief and pithy, but it can easily cause confusion and obscurity and must be used with skill" (*A Dictionary of Contemporary American Usage* [New York: Random House, 1957]).

QUOTATION ABOUT WRITING

I only wish I could write with both hands, so as not to forget one thing while I am saying another.

         —Teresa of Avila

15e
cont.

sions blur your meaning, and your reader has to work too hard to understand your message.

15e-1

Using elliptical constructions carefully

An **elliptical construction** deliberately leaves out, rather than repeats, one or more words that appear elsewhere in the sentence. *I have my book and Joan's,* for example, is an acceptable way to express *I have my book and Joan's book.* An elliptical construction is correct only if the sentence contains the exact word or words omitted from the elliptical construction. Thus, *I have my book and Joan's* cannot be used to express the thought that Joan, for example, has many *books*.

NO   During the 1920s in Chicago, the cornetist Manuel Perez **was leading** one outstanding jazz group, Tommy and Jimmy Dorsey another. [The words *was leading* cannot take the place of *were leading,* which the subject *Tommy and Jimmy Dorsey* requires.]

YES   During the 1920s in Chicago, the cornetist Manuel Perez **was leading** one outstanding jazz group; Tommy and Jimmy Dorsey **were leading** another.

YES   During the 1920s in Chicago, the cornetist Manuel Perez **led** one outstanding jazz group, Tommy and Jimmy Dorsey another. [The verb *led* is correct both with *Manuel Perez* and with *Tommy and Jimmy Dorsey* and thus can be omitted after *Dorsey.*]

NO   The period of the big jazz dance bands **began** and **lasted through** World War II. [This sentence implies *through* after *began,* but *began* requires *in,* not *through.*]

YES   The period of the big jazz band **began in** and **lasted through** World War II.

15e-2

Making comparisons complete, unambiguous, and logical

In writing a comparison, be sure to include all words needed to make clear the relationship between the items or ideas being compared.

NO   Individuals with high concern for achievement make **better** business executives. [*Better* implies a comparison, but none is stated.]

YES   Individuals with high concern for achievement make **better** business executives **than** do people with little interest in personal accomplishments.

NO   Most personnel officers value high achievers more than risk takers. [Unclear: more than risk takers value high achievers, or more than personnel officers value risk takers?]

YES   Most personnel officers value high achievers more than they value risk takers.

YES   Most personnel officers value high achievers more than risk takers do.

NO   A risk taker's chance of success is very different. [Different from what?]

YES   A risk taker's chance of success is very different **from a high achiever's**.

NO   Achievers value success **as much,** if not more than, a high salary. [Comparisons using *as . . . as* require the second *as*.]

YES   Achievers value success **as much as,** if not more than, a high salary.

In speech, sentences such as *That was such a difficult exam, You're so smart,* or *I'm too upset* are common. These constructions using *so, too,* and *such* as intensifiers imply that a completing thought has been omitted, and listeners can simply ask for more information if they need it. In academic writing, however, be sure to supply the completing information or take out the intensifier.

NO   Risk takers are often **such** innovative people.

YES   Risk takers are often **such** innovative people **that some businesses seek them out as employees**.

YES   Risk takers are often innovative people.

Proofreading for inadvertently omitted articles, pronouns, conjunctions, and prepositions

15e-3

Small words—ARTICLES, PRONOUNS, CONJUNCTIONS, and PREPOSITIONS—needed to make sentences complete tend to drop out when a writer is rushing or is distracted. If you tend to omit small words, proofread your work an extra time exclusively to discover the missing words.

NO   On May 2, 1808, citizens Madrid rioted against French soldiers.

YES   On May 2, 1808, **the** citizens **of** Madrid rioted against French soldiers.

QUOTATION ABOUT WRITING

The secret of good writing is to say an old thing a new way or to say a new thing an old way.

—Richard Harding Davis

QUOTATION ABOUT WRITING

I love being a writer. What I can't stand is the paperwork.

—Peter DeVries

ANSWERS AND COVERAGE: EXERCISE 15–8

Answers may vary somewhat. One set of possibilities is the following.

(1) Engineering students use innovative thinking to solve difficult problems as much as <u>they use</u> [15e-2, ambiguous comparison] theoretical knowledge. (2) One group <u>of</u> students at the University <u>of</u> California <u>at</u> Berkeley received a <u>chal</u>lenging assignment. [15e-3, small words omitted] (3) They had to create a package that would allow an egg to be dropped as much <u>as</u>, [15e-2, incomplete comparison] but not more than, eighty feet on <u>to</u> [15e-3, small word omitted] cement without breaking. (4) This complex problem was considered and possible solutions <u>were</u> [15e-1, incorrect elliptical] analyzed by fourth-year chemical engineering student Carla St. Laurent. (5) She gave so much thought to <u>her</u> professor's challenge <u>that she came up with the winning solution</u>. [15e-3, 15e-2: small word omitted, incomplete comparison] (6) She created a mother hen made of papier-maché that kept safe <u>the</u> egg dropped from a fourth-floor window. [15e-3, small words omitted]

15e-3
cont.

| NO | On following day, captured rioters were taken into country and shot. |
| YES | On **the** following day, captured rioters were taken into **the** country and shot. |

| NO | The Spanish painter Francisco Goya recorded both the riot the execution in a pair of pictures painted 1814. |
| YES | The Spanish painter Francisco Goya recorded both the riot **and** the execution **in** a pair of pictures painted in 1814. |

EXERCISE 15-8

Consulting section 15e, revise this paragraph to create correct elliptical constructions, to complete comparisons, and to insert any missing words.

(1) Engineering students use practical thinking to solve difficult problems as much as academic training. (2) One group students at the University California Berkeley received challenging assignment. (3) These students had to create a package that would allow an egg to be dropped as much, but not more than eighty feet onto cement without breaking. (4) This complex problem was considered and possible solutions analyzed by fourth-year chemical engineering student Carla St. Laurent. (5) She gave so much thought to professor's challenge. (6) She created a mother hen made papier-maché that kept safe egg she dropped from fourth-floor window.

Focus on Revising

REVISING YOUR WRITING

If you write sentences that send unclear messages, go back to your writing and locate the errors. Using this chapter as a resource, revise your writing to eliminate unnecessary shifts (15a), misplaced modifiers (15b), dangling modifiers (15c), mixed sentences (15d), and incomplete sentences (15e).

CASE STUDIES: REVISING TO CORRECT SENTENCES THAT SEND UNCLEAR MESSAGES

In these case studies, you can observe a student writer revising. Then you have the chance to revise other student writing on your own.

Observation

A student wrote the following draft for a course called Freshman Composition. The assignment was to compose a narrative of a personal experience with which other students in the class might sympathize. This narrative explains the experience clearly, uses specific examples well to illustrate the story, and draws on the writer's voice effectively. The draft's effectiveness is diminished, however, by the presence of sentences that send unclear messages by unnecessary shifts, misplaced modifiers, dangling modifiers, mixed sentences, and incomplete sentences.

Read through the draft. The unclear messages are highlighted and explained. Before you look at the student's revision, revise the material yourself. Then compare what you and the student did.

dangling modifier:
15c

Moving to a different part of the United States was one of the most difficult experiences of my life. Looking forward to my senior year in high school, my father's company informed him that he had been transferred to Colorado Springs, and would we be ready to move in a month? I liked Boston much better than my father, so I was less than thrilled about having to leave. But

shift from direct to indirect discourse: 15a-4

ambiguous comparison: 15e-2

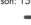

FOCUS ON REVISING   **FOCUS ON REVISING**   **FOCUS ON REVISING**   **FOCUS ON REVISING**

COVERAGE: PARTICIPATION ESSAY, pages 327–328

Most job hunters *enter business* [15e-3: missing word] world through a door labelled "Job Interviews." *Regardless of training and experience* [15c: dangling modifier], the interview is the occasion when an employer gets an impression of the candidate. What can a person do so that *you* [15a-1: shift in person] perform successfully at what is likely to be a fifteen-minute interview?

By understanding the objectives of the interview will help an applicant prepare [15d-1: mixed construction]. *An applicant who knows the company's needs is better equipped* [15e-2: incomplete comparison]. Most businesses with a position to fill interview with three basic questions in mind: Is this applicant qualified to do the job? Will this applicant perform if hired? Will *you* [15a-1: shift in person] fit into the work environment?

A job applicant can use a well-prepared résumé to present information about experience and training. At the interview, *applicants* [15a-1: shift in number] should be prepared to talk about courses taken, jobs held, and capabilities demonstrated. *Probing for specific details* [15c: dangling modifier], the applicant's abilities will be judged by the employer. *Job applicants will be judged by*

➡

---

after days of arguing and talking to my parents, I knew that the decision was final.

When our family arrived in Colorado Springs, I was depressed. Our house was comfortable, about twice the size of our Boston apartment, but you had the feeling that it was in the middle of nowhere. Living in the outskirts of the city, I couldn't go anywhere without car. In Boston, all I have to do is hop on the "T" to go anywhere in the city.

Also, by discovering that the expressions for some everyday things were different than in Boston was the place that I wanted to be. When I asked for a submarine, a thick sandwich on a long roll, the convenience store clerk said she didn't have kits for making model ships with a confused look. When buying something in Colorado, salespeople offered me what they called "a sack" instead of a bag. As far as I knew, a sack means that the quarterback has been tackled in football game.

Slowly, however, I began to realize that in Colorado even there are movies, fast-food restaurants, and shopping malls. Mostly, the people made the big difference for me. It didn't happily take long for me to get to know some students in my high school, and to, much to my surprise, find that most were eager to make me feel at home. By now, I can't imagine a better place to live than Colorado Springs.

incorrect elliptical construction: 15e-1

unnecessary shift in person and number: 15a-1

omitted word: 15e-3

mixed construction: 15d-1

unnecessary shift in tense: 15a-3

dangling modifier; 15c

dangling modifier: 15c

omitted word: 15e-3

ambiguous placement: 15b-1

awkward placement: 15b-2

Here is how the student revised the draft to correct the errors. In a few places, the student could correct the errors in more than one way. Your revision, therefore, might not be exactly like this one, but it should deal with each error highlighted on the draft.

Moving to a different part of the United States was one of the most difficult experiences of my life. At the time that I was looking forward to my senior year in high school, my father's company informed him that he had been transferred to Colorado Springs, and we would need to be ready to move in a month. I liked Boston much better than my father did, so I was less than thrilled about having to leave. But after days of arguing with and talking to my parents, I knew that the decision was final.

When our family arrived in Colorado Springs, I was depressed. Our house was comfortable, about twice the size of our Boston apartment, but I had the feeling that it was in the middle of nowhere. Living in the outskirts of the city, I couldn't go anywhere without a car. In Boston, all I had to do was hop on the "T" to go anywhere in the city.

Also, when I discovered that the expressions for some everyday things were different, Boston was the place that I wanted to be. When I asked for a submarine, a thick sandwich on a long roll, the convenience store clerk looked confused and said she didn't have kits for making model ships. When I would buy something in Colorado, salespeople offered me "a sack" instead of a bag. As far as I knew, a sack means that the quarterback has been tackled in a football game.

Slowly, however, I began to realize that even in Colorado there are movies, fast-food restaurants, and shopping malls. Mostly, the people made the big difference for me. Happily, it didn't take long for me to get to know some students in my high school, and to find, much to my surprise, that most were eager to make me feel at home. By now, I can't imagine a better place to live than Colorado Springs.

Participation

A student working in the college peer counseling program for job hunters wrote the following draft for an article in the campus newspaper. This material shows a very good awareness of audience, and it contains well-organized, useful information. The draft's effectiveness is diminished, however, by the presence of sentences that send unclear messages because of unnecessary shifts, misplaced modifiers, dangling modifiers, mixed sentences, and incomplete sentences.

Read through the draft. Then revise it to eliminate the errors. Also, make any additional revisions that you think would improve the content, organization, and style of the material.

Most job hunters enter business world through a door labeled "Job Interviews." Regardless of training and experience the interview is

COVERAGE: PARTICIPATION ESSAY, cont.

the employer. Job applicants should be aware that personal questions about marital status or plans to have children are illegal; however, such matters might be raised by some interviewers anyway [15a-2: shift from passive to active voice]. By preparing an answer like "Those areas of my life are personal," or "I make it a rule never to let my personal life interfere with business" will help an applicant's confidence [15d-1: mixed construction].

A major concern of an interviewer is focused on whether the applicant would fit into the company [15d-2: faulty construction]. An applicant who plays merely [15b-1: ambiguous placement of modifier] a role to impress an interviewer is making a mistake, particularly if you [15a-1: shift in person used in rest of essay] are offered a job that you [15a-1: shift in person used in rest of essay] are not suited for. Present a natural image. Use the interview to find out how the company's work environment will fit your [15a-1: shift in person used in rest of essay] personal style [15a-3: shift in mood, with two imperative sentences].

ANSWER: PARTICIPATION ESSAY

This version is revised to eliminate errors that cause sentences to send unclear messages. Because options are available for handling corrections, answers will vary somewhat. Also, answers will vary if students have revised for content, organization, or style.

Most job hunters enter the business world through a door labelled "Job Interviews." Regardless of training and experience, the job candidate makes an impression on an employer during an

→

ANSWER: PARTICIPATION ESSAY, cont.

interview. What can a person do so that he or she can perform successfully at what is likely to be a fifteen-minute interview?

Understanding the objectives of the interview will help an applicant prepare. An applicant who knows the company's needs is better equipped than someone who does not have such information. Most businesses with a position to fill interview with three basic questions in mind: Is this applicant qualified to do the job? Will this applicant perform if hired? Will this applicant fit into the work environment?

A job applicant can use a well-prepared résumé to present information about experience and training. At the interview, an applicant should be prepared to talk about courses taken, jobs held, and capabilities demonstrated. Probing for specific details, the employer will judge the applicant's abilities. Job applicants should be aware that personal questions about marital status or plans to have children are illegal; however, some interviewers might raise such matters anyway. Preparing an answer like "Those areas of my life are personal" or "I make it a rule never to let my personal life interfere with business" will help an applicant's confidence.

A major concern of an interviewer is whether the applicant would fit into the company. An applicant who merely plays a role to impress an interviewer is making a mistake, particularly if the person is offered a job that he or she is not suited for. A wise job candidate presents a natural image and finds out whether the company's work environment fits his or her personal style.

the occasion when an employer gets an impression of the candidate. What can a person do so that you perform successfully at what is likely to be a fifteen-minute interview?

By understanding the objectives of the interview will help an applicant prepare. An applicant who knows the company's needs is better equipped. Most businesses with a position to fill interview with three basic questions in mind: Is this applicant qualified to do the job? Will this applicant perform if hired? Will you fit into the work environment?

A job applicant can use a well-prepared résumé to present information about experience and training. At the interview, applicants should be prepared to talk about courses taken, jobs held, and capabilities demonstrated. Probing for specific details, the applicant's abilities will be judged by the employer. Job applicants should be aware that personal questions about marital status or plans to have children are illegal; however, such matters might be raised by some interviewers anyway. By preparing an answer like "Those areas of my life are personal," or "I make it a rule never to let my personal life interfere with business" will help an applicant's confidence.

A major concern of an interviewer is focused on whether the applicant would fit into the company. An applicant who plays merely a role to impress an interviewer is making a mistake, particularly if you are offered a job that you are not suited for. Present a natural image. Use the interview to find out how well the company's work environment will fit your personal style.

Writing Effective Sentences

When you write effective sentences, you move beyond correctness to writing characterized by style and grace. Part Four shows you various techniques of writing style that can enhance the delivery of your message. As you use Chapters 16 through 19, remember that writers can make choices to help form and content work together to create memorable prose.

16 *Conciseness*

Conciseness describes writing that is direct and to the point. Wordy writing is not concise. Wordiness irritates readers, who must clear away excess words before sentences can deliver their messages. Concise writing can be achieved by eliminating wordy sentence structures (see 16a); dropping unneeded words (see 16b); and omitting redundancies (see 16c).

16a Eliminating wordy sentence structures

Wordy sentence structures make writing seem abstract and uninteresting. Whenever possible, revise to achieve conciseness.

16a-1 Revising unnecessary expletive constructions

An **expletive construction** consists of *it* or *there* along with a form of the VERB* *be* placed before the SUBJECT in a sentence. In some contexts, an expletive construction can create anticipation and provide emphasis, but usually expletive constructions are merely wordy. Removing the expletive and revising slightly eliminates wordy sentence structures.

NO	**It was** on Friday that we missed class.
YES	On Friday, we missed class.
YES	We missed class on Friday.
NO	**There was** a new teacher waiting for us.
YES	A new teacher was waiting for us.

ESL ❖ ESL NOTE: The *it* in an expletive construction is not a PRONOUN referring to a specific ANTECEDENT. The *it* is an "empty" word that fills the subject position in a sentence but does not function as the actual subject. The actual subject appears after the expletive construction: **It** *was* the **teacher** *who answered the question.* (A more concise version is *The* **teacher** *answered the question.*) ❖

*You can find the definition of a word printed in small capital letters (such as VERB) in the Glossary of Terms toward the back of this handbook.

❖ ESL NOTE: The *there* in an expletive construction does not designate a place. The *there* indicates merely that something exists. Expletive constructions with *there* shift the sequence of the subject and verb in a sentence, so that the actual subject appears after the expletive construction: ***There** are many **teachers** who can answer the question.* (A more concise version is *Many **teachers** can answer the question.*) ❖

Revising unnecessary passive constructions

In the **active voice,** the subject of a sentence *does* the action named by the verb.

ACTIVE	**Professor Higgins teaches** public speaking. [*Professor Higgins* is the subject, and he does the action: he *teaches.*]

In the **passive voice,** the subject of a sentence receives the action named by the verb.

PASSIVE	**Public speaking is taught** by Professor Higgins. [*Public speaking* is the subject, which receives the action *taught.*]

The active voice adds liveliness as well as conciseness, so it is usually preferable. The simplest way to revise from the passive voice to the active voice is to make the doer of the action the subject of the sentence. (In a passive construction, the doer of an action is usually identified in a phrase starting with *by.*) When you want to switch from passive to active, turn the NOUN or PRONOUN in the *by* phrase into the sentence subject.

NO	Volunteer work **was done by the students** for extra credit in sociology. [The students are doers of the action, but they are not the subject of the sentence.]
YES	The students did volunteer work for extra credit in sociology.
NO	The new spending bill **was vetoed by the governor**. [The governor is the doer of the action, but he is not the subject of the sentence.]
YES	The **governor vetoed** the new spending bill.

Sometimes you can revise a sentence from passive voice to active voice by using a new verb. This method works especially well when you want to keep the same subject.

PASSIVE	**Britain was defeated** by the United States in the War of 1812.
ACTIVE	**Britain lost** the War of 1812 to the United States.

331

ESL

16a-2

QUOTATION ABOUT WRITING
There is no artifice as good and desirable as simplicity.
—Francis de Sales

TEACHING TIP
You might find it effective to take a passage of good prose (professional or student writing) and clutter it up. Then distribute copies, and ask students to delete all unnecessary words, phrases, and clauses. Discuss their cuts. End by distributing copies of the original for students to compare with their versions. The discussion can become particularly lively if students question the conciseness of the original or champion the value of your padding.

TEACHING TIP
A computer style-checker can be a great help to writers revising their sentences, but writers cannot expect the computer program to edit their papers for them. Most style-checkers flag words and phrases such as "to be" verbs and nominalizations often associated with wordiness, imprecision, and other problems, but the writer must decide whether to revise a flagged sentence and how to revise it. Many programs are easy to customize to deal with the writer's habitual problems.

TEACHING TIP
Joseph M. Williams (*Style: Ten Lessons in Clarity and Grace*, 4th ed. [New York: HarperCollins, 1994]) writes that "the first principle of clear writing" can be stated in two parts:

1. In the subjects of your sentences, name your cast of characters.

2. In the verbs of your sentences, name the crucial actions in which you involve those characters (9).

QUOTATION ABOUT WRITING

QUOTATION ABOUT WRITING

What I like in a good author is not what he says, but what he whispers.

—Logan Pearsall Smith

TEACHING TIP

One way to demonstrate how conciseness is achieved is to show students how you as a writer work toward it in your own work. Telling a student "I always revise to eliminate wordiness" rarely works. Instead, you might try one of these two approaches:

1. Distribute copies of a first, messy draft and a final version of one of your current projects. Invite students to trace the changes you made as you took out unnecessary words and passages, wavered between synonyms, adjusted verb tenses, and so forth. If you are using an anthology of essays that includes facsimile pages from writers' early drafts, students can also look for changes there. Students are likely to take the process more seriously, however, if they see your work. A page from Keats or Faulkner is not as immediate as one from their own teacher's current project.

2. You might distribute three or four versions of a piece (each successively more concise) without noting their order of composition. Ask the students to guess which came earlier or later, and how they know. This activity helps prove that revising for conciseness produces noticeable results.

QUOTATION ABOUT WRITING

The misfortune of writing fast is that one cannot at the same time write concisely.

—Walter Scott

QUOTATION ABOUT WRITING

People seldom write simply to be clear. . . . Pure prose is as rare as pure virtue, and for the same reasons.

—Richard A. Lanham

16a-2
cont.

PASSIVE	Many **soldiers were stricken** with yellow fever.
ACTIVE	Many **soldiers caught** yellow fever.

Writers may sometimes have no choice but to use the passive voice, as when the doer of an action is unknown or when naming the doer would disrupt the focus of a sentence (see 8n-8o).

Writers sometimes, however, deliberately use the passive voice in sentence after sentence in the mistaken belief that it sounds "mature" or "academic."

NO	One very important quality developed by an individual during a first job is self-reliance. This strength was gained by me when I was allowed by my supervisor to set up and conduct my own survey project.
YES	During their first job, many individuals develop the very important quality of self-reliance. I gained this strength when my supervisor allowed me to set up and conduct my own survey project.
YES	During a first job, many people develop self-reliance, as I did when my supervisor let me set up and conduct my own survey project.

Be particularly alert for the passive voice that misleads readers because it hides information about who acts: *Cracks in the foundation of the structure had been found, but they were not considered serious.* Left out of the sentence is important information telling who found cracks and who decided that they were not serious.

16a-3

Combining sentences and reducing clauses and phrases

As you revise, check your writing for conciseness. To counteract wordiness, you can often combine sentences and reduce CLAUSES and PHRASES.

Combining sentences

Look carefully at sets of sentences in your writing. You may be able to fit the information in one sentence into another sentence.

TWO SENTENCES

The *Titanic* was discovered seventy-three years after being sunk by an iceberg. The wreck was located in the Atlantic by a team of French and American scientists.

COMBINED SENTENCE

Seventy-three years after being sunk by an iceberg, the *Titanic* was located in the Atlantic by a team of French and American scientists.

TWO SENTENCES

The stern of the ship was missing and there was some external damage to the hull. Otherwise, the *Titanic* seemed to be in excellent condition.

COMBINED SENTENCE

Aside from its missing stern and external damage to its hull, the *Titanic* seemed to be in excellent condition.

For more advice about combining sentences, see Chapter 17.

Reducing clauses

You can sometimes reduce an ADJECTIVE CLAUSE simply by dropping the opening RELATIVE PRONOUN and VERB.

The *Titanic*, **which was a huge ocean liner,** sank in 1912.

The *Titanic*, **a huge ocean liner,** sank in 1912.

Sometimes you can reduce a clause to a single word.

The scientists held a memorial service for the passengers and crew members **who had died.**

The scientists held a memorial service for the **dead** passengers and crew members.

You can create ELLIPTICAL CONSTRUCTIONS to reduce clauses. Be sure to omit only words that are clearly implied (see 15e-1).

When they were confronted with disaster, some passengers behaved heroically, **while others behaved selfishly.**

Confronted with disaster, some passengers behaved heroically, **others selfishly.**

Keep your meaning clear when you reduce clauses. Removing words should never get in the way of clarity.

Reducing phrases

Sometimes you can reduce phrases to shorter phrases or to single words.

More than fifteen hundred **travelers on that voyage** died in the shipwreck.

More than fifteen hundred **passengers** died in the shipwreck.

Objects found inside the ship **included unbroken** bottles of wine and expensive **undamaged** china.

Found undamaged inside the ship were bottles of wine and expensive china.

EXTRA EXERCISE

Rewrite each of the following groups of sentences as a single statement by reducing the information in one of them to a group of words that you can include in the other.

1. William Shakespeare had seven brothers and sisters. He was the third child.

2. He attended Stratford's free grammar school until he was about thirteen. Later he apprenticed to a local tradesperson.

3. Anne Hathaway was eight years older than Shakespeare. He married her in 1582.

4. Their first child was born the next year. They named her Susanna.

5. In 1585 Anne bore twins. They were named Hamnet and Judith.

6. In 1597 Shakespeare moved from London back to Stratford. He bought a large house called New Place.

ANSWERS: EXTRA EXERCISE

Answers will vary, but here are some possibilities.

1. William Shakespeare was the third of eight children.

2. He attended Stratford's free grammar school until he was about thirteen, when he was apprenticed to a local tradesperson.

3. Shakespeare married Anne Hathaway, who was eight years his senior, in 1582.

4. Susanna, their first child, was born the next year.

5. In 1585 Anne bore the twins Hamnet and Judith.

6. In 1597 Shakespeare moved back from London to New Place, a large house in Stratford.

Truman Capote, known for a prose style marked by clarity and lucidity, never relented in his efforts to delete everything that marred the lean simplicity of his work. In *Music for Chameleons*, a book of essays published toward the end of his life, he included a description of an experience he had in a Moscow subway. To Capote's surprise, he recognized a man who had lived in Capote's apartment building in New York ten years earlier. Blind, crippled, and dignified, Mr. Jones never left his apartment but received a steady stream of visitors and telephone calls. Suddenly he disappeared. Using the following excerpt from Capote's remembrance, you might ask students if they can find any words that can be deleted or phrases that can be reduced and revise the passage to be more concise.

—Ten years pass.

Now it is a zero-cold December afternoon, and I am in Moscow. I am riding in a subway car. There are only a few other passengers. One of them is a man sitting opposite me, a man wearing boots, a thick long coat and a Russian-style fur cap. He has bright eyes, blue as a peacock's.

After a doubtful instant, I simply stared, for even without the black glasses, there was no mistaking that lean distinctive face, those high cheekbones with the single scarlet star-shaped birthmark.

I was just about to cross the aisle and speak to him when the train pulled into a station, and Mr. Jones, on a pair of fine sturdy legs, stood up and strode out of the car. Swiftly, the train door closed behind him.

Using strong verbs and avoiding nouns formed from verbs

Your writing will have more impact when you choose VERBS that are strong because they directly convey an action. *Be* and *have* are not strong verbs, and they tend to create wordy structures. When you revise weak verbs to strong ones, often you can reduce the number of words in your sentences.

WEAK VERB

The proposal before the city council **has to do with** locating the sewage treatment plant outside city limits.

STRONGER VERBS

The proposal before the city council **suggests** locating the sewage treatment plant outside city limits.

The proposal before the city council **argues against** locating the sewage treatment plant outside city limits.

WEAK VERBS

The board members **were of the opinion** that the revisions in the code were not changes they could accept.

STRONGER VERBS

The board members **said** that they **could not accept** the revisions in the code.

❖ ALERT: When you revise, look carefully at verbs with the pattern *be* + ADJECTIVE + *of* (*be aware of, be capable of, be fearful of*). Many of these phrases can be replaced with one-word verbs: *I envy* [not *am envious of*] *the council president's ability to speak in public.* Always avoid certain of these phrases: for example, always use ***appreciate*** (not *be appreciative of*), ***illustrate*** (not *be illustrative of*), and ***support*** (not *be supportive of*).

NO	The council president **was supportive of** the council's attempts to lower property taxes.
YES	The council president **supported** the council's attempts to lower property taxes. ❖

When you look for weak verbs to revise, look also for nominals (nouns derived from verbs, usually by added suffixes such as *-ance*, *-ment*, or *-tion*). Turning a nominal back into a verb reduces words and increases impact.

NO	We **oversaw the establishment of** a student advisory committee.
YES	We **established** a student advisory committee.

NO   The building **had the appearance of** having been renovated.

YES   The building **appeared** to be renovated.

Using pronouns for conciseness

Replacing NOUNS with PRONOUNS can reduce wordiness. When changing nouns to pronouns, be sure that each pronoun's antecedent is unambiguous (see 10a-10c) and that each pronoun agrees with its antecedents (see 11m-11p).

NO   Queen Elizabeth II served as a driver and mechanic in World War II. **Elizabeth** joined the Auxiliary Territorial Service in 1944, while **the future queen** was still a princess. Although **Princess Elizabeth** did not know how to drive, she quickly learned how to strip and repair many kinds of engines.

YES   Queen Elizabeth II served as a driver and mechanic in World War II. **She** joined the Auxiliary Territorial Service in 1944, while **she** was still a princess. Although she did not know how to drive, she quickly learned how to strip and repair many kinds of engines.

EXERCISE 16-1

Consulting section 16a, combine each set of sentences to eliminate wordy constructions.

EXAMPLE   A creative idea, says psychologist Robert Epstein, can be like a rabbit. The rabbit runs by fast. We glimpse only the rabbit's ears or tail.

A creative idea, says psychologist Robert Epstein, can be like a rabbit that runs by so fast we glimpse only its ears or tail.

1. There is evidence that suggests that there is only one difference between creative people and the rest of us. It is creative people who are always poised to capture the new ideas we might not catch right away.

2. Creative thinking has to do with seizing opportunities. Creative thinking has to do with staying alert. Creative thinking has to do with seeking challenges and pushing boundaries.

3. The goal is that the idea be caught first and that the idea be evaluated later. A fleeting thought is captured by the alert person by writing it down at once. The goal is not to worry whether the thought will have eventual value.

4. There is an important part of creativity, and that is daydreaming, which is an activity allowing thoughts to bubble up spontaneously. These creative thoughts surprise us with their freshness.

ANSWERS AND COVERAGE: EXERCISE 16–1

Answers will vary. Here is one set of possibilities.

1. Evidence suggests that the only difference between creative people and the rest of us is that they are always poised to capture the new ideas we might not catch right away. [16a-1, unnecessary expletives; 16a-5, using pronouns]

2. Creative thinking involves seizing opportunities, staying alert, seeking challenges, and pushing boundaries. [16a-4, using stronger verbs]

3. Because the goal is to catch the idea first and evaluate it later, the alert person captures a fleeting thought by writing it down at once without worrying about its eventual value. [16a-2, unnecessary passive; 16a-5, using pronouns; 16a-3, reducing phrases]

4. An important part of creativity is daydreaming, which allows thoughts to bubble up spontaneously and surprise us with their freshness. [16a-1, unnecessary expletive; 16a-3, reducing clauses]

5. We can sometimes unlock our creativity by trying something different, such as turning pictures sideways or upside down to see them in new ways or molding clay while thinking about a difficult writing problem. [16a-2, unnecessary passive; 16a-3, reducing clauses to phrases and phrases to words; 16a-1, unnecessary expletive]

6. Robert Epstein stresses that many exciting advances in fields from astrophysics to car design to dance combine creative ideas from widely different sources. [16a-2, unnecessary passive; 16a-3, reducing clauses]

7. Epstein assigned his students the problem of retrieving a ping-pong ball

➡

ANSWERS AND COVERAGE:
EXERCISE 16–1, cont.

at the sealed bottom of a vertical
drainpipe. [16a-4, using strong verbs
and avoiding nouns formed from verbs;
16a-3, reducing phrases to words and
clauses to phrases]

8. Epstein gave the students tools
that were too short to reach the ball or
too wide to fit into the pipe. [16a-3,
reducing phrases]

9. Stumped at first, the students tried
unsuccessfully to capture the ball with
the tools before stepping back from the
immediate situation, seeing the big
picture, and thinking creatively. [16a-3,
reducing clauses to phrases and
reducing phrases to words]

10. The students poured water down
the drainpipe and the ball floated to
the top, where they retrieved it. [16a-
2, unnecessary passive; 16a-4, strong
verbs; 16a-5, using pronouns]

REFERENCE TO SUPPLEMENTS

This topic is included in the TASP writing competency test. Refer students to
Preparing for the TASP by M. Saenz and
to ch. 1, Section B1c of *Preparing for the
CLAST* by S. Patterson.

TEACHING TIP

In class you might ask the students to exchange papers and look for unnecessary
words. As a courtesy, you should notify
students ahead of time that their classmates are going to read their work. You
can structure this lesson in several ways:

1. Have pairs of students write directly
on one another's papers. You can then
collect the paragraphs, add your own
comments, and return the material at the
next class.

2. Have pairs or trios of students confer
on papers one at a time and arrive at a
consensus. You can circulate around the

➔

5. Creativity can be unlocked in us by our trying something different. It is possible to turn pictures sideways or upside down to see them in new ways.
We can mold clay while we think about a writing problem that is difficult.

6. It is stressed by the psychologist Robert Epstein that there are many exciting
advances in everything. The advances are in fields from astrophysics to
car design to dance. The advances creatively combine ideas that are from
widely different sources.

7. Epstein gave his students the assignment of a problem. The problem called
for the retrieval of a ping-pong ball. It was located at the bottom of a
vertical drainpipe that was sealed at the bottom.

8. Some of the tools that the students had been given by Epstein were too
short to reach the ball. Other tools that the students had been given were
too wide to fit into the pipe.

9. The students were stumped at first. The students tried unsuccessfully to
capture the ball with the tools. Then the students stepped back from the
immediate situation. The students saw the big picture and began thinking
creatively.

10. Water was poured down the drainpipe by the students. The ball achieved
flotation and rose to the top. The ball was retrieved by the students there.

16b   Eliminating unneeded words

To achieve conciseness, eliminate unneeded words that clutter
sentences. Also, revise imprecise language so that six inexact words do
not take the place of one precise word.

When a writer tries to write very formally or tries to reach an
assigned word limit, **padding** usually results. Sentences loaded with
deadwood contain empty words and phrases that increase the word
count but lack meaning. If you find deadwood, clear it away.

PADDED

~~In fact,~~ the television station ~~which is situated in the local area~~ has
won ~~a great~~ many awards ~~as a result of its having been involved in the~~
coverage of ~~all kinds of~~ controversial issues.

CONCISE

The local television station has won many awards for its coverage of
controversial issues.

PADDED

The bookstore ~~entered the order for~~ the books ~~that the instructor has
said will be utilized in~~ the course ~~sequence.~~

CONCISE

The bookstore ordered the books for the course.

Chart 89 lists typical empty words that are among the worst offenders. The chart also offers revised versions. Apply what is here to similar items not listed.

GUIDE FOR ELIMINATING EMPTY WORDS AND PHRASES 89

EMPTY WORD OR PHRASE	WORDY EXAMPLE	REVISION
as a matter of fact	As a matter of fact, statistics show that many marriages end in divorce.	Statistics show that many marriages end in divorce.
due to the fact that	Mary Stuart did not say the monarch's oath when she became queen of Scotland due to the fact that she was just six days old.	Mary Stuart did not say the monarch's oath when she became queen of Scotland because she was just six days old.
in a very real sense	In a very real sense, the drainage problems caused the house to collapse.	The drainage problems caused the house to collapse.
factor	The project's final cost was an essential factor to consider.	The project's final cost was essential to consider.
manner	The child touched the snake in a reluctant manner.	The child touched the snake reluctantly.
nature	His comment was of an offensive nature.	His comment was offensive.
type of	Gordon took a relaxing type of vacation.	Gordon took a relaxing vacation.
seems	It seems that the union called a strike over health benefits.	The union called a strike over health benefits.
tendency	The team had a tendency to lose home games.	The team often lost home games.
in the process of	We are in the process of reviewing the proposal.	We are reviewing the proposal.
exist	The crime rate that exists is unacceptable.	The crime rate is unacceptable.

→

TEACHING TIP, cont.

room, answering questions, and give credit for each paragraph completed.

3. Have authors number their lines in the margin. Ask students to pass their assignments to the left. The students write comments on a separate sheet of paper, keying each comment to line number. After five minutes, students sign their comments and pass the paragraphs and comment sheets to the left again. Repeat as time and class interest allow. At the end of the class, give the comment sheets to the authors. For homework, students can review the responses to their work and incorporate whichever comments they feel are valid. At the next class, you can collect the revised paragraphs and comment sheets.

TEACHING TIP

You might want to provide students with wordy phrases that commonly inflate and obscure English prose, asking them to find replacements that are more direct and effective. Here are some you can use, with suggested replacements; you can easily find others.

at this point in time	now
free up some space	make room
in the event that	if
my personal physician	my doctor
thunderstorm activity	thunderstorm
it is believed by many that	many believe
head up a committee	head a committee
experience some discomfort	hurt
in order to	to
making an effort to	trying to

QUOTATION ABOUT WRITING

Proper words in proper places, make the true definition of a style.

—Jonathan Swift

QUOTATION ABOUT WRITING

The language must be careful and must appear effortless. It must not sweat. It must suggest and be provocative at the same time.

—Toni Morrison

ANSWERS: EXERCISE 16–2

Answers will vary. Here is one set of possibilities.

(1) <u>As a matter of fact</u>, it seems like a great many folk beliefs that are popular are, <u>in a very real sense,</u> dead wrong. (2) For example, the American Academy of Ophthalmology <u>makes the statement that</u> reading in the dark will not <u>have the effect of</u> ruining a person's eyes. (3) <u>In the case of</u> spicy foods, specialists have proven that foods <u>of this sort</u> are not <u>necessarily</u> bad for the stomach, even for people who have been treated as ulcer patients. (4) What about our mothers' warning <u>that exists</u> about catching colds when we are <u>in the process of</u> becoming chilled?

(5) <u>It is certainly quite true</u> that more people <u>have a tendency</u> to get sick in winter than <u>people do</u> in summer. (6) <u>It seems that</u> lower temperatures are not <u>the blame factor</u>, however. (7) <u>In view of the fact</u> that cold weather often <u>has a tendency</u> to drive people indoors and to bring people together inside, <u>this factor has the appearance</u> of increasing our odds of infecting one another. (8) Finally, <u>there has been</u> a long-standing tradition <u>that states</u> that the full moon <u>has the effect on people</u> of making them crazy. (9) Investigations <u>that were made</u> by researchers <u>who were</u> tireless and careful <u>came to the ultimate conclusion</u> that <u>there is</u> no such relationship <u>in existence</u>.

GUIDE FOR ELIMINATING EMPTY WORDS AND PHRASES (continued)

89

in light of the fact that	*In light of the fact that* jobs are scarce, I am going back to school.	Because jobs are scarce, I am going back to school.
for the purpose of	Work crews were dispatched *for the purpose of* fixing the potholes.	Work crews were dispatched to fix the potholes.
in the case of	*In the case of* the proposed water tax, residents were very angry.	Residents were very angry about the proposed water tax.
in the event that	*In the event that* you are late, I will leave.	If you are late, I will leave.
the point I am trying to make	*The point I am trying to make* is that news reporters should not invade people's privacy.	News reporters should not invade people's privacy.

EXERCISE 16-2

Consulting section 16b, eliminate unnecessary words or phrases. Be especially alert for empty words that add nothing to meaning.

EXAMPLE   Folk wisdom has a tendency to be untrue.

Folk wisdom is often untrue.

(1) As a matter of fact, it seems as though a great many folk beliefs that are popular are, in a very real sense, dead wrong. (2) For example, the American Academy of Ophthalmology makes the statement that reading in the dark will not have the effect of ruining a person's eyes. (3) In the case of spicy foods, specialists have proven that foods of this sort are not necessarily bad for the stomach, even for people who have been treated as ulcer patients. (4) What about our mothers' warning that exists about catching colds when we are in the process of becoming chilled? (5) It is certainly quite true that more people have a tendency to get sick in winter than people do in summer. (6) It seems that lower temperatures are not the factor that deserves the blame, however. (7) In view of the fact that cold weather often has a tendency to drive people indoors and to bring people together inside, this factor has the appearance of increasing our odds of infecting one another. (8) Finally, there has been a long-standing tradition that states that the full moon has the effect on

people of making them crazy. (9) Investigations that were made by researchers who were tireless and careful came to the ultimate conclusion that there is no such relationship in existence.

Revising redundancies   16c

Planned repetition can create a powerful rhythmic effect (see 19g). The dull drone of unplanned repetition, however, can bore a reader and prevent the delivery of your message. Unplanned repetition, called **redundancy,** says the same thing more than once.

Certain redundant word pairs are very common. Avoid expressions like *each and every, null and void, forever and ever,* and *final and conclusive.* Other common redundancies are *perfectly clear, few* (or *many*) *in number, consensus of opinion,* and *reason is because.*

NO	Bringing the project to **final completion** three weeks early, the new manager earned our **respectful regard** when **the project was completed.**
YES	**Completing** the project three weeks early, the new manager earned our **respect.**
YES	The new manager earned our **respect** for **completing** the project three weeks early.
NO	**Astonished,** the architect **circled around** the building in **amazement.**
YES	**Astonished,** the architect **circled** the building.
YES	The architect **walked around** the building **in amazement.**

Notice how redundancies deaden a sentence's impact.

NO	The council members **proposed a discussion** of the amendment, but that **proposal for a discussion** was voted down after they had **discussed** it for a while.
YES	The council members' proposal to discuss the amendment was eventually voted down.
NO	The **consensus of opinion** among those of us who saw it is that the carton was **huge in size.**
YES	Most of us who saw the carton agree that it was huge.

❖ ESL NOTE: In all languages, words often carry an unspoken message—an *implied meaning*—that is assumed by native speakers of the language. Implied meaning can cause redundancy in writing. For exam-

ESL

339

ANSWERS: EXERCISE 16–3

Answers will vary. Here is one set of possibilities.

(1) Now is the time to interview <u>and talk to</u> each <u>and every</u> family elder about the events <u>and happenings</u> of their lives. (2) <u>The reason for</u> the urgency <u>is because</u> the aging process of growing older can interrupt our dialogue with elderly relatives faster and <u>more rapidly</u> than we <u>could or should be able to</u> imagine. (3) <u>To give just one example,</u> in the 1980s, Ellen Miller, a woman in her forties, <u>started to begin</u> audiotaping her mother's <u>memories and reminiscences</u> of Berlin during <u>the era of</u> the early 1900s. (4) Before Miller <u>could have the chance</u> to videotape some sessions, however, Alzheimer's disease had robbed her mother of speech and memory. (5) <u>Upon her mother's death at the age of eighty-eight years,</u> Miller sat down, <u>listened again,</u> and heard once more the familiar gentle voice telling <u>stories and tales</u> of <u>far-off days on another continent</u> that vividly evoked those times. (6) <u>Then and there</u> Miller decided <u>on the spot</u> to make a film that would <u>bring together</u> these audiotapes combined with family photographs, her own narration, and her mother's favorite Beethoven piano sonata. (7) Ellen Miller advises those who want to <u>capture and preserve</u> their family history on tape to bring family heirlooms and photographs when the recording sessions <u>are being held.</u> (8) The interviewer should ask questions that are <u>specific and particular and not vague,</u> and <u>the interviewer</u> should keep his or her own comments to a minimum.

ple, *I sent a letter **by mail*** is redundant; in American English, *to send a letter* implies *by mail*. A good dictionary gives information about implied meaning of words (see the list of dictionaries in 20a). *Webster's New World Dictionary, Fourth College Edition*, for example, defines the verb *send* this way: "to dispatch, convey, or transmit (a letter, message, etc.) by mail, radio, etc." ❖

EXERCISE 16-3

Consulting section 16c, eliminate redundant words and phrases. Then revise the paragraph so that it is concise.

EXAMPLE   Oral history is an important legacy that can be handed down to future generations who come later.

Oral history is an important legacy for future generations.

   (1) Now is the time to interview and talk to each and every family elder about the events and happenings of their lives. (2) The reason for the urgency is because the aging process of growing older can interrupt our dialogue with elderly relatives faster and more rapidly than we could or should be able to imagine. (3) To give just one example, in the 1980s, Ellen Miller, a woman in her forties, started to begin audiotaping her mother's memories and reminiscences of Berlin during the era of the early 1900s. (4) Before Miller had the chance to videotape some sessions, however, Alzheimer's disease had robbed her mother of speech and memory. (5) Upon her mother's death at the age of eighty-eight years, Miller sat down, listened again and heard once more the familiar gentle voice telling stories and tales of far-off days on another continent that vividly evoked those times. (6) Then and there Miller decided on the spot to make a film that would bring together these audiotapes combined with family photographs, her own narration, and her mother's favorite Beethoven piano sonata. (7) Ellen Miller advises those who want to capture and preserve their family history on tape to bring family heirlooms and photographs when the recording sessions are being held. (8) The interviewer should ask questions that are specific and particular and not vague, and the interviewer should keep his or her own comments to a minimum.

Focus on Revising

REVISING YOUR WRITING

If you need to write more concisely, go back to your writing and locate wordy material. Using this chapter as a resource, revise your writing to eliminate wordiness in sentences (see 16a) and to avoid unneeded words (see 16b) and redundancy (see 16c).

CASE STUDY: REVISING FOR CONCISENESS

In these case studies, you can observe a student writer revising. Then you have the chance to revise other student writing on your own.

Observation

A student wrote the following draft for a course called Business Management. The assignment was to write a summary of a research study related to the course. This material summarizes the source material thoroughly, but the draft's effectiveness is diminished by a lack of conciseness.

Read through the draft. The wordy material is highlighted and explained. Before you look at the student's revision, revise the material yourself. Then compare what you and the student did.

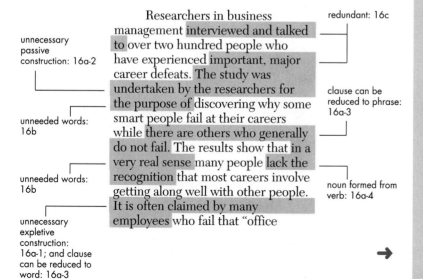

unnecessary passive construction: 16a-2

unneeded words: 16b

unneeded words: 16b

unnecessary expletive construction: 16a-1; and clause can be reduced to word: 16a-3

Researchers in business management interviewed and talked to over two hundred people who have experienced important, major career defeats. The study was undertaken by the researchers for the purpose of discovering why some smart people fail at their careers while there are others who generally do not fail. The results show that in a very real sense many people lack the recognition that most careers involve getting along well with other people. It is often claimed by many employees who fail that "office

redundant: 16c

clause can be reduced to phrase: 16a-3

noun formed from verb: 16a-4

➔

QUOTATION ABOUT WRITING

The true artist declares himself by leaving out a lot. The artist alone sees spirits. But after he has told of their appearing to him, everybody sees them.

—Goethe

COVERAGE: PARTICIPATION ESSAY, page 343

College students seeking alternatives to dormitories, young adults moving out on their own, and newcomers to an area often rent apartments or houses. All of these potential renters should keep in mind that *renting or leasing* [16c: redundancy] involves a legal agreement between landlord and tenant. *It is recommended* [16a-1: expletive construction; also 16a-2: unnecessary passive] that anyone preparing to rent conduct *thorough and extensive* [16c: redundancy] *evaluations* [16a-4: noun from a verb] *of the entire situation* [16b: unneeded word] before making any decisions. *One major area to investigate is the evaluation of the type of landlord* [16b: unneeded words]. *It is also recommended* [16a-1: expletive construction; also 16a-2: unnecessary passive] that renters carefully examine the *condition and nature* [16c: redundancy] of the premises before any lease *is signed by them* [16a-2: unnecessary passive].

An initial step in the rent process is the investigation of the landlord [16b: unneeded words]. *Renters can determine the nature of* [16b: unneeded words] the landlord's management style by several strategies. A list of current and former tenants *of the facility* [16b: unneeded words] can *be requested* [16a-2: unnecessary passive] from the landlord.

➔

COVERAGE: PARTICIPATION ESSAY, page 343, cont.

Renters should not hesitate to contact a reasonable number of parties on the list. Renters should ask all of those with whom they come in contact whether the management of the property, in particular the landlord, is easy to contact if problems should arise and whether the landlord is willing to handle such problems without delay [16a-3: combine sentences]. If anyone is *of the opinion* [16b: unneeded words] that the landlord has a poor reputation for handling problems properly, *it is better* [16a-1: expletive construction; also 16a-2: unnecessary passive] to find out before signing a lease or deposit check.

Also, *for the purpose of being* [16b: unneeded words] protected *in the event of* [16b: empty phrase] future disagreements, *it is recommended* [16a-1: expletive construction; also 16a-2: unnecessary passive] that renters inspect the premises carefully. If there is any *type of* [16b: empty words] damage in the apartment, the details should be *written down in a written inventory* [16c: redundancy] by the renters, and *it should be signed and dated by the renters and the landlord* [16a-2: unnecessary passive]. If any damages are to be repaired by the landlord, those promises should also be put in writing. *In the event that* [16b: empty words] any damage is present when renters leave the property, *it is* [16a-1: expletive construction] the renters who will probably be held legally liable for repairs since the landlord would be able to claim that the damage was done during the term of the renters' lease.

In short, only after careful *consideration of the landlord and the premises should the renter even consider* [16c: redundancy] *signing a lease or leaving a deposit or signing anything that might be legally binding* [16c: redundancy].

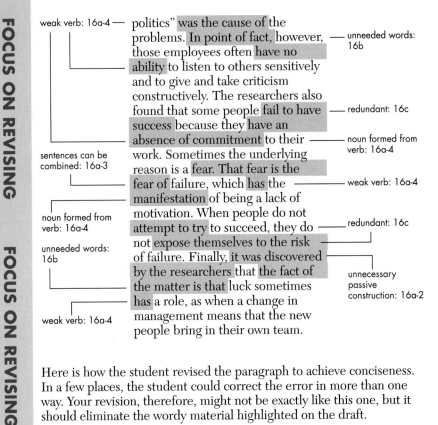

weak verb: 16a-4 — politics" was the cause of the problems. In point of fact, however, — unneeded words: 16b
those employees often have no ability to listen to others sensitively and to give and take criticism constructively. The researchers also found that some people fail to have — redundant: 16c
success because they have an absence of commitment to their — noun formed from verb: 16a-4
sentences can be combined: 16a-3 — work. Sometimes the underlying reason is a fear. That fear is the fear of failure, which has the — weak verb: 16a-4
manifestation of being a lack of motivation. When people do not — redundant: 16c
noun formed from verb: 16a-4 — attempt to try to succeed, they do not expose themselves to the risk of failure. Finally, it was discovered
unneeded words: 16b — by the researchers that the fact of the matter is that luck sometimes — unnecessary passive construction: 16a-2
has a role, as when a change in
weak verb: 16a-4 — management means that the new people bring in their own team.

Here is how the student revised the paragraph to achieve conciseness. In a few places, the student could correct the error in more than one way. Your revision, therefore, might not be exactly like this one, but it should eliminate the wordy material highlighted on the draft.

Researchers in business management interviewed over two hundred people who have experienced major career defeats. The researchers wanted to discover why some smart people fail at their careers while others do not. The results show that many people do not recognize that most careers involve getting along well with other people. Many employees who fail claim that "office politics" caused the problem. However, those employees often do not listen to others sensitively and do not give and take criticism constructively. The researchers also found that some people fail because they are not committed to their work. Sometimes the underlying reason is a fear of failure, which manifests itself as a lack of motivation. When people do not try to succeed, they do not risk failure. Finally, the researchers discovered that luck sometimes plays a role, as when a change in management means that the new people bring in their own team.

Participation

A student wrote the following draft for a journalism class called Feature Writing. The material is logically presented and informative, but the draft's effectiveness is diminished by wordy constructions, padding, and redundancies.

Read through the draft. Then revise it to eliminate the errors. Also, make any additional revisions you think would improve the content, organization, and style of the material.

College students seeking alternatives to dormitories, young adults moving out on their own, and newcomers to an area often rent apartments or houses. All of these potential renters should keep in mind that renting or leasing involves a legal agreement between landlord and tenant. It is recommended that anyone preparing to rent conduct careful and extensive evaluations of the entire situation before making any decisions. One major area to investigate is the evaluation of the type of landlord. It is also recommended that renters carefully examine the condition and nature of the premises before any lease is signed by them.

An initial step in the rent process is the investigation of the landlord. A list of current and former tenants of the facility can be requested from the landlord. Renters should not hesitate to contact a reasonable number of parties on the list. Renters should ask all of those with whom they come in contact whether the management of the property, in particular the landlord, is easy to contact if problems should arise and whether the landlord is willing to handle such problems without delay. If anyone is of the opinion that the landlord has a poor reputation for handling problems properly, it is better to find out before signing a lease or deposit check.

Also, for the purpose of being protected in the event of future disagreements, it is recommended that renters inspect the premises carefully. If there is any type of damage in the apartment, the details should be written down in a written inventory by the renters, and it should be signed and dated by the renters and the landlord. If any damages are to be repaired by the landlord, those promises should also be put in writing. In the event that any damage is present when renters leave the property, it is the renters who will probably be held legally liable for repairs since the landlord would be able to claim that the damage was done during the term of the renters' lease.

In short, only after careful consideration should the renter even consider signing a lease or leaving a deposit or signing anything that might be legally binding.

ANSWER: PARTICIPATION ESSAY

This version is revised for conciseness. Answers will vary but here is one possible revision. Also, answers will vary if students have revised content, organization, or style.

College students seeking alternatives to dormitories, young adults moving out on their own, and newcomers to an area often rent apartments or houses. All of these potential renters should keep in mind that renting involves a legal agreement between landlord and tenant. Anyone preparing to rent should thoroughly evaluate the situation before making any decisions. One factor to investigate is the landlord. Renters should also examine the condition of the premises carefully before they sign a lease.

First, renters should investigate the landlord. Renters can determine the landlord's management style by several strategies. They can ask the landlord for a list of current and former tenants. Renters should not hesitate to contact a reasonable number of parties on the list to ask them whether the landlord is easy to contact and prompt about handling problems. If anyone thinks that the landlord has a poor reputation, renters are better off knowing before they sign a lease or deposit check.

Also, to be protected against future disagreements, renters should inspect the premises carefully. If there is any damage in the apartment, the renters should make a written inventory, and they and the landlord should sign and date it. Also, renters should get in writing all promises of repairs. If any damage is present when renters leave the property, they will probably be held legally liable for repairs since the landlord would be able to claim that they caused the damage.

In short, only after carefully considering the situation should renters sign a lease or leave a deposit.

17 *Coordination and Subordination*

You can include **coordination** and **subordination** in your writing style to help you communicate relationships between two or more ideas. These techniques help your stylistic choices work in concert with the meaning that you want your sentences to deliver. While you are DRAFTING, concentrate on getting your ideas onto paper. When you are REVISING, you can explore the full potential of coordination and subordination for enriching your writing style.

TWO IDEAS	The sky turned dark gray. The wind died suddenly.
COORDINATED VERSION	The sky turned dark gray, and the wind died suddenly.
SUBORDINATED VERSION	As the sky turned dark gray, the wind died suddenly. [The *wind* is the focus.]
SUBORDINATED VERSION	As the wind died suddenly, the sky turned dark gray. [The *sky* is the focus.]

COORDINATION

17a | ## Understanding coordination

Coordination can produce harmony by bringing together related but separate elements to function smoothly in unison. Sections 17a through 17d explain coordination of INDEPENDENT CLAUSES. Coordinate sentences communicate balance in, or sequence of, the ideas that they contain. You can apply these same principles to the coordination of words, PHRASES, and DEPENDENT CLAUSES (see also the explanation of parallelism, Chapter 18).

344

Patterns for coordinate sentences, also known as *compound sentences,* are shown in Chart 90. When you choose to coordinate sentences in your writing, keep these principles in mind:

- A coordinate sentence consists of two grammatically equivalent independent clauses.

- Coordinating independent clauses must be justified by the meaning that you want your sentence to communicate.

- The independent clauses must be joined either by a coordinating conjunction (see Chart 90) or by a semicolon (see 25a and 25b).

- The coordinating conjunction must accurately express the relationship (see Chart 91) between the ideas in the independent clauses.

- If you are tempted to coordinate more than two independent clauses, do so with much care (see 17d-1 and 19b-2).

❦ CONJUNCTION ALERT: Do not confuse coordinating conjunctions with conjunctive adverbs such as *also, however*, and *therefore* (for a complete list, see Chart 49 in section 7f). When conjunctive adverbs connect independent clauses, they function as explained in 7f and 14e.❦

❦ PUNCTUATION ALERT: You will never be wrong if you use a comma before a coordinating conjunction that joins two independent clauses (see 24a).

The sky turned dark gray, **and** the wind died suddenly.
The November morning had just begun, **but** it looked like dusk. ❦

PATTERNS FOR COORDINATE (COMPOUND) SENTENCES   90

Independent clause	{ , and , but , for , nor , or , so , yet ; }	independent clause

---

REFERENCES TO SUPPLEMENTS, *cont.*
Drafts by K. S. Cain, Part III, Exercise 4.

See transparency 5–2 on revising for coordination/subordination in the *Prentice Hall/Simon & Schuster Transparencies for Writers* by D. Carter.

TEACHING TIP

Here is an alternate example and a discussion of how it illustrates the contrast between coordination and subordination.

When we toss a handful of good-luck rice at newlyweds, we're gracing them with one of the world's most important and versatile foods.

—Jack Denton Scott,
"Rice: A Food for All Reasons"

This sentence mentions (1) the idea of tossing rice at a wedding and (2) the fact that rice is an essential grain with many uses. Scott wants to stress the importance of rice as food because he puts that information in the independent clause. Rice as a ceremonial custom gives an ironic context to the main idea, but according to the way the sentence is written, it is a less important idea.

On the other hand, if Scott had been writing on marriage customs, he could have used subordination to provide a different emphasis:

Although rice is one of the world's most important and versatile foods, many Americans value it most as a good-luck symbol for newlyweds.

Here the independent clause stresses the connection of rice with weddings, and the food value of rice is mentioned as a less central point.

PATTERNS FOR COORDINATE (COMPOUND) SENTENCES

TEACHING TIP

You might want to ask your students to consider these two versions of the same passage from the opening of the twenty-second chapter of Genesis, marking the instances of coordination and subordination, then considering the differences in style and meaning that result. The first, from the King James translation of 1611, uses coordination heavily; the second, from the Revised Standard Version of 1971, uses much less.

King James Version

And it came to pass after these things, that God did tempt Abraham, and said unto him, Abraham: and he said, Behold, here I am. And he said, Take now thy son, thine only son Isaac, whom thou lovest, and get thee into the land of Moriah; and offer him there for a burnt offering upon one of the mountains which I will tell thee of. And Abraham rose up early in the morning, and saddled his ass, and took two of his young men with him, and Isaac his son, and clave the wood for the burnt offering, and rose up, and went unto the place of which God had told him. Then on the third day Abraham lifted up his eyes, and saw the place afar off. And Abraham said unto his young men, Abide ye here with the ass; and I and the lad will go yonder and worship, and come again to you. And Abraham took the wood for the burnt offering, and laid it upon Isaac his son; and he took the fire in his hand, and a knife; and they went both of them together.

Revised Standard Version

After these things God tested Abraham, and said to him, "Abraham!" And he said, "Here am I." He said, "Take your son, your only son Isaac, whom you love, and go to the land of Moriah, and offer him there as a burnt offering upon one of the mountains of which I shall

➜

COORDINATING CONJUNCTIONS AND THE RELATIONSHIPS THEY EXPRESS   91

RELATIONSHIPS	WORDS
addition	*and*
contrast	*but, yet*
result or effect	*so*
reason or choice	*for*
choice	*or*
negative choice	*nor*

17b Using coordinate sentences to show relationships

You can choose to use a string of short sentences for the impact that such style creates. In most cases, however, a series of short sentences does not communicate well the relationships among the ideas. In such situations, coordination can help you avoid writing a series of short sentences that have unclear relationships.

UNCLEAR RELATIONSHIPS

We decided not to go to class. We planned to get the notes. Everyone else had the same plan. Most of us ended up failing the quiz.

CLEAR RELATIONSHIPS

We decided not to go to class, **but** we planned to get the notes. Everyone else had the same plan, **so** most of us ended up failing the quiz.

Overuse of coordination, however, can bore a reader with its unbroken rhythm (see 17d-2). For another technique to help you avoid an unwanted series of short sentences, see the discussion of subordination in 17e through 17i.

17c Using coordinate sentences for effect

Coordinate sentences can help you effectively communicate an unfolding of events.

The first semester of my junior year at Princeton University is a disaster, **and** my grades show it. D's and F's predominate, **and** a note from the dean puts me on academic probation. Flunk one more course, **and** I'm out.

—JOHN A. PHILLIPS AND DAVID MICHAELS, "Mushroom: The Story of an A-Bomb Kid"

F. Scott Fitzgerald, a U.S. writer of fiction and screenplays (1896–1940), often used coordination to achieve dramatic effect. In this passage, coordination underlines the contrasts that Fitzgerald draws:

It was a hidden Broadway restaurant in the dead of night, **and** a brilliant and mysterious group of society people, diplomats, and members of the underworld were there. A few minutes ago the sparkling wine had been flowing, **and** a girl had been dancing gaily upon a table, **but** now the whole crowd were hushed and breathless.

—F. SCOTT FITZGERALD, "The Freshest Boy"

Avoiding the misuse of coordination   **17d**

Avoiding illogical coordination   **17d-1**

Coordination is illogical when ideas in the compounded INDEPENDENT CLAUSES are not related. Your reader expects one part of a coordinate construction to lead logically to the other.

NO   Computers came into common use in the 1970s, and they sometimes make costly errors.

The statement in each independent clause is true, but the ideas are not related closely enough. The date computers became commonly used is unrelated to their making errors. The two ideas should not be coordinated. Here are ideas that do coordinate logically.

YES   Computers came into common use in the 1970s, and they are now indispensable for conducting business.

YES   Modern computer systems are often very complex, and they sometimes make costly errors.

Avoiding the overuse of coordination   **17d-2**

Overused coordination creates writing that reads as if it were whatever came into the writer's head. Readers become impatient with "babble" and quickly lose interest. When you are REVISING, be sure to check that your intended meaning justifies the use of coordination.

TEACHING TIP

In *Style: An Anti-Textbook* (New Haven: Yale UP, 1974), Richard Lanham attacks the pragmatic insistence "that words are for use, not enjoyment" and "that expression is a duty, not a pleasure" (10) to urge instructors to teach style as wordplay. "Prose written without joy," he warns, "can only be read in the same spirit" (10). Given the opportunity to play with new sentence patterns, students may surprise themselves with the ideas that they can express and the effects that they can create. Ask students to compose sentences following patterns such as "not only/but also" and then to share their favorite sentences with the class.

ANSWERS AND COVERAGE: EXERCISE 17-1

Answers will vary somewhat. Here is one set of possibilities.

1. In 1994, a bill was signed by the California legislature that eliminated laws regulating elaborate hood ornaments for cars, dropped laws against horse and donkey mating, and repealed dozens of other ancient regulations [17d-2, overused].

2. Some of the laws date back to Old West days, and one of these was the prohibition on dueling. [17d-1, illogical]

➜

17d cont.

NO   Dinosaurs could have disappeared for many reasons, and one theory holds that the climate suddenly became cold, and another theory suggests that a sudden shower of meteors and asteroids hit the earth, so the impact created a huge dust cloud that caused a false winter. The winter lasted for years, and the dinosaurs died, for most of the vegetation they lived on died out.

YES   Dinosaurs could have disappeared for many reasons. One theory holds that the climate suddenly became cold, and another suggests that a sudden shower of meteors and asteroids hit the earth. The impact created a huge dust cloud that caused a false winter. The winter lasted for years, killing most of the vegetation that dinosaurs used for food.

In the revised version, the sentences deliver their meanings clearly.

Writers also overuse coordination if they fail to feature some ideas more prominently than others. Such writing tends to drone on monotonously.

NO   Laughter seems to help healing, so many doctors are prescribing humor for their patients, and some hospitals are doing the same. Comedians have donated their time to several California hospitals, and the nurses in one large hospital in Texas have been trained to tell each patient a joke a day.

YES   Laughter seems to help healing. Many doctors and hospitals are prescribing humor for their patients. Comedians have donated their time to several California hospitals, and the nurses in one large hospital in Texas have been asked to tell each patient a joke a day.

In the revised version, some ideas are kept separate and some are put into a coordinate sentence. (For another way to revise overused coordination, see the discussion of subordination, 17e through 17h.)

ESL   ❖ ESL NOTE: If your instructor tells you that your sentences are too long and complex, practice limiting them. When you write your next paper, follow the advice of many ESL teachers: Revise any sentence containing a combination of more than three independent and dependent clauses. ❖

EXERCISE 17-1

Consulting sections 17a through 17d, revise these sentences to eliminate illogical or overused coordination. If you think a sentence needs no revision, circle its number.

EXAMPLE   Laws become outdated as time passes, but just how outdated they get can be a surprise, and frequently, legislators have to wipe old laws off the books.

Laws become outdated as time passes, but just how outdated they get can be a surprise. Frequently, legislators have to wipe old laws off the books.

1. In 1994, a bill was signed by the California legislature, and it eliminated laws regulating elaborate hood ornaments for cars, and it dropped the laws against the mating of horses and donkeys, and it also repealed dozens of other ancient regulations.

2. Some of the laws date back to Old West days, but one of these was a prohibition on dueling.

3. Dueling is not a common practice today, but lawmakers decided that it was enough of a problem to be declared illegal in 1872.

4. There was another old law, and it dealt with the capture and possession of frogs used in jumping contests, but it was not repealed, and so why then is it staying on the books?

5. Calaveras County fair officials were upset, and they pleaded with state lawmakers to let the law stand, for in his story "The Celebrated Jumping Frog of Calaveras County," Mark Twain made the contest famous, and this happened more than a century ago, and the event still draws huge crowds every year.

EXERCISE 17-2

Consulting sections 17a through 17d, revise this paragraph. Decide which ideas seem to have equal weight and could therefore be contained in compound sentences. Your final version should have no more than two compound sentences—all other sentences should be left as they are.

   Kudzu is the Asian vine that is choking out other vegetation in the southern United States. It can grow a foot a day. It can cover a car in a few weeks. Kudzu seems to have no redeeming qualities whatsoever. A few clever people have come up with commercial uses. The following are some of their suggestions. The Kudzu Cafe in Atlanta serves kudzu leaves in salads. A teacher at Georgia Tech University has his students make paper from kudzu. Craftspeople make baskets and sculptures from the vine. Finally, when hamsters in laboratories are made chemically dependent on alcohol, kudzu has been found to help control their addiction. Maybe what is good for hamsters will work for humans some day.

QUOTATION ABOUT WRITING

In stating as fully as I could how things really were, it was often very difficult and I wrote awkwardly and the awkwardness is what they called my style. All mistakes and awkwardness are easy to see, and they called it style.

—Ernest Hemingway

QUOTATION ABOUT WRITING

(i)   Never use a metaphor, simile or other figure of speech which you are used to seeing in print.

(ii)   Never use a long word where a short one will do.

(iii)   If it is possible to cut a word out, always cut it out.

(iv)   Never use the passive where you can use the active.

(v)   Never use a foreign phrase, a scientific word or jargon word if you can think of an everyday English equivalent.

(vi)   Break any of these rules sooner than say anything barbarous.

—George Orwell

QUOTATION ABOUT WRITING

Advice to young writers? Always the same advice: learn to trust your own judgment, learn inner independence, learn to trust that time will sort the good from the bad—including your own bad.

—Doris Lessing

SUBORDINATION

17e   Understanding subordination

Subordination expresses the relative importance of ideas in a sentence by making a less important idea grammatically less prominent than a more important one. Sections 17e through 17h explain subordination of DEPENDENT and INDEPENDENT CLAUSES: The more important idea appears in the independent clause—a group of words that can stand alone as a grammatical unit; the subordinated idea appears in the dependent clause—a group of words that cannot stand alone as a grammatical unit. What information you choose to subordinate depends on the meaning that you want a sentence to deliver.

Major patterns of subordination with dependent clauses are shown in Chart 92. Two types of dependent clauses are adverb clauses and adjective clauses (see Chart 92). An **adverb clause** is a dependent clause that starts with a SUBORDINATING CONJUNCTION. Each subordinating conjunction has a specific meaning that expresses a relationship between the dependent clause and the independent clause, as shown in Chart 93.

An **adjective clause** is a dependent clause that can start with a RELATIVE PRONOUN (*who, which, that*), a RELATIVE ADVERB (such as *where*), or a PREPOSITION before a "relative" word (for example, **to** *whom*, **above** *which*).

PATTERNS OF SUBORDINATION WITH DEPENDENT CLAUSES   92

SENTENCES WITH ADVERB CLAUSES

- **Adverb clause,** independent clause.
    After the sky grew dark, the wind died suddenly.

- Independent clause, **adverb clause.**
    Birds stopped singing, **as they do during an eclipse.**

- Independent clause **adverb clause.**
    The shops closed **before the storm began.**

PATTERNS OF SUBORDINATION WITH DEPENDENT CLAUSES (continued)

92

SENTENCES WITH ADJECTIVE CLAUSES

■ Independent clause **restrictive (essential)* adjective clause.**

> The weather forecasts warned of a storm **that might bring a thirty-inch snowfall.**

■ Independent clause, **nonrestrictive (nonessential)* adjective clause.**

> Spring is the season for tornadoes, **which rapidly whirl their destructive columns of air.**

■ Beginning of independent clause **restrictive (essential)* adjective clause** end of independent clause.

> Anyone **who lives through a tornado** recalls the experience.

■ Beginning of independent clause, **nonrestrictive (nonessential)* adjective clause,** end of independent clause.

> The sky, **which had been clear,** was turning gray.

*For an explanation of restrictive (essential) and nonrestrictive (nonessential) elements, see 24e.

SUBORDINATING CONJUNCTIONS AND THE RELATIONSHIPS THEY EXPRESS

93

RELATIONSHIPS	WORDS
time	after, before, once, since, until, when, whenever, while
reason or cause	as, because, since
purpose or result	in order that, so, so that, that
condition	even if, if, provided that, unless
contrast	although, even though, though, whereas
location	where, wherever
choice	rather than, whether

QUOTATION ABOUT WRITING

Coordination is simply a way to show ideas that are equal in importance, but subordination indicates what's powerful and what isn't.

—Betty Jean Goodwin

QUOTATION ABOUT LANGUAGE

As I remained in the Third Form three times as long as anyone else, I had three times as much of it [sentence analysis]. I learned it thoroughly. Thus I got into my bones the essential structure of the ordinary British sentence—which is a noble thing.

—Winston Churchill

QUOTATION ABOUT WRITING

> Blot out, correct, insert, refine,
> Enlarge, diminish, interline;
> Be mindful, when invention fails,
> To scratch your head, and bite your nails.

—Jonathan Swift

QUOTATION ABOUT LANGUAGE

American speech is conceded to be energetic and picturesque, possibly as an expression or reflection of national activity and variety.

—William Eben Schultz

BACKGROUND
Sentence-combining exercises such as exercises 3, 4, 6, and 8 in this chapter, in which students are given two or more sentences and are asked to combine them into a single effective sentence to practice a specific sentence structure, were developed in the 1960s and 1970s by teachers applying principles of transformational grammar to writing instruction. Dozens of studies have found that while sentence combining has limitations, students who receive intensive instruction in sentence combining normally increase the complexity of their sentences and the overall quality of their writing (*Sentence Combining: A Rhetorical Perspective*, ed. Donald A. Daiker, Andrew Kerek, and Max Morenberg [Carbondale, IL: Southern Illinois UP, 1985]). Even brief use of sentence combining has been found to help improve the sentence complexity of some students. Several textbooks are devoted entirely to sentence combining, including *The Writer's Options* by Daiker, Kerek, and Morenberg, 2nd ed. (New York: Harper & Row, 1982) and *Sentence Combining: A Composing Book* by William Strong, 2nd ed. (New York: Random House, 1983).

17f Choosing the subordinate conjunction appropriate to your meaning

Subordinating conjunctions express the relationship between major and minor ideas in sentences (see Chart 93). Consider the influence of the subordinating conjunction in each of the following sentences.

After you have handed it in, you cannot make any changes in your report. [time]

Because you have handed it in, you cannot make any changes in your report. [reason]

Unless you have handed it in, you cannot make any changes in your report. [condition]

Although you have handed it in, you can make changes in your report. [contrast]

I want to read your report **so that I can evaluate it.** [purpose]

Since you handed in your report, three more people have handed in theirs. [time]

Since I have seen the report, I can comment on it. [cause]

17g Using subordination to show relationships

Subordination directs your reader's attention to the idea in the INDEPENDENT CLAUSE while at the same time using the idea in the DEPENDENT CLAUSE to provide context and support. Consider these examples (dependent clauses are in boldface).

As soon as I saw the elephant, I knew with perfect certainty that I ought not to shoot it.

—GEORGE ORWELL, "Shooting an Elephant"

If they are very lucky, the passengers may catch a glimpse of dolphins playfully breaking water near the ship.

—ELIZABETH GRAY, student

Subordination usually communicates relationships among ideas more effectively than does a group of separate sentences, although you may occasionally use a string of short sentences for impact.

UNCLEAR RELATIONSHIPS

In 1888, two cowboys had to fight a dangerous Colorado snowstorm. They were looking for cattle. They came to a canyon. They saw outlines of buildings through the snow. Survival then seemed certain.

CLEAR RELATIONSHIPS

In 1888, two cowboys had to fight a dangerous Colorado snowstorm **while they were looking for cattle. When they came to a canyon,** they saw outlines of buildings through the snow. Survival then seemed certain.

In the clear version, the first four short sentences have been combined into two COMPLEX SENTENCES. The last sentence is left short.

EXERCISE 17-3

Consulting sections 17e through 17g, combine each pair of sentences, using an adverb clause to subordinate one idea. Then revise each sentence so that the adverb clause becomes the independent clause. Refer to the list of subordinating conjunctions in Chart 92.

EXAMPLE   Shoes can be colorful, glamorous, or even witty. They are meant to protect the foot from some of the dangers of walking.

        a: *Although shoes can be colorful, glamorous, or even witty, they are meant to protect the foot from some of the dangers of walking.*

        b: *Although they are meant to protect the foot from some of the dangers of walking, shoes can be colorful, glamorous, or even witty.*

1. Sandals are worn primarily to protect the sole of the foot. They are also worn for comfort and style.
2. Ornamentation was added to sandals worn by ancient peoples. Footwear became a stylish article of clothing.
3. Sandalmakers were constrained by certain requirements in ancient Egyptian society. They had to cater to their clients' fashion whims.
4. For example, the nobility demanded sandals with turned-up toes. Peasants were expected to wear sandals with rounded or pointed toes.
5. Clothing had to be made from available materials. Ancient Egyptian sandals were made of leather, woven palm leaves, or papyrus stalks.

ANSWERS: EXERCISE 17-3

Answers will vary. Here is one set of possibilities.

1a. Although sandals are worn primarily to protect the sole of the foot, they are also worn for comfort and style.

1b. Whereas they are also worn for comfort and style, sandals are worn primarily to protect the sole of the foot.

2a. After ornamentation was added to sandals worn by ancient peoples, footwear became a stylish article of clothing.

2b. When footwear became a stylish article of clothing, ornamentation was added to sandals worn by ancient people.

3a. Although sandalmakers were constrained by certain requirements in ancient Egyptian society, they had to cater to their clients' fashion whims.

3b. Because they had to cater to their clients' fashion whims, sandalmakers were constrained by certain requirements in ancient Egyptian society.

4a. For example, when the nobility demanded sandals with turned-up toes, peasants were expected to wear sandals with rounded or pointed toes.

4b. For example, whereas peasants were expected to wear sandals with rounded or pointed toes, the nobility demanded sandals with turned-up toes.

5a. As clothing had to be made from available materials, ancient Egyptian sandals were made of leather, woven palm leaves, or papyrus stalks.

5b. Clothing had to be made from available materials, so ancient Egyptian sandals were made of leather, woven palm leaves, or papyrus stalks.

EXERCISE 17-4

Consulting sections 17e through 17g, combine each pair of sentences, using an adjective clause to make one idea subordinate to the other. Then revise each sentence so that the adjective clause becomes the independent clause. Use the relative pronoun given in parentheses.

EXAMPLE   The artist Joseph Cornell died in 1972 at the age of 69. He is best known for his small boxes arranged with stuffed birds, buttons and toys, and pieces of old posters. (who)

> a: *The artist Joseph Cornell, who died in 1972 at the age of 69, is best known for his small boxes arranged with stuffed birds, buttons and toys, and pieces of old posters.*
>
> b: *The artist Joseph Cornell, who is best known for his small boxes arranged with stuffed birds, buttons and toys, and pieces of old posters, died in 1972 at the age of 69.*

1. Cornell was a textiles salesperson. He explored the junk shops and secondhand bookstores of Manhattan between business appointments. (who)
2. Old books, records, prints, and bits of trash fascinated Cornell. They became the raw material for his unique collages and boxes. (that)
3. In 1931, a gallery owner named Julius Levy included Cornell's collages in an exhibition of surrealist art. Levy encouraged Cornell to keep producing his art. (who)
4. Cornell's boxes won international acclaim. They often contained the same kinds of objects, such as brass rings and foreign postage stamps. (which)
5. Cornell rarely left his home in New York and never ventured outside the United States. He was deeply influenced by European art. (who)

17h   Avoiding the misuse of subordination

17h-1   Avoiding illogical subordination

Subordination is illogical when the subordinating conjunction does not make clear the relationship between the INDEPENDENT and DEPENDENT CLAUSE (see Chart 93).

> **NO**   Because Beethoven was deaf when he wrote his final symphonies, they are musical masterpieces.

The above sentence is illogical because it was not Beethoven's deafness that led to his writing symphonic masterpieces. Revising from *because* to *although* creates logical subordination:

YES   Although Beethoven was deaf when he wrote his final symphonies, they are musical masterpieces.

Avoiding the overuse of subordination

17h-2

Overused subordination occurs when too many images or ideas crowd together, making your reader lose track of your intended message. If you have used more than two subordinating conjunctions or RELATIVE PRONOUNS in a sentence, be skeptical about whether your meaning is clear.

NO   A new technique for eye surgery, which is supposed to correct nearsightedness, which previously could be corrected only by glasses, has been developed, although many doctors do not approve of it because it can create unstable eyesight.

YES   A new technique for eye surgery, which is supposed to correct nearsightedness, has been developed. Previously, nearsightedness could be corrected only by glasses. Because it can create unstable eyesight, many doctors do not approve of it, however.

In the revised version the first sentence has a RELATIVE CLAUSE, the second is a SIMPLE SENTENCE, and the third has a dependent clause starting with *Because*. Some words have been moved to new positions. The revision communicates its message more clearly because it provides a variety of sentence structures (see 19a) while avoiding the clutter of overused subordination.

EXERCISE 17-5

Consulting section 17h, correct illogical or excessive subordination in this paragraph. As you revise, use not only some short sentences but also some correctly constructed adverb clauses. Also, apply the principles of coordination discussed in 17a through 17d, if you wish.

Because too many young ape mothers in zoos were rejecting or abusing their infants, zoo keepers decided to stop their usual practice of separating mother and infant from the rest of the ape community which was done so that the infant would supposedly be safe from harm from other apes. In the new arrangement, group settings were established that included older, experienced, loving ape mothers as well as other infants and young mothers so that the abusive mothers could learn from good role models how to love and care for their infants and so that each mother would have childrearing support from the equivalent of aunts and cousins. The experiment was successful, and some pediatricians, who are doctors who specialize in child care, tried a similar program for abusive human mothers, which worked well even though the human mothers took far longer than the ape mothers to learn and use good mothering techniques.

ANSWERS: EXERCISE 17–4, cont.
5b. Cornell, *who* was deeply influenced by European art, rarely left his home in New York and never ventured outside the United States.

ANSWERS AND COVERAGE: EXERCISE 17–5

Each sentence contains illogical and overused subordination. Answers will vary considerably. Here is one possibility.

Because too many young ape mothers in zoos were rejecting or abusing their infants, zoo keepers decided to stop their usual practice of separating mother and infant from the rest of the ape community. This practice was done so that the infant would supposedly be safe from harm from other apes. In the new arrangement, group settings were established that included older, experienced, loving ape mothers, as well as other infants and young mothers. The abusive mothers could learn from good role models how to love and care for their infants, and each mother would have childrearing support from the equivalent of aunts and cousins. The experiment was successful. When some pediatricians, who are doctors who specialize in child care, tried a similar program for abusive human mothers, it worked well even though the human mothers took far longer than the ape mothers to learn and use good mothering techniques.

ANSWERS: EXERCISE 17–6
Answers will vary. Here is one set of possibilities.

1. Owl pellets are the latest teaching tool in biology classrooms around the country because they provide an alternative to dissecting frogs and other animals.

2. Inside the pellets are the remains of the owl's nightly meal, which include beautifully cleaned hummingbird skulls, rat skeletons, and lots of bird feathers.

3. The owl pellet market has been cornered by companies in New York, California, and Washington that distribute pellets to thousands of biology classrooms all over the world.

4. Company workers scour barns and the ground under trees where owls nest to pick up the pellets, which retail for $1 each.

5. The owl pellet business may have a short future because the rural areas of the United States are vanishing. Old barns are being bulldozed. When all the barns are torn down, the owls will be gone, too.

ANSWERS: EXERCISE 17–7, page 357

Students use a topic of their own to imitate the styles of three different examples shown in this chapter. Imitation has a proud tradition as a learning tool. The classic rhetoricians said that versatility in style came from (1) a study of principles, (2) practice in writing, and (3) imitation of the practice of others. For a modern interpretation of classical rhetoric, see Edward P. J. Corbett, *Classical Rhetoric for the Modern Student* (New York: Oxford UP, 1971), especially pp. 416 and 496–538.

17i Balancing subordination and coordination

Coordination and subordination can sometimes be used in concert with each other.

> **When two Americans look searchingly into each other's eyes,** emotions are heightened, and the relationship is tipped toward greater intimacy.
>
> —FLORA DAVIS, "How to Read Body Language"

Varying sentence types can improve your ability to emphasize key points in your writing. Consider the following paragraph, which demonstrates a good balance in the use of coordination and subordination. It contains compound sentences (see 17a-17d), sentences that consist of dependent and independent clauses (see 17e-17h), and SIMPLE SENTENCES.

> **When I was growing up,** I lived on a farm just across the field from my grandmother. My parents were busy trying to raise six children and to establish their struggling dairy farm. It was nice to have Grandma so close. **While my parents were providing the necessities of life,** my patient grandmother gave her time to her shy, young granddaughter. I always enjoyed going with Grandma and collecting the eggs that her chickens had just laid. Usually she knew which chickens would peck, **and** she was careful to let me gather the eggs from the less hostile ones.
>
> —PATRICIA MAPES, student

Avoid using both a coordinate and a subordinate conjunction to express one relationship.

NO	**Although** the story was well-written, **but** it was too unbelievable.
YES	**Although** the story was well-written, it was too unbelievable.
YES	The story was well-written, **but** it was too unbelievable.

EXERCISE 17-6

Consulting all sections of this chapter, use subordination and coordination to combine these sets of short, choppy sentences.

EXAMPLE   Owls cannot digest the bones and fur of the mice and birds they eat. They cough up a furry pellet every day.

Because owls cannot digest the bones and fur of the mice and birds they eat, they cough up a furry pellet every day.

1. Owl pellets are the latest teaching tool in biology classrooms around the country. The pellets provide an alternative to dissecting frogs and other animals.

2. Inside the pellet are the remains of the owl's nightly meal. They include beautifully cleaned hummingbird skulls, rat skeletons, and lots of bird feathers.

3. The owl pellet market has been cornered by companies in New York, California, and Washington. These companies distribute pellets to thousands of biology classrooms all over the world.

4. Company workers scour barns and the ground under trees where owls nest to pick up the pellets. The pellets sell for $1 each.

5. The owl pellet business may have a short future. The rural areas of the United States are vanishing. Old barns are being bulldozed. All the barns are torn down. The owls will be gone, too.

EXERCISE 17-7

Using topics you choose, imitate the style of three different examples shown in this chapter. Select from the quotations by Fitzgerald, Orwell, Gray, Davis, and Mapes.

EXERCISE 17-8

Consulting all sections of this chapter, revise this passage by using coordination and subordination.

Few people have ever seen a manatee. Only about 2,000 of these seagoing mammals are left in the world. In the South Pacific, manatees are known as dugongs. They are smaller than sea lions and bigger than seals. They bear an uncanny resemblance to humans. They are thought to be the source of sailors' mermaid legends. Researchers are trying to preserve and protect the dying manatee population in every way they can. Divers at the Sea World amusement park in Florida rescued one manatee female they named Fathom. She was severely injured, possibly by a boat's propeller. She would have died in the wild. She was unable to float or breathe properly. At Sea World, Fathom was given a tailor-made wet suit. She recovered nicely.

ANSWERS: EXERCISE 17–8

Answers may vary. Here are two possibilities that students might enjoy comparing with their own.

1. Few people have ever seen a manatee because only about 2,000 of these seagoing mammals, known as dugongs in the South Pacific, are left in the world. Smaller than sea lions and bigger than seals, manatees bear an uncanny resemblance to humans, and they are thought to be the source of sailors' mermaid legends. Researchers are trying to preserve and protect the dying manatee population in every way they can. Divers at the Sea World amusement park in Florida rescued one manatee female they named Fathom. Severely injured, possibly from a boat's propeller, and unable to float or breathe properly, Fathom would have died in the wild. At Sea World, Fathom was given a tailor-made wet suit, and she recovered nicely.

2. Only about 2,000 manatees are left in the world, and few people have ever seen one of these seagoing mammals. Known as dugongs in the South Pacific, manatees are smaller than sea lions and bigger than seals. Because manatees bear an uncanny resemblance to humans, they are thought to be the source of sailors' mermaid legends. Researchers are trying to preserve and protect the dying manatee population in every way they can. When divers at the Sea World amusement park in Florida rescued one manatee female they named Fathom, she was severely injured, possibly from a boat's propeller. Unable to float or breathe properly, she would have died in the wild. Fathom was given a tailor-made wet suit at Sea World, where she recovered nicely.

18 *Parallelism*

This chapter advises you how to avoid **faulty parallelism** (18b through 18e) and how to use the grace and power of **parallelism** to strengthen your writing (18f and 18g). It also explains parallelism in outlines and lists (18h).

Many writers attend to parallelism when they are REVISING. If while you are DRAFTING you think that your parallelism is faulty or that you can enhance your writing style by using parallelism, underline or highlight the material and keep your focus on getting ideas onto paper. When you revise, you can work on the places that you marked.

18a Understanding parallelism

Parallelism in writing, related to the concept of parallel lines in geometry, calls for the use of equivalent grammatical forms to express ideas of equal importance. An **equivalent grammatical form** is a word or group of words that matches—is parallel to—the structure of a corresponding word or group of words, as explained in Chart 94.

Also, when you are expressing ideas of equal weight in your writing, parallel sentence structures can echo that fact and offer you a writing style that uses balance and rhythm to help deliver your meaning.

> **The deer** often come **to eat their grain, the wolves to destroy their sheep, the bears to kill their hogs, the foxes to catch their poultry.** [The message of the multiple, accumulating assaults is echoed by the parallel structures.]
>
> —J. HECTOR ST. JEAN DE CRÈVECOEUR, Letters from an American Farmer

REFERENCES TO SUPPLEMENTS

For this topic in the CLAST writing competency test, refer students to ch. 1, section B2c of *Preparing for the CLAST* by S. Patterson.

This topic is included in the TASP writing competency test. Refer students to *Preparing for the TASP* by M. Saenz.

For revising for parallelism, refer students to *Rough Drafts* by K. S. Cain, Part III, Exercise 5.

See transparency 5–3 on revising for parallelism in the *Prentice Hall/Simon & Schuster Transparencies for Writers* by D. Carter.

TEACHING TIP

Classical rhetoric teaches that successful speaking or writing comes, in part, from the imitation of good examples. This imitation can take the form of copying passages verbatim or of imitating particular sentence patterns. Classical rhetoricians are not the only ones who have written about the benefits of imitation. Benjamin Franklin writes in his *Autobiography* (1771) of using essays in *The Spectator* as models for organization, sentence structure, and vocabulary. Malcolm X writes in his *Autobiography* of the benefits he

➜

358

PARALLEL STRUCTURES 94

PARALLEL WORDS

Recommended exercise includes **running,** **swimming,** and **cycling.** [The *-ing* words are parallel in structure and equal in importance.]

PARALLEL PHRASES

Exercise helps people **to maintain healthy bodies** and **to handle mental pressures.** [The *to* phrases are parallel in structure and equal in importance.]

PARALLEL CLAUSES

People exercise **because they want to look healthy,** **because they need to have stamina,** or **because they hope to live longer.** [The *because* clauses are parallel in structure and equal in importance.]

Using words in parallel forms 18b

To avoid faulty parallelism, be sure that words in parallel structures occur in the same grammatical form.

NO   The strikers had tried **pleading, threats,** and **shouting.**

YES   The strikers had tried **pleading, threatening,** and **shouting.**

YES   The strikers had tried **pleas, threats,** and **shouts.**

Using words in parallel form can also enhance the impact of the meaning that you want your material to deliver (see 18f and 18g).

Using phrases and clauses in parallel forms 18c

To avoid faulty parallelism, be sure that PHRASES and CLAUSES in parallel structures occur in the same grammatical form.

TEACHING TIP, cont.

gained from simply copying the dictionary in longhand. Winston Churchill and Somerset Maugham also write of the lessons they learned by imitating written models.

A possible first step in imitation is copying passages from favorite writers verbatim. This is not as brainless as it seems, for done properly it enables students to observe the details of an author's style. For this exercise to succeed, students should follow these guidelines adapted from Corbett, *Classical Rhetoric for the Modern Student* (New York: Oxford UP, 1990):

1. Students should read a piece through before beginning to copy it, in order to see the purpose and style of the whole. While working, they should read each sentence before beginning to write it. Once the passage has been completed, students should read their transcriptions in order again to "get a sense of the passage as a whole."

2. Students should copy for fifteen minutes per session. If they copy much longer, their minds will no longer focus on the work and the copying will become mechanical.

3. Students should copy by hand. Typing is too fast to allow students to see the qualities of a writer's style. Writing lets students work slowly enough to see the selection and placement of words, and the lengths and types of sentences.

4. Students should copy from a variety of authors. If they concentrate on one author to the exclusion of others, they may end up aping a single style rather than getting the feel of a variety of styles.

5. Students should copy patiently and with care. Too much speed can make the

→

TEACHING TIP, *cont.*
exercise meaningless. One way of controlling speed is to require that work be legible.

A second kind of imitation exercise uses sentences as patterns. The students duplicate the *kind, number,* and *order* of clauses and phrases in the model. The aim of this exercise is not to achieve a word-for-word correspondence with the model but rather to achieve an awareness of the variety of sentence structures of which the English language is capable (Corbett, 495).

Parody can be an enjoyable imitation exercise for students. Writing a "restaurant review" of the cafeteria or a literary analysis of a comic book not only engages students in wordplay, but requires them to notice the stylistic and structural conventions of the model in order to make fun of them.

QUOTATION ABOUT WRITING
It doesn't matter how you write the first draft or even the second draft, but it makes all the difference in the world how you write the *final* draft.
—Elizabeth White

BACKGROUND
In "Symmetrical Form and the Rhetoric of the Sentence" (*Essays on Classical Rhetoric and Modern Discourse*, ed. Robert J. Connors, Lisa S. Ede, and Andrea A. Lunsford [Carbondale, IL: Southern Illinois UP, 1984]), Richard Graves writes that parallel and balanced sentences are "part of the continuing human concern with the idea of symmetry, an idea which is rooted in our physiological being and touches many aspects of our collective lives" (171). The satisfaction that audiences have always taken from symmetry in language—as well as

➤

18c
cont.

NO	The committee members **read the petition, discussed its major points,** and **the unanimous decision was to ignore it.**
YES	The committee members **read the petition, discussed its major points,** and **unanimously decided to ignore it.** [revised to parallel phrases]

NO	**The signers heard that their petition had not been granted, they became very upset,** and then **staged a protest demonstration.**
YES	**The signers heard that their petition had not been granted, they became very upset,** and then **they staged a protest demonstration.** [revised to parallel clauses]
YES	**The signers heard that their petition had not been granted, became very upset,** and then **staged a protest demonstration.** [revised to parallel phrases]

Using phrases and clauses in parallel form can also serve to enhance the impact of the meaning that you want your material to deliver (see 18f and 18g).

18d Using parallel structures with coordinating and correlative conjunctions and with *than* and *as*

18d-1 Using parallel forms with coordinating conjunctions

The coordinating conjunctions are *and, but, or, nor, for, yet,* and *so* (for the relationship each expresses, see Chart 91 in section 17a). To avoid faulty parallelism, be sure that elements joined by coordinating conjunctions are parallel in grammatical form.

NO	**Love and being married** go together.
YES	**Love and marriage** go together.
YES	**Being in love and being married** go together.

18d-2 Using parallel forms with paired words (correlative conjunctions)

The correlative conjunctions are pairs of words that work in unison, such as *not only...but (also), either...or,* and *both...and* (for more, see 7h). To avoid faulty parallelism, be sure that elements joined by correlative conjunctions are parallel in grammatical form. As you check your writing, pay particular attention to the correct placement of each half of the pair.

NO Differing expectations for marriage **not only** can lead to disappointment **but also** to anger. [The words *can lead* apply to *disappointment* and to *anger,* so they belong before *not only.*]

YES Differing expectations for marriage can lead **not only** to disappointment **but also** to anger.

—NORMAN DuBois, student

Using parallel forms with *than* and *as*

18d-3

To avoid faulty parallelism when you use *than* and *as* for comparisons, be sure that elements are parallel in grammatical form. Also, make sure that these comparisons are complete (see 15e-2).

NO **Having a solid marriage** can be more satisfying **than** the **acquisition of wealth.**

YES **Having a solid marriage** can be more satisfying **than acquiring wealth.**

YES A **solid marriage** can be more satisfying **than wealth.**

—EUNICE FERNANDEZ, student

Repeating function words in parallel elements

18e

In a series of two or more parallel elements, be consistent in the second and subsequent elements about repeating or omitting function words. These include articles (*the, a, an*); the *to* of the INFINITIVE (for example, *to* love) and PREPOSITIONS (for example, *of, in, about*). If you think that repeating such words clarifies your meaning or might help your reader catch the parallelism that you intend, use them.

NO **To assign** unanswered letters their proper weight, **free us** from the expectations of others, **to give us** back to ourselves—here lies **the great, the singular** power of self-respect.

YES **To assign** unanswered letters their proper weight, **to free us** from the expectations of others, **to give us** back to ourselves—here lies **the great, the singular** power of self-respect.

—JOAN DIDION, "On Self-Respect"

BACKGROUND, cont.

from symmetry in music, art, and architecture—is closely connected to the rhythms of the body, of walking, breathing, and the beating heart. Psychological studies suggest that symmetrical patterns are powerful aids for memory and comprehension. Even "the idea of justice carries with it the idea of balance and symmetry" (171).

TEACHING TIP

In *Style: Ten Lessons in Clarity and Grace*, 4th ed. [New York: Harper Collins, 1994], Joseph M. Williams suggests two simple ways to "enhance the rhythm and grace of coordination." First, a series of parallel clauses or phrases "will move more gracefully if each . . . is longer than the one before it." Second, writers can enhance parallel elements if they "consciously balance parts of phrases and clauses against one another."

BACKGROUND

Although parallelism is the best known of the balanced sentence patterns, some others are also available. *Antithesis*, for one, juxtaposes contrasting ideas, often in parallel structure. Neil Armstrong was using antithesis when he made his famous comment as he stepped on the moon in 1969: "That's one small step for a man, one giant leap for mankind." *Chiasmus*, sometimes called "the crisscross," reverses grammatical structures in successive phrases or clauses. One of John Kennedy's well-known statements in his inaugural address, for example, uses chiasmus: "Ask not what your country can do for you, ask what you can do for your country."

QUOTATION ABOUT WRITING

Writers should be read—but neither seen nor heard.

—Daphne du Maurier

18e cont. To avoid faulty parallelism when you use *who, which,* or *that* to start a series of CLAUSES, be sure to repeat or omit the words consistently in subsequent clauses.

> I have in my own life a precious friend, a woman of 65 **who has** lived very hard, **who is** wise, **who listens** well, **who has** been where I am and can help me understand it; and **who represents** not only an ultimate ideal mother to me but also the person I'd like to be when I grow up.
>
> —JUDITH VIORST, "Friends, Good Friends—and Such Good Friends"

> We looked into the bus, **which was** painted blue with orange daisies, **had** picnic benches instead of seats, and **showed** yellow curtains billowing out its windows.
>
> —KERRIE FALK, student

18f Using parallel, balanced structures for impact

Parallel structures characterized by balance serve to emphasize the meaning that sentences deliver. Balanced, parallel structures can be words, PHRASES, CLAUSES, or sentences.

Deliberate, rhythmic repetition of parallel, balanced word forms and word groups reinforces the impact of a message. (For information about misused repetition, see 16c.) Consider the impact of this famous passage:

> **Go back to** Mississippi, **go back to** Alabama, **go back to** South Carolina, **go back to** Georgia, **go back to** Louisiana, **go back to** the slums and ghettos of our northern cities, knowing that somehow this situation can and will be changed.
>
> —MARTIN LUTHER KING, JR., "I Have a Dream"

If King had expressed the same idea with only minimal or no parallelism, his message would have been weaker. His structures reinforce the power of his message. An ordinary sentence would have been less effective: "Return to your homes in Mississippi, Alabama, South Carolina, Georgia, Louisiana, or the cities, and know that the situation will be changed."

A **balanced sentence** has two parallel structures, usually sentences, with contrasting content. A balanced sentence is a coordinate sentence (see 17a), characterized by opposition in the meaning of the two structures, sometimes with one cast in the negative: *Mosquitos do not bite, they stab.* Consider the impact of this sentence:

By night, the litter and desperation disappeared as the city's glittering lights came on; by day, the filth and despair reappeared as the sun rose.

—JENNIFER KIRK, student

Similarly, consider the impact of this famous sentence, which adds unusual word order (*ask not*, instead of *do not ask*) to its parallelism and balance.

Ask not what your country can do for you, ask what you can do for your country.

—JOHN F. KENNEDY

♣ COMMA ALERT: Authorities differ about using a comma or semicolon between the parts of a balanced sentence. In college, to prevent seeming to make the error of a comma splice (see Chapter 14), you are safer if you use a semicolon (or revise in other ways).♣

!

Using parallel sentences in longer passages for impact

18g

Parallel, balanced sentences in longer passages can create a dramatic unity through carefully controlled repetition of words and word forms. Consider this rich passage of repeated words, concepts, and rhythms.

You ask me what is **poverty? Listen** to me. Here I am, dirty, **smelly,** and with no "proper" underwear on and with the **stench** of my rotting teeth near you. I will tell you. **Listen** to me. **Listen** without pity. I cannot use your pity. **Listen** with understanding. Put yourself in my dirty, worn-out, ill-fitting shoes, and hear me.

Poverty is getting up every morning from a dirt- and illness-stained mattress. The sheets have long since been used for diapers. **Poverty** is living in a **smell** that never leaves. **This is a smell** of urine, sour milk, and spoiling food sometimes joined with the strong **smell** of long-cooked onions. Onions are cheap. If you have **smelled** this **smell,** you did not know how it came. **It is the smell** of the outdoor privy. **It is the smell** of young children who cannot walk the long dark way in the night. **It is the smell** of the mattresses where years of "accidents" have happened. **It is the smell** of the milk which has gone sour because the refrigerator long has not worked, and it costs money to get it fixed. **It is the smell** of rotting garbage. I could bury it, but where is the shovel? Shovels cost money.

—JO GOODWIN PARKER, "What Is Poverty?"

TEACHING TIP

You may want to ask your students to identify the various techniques by which parallelism is set up in the following sentences.

1. Standing on a concrete jetty at seven-thirty of a drizzly morning, looking across the gray Hudson at the shore softened by fog, one can just make out an endless miniature procession of Manhattan-bound cars going down the ramp to the Lincoln Tunnel.

"Gray Manhattan," *The New Yorker*

2. There is a crazy restaurant in the south of France where you are expected to eat well and copiously, to drink to excess, to listen to music and perhaps to spin to it—and also to break up the joint before you leave.

—Richard Atcheson *"Le Pirate"*

3. On one side of this line are They: the bribers, the cheaters, the chiselers, the swindlers, the extortioners. On the other side are We. . . .

—Marya Mannes *"The Thin Grey Line"*

BACKGROUND

Joseph M. Williams points out that some nonparallel constructions are acceptable at times. Skilled writers often join a noun phrase with a *how*-clause ("The debater knew the facts and how to use them to her best advantage") or an adjective or adverb with a prepositional phrase ("The young team played aggressively, intelligently, and with surprising poise"). Many editors and teachers, however, do not accept these constructions.

ANSWERS: EXERCISE 18–1

Elements of parallelism in Parker's passage not shown in boldface are: *Repetitions*: you, me, I, dirty (dirt), pity, onions, mattress(es), urine (privy, "accidents"), long, it, shovels. *Paired words*: with / with. *Imperatives* (*mild commands*): Listen, Put, hear. *Contrasts*: pity and understanding, with / without. *Words in a series*: my dirty, worn-out, ill-fitting shoes; smell of urine, sour milk, and spoiling food.

ANSWERS: EXERCISE 18–2

Students use topics of their own to imitate the parallel style of three of the passages shown in this chapter: by Didion, Viorst, King, Kennedy, or Parker. Style imitation has a proud tradition as a learning tool. The classical rhetoricians said that versatility in style came from (1) a study of principles, (2) practice in writing, and (3) imitation of the practice of others. For a modern interpretation of classical rhetoric see Edward P. J. Corbett, *Classical Rhetoric for the Modern Student* (New York: Oxford UP, 1971), especially pp. 416 and 496–538.

ANSWERS AND COVERAGE: EXERCISE 18–3

Answers will vary. Here is one set of possibilities.

1. According to psychologist Harry Levinson, the five main types of bad boss are *the workaholic, the bully, the bad communicator, the jellyfish, and the perfectionist.* [18b, words]

2. *To get ahead, to keep their self-respect, and simply to survive,* wise employees handle problem bosses with a variety of strategies. [18c, phrases]

3. To cope with a bad-tempered employer, workers can both *stand up for themselves* and *reason with a bullying boss.* [18d-2, correlative conjunctions]

➡

18g
cont.

EXERCISE 18-1

Reread the Jo Goodwin Parker passage above. Then, consulting sections 18a through 18e, discover all parallel elements in addition to those shown in boldface.

EXERCISE 18-2

Using topics you choose, imitate the writing style of three different passages shown in this chapter. Select from the quotations from Crèvecoeur, Didion, Viorst, King, Kennedy, or Parker.

EXERCISE 18-3

Consulting sections 18a through 18e, revise these sentences to eliminate errors in parallel structure.

EXAMPLE   Difficult bosses not only affect their employees' performances but their private lives are affected as well.

         Difficult bosses affect *not only their employees' performances but their private lives as well.*

1. According to psychologist Harry Levinson, the five main types of bad boss are the workaholic, the kind of person you would describe as bullying, a person who communicates badly, the jellyfish type, and someone who insists on perfection.

2. As a way of getting ahead, to keep their self-respect, and for simple survival, wise employees handle problem bosses with a variety of strategies.

3. To cope with a bad-tempered employer, workers can both stand up for themselves and reasoning with a bullying boss.

4. Often bad bosses communicate poorly or fail to calculate the impact of their personality on others; being a careful listener and to be sensitive to others' responses are qualities that good bosses possess.

5. Employees who take the trouble to understand what makes their boss tick, engage in some self-analysis, and staying flexible are better prepared to cope with a difficult job environment than suffering in silence like some employees.

EXERCISE 18-4

Consulting sections 18a through 18e, combine the sentences in each numbered item, using techniques of parallelism.

EXAMPLE   New York City is an urban zoo of stone animals that decorate many buildings. These stone creatures serve as waterspouts. They guard museums and libraries. They act as the city's unofficial watchdogs.

New York City is an urban zoo of stone animals *that decorate many buildings, serve as waterspouts, guard museums and libraries, and act as the city's unofficial watchdogs.*

1. A bulldog glares at pedestrians from the door of a fancy apartment building. The Fifth Avenue entrance to the New York Public Library is guarded by a pair of magnificent lions. Perched high on a rooftop a couple of thoughtful pelicans regards the passing parade of life.

2. These architectural animals not only were made of stone but also there are terra cotta and metal ones. They come in other more unusual materials too.

3. A group of stone animal lovers is cataloguing New York City's stone zoo. It stretches across five boroughs. It includes such rare specimens as quahogs, crocodiles, and vultures.

4. Once, the stone animals were thought to provide protection. They warded off evil spirits. They provide decoration today.

5. Some of New York City's stone animals are puzzling, such as a monkey holding a camera on one Victorian-style building. A fish smiles on the front of a restaurant. A doctor's office door has a squirrel chewing a nut on it.

Using parallelism in outlines and lists   **18h**

Items in formal outlines and lists must be parallel in grammar and structure. (For information about other issues of outline format and about how to develop an outline, see 2n.)

FORMAL OUTLINE NOT IN PARALLEL FORM

Reducing Traffic Fatalities

I. Stricter laws

    A. Top speed should be 50 m.p.h. on highways.

    B. Higher fines

    C. Requiring jail sentences for repeat offenders

II. The use of safety devices should be mandated by law.

FORMAL OUTLINE IN PARALLEL FORM

Reducing Traffic Fatalities

I. **Passing** stricter speed laws

    A. **Making** 50 m.p.h. the top speed on highways

    B. **Raising** fines for speeding

    C. **Requiring** jail sentences for repeat offenders

II. **Mandating** by law the use of safety devices

ANSWERS AND COVERAGE: EXERCISE 18–3, cont.

4. Often bad bosses communicate poorly or fail to calculate the impact of their personality on others; *good bosses listen carefully and are sensitive to others' responses.* [18f, parallel sentence structures]

5. Employees *who take the trouble to understand what makes their boss tick, who engage in some self-analysis, and who stay flexible* [18e, repeating parallel function words] are better prepared to cope with a difficult job environment than employees *who suffer in silence.* [18d–3, parallel form with *than*]

ANSWERS AND COVERAGE: EXERCISE 18–4

Answers may vary. Here is one set of possibilities.

1. A bulldog glares at pedestrians from the door of a fancy apartment building, *a pair of magnificent lions guards* the Fifth Avenue entrance to the New York Public Library, *and a couple of thoughtful pelicans perched high on a rooftop regard* the passing parade of life. [18f, parallelism among sentences]

2. These architectural animals were made not only of stone, *but also of terra cotta, metal, and other more unusual materials.* [18d–2, parallelism with correlative conjunction *not only*]

3. A group of stone animal lovers is cataloguing New York City's stone zoo *that stretches across five boroughs and that includes* such rare specimens as quahogs, crocodiles, and vultures. [18e, repeating function words]

4. Once, the stone animals were thought to provide protection by warding off evil spirits; today, they provide decoration. [18f, balanced sentences]

➜

5. Some of New York City's stone animals are puzzling, such as a monkey holding a camera on one Victorian-style building, a *fish smiling on the front of a restaurant, and a squirrel chewing a nut on a doctor's office door.* [18e, clauses]

TEACHING TIP

Parallelism is easily found in advertising, public speeches, and promotional letters. You might ask students to bring to class examples that they see on television, or find in advertisements in magazines, newspapers, or their mail. You can then analyze the parallelism and discuss the effectiveness of the examples, including any instances of faulty parallelism (which appear in published material with surprising frequency).

ANSWERS AND COVERAGE: EXERCISE 18–5

Reducing Traffic Fatalities

I. Passing stricter speed laws
   A. Making 50 m.p.h. top speed on any highway
   B. Raising fine for first-time speeding offenders
   C. Requiring jail sentences for repeat offenders

II. Legislating installation and use of safety devices
   A. Requiring all automobiles to have safety belts in front and back seats
   B. Making seat belt use mandatory for all drivers
   C. Forcing auto manufacturers to offer airbags as an option in all cars

---

ANSWERS: EXERCISE 18–6

Answers will vary. See the answer to Exercise 18–2 for commentary on imitation as a learning device.

18h
cont.

Although a nonparallel outline might serve as an informal, scratch outline for a writer's private purposes in the early stages of the writing process, only a parallel outline is acceptable as a final draft.

FORMAL LIST NOT IN PARALLEL FORM

Workaholics share these characteristics:

1. They are intense and driven.
2. Strong self-doubters
3. Labor is preferred to leisure by workaholics.

FORMAL LIST IN PARALLEL FORM

Workaholics share these characteristics:

1. **They are** intense and driven.
2. **They have** strong self-doubts.
3. **They prefer** labor to leisure.

EXERCISE 18-5

Consulting section 18h, revise this outline into parallel form.

Reducing Traffic Fatalities

I. Stricter laws
   A. Top speed on any highway should be 50 m.p.h.
   B. Higher fines
   C. Repeat offenders sentenced to jail

II. Legislating installation of safety devices
   A. All automobiles should be required to have safety belts in both front and back seats.
   B. Making seat belt use mandatory for all drivers
   C. We should force auto manufacturers to offer airbags as an option in all cars.

EXERCISE 18-6

Find the parallel elements in the following examples. Next, using your own topics, imitate the style of two of the examples.

1. Our earth is but a small star in a great universe. Yet of it we can make, if we choose, a plane unvexed by war, untroubled by hunger or fear, undivided by senseless distinctions of race, color, or theory.

—STEPHEN VINCENT BENÉT

2. Some would recover almost entirely. Some would die. Some would come through unable to move their legs, or unable to move arms and legs; some could move nothing but an arm, or nothing but a few fingers and their eyes. Some would leave the hospital with a cane, some with crutches, crutches and steel leg braces, or in wheelchairs—white-faced, shrunken, with frightened eyes, light blankets over their legs. Some would remain in an iron lung—a great, eighteen-hundred-pound, casket-like contraption, like the one in which the woman in the magic show (her head and feet sticking out of either end) is sawed in half.

—CHARLES L. MEE, JR., "The Summer Before Salk"

3. I am lonely only when I am overtired, when I have worked too long without a break, when for the time being I feel empty and need filling up. And I am lonely sometimes when I come back home after a lecture trip, when I have seen a lot of people and talked a lot, and am full to the brim with experience that needs to be sorted out.

—MAY SARTON, "The Rewards of a Solitary Life"

4. What does it mean to be a man? What does it mean to be an Indian? What does it mean to be an Indian man?

—SHERMAN ALEXIE, "White Men Can't Drum"

5. Marlon Brando, mumbling and muttering and flashing with bolts of barbaric energy, freed theatrical emotion from its enslavement by words. He brought American nature to American acting. And he brought American personality to the world.

—CAMILLE PAGLIA, "Brando Flashing"

ALTERNATE EXAMPLES

Because parallelism gives statements a stately, dignified sound, it appears often in official declarations, as in the following.

1. . . . for the support of this declaration, with a firm reliance on the protection of Divine Providence, we mutually pledge to each other our Lives, our Fortunes, and our sacred Honor.
—The Declaration of Independence

2. It is rather for us to be here dedicated to the great task remaining before us—that from these honored dead we take increased devotion to that cause for which they gave the last full measure of devotion; that we here highly resolve that these dead shall not have died in vain; that this nation, under God, shall have a new birth of freedom; and that government of the people, by the people, for the people, shall not perish from the earth.
—Abraham Lincoln, from the Gettysburg Address

3. We are saddened; we are stunned; we are perplexed.
—Earl Warren, on the death of John Kennedy

19 *Variety and Emphasis*

REFERENCES TO SUPPLEMENTS

For this topic in the CLAST writing competency test, refer students to ch. 2, section B3a of *Preparing for the CLAST* by S. Patterson.

This topic is included in the TASP writing competency test. Refer students to *Preparing for the TASP* by M. Saenz.

For revising for variety and emphasis, refer students to *Rough Drafts* by K. S. Cain, Part III, Exercise 6.

See transparency 5–4 for revising for variety in the *Prentice Hall/Simon & Schuster Transparencies for Writers* by D. Carter.

TEACHING TIP

Students sometimes cannot perceive the contrast between short and long sentences. One helpful technique is to use highlighter pen on typewritten material to make either the short or the long sentences stand out from the rest of the passage. Another method is to make a transparency of your typewritten copy and ask the students to participate in deciding which sentences are long and which are short—and then underline or circle one type. Also, many computer style-checkers point out passages' variety or lack of variety in sentence length.

TEACHING TIP

In *Classical Rhetoric for the Modern Student*, 3rd ed. (New York: Oxford UP, 1990), pp. 415–416, Edward P. J. Corbett provides a simple chart enabling students to compare their sentences and paragraphs to the sentences and paragraphs in a piece by a professional writer:

➜

19a Understanding variety and emphasis

Your writing style has **variety** when your sentence lengths and patterns vary; see 19b and 19c. Your writing style is characterized by **emphasis** when your sentences are constructed to communicate the relative importance of their ideas. Strategies include choosing the subject of a sentence to highlight meaning (see 19d); adding MODIFIERS to basic sentences (see 19e); inverting standard word order (see 19f); and repeating important words or ideas (see 19g).

Consider the following passage, which successfully employs key techniques of variety and emphasis. The authors vary their sentence length (see 19b), include a variety of structures (see 19c), and use different kinds of modifiers in various positions (see 19e).

> Henri Poincaré, a famous mathematician who lived in the nineteenth century, devised an exercise in imagination to help people understand the relativity of measures. Imagine that one night while you were asleep everything in the universe became a thousand times larger than before. Remember this would include electrons, planets, all living creatures, your own body, and all the rulers and other measuring devices in the world. When you awoke, could you tell that anything had changed? Is there any experiment you could make to prove that some change had occurred? According to Poincaré there is no such experiment.
>
> —JUDITH AND HERBERT KOHL, *The View from the Oak*

The techniques of variety and emphasis can move your writing beyond being correct to having style and grace. Rarely do variety and emphasis emerge during DRAFTING. Until you are a very experienced writer, you might not be able to apply the principles in this chapter until you are REVISING.

19b Varying sentence length

When you use a variety of sentence lengths, you communicate clear distinctions among ideas. Such a style can help your readers understand the focus of your material. Also, such a style avoids the

368

unbroken rhythm of monotonous sentence length, which can lull your reader into inattention.

Revising strings of too many short sentences

Strings of too many short sentences rarely establish relationships and levels of importance among ideas. Readers cannot easily make distinctions between major and minor points. Such strings, unless deliberately planned in a longer piece of writing for occasional impact (see 19b-3), suggest that the writer has not thought through the material and decided what to emphasize. The style tends to read like that of young children.

NO There is a legend. This legend is about a seventeenth-century Algonquin Indian. It says that he was inspired. He had an idea about popcorn. He transformed it into a gift. It was the first gift to a hostess in American history. He was invited to the Pilgrims' harvest meal. He brought along a bag of popcorn. This was a demonstration of good will. The occasion is honored to this day with Thanksgiving dinner.

YES According to legend, in the seventeenth century an inspired Algonquin transformed popcorn into the first hostess gift in history. Invited to the Pilgrims' harvest meal, the Indian brought along a bag of popcorn as a demonstration of good will. The occasion is honored today with Thanksgiving dinner.

—Patricia Linden, "Popcorn"

In the revised version, the sentence structures permit key ideas to be featured. The two versions use almost the same short last sentence, but because the revised version leads up to it with longer sentences, the message in the last sentence is emphasized. In the revised version, ten sentences reduce to three and 74 words reduce to 47. (See also the explanation of conciseness, Chapter 16.)

Revising a string of too many compound sentences

A **compound sentence** consists of two or more INDEPENDENT CLAUSES that are grammatically equivalent and that communicate balance or sequence in the ideas that they contain (see 17a). Too often, compound sentences are short sentences only strung together with *and* or *but*, without consideration of the relationships among the ideas.

NO Science fiction writers are often thinkers, and they are often dreamers, so they let their imaginations wander. Jules Verne was such a writer, and he predicted space ships and atomic submarines, but most people did not believe airplanes were possible.

369

19b-1

19b-2

TEACHING TIP, cont.

Evaluation	Professional	Student
A. Total number of words in the piece studied	_____	_____
B. Total number of sentences in the piece studied	_____	_____
C. Longest sentence (in no. of words)	_____	_____
D. Shortest sentence (in no. of words)	_____	_____
E. Average sentence (in no. of words)	_____	_____
F. Number of sentences that contain more than 10 words *over* the average sentence	_____	_____
G. Percentage of sentences that contain more than 10 words *over* the average sentence	_____	_____
H. Number of sentences that total 5 words or more *below* the average	_____	_____
I. Percentage of sentences that total 5 words or more below the average	_____	_____
J. Paragraph length longest paragraph (in no. of sentences)	_____	_____

→

19b-2
cont.

TEACHING TIP, cont.

shortest
paragraph
(in no. of
sentences)   ____   ____

average
paragraph
(in no. of
sentences)   ____   ____

You might want to try Corbett's analysis on a piece that you have written and share the results with the class.

TEACHING TIP

You might want to read aloud the following passage from Truman Capote's "A Christmas Memory," using a single breath for each sentence. In a second reading, you might pause after each sentence for students to guess how many words are in it. After the number of words in each has been announced, students can try drawing a graph of the paragraph based on the length of the sentences. (The word count follows each sentence in brackets.)

Morning. [1] Frozen rime lusters the grass; the sun, round as an orange and orange as hot-weather moons, balances on the horizon, burnishes the silvered winter woods. [26] A wild turkey calls. [4] A renegade hog grunts in the undergrowth. [7] Soon, by the edge of knee-deep, rapid-running water, we have to abandon the buggy. [16] Queenie wades the stream first, paddles across barking complaints at the swiftness of the current, the pneumonia-making coldness of it. [21] We follow, holding our shoes and equipment (a hatchet, a burlap sack) above our heads. [15] A mile more: of chastising horns, burs and briers that catch at our clothes; of rusty pine needles brilliant with gaudy fungus and molted feathers. [25] Here, there, a flash, a flutter, an ecstasy of shrilling remind us that not all the birds have flown south. [20]

19b-3

YES   Science fiction writers are often thinkers and dreamers who let their imaginations wander. Jules Verne was one such writer. He predicted space ships and atomic submarines before most people believed airplanes were possible.

In the revised version, the relationships among the ideas are clear and key ideas are featured. In the last sentence, a particularly obscure connection is clarified. For conciseness, one independent clause is reduced to a word, *dreamers;* another is reduced to a RELATIVE CLAUSE, *who let their imaginations wander;* another starts a new sentence, *He predicted . . . ;* and another is reduced to a SUBORDINATE CLAUSE, *before most people . . . possible.*

Revising for a suitable mix of sentence lengths

To emphasize one idea among many others, you can express it in a sentence noticeably different in length or structure from the sentences surrounding it. Consider this passage, which carries its emphasis in one short sentence among longer ones:

Today is one of those excellent January partly cloudies in which light chooses an unexpected landscape to trick out in gilt, and then shadow sweeps it away. **You know you are alive.** You take huge steps, trying to feel the planet's roundness arc between your feet. Kazantzakis says that when he was young he had a canary and a globe. When he freed the canary, it would perch on the globe and sing. All his life, wandering the earth, he felt as though he had a canary on top of his mind, singing.

—ANNIE DILLARD, *Pilgrim at Tinker Creek*

A long sentence among shorter ones is equally effective.

Mistakes are not believed to be part of the normal behavior of a good machine. **If things go wrong, it must be a personal, human error, the result of fingering, tampering, a button getting stuck, someone hitting the wrong key.** The computer, at its normal best, is infallible. I wonder whether this can be true.

—LEWIS THOMAS, "To Err Is Human"

EXERCISE 19-1

Consulting sections 19a and 19b, revise these sets of sentences to vary the sentence lengths effectively.

1. Secondhand jeans have become international status symbols. A new generation of teenagers around the world embraces U.S. pop culture. The entrepreneurs are ready. West of the Mississippi River a thriving

underground industry has emerged. This industry buys, washes, and repairs vintage Levi's. These jeans are resold in many countries. Japan provides the largest market for them.

2. United States rock-and-roll clothes from the 1960s are also popular throughout the world, and so are used Air Jordan sneakers from the 1980s, but the big winner is still blue jeans. The most popular brand is the Levi's 501, and Levi's 501s have been made by Levi Strauss & Company since 1873, and the Levi's 501 button-fly style is no longer made and it is the biggest winner of them all. Most used button-fly Levis are found in the western United States, and the reason for this is that people who lived in the eastern states with long, cold winters have always preferred the zipper fly, it doesn't let in chilly air.

3. Even though the business is highly profitable, the cultural history of old clothes hooks most dealers, some of whom can tell fascinating tales of their collecting adventures. One dealer spent a week buying clothes of the Great Depression from a woman in Oklahoma whose mother had saved the family wardrobe, which clearly showed the economic hardships they had endured since all the jeans were covered with patches, more than a hundred on one pair alone.

Using an occasional question, mild command, or exclamation   19c

To vary your sentence structure and to emphasize material, you can call on four basic sentence types. The most common English sentence is **declarative.** A declarative sentence makes a statement—it declares something. Declarative sentences offer an almost infinite variety of structures and patterns.

A sentence that asks a question is called **interrogative.** Occasional questions can help you involve your reader. A sentence that issues a mild or strong command is called **imperative.** Occasional mild commands are particularly helpful for gently urging your reader to think along with you. A sentence that makes an exclamation is called **exclamatory.**

❖ PUNCTUATION ALERT: A mild command ends with a period. A strong command or an exclamation ends with an exclamation mark. (see 23e)❖

Consider the following paragraph, which uses the three basic sentence types found most frequently in academic writing: declarative, interrogative, and imperative.

Imagine what people ate during the winter as little as seventy-five years ago. They ate food that was local, long-lasting, and dull, like acorn squash, turnips, and cabbage. Walk into an American super-

!

In this exercise, the first item has too many short sentences, the second too many compounds, the third long and complicated sentences. Students will revise in various ways. Here is one set of possibilities.

1. Secondhand jeans have become international status symbols as a new generation of teenagers embraces U.S. pop culture. The entrepreneurs are ready. West of the Mississippi River a thriving underground industry has emerged that buys, washes, and repairs vintage Levi's. The jeans are resold in many countries, with Japan providing the largest market.

2. United States rock-and-roll clothes from the 1960s are also popular throughout the world. So are used Air Jordan sneakers from the 1980s. However, the big winner is still blue jeans. The most popular brand is the Levi's 501, made by Levi Strauss & Company since 1873. The Levi's 501 button-fly style, which is no longer made, is the biggest winner of them all. Most used button-fly Levis are found in the western U.S. People who lived in the eastern states with long, cold winters have always preferred the zipper fly that doesn't let in chilly air.

3. Even though the business is highly profitable, the cultural history of old clothes hooks most dealers. Some can tell fascinating tales of their collecting adventures. One dealer spent a week buying clothes of the Great Depression from a woman in Oklahoma whose mother had saved the family wardrobe. The clothes clearly showed the economic hardships they had endured. All the jeans were covered with patches; one pair alone had more than a hundred.

ANSWERS: EXERCISE 19–2

Answers may vary. Ask students to explain their choices. Here is one set of possibilities.

1. Easy Jet, a multi-race winner, was sold for 30 million dollars. That is more than the average combined yearly income of a town of 2,000 people!

2. What might the popularity of horse racing suggest about the American national character? We may be a nation of gamblers. On the other hand, we simply may want financial independence.

3. Tradition holds that no race horse can have a name that contains more than eighteen letters. Apostrophes, hyphens, and spaces count in the total! Longer names would take up too much room on written records.

4. Lotteries have become as popular as horse racing. Many states run lotteries to raise money for basic services earlier provided from taxes. Did you know that in many states school books are purchased with funds gambled on lottery tickets?

5. Some television commercials for lotteries show winners riding in limousines. Most lottery ticket holders lose, though. That tempting chance to win a million dollars has odds worse than a million to one!

TEACHING TIP

In *Revising Prose*, 3rd ed. (New York: Macmillan, 1992), Richard A. Lanham lays out the eight-step "Paramedic Method" to help writers to revise sentences for emphasis, clarity, and conciseness.

1. Circle the prepositions.
2. Circle the "is" forms.
3. Ask, "Where's the action?" "Who's kicking who?"

➡

19c
cont.

market in February and the world lies before you: grapes, melons, artichokes, fennel, lettuce, peppers, pistachios, dates, even strawberries, to say nothing of ice cream. Have you ever considered what a triumph of civilization it is to be able to buy a pound of chicken livers? If you lived on a farm and had to kill a chicken when you wanted to eat one, you wouldn't ever accumulate a pound of chicken livers.

—Phyllis Rose, "Shopping and Other Spiritual Adventures in America Today"

EXERCISE 19-2

The paragraph below effectively varies sentence lengths and uses a question and a command. The result emphasizes the key points. Write an imitation of this paragraph, closely following all aspects except the topic. Choose your own topic.

EXAMPLE   If your topic were gardens, your first sentence might be: *Why do most people plant tomatoes in their gardens when they know they will harvest many more tomatoes than the average family wants to eat in a whole year?*

Why do most Americans spend $95 a year to operate their clothes dryers when Nature provides free energy for the same task? Consider the humble clothesline and clothespins. They cost about $30 for a lifetime and solar power is free, unlike an electric dryer, which can cost as much as $500. In an increasingly mechanized indoor life, people who hang their clothes on the line are obliged to notice the weather. Today is a perfect morning for drying, they think. Or: Will it rain this afternoon? Another line in the basement or spare room works well in rainy weather and in winter. Indoor drying has the further benefit of humidifying the house; twenty pounds of wet wash contributes about one gallon of water to the air.

19d

Choosing the subject of a sentence according to your intended emphasis

The SUBJECT of a sentence establishes the focus for that sentence. The subject you choose should correspond to the emphasis that you want to communicate to your reader.

Each of the following sentences, all of which are correct grammatically, contains the same information. Consider, however, how changes of the subject (and its VERB) influence meaning and impact.

Our study showed that 25 percent of college students' time is spent eating or sleeping. [Focus is on the study.]

College students eat or sleep 25 percent of the time, according to our study. [Focus is on the student.]

Eating or sleeping occupies 25 percent of college students' time, according to our study. [Focus is on eating and sleeping.]

Twenty-five percent of college students' time is spent eating or sleeping, according to our study. [Focus is on the percentage of time.]

Adding modifiers to basic sentences for variety and emphasis   19e

Adding MODIFIERS to basic sentences can provide you with a rich variety of sentence patterns.

Expanding basic sentences with modifiers   19e-1

Sentences that consist only of a subject and verb usually seem very thin. You might use a very short sentence for its dramatic effect in emphasizing an idea (see 19b-3). When you want to avoid a very short sentence, however, you can expand the basic sentence as illustrated in Chart 95. Your decision to expand a basic sentence will depend on the focus of each sentence and how it works in concert with its surrounding sentences.

WAYS TO EXPAND A BASIC SENTENCE		95
BASIC SENTENCE	The river rose.	
ADJECTIVE	The **swollen** river rose.	
ADVERB	The river rose **dangerously.**	
PREPOSITIONAL PHRASE	**In April,** the river rose **above its banks.**	
PARTICIPIAL PHRASES	**Swollen by melting snow,** the river rose, **flooding the farmland.**	
ABSOLUTE PHRASE	**Trees swirling away in the current,** the river rose.	
ADVERB CLAUSE	**Because the snows had been heavy that winter,** the river rose.	
ADJECTIVE CLAUSE	The river, **which runs through vital farmland,** rose.	

WAYS TO EXPAND A BASIC SENTENECE

TEACHING TIP, cont.

4. Put this "kicking" action in a simple (not compound) active verb.

5. Start fast—no slow windups.

6. Write out each sentence on a blank sheet of paper and mark off its basic rhythmic units with a "/".

7. Read the passage aloud with emphasis and feeling.

8. Mark off sentence lengths in the passage with a "/" (47).

REFERENCES TO SUPPLEMENTS

For this topic in the CLAST writing competency test, refer students to ch. 1, section B4e of *Preparing for the CLAST* by S. Patterson.

This topic is included in the TASP writing competency test. Refer your students to *Preparing for the TASP* by M. Saenz.

BACKGROUND

Adding modifiers to basic sentences is the central feature of the "generative rhetoric" developed by Francis Christensen in *Notes Toward a New Rhetoric* (New York: Harper & Row, 1967) and *The Christensen Rhetoric Program* (New York: Harper & Row, 1968). The Christensen program teaches students various ways to expand a sentence by showing them model sentences, giving students a basic sentence and having them expand it following the pattern of the models, and then having students compose their own sentences according to that pattern. These exercises not only develop the style of students but also teach them ways of elaborating their ideas.

ANSWERS AND COVERAGE: EXERCISE 19–3

Students are to expand each sentence by adding (a) an adjective, (b) an adverb, (c) a prepositional phrase, (d) a participial phrase, (e) an absolute phrase, (f) an adverb clause, and (g) an adjective clause. They can refer for guidance to the expansion techniques shown in Chart 104. Here is a possible set of answers for item 1:

a. We went to the *county* fair.

b. We went *happily* to the fair.

c. We went to the fair *in the park.*

d. *Tired of studying*, we went to the fair, *looking for a good time.*

e. *Textbooks left open on our desks*, we went to the fair.

f. After we *finished studying*, we went to the fair.

g. We went to the fair, *which had just opened.*

BACKGROUND

Periodic and cumulative sentences work by placing the weight of a sentence's message at one end. On the other hand, the balanced sentence, using the concept of parallel structure, presents two equally weighted pieces of meaning. Usually a punctuation mark and/or a coordinating conjunction acts as a centerpoint upon which the meaning balances, much like a see-saw on its base.

Freedom is the right to be wrong, not the right to do wrong.

—John Diefenbaker

QUOTATION ABOUT WRITING

I think the single most important factor in any writing is its rhythm. A badly balanced sentence jars on me with something like physical pain!

—Helen Cresswell

19e-1
cont.

EXERCISE 19-3

Consulting section 19e-1, expand each sentence by adding (a) an ADJECTIVE, (b) an ADVERB, (c) a PREPOSITIONAL PHRASE, (d) a PARTICIPIAL PHRASE, (e) an ABSOLUTE PHRASE, (f) an ADVERB CLAUSE, and (g) an ADJECTIVE CLAUSE.

1. We went to the fair.
2. The ride was full.
3. I won a basketball.
4. Rain poured from the sky.
5. Both of us got our clothes wet.

19e-2

Positioning modifiers to create variety and emphasis

Research on learning suggests that readers are more likely to retain the message that is at the very beginning or the very end of a sentence. Although you do not have unlimited choices about where to place modifiers, you often have options. Try to place a modifier according to the emphasis that you want to achieve. At the same time, be sure to place a modifier precisely within a sentence so that you avoid the error of misplaced modifiers (see 15b).

A sentence that starts with a SUBJECT and VERB and then provides additional information with modifiers that appear after the subject and verb is called a **cumulative sentence.** The cumulative sentence is the most common sentence structure in English; it is called "cumulative" because information accumulates. Sometimes the cumulative sentence is referred to as a **loose sentence** because it lacks the tightly planned structure of other sentence varieties. Such sentences, easy to read because they reflect how humans receive and pass on information, often do not provide impact, however.

In contrast, a **periodic sentence,** also called a *climactic sentence,* is highly emphatic. It builds up to the period, reserving the main idea for the end of the sentence. It draws the reader in as it builds to its climax. Periodic sentences can be very effective, but if they are overused they lose their punch.

PERIODIC At midnight last night, on the road from Las Vegas to Death Valley Junction, **a car hit a shoulder and turned over.**

—JOAN DIDION, "On Morality"

CUMULATIVE **A car hit a shoulder and turned over** at midnight last night on the road from Las Vegas to Death Valley Junction.

Another way to vary sentence structures is to start sentences with introductory words, PHRASES, or CLAUSES. (For a discussion of commas with introductory material, see 24b.)

WORD	**Fortunately,** I taught myself to read before I had to face boring reading drills in school.

—ANDREW FURMAN, student

PHRASE	**Along with cereal boxes and ketchup labels,** comic books were the primers that taught me how to read.

—GLORIA STEINEM

CLAUSE	**Long before I wrote stories,** I listened for stories.

—EUDORA WELTY, *One Writer's Beginnings*

Often, modifiers may appear in several different positions within a sentence. Positioning modifiers offers you a chance to enhance your writing style with variety and emphasis. Here are sentences with the same modifiers in various positions. If you use this technique, be very careful to avoid placing modifiers in positions that create ambiguous meaning (see 15b-1).

Angrily the physician slammed down the chart, **sternly** speaking to the patient.

The physician slammed down the chart **angrily,** speaking **sternly** to the patient.

The physician **angrily** slammed down the chart, speaking to the patient **sternly.**

EXERCISE 19-4

Consulting section 19e, combine each set of sentences by changing one sentence to a clause, phrase, or word that will modify the other sentence.

EXAMPLE   The ancestor of our pencil was the penicillum. The penicillum was a brush made of animal hairs that the Romans used for writing and drawing.

The ancestor of our pencil was the penicillum, *a brush made of animal hairs that the Romans used for writing and drawing.* [sentence changed to phrase]

375

ANSWERS AND COVERAGE: EXERCISE 19–4

Answers will vary. Here is one set of possibilities.

1. *According to the 1771 edition of the Encyclopedia Britannica* [phrase], these early writing implements were made of boar bristles, the hair of camels, badgers, and squirrels, and the down feathers of swans.

2. Graphite, a form of the element carbon, was to become the *main* [word] component of pencil lead.

3. *In the late 1600s* [phrase], cabinetmakers were producing the first version of the modern pencil by encasing strips of graphite in wood.

4. *Following the sandwich-making principle,* [phrase] they sliced a strip of wood, cut a groove down the middle, glued the lead into the groove, then glued the two halves together.

5. At one time the ingredients of a fine pencil came from the geographically diverse areas of Siberia, *where the purest graphite was mined* [clause] and Florida, *where the best red cedar was grown.* [clause]

6. When an acute shortage of Southern red cedar developed in the United States during the early 1900s, *desperate* [word] pencil manufacturers bought old cedar fence posts.

7. The pencil makers had to substitute another kind of cedar, *so they dyed and perfumed it to match people's expectations of how a pencil should look and smell.* [clause]

8. Pencils have had some unlikely promoters, such as the naturalist and writer Henry David Thoreau, *who helped his father produce the highest-quality pencils in America during the 1840s.* [clause]

9. The inventor Thomas Edison engaged a pencil factory to produce specially made stubby pencils just for him *because he preferred short pencils.* [clause]

➡

10. *Lacking a pencil,* [phrase] the Scottish poet Robert Burns once used his diamond ring to scratch verses on a windowpane.

ALTERNATE EXAMPLE

The following passage from a student paper employs different sentence types. You may want to discuss with students the effect of the mixture.

I froze when the voice said "Stop!" What did it want, I wondered, this voice that came from out of the shadows to my left? Although my knees were shaking, I hoped my voice would be steady. "What for?" I asked. "Because I said so, that's why. Don't go anywhere—yet." I didn't move, except that my eyes were almost popping out of my head trying to see the person with the voice. "Where's your car?" the voice asked. "Take me to it." "It's parked several blocks away," I objected. "Then go get it. Now!" "How do you know I'll come back?" I asked. "Because," the voice groaned, "I don't think you'd leave your best friend sitting in the street with a sprained ankle." "Well why didn't you say that in first place!" I shouted, then went to see if I could help Mike, the voice I thought I would know anywhere.

ALTERNATE EXAMPLES

You might ask your students to explain the differences in emphasis in these sentences, which contain the same information presented in various ways.

1. Revelers wear bizarre costumes and dance in the streets on Mardi Gras, a day of carefree indulgence.

2. The bizarre costumes and dancing of revelers attract attention on Mardi Gras, a day of carefree indulgence.

3. Mardi Gras is a day of carefree indulgence marked by revelers' bizarre costumes and street dancing.

19e-2
cont.

1. These early writing implements were made of boar bristles, the hair of camels, badgers, and squirrels, and the down feathers of swans. This is according to the 1771 edition of the *Encyclopaedia Britannica*.

2. Graphite, a form of the element carbon, was to become a component of pencil lead. It would be the main component.

3. Cabinetmakers were producing the first version of the modern pencil by encasing strips of graphite in wood. This happened in the late 1600s.

4. They followed the sandwich-making principle. They sliced a strip of wood, cut a groove down the middle, glued the lead into the groove, then glued the two halves together.

5. At one time the ingredients of a fine pencil came from the geographically diverse areas of Siberia and Florida. Siberia is where the purest graphite was mined. Florida is where the best red cedar was grown.

6. When an acute shortage of southern red cedar developed in the United States during the early 1900s, pencil manufacturers bought old cedar fence posts. They were desperate.

7. The pencil makers had to substitute another kind of cedar. They dyed and perfumed it to match people's expectations of how a pencil should look and smell.

8. Pencils have had some unlikely promoters, such as the naturalist and writer Henry David Thoreau. He helped his father produce the highest-quality pencils in America during the 1840s.

9. The inventor Thomas Edison engaged a pencil factory to produce specially made stubby pencils just for him. He preferred short pencils.

10. The Scottish poet Robert Burns once lacked a pencil. He used his diamond ring to scratch verses on a windowpane.

19f   **Inverting standard word order**

Standard word order in the English sentence places the SUBJECT before the VERB. Because this pattern is so common, it is set in people's minds, so any variation creates emphasis. Inverted word order places the verb before the subject. Used too often, inverted word order can be distracting; but used sparingly, it can be very effective.

STANDARD	**The mayor walked** in. **The governor walked** out.
INVERTED	In **walked the mayor.** Out **walked the governor.**
STANDARD	**Responsibilities begin** in dreams.
INVERTED	In dreams **begin responsibilities.**

—DELMORE SCHWARTZ, "In Dreams Begin Responsibilities"

Repeating important words or ideas to achieve emphasis

You can repeat some words to help emphasize meaning, but choose the words carefully. Repeat only those words that contain a main idea or that use rhythm to focus attention on a main idea. Consider this passage, which uses deliberate repetition along with a variety of sentence lengths to deliver its meaning.

> Coal is **black** and it warms your house and cooks your food. The night is **black,** which has a moon, and a million stars, and is beautiful. Sleep is **black** which gives you rest, so you wake up **feeling good.** I am **black.** I feel very **good** this evening.
>
> —LANGSTON HUGHES, "That Word *Black*"

Hughes repeats the word *black,* each time linking it to something related to joy and beauty. The rhythm that results from the deliberate repetition of *black* and *good* emphasizes Hughes's message and helps the reader remember it.

Be sure to use deliberate repetition sparingly, with central words, and only when your meaning justifies such a technique. Consider this passage, which is the result of limited vocabulary and a dull, unvaried style. Although few synonyms exist for the words *an insurance agent, car,* and *model,* some do. Also, the sentence structure has no variety.

NO   **An insurance agent** can be an excellent advisor when you want to buy a **car. An insurance agent** has records on most **cars. An insurance agent** knows which **models** tend to have most accidents. **An insurance agent** can tell you which **models** are the most expensive to repair if they are in a collision. **An insurance agent** can tell you which **models** are most likely to be stolen.

YES   If you are thinking of buying a new car, an insurance agent can be an excellent advisor. An insurance broker has complete records on most automobiles. For example, he or she knows which models are accident prone. Did you know that some car designs suffer more damage than others in a collision? If you want to know which automobiles crumple more than others and which are least expensive to repair, ask an insurance agent. Similarly, some models are more likely to be stolen, so find out from the person who specializes in dealing with claims.

EXERCISE 19-5

Consulting all sections of this chapter, revise this paragraph to achieve emphasis through varied sentence length and deliberate repetition. You can

ANSWERS AND COVERAGE: EXERCISE 19–5

Answers will vary. One possible revision is shown here.

One of civilization's great technological innovations, [19e, sentence converted into appositive to modify] the chimney represents a major step up from a hole in the roof or a slit in the wall. *In the warm climates of ancient Egypt and Mesopotamia* [19e-2, modifiers positioned for effect] the heating of houses was not an urgent problem. *So scholars believed* [19e-2, positioning modifiers for effect, with *this* changed to *so*] until a *4000-year-old palace that was peppered with chimneys* was uncovered during a recent excavation of the great lost city of Mari on the upper Euphrates River in ancient Persia. [19b-1, short sentences combined] Along came the Romans two thousand years later. [19f, inverting standard word order] The Romans, *who* were [19b-2, sentence converted into relative clause] engineering geniuses, developed elaborate chimneys as part of their heating systems. *After the Roman empire fell in the fourth century* A.D., *nobody* [19b-1, short sentences combined into one] from the former colonies knew how to make chimneys. For four centuries, western Europe had no chimneys. *How did chimneys finally get to western Europe?* [19c, revised to question] Nobody is quite sure. [19b-3, revised for short sentence] *A current theory holds that* around A.D. 800, chimneys were brought *by* Syrian and Egyptian traders from the East. [19b-3, short sentences combined into one long sentence for mix of sentence lengths]

ANSWERS AND COVERAGE: EXERCISE 19–6

Answers will vary. This is a summary exercise, so it should reflect many of the techniques of variety and emphasis discussed in this chapter. Here is one answer; many others are possible.

Born in 1809 [19e-1, participial phrase to modify] French educator Louis Braille became blind at three years of age [19b-1, combined two short sentences], and he was enrolled at the Institute for the Blind [19b-3, compound sentence to vary sentence lengths] in Paris [19e-1, prepositional phrase to modify] when he was ten [19e-1, adverb clause to modify]. Braille devised for blind people a writing system that consisted of raised dots on paper [19e-1, adjective clause to modify]. At the time of this accomplishment of enormous benefit to humanity, Braille was only twenty [19e-2, periodic sentence]. Braille's system used 43 configurations of raised dots to represent individual letters of the alphabet, some combinations of letters, and some punctuation marks [19b-1, revised string of too many short sentences]. A modified version is still used today [19b-3, no change because effective short sentence among long sentences]. Did you know that Louis Braille was also a distinguished musician [19c, a question to vary sentence structures]? So talented was he [19f, inverted word order] that as an adult he played the violoncello and the organ to great acclaim throughout Paris [19e-1, prepositional phrases to modify]. Sadly, Braille died when only 43 years of age [no change].

ANSWERS: EXERCISE 19–7

Using their own topics, students imitate the variety and emphasis of two different passages shown in this chapter. They can choose from the Kohls, Dillard, Thomas, or Hughes. For a discussion of the technique of imitation, see the answer to Exercise 18–2.

reduce or increase the number of sentences, and you can drop words to reduce unneeded repetition. Each writer's revision will vary somewhat, but try to include at least one revision to a question or exclamation (19c) and one revision to an inverted word order (19f).

The chimney is one of civilization's great technological innovations. The chimney represents a major step up from a hole in the roof or a slit in the wall. The heating of houses was not an urgent problem in the warm climates of ancient Egypt and Mesopotamia. Scholars believed this until a palace was uncovered during a recent excavation of the great lost city of Mari on the upper Euphrates River in ancient Persia. The palace, which was 4,000 years old, was peppered with chimneys. Two thousand years later the Romans came along. The Romans were engineering geniuses. The Romans developed elaborate chimneys as part of their hot-air heating systems. The Roman empire declined in the fourth century A.D., and after then no one from the former colonies knew how to make chimneys. For four centuries western Europe had no chimneys. So the simple question has always been how chimneys finally got to western Europe. Nobody is quite sure, but here is what a current theory holds. Around A.D. 800, chimneys were brought by Syrian and Egyptian traders. They were from the East.

EXERCISE 19-6

Consulting all sections of this chapter, use techniques of variety and emphasis to revise the following paragraph.

French educator Louis Braille was born in 1809. He became blind at three years of age. He was enrolled at the Institute for the Blind when he was ten. The Institute was in Paris. Braille devised a writing system for blind people consisting of raised dots on paper. Braille's accomplishment was of enormous benefit to many people. At the time, he was only twenty years old. Braille's system used 43 configurations of raised dots. Some symbols represented individual letters of the alphabet. Other symbols stood for some combinations of letters. Still other symbols stood for some punctuation marks. A modified version is still used today. Few people know that Louis Braille was also a distinguished musician. He was so talented that as an adult he played the violoncello and the organ to great acclaim. He was known throughout Paris for his playing. Sadly, Braille died when only 43 years of age.

EXERCISE 19-7

Using topics you choose, imitate the variety and emphasis of two different passages shown in this chapter. Select from the quotations from the Kohls, Dillard, Thomas, or Hughes.

Using Effective Words

When you use words effectively, you choose words that communicate your message precisely. Part Five alerts you to the meanings that reside in words and the effect that words have on your readers. As you use Chapters 20 through 22, keep in mind that words work in concert with effective sentence structures and paragraphs to create good writing.

20 *Understanding the Meaning of Words*

BACKGROUND

The earliest dictionary, really a combination grammar and dictionary, was a tablet from Sumerian Nippur that attempted to enunciate the rules of language use. Not until the early seventeenth century was the first English dictionary produced by Henry Cockeram. The earliest attempt to list all the words in the English language was Nathaniel Bailey's *Universal Etymological English Dictionary* of 1721. Mulcaster had urged such a compilation as far back as 1582, but the only result was Robert Cawdrey's *Table Alphabeticall of Hard Words* (about 3,000 of them) published in 1604. Following Bailey's effort, dictionary makers dutifully tried to include all words, not just the difficult ones. Consequently, the seventeenth and eighteenth centuries saw the size of dictionaries grow substantially. Further innovations included Samuel Johnson's use of quotations to exemplify usage in his *Dictionary of the English Language* (1755) and Noah Webster's inclusion of quotations from the Founding Fathers in his *An American Dictionary of the English Language* (1828). Webster's nationalistic feelings were also evident in his insistence on American spellings.

American English, evolving over centuries into a rich language, reflects the many cultures that have merged in our melting-pot society. The earliest varieties of American English can be traced from sixteenth-century Elizabethan English—the language of Shakespeare. As the United States expanded, so did American English. Changes from Elizabethan forms occurred in vocabulary, spelling, and syntactic patterns. Distinctly American words originated colloquially—in spoken language—and words from all the cultures settling the United States became part of the language. Food names, for example, show how other languages and cultures loaned words to English. Africans brought the words *okra, gumbo,* and *goober* (peanut); Spanish and Latin American peoples contributed *tortilla, taco, burrito,* and *enchilada.* Greek gave us *pita,* Cantonese *chow* and *chop suey,* and Japanese *sushi.* American English creates a truly international *smorgasbord,* a Swedish word meaning "a wide variety of appetizers and other tasty foods."

Etymology is the study of the origins and historical development of words, including changes in form and meaning. For example, *alphabet* originates from the names of the first two letters in Greek: *a = alpha, b = beta.* The meanings of some words change with time. For example, W. Nelson Francis points out in *The English Language,* the word *nice* "has been used at one time or another in its 700-year history to mean . . . foolish, wanton, strange, lazy, coy, modest, fastidious, refined, precise, subtle, slender, critical, attentive, minutely accurate, dainty, appetizing, agreeable."

To use American English well, you want to be aware of the kinds of information that dictionaries offer (20a), to know how to choose exact words (20b), and to use strategies that actively build your vocabulary (20c).

Using dictionaries

20a

Good dictionaries show how language has been used and is currently being used. Each dictionary entry gives the meaning of the word and much additional important information. Many dictionaries also include essays on the history and use of language.

Understanding all parts of a dictionary entry

20a-1

A dictionary entry usually includes items 1 through 11, and sometimes 12 and 13, in the list that starts below. As you use the list, consult the entry shown here for *celebrate*, from *Webster's New World Dictionary*, Third College Edition.

Dictionary Entry for *Celebrate*

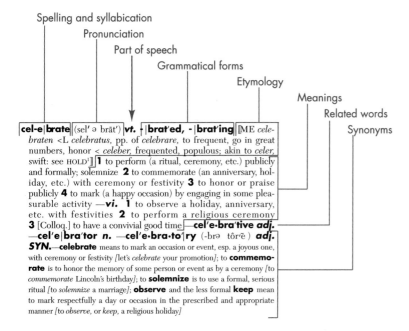

1. **Spelling.** If more than one spelling is shown, the first is the most commonly used, and the others are acceptable.

    Celebrate has only one spelling.

2. **Word Division.** Dots (or bars, in some dictionaries) separate the syllables of a word. Writers can hyphenate at syllables as long as the rules in section 22d are not violated. To help writers, *Webster's New*

20a-1
cont.

TEACHING TIP

Words dealing with cooking or food are often put to other uses. You can ask students to find the original meanings of the following words, then to write sentences in which they are used in situations that have nothing to do with food.

1. hodgepodge (a pot of beans, meat, and barley)
2. goulash (a Hungarian stew)
3. mishmash (an English stew dating back to the fifteenth century)
4. pastiche (a meat pie)
5. smorgasbord (a Swedish buffet)

TEACHING TIP

Students may find it interesting to discover that different dictionaries do not always provide the same information about specific words. To identify some differences (and even contradictions), you can ask students to bring to class their findings about the spelling, pronunciation, syllabification, etymology, and usage of the following words. Where differences appear, students can question and discuss the reasons for them.

1. gumbo
2. cab
3. broadcast
4. rhetoric
5. nachos

WORD DERIVATION

Georgia was named for King George II of England. *Virginia* was named for Elizabeth I, who was known as the Virgin Queen. Naming new territories after monarchs and their family members was a common practice among explorers who wanted to gain favor or give thanks for patronage.

World Dictionary, Third College Edition, uses a hairline (a thin vertical line) to indicate any syllable that should not be used for hyphenating.

> *Cel•e|brate* has three syllables: *cel, e,* and *brate.* This dictionary recommends hyphenating the word *cel-ebrate* but not *cele-brate.*

3. **Pronunciation.** The symbols in parentheses show pronunciation. If more than one pronunciation is given, the first is the most common, and the others are acceptable. A guide to the pronunciation of the symbols appears in the front of most dictionaries, and some dictionaries provide a brief guide to the most common symbols at the bottom of pages.

> *Celebrate* is pronounced *sel' ə brāt.* The accent mark after the *l* shows that the stressed syllable is *sel.* The unusual looking symbol ə, called a *schwa,* is pronounced "uh," as in *ago.* The line over the **a** indicates the long **a** sound, as in *ate.*

4. **Part of Speech Labels.** Abbreviations, explained in the front of the dictionary, indicate parts of speech. Many words can function as more than one part of speech.

> *Celebrate* is a TRANSITIVE VERB* **(vt.),** for which four definitions are given; also, it is an INTRANSITIVE VERB **(vi.),** for which three definitions are given.

5. **Grammatical Forms.** This information tells of variations in grammar: for a VERB, its principal parts and form variations; for a NOUN, its plural if formed other than by adding only -*s;* for an ADJECTIVE or ADVERB, its comparative and superlative forms.

> The principal parts of the verb *celebrate* are *celebrated* and *celebrating.*

6. **Etymology.** This information traces the way that the word has evolved through other languages over the years to become the word and meaning in current use.

> *Celebrate* comes from a Middle English (ME) word that is derived from the Latin (L). The meaning evolved from the idea of "going in great numbers, honoring," a meaning reflected by the first definition in the entry.

7. **Definitions.** If a word has more than one meaning, the definitions are numbered in most dictionaries from the oldest to the newest meaning. A few dictionaries start with the most common use.

*You can find the definition of a word printed in small capital letters (such as TRANSITIVE VERB) in the Glossary of Terms toward the back of this handbook.

The oldest meaning of *celebrate* is given first, and its most recent use is given last (item 4 in the **vt.** list and item 3 in the **vi.** list).

8. **Usage Labels.** If the use of a word is special, a usage label explains how the word should be used. Chart 96 explains the most common usage labels in dictionaries.

> The most recent meaning of *celebrate* as an intransitive verb (**vi.**) is *colloquial.* Therefore, such use is informal (and probably should be avoided in academic writing).

9. **Field Labels.** When a word applies to a specialized area of study, such as chemistry or law, an abbreviation alerts a reader to the specialized meaning. For example, along with its everyday meanings, the word *center* has specialized meanings in these fields: sports, mechanics, the military, and politics.

10. **Related Words.** Words based on the defined word appear, with their part of speech, at the end of the definitions.

> Words related to *celebrate* are *celebrative* (adjective), *celebrator* (noun), and *celebratory* (adjective).

11. **Synonyms and Antonyms,** if any. Synonyms are words that are close in meaning. They are listed and their subtle differences are explained. Also, for each word in the list of synonyms, a cross-reference appears at that word's entry so that the reader can tell where to find the complete list. For example, at the entry *commemorate,* this information appears: SYN. CELEBRATE. It means that synonyms for *commemorate* can be found at the entry for *celebrate.* Antonyms are words that are opposite in meaning to the word defined. Any antonyms are listed after any synonyms.

> *Celebrate* and four of its synonyms are listed and explained; it has no antonyms.

12. **Idioms,** if any. When the defined word is an idiom, either in itself or when combined with other words, it has a meaning that differs from its usual meaning. For example, in *Webster's New World Dictionary,* the entry for *ceiling* lists and defines the idiom *hit the ceiling.* If an idiom is considered slang or colloquial, a usage label (see item 8 above and section 20a-2) alerts the reader.

13. **Examples.** Some definitions provide an example sentence that illustrates the defined word in use.

Understanding usage labels

20a-2

Usage refers to the customary manner of using particular words or phrases. As a writer, you can refer to the **usage labels** in a dictionary

---

TEACHING TIP

Many commonly used English words come directly from classical mythology. Maxwell Nurnberg and Morris Rosenblum suggest that students will enjoy finding the stories that have given us such words as *aegis, chimerical, cornucopia, protean, stentorian, stygian,* and *titanic.* They will add words to their vocabularies at the same time (*All About Words: An Adult Approach to Vocabulary Building* [New York: The New American Library, 1966]).

WORD DERIVATION

Nevada is a shortening of the Spanish *Sierra Nevada* ("snowy range"), a mountain range in eastern California.

WORD DERIVATION

New Mexico is a literal translation of the Spanish *Nuevo Méjico. Méjico* is the Spanish rendering of *Mexitli,* the name of an Aztec war god.

WORD DERIVATION

The state of *Pennsylvania* is named after a man and the local geography. *Sylvania* means "wooded land" in Latin. The *Penn* part is less clear. Some say that the *Penn* is William Penn, the colonist to whom King Charles II of England gave the land. Others say that under orders from King Charles, Penn named the land after his own late father, an English admiral. In either case, the admiral had died before the king could repay a debt of 16,000 pounds. The king gave the land to William Penn in settlement of the debt— and to keep the religious activist out of England.

EXTRA EXERCISE A

Find the answers to the following questions in the dictionary you commonly use. Name the sections consulted for any answers you are unable to find.

1. When was the University of the South (in Tennessee) founded?

2. What is the population of Midland, Texas?

3. What was George Eliot's real name?

4. Who took the Elgin marbles to England?

5. When did Mary Cassatt live?

6. What is the highest peak in the Elk Mountains?

7. Where is the Bonneville Dam?

8. What large city is near Evanston?

9. What is the meaning of the abbreviation *e.g.*?

10. Where does a cockney live?

11. What is the zip code for Auburn University?

12. What is the mathematical symbol for infinity?

13. To what genus does the mandrill belong?

14. What is the size (in square miles) of Manitoba?

15. What is the etymology of *helicopter*?

ANSWERS: EXERCISE 20–1

Answers will vary.

BACKGROUND

In an interesting examination of the objectivity of dictionaries, Sidney Landau argues that many American dictionaries present misleading definitions of the word *abortion* ("A Matter of Life and Death," *English Today 4* [October 1988]: 43–46).

20a-2
cont.

to help you decide when a word is appropriate for use. For example, a word labeled *slang* usually is not suitable for academic writing unless you are writing about the word itself. A word labeled *poetic* is likely to be found in poetry, not in prose.

The concept of usage also applies to the customary manner of using certain words (for example, *among* versus *between*). For a list and explanation of such words, see the Usage Glossary toward the back of this handbook.

USAGE LABELS			96
LABEL	*DEFINITION*		*EXAMPLE*
COLLOQUIAL	Characteristic of conversation and informal writing		**pa** [father] **ma** [mother]
SLANG	Not considered part of standard language, but sometimes used in informal conversation		**whirlybird** [helicopter]
OBSOLETE	No longer used; occurred in earlier writing		**betimes** [promptly, quickly]
POETIC	Found in poetry or poetic prose		**o'er** [for *over*]
DIALECT	Used only in some geographical areas		**poke** [Southern: a bag or sack]

EXERCISE 20-1

Consulting sections 20a-1 and 20a-2, use a dictionary with entries that include a list of synonyms and some labels, as in the entry for *celebrate* on page 381. Then, write an explanation of each part, assuming that your audience is a student unfamiliar with such entries.

20a-3

Using unabridged dictionaries

Unabridged means "not shortened." Of the various kinds of dictionaries, unabridged dictionaries have the most in-depth, accurate, complete, and scholarly entries. They give many examples of current uses and changes in meanings of the word over time. They include infrequently used words that abridged dictionaries (see 20a-4) often omit.

The most comprehensive, authoritative unabridged dictionary of English is the *Oxford English Dictionary (OED)*. Its second edition has twenty volumes defining more than 616,500 words and terms. The *OED* traces each word's history, using quotations to illustrate changes in meaning and spelling over the life of the word. The second edition consists of three parts: (1) the first edition of the *OED*, which is largely unchanged; (2) the contents of the four supplements that accompanied the first edition; and (3) approximately 5,000 words or terms new in the second edition.

Its comprehensive historical information and examples about English words make the *OED* a specialized dictionary (20a-5) as well as an unabridged dictionary. The following small excerpt from the second edition's entry for *celebrate* shows the kinds of information that you can get from the *OED*. Compare it with the entry for *celebrate* on page 381 taken from *Webster's New World Dictionary,* Third College Edition. In addition to the usual dictionary features, the *OED* offers a history of the word (*celebrate*'s first recorded use was in 1656). Note the historical examples of *celebrate* following its third meaning.

Sample OED Entry

celebrate ('sɛlibreit), *v.* [f. prec., or on analogy of vbs. so formed. See -ATE³.]
(**1656** BLOUNT *Glossogr., Celebrate,* to frequent, to solemnize with an Assembly of men, to make famous, also to keep a festival day or other time with great solemnity.)

3. To observe with solemn rites (a day, festival, season); to honour with religious ceremonies, festivities, or other observances (an event, occasion). Also *absol.* (see quot. 1937).
    1560 BIBLE (Genev.) *Lev.* xxiii. 32 From euen to euen shall ye celebrate [WYCL. halowe, COVERD. kepe] your Sabbath. **1591** SHAKS. I *Hen. VI,* I. VI. 14 Feast and banquet in the open streets, To celebrate the joy that God hath given us. **1672** DRYDEN *Conq. Granada* 1. i, with Pomp and Sports my Love I celebrate. **1697** — *Virg. Georg.* I. 466 Celebrate the mighty Mother's Day. **1737** L. CLARKE *Hist. Bible* IX. (1840) I. 376 The Feast of Tabernacles being then celebrating. **1841** Lane *Arab. Nts.* I. 71 The Minor Festival . . is celebrated with more rejoicing than the other. **1929** *Randolph Enterprise* (Elkins, W. Va.) 26 Sept. 3/2 [He] came over . . Sunday night to celebrate a little. **1937** PARTRIDGE *Dict. Slang* 136/1 *Celebrate,* v.i., to drink in honour of an event or a person; hence, to drink joyously. **1963** J. T. STORY *Something for Nothing* i. 40 It's Treasure's wedding day. Somebody's got to celebrate.

For most college students, *Webster's Third New International Dictionary of the English Language* provides any needed information. This highly respected, one-volume work has more than 470,000 entries and is especially strong in new scientific and technical terms. It uses quotations to show various meanings, and its definitions are given in chronological order of their appearance in the language.

WORD DERIVATION

Rhode Island's etymology is a mystery. There are two theories. According to one, Italian explorer Giovanni da Verrazano saw a resemblance between the island on which the city of Newport is now located and the Greek island of Rhodes. According to the second, Dutch explorers named the area *Roode Eylandt* ("red island") because of its red clay soil.

EXTRA EXERCISE B

List two synonyms for each of the following words. On the basis of information that you can find about them in a dictionary, explain the differences between the pairs of synonyms.

1. indulge
2. egotism
3. lazy
4. fame
5. friendly
6. frugal
7. red
8. good
9. govern
10. industry

TEACHING TIP

You may want to ask students to work in groups to research the origins of a slang expression, a commonly used phrase, or a regional expression of their own choice. The results can take the form of an oral report to the rest of the class.

WORD DERIVATION

Florida was named by explorer Ponce de Leon. The name is Spanish for "abounding in flowers."

BACKGROUND

In "English Language Teaching Dictionaries: Past, Present, and Future" (*English Today* 4 [April 1988]: 10–14), Della Summers reviews the development of English dictionaries for foreign students. She goes on to compare the coverage provided by three monolingual English language teaching dictionaries.

BACKGROUND

In 1989 Oxford University published a second edition of the *Oxford English Dictionary*, commonly known as the *OED*. The idea for the first edition came from a paper delivered in 1857 to Britain's Philological Society by Richard Trench, Dean of Westminster; it was entitled "On Some Deficiencies in Our English Dictionaries." His concerns led the Society to make plans for compiling a completely new dictionary that would include "every word occurring in the literature of the language." In 1859 Herbert Coleridge, a grandson of the poet, became editor of the new work, expecting to publish it in two years. After his untimely death, he was succeeded by Frederick J. Furnivall, who agreed to devote four or five years to producing the first part of the dictionary. Overburdened by work, Furnivall in 1876 turned over his duties to James Murray, who agreed to produce a dictionary of between 6,000 and 7,000 pages within ten years. Beginning with one and three-quarters tons of materials collected by Furnivall, he made a public appeal for a thousand readers of English to assist with finding quotations for unusual as well as ordinary words. Working twelve to fifteen hours a day, with the help of his eleven children, Murray had, by 1894, completed sections A, B, C, and D, whereupon the work was first called *The Oxford English Dictionary*. Murray died in 1915 with a sixth of the work unfinished. The completed dictionary emerged in 1928 after 70 years of work by a series of devoted researchers. Since that time four supplements to the original work have been published.

The new edition combines the original *OED* and the supplements, which add 5,000 new words as well as revised, corrected, and updated information. Revision will continue, and new supplements will appear as time goes on. Meanwhile, the first edition is now available in a CD-ROM (Compact Disk—Read Only Memory) version that presents not only the full text of the *OED*, but also eight indexes.

20a-4

Using abridged dictionaries

Abridged means "shortened." Abridged dictionaries contain the most commonly used words. They are convenient in size and economical to buy, and they serve as practical reference books for writers and readers. Many good abridged dictionaries are referred to as "college" editions because they serve the needs of most college students. Typical of these is *Webster's New World Dictionary of American English*, Revised College Edition, which has more than 170,000 entries and gives detailed etymologies. Names of people, places, abbreviations, and foreign expressions appear in the main body of the work (rather than in appendixes). Definitions appear in chronological order of their acceptance into the language. *Webster's New World Dictionary* has a contemporary American emphasis. It uses a star symbol (★) for Americanisms—words that first became part of the language in the United States. It gives the origins of American place names (cities, states, rivers, and so on). It supplies usage labels for many words and gives synonyms, often in lists that explain distinctions among closely related words. An appendix covers punctuation, italics, numbers, capitalization, abbreviations, and source documentation. Its introductory material includes essays on the English language and etymology. *Webster's New World Compact School and Office Dictionary* is based on *Webster's New World Dictionary,* Third College Edition. More complete than a "pocket" dictionary, it has 56,000 entries.

ESL

❖ ESL NOTE: A useful dictionary for students who speak English as a second language is the *Dictionary of American English* published by Longman. For a list of specialized dictionaries, see 20a 5. ❖

20a-5

Using specialized dictionaries of English

A specialized dictionary focuses on a single area, such as slang, word origins, synonyms, antonyms, usage, or almost any other aspect of language. Most college libraries include all or some of the volumes listed here:

SPECIALIZED DICTIONARIES

SYNONYMS	*New Roget's Thesaurus of the English Language in Dictionary Form*
SLANG AND COLLOQUIALISMS	*Dictionary of Slang and Unconventional English,* ed. Eric Partridge
	Dictionary of American Slang, ed. Harold Wentworth and Stuart Berg Flexner [out of print, but available in many libraries]

The Thesaurus of Slang, by Esther Lewin and Albert E. Lewin

NTC's Dictionary of American Slang and Colloquial Expressions, by Richard A. Spear

ETYMOLOGIES   *Dictionary of Word and Phrase Origins,* ed. William Morris and Mary Morris

Origins: A Short Etymological Dictionary of Modern English, ed. Eric Partridge [out of print, but available in many libraries]

USAGE   *Modern American Usage,* ed. Jacques Barzun

REGIONALISMS   *Dictionary of American Regional English,* ed. Frederic Cassidy

IDIOMS   *A Dictionary of American Idioms,* by Adam Makkai

Dictionary of English Idioms, published by Longman Inc.

Using CD-ROM dictionaries   20a-6

Several major dictionaries are available on CD-ROM disks, including *The Merriam Webster Collegiate Dictionary, The Random House College Dictionary, The American Heritage Dictionary* (in a "talking" edition), and the second edition of the *Oxford English Dictionary* (the *OED*).

Choosing exact words   20b

The English language offers a wealth of words to choose from as a writer. **Diction,** the term for choice of words, affects the clarity and impact of the message that you want your sentences to deliver. As a writer, you want to use words that exactly fit the particular context of each piece of writing.

Understanding denotation and connotation   20b-1

When you look up a word in the dictionary to find out what it means, you are looking for its **denotation.** For example, the one denotation of the word *semester* is "a period of time of about eighteen weeks that makes up part of a school or college year."

BACKGROUND

20b-1
cont.

The roots of the *Dictionary of American Regional English* (*DARE*) go back to 1889 and the founding of the American Dialect Society. The society's purpose was to sponsor and record data for an American dialect dictionary. It had its own journal, which continues today as *The Publication of the American Dialect Society*. Compilation of a master file of entries for the dictionary began in 1917, and the society participated along the way in several other, smaller dialect dictionaries (the incomplete *Linguistic Atlas of the United States and Canada* and the *American Dialect Dictionary* [1944]).

In 1963 the society appointed Frederic G. Cassidy (editor of *The Dictionary of Jamaican English*) the *DARE* editor. He and his staff had at their disposal a hundred years of accumulated scholarship: the files of the American Dialect Society, linguistic and folklore journals, regional publications, diaries and other materials in library archives, records of folk speech, historical dictionaries, and linguistic atlases.

Astonishingly, Cassidy chose to go beyond the written word, and the *DARE* benefits from five years of original fieldwork aimed at finding out how people speak in their daily lives. Eighty-two trained field-workers, most of them graduate students in linguistics or the history of English, went across the United States conducting personal interviews.

The 2,777 informants represented 1,002 communities across the United States. The informants were chosen to create a balance of male and female, city and country, black and white, North and South. However, in order to preserve vanishing words, about two-thirds of the informants were 60 years old or older. Each questionnaire contained 1,847 questions. One questionnaire was filled in for each community. In some cases, one informant answered all the ques-

→

Readers expect words to be used according to their established meanings for their established functions. Exactness is essential. When you use a thesaurus or dictionary of synonyms, be aware that subtle shades of meaning create distinctions among words that have the same general definition. These small differences in meaning allow you to be very precise in choosing just the right word, but they also oblige you to make sure that you know what precise meanings your words convey. For instance, describing a person famous for praiseworthy achievements in public life as *notorious* would be wrong. Although *notorious* means "well-known" and "publicly discussed"—which famous people are likely to be—*notorious* also carries the meaning "unfavorably known or talked about." George Washington is *famous*, not *notorious*. Al Capone, on the other hand, is *notorious*.

Here is another example. *Obdurate* means "not easily moved to pity or sympathy," and its synonyms include "inflexible, obstinate, stubborn, hardened." The synonym *hardened* for *obdurate,* however, might prompt someone unfamiliar with *obdurate* to use the word incorrectly.

NO   Footprints showed in the *obdurate* concrete.

Here are two correct uses of *obdurate:*

YES   The supervisor remained *obdurate* in refusing to accept excuses.

YES   My *obdurate* roommates will not let my pet boa constrictor live in the bathtub.

! ❖ COMPUTER ALERT: Be especially careful about using a software program's thesaurus. Recent versions of sophisticated programs have thesauruses that offer synonyms for many words and that make substitutions easy. However, unless you know the exact meaning of an offered synonym, as well as its part of speech, you may introduce a grammatical error or a "wrong word" error into your writing. For example, one word-processing program's thesaurus offers the choices *low, below, beneath,* and *subterranean* as synonyms for *deep* with the sense of low (down, inside). None of these words, however, could replace *deep* in many sentences, including this one: *Mine shaft #4 is too deep* [not too *low, below, beneath,* or *subterranean*] *to be filled with sand or rocks.* ❖

Connotation refers to ideas implied, but not directly indicated, by a word. Connotations convey associations as emotional overtones beyond the direct, explicit definition of a word. For example, the word *home* usually evokes more emotion than does its denotation "a dwelling place" or its synonym *house*. *Home* may have very pleasant connotations of warmth, security, the love of family. Or *home* may have unpleasant connotations of an institution for elderly or sick people. As a student writer, be aware of the potential of connotation to help your words deliver their meaning. Connotations are never completely fixed, for they can vary with different contexts for a word. Still, people can communicate effectively because most words have relatively stable connotations and denotations in most contexts.

Being sensitive to the differences between the denotation and connotation of a word is essential for critical thinking. Critical thinkers must first consider material at its literal level (see 5d-1). Doing so calls for dealing with the denotation of words. Next, critical thinkers must move to the inferential level (see 5d-2)—to what is implied although not explicitly stated. Connotations of words often carry the inferential message, as illustrated in Chart 97.

COMPARING DENOTATION AND CONNOTATION		97
SAMPLE WORD	DENOTATION	CONNOTATION
ADDITIVE	an added substance	something unnatural, especially in food; perhaps harmful to health
CHEAP	inexpensive	of products, low quality; of people, stingy
NUCLEAR REACTOR MELTDOWN	melting of fuel rods in a nuclear reactor, releasing dangerous radiation	specter of imminent death or eventual cancer; poisoning of food chain

EXERCISE 20-2

Consulting section 20b-1, separate the words in each set into one of three groups: *Neutral* if you think the word has no connotations; *Positive* if you think it has good connotations; *Negative* if you think it has bad connotations. If you think a word fits in more than one group, put it under each heading that applies, and be ready to explain your choices. If you are unsure of a word, consult your dictionary.

EXAMPLE   sensitive, touchy, tender, thin-skinned, impressionable

           Neutral: impressionable; *Positive:* sensitive; *Negative:* touchy, thin-skinned

1.   carefree, exuberant, light-hearted, frivolous, rash, high-spirited, riotous, animated, reckless, joyful

COMPARING DENOTATION AND CONNOTATION

BACKGROUND, *cont.*

tions; in others, the questions were divided among a number of informants. The fieldworkers also brought back 1,843 tape recordings of conversations: a total of two million oral responses and 900 hours of tape recordings.

WORD DERIVATION

Kentucky comes from the Iroquoian words for "level land."

ANSWERS AND COVERAGE: EXERCISE 20–2

The response to this exercise is likely to elicit much debate, given that shades of connotative meaning are often fairly personal. The following are some possible answers.

1. *Positive*: exuberant, light-hearted, high-spirited, joyful; *Neutral*: carefree, animated; *Negative*: frivolous, rash, riotous, reckless.

2. *Positive*: prudent, foresighted; *Neutral*: thrifty, economical, frugal, money-conscious; *Negative*: stingy, tight-fisted, penny-pinching.

3. *Positive*: learned counsel, advocate; *Neutral*: lawyer, attorney, legal practitioner, public defender, prosecutor; *Negative*: shyster, ambulance chaser.

4. *Positive*: fragrance, scent, perfume, incense; *Neutral*: smell, aroma, scent, whiff; *Negative*: odor, stink, stench, smoke.

5. *Positive*: flexible, tolerant, adaptable; *Neutral*: yielding, undemanding; *Negative*: wishy-washy, indulgent, weak, submissive, imitative.

WORD DERIVATION

Louisiana comes from *La Louisianne.* The French, who had controlled the Mississippi Valley before selling the area to the United States in 1803, had named the area after their king, Louis XIV.

REFERENCE TO SUPPLEMENTS

See transparency 6–1 on diction: general/specific and abstract/concrete in the *Prentice Hall/Simon & Schuster Transparencies for Writers* by D. Carter.

EXTRA EXERCISE D

Be prepared to discuss differences in the connotations of the following pairs of words.

1. passive—shy
2. giggle—snicker
3. buddy—cohort
4. brave—foolhardy
5. wise—intelligent

TEACHING TIP

To underscore the importance of subtle shades of meaning and connotation, you might ask your students how they would react to each of the statements below. Once their egos are involved, students will quickly see that not all synonyms are created equal.

You are wrong.
You are incorrect.
What you say is false.
You are inaccurate.
You are imprecise.
You are evil.
You are improper.
You are unethical.
You are unrighteous.
You are bad.
You are willfully misleading.

20b-1 cont.

2. thrifty, economical, frugal, stingy, tight-fisted, prudent, foresighted, penny-pinching, money-conscious
3. lawyer, attorney, shyster, learned counsel, ambulance chaser, advocate, legal practitioner, public defender, prosecutor
4. smell, odor, fragrance, stink, aroma, scent, stench, whiff, perfume, smoke, incense
5. flexible, yielding, wishy-washy, adaptable, tolerant, indulgent, undemanding, weak, submissive, imitative
6. loyal, dedicated, devoted, determined, stubborn, firm, unyielding

20b-2

Using specific and concrete language to bring life to general and abstract language

Specific words identify individual items in a group (*Oldsmobile, Honda, Ford*). **General** words relate to an overall group (*car*). **Concrete** words identify persons and things that can be perceived by the senses—seen, heard, tasted, felt, smelled (the *black padded vinyl dashboard* of my car). **Abstract** words denote qualities, concepts, relationships, acts, conditions, ideas (*transportation*).

As a writer, you want to choose words suitable for your writing PURPOSE and your AUDIENCE. Usually, specific and concrete words bring life to general and abstract words. Whenever you choose general and abstract words, be sure to supply enough specific, concrete details and examples to illustrate effectively your generalizations and abstractions. Consider how sentences with general words come to life when they are revised with words that refer to specifics.

GENERAL	My car has a great deal of power, and it is very quick.
SPECIFIC	My Trans Am with 220 horsepower can go from zero to fifty in six seconds.
GENERAL	The car gets good gas mileage.
SPECIFIC	The Dodge Lancer gets about 35 mpg on the highway and 30 mpg in the city.
GENERAL	Her car is comfortable and easy to drive.
SPECIFIC	When she drives her new Buick Regal on a five-hour trip, she arrives refreshed and does not need a long nap to recover, as she did when she drove her ten-year-old Upusho.

Specific language is not always preferable to general language, nor is concrete language always preferable to abstract language. Effective writing usually combines them. Consider the following from an effective essay comparing cars:

GENERAL AND SPECIFIC COMBINED

GENERAL   SPECIFIC   SPECIFIC   GENERAL
My car, a **220-horsepower Trans Am,** is **quick.** It accelerates from

SPECIFIC   SPECIFIC   SPECIFIC
0 to 50 miles per hour in **6 seconds**—but it gets only **18 miles** per

               SPECIFIC   GENERAL
gallon. The **Dodge Lancer,** on the other hand, gets **very good** gas

GENERAL   SPECIFIC   GENERAL   SPECIFIC
mileage: about **35 mpg** in **highway driving** and **30 mpg** when

GENERAL   SPECIFIC   GENERAL   SPECIFIC
traffic is **bumper-to-bumper** or when **car trips** are **frequent and short.**

Do not overdo being specific and concrete. If you want to inform a nonspecialist reader about possible automobile fuels other than gasoline, *do* name the fuels and be very specific about their advantages and drawbacks. *Do not* go into a detailed, highly technical discussion of the chemical profiles of the fuels. Always base your choices on an awareness of your purpose for writing (see 1b) and your audience (see 1c).

EXERCISE 20-3

Consulting section 20b-2, revise the following paragraph by providing specific and concrete words and phrases to explain and enliven the ideas presented here in general and abstract language. As needed, you can revise these sentences to accommodate your changes in language.

The car was exactly what we were looking for. It was the right color, size, and, best of all, price. It had nice seats, and it had many features we wanted. We were especially pleased by the average miles per gallon it got on the highway. The dealer said that we could have it right away. The only problem was that he would not take our broken-down old car as a trade-in.

Increasing your vocabulary   20c

The benefits of increasing your vocabulary are many. The more words you know, the more easily and the faster you can read. A large, rich vocabulary also helps you understand ideas and communicate them clearly and effectively in your writing. Use the techniques described in Chart 98.

BACKGROUND

Over time words change their meanings in several different ways. In *The Story of Our Language* (New York: Doubleday, 1962), Henry Alexander points out that a word may undergo a widening, in which it expands its range of meaning and is applied to new situations; a narrowing, by which it comes to refer to only a portion of the idea or objects it originally covered; a lowering of meaning, wherein it takes on pejorative aspects; and a raising of meaning, by which it loses its unpleasant associations and acquires more positive ones. For example, *meat* has undergone a narrowing of meaning; it originally referred to all kinds of food, but now denotes what was earlier called flesh. The word *hussy*, with its contemporary uncomplimentary meaning, has experienced a lowering; it originally denoted a housewife.

ANSWERS: EXERCISE 20–3

Because of the many possibilities for rewording posed by this exercise, the answers are likely to vary widely. Students may enjoy comparing the different choices they have made. The important principle for revision is that the new versions should have a high degree of specificity and concreteness. Here is one set of possibilities.

The used 1988 Buick was exactly what we were looking for. It was a maroon two-door model with a vinyl top, and it was priced at several hundred dollars less than we were expecting to pay. The seats were covered in black fabric that looked brand new. It had a tape player, air conditioning, and automatic transmission. We were especially pleased that it could get 28 miles per gallon on the highway. The dealer said we could drive it off the lot that very day. The only problem was that he would not take our 1956 Chevrolet with the cracked windshield and bent right fender as a trade-in.

EXTRA EXERCISE E

Working in groups and without a dictionary, compile a list of as many words as you can think of that begin with the following prefixes. How does the prefix affect the meaning of each of the words on your list? The group with the longest list can be declared the winner.

1. mono	**6.** auto
2. retro	**7.** super
3. contra	**8.** un
4. sub	**9.** re
5. pre	**10.** poly

EXTRA EXERCISE F

Using the following prefixes, devise new words, being prepared to explain their meaning.

1. inter

2. ante

3. anti

4. post

5. uni

TEACHING TIP

Following Henry Alexander's discussion of four ways in which words change their meaning over time, students can be asked to discover what types of change have occurred with the following words. Their findings will make an interesting report to the class.

1. chagrin	**6.** wanton
2. picture (n.)	**7.** nice
3. miscreant	**8.** stench
4. place	**9.** fond
5. cafeteria	**10.** wife

TECHNIQUES FOR BUILDING YOUR VOCABULARY 98

TO FIND WORDS

■ Use a highlighter pen to mark all unfamiliar words in textbooks and other reading material. Then define the words in the margin so that you can study the meaning in context. Use context clues (see 20c-2) to figure out definitions, or look up the words in a dictionary. Write each word and its definitions on an index card or in a notebook.

■ Listen carefully to learn how speakers use the language. Jot down new words to look up later. Write each word and its definitions on an index card or in a notebook.

TO STUDY WORDS

■ Select some words that you intend to study each week. Put the date next to the word so that you can keep track of your goals. Whenever you look up a word in your dictionary, put a small checkmark next to it. When you accumulate three checkmarks next to a word, it is time to learn that word.

■ Set aside time each day to study your selected words. Carry your cards or notebook to study in spare moments each day.

■ Use mnemonics (see 22b) to help you memorize words. Set a goal of learning eight to ten new words a week. Use the words in your writing and, when possible, in conversation.

■ Go back to words from previous weeks, whenever possible. List any words you have not learned well. Study them again, and use them.

20c-1

Knowing prefixes and suffixes

Prefixes are syllables in front of a **root** word that modify its meaning. *Ante-* (before) placed before the root *bellum* (war) gives *antebellum,* which means "before the war." In American English, *antebellum* refers to the time before the Civil War.

Suffixes are syllables added to the end of a root word that modify its meaning. For example, *excite* is formed by adding the prefix *ex-* (out) to the past participle of *cierce* (to summon). It has various forms when suffixes are added: *excited, exciting, excitedly, excitement.* The part of speech of a word is often signaled by the suffix.

Knowing common prefixes and suffixes is an excellent way to learn to decode unfamiliar words and increase your vocabulary.

PREFIXES

PREFIX	MEANING	EXAMPLE
ante-	before	*antebellum*
anti-	against	*antiballistic*
auto-	self	*autobiography*
contra-	against	*contradict*
dis-	not	*disagree*
extra-	more	*extraordinary*
hyper-	more	*hyperactive*
il-	not	*illegal*
im-	not	*immoral*
in-	not	*inadequate*
inter-	between	*interpersonal*
intra-	inside	*intravenous*
ir-	not	*irresponsible*
mal-	poor	*malnutrition*
mis-	wrongly, badly	*misunderstood*
mono-	one	*monopoly*
non-	not	*noninvolvement*
poly-	many	*polygamy*
post-	after	*postscript*
pre-	before	*prehistoric*
re-	back	*return*
retro-	back	*retroactive*
semi-	half	*semicircle*
sub-	under	*submissive*
super-	more	*supernatural*
trans-	across	*transportation*
ultra-	more	*ultraconservative*
un-	not	*unhappy*
uni-	one	*uniform*

TEACHING TIP

Knowledge of prefixes and suffixes can help students figure out the meanings of many words. If this skill is coupled with the ability to recognize root words, however, many students' power to decipher new words can increase dramatically. Fundamentally, a root word is a base to which prefixes and suffixes can be added. For example, -*graph* (from the Greek -*graphos*, "to write") refers to something that writes or records, as in *telegraph* or *graphite*; or to something written, as in *paragraph* or the *graphic arts*; *graphology* is the study of handwriting.

Here are a few of the most common Greek and Latin roots, their meanings, and a sample word built from each root.

LATIN

aequs	equal (equivalent)
amare, amatum	to love (amiable)
dicere, dictum	to say, to speak (diction)
manus	hand (manuscript)
omnis	all (omnipotent)
portare, portatum	to carry (porter)
scribere, scriptum	to write (scribble)
sentire, sensum	to feel (sense)
spirare, spiratum	to breathe (inspiration)
verbum	word (verb)

GREEK

bios	life (biology)
chronos	time (chronology)
gamos	marriage (bigamy)
geo-	earth (geology)
krates (-crat)	member of a group (democrat)
metron	to measure (thermometer)
pathos	suffering, feeling (sympathy)
phobos	fear (agoraphobia)
photos	light (photograph)
podos	foot (tripod)

20c-1
cont.

QUOTATION ABOUT WRITING

For your born writer, nothing is so healing as the realization that he [or she] has come upon the right word.
— Catherine Drinker Bowen

QUOTATION ABOUT WRITING

Short words are best and the old words are best of all.
— Winston Churchill

QUOTATION ABOUT WRITING

I hear things in a kinesthetic way. I tap into a rhythm of language to portray what I feel.
— Mary Gordon

EXTRA EXERCISE G

Working in groups and without a dictionary, compile a list of as many words as you can think of that end with the suffixes in the accompanying chart. What does the suffix tell you about the meaning of each word?

ANSWERS AND COVERAGE: EXERCISE 20–4

1. impossible [im-]
2. reexamine [re-]
3. malfunction [mal-]
4. interstate [inter-]
5. irreversible [ir-]
6. semiconscious [semi-]
7. misstated [mis-]
8. unbelievable [un-]
9. preconceived [pre-]
10. hypersensitive [hyper-]

SUFFIXES

NOUNS

SUFFIX	MEANING	EXAMPLE
-dom	state of	*freedom*
-hood	state of	*childhood*
-ness	state of	*kindness*
-ship	state of	*friendship*
-tion	act of	*integration*
-tude	state of	*solitude*

VERBS

SUFFIX	MEANING	EXAMPLE
-ate	to make	*integrate*
-ify	to make	*unify*
-ize	to make	*computerize*

ADJECTIVES

SUFFIX	MEANING	EXAMPLE
-able	able to be	*comfortable*
-ate	full of	*fortunate*
-ible	able to be	*compatible*
-ful	full of	*tactful*
-less	without	*penniless*
-ous	full of	*pompous*
-y	full of	*gloomy*

EXERCISE 20-4

Consulting section 20c-1, add a prefix to each italicized word to match the definition given. Use a dictionary if necessary.

EXAMPLE   not a *citizen* = noncitizen

1. not *possible*
2. *examine* again
3. poor *function*
4. between *states*
5. not *reversible*
6. half *conscious*
7. *stated* incorrectly
8. not *believable*
9. *conceived* before
10. more *sensitive*

EXERCISE 20-5

Consulting section 20c-1, add a suffix to each italicized word to match the definition given. Notice that the form of the word should change to match the exact definition. Consult a dictionary to verify your spelling.

EXAMPLE   act of *communicating* = communication

1. lacking *children*
2. to make *objective*
3. to make *beautiful*
4. to make *harmony*
5. state of being *kin*
6. able to be *touched*
7. without *care*
8. full of *mercy*
9. state of being a *bachelor*
10. full of *compassion*

Using context clues to figure out word meanings   20c-2

The familiar words that surround an unknown word can give you hints about the meaning of the new word. Such context clues include four main types.

1. **Restatement context clue.** You can figure out an unknown word when a word you know repeats the meaning: *He jumped into the* fray *and enjoyed every minute of the fight. Fray* means "fight." Sometimes a restatement is set off by punctuation. For example, parentheses contain a definition in this sentence: *Fatty deposits on artery walls combine with calcium compounds to cause* arteriosclerosis *(hardening of the arteries).* Sometimes a technical term is set off by punctuation after the definition of a term is given. For example, dashes set off a term after it is defined in this sentence: *The upper left part of the heart—the left* atrium—*receives blood returning from circulation.*

2. **Contrast context clue.** You can figure out an unknown word when an opposite or contrast is presented: *We feared that the new prime minister would be a* menace *to society, but she turned out to be a great peacemaker. Menace* means "threat"; the contrast that explains *menace* is *but she turned out to be a great peacemaker.* As you read, watch for words that express contrast (such as *but, however, nevertheless;* for a complete list see Chart 23 in 4d-1).

3. **Example context clue.** You can figure out an unfamiliar word when an example or illustration relating to the word is given: *They were* conscientious *workers, making sure that everything was done correctly and precisely.* A dictionary defines *conscientious* as "motivated by a desire to do what is right." The words "done correctly and precisely" are close to that meaning.

➡

ANSWERS AND COVERAGE: EXERCISE 20–5

1. childless [-less, adjective]
2. objectify [-ify, verb]
3. beautify [-ify, verb]
4. harmonize [-ize, verb]
5. kinship [-ship, noun]
6. touchable [-able, adjective]
7. careless [-less, adjective]
8. merciful [-ful, adjective]
9. bachelorhood [-hood, noun]
10. compassionate [-ate, adjective]

QUOTATION ABOUT WRITING

Many writers confess to observing certain professional superstitions which the non-writer would find absurd. Some break off a day's writing in mid-sentence, sure of how the sentence is to continue, so that the next day they can complete it, and thus find themselves in an already forward-moving phase of work. Others make a great fuss over having their materials arranged on their desks in exactly the same way throughout the writing of a work: the completed pages, the notes for those to come, the position of the dictionaries, the very direction of the lie of the bundle of pencils beside the typewriter, or the way the pen is pointing in its rack . . . all these are more than matters of simple convenience or efficiency. They signify continuity. They seem like a promise that what has gone well so far will continue to do so if the proper acts of propitiation are made . . .

—Paul Horgan

QUOTATION ABOUT WRITING

Why shouldn't we quarrel about a word? What is the good of words if they aren't important enough to quarrel over? Why do we choose one word more than another if there isn't any difference between them?

—G. K. Chesterton

BACKGROUND

The growing public awareness of sexism in the English language has resulted in the appearance of numerous books and articles that examine the problem from a variety of viewpoints: those of the sociologist, the psychologist, and the anthropologist, as well as those of the linguist, the writer, and the historian. One of the most perceptive and comprehensive of these books is *Sexism and Language* by Nilsen, Bosmajiam, Gershuny, and Stanley (NCTE, 1977). It addresses such matters as sexism in English vocabulary, in literature, in dictionaries, and in children's books. It concludes with the NCTE Guidelines for Nonsexist Use of Language.

20c-2
cont.

4. **General sense context clue.** You can use an entire passage to get a general sense of difficult words. For example, in *Nearly forty million Americans are overweight; obesity has become an epidemic*, chances are good that *epidemic* refers to something happening to many people. Sometimes a "general sense context clue" will not make clear a word's exact denotation. For example, you might guess that *epidemic* indicates a widespread threat, but you might miss the connection of the word *epidemic* with the concept of disease. Interpreting the meaning of a word from the general sense carries the risk of allowing subtle variations that distinguish one word from another to slip by. You might want, therefore, to check the exact definition in a dictionary.

21 *Understanding the Effect of Words*

As words communicate meaning (see Chapter 20), they have an effect on the people reading or hearing them. As a writer, you want to choose words carefully. Sometimes the choices available to you are clearly either right or wrong, but often the choices are subtle. The guidelines discussed in this chapter can help you make good choices: using the right level of formality (see 21a-1); using edited American English (see 21a-2); avoiding slang or inappropriate colloquial words or regional words (see 21a-3); avoiding slanted language (see 21a-4); avoiding sexist language (see 21b); using figurative language appropriately (see 21c); avoiding clichés (see 21d); and avoiding artificial language (see 21e).

Using appropriate language

21a

As a writer, you need to pay special attention to **tone** (see 1d) and **diction** (see 20b). You want the words that you use to communicate your meaning as clearly and effectively as possible. Equally important, your choice of words should work in concert with the effectiveness of your sentence style (see Chapters 16–19) to create your individual style of writing.

Using appropriate levels of formality

21a-1

Informal and highly formal levels of writing differ clearly in tone. They use different vocabulary and sentence structures. Tone in writing indicates the attitude of the writer toward the subject and toward the audience. Tone may be highly formal, informal, or somewhere in between.

Different tones are appropriate for different AUDIENCES, different subjects, and different PURPOSES. An informal tone occurs in casual conversation or letters to friends. A highly formal tone, in contrast, occurs in sermons and proclamations.

REFERENCES TO SUPPLEMENTS

For this topic in the CLAST writing competency test, refer students to ch. 2, section B1b of *Preparing for the CLAST* by S. Patterson.

For editing for appropriate diction, refer students to *Rough Drafts* by K. S. Cain, Part IV, Exercise 11.

REFERENCE TO SUPPLEMENTS

This topic is included in the TASP writing competency test. Refer students to *Preparing for the TASP* by M. Saenz.

TEACHING TIP

Because language varies from one geographic area to another, students who have lived in several different parts of the country often know expressions that are used in one region but not in another. Other members of a class may find it interesting to hear some of those regionalisms, afterwards compiling a list of words and phrases peculiar to their own area.

21a-1 cont.

Informal language, which creates an informal tone, may include slang, colloquialisms, and regionalisms (see 21a-3). In addition, informal writing often includes sentence fragments (see Chapter 13), contractions, and other forms that approximate casual speech. **Medium** language level uses general English: not too casual, not too scholarly. Unlike informal language, medium-level language is acceptable for academic writing. This level uses standard vocabulary (for example, *learn* instead of *wise up*), conventional sentence structure, and few or no contractions. A **highly formal** language level uses a multisyllabic Latinate vocabulary (*edify* instead of *teach*) and often stylistic flourishes such as extended or complex figures of speech. Academic writing, along with most writing for general audiences, should range from medium to somewhat formal levels of language.

INFORMAL	Ya know stars? They're a gas!
MEDIUM	Gas clouds slowly changed into stars.
FORMAL	The condensations of gas spun their slow gravitational pirouettes, slowly transmogrifying gas cloud into star.

—CARL SAGAN, "Starfolk: A Fable"

The informal example would be appropriate in a letter to a close friend or in a journal. The writer's attitude toward the subject is playful and humorous; the word choice and sentence structure assume great familiarity between writer and audience. The medium example would be appropriate in most academic and professional situations. The writer's attitude toward the subject is serious and straightforward. The formal example is addressed to an audience with considerable interest in and knowledge of scientific phenomena, such as readers of a science journal.

21a-2

Using edited American English for academic writing

The language standards that you are expected to use in academic writing are those of **edited American English:** the accepted written language of a book like this handbook or a magazine like *U.S. News & World Report* or *National Geographic*. Such language conforms to widely established rules of grammar, sentence structure, punctuation, and spelling. Because advertising language and other language intended to reach and sway a large audience often ignore conventional usage, readers often encounter written English that varies from the standard. Do not let these published departures from edited American English influence you to believe that they are acceptable in academic writing.

Edited English is not a fancy dialect for the elite. It is a practical form of the language that educated people use. As a student writer, you might find that early drafts of your essays contain language that departs from edited American English. When you use edited American English in your academic writing, you will not risk distracting your readers from the message you want to communicate. Do not, however, REVISE your words too early in the WRITING PROCESS, or you will risk being distracted from getting your ideas onto paper.

Avoiding slang and colloquial or regional language for most academic writing

21a-3

Slang consists of coined words and new meanings attached to established terms. Slang words and phrases usually pass out of use quickly, although occasionally they become accepted into standard usage. A reasonable guideline is to reserve slang for very informal situations. **Colloquial language** is characteristic of casual conversation and informal writing: *The student flunked chemistry,* instead of *the student failed chemistry.*

Slang varies according to time and place. For example, mid-1990s slang in New York City has included *be sword* for "relax, be cool" and *say what?* for "excuse me?" These expressions might not communicate the same meanings to contemporary teenagers in California or to teenagers anywhere by the year 2000. At no time, however, does slang communicate accurate meanings in academic or business writing.

Regional language (also called *dialectal language*) is specific to some geographic areas. A *dragonfly* is a *snake feeder* in parts of Delaware, a *darning needle* in parts of Michigan, and a *snake doctor* or an *ear sewer* in parts of the southern United States. Dialects are different from slang because dialectical differences reflect geographical regions and socioeconomic status. Using a dialect when writing for the general reading public tends to shut some people out of the communication. Except when dialect is the topic of the writing, academic writing rarely accommodates dialect well.

Although slang, colloquial words, and regional language are neither substandard nor illiterate, they are usually not appropriate for academic writing. Replacing them in your college writing allows you to communicate clearly with the large number of people who speak and write in medium or somewhat formal levels of language (see 21a-1).

Avoiding slanted language

21a-4

To communicate clearly, you will want to choose words that convince your audience of your fairness as a writer. When you are writing about a subject on which you hold strong opinions, it is easy to slip into biased or emotionally loaded language. Such **slanted language** usually does not convince a careful reader to agree with your point. Instead, it makes the reader wary or hostile. For example, suppose you are arguing of style and tradition. And imbued with the spirit of a place you once knew, and want to find again.

Eddie Bauer
The New Yorker, September 2, 1991

3. Quite simply, Hartmann is dedicated to building the best case. With the best leathers. The best tweed. The best vinyl. And the best locks. Hartmann. No one builds a better a case.

Hartmann Luggage
The New Yorker, May 29, 1989

4. Getting to gate 87 in two minutes isn't always easy. Anyone who travels on business knows how hard it can be. Which is why we've made getting AT&T so easy. Even at public phones that aren't automatically connected to AT&T. If you're calling long distance and you don't hear "AT&T" after the bong, simply hang up.

AT&T
The New Yorker, December 30, 1991

REFERENCES TO SUPPLEMENTS

This topic is included in the TASP writing competency test. Refer students to *Preparing for the TASP* by M. Saenz.

See transparency 6–3 for avoiding sexist references in the *Prentice Hall/Simon & Schuster Transparencies for Writers* by D. Carter.

TEACHING TIP

Discussions about slanted language make students more aware of biased writing. A logical follow-up assignment is to ask them to be alert to loaded diction in news articles and television broadcasts. Examples are particularly abundant during an election year. The words and phrases students collect can be the basis of another lesson, this one specific and close to home.

21a-4
cont.

against the practice of scientific experimentation on animals. If you use language such as "laboratory Frankensteins" who "routinely and viciously maim helpless kittens and puppies," you are using slanted language. You want to use words that make your side of an issue the more convincing one. Once you start using slanted, biased language, readers feel manipulated rather than reasoned with.

21b Avoiding sexist language

Sexist language assigns roles or characteristics to people on the basis of gender. Most women *and* men today feel that sexist language unfairly discriminates against both sexes. Sexist language inaccurately assumes all nurses and homemakers are female (and therefore refers to them as "she") and all physicians and wage earners are male (and therefore refers to them as "he"). One of the most widespread occurrences of sexist language is the use of the pronoun *he* to refer to someone of unidentified sex. Although tradition holds that *he* is correct in such situations, using only masculine pronouns to represent the human species excludes women and thereby distorts reality.

If you want to avoid sexist language in your writing, follow the guidelines in Chart 99. Also, you can avoid sexism by avoiding demeaning, outdated stereotypes, such as *women are bad drivers* or *men are bad cooks*. Do not describe a woman by her looks, clothes, or age (unless you do the same for men). Do not use the first name of one spouse when you use a title (such as *Mr.* or *Mrs.*) and the last name for the other spouse: *Phil Miller* [not *Mr. Miller*] *and his wife, Jeannette, travel on separate planes* or *Jeannette and Phil Miller live in Idaho.*

HOW TO AVOID SEXIST LANGUAGE	99

■ Avoid using only the masculine pronoun to refer to males and females together. Use a pair of pronouns.

NO A doctor has little time to read outside **his** specialty.

YES A doctor has little time to read outside **his** or **her** specialty.

The "he or she" construction acts as a singular pronoun, and it therefore calls for a singular verb when it serves as the subject of a sentence. Try to avoid using the "he or she" construction, especially more than once in a sentence or in consecutive sentences. Revising into the plural may be a better solution:

HOW TO AVOID SEXIST LANGUAGE (continued)   99

NO   A successful doctor knows that **he** has to work long hours.

YES   Successful doctors know that **they** have to work long hours.

You may also recast a sentence to omit the gender-specific pronoun.

NO   Everyone hopes that **he** will win the scholarship.

YES   Everyone hopes to win the scholarship.

■ Avoid the use of *man* when men and women are clearly intended in the meaning.

NO   **Man** is a social animal.

YES   **People** are social animals.

NO   Dogs are **man's** best friend.

YES   Dogs are **humans'** best friends.

Dogs are **people's** best friends.

Dogs are **our** best friends.

■ Avoid stereotyping jobs and roles by gender when men and women are included.

NO	YES
chairman	chair, chairperson
policeman	police officer
businessman	businessperson, business executive
statesman	diplomat, prime minister, statesperson

NO   teacher . . . **she**; principal . . . **he**

YES   teachers . . . **they**; principals . . . **they**

■ Avoid expressions that exclude either sex.

NO	YES
mankind	humanity
the common man	the average person
man-sized sandwich	huge sandwich
old wives' tale	superstition

➜

TEACHING TIP

If you have any doubts about whether encouraging nonsexist language is worth the effort, consider this passage from the introduction to "Guidelines for Nonsexist Use of Language in NCTE [National Council Teachers of English] Publications":

"Sexism" may be defined as words or actions that arbitrarily assign roles or characteristics to people on the basis of sex. Originally used to refer to practices that discriminated against women, the term now includes any usage that unfairly delimits the aspirations or attributes of either sex. Neither men nor women can reach their full potential when men are conditioned to be only aggressive, analytical, and active and women are conditioned to be only submissive, emotional, and passive. The man who cannot cry and the woman who cannot command are equally victims of their socialization.

Language plays a central role in socialization, for it helps teach children the roles that are expected of them. Through language, children conceptualize their ideas and feelings about themselves and their world. Thought and action are reflected in words, and words in turn condition how a person thinks and acts. Eliminating sexist language will not eliminate sexist conduct, but as the language is liberated from sexist usages and assumptions, women and men will begin to share more equal, active, caring roles.

21b
cont.

HOW TO AVOID SEXIST LANGUAGE (continued)   99

■ Avoid using demeaning and patronizing labels.

NO	YES
lady lawyer	lawyer
male nurse	nurse
gal Friday	assistant
coed	student

NO	My **girl** will send it.
YES	My **secretary** will send it.
	Ida Morea will send it.

EXERCISE 21-1

Consulting section 21b, revise the following sentences by changing sexist language to nonsexist language.

1. Man's sense of space and distance is variable.
2. Everyone establishes his own "personal space" by what he can do, not what he can see, in a given area.
3. A mother is usually seen standing very close to her children.
4. A lady politician, too, usually stands close to talk with one or two of her constituents but many feet away from large groups of people to whom she is talking.
5. The size of a person's "bubble" of personal space varies with his culture or ethnicity.
6. A German will go to great lengths to preserve his "private sphere" at home and at work.
7. An Englishman, however, is used to a common work space at the office.
8. For that reason, he is willing to exist close to his fellow workers.
9. Some U.S. businessmen use the ladies who work in the office to help protect their personal bubbles.
10. They have the office girls announce all visitors and screen all phone calls.

21c

Using figurative language

Figures of speech use words for more than their literal meanings, yet they are not merely decorative. **Figurative language** enhances meaning. It makes comparisons and connections that draw on one idea or image to explain another, as shown in Chart 100.

ANSWERS: EXERCISE 21-1

Answers will vary. Here are some possible nonsexist versions.

1. An individual's sense of space and distance is variable.
2. People establish their own "personal space" by what they can do, not what they can see, in a given area.
3. A parent is usually seen standing very close to his or her children. [*or* Parents are usually . . . to their children.]
4. Politicians, too, usually stand close to talk with one or two constituents but many feet away from large groups of people to whom they are talking.
5. The sizes of people's "bubbles" of personal space vary with their culture or ethnicity.
6. Germans will go to great lengths to preserve their "private sphere" at home and at work.
7. English businesspeople, however, are used to a common work space at the office.
8. For that reason, they are willing to exist close to their co-workers.
9. Some U.S. business executives use other people in the office to help protect their personal bubbles.
10. They have assistants [or *secretaries* or *receptionists*] announce all visitors and screen all phone calls.

REFERENCE TO SUPPLEMENTS

See transparency 6–2 for figurative language in the *Prentice Hall/Simon & Schuster Transparencies for Writers* by D. Carter.

- **Analogy:** a comparison of similar traits between dissimilar things (The length of an analogy can range from one sentence to a paragraph to an entire essay; see 4f-8 .)

    A cheetah sprinting across the dry plains after its prey, the base runner dashed for home plate.

- **Irony:** the use of words to suggest the opposite of their usual sense

    Told that the car repair would cost $2,000 and take at least two weeks, she said, "Oh, that would be wonderful!"

- **Metaphor:** a comparison between otherwise dissimilar things without using the word *like* or *as* (Be alert to avoid the error of a mixed metaphor, explained in the text.)

    The rush-hour traffic bled out of all the city's major arteries.

- **Overstatement** (also called *hyperbole*): deliberate exaggeration for emphasis

    Andrew Marvell said praising his love's eyes and forehead could take 100 years.

- **Personification:** the assignment of a human trait to a nonhuman thing

    The book begged to be read.

- **Simile:** a direct comparison between otherwise dissimilar things, using the word *like* or *as*

    Langston Hughes said that a deferred dream dries up like a raisin in the sun.

- **Understatement:** deliberate restraint for emphasis

    It gets a little warm when the temperature reaches 105 degrees.

A mixed metaphor combines images that do not work well together. Consider this sentence, for example: *Milking the migrant workers for all they were worth, the supervisors barked orders at them.* Here the initial image is of taking milk from a cow, but the final image has supervisors barking, an action suggesting dogs. Avoid confusing your reader by combining two or more images that do not blend well.

TEACHING TIP

In addition to the techniques given in Chart 112, How to Avoid Sexist Language, here are a few additional tactics.

   1. When appropriate, use the first person or the second person.

No *A person should always keep an eye on his luggage in airports.*

Yes *I should always keep my eye on my luggage in airports.*

Yes *We should always keep an eye on our luggage in airports.*

Yes *Keep an eye on your luggage in airports.*

   2. Repeat a noun or use a synonym in place of the troublesome pronoun.

No *A preoccupied traveler is an easy target for thieves, who can pick his pocket in a second.*

Yes *A preoccupied traveler is an easy target for thieves, who pick a traveler's pocket in a second.*

Yes *A preoccupied traveler is an easy target for thieves, who can pick a tourist's pocket in a second.*

   3. Use *who.*

No *A traveler has little to worry about, if he stays alert.*

Yes *A traveler who stays alert has little to worry about.*

WORD DERIVATIONS

Metaphor comes from *metapherein* (Greek for "to transfer"), a combination of *pherein* ("to carry") and *meta* ("over"). A metaphor carries over the meaning. *Simile* comes from *similis* (Latin for "like"). Similes always contain *like* or *as*, making the comparison explicit. *Simile* was first used in 1393 in William Langland's "Piers Plowman."

21c
cont.

EXERCISE 21-2

Consulting section 21c, identify each figure of speech. Also, revise any mixed metaphors.

1. In the 1990s we stand with one foot in the twentieth century while we set sail on the seas of a new era.
2. Having spent the whole day on the beach, he came home as red as a lobster.
3. If I eat one more bite of that chocolate cake, I'll explode.
4. What I love best about you is that you use all the hot water every time you take a shower.
5. The daisies nodded their heads in the hot sun.
6. Beginning to testify in the courtroom, the defendant was as nervous as a cat in a roomful of rocking chairs.
7. Think of the environment as a human body, where small problems in one part do not much affect other parts, any more than a paper cut causes most of us more than an instant's pain and a heartfelt "Ouch!" Problems throughout a system like the air or the oceans, however—say, pollution building up beyond the system's ability to cleanse itself—can kill the entire organism just as surely as cholesterol building up in arteries can kill you or me.
8. That actor displayed the entire range of human emotions from A to B.
9. My heart stopped when I opened the gift my parents gave me.
10. Our supervisor said that reorganizing the department according to our recommendations would be trading a headache for an upset stomach.

21d   **Avoiding clichés**

A **cliché** is a worn-out expression that has lost its capacity to communicate effectively. Many clichés are similes or metaphors, once clever, that have grown trite from overuse: *dead as a doornail, gentle as a lamb, straight as an arrow.* If you have heard words over and over again, so has your reader. If you cannot think of a way to rephrase a cliché, delete the phrase entirely.

English is full of frequently used word groups that are not clichés (for example, *up and down* and *in and out*). Common patterns are not clichés and need not be avoided.

EXERCISE 21-3

Consulting section 21d, revise these clichés. Use the idea in each cliché for a sentence of your own in plain English.

1. The bottom line is that Carl either raises his grade point average or finds himself in hot water.

2. Carl's grandfather says, "When the going gets tough, the tough get going."

3. Carl may not be the most brilliant engineering major who ever came down the pike, but he has plenty of get-up-and-go.

4. When they were handing out persistence, Carl was first in line.

5. The $64,000 question is: Will Carl make it safe and sound, or will the college drop him like a hot potato?

Avoiding artificial language   **21e**

Sometimes student writers think that ornate words and complicated sentence structures make writing impressive. Experienced writers, however, work hard to communicate as clearly and directly as they can. As a student writer, avoid long, fancy words to explain a point. Try to make what you write as accessible as possible to your readers. Extremely complex ideas or subject areas may require complex terms or phrases to explain them, but in general the simpler the language, the more likely it will be understood.

Avoiding pretentious language   **21e-1**

Pretentious language is too showy, calling undue attention to itself with complex sentences and polysyllabic words. Academic writing does not call for big words used for their own sake. Overblown words are likely to obscure your message.

As I alighted from my vehicle, my clothing was besmirched with filth. [*Translation:* My coat got dirty as I got out of my car.]

I hate it when he tries ostentatiously to flaunt his accouterments recently acquired in the haberdashery shop. [*Translation:* I hate it when he tries to show off his new clothes.]

Avoiding unnecessary jargon   **21e-2**

Jargon is specialized vocabulary of a particular group. It consists of words that an outsider might not understand. As you write, consider your PURPOSE and AUDIENCE to decide whether a word is jargon in the context of your material. For example, a football fan easily understands a sportswriter's use of words such as *punt, sacked,* and *safety,* but they are jargon to people not familiar with football. Specialized language evolves in every field: professions, academic disciplines (see Chapters 36–38), business, and even hobbies. Avoid using jargon unnecessarily. When you must use jargon for a general audience, be sure to explain the specialized meanings.

TEACHING TIP

Sports have been a fertile field for metaphor in America. You might remind your students of these common metaphors. What does each mean within its sport? What does each mean in a general context? You might also ask students if they can add to the lists or start lists for other sports or interests. Many metaphors listed here are discussed in Tim Considine's "Starting from Scratch" (*New York Times*, June 8, 1985).

Soccer	*Football*
kick off	huddle
get the ball rolling	chalk talk
Baseball	a flag on the play
right off the bat	all-American
off base	*Boxing*
touch base with	answer the bell
go to bat for	a low blow
out of left field	below the belt
drop the ball	on the ropes

TEACHING TIP

Because every professional discipline has its own jargon, your students may find it interesting to investigate the language used by people in a particular field of work. They can do so by interviewing individuals active in that profession, talking to those who teach courses preparing people to enter a field, reading professional literature, or observing (if possible) someone at work.

REFERENCE TO SUPPLEMENTS

This topic is included in the TASP writing competency test. Refer students to *Preparing for the TASP* by M. Saenz.

BACKGROUND

BACKGROUND

Jargon and euphemisms are not forms of language often recommended by teachers. However, Stephen Fry and David Shults have taken unusual positions in their articles on these kinds of expressions. Fry argues that jargon is sometimes preferable to plain language because people today lack a common understanding of many words ("Who Knows?: Purchasing Comprehension with Linguistic Currency," *ETC: A Review of General Semantics* 45 [Fall 1988]: 256–257). In "Soothespeak" Shults defends the use of some euphemisms (*Quarterly Review of Doublespeak* 15 [October 1988]: 11–12).

TEACHING TIP

Students who are interested in finding examples of doublespeak should refer to *Quarterly Review of Doublespeak*, published by the National Council of Teachers of English. The journal publishes articles that report doublespeak in business, education, government, law, medicine, and the military. See, for example, Michael Johanel's "Edspeak 1988," an examination of doublespeak in education which was published in *QRD* in January 1988, or "Campaign '88 Doublespeak," which appeared in April of the same year. In addition, *QRD* makes annual awards for the most notable instances of doublespeak that have appeared in a given year.

BACKGROUND

What constitutes "correct" usage is not as easy to define as it might seem. In a study of what university teachers accept as correct, Herb Smith discovered wide variation. He reports his findings in "The Fallacy of 'Correct' Usage: An Empirical Study" (*English Quarterly* 17 [Spring 1984]: 102–108).

21e-2 cont.

This example, showing specialized language used appropriately, is from a college textbook. The writers assume students know or can decipher the meaning of *eutrophicates, terrestrial,* and *eutrophic.*

> As the lake eutrophicates, it gradually fills until the entire lake will be converted into a terrestrial community. Eutrophic changes (or eutrophication) is the nutritional enrichment of the water, promoting the growth of aquatic plants.
>
> —DAVIS and SOLOMON, *The World of Biology*

21e-3

Avoiding euphemisms

Euphemisms attempt to avoid the harsh reality of truth by using more pleasant-sounding, "tactful" words. The word *euphemism* comes from the Greek meaning "words of good omen" (*eu-,* "good" + *pheme,* "voice").

Euphemisms are, of course, sometimes necessary for tact in social situations (using *passed away* instead of *died* when offering condolences, for example). In other situations, euphemisms drain meaning from truthful writing. Unnecessary euphemisms might describe socially unacceptable behavior (for example, *Johnny has a wonderfully vivid imagination* instead of *Johnny lies*). Unnecessary euphemisms might try to hide unpleasant facts (*She is between assignments* instead of *She lost her job*).

21e-4

Avoiding "doublespeak"

Doublespeak is artificial, evasive language. It aims to distort and deceive. For example, many automobile dealerships today have renamed "used cars" as "pre-owned cars" or "previously distinguished cars." A major corporation has described its notice that laid off 5,000 workers as a "career alternative enhancement package." The Pentagon has used "collateral damage" for unintended killing of innocent civilians.

To use doublespeak is to try to hide the truth, a highly unethical practice that seeks to control people's thoughts. So severe has the doublespeak problem become in our society that the National Council of Teachers of English yearly announces a Doublespeak Award to the "best" example of language that purposely misleads. A recent nominee for the award went to a foreign government for calling hostages "foreign guests" whose guards are "hosts." An award went to a U.S. Representative for saying the Congress "did not raise taxes" it "sought new revenues." Such misuses of language have devastating social and political consequences in a free society. As a writer, always avoid using doublespeak; use language truthfully.

Avoiding bureaucratic language

Bureaucratic language is stuffy and overblown.

You can include a page that also contains an Include instruction. The page including the Include instruction is included when you paginate the document but the included text referred to in its Include instruction is not included.

The irony in this example is that the writer seems to be trying to communicate very precisely. Bureaucratic language (or *bureaucratese,* the coined word to describe the style) is marked by unnecessary complexity. Always avoid such meaningless writing.

EXERCISE 21-4

Consulting section 21e, revise these examples of pretentious language, jargon, euphemism, "doublespeak," and bureaucratic language.

1. In-house employee interaction of a nonbusiness nature is disallowed.
2. An index card posted on the bulletin board advertised a gently worn bridal gown for sale.
3. Shortly after Mrs. Harriman went to her reward, Mr. Harriman moved to Florida to be near his son, daughter-in-law, and their bundle of joy.
4. It is with grave misgivings that I undertake this endeavor to instruct myself in the intricacies of computer programming.
5. My male sibling concocted a tale that was entirely fallacious.
6. An individual's cognitive and affective domains are at the center of his or her personality.
7. He told the police officer that the unanticipated collision occurred as the result of a sudden, involuntary explosive action from his nose and mouth that caused him to momentarily close his eyes, which prevented him from seeing the other motorist's automobile.
8. When the finalization of this negotiation comes through, it will clarify our position in a positive manner.
9. The refuse has accumulated because the sanitation engineers were on strike last month.
10. Employees who are employed by the company for no less than five years in a full-time capacity fulfill the eligibility requirements for participation in the company's savings program.

22 *Spelling and Hyphenation*

REFERENCES TO SUPPLEMENTS

For this topic in the CLAST writing competency test, refer students to ch. 1, section B5a of *Preparing for the CLAST* by S. Patterson.

This topic is included in the TASP writing competency test. Refer students to *Preparing for the TASP* by M. Saenz.

For revising for coherence, refer students to *Rough Drafts* by K. S. Cain, Part II, Exercise 4.

BACKGROUND

The earliest writing systems were developed not much more than 6,000 years ago to meet the needs of increasingly complex cultures. In particular, the Egyptians and Babylonians contrived ways of recording their sacred records, commercial transactions, and royal decrees by pictographs—drawings that attempted to convey a general idea by visually reproducing the major elements in it. Writing can be said to have begun when a method for making a linguistic statement of the facts was devised. The earliest of such systems did not make use of the *phonology*, or sounds of language. Instead, they used signs to represent *morphemes* (roots and affixes). Chinese is the only language that continues to use this system. The Egyptians and other Middle East cultures based their writing systems on the sounds of the syllables that made up words. Alphabetic writing

➔

You might be surprised to know this about good spellers: They do not always remember how to spell every word they write, but they are very skilled at sensing when they should check the spelling of a word. Try, therefore, not to ignore your quiet inner voice that doubts a spelling; listen to it and look up the word. At the same time, do not allow spelling doubts to interrupt the flow of your writing during drafting (see 3b). Underline or circle words you want to check, and go back to them when you are editing (see 3d) your writing.

How do you look up a word in the dictionary if you do not know how to spell it? If you know the first few letters, find the general area for the word and browse for it. If you do not know how a word begins, try to find it listed in a thesaurus under an easy-to-spell synonym. When you are writing on a computer, you can usually use a program that checks spelling. Be careful, though, to proofread for spelling errors that result when you substitute another correctly spelled word for the word that you intend (for example, *whole* if you mean *hole*).

As you spell, be aware that the various origins and ways English-speaking people pronounce words make it almost impossible to rely solely on pronunciation to spell a word. What you can rely on is using a system of proofreading and using spelling rules.

22a   Eliminating careless spelling errors

Many spelling errors are the result of illegible handwriting, slips of the pen, or typographical mistakes. Catching "typos" requires especially careful proofreading, using these techniques:

TECHNIQUES FOR PROOFREADING FOR SPELLING

1. Slow down your reading speed so that you can concentrate on individual letters of words rather than on the meaning of the words.
2. Stay within your "visual span," the number of letters you can identify with a single glance (for most people, about six letters).

3. Put a ruler or large index card under each line as you proofread, to focus your concentration and vision.
4. Read each paragraph *backwards*, from the last sentence to the first. This method helps to prevent your being distracted by the meaning of the material.

Spelling homonyms and commonly confused words

22b

Homonyms are words that sound exactly like others (*its, it's; morning, mourning*). There are also many words that sound so much alike that they are often confused with each other. A comprehensive list appears here (also, the most common sets are included in the Usage Glossary at the back of this handbook).

One source of confusion not covered by this list is "swallowed" pronunciation. For example, if a speaker fails to pronounce the letter *-d* at the end of words ("swallows" it), a writer may put down *use to, suppose to,* or *prejudice* when *used to, supposed to,* or *prejudiced* is required.

Another source of confusion is expressions that are always written as two words, not one: for example, *all right,* [not *alright*] and *a lot* [not *alot*].

The best way to remember how to distinguish between homonyms and between other commonly confused words is to use memory devices (mnemonics). For example, if you have trouble with the homonyms *stationary* and *stationery,* try this: *Stationary* means *standing* (*a* is in both) still while *stationery* is *written* (*e* is in both) on.

HOMONYMS AND COMMONLY CONFUSED WORDS

accept	to receive
except	with the exclusion of
advice	recommendation
advise	to recommend
affect	to produce an influence on (VERB); an emotional response (NOUN)
effect	result (NOUN); to bring about or cause (VERB)
aisle	space between rows
isle	island

→

409

BACKGROUND, cont.

was invented by the peoples of the Eastern Mediterranean. At first they used only consonants, depending on readers to fill in the vowels as well as to supply such missing information as intonation and stress. When the Greeks took over a Semitic alphabet, they used the unneeded consonants to represent vowels. That tradition is the basis of all modern alphabets used in the West today.

REFERENCE TO SUPPLEMENTS

For this topic in the CLAST writing competency test, refer students to ch. 1, section B4a of *Preparing for the CLAST* by S. Patterson.

WORDS OFTEN MISSPELLED

Here is a collection of commonly misspelled words. To help you locate the words your students have difficulty with, the lists are organized in these categories: Word Endings (Suffixes), Double Consonants, Unstressed Syllables, Silent Letters and Blended Sounds, *ei/ie,* and Other Commonly Misspelled Words. It's a good idea to assign words for study in groups of 25 at a time.

Double Consonants

accommodate	committee	missile
accompanied	controlled	occasion
accomplish	different	occurred
accordion	disappear	parallel
accustomed	disappoint	processes
address	disapprove	quizzes
annihilate	efficient	satellite
appoint	equipped	stepped
appreciate	fulfill	succeed
appropriate	happened	suppose
arrest	harass	surround
bulletin	interrupt	tyranny
commercial	mirror	villain

WORDS OFTEN MISSPELLED
Word Endings (Suffixes)

acceptable	characteristic
accessible	Christianity
accidentally	commitment
accuracy	competent
acreage	competition
actually	completely
admission	confident
affectionately	consistent
aggression	continuous
announcement	convenient
apparent	coolly
appearance	criticism
approximately	criticize
arguing	cruelty
argument	curiosity
assassination	decision
attendance	definitely
barbarous	description
basically	desirable
beautiful	desperate
beginning	despicable
beneficial	disastrous
biggest	discussion
bureaucracy	dormitory
business	easily
calculator	elaborately
carrying	entirely
changeable	environment
changing	equipment
especially	insurance
evidently	intelligent
existence	interference
experiment	irrelevant
explanation	irresistible
extremely	irritated
finally	likelihood
financially	listening
generally	liveliest
government	livelihood
governor	lying
guidance	magnificent

→

allude	to make indirect reference to
elude	to avoid
allusion	indirect reference
illusion	false idea, misleading appearance
already	by this time
all ready	fully prepared
altar	sacred platform or place
alter	to change
altogether	thoroughly
all together	everyone or everything in one place
are	plural form of *to be*
hour	sixty minutes
our	plural form of *my*
ascent	the act of rising or climbing
assent	consent
assistance	help
assistants	helpers
bare	nude, unadorned
bear	to carry; an animal
board	piece of wood
bored	uninterested
breath	air taken in
breathe	to take in air
brake	device for stopping
break	destroy, make into pieces
buy	to purchase
by	next to, through the agency of
capital	major city
capitol	government building
choose	to pick
chose	past tense of *to choose*
cite	to point out
sight	vision
site	a place
clothes	garments
cloths	pieces of fabric

coarse	rough
course	path; series of lectures
complement	something that completes
compliment	praise, flattery
conscience	sense of morality
conscious	awake, aware
council	governing body
counsel	advice
dairy	place associated with milk production
diary	personal journal
descent	downward movement
dissent	disagreement
dessert	final, sweet course in a meal
desert	to abandon (VERB); dry, sandy area (NOUN)
device	a plan; an implement
devise	to create
die	to lose life (VERB) (*dying*); one of a pair of dice (NOUN)
dye	to change the color of something (*dyeing*)
dominant	commanding, controlling
dominate	to control
elicit	to draw out
illicit	illegal
eminent	prominent
immanent	living within; inherent
imminent	about to happen
envelop	to surround
envelope	container for a letter or other papers
fair	light-skinned; just, honest
fare	money for transportation; food
formally	conventionally, with ceremony
formerly	previously
forth	forward
fourth	number four

→

happily	maintenance
hindrance	manageable
hoping	management
humorous	marriage
hungry	meanness
hurriedly	mischievous
hypocrisy	mysterious
ideally	narrative
idiosyncrasy	naturally
ignorant	necessary
illogical	noticeable
imaginary	noticing
immediately	nuisance
immensely	numerous
incalculable	occasionally
incidentally	occurrence
incredible	occurring
independent	official
indispensable	omission
individually	omitting
influential	opponent
innocuous	questionnaire
opportunity	rarity
opposite	reality
oppression	realize
optimism	really
ordinarily	recession
originally	recommend
particularly	referring
peaceable	regulate
peculiar	rehearsal
performance	religious
permanence	remembrance
permissible	repetition
politician	representative
possession	resemblance
practicality	ridiculous
predominant	scarcity
preparation	scenery
prevalent	secretary
prisoner	senseless
probably	shining
professor	shrubbery
prominent	significant

→

WORDS OFTEN MISSPELLED, cont.

pronunciation	simply
publicly	sincerely
pursuing	tragedy
skiing	tremendous
strenuous	truce
stubbornness	unanimous
studying	unconscious
suburban	undoubtedly
succession	usage
sufficient	using
summary	usually
superintendent	valuable
supersede	various
suppress	vegetable
surely	vengeance
susceptible	violence
suspicious	visible
swimming	writing
technical	written
temporary	
tendency	

BACKGROUND

J. Richard Gentry reports that learning to spell may not be as difficult as it often seems to be, but that teaching it is not a simple matter. He points out that children who are encouraged to invent spelling spontaneously in the context of writing find the process relatively simple. Words removed from their context and isolated in formal lessons are harder to master. Learning to spell becomes more difficult and less successful (*Spel . . . Is a Four-Letter Word* [Portsmouth, NH: Heinemann Books, 1978]).

QUOTATION ABOUT WRITING

Bad spellers of the world, untie!

(Graffito)

gorilla	animal in ape family
guerrilla	soldier specializing in unconventional, surprise attacks
hear	to sense sound by ear
here	in this place
hole	opening
whole	complete; an entire thing
human	relating to the species *homo sapiens*
humane	compassionate
insure	buy or give insurance
ensure	guarantee, protect
its	possessive form of *it*
it's	contraction for *it is*
know	to comprehend
no	negative
later	after a time
latter	second one of two things
lead	heavy metal substance; to guide
led	past tense of *to lead*
lightning	storm-related electricity
lightening	making lighter
loose	unbound, not tightly fastened
lose	to misplace
maybe	perhaps
may be	might be
meat	animal flesh
meet	to encounter
miner	a person who works in a mine
minor	under age
moral	distinguishing right from wrong; the lesson of a fable, story, or event
morale	attitude or outlook, usually of a group
of	preposition indicating origin
off	away from
passed	past tense of *to pass*
past	at a previous time

patience	forbearance
patients	people under medical care
peace	absence of fighting
piece	part of a whole; musical arrangement
personal	intimate
personnel	employees
plain	simple, unadorned
plane	to shave wood; aircraft
precede	to come before
proceed	to continue
presence	being at hand; attendance at a place or in something
presents	gifts
principal	foremost (ADJECTIVE); school head (NOUN)
principle	moral conviction, basic truth
quiet	silent, calm
quite	very
rain	water drops falling to earth (NOUN); to fall like rain (VERB)
reign	to rule
rein	strap to guide or control an animal (NOUN); to guide or control (VERB)
raise	to lift up
raze	to tear down
respectfully	with respect
respectively	in that order
right	correct; opposite of *left*
rite	ritual
write	to put words on paper
road	path
rode	past tense of *to ride*
scene	place of an action; segment of a play
seen	viewed
sense	perception, understanding
since	measurement of past time; because

➜

TEACHING TIP

A sophisticated relative of the spelling test is the dictation exercise. Passages can be created to test student ability to spell, punctuate, or capitalize. Here is a sample dictation passage aimed at testing whether students can distinguish among homonyms and commonly confused words. The context gives students clues to which word is intended (much as the sentences normally given as part of a spelling test do); at the same time, the paragraph format is more interesting than random illustrative sentences. (Homonyms and commonly confused words are in italics.)

The institution of marriage has received *its* share of public attention over the past few years. Rising divorce rates, *seen* as a symptom of a troubled society, have *led* people to question why *some* marriages *break* up and others succeed. One reason may be that the *effect* of courtship is to cause the bride and groom to *lose sight* of reality. Researchers *cite* evidence that some couples are *too* unrealistic. They *proceed* to the *altar* carrying romantic *illusions* about themselves, each other, and marriage itself. Having grown accustomed to *compliments* and *presents*, they find themselves walking down the *aisle* expecting a lifetime of romantic bliss to follow. The groom may assume that his bride is an *angel*, and she may *choose* to think of him as a *knight* on a white horse. They may fail to realize that one expects to *dominate* rather than *complement* the other, or that he lacks *patience* and she is not as *quiet* as she seems. *They're* reluctant to look at the *whole* situation until *later*, when they *are* called on to *accept* the serious responsibilities of marriage. The best *advice*, of *course*, is for husbands and wives to live by *principles* that *lead* them to treat each other *respectfully*, *lightening* each other's troubles and acknowledging each other's *rights*.

QUOTATION ABOUT WRITING

English orthography satisfies all the requirements of the canons of reputability under the law of conspicuous waste. It is archaic, cumbrous, and ineffective; its acquisition consumes much time and effort; failure to acquire it is easy of detection.

—Thorstein Veblen,
Theory of the Leisure Class

TEACHING TIP

Much of the recent research on spelling improvements stresses the importance of using as many of the senses as possible during word study. You may want to suggest to students that they try to improve their visual memory by writing a word in the air, using a finger to make the troublesome letters especially large. Ask them to try to imagine a word as if it were on an outdoor movie screen. Then they can try to write the word mentally in "longhand." The auditory sense can be invoked by making exaggerated pronunciations. That is, the speaker emphasizes the problem portion of a word when saying it. For example, the person who habitually leaves off the final *-d* of *used* should practice pronouncing the word as "you said." The kinesthetic and tactile senses are combined when a writer records a problem word on paper using a different kind of medium to write the difficult spots, changing from a ball-point pen, for instance, to a crayon. This technique can include a visual element if the student puts the problem letters in red or some other bright color.

BACKGROUND

In "English Spelling and Pidgin" (*English Today* [July 1988]: 29–35), Valerie Yule discusses how spelling systems are developed for English pidgins. She analyzes the factors that determine how closely pidgin spelling correlates with English spelling.

22b
cont.

stationary	standing still
stationery	writing paper
than	in comparison with; besides
then	at that time; next; therefore
their	possessive form of *they*
there	in that place
they're	contraction for *they are*
through	finished; into and out of
threw	past tense of *to throw*
thorough	complete
to	toward
too	also; indicates degree (*too much*)
two	number following one
waist	midsection of the body
waste	discarded material (NOUN); to squander, to fail to use up (VERB)
weak	not strong
week	seven days
weather	climatic condition
whether	if
where	in which place
were	past tense of *to be*
which	one of a group
witch	female sorcerer
whose	possessive form of *who*
who's	contraction for *who is*
your	possessive form of *you*
you're	contraction for *you are*
yore	long past

EXERCISE 22-1

Consulting section 22b, select the appropriate homonym from each group in parentheses.

According to the (Council, Counsel) on Aging, the U.S. population over 85 is growing faster (than, then) any other segment of society. The (council, counsel) (cites, sites) statistics indicating that elderly people who have access (to, too, two) good health care (are, our) likely to outlive (their, there, they're) parents. If elderly parents grow (to, too, two) (weak, week) to care for themselves, responsibility for them (maybe, may be) (passed, past) to children (know, no) longer young themselves. (Formally, Formerly) (use to, used to) (their, there) parents making independent decisions, adult children must now learn to (accept, except) that parents may need (assistance, assistants) with some decisions. Aging parents must be treated with courtesy and handled with (patience, patients). Frequent (personal, personnel) visits help to keep parents' (moral, morale) high or to (raise, raze) low spirits. In (principal, principle), adult children (all ready, already) (know, no) how to behave with aging parents; they must sometimes be prepared to reverse their (respectful, respective) roles.

Using spelling rules for plurals, suffixes, and *ie, ei* words

22c

Knowing the rules in Chart 101 will help you spell plurals, add suffixes, and spell words that contain *ie* or *ei* combinations.

SPELLING RULES FOR PLURALS, SUFFIXES, AND *IE, EI* WORDS 101

PLURALS

- **Adding *-s* or *-es*:** Most plurals are formed by adding *-s*, including words that end in "hard" *-ch* (sounding like *k*): *leg, legs; shoe, shoes; stomach, stomachs.* For words ending in *-s, -sh, -x, -z,* or "soft" *-ch* (as in *beach*), add *-es* to the singular: *beach, beaches; tax, taxes; coach, coaches.*

- **Words Ending in *-o*:** Add *-s* if the *-o* is preceded by a vowel (*radio, radios; cameo, cameos*). Add *-es* if the *-o* is preceded by a consonant (*potato, potatoes*). A few words can be pluralized either way: *cargo, volcano, tornado, zero.*

- **Words Ending in *-f* or *-fe*:** Some *-f* and *-fe* words are made plural by adding *-s: belief, beliefs.* Others require changing *-f* or *-fe* to *-ves: life, lives; leaf, leaves.* Words ending in *-ff* or *-ffe* simply add *-s: staff, staffs; giraffe, giraffes.*

- **Compound Words:** For most compound words, add *-s* or *-es* at the end of the last word: *checkbooks, player-coaches.* For a few, the word to make plural is not the last one: *sister-in-law, sisters-in-law; mile per hour, miles per hour.* (For hyphenating compound words, see Chart 103 in 22d.)

→

ANSWERS: EXERCISE 22–1

1. Council
2. than
3. council
4. cites
5. to
6. are
7. their
8. too
9. weak
10. may be
11. passed
12. no
13. Formerly
14. used to
15. their
16. accept
17. assistance
18. patience
19. personal
20. morale
21. raise
22. principle
23. already
24. know
25. respective

WORDS OFTEN MISSPELLED

Unstressed Syllables (including syllables frequently not pronounced)

adolescent	category
alcohol	cemetery
amateur	census
analysis	certain
angel	challenge
apology	channel
article	children
aspirin	chocolate
average	chosen
bargain	coarsely
boundary	concentrate
cafeteria	controversial
calendar	curious

→

WORDS OFTEN MISSPELLED, cont.

decorate	poison
delicate	practical
despair	prepare
destroy	privilege
develop	propaganda
disease	pumpkin
dispel	purpose
divide	pursue
divine	pursuit
ecstasy	quandary
embarrass	rebel
enemy	recognize
escape	regular
everything	remember
exercise	reproduce
family	resources
favorite	restaurant
grammar	sacrifice
heroes	saxophone
holiday	sentence
hundred	separate
imagine	several
imitate	sheriff
integrate	similar
interest	sophomore
introduce	specimen
laboratory	sponsor
liable	statistics
luxury	strategy
magazine	surprise
manual	temperature
mathematics	therefore
medicine	thorough
miniature	tobacco
particle	together
perhaps	tomorrow
persuade	typical
physical	vitamins
pigeon	Wednesday
pitiful	woman
pleasant	women

SPELLING RULES FOR PLURALS, SUFFIXES, AND *IE, EI* WORDS (continued)

- **Internal Changes and Endings Other Than *-s*:** A few words change internally or add endings other than *-s* to become plural: *foot, feet; man, men; mouse, mice; child, children.*

- **Foreign Words:** Plurals other than *-s* or *-es* are listed in good dictionaries. In general, for many Latin words ending in *-um*, form plurals by changing *-um* to *-a: curriculum, curricula; datum, data; medium, media; stratum, strata.* For Latin words that end in *-us*, the plural is often *-i: alumnus, alumni; syllabus, syllabi.* For Greek *-on* words, the plural is often *-a: criterion, criteria; phenomenon, phenomena.*

- **One-Form Words:** A few spellings are the same for the singular and plural: *deer, elk, quail.* The differences are conveyed by adding words, not endings: *one deer, nine deer; rice, bowls of rice.*

SUFFIXES

- **-y Words:** If the letter before the final *y* is a consonant, change the *y* to *i* unless the suffix begins with an *i* (for example, *-ing*): *fry, fried, frying.* If the letter before the *-y* is a vowel, keep the final *y: employ, employed, employing.* These rules do not apply to irregular verbs (see Chart 59 in section 8d).

- **-e Words:** Drop a final *e* when the suffix begins with a vowel unless doing so would cause confusion (for example, *be + ing* does not become *bing*): *require, requiring; like, liking.* Keep the final *e* when the suffix begins with a consonant: *require, requirement; like, likely.* Exceptions include *argument, judgment,* and *truly.*

- **Words That Double a Final Letter:** If the final letter is a consonant, double it only if it passes all three of these tests: (1) Its last two letters are a vowel followed by a consonant; (2) it has one syllable or is accented on the last syllable; and (3) the suffix begins with a vowel: *drop, dropped; begin, beginning; forget, forgetful, forgettable.*

- **-cede, -ceed, -sede Words:** Only one word ends in *-sede: supersede.* Three words end in *-ceed: exceed, proceed, succeed.* All other words whose endings sound like "seed" end in *-cede: concede, intercede, precede.*

- **-ally and -ly Words:** The suffixes *-ally* and *-ly* turn words into ADVERBS. For words ending in *-ic*, add *-ally: logically, statistically.* Otherwise, add *-ly: quickly, sharply.*

SPELLING RULES FOR PLURALS, SUFFIXES, AND *IE, EI* WORDS (continued)   101

■ **-ance, -ence,** and **-ible, -able:** No consistent rules govern words with these suffixes. The best advice is "When in doubt, look it up."

THE IE, EI RULE: The old rhyme for *ie* and *ei* is usually true:

"*I* before *e* [bel**ie**ve, f**ie**ld, gr**ie**f]
Except after *c* [c**ei**ling, conc**ei**t],
Or when sounded like *ay* [**ei**ght, v**ei**n],
As in n**ei**ghbor and w**ei**gh."

You may want to memorize these major exceptions:

ie	conscience	financier	science	species
ei	either	neither	leisure	seize
	counterfeit	foreign	forfeit	sleight
	weird			

EXERCISE 22-2

Consulting section 22c and Chart 101, form the plurals of these words.

1. scarf
2. species
3. rodeo
4. moose
5. leech
6. datum
7. log
8. brother-in-law
9. phenomenon
10. self
11. nacho
12. fungus
13. loaf
14. push-up
15. thesis

EXERCISE 22-3

Consulting section 22c, Chart 101, and a dictionary, follow the directions for each group of words.

1. Add *-able* or *-ible:* (a) profit; (b) reproduce; (c) control; (d) coerce; (e) recognize.
2. Add *-ance* or *-ence:* (a) luxuri _____ ; (b) prud _____ ; (c) devi _____ ; (d) resist _____ ; (e) independ _____ .
3. Drop the final *e* as needed: (a) true + ly; (b) joke + ing; (c) fortunate + ly; (d) appease + ing; (e) appease + ment.
4. Change the final *y* to *i* as needed: (a) happy + ness; (b) pry + ed; (c) pry + ing; (d) dry + ly; (e) beautify + ing.

WORDS OFTEN MISSPELLED
ei/ie

achievement	conscientious	relief
apiece	eighth	relieve
atheist	foreign	review
belief	forfeit	seize
believed	height	view
ceiling	leisure	weird
chief	lenient	
conceited	niece	
conceive	receive	

TEACHING TIP

Carol Chomsky suggests an exercise that can be used to clarify the spellings of words with silent consonants. She points out that it is helpful to associate each one with a root word in a different form that does not silence the letter. For instance, the *g* in *sign* is easily heard in *signature;* the silent *c* in *muscle* is apparent in *muscular.* Groups of words that have consonant alternation become easier to spell after the exchange is noted and discussed—as in *coincidental* and *coincidence, pirate* and *piracy,* in which the *t* and *c* are alternated ("Reading, Writing, and Phonology," *Harvard Educational Review* 40 [1970]: 287–309).

ANSWERS: EXERCISE 22–2

1. scarves
2. species
3. rodeos
4. moose
5. leeches
6. data
7. logs
8. brothers-in-law
9. phenomena
10. selves
11. nachos
12. fungi
13. loaves
14. push-ups
15. theses

ANSWERS: EXERCISE 22–3

1. (a) profitable
   (b) reproducible
   (c) controllable
   (d) coercible
   (e) recognizable
2. (a) luxuriance
   (b) prudence
   (c) deviance
   (d) resistance
   (e) independence
3. (a) truly
   (b) joking
   (c) fortunately
   (d) appeasing
   e) appeasement
4. (a) happiness
   (b) pried
   (c) prying
   (d) dryly
   (e) beautifying
5. (a) committed
   (b) commitment
   (c) dropped
   (d) occurred
   (e) regretful
6. (a) relief
   (b) achieve
   (c) weird
   (d) niece
   (e) deceive

WORDS OFTEN MISSPELLED

Silent Letters and Blended Sounds

acquainted	muscle
acquire	pamphlet
condemn	psychology
contradict	quantity
courteous	receipt
crowd	reminisce
dealt	rhythm
descend	safety
distinct	sandwich

➡

22c
cont.

5. Double the final consonant as needed: (a) commit + ed;
   (b) commit + ment; (c) drop + ed; (d) occur + ed; (e) regret + ful.
6. Insert *ie* or *ei* correctly: (a) rel _____ f; (b) ach _____ ve; (c) w _____ rd;
   (d) n _____ ce; (e) dec _____ ve.

22d   # Using hyphens correctly

22d-1   ## Hyphenating at the end of a line

Unless the last word on a line would use up most of the right margin of your paper, do not divide it. If you must divide a word, try not to divide the last word on the first line of a paper, the last word in a paragraph, or the last word on a page. When you have to hyphenate, break the word only at a syllable, using the guidelines in Chart 102. If you are unsure of how to divide a word into syllables, consult a dictionary (see 20a).

GUIDELINES FOR END-OF-LINE HYPHENATION

GUIDELINES FOR END-OF-LINE HYPHENATION   102

- **Do not divide very short words, one-syllable words, or words pronounced as one syllable.**

NO	we-alth	en-vy	scream-ed
YES	wealth	envy	screamed

- **Do not leave or carry over only one or two letters.**

NO	a-live	tax-i	he-licopter	helicopt-er
YES	alive	taxi	heli-copter	helicop-ter

- **Divide words only between syllables.**

NO	proc-ede
YES	pro-cede

- **Always follow rules for double consonants.**

NO	ful-lness	omitt-ing	asp-halt
YES	full-ness	omit-ting	as-phalt

➡

418

GUIDELINES FOR END-OF-LINE HYPHENATION (continued)   102

- ■ **Divide hyphenated words after the hyphen, if possible, rather than at any other syllable.**

NO	self-con-scious	good-look-ing report
YES	self-conscious	good-looking report

Hyphenating prefixes, suffixes, compound words, and numbers

Prefixes and **suffixes** are syllables attached to root words. **Compound words** use two or more words together to express one concept. Some prefixes and suffixes are hyphenated; others are not. Compound words can be written as separate words (*night shift*), hyphenated words (*tractor-trailer*), or one word (*handbook*). Chart 103 gives basic guidelines for word hyphenation.

HYPHENATING PREFIXES, SUFFIXES, COMPOUND WORDS, AND NUMBERS   103

PREFIXES AND SUFFIXES

- ■ **Use hyphens after the prefixes *all-, ex-, quasi-,* and *self-*.**

  all-inclusive   self-reliant

- ■ **Do not use a hyphen when *self* is a root word, not a prefix.**

NO	self-ishness	self-less
YES	selfishness	selfless

- ■ **Use a hyphen to avoid a distracting string of letters.**

NO	antiintellectual	belllike
YES	anti-intellectual	bell-like

- ■ **Use a hyphen before the suffix *-elect*.**

NO	presidentelect
YES	president-elect

➡

WORDS OFTEN MISSPELLED, cont.

empty	schedule
fascinate	sergeant
February	shoulder
foresee	source
foretell	souvenir
gauge	straight
group	strength
gruesome	stretch
guaranteed	strict
guard	technique
initiative	themselves
instead	though
knowledge	thought
length	through
library	trouble
meant	twelfth
mortgage	vacuum

BACKGROUND

Some grammarians point out that context usually clarifies whether a writer means *research* or *re-search, re-creation* or *recreation,* and other words beginning with the *re-* prefix. Carl Kane, writing in *The Cedar Rapids Gazette* (August 20, 1986), contends that hyphens should not be neglected. "Anything that might even temporarily mislead a reader should be eliminated. Throw in a hyphen. It can't hurt."

WORDS OFTEN MISSPELLED
Other Commonly Misspelled Words

absence	material
across	mere
always	minutes
among	morning
ancestry	nevertheless
anxiety	nineteen
anywhere	ninety
authentic	ninth
awkward	nuclear

➡

HYPHENATING PREFIXES, SUFFIXES, COMPOUND WORDS, AND NUMBERS (continued)

WORDS OFTEN MISSPELLED, cont.

bachelor	omit
benefited	opinion
birthday	paid
compel	parole
consensus	pastime
cylinder	penetrate
defer	pertain
disagree	phase
disturb	prairie
exceed	pretty
expense	prevail
familiar	restaurant
forty	science
forward	speak
furniture	speech
grandeur	temperature
hesitate	until
hypocrite	vicious
intercede	wherever
laid	whether
license	wholly

TEACHING TIP

Because hyphenation of compound words is subject to change, students sometimes have trouble knowing whether to use hyphens with them or not. Words used consecutively over a considerable period of time often move closer together through hyphenation, then later become a single word. *Steamboat*, for example, was once *steam boat*, then *steamboat*, and finally took the form in which it appears today. *Wristwatch* was, earlier, *wrist watch* and later *wrist-watch*. To be sure of current usage, students need to use a dictionary.

QUOTATION ABOUT WRITING

Hooray for the hyphen! Or, rather, Hoo-ray!

—George Plimpton

22d-2 cont.

HYPHENATING PREFIXES, SUFFIXES, COMPOUND WORDS, AND NUMBERS (continued)   103

■ **Use a hyphen when a prefix comes before a number or a word that starts with a capital letter.**

NO	post1950s	proAmerican
YES	post-1950	pro-American

■ **Use a hyphen between a prefix and a compound word.**

NO	antigun control
YES	anti-gun control

■ **Use a hyphen to prevent confusion in meaning or pronunciation.**

YES	re-dress ("dress again")	redress ("set right")
	un-ionize	unionize ("form a union")
	("remove the ions")	

■ **Use a hyphen when two or more prefixes apply to one root word.**

YES	pre- and post-war eras	two-, three-, or four-year program

COMPOUND WORDS

■ **Use a hyphen for most compound modifiers that precede the noun. Do not use a hyphen for most compound modifiers after the noun.**

YES	well-researched report	two-inch clearance
	report is well researched	clearance of two inches

■ **Use a hyphen between compound nouns joining two units of measure.**

YES	light-year	kilowatt-hour	foot-pound

■ **You do not need to use a hyphen when a compound modifier starts with an *-ly* adverb.**

YES	happily married couple	loosely tied package

➡

420

HYPHENATING PREFIXES, SUFFIXES, COMPOUND WORDS, AND NUMBERS (continued)

103

■ **Do not use a hyphen when a compound modifier is in the comparative or superlative form.**

NO	better-fitting shoe	least-welcome guest most-significant factor
YES	better fitting shoe	least welcome guest most significant factor

■ **Do not use a hyphen when a compound modifier is a foreign phrase.**

YES	post hoc fallacies

■ **Do not use a hyphen with a possessive compound modifier.**

NO	a full-week's work	eight-hour's pay
YES	a full week's work	eight hours' pay

SPELLED-OUT NUMBERS

■ **Use a hyphen between two-word numbers from twenty-one through ninety-nine.**

YES	thirty-five (35)	two hundred thirty-five (235)

■ **Use a hyphen in a compound-word modifier formed from a number and a word.**

YES	fifty-minute class [also 50-minute class]	three-to-one odds [also 3-to-1 odds]

■ **Use a hyphen between the numerator and the denominator of two-word fractions.**

YES	one-half	two-fifths	seven-tenths

❖ ALERT: Use figures rather than words for any fraction that needs more than two words to express. If you cannot use figures (for example, if you cannot rearrange a sentence that starts with a multiword fraction), use hyphens between the words of the numerator's number and the words of the denominator's number but not between the numerator and the denominator: two one-hundredths (2/100), thirty-three ten-thousandths (33/10,000). ❖

HYPHENATING PREFIXES, SUFFIXES, COMPOUND WORDS, AND NUMBERS (continued)

LANGUAGE HISTORY

During the period of colonization, English continued to expand. From Native Americans we learned *tomahawk, wigwam, squaw,* and place names, such as *Nebraska, Allegheny, Kentucky, Seattle,* and *Dakota.* From the Spanish in the New World: *mustang, ranch, patio, bonanza, rodeo, vigilante, sombrero.* From India: *thug, loot, pajamas, bandana.* From Germany: *kindergarten, semester, delicatessen, frankfurter, hamburger.*

Borrowing continues unabated. Recent borrowings have come from Italian (*casino, malaria, studio*); Spanish (*cigar, canyon, cafeteria*); German (*pumpernickel, iceberg, protein*); Slavic (*pogrom, soviet, robot*); Arabic (*genie, candy, safari*); Hebrew (*hallelujah, kosher*); Persian (*spinach, lilac, bazaar*); Tibeto-Chinese (*tea, ketchup*); and Japanese (*zen, karate*).

Over the centuries, the Anglo-Saxons' vocabulary of 50,000 words has expanded to more than 600,000 words. Irregular spellings are the price we pay for this acquired richness and flexibility.

BACKGROUND

A single missing hyphen cost U.S. citizens $18.5 million in 1962. *Mariner I*, a U.S. space exploration rocket, went off course and had to be destroyed. The reason: a missing hyphen in its computer-run flight program.

ANSWERS: EXERCISE 22–4

1. all-powerful
2. Comparison-contrast; more agile
3. boldly striped; underbody
4. eleven feet; one-quarter; five hundred
5. self-confident
6. village destroyer; into
7. terror-stricken
8. spring-loaded; poisoned arrows
9. cattle killers
10. animal shows; pro-animal

COVERAGE: EXERCISE 22–4

1. *all-* prefixes hyphenated
2. hyphenated compound; open
3. *-ly* adverb as first word of compound; *under* prefixes spelled closed
4. not a double digit; fraction; not a double digit
5. *self-* prefixes hyphenated
6. open compound; closed compound
7. hyphenated compound
8. hyphenated compound; open compound
9. open compound
10. open compound; *pro-* prefix hyphenated before a vowel

ANSWERS AND COVERAGE: EXERCISE 22–5

Incorrect	Correct	Section & Chart
1. beautyful	beautiful	22c, Chart 101
2. envelop	envelope	22b
3. rite	right	22b
4. recieve	receive	22c, Chart 101
5. through	threw	22b
6. tryed	tried	22c, Chart 101
7. practiceing	practicing	22c, Chart 101
8. freinds	friends	22c, Chart 101
9. insure	ensure	Usage Glossary
10. publically	publicly	22c, Chart 101
11. heart-ache	heartache	22d, Chart 103

22d cont.

EXERCISE 22-4

Consulting section 22d, in the blanks write the correct form of the word in parentheses according to the way it is used in the sentence.

1. The tiger is (all powerful) _____ in the cat family.
2. (Comparison contrast) _____ studies of tigers and lions show that the tiger is the (more agile) _____ and powerful.
3. The tiger's body is a (boldly striped) _____ yellow, with a white (under body) _____ .
4. The tiger's maximum length is about (eleven feet) _____ , about (one quarter) _____ of which is accounted for by its tail, and its maximum weight is up to (five hundred) _____ pounds.
5. The Bengal tiger, the largest of the family, is aggressive and (self confident) _____ .
6. In India, where the Bengal is called a (village destroyer) _____ , it has a reputation for going (in to) _____ villages to hunt for food.
7. Entire villages have been temporarily abandoned by (terror stricken) _____ people who have seen a Bengal tiger nearby.
8. Villagers seek to protect their homes by destroying tigers with traps, (spring loaded) _____ guns, and (poisoned arrows) _____ .
9. Bengal tigers are also called (cattle killers) _____ , although they attack domestic animals only when wild ones cannot be found.
10. Many people who do not live near a zoo get to see tigers only in (animal shows) _____ , although (pro animal) _____ activists try to prevent tigers' being used this way.

EXERCISE 22-5

The following paragraph contains eleven misspelled words. Circle the words, correct them, and match them to a section in this chapter. If the error does not fall under any particular section, describe the cause of the error in your own words.

An invitation arrived last week in a beautyful, crisp white envelop. I knew rite away it was a peace of important mail, unlike all the junk mail I usually recieve. It seemed that the local chapter of the Falcon Club of America wanted to hear my thoughts on American car collecting. The prospect of giving a speech through me into a nervous frenzy as I tryed to prepare at the last minute—getting a haircut, memorizing my notes, practiceing in front of my freinds—all designed to insure that I would not humiliate myself publically. As it turned out, my heart-ache was pointless. The club really just wanted the opportunity to inspect my 1965 navy blue Ford Falcon.

Using Punctuation and Mechanics

When you use punctuation and mechanics according to currently accepted practice, you avoid errors that interfere with the delivery of the meaning that you want to communicate. Part Six presents and explains the rules and conventions that readers have come to expect. As you use Chapters 23 through 30, remember that punctuation and mechanics are tools that help you deliver your message clearly to your readers.

23 The Period, Question Mark, and Exclamation Point

The period, question mark, and exclamation point are called **end punctuation** because they occur at the end of sentences.

I love you. Do you love me? I love you!

THE PERIOD

Using a period at the end of a statement, a mild command, or an indirect question

Unless a sentence asks a DIRECT QUESTION* (23c) or issues a strong command or emphatic declaration (23e), it ends with a period.

STATEMENT

A journey of a thousand leagues begins with a single step.

—LAO-TSU

MILD COMMAND

Put a gram of boldness into everything you do.

—BALTASAR GRACIAN

INDIRECT QUESTION

I asked if they wanted to climb Mt. Everest. [A direct question would end with a question mark: I asked, *"Do you want to climb Mt. Everest?"*]

---

*You can find the definition of a word printed in small capital letters (such as DIRECT QUESTION) in the Glossary of Terms toward the end of this handbook.

REFERENCE TO SUPPLEMENTS

For this topic in the CLAST writing competency test, refer students to ch. 1, section B5b of *Preparing for the CLAST* by S. Patterson.

REFERENCE TO SUPPLEMENTS

This topic is included in the TASP writing competency test. Refer students to *Preparing for the TASP* by M. Saenz.

BACKGROUND

R. Baird Shuman addresses the on-going debate about the value of grammar instruction and provides exercises designed to help students both understand the vocabulary of grammar and develop a repetoire of strategies related to recognizing options of style. ("Grammar for Writers: How Much Is Enough?" in *The Place of Grammar in Writing Instruction: Past, Present, Future*, Susan Hunter and Ray Wallace, Portsmouth, NH: Boynton-Cook, 1995).

Using periods with most abbreviations   **23b**

Most **abbreviations** call for periods, but some do not. Typical abbreviations with periods include *Mt., St., Dr., Mr., Ms., Mrs., Ph.D., M.D.,* and *R.N.* In general, the word *professor* is spelled out, not abbreviated. Also, *a.m.* and *p.m.* are appropriate with exact times (such as 2:15 *p.m.*) but should not be used instead of the word *morning, evening,* or *night*. Abbreviations without periods include the names of some organizations and government agencies (such as CBS and NASA). For more information about abbreviations, see 30h and 30i.

> Ms. Yuan, who works at NASA, lectured to Dr. Garcia's physics class at 9:30 a.m.

❖ PUNCTUATION ALERT: When the period of an abbreviation falls at the end of a sentence, the period serves also to end the sentence. ❖   **!**

THE QUESTION MARK

Using a question mark after a direct question   **23c**

A **direct question** asks a question and ends with a question mark. In contrast, an **indirect question** reports a question and ends with a period (see 23a).

> How many attempts have been made to climb Mt. Everest?
> [An indirect question would be: *The tourists wanted to know how many attempts had been made to climb Mt. Everest.*]

❖ PUNCTUATION ALERT: Do not combine a question mark with a comma, a period, or an exclamation point. ❖   **!**

> **NO**   She asked, "How are you**?**."
> **YES**   She asked, "How are you?"

Questions in a series are each followed by a question mark, whether or not each question is a complete sentence.

❖ CAPITALIZATION ALERT: When questions in a series are not complete sentences, you can choose whether or not to capitalize the first letter, as long as you are consistent in each piece of writing. ❖   **!**

> After the fierce storm had passed, the mountain climbers debated what to do next. Turn back? Move on? Rest for a while?

QUOTATION ABOUT WRITING

GREEKANDLATINMANUSCRIPTS WEREUSUALLYWRITTENWITHNOSPACEBETWEENWORDSUNTIL AROUND THE NINTH CENTURY AD ALTHOUGH·ROMAN·INSCRIPTIONS·LIKE·THE·FAMOUS·TRAJAN· COLUMN·SOMETIMES·SEPARATED·WORDS·WITH·A·CENTERED· DOT·EVEN AFTER SPACING BECAME COMMON IT REMAINED HAPHAZARD FOREXAMPLE OFTEN A PREPOSITION WAS LINKEDTO ANOTHER WORD

    A CENTERED DOT DIVIDED WORDS WHICH FELL AT THE END OF A LINE IN EARLY GREEK AND LATIN MANUSCRIPTS AND THE MORE VISUALLY DISTINCT HYPHEN WAS INTRODUCED IN THE ELEVENTH CENTURY MEDIEVAL SCRIBES OFTEN PUT MARKS AT THE END OF SHORT LINES TO MAKE A SOLID TEXT

—*Period Styles: A History of Punctuation,* catalog, The Cooper Union for the Advancement of Science and Art

QUOTATION ABOUT WRITING

Punctuation is a group of supplementary visual cues which organize letters on a two-dimensional surface. Some kinds of punctuation merely format a text, without affecting its basic meaning: for example, abbreviations, hyphenated line breaks, word spacing, and the left-to-right direction of reading. Other forms affect the meaning of a text, like the comma, colon, period, and question mark, which stand in place of spoken pauses and intonations.

—*Period Styles: A History of Punctuation,* catalog, The Cooper Union for the Advancement of Science and Art

23c cont. **When a request is phrased as a question,** it does not always require a question mark, especially when the request is phrased as a question to achieve a polite tone: *Would you please send me a copy.*

23d Using a question mark in parentheses

When a date or number is unknown or doubtful even after your very best research, you can use (?).

Mary Astell, an English author who wrote pamphlets on women's rights, was born in 1666 (**?**) and died in 1731.

The word *about* is often a graceful substitute for (?): *Mary Astell was born about 1666.*

Do not use (?) to communicate that you are unsure of information: *It might rain* [not *will rain* (?)] today. Also, your choice of words, not (?), should communicate irony or sarcasm.

NO Having the flu is a delightful (**?**) experience.

YES Having the flu is as pleasant as almost drowning.

THE EXCLAMATION POINT

23e Using an exclamation point for a strong command or an emphatic declaration

An **exclamation point** can end a strong command or an emphatic declaration. A strong command gives a very firm order: *Look out behind you!* An emphatic declaration makes a shocking or surprising statement: *There's been an accident!*

! ❧ PUNCTUATION ALERT: Do not combine an exclamation point with a comma, a period, or a question mark. ❧

NO "There's been an accident**!,**" cried my mother.

YES "There's been an accident**!**" cried my mother.

23f Avoiding the overuse of exclamation points

In academic writing, your words, rather than exclamation points, should communicate the strength of your message. Reserve exclamation points for occasional emphatic dialogue. Use them only very rarely for a short emphatic declaration within a longer passage.

When we were in Nepal, we tried each day to see Mt. Everest. But each day we failed to see it. Clouds defeated us! The summit never emerged from a heavy overcast.

If you use exclamation points too often in academic writing, your reader will think that your judgment of urgency is exaggerated.

NO Mountain climbing can be dangerous! You must learn correct procedures! You must have the proper equipment. Take rope! Wear spiked boots! Carry special picks designed for mountaineering.

YES Mountain climbing can be dangerous. Without knowing correct procedures, climbers quickly can turn an outing into a disaster. Required mountaineering gear includes rope, spiked boots, and special picks.

Your choice of words, not (*!*), should communicate amazement or sarcasm.

NO At 29,141 feet (!), Mt. Everest is the world's highest mountain. I heard that Chris (!) wants to climb it.

YES At a majestically staggering 29,141 feet, Mt. Everest is the world's highest mountain. Surely, Chris lacks the stamina to climb it.

EXERCISE 23-1

Consulting sections 23a–23f, insert any needed periods, question marks, and exclamation points. Also delete any unneeded ones.

EXAMPLE The paintings of the great El Greco are associated with Spain, but he was actually born in 1541 on the island of Crete!

The paintings of the great El Greco are associated with Spain, but he was actually born in 1541 on the island of Crete.

1. After studying art in Crete, El Greco moved to Venice, Italy, before 1567 (?), apparently to study with the famous Venetian artist Titian.
2. Scholars wonder if Titian was referring to El Greco when Titian mentioned "a talented young pupil" in a letter to King Philip II?
3. El Greco later moved to Rome with a letter of introduction (dated Nov 19, 1570) to a rich, influential art patron, Cardinal Alessandro Farnese.
4. Cardinal Farnese introduced El Greco to the outstanding (!) people of the city.
5. By 1572, El Greco had moved to the city of Toledo in Spain, where he spent the rest of his life!
6. Toledo was a rich, cultured, and intellectual city where El Greco worked as a sculptor, painter, and architect

QUOTATION ABOUT WRITING

Without some convention for showing the groupings and relationships of words, for suggesting pace and intonation, the written sentence becomes a puzzle to the modern reader, and the writer, with freedom to do *anything* in the way of charting his reader's course through lines of words, must set about doing *something*, selecting some kind of systematic spacing or marking arrangement that will clarify his meaning.

—Mina Shaughnessy,
Errors and Expectations

ANSWERS AND COVERAGE: EXERCISE 23–1

1. After studying art in Crete, El Greco moved to Venice, Italy, probably before 1567 [23d, question mark deleted and *probably* added], apparently to study with the famous Venetian artist Titian.

2. Scholars wonder if Titian was referring to El Greco when Titian mentioned "a talented young pupil" in a letter to King Philip II. [23a, question mark deleted and replaced with period]

3. El Greco later moved to Rome with a letter of introduction (dated Nov. [23a, period added] 19, 1570) to a rich, influential art patron, Cardinal Alessandro Farnese.

4. Cardinal Farnese introduced El Greco to the outstanding [23e, exclamation point deleted] people of the city.

5. By 1572, El Greco had moved to the city of Toledo in Spain, where he spent the rest of his life. [23e, exclamation point deleted and replaced with period]

6. Toledo was a rich, cultured, and intellectual city where El Greco worked as a sculptor, painter, and architect. [23a, period added]

→

ANSWERS AND COVERAGE:
EXERCISE 23–1, cont.

7. Toward the end of his life, El Greco suffered from a mysterious [23d, question mark deleted] illness that reduced his capacity for work. [23a, period added]

8. "Was El Greco's eyesight affected by the illness? [23c, question mark added]" is a question that has been asked for centuries. [23a, question mark deleted and replaced with period]

9. Visual problems might explain the elongated bodies in El Greco's portraits. [23a, question mark deleted and replaced with period]

10. From time to time, physicians write articles diagnosing [23d, question mark deleted] El Greco's illness based on this artist's paintings! [23e, acceptable exclamation point]

ANSWERS: EXERCISE 23–2

During World War II, U.S. soldiers' mail was censored. Specially trained people read the mail. Many people wanted to know why this was necessary. The censors had to make sure that no military information was disclosed. Return addresses often read "Somewhere in the Pacific Area" to keep strategic positions secret. Have you ever heard the story about the soldier who could not write his sweetheart for many months but finally had time? He wrote her a long letter explaining the delay and telling her that he loved her very much. All the woman received, however, was a tiny slip of paper that read: "Your boyfriend is fine. He loves you. He also talks too much! Sincerely, The Censor."

7. Toward the end of his life, El Greco suffered from a mysterious (?) illness that reduced his capacity for work

8. "Was El Greco's eyesight affected by the illness" is a question that has been asked for centuries?

9. Visual problems might explain the elongated bodies in El Greco's portraits?

10. From time to time, physicians write articles diagnosing (?) El Greco's illness based on this artist's paintings!

EXERCISE 23-2

Insert needed periods, question marks, and exclamation points.

During World War II, US soldiers' mail was censored Specially trained people read the mail Many people wanted to know why this was necessary The censors had to make sure that no military information was disclosed Return addresses often read "Somewhere in the Pacific Area" to keep strategic positions secret Have you ever heard the story about the soldier who could not write his sweetheart for many months but finally had time He wrote her a long letter explaining the delay and telling her that he loved her very much All the woman received, however, was a tiny slip of paper that read: "Your boyfriend is fine He loves you He also talks too much Sincerely, The Censor."

24 *The Comma*

The comma is the most frequently used mark of punctuation, occurring twice as often as all other marks of punctuation combined. Rules for the comma are many: The comma *must* be used in certain places, it *must not* be used in other places, and it is *optional* in still other places. This chapter will help you sort through the various rules and uses of the comma: before a COORDINATING CONJUNCTION linking INDEPENDENT CLAUSES, 24a; after an INTRODUCTORY CLAUSE, PHRASE, or word, 24b; to separate items in a series, 24c; to separate COORDINATE ADJECTIVES, 24d; with NONRESTRICTIVE (nonessential) elements, 24e; with PARENTHETICAL and TRANSITIONAL EXPRESSIONS, contrasts, words of DIRECT ADDRESS, and TAG SENTENCES, 24f; with quoted words, 24g; in names, dates, addresses, and numbers, 24h; to clarify meaning, 24i; to avoid misuse or overuse, 24j.

The role of the comma is to group and separate sentence parts, helping to create clarity for readers. Consider the clarity of the following paragraph, which contains all needed punctuation except commas.

> **NO** Among publishers typographical errors known as "typos" are an embarrassing fact of life. In spite of careful editing reviews and multiple readings few books are perfect upon publication. Soon after a book reaches the marketplace reports of errors embarrassments to authors and editors alike start to come in. Everyone laughed therefore although no one thought it was funny when an English textbook was published with this line: "Proofread your writing carefullly."

Here is the same paragraph with commas included.

> **YES** Among publishers, typographical errors, known as "typos," are an embarrassing fact of life. In spite of careful editing, reviews, and multiple readings, few books are perfect upon publication. Soon after a book reaches the marketplace, reports of errors, embarrassments to authors and editors alike, start to come in. Everyone laughed, therefore, although no one thought it was funny, when an English textbook was published with this line: "Proofread your writing carefullly."

In the Yes paragraph, the meaning is clear. Each comma in it is used for a specific reason according to a comma rule.

REFERENCES TO SUPPLEMENTS

For this topic in the CLAST writing competency test, refer students to ch. 1, section B5b of *Preparing for the CLAST* by S. Patterson.

This topic is included in the TASP writing competency test. Refer students to *Preparing for the TASP* by M. Saenz.

For editing for correct use of commas, refer students to *Rough Drafts* by K. S. Cain, Part V, Exercise 13.

See transparency 7–12 for common problems with comma usage in the *Prentice Hall/Simon & Schuster Transparencies for Writers* by D. Carter.

QUOTATION ABOUT WRITING

Next in importance to the longest pause of all, the period or full stop, comes the shortest, the comma. The practice does not seriously differ from the theory implied by the etymology: *comma*, the Latin transliteration of Greek *komma*, related to *keptein*, to cut, means literally "a cutting," hence "a cutting-off," hence a clause, which after all, is nothing but a part, especially a (comparatively) short part, cut off from the rest of the sentence; hence the sign that indicates the division. In modern practice, the comma serves to separate not only clauses but phrases and words; more precisely, certain kinds of clauses and certain kinds of phrases and certain groupings of words.

—Eric Partridge,
You Have a Point There

1. England, Scotland and Wales are located on the same island.

2. Wales is located on the western peninsula of the island and England and Scotland occupy the rest of it.

3. It is bounded on the east by the North Sea and on the south by the English Channel.

4. The Teutonic invaders of the fifth century had to struggle with native Britons for possession of the island for the Romans had virtually abandoned the island by that time.

5. Britain is the proper name of the whole island but England is the political name of the part conquered by the Angles.

6. Neither the Jutes nor the Saxons moved north for they chose to settle in what is today Kent or they moved on to Sussex, Wessex, and Essex.

7. The Scots were actually the people of Ireland yet a small colony they established in the northern part of the island eventually gave it its name.

8. The Norman Conquest of Britain was begun under William the Conqueror and was continued by his sons.

9. With few exceptions all the existing shires of England had been established at the time of the Norman Conquest but the boundaries were not always exactly the same as they are now.

10. Since the eleventh century the map of Britain has remained little changed yet the reins of power have shifted many times.

Avoid two practices that can get writers into trouble with commas: (1) As you are writing, do not insert a comma just because you happen to pause to think before moving on. (2) As you reread your writing, do not insert commas according to your personal habits of pausing. Although a comma alerts a reader to a slight pause (except in dates and other conventional material), pausing is not a reliable guide for writers, because people's breathing rhythms, accents, and thinking spans vary greatly.

24a Using a comma before a coordinating conjunction that links independent clauses

When **coordinating conjunctions** (*and, but, for, or, nor, so,* and *yet*) link INDEPENDENT CLAUSES, they create COMPOUND SENTENCES. Use a comma before the coordinating conjunction.

PATTERN FOR COMMAS WHEN COORDINATING CONJUNCTIONS LINK INDEPENDENT CLUASES

PATTERN FOR COMMAS WHEN COORDINATING CONJUNCTIONS LINK INDEPENDENT CLAUSES 104

Independent clause, { and / but / for / or / nor / so / yet } independent clause.

The sky turned dark gray, **and** the wind died suddenly.

The November morning had just begun, **but** it looked like dusk.

Shopkeepers closed their stores early, **for** they wanted to get home.

Soon high winds would start, **or** thick snow would begin silently.

Farmers had no time to continue harvesting, **nor** could they round up their animals in distant fields.

The firehouse whistle blew four times, **so** everyone knew a blizzard was closing in.

People on the road tried to reach safety, **yet** a few unlucky ones were stranded.

When the two independent clauses in a compound sentence are very short, some authorities omit the comma before the coordinating conjunction. However, you will never be wrong, and you avoid the risk of error, if you always use a comma in your college writing.

❖ COMMA CAUTION: Do not put a comma after a coordinating conjunction that links independent clauses.

NO	The sky turned dark gray **and,** the wind died suddenly.
YES	The sky turned dark gray, **and** the wind died suddenly. ❖

❖ COMMA CAUTION: Do not use a comma when a coordinating conjunction links two words, PHRASES, or DEPENDENT CLAUSES only. Use commas for a series of three or more items (see 24c).

NO	Learning a new language demands **time, and patience.** [Two words linked by *and* use no comma.]
YES	Learning a new language demands **time and patience.**

NO	Each language has **a beauty of its own, and forms of expression** which are duplicated nowhere else. [Two phrases linked by *and* use no comma.]
YES	Each language has **a beauty of its own and forms of expression** which are duplicated nowhere else.

—MARGARET MEAD, "Unispeak" ❖

❖ COMMA CAUTION: To avoid creating a comma splice, do not use a comma to separate independent clauses unless they are linked by a coordinating conjunction (see 14c).

NO	Five inches of snow fell in two hours, one inch of ice built up when the snow turned to freezing rain. [The comma alone is insufficient. A coordinating conjunction must follow when the comma is used here.]
YES	Five inches of snow fell in two hours, **and** one inch of ice built up when the snow turned to freezing rain. [The coordinating conjunction *and* links the two independent clauses.]
YES	Five inches of snow fell in two hours. One inch of ice built up when the snow turned to freezing rain. [Independent clauses can become two separate sentences.] ❖

431

ANSWERS: EXTRA EXERCISE A

1. correct
2. comma before *and England*
3. correct
4. comma before *for the Romans*
5. comma before *but England*
6. comma before *for they chose* and comma before *or they moved*
7. comma before *yet a small colony*
8. correct
9. comma before *but the boundaries*
10. comma before *yet the reins*

BACKGROUND

In a letter to the editors of *Time*, Michael Priestley wrote about that magazine's policy of omitting the final comma before the conjunction in a series of words or phrases (July 4, 1988, pp. 6–7). "This omission," he wrote, "reminds me of my fifth-grade teacher's lesson on the subject. A father's will stipulated that his estate be shared equally by his three sons: 'Tom, Dick and Harry.' Tom took the matter to grammar court and won the case: he inherited half the estate, and Dick and Harry split the other half."

TEACHING TIP

How to call attention to punctuation errors so that students avoid making them in subsequent pieces of writing is a dilemma for many teachers. Theresa Cullen Timmons suggests using a highlighter to emphasize problem passages. In "Marking Errors: A Simple Strategy" (*Teaching English in the Two-Year College* 14 [February 1987]: 18–21), she reports that the technique helps students to proofread their work more effectively.

ANSWERS: EXERCISE 24-1

Answers may vary slightly. Here is one set of possibilities.

1. Immigrants from Eastern Europe came to New York City, and they sold meat patties in stands all over the city to hungry passersby.

2. The patties were too messy to carry around, so some German sailors on shore leave asked that the meat patties be placed on soft rolls of bread.

3. The combination of meat and bread came to be known as hamburger, for the German sailors named the portable snack after their hometown of Hamburg.

4. The hamburger went national in 1903 at the United States Louisiana Purchase Exposition in St. Louis, and it was an instant success.

5. A patty served with no roll and on a plate is not a true hamburger, nor can a true hamburger be any shape but round.

6. Many burger lovers pile onions and pickles on their hamburgers and smother them with ketchup, yet others insist the only authentic hamburger is served plain.

7. Some cooks put a slice of cheese on their burger, or they place slices of bacon on top for a special treat.

8. Some people prefer not to eat red meat, but U.S. cooks used only beef until a decade ago.

9. People not willing to eat beef missed their burgers, so a variety of ingredients are now available for making different kinds of burgers.

10. Most supermarkets carry the ingredients for turkey burgers and pork burgers, and some also carry ground tofu for tofu burgers.

24a
cont.

When independent clauses containing other commas are linked by a coordinating conjunction, you can choose to use a semicolon before the coordinating conjunction (see 25b). Base your decision on what would help your reader understand the material most easily.

Because temperatures remained low all winter, the snow could not melt until spring**; and** some people wondered when they would see grass again.

EXERCISE 24-1

Consulting section 24a, combine each pair of sentences using the coordinating conjunction shown in parentheses. When necessary, rearrange words. Insert commas before coordinating conjunctions that separate independent clauses.

EXAMPLE Sailors in U.S. ports put chopped meat patties between slices of bread at the turn of the century.   A U.S. classic was born. (and)

Sailors in U.S. ports put chopped meat patties between slices of bread at the turn of the century, and a U.S. classic was born.

1. Immigrants from Eastern Europe came to New York City. They sold meat patties in stands all over the city to hungry passersby. (and)

2. The patties were too messy to carry around. Some German sailors on shore leave asked that the meat patties be placed on soft rolls of bread. (so)

3. The combination of meat and bread came to be known as a hamburger. The German sailors named the portable snack after their hometown of Hamburg. (for)

4. The hamburger went national in 1903 at the United States Louisiana Purchase Exposition in St. Louis. It was an instant success. (and)

5. A patty served with no roll and on a plate is not a true hamburger. A true hamburger cannot be any shape but round. (nor)

6. Many burger lovers pile onions and pickles on their hamburgers and smother them with ketchup.   Others insist the only authentic hamburger is served plain. (yet)

7. Some cooks put a slice of cheese on their burger. They place slices of bacon on top for a special treat. (or)

8. Some people prefer not to eat red meat. U.S. cooks used only beef until a decade ago. (but)

9. People not willing to eat beef missed their burgers. A variety of ingredients are now available for making different kinds of burgers. (so)

10. Most supermarkets carry the ingredients for turkey burgers and pork burgers. Some also carry tofu for tofu burgers. (and)

Using a comma after an introductory clause, phrase, or word

24b

Use a comma to signal the end of an introductory element and the beginning of an independent clause.

PATTERN FOR COMMAS WITH INTRODUCTORY CLAUSES, PHRASES, AND WORDS 105

- Introductory clause,
- Introductory phrase, ——————— independent clause.
- Introductory word,

Some authorities omit the comma when an introductory element is very short and the sentence is clear without a comma. However, you will never be wrong if you use a comma after an introductory clause, phrase, or word in your college writing.

Using a comma after an introductory adverb clause

24b-1

An **adverb clause** is a dependent clause (see 7o-2). It cannot stand alone as an independent unit because it starts with a subordinating conjunction (for example, *although, because, if*; for a complete list, see 7h). When an adverb clause precedes an independent clause, separate the clauses with a comma.

> **When it comes to eating,** you can sometimes help yourself more by helping yourself less.
>
> —RICHARD ARMOUR

Using a comma after an introductory phrase

24b-2

A **phrase** is a group of words that cannot stand alone as an independent unit. It lacks a SUBJECT, a PREDICATE, or both. Use a comma to set off a phrase that introduces an independent clause. (Types of phrases are explained in 7n.)

> **Between 1544 and 1689,** sugar refineries appeared in London and New York. [PREPOSITIONAL PHRASE]
>
> **Obtained mainly from sugar cane and sugar beets,** sugar is also developed from the sap of maple trees. [PAST PARTICIPLE PHRASE]
>
> **Beginning in infancy,** we develop lifelong tastes for sweet and salty foods. [PARTICIPIAL PHRASE]

PATTERN FOR COMMAS WITH INTRODUCTORY CLAUSES, PHRASES, AND WORDS

24b-2
cont.

To satisfy a craving for ice cream, timid people sometimes brave midnight streets. [INFINITIVE PHRASE]

Eating being enjoyable, we tend to eat more than we need for fuel. [ABSOLUTE PHRASE]

24b-3

Using a comma after introductory words

Transitional expressions and **conjunctive adverbs** carry messages of a relationship between ideas in sentences and paragraphs. Transitional expressions include *for example* and *in addition* (for a complete list, see Chart 23 in section 4d-1). Conjunctive adverbs include *therefore* and *however* (for a complete list, see Chart 49 in section 7f). When these introductory words appear at the beginning of a sentence, most writers follow them with a comma.

> **For example,** fructose is fruit sugar that is metabolized as a blood sugar.

Interjections are introductory words that convey surprise or other emotions. Use a comma after an interjection at the beginning of a sentence: **Oh,** *we did not realize that you are allergic to cats.* **Yes,** *your sneezing worries me.*

❖ PUNCTUATION ALERT: Use a comma before and a comma after a transitional expression, conjunctive adverb, or interjection that falls within a sentence. Use a comma before such words that fall at the end of a sentence. ❖

EXERCISE 24-2

Consulting section 24b, insert commas where needed after introductory words, phrases, and clauses. If a sentence is correct, circle its number.

EXAMPLE   In 1876 Dr. John Kellogg created a precooked food made of dried wheat for the patients at his vegetarian health institute in Battle Creek, Michigan.

In 1876, Dr. John Kellogg created a precooked food made of dried wheat for the patients at his vegetarian health institute in Battle Creek, Michigan.

(1) Although he meant it to serve as a between-meals snack Kellogg's new "cereal" was quickly put to other uses. (2) Eaten with milk and sugar it became a breakfast food in the United States from coast to coast. (3) Not long after his brother Will Kellogg created cornflakes. (4) As other types of cereal such as shredded wheat and puffed rice flooded the market the United States breakfast took on its present identity. (5) Other reasons besides perceived health benefits accounted for the sudden popularity in packaged dry food at the turn of this century. (6) To save time in the morning the growing population

of office workers abandoned heavy cooked breakfasts for quick "convenience" foods. (7) By the late 1800s the improvement of food preservation techniques and the introduction of railroad refrigerator cars radically changed breakfast choices in the United States. (8) For the first time perishable food could be transported across North America without spoiling. (9) When the benefits of Vitamin C were discovered in 1913 orange juice and grapefruits were added to the breakfast menu. (10) Consequently today's balanced breakfast consists of a glass of juice along with a bowl of cereal and milk.

EXERCISE 24-3

Consulting section 24b, combine each set of sentences into one sentence that starts according to the directions in parentheses. You can add, delete, and rearrange words as needed. Be sure to use commas after introductory elements in the combined sentences.

EXAMPLE   The term cyberspace was introduced a decade ago by the science-fiction writer William Gibson. The idea of a total electronic environment seemed highly fanciful. (clause beginning *when*)

When the term cyberspace was introduced a decade ago by the science-fiction writer William Gibson, the idea of a total electronic environment seemed highly fanciful.

1. It began as a flight of sheer fantasy. Virtual reality is turning out to be one of the most versatile technological applications of this century. (clause beginning *although*)

2. Computer-generated environments are now known as "virtual reality." Computer-generated environments now have many important applications ranging from medicine and space exploration to entertainment. (phrase beginning *now known*)

3. Surgeons can use virtual scalpels to practice difficult operations. They can predict their effects on the patient's total body system. (begin with *for example*)

4. Astronauts have been using virtual reality space walks to train themselves to function in the demanding zero-gravity environment of orbiting space satellites. They have been using virtual reality recently. (begin with *recently*)

5. You can also enter the world of virtual reality for entertainment. You can use a glove and a specially equipped helmet. (phrase beginning *to enter*)

6. The computer operator punches a few keys on the computer in a virtual reality room. She transports you into a colorful make-believe world. (phrase beginning *by punching*)

7. Two tiny television screens in the helmet's visor provide startlingly realistic three-dimensional vision. You can interact with objects in the virtual world by moving your glove. (clause beginning *while*)

ANSWERS AND COVERAGE: EXERCISE 24–3

Answers may vary, but the following versions are possibilities.

1. Although it began as a flight of sheer fantasy, virtual reality is turning out to be one of the most versatile technological applications of this century. [adverb clause]

2. Now known as "virtual reality," computer-generated environments have many important applications ranging from medicine and space exploration to entertainment. [participial phrase]

3. For example, surgeons can use virtual scalpels to practice difficult operations and predict their effects on the patient's total body system. [introductory words—transitional expression]

4. Recently, astronauts have been using virtual reality space walks to train themselves to function in the demanding zero-gravity environment of orbiting space satellites. [introductory word—transitional expression]

5. To enter the world of virtual reality for entertainment, you can use a glove and a specially-equipped helmet. [infinitive phrase]

6. By punching a few keys on the computer in a virtual reality room, the computer operator transports you into a colorful make-believe world. [prepositional phrase]

7. While two tiny television screens in the helmet's visor provide startlingly realistic three-dimensional vision, you can interact with objects in the virtual world by moving your glove. [adverb clause]

24b-3 cont.

8. You look up at the deep blue sky. You see a large prehistoric bird soaring above your head. (phrase beginning *looking*)

9. The ground quakes and splits under your feet. It becomes an ocean with a shark circling nearby. (begin with *under your feet*)

10. You can repel the shark with your virtual spear. You will not be hurt if it attacks. (begin with *fortunately*)

ANSWERS AND COVERAGE:
EXERCISE 24–3, cont.

8. Looking up at the deep blue sky, you see a large prehistoric bird soaring above your head. [participial phrase]

9. Under your feet, the ground quakes and splits and becomes an ocean with a shark circling nearby. [prepositional phrase]

10. Fortunately, you can repel the shark with your virtual spear and you will not be hurt if he attacks. [introductory word—conjunctive adverb]

TEACHING TIP

Group work in the writing classroom has become an increasingly popular teaching strategy in the last few years. Called by a variety of names (Reading-Response Groups, Peer Response Groups, Writing-in-Progress, for example), in all its forms the technique emphasizes sharing writing so that an audience besides the teacher can offer suggestions for improvement. Such groups can focus on any stage of the writing process, including editing. An article that discusses their use in classes for basic writers, "Ideas in Practice: Why Come to Class? Productive Class Time in a Developmental Writing Course" was published by Debra Gomez (*Journal of Developmental Education* 8 [1985]: 20–21). A more comprehensive view of why and how to organize writing groups for a writing class is offered by Anne Ruggles Gere in her book *Writing Groups* (Carbondale, IL: Southern Illinois UP, 1987).

QUOTATION ABOUT WRITING

In conversation you can use timing, a look, inflection, pauses. But on the page all you have is commas, dashes, the amount of syllables in a word. When I write, I read everything out loud to get the right rhythm.

—Fran Lebowitz

24c   # Using commas to separate items in a series

A **series** is a group of three or more elements—words, PHRASES, or CLAUSES—that match in grammatical form as well as in importance in the same sentence.

PATTERN FOR COMMAS IN A SERIES

PATTERN FOR COMMAS IN A SERIES   106

- word, word, and word
- word, word, word

- phrase, phrase, and phrase
- phrase, phrase, phrase

- clause, clause, and clause
- clause, clause, clause

Marriage requires **sexual, financial, and emotional** discipline.

—Anne Roiphe, "Why Marriages Fail"

Culture is a way of **thinking, feeling, believing.**

—Clyde Kluckhohn, *Mirror for Man*

My love of flying goes back to those early days **of roller skates, of swings, of bicycles.**

—Teresa Wiggins, student

The big world of action is both dangerous and mysterious; you'll never really understand it. **Stay out of it, sit still, don't try.**

—Elizabeth Janeway, "Soaps, Cynicism, and Mind Control"

We have been taught **that children develop by ages and stages, that the steps are pretty much the same for everybody, and that to grow out of the limited behavior of childhood,** we must climb them all.

—GAIL SHEEHY, *Passages*

Some authorities omit the comma before the coordinating conjunction between the last two items of a series. This handbook does not recommend omitting this comma, for its absence can distort meaning and confuse a reader. If you never omit the comma in your academic writing, you will never be wrong.

When the items in a series contain commas or other punctuation, separate them with semicolons instead of commas (see 25d). This practice ensures that your sentence will deliver the meaning you intend.

If it's a bakery, they have to sell cake; if it's a photography shop, they have to develop film; **and** if it's a dry-goods store, they have to sell warm underwear.

—ART BUCHWALD, "Birth Control for Banks"

Numbered or lettered lists within a sentence are items in a series. Use commas (or semicolons if the items are long) to separate them when there are three or more items.

To file your insurance claim, please enclose (1) a letter requesting payment, (2) a police report about the robbery, and (3) proof of purchase of the items you say are missing.

✤ COMMA CAUTION: Do not use a comma before the first item or after the last item in a series unless a different rule makes it necessary.

NO   Many artists, writers, and composers, have indulged in daydreaming and reverie.

YES   Many artists, writers, and composers have indulged in daydreaming and reverie.

NO   Such dreamers include, Miró, Debussy, Dostoevsky, and Dickinson.

YES   Such dreamers include Miró, Debussy, Dostoevsky, and Dickinson.

YES   Such dreamers include, of course, Miró, Debussy, Dostoevsky, and Dickinson. [The comma after *of course* is necessary to set off the phrase from the rest of the sentence.] ✤

!

437

24c
cont.

ANSWERS: EXERCISE 24–4

1. Rabbits, squirrels, raccoons, and other small game; Shawnees, Cherokees, and European pioneers
2. weight, buffalo tracks . . . highways, and
3. the hunters, trappers, and scouts; vertical mountains, overgrown forests, and lush meadows.
4. Virginia, North Carolina, Pennsylvania, and other . . .
5. Correct

BACKGROUND

The placement of a comma can have consequences that are highly important. Consider the following examples:

1. A comma once saved a man's life. Czar Alexander III had signed a death warrant reading: "Pardon impossible, to be sent to Siberia." Being sent to Siberia inevitably led to death. However, Czarina Maria Fyodorovna saved the man by altering the message to read: "Pardon, impossible to be sent to Siberia."

2. Elizabeth Langmore (Letters, *Time*, July 4, 1988) points out how very different it is to ask, "Have you seen the elephant eating Tom?" and "Have you seen the elephant eating, Tom?"

3. In the same publication, Grover Reynolds points out the difference between "Woman without her man has no reason for living," and "Woman: without her, man has no reason for living."

4. In another letter to *Time*, Leslie Bryant asks readers to decipher "That that is is that that is not is not is that it it is." With commas and periods, it reads "That that is, is. That that is not, is not. Is that it? It is."

24c
cont.

EXERCISE 24-4

Consulting section 24c, insert commas to separate items in a series. If a sentence needs no commas, circle its number.

EXAMPLE   In the fertile Kentucky mountain country of the late 1700s deer elk and black bears were abundant.

> *In the fertile Kentucky mountain country of the late 1700s, deer, elk, and black bears were abundant.*

1. Rabbits squirrels raccoons and other small game were so common that they were simply taken for granted by the Shawnees Cherokees and European pioneers who settled there.
2. An alert observer noted that wild turkeys were so fat that the branches of trees could not hold their weight buffalo tracks were wide as highways and everybody wore a cap made of raccoon skin.
3. The farmers followed close on the heels of the hunters trappers and scouts despite the difficulties of making their way through a wilderness of vertical mountains overgrown forests and lush meadows.
4. The year 1788 marked the beginning of a mass migration of farmers from Virginia North Carolina Pennsylvania and other long-settled areas over the mountains to Kentucky.
5. Kentucky had so many new inhabitants in five short years that it became the first "western" state to be admitted to the Union.

24d

Using a comma to separate coordinate adjectives

Coordinate adjectives are two or more ADJECTIVES that equally modify a NOUN. Separate coordinate adjectives with commas (unless the coordinate adjectives are joined by a coordinating conjunction such as *and* or *but*).

PATTERN FOR COMMAS WITH COORDINATE ADJECTIVES   107

coordinate adjective, coordinate adjective noun

COORDINATE ADJECTIVES

The **huge, restless** crowd waited for the concert to begin. [Both *huge* and *restless* modify *crowd*.]

The audience cheered happily when the **pulsating, rhythmic** music filled the stadium. [Both *pulsating* and *rhythmic* modify *music*.]

PATTERN FOR COMMAS WITH COORDINATE ADJECTIVES

438

CUMULATIVE (NONCOORDINATE) ADJECTIVES

The concert featured **several new** bands. [*New* modifies *bands; several* modifies *new bands.*]

Each had a **distinctive musical** style. [*Musical* modifies *style; distinctive* modifies *musical style.*]

If you are not sure whether adjectives need a comma between them, use the Tests for Coordinate Adjectives in Chart 108. ❖ COMMA CAUTIONS: (1) Do not put a comma after a final coordinate adjective and the noun it modifies. (2) Do not put a comma between adjectives that are not coordinate.❖

TESTS FOR COORDINATE ADJECTIVES   108

If either test given here works, the adjectives are coordinate and need a comma between them.

■ Can the order of the adjectives be reversed without changing the meaning or creating nonsense? If yes, use a comma.

NO	The concert featured **new several** bands. (Only *several new* makes sense.)
YES	The **huge, restless** (or *restless, huge*) crowd waited for the concert to begin.

NO	Each had a **musical distinctive** style. (Only *distinctive musical* makes sense.)
YES	The audience cheered happily as the **rhythmic, pulsating** (or *pulsating, rhythmic*) music filled the stadium.

■ Can the word *and* be inserted between the adjectives? If yes, use a comma.

NO	The concert featured **new and several** bands.
YES	The **large and restless** crowd waited.

EXERCISE 24-5

Consulting section 24d, insert commas to separate coordinate adjectives. If a sentence needs no commas, circle its number.

EXAMPLE   The lively bright bird known as the parakeet was first imported to England from Australia in 1840.

The lively, bright bird known as the parakeet was first imported to England from Australia in 1840.

!

QUOTATION ABOUT WRITING

A world that has only periods is a world without inflections. It is a world without shade. It has a music without sharps and flats. It is a martial music. It has a jackboot rhythm. Words cannot bend and curve. A comma, by comparison, catches the gentle drift of the mind in thought, turning in on itself and back on itself, reversing, redoubling and returning along the course of its own sweet river music; while the semicolon brings clauses and thoughts together with all the silent discretion of a hostess arranging guests around her dinner table.

—Pico Iyer,
"In Praise of the Humble Comma"

BACKGROUND

Carl Singleton calls for increased attention to the teaching of punctuation and usage based on the premise that without an understanding of the basic mechanics of the language, students cannot communicate in writing. He underscores the importance of helping them to master standard conventions ("We Can Never Teach Students to Write If They Can't Use Standard Grammar," *Chronicle of Higher Education* 33 [20 May 1987]: 40–41).

24d
cont.

ANSWERS: EXERCISE 24–5

1. small, colorful
2. correct
3. small, sturdy; strong, curved
4. effortless, efficient
5. short, simple

1. Small colorful parakeets were one of the best-loved pets of the nineteenth century.
2. No upper-class British parlor was considered fashionable without a cage of several singing parakeets.
3. Parakeets are small sturdy parrots who use their strong curved beaks for husking seeds.
4. Their feet have two toes pointing forward and two toes pointing backward, a highly unusual feature that makes for effortless efficient climbing—even in a cage.
5. Some parakeet owners report that their birds are able to speak a few short simple words after some persistent coaching.

TEACHING TIP

The words *restrictive* and *nonrestrictive* are being replaced in many classrooms with the word *essential* and *nonessential*. For this reason, this chapter uses the more grammatically descriptive terms and then gives in parentheses the terms more accessible to nongrammarians. No matter what words you use in your teaching, the concept of restriction is a helpful one for students to understand. To illustrate this concept, you might focus on the differences between the words *the* and *a* in these sentences, as they affect restriction and the role of the commas:

I took the bus, which made many stops, to get here.

I took a bus that made many stops to get here.

QUOTATION ABOUT WRITING

Anyone who undervalues the use of the comma in creating meaning should compare the statement "God rest you, merry gentlemen" with its older form, "God rest you merry, gentlemen."

—Carolyn Good

24e

Using commas to set off nonrestrictive (nonessential) elements; not setting off restrictive (essential) elements

Perhaps the most difficult comma decisions are those related to **restrictive (essential)** elements and **nonrestrictive (nonessential)** elements. The comma usage rules themselves are easy. The difficult part comes in understanding what *restrictive, essential, nonrestrictive,* and *nonessential* mean. Before trying to master the rules, use Chart 109 to become familiar with the meaning of these terms. Then apply the definitions as you closely reread your writing and analyze what you want your reader to understand from your sentences.

DEFINITIONS OF "RESTRICTIVE" AND "NONRESTRICTIVE"

DEFINITIONS OF "RESTRICTIVE" AND "NONRESTRICTIVE"   109

■ A **restrictive element** contains information **essential** for the reader to understand fully the meaning of the word or words that it modifies. It limits ("restricts") what it modifies.

Some states retest drivers **over age 65** to check their driving competency.

The PREPOSITIONAL PHRASE *over age 65* limits the word *drivers* so that a reader understands which drivers are being retested (not all drivers, only those over age 65). Therefore, *over age 65* is restrictive.

DEFINITIONS OF "RESTRICTIVE" AND "NONRESTRICTIVE" (continued)

109

■ A **nonrestrictive element** is **not essential** for a reader to understand fully the word or words that it modifies. It describes but does not limit (does not "restrict") what it modifies.

My parents, **who are both over age 65,** took a defensive driving course last year.

The RELATIVE CLAUSE *who are both over age 65* describes my parents, but it is not essential to a reader's understanding which parents took a defensive driving course last year. Therefore, *who are both over age 65* is nonrestrictive.

Here are additional examples of restrictive and nonrestrictive elements.

RESTRICTIVE ELEMENTS

Some people **in my neighborhood** enjoy jogging. [The reader needs the information *in my neighborhood* to know which people enjoy jogging. The information is essential, so commas are not used.]

Some people **who are in excellent physical condition** enjoy jogging. [The reader needs the information *who are in excellent physical condition* to know which people enjoy jogging. The information is essential, so commas are not used.]

NONRESTRICTIVE ELEMENTS

An energetic person, Anna Hom enjoys jogging. [Without knowing that Anna Hom is energetic, the reader can understand that Anna Hom enjoys jogging. The information is not essential, so commas are used.]

Anna Hom**, who is in excellent physical condition,** enjoys jogging. [Without knowing that Anna Hom is in excellent physical condition, the reader can understand the information that Anna Hom enjoys jogging. The information is not essential, so commas are used.]

Anna Hom enjoys jogging**, which is also my favorite pastime.** [Without knowing about my favorite pastime, the reader can understand the information that Anna Hom enjoys jogging. The information is not essential, so commas are used.]

BACKGROUND

Punctuating relative clauses correctly is easier for many teachers to do than to explain. Students, they find, seem especially resistant to understanding when a clause is restrictive and when it is nonrestrictive. Paul Arakelian asserts that English speakers generally assume that "all relative clauses are restrictive." He concludes that "pause or intonation have very little to do with the restrictiveness of a modifier" ("Prescriptive Nonsense: The Nonrestrictive Relative Clause," *Freshman English News* 14 [Spring 1985]: 18–20).

ALTERNATE EXAMPLES

Restrictive Clauses and Phrases

1. People *who travel abroad* should be willing to alter their eating habits.

2. Tours *that make dining decisions for travelers* sometimes provide surprises.

3. Diners *with conservative tastes* are sometimes offended.

4. For example, the evening meal *in Spain* is usually served after 9 P.M.

5. The restaurant *where I often had dinner in Madrid* was never filled until after 10:00.

Nonrestrictive Clauses and Phrases

1. My aunt, *who often travels abroad*, enjoys experimenting with unusual foods.

2. Holiday Tours, *which makes all the dining decisions for its travelers*, provides too few surprises for her.

3. Her tastes, *after her many excursions to exotic places*, are still adventuresome.

4. For example, eating in Spain, *which is always a late evening affair*, is one of her favorite excursions.

5. Las Tres Encinas, *where she often dines when she is in Madrid*, is never filled until after 10 P.M.

EXTRA EXERCISE B

Circle unnecessary commas and add needed commas where restrictive and nonrestrictive phrases, clauses, and appositives appear in the following sentences.

1. Elizabeth II, who is queen of the United Kingdom, was born in London in 1926.

2. She is the elder daughter of King George VI and Queen Consort Elizabeth, who is now known as the Queen Mother.

3. Her education, administered at home by private tutors, covered a wide variety of subjects.

4. She was married at Westminster Abbey to Philip Mountbatten, who was formerly Prince Philip of Greece.

5. He was created Duke of Edinburgh, with all the rights and privileges of the title, on the eve of the marriage.

6. Prince Charles Elizabeth's first child was born on November 14, 1948.

7. Princess Anne the second child was born on August 15, 1950.

8. Elizabeth's father George VI died in 1952.

9. She was crowned, Queen of England, in Westminster Abbey a historic site on June 2, 1953.

10. Prince Charles, now heir apparent, thus became, the Duke of Cornwall.

Once you understand the terms *restrictive, essential, nonrestrictive,* and *nonessential,* use Chart 110 to get to know the patterns for commas with nonrestrictive (nonessential) elements.

PATTERN FOR COMMAS WITH NONRESTRICTIVE ELEMENTS	110

- **Nonrestrictive element,** independent clause.
- Beginning of independent clause, **nonrestrictive element,** end of independent clause.
- Independent clause, **nonrestrictive element.**

❖ COMMA CAUTION: Remember, a restrictive element is essential. Do not set it off with commas (or any other punctuation) from the rest of the sentence. ❖

24e-1

Using commas to set off nonrestrictive (nonessential) clauses and phrases

Adjective clauses usually begin with relative pronouns or relative adverbs, such as *who, whom, that, which,* and *where.* Set nonrestrictive (nonessential) adjective clauses off with commas.

NONRESTRICTIVE CLAUSES

Farming**, which is a major source of food production,** may not always be dependent on the weather. [*Farming* in this sentence is not meant to be restricted by *which is a major source of food production,* so the information is not essential and commas are used.]

Organic farmers**, who use only natural substances to produce food,** disapprove of the widespread use of chemicals in commercial agriculture. [*Organic farmers* in this sentence is not meant to be restricted by *who use only natural substances to produce food,* so the information is not essential and commas are used.]

RESTRICTIVE CLAUSES

Much food **that is canned or frozen** is grown by the same large companies **that process it for consumption.** [The first restrictive clause limits the general word *food* to only food that is canned or frozen; the second one restricts the large companies to only those that process the food for consumption. The information in both cases is essential, and so commas are not used.]

❖ USAGE ALERT: In adjective clauses, use the relative pronouns *who* or *whom* to refer to people. To refer to animals or things, some writers use the relative pronoun *which* both for restrictive and for nonrestrictive clauses. Other writers reserve *which* for nonrestrictive clauses and use *that* for restrictive clauses. You can follow either practice as long as you are consistent in each piece of writing.❖

A **phrase** is a group of related words without a SUBJECT, a PREDICATE, or both. Set nonrestrictive (nonessential) phrases off with commas.

NONRESTRICIVE PHRASES

Farmers**, wanting the best possible yields,** use many techniques to enhance their crops' growth. [*Farmers* in this sentence is not meant to be limited by the phrase *wanting the best possible yields,* so the information is not essential and commas are used.]

RESTRICTIVE PHRASES

Farmers **retaining complete control over their land** are very hard to find these days. [*Farmers* in this sentence is meant to be narrowed to only those retaining complete control over their land, so the information is essential and commas are not used.]

Using commas to set off nonrestrictive appositives   24e-2

An **appositive** is a word or group of words that renames the NOUN or noun group preceding it. A **nonrestrictive appositive** is not essential for the identification of what it is renaming; it is set off by commas.

NONRESTRICTIVE APPOSITIVE

The agricultural scientist, **a new breed of farmer,** controls the farming environment. [The appositive *a new breed of farmer* is not essential in identifying who controls the farming equipment, so the nonrestrictive appositive is set off with commas.]

Most appositives are nonrestrictive (nonessential). Once the name of something is given, words renaming it are not usually necessary to specify or limit it even more. In some cases, however, appositives are restrictive (essential) and are not set off with commas.

RESTRICTIVE APPOSITIVE

The agricultural scientist **Wendy Singh** has helped develop a new fertilization technique. [The appositive *Wendy Singh* is essential in identifying exactly which agricultural scientist has developed the new fertilization technique, so the restrictive appositive is not set off with commas.]

!

ANSWERS: EXTRA EXERCISE B

1. Correct

2. She is the elder daughter of King George VI and Queen Consort Elizabeth, who is now known as the Queen Mother.

3. Her education, administered at home by private tutors, covered a wide variety of subjects.

4. She was married at Westminster Abbey to Philip Mountbatten, who was formerly Prince Philip of Greece.

5. Correct

6. Prince Charles, Elizabeth's first child, was born on November 14, 1948.

7. Princess Anne, the second child, was born on August 15, 1950.

8. Elizabeth's father, George VI, died in 1952.

9. She was crowned Queen of England in Westminster Abbey, a historic site, on June 2, 1953.

10. Prince Charles, now heir apparent, thus became the Duke of Cornwall.

QUOTATION ABOUT WRITING

The most important fact about a comma is that there are places where it must not be used. That is, there are places where a comma alters the meaning of a statement. Max Beerbohm was being witty when he used a comma in writing about *Frank Harris, and many good writers*. There are also a few places where a comma must be used in order to protect the meaning.

—Bergen and Cornelia Evans,
A Dictionary of Contemporary American Usage

ANSWERS AND COVERAGE: EXERCISE 24–6

1. Elena Piscopia, a resident of Venice, was the first woman to receive a doctoral degree. [nonrestrictive appositive]

2. Many university officials, reflecting the beliefs of their time, opposed Elena's goal of higher education. [nonrestrictive participial phrase]

3. The doctoral examination of a woman, a unique phenomenon in 1678, drew crowds of curious spectators. [nonrestrictive appositive]

4. Elena Piscopia, who had prepared carefully for her questioners, completed the examination easily. [nonrestrictive relative clause]

5. Her replies, which were given entirely in Latin, amazed her examiners with their clarity and brilliance. [nonrestrictive relative clause]

6. Elena Piscopia's father, who was an exceptionally enlightened man for his time, supported and encouraged his daughter's education. [nonrestrictive relative clause]

7. None. [restrictive relative clause]

8. Christine de Pisane, widowed at twenty-five, turned to writing to support herself and her three children. [nonrestrictive participial phrase]

9. She found herself unprepared and taught herself a complete course of study, which included Latin, history, philosophy, and literature. [nonrestrictive relative clause]

10. She later wrote *The City of Ladies*, a book about women leading creative lives.

24e-2
cont.

EXERCISE 24-6

Consulting section 24e and using your knowledge of restrictive and nonrestrictive clauses and phrases, insert commas as needed. If a sentence is correct, circle its number.

EXAMPLE   Elena Piscopia who began to study Aristotle at the age of seven took the examination for her doctoral degree.

Elena Piscopia, who began to study Aristotle at the age of seven, took the examination for her doctoral degree.

1. Elena Piscopia a resident of Venice was the first woman to receive a doctoral degree.

2. Many university officials reflecting the beliefs of their time opposed Elena's goal of higher education.

3. The doctoral examination of a woman a unique phenomenon in 1678 drew crowds of curious spectators.

4. Elena Piscopia who had prepared carefully for her questioners completed the examination easily.

5. Her replies which were given entirely in Latin amazed her examiners with their clarity and brilliance.

6. Elena Piscopia's father who was an exceptionally enlightened man for his time supported and encouraged his daughter's education.

7. Other women who lived in the 1600s were not so lucky.

8. Christine de Pisane widowed at 25 turned to writing to support herself and her three children.

9. She found herself unprepared and taught herself a complete course of study which included Latin, history, philosophy, and literature.

10. She later wrote *The City of Ladies* a book about women leading creative lives.

24f

Using commas to set off transitional and parenthetical expressions, contrasts, words of direct address, and tag sentences

Words, PHRASES, or CLAUSES that interrupt a sentence but do not change its essential meaning should be set off, usually with commas. (Dashes or parentheses can also set material off; see sections 29a and 29b.)

Conjunctive adverbs such as *however* and *therefore* (for a complete list, see Chart 49 in section 7f) and **transitional expressions** such as *for example* and *in addition* (for a complete list, see Chart 23 in section 4d-1) can express connections within sentences. When they do, set them off with commas.

The American Midwest, **therefore,** is considered the world's breadbasket.

California and Florida are important food producers, **for example.**

❖ COMMA CAUTION: Use a semicolon or a period—not a comma— before the conjunctive adverb or a transitional expression that falls between independent clauses. If you use a comma, you will create the error known as a comma splice (see Chapter 14). ❖

!

Parenthetical expressions are "asides," additions to sentences that the writer thinks of as extra. Set them off with commas.

American farmers, **according to U.S. government figures,** export more wheat than they sell at home.

A major drought, **sad to say,** reduces wheat crops drastically.

Expressions of contrast describe something by stating what it is not. Set them off with commas.

Feeding the world's population is a serious problem, **but not an intractable one.**

We must work against world hunger continuously, **not just when emergencies develop.**

Words of **direct address** indicate the person or group spoken to. Set them off by commas.

Join me, **brothers and sisters,** to end hunger.

Your contribution to the Relief Fund, **Steve,** will help us greatly.

Tag sentences consist of a VERB, a PRONOUN, and often the word *not,* generally contracted. Set off tag sentences with commas. If the tag sentence is a question, end it with a question mark.

Worldwide response to the Ethiopian famine was impressive, **wasn't it?**

Response to the next crisis will be as generous, **I hope.**

BACKGROUND
Erika Lindemann, in *A Rhetoric for Writing Teachers,* 2nd ed. (Oxford UP, 1987, p. 135) discusses how sentence combining can improve comma usage in student writing.

Students who have learned to be careful about commas understandably "write around" the problem. Sentence-combining exercises not only illustrate how punctuation organizes sentence elements for a reader but also how to solve punctuation problems which for years have limited a student's range of syntactic options. Furthermore, the exercises sometimes expose misunderstood punctuation rules discussed in previous English classes . . . [and] grammatical labels [that] sometimes create punctuation problems. Sentence combining allows teachers to dispense with terminology altogether or, if they wish, to name constructions *after* students have practiced them.

QUOTATION ABOUT WRITING
Unlike the period, question mark, exclamation, colon, dash, and parentheses, the comma has no clear special quality. . . It is not a terminal marking like the period, a specialized coordinating mark like the semicolon, or an anticipatory mark like the colon. Even the dash, which comes nearest the comma in variety of uses, has a characteristic quality, and all the points except the dash have a much more limited number of uses. The comma may be used alone or in pairs; it may stand between coordinate expressions or may separate expressions of different grammatical rank; it may set off a group for emphasis or clearness even when the grammatical relation is close.
—George Summey, Jr., *American Punctuation*

ANSWERS AND COVERAGE: EXERCISE 24–7

Answers may vary slightly. Here is one set of possibilities.

1. Inability to write, some say, [parenthetical expression] stems from lack of discipline and a tendency to procrastinate.

2. Therefore, [transitional word] according to this thinking, [parenthetical expression] the only way to overcome writer's block is to exert more willpower.

3. But writer's block can be a complex psychological event that happens to conscientious, hard-working people, not just the procrastinators. [expression of contrast]

4. Strange as it may seem, [parenthetical phrase] such people are often unconsciously rebelling against their own self-tyranny and rigid standards of perfection.

5. If I told you, my fellow writer, [direct address] that all it takes to start writing again is to quit pushing yourself, you would think I was crazy, wouldn't you? [tag sentence]

EXERCISE 24-7

Consulting section 24f, add necessary commas to set off transitional, parenthetical, and contrasting elements, words of direct address, and tag sentences.

EXAMPLE   Writer's block it seems to me is a misunderstood phenomenon.

Writer's block, it seems to me, is a misunderstood phenomenon.

1. Inability to write some say stems from lack of discipline and a tendency to procrastinate.

2. Therefore according to this thinking the only way to overcome writer's block is to exert more willpower.

3. But writer's block can be a complex psychological event that happens to conscientious and hard-working people not just the procrastinators.

4. Strange as it may seem such people are often unconsciously rebelling against their own self-tyranny and rigid standards of perfection.

5. If I told you my fellow writer that all it takes to start writing again is to quit punishing yourself you would think I was crazy wouldn't you.

24g

Using commas to set off quoted words from explanatory words

Use a comma to set off quoted words from short explanations in the same sentence. This rule holds whether the explanatory words come before, between, or after the quoted words.

PATTERNS FOR COMMAS WITH QUOTED WORDS 111

■ Explanatory words, "Quoted words."

■ "Quoted words," explanatory words.

■ "Quoted words begin," explanatory words, "quoted words continue."

Speaking of ideal love, the poet William Blake wrote, "Love seeketh not itself to please."

"My love is a fever," said William Shakespeare about love's passion.

"I love no love," proclaimed poet Mary Coleridge, "but thee."

This use of commas is especially important in communicating conversations or other direct discourse. Explanatory words like *she said*, *they replied*, and *he answered* are called **speaker tags,** and they are always set off from immediately following words of direct discourse in the ways shown in the pattern chart.

Because explanatory words such as *that* or *as* create a different kind of grammatical setting (such as a NOUN CLAUSE or a SUBJECT COMPLEMENT) for the quoted words, do not separate the explanatory words from the quoted words with a comma. (For capitalization in quotations, see 30c.)

Shakespeare also wrote that "Love's not Time's fool."

The duke describes the duchess as being "too soon made glad."

Shaw's quip "Love is a gross exaggeration of the difference between one person and everybody else" delights me.

Sometimes words a person has spoken or written are conveyed through indirect discourse. The writer does not use direct quotation but instead paraphrases material. Do not use a comma after *that* in indirect discourse.

Shakespeare also wrote that people should be true to themselves.

❖ COMMA CAUTION: When quoted words end with a question mark or an exclamation point, keep that punctuation even if explanatory words follow.

QUOTED WORDS *"O Romeo! Romeo!"*

NO "O Romeo! Romeo**!,**" called Juliet as she stood at her window.

NO "O Romeo! Romeo**,**" called Juliet as she stood at her window.

YES "O Romeo! Romeo**!**" called Juliet as she stood at her window.

QUOTED WORDS *"Wherefore art thou Romeo?"*

NO "Wherefore art thou Romeo**?,**" continued Juliet as she yearned for her new-found love.

NO "Wherefore art thou Romeo**,**" continued Juliet as she yearned for her new-found love.

YES "Wherefore art thou Romeo**?**" continued Juliet as she yearned for her new-found love. ❖

447

ANSWERS: EXERCISE 24–8

1. "His father," replied the ambulance driver, "but he's unconscious."

2. "This boy looks like he needs surgery, but he is the son of the surgeon now on duty," said the clerk.

3. She explained in an agitated voice, "Surgeons do not operate on their own family members."

4. Correct

5. With a disgusted look, the clerk told the driver, "The surgeon is the boy's mother."

COVERAGE: EXERCISE 24–8

1. explanatory words in the middle of a quotation

2. explanatory words at the end of a quotation

3. explanatory words at the beginning of a quotation

4. Correct (no comma should follow the question mark)

5. explanatory words at the beginning of a quotation

BACKGROUND

In an article entitled "Pain and Suffering: Apostrophes and Academic Life" (*Journal of Basic Writing* 7 [Fall 1988]: 91–98), Irvin Hashimoto argues for tolerance on the part of teachers towards students' punctuation errors. He describes what happens when writers "wade into the wonderful sea of arbitrary punctuation."

24g cont.

EXERCISE 24-8

Consulting section 24g, punctuate the following dialogue correctly. If a sentence is correct, circle its number.

EXAMPLE   "Was anyone with the injured boy?," asked the admissions clerk.

"Was anyone with the injured boy?" asked the admissions clerk.

1. "His father" replied the ambulance driver "but he's unconscious."

2. "This boy looks like he needs surgery, but he is the son of the surgeon now on duty" said the clerk.

3. She explained in an agitated voice "Surgeons do not operate on their own family members."

4. "How can he be the surgeon's son when his father is still in the ambulance?" asked the driver.

5. With a disgusted look, the clerk told the driver "The surgeon is the boy's mother."

24h

Using commas in dates, names, addresses, and numbers according to accepted practice

When you write dates, names, and numbers, be sure to use commas according to accepted practice.

RULES FOR COMMAS WITH DATES	112

- Use a comma between the date and the year: **July 20,** 1969.

- Use a comma between the day and the date: **Sunday,** July 20, 1969.

- Within a sentence, use a comma on both sides of the year in a full date.

  Everyone wanted to be near a television set on **July 20,** 1969, to watch Armstrong emerge from the lunar landing module.

- Do not use a comma in a date that contains the month with only a day or the month with only a year. Also, do not use a comma in a date that contains only the season and year.

  The major news story during **July 1969** was the moon landing; news coverage was especially heavy on **July 21**.

- An inverted date takes no commas: **20 July 1969.**

  People stayed near their television sets on **20 July 1969** to watch the moon landing.

RULES FOR COMMAS WITH NAMES, PLACES, AND ADDRESSES   113

- When an abbreviated title (Jr., M.D., Ph.D.) comes after a person's name, use a comma between the name and the title—**Rosa Gonzales,** M.D.—and also after the title if it is followed by the rest of the sentence:

  The jury listened closely to the expert testimony of **Rosa Gonzales,** M.D., last week.

- When you invert a person's name, use a comma to separate the last name from the first: **Troyka,** David.

- Use a comma to separate the names of a city and state: **Philadelphia, Pennsylvania.** If the city and state fall within a sentence, use a comma after the state as well, unless the state name ends the sentence and thus is followed by a period, question mark, or exclamation point.

  The Liberty Bell has been on display in **Philadelphia, Pennsylvania,** for many years.

- When you write a complete address as part of a sentence, use a comma to separate all the items, with the exception of the zip code. The zip code follows the state after a double space but no comma. Also, do not follow the zip code with a comma.

  I wrote to **Mr. U. Lern, 10-01 Rule Road, Englewood Cliffs, New Jersey 07632** for the instruction manual.

RULES FOR COMMAS WITH LETTERS   114

- For the opening of an informal letter, use a comma:

  Dear Betty,

  For the opening of a business or formal letter, use a colon (:).
- For the close of a letter, use a comma.

  Sincerely yours,   **Best regards,**

  Love,   **Very truly yours,**

BACKGROUND

One of the most disputed topics in the teaching of composition concerns the effectiveness of formal grammar instruction in improving student writing. Opinions, many of them supported by research and experience, range from those that insist on the necessity for writers to understand the rules of grammar to those that would replace all such instruction with writing experience. Typical of the dialogue to be found in professional journals is a series of articles published in *College English* in 1985. Patrick Hartwell began the discussion by claiming that because teaching grammar does not improve student writing, teachers should look for more effective means of instruction ("Grammar, Grammars, and the Teaching of English" 47 [February 1985]: 105–127). The article was rebutted by Martha Kolln in "Comment on 'Grammar, Grammars, and the Teaching of Grammar' 47 (February 1985) and a Response," also published in *College English* 47 [December 1985]: 874–879). Additional comments from four theorists appeared, along with a final commentary from Hartwell, in the same journal, in October 1985 (641–650).

Another article dealing with the controversy is "John S. Mayher's "Grammar and Consciousness" (*Connecticut English Journal* 15 [Spring 1984]: 29–30), in which Mayher reports research to support his argument against teaching grammar to improve writing. Also, in "Three Reasons Why We Shouldn't Teach Grammar and One Why We Should (Sort Of)" (*Connecticut English Journal* 18 [Spring 1985]: 1–4), Robert C. Small argues that because grammar instruction is abstract, time-consuming, and ineffective, it should not be included in composition classes, but he suggests that it has a more appropriate place in linguistics courses.

BACKGROUND

The power of the comma was demonstrated at the 1984 Republican National Convention. An item proposed for the party platform read "The Convention opposes any form of tax increase which would hurt the economy." Someone called for the addition of a comma, so that the item would read, "The Convention opposes any form of tax increase, which would hurt the economy."

That comma was a reflection of the conservative economic position of its proposer. In the first version of the sentence, *which* begins a restrictive clause. The author of the proposal was talking only of harmful tax increases and implying that nonharmful increases would be acceptable. In the second version, *which* begins a nonrestrictive clause. This author saw all tax increases as the same—harmful.

ANSWERS AND COVERAGE: EXERCISE 24–9

1. Made by the noted German director Wim Wenders, *Paris, Texas* [comma after city in title] was set in an actual town in Lamar County, Texas, [comma after county and state] with a population of 24,699. [comma with numbers]

2. Correct

3. The custom of naming little towns in the United States after cosmopolitan urban centers in the Old World has resulted in such places as Athens, Georgia, and St. Petersburg, Florida. [commas after cities]

4. As of December 31, 1990, [comma with dates] the U.S. St. Petersburg had 238,629 [comma with numbers] citizens and the U.S. Athens had 45,734. [comma with numbers]

5. By comparison, St. Petersburg, Russia, and Athens, Greece, [commas after cities] have populations of approximately 4 million and 1 million, respectively.

RULES FOR COMMAS WITH NUMBERS

- Counting from the right, put a comma after every three digits in numbers over four digits: **72,867**   **156,567,066**

- A comma is optional for most four-digit numbers. Use a consistent style within a given piece of writing.

  $1776   **$1,776**

  1776 miles   **1,776 miles**

  1776 potatoes **1,776 potatoes**

- Do not use a comma for a four-digit year: **1990** (a year of five digits or more gets a comma: **25,000** B.C.); in an address of four digits or more: **12161 Dean Drive;** or in a page number of four digits or more: **see page 1338**

- Use a comma to separate related measurements written as words: **five feet, four inches**

- Use a comma to separate a scene from an act in a play: **Act II, scene iv**

- Use a comma to separate a reference to a page from a reference to a line: **page 10, line 6**

EXERCISE 24-9

Consulting section 24h, insert commas where they are needed. If a sentence is correct, circle its number.

EXAMPLE   On June 1 1984 the small German-French production company Road Movies released a feature film called *Paris Texas*.

On June 1, 1984, the small German-French production company Road Movies released a feature film called *Paris*, *Texas*.

1. Made by the noted German director Wim Wenders, *Paris Texas* was set in an actual town in Lamar County Texas with a population of 24699.

2. The movie's title was clearly intended to play off the slightly more famous Paris in France.

3. The custom of naming little towns in the United States after cosmopolitan urban centers in the Old World resulted in such places as Athens Georgia and St. Petersburg Florida.

4. As of December 31 1990 the American St. Petersburg had 238629 citizens and the American Athens had 45734.

5. By comparison, St. Petersburg Russia and Athens Greece have populations of approximately 4 million and 1 million, respectively.

Using commas to clarify meaning **24i**

Sometimes you will need to use a comma to clarify the meaning of a sentence, even though no other rule calls for one.

NO   Of the gymnastic team's twenty five were injured.
YES Of the gymnastic team's twenty, five were injured.

NO   Those who can practice many hours a day.
YES Those who can, practice many hours a day.

NO   George dressed and performed for the sellout crowd.
YES George dressed, and performed for the sellout crowd.

EXERCISE 24-10

Consulting section 24i, insert commas to prevent misreading. If a sentence is correct, circle its number.

EXAMPLE   Though controversial subliminal learning appeals to many people.

Though controversial, subliminal learning appeals to many people.

1. Using specially prepared tape recorders communicate hidden messages to listeners.
2. Some people who want to learn supposedly without effort by listening to the tape.
3. To prevent shoplifting twenty major department stores started using subliminal tapes.
4. Of the twenty nine reported pilferage had decreased by about 37 percent.
5. Many people worry that governments or businesses might use subliminal learning to control people against their will.

Avoiding misuse of the comma **24j**

Using commas correctly helps you deliver your meaning to your reader. As a writer, you frequently have to make decisions about

---

QUOTATION ABOUT WRITING

A novel is a piece of architecture. It's not random wallowings or confessional diaries. It's a building—it has to have walls and floors and the bathrooms have to work.

—John Irving

QUOTATION ABOUT WRITING

I think I did pretty well, considering I started out with nothing but a bunch of blank paper.

—Steve Martin

QUOTATION ABOUT WRITING

I have performed the necessary butchery. Here is the bleeding corpse.
—Henry James,
following a request to cut three lines from a 5,000 word article

ANSWERS: EXERCISE 24–10

1. Using specially prepared tape, recorders communicate hidden messages to listeners.
2. Some people who want to, learn supposedly without effort by listening to the tape.
3. To prevent shoplifting, twenty major department stores started using subliminal tapes.
4. Of the twenty, nine reported pilferage had decreased by about 37 percent.
5. Correct

BACKGROUND

From a study of 100 basic writers, Carole McAllister and Richard Louth concluded that the use of a word processor raises the quality of students' revisions (ERIC ED 281 232).

Behind him the white man was shouting, "My horse! Fetch my horse!" and he thought for an instant of cutting across the park and climbing the fence into the road, but he did not know the park nor how high the vine-massed fence might be and he dared not risk it. So he ran on down the drive, blood and breath roaring; presently he was in the road again though he could not see it. He could not hear either: the galloping mare was almost upon him before he heard her, and even then he held his course, as if the very urgency of his wild grief and need must in a moment more find him wings, waiting until the ultimate instant to hurl himself aside and into the weed-choked roadside ditch as the horse thundered past and on, for an instant in furious silhouette against the stars, the tranquil early summer night sky which, even before the shape of the horse and rider vanished, strained abruptly and violently upward: a long, swirling roar incredible and soundless, blotting the stars, and he springing up and into the road again, running again, knowing it was too late yet still running even after he heard the shot an instant later, two shots, pausing now without knowing he had ceased to run, crying "Pap! Pap!," running again before he knew he had begun to run, stumbling, tripping over something and scrabbling up again without ceasing to run, looking backward over his shoulder at the glare as he got up, running on among the invisible trees, panting, sobbing, "Father! Father!"

whether a comma is needed. If as you are DRAFTING you are in doubt about a comma, insert and circle it clearly so that you can go back to it later when you are REVISING and think through whether it is correct. Throughout this chapter, most sections that discuss a correct use of the comma include a comma caution to alert you to a related misuse of the comma. This section summarizes the most frequent misuses of the comma.

24j-1　Avoiding misuse of a comma with coordinating conjunctions

Section 24a discusses the correct use of commas with sentences joined by COORDINATING CONJUNCTIONS. Do not put a comma *after* a coordinating conjunction that joins two INDEPENDENT CLAUSES unless another rule makes it necessary. Also, do not use commas to separate two items joined with a coordinating conjunction.

NO	The sky was dark gray **and,** it looked like dusk.
YES	The sky was dark gray, **and** it looked like dusk.
NO	**The moon, and the stars** were shining last night.
YES	**The moon and the stars** were shining last night.

24j-2　Avoiding misuse of a comma with subordinating conjunctions and prepositions

Do not put a comma *after* a SUBORDINATING CONJUNCTION or a PREPOSITION unless another rule makes it necessary.

NO	**Although, the storm brought high winds,** it did no damage.
YES	**Although the storm brought high winds,** it did no damage.
NO	The storm did no damage **although, it brought high winds.**
YES	The storm did no damage **although it brought high winds.**
NO	People expected worse **between, the high winds and the heavy downpour.**
YES	People expected worse **between the high winds and the heavy downpour.**

24j-3　Avoiding misuse of commas to separate items

Section 24c discusses the correct use of commas with items in a series. Do not use a comma *before* the first or *after* the last item in a series, unless another rule makes it necessary.

NO	The gymnasium was decorated with, **red, white, and blue ribbons** for the Fourth of July.
NO	The gymnasium was decorated with **red, white, and blue,** ribbons for the Fourth of July.
YES	The gymnasium was decorated with **red, white, and blue** ribbons for the Fourth of July.

Section 24d discusses the correct use of commas with COORDI-NATE ADJECTIVES. Do not put a comma after the final coordinate adjective and the noun it modifies. Also, do not use a comma between noncoordinate adjectives.

NO	The **huge, restless,** crowd waited.
YES	The **huge, restless** crowd waited.

NO	The concert featured **several, new** bands.
YES	The concert featured **several new** bands.

Avoiding misuse of commas with restrictive elements

Section 24e discusses the correct use of commas with RESTRICTIVE (essential) ELEMENTS and NONRESTRICTIVE (nonessential) ELEMENTS. Do not use a comma to set off a restrictive (essential) element from the rest of a sentence.

NO	Vegetables, **stir-fried in a wok,** are uniquely crisp and flavorful. [The information about being stir-fried in a wok is essential, so it is not set off with commas.]
YES	Vegetables **stir-fried in a wok** are uniquely crisp and flavorful.

Avoiding misuse of commas with quotations

Section 24g discusses the correct use of commas with quoted material. Do not use a comma to set off INDIRECT DISCOURSE (often signaled by *that* or *as*).

NO	Jon **said that, he likes stir-fried vegetables.**
YES	Jon **said that he likes stir-fried vegetables.**
YES	Jon **said, "I like stir-fried vegetables."**

24j-4

24j-5

QUOTATION ABOUT WRITING

The commas are the most useful and usable of all the stops. It is highly important to put them in place as you go along. If you try to come back after doing a paragraph and stick them in the various spots that tempt you you will discover that they tend to swarm like minnows into all sorts of crevices whose existence you hadn't realized and before you know it the whole long sentence becomes immobilized and lashed up squirming in commas. Better to use them sparingly, and with affection, precisely when the need for each one arises, nicely, by itself.
—Lewis Thomas

QUOTATION ABOUT WRITING

When I stepped from hard manual work to writing, I just stepped from one kind of hard work to another.
—Sean O'Casey

QUOTATION ABOUT WRITING

The most important sentence in a good book is the first one; it will contain the organic seed from which all that follows will grow.

—Paul Horgan

ANSWERS AND COVERAGE: EXERCISE 24-11

1. In the 1920s, [keep: introductory phrase] the Harlem Renaissance [omit: do not separate subject from its verb, 24j-6] was not confined to New York City; Harlem was only one of several [omit: comma between noncoordinate adjectives or modifiers, 24j-3] African-American urban districts where the arts flourished during this decade.

2. Black urban singers began to attract a national audience, and [omit: comma after coordinating conjunction, 24j-1; position between independent clauses] Harlem surpassed Broadway in the originality of its musical revues, poetry, and fiction. [keep: commas to separate items, 25j-3]

3. One of the leading poets of the Harlem Renaissance [omit: do not separate subject from its verb, 24j-6] was Claude McKay, who [keep: nonrestrictive clause] arrived in the United States from Jamaica in 1912 at the age of twenty-three.

4. He studied briefly at Booker T. Washington's [omit: noncoordinating adjectives or modifiers] famous Tuskegee Institute in Alabama.

5. In 1917, [keep: introductory phrase] he moved to Harlem, [keep: nonrestrictive clause, 24j-4] where he published his first poem.

6. McKay said that [omit: comma in indirect discourse, 24j-5] poetry was his vehicle of protest, and [keep: comma linking independent clauses, 24a] he wrote his 1919 poem "If We Must Die" in response to [omit: do not separate a preposition from its object, 24j-6] the race riots of that year.

7. In fact, [keep: introductory phrase] Harlem was a neighborhood seething in revolt [omit: coordinating conjunction joining two nouns, 24j-1] and racial pride.

➔

24j-6

Avoiding use of a comma to separate a subject from its verb, a verb from its object, a verb from its complement, and a preposition from its object

NO **Orville and Wilbur Wright,** **made** their first successful airplane flights on December 17, 1903. [As a rule, do not let a comma separate a SUBJECT from its VERB.]

YES **Orville and Wilbur Wright made** their first successful airplane flights on December 17, 1903.

NO These inventors enthusiastically **tackled, the problems** of powered flight and aerodynamics. [As a rule, do not let a comma separate a verb from its OBJECT.]

YES These inventors enthusiastically **tackled the problems** of powered flight and aerodynamics.

NO Flying has **become, both** an important industry and a popular hobby. [As a rule, do not let a comma separate a verb from its COMPLEMENT.]

YES Flying has **become both** an important industry and a popular hobby.

NO Airplane hobbyists visit Kitty Hawk's flight museum **from, all over the world.** [As a rule, do not let a comma separate a PREPOSITION from its object.]

YES Airplane hobbyists visit Kitty Hawk's flight museum **from all over the world.**

Because the comma occurs so frequently, advice against overusing it sometimes clashes with a rule requiring it. In such cases, follow the rule that calls for the comma.

The town of Kitty Hawk, North Carolina, attracts thousands of tourists each year. [Although the comma after *North Carolina* separates the subject and verb, it is required because the state is set off from the city and from the rest of the sentence; see 24h.]

EXERCISE 24-11

Some deliberately misused commas have been added in these sentences. Consulting 24j and the other sections in this chapter that are referred to in 24j, delete unneeded commas. If a sentence is correct, circle its number.

EXAMPLE   Large U.S. cities experienced a cultural flowering during the 1920s, and nurtured a diversity of cultures.

Large U.S. cities experienced a cultural flowering during the 1920s and nurtured a diversity of cultures.

1. In the 1920s, the Harlem Renaissance, was not confined to New York City; Harlem was only one of several, African-American urban districts where the arts flourished during this decade.

2. Black urban singers began to attract a national audience and, Harlem surpassed Broadway in the originality of its musical revues, poetry, and fiction.

3. One of the leading poets of the Harlem Renaissance, was Claude McKay, who arrived in the United States from Jamaica in 1912 at the age of twenty-three.

4. He studied briefly at Booker T. Washington's, famous Tuskegee Institute in Alabama.

5. In 1917, he moved to Harlem, where he published his first poem.

6. McKay said that, poetry was his vehicle of protest, and he wrote his 1919 poem "If We Must Die" in response to, the race riots of that year.

7. In fact, Harlem was a neighborhood seething in revolt, and racial pride.

8. Marcus Garvey, and his Universal Negro Improvement Association sought to transport blacks to, a new and better life in Africa.

9. Garvey, who was born in Jamaica like Claude McKay, was one of the first people, who taught African Americans that black is beautiful.

10. The Harlem Renaissance continued through 1945, when writers from Langston Hughes and Richard Wright to Zora Neale Hurston and Margaret Walker launched their great literary careers.

ANSWERS AND COVERAGE: EXERCISE 24–11, cont.

8. Marcus Garvey [omit: coordinating conjunction joining two nouns, 24j-1] and his Universal Negro Improvement Association sought to transport blacks to [omit: do not separate a preposition from its object, 24j-6] a new and better life in Africa.

9. Garvey, who was born in Jamaica like Claude McKay, [keep: nonrestrictive clause] was one of the first people [omit: restrictive clause] who taught African Americans that black is beautiful.

10. The Harlem Renaissance continued through 1945, [keep: nonrestrictive clause] when writers from Langston Hughes and Richard Wright to Zora Neale Hurston and Margaret Walker launched their great literary careers.

Focus on Revising

REVISING YOUR WRITING

If you make comma errors when you write, go back to your writing and locate the errors. Using this chapter as a resource, revise your writing to correct the errors.

CASE STUDY: REVISING FOR CORRECT USE OF COMMAS

In these case studies, you can observe a student writer revising. Then you have the chance to revise other student writing on your own.

Observation

A student wrote the following draft for a course called Introduction to Sociology. The assignment was to write about a person who organizes group efforts to improve society. This material is well organized and includes excellent specific details, but the draft's effectiveness is diminished by the presence of comma errors.

Read through the draft. The errors are highlighted and explained. Before you look at the student's revision, revise the material yourself. Then compare what you and the student did.

COVERAGE: PARTICIPATION ESSAY, page 458

Consumers often feel that choosing a new car is a *difficult time-consuming* [24d: commas for coordinate adjectives] matter. Most automobile customers tend to concentrate on *the price, the special features the look and the reputation* [24c: commas in a series] of the car. Truly *experienced informed* [24d: commas for coordinate adjectives] car buyers *however* [24f: commas for transitional word in middle of a sentence] carefully investigate the car manufacturer's grievance procedures.

A common mistake that consumers make is to assume that the *helpful*

Millard Fuller, executive director of Habitat for Humanity, believes that all people have a right to decent housing. Habitat for Humanity an organization that depends on volunteer labor and donations of money and materials builds modest sturdy homes that are sold at cost to low-income families. Previously these families had rented substandard housing without plumbing or heat. The full cost of each Habitat home is approximately $28000. To buy a home each family has to make a small down payment and support a mortgage. The monthly mortgage payment is

comma missing to set off nonrestrictive phrase: 24e-1

comma missing between coordinate adjectives: 24d

comma missing in a number of five digits: 24h

comma missing to set off nonrestrictive phrase: 24e-1

comma missing after introductory word: 24b-3

comma missing after introductory phrase: 24b-2

comma missing after introductory word: 24b-3

comma missing between items in a series: 24c

comma missing after introductory clause: 24b-1

comma missing between independent clauses joined by for: 24a

usually about $150 an amount less than the monthly rent that the family had been paying for their indecent housing. Nevertheless Habitat for Humanity is not a charitable organization. The families offered the homes must be able to take on the financial responsibility involved participate in the labor of building their house and donate time to help build other houses.

When Fuller asks people to help he says "It's not your blue blood your pedigree or your college degree. It's what you do with your life that counts." One famous volunteer recruited to take on a yearly assignment is Jimmy Carter former President of the United States. The concept of Habitat for Humanity is catching on for the number of new Habitat U.S. affiliates increased from 11 to 171 between 1980 and 1986 and continues to increase today. This seems like an excellent way to fight poverty housing doesn't it?

comma missing to set off nonrestrictive appositive: 24e-2

commas missing between items in a series: 24c

comma missing before quoted words: 24g

comma missing between items in a series: 24c

comma missing to set off nonrestrictive appositive: 24e-2

comma missing to set off tag sentence: 24f

Here is how the student revised to correct the comma errors. Compare it with your revision. Make sure that your revision has eliminated each of the errors highlighted in the draft.

Millard Fuller, executive director of Habitat for Humanity, believes that all people have a right to decent housing. Habitat for Humanity, an organization that depends on volunteer labor and donations of money and materials, builds modest, sturdy homes that are sold at cost to low-income families. Previously, these families had rented substandard housing without plumbing or heat. The full cost of each Habitat home is approximately $28,000. To buy a home, each family has to make a small down payment and support a mortgage. The monthly mortgage payment is usually about $150, an amount less than the monthly rent that the family had been paying for their indecent housing. Nevertheless, Habitat for Humanity is not a charitable organization. The families offered the homes must be able

---

COVERAGE: PARTICIPATION ESSAY, *cont.*

friendly [24d: commas for coordinate adjectives] car salesperson will help resolve problems with the automobile after it is purchased. In fact [24b: comma after introductory words] the salesperson's job is essentially finished once the car is *sold so a consumer* [24a: comma before coordinating conjunction that joins two independent clauses] with a complaint will usually *hear* "You'll [24g: comma before quoted words] have to talk to the service department."

If a car salesperson offers little or no help [24b: comma after introductory clause] consumer may feel cheated by the indifference. One reaction *one felt by many people who end up with a lemon of a car* [24e: commas for nonrestrictive appositive] is to write an angry letter to the chief executive officer of the automobile manufacturer. *Before writing* [24b: comma after introductory phrase; also 24i: comma needed for clarity] the consumer should realize that complaints to the manufacturer are referred back to the dealership. *After all* [24b: comma after introductory words; also 24i: comma needed for clarity] dealerships and manufacturers are not owned and managed by the same people.

In some cases [24b: comma after introductory words] consumers may benefit from legal advice. States have varying "lemon laws" to help consumers who purchase defective cars. In some states *for example* [24f: commas for transitional word in middle of a sentence] the existence of a problem, *that is unresolved*, [24e: drop commas with restrictive element] after six repair attempts by the dealership's service department can require a dealer to substitute a new vehicle. Chrysler Motors has the Customer Arbitration Board (CAB), which consists of a consumer advocate, a member of the general public, and *an independent, technical expert* [24d: drop comma with non-

COVERAGE: PARTICIPATION ESSAY, cont.

coordinate adjectives]. Any solution that the CAB proposes is binding on the dealer and Chrysler Motors.

It is comforting to know that a consumer, *who buys a lemon of a car,* [24e: drop commas with restrictive clause] is not always *helpless isn't it?* [24h: comma for tag question] Sometimes a lemon can be made into lemonade, right?

ANSWER: PARTICIPATION ESSAY, page 458

This version revises the comma errors. Answers will vary if students have revised content, organization, or style.

Consumers often feel that choosing a new car is a difficult, time-consuming matter. Most automobile customers tend to concentrate on the price, the special features, the look, and the reputation of the car. Truly experienced, informed car buyers, however, carefully investigate the car manufacturer's grievance procedures.

A common mistake that consumers make is to assume that the helpful, friendly car salesperson will help resolve problems with the automobile after it is purchased. In fact, the salesperson's job is essentially finished once the car is sold, so a consumer with a complaint will usually hear, "You'll have to talk to the service department."

If a car salesperson offers little or no help, a consumer may feel cheated by the indifference. One reaction, one felt by many people who end up with a lemon of a car, is to write an angry letter to the chief executive officer of the automobile manufacturer. Before writing, the consumer should realize that complaints to the manufacturer are referred back to the dealership. After all, dealerships and manufacturers are not owned and managed by the same people.

→

to take on the financial responsibility involved, participate in the labor of building their house, and donate time to help build other houses.

When Fuller asks people to help, he says, "It's not your blue blood, your pedigree, or your college degree. It's what you do with your life that counts." One famous volunteer recruited to take on a yearly assignment is Jimmy Carter, former President of the United States. The concept of Habitat for Humanity is catching on, for the number of new Habitat U.S. affiliates increased from 11 to 171 between 1980 and 1986 and continues to increase today. This seems like an excellent way to fight poverty housing, doesn't it?

Participation

A student wrote the following draft for a course called Introduction to Political Science. The assignment was to discuss an example of the power of consumers. The material is clear and logically presented, but the draft's effectiveness is diminished by comma errors.

Read through the draft. Then revise it to eliminate the errors. Also, make any additional revisions you think would improve the content, organization, and style of the material.

Consumers often feel that choosing a new car is a difficult time-consuming matter. Most automobile customers tend to concentrate on the price, the special features the look and the reputation of the car. Truly experienced informed car buyers however carefully investigate the car manufacturer's grievance procedures.

A common mistake that consumers make is to assume that the helpful friendly car salesperson will help resolve problems with the automobile after it is purchased. In fact the salesperson's job is essentially finished once the car is sold so a consumer with a complaint will usually hear "You'll have to talk to the service department."

If a car salesperson offers little or no help a consumer may feel cheated by the indifference. One reaction often felt by many people who end up with a lemon of a car is to write an angry letter to the chief executive officer of the automobile company. Before writing the consumer should realize that complaints to the manufacturers are referred back to the dealership. After all dealerships and manufacturers are not owned and managed by the same people.

In some cases consumers may benefit from legal advice. States have varying "lemon laws" to help consumers who purchase defective cars. In some states for example the existence of a problem, that is unresolved, after six repair attempts by the dealership's service department can require a dealer to substitute a new vehicle. Chrysler Motors has the Customer Arbitration Board (CAB), which consists of a consumer advocate, a member of the general public, and an independent, technical expert. Any solution that the CAB proposes is binding on the dealer and Chrysler Motors.

It is comforting to know that a consumer, who buys a lemon of a car, is not always helpless isn't it? Sometimes a lemon can be made into lemonade, right?

COVERAGE: PARTICIPATION ESSAY,
cont.

In some cases, consumers may benefit from legal advice. States have varying "lemon laws" to help consumers who purchase defective cars. In some states, for example, the existence of a problem that is unresolved after six repair attempts by the dealership's service department can require a dealership to substitute a new vehicle. Chrysler Motors has the Customer Arbitration Board (CAB), which consists of a consumer advocate, a member of the general public, and an independent technical expert. Any solution that the CAB proposes is binding on the dealer and Chrysler Motors.

It is comforting to know that a consumer who buys a lemon of a car is not always helpless, isn't it? Sometimes a lemon can be made into lemonade, right?

25 *The Semicolon*

REFERENCES TO SUPPLEMENTS

For this topic in the CLAST writing competency test, refer students to ch. 1, sections B2d and B5b of *Preparing for the CLAST* by S. Patterson.

This topic is included in the TASP writing competency test. Refer students to *Preparing for the TASP* by M. Saenz.

For editing for correct use of semicolons, refer students to *Rough Drafts* by K. S. Cain, Part V, Exercise 14.

See transparency 7–13 for correct use of the semicolon in the *Prentice Hall/Simon & Schuster Transparencies for Writers* by D. Carter.

BACKGROUND

Beginning in the eighth century, the inverted semicolon served as a pause somewhere between a comma and a colon. After about 700 years of use, it was discarded. The semicolon as it is known today dates from the seventeenth century.

QUOTATION ABOUT WRITING

It is almost always a greater pleasure to come across a semicolon than a period. The period tells you that that is that; if you didn't get all the meaning you wanted or expected, anyway you got all the writer intended to parcel out and now you have to move along. But with a semicolon there, you get a pleasant little feeling of expectancy; there is more to come; read on; it will get clearer.

—Lewis Thomas,
"Notes on Punctuation"

SEMICOLON PATTERN I

25a Using a semicolon between closely related independent clauses

When INDEPENDENT CLAUSES are clearly related in meaning, you can separate them with a semicolon instead of a period. The choice is yours in relation to the meaning you want your material to deliver. A period signals complete separation between independent clauses; a semicolon tells readers that the separation is softer.

SEMICOLON PATTERN I   116

Independent clause; independent clause.

> This is my husband's second marriage; it's the first for me.
>
> —RUTH SIDEL, "Marion Deluca"
>
> Our Constitution is in actual operation; everything appears to promise that it will last; but in this world nothing is certain but death and taxes.
>
> —BENJAMIN FRANKLIN

! ♣ COMMA CAUTION: Do not use only a comma between independent clauses, or you will create the error called a comma splice (see Chapter 14). ♣

25b Using a semicolon before a coordinating conjunction joining independent clauses containing commas

When INDEPENDENT CLAUSES are linked by a coordinating conjunction (*and, but, or, nor, for, yet, so*), a comma should separate them (see 24a), but there is one exception. When one of the independent clauses contains a comma, you can use a semicolon before the coordinating conjunction. Choose according to what would be easier for your reader.

SEMICOLON PATTERN II 117

- Independent clause, one that contains a comma; coordinating conjunction independent clause.

- Independent clause; coordinating conjunction independent clause, one that contains a comma.

- Independent clause, one that contains commas; coordinating conjunction independent clause, one that contains a comma.

When the peacock has presented his back, the spectator will usually begin to walk around him to get a front view; but the peacock will continue to turn so that no front view is possible.

—FLANNERY O'CONNOR, "The King of the Birds"

For anything worth having, one must pay the price; and the price is always work, patience, love, self-sacrifice.

—JOHN BURROUGHS

Using a semicolon when conjunctive adverbs or other transitional expressions connect independent clauses

25c

You can use a semicolon between two INDEPENDENT CLAUSES when the second clause begins with a conjunctive adverb (*therefore, however;* for a complete list, see Chart 49 in 7f) or other transitional expression (*in fact, as a result;* for a complete list, see Chart 23 in 4d-1). Your other option is to use a period, creating two sentences.

SEMICOLON PATTERN III 118

- Independent clause; conjunctive adverb, independent clause.

- Independent clause; transitional expression, independent clause.

The average annual rainfall in Death Valley is about two inches; **nevertheless,** hundreds of plant and animal species survive and even thrive there.

Patient photographers have spent years recording desert life cycles; **as a result,** all of us have watched barren sands flower after a spring storm.

QUOTATION ABOUT WRITING

From the reader's point of view, punctuation provides a map for one who must otherwise drive blindly past the by-ways, intersections, and detours of a writer's thought.

—Mina Shaughnessy,
Errors and Expectations

QUOTATION ABOUT WRITING

Punctuation contributes to art as well as to correctness, to style as well as to styling. Make it work for you, not just to develop prose that is "clear enough"— not just to prevent confusion—but to help you express yourself, or your characters express themselves. Don't lean on it; don't shy away from it; just *use* it—and in doing so, let it help you convey nuances too subtle for words alone to convey; let it help you evoke effects so delicate that talk would shatter them. And remember that if you frequently use more marks than usual—or fewer than usual—you will call attention to your craft, with the results possibly seeming artful rather than artistic, posturing rather than expressive. Nor do I for a moment suggest that punctuation can, or should, be charged with sole responsibility for effectiveness: descriptive detail, diction, sentence length, sentence rhythm, paragraph structure, timing— these and other elements of style can and must share the load.

—Robert M. Pierson,
"Punctuation as Art"

QUOTATION ABOUT WRITING

I think of myself as a stylist, and stylists can become notoriously obsessed with the placing of a comma, the weight of a semicolon.

—Truman Capote

ALTERNATE EXAMPLES

1. Each year people from all over the world visit the Tower of London; for centuries, it served as a prison for famous persons who were deemed to be enemies of the crown.

2. The Tower is located in the Borough of Stepney; it covers about eighteen acres.

3. The central portion, called the White Tower, was begun in 1078; it was modernized by Christopher Wren.

4. The Beauchamp Tower has 91 inscriptions of prisoners in it; the Bloody Tower served as the prison of Sir Walter Raleigh, who wrote an incomplete *History of the World* during his stay there in 1614.

5. The place of execution within the walls was Tower Green; there Anne Boleyn was beheaded in 1536.

ALTERNATE EXAMPLES

1. Black varieties of the leopard are common in humid parts of India; however, they are rare in Africa.

2. Leopards prey on monkeys, birds, and reptiles; consequently, they must hunt both in trees and on the ground.

3. A leopard begins its meal by tearing at the forequarters of its prey; in contrast, the tiger starts with the hindquarters of its victim.

4. One Indian leopard was alleged to have killed 200 human beings in two years before it was shot; similarly, a leopard in Ceylon used to lie in wait for passers-by on a main road.

5. The leopard's roar of belligerence is different from its mating call; nevertheless, both sound fierce to the human ear.

♣ COMMA ALERTS: (1) Do not use *only* a comma between independent clauses connected by a conjunctive adverb or other words of transition, or you will create the error called a comma splice; see Chapter 14. (2) Usually use a comma *after* a conjunctive adverb or a transitional expression that begins an independent clause, although some writers omit the comma after short words, such as *then, next, soon*. ♣

25d   Using a semicolon between long or comma-containing items in a series

When a sentence contains a series of PHRASES or CLAUSES that are long or that contain commas, use a semicolon, not a comma, to separate the items. This practice enables your reader to read without having to stop to figure out where one item in the series ends and the next begins. (For information on using commas in a series, see 24c.)

SEMICOLON PATTERN IV

SEMICOLON PATTERN IV 119

Independent clause containing a series of items, any of which contain a comma; another item in the series; another item in the series.

Functioning as assistant chefs, the students chopped onions, green peppers, and parsley; sliced chicken and duck meat into strips; started a broth simmering; and filled a large, low, copper pan with oil before the head chef stepped to the stove.

25e   Avoiding misuse of the semicolon

25e-1   Not using a semicolon after an introductory phrase or between a dependent clause and an independent clause

NO   Once opened; the computer lab will be well used.

YES   Once opened, the computer lab will be well used.

NO   Although the new computers had arrived at the college; the computer lab was still being built.

YES   Although the new computers had arrived at the college, the computer lab was still being built.

Using a colon, not a semicolon, to introduce a list

NO   The newscast featured three major stories; the latest pictures of Uranus, a speech by the president, and a series of brush fires in Nevada.

YES   The newscast featured three major stories: the latest pictures of Uranus, a speech by the president, and a series of brush fires in Nevada.

EXERCISE 25-1

Consulting sections 25a–25e, insert semicolons where they are needed, and change any incorrectly used semicolons to correct punctuation. If a sentence is correct, circle its number.

EXAMPLE   In the seventeenth century, the citizens of Holland became victims of tulip madness, this mania became so intense that regular businesses were neglected while people bought and sold tulips.

In the seventeenth century, the citizens of Holland became victims of tulip madness; this mania became so intense that regular businesses were neglected while people bought and sold tulips.

1. Tulips were first noted in Holland by Conrad Gesner in 1559, he saw them in the garden of Counsellor Herwart, a person famous for growing exotic plants.
2. Herwart had gotten the onionlike bulbs from a friend traveling in Turkey, where tulips were a favorite flower, in fact, the tulip's name comes from a Turkish word for *turban.*
3. Growing tulips quickly became popular throughout Dutch society, it became a mark of good taste to have a garden full of them.
4. Soon, merchants and shopkeepers were competing to find the rarest specimens, consequently, prices for these prized bulbs soared.
5. As tulip bulb prices reached preposterous heights, Dutch businesses of all kinds began to suffer because money needed for other goods was tied up in tulip purchases.
6. In 1635, a person might invest 100,000 florins to buy forty bulbs, but four tons of beer cost 32 florins, twelve sheep 120 florins, a thousand pounds of cheese 100 florins, and a silver cup 60 florins.
7. In Amsterdam, a very rare tulip was exchanged for the following items; 4,600 florins, an expensive, gilded carriage, and two gray horses, complete with harnesses, bridles, and bells.
8. Brokers began to trade tulips on the stock exchanges, therefore, Dutch nobles, farmers, merchants, servants, and street-sweepers alike found themselves growing richer as prices rose.

ANSWERS AND COVERAGE: EXERCISE 25–1

1. . . . Conrad Gesner in 1559; he saw them . . . [25a, closely related independent clauses] person famous for growing exotic plants.

2. . . . a favorite flower; in fact, the tulip's name . . . [25c, transitional expression connecting independent clauses] comes from a Turkish word for *turban.*

3. . . . throughout Dutch society; it became a . . . [25a, closely related independent clauses] mark of good taste to have a garden full of them.

4. . . . the rarest specimens; consequently, prices . . . [25c, conjunctive adverb connecting independent clauses]

5. Correct.

6. . . . to buy forty bulbs; but four tons . . . [25b, coordinating conjunction joining independent clauses]

7. . . . following items: [25e-2, list introduced by colon, not semicolon] 4,600 florins; an expensive, gilded carriage; and two gray horses, complete with harnesses, bridles, and bells [25d, between comma-containing items in a series].

8. . . . on the stock exchanges; therefore, [25c, conjunctive adverb joining independent clauses] Dutch nobles, farmers, merchants, servants, [note that commas should be used between the items in the series here] and street-sweepers alike found themselves growing richer as prices rose.

➜

9. made . . . a delivery; an hour later he found the messenger finishing lunch, which included the "onion" he had taken from the merchant's office [25a, closely related independent clauses containing one or more commas]

10. Although Holland's tulip madness has calmed down considerably today, growing tulips . . . [25e-1, use a comma, not a semicolon, to separate a dependent clause from an independent clause]

ANSWERS: EXERCISE 25–2

1. The first roller coaster in the United States, installed in the late nineteenth century, was part of an amusement park in the Coney Island section of New York City; it was named the "Switchback Gravity Pleasure Railway."

2. The first roller coaster was extremely primitive; it was built of wood, had only two inclines, and reached a downhill speed of a mere six miles per hour.

3. Riders got on at the top of the first incline and climbed out when the train reached the bottom; then the riders walked up the hill to the top of the second incline and climbed in for the ride to the bottom.

4. Soon a chain drive for roller coasters was developed to power the train on the uphill parts; therefore, higher inclines could be built to give riders a greater thrill.

5. Major breakthroughs in roller-coaster design occurred in the 1970s, when roller coaster designers drew on advanced knowledge from physics, mathematics, and human physiology; and the designers used computer simulations to check their work.

9. One merchant discovered that a rare bulb was missing after a messenger had made a delivery, an hour later he found the messenger finishing lunch, which included the "onion" he had taken from the merchant's office.

10. Although Holland's tulip madness has calmed down considerably today; growing tulips is an important industry in that country.

EXERCISE 25-2

Combine each set of sentences into one sentence containing two independent clauses. Use a semicolon between the two clauses. You may add, omit, revise, and rearrange words. Try to use all the patterns in this chapter. More than one revision may be correct, so be ready to explain the reasoning behind your decisions.

EXAMPLE   Roller coasters have been around for a long time. Today's roller coasters barely resemble their ancestors. Today's roller coasters are scientifically designed.

Roller coasters have been around for a long time; however, today's scientifically designed roller coasters barely resemble their ancestors.

1. The first roller coaster in the United States was installed in the late nineteenth century. It was installed as part of an amusement park. The park was in the Coney Island section of New York City. It was named the "Switchback Gravity Pleasure Railway."

2. The first roller coaster was extremely primitive. It was built of wood. It had only two inclines. It reached a downhill speed of a mere six miles per hour.

3. Riders got on at the top of the first incline. Riders climbed out when the train reached the bottom. Then the riders walked up the hill to the top of the second incline. Once again they climbed in for the ride to the bottom.

4. Soon a chain drive for roller coasters was developed. The chain drive powered the train on the uphill parts. Higher inclines could be built. The higher inclines gave riders a greater thrill.

5. Major breakthroughs in roller-coaster design occurred in the 1970s. Roller coaster designers drew on advanced knowledge from physics, mathematics, and human physiology. The designers used computer simulations to check their work.

26 *The Colon*

Using a colon after an independent clause to introduce a list, an appositive, or a quotation

You can use a colon to introduce statements that summarize, restate, or explain what is said in an INDEPENDENT CLAUSE.

COLON PATTERN I 120

- Independent clause: list.

- Independent clause: appositive.

- Independent clause: "Quoted words."

A colon can introduce a list only when the words before the colon are an independent clause. After phrases such as *the following* or *as follows*, a colon is usually required. A colon is not called for with the words *such as* or *including* (see 26d).

LISTED ITEMS

If you really want to lose weight, you need give up only three things: breakfast, lunch, and dinner.

The students' demands included the following: an expanded menu in the cafeteria, improved janitorial services, and more up-to-date textbooks.

A colon can introduce an appositive—a word or words that rename a NOUN or PRONOUN—but only if the introductory words are an independent clause.

APPOSITIVE

The Metropolitan Museum in New York City now owns the best-known works of Louis Tiffany's studio: those wonderful stained-glass windows. [Stained-glass windows renames best-known works.]

465

REFERENCES TO SUPPLEMENTS

For this topic in the CLAST writing competency test, refer students to ch. 1, section B5b of *Preparing for the CLAST* by S. Patterson.

This topic is included in the TASP writing competency test. Refer students to *Preparing for the TASP* by M. Saenz.

For editing for correct use of colons, refer students to *Rough Drafts* by K. S. Cain, Part V, Exercise 15.

COLON PATTERN I

BACKGROUND

A *colon* (in Greek *kōlon*) was originally a person's or an animal's limb. As such it came to be used to refer to a portion of a strophe in choral dancing, then to a division in prosody, and later to a principal clause in a sentence. Finally it became the sign marking the breathing space at the end of a clause.

Historically the colon as a mark of punctuation was preceded by the semicolon, but in English it had more use than the semicolon until the nineteenth century, when it was employed almost solely as a mark of anticipation. It began to regain prestige with the publication of Fowler's *A Dictionary of Modern English Usage* in 1926 and has experienced increased usage since that time.

QUOTATION ABOUT WRITING

An unnecessary mark is worse than useless. It is an interruption.

—George Summey, *American Punctuation*

26a cont.

A colon can introduce a quotation, but only if the introductory words are an independent clause. Use a comma, not a colon, if the introductory words are not an independent clause (see 24b).

QUOTATION

The little boy in *E.T.* did say something neat: "How do you explain school to a higher intelligence?"

—GEORGE F. WILL, "Well, *I* Don't Love You, E.T."

! ♣ QUOTATION ALERT: When a quotation is more than four lines, it must be *displayed* on lines indented ten spaces (see 28a). ♣

26b

Using a colon between two independent clauses

When the first INDEPENDENT CLAUSE explains or summarizes the second independent clause, a colon can separate them.

COLON PATTERN II   121

Independent clause: Independent clause.

! ♣ CAPITALIZATION ALERT: You can use a capital letter or a lower-case letter for the first word of an independent clause that follows a colon. Whichever you choose, be consistent in each piece of writing. This handbook uses a capital letter.

We will never forget the first time we made dinner at home together: He got stomach poisoning and for four days was too sick to go to work.

—LISA BALADENDRUM, student ♣

26c

Using a colon to separate standard material

TITLE AND SUBTITLE
A Brief History of Time: From the Big Bang to Black Holes

HOURS, MINUTES, AND SECONDS
The plane took off at 7:15 p.m.
The track star passed the halfway point at 1:23:02.

COLON PATTERN II

In the military services, hours and minutes are written without colons (and always use four digits):

> The staff meeting originally scheduled for Tuesday at 0930 will be held Tuesday at 1430 instead.

CHAPTERS AND VERSES OF THE BIBLE

Psalms 23:1–3   Luke 3:13

MEMO FORM

To: Dean Kristen Olivero
From: Professor Daniel Black
Re: Student Work-Study Program

SALUTATION OF FORMAL OR BUSINESS LETTER

Dear Ms. Morgan:

For the use of colons in documenting sources, see 33c–33d.

Avoiding misuse of the colon

A complete INDEPENDENT CLAUSE must precede a colon, except with standard material (see 26c). When you have not written an independent clause, do not use a colon.

NO   The cook bought: eggs, milk, cheese, and bread.

YES   The cook bought eggs, milk, cheese, and bread.

The words *such as, including, like,* and *consists of* can be tricky: Do not let them lure you into using a colon incorrectly (see 26a).

NO   The health board discussed a number of problems, **such as:** poor water quality, an aging sewage treatment system, and the lack of an alternate water supply.

YES   The health board discussed a number of problems, **such as** poor water quality, an aging sewage treatment system, and the lack of an alternate water supply.

YES   The health board discussed a number of problems: poor water quality, an aging sewage treatment system, and the lack of an alternate water supply.

Do not use a colon to separate a PHRASE or DEPENDENT CLAUSE from an independent clause.

ALTERNATE EXAMPLES

1. To introduce quotations, summaries, lists:

a. Alice Roosevelt Longworth's colorful reputation is exemplified by this remark: "I have a simple philosophy. Fill what's empty. Empty what's full. And scratch where it itches."

b. Greek mythology comprises the description of the gods and the various stories told about them: it is a series of narratives depicting their personalities, functions, and relationships.

c. Zeus, the supreme god of the Greeks, served in a number of capacities: as weather god, sender of rain and lightning, and ruler over the other gods.

2. To separate material:

a. Eric Partridge is the author of *You Have a Point There: A Guide to Punctuation and Its Allies* as well as *Usage and Abusage: A Guide to Good English.*

b. I will cite the work in the bibliography as follows:
O'Connor, Flannery. "The Life You Save May Be Your Own." *The Realm of Fiction: Seventy-Four Stories.* Ed. James B. Hall and Elizabeth Hall. 3rd ed. New York: McGraw, 1977. 479–88.

c. To: Professor Dorothy Bankston
From: Professor Sylvia Iskander
Re: Selection of textbooks

TEACHING TIP

Of all the elements of writing, punctuation is probably the most rule-bound. It makes more demands on a writer to be acquainted with the conventions governing its use. Edgar Schuster takes up the issue of writing rules in "Let's Get Off the Mythmobile" (*English Journal* 74 [October 1985]: 40–43), in which he refutes five commonly accepted requirements of grammar by citing examples from the work of several established authors who deviated from them.

QUOTATION ABOUT WRITING

For what is Punctuation, and what its aim? It is the art of dividing a literary composition into sentences, and parts of sentences, by means of points, for the purpose of exhibiting the various combinations, connections, and dependencies of words. And what is this process but a means of facilitating that analysis and combination which must be made, consciously or unconsciously, before we can penetrate to the very core of an author's thoughts, and appropriate them as food for the life and growth of our own minds?
—John Wilson,
A Treatise on English Punctuation,
32nd ed., 1899

ANSWERS AND COVERAGE: EXERCISE 26–1

1. craze: chocolate cake [26a, appositive]

2. Correct

3. both: chocolate [26a, list]

4. Unfortunately, lots [26d, not an independent clause]

5. *Ethics: Concepts* [26c, separate standard material]

6. words: "To [26a, quotation]

7. fame: Lee [26a, list]

8. such as astronauts [26a, not an independent clause]

9. Calling, "Max [26a, not an independent clause]

10. Cadets: [26c, formal salutation]

11. broken: Henry [26b, between two independent clauses]

12. diseases: diphtheria [26a, list]

13. To: All; From: Management; Re: Vacation [26c, memo form]

14. pollution: "The [26a, quotation]

15. message: How [26b, between two independent clauses]

26d
cont.

NO	Day after day: the drought dragged on.
YES	Day after day, the drought dragged on.
NO	After the drought ended: the farmers celebrated.
YES	After the drought ended, the farmers celebrated.

EXERCISE 26-1

Consulting sections 26a–26d, insert colons where they are needed and delete unnecessary ones. If a sentence is correct, circle its number.

EXAMPLE   Most runners ignore how slim their chances are of winning the New York Marathon, about 1 in 26,000.

Most runners ignore how slim their chances are of winning the New York Marathon: about 1 in 26,000.

1. Chefs in the most fashionable restaurants in large cities report a new dessert craze; chocolate cake with a melting chocolate center.

2. The chefs describe two principal types of cake: (1) those with a solid chocolate layer that melts in the oven and (2) those that are underbaked so the center stays semiliquid.

3. Although ingredients for the two versions of the cake vary, three are common in recipes for both, chocolate, sugar, and butter.

4. Unfortunately: lots of calories are common to both.

5. A book used in many business courses today is *Business Ethics; Concepts and Cases.*

6. Its author describes the primary aim of the book in these words "To introduce the reader to the ethical concepts that are relevant to resolving moral issues in business."

7. Among artists married to artists, two couples illustrate some interesting dynamics of fame, Lee Krasner and Jackson Pollack, both respected today, although Pollack is far more famous; and Georgia O'Keeffe and photographer Alfred Stieglitz, with O'Keeffe more famous than Stieglitz, at least in the last years of the twentieth century.

8. Insurance companies classify adventurous people such as: astronauts, drivers of hydroplanes, and auto race drivers, as bad risks.

9. Calling: "Max, Max," Belinda ran through the forest.

10. Cadets;
This year's graduation ceremony begins at 1400 hours, but tell your parents 200 p.m., so that no one will be confused.

11. On April 8, 1974, Babe Ruth's home-run record was finally broken. Henry Aaron became the new home-run king.

12. In the past century, vaccines have been developed for five diseases, diphtheria, measles, polio, typhoid fever, and whooping cough.

13. To;   All Employees
From;   Management
Re;   Vacation Schedules

14. In *Silent Spring,* the environmentalist Rachel Carson wrote these words about pollution, "The chemical barrage has been hurled against the fabric of life."

15. The city's budget crisis carries a message, How long can government continue to spend beyond its means?

ALTERNATE EXERCISE

You may want to ask your students to rewrite the following sentences, omitting the colons. The students will probably have to divide each into several sentences.

1. The institution of marriage is generally divided by sociologists into four main types: monogamy, polygyny, polyandry, and group marriage.

2. An early reference to group marriage was made by Julius Caesar concerning the early Britons: "Ten and even twelve have wives common to them, and particularly brothers among brothers, and parents among their children."

3. Monogamy, the marriage of one man with one woman, is the most widely approved form in contemporary society: it is the basis of the modern family.

4. Polygyny is practiced by some religious sects: it is acceptable, for example, in some Arab countries.

5. Most American women do not generally favor such an arrangement: they have no desire to be one of several wives.

QUOTATION ABOUT WRITING

The colon is usually a mark of addition or expectation, with emphasis on a following explanation, list, table, or quotation. With formal words (*as follows* or the like) it raps for attention; with easy wording it is little more formal than the somewhat lighter semicolon. It is not a series or balancing point like the semicolon; it seems to say "Watch carefully what comes next."

—George Summey,
American Punctuation

27 *The Apostrophe*

The apostrophe plays three roles: It helps to form the possessive of nouns and some pronouns; it stands for one or more omitted letters; and it can be used to help form the plurals of letters and numerals. It does *not* help form plurals of nouns or the possessive case of personal pronouns.

REFERENCES TO SUPPLEMENTS

For this topic in the CLAST writing competency test, refer students to ch. 1, section B5b of *Preparing for the CLAST* by S. Patterson.

This topic is included in the TASP writing competency test. Refer students to *Preparing for the TASP* by M. Saenz.

For editing for correct spelling and hyphenation, refer students to *Rough Drafts* by K. S. Cain, Part V, Exercise 16.

See transparency 7–11 for problems with possessives in the *Prentice Hall/Simon & Schuster Transparencies for Writers* by D. Carter.

QUOTATION ABOUT WRITING

It's my experience that very few writers, young or old, are really seeking advice when they give out their work to be read. They want support; they want someone to say, "Good job."

—John Irving

QUOTATION ABOUT WRITING

I read about writers who have routines. They write at certain times of the day. I can't do that. I am always writing—but in my head.

—Jamaica Kincaid

27a

Using an apostrophe to form the possessive case of nouns and indefinite pronouns

The **possessive case** serves to communicate ownership or close relationship.

| OWNERSHIP | The writer's pen |
| CLOSE RELATIONSHIPS | The novel's plot |

Possession in NOUNS and certain INDEFINITE PRONOUNS can be communicated by PHRASES beginning with *of* (*comments of the instructor, comments of Professor Montana*) or by an apostrophe in combination with an *s* (*instructor's comments*).

27a-1

Adding 's to show possession when nouns and indefinite pronouns do not end in 's

The **dean's** duties included working closely with the resident assistants. [*dean* = singular noun not ending in *s*]

In one more year I will receive my **bachelor's** degree. [*bachelor* = singular noun not ending in *s*]

They care about their **children's** futures. [*children* = plural noun not ending in *s*]

An **indefinite pronoun** refers to nonspecific persons or things (for example, *any, few, someone, no one;* see 7b and 11p).

The accident was really **no one's** fault. [*no one* = indefinite pronoun not ending in *s*]

Adding *'s* to show possession when singular nouns end in *s*

Most academic writers today use *'s* to show possession when singular nouns end in *s*, although some writers prefer to use only the apostrophe. Be consistent in each piece of writing. This handbook uses *'s*.

That **business's** system for handling complaints is inefficient.
Chris's ordeal ended.
Lee **Jones's** insurance is expensive.

When adding *'s* could lead to tongue-twisting pronunciation, practice varies. All writers use the apostrophe. Some writers do not add the *s*; others do, for consistency with other practices.

Charles **Dickens's** story "A Christmas Carol" is a classic tale.

Using only an apostrophe to show possession when a plural noun ends in *s*

The **boys'** statements were recorded.
The newspapers have publicized several **medicines'** severe side effects recently.
Three **months'** maternity leave is in the **workers'** contract.

Adding *'s* to the last word in singular compound words and phrases

His **mother-in-law's** corporation just bought out a competitor.
The **tennis player's** strategy was brilliant.
They wanted to hear **somebody else's** interpretation of the rule.

Adding *'s* to only the last noun in joint or group possession

Olga and Joanne's books are valuable. [Olga and Joanne own the books together.]
Anne Smith and Glen Smith's article on solar heating interests me. [Anne Smith and Glen Smith wrote the article together.]

27a-2
27a-3
27a-4
27a-5

ALTERNATE EXERCISE

The questions that follow this brief paragraph are designed to point out how much information about the situation has been provided by the apostrophes. You may want to use the questions in a class discussion of apostrophe usage.

The jury's deliberations were over. Charles's lawsuit had at last come to an end. The defendants' lawyers seemed calm as they waited, but the prosecuting attorney's hands twitched with nervousness. Charles's and Robert's businesses would be either ruined or saved by the verdict of the court. Charles and his family's holdings would be seriously affected. The judge's face was impassive as he addressed the jury about its verdict. The jury foreman's voice trembled as he began to speak.

1. Does the writer think of the jury as a single body or as individuals?
2. Is there one defendant, or are there several?
3. Is there one prosecuting attorney, or are there several?
4. Do Charles and Robert own businesses together or separately?
5. Does Charles share in his family's holdings?
6. Why is there no apostrophe in *its verdict*?
7. Why do the words *jury's* (first sentence), *judge's* (next to last sentence), and *foreman's* (last sentence) end in *'s*?

ANSWERS: ALTERNATE EXERCISE

(1) a single body; (2) several; (3) one; (4) separately; (5) yes; (6) the personal pronoun is possessive without an apostrophe; (7) each word is a singular noun that does not end in -*s*

27a-6

Adding 's to each noun in individual possession

Olga's and Joanne's books are valuable. [Olga and Joanne each own some of the valuable books, but they do not own the books together.]

After the fire, **the doctor's and the lawyer's** offices had to be rebuilt. [The doctor and the lawyer had separate offices.]

! ♣ APOSTROPHE CAUTION: Do not use an apostrophe to indicate the plural form of a noun, unless you want to indicate possession or close relationship as explained in 27a-1 and 27a-3. ♣

27b

Not using an apostrophe with the possessive forms of personal pronouns

Some pronouns have specific possessive forms, which do not include an apostrophe. Contrast them with contractions, discussed in 27c.

PRONOUN	POSSESSIVE FORM(S)
he	his
she	her, hers
it	its
we	our, ours
you	your, yours
they	their, theirs
who	whose

Be especially alert to *it's* and *its,* as well as *who's* and *whose,* which are frequently confused. (*It's* stands for *it is; its* is a personal pronoun showing possession. *Who's* stands for *who is; whose* is a personal pronoun showing possession.)

NO   The government has to balance **it's** budget.

YES   The government has to balance **its** budget.

NO   The professor **who's** class was canceled is at a meeting of bird watchers.

YES   The professor **whose** class was canceled is at a meeting of bird watchers.

❦ **APOSTROPHE CAUTION:** The following forms are nonstandard, so do not use them: *its', his', hers', her's, yours', your's, theirs', their's, whos',* and *our's.* ❦

!

Using an apostrophe to stand for omitted letters, numbers, or words in contractions

27c

Contractions are words from which one or more letters have been intentionally omitted and in which apostrophes are inserted to signal the omission. Contractions are common in speaking and in informal writing, but many readers dislike them in academic writing. A major exception is *o'clock* (which stands for *of the clock*). To choose between a contraction and the full phrase, consider your audience and the level of formality you want. Here is a list of some common contractions.

SOME COMMON CONTRACTIONS

aren't = are not	*she's* = she is
can't = cannot	*there's* = there is
didn't = did not	*they're* = they are
don't = do not	*wasn't* = was not
he's = he is	*we're* = we are
it's = it is	*weren't* = were not
I'd = I would, I had	*we've* = we have
I'm = I am	*who's* = who is
isn't = is not	*won't* = will not
let's = let us	*you're* = you are

Contractions can help to show informal speech or dialect, especially in dramatic or fiction writing.

> Scout **yonder's** been **readin'** ever since she was born, and she **ain't** even started school yet. You look right puny for **goin'** on seven.
>
> —HARPER LEE, *To Kill a Mockingbird*

Apostrophes also indicate the omission of the first two numerals in years. Avoid this contraction in academic writing.

The class of **'50** is having a reunion this year.

They moved from Vermont to Florida after the blizzard of **'78**.

BACKGROUND

In a study of contractions in writing, Rose-Marie Weber concluded that they do not corrupt the writing system, but, instead, offer a means for making writing informal ("Variations in Spelling and the Special Case of Colloquial Contractions," *Visible Language* 20 [Autumn 1986]: 413–425).

ALTERNATE EXERCISE

You may want to see if students can locate all the unnecessary and misplaced apostrophes in the following paragraph.

(1) A good cook stay's busy doing many tasks that make cooking possible. (2) The oven's interior has to be cleaned, the pots' and pans' scrubbed, and the knives sharpened. (3) Once the kitchen is tidy, the grocery list's have to be made and menu's planned. (4) Then comes the shopping so that the pantry's shelves will be full. (5) When the chopping and stirring actually begin, most cook's pleasure begins. (6) The aromas' that come from the kitchen are a sign that someone is having a good time.

COVERAGE: ALTERNATE EXERCISE

(1) stay's (present-tense verb); (2) oven's is correct; pots', pans' (nonpossessive nouns ending in -s); (3) list's (nonpossessive plural noun); menu's (nonpossessive plural noun); (4) pantry's is correct; (5) cook's (possessive plural noun); (6) aromas' (nonpossessive plural noun)

27d ## Using 's to form plurals of letters, numerals, symbols, and words when used as terms

Some writers use 's to form plurals of letters, numerals, years, symbols, and words used as terms. Others use *s* alone. Either style is acceptable as long as one style is used throughout a piece of writing.

WITH 'S

Billie always has trouble printing **W's.**

The address includes six **6's.**

These trends should continue through the **1990's.**

The *for's* in the paper were all misspelled as *four's.*

When the keys jammed, a series of **⅋'s** showed on the screen.

WITH S ALONE

Billie always has trouble printing **Ws.**

The address includes six **6s.**

These trends should continue through the **1990s.**

The *fors* in the paper were all misspelled as *fours.*

When the keys jammed, a series of **⅋s** showed on the screen.

! ❖ UNDERLINING ALERT: Always underline (or use italic type for) letters, numbers, symbols, and words referred to as in the examples above. For plurals, do not underline (or use italics for) the 's or s.

```
Many first-graders had trouble writing 8's and pronouncing
eight's phonetically.

Many first-graders had trouble writing 8s and pronouncing
eights phonetically. ❖
```

27e ## Avoiding misuse of the apostrophe

Do not overuse apostrophes by inserting them where they do not belong. Chart 122 lists the major causes for apostrophe errors. If you tend to make apostrophe errors, use Chart 122 to diagnose the causes of your problem; then stay conscious of them as you edit (see 3d) your writing.

LEADING CAUSES OF APOSTROPHE ERRORS 122

1. Do not use an apostrophe with the present-tense verb form.

   NO   Cholesterol **plays'** an important role in how long we live.

   YES   Cholesterol **plays** an important role in how long we live.

2. Do not add an apostrophe at the end of a nonpossessive noun ending in *s*.

   NO   Medical **studies'** reveal that cholesterol is the primary cause of coronary heart disease.

   YES   Medical **studies** reveal that cholesterol is the primary cause of coronary heart disease.

3. Use an apostrophe after the *s* in the possessive plural of a noun.

   NO   The medical community is seeking more information from **doctor's** investigations into heart disease.

   YES   The medical community is seeking more information from **doctors'** investigations into heart disease.

4. Do not use an apostrophe to form a nonpossessive plural.

   NO   **Team's** of doctors are trying to predict who might be most harmed by cholesterol.

   YES   **Teams** of doctors are trying to predict who might be most harmed by cholesterol.

QUOTATION ABOUT WRITING

Punctuation marks are one means of helping us get our exact meaning on the page. They do more than mark such obvious facts of language as "This is a sentence." "This is a question." They help us separate words (and thoughts) and so present them distinctly to a reader; they help group and keep together related ideas; they set off certain words for emphasis. Their use affects the tempo of writing.

—Porter Perrin,
Writer's Guide and Index to English,
1942

EXERCISE 27-1

Consulting sections 27a and 27e, rewrite these sentences to insert -'s or an apostrophe alone to make the words in parentheses show possession. Delete the parentheses.

EXAMPLE   Born in 1732, Franz-Josef Haydn, one of (Austria) most notable musicians, sang in (St. Stephan) Choir until, at age 16, his voice changed.

Born in 1732, Franz-Josef Haydn, one of Austria's most notable musicians, sang in St. Stephan's choir until, at age 16, his voice changed.

ANSWERS: EXERCISE 27–1

1. Haydn's; music lovers'
2. composer's; children's
3. Haydn's; today's; orchestra's
4. musicians'
5. musicians'; women's; men's; concertgoers'; Brahms's; Beethoven's; Ives's; Strauss's
6. players'
7. singer-composer's
8. Esterhazy's; life's
9. patron's; London's
10. music-maker's; homeland's

ANSWERS: EXERCISE 27–2

1. Athletic competition is encouraged in accordance with the participants' age and ability.
2. These athletes' training takes place in schools and other institutions.
3. Participants' handicaps do not prevent them from competing in sports from basketball to gymnastics and ice skating to wheelchair exercise.
4. The program's sponsor is the Joseph P. Kennedy, Jr., Foundation, which first sponsored the event in 1968.
5. The foundation's true beneficiary is American society, for a democracy's aim is equal opportunity and participation for all its members.

ANSWERS: EXERCISE 27–3

(1) One of Albert Einstein's biographers tells about the famous physicist's encounter with a little girl in his neighborhood. (2) The little girl stared at Einstein's soaking wet feet and said, "Mr. Einstein, you've come out without your boots again!" (3) Einstein laughed and, pulling up his trousers, replied, "Yes, and I've forgotten my socks, too." (4) Most people aren't as forgetful as Einstein, but ➡

27e
cont.

1. (Haydn) music has delighted (music lovers) ears for more than two centuries.
2. The (composer) symphonies are still performed frequently, with the "Surprise Symphony" a favorite at (children) concerts.
3. Apart from recognizing (Haydn) music, however, (today) concertgoers would find little else familiar at an eighteenth-century (orchestra) performance.
4. Eighteenth-century (musicians) powdered wigs, satin breeches, and white stockings, colorful and elegant, were meant to be noticed.
5. Contemporary orchestral (musicians) black garb, usually (women) dresses and (men) tuxedos, is meant to keep (concertgoers) attention focused on (Brahms), (Beethoven), (Ives), or (Strauss) music, not on the people playing it.
6. Also, eighteenth-century (players) musical instruments differed from modern ones, in both appearance and sound.
7. In fact, 163 of the Austrian (singer-composer) compositions were written for the *baryton*, a now-obsolete instrument similar to a viola or cello.
8. In 1760, Prince Paul (Esterhazy) offer to hire Haydn as court musician freed him to pursue his (life) main purpose: composing.
9. After his (patron) death, Haydn left Austria to visit (London) musical world.
10. Although he died in 1809, this brilliant (music-maker) special legacy to Austria lives on because Haydn wrote his (homeland) national anthem.

EXERCISE 27-2

Consulting sections 27a, 27b, and 27e, rewrite these sentences so that each contains a possessive noun.

EXAMPLE   The Special Olympics is an international program promoting the physical fitness of mentally challenged children and adults.

The Special Olympics is an international program promoting mentally challenged children's and adults' physical fitness.

1. Athletic competition is encouraged in accordance with the age and ability of the participants.
2. The training of these mentally challenged athletes takes place in schools and other institutions.
3. Handicaps of the participants do not prevent them from competing in sports from basketball to gymnastics and ice skating to wheelchair exercise.
4. The sponsor of the program is the Joseph P. Kennedy, Jr., Foundation, which first sponsored the event in 1968.
5. The true beneficiary of the foundation is American society, for the aim of a democracy is equal opportunity and participation for all its members.

EXERCISE 27-3

Consulting all sections in this chapter, correct any errors in the use of apostrophes in the paragraph below.

(1) One of Albert Einsteins biographers tells about the famous physicists encounter with a little girl in his' neighborhood. (2) The little girl stared at Einstein's soaking wet feet and said, "Mr. Einstein, youve come out without you'r boots again!" (3) Einstein laughed and, pulling up his trousers, replied, "Yes, and Ive forgotten my socks, too." (4) Most people arent as forgetful as Einstein, but sometimes our memories' let all of us down. (5) We may not be able to remember if our first job started in '81 or 82; we may forget whether our employers' husband spells his name with two *t*s or with one. (6) No one is absolutely sure how memory works. (7) Dr. Barbara Jones study of memory suggests that personality style's affect memory. (8) People with rigid personalities who's livelihoods depend on facts tend to have good memories. (9) Mr. Harry Lorayne and Dr. Laird Cermak's studies of memory each provide a different approach to improving that useful faculty. (10) Mr. Lorayne suggest's relating what you want to remember to something verbal or visual. (11) For instance, if you want to remember that your sister's-in-law's name is Rose, you would picture her wearing a rose corsage. (12) Dr. Cermaks suggestions include consideration of physiological factors. (13) He notes that doctors' are currently developing drugs that will prevent older people from losing the memories that are rightfully their's.

EXERCISE 27-4

Consulting all sections of this chapter, correct any errors in the use of apostrophes in the paragraph below.

(1) Every summer Twinsburg, Ohio, comes to life when over one thousand pair's of twins gather for the towns annual festival. (2) The conversation at the gathering usually involves twin's stories about tricking people by exchanging identities, about knowing each others thoughts, and about sharing secret's. (3) The stories' are entertaining, but many psychologists' find them informative as well. (4) Many studies' have involved identical twins' who were separated at birth. (5) Identical twins come from a single fertilized egg that split's soon after conception, resulting in two fetuses' with identical genes. (6) Although identical twins may look like carbon copies of each other, theyre like snowflakes: No pair is exactly alike.

ANSWERS: EXERCISE 27–3, cont.

sometimes our memories let all of us down. (5) We may not be able to remember if our first job started in '81 or '82; we may forget whether our employer's husband spells his name with two *t*'s or with one. (6) No one is absolutely sure how memory works. (7) Dr. Barbara Jones's study of memory suggests that personality styles affect memory. (8) People with rigid personalities whose livelihoods depend on facts tend to have good memories. (9) Mr. Harry Lorayne's and Dr. Laird Cermak's studies of memory each provide a different approach to improving that useful faculty. (10) Mr. Lorayne suggests relating what you want to remember to something verbal or visual. (11) For instance, if you want to remember that your sister-in-law's name is Rose, you would picture her wearing a rose corsage. (12) Dr. Cermak's suggestions include consideration of physiological factors. (13) He notes that doctors are currently developing drugs that will prevent older people from losing the memories that are rightfully theirs.

ANSWERS: EXERCISE 27–4

(1) Every summer Twinsburg, Ohio, comes to life when over one thousand pairs of twins gather for the town's annual festival. (2) The conversation at the gathering usually involves twins' stories about tricking people by exchanging identities, about knowing each other's thoughts, and about sharing secrets. (3) The stories are entertaining, but many psychologists find them informative as well. (4) Many studies have involved identical twins who were separated at birth. (5) Identical twins come from a single fertilized egg that splits soon after conception, resulting in two fetuses with identical genes. (6) Although identical twins may look like carbon copies of each other, they're like snowflakes: no pair is exactly alike.

28 *Quotation Marks*

Most commonly, quotation marks enclose **direct quotations**—spoken or written words from an outside source (see 28a). Quotation marks also set off some titles (see 28b), and they can call attention to words used in special senses (see 28c).

Always use quotation marks in pairs, and be especially careful not to omit the second (closing) quotation mark. **Double quotation marks** (" ") are standard. **Single quotation marks** (' ') are used only for quotation marks within quotation marks. In print, opening and closing quotation marks look slightly different from each other, but they look identical on a typewriter or computer printer. Examples of both print and typewritten quotation marks are in this chapter. For information about using brackets in quotations, see 29c; for the ellipsis, see 29d; for the slash, see 29e. For information about commas with quoted words, see 24g; for capitalizing letters with quotations, see 30c.

REFERENCES TO SUPPLEMENTS

For this topic in the CLAST writing competency test, refer students to ch. 1, section B5b of *Preparing for the CLAST* by S. Patterson.

This topic is included in the TASP writing competency test. Refer students to *Preparing for the TASP* by M. Saenz.

For editing for correct use of quotation marks, refer students to *Rough Drafts* by K. S. Cain, Part V, Exercise 18.

BACKGROUND

Quotation marks did not come into use until the seventeenth century. Before that time quotations and direct speech were simply tagged with comments such as *he said* to set them off. Early use of marks to indicate quoted matter included arrowheads in the margin of the manuscript and double commas placed before a sentence of quoted matter; later the double commas were used to enclose quotations. The scholarly printer Theodore Low De Vinne lamented the decision of English printers to refuse the French form of marking quotations (a reversible mark that occupies the middle of the type face), since he found it more esthetically pleasing than the one they adopted, that of a pair of reversed commas for the beginning of a quotation and a pair of apostrophes for its closing.

28a Using quotation marks to enclose direct quotations of not more than four lines

Direct quotations are exact words from a print or nonprint source. When you use a quotation, always check carefully that you have recorded it precisely as it appeared in the original (see also 31c-1).

28a-1 Using double quotation marks to enclose short quotations

A quotation is considered "short" if it can be typed or handwritten to occupy no more than four lines on a page. Short quotations are enclosed in double quotation marks. Longer quotations are usually set off ("displayed") by indentation and line spacing, and they are not enclosed in quotation marks. The requirements for setting quotations off vary with different documentation styles. For advice about setting off quotations in specific documentation styles, see Chart 142 (MLA), Chart 143 (APA), Chart 144 (CM), and Chart 145 (CBE) in Chapter 33.

Whether a quotation is one word or many lines, it must be documented; see Chapter 33. The examples in this chapter are in MLA-parenthetical documentation.

SHORT QUOTATIONS

Hall explains the practicality of close conversational distances: "If you are interested in something, your pupils dilate; if I say something you don't like, they tend to contract" (47).

Personal space "moves with us, expanding and contracting according to the situation in which we find ourselves" (Fisher, Bell, and Baum 149).

Any quotation marks that appear in the original source should also be used in a long (displayed) quotation.

LONG QUOTATION (MORE THAN FOUR LINES)

Robert Sommer, an environmental psychologist, uses literary and personal analogies to describe personal space:

> Like the porcupines in Schopenhauer's fable, people like to be close enough to obtain warmth and comradeship but far enough away to avoid pricking one another. Personal space . . . has been likened to a snail shell, a soap bubble, an aura, and "breathing room." (26)

✤ PUNCTUATION ALERT: In MLA documentation style, the period goes after the parenthetical reference for a short quotation (not displayed); the period goes before the parenthetical reference for a displayed quotation. ✤

Using single quotation marks for quotations within quotations

28a-2

When you quote four lines or less and the original words already contain quotation marks, use double quotation marks at the start and end of the directly quoted words. Then, substitute single quotation marks (' ') wherever there are double quotation marks in the original source.

QUOTATION ABOUT WRITING

Like italics and hyphens, quotation marks are to be used as sparingly as possible. They should light the way, not darken it.

—Eric Partridge,
You Have a Point There

TEACHING TIP

You might point out to your students that typewriter face is used in 28a-1 so that writers can see how such material should look on their typed papers. All material is double spaced. A short quotation is "run in" with the writer's prose; a long quotation is displayed. For additional examples in typewriter face, you might direct your students' attention to the student research paper in Chapter 34. In particular, you might point out that paragraphs are indented five spaces and displayed quotations are indented ten spaces for all lines.

TEACHING TIP

As the study summarized in the margins of Chapter 31 points out, many students think that they are not plagiarizing as long as they use quotation marks to indicate material taken from sources. These students do not realize that they must also document the source. Now that MLA recommends a system of parenthetical references, the direction to "use footnotes" no longer can help college instructors deal easily with documentation. You might find it useful, therefore, to take some time to explain the word *documentation*, which, in contrast to *footnotes*, is not widely known to students inexperienced in writing research papers. You might also explain that the placement of the parenthetical reference depends on the length of the quotation. If the quotation is "run in," the parenthetical reference comes before the period; if the quotation is displayed, the parenthetical reference comes after the period.

28a-2
cont.

28a-3

ORIGINAL SOURCE
Personal space . . . has been likened to a snail shell, a soap bubble, an aura, and "breathing room."
—ROBERT SOMMER, *Personal Space: The Behavioral Bases of Design,* page 26

SINGLE QUOTATION MARKS WITHIN DOUBLE QUOTATION MARKS
Robert Sommer, an environmental psychologist, compares personal space to "a snail shell, a soap bubble, an aura, and 'breathing room' " (26).

Using quotation marks correctly for short quotations of poetry and for direct discourse

A quotation of poetry is "short" if it is no more than three lines of the poem. As with short prose quotations, use double quotation marks to enclose the material. If you quote more than one line of poetry, use a slash with one space on each side to show the line divisions (see 29e).

> As Auden wittily defined personal space, "some thirty inches from my nose / The frontier of my person goes. . . . "

! ✤ CAPITALIZATION ALERT: When you quote lines of poetry, follow the capitalization of your source. ✤

Quotation marks are also used to enclose speakers' words in DIRECT DISCOURSE. Whether you are reporting the exact words of a real speaker or making up dialogue in, for example, a short story, quotation marks let your readers know which words belong to the speaker and which words do not. Use double quotation marks at the beginning and end of a speaker's words, and start a new paragraph each time the speaker changes.

> "I don't know how you can see to drive," she said.
>
> "Maybe you should put on your glasses."
>
> "Putting on my glasses would help you to see?"
>
> "Not me; you," Macon said. "You're focused on the windshield instead of the road."
>
> —ANNE TYLER, *The Accidental Tourist*

If one speaker's words require two or more paragraphs, use double quotation marks at the start of each paragraph *but* double quotation marks at the end of the last quoted paragraph *only*.

Indirect discourse reports what a speaker said. In contrast, direct discourse presents a speaker's exact words. Note that the difference between direct and indirect discourse is not only a matter of punctuation; usually the verb tenses differ. Do not enclose indirect discourse in quotation marks.

DIRECT DISCOURSE

The mayor said, "I intend to veto that bill."

INDIRECT DISCOURSE

The mayor said that he intended to veto that bill.

For advice on revising incorrect shifts between direct and indirect discourse, see 15a-4.

EXERCISE 28-1

Consulting section 28a, correct the use of double and single quotation marks. If a sentence is correct, circle its number.

EXAMPLE   According to J. F. Perkins, "O. Henry "solves" most of his short story plots with surprise endings.

According to J. F. Perkins, "O. Henry 'solves' most of his short story plots with surprise endings."

1. Canfield and Lebson write, No one understands the sleeping habits of these sharks.
2. In the last two lines of the poem, Dickinson creates a powerful contrast: Parting is all we know of heaven, / And all we need of hell.
3. "One can put up with "Service with a Smile" if the smile is genuine and not mere compulsory toothbaring," wrote Cornelia Otis Skinner. She did not, on the other hand, advocate "Service with a Snarl."
4. "Promises," said Hannah Arendt, are the uniquely human way of ordering the future.
5. According to Henry James, "Nothing . . . will ever take the place of the good old fashion of "liking" a work of art or not liking it."
6. Pauline Kael, the movie critic, notes that "certain artists can, at moments in their lives, reach out and unify the audience" and in so doing give people the opportunity for "a shared response.
7. Don't let anyone convince you that you can't fulfill your ambitions, warned the speaker, or you surely won't.
8. Why have women passion, intellect, moral activity—these three—and a place in society where no one of the three can be exercised? asked Florence Nightingale in the 1850s.

ANSWERS: EXERCISE 28–1

1. Canfield and Lebson write, "No one understands the sleeping habits of these sharks."

2. In the last two lines of the poem, Dickinson creates a powerful contrast: "Parting is all we know of heaven. And all we need of hell."

3. "One can put up with 'Service with a Smile' if the smile is genuine and not mere compulsory toothbaring." wrote Cornelia Otis Skinner. She did not, on the other hand, advocate "Service with a Snarl."

4. "Promises," said Hannah Arendt, "are the uniquely human way of ordering the future."

5. According to Henry James, "Nothing . . . will ever take the place of the good old fashion of 'liking' a work of art or not liking it."

6. Pauline Kael, the movie critic, notes that "certain artists can, at moments in their lives, reach out and unify the audience" and in so doing give people the opportunity for "a shared response."

7. "Don't let anyone convince you that you can't fulfill your ambitions," warned the speaker, "or you surely won't."

8. "Why have women passion, intellect, moral activity—these three—and a place in society where no one of the three can be exercised?" asked Florence Nightingale in the 1850s.

➜

ANSWERS: EXERCISE 28–1, cont'd.

9. "In seven cases," the report continued, "outlets with the lowest prices had the highest percentages of defective merchandise."

10. Leslie Hanscom reports about the latest volume of the *Oxford English Dictionary*. "Most of the new words are originating in the USA."

COVERAGE: EXERCISE 28–1
(1) direct discourse; (2) short poetry quotation; (3) quotation within a quotation; short quotation; (4) direct discourse following an interruption; (5) quoted word within a quotation; (6) closing quotation marks needed; (7) interrupted direct discourse; (8) direct discourse; (9) interrupted short quotation; closing quotation marks needed; (10) short quotation

---

**ANSWERS AND COVERAGE;
EXERCISE 28–2**

1. "What's the problem?" Charlie Chaplin asked him. [indirect discourse]

2. MacArthur asked Chaplin how he could show a fat man slipping on a banana peel and still get a laugh. [direct discourse]

3. "Should I show the banana peel first, then the man approaching and slipping on it? Or should I show the fat man first, next the banana peel, and then the man slipping on it?" he wondered. [indirect discourse]

4. "Neither one," Chaplin said. [indirect discourse]

5. Chaplin told him to show the fat man approaching, then the banana peel. Next he should show the fat man and the banana peel together. Then he should have the fat man step over the banana peel and disappear down a manhole. [direct discourse]

9. "In seven cases, the report continued, outlets with the lowest prices had the highest percentages of defective merchandise.

10. Leslie Hanscom reports about the latest volume of the *Oxford English Dictionary*, Most of the new words are originating in the United States.

EXERCISE 28-2

Consulting section 28a, decide whether each sentence is direct or indirect discourse. Then rewrite each sentence in the other form. Be sure to make any changes needed for grammatical accuracy.

EXAMPLE   Clifton Fadiman once wrote that the playwright Charles MacArthur was having a hard time writing a visual joke for the movies. (indirect discourse)

"The playwright Charles MacArthur was having a hard time writing a visual joke for the movies," Clifton Fadiman once wrote.

1. Charlie Chaplin asked him what the problem was.

2. "How can I show a fat man slipping on a banana peel and still get a laugh?" MacArthur asked.

3. MacArthur wondered if he should show the banana peel first, and then the man approaching and slipping on it. Or should he show the fat man first, the banana peel next, and then the man slipping on it?

4. Chaplin advised against either one.

5. Chaplin told him, "Show the fat man approaching, then the banana peel. Next, show the fat man and the banana peel together. Then have the fat man step over the banana peel and disappear down a manhole."

28b ## Using quotation marks to enclose certain titles

When you refer to certain types of works by their titles, enclose the titles in quotation marks. Use quotation marks around the titles of short published works, like poems, short stories, essays, articles from periodicals, pamphlets, and brochures. Also use them around song titles and individual episodes of television or radio series.

Discuss the rhyme scheme of Andrew Marvell's "Delight in Disorder." [poem]

Have you read "Young Goodman Brown"? [short story]

One of the best sources I have found is "The Myth of Political Consultants." [magazine article]

"Shooting an Elephant" describes George Orwell's experience in Burma. [essay]

Underlining is used for titles of many other types of works, such as books and plays. A few titles are neither underlined nor enclosed in quotation marks. (For useful lists showing how to present titles, see Chart 123 in 30e and Chart 124 in 30f).

♣ UNDERLINING ALERT: Underlining in typed or handwritten papers signals words that would appear in **italic type** if the paper were to be typeset. (Printed books, magazines, newspapers, and similar documents are "typeset.") If you use a computer and can produce italic type, you may choose either underlining or italics. Be consistent in each piece of writing. ♣

Do not put the title of your own paper in quotation marks when you place it on a title page or at the top of a page (see 28d).

EXERCISE 28-3

Consulting section 28b, correct any quotation mark errors. If a sentence is correct, circle its number.

1. Almost everyone who has had to make a difficult choice in life can relate to Robert Frost's poem The Road Not Taken.
2. On a *Twilight Zone* episode called Healer, the main character steals a magic artifact.
3. In her essay titled "In Search of Our Mothers' Gardens, Alice Walker says that she found her own garden because she was guided by a "heritage of a love of beauty and a respect for strength."
4. Unable to get enough peace and quiet to write songs, such as his famous Over There and You're a Grand Old Flag, George M. Cohan would sometimes hire a Pullman car drawing room on a train going far enough away to allow him to finish his work.
5. A snake gives Sherlock Holmes the clue he needs to solve a puzzling murder in the mystery story The Speckled Band.

Using quotation marks for words used in special senses or for special purposes

28c

Writers sometimes enclose in quotation marks words or phrases meant ironically or in some other nonliteral way.

The proposed tax "reform" is actually a tax increase.
The "wonderful companion for children" snarled menacingly.

Writers sometimes put technical terms in quotation marks and define them the first time they are used. No quotation marks are used once such terms have been introduced and defined.

!

ANSWERS AND COVERAGE: EXERCISE 28–3

1. Almost everyone who has had to make a difficult choice in life can relate to Robert Frost's poem "The Road Not Taken" [title of poem].

2. On a *Twilight Zone* episode called "Healer," the main character steals a magic artifact [television episode].

3. In her essay titled "In Search of Our Mothers' Gardens," Alice Walker says that she found her own garden because she was guided by a "heritage of a love of beauty and a respect for strength" [essay title; closing quotation marks needed].

4. Unable to get enough peace and quiet to write songs, such as his famous "Over There" and "You're a Grand Old Flag," George M. Cohan would sometimes hire a Pullman car drawing room on a train going far enough away to allow him to finish his work [song titles].

5. A snake gives Sherlock Holmes the clue he needs to solve a puzzling murder in the mystery story "The Speckled Band" [short story title].

TEACHING TIP

Lewis Thomas objects to the misuse and overuse of quotation marks in ordinary prose. He cites advertising as a prime culprit in the practice. You might want to ask students to bring to class examples of questionable uses of quotation marks that they find in stores, newspapers, billboards, and other advertising spaces. What point was the advertiser trying to make by using quotation marks? Was the advertiser successful?

BACKGROUND
Classical Greek and Latin manuscripts usually had no word separation, but in inscriptions and nonliterary works, dots or apostrophes were often used to set off individual words. The custom of separating words by spacing was used off and on, beginning in the seventh century, becoming systematic only in the eleventh.

QUOTATION ABOUT QUOTATIONS
It is a good thing for an uneducated man to read books of quotations.
—Winston Churchill

BACKGROUND
In an article published in 1988 ("My Words of an Other," *College English* 50 [January 1988]: 63–73), George Dillon considered the use of quotation marks in terms of Bakhtin's theories. Quotation marks, according to Dillon's application of Bakhtin, point out the intersections of a writer's language and another's language.

ALTERNATE EXAMPLES
  1. Virginia Woolf was a member of the "Bloomsbury group," the name taken from the district of London in which she and her sister lived after the death of their father.
  2. She was the author of many short stories, essays, and sketches, such as "The Mark on the Wall."
  3. She was an early user of "stream of consciousness": an attempt to capture the truth of human experience by depicting aspects of an individual's personality.
  4. Have you read her long essay called "A Room of One's Own"?

28c
cont.

"Plagiarism"—the unacknowledged use of another person's words or ideas—can result in expulsion. Plagiarism is a serious offense.

The translation of a word or phrase can be enclosed in quotation marks. (Also underline any words or phrases that require translation.)

My grandfather usually ended arguments with *de gustibus non disputandum est* ("there is no disputing about tastes").

Words being referred to as words can be either enclosed in quotation marks or underlined. Follow consistent practice throughout a paper.

NO	Many people confuse "affect" and *effect*.
YES	Many people confuse "affect" and "effect."
YES	Many people confuse *affect* and *effect*.

28d

Avoiding the misuse of quotation marks

Writers sometimes enclose in quotation marks words they are uncomfortable about using, such as slang in formal writing or a cliché. Do not use quotation marks around language you sense is inappropriate to your audience or your purpose. Take the time to find accurate, appropriate, and fresh words instead.

NO	They "eat like birds" in public, but they "stuff their faces" in private.
YES	They eat very little in public, but they consume enormous amounts of food in private.

Do not enclose a word in quotation marks merely to call attention to it.

NO	"Plagiarism" can result in expulsion.
YES	Plagiarism can result in expulsion.

When you refer to published or performed works by title, you often need quotation marks (see 28b) or underlining (see 30f) to set the title off. When you put your paper's title at the top of a page or on a title page, however, do not enclose it in quotation marks or underline it.

NO	"The Elderly in Nursing Homes: A Case Study"
YES	The Elderly in Nursing Homes: A Case Study

The only exception is if the title of *your* paper refers to another title or a word that requires setting off in quotation marks.

NO   Character Development in Shirley Jackson's Story The Lottery

YES   Character Development in Shirley Jackson's Story "The Lottery"

Do not put a nickname in quotation marks unless you are giving a nickname with a full name. When a person's nickname is widely known and used, you do not have to give both the nickname and the full name. For example, use *Senator Ted Kennedy* or *Senator Edward Kennedy*, whichever is appropriate to your audience and purpose. You do not have to write Senator Edward "Ted" Kennedy.

EXERCISE 28-4

Consulting section 28d, correct any incorrect use of quotation marks. If a sentence is correct, circle its number.

EXAMPLE   Many people confuse the spellings of "there," *their,* and *they're.*

Many people confuse the spellings of "there," "their," and "they're."

1. "Accept" and *except* sound enough alike to confuse many listeners.
2. "Mickey" Mantle, "Yogi" Berra, and "Whitey" Ford helped make the Yankees champions in the 1950s.
3. Although the district attorney thought it would be an "open and shut case," she found out that "life is full of surprises."
4. An "antigen" is any substance from outside the body that activates the body's immune system. Today scientists are focusing intensive research on "antigens."
5. *Valross,* whale-horse, is the Norwegian word from which we get *walrus.*

Following accepted practices for other punctuation with quotation marks   28e

Placing commas and periods inside closing quotation marks   28e-1

Because the class enjoyed F. Scott Fitzgerald's "The Freshest Boy," they were looking forward to his longer works.
Ms. Rogers said, "Don't stand so close to me."
Edward T. Hall coined the word "proxemics."

For information about commas before quotations, see 24g.

QUOTATION ABOUT WRITING
How to read writers on writing: With respect, amusement, and skepticism. They will contradict one another—as they should—for each writer brings an individual history to the writing task. There is no single theology here.
—Donald M. Murray

ANSWERS: EXERCISE 28–4
  1. "Accept" and "except" sound enough alike to confuse many listeners. (or *Accept* and *except* sound enough alike to confuse many listeners.)
  2. Mickey Mantle, Yogi Berra, and Whitey Ford helped make the Yankees champions in the 1950s.
  3. Correct
  4. An "antigen" is any substance from outside the body that activates the body's immune system. Today scientists are focusing intensive research on antigens.
  5. *Valross,* "whale-horse," is the Norwegian word from which we get *walrus.*

COVERAGE: EXERCISE 28–4
(1) consistent treatment needed; (2) nicknames; (3) correct; (4) second use of a technical term; (5) translation of a term

ANSWERS: EXERCISE 28–5

1. One of the most famous passages in Shakespeare is Hamlet's soliloquy, which begins with the question "To be, or not to be?"

2. "Take this script," Rudyard Kipling said to the nurse who had cared for his first-born child, "and someday if you are in need of money you may be able to sell it at a handsome price."

3. Ernest Hemingway claimed this was the source of his famous phrase "a lost generation": in conversation with Papa Hemingway, a garage owner used the words to describe the young mechanics he employed.

4. After lulling the reader with a description of a beautiful dream palace in his poem "Kubla Khan," Coleridge changes the mood abruptly: "And 'mid this tumult Kubla heard from far   / Ancestral voices prophesying war."

5. The words of Emma Lazarus, "Give me your tired, your poor, your huddled masses yearning to breathe free," open the inscription on the Statue of Liberty.

COVERAGE: EXERCISE 28–5

(1) quotation is a question; (2) commas always placed inside closing quotation marks; (3) colon always placed outside closing quotation marks; (4) title of poem; quotation from poem; (5) commas always placed inside closing quotation marks

QUOTATION ABOUT WRITING

If we had to say what writing is, we would have to define it essentially as an act of courage.

—Cynthia Ozick

28e-2

Placing colons and semicolons outside closing quotation marks

We have to know "how close is close": We do not want to offend.

Some experts claim that the job market now offers "opportunities that never existed before"; others disagree.

28e-3

Placing question marks, exclamation points, and dashes inside or outside closing quotation marks, according to the context

If a question mark, exclamation point, or dash belongs with the words enclosed in quotation marks, put that punctuation mark inside the closing quotation mark.

"Did I Hear You Call My Name?" was the winning song.

"I've won the lottery!" he shouted.

"Who's there? Why don't you ans—"

If a question mark, exclamation point, or dash belongs with words that are *not* included in quotation marks, put the punctuation outside the closing quotation mark.

Have you read Nikki Giovanni's poem "Knoxville, Tennessee"?

If only I could write a story like Erskine Caldwell's "The Rumor"!

Weak excuses—a classic is "I have to visit my grandparents"—change little from year to year.

EXERCISE 28-5

Consulting section 28e, correct any errors in quotation marks and other punctuation with quotation marks. If a sentence is correct, circle its number.

1. One of the most famous passages in Shakespeare's plays is Hamlet's soliloquy, which begins with the question "To be, or not to be"?

2. "Take this script", Rudyard Kipling said to the nurse who had cared for his first-born child", and someday if you are in need of money you may be able to sell it at a handsome price."

3. Ernest Hemingway claimed this was the source of his famous phrase "a lost generation:" In conversation with "Papa" Hemingway, a garage owner used the words to describe the young mechanics he employed.

4. After lulling the reader with a description of a beautiful dream palace in his poem Kubla Khan, Coleridge changes the mood abruptly: And 'mid this tumult Kubla heard from far / Ancestral voices prophesying war.

5. The words that Emma Lazarus wrote, "Give me your tired, your poor, your huddled masses yearning to breathe free", open the inscription on the Statue of Liberty.

29 *Other Marks of Punctuation*

This chapter explains the uses of the dash (see 29a), parentheses (see 29b), brackets (see 29c), ellipsis (see 29d), and slash (see 29e).

THE DASH

Using the dash

The dash, or a pair of dashes, lets you interrupt a sentence's structure to add information. Such interruptions can fall in the middle or at the end of a sentence. Use dashes sparingly—if you do use them—so that their impact is not diluted by overexposure.

In typed papers, make a dash by hitting the hyphen key twice (--). Do not put a space before, between, or after the hyphens. In print, the dash is an unbroken line that is approximately the length of two hyphens joined together (—). In handwritten papers, make a dash slightly longer than a hyphen, using one unbroken line.

Using a dash or dashes to emphasize an example, a definition, an appositive, or a contrast

EXAMPLE

The care-takers—those who are helpers, nurturers, teachers, mothers—are still systematically devalued.

—ELLEN GOODMAN, "Just Woman's Work?"

DEFINITION

Although the emphasis at the school was mainly language—speaking, reading, writing—the lessons always began with an exercise in politeness.

—ELIZABETH WONG, *Fifth Chinese Daughter*

REFERENCES TO SUPPLEMENTS

For this topic in the CLAST writing competency test, refer students to ch. 1, section B5b of *Preparing for the CLAST* by S. Patterson.

For editing for correct use of other punctuation marks, refer students to *Rough Drafts* by K. S. Cain, Part V, Exercise 18.

QUOTATION ABOUT WRITING

A *dash* derives from "to *dash*," to shatter, strike violently, to throw suddenly or violently, hence to throw carelessly in or on, hence to write carelessly or suddenly, to add or insert suddenly or carelessly to or in the page. "To *dash*" comes from Middle English *daschen*, itself probably from Scandinavian—compare Danish *daske*, to beat, to strike. Ultimately the word is—rather obviously—echoic.

—Eric Partridge,
You Have a Point There

REFERENCE TO SUPPLEMENTS

This topic is included in the TASP writing competency test. Refer students to *Preparing for the TASP* by M. Saenz.

29a-1
cont.

ALTERNATE EXAMPLES: DASH

Appositive
Elizabeth Barrett Browning—the wife of Robert Browning—was probably a more popular poet than her husband in the nineteenth century.

Example
Many students—elementary school, high school, and college students—find themselves taking required courses that they would not choose for themselves.

Definition
A meaningful relationship—one that is satisfying to those involved and promises to last—is sought by most single people.

Futuristic novels with a bleak vision of the prospects for the free individual characteristically portray a society in which history—knowledge of the past—has been systematically eliminated.
—Diane Ravitch,
"Decline and Fall of Teaching History"

Dinner at the Huntercombe's possessed only two dramatic features—the wine was a farce and the food a tragedy.
—Anthony Powell

ALTERNATE EXAMPLES: DASH

Contrast
It's not right or wrong—it's just fattening.

An Aside
If you choose to vote for that candidate—and I don't care whether you do or not—then you have put yourself in the conservative camp.

Broken-Off Speech
"It's not that I don't love you, Tom, it's just that—"

APPOSITIVE

Two of the strongest animals in the jungle are vegetarians—the elephant and the gorilla.

—DICK GREGORY, *The Shadow that Scares Me*

CONTRAST

Tampering with time brought most of the house tumbling down, and it was this that made Einstein's work so important—and controversial.

—BANESH HOFFMANN, "My Friend, Albert Einstein"

Always place the words that you set off in dashes next to or near the words they explain. Otherwise, the interruption will confuse your reader.

NO   The current argument **is—one that parents, faculty, students, and coaches all debate fiercely—whether** athletes should have to meet minimum academic standards to play their sports.

YES   The current **argument—one that parents, faculty, students, and coaches all debate fiercely—is whether** athletes should have to meet minimum academic standards to play their sports.

29a-2

Using a dash or dashes to emphasize an "aside"

"Asides" are writers' comments within the structure of a sentence or a paragraph. In writing meant to seem objective, asides help writers convey their personal views. Consider your PURPOSE and AUDIENCE when deciding whether to insert an aside.

Television showed us the war. It showed us the war in a way that was—if you chose to watch television, at least—unavoidable.

—NORA EPHRON, *Scribble Scrabble*

❖ PUNCTUATION ALERTS: (1) If the words within a pair of dashes would take a question mark or an exclamation point if they were a separate sentence, use that punctuation before the second dash: *A first date—do you remember?—stays in the memory forever.* (2) Do not use commas, semicolons, or periods next to dashes. When such a possibility comes up, revise the sentence to avoid it. (3) Do not enclose dashes in quotation marks except when the words require them: *Many of George*

Orwell's essays—"A Hanging," for example—draw on his experiences as a civil servant. "Shooting an Elephant"—another Orwell essay—appears in many anthologies. ❧

EXERCISE 29-1

Consulting section 29a, write a sentence about the italicized subject. In your sentence, use dashes to set off the contrast, appositive, aside, example, or definition called for.

EXAMPLE   (*health*, definition) Anorexia nervosa—an eating disorder characterized by an aversion to eating and an obsession with losing weight—is extremely common among young female gymnasts and ballet dancers.

1. (*television program*, contrast)
2. (*politician*, appositive)
3. (*food*, aside)
4. (*music*, example)
5. (*recreational sport*, definition)

PARENTHESES

Using parentheses   29b

Parentheses allow writers to interrupt a sentence's structure to add information of many kinds. Parentheses are like dashes in this function of setting off extra or interrupting words. Unlike dashes, which tend to make interruptions stand out, parentheses tend to deemphasize what they enclose.

Use parentheses sparingly, because their overuse can be very distracting for readers.

Using parentheses to enclose interrupting words   29b-1

EXPLANATION

After they've finished with the pantry, the medicine cabinet, and the attic, they will throw out the red geranium (too many leaves), sell the dog (too many fleas), and send the children off to boarding school (too many scuffmarks on the hardwood floors).

—SUZANNE BRITT, "Neat People vs. Sloppy People"

In *division* (also known as *partition*) a subject commonly thought of as a single unit is reduced to its separate parts.

—DAVID SKWIRE, *Writing with a Thesis*

QUOTATION ABOUT WRITING

This morning I deleted the hyphen from "hell-bound" and made it one word; this afternoon I redivided it and restored the hyphen.

—Edwin Arlington Robinson

QUOTATION ABOUT WRITING

The dash has been described as the interruption, the mark of abruptness, the sob, the stammer, and the mark of ignorance. The last name—which might be equally well applied to the comma as crude writers use it—records the fact that the uninformed mistake the dash for an all-purpose mark for every possible occasion.

—George Summey,
American Punctuation

QUOTATION ABOUT WRITING

Writers kid themselves—about themselves and other people. Take the talk about writing methods. Writing is just work—there's no secret. If you dictate or use a pen or type or type with your toes—it is just work.

—Sinclair Lewis

QUOTATION ABOUT WRITING

It [the dash] is a comfortable punctuation mark since even the most rigorous critic can seldom claim that any particular example of it is a misuse. Its overuse is its greatest danger, and the writer who can't resist dashes may be suspected of uncoordinated thinking.

—Cornelia and Bergen Evans

ALTERNATE EXAMPLES: PARENTHESES

Explanations
Most Americans try to be honest about filing their income tax returns (no matter how much it hurts to pay).

Examples
Many modern zoos (such as the Santa Barbara Zoo) try to present the animals so that young children can easily see them.

Asides
House plants are subject to bug infestations (at least mine are) which require special treatment if the attack is to be repelled.

ALTERNATE EXAMPLES: PARENTHESES

Numbers and letters
There are five basic ingredients in a good gumbo: (1) a roux, (2) chopped vegetables, (3) water, (4) seafood or chicken, and (5) seasonings.

Numerical repetition
A freshman is required to take twelve (12) hours of course work to be in regular status.

Expression of doubt
We have $900 (?) in the bank.

QUOTATION ABOUT WRITING

Though parentheses seem to say "here it is if you wish it; it's only an aside," such an aside may be intended for special notice—like many a remark that begins with the disarming *by the way* or *incidentally*.

—George Summey,
American Punctuation

29b-1
cont.

EXAMPLE
Though other cities (Dresden, for instance) had been utterly destroyed in World War II, never before had a single weapon been responsible for such destruction.

—Laurence Behrens and Leonard J. Rosen,
Writing and Reading Across the Curriculum

ASIDE
The older girls (non-graduates, of course) were assigned the task of making refreshments for the night's festivities.

—Maya Angelou, *I Know Why the Caged Bird Sings*

The sheer decibel level of the noise around us is not enough to make us cranky, irritable, or aggressive. (It can, however, affect our mental and physical health, which is another matter.)

—Carol Tavris, *Anger: The Misunderstood Emotion*

29b-2

Using parentheses for certain numbers and letters of listed items

When you number listed items within a sentence, enclose the numbers (or letters) in parentheses.

❖ PUNCTUATION ALERTS: (1) Use a colon before a list only if the list is preceded by an independent clause; see 26b. (2) You can use commas or semicolons to separate items in a list that falls within a sentence, as long as you are consistent within a piece of writing. When any item itself contains punctuation, use a semicolon to separate the items so that your material is easily read. ❖

Four items are on the agenda for tonight's meeting: (1) current membership figures, (2) current treasury figures, (3) the budget for renovations, and (4) the campaign for soliciting additional public contributions.

In legal and some business writing, you can use parentheses to enclose a numeral that repeats a spelled-out number.

The monthly rent is three hundred fifty dollars ($350).
Your order of fifteen (15) gross was shipped today.

29b-3

Using other punctuation with parentheses

Do not put a **comma** before an opening parenthesis even if what comes before the parenthetical material requires a comma.

NO   Although clearly different from my favorite film, (*The Wizard of Oz*) *Gone with the Wind* is an important film worth studying.

YES   Although clearly different from my favorite film (*The Wizard of Oz*), *Gone with the Wind* is an important film worth studying.

You can use a **question mark** or an **exclamation point** with parenthetical words that occur within the structure of a sentence.

Looking for clues (what did we expect to find?) wasted four days.

A complete sentence enclosed in parentheses sometimes stands alone and sometimes falls within the structure of another sentence. Those that stand alone start with a capital and end with a period. Those that fall within the structure of another sentence do not start with a capital and do not end with a period.

NO   Looking for his car keys (he had left them at my sister's house.) wasted an entire hour.

YES   Looking for his car keys wasted an entire hour. (He had left them at my sister's house.)

YES   Looking for his car keys (he had left them at my sister's house) wasted an entire hour.

Place quotation marks to enclose words that require them, but do not use quotation marks around parentheses that come before or after those words.

NO   Alberta Hunter **"(Down Hearted Blues)"** is better known for her jazz singing than for her poetry.

YES   Alberta Hunter (**"Down Hearted Blues"**) is better known for her jazz singing than for her poetry.

EXERCISE 29-2

Consulting section 29b, supply needed or useful parentheses.

EXAMPLE   The world's largest and only? camel hospital was set up by the Israeli government in 1978.

The world's largest (and only?) camel hospital was set up by the Israeli government in 1978.

1. Railroad entrepreneur George Francis Train his real name dreamed of creating a chain of great cities across the country connected by his Union Pacific Railroad.

EXAMPLES OF PARENTHESES WITH OTHER PUNCTUATION

When eating at a formal restaurant (such as Chez Marcelle), a man is expected to wear a coat and tie.

Although the rain kept falling (and the river rising!), we decided to wait for the rescue boat instead of striking out on our own.

Casablanca has become a favorite film of many people too young to have seen it when it was originally released (or to have seen Bogart and Bergman in their other films).

QUOTATION ABOUT WRITING

Writing is my vacation from living.
—Eugene O'Neill

BACKGROUND

Literally *parenthesis* indicates "an insertion beside" the basic meaning of the sentence because etymologically the Greek from which it comes (by way of Medieval Latin) is composed of *para*, beside, *en*, meaning in, and *thesis*, a placing, from *tithenai*, to place or put. Hence a parenthesis is a placing beside the principal meaning.

ANSWERS AND COVERAGE: EXERCISE 29–2

1. Railroad entrepreneur George Francis Train (his real name) dreamed of creating a chain of great cities across the country connected by his Union Pacific Railroad. [29b-1, interruptive aside]

ANSWERS AND COVERAGE:
EXERCISE 29–2, cont.

2. Nowadays you can order almost anything (clothing, toys, greeting cards, and even meat) through mail-order catalogs. [29b-1, interruptive examples]

3. W.C. Fields offered two pieces of advice on job hunting: (1) never show up for an interview in bare feet, and (2) do not read your prospective employer's mail while he is questioning you about your qualifications. [29b-2, numbers of listed items]

4. Patients who pretend to have ailments are known to doctors as "Münchausens" after Baron Karl Friedrich Hieronymous von Münchausen. (He was a German army officer who had a reputation for wild and unbelievable tales.) [29b-1, interruptive explanation]

5. The questions raised by China's struggles to integrate capitalism with communism during the 1980s and 1990s (Will the country disintegrate into civil war? Can the present economic boom be sustained? What will emerge from the chaos?) cannot yet be clearly answered, even by those who follow the country's progress closely. [29b-1, interruptive examples; 29b-3, punctuation with parentheses]

BACKGROUND

A Comprehensive Grammar of the English Language (White Plains, NY: Longman, 1985) is a long (1,779 pages) report from Randolph Quirk, Sidney Greenbaum, Geoffrey Leech, and Jan Svartik on current research on American and British English. Punctuation is covered in one of the three appendixes.

QUOTATION ABOUT WRITING

The author must keep his mouth shut when his work starts to speak.
—Friedrich Nietzsche

29b-3
cont.

2. Nowadays you can order almost anything clothing, toys, greeting cards, and even meat through mail-order catalogs.

3. W. C. Fields offered two pieces of advice on job hunting: 1 never show up for an interview in bare feet, and 2 do not read your prospective employer's mail while he is questioning you about your qualifications.

4. Patients who pretend to have ailments are known to doctors as "Munchausen" after Baron Karl Friedrich Hieronymous von Münchhausen, he was a German army officer who had a reputation for wild and unbelievable tales.

5. The questions raised by China's struggles to integrate capitalism with communism during the 1980s and 1990s Will the country disintegrate into civil war? Can the present economic boom be sustained? What will emerge from the chaos? cannot yet be clearly answered, even by those who follow the country's progress closely.

BRACKETS

29c   ## Using brackets

29c-1   ### Using brackets to enclose words you insert into quotations

When you work quoted words into your own sentences (see 31c), you may have to change the form of a word or two to make the quoted words fit into the structure of your sentence. Enclose any changes you make in square brackets. (The examples with brackets in this section use MLA STYLE of parenthetical references; see 33b-1.)

ORIGINAL SOURCE

Surprisingly, this trend is almost reversed in Italy, where males interact closer and display significantly more contact than do male/female dyads and female couples.
—ROBERT SHUTER, "A Field Study of Nonverbal Communication in Germany, Italy, and the United States," page 305

QUOTATION WITH BRACKETS

Although German and American men stand farthest apart and touch each other the least, Shuter reported "this trend [to be] almost reversed in Italy" (305).

Enclose your words in brackets if you need to add explanations and clarifications to quoted material.

ORIGINAL SOURCE

This sort of information seems trivial, but it does affect international understanding. Imagine, for example, a business conference between an American and an Arab.

—CHARLES G. MORRIS, *Psychology: An Introduction,* page 516

QUOTATION WITH BRACKETS

"This sort of information [about personal space] seems trivial, but it does affect international understanding" (Morris 516).

Now and then you may find that an author or a typesetter has made a mistake in something you want to quote—a wrong date, a misspelled word, an error of fact. You cannot change another writer's words, but you want your readers to know that you did not make the error. To show that you see the error, insert the Latin word *sic* in brackets, right after the error. Meaning "so" or "thus," *sic* in brackets says to a reader, "It is thus in the original."

The construction supervisor points out one unintended consequence of doubling the amount of floor space: "With that much extra room per person, the tennants [*sic*] would sublet."

Using brackets to enclose very brief parenthetical material inside parentheses

29c-2

From that point on, Thomas Parker simply disappears. (His death [c. 1441] is unrecorded officially, but a gravestone marker is mentioned in a 1640 parish report.)

The abbreviation "c." means "about" when placed next to numerals that refer to time (see Chart 125 in section 30j).

THE ELLIPSIS

Using the ellipsis

29d

An **ellipsis** is a set of three spaced dots (use the period key on a keyboard or a typewriter). Its most important function is to show that you have left out some of the original writer's words in material you are quoting.

ORIGINAL SOURCE

Personal space is not necessarily spherical in shape, nor does it extend equally in all directions. (People are able to tolerate

---

ALTERNATE EXAMPLES: BRACKETS

Insertion of words
   Describing the end of grief, Marjorie Waters wrote, "[it] was a homecoming, a returning to myself made sweeter by the long separation."

—Marjorie Waters, "Coming Home"

   To be reasonably comfortable for even short walks outdoors [in Moscow during the winter] it is necessary to wear coats of natural fur.

—Leona P. Schecter, "Moscow"

   We hold these truths to be self-evident, that all men are created equal, that they are endowed by their Creator with certain unalienable [sic] Rights, that among these are Life, Liberty and the pursuit of Happiness.

—The Declaration of Independence

Brief parenthetical material inside parentheses
   "The Declaration of Independence" (subtitled "The Unanimous Declaration of the Thirteen United States of America" [and published by Congress in 1776]) is an eloquent assertion of human rights.

QUOTATION ABOUT WRITING
Surely the unnecessary profusion of straight lines, particularly on a printed page, is offensive to good taste, is an index of the *dasher's* profound ignorance of the art of punctuation, and, so far from helping to bring out the sense of an author, is better adapted for turning into nonsense some of his finest passages.

—John Wilson, *A Treatise on English Punctuation,* 32nd ed., 1871

ALTERNATE EXAMPLES: ELLIPSIS

Give me liberty or . . . death!
—Patrick Henry

As a recommendation for raising children in the future, Elizabeth Janeway urges "the establishment of enriching and exciting child-care facilities at industrial plants, commercial centers, educational establishments . . ."
—"Raising Children in the Year 2000"

In a comment about Dashiell Hammett, Lillian Hellman says, "He had made up honor early in his life and stuck with his rules . . ." (*An Unfinished Woman* 126), and then she cites examples of that honor from his own acts.

BACKGROUND

Ellipsis is the descendant of one of the classical rhetorician's schemes of omission, the deliberate dropping of a word or words that are readily implied by the context. Edward P. J. Corbett points out that ellipsis can be "an artful and arresting means of securing economy of expression. We must see to it, however, that the understood words are grammatically compatible."
—Edward Corbett,
Classical Rhetoric for the Modern Student

QUOTATION ABOUT WRITING

Speech is highly elliptical. It would scarcely be endurable otherwise. Ellipsis is indispensable to the writer or speaker who wants to be brief and pithy, but it can easily cause confusion and obscurity and must be used with skill.
—Cornelia and Bergen Evans,
A Dictionary of Contemporary American Usage

closer presence of a stranger at their sides than directly in front.) It has been likened to a snail shell, a soap bubble, an aura, and "breathing room."

—ROBERT SOMMER, *Personal Space: The Behavioral Bases of Design*, page 26

Because ellipses signal readers that you have left out some of the source's words, you do not need an ellipsis to quote a single word. You can also quote a phrase without using an ellipsis as long as you do not omit any words between the first one and the last one that you quote.

> Describing how personal space varies, Sommer says that it "is not necessarily spherical" for it does not "extend equally in all directions" (26).

If you do omit any of the original source's words between the first and the last word you quote, use an ellipsis at each omission.

> Other descriptions of personal space include a "shell . . . and 'breathing room' " (Sommer" 26).

! ❖ PUNCTUATION ALERT: When you omit words from a source you are quoting, omit punctuation that accompanies the omitted words unless it correctly punctuates your sentence.

> Other descriptions of personal space include a "shell . . . and 'breathing room' " (Sommer 26). [comma omitted after *shell*]

> Other descriptions of personal space include a "shell, . . . a . . . bubble, . . . and 'breathing room' " (Sommer 26). [commas kept after *shell* and *bubble* to separate three items in a series] ❖

In two situations, use a fourth dot—a sentence-ending period—along with an ellipsis.

1. When an ellipsis falls at the end of your sentence, add a sentence-ending period after the ellipses.

> Sommer goes on to say that people have described personal space as "a snail shell, a soap bubble, an aura. . . ."

! ❖ DOCUMENTATION ALERT: In MLA documentation style, if a parenthetical reference is needed, put it after the ellipsis and closing quotation mark and before the sentence-ending period.

> Sommer goes on to say that people have described personal space as "a snail shell, a soap bubble, an aura . . . " (26).❖

2. When you omit a sentence or more from a source's words and the quoted words before and after the omission are independent clauses, add a fourth dot to the ellipsis.

> Using similes to define its dimensions, Sommer explains that "personal space is not necessarily spherical in shape. . . . It has been likened to a snail shell, a soap bubble, an aura, and 'breathing room' " (26).

These rules apply to omissions of words from both prose and poetry. If you omit a line or more from poetry, however, use a full line of spaced dots.

ORIGINAL SOURCE

> Sing a song of sixpence,
> A pocket full of rye.
> Four and twenty blackbirds
> Baked in a pie.
> When the pie was opened,
> The birds began to sing.
> Wasn't that a pleasant dish
> To set before the king?

POEM WITH OMITTED LINES

> Sing a song of sixpence,
> A pocket full of rye.
> Four and twenty blackbirds
> Baked in a pie.
>
> . . . .
>
> Wasn't that a pleasant dish
> To set before the king?

THE SLASH

Using the slash   29e

The **slash** (/) is a diagonal line also known as a *virgule* or *solidus*.

Using the slash to separate quoted lines of poetry   29e-1

If you quote more than three lines of a poem in writing, set the poetry off with space and indentations as you would a prose quotation of more than four lines (see 28a). For three lines or less, use a sentence

ANSWERS AND COVERAGE: EXERCISE 29–3

Answers may vary somewhat, especially in usage of dashes and parentheses.

1. In 1994, Neil Yerman—a scribe and artist who writes with a turkey feather quill—[29a-1, dash for appositive] copied one letter at a time (304,805 of them, to be exact) to create a Torah scroll for Congregation Emanu-El in Manhattan. [29b-1, parentheses for an aside]

2. If we change our thoughts, we can change our moods: (1) Get up and go. When you most feel like moping, do something, anything. Try cleaning up a drawer. (2) Reach out. Make contact with people you care about. (3) Start smiling. Studies show that people send the same signals to their nervous system when they smile as they do when they are genuinely happy. [29b-2, parentheses for numbers of listed items]

3. A series of resolutions was passed 11-0 (with one council member abstaining) calling on the mayor and the district attorney to improve safety conditions and set up law enforcement on city buses. [29b-1, parentheses for interruptive explanation]

4. Whatever it is you're doing—writing, painting or performing—art should not be hard to understand. Art is communication. [29a-1, dashes for interruptive example]

5. Thunder is caused when the flash of lightning heats the air around it to temperatures up to 30,000 F (16,666 C). [29b-2, numbers]

➡

29e-1 cont. format and enclose the poetry lines in quotation marks, with a slash to divide one line from the next. Leave a space on each side of the slash.

> Consider the beginning of Anne Sexton's poem "Words": "Be careful of words, /even the miraculous ones."

Capitalize and punctuate each line as it is in the original, with this exception: End your sentence with a period if the quoted line of poetry does not have other end punctuation. If your quotation ends before the end of the line, use an ellipsis (see 29d).

29e-2

Using the slash for numerical fractions in typed manuscripts

If you have to type numerical fractions, use the slash (with no space before or after the slash) to separate numerator and denominator and a hyphen to tie a whole number to its fraction: *1/16, 1-2/3, 2/5, 3-7/8* (For advice on using spelled-out and numerical forms of numbers, see section 30l.)

29e-3

Using the slash for *and/or*

Try not to use word combinations like *and/or* for writing in the humanities. In academic disciplines where use of such combinations is acceptable, separate the words with a slash. Leave no space before or after the slash. In the humanities, listing both alternatives in normal sentence structure is usually better than separating choices with a slash.

NO The best quality of reproduction comes from 35mm slides/direct-positive films.

YES The best quality of reproduction comes from 35mm slides or direct-positive films.

EXERCISE 29-3

Consulting all sections in this chapter, supply needed dashes, parentheses, brackets, ellipses, and slashes. If a sentence is correct as written, circle its number. In some sentences you can choose between dashes and parentheses; when you make your choice, be ready to explain it.

EXAMPLE   Clarence Darrow's legal writings forceful, humane, and written with remarkable clarity express his judicial philosophy.

Clarence Darrow's legal writings—forceful, humane, and written with remarkable clarity—express his judicial philosophy.

1. In 1994, Neil Yerman a scribe and artist who writes with a turkey feather quill copied one letter at a time 304,805 of them, to be exact to create a Torah scroll for Congregation Emanu-El in Manhattan.

2. If we change our thoughts, we can change our moods: 1 Get up and go. When you most feel like moping, do something anything. Try cleaning up a drawer. 2 Reach out. Make contact with people you care about. 3 Start smiling. Studies show that people send the same signals to their nervous system when they smile as they do when they are genuinely happy.

3. A series of resolutions was passed 11–0 with one council member abstaining calling on the mayor and the district attorney to improve safety conditions and step up law enforcement on the city buses.

4. Whatever it is you're doing writing, painting, or performing art should not be hard to understand. Art is communication.

5. Thunder is caused when the flash of lightning heats the air around it to temperatures up to 30,000 F 16,666 C.

6. I love Ogden Nash's limericks about animals, especially his lines about the many limbs of a certain sea creature: "I marvel at thee, Octopus; If I were thou, I'd call me Us."

7. After the internationally famous racehorse Dan Patch died suddenly from a weak heart, his devoted owner Will Savage died of the same condition a mere 32-1/2 hours later.

8. In his famous letter from the Birmingham jail on April 16, 1963, Martin Luther King, Jr., wrote: "You the eight clergymen who had urged him not to hold a protest deplore the demonstrations taking place in Birmingham."

9. The world's most expensive doll house sold for $256,000 at a 1978 London auction contains sixteen rooms, a working chamber organ, and a silver clothes press but no toilet.

10. Excavating, removing, or trafficking in artifacts from federal or Indian land can be a felony punishable by up to five years' imprisonment and two hundred and fifty thousand dollars $250,000 in fines under the Archaeological Resources Protection Act.

EXERCISE 29-4

Follow the directions for each item. Consulting sections 29a, 29b, 29d, and 29e, use dashes, parentheses, ellipses, and slashes as needed.

EXAMPLE   Write a sentence using dashes that exclaims about getting something right.

I tried and failed, I tried and failed again—and then I did it!

1. Write a sentence that quotes only three lines of the following sonnet by William Shakespeare:

ANSWERS AND COVERAGE: EXERCISE 29–3, cont.

6. I love Ogden Nash's limericks about animals, especially his lines about the many limbs of a certain sea creature: "I marvel at thee, Octopus; / If I were thou, I'd call me Us." [29e-1, slash between lines of quoted poetry]

7. Correct

8. In his famous letter from the Birmingham jail on April 16, 1963, Martin Luther King, Jr., wrote: "You (the eight clergymen who had urged him not to hold a protest) deplore the demonstrations taking place in Birmingham." [29c-1, brackets for words inserted into quotation]

9. The world's most expensive doll house (sold for $256,000 at a 1978 London auction) [29b-1, interruptive explanation] contains sixteen rooms, a working chamber organ, and a silver clothes press—but no toilet. [29a-1, contrast]

10. Pillaging (excavating, removing, or trafficking [buying or selling]) [29c-1, brackets within parentheses for explanation within an explanation] artifacts from federal or Indian land can be a felony punishable by up to five years' imprisonment and two hundred and fifty thousand dollars ($250,000) in fines under the Archaeological Resources Protection Act. [29b-2, repetition of a spelled-out number]

ANSWERS: EXERCISE 29–4

Answers will vary greatly. When checking them, note whether the directions were followed.

1. any three lines of the poem—with quotation marks and with slash marks between the first and second and between the second and third lines—in the sentence

➜

29e-3
cont.

ANSWERS: EXERCISE 29–4, *cont.*

2. parentheses to enclose a brief example in a sentence

3. dashes to set off the definition in the sentence

4. parentheses to enclose the numbers 1-4 that label the list within a sentence

5. ellipsis to indicate an omission from a quotation, with the meaning of the whole still clear

Let me not to the marriage of true minds
Admit impediments. Love is not love
Which alters when it alteration finds,
Or bends with the remover to remove.
O no, it is an ever-fixed mark
That looks on tempests and is never shaken;
It is the star to every wand'ring bark
Whose worth's unknown, although his height be taken.
Love's not Time's fool, though rosy lips and cheeks
Within his bending sickle's compass come.
Love alters not with his brief hours and weeks,
But bears it out even to the edge of doom.
If this be error and upon me proved,
I never writ, nor no man ever loved.

2. Write a sentence in which you use parentheses to enclose a brief example.

3. Write a sentence in which you use dashes to set off a definition.

4. Write a sentence that includes a list of four numbered items.

5. Quote a few sentences from a source. Choose one from which you can omit a few words without losing meaning. Correctly indicate the omission. At the end, give the source of the quotation.

30 *Capitals, Italics, Abbreviations, and Numbers*

CAPITALS

Capitalizing the first word of a sentence

30a

Always capitalize the first letter of the first word in a sentence: *Records show that four inches of snow fell last year.* Practice varies for using a capital letter to start each question in a series of questions. Whichever practice you choose, be consistent throughout a piece of writing. Of course, if the questions are complete sentences, start each with a capital letter.

> **YES** What facial feature would most people change if they could? Their eyes? Their ears? Their mouth?

> **YES** What facial feature would most people change if they could? their eyes? their ears? their mouth?

Practice varies for using a capital letter for a complete sentence following a colon (see 26b). Whichever practice you choose, be consistent throughout a piece of writing. This handbook uses a capital letter after the colon.

A complete sentence enclosed in parentheses sometimes stands alone and sometimes falls within the structure of another sentence. Those that stand alone start with a capital letter and end with a period. Those that fall within the structure of another sentence do not start with a capital letter and do not end with a period.

> I did not know till years later that they called it the Cuban Missile Crisis. But I remember Castro. (We called him Castor Oil and were awed by his beard.) We might not have worried so much (what would the Communists want with our small New Hampshire town?) except that we lived 10 miles from an air base.

> —JOYCE MAYNARD, "An 18-Year-Old Looks Back on Life"

REFERENCES TO SUPPLEMENTS
For this topic in the CLAST writing competency test, refer students to ch. 1, section B5c of *Preparing for the CLAST* by S. Patterson.

For editing for correct use of capitals, italics, abbreviations, and numbers, refer students to *Rough Drafts* by K. S. Cain, Part V, Exercise 19.

This topic is included in the TASP writing competency test. Refer students to *Preparing for the TASP* by M. Saenz.

For more on the special needs of some ESL students, see C. Myers, "ESL Writers in the Composition Class" in L. Julian, et al., *Strategies and Resources for Teaching Writing with the Simon & Schuster Handbook for Writers*.

TEACHING TIP

Because capitalization practice sometimes varies from one publisher to another, and even from one instructor to another, writers should be aware of the basic rules that are in general use but also should stand prepared to adjust minor matters, depending on the guidelines under which they are working at the time. Students should also be aware that capitalization (as well as research documentation and other conventions regarding the mechanics of writing) varies from one discipline to another, making it necessary for students to be alert to the requirements of the situation in which they are writing.

ESL students may need special attention in learning capitalization conventions in English, since practices are not the same in all languages. German, for instance, capitalizes all nouns, and English does not.

QUOTATION ABOUT WRITING

Some readers think my writing is a capital offense. Others think it is capital fun. I hope it converts into capital.
—Diana Davis

BACKGROUND

The terms *uppercase* and *lowercase* originally referred to the drawers, or cases, that held the fonts in a print shop. Although the use of capital letters is still not entirely standardized, by the seventeenth century the spread of printing had made it regular practice to place capital letters at the beginnings of sentences and of proper names and titles. Before the advent of printing, lowercase characters, a full set of which existed by the sixth century, were generally mixed with uppercase ones, and large letters, though not necessarily uppercase letters, were used to mark the beginning of a sentence.

30b Capitalizing listed items correctly

In a **run-in list,** the items are worked into the structure of a sentence or a paragraph rather than arranged with each item on a new line. When the items in a run-in list are complete sentences, capitalize the first letter of each item.

> We found three reasons for the delay: (1) Bad weather held up delivery of raw materials. (2) Poor scheduling created confusion and slowdowns. (3) Lack of proper machine maintenance caused an equipment failure.

When the items in a run-in list are not complete sentences, begin each with a lower-case letter.

> The reasons for the delay were (1) bad weather, (2) poor scheduling, and (3) equipment failure.

In a **displayed list,** the items are set up vertically, one below the other. If the items are sentences, capitalize the first letter. If the items are not sentences, you may start each with a capital letter or a lower-case letter. Whichever you choose, be consistent in each piece of writing.

! ❦ PARALLELISM ALERT: Make list items parallel in structure; for example, if one item is a sentence, use sentences for all the items (see 18h). ❦

In a **formal outline,** each item must start with a capital letter (see 2n).

30c Capitalizing the first letter of an introduced quotation

If you have made quoted words part of the structure of your own sentence, do not capitalize the first quoted word.

> Mrs. Enriquez says that when students visit a country whose language they are trying to learn, they "absorb a good accent with the food."

If the words in your sentence serve only to introduce quoted words or if you are directly quoting speech, capitalize the first letter of the quoted words if it is capitalized in the original.

> Mrs. Enriquez says, "Students should always visit a country when they want to learn its language. They'll absorb a good accent with the food."

Do not capitalize the continuation of a one-sentence quotation within your sentence, and do not capitalize a partial quotation.

"Of course," she added, "the accent lasts longer than the food."
Smiling, she encouraged me to "travel—and eat—to learn to speak Spanish."

Capitalizing *I* and *O*   30d

Always capitalize the PRONOUN *I*, no matter where it falls in a sentence or in a group of words or when it stands alone: *I love you, even though I do not want to marry you.* Always capitalize the INTERJECTION *O: You are, O my fair love, a burning fever.* Do not capitalize the interjection *oh* unless it starts a sentence or is capitalized in material that you are quoting.

Capitalizing nouns and adjectives according to standard practice   30e

Capitalize **proper nouns** (NOUNS that name specific people, places, and things): *Mexico, Rome.* Also capitalize **proper adjectives** (ADJECTIVES formed from proper nouns): *a Mexican entrepreneur, the Roman street.* Do not capitalize articles (*the, a, an*) accompanying proper nouns or proper adjectives.

A proper noun or adjective sometimes takes on a "common" meaning, losing its very specific "proper" associations. When this happens, the word loses its capital letter as well: *french fries, pasteurize.*

Many common nouns are capitalized when names or titles are added to them. For example, *lake* is not ordinarily capitalized, but when a specific name is added, it is: *Lake Mead.*

In your reading, expect sometimes to see capitalized words that this book says not to capitalize. How writers capitalize can sometimes depend on audience and purpose. For example, a corporation's written communications usually use *the Board of Directors* and *the Company,* not *the board of directors* and *the company.* Similarly, the administrators of your school might write *the Faculty* and *the College* or *the University,* words you would not capitalize in a paper. In specific contexts, adapt to the situation.

Chart 123 is a Capitalization Guide. Apply what you find in it to similar items not listed. Also, for information about using capital letters in addresses on envelopes, see section 39a.

Also, for information about using capital letters in addresses on envelopes, see section 39a.

ALTERNATE EXAMPLES

Can your students cite the rules governing the following uses of capital letters?

1. I spent my last vacation in Santa Barbara, California.

2. My father has retired from the First National Bank.

3. I didn't know that she is British.

4. Marjorie Brewster is the Chief Executive Officer.

5. I am reading a biography of Queen Elizabeth I.

6. It is written by Martha Patterson.

7. The guests are to arrive early: They should be here by 6 P.M.

8. Before next week those involved must complete several tasks: (1) Painters must finish with the living room. (2) Apartment owners must move their furniture back into their rooms. (3) Carpet cleaners must erase the marks left by the renovation efforts.

9. Who was it that wrote, "They also serve who only stand and wait"?

10. You are quoting John Milton's sonnet "When I Consider How My Light is Spent."

TEACHING TIP

A useful capitalization activity is to dictate a passage containing a mix of proper and common nouns, leaving capitalization up to the students. Grading can be based either on use of capitals only or on overall correctness. If you do not want to test punctuation, read all punctuation marks as you go along; this practice helps students focus their attention on capitalization. You can easily find passages appropriate for dictation in newspaper articles about people currently making news.

ALTERNATE EXERCISE

To point out the importance of capitalization, you might want to give your students a paragraph that has been typed with only lowercase letters. Then ask them to sort out the sentences and meaning, placing capital letters where they are needed. Here is a paragraph you can use:

> drugs are one of the techniques of western therapy of which we are most proud. however, drugs are used by healers in other cultures as well. rauwulfia root, for example, which was introduced into western psychiatry in the 1950s as reserpine, a major tranquilizer, has been used in india for centuries as a tranquilizer and has also been in wide use in west africa for many years. another example is shock therapy. when electric shock therapy was introduced by cerletti in the 1930s, he was not aware that it had been used in some cultures for up to 4,000 years. the technique of applying electrical eels to the head of a patient is referred to in the writings of aristotle, pliny, and plutarch. what kind of results do therapists in other cultures—witch doctors—achieve? a canadian psychiatrist, dr. raymond prince, spent 17 months studying 46 nigerian witch doctors and judged that the therapeutic results were about equal to those obtained in north american clinics and hospitals.
>
> —Edwin Fuller Torrey,
> *The Mind Game*

ANSWERS TO ALTERNATE EXERCISE

The words capitalized in the original paragraph, grouped by sentences, are: Drugs, Western; However; Rauwulfia, Western, India, West Africa; Another; When, Cerletti; The, Aristotle, Pliny, Plutarch; What; A, Canadian, Dr. Raymond Prince, Nigerian, North American.

30e
cont.

CAPITALIZATION GUIDE

CAPITALIZATION GUIDE   123

		CAPITALS	LOWER-CASE LETTERS
NAMES		Mother Teresa (*also*, used as names: Mother, Dad, Mom, Pa, etc.)	my mother (*relationship*)
		Doc Holliday	the doctor (*role*)
TITLES		President Truman the President (*now in office*)	a president
		Democrat (*a party member*)	democrat (*a believer in democracy*)
		Representative Patsy Mink	the congressional representative
		Senator Mark Hatfield	the senator
		Queen Elizabeth II	the queen
GROUPS OF HUMANITY		Caucasian (*race*)	white (*also* White)
		Negro (*race*)	black (*also* Black)
		Hispanic, African-American (*ethnic group*)	
		Jew, Catholic, Protestant, Buddhist (*religious affiliation*)	
ORGANIZATIONS		Congress	congressional
		the Ohio State Supreme Court	the state supreme court
		the Republican Party	the party
		National Gypsum Company	the company
PLACES		Los Angeles	the city
		the South (*a region*)	turn south (*a direction*)
		Main Street	the street
		Atlantic Ocean (*also* the Atlantic)	the ocean
		the Black Hills	the hills

CAPITALIZATION GUIDE (continued) 123

BUILDINGS	the Capitol (in Washington, D.C.)	the state capitol
	Ace High School	the high school
	China West Cafe	the restaurant
	Highland Hospital	the hospital
SCIENTIFIC TERMS	Earth (the planet)	the earth (where we live)
	the Milky Way	the galaxy
		the moon, the sun
	Streptococcus aureus	a streptococcal infection
	Gresham's law	the theory of relativity
LANGUAGES, NATIONALITIES	Spanish	
	Chinese	
SCHOOL COURSES	Chemistry 342	a chemistry course
	my English class	
NAMES OF THINGS	the *Boston Globe*	the newspaper
	Time	the magazine
	Purdue University	the university
	Heinz Ketchup	ketchup
	the Dodge Colt	the car
TIMES AND SEASONS	Friday	spring, summer, fall, autumn, winter
	August	
HISTORICAL PERIODS	World War II	the war
	the Great Depression (*in the 1930s*)	the depression (*any economic depression*)
	the Reformation	an era, an age
		the eighteenth century
		fifth-century manuscripts
		the civil rights movement

➡

TEACHING TIP

You might find that students overcapitalize in their writing. Comparison can be a useful tool in getting them to distinguish between common and proper nouns. First, review the basic rule: proper (capitalized) nouns name specific people, places, or things; common (uncapitalized) nouns refer to nonspecific people, places, or things. Then give students pairs of noun phrases, one of which contains a proper noun and one a common noun. Omit all capitals. Ask students to identify and capitalize the proper noun; president Washington, the president of the country; hunter high school, the high school band; a new car, a lincoln continental; psychological testing, psychology 101. Augment this list with pairs representing your students' most common errors.

Your students will probably find this rather easy, because contrast highlights the specific nouns. The next step can be to make up or edit a paragraph to eliminate all capital letters except those that begin sentences. Ask students to capitalize the first letters of all proper nouns. Upon completion, you might have students exchange papers and discuss the correct answers. Then students can correct one another's exercises and you can collect the papers to review or record grades.

TEACHING TIP

To draw students' attention to standard (and perhaps nonstandard) capitalization practice, you may want to ask them to bring to class examples from advertising and newspapers that demonstrate the use of capital letters for a variety of purposes. The examples can be the basis for discussing reasons for using capital letters and the effectiveness with which they are used.

ANSWERS: EXERCISE 30–1, page 505

A slash indicates no capital is needed. A capitalized italicized word indicates that a capital is needed.

1. President Abraham Lincoln's S̶ecretary, whose name was Kennedy, and President John F. Kennedy's S̶ecretary, whose name was Lincoln, advised these ill-fated presidents not to go out just before their assassinations.

2. The first child of *European* P̶arents to be born in *North America* was Snorro, whose M̶other was the W̶idow of Leif Erickson's B̶rother.

3. The A̶ncient *Egyptians*, the first to embalm their D̶ead C̶itizens, also embalmed their D̶ead C̶rocodiles.

4. In 1659 *Massachusetts* outlawed *Christmas* and fined anyone celebrating the H̶oliday five S̶hillings.

5. Mark Twain, the author of "*The Celebrated Jumping Frog of Calaveras County*," once refused to invest in a friend's invention, calling a "W̶ildcat speculation." The invention was the telephone!

➡

30e
cont.

CAPITALIZATION GUIDE (continued)

RELIGIOUS TERMS	God Buddhism the Torah the Koran the Bible	a god, a goddess a religion
LETTER PARTS	Dear Ms. Tauber: Sincerely, Yours truly,	
TITLES OF PUBLISHED AND RELEASED MATERIAL	"The Lottery" *A History of the United States to 1877* *Jazz on Ice*	[Capitalize the first letter of the first word and all other words except ARTICLES, short PREPOSITIONS, and short CONJUNCTIONS]
COMPOUND WORDS	African-American post-Victorian Mexican-American Indo-European	
ACRONYMS AND INITIALISMS	NATO FBI AFL-CIO UCLA NAACP IBM	
SOFTWARE	Microsoft Word DOS WordPerfect	[Capitalize software names as shown in the program documentation. Do not underline these titles or enclose them in quotation marks.]

ESL

❖ ESL NOTE: When the subject of your paragraph or essay is a proper noun, capitalize that word or those words. ❖

EXERCISE 30-1

Consulting sections 30a through 30e, add capital letters as needed.

1. President Abraham Lincoln's secretary, whose name was Kennedy, and President John F. Kennedy's secretary, whose name was Lincoln, advised these ill-fated presidents not to go out just before their assassinations.

2. The first child of european parents to be born in north america was Snorro, whose mother was the widow of Leif Erickson's brother.

3. The ancient egyptians, the first to embalm their dead citizens, also embalmed their dead crocodiles.

4. In 1659 massachusetts outlawed christmas and fined anyone celebrating the holiday five shillings.

5. Mark Twain, the author of "the celebrated jumping frog of calaveras county," once refused to invest in a friend's invention, calling it a "wildcat speculation." The invention was the telephone!

6. An artificial hand invented in 1551 by a frenchman (his name was Ambroise Tare) had fingers that moved by cogs and levers, thus enabling a handless member of the cavalry to grasp the reins of his horse.

7. "Take care, o traitor," roared the hero, "Or your villainy will do you in!"

8. Researchers at the institute for policy studies of harvard university discovered that the following jobs are considered most boring by those who hold them: (1) assembly line worker, (2) elevator operator, (3) pool typist, (4) bank guard, (5) housewife.

9. What is the most common item in a family medicine chest? Is it aspirin? adhesive bandages? a thermometer? an antibacterial agent?

10. "I don't care what you do, my dear," the actress mrs. Patrick Campbell is supposed to have said, "as long as you don't do it in the street and frighten the horses!"

11. The letter announcing that the company was closing its doors and all employees were losing their jobs ended with the words "have a happy day."

12. The book that has sold the most copies of any book throughout the world is the bible.

13. I registered for biology 101 and history 121, but the courses I wanted in psychology and in art were filled by the time I got to registration.

14. The capitol building is located in the nation's capital.

15. The sun does not shine for 186 days at the north pole.

ANSWERS: EXERCISE 30–1, *cont.*

6. An artificial hand invented in 1551 by a *Frenchman* (his name was Ambroise Tare) had Fingers that moved by cogs and levers, thus enabling a handless member of the Cavalry to grasp the reins of his horse.

7. "Take care, *O* traitor," roared the hero, "Or your Villainy will do you in!"

8. Researchers at the *Institute* for *Policy Studies of Harvard University* discovered that the following jobs are considered most boring by those who hold them: (1) Assembly line worker, (2) elevator operator, (3) pool typist, (4) Bank Guard, (5) Housewife.

9. What is the most common item in a family medicine chest? Is it Aspirin? *Adhesive* bandages? A thermometer? *An* antibacterial agent? [lower case for *adhesive, a,* and *an* also acceptable]

10. "I don't care what you do, my dear," the Actress *Mrs.* Patrick Campbell is supposed to have said, "as long as you don't do it in the Street and frighten the horses!"

11. The letter announcing that the company was closing its doors and everyone was losing their jobs ended with the words "*Have* a happy day."

12. The book that has sold the most copies of any book throughout the world is the *Bible*.

13. I registered for *Biology* 101 and *History* 121, but the courses I wanted in psychology and in art were filled by the time I got to registration.

14. The *Capitol* building is located in the nation's capital.

15. The sun does not shine for 186 days at the *North Pole*.

BACKGROUND

The three basic type forms are gothic, old-style roman, and modern roman. (There are many variations of these basic ones.) Italic type is a companion form of modern roman, one that is lighter and slopes to the right. The earliest type forms were based on contemporary manuscript hands, for the printer was replacing the scribe. The old-style roman form reached its zenith in the fifteenth century, and in 1501 Aldus Manutius of Venice produced and used the first italic form in the printing of a series of Latin texts, the first volume of which was called "Aldine Virgil." The "modern" roman form, the kind of type most used in Western publishing today, originated about 1693 with Philippe Grandjean. Benjamin Franklin was responsible for introducing a variety of roman type, designed by William Caslon, to the American colonies. The Declaration of Independence was printed using it. The early type founders were artists who were concerned about the esthetics of their type faces. In the nineteenth century, however, emphasis shifted from artistry to quantity, and attention to the beauty of printed letters suffered a decline.

ALTERNATE EXAMPLES

Can your students cite the rule governing the following italicized words?

1. *Hamlet* is still one of the world's most frequently produced plays.

2. Several magazines, such as *Life* and *The Saturday Evening Post*, have significantly changed their format in recent years.

3. Some people prefer to keep up with current events by watching *CBS Evening News* instead of reading *USA Today*.

➡

ITALICS (UNDERLINING)

In printed material, **roman type** is the standard; type that slants to the right is called **italic.** Words in italics indicate material that is underlined when typewritten or written by hand.

Catch 22 [roman]

Catch 22 [italic]

<u>Catch 22</u> [underlined]

30f   **Using standard practice for underlining titles and other words, letters, or numbers**

Chart 124 provides a guide for making decisions about whether to underline. Apply what you find in it to similar items not listed.

GUIDE TO UNDERLINING	124

TITLES

UNDERLINE	DO NOT UNDERLINE
<u>The Bell Jar</u> [a novel]	your own paper's title
<u>Death of a Salesman</u> [a play]	
<u>Collected Works of O. Henry</u> [a book]	"The Last Leaf" [one story in the book]
<u>Simon & Schuster Handbook for Writers</u> [a book]	"Writing Research" [one chapter in the book]
<u>Contexts for Composition</u> [a collection of essays]	"Science and Ethics" [one essay in the collection]
<u>The Iliad</u> [a long poem]	"Nothing Gold Can Stay" [a short poem]
<u>The African Queen</u> [a film]	

GUIDE TO UNDERLINING (continued)   124

UNDERLINE	DO NOT UNDERLINE
<u>Scientific American</u> [a magazine]	"The Molecules of Life" [an article in a magazine]
<u>The Barber of Seville</u> [title of an opera]	Concerto in B-flat Minor
<u>Symphonie Fantastique</u> [title of a long musical work]	[identification of a musical work by form, number, and key. Use neither quotation marks *nor* underlining.]
<u>Twilight Zone</u> [a television series]	"Terror at 30,000 Feet" [an episode of a television series]
<u>The Best of Bob Dylan</u> [a record album or a tape]	"Mr. Tambourine Man" [a song or a single selection on an album or a tape]
	Lotus 1-2-3 [software program names are neither underlined nor enclosed in quotation marks]

the <u>Los Angeles Times</u> [a newspaper. Note: Even if *The* is part of the title printed on a newspaper, do not use a capital letter and do not underline it in your writing. In MLA and CM DOCUMENTATION, omit the word *The*. In APA and CBE documentation, keep *The*.]

OTHER WORDS

the <u>Intrepid</u> [a ship; don't underline preceding initials like U.S.S. or H.M.S.]	aircraft carrier [a general class of ship]
<u>Voyager 2</u> [names of specific aircraft, spacecraft, and satellites]	Boeing 747 [general names shared by classes of aircraft, spacecraft, and satellites]
<u>summa cum laude</u> [term in a language other than English]	burrito, chutzpah [widely used and commonly understood words from languages other than English]

What does <u>our</u> imply? [a word referred to as such]

the <u>abc</u>'s; confusing <u>3</u>'s and <u>8</u>'s [letters and numbers referred to as themselves]

ALTERNATE EXAMPLES, cont.

4. The reruns of *Star Trek* continue to attract viewers.

5. The *Challenger* disaster will be long remembered.

6. Children should know their *abc*'s before starting first grade.

7. The literary works of the *fin de siècle* were shocking to many readers.

8. English has borrowed many words from other languages, such as *chauffeur*, *taco*, and *moccasin*.

9. *The Red Badge of Courage* is a modern epic.

10. The *Titanic* was thought to be invulnerable.

ALTERNATE EXERCISE
What is the difference in meaning suggested by the following changes in the italicized words?

1. a. *Six* different bodies compose the United Nations.

   b. Six different bodies compose the *United Nations*.

2. a. All members of the U.N. can send *five* representatives to the General Assembly.

   b. All members of the U.N. can send five representatives to the *General Assembly*.

3. a. The *primary* responsibility of the Security Council is to maintain international peace and security.

   b. The primary responsibility of the Security Council is to maintain *international* peace and security.

ANSWERS: EXERCISE 30–2

1. The first rule in an old book about rules of etiquette reads, "Do not eat in mittens."

2. When he originated the role of Fonzie in the television series *Happy Days*, Henry Winkler earned about $750 per episode.

3. The *Monitor* and the *Merrimac* were the first iron-hulled ships to engage in battle.

4. Iowa's name comes from the Indian word *ayuhwa*, which means "sleepy ones."

5. The *New York Times* does not carry comic strips.

6. Judy Garland was the second lowest paid star in the film classic *The Wizard of Oz*; only the dog who portrayed Toto was paid less.

7. For distinguished accomplishments of people over age 70, we can look to Verdi, who wrote the song "Ave Maria" at age 85, and Tennyson, who wrote the short poem "Crossing the Bar" at age 80.

8. Handwriting experts say personality traits affect the way an individual dots an *i* and crosses a *t*.

9. The Italian word *ciao* is both a greeting and a farewell.

10. A sense of danger develops slowly in Shirley Jackson's short story "The Lottery."

COVERAGE: EXERCISE 30–2

(1) underlining not needed because title is not cited; (2) omit underlining with proper name: underline title of television show; (3) underline names of ships; (4) omit underlining with proper name; (5) underline title of a newspaper (does not include *the*); (6) underline movie title, underlining not needed for proper name;

➡

30g   Underlining sparingly for special emphasis

Professional writers sometimes use italics to clarify a meaning or stress a point.

> Many people we *think* are powerful turn out on closer examination to be merely frightened and anxious.
>
> —MICHAEL KORDA, *Power!*

In your academic writing, rely on choice of words and sentence structures to convey emphasis.

EXERCISE 30-2

Consulting section 30f, eliminate unneeded underlining and quotation marks, and add needed underlining. Correct capitalization as necessary.

1. The first rule in an old book about <u>Rules of Etiquette</u> reads, "Do not eat in mittens."
2. When he originated the role of <u>Fonzie</u> in the television series "Happy Days," Henry Winkler earned about $750 per episode.
3. The Monitor and the Merrimac were the first iron-hulled ships to engage in battle.
4. <u>Iowa's</u> name comes from the Indian word <u>ayuhwa</u>, which means "sleepy ones."
5. The New York Times does not carry comic strips.
6. Judy Garland was the second-lowest-paid star in the film classic The Wizard of Oz; only the dog who portrayed <u>Toto</u> was paid less.
7. For distinguished accomplishments of people over age 70, we can look to Verdi, who wrote the song "Ave Maria" at age 85, and Tennyson, who wrote the short poem "Crossing the Bar" at age 80.
8. Handwriting experts say personality traits affect the way an individual dots an i and crosses a t.
9. The <u>Italian</u> word <u>ciao</u> is both a greeting and a farewell.
10. A sense of danger develops slowly in Shirley Jackson's short story <u>The Lottery</u>.

ABBREVIATIONS

30h   Using abbreviations with time and symbols

Some abbreviations are standard in all writing circumstances. In some situations, you may choose whether to abbreviate or spell out a word. When choosing, consider your purpose for WRITING and your AUDIENCE. Then be consistent in each piece of writing.

❧ PUNCTUATION ALERT: Most abbreviations call for periods: *Mr.*, *R.N.*, *a.m.* Some do not, including names of organizations, government agencies, and postal service abbreviations (see 39a): *IBM*, *FBI*, *AZ*. When the period of an abbreviation falls at the end of a sentence, the period serves also to end the sentence. ❧

TIME

The abbreviations a.m. (A.M.) and p.m. (P.M.) can be used only with exact times, such as *7:15 A.M.*, *7:15 a.m.*; *3:47 P.M.*, *3:47 p.m.* You can use capital or lower-case letters, but be consistent in each piece of writing.

❧ USAGE ALERT: Use *a.m.* and *p.m.* only with numbers indicating time. Do not use them instead of the words *morning, evening,* and *night.* ❧

In abbreviations for years, A.D. precedes the year: *A.D. 977.* Conversely, B.C. (or B.C.E.) follows the year: *12 B.C.* (or *12 B.C.E.*).

SYMBOLS

Symbols are seldom used in the body of papers written for courses in the humanities, but they are used in charts or similar formats. Also, symbols can be appropriate in the sciences.

In the humanities, spell out *percent* and *cent* rather than using the symbols % and ¢. You can use a dollar sign with specific dollar amounts: *$23 billion, $7.85.* Let common sense and your readers' needs guide you.

Using abbreviations with titles, names and terms, and addresses

30i

TITLES

Use either a title of address before a name (**Dr.** *Daniel Gooden*) or an academic degree after a name (*Daniel Gooden,* **Ph.D.**). Do not use both. Because *Jr., Sr., II, III,* and the like are considered part of the name, they can be used with both titles of address and academic degree abbreviations: *Dr. Martin Luther King, Jr.; Arthur Wax, Sr., M.D.* (The title *Professor* is usually not abbreviated.)

❧ COMMA ALERT: When you use an academic degree or *Jr.* or *Sr.*, insert a comma both before it and after it if it falls before the end of a sentence: *Martin Luther King, Jr., was a superb orator.* ❧

COVERAGE: EXERCISE 30–2, cont.

(7) do not underline title of short literary or musical works; (8) underline letters used as themselves; (9) omit underlining with proper name; underline foreign word; (1) use quotation marks for titles of short works

TEACHING TIP

William Safire, essayist on language for the *New York Times*, pointed out in his column of April 23, 1986, that practice varies greatly on how to write *noon* or *midnight* when the number 12 is involved. Some people use 12:00 A.M. for midnight while others use 12:00 P.M. The same is true for noon. Safire suggests using *12 noon* and *12 midnight* for greater clarity.

30i
cont.

NAMES AND TERMS

If you use a long name or term frequently in a paper, you may abbreviate it using these guidelines: The first time, give the full term, with the abbreviation in parentheses immediately after the spelled-out form. After that, you can use the abbreviation alone.

Spain voted to continue as a member of the **North Atlantic Treaty Organization (NATO),** to the surprise of other **NATO** members.

You can abbreviate *U.S.* as a modifier (*the U.S. ski team*), but spell out *United States* when you use it as a noun.

NO   The **U.S.** has many different climates.

YES   The **United States** has many different climates.

ADDRESSES

If you include a full address—street, city, and state—in the body of a paper, you can use the state abbreviation (for a list, see Chart 127) for the state name. Spell out any other combination of a city and a state or a state by itself.

❖ COMMA ALERT: Use a comma before *and* after the state. ❖

NO   The Center for Disease Control in **Atlanta, GA,** sometimes quarantines livestock.

YES   The Center for Disease Control in **Atlanta, Georgia,** sometimes quarantines livestock.

YES   The Center for Disease Control in **Georgia** sometimes quarantines livestock.

30j   **Using abbreviations in documentation according to standard practice**

Documentation means giving the source of any material that you quote (see 31c), paraphrase (see 31d), or summarize (see 31e). Styles of documentation are discussed in Chapter 33. Chart 125 gives scholarly abbreviations that you might find in the sources that you consult, as well as those that you need for documentation in your writing.

COMMON SCHOLARLY ABBREVIATIONS

125

anon.	anonymous	i.e.	that is
b.	born	ms., mss.	manuscript, manuscripts
c. *or* ©	copyright	n.b.	note carefully
c. *or* ca.	about (with dates)	n.d.	no date (of publication, for a book)
cf.	compare		
col., cols.	column, columns	p., pp.	page, pages
d.	died	pref.	preface
ed.; eds.	edited by; editors	rept.	report, reported by
e.g.	for example	sec., secs.	section, sections
esp.	especially	v. *or* vs.	versus (legal case)
et al.	and others	vol., vols.	volume, volumes
f., ff.	and the following page or pages		

MONTH ABBREVIATIONS USED IN MLA STYLE DOCUMENTATION

126

Jan.	January	May	(none)	Sept.	September
Feb.	February	June	(none)	Oct.	October
Mar.	March	Jl.	July	Nov.	November
Apr.	April	Aug., Ag.	August	Dec.	December

QUOTATION ABOUT WRITING

The most famous abbreviation of antiquity, perhaps of all time, was SPQR—Senatus Populusque Romanus—the great insigne of Rome.

—Cornelia and Bergen Evans

TEACHING TIP

The letters B.C. follow a date, while the letters A.D. precede a date. William Safire, essayist on language for the *New York Times*, reports in his column of June 22, 1986 that a plaque left on the moon by the first Americans to land there reads: "July 1969, A.D." He further reports that at the time he was a speechwriter at the White House and he approved the wording. He writes:

In a century or so, I hope some descendant of mine will take a sharp stylus on some weekend rocket to the moon and, while awaiting a transfer rocket to Mars, will draw a little circle around the A.D and put an arrow placing it in front of the word *July*. This will show that human beings in the early days of space were grammatically fallible; that mankind (since changed to *humankind*, but you can leave it the old way on the plaque, Junior) is forever editing, and that a little precision is a dangerous thing.

You may want to organize your class into competing teams, giving each in turn a postal abbreviation to which a member is to respond by naming a city in that state. For example, an acceptable answer for a player who is given the abbreviation MN would be Minneapolis. When a player cannot answer, the abbreviation is given to a player on the other team.

30j cont.

POSTAL ABBREVIATIONS

127

POSTAL ABBREVIATIONS

AL	Alabama		MT	Montana
AK	Alaska		NB	Nebraska
AZ	Arizona		NV	Nevada
AR	Arkansas		NH	New Hampshire
CA	California		NJ	New Jersey
CO	Colorado		NM	New Mexico
CT	Connecticut		NY	New York
DE	Delaware		NC	North Carolina
DC	District of Columbia		ND	North Dakota
FL	Florida		OH	Ohio
GA	Georgia		OK	Oklahoma
HI	Hawaii		OR	Oregon
ID	Idaho		PA	Pennsylvania
IL	Illinois		RI	Rhode Island
IN	Indiana		SC	South Carolina
IA	Iowa		SD	South Dakota
KS	Kansas		TN	Tennessee
KY	Kentucky		TX	Texas
LA	Louisiana		UT	Utah
ME	Maine		VT	Vermont
MD	Maryland		VA	Virginia
MA	Massachusetts		WA	Washington (state)
MI	Michigan		WV	West Virginia
MN	Minnesota		WI	Wisconsin
MS	Mississippi		WY	Wyoming
MO	Missouri			

Using *etc.* 30k

The abbreviation *etc.* is from Latin *et cetera*, which means "and the rest." Do not use *etc.* in writing in the humanities. Acceptable substitutes are *and the like, and so on*, and *and so forth*.

EXERCISE 30-3

Consulting sections 30h, 30i, and 30j, revise this material so that abbreviations are used correctly.

1. In 1665, Harvard U. graduated its first N. American Indian, Caleb Cheeshateaumuck.
2. The first swim across the Eng. Channel took twenty-one hrs., forty-five mins.
3. According to most drs., the best places in the U.S. for allergy sufferers to live in are the deserts of AZ.
4. When Sandra Day O'Connor was appt. to the Supreme Ct. by Pres. R. Reagan in 1981, she became the 1st woman Supreme Ct. justice in Amer. history.
5. Many coll. students today are required to take courses in lit., soc. sci., and lang.
6. The energy crisis of 1973 prompted enforcement of a natl. speed limit of 55 mph.
7. It seems ironic that the paintings of Vincent van Gogh, who died penniless, now sell for millions of $.
8. The route of the Boston Marathon, run every Apr., covers twenty-six mi. between Hopkinton, MA, and Boston, MA.
9. At fifty mins. before the liftoff, the Sat. launch was postponed.
10. The UN bldg. in NYC has been a popular tourist attraction for yrs.

NUMBERS

Using spelled-out numbers 30l

Depending on how often numbers occur in a paper and what they refer to, you will sometimes express the numbers in words and sometimes in figures. The guidelines here, like those in the *MLA Handbook for Writers of Research Papers*, Third Edition, are suitable for writing in the humanities. For the guidelines other disciplines follow, consult their style manuals.

ANSWERS: EXERCISE 30–3

1. In 1665, Harvard University graduated its first North American Indian, Caleb Cheeshateaumuck.

2. The first swim across the English Channel took twenty-one hours, forty-five minutes.

3. According to most doctors, the best places in the United States for allergy sufferers to live in are the deserts of Arizona.

4. When Sandra Day O'Connor was appointed to the Supreme Court by President Ronald Reagan in 1981, she became the first woman Supreme Court justice in American history.

5. Many college students today are required to take courses in literature, social science, and language.

6. The energy crisis of 1973 prompted enforcement of a national speed limit of 55 mph.

7. It seems ironic that the paintings of Vincent van Gogh, who died penniless, now sell for millions of dollars.

8. The route of the Boston Marathon, run every April, covers twenty-six miles between Hopkinton, Massachusetts, and Boston, Massachusetts.

9. At fifty minutes before the scheduled liftoff, the Saturday launch was postponed.

10. The United Nations building in New York City has been a popular tourist attraction for years.

TEACHING TIP

William Karis suggests a proofreading method that operates as a class activity. After students mark mechanical errors in an "intentionally mangled" text, they rewrite a passage that has serious content errors. In a subsequent discussion, they examine the differences in the two processes ("TWI Resource File: Contrasting Proofreading and Revision," *Writing Instructor* 6 [Winter 1987]: 97).

BACKGROUND

Conventions regarding written numbers differ from place to place and from one institution to another. Where Americans use a decimal point to separate numbers, for example, Europeans use a comma; in Britain an earlier practice called for a raised dot in that position. The traveler should also be aware that dates are cited in a different way in some other countries. The American who invites a British friend to a spring picnic on 6/1/93, the first day of June, will cause some confusion, because the invited person will assume the event is to take place in the snow, planned as it seems to be for January 6. The American military follows the European practice, even in letters, using as a heading, for instance, 2 July 1992 instead of July 2, 1992.

TEACHING TIP

Some students may need a review of Roman numerals. The major ones are: I = 1; V = 5; X = 10; L = 50; C = 100; D = 500; M = 1,000.

In academic writing, Roman numerals have few uses. They designate the major divisions in outlines; sometimes they are used in lists. They are used as parts of names and titles: *Peter Brown III*, *Queen Elizabeth II*, *Rocky IV*. You might remind students that Roman numerals are not interchangeable with arabic (regular) numeral in addresses, dates, or measurements.

30l
cont.

If conveying numerical exactness to your readers is not a prime purpose in your paper, and if you mention numbers only a few times, spell out numbers that can be expressed in one or two words: *Iceland's population increases by more than **one** percent a year, but that gain translates into fewer than **three thousand** individuals.*

! ❧ HYPHENATION ALERT: Use a hyphen between spelled-out two-word numbers from *twenty-one* through *ninety-nine*. (see 22g-4). ❧

If you use numbers fairly frequently in a paper, spell out numbers from *one* to *nine*, and use figures for numbers *10* and above. In the humanities, never start a sentence with a figure; spell out the number. In practice, you can usually revise a sentence so that the number does not come first.

> **Three hundred seventy-five dollars** per credit is the tuition rate for nonresidents.

> The tuition rate for nonresidents is **$375** per credit.

If you are using specific numbers often in a paper (temperatures in a paper about climate, for example, or percentages, or any specific measurements of time, distance, or other quantities) use figures. If you are using an occasional approximation, spell out the numbers: *about five inches of snow.*

Do not mix spelled-out numbers and figures in a paper when they both refer to the same thing.

> **NO**   In four days, our volunteers increased from **five** to **eight** to **17** to **233**.

> **YES**   In four days, our volunteers increased from **5** to **8** to **17** to **233**. [All the numbers referring to volunteers are given in figures, but *four* is still spelled out because it refers to a different quantity—days.]

30m Using numbers according to standard practice

Standard practice requires figures for numbers in the cases covered in Chart 128.

GUIDE FOR USING SPECIFIC NUMBERS 128

DATES	August 6, 1941; 1732–1845; 34 B.C. to A.D. 230
ADDRESSES	10 Downing Street 237 North 8th Street Export Falls, MN 92025
TIMES	8:09 A.M.; 6:00 P.M.; six o'clock, *not* 6 o'clock; four in the afternoon (or 4 P.M.), *not* four P.M.
DECIMALS AND FRACTIONS	5:55; 98.6; 3.1416; 7/8; 12-1/4 three quarters, *not* 3 quarters; one-half
CHAPTERS AND PAGES	Chapter 27, page 245
SCORES AND STATISTICS	a 6–0 score; a 5 to 3 ratio; 29 percent
IDENTIFICATION NUMBERS	94.4 on the FM dial; call 1-212-555-XXXX
MEASUREMENTS	2 feet; 67.8 miles per hour; 1.5 gallons; 2 level teaspoons; 3 liters; 8-1/2″ × 11″ paper, *or* 8-1/2 × 11-inch paper
ACT, SCENE, AND LINE NUMBERS	act II, scene 2, lines 75–79
TEMPERATURES	43° F; 4° C
MONEY	$1.2 billion; $3.41; 25 cents *or* 25¢

EXERCISE 30-4

Consulting sections 30l and 30m, revise this material so that the numbers are in correct form, either spelled out or in figures.

1. The film *Quo Vadis* used thirty thousand extras and 63 lions.
2. The best time to use insecticides is four p.m. because that is when insects are most susceptible.

TEACHING TIP

Some writers mix suffixes with numerals: *1st*, *33rd*. Traditional practice calls for the spelled-out word (the *first* robin), except for days, when only the numeral without a suffix should be used (November 1). When you clarify this issue for students, you might also want to point out that this is among the few cases in English in which formal spoken practice differs from formal written practice. That is, a person can say in a formal talk: "The crisis occurred on November 21st." In written form, however, the formal convention is November 21.

ANSWERS: EXERCISE 30–4

1. The film *Quo Vadis* used 30,000 extras and 63 lions. (or thirty thousand extras and sixty-three lions.)
2. The best time to use insecticides is 4:00 P.M. because that is when insects are most susceptible.
3. People in the United States spend $600 million a year on hot dogs. (Also correct are the spelled-out form, $600,000,000 and 600,000,000 dollars, but $600 million is most appropriate for academic writing.)
4. Four-fifths of everything alive on this earth is in the sea.
5. The earliest baseball game on record was played in 1846 on June 19 (*or* 19th) for a final score of 23 to 1 in four innings.
6. Aaron Montgomery Ward started the first mail order company in the United States in 1872 at 825 North Clark Street in Chicago.

➜

30m
cont.

7. The record for a human's broad jump is about 28 feet, one-quarter inch, and the record for a frog's broad jump is 13 feet, 5 inches.

8. Two hundred fifty words per minute is the reading speed of the typical reader. (*or:* The typical reader reads 250 words per minute.)

9. The yearly income of the average family in the United States in 1915 was $687. (Spelled-out form for money is also correct.)

10. Three out of four people who wear contact lenses are between 12 and 23 years of age.

11. Vine Deloria counts 315 Native American "tribes" in the United States today.

12. It will be about thirty degrees warmer in April.

13. Her date of birth may have been 27 B.C.E.

14. One teaspoon of baking soda will neutralize the acid in the 1½ cups of lemon juice.

15. They were born at 3:17 A.M. in 1900.

COVERAGE: EXERCISE 30–4
(1) numbers over 10 expressed in words and figures; (2) time; (3) money; (4) fraction; (5) date, words and figures mixed in statistics; (6) address; (7) statistics expressed with mixed figures and words; (8) sentence opened with figures; (9) date and money; (10) sentence opened with figures; (11) number over 10 expressed in words; (12) number over 10 expressed in words; (13) year expressed in words; (14) sentence opened with figures; measurement expressed in words; (15) time and date expressed in words

3. People in the United States spend six hundred million dollars a year on hot dogs.

4. 4/5 of everything alive on this earth is in the sea.

5. The earliest baseball game on record was played in 1846 on June nineteenth for a final score of 23 to one in 4 innings.

6. Aaron Montgomery Ward started the first mail-order company in the United States in 1872 at eight hundred twenty-five North Clark Street in Chicago.

7. The record for a human's broad jump is about twenty-eight feet, one-quarter inch, and the record for a frog's broad jump is 13 feet, 5 inches.

8. 250 words per minute is the reading speed of the typical reader.

9. The yearly income of the average family in the United States in nineteen fifteen was six hundred and eighty-seven dollars.

10. 3 out of 4 people who wear contact lenses are between 12 and 23 years of age.

11. Vine Deloria counts three hundred fifteen Native American "tribes" in the United States today.

12. It will be about 30 degrees warmer in April.

13. Her date of birth may have been twenty-seven B.C.E.

14. 1 teaspoon of baking soda will neutralize the acid in the one and one-half cups of lemon juice.

15. They were born at three seventeen a.m. in nineteen hundred.

Writing Research

When you write research, you engage in two processes: doing research and writing a research paper. Part Seven explains how to find, evaluate, and write from sources; how to conduct research, understand its results, and write a paper based on your findings; and how to document your sources completely and accurately. As you use Chapters 31 through 35, be aware that writing research fosters habits of mind to draw upon in college and throughout your life.

REFERENCE TO SUPPLEMENTS

For revising for proper use of sources, refer students to *Rough Drafts* by K. S. Cain, Part II, Exercise 6.

TEACHING TIP: STOPPING PLAGIARISM BEFORE IT HAPPENS

All of us, unfortunately, have to deal with plagiarism from time to time. Techniques for plagiarism-proofing assignments are plentiful: requiring the submission in the student's own hand of working bibliographies, note cards, outlines, and rough drafts; assigning unusual topics and changing them every semester; replacing the semester-long research project with several shorter ones to prevent students from having time to contact research paper mills; limiting research to the use of a particular casebook. All of these work to some degree, but at the price of turning us into thought-police, ever on the alert for the student who might find a way around our system. We take on extra stress and extra paperwork—students continue to think of us as fussy creatures who demand they follow rituals peculiar to English classes. If we are not to continue to waste our energies tracking down plagiarized passages in the library stacks, we need to take steps to counter the mixed signals about plagiarism that our students have received over the years—and continue to receive.

Doris R. Dant, in "Plagiarism in High School: A Survey" (*English Journal* [Feb. 1986]: 81–84), makes several points about how students are taught to write reports in high school and the impact of this on plagiarism in college. In a survey of fourteen freshman composition classes at Brigham Young University (1984), she found that 17 percent of the students reported being advised by their high school teachers to copy "the information word

➜

31 *Using Sources: Avoiding Plagiarism and Quoting, Paraphrasing, and Summarizing*

In writing essays and other papers outside your personal experience, you are usually expected to consult such sources as books, articles, videos, interviews, or even computer bulletin boards. Your assignment might require you to analyze, summarize, synthesize (see 5b and 5f), and react to a single source, in which case you draw on only that one source; or your assignment might require you to write a research paper, in which case you draw on many sources. Using outside sources well takes practice, so become familiar with what is involved. And then get started. The more you follow the guidelines in Chart 129, the better you will meet the challenge.

GUIDELINES FOR USING OUTSIDE SOURCES IN YOUR WRITING   129

1. Apply the concepts and skills of thinking critically (see 5a–5b), reading critically (see 5c–5f), and writing critically (see 5h–5k).
2. Avoid PLAGIARISM* by always crediting the source for any ideas and words not your own.
3. Use documentation (see Chapter 33) to credit sources accurately and completely.

➜

*You can find the definition of a word printed in small capital letters (such as PLAGIARISM) in the Glossary of Terms toward the end of this handbook.

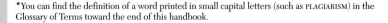
GUIDELINES FOR USING OUTSIDE SOURCES IN YOUR WRITING

GUIDELINES FOR USING OUTSIDE SOURCES IN YOUR WRITING (continued)   129

4. Know how and when to use these techniques for incorporating material from sources into your own writing:

- **Quotation:** the exact words of a source set off in quotation marks (see 31c)
- **Paraphrase:** a detailed restatement of someone else's statement expressed in your own words and your own sentence structure (see 31d)
- **Summary:** a condensed statement of the main points of someone else's passage expressed in your own words and sentence structure (see 31e)

Avoiding plagiarism   31a

To **plagiarize** is to present another person's words or ideas as if they were your own. Plagiarism is like stealing. The word *plagiarize* comes from the Latin word for kidnapper and literary thief. Plagiarism is a serious offense that can be grounds for failing a course or expulsion from a college. Plagiarism can be intentional, as when you submit as your own work a paper you did not write. Plagiarism is also intentional when you deliberately incorporate the work of other people into your writing without acknowledging those sources and the use you have made of them. Plagiarism can also be unintentional—but no less serious an offense—if you are unaware of what must be acknowledged and how to do it. College students are expected to know what plagiarism is and how to avoid it.

Knowing what not to document   31a-1

When you write a paper that draws on outside sources, you are not expected to document common knowledge (if there is any on your topic) or your own thinking about the subject.

Common knowledge

You do not have to document **common knowledge**. Common knowledge is information that most educated people know, although they might need to remind themselves of certain facts by looking up information in a reference book. For example, it is common knowledge

TEACHING TIP

To give your students practice in note taking before they are assigned research paper topics, you might distribute copies of a newspaper or magazine article on a popular subject and ask your students to take notes in support of a particular thesis.

Once they (and you) are sure of their skills, the students can move on to more complex issues with confidence, but at first keeping to popular subjects will help interest students.

Encourage students to paraphrase, summarize, and quote as they feel necessary, and to take as many (or as few) notes as they feel would be useful in supporting a thesis. Then collect their notes and distribute copies of all or some sets of notes. As a class (or in groups), discuss the notes one set at a time.

1. Do all the notes support the thesis?

2. Are paraphrases accurate?

3. Are summaries accurate?

4. Are quotations appropriate and accurate?

5. Are quoted words within paraphrases and summaries placed in quotation marks?

6. Would any material be better presented in a different kind of note?

QUOTATION ABOUT WRITING

Usually I try to be there by six. Everything has been taken off the walls so that there's nothing to arrest my sight. On the bed I have *Roget's Thesaurus*, a dictionary, a Bible, and a deck of playing cards.
—Toni Morrison

that the U.S. space program included moon landings. Even though you might have to look in a reference book to recall that Neil Armstrong was the first person to set foot on the moon on July 20, 1969, those facts are common knowledge and do not have to be documented. You move into *the realm of research and the need to document* as soon as you get into less commonly known details about the moon landing: the duration of the stay on the moon, the size and capabilities of the spaceship, what the astronauts ate during their journey, and similar details. If you feel that you are walking a thin line between knowledge held in common and knowledge learned from research, be safe and document.

Sometimes, of course, a research paper does not happen to contain common knowledge. For example, Amy Brown, whose research paper appears in Chapter 34, had no common knowledge about her topic of personal space. (In fact, Brown deliberately chose to write about a subject new to her.) Brown's research paper, therefore, consists of documented material from sources and her own thinking about the subject.

Your own thinking

You do not have to document **your own thinking** about your subject. As you conduct your research, you learn new material by building on your *prior knowledge*—what you already know. You are expected to think about that new material, using the sequence for critical thinking in Chapter 5 and summarized in Chart 28. It is your thinking when you synthesize what you have learned from the sources you are using. But it is your sources' material that you must document. When in doubt, document.

Be particularly careful about allowing plagiarism to slip into a THESIS STATEMENT and TOPIC SENTENCES. It is plagiarism to put a source's main idea into your words and pass that off as yours in your thesis statement or topic sentences. Similarly, it is plagiarism to combine the main ideas of several sources, put them into your own words, and pass that off as your own idea. Your thesis statement and topic sentences must reflect your synthesis of material to make them into your own thinking.

Here are illustrations of a student's own thinking, drawn from the research paper by Amy Brown in Chapter 34:

■ the thesis statement: see paragraph 1

■ most topic sentences: see, for example, the opening sentences of many paragraphs after paragraph 2; also see comment F

■ comments: see, for example, the sentence in paragraph 1 after the parenthetical reference; also the sentence in paragraph 4 introducing the quotation from poet W. H. Auden.

■ transitional sentences: for example, the sentence in paragraph 13 after the summary of information from Remland, Jones, and Brinkman and the parenthetical reference

■ the conclusion: see paragraph 14

Knowing what to document

31a-2

What should you document? Everything that is not common knowledge or your own thinking. Document any material that you quote (see 31c), paraphrase (see 31d), or summarize (see 31e). Remember that writing the words of others in your own words does not release you from the obligation to document.

To prevent plagiarism in your writing, take careful notes as you conduct research using outside sources. Here are practices that help researchers avoid plagiarism.

■ **Record complete documentation information.** Become entirely familiar with the documentation style you will use in your paper (see 31b) so that you know what information you will need and in what form.

Make a master list of the documentation facts required for each type of source. For example, a master list for recording the data needed to document articles in print (not electronic) academic journals includes (1) author or authors' names; (2) article title; (3) journal title; (4) journal volume number; (5) issue number, if any; (6) date of publication; (7) page numbers. For an electronically accessed version, the master list has at least four more items: (8) database title; (9) publication medium; (10) name of CD-ROM producer or of online computer service or network; (11) publication date of CD-ROM or online access date. (For more about the categories of information needed for master lists, see Chapter 33.)

Write a bibliography card for each source, recording on it all the information on the master list for the type of source, as well as any information you might need to locate the source again (see 33b).

■ **Record documentation information as you go along.** Never forget to write down complete documentation facts. Use your clearest, most readable handwriting. *When you write a research paper, your chances of unintentional plagiarism decrease sharply if you can easily figure out what you found and where you found it. Never expect to relocate your sources (others might be using them) or to reconstruct what came from the source and what is the result of your own thinking.*

■ **Use a consistent note-taking system.** Always use different colors of ink or a code system to keep three things separate: (1) material

---

EXTRA EXERCISE A

Which of the following statements should be documented and which need not be documented?

1. The Declaration of Independence was issued in 1776.

2. The sediments on the ocean floor are the accumulation of silt carried by rivers to the sea, volcanic dust, coastal sands, and discarded shells of living creatures.

3. Levi Strauss, the inventor of blue jeans, came to the United States from Germany in 1848.

4. Coca-Cola is a popular soft drink all around the world.

5. According to Germaine Greer, the reason few women artists have achieved greatness is that they have historically internalized their oppression, thereby draining the energy required for creative work.

6. The United States is a substantially less secure society today than it was forty years ago.

7. The Olympic Games are held every four years.

8. The initials GNP stand for the term *gross national product*.

9. As a society we should read poetry because it makes us live more fully and live more deeply.

10. Henry David Thoreau lived at Walden Pond for two years.

ANSWERS: EXTRA EXERCISE A

1. No. Common knowledge.

2. Yes. Not common knowledge.

3. Yes. Not common knowledge.

4. No. Common knowledge.

5. Yes. Opinion of someone besides the writer.

6. No, if opinion of the writer. Yes, if opinion of someone besides the writer.

➜

31a-2
cont.

paraphrased or summarized from a source; (2) quotations from a source; and (3) your own thoughts. For quotations, always write clear, perhaps oversize, quotation marks so that you are certain to see them later.

31b Understanding the concept of documentation

Documentation means acknowledging your sources by giving full and accurate information so that readers can find your sources if they choose to. This information includes the author, title, publication information, or electronic accessing information, and related facts. Whenever you quote (see 31c), paraphrase (see 31d), or summarize (see 31e), you must document your source correctly according to the DOCU-MENTATION STYLE you are using.

Documentation styles vary among the academic disciplines. When you write using outside sources, ask your instructor what documentation style you are expected to use. Chapter 33 explains and illustrates four documentation styles. It is easy to find the section for the style you need because each style has a different-colored bar on the long outer edge of the pages: a blue bar for Modern Language Association (MLA) style; a red bar for American Psychological Association (APA) style; a brown bar for Chicago Manual (CM) style; and a gray bar for Council of Biology Editors (CBE) style.

31c Using quotations effectively

Quotations are the exact words of a source set off in quotation marks (see 28a). In contrast to paraphrases (see 31d) and summaries (see 31e), which present your sources' ideas in your words, quotations give your reader the chance to encounter your source's words directly. Chart 130 gives guidelines for using quotations.

GUIDELINES FOR USING QUOTATIONS

GUIDELINES FOR USING QUOTATIONS 130

1. Use quotations from authorities in your subject to *support* what you say, not for your THESIS STATEMENT or main points.
2. Select quotations that fit your message.
3. Choose a quotation only if
   a. its language is particularly appropriate or distinctive;
   b. its idea is particularly hard to paraphrase accurately;

QUOTATION ABOUT WRITING

You could compile the worst book in the world entirely out of selected passages from the best writers in the world.

—G. K. Chesterton

BACKGROUND

In a lively, ironic article, Geraldine Mc-Nenny and Duane Roen address the controversies that often surround the use of collaboration in academic settings. In addition, the authors provide an extensive and useful bibliography. ("Collaboration or Plagiarism—Cheating Is in the Eye of the Beholder" in *Dialogue: A Journal for Writing Specialists* 1: Fall 1993, 6–27).

QUOTATION ABOUT WRITING

I've never discussed my writing with others much, but I don't believe it can do any harm. I don't think that there's any risk that ideas or materials will evaporate.

—Aldous Huxley

QUOTATION ABOUT WRITING

Nothing is said that has not been said before.

—Terence

QUOTATION ABOUT WRITING

Be sure you go to the author to get at his meaning, not to find yours.

—John Ruskin

GUIDELINES FOR USING QUOTATIONS

    c. the authority of the source is especially important to support your material;

    d. the source's words are open to more than one interpretation, so your reader needs to see the original.

4. Do not use quotations in more than a quarter of your paper; rely mostly on paraphrase and summary.

5. Quote accurately.

6. Integrate quotations smoothly into your prose (see 31c-4), paying special attention to the verbs that help you to do so effectively (see 31f).

7. **Avoid plagiarism** (see 31a). Always document your source. Enclose quotations in quotation marks. Even if you do not use the entire quotation in your paper, the quotation marks signal that all the words they enclose are words quoted directly from a source.

Two conflicting demands confront you when you use quotations in your writing. Along with the effect and support of quotations, you also want your writing to be coherent and readable. You might seem to gain authority by quoting experts on your topic, but if you use too many quotations, you lose coherence as well as control of your own paper. If more than a quarter of your paper consists of quotations, you may have written what some people call a "scotch tape special." Having too many quotations gives readers—including instructors—the impression that you have not synthesized what your sources say and are letting other people do your talking. Use quotations sparingly, therefore. When you draw on support from an authority, rely mostly on paraphrase (see 31d) and summary (see 31e).

Quoting accurately

31c-1

When you use quotations, be very careful to quote a source exactly. Always check your quotations against the originals—and then recheck. Mistakes are extremely easy to make when you are copying from a source into your notes or from your notes into your paper. If you can do so, photocopy a source's words that you think you might want to quote. If you photocopy material that you intend to quote directly, mark off on the copy the exact place that caught your attention; otherwise, you might forget your impressions and have to spend time trying to reconstruct your thought processes.

TEACHING TIP

In the belief that most students who plagiarize from their sources do so because they don't know how to avoid the problem, Kathleen Mouton has devised a technique that can be demonstrated in class to help students avoid taking notes that are too close to the words of the source. She suggests that instructors ask students to read a short, informative passage of material, then put it away and make notes from memory. Students can check afterwards to make sure that facts (such as dates and names) are correct. With larger amounts of material, students can stop frequently to make their notes, still being careful not to look at the source while recording the note.

TEACHING TIP

Sometimes students fall into the habit of using summaries to take notes, forgetting that they can also be used in developing the thesis of a paper. You may find it helpful to remind students that when they want to introduce ideas from sources but have no need to use direct quotation, summaries are a useful strategy to employ. In them the writer can provide unusual facts, background information, and even other points of view regarding the subject. When summaries are used in this way, however, it is important to make sure that they fit smoothly and easily into the text. A series of unconnected summaries will not make an effective piece of writing.

QUOTATION ABOUT WRITING

The wisdom of the wise and the experience of the ages are perpetuated by quotations.

—Benjamin Disraeli

QUOTATION ABOUT WRITING

I often quote myself. It adds spice to my conversation.

—George Bernard Shaw

BACKGROUND
Only in the last century has the paraphrase been taught mainly for research. For 2,000 years the paraphrase was an important exercise for developing style and teaching structure. In his *Institutio Oratoria* (A.D. 95), Roman educator Quintilian described a curriculum in which young boys began paraphrasing simple stories such as Aesop's fables and, as they grew older, were required to paraphrase longer and more complex texts by great writers. Quintilian believed that paraphrasing also improved students' appreciation for great writing and their ability to critique their own work.

31c-1 cont.

If you have to add a word or two to a quotation so that it fits in with your prose, put those words in brackets (see 29c). Make sure that your additions do not distort the meaning of the quotation. The quotation below is taken from original material shown in section 31d-2. The bracketed material replaces the word *he* in the original quotation. The meaning of *he* is clear in the context of the original source but would not be clear as excerpted here. The bracketed information supplies words to clarify the material.

> "If you hail from western Europe, you will find that [the person you are talking to] is at roughly fingertip distance from you" (Morris 131).*

If you delete a portion of a quotation, indicate the omission with an ellipsis (see 29d). When using ellipses, make sure that the remaining words accurately reflect the source's meaning. Also, make sure that your omission does not create an awkward sentence structure.

ORIGINAL

Like the porcupines in Schopenhauer's fable, people like to be close enough to obtain warmth and comradeship but far enough away to avoid pricking one another. Personal space is not necessarily spherical in shape, nor does it extend equally in all directions. (People are able to tolerate closer presence of a stranger at their sides than directly in front of them.) It has been likened to a snail shell, a soap bubble, an aura, and "breathing room" (Sommer 26).

WITH ELLIPSES

Like the porcupines in Schopenhauer's fable, people like to be close enough to obtain warmth and comradeship but far enough away to avoid pricking one another. Personal space . . . has been likened to a snail shell, a soap bubble, an aura, and "breathing room" (Sommer 26).

31c-2

Selecting quotations from accepted authorities that fit your meaning

Quotations from authorities on your subject can bring credibility to your discussion. You must be able to justify every quotation that you decide to use. If you are unsure whether to quote, follow the criteria in Chart 130, item 3. If you decide not to quote, either paraphrase (see 31d) or summarize (see 31e) the material. For example, Amy Brown, author of the student research paper in Chapter 34 about personal space, quoted Edward T. Hall because he is an accepted authority on her topic. (See Chart 138 in 32f–3.)

*Source information is in MLA style throughout this chapter (see 33c).

Similarly, choose words to quote that fit your context. If you force a quotation to fit your material, most readers will quickly discern the manipulation. Also, if you have to hunt for a quotation simply because you want to include a particular authority's words, chances are that the quotation will seem tacked on, not integrated.

Keeping long quotations to a minimum

31c-3

When you use a quotation, your purpose is to supply evidence or support your assertion, not to reconstruct someone else's argument. If you need to present a complicated argument in detail and thus quote long passages, make absolutely *sure* every word in the quotation counts. Edit out irrelevant parts (using an ellipsis to indicate deleted material; see 31c-1).

If you quote a long passage, you should be able to defend your decision to use it by explaining the quotation's significance. Otherwise, your readers will likely skip over the long quotation—and your instructor will assume that you did not want to take the time to paraphrase (see 31d) or summarize (see 31e) the material.

✤ FORMAT ALERT: For instructions on how to format the layout of a prose quotation more than four lines long (or more than three quoted lines of poetry) in "MLA style," see page 582. For formatting more than 40 quoted words in "APA style," see pages 608–609. ✤

Integrating quotations smoothly into your prose

31c-4

When you use quotations, you *must* integrate them smoothly into your sentences to avoid choppy, incoherent sentences in which quotations do not mesh with the grammar, style, or logic of your prose. Consider these examples based on the original material in section 31c-1.

NO   Sommer says personal space for people "like the porcupines in Schopenhauer's fable, people like to be close enough to obtain warmth and comradeship but far enough away to avoid pricking one another" (26). [grammar problem]

YES   Sommer says concerning personal space that "like the porcupines in Schopenhauer's fable, people like to be close enough to obtain warmth and comradeship but far enough away to avoid pricking one another" (26).

Perhaps the biggest complaint instructors have about student research papers is that sometimes quotations are simply stuck in without any reason for their inclusion. Without context-setting information, the reader cannot know how the writer connects the quotation with its surroundings. When words are placed between quotation marks, they take on special significance concerning message as well as language.

EXTRA EXERCISE B

Working in small groups or in pairs, students can learn good techniques of paraphrasing by trying to find acceptable synonyms for key words in a passage. The italicized words and phrases in the following excerpts can be used for the exercise.

(1) It is clear that between what a man calls (a) *"me"* and what he simply calls (b) *"mine,"* the line is difficult to draw. We (c) *feel and act* about certain things that are ours very much as we (c) *feel and act* about ourselves. . . . In its widest possible sense, a man's Self is the sum total of all that he can call his, not only his (d) *body* and his (e) *psychic powers,* but his (f) *clothes* and his (g) *house,* his (h) *wife and his children,* his (i) *ancestors* and his (j) *friends,* his (k) *reputation* and his (l) *works,* his (m) *land and horses and yacht and bank account.* If they (n) *wax and prosper,* he feels triumphant, if they (o) *dwindle and die away,* he feels (p) *cast down*—not necessarily in the same degree for each thing, but in much the same way for all.

—William James,
Principles of Psychology

(2) Subject to (a) *infinite variables* of winds and currents, of (b) *supply and demand,* of crops and markets, trade has a way of (c) *carving its own paths* not always obedient to (d) *the mercantilist faith.* The faith (e) *was embodied* in Britain's Navigation Act, enacted under Oliver Cromwell in 1651 in the interests of the (f) *rising middle class* and the industrial towns and major trading ports—the so-called Cinque Ports, so long (g) *influential* in British history. Aimed specifically at the Dutch to protect British trade against its (h) *most dangerous rival,* the Act raised (i) *a wall of customs duties,* and permitted (j) *transshipment of goods* only in British (k) *bottoms* calling at British ports. The natural result had been (l) *maritime war* with Holland and (m) *bitter resentment* of customs du-

→

EXTRA EXERCISE B, cont.

ties in the Colonies, feeding the (n) *spirit of rebellion* which led to the American war. For Britain, the expense of fighting the Dutch and trying to (o) *suppress the American revolt* was more costly than anything that could be gained by the trade laws, causing (p) *higher taxes* at home and their natural consequence, a rise in (q) *domestic disaffection*. That was not the least of Britain's (r) *afflictions* in her (s) *embattled time*.

—Barbara W. Tuchman,
The First Salute

ANSWERS: EXTRA EXERCISE B

Answers will vary, but here are possible responses.

(1) (a) my self, (b) my people and my things, (c) respond to and behave, (d) physical substance, (e) spiritual capacities, (f) dress, (g) home, (h) family, (i) lineage, (j) favored companions, (k) general character estimation by others, (l) accomplishments, (m) possessions, (n) increase and thrive, (o) decrease and disappear, (p) undone.

(2) (a) unlimited possibilities, (b) resources and desires, (c) going its own way, (d) commercial assumptions, (e) was contained, (f) growing bourgeois class, (g) a force, (h) greatest enemy, (i) tariff barriers, (j) transfer of merchandise, (k) ships, (l) naval battles, (m) animosity, (n) defiant temper, (o) put down the American revolution, (p) greater levies, (q) discontent among the people, (r) ills, (s) period of struggle.

Also, make sure your readers know *who* said the quoted words; otherwise, you have disembodied quotations (some instructors call them "ghost quotations"). Revise so that more than quotation marks differentiates a quotation from your prose. A quotation seldom should begin a paragraph; rely on your own TOPIC SENTENCE to begin. Then use the quotation if it supports or extends what you have said.

Citing the author's name and the title of the work as you introduce a quotation helps to create a context for the quotation. Moreover, if the author is noteworthy, you give additional authority to your message by referring to his or her credentials as part of this introduction. Consider the following treatments of source material:

SOURCE

Hall, Edward T. *The Hidden Dimension.* New York: Doubleday, 1966: 171.*

ORIGINAL MATERIAL

Therefore, people from different cultures, when interpreting each other's behavior, often misinterpret the relationship, the activity, or the emotions.

AUTHOR'S NAME

Edward T. Hall claims that "people from different cultures, when interpreting each other's behavior, often misinterpret the relationship, the activity, or the emotions" (171).

AUTHOR'S NAME AND SOURCE TITLE

Edward T. Hall claims in *The Hidden Dimension* that "people from different cultures, when interpreting each other's behavior, often misinterpret the relationship, the activity, or the emotions" (171).

AUTHOR'S NAME, CREDENTIALS, AND SOURCE TITLE

Edward T. Hall, an anthropologist who was a pioneer in the study of personal space, claims in *The Hidden Dimension* that "people from different cultures, when interpreting each other's behavior, often misinterpret the relationship, the activity, or the emotions" (171).

Occasionally quotations speak for themselves, but at times they do not. Usually the words you are quoting are part of a larger piece, and you know the connection that the quotation has to the original material. Your reader may puzzle over why you included the quotation, so a brief introductory remark provides the needed information.

AUTHOR'S NAME AND INTRODUCTORY ANALYSIS

Anthropologist Edward T. Hall believes that people from different societies perceive personal space in varying ways, claiming that

*Source information is in MLA style throughout this chapter (see 33c).

"people from different cultures, when interpreting each other's behavior, often misinterpret the relationship, the activity, or the emotions" (171).

Another technique for fitting a quotation into your own writing involves interrupting the quotation with your own words.

✤ **ALERT:** To insert bracketed words into a quotation to make the grammar of the quotation fit the structure of your sentence, see 29c. ✤

"Therefore," claims Edward T. Hall, "people from different cultures, when interpreting each other's behavior, often misinterpret the relationship, the activity, or the emotions" (171).

✤ **ALERT:** After using an author's full name in the first reference, in subsequent references you can use the author's last name only, unless another source has that same last name. ✤

EXERCISE 31-1

Read the original material. Then evaluate the passages that show unacceptable uses of quotations. Describe the problems, and then revise each passage. End the quotations with this MLA parenthetical reference: (Siwolop 111).

ORIGINAL MATERIAL

This is from "Helping Computer Chips to Keep Their Cool" by Sana Siwolop in *Business Week*, January 25, 1988.

Engineers could improve the efficiency of engines, chemical reactors, furnaces, and other equipment if only they could supply them with electronic sensors. But computer chips can't take the heat. Most microchips develop amnesia long before the temperature climbs to the boiling point of water. But that may change. Researchers at North Carolina State University in Raleigh have successfully made microelectronic transistors that operate at temperatures of up to 1,200 F. The key: using silicon carbide, a material familiar to most people as the grit on sandpaper, instead of the crystalline silicon usually used for computer chips.

UNACCEPTABLE USES OF QUOTATIONS

A. Many problems are caused when sensitive equipment overheats. "Most microchips develop amnesia long before the temperature climbs to the boiling point of water" (Siwolop 111).

B. Many researchers believe that they would be able to "improve the efficiency of engines and other equipment if only they could supply them with electronic sensors" (Siwolop 111).

C. Several new developments have taken place at North Carolina State University in Raleigh "have successfully made microelectronic transistors that operate at temperatures of up to 1,200 F" (Siwolop 111).

ANSWERS: EXERCISE 31-1

A. *Analysis:* The quotation does not relate clearly to the sentence it follows. A transitional introduction to the quotation is needed. *Acceptable* (answers will vary): Many problems are caused when sensitive equipment overheats. Until now, researchers have failed to develop sensors that would warn of such overheating mainly because nearly all "microchips develop amnesia long before the temperature climbs to the boiling point of water" (Siwolop 111).

B. *Analysis:* The quotation omits several words but does not provide an ellipsis to indicate where material has been deleted. *Acceptable* (answers will vary): Many researchers believe that they would be able to "improve the efficiency of engines . . . if only they could supply them with electronic sensors" (Siwolop 111).

C. *Analysis:* The sentence is grammatically incorrect. The quotation does not fit with the rest of the sentence. Words need to be added so that the information flows smoothly. *Acceptable* (answers will vary): Several new developments have taken place at North Carolina State University in Raleigh where researchers "have successfully made microelectronic transistors that operate at temperatures of up to 1,200° F" (Siwolop 111).

D. *Analysis:* The tense of the verb in the quotation shifts from the tense of the verb in the previous sentence. Brackets can be used to change the tense of the verb in the quotation so that it agrees grammatically with the previous verb. *Acceptable* (answers will vary): In the past, there have been serious problems with sensors designed to detect heat. Until recently, "computer chips [couldn't] take the heat" (Siwolop 111) but now that problem may be solved.

E. *Analysis:* The quotation is inaccurate; the word "long" is omitted while "up" is added. *Acceptable* (answers may vary):

➜

ANSWERS: EXERCISE 31–1, cont.

One of the problems in designing a heat sensor is that many "microchips develop amnesia long before the temperature climbs to the boiling point of water" (Siwolop 111).

ANSWERS: EXERCISE 31–2

A. Answers will vary; here is one possibility:

Because genetic research is becoming increasingly important, scientists are seeking twins who are willing to participate in experiments either for pay or as volunteers. The Twins Foundation is confident that researchers will find the subjects they need because "there are approximately 4.5 million twin individuals in the United States alone, and about 70,000 more are born each year," (Begley 84).

B. Answers will vary; here is one possibility:

It is becoming increasingly difficult to assure that large-scale testing will be taken honestly. For example, in New York State students stole copies of the Regents exam, and because of their actions "1,200 principals received instructions from the State Education Commissioner to look for *unusual scoring patterns* that would show that students had the answers beforehand" (Robbins 12).

C. Answers will vary.

D. In the past, there have been serious problems with sensors designed to detect heat. Until recently, "computer chips can't take the heat" (Siwolop 111), but now that problem may be solved.

E. One of the problems in designing a heat sensor is that many "microchips develop amnesia before the temperature climbs up to the boiling point of water" (Siwolop 111).

EXERCISE 31-2

A. For a paper describing how and why twins make important contributions to scientific research, write a three- to four-sentence passage that includes your own words and a quotation from this material. After the quoted words, use this parenthetical reference: (Begley 84).

> For over a century twins have been used to study how genes make people what they are. Because they share precisely the same genes but live in different surroundings under different influences, identical twins reared apart are helping science sort out which qualities of body and mind are shaped by our genes, and which by upbringing. Researchers needn't worry about running out of subjects: according to the Twins Foundation, there are approximately 4.5 million twin individuals in the United States alone, and about 70,000 more are born each year.
>
> —SHARON BEGLEY, "Twins"

B. For a paper arguing that it is difficult, if not impossible, to assure honesty in large-scale testing, quote from the Robbins material in Exercise 31-6. Be sure to include at least one numerical statistic in your quotation.

C. Write a three- to four-sentence passage that includes your own words and a quotation from a source you are using for a paper assigned in one of your courses. If you have no such assignment, choose any material suitable for a college-level paper. Your instructor might request a photocopy of the material from which you are quoting.

31d Paraphrasing accurately

When you **paraphrase,** you precisely restate in your own words a passage written (or spoken) by another person. The word *paraphrase* combines the Greek word for "tell" with the Greek prefix *para-*, meaning "alongside." Thus, *paraphrase* describes a parallel text, one that goes alongside an original writing. Your paraphrases offer an account of what various authorities have to say, not in their words but in yours. The ideas of authorities can give substance and credibility to your message and can offer support for your material. Equally important, the process of writing a paraphrase helps you untangle difficult passages and come to understand them. Paraphrasing forces you to read closely and to extract precise meaning from complex passages. Guidelines for writing a paraphrase are in Chart 131.

GUIDELINES FOR WRITING A PARAPHRASE	131

1. Say what the source says, but no more.
2. Reproduce the source's emphases.
3. Use your own words, phrasing, and sentence structure to restate the message. If certain synonyms are awkward, quote the material—but resort to quotation very sparingly.
4. Read over your sentences to make sure that they do not distort the source's meaning.
5. Expect your material to be as long as, and possibly longer than, the original.
6. Use verbs that help you integrate paraphrases smoothly into your prose (see 31f).
7. **Avoid plagiarism** (see 31a).
8. As you take notes, record all documentation facts about your source so that you can acknowledge your source accurately to prevent plagiarism.

Restating material completely using your own words   31d-1

When you paraphrase, restate the material—and no more. Do not skip points. Do not guess at meaning. Do not insert your own opinions or interpretations. If the source's words trigger your own thinking, preserve your thought right away because you might not recall it later. However, *when you write down your thought, make sure it is physically separate from your paraphrase:* in the margin, in a different color ink, or circled.

As you paraphrase, use your own words; otherwise you will be quoting. Use synonyms wherever you can, and use your own sentence structures. When you finish, read over your paraphrase to check that it makes sense and does not distort the meaning of the source.

In paraphrasing, the farther you get from the original phrasing, the more likely you are to sound like yourself. Do not be surprised to find that when you change language and sentence structure you might also have to change punctuation, VERB TENSE, and VOICE.

Sometimes, synonyms or substitute phrases are not advisable. Consider how each synonym fits into the flow of your sentence. For example, for a basic concept such as *people*, the phrase *homo sapiens*

Following the guidelines for writing a summary, summarize one of the following paragraphs.

1. The Elizabethan Age takes its name from the queen who reigned over England and Ireland from 1558 to 1603. She was an intelligent and gifted ruler, managing for decades to escape political disasters at home and abroad. Always an insightful judge of character, she achieved her success in large part because of her tendency to make use of the shrewdest people around her. However, her clear awareness of what she wanted and why she wanted it sometimes led her to go her own way, using a variety of means to reach the ends she desired. She was on occasion devious, even false, but she managed to outwit her opposition time after time. As a result, it was a glorious time in the history of Britain, for under her rule the nation rose from a relatively weak position among the nations of Europe to the highest rank. England's power and success grew rapidly in the sixteenth century, leaving it, at the death of Elizabeth I, a leader in navigation and exploration, in literary productivity— particularly in the drama—and in colonization of the New World.

2. When she died in 1986, Georgia O'Keeffe the person generated almost as much interest among the public as Georgia O'Keeffe the artist. Sometimes she was thought of as the wife and often-photographed model of Alfred Stieglitz, but more often she was pictured as a romantic recluse who, when she grew older, moved increasingly away from the world of art critics and historians and closer to the rugged but exotic New Mexico countryside and culture. In the long run, however, it will be for her art that she will be best remembered. Some viewers admire her abstractions, others her figurative works. Even those who disagree about the relative quality of her paintings agree that her art is memorable, clear, and strong. She painted with

→

EXTRA EXERCISE C, cont.

a distinctive, powerful, personal vision, one that continues to speak strongly to viewers today. Her red poppies, purple hills, and bleached skulls fix themselves in the mind's eye not to be easily erased.

3. To the non-Scot, the tartan is perhaps the most picturesque and original costume in Europe. To a Scot, it is a costume of national distinction. Even without considering the causes for the veneration paid to it by the Highlanders, its merits are several. For one, it bears extraordinarily well the inclemency of weather. It also is economical, light, and unencumbering to the wearer, making it comfortable to wear in a variety of situations. In addition, the plaid of the tartan designates the clan, or family, of the wearer. In the mid-eighteenth century it came to be such a powerful symbol of Scottish culture that it was banned by the English in a law that was not repealed until 1782.

ANSWERS: EXTRA EXERCISE C

Here are possible summaries.

1. An "insightful judge of character," a clever and sometimes deceitful politician, and an independent and purposeful ruler, Elizabeth I, queen of England from 1558 to 1603, continually triumphed over her enemies and weathered political crises to help make England into one of the most powerful countries of Europe.

2. Although people occasionally identify Georgia O'Keeffe as photographer Alfred Stieglitz's model and wife or as a hermit artist from New Mexico, people will recall her finally for her paintings. Whatever their opinions of her art, all find it original, personal, forceful, and unforgettable.

3. The tartan is not only an important emblem of the Scottish people, but also an inexpensive, comfortable, and durable piece of clothing that Scots may wear for most occasions. Each plaid represents a different clan.

31d-1 cont.

31d-2

might make the material seem strained. Also, do not rename terms that the author identifies as coined; quote them. For example, in the student research paper in Chapter 34, no synonym appears for Edward Hall's word "proxemics" because Hall originated it.

Avoiding plagiarism when you paraphrase

You must **avoid plagiarism** (see 31a) when you paraphrase. Even though a paraphrase is not a direct quotation, you *must* use DOCUMENTATION to credit your source. Also, you *must* reword your source material, not merely change a few words. Compare these passages, based on a source used in the student research paper in Chapter 34:

SOURCE

Morris, Desmond. *Manwatching.* New York: Abrams, 1977: 131.*

ORIGINAL

> Unfortunately, different countries have different ideas about exactly how close is close. It is easy enough to test your own "space reaction": when you are talking to someone in the street or in any open space, reach out with your arm and see where the nearest point on his body comes. If you hail from western Europe, you will find that he is at roughly fingertip distance from you. In other words, as you reach out, your fingertips will just about make contact with his shoulder. If you come from eastern Europe, you will find you are standing at "wrist distance." If you come from the Mediterranean region, you will find that you are much closer to your companion, at little more than "elbow distance."

UNACCEPTABLE PARAPHRASE (UNDERSCORED WORDS ARE PLAGIARIZED)

> Regrettably, different nations think differently about <u>exactly how close is close.</u> Test yourself: <u>when you are talking to someone in the street or in any open space,</u> stretch your arm out to measure how close that person is to you. If you are from western Europe, you will find that <u>your fingertips will just about make contact with the person's shoulder.</u> If you are from eastern Europe, your wrist will reach the person's shoulder. If you are from <u>the Mediterranean region, you will find that you are much closer to your companion,</u> when your elbow will reach that person's shoulder (Morris 131).

ACCEPTABLE PARAPHRASE

> People from different nations think that "close" means different things. You can easily see what your reaction is to how close to you people stand by reaching out the length of your arm to measure how close someone is as the two of you talk. When people from western Europe stand on the street and talk together, the space between

---

*Source information is in MLA style throughout this chapter (see 33c).

them is the distance it would take one person's fingertips to reach to the other person's shoulder. People from eastern Europe converse at a wrist-to-shoulder distance. People from the Mediterranean, however, prefer an elbow-to-shoulder distance (Morris 131).

The first attempt to paraphrase is not acceptable. All that the writer has done is simply change a few words. What remains is plagiarized because the passage keeps most of the original's language, has the same sentence structure, and uses no quotation marks. The documentation is correct, but its accuracy does not make up for the unacceptable paraphrasing.

The second paraphrase is acceptable. It captures the essence of the original in the student's own words.

EXERCISE 31-3

Read the original material and then the unacceptable paraphrase. Point out each example of plagiarism. Then write your own paraphrase. End it with this parenthetical reference: (Jacobs 141).*

ORIGINAL MATERIAL

This paragraph is from *The Death and Life of Great American Cities* by Jane Jacobs, published by Random House in 1961, page 141.

A good street neighborhood achieves a marvel of balance between its people's determination to have essential privacy and their simultaneous wish for differing degrees of contact, enjoyment, or help from the people around. This balance is largely made up of small, sensibly managed details, practiced and accepted so casually that they normally seem taken for granted.

UNACCEPTABLE (PLAGIARIZED) PARAPHRASE

A good neighborhood maintains an impressive balance between the people being determined to have privacy and wishing for varying degrees of contact, pleasure, or assistance from others nearby. People manage this with small details that are normally taken for granted (Jacobs 141).*

EXERCISE 31-4

A. For a paper on economic conditions in Third World countries, paraphrase this paragraph. End your paraphrase with this parenthetical reference: (Ehrenreich and Fuentes 87).*

For many Third World women, electronics is a prestige occupation, at least compared to other kinds of factory work. They are unlikely to know

*Source information is in MLA style throughout this chapter (see 33c).

531

Analysis: This paraphrase is unacceptable because it uses many words and phrases from the original. Also, the first sentence uses the same sentence structures. *Acceptable paraphrase* (answers will vary considerably): When people want to create a sense of neighborhood where they live, they need to balance their interest in privacy with their desire for knowing their neighbors. Practically without being conscious of it, people manage the details of their lives to achieve the balance they need (Jacobs 141).

ANSWERS: EXERCISE 31–4
A. Answers will vary; here is one acceptable paraphrase:

Women who live in underdeveloped or emerging countries frequently regard working with electronics as giving them higher status than other assembly line work. Most of these women are unaware that the electronics occupation may pose significant threats to their physical well-being. They have no way of knowing that NIOSH (National Institute on Occupational Safety and Health) has identified electronics plants in the United States as employing the largest amount of poison materials that may have a negative effect on workers' health in any industry. Certainly the dangers here in the United States are twice as threatening when they exist in Third World nations, which have no organization like NIOSH to act as watchdogs. In underdeveloped countries, the air in factories is often polluted with toxic vapors that arise from poisonous materials that are stored in uncovered vessels. The gas created by these chemicals and other substances is strong enough to make a worker lose consciousness (Ehrenreich and Fuentes 87).

EXTRA EXERCISE D

Practice working quotations smoothly into your own writing by devising introductions to the following statements.

1. "Boys and girls grow up in different worlds, but we think we're in the same one, so we judge each other's behavior by the standards of our own."

—Deborah Tannen,
You Just Don't Understand: Men and Women in Conversation

2. "Science does not aim at establishing immutable truths and eternal dogmas: its aim is to approach the truth by successive approximations, without claiming that at any stage final and complete accuracy has been achieved."

—Bertrand Russell,
The ABC of Relativity

3. "Femininity, in essence, is a romantic sentiment, a nostalgic tradition of imposed limitations."

—Susan Brownmiller,
"Femininity"

4. "In books I've read since I was young I've searched for heroines who could serve as ideals, as models, as possibilities."

—Judith Viorst,
"How Books Helped Shape My Life"

5. "Every gift we give carries with it our idea of what a present is. Perhaps it expresses our personality; perhaps, on the contrary, it is what we believe the recipient really wants, a choice based on careful listening for the slightest hint of what he longs for or needs or should have, even though he may not realize it."

—Margaret Mead and Rhoda Metraux,
"The Gift of Autonomy"

that in the United States the National Institute on Occupational Safety and Health (NIOSH) has placed electronics on its select list of high health-risk industries using the greatest number of toxic substances. If electronics assembly work is risky here, it is doubly so in countries where there is no equivalent of NIOSH to even issue warnings. In many plants toxic chemicals and solvents sit in open containers, filling the work area with fumes that can literally knock you out.

—BARBARA EHRENREICH AND ANNETTE FUENTES,
"Life on the Global Assembly Line"

B. Write a paraphrase of a paragraph of at least 150 words from one of the sources you are using for a paper assigned in one of your courses. If you have no such assignment, choose any material suitable for a college-level paper. Your instructor may request that you submit a photocopy of the original material to accompany your paraphrase.

31e Summarizing accurately

A **summary** reviews the main points of a passage and gets at the gist of what an author or speaker says. A summary condenses the essentials of someone else's thought into a few statements. Guidelines for writing a summary are in Chart 132.

Summaries and paraphrases (see 31d) differ in one primary way. A paraphrase restates the original material completely; a summary is much shorter and provides only the main point of the original source.

Here is a summary based on the original material shown in section 31d-2. Compare it with the acceptable paraphrase in that section.

GUIDELINES FOR WRITING A SUMMARY   132

1. Identify the main points and condense them without losing the essence of the material.
2. Use your own words to condense the message.
3. Keep your summary short.
4. Use verbs effectively to integrate summaries into your prose (see 31f).
5. **Avoid plagiarism** (see 31a).
6. As you take notes, record all documentation facts about your source so that you can acknowledge your source accurately to prevent plagiarism.

---

*Source information is in MLA style throughout this chapter (see 33c).

SUMMARY

Expected amounts of space between people when they are talking differs among cultures: in general, people from western Europe prefer fingertip to shoulder distance, from eastern Europe wrist to shoulder, and from the Mediterranean elbow to shoulder (Morris 131).*

Summarizing forces you to read closely and to comprehend clearly. By writing summaries, you can learn the material because that process helps lock information into your memory. Summarizing is probably the most frequently used technique for taking notes and for incorporating sources into papers.

Isolating the main points and condensing without losing meaning

A summary captures the entire sense of a passage in very little space, so you must read through all the content before you write. Then isolate the main points by asking these questions: What is the subject? What is the central message on the subject? A summary excludes more than it includes, so you must make substantial deletions.

As you summarize, you trace a line of thought. Doing this involves deleting less central ideas and sometimes transposing certain points into an order more suited to summary. A summary should reduce the original by at least half. In summarizing a longer original—about ten pages or more—you may find it helpful to first divide the original into subsections and summarize each. Then group your subsection summaries and use them as the basis for further condensing the material into a final summary. Until you are experienced at writing summaries, you will likely have to revise them more than once. Always make sure that a summary accurately reflects the source and its emphases.

Condensing information into a table is another option for summarizing, particularly when you are working with numerical data. (For an example, see the student research paper in Chapter 34: Table 1 summarizes ten pages of a source.)

As you summarize, you may be tempted to interpret something the author says or make a judgment about the value of the author's point. Your own opinions do not belong in a summary, but do jot them down immediately so that you can recall your reactions later. *Be sure to place your own ideas in your notes so that they are physically separate from your summary:* in the margin, in a different color ink, or circled.

*Source information is in MLA style throughout this chapter (see 33c).

QUOTATION ABOUT WRITING

Originality consists in thinking for yourself, and not in thinking unlike other people.

—J. Fitzjames Stephen

QUOTATION ABOUT WRITING

Stay at home in your mind. Don't recite other people's opinions. I hate quotations. Tell me what you know.

—Ralph Waldo Emerson

QUOTATION ABOUT WRITING

31e-1

I quote others only the better to express myself.

—Montaigne

TEACHING TIP: PLAGIARISM

ESL students may have more problems than native speakers understanding the concept of plagiarism. In many cultures, copying and memorizing are respected forms of learning. Originality and creativity are not valued as highly in all cultures as they are in the United States, where uniqueness in many forms (fashion, language, behavior) is often prized. ESL students may say they understand rather than question anything the teacher explains; therefore, difficult, culture-bound concepts like plagiarism may have to be explained and demonstrated repeatedly.

TEACHING TIP

Many activities in other courses require students to write about readings and employ paraphrasing and summarizing. Students are often asked to synthesize, analyze, respond to, and critique readings in exams and papers. They may compose book reviews, interpret literature, analyze arguments, and relate textbook material to experiments in lab reports. Paraphrasing and summarizing are also effective study techniques that can be applied to any reading assignment. They are particularly helpful to students trying to identify the main points of a piece of writing and relate them to each other. Students often disagree in identifying the main points of a text. For that reason, they often find it informative to compare their paraphrases and summaries, discussing why they made certain choices.

31e-2

Avoiding plagiarizing when you summarize

Even though a summary is not a direct quotation, you *must* use DOCUMENTATION to credit your source. Also, you *must* use your own words. Compare these passages, based on a source used in the student research paper in Chapter 34.

SOURCE

Hall, Edward T. *The Hidden Dimension.* New York: Doubleday, 1966: 109.*

ORIGINAL

The general failure to grasp the significance of the many elements that contribute to man's sense of space may be due to two mistaken notions: (1) that for every effect there is a single and identifiable cause; and (2) that man's boundary begins and ends with his skin. If we can rid ourselves of the need for a single explanation, and if we can think of man as surrounded by a series of expanding and contracting fields which provide information of many kinds, we shall begin to see him in an entirely different light. We can then begin to learn about human behavior, including personality types. . . . Concepts such as these are not always easy to grasp, because most of the distance-sensing process occurs outside the awareness. We sense other people as close or distant, but we cannot always put our finger on what it is that enables us to characterize them as such. So many different things are happening at once it is difficult to sort out the sources of information on which we base our reactions.

UNACCEPTABLE SUMMARY (UNDERSCORED WORDS ARE PLAGIARIZED)

<u>Concepts such as</u> identifying causes and determining boundaries <u>are not always easy to grasp</u> (Hall 109).*

ACCEPTABLE SUMMARY

Human beings make the mistake of thinking that an event has a "single and identifiable cause" and that people are limited by the boundaries of their bodies. Most people are unaware that they have a sense of interpersonal space, which contributes to their reactions to other people (Hall 109).*

The unacceptable summary does not isolate the main point, and it plagiarizes by using almost all language used in the source.

The second summary is acceptable because it not only isolates the main idea but also recasts it in the student's words. One phrase (*single and identifiable cause*) is borrowed, but it is set off in quotation marks. No one would charge this student with plagiarism.

*Source information is in MLA style throughout this chapter (see 33c).

EXERCISE 31-5

Read the original material and then the unacceptable summary. Point out each example of plagiarism. Then write your own summary. End it with this parenthetical reference: (Friedman 69).*

ORIGINAL MATERIAL

This is from *Overcoming the Fear of Success* by Martha Friedman, published by Seaview Books in 1980, page 69.

The manner in which we respond to negative criticism is a clue to the level of our self-esteem, which in turn is a good index to the degree of our fear of success. If we harbor a feeling of inadequacy, as many of us do, about something, no matter how slight, negative criticism can wipe us out. Many of us carry too many internalized low-esteem messages from the past, negative things our parents or siblings or teachers or schoolday peers said to us.

UNACCEPTABLE SUMMARY

Many people harbor feelings of low self-esteem as a result of internalized negative messages from the past, and if people respond badly to negative criticism, no matter how slight, it indicates a low level of self-esteem, which is also an excellent index of their fear of success (Friedman 69).*

EXERCISE 31-6

A. For a paper explaining the problems of large-scale competency testing, summarize this material. End your summary with this parenthetical reference: (Robbins 12).*

More and more states are requiring students to pass competency tests in order to receive their high school diplomas. And many educators fear that an increase in the use of state exams will lead to a corresponding rise in cheating. They cite the case of students in New York State who faced criminal misdemeanor charges for possessing and selling advance copies of state Regents examinations. Approximately 600,000 students take the Regents exams. And it proved impossible to determine how many of them had seen the stolen tests. As a result, 1,200 principals received instructions from the State Education Commissioner to look for *unusual scoring patterns* that would show that students had the answers beforehand. This put a cloud over the test program.

—STACIA ROBBINS, "Honesty: Is It Going Out of Style?"

B. Write a summary of your paraphrase of the Ehrenreich and Fuentes material in Exercise 31-4. End it with the parenthetical reference given.

*Source information is in MLA style throughout this chapter (see 33c).

ANSWERS: EXERCISE 31–5
Analysis: This summary is unacceptable because it uses many words and phrases from the original. *Acceptable summary* (answers will vary considerably): When people respond badly to negative criticism, they are revealing poor self-esteem that usually results from childhood experience and that also indicates that they are afraid of success (Freidman 69).

ANSWERS: EXERCISE 31–6
A. Answers will vary, but here is one possible summary:

A cloud hangs over testing programs because of an increase in cheating, as when students in New York State sold the state Regents examination in advance. This led to warnings that educators should watch for student scores that appear in unusual patterns (Robbins 12).

B. Answers will vary, but here is one possible summary:

Many women in underdeveloped countries regard electronics as a desirable career, but they are usually unaware that this industry has been identified by experts in the United States as posing serious threats to the health of workers (Ehrenreich and Fuentes 87).

C. Answers will vary.

31e-2
cont.

C. Write a one- or two-paragraph-long summary of a source you are using for a paper assigned in one of your courses, or select material suitable for a college-level paper. Your instructor may request that you submit a photocopy of the original material to accompany your summary.

31f ## Using verbs effectively to integrate source material into your prose

Many verbs can help you work quotations, paraphrases, and summaries smoothly into your writing. They are listed in Chart 133. Always try to use them without any strain of style. Also, be aware that some of these verbs imply your position toward the source material (for example, *argue, complain, concede, deny, grant, insist,* and *reveal*); others are general or neutral in meaning (*comment, describe, explain, note, say,* and *write*). Choose them according to the meaning that you want your sentences to deliver. (For examples of verbs being used well in student research papers, see Chapters 34, 35, and 38.)

VERBS USEFUL FOR INTEGRATING QUOTATIONS, PARAPHRASES, AND SUMMARIES   133

agree	complain	emphasize	note	see
analyze	concede	explain	observe	show
argue	conclude	find	offer	speculate
ask	consider	grant	point out	state
assert	contend	illustrate	refute	suggest
believe	declare	imply	report	suppose
claim	deny	insist	reveal	think
comment	describe	maintain	say	write

32 *The Processes of Research Writing*

Understanding research writing

Research writing involves three processes: conducting research, understanding the results of your research, and writing a paper on your understanding. The processes of researching, understanding, and writing are interwoven throughout a research project; they utilize all the skills of critical thinking, critical reading, and critical writing discussed in Chapter 5. The **writing process** for a research paper is much like that for all academic papers (see Chapters 1-3), but the **research process** adds a new dimension. In planning, you choose a suitable topic; refine the topic into a research question; use a search strategy to locate, understand, and evaluate sources; and take note. In drafting and revising, you present your synthesis (see sections 5b and 5f) of the material and support it by quoting, paraphrasing, and summarizing your sources (see Chapter 31).

Research writing seeks to answer questions. Few research assignments are stated as questions, but all assignments imply the need to search for answers. Seeing research as a quest for answers makes clear that you cannot know whether you have located useful material unless you know what you are looking for. Research questions, whether stated or implied, and the processes needed to answer them vary widely. You might explain or otherwise present information: "How does penicillin destroy bacteria?" You might argue one side of an issue: "Is Congress more important than the Supreme Court in setting social policy?" To attempt to find answers, you must track down information from varied sources. *Attempt* is an important word in relation to research. Some research questions lead to a final, definitive answer, but some do not. In the preceding paragraph, the question about penicillin leads to a definitive answer (the antibiotic destroys the cell walls of some bacteria); the question about social policy, on the other hand, leads not to a definitive answer but rather invites an informed opinion based on information gathered from research.

REFERENCES TO SUPPLEMENTS

For more on effective researching skills, see *Teaching Writing: Prentice Hall Resources for Composition* by P. Hastings, ch. 4, "Learning to Use Resources."

For additional help with the research writing process, from search strategy to final draft, refer students to *The Research Organizer: Prentice Hall Resources for Composition* by S. Hopke.

See transparencies 8–1 through 8–5a for useful research skills classroom activities in the *Prentice Hall/Simon & Schuster Transparencies for Writers* by D. Carter.

QUOTATION ABOUT RESEARCH

The beginning of research is curiosity, its essence is discernment, and its goal truth and justice.

—Isaac H. Satanov

QUOTATION ABOUT RESEARCH

Research is a way of life dedicated to discovery.

—Anonymous

QUOTATION ABOUT RESEARCH

Research is formalized curiosity. It is poking and prying with a purpose.

—Zora Neale Hurston

QUOTATION ABOUT RESEARCH

The search should take place because somebody needs to find out something or wants to satisfy an itch of curiosity as insistent as athlete's foot.

—Ken Macrorie,
The I-Search Paper

32a
cont.

Research can be an engrossing, creative activity. By gathering information, analyzing its separate components, and composing a synthesis of it, you can come to know your subject deeply. As you write, you can make fresh connections and gain unexpected insights. Equally important, you can sample the pleasures of being a self-reliant learner, someone with the self-discipline and intellectual resources to locate and learn information independently.

If you are among those who feel overwhelmed by the prospect of research writing, you are not alone. Many researchers, whether inexperienced or experienced, share such feelings. When you break research writing into the series of steps described in this chapter, however, the project becomes far less intimidating.

32b

Scheduling for research writing

Research writing takes time. Once you are aware of what is involved, you can plan ahead and budget your time intelligently. As soon as your instructor gives a research-paper assignment, work out a schedule for finishing each step. You might need only one day for some steps but two weeks each for others.

The more you do research-paper projects, the more skilled you will become at scheduling the work and handling it efficiently. The schedule in Chart 134 lists typical research steps (the parentheses give the section in which each step is discussed). No two research-paper projects are alike, so adapt the schedule to your needs. Also, you might find that all steps do not proceed in a straight line, but rather loop back and forth. Be flexible, but always keep an eye on the calendar.

SAMPLE SCHEDULE FOR A RESEARCH PAPER PROJECT   134

Assignment received (date) _____   **FINISH BY**

PLAN

   1. Keep a research log (see 32c).   _____

   2. Choose a suitable topic (see 32d).   _____

   3. Decide on purpose and audience (see 32e).   _____

   4. Gather needed equipment (see 32f-1).   _____

   5. Know how to evaluate sources (see 32f-3).   _____

   6. Determine documentation style (see 32f-4).   _____

   7. Decide whether to do field research (see 32g).   _____

SAMPLE SCHEDULE FOR A RESEARCH PAPER PROJECT (continued)

134

SEARCH   **FINISH BY**

8. Use a search strategy (see 32h) to compile a working bibliography (see 32j-1).   _____

9. Consult the LCSH [Library of Congress Subject Headings] and start compiling a list of key words (see 32i).   _____

10. Know how to make bibliographic cards (see 32j-1 and 33b) and take content notes (see 32j-2).   _____

11. Draft a preliminary research question or thesis statement (see 32r).   _____

12. Use general reference works (see 32k) and specialized reference works (see 32l).   _____

13. Use the book catalog and read books (see 32m).   _____

14. Use indexes to periodicals and read periodicals (see 32n).   _____

15. Use electronic resources (see 32o).   _____

16. Know what resources are available in government documents (see 32p).   _____

17. Know how to interview an expert (see 32q).   _____

WRITE

18. Draft and revise a final thesis statement (see 32r).   _____

19. Outline as required (see 32s).   _____

20. Draft paper (see 32t).   _____

21. Use accurate and appropriate in-text citations (see 33c through 33f).   _____

22. Revise paper (see 32t).   _____

23. Compile a final Works Cited or References list (see 33c through 33f).   _____

Assignment due (date) _____

TEACHING TIP, cont.

The next step is a "researched paper," using more thorough research and fuller documentation. This time students are asked to imagine that they have been invited to expand their Sunday newsmagazine piece into a full-size article (14–24 pages) for a major national magazine. Each student serves as "editor" to another student, in addition to writing his or her own article. The editor's job is to point out places in the essay where additional evidence is needed or where logic is unclear or faulty. The students explore a variety of heuristics as they seek to fill developmental gaps and correct logical flaws.

Overall, Strickland feels, the sequence has resulted in superior papers, exhibiting better documentation skills than papers written by students before he used this sequence. Student attitude has also changed in a positive way: students are more willing to go to the library, are more confident in their ability to do research, and complain less about assignments.

TEACHING TIP

A research log can become the basis for an "I-Search paper" describing the search conducted for the research paper. According to Ken Macrorie (*The I-Search Paper* [Portsmouth, NH: Boynton/Cook, 1988]), an I-Search paper tells the story of what the writer went through to learn something that he or she needed to know. Writing an I-Search paper encourages writers to reflect about the process of conducting their research, allows writers to describe the satisfactions and frustrations of their research, and, when well written, can tell an entertaining, suspenseful tale. Many I-Search papers follow a four-part outline:

1. What I Knew (and didn't know about my topic when I started out).

2. Why I'm Writing This Paper. . . .

3. The Search (story of the hunt).

4. What I Learned (or didn't learn . . .) (64).

BACKGROUND

The research paper originated when American universities adopted the research ideal and began developing a curriculum to educate students for careers in specialized disciplines. According to David R. Russell (*Writing in the Academic Disciplines, 1870–1990* [Carbondale, IL: Southern Illinois UP, 1991]), young college instructors who had studied in research-oriented German universities began occasionally to assign a "scholarly thesis" in U.S. colleges around 1870. Ten years later many colleges began to require seniors to write a "graduating thesis" of 1,000 to 3,000 words, and by the 1890s these were frequently required in the new seminar courses for advanced students. At first instructors required little formal documentation in a thesis, but by the turn of the century, the typical thesis paper provided a bibliography, extensive footnotes, and charts and diagrams. Faculty regarded students as "apprentices" in a profession, and the thesis was an opportunity for students to develop the investigative skills needed to become experts in their fields, and to learn to address readers in their professions. The research paper soon moved into lower-level courses, and by 1931 high school students often were required to write a term paper in their junior or senior year.

Research paper instruction began to be offered in freshman composition courses in the 1920s. By the early 1980s, according to James E. Ford and Dennis R. Perry ("Research Paper Instruction in the Undergraduate Writing Program," *College English* [December 1982]: 825–831), 84 percent of freshman writing programs and 40 percent of advanced composition programs were teaching the research paper, and the research paper was a requirement in 78 percent of the freshman programs and 42 percent of the advanced programs.

32c   Using a research log

A research log is like a diary. It becomes a record of your research process, especially your evolving thoughts about your work. Start a research log as soon as you get your assignment. Begin by entering the schedule (see 32b) you intend to follow. Use a separate notebook for the log, one that you can take to the library and wherever else you conduct research.

Although much of your research log will never find its way into your research paper itself, its entries become invaluable aids as you progress from choosing a topic to gathering material to organizing information and finally to writing the paper. As a student expected to concentrate simultaneously on various courses, you can use a research log to enhance your efficiency. A well-kept log traces your line of reasoning as your project evolves, tells where you ended each work session, and suggests what your next steps should be. Such a record means much

Excerpts from Amy Brown's Research Log

> Nov. 1: The assigned subject is communication. Must narrow! I've always wondered about "unspoken" communication, like the messages of body language or the idea of being comfortable when I have "my own space." My psychology textbook has the term "nonverbal communication." Check what it means.

> Nov. 15: Found Sommer's book, made a biblio. card, and photocopied p. 26. Excellent source. He is an environmental psychologist. Tone is calm; seems unbiased. I see I was overlapping two concepts: territory and personal space. Territory refers to places we carve out as our own — a chair in a classroom, a room in a house. Personal space is the "bubble" of space we carry around with us. We don't like intrusions in our bubbles.

less wasted time retracing a research path or reconstructing your thinking. Also, a research log serves as a journal (see section 2e) in which you can "think on paper" by using the critical-thinking sequence in Chart 28, section 5b. Most particularly, as you seek to synthesize the various elements in your material, your log helps you discover insights that only the physical act of writing makes possible. The excerpts from a research log shown here are by Amy Brown, the student whose research paper about personal space appears in Chapter 34.

Choosing and narrowing a topic for research writing

Instructors assign topics for research papers in a variety of ways. Some assign the specific topic. Others assign a general subject area and require you to narrow it to a topic that can be researched within the constraints of time and length imposed by the assignment. Still other instructors expect you to choose a topic on your own.

What if you have free choice of a research topic, but you develop what might be called "research topic block" because the task seems overwhelming? First, stay calm so that you can think clearly. Next, force yourself to get started. One way is to use the "BLB" system, explained in Chart 135.

OVERCOMING RESEARCH TOPIC BLOCK USING "BLB" 135

Use this system by taking one step at a time, without focusing on the entire project right away. Think positively and assure yourself that you can find a topic in the allotted time. For best results, if you do not already know how your college library is organized, devote one visit to learning where things are (see 32i).

1. B-BROWSE for a subject where ideas can be found.

■ The **Library of Congress Subject Headings (LCSH)** is a multivolume collection that shows the terms used to classify and organize information in the library. LCSH is in conventional books and/or online. The headings are updated frequently, so most current topics are listed. Browsing the LCSH lists is a first-rate way to get ideas for topics—and to see how topics are broken down in subcategories. LCSH also tells you what terms librarians use for various subjects, knowledge that helps you to communicate with librarians about your topic. LCSH lists each subject's call letters and numbers, information that makes you more efficient in locating library sources.

➡

TEACHING TIP
Saying something original based on several sources is an imposing challenge for most students. Many instead treat the research paper as a knowledge-telling exercise in which they restate what they have read. The research paper becomes a string of quotations, paraphrases, and summaries that drown out the student's voice, lack purpose and focus, and often invite plagiarism. According to Margaret Kantz ("Helping Students Use Textual Sources Persuasively," *College English* [January 1990]: 74–91), "Writing an original persuasive argument based on sources requires students to apply material to a problem or to use it to answer a question, rather than simply to repeat it or evaluate it" (78). But students "have learned to see texts statically, as descriptions of truths, instead of as arguments" (79). This view encourages students simply to collect facts into a research paper in the belief that the facts will settle any disagreements and reveal the truth. Kantz recommends that teachers encourage students to regard the research paper and its sources "as existing to solve problems" (84). Students should try to understand what the author of a source was trying to accomplish and what audience was being addressed. They should treat facts as claims that could be challenged or interpreted differently. And they should write their research paper in order to solve a problem or answer a question for a particular audience.

BACKGROUND

As we struggle to teach the Research Paper, we may sometimes wonder if we are struggling alone. According to James E. Ford and Dennis R. Perry ("Research Paper Instruction in the Undergraduate Writing Program," *College English*, Dec. 1982, 825–31), we are definitely not alone.

Research paper instruction is currently being offered in 84.09% of freshman composition programs and in 40.03% of advanced composition programs. In general this high level of occurrence is fairly uniform in all types and sizes of institutions and in all regions of the country. There is, however, a slight tendency for research paper instruction to decrease as the size of the school increases (down to 71.06% in the large schools). Also, occurrence is highest in the Rocky Mountain region (91.66%) and . . . lowest on the Pacific coast (72.40%). Instruction in the research paper is required in 78.11% of freshman composition programs offering it and 42.35% of advanced writing programs where it is offered. Although 4.16% of the schools not offering instruction in the research paper at the basic level indicated their reason for omitting it as "faculty think it unnecessary," the most common reason given for not offering it came under the "other" category, checked by 12.12%. About half of these (that is, about 6% of the total respondents) said the course was already too full to allow time for such instruction.

. . . No institution surveyed had eliminated a research paper requirement during the past five years and only two now have plans to do away with it. (827)

Ford and Perry also say:

Not surprisingly, research paper instruction is offered more in freshman

- **General Encyclopedias** contain articles on many subjects. Most college libraries maintain up-to-date editions of general encyclopedias with articles on current topics. Skimming articles may stimulate you to think about a variety of research topic ideas. The index volume of a general encyclopedia is also a good place to browse for topics because it lists every subject covered in the encyclopedia and also cross-references information.
- **Specialized or subject encyclopedias** frequently have chapter headings that read like titles, which can sometimes help you identify issues and controversies that might be interesting to research in particular fields.
- **"Open stacks"** (book collections that libraries give users free access to) or perhaps the library's book catalog (see 32m) or indexes to periodicals (see 32n).
- **Textbooks**—especially in subjects that relate to an assigned research topic. (College libraries sometimes have copies of textbooks on reserve, or you might look at one in the bookstore.)
- A **"vertical file"** in some college and public libraries stores materials too short or informal to be catalogued. The file may also contain reports from nonprofit organizations and government offices.

2. **L-LOOK OVER all the items that interest you.** Focus especially on major headings (often in larger and/or darker print than the rest of the material) and the first few pages. To avoid too broad a topic, look at its subdivisions in LCSH. If there are many, the subject is probably too broad. You can use one of the subdivisions marked NT (for "narrower topic") in LCSH to suggest an aspect for you to research.

3. **B-BRAINSTORM as soon as you think that an idea might have potential.** Use the techniques for gathering ideas explained in sections 2d through 2k: freewrite, make lists, draw clusters of ideas, or whatever else helps you scan ideas in what you have found or what comes to mind. Also, carry pen and paper at all times so that you can jot down thoughts if a topic or related ideas suddenly occur to you.

Before deciding on a topic, check it using the guidelines for choosing a topic in Chart 136.

What if you have been assigned a general subject area for your research, but you are not sure how to narrow the subject into a topic appropriate for a research paper? Use the guidelines in Chart 136.

Communication was the general topic assigned to Amy Brown, the student whose research paper appears in Chapter 34. Her instructor required a paper of 1,800 to 2,000 words to be written in six weeks based on about twelve sources. To get started, Brown borrowed two textbooks from a friend, one an introduction to psychology and the other an introduction to business communication. Browsing through the textbooks helped Brown make her first major choice. She decided to focus on nonverbal communication. To further narrow her topic, Brown went to her college library and looked up the term *nonverbal communication* in the LCSH. She discovered several subdivisions under *Nonverbal communication,* including *personal space,* a topic that particularly caught her interest. Her next step was to check the general encyclopedias and specialized encyclopedias for further information on her topic. She was fascinated to learn that cultures have unspoken standards for the accepted distances between people who are conversing and interacting. Brown also liked the topic of personal space because her college had many sources to which she could refer. As she began to read closely on the topic, Brown evolved her research question: "How do standards for personal space differ among cultures?" The flow chart on page 544 illustrates Brown's process of narrowing the topic. Although each decision seems to flow smoothly from the one before, the process is rarely neat and tidy. It looks clearcut only after all the thinking, debating, and choosing end. Do not be surprised if you back out of dead ends and make some sharp turns as you define your choices and find a suitable path to a research question. To clarify your thinking, try charting your decision process as you go along.

GUIDELINES FOR CHOOSING A TOPIC FOR A RESEARCH PAPER 136

1. **Expect to think through various topics before making your final choice.** Avoid rushing; give yourself time to think. Keep your mind open to flashes of insight and to alternative ideas. Conversely, avoid allowing indecision to block you.

2. **Be practical.** Plan to do the work within the established time limit and paper length. Be sure that sufficient resources on your topic are available and accessible to you.

➜

BACKGROUND, cont.

programs (50.56%) during the second semester of the freshman year, but it also is included in a significant number of courses offered during the first semester (41.57%). It is a feature in both semesters at 15.17% of the institutions. Such instruction on the advanced level most often comes during the sophomore year (63.83%), but it is common also during the junior year (46.81%) . . . . Whenever it is offered, research paper instruction constitutes, on the average, a very considerable 34.66% of one basic course and 36.71% of an advanced course. (828)

Post Script: we cannot find an update of this information (in the 1990's). Please write LQT if you know of any published or unpublished. Thank you.

TEACHING TIP

Students usually write more effective research papers if they formulate a tentative thesis after they have read and taken notes on a wide selection of sources but well before they begin drafting the paper, according to Sandra Stotsky ("On Developing Independent Critical Thinking: What We Can Learn from Studies of the Research Process," *Written Communication* [April 1991]: 193–212). "Finding a focus, or controlling idea," Stotsky suggests, "may well depend on how much information is gathered in an initial search process and how students organize and evaluate their initial notes. Categorizing, organizing, recategorizing, and reorganizing may be the most significant generative activities in the search process" (207).

TEACHING TIP

In a three-year study of students in the Developmental Writing course at Augsburg College ("Basic Writers and the Library: A Plan for Providing Meaningful Bibliographic Instruction," *Journal of Basic Writing* [Spring 1990]: 56–74), Boyd Koehler and Kathryn Swanson found that a "hands-on approach" to teaching students basic research skills was more effective than the traditional library lecture tour. Students in the study worked in groups of four on exercises that required them to use the online library catalog to search out books and articles on assigned topics. Topics such as AIDS, date rape, and student privacy were chosen for their current popularity or practical relevance to the lives of college students.

QUOTATION ABOUT RESEARCH

[Research] method is so central to the understanding and evaluation of the final written product that in many disciplines a writer is obliged to describe as part of the statement the method used to produce and analyze the data. In this way, many articles contain stories of how they were made.

—Charles Bazerman,
The Informed Writer

QUOTATION ABOUT WRITING

It's not a bad idea to get in the habit of writing down one's thoughts. It saves one having to bother anyone else with them.
—Isabel Colegate

GUIDELINES FOR CHOOSING A TOPIC FOR A RESEARCH PAPER (continued)

136

3. **Choose a topic worth researching.** Trivial topics prevent you from doing what student researchers are expected to do—use critical thinking: Investigate related ideas; analyze, summarize, and interpret them; synthesize complex, perhaps conflicting, concepts; and assess them critically.

4. **Try to select a topic that interests you.** Know that your topic will be a companion for a while, sometimes most of a semester. Select a topic that arouses your interest and allows you the pleasure of satisfying your intellectual curiosity.

5. **Narrow the topic sufficiently.** Avoid topics that are too broad, such as communication or even nonverbal communication. Conversely, avoid topics that are too narrow to allow a suitable mix of generalizations and specific details.

6. **Confer briefly with a professor in your field of interest.** Ask for advice in narrowing your topic. Also, ask for the names of the major books and authorities on your topic.

Flow Chart of Amy Brown's Narrowing Process

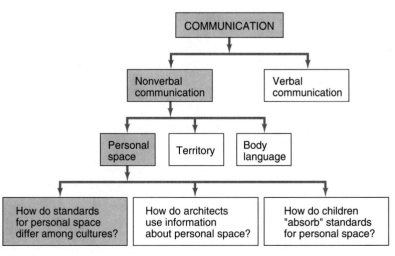

Determining the purpose and audience for your research paper

The question that guides your research process (see 32a) can help you determine your paper's purpose. If your question asks for facts, information and/or explanation, your purpose is to inform. For example, the question "How do standards for personal space differ among cultures?" requires an answer that calls for informative writing.

On the other hand, if the question raised by a topic asks for an informed opinion *based* on information and other evidence, your purpose is to persuade. For example, the question "Why should people be aware of intercultural differences in standards for personal space?" calls for persuasive writing. You may find that your paper's purpose shifts during the research process, as Amy Brown's purpose changed (Chapter 34). Remain open-minded as you work. By the time you start to write, however, be sure to have defined your purpose.

The **audience** for your college writing is primarily, but perhaps not exclusively, your instructor (see section 1c). When you think of writing for your instructor, remember that he or she plays two roles: a surrogate for the general reading public or a specialized reader as well as a person responsible for judging how well you have understood your material and the forms for presenting it. Sometimes the audience for a research paper includes other people—students in your class or perhaps specialists on your topic. Your reader's expertise on your topic helps you make decisions about content, specific details in explanations, and word choice.

Preparing to undertake research

Gathering equipment needed for research

Experienced researchers use equipment that helps them work efficiently. Gather the materials listed in Chart 137. Keep them separate from your regular books and materials so that you can locate them easily.

Color coding often helps researchers organize categories of information. For example, you might use one color of index cards or colored clips for notes and another for bibliographic information. You might use one color ink for quotations (see section 31c), another for paraphrases and summaries (see sections 31d and 31e), and a third for your thoughts about and synthesis of sources.

QUOTATION ABOUT RESEARCH

Research is a way of learning, important in formal study, which we can use for the rest of our lives: we can research the voting records of congressmen, recipes, genealogy, precedents in zoning for the neighborhood, or types of schooling for information of the PTA. Research is a method. The research paper is a particular embodiment of the general method.

—Donald Hall

TEACHING TIP

You may find it helpful to ask students to bring to class research assignments made in other classes. Working in groups, they can analyze the assignments in terms of audience, purpose, and scope of topic. Given sufficient time, they may be able to discuss a search strategy for carrying out the assignment that will be helpful to the student charged with doing the work.

QUOTATION ABOUT WRITING

All I needed was a steady table and a typewriter . . . a marble-topped bedroom washstand table made a good place; the dining-room table between meals was also suitable.

—Agatha Christie

TEACHING TIP

The entire process of writing a research paper can be facilitated by computers for those students who have access to a battery-operated "notebook" or portable computer. They can use it to take notes by saving information in separate files for each section, as well as for drafting, organizing, and revising. The latter steps will be easier because sources will be readily accessible in the computer's memory.

TEACHING TIP

Students might feel overwhelmed if they had to do a research paper on, say, the role of the media in shaping public attitudes toward the Vietnam war or the impact of wheat sales to Russia on the American farmer. The problem has more to do with students' fears than the actual complexity of such assignments. Students' confidence can be built as research skills are developed if "accessible" topics are assigned—especially for preliminary exercises in library skills and note taking. Here are a few possibilities.

1. Write a biography of someone you would like to know more about: a sports figure, a cartoonist, a movie director, a state legislator, a deposed dictator.

2. Write an essay recommending a particular type or model of some fairly expensive consumer item that you are interested in buying yourself, such as a car, a VCR, or a microwave oven.

3. Write an essay recommending and explaining an eating regimen that can help someone lose weight, train for a sport, or control a health problem (e.g., diabetes or high blood pressure).

4. Imagine you are a travel agent who has been asked to plan a tour of Asia or Africa. Money is no object. You have been told to arrange stops in all countries with which the United States has friendly relations. Advise your clients of (1) entry requirements such as a visa and limitations on what they may bring into each country; (2) health precautions that they ought to take, including inoculations; and (3) local laws or customs that they must not violate, such as the non-use of alcohol or drugs.

5. If you have not chosen a career or major, write an essay exploring the pros and cons of a particular career or major that you are considering. If you have chosen your field, write an essay exploring a particular job in that field or arguing a position about an ethical or political problem in the field.

32f-1
cont.

1. A copy of your assignment.
2. A separate notebook for your research log (see 32c).
3. Pens of several different colors for taking notes. (Pencil tends to blur when notes are shuffled and handled often.)
4. Index cards to give you flexibility in moving information around. Use one index card per source to record bibliographic data (see 33b). Always use a separate index card for each idea you take down in notes.
5. This handbook, the *Simon & Schuster Handbook for Writers*. Refer to sections 32j-1 and 33b when you make bibliographic cards. Write down bibliographic information while you have your sources in hand.
6. Whatever coins you need for the library's copy machines or downloading from a database to a printer.
7. Paper clips, a small stapler, and rubber bands to help you organize index cards and other papers.
8. A separate book bag for you to check out books from the library. Librarians joke about researchers with wheelbarrows. You might need a backpack.

32f-2

Learning how the library is organized

Before you begin researching a subject, familiarize yourself with your college library. Although public and community libraries often provide additional sources for student researchers, their mission is nonacademic, so plan to do the bulk of your research at your college or university library. Some college libraries provide in-class tours, others offer training sessions, and some distribute informative pamphlets to help you learn the library layout and materials. Regardless of the size of your library, be sure to get the answers to these basic questions:

1. Where is the general reference collection?

2. Where is the special reference collection? Is the book catalog computerized or on cards? (Some libraries use both systems.)

3. What periodical indexes does the library have, and are they print or electronic?

4. Are the book and journal stacks open (you can go where materials are shelved and can browse) or closed (you must request each shelved or archived item, which library personnel obtain for you)?

5. How are the magazines and journals stored? At some libraries, current periodicals published in the last year are usually on display in bins or racks for easy browsing. Older issues may be put into binders and shelved with the book collection.

6. Does the library have any special collections such as newspapers on microfilm, local historical works, and state and federal government documents? Remember, using the library takes time, so before you start a project that involves library research, become familiar with the library's possibilities.

Being ready to evaluate sources

32f-3

A **source** can be a book, article, videotape, or any other form of communication. Sources are rarely equally valuable. Before you start to gather information from sources, learn the criteria for evaluating research material given in Chart 138. Evaluate them with a critical eye. Also, as you read, apply the principles of critical reading discussed in sections 5d and 5e.

CRITERIA FOR EVALUATING SOURCES FOR RESEARCH   138

1. **Authoritative:** Check encyclopedias, textbooks, articles in academic journals, bibliographies, electronic indexes, databases, and ask experts. If a particular name or a specific work is mentioned often, that source is probably recognized as an authoritative one on your topic. To see whether the author of a source has a background that makes him or her an authority, consult one of the biographical references listed in 32k. Also, look for the author's name in bibliographies of reference articles on your topic.

2. **Reliable:** Material published in academic journals (see 32n-2), by university presses, or by presses that specialize in scholarly books is considered reliable. Material published in newspapers, general readership magazines, and by large commercial publishers usually can be considered reliable, though cross-checking is advisable when possible.

3. **Well known:** Check several different sources. If the same information appears, it is probably reliable.

4. **Well supported:** Check that each source supports assertions or information with sufficient evidence (see 5h). If the material expresses the source's point of view but offers little to back up that position, turn to another source.

→

CRITERIA FOR EVALUATING SOURCES FOR RESEARCH

BACKGROUND

Before it was burnt down in the third century A.D., the famous library at Alexandria, Egypt contained as many as 700,000 scrolls. Under the Ptolemies (third century B.C. on) the library became a depository for copies of all important texts. Books were edited into a standard format, and systems of punctuation and accents were introduced. Textual scholarship, revisions of books to incorporate new knowledge, and the writing of new books went on constantly. Most of the books have been lost. Only those works which were widely copied and distributed have managed to survive. For example, evidence indicates that Aeschylus, Sophocles, Euripides, and Aristophanes wrote about 330 plays in total; only 43 remain.

TEACHING TIP: COLLABORATION

Working together, students can undertake more extensive primary research than the student working alone. A student group can develop together a list of interview questions to ask in individually conducted interviews. The identical question set assures that the information from each interview can be compared with the others. On the other hand, some projects may benefit from members of the group asking different questions so that each gathers information on a different aspect of the topic. Students also need to know that sometimes during an interview, the person being interviewed may open new and intriguing subjects that do not appear on the list of questions. Flexibility by the interviewer usually pays off in such situations.

BACKGROUND

During the Middle Ages, the libraries of Western Europe were affiliated with religious houses and cathedrals. The few private libraries belonged to bishops. The clergy were the only people who could read, and even if the level of literacy was sometimes low, the church maintained the tradition of schools and libraries. These religious libraries were quite small by twentieth-century standards. The largest (at Canterbury and Bury St. Edmunds) had 2,000 volumes each, but libraries of only a few hundred volumes were the rule. The libraries contained theological and biblical works, law books, classical texts, medical and historical works. Contemporary histories, written in monasteries, remain the best records of what happened during the period. In the thirteenth and fourteenth centuries, the rise of the new universities, the rediscovery of Aristotle (from Arabic), and the position of the friars as university teachers undermined the dominance of the monastic libraries. Although the university libraries were not open to undergraduates, the Franciscan friars opened their own libraries (some still survive in England), and they printed small, portable books which contrasted with the bulky illuminated manuscripts of the monasteries. The monastic libraries of England were destroyed in 1536–1540 (during Henry VIII's reign) and their books dispersed. In 1550, university libraries, schools, and churches were purged. Many treasures saved during the 1,000 years of the Dark Ages were lost.

Medieval libraries apparently were noisier than libraries today. Silent reading was not a common practice until the Renaissance. Until then, most people mumbled as they read. Carrels (small private enclosures) were invented so that readers would not disturb other people in the library with their noise.

32f-3
cont.

CRITERIA FOR EVALUATING SOURCES
FOR RESEARCH (continued)

CRITERIA FOR EVALUATING SOURCES
FOR RESEARCH (continued)

138

5. **Balanced tone:** Read a source critically (see 5d through 5h). If the tone is unbiased and if the reasoning is logical, the source is probably well balanced.

6. **Current:** Check that the information is up-to-date. Sometimes long-accepted information is replaced or modified by new research. Check indexes to journals or computerized databases to see if anything newer has come along.

As you evaluate sources, be aware of the difference between **primary** and **secondary sources.** Secondary sources report, describe, comment on, or analyze someone else's work. The information comes to you secondhand, influenced by the intermediary between you and the primary source. Secondary sources explain events, analyze information, and draw conclusions. Consulting secondary sources gives you the opportunity to understand what scholars and other experts know about your subject.

Primary sources include original works—novels, poems, short stories, autobiographies, diaries, firsthand reports of observations and of research, and so on. When you use primary sources, no one comes between you and your direct exposure to the author's own words. Also, you can create a primary source by conducting primary research such as a scientific experiment or an observation, survey, or interview of field research (see 32g).

32f-4

Determining your documentation style

The term **documentation style** refers to a specific system for providing information about each source you have used in a research paper. Documentation styles vary among the disciplines. The **Modern Language Association (MLA)** has developed a style often used in the humanities (see 33c). The **American Psychological Association (APA)** has developed a style often used in the social sciences (see 33d). **Chicago Manual (CM)** style is used in the humanities and other disciplines (see 33e), and **Council of Biology Editors (CBE)** style is used in the life and physical sciences and in mathematics (see 33f).

Before you start consulting sources, know what documentation style you need to use. (If your assignment does not specify a documentation style, ask your instructor which to use.) Then as you take notes on each source, you will know precisely what sorts of information your documentation style demands so you will write down the correct, full facts from the start.

Deciding whether to conduct field research 32g

Field research is primary research. It involves going "into the field" to observe, survey, interview, or engage in other activities. Field research yields original (primary) data. It is not the same as library research, in which you assimilate data and information that others have gathered. Information produced by your observations, questionnaires, or surveys is primary data. Unlike secondary data, primary data do not require documentation with these exceptions: Interviews (see 32q) and some performances involve other persons' words, which must be documented if you use them. The guidelines in Chapter 31 for documenting quotations, paraphrases, and summaries apply to spoken as well as written words.

If you intend to do field research, plan time to gather the original (primary) data or information you need as well as to analyze your gathered information and to synthesize (see sections 5b and 5f) it with any other material. Also allow extra time if you think you might want to interview an expert on your topic. First, you must gain enough control of your topic to learn who the authorities are and whom you might be able to interview. Then, you must have your research question in clear focus so that you can ask worthwhile questions of an expert during the interview. For detailed information about conducting an interview, see 32q.

If you want to survey a group of people on an issue your topic involves, allow time to write, reflect on, and revise a questionnaire. Test the questionnaire on a few people you do not intend to survey so that you can revise any ineffective or ambiguous questions. For detailed information on creating a questionnaire, see Chart 166 in section 38a.

If you need to get tickets to an event such as a concert or play, plan ahead. Be ready to suggest alternate dates if you can not get your first choice. If you need to visit a museum, plan the dates right away.

Field research often involves events that cannot be revisited, so expect to record detailed information during an observation or interview and to decide later whether to use the information. If conditions make it impossible to take notes (for example, darkness in a performance hall), as soon as you have an opportunity, find a quiet place and write down notes as fully as you can.

Decide what is important in your notes. Often, field research conditions make selective note-taking difficult, so go over your notes while your memory is fresh to highlight major categories of information. Again, take the opportunity to fill in details.

BACKGROUND

An innovative approach to research paper assignments is suggested by Jennie C. Cooper in "Writing for Real People: A Client-Centered Approach." Cooper describes her process of contacting local journalists, government officials, faculty members, and business leaders (among others) and asking them whether they had any research projects they would like her students to pursue. Evaluations of the project both by those to whom she submitted requests and by initially-reluctant students were overwhelmingly positive. (*College Composition and Communication*, 44:3, Oct. 1993, 386–388)

TEACHING TIP

Students need to know that librarians are experts who can (and will) assist the confused or lost researcher in finding helpful materials. You can make students aware of the help libraries provide by arranging a guided tour of your university's facilities, or it may be more appropriate to urge individual students to join regularly scheduled tours. In either case, novice researchers will be helped because knowledgeable people will provide information about how to go about finding the sources they need. Such tours are usually boring if they are an end in themselves, but when they serve a purpose, such as pointing out where students can find information for a particular assignment, they become vastly more interesting.

BACKGROUND

"Strategy for a Cross-Disciplinary Research Paper" (Marilyn D. Jensen, *Teaching English in the Two Year College*, 19:2, May 1992, 136–138) describes a process for original research that requires interviewing an expert before beginning library research.

32h

Using a search strategy for conducting research

A **search strategy** is an organized procedure that leads step-by-step from general to specific sources that can help you answer your research question (see 32a). A productive search allows you to compile a **working bibliography**. A working bibliography is a list of possible sources, which may or may not be useable for your paper or available to you at the time you do your research. A working bibliography is generally about twice as long as the list of sources that you actually refer to in your finished paper. If your assignment is to write an 8-to-10 page paper with a minimum of 10 to 12 sources, then your working bibliography should be at least 20 to 25 items.

When you search for sources according to a plan, you can avoid feeling either at a loss for useful sources or overwhelmed by a seemingly limitless choice of sources. When your search strategy is effective, it structures your work so that you do not mistake activity for productivity. Spending days in the library to locate anything even remotely related to a topic is as fruitless as it is exhausting. No two research processes are exactly alike, so expect to adapt the search strategy explained in this section through section 32q to your needs. As you work, be aware that search strategy is rarely as tidy as it seems it will be when described in this handbook.

Useful search strategies include the "expert" method, which starts with an expert in the field; the "chaining" method, which uses bibliographies from current articles to "chain" back to older sources; and the "layering" method, which layers information from general sources to increasingly specific sources. The layering method is especially useful for student researchers and for anyone researching in an unfamiliar field; it is discussed below and illustrated on the opposite page.

The **layering strategy** moves from general to specialized reference materials to uncover the most credible authors and sources in a specific subject area. Each time you locate a source about your topic, try to use it to find other sources, so that you layer the information from one source to another. You want the most credible authors and articles to help you answer your research question.

Moreover, having background information and possible author names from general and specialized reference articles makes your searches in the catalogs, indexes, and computer databases faster and more purposeful. Remember, you should complete this phase of the research project as soon as possible after the research paper assignment has been given. Discovering early in the process which sources you need allows you time to find those that are hard to locate, to use interlibrary loan, and to wait for others to return books that you want.

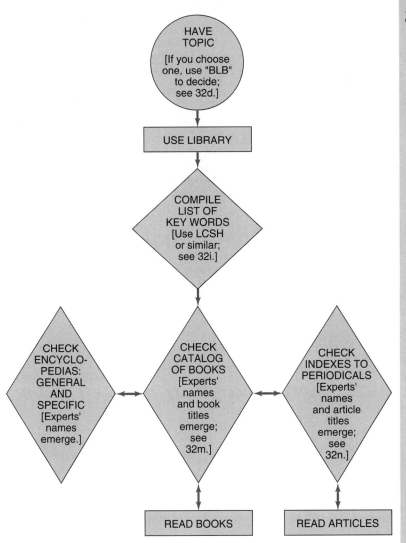

One Option for a Search Strategy: The Layering Method

BACKGROUND

Benjamin Franklin organized the Library Company of Philadelphia in 1731. It was the first American subscription library. Its original purpose was to provide ready access to books for members of the Junto Club, a public service group to which Franklin belonged. Franklin himself said that he spent time at the library almost daily, learning foreign languages or reading for general knowledge.

Until the founding of the Library Company of Philadelphia in 1731, there were few public libraries in the American colonies. The earliest one was the library of Harvard College, founded in 1638 with around 400 volumes bequeathed by John Harvard. Libraries were established at Yale and at William and Mary around 1700. In the Southern colonies the Reverend Thomas Bray (1656–1730), working by appointment of the Bishop of London as commissary of the Anglican Church, established parochial libraries. In 1876 a report on *Public Libraries in the United States* stated: "So far as is known, there were, in 1776, twenty-nine public libraries in the thirteen American colonies, and they numbered altogether 45,623 volumes; in the year 1800 the number of libraries had increased to forty-nine, and the number of volumes to about 80,000." The Library of Congress, which contains over 72 million pieces of material (among them 16.5 million books and 31 million manuscripts), was begun by Congress in 1800 with a budget of $5,000. Today it costs over $150 million per year to operate.

Using LCSH and compiling a list of headings or key words

The Library of Congress cataloging system is one widely used system for organizing a library's materials. The categories into which this system groups materials are laid out in the *Library of Congress Subject*

BACKGROUND

Elaine E. Whitaker describes a hands-on exercise that leads to students to understand both the practical and philosophical issues related to academic integrity. ("A Pedagogy to Address Plagiarism," *College Composition and Communication*, 44:4, Dec. 1993, 509–514)

QUOTATION ABOUT WRITING

If you copy from one author it's plagiarism. If you copy from two, it's research.
—Wilson Mizner

EXTRA EXERCISE A

To practice methods of preventing unconscious plagiarism, paraphrase or summarize the following paragraphs.

(1) Jane Austen, an English novelist, was born in 1775 the daughter of the Reverend George Austen, rector of Steventon and Deane, and Cassandra Leigh Austen. She was the youngest of seven children. Her childhood at Steventon was quiet, domestic, and moderately studious. Much of her spare time was spent in writing, mostly for her own amusement. In 1801 the family moved to Bath. After the death of her father in 1805, she settled in Chawton, where she remained until shortly before her death.

(2) Jane Austen began writing stories at an early age, and by the time she was twenty-two had completed one of her best known novels, *Pride and Prejudice*. Other works for which she is remembered include *Sense and Sensibility* and *Northanger Abbey*, which was published by her family after her death. The novels were not especially popular in Jane Austen's lifetime, but today are regarded as among the best novels in the English language. Although her people are neither intellectual nor heroic, and her plots are not elaborate, her skill at storytelling and drawing characters continues to please her readers.

➔

Headings (LCSH). LCSH is a multivolume catalog available online or in book form in the reference section of the library. This valuable resource is a catalog of subject headings only—not authors and titles. Beginning a search strategy with the LCSH can help you narrow your topic (see 32d). Also, in LCSH you find the words and library codes used to organize and classify relevant source materials. LCSH is one of the best places to look for the **search keys** that you need to look for other sources because many computer catalogs and indexes classify their contents by subject with LCSH terms. You may need specific LCSH words and phrases to access computerized information.

Amy Brown, whose research paper appears in Chapter 34, found the LCSH excerpt shown below when she looked up *nonverbal communication*. In addition to the subject headings, you can find related headings that can lead to additional sources marked with such codes as RT (related topic), BT (broader topic), and NT (narrower topic).

May Subdivide Geographically

indicates that a geographic location may follow the heading or subdivision

Nonverbal communication (Psychology)
(May Subd Geo)
Call number — *[BF637.N66]*
Used for — UF Body language
    Kinesics
Broader topic — BT Interpersonal communication
Narrower topic — NT Eye contact
    Gaze—Psychology aspects
    Hugging
    Personal space — Amy Brown selected the narrower topic of Personal Space for her research paper that appears in Chapter 34.

Excerpt from Library of Congress Subject Headings

Researchers use headings and key words to look up information. **Headings** are subject categories in books and periodicals. **Key words**, sometimes called descriptors or identifiers, identify subject categories in periodicals and electronic databases. Knowing how to locate headings and key words is central to the research process. The people who compile reference books, library catalog information, and indexes to periodicals cannot accommodate an infinite number of headings, so they group information into categories and then base the retrieval systems on key terms.

As you search for sources, you have to compile a list of the headings and key words that will lead you to books and articles on your topic. For example, the topic *nuclear energy* is identified with various headings or key words: *energy, nuclear; atomic energy; energy, atomic; nuclear power; power, nuclear;* and so on. You have to "break the code" to figure out what words identify the category you are seeking in each source. As you work on your research, keep an ongoing list in your research log of headings and key words that relate to your topic. Then whenever you approach a new source, you can use it efficiently.

Understanding how to take notes

32j

Your research process includes taking notes as you consult sources. Notetaking has two phases. First, you write preliminary bibliography and summary cards when you think you have located a useful source for your working bibliography. Second, you write content notes once you have moved from searching to reading your selected sources carefully.

Notetaking is a decision-making process. The criteria in Chart 138 in 32f can help you decide if a particular source is worth notetaking—or photocopying, or printing out from the computer. Even if the source does not appear to be useful, note it in your research log with the title, author, date, and call number. Add a message to yourself about why you rejected it. What seems useless one day might have potential if you revise the focus of your paper or slightly reshape your topic.

Taking preliminary notes

32j-1

As you find useable sources, write bibliography cards for them immediately while you have each source in front of you (see 33b). For greatest efficiency, record the information exactly as it will be listed in your finished paper in the documentation style that your instructor has specified (see 32f-4). Doing this can save endless hours of grief later on, because when you compile the list of sources you have referred to in your paper, you have only to put the cards in alphabetical order and type directly from them.

Also, each time you find a useful source, at the bottom of its bibliography card summarize it briefly according to the criteria for evaluating sources in Chart 138. An evaluation might read: "This article is by one of the most credible authors writing about my subject" or "Although this book is old, it has good background information and gives good definitions and interesting historical data" or "This article was published only two months ago—it appeared in a scholarly journal and answers my research question perfectly!" Such evaluative statements can provide direction later for your reading and for further notetaking.

32j-2

Taking content notes

In content notes, record information and ideas that relate specifically to your paper. Also, record any understanding you have gained from your readings, using a different color ink so you do not confuse an author's ideas with yours (also see 5e-2). Although researchers vary in the approaches and methods they use in taking content notes, they agree that it is essential to have a reliable system for synthesizing information. Use your critical reading skills (see 5d) to sort major information from minor information as it relates to your topic.

One option is to decide to take content notes as you go along, right after making a bibliography card for a source and before you try to locate another source. By the time you have worked through the entire layering strategy, you have isolated useable sources, created a working bibliography, and completed a major part of your reading and notetaking.

Another option is to use the layering strategy as a survey process to find out what is available on a particular subject before you commit to extensive reading and notetaking. For this process, set aside two to three hours to go through all the collections on a given subject, writing data and information in your research log and creating an index of available materials on your topic. If you feel comfortable in the early stages of searching that your topic is going to work, you can begin to photocopy useful articles and make preliminary notecards as you go along. Also, keep an author list and a title list to look for specific authors and sources in the catalogs and periodical indexes. The goals for this first block of time in the library are to have a complete working bibliography and perhaps a few articles and books and to know which sources, if any, you need to get through interlibrary loan or from a community library. Researching this way, you start compiling content notes only after the library search is almost complete.

Whatever method works best for you, remember that notetaking has a threefold purpose: first, to help you understand and narrow your topic; second, to find answers to your research question; and third, to help you guard against plagiarism. The third matter is so important that Chapter 31 is devoted to **avoiding plagiarism** and to the skills of quoting, paraphrasing, and summarizing. To **plagiarize** is to steal someone else's words and pass them off as your own. To avoid the risk of plagiarism, take notes in such a way that you will always be able to tell from your notes what is yours and what belongs to a source. You might want to use one color ink for your thoughts and another color ink for words that you take from sources in the form of quotations, paraphrases, or summaries.

Use index cards for content notes. In contrast to pages in a notebook, cards provide flexibility for organizing material to use in writing your paper. Never put notes from more than one source on the same index card. If your notes on a source require more than one index card, number the cards sequentially. Using such labels as "1 of 2" for the first card on a source and "2 of 2" for the second card on that same source helps you to work efficiently from your content notecards. If you take notes on more than one idea or topic from a particular source, start a new card for each new area of information. Put a heading on each index card that shows a precise link to one of your bibliographic cards (see section 33b). Include in your content notes the source's title and the number of the page or pages from which you are taking notes. Also, clearly identify the type of note on the card: quotation, paraphrase, or summary. A summary note card written by Amy Brown, the student whose paper is in Chapter 34, is shown below.

> Hall and Hall, *Understanding*, p. 39
> *Cultural variations in amounts of touching*
>
> Summary: Germans keep eye contact but avoid any deliberate or unintentional touching.

Note Card Summarizing a Source

Sommer p. 26

The best way to learn the location of invisible boundaries is to keep walking until somebody complains. Personal space refers to an area with invisible boundaries surrounding a person's body into which intruders may not come. [Like the porcupines in Schopenhauer's fable, people like to be close enough to obtain warmth and comradeship but far enough away to avoid pricking one another. Personal space ~~is not necessarily spherical in shape, nor does it extend equally in all directions. (People are able to tolerate closer presence of a stranger at their sides than directly in front.)~~ It has been likened to a snail shell, a soap bubble, an aura, and "breathing room."] There are major differences between cultures in the distances that people maintain–Englishmen keep further apart than Frenchmen or South Americans. Reports

I'll paraphrase this

I'll quote this with ellipses

Photocopy of Source, with Annotations

BACKGROUND

The Nuremberg Chronicle (1493) was the world's first encyclopedia. Its three volumes were written by one man, Hartmann Schedel, using his extensive personal library for most of his research. Schedel did overlook one event, though: Columbus's discovery of the New World one year earlier.

BACKGROUND

Denis Diderot spent over twenty years writing and editing his *Encyclopédie*. In twenty-eight volumes, he and famous contributors, such as Rousseau and Voltaire, collected all the scientific thinking of the Age of Reason. The project began as a commission from a French publisher to translate a one-volume British encyclopedia into French. Diderot earned about $12 a week while working on the encyclopedia. When the project was complete, he was forced to sell his library in order to provide his daughter with a dowry. Catherine II, Empress of Russia, paid him $5,000—and also allowed him access to the books for the rest of his life.

32j-2
cont.

Photocopying can save you time, and having the original copy of articles or book chapters in your research file can be helpful. For instance, you might have paraphrased in your notes and then revised what you have said in later drafts of your paper. Having the original source allows you to check how close your revised comments are to the actual writing, and whether you have inadvertently plagiarized by restating the information. Also, some instructors require you to submit copies of any material you have used in your research. Be sure each photocopied source is labeled with the author's name and other bibliographic information.

Many students try to substitute underlining and annotating on photocopied articles for more detailed notetaking on notecards, only to find that synthesizing the material into their research papers at the drafting stage is far more difficult without paraphrases and summaries to work with. Taking short cuts on notetaking also risks inadvertent plagiarism.

32k   **Using general reference works**

The general reference collection is the starting point for many research studies. The works in this collection are interdisciplinary; they provide basic summaries on vast amounts of information. This collection is also one of the best places to learn the search key words that are so critical to the successful use of the modern library. You will be hearing a great deal about "search keys," also called "key words," as we work through the different library collections.

Most widely used reference works are available in computerized CD-ROM versions. Many libraries give students access to computer-based dictionaries, thesauruses, encyclopedias, bibliographies, and even atlases. Almanacs and statistical works on computer often are kept more up-to-date than their printed counterparts, and can often present information in several different ways.

General Encyclopedias

General encyclopedia articles can help you get started but usually are not suitable as major sources for college-level papers. Articles in general encyclopedias such as *Encyclopaedia Britannica* summarize information about a wide variety of subjects. The articles can give you background information and authors' names. General encyclopedias are not the place to look for information on recent events or current research, although sometimes controversies about the field are summarized. Many articles end with a brief bibliography of major works on the subject, which may lead you to the authors' names and their most current works. To locate the information, start with the Index volume, which will give you volume and page numbers related to your topic. The letters "bib" at the end of an index listing means that article contains a bibliography and so might be worth checking. If you cannot find what you are looking for, try alternate headings or key words.

One-volume general encyclopedias, such as *The New Columbia Encyclopedia* or the *Random House Encyclopedia*, may cover subjects very briefly. For college-level work these sources are useful only for you to see whether a general subject area interests you enough for further research.

Almanacs, Yearbooks, Fact Books

Almanacs—books such as *The World Almanac and Book of Fact*—briefly present a year's events and data in government, politics, sports, economics, demographics, and many other categories. *Facts on File* covers world events in a weekly digest and in an annual one-volume Yearbook.

The *Statistical Abstract of the United States* contains a wealth of data about the United States. *Demographic Yearbook* and *United Nations Statistical Yearbook* carry worldwide data. (Other specialized yearbooks and handbooks are named in 32l.) These reference books provide additional resources for key word lists as well as give statistical data that can verify or support the problem you may be investigating.

Atlases

Atlases contain maps—and remember that seas and skies and even other planets have been mapped. These comprehensive sources, many of which have been computerized, contain much geographic information: topography, climates, populations, migrations, natural resources, crops, and so on.

Dictionaries

Dictionaries define words and terms (see Chapter 20).In addition to general dictionaries, specialized dictionaries exist in many academic disciplines to define words and phrases specific to a field (see 32l). Many dictionaries are available on computer.

Biographical Reference Works

Biographical reference books give brief factual information about many famous people. They are good places to find dates and brief listings of major events or accomplishments in noted people's lives. (Do not confuse these works with full-length biographies or bestseller accounts about noted people.) Various *Who's Who* series cover noteworthy people. *Current Biography: Who's News and Why* is published

BACKGROUND

The Guinness Book of Records was founded as a result of the curiosity of Sir Hugh Beaver, the managing director of Arthur Guinness, Son and Co., Ltd. One day in 1954, Sir Hugh went bird hunting. He shot at some plovers—and missed. He started wondering if plovers were the fastest game birds, and he tried to satisfy his curiosity in the encyclopedia. Neither it nor any other reference work had the answer.

As a result, Sir Hugh decided that people needed a book that would accurately list record sizes, speeds, and durations. His plan was to have a copy of the book in every pub that sold Guinness stout, as an aid in settling bets. He set about finding someone to author such a book, and one of his executives recommended the McWhirter brothers. Trivia history was made.

Norris and Ross McWhirter, identical twin sons of a newspaper writer, had grown up around newspapers, magazines, and reference books. Their childhood hobby had been to collect information of the very type Sir Hugh was seeking. They had frequently found contradictions in their sources, and so as adults they had founded a company to verify these statistics and to "supply facts and figures to newspapers, yearbooks, encyclopedias, and advertisers."

Four months after Sir Hugh had interviewed them, the McWhirters published the first book in the series. The 198-page bet-settler became England's number one nonfiction best-seller in only four months. Immediately, readers began submitting their own fantastic facts. The McWhirters collected and checked these submissions, and soon an updated volume was on the way. Norris and Ross McWhirter acted as coeditors until 1975.

BACKGROUND

Libraries are as old as recorded history. In fact, they were the repository of the records of past civilizations. In what was ancient Mesopotamia, for example, temples and princely houses have been excavated that held thousands of clay tablets inscribed with epic poems, liturgic and magic texts, and commercial records. The palace of Ashurbanipal, who reigned from 668–633 B.C. in Nineveh, has provided tablets bearing stamps of ownership, catchwords, and sometimes source and place indications, thereby testifying to the existence of a well-developed cataloging system. In Egypt every temple had its library and school. Although the Egyptian collections were made on papyrus (and thus have been found mostly in graves and tombs rather than in temples), the content was similar. Much has been lost, but records often remain. In the temple at Edfu, for instance, a full catalogue of all the hieratical works the library contained was incised on the walls, bearing witness to what was once there.

monthly, with six-month and annual cumulative editions. *Dictionary of American Biography* and *Webster's Biographical Dictionary* are also widely available. These sources, as well as specialized biographical reference works on famous people in various fields, also list Nobel Peace Prize and Pulitzer Prize winners.

Because of the many different biographical sources, you may want to ask a librarian for assistance in locating biographical references.

Bibliographies

Bibliographies list books. *Books in Print* lists all books that are available through their publishers and sometimes other sources in the United States. This multivolume work classifies its entries by author name, title, and general subject headings, but it does not describe a book's content.

The *Book Review Digest* excerpts book reviews that have appeared in major newspapers and magazines. These excerpts of critics' opinions can help you evaluate a source (see 32f-3). This digest is published every year. The reviews appear in the volume that corresponds either to the year a book was published or to the one immediately following. The *Book Review Index* lists where reviews have appeared but does not carry the actual reviews. Other book reviews are available in specialized areas, and some book reviews are available as computerized sources.

Consulting specialized bibliographies—ones that list many books on a particular subject—can be very helpful in your research process (see 32l). Annotated or critical bibliographies describe and evaluate the works that they list and are therefore especially useful.

Using specialized reference works

Specialized or subject encyclopedias, which provide more authoritative and specific information than general reference works, are usually appropriate for college-level research. As you work with the layering strategy (see 32h) in your search for sources, you will soon need to become more focused in your research. The specialized reference collection can assist you at this point. It is an area many students overlook in their preliminary searches Specialized encyclopedia usually contain short summaries that introduce you to the controversies, the experts, and the key words for searching that are specific to your topic. Be sure to look for authors' names in the article or in the bibliography so that you can begin to accumulate a list of credible authors. Those names become invaluable as you search book and periodical catalogs. You may wish to photocopy articles you find, and in particular, any bibliographies that are listed. You will want to start your notetaking process with these sources. Here are selected titles of some of the more commonly used specialized materials categorized by subject area.

BUSINESS AND ECONOMICS

A Dictionary of Economics
Encyclopedia of Advertising
Encyclopedia of Banking and Finance
Handbook of Modern Marketing

FINE ARTS

Crowells' Handbook of World Opera
International Cyclopedia of Music and Musicians
The New Grove Dictionary of Music and Musicians
Oxford Companion to Art

HISTORY

Dictionary of American Biography
Encyclopedia of American History
An Encyclopedia of World History
New Cambridge Modern History

LITERATURE

Cassell's Encyclopedia of World Literature
Dictionary of Literary Biography
A Dictionary of Literary Terms
MLA International Bibliography of Books and Articles on the Modern Languages and Literature
The Oxford Companion to American Literature
The Oxford Companion to English Literature

PHILOSOPHY AND RELIGION

Dictionary of the Bible
Eastern Definitions: A Short Encyclopedia of Religions of the Orient
Encyclopedia of Philosophy
Encyclopedia of Religion

POLITICAL SCIENCE

Foreign Affairs Bibliography
Political Handbook and Atlas of the World
Political Science Bibliographies

BACKGROUND

The first general index of magazine articles was *Poole's Index of Periodical Literature*, which lists articles from the years 1802 through 1906 and is still a valuable reference tool. The idea for *Poole's Index* originated in the 1840s when a college student from Yale, William Frederick Poole, noticed that the many periodicals in the Yale library were going unused because people could not find the articles they wanted except by going through the journals one by one. Poole decided to scan the periodicals himself, compile a list of articles, and organize the list under subject headings. At first he wrote out a single copy which he shared with others, but the demand for the list was so great that Poole published it in 1848. For many years Poole updated and expanded the index himself, until 1876, when he asked the American Library Association to sponsor the index and assign fifty librarians from across the United States to the project. Receiving no pay, each librarian went through a list of assigned magazines to record and classify the articles and then sent this information to Poole for the next volume of the index.

SCIENCE AND TECHNOLOGY
Encyclopedia of Chemistry
Encyclopedia of Computer Science and Technology
Encyclopedia of Physics
The Encyclopedia of the Biological Sciences
The Larousse Encyclopedia of Animal Life
The McGraw-Hill Encyclopedia of Science and Technology

SOCIAL SCIENCES
Dictionary of Anthropology
Dictionary of Education
Encyclopedia of Psychology
International Encyclopedia of the Social Sciences

FILM, TELEVISION, THEATER
International Encyclopedia of Film
International Television Almanac
The Oxford Companion to the Theatre

! ❖ ALERTS: (1) Very specific one-volume works are available that have not been listed here. For example, under Social Science you would find the *Encyclopedia of Divorce, Encyclopedia of Aging,* or *The Encyclopedic Dictionary of Psychology.* (2) New specialized reference works are published throughout the year. Find the call number for your subject area and browse the collection to see what special references are available in your own library. ❖

BACKGROUND
Under the strong influence of the Renaissance, Italy became the center of book collecting in the Western world. Florence was one of the major trading cities, because of the support of the princes, who served as patrons to scholars who searched for lost treasures of Greek and Latin literature. The scholars' efforts were in large measure responsible for transmitting classical learning to a new age through the works they found, translated, recopied, and sold. Among the princes of that time, Cosimo de Medici (1389–1464) is especially notable for building the Medici Library, the first public library in Europe to have been opened since the Romans. The Medicis invested $15 million from 1434 to 1469, collecting and commissioning copies of manuscripts. The collection acquired under their patronage, especially that of Cosimo and his successor, Lorenzo the Magnificent (1449–1492), are now housed in the Laurentian and National libraries of Florence.

32m

Using a library's book catalog

A book catalog is a list of all the books in a library. Years ago, all libraries used a card catalog to list all their holdings. Then some libraries switched to microfiched catalogs. Today, most libraries have computerized the catalog.

An online catalog typically can be accessed in three ways: by author, by title, and by subject. The layering strategy helps you find specific author's names and titles to use in an online catalog. To use the subject listings, you must use the correct words as search keys. Usually, these are the ones listed in the LCSH (Library of Congress Subject Headings). Many students become discouraged when they type in a topic on a computerized catalog only to have "nothing on this subject" appear on the computer screen. For instance, if you type "ghost towns" into the computer, the screen might read "no works found." Under "ghosts towns," the LCSH says "see Cities and Towns: Ruined and Extinct." Unless you use the specific phrase a topic is classified under in the system, you might not be able to access the information you are looking for. If you are having difficulty in locating key words, ask a reference librarian to help you.

Many libraries are connected electronically to other libraries' catalogs, giving you access to the holdings of those libraries. Some states link all their state colleges and universities into one system and, through the Internet, connect to colleges and universities outside their state systems. If you need materials not available in your own library, accessing a network can tell you where to find them. Librarians can request materials from other libraries through interlibrary loan.

Whether a catalog is on cards, microfiche, or computer, the same information is offered. Catalog information is organized alphabetically in three categories: authors' names, book titles, and subjects. In some libraries, authors and titles are in one file, subjects in another. In other libraries, the three types of information are filed together.

Library of Congress Catalog Cards

32m
cont.

Each card in the card catalog or on microfiche contains much useful information. The call number is most important. Be sure to copy it down exactly as it appears, with all numbers, letters, and decimal points. The call number tells where the book is located in the stacks. If you are researching in a library with open stacks (you can go where books are shelved), the call number leads you to the area in the library where all books on the same subject can be found. Being there can help you search for sources, even though some books might have been checked out and other books might be at the reserve desk. The call number is also crucial in a library with closed stacks, where, to get a book, you must fill in a call slip, hand it in at the call desk, and wait for the book to arrive. If you fill in the wrong number or an incomplete number, your wait will be in vain. No matter what medium is used for the book catalog, write down all call number information on your preliminary notecards to make it easier to locate your books and periodicals.

Tracings are an important feature of card-catalog cards. Tracings are words, numbered and in fine print below a book's publication data, that give other headings used to classify information related to the subject of the card. Tracings are valuable hints for other topics to look up in the subject file of the card catalog when you want to find more about a subject. As you find tracings, be sure to add them to your list of headings and key words (see 32i).

see 32i

32n

Using periodicals

Periodicals are magazines and journals published at set periods during a year. The key to using periodicals is to locate **indexes to periodicals**. These indexes list articles written between the dates listed on the cover on each edition. Many indexes are kept up-to-date with supplements between editions. Some but not all indexes include abstracts, which are brief summaries of each article. Classification systems vary among indexes, so take time to learn how to decipher the codes and abbreviations in the index that you need. Most indexes include a guide for readers in the front or back of each volume and supplement, and the guide is usually also in a computerized database, if available. As you learn to use an index, update your list of headings and key words (see 32i) for future reference.

see 32i

Indexes are packaged in a variety of ways. Some indexes are in yearly bound volumes and interim paperback updates. Depending on the systems at your library, some indexes may be on microfilm or microfiche. These may have to be accessed through computer terminals. Before you start using periodicals, get to know the systems at your library.

Almost all periodical indexes are available on computerized databases, either locally on CD-ROM or through remote access via the Internet. Most of the systems have different access methods. To access the computer indexes, it is essential to have the specific key words for your topic. A list of author names can also be useful.

Using general indexes to periodicals

General indexes list articles in magazines and newspapers. Headings and key words on the same subject vary among indexes, so think of every possible way to look up the information you seek. Large libraries have many general indexes, among them these two major ones:

- The *New York Times Index* catalogs all articles that have been printed in this encyclopedic newspaper since 1851. Supplements are published every two weeks in paperbound volumes. The supplements are organized into volumes (bound, in computerized databases, or on microfilm) periodically.

- The *Readers' Guide to Periodical Literature* is the most widely used index to over 100 magazines and journals for general (rather than specialized) readers. Paperback supplements are published every two weeks. These supplements are organized into volumes (bound, in computerized databases, or on microfilm) periodically. This index does not include scholarly journals, so its uses are often very limited for college-level research. It can be useful for getting a broad overview and for thinking of ways to narrow a subject. An entry from *Readers' Guide* showing listings for Communication, the subject of Amy Brown's research paper assignment, appears below.

COMMUNICATION, Nonverbal ————————— Subject heading
Does your body *parle francais?*/French body —— Title of article
language; teaching methods of (L. Wylie)pors —— Author
(Time)113:107 + My 14 '79 ———————— Periodical title
Watching your every move: what you reveal
about yourself without saying a word. J. Marks.
Teen(23:36 + Jl '79)———————————— Vol. 23, p. 36 +, July 1979
When tensions talk—listen! Subtle motion tells a
story. E. Hamilton.(por)Sci Digest 85:30–2 + Ap
'79 ——————————————————— Has portrait
Women smile less for success; study of job success
by Wendy McKenna and Florence Denmark.
M. B. Parlee, Psychol Today 12:16 Mr '79
   See also
Eye—Movements
Gesture ———————————————— Related subject
Sign language   headings
Touch

Annotated Excerpt from *Readers' Guide to Periodical Literature*

TEACHING TIP
Donnelyn Curtis and Stephen A. Bernhardt ("Keywords, Titles, Abstracts, and Online Searches: Implications for Technical Writing," *Technical Writing Teacher* [1991]: 142–161) write that a student who knows the title of one helpful book or article for his or her research paper can employ a popular "backdoor approach" (151) that librarians often use with difficult subjects. The database entry for that title will provide the student with subject headings that should be fruitful key terms for the search. Curtis and Bernhardt also recommend that students consult a thesaurus for alternative terms.

BACKGROUND
Christine Neuwirth reviews Myron C. Tuman's *Literacy Online: The Promise (and Peril) of Reading and Writing with Computers*, a collection of essays based on the premise that computer technology is likely to revolutionize literacy. Tuman suggests that "computers will reshape not just how we read and write, and, by extension, how we teach these skills, but our very understanding of basic terms such as *reading, writing,* and *text.*" (*College Composition and Communication*, 44:1, Feb. 1993, 404–406)

BACKGROUND

According to Curtis and Bernhardt, computers and the information explosion are changing the nature of indexing. Books and articles increasingly are indexed by title and keywords instead of by subject. Subject indexing requires readers to scan and classify each item for the index and is a slower, more expensive process than indexing by title and keywords, which can be done by computers. The process of having readers scan and classify makes it difficult and more expensive for indexes to adjust to the present rapid increase in journals and the development of new subject areas. Curtis and Bernhardt argue that the new emphasis on titles and keywords in indexes and computer searches means that writing teachers and students need to give more attention to composing titles.

QUOTATION ABOUT WRITING

Adam was the only man who, when he said a good thing, knew that nobody had said it before him.

—Mark Twain

QUOTATION ABOUT WRITING

Plagiarists are always suspicious of being stolen from.

—Samuel Taylor Coleridge

32n-1
cont.

Computerized general indexes include the *Academic Abstracts* and *Info-trac*. Although they sometimes list more scholarly articles and journals, the majority of these listings serve broad general subjects. *Academic Abstracts* might be compared to a computerized version of *Reader's Guide*. These indexes will print out the information listed on the screen. Some articles are available from the computer in whole text form.

32n-2

Using specialized indexes to periodicals

Specialized indexes are much more helpful for most college-level research than are general indexes (see 32n-1). Specialized indexes help a researcher become a specialist in a particular topic. These indexes list articles published in academic and professional periodicals. Many specialized indexes carry an abstract (a summary) of each listed article.

Depending on their resources, libraries have many or few specialized indexes in book form and in paperback supplements. Some libraries make available a computerized database that includes many different, specialized indexes. Specialized indexes are usually classified under the same subject headings as the specialized encyclopedia. In larger libraries, both print and computer indexes will be located on the floors with other materials for that subject area. Commonly available specialized indexes (some on CD-ROM or online) include:

> *Business and Economics*
> *Business Periodicals Index*
> *ABI-Inform*
> *Humanities and Fine Arts*
> *Art Index*
> *Essay and General Literature Index*
> *Humanities Index*
> *MLA International Bibliography of Books and Articles in the Modern Languages and Literatures*
> *Music Index*
> *Medicine and Nursing*
> *Cum Index of Nursing and Allied Health Lit (CINAHL)*
> *Medline* (computer only)
> *Religion and History*
> *Religious Index*
> *Historical Abstracts*
> *America: History and Life*

Social Science

Education Index

Psychological Abstracts

Social Science Index

PAIS (Public Affairs Information Service)

Science and Technology

General Science Index

Applied Science and Technology Index

Biological Abstracts

Biological and Agricultural Index

Here is an entry from the *Humanities Index* that Amy Brown used in her research for the paper in Chapter 34. The abbreviations have the same meaning as those in the excerpt from the *Reader's Guide to Periodical Literature*. Entries from the computerized edition of the *Humanities Index* will appear a little different on the screen, but the information given will be similar.

> Nonverbal communication
> > *See also*
> > Expression
> > Gesture
> Background to kinesics. R. L., Birdwhistell. *Etc* 40:352-61
> > Fall '83
> Mediated interpersonal communication: toward a new
> > typology. R. Cathcart and G. Gumpert. *QJ Speech*
> > 69:267-77 Ag '83

Excerpt from *Humanities Index*

Few libraries subscribe to all the periodicals that are listed in these specialized indexes. Most libraries list the periodicals they carry; some libraries list the titles of their magazines on their computer catalog under the title access key. Consult those lists to find out if your library has the magazine or journal you are looking for.

Although it may not be possible to locate every article you find listed in the indexes, Internet and interlibrary loan systems allow you to request articles from other locations. Check your library to see what services are available. Many colleges have reciprocal agreements to allow students access to each other's libraries. Find out what major colleges and universities are in your area.

Other places to look include the many community libraries and professional agencies that subscribe to assorted periodicals. Medical centers often have small libraries and reading rooms for their doctors

---

and nurses. Some permit students to use their facilities. When you know a book or periodical is just what you need to pull your paper together, take the time to try to find it. The longer you give yourself to complete the process, the more opportunity there will be for tracking down good sources.

32o

Using electronic resources

32o-1

Knowing about online and CD-ROM databases

Electronic databases include bibliographic files of articles, reports, and—less often—books. Each item in these databases provides information about title, author, and publisher. If a database catalogs articles from scholarly journals, the entry might also provide an abstract (a summary) of the material. Once you locate an entry that seems promising for your research, however, you must then track down the source itself. Some databases, including ERIC and NEWSBANK, provide the full texts of cited articles on microfiche. With such a system, each citation contains an abstract as well as a catalog number (for example, ERIC ED 139 580) which allows you to look up the microfiche—ask a librarian where this is stored—that contains the entire article. ERIC is also online now.

Key words are essential for searching electronic databases, some of which contain as many as 100 million references. You must, therefore, choose which databases will be most helpful before you can begin to search. The DIALOG Information System, one of the largest databases, is a compilation of over 200 smaller databases likely in the humanities, the social sciences, business, science and technology, medicine, economics, and current events. Restrict your search to one database at a time. A reference librarian usually can help you choose the databases best suited to your research, but first you must be able to provide a specific, not vague, description of your research.

Electronic databases may be online (such as DIALOG) or on CD-ROM. CD-ROM is cheaper and easier to use—generally an inexperienced user may follow simple on-screen instructions to search for entries. In contrast, online systems often must be used by trained librarians. Online databases require the library to pay a fee for the time used and the number of entries requested, and your library may pass the fee on to you when you use such a system. Find out whether the service is free for students and, if not, what the charge is. (Some charges are a dollar or more per entry). Narrowing your search with key words is important to avoid having to pay for a list of useless sources.

Recently, many databases previously available only online have been transferred to CD-ROM. The most popular databases on the DIALOG system, (such as the business, psychology, and scientific databases) are now available in this format. CD-ROM databases tend to be smaller than those online and are updated less frequently.

Amy Brown, the student who wrote the research paper in Chapter 34, used a CD-ROM database to search for sources. After consulting a librarian and determining which specific databases were available at her college library, she decided to use the PsychLIT database (a computerized version of *Psychological Abstracts*, which includes about a dozen major journals related to psychology). With the help of a librarian, Brown chose key words such as *cross cultural differences*, *social perception*, and *labor force*. She combined these words with others to come up with a list of citations that she could manage to look up in a reasonable amount of time. One of those she found is shown on page 568; its numbered parts are explained on page 569. In addition to the specific databases Amy Brown was able to access, many traditional print indexes such as the *Wilson Indexes for Humanities, Social Science, and Business* are now available in electronic forms.

Knowing about the Internet

32o-2

The **Internet** is a network of networks linking computers at universities, research centers, government facilities, and businesses around the world. People with personal computers, modems, and a connecting service can also access the Internet. Nicknamed "the information highway," the Internet contains vast numbers of databases that offer a wide variety of information, from company reports, statistical information, and copies of speeches to treaties and government documents. **Gophers** are menus of databases that can be accessed through the Internet. As a researcher, you can use gopher menus to do subject searches.

Also, the Internet enables e-mail, bulletin boards, and other public access between individuals. It contains numerous discussion groups and newsgroups that you can browse or query.

The **World Wide Web** is another Internet function connecting computers around the world. It has the capability to transmit graphics and other images as well as text.

Most important, the Internet is developing and changing very quickly. If you are interested in exploring this resource, ask a reference librarian for assistance. Many colleges and universities offer training courses on how to navigate the Internet, and dozens of books have been published about getting into and around it. This network can be your path into a vast world of electronic information.

QUOTATION ABOUT RESEARCH

Research is the ability to investigate systematically and truly all that comes under your observation in life.
—Marcus Aurelius

QUOTATION ABOUT RESEARCH

. . . You should always collect more material than you will eventually use. Every article is strong in proportion to the surplus of details from which you can choose the few that will serve you best—if you don't go on gathering facts forever. At some point you must decide to stop researching and start writing.
—William Zinsser, *On Writing Well*

QUOTATION ABOUT RESEARCH

The process of doing research is not dissimilar from the process of writing anything else. It starts with a question, a problem, a topic which the writer examines, probes, and analyzes. The difference is that the writer is not alone in this game. When doing research, the writer participates with others who have also been taken with the subject.
—Ann Sullivan

TEACHING TIP

Since the processes of drafting and revising vary from one writer to another, students may gain insight into their own processes by interviewing one another about how they approach these stages of writing a research paper. They can base their interviews on the following questions.

1. Do you organize your note cards in piles?

2. Do you work with your notes in front of you?

3. Do you write the first draft without referring to your note cards?

4. Is your first draft a complete draft?

5. When do you insert parenthetical references?

6. Is your first draft composed slowly and carefully? Or quickly and sketchily?

7. Do you proceed immediately to a second draft, or do you let some time elapse between drafting and revising?

8. Do you show your work to other people for responses and suggestions?

(1) Silver Platter   2.01   (2) PsycLIT Disc 2 (1/83   9/91)
  TI   DOCUMENT TITLE:Culture and the Self: Implications for cognition, emotion, and motivation.
  AU   AUTHOR(S) : Marcus, Hazel R., Kitayamo, Shinobu
  IN   INSTITUTIONAL AFFILIATION OF FIRST AUTHOR: U Michigan, Research Ctr for Group Dynamics, Ann Arbor, US
(3) JN   JOURNAL NAME: PSYCHOLOGICAL REVIEW, 1991 Apr Vol 88(2)   224 253
(4) CC   CODEN: PORVAX
(5) IS   ISSN:0033295X
  LA   LANGUAGE: English
  PY   PUBLICATION YEAR : 1991
(6) AB   ABSTRACT: People in different cultures have strikingly different construals of the self, of others, and of the interdependence of the 2. These construals can influence, and in many cases determine, the very nature of the individual experience, including cognition, emotion, and motivation. Many Asian cultures have distinct conceptions of individuality that insist on the fundamental relatedness of individuals to each other. The emphasis is on attending to others, fitting in, and harmonious interdependence with them. American culture neither assumes nor values such overt connectedness among individuals. In contrast, individuals seek to maintain that independence from others by attending to the self and by discovering and expressing their unique inner attributes. As proposed herein, these construals are even more powerful than previously imagined. Theories of the self from both psychology and anthropology are integrated to define in detail the difference between a construal of the self as independent and a construal of the self as interdependent. Each of these divergent construals should have a set of specific consequences for cognition, emotion, and motivation; these consequences are proposed and relevant empirical literature is reviewed. (PsycLIT Database Copyright 1991 American Psychological Assn, all rights reserved)
(7) KP   KEY PHRASE:cultural construals of self and others; individual experience and cognition and emotion and motivation
(8) DE   DESCRIPTORS:CROSS CULTURAL DIFFERENCES; SELF PERCEPTION; SOCIAL PECEPTION; COGNITION; EMOTIONAL STATES; LIFE EXPERIENCES; MOTIVATION
(9) CC   CLASSIFICATION CODE(S):   2830
(10) PO   POPULATION: Human
(11) UD   UPDATE CODE: 9109
(12) AN   PSYC ABS. VOL. AND ABS. NO.: 78   23878
(13) JC   JOURNAL CODE: 1838

A CD—ROM Database Entry

32p

Using the government documents collection

     United States government publications are available in astounding variety. Information is available on population figures, weather patterns, agriculture, national parks, education, welfare, and many other topics. Government document collections are available in reference libraries throughout the country, and these collections are often made available to the public even in libraries whose other collections are restricted. Ask your reference librarian if your library contains government publications; and if not, ask what library nearest you houses government documents.

① The brand name of the CD ROM system. Another common name is DIALOG OnDisc.

② The name of the database. The dates in parentheses list the earliest and latest dates covered on the disk.

③ The journal name, date, and volume, and inclusive page numbers for the full text of the article.

④ Numerical codes for the journal in which the article appears.

⑤ The journal's standard identification number.

⑥ The abstract of the article. An abstract provides just enough information to let a researcher decide whether to read the article itself. As a responsible researcher, you should always read an article yourself, quoting from it or paraphrasing or summarizing it in your own words, rather than quoting an abstract of the article.

⑦ The key phrases that very briefly sum up what the article is about and that can be very useful for scanning through large numbers of database entries for useful material.

⑧ The descriptors, or subject words under which the entry is listed, like subject cards in a card catalog. The underlined descriptors cross-cultural differences and self-perception are the words that were entered to start the search that found this entry.

⑨ A code for the subject of the article.

⑩ The group to which the article applies. This article is about humans in general. Other articles may be about more specific groups, such as Americans, dysfunctional families, paranoid schizophrenics, etc.

⑪ A code for when this article was added to the database.

⑫ The volume and abstract number where this entry can be found in the print version of Psychological Abstracts.

⑬ Numerical codes for the journal in which the article appears.

A Key for the CD—ROM Database Entry

You can order government publications that are not available to you through your library system by consulting one of the directories below. Many of these publications are now also available on either computer databases or CD-ROM. Using a computer will eliminate the mailing time and can provide you with the most current information available. Ask a reference librarian if the publications you need are accessible by computer.

- The *Monthly Catalog of United States Government Publications* is an up-to-date listing of all offerings. Items are cataloged according to subject.

32p
cont.

■ *American Statistics Index (ASI)* is published in two volumes: the index, which catalogs all statistical documents produced by government departments, and the *Abstracts*, which gives concise summaries of the contents of the documents.

■ The *Congressional Information Service (CIS)* indexes all papers produced by U.S. congressional panels and committees. These documents include the texts of hearings (for example, testimony about the plight of the homeless) and reports (for example, a comparative study of temporary shelters for the homeless.)

32q   ## Interviewing an expert

An expert can often offer valuable information, points of view concerning your topic, or advice. The faculty at your college or nearby colleges have special expertise about many topics. Corporations and professional organizations can often suggest experts in many fields; a customer service department or public relations office is a good place to begin. Public officials are sometimes available for interviews. Many federal and state government offices have employees who specialize in providing information to the public. If your topic relates to an event that your family or friends experienced, they qualify as experts.

If you think you might want to interview other people, plan ahead. It takes time to set up appointments and fit your research needs into other people's schedules. You may not always be granted the interviews you seek, but many people remember their own experiences doing academic research and try to help. If you are following the layering strategy, conduct an interview only after you have solid control of your topic. The layering strategy leads you from the most general to the most specific sources on your topic, and you gradually become an expert on your research question. Wait to interview an expert until you have a solid foundation of knowledge about your topic and you know the specific focus your paper is going to take. Do not expect an interview with an expert to save you the work of researching your topic.

Know why you are interviewing the person and what you want to know. Ask questions that elicit information, not merely a "yes" or "no" answer. Be constructive; avoid language that shows bias or a hostile attitude. Keep in mind some basic rules to follow in arranging an interview:

1. Call for an appointment during office hours.
2. Ask permission to use a tape recorder at the time you make the appointment.
3. Be on time for the interview.

4. If you are tape recording, know your equipment and have it ready when you arrive. Set it up and leave it running until the end of the interview. (No periodic checks to see if it is running.)

5. Go to the appointment prepared with specific questions. The more you know about the subject already, the more specific your questions can be.

6. Pace the interview to the time you have been allotted. Be courteous and appreciative and be prepared to leave promptly at the end of your appointment time.

7. Ask permission to use quotes in your paper.

8. If a secretary or other assistant set up the interview for you, thank him or her at the end of the interview.

9. Follow up an interview, no matter how short, with a brief thank-you note. A note is not just polite; it helps pave the way for the next student who might ask for an interview.

10. After the interview, allow yourself time to fill in any notes you didn't have time to finish. Write a bibliography entry, and on notecards summarize and evaluate your experience. An expert may have a slanted point of view in line with vested interests.

For details about creating and using questionnaires to gather research data, see section 38a.

Drafting a thesis statement for a research paper

Drafting a **thesis statement** for a research paper is the beginning of the transition between the research process and the writing process. A thesis statement in a research paper is like the thesis statement in any essay: it tells the central theme (see section 2m, especially Chart 9). Any paper must fulfill the promise of its thesis statement. Because readers expect unified material, the theme of the thesis must be sustained throughout a research paper.

Most researchers draft a **preliminary thesis statement** before or during their research process. They expect that they will revise the thesis somewhat after their research, because they know that the sources they will consult will enlarge their knowledge of a subject. Other researchers draft a thesis statement after the research process.

No matter when you draft your thesis statement, expect to write many alternatives. Your goal is to draft the thesis carefully so that it delivers the message you intend. In writing a **revised thesis statement**, take charge of your material. Reread your research log (see 32c). Reread your notes (see 32j). Look for categories of information. Rearrange your note cards into logical groupings. Begin to impose a structure on your material. As you draft a thesis statement, remember that one of your major responsibilities in a research paper is to support the thesis. Be sure that the material you gathered during the research process offers effective support. If it does not, revise your thesis statement, or conduct further research, or both.

Amy Brown, whose research paper appears in Chapter 34, drafted two different preliminary thesis statements before she composed one that worked well with her material.

FIRST PRELIMINARY VERSION	Standards for personal space vary among cultures.
NEXT PRELIMINARY VERSION	These different norms can lead to intercultural misunderstandings when people from different countries come together unaware of how their expectations concerning interpersonal distances can affect their reactions to each other.
FINAL VERSION	Everyone has expectations concerning the use of personal space, but accepted distances for that space are determined by each person's culture.

Brown knew that the first version of her thesis statement was too broad. Still, she used it as she wrote the first draft of her paper because she knew she would revise it once she saw how the material from her research would come together in her paper. Brown wrote the second version of her thesis statement in the middle of her revising process, after she had written a few drafts of her paper. She knew that her second version was wordy and complicated. She composed her final thesis statement after she put her drafts aside for a few days and got some distance from her material.

As you revise your thesis statement, go back to the research question that guided your research process (see 32a). Your thesis statement should be one answer to the question. Here are examples of subjects narrowed to topics, focused into research questions, and then cast as thesis statements.

SUBJECT	*Rain Forests*
TOPIC	The importance of rain forests
RESEARCH QUESTION	What is the importance of rain forests?

EXTRA EXERCISE B

For each of the following subjects devise a narrowed topic, then a research question, followed by a thesis statement, noting its purpose.

1. Fishing
2. Large families
3. Retirement communities
4. Competitive swimming
5. Study habits
6. Current clothing styles
7. Contemporary American novels
8. Olympics
9. Professional football
10. Diets

INFORMATIVE THESIS STATEMENT	Rain forests provide the human race with many irreplaceable resources.
PERSUASIVE THESIS STATEMENT	Rain forests must be preserved because they offer the human race many irreplaceable resources.

SUBJECT	*Nonverbal Communication*
TOPIC	Personal space
RESEARCH QUESTION	How do standards for personal space differ among cultures?
INFORMATIVE THESIS STATEMENT	Everyone has expectations concerning the use of personal space, but accepted distances for that space are determined by each person's culture.
PERSUASIVE THESIS STATEMENT	To prevent intercultural misunderstandings, people must be aware of cultural differences in standards for personal space.

SUBJECT	*Smoking*
TOPIC	Curing nicotine addiction
RESEARCH QUESTION	Are new approaches being used to cure nicotine addiction?
INFORMATIVE THESIS STATEMENT	Some approaches to curing nicotine addiction are themselves addictive.
PERSUASIVE THESIS STATEMENT	Because some methods of curing addiction are themselves addictive, doctors should prescribe them with caution.

Outlining a research paper   32s

Some instructors require an outline of a research paper. To begin organizing your material for an outline, you might write an **informal outline**. Group the subcategories in your material until you are ready to write a formal outline.

A **formal outline** should be in the form discussed in section 2o. Head it with the paper's thesis statement. You can use a **topic outline** (a format that requires words or phrases for each item) or a **sentence outline** (a format that requires full sentences for each item). Do not mix the two types. For a sentence outline of a student's research paper, see Chapter 34.

REFERENCE TO SUPPLEMENTS

For additional help with outlining, refer students to *The Research Organizer: Prentice Hall Resources for Composition* by S. Hopke.

REFERENCE TO SUPPLEMENTS

For additional help with drafting, revising, and completing the final draft of a research paper, refer students to *The Research Organizer: Prentice Hall Resources for Composition* by S. Hopke.

32t

Drafting and revising a research paper

Drafting and revising a research paper have much in common with the writing processes for writing any type of paper (see Chapters 2 and 3). But more is demanded. You must demonstrate that you have followed the research steps in this chapter. You must demonstrate an understanding of the information you have located, and you must organize for effective presentation. Additionally, you must integrate sources into your writing without plagiarizing (see section 31a) by properly using the techniques of quotation (see section 31c), paraphrase (see section 31d), and summary (see section 31e). Also, you must use parenthetical references (see section 33a) to document your sources. So many special demands take extra time for drafting, thinking, redrafting, and rethinking.

Expect to write a number of drafts of your research paper. Successive drafts help you gain authority over the information that you have learned from your research. The **first draft** is your initial attempt to structure your notes into a unified whole. It is also a chance to discover new insights and fresh connections. Only the act of writing makes such discovery possible. A first draft is a rough draft. It is a prelude to later work at revising and polishing. Chart 139 suggests some alternative ways to write the first draft of a research paper.

A **second and subsequent drafts** are the results of reading your first draft critically and revising it. If at all possible, get some distance from your material by taking a break of a few days (or a few hours, if you are pressed for time). Then, reread your first draft and think how it can be improved. You also might ask friends or classmates to read it and react.

SUGGESTIONS FOR DRAFTING A RESEARCH PAPER

SUGGESTIONS FOR DRAFTING A RESEARCH PAPER   139

- Some researchers work with their notes in front of them. They use the organized piles made for drafting a thesis statement (see 32r) and for outlining (see 32s). They spread out each pile and work according to the categories of information that have emerged from their material. They proceed from one pile to the next. They expect this process to take time, but they are assured of a first draft that includes much of the results of their research.

- Some researchers gather all their information and then set it aside to write a **partial first draft**, a quickly written first pass at getting the material under control. Writing this way helps researchers get a broad view of the material. The second step is to go back and write

---

SUGGESTIONS FOR DRAFTING A RESEARCH PAPER (continued)   139

a **complete first draft** with research notes at hand. The researchers go over their partial draft slowly to correct information, add material left out, and—most important—insert in-text references (see Chapter 33).

■ Some researchers write their first draft quickly to get words down on paper when they feel "stuck" about what to say next. When they have a clear idea of how to proceed, they slow down and use their notes. These researchers draw on their experiences with gathering ideas (see 2d through 2j), shaping ideas (see 2l), getting started (see 3a), and drafting (see 3b).

■ Some researchers photocopy their first drafts and cut up the paper to move paragraphs and sentences around. If a new order suggests itself, the researchers tape the paper together in its new form. Researchers who have access to a computer will find this process considerably easier.

As you work, pay attention to any uneasy feelings you have that hint at the need to rethink or rework your material. Experienced writers expect to revise; they know that writing is really rewriting. Research papers are among the most demanding composing assignments, and most writers have to revise their drafts more than a few times. As you revise, consult the Revision Checklists in section 3c to remind yourself of general principles of writing. Also, consult the revision checklist in Chart 140 designed especially for a research paper.

REVISION CHECKLIST FOR A RESEARCH PAPER   140

If the answer to any question in the list is "no," revise your draft.
1. Does the introductory paragraph lead effectively into the material (see 4g)?
2. Are you fulfilling the promise of the thesis statement (see 32r)?
3. Do the ideas follow from one another?
4. Do you stay on the topic?
5. Are important questions answered?
6. Do you avoid bogging down the paper with irrelevant or insignificant information?

➡

TEACHING TIP

Using the Revision Checklists in 3c and their own previously written and marked papers, students can devise individualized checklists for themselves to serve as reminders of their own problem areas. If, for example, they consistently leave the -s off third-person singular verbs, they should make that instance an item to be checked during the editing stage. Compiling such a checklist not only provides students with an efficient means of self-editing, it also makes them more conscious of where they need to exercise the greatest concern about mechanics.

QUOTATION ABOUT WRITING

Language exists only when it is listened to as well as spoken. The hearer is an indispensable partner.

—John Dewey

REVISION CHECKLIST FOR A RESEARCH PAPER (continued)   140

7. Do you avoid leaving gaps in information?

8. Have you integrated source material without plagiarizing (see 31a)?

9. Have you used quotations, paraphrases, and summaries well (see Chapter 31)?

10. Have you used parenthetical references (see 33c–1 and 33d–1) correctly, and has each tied in with a source listed in the Works Cited (or References) list at the end of the paper (see 33c–3 and 33d–3)?

11. Have you used correct documentation forms (see Chapter 33)?

12. Does the concluding paragraph end the material effectively (see 4g)?

The **final draft** shows that you have revised well. It shows also that you have edited (see section 3d) and proofread (see section 3e) for correct grammar, spelling, and punctuation. No amount of careful research and good writing can make up for a sloppy manuscript. Strive to make the paper easy to read. If any page is messy with corrections, retype it. If your instructor accepts handwritten papers, use ruled white paper that has not been torn out of a spiral notebook. (If at all possible, however, type your work because it will present itself better.) Use black or blue ink and write very legibly.

For a case study of a student writing an MLA-style research paper, including a narrative of the writing process in action, and a sample student research paper, see Chapter 34. For a case study and a sample student research paper using APA style, see Chapter 35.

33 *Documenting in MLA, APA, CM, and CBE Styles*

When you write a research paper, you must **document** your sources. If you do not, you are plagiarizing, which is a serious offense (see 31a). The purpose of documenting sources is to inform your reader of exactly which sources you have taken information from. To prepare to document, you want to create a working bibliography on cards (see 33b), to keep careful track of all the sources on which you take notes. In your research paper itself, you are expected to use the style of documentation required by your instructor—four major styles are presented in this chapter.

Understanding the concept of documentation   33a

Documentation involves marking the exact place in a paper where source material has been used *and* presenting bibliographic information (for example, a book's author, title, year of publication, publisher, and any other required information). Although *bibliography* literally means "description of books," for your research projects you might find yourself compiling a list of sources that includes live interviews, CDs, online information, and films, as well as books and articles.

Bibliographic information is given in a **list of sources** at the end of the paper or in bibliographic notes. When a list of sources includes only the sources actually referred to in a paper, it is called *Works Cited* or *References.* A source list that includes all the works a writer looks at, not just those referred to in the paper, is called *Works Consulted, Bibliography,* or *References.*

REFERENCES TO SUPPLEMENTS

For revising for proper use of sources, refer students to *Rough Drafts* by K. S. Cain, Part II, Exercise 6.

For additional help with the research writing process, from search strategy to final draft, refer students to *The Research Organizer: Prentice Hall Resources for Composition* by S. Hopke.

See transparencies 8–1 through 8–5a for useful research skills classroom activities in the *Prentice Hall/Simon & Schuster Transparencies for Writers* by D. Carter.

TEACHING TIP

Students often wonder why they need to be scrupulous in their documentation of information, sometimes thinking of the process as just another pointless but difficult exercise devised by the teacher. It may help them to understand the demands of documentation if you point out to them the reasons behind it. You will probably think of additional reasons, but here are some that you might find useful.

1. Using someone else's ideas or words is like using anything else that belongs to another person: The borrower has an ethical obligation to the owner not to claim the article as his or her own. Thus, the writer must acknowledge that the ideas or words of someone else belong to another person. In the case of long quotations—e.g., the reprinting of an entire work or a substantial portion of it—the writer must request and receive permission from the original author or publisher to use it.

2. Other researchers of the same subject may be intrigued by a reference to a particular work or author, causing them to look for the original so that they can read the entire piece. Citation of complete publication information will greatly simplify finding the original work or even the original passage.

3. Documentation protects the researcher from any charges of plagiarism. When all sources are acknowledged, there can be no doubt about what the researcher has gleaned from others and what is original.

4. References to sources inform the reader that the researcher has been thorough. The study which does not indicate that standard work in the field has been considered will be taken less seriously than the one that shows that the researcher is aware of what has already been written about the topic.

➡

33a

cont.

Four documentation styles are featured in this chapter. Never mix documentation styles. The most frequently used style in the humanities was developed by the Modern Language Association (**MLA**). It is a **parenthetical citation system** that calls for a source name and page reference to be entered at each place you use a source in your paper. Also, at the end of your paper you include a Works Cited list giving full bibliographic details about each cited source. For full coverage of MLA documentation based on the Fourth Edition of the *MLA Handbook for Writers of Research Papers* by Joseph Gibaldi (1995), see section 33c.

The documentation style used in most social sciences was developed by the American Psychological Association (**APA**). It is a parenthetical citation system that calls for a source name and a publication year, and sometimes a page reference, to be entered at each place you use a source in your paper. Also, at the end of your paper, you include a References list of all cited and "recoverable" sources. (A recoverable source is one that a reader can expect to be able to locate, like a book, and unlike a personal letter.) For full coverage of APA documentation based on the Fourth Edition of the *Publication Manual of the American Psychological Association* (1994), see section 33d.

A third style, also used in the humanities and other disciplines, is described in the style manual of the University of Chicago Press and is known as Chicago Manual (**CM**) style. *The Chicago Manual of Style* describes two very different documentation systems: (1) a name-year parenthetical citation system and References list similar to APA's and (2) a system using bibliographic notes containing full source information. (A separate list of references is usually unnecessary with bibliographic notes.) For full coverage of the CM bibliographic note style of documentation as described in the Fourteenth Edition of *The Chicago Manual of Style* (1993), see section 33e.

The Council of Biology Editors (**CBE**) has compiled a manual of style and documentation guidelines for mathematics, the physical sciences, and the life sciences. In it, the CBE describes two documentation systems: (1) a **name-year parenthetical citation system** and References list and (2) a **"numbered reference" system** using numbers in the paper to cite a source and a numbered References list giving full bibliographic details for each source. For coverage of CBE recommendations for citing sources in a paper and for a References list as described in the sixth edition of *Scientific Style and Format: The CBE Manual for Authors, Editors, and Publishers* (1994), see section 33f.

Careful, responsible documentation is an academic obligation. To help you fulfill this obligation, this handbook presents MLA, APA, CM, and CBE documentation guidelines in separate sections, each with a different identifying color bar down the outside of the pages. Chart 141 gives a handy list of where in this handbook you can find information on each style.

WHERE TO FIND THE MLA, APA, CM, AND CBE 141
INFORMATION YOU NEED

MLA STYLE: BLUE BAR ON PAGES—SECTION 33C

■ Parenthetical citations—section 33c-1
■ Guidelines for Compiling an MLA-Style Works Cited List
  (Chart 142)—section 33c-2
■ Directory of MLA Works Cited List Models—section 33c-3
■ Content or other notes with MLA's parenthetical documentation—
  section 33c-4

APA STYLE: RED BAR ON PAGES—SECTION 33D

■ In-text style and parenthetical citations—section 33d-1
■ Guidelines for Compiling an APA-Style References List
  (Chart 143)—section 33d-2
■ Directory of APA References List Models—section 33d-3
■ Abstracts and notes—section 33d-4

*CM (CHICAGO MANUAL) STYLE: BROWN BAR ON PAGES—
SECTION 33E*

■ Guidelines for Compiling CM-Style Bibliographic Notes
  (Chart 144)—section 33e-1
■ Directory of CM-Style Bibliographic Notes and References Models—
  section 33e-2

*CBE (COUNCIL OF BIOLOGY EDITORS) STYLE: GRAY BAR ON
PAGES—SECTION 33F*

■ Guidelines for Compiling a CBE-Style References List
  (Chart 145)—section 33f-1
■ Directory of CBE-Style References List Models—section 33f-2

Creating a working bibliography   **33b**

To create a working bibliography, write out a bibliographic card
for every source you take notes on. Include all the information you need
to fulfill the requirements of the documentation style you are using.
Also, for each card on a library source, write the call number in the
upper left corner, being careful to copy it exactly. (Depending on how

---

TEACHING TIP, cont.

5. Particularly in science, the test of research findings is the replication of experiments by other researchers. They can repeat such work only if the steps of the process have been clearly documented, with careful reference to the work of others in the field.

BACKGROUND

The term *bibliography* is derived from two Greek roots. The first is *biblia,* the plural form of the word meaning book or papyrus, so named after the Phoenician city *Byblos* (now Jubayl) from which papyrus was exported. *Biblia* has been responsible for many words in the English language dealing with books. For example, a *biblioclast* is a destroyer of books, and *bibliognost* refers to one who is knowledgeable about books. A *bibliolater* is a lover of books. A *bibliopegist* is a bookbinder.

The second Greek root is *graphos,* meaning *to write.* At one time *bibliography* meant *the writing of books,* but in the seventeenth century the term came to meaning *writing about books.* At the same time, *bibliography* began to receive wide usage in Latin and began to replace such words as *catalogus* and *bibliotheca* in the titles of bibliographies, the making of which became increasingly important as bibliographers struggled to devise some type of organization for keeping track of the flood of publications that resulted from the invention of printing. Nevertheless, the term *bibliography* was not included in Samuel Johnson's dictionary of 1755 and was not found in the *Encyclopaedia Britannica* until its third edition in 1797. According to the *Oxford English Dictionary,* not until the early nineteenth century was the word *bibliography* first used to refer to "the systematic description and history of books, their authorship, printing, publication, editions, etc." or to a book about such matters.

As commonly used, the term *bibliography* sometimes refers to a science, sometimes to an art, and sometimes to the product of the art. As a science, it is an organized body of knowledge dealing with all aspects of books, both as physical objects and as the expression of ideas. Bibliography as an art consists of the techniques for finding, organizing, and presenting information about books. The bibliography that is produced by that art is a systematic listing of books that share common characteristics.

The objectives of bibliography may be analytical or systematic. Analytic bibliography tries to discover information about authorship, publication, and derivation of a text. Systematic bibliography, on the other hand, produces systematic lists of books. The result is many different kinds of bibliographies. For example, bibliographies may be critical (critically appraising the books they list), current or retrospective, comprehensive or selective, annotated or not, enumerative (presenting an inventory) or subject oriented (presenting content). In all their varied forms, they provide the modern researcher with invaluable assistance in finding out where to look to learn what is already known about a subject.

The Bibliographical Society of America was organized at the American Library Association's St. Louis Conference in 1904. It succeeded the Bibliographical Society of Chicago, which had been in existence for the preceding five years. The object of the society is "to promote bibliographical research and to issue bibliographical publications." Its membership is made up of professors, librarians, instructors, rare book dealers, collectors, and other bibliophiles. It is responsible for many publications dealing with published American writing.

33b
cont.

recent they are and how the library you are using stores them, magazines and journals may not have call numbers.) If you conduct research at more than one library, also note on the card the library where you found each source.

Be especially careful with online sources: Include on the bibliographic card for each online source the date on which you access the material. Because some information in online databases is updated periodically, documentation for an online source must include both any date related to the source (such as the date of publication for a print form of the source, if any) and the date you access the material. If you download the source, the date you download is the access date to use even if you take notes on it later. If you take notes from the screen, use the date you take notes.

When the time comes to compile bibliographic information for your research paper, you can easily arrange your bibliographic cards in the order required by your documentation style (for example, in alphabetical order for an MLA-style Works Cited list). The bibliographic cards shown here are for a source cited in the research paper in Chapter 34.

Kenner, Andrew N., and George Katsimaglis. "Gender Differences in Proxemics: Taxi-Seat Choice." *Psychological Reports* 72 (1993): 625-626.
(I found this in Social Science Index.)

HD31.H229-1990

Hall, Edward and Hall, Mildred Reed. *Understanding Cultural Differences: Germans, French, and Americans.* Yarmouth, ME: Intercultural Press, 1990.

33c   **Using MLA-style documentation**

In MLA (Modern Language Association) documentation, you are expected to document any source that you quote, paraphrase, or summarize with a two-part system.

1. Within the body of the paper, use in-text citations, as described in 33c-1.

2. At the end of the paper, provide a list of sources titled Works Cited; see 33c-2 and 33c-3.

(For information about using notes for additional content or for extensive citations of sources when you are using MLA-style parenthetical citations, see 33c-4.)

Citing sources in the body of a paper in MLA style

For most in-text citations, wherever you use ideas or information you have found in a source, you give a name or a title (whichever is the first information in the source's entry in the Works Cited list) to identify the source and page numbers to show the exact location in the source of the material you are using. In your sentences that set the context for your use of source material, try to include author names and, when relevant, credentials of authors who are authorities. In such cases, the only part of a citation to put in parentheses is the page number(s). If you cannot incorporate author names into your sentences, give them as part of the parenthetical citation. In a parenthetical citation, use one space between an author name (or title) and page number; do not use a comma or other punctuation between name and page number.

❖ MLA FORMAT ALERT: Position a parenthetical citation at the end of the material it refers to, even at the end of a sentence, if that is not too far away from the material. At the end of a sentence, place a parenthetical reference before the sentence's end punctuation. ❖

The examples in this section show how to handle various parenthetical citations in the body of your paper. Remember, however, that you can usually integrate the names and titles of sources into your sentences.

1. CITING A PARAPHRASED OR SUMMARIZED SOURCE—MLA

Desmond Morris notes that people from the Mediterranean prefer an elbow-to-shoulder distance from each other (131). [Author name cited in text; page number cited in parentheses.]

In <u>Manwatching: A Field Guide to Human Behavior</u>, zoologist Desmond Morris notes that people from the Mediterranean prefer an elbow-to-shoulder distance from each other (131). [Title of source, author name, and author credentials cited in text; page number cited in parentheses.]

On the other hand, people from the Mediterranean prefer an elbow-to-shoulder distance from each other (Morris 131). [Author name and page number cited in parentheses.]

2. CITING THE SOURCE OF A SHORT QUOTATION—MLA

Hall observes that "if you are interested in something, your pupils dilate; if I say something you don't like, they tend to contract" (47), thus suggesting why in some cultures people stand close to each other when they speak. Personal space "moves with us," according to Fisher,

33c-1

EXTRA EXERCISE A

Devise parenthetical references for the following quotation, paraphrase, and summary. The source is provided at the end of each selection.

1. "If indeed we note in his [Thomas Carlyle's] writings those passages in which the words and rhythms are most resonant, and the accent falls with the strongest emphasis, we shall find they are the expression of the cosmic wonder and terror which formed the darkly flaming background of all his thoughts." (Logan Pearsall Smith, "Thomas Carlyle: The Rembrandt of English Prose," *Reperusals and Re-Collections,* Harcourt, Brace and Company, Inc., 1936, p. 115.)

2. Ethologists study the traits that distinguish a group—a group of people or a group of animals. They try to discover how the group usually acts by observing its members in their natural surroundings, and to understand their behavior by testing it, when possible, in the laboratory. (Sally Carrighar, "Ethology," from *Wild Heritage,* Houghton Mifflin Company, 1965, pp. 174–175.)

3. May Sarton, who lives in Maine, is the author of over forty books of poetry, fiction, journals, and memoirs. Since her first book of poetry appeared in 1937, and her first novel the year following, she has been known to the reading public as one who explores the solitary life and different forms of female creativity. She has been an influential figure in the Women's Movement. (Karen Saum, "May Sarton", *Writers at Work,* ed. George Plimpton, Viking Penguin Inc., p. 71.)

ANSWERS: EXTRA EXERCISE A

1. (Smith 115).
2. (Carrighar 174–75).
3. (Saum 71).

Bell, and Baum, "expanding and contracting according to the situation in which we find ourselves" (149).

✤ MLA FORMAT ALERT: When a quotation is no longer than four handwritten or typed lines, enclose the quoted words in quotation marks to distinguish them from your own words in the sentence. Place the parentheses after the closing quotation mark but before sentence-ending punctuation. If a quotation ends in an exclamation point or a question mark, however, put that punctuation mark before the closing quotation mark, put the parenthetical citation next, and then put a period after the parenthetical citation. ✤

Coles asks, "What binds together a Mormon banker in Utah with his brother, or other coreligionists in Illinois or Massachusetts?" (2).

3. CITING THE SOURCE OF A LONG QUOTATION—MLA

Robert Sommer, an environmental psychologist, uses literary and personal analogies to describe personal space:

Like the porcupines in Schopenhauer's fable, people like to be close enough to obtain warmth and comradeship but far enough away to avoid pricking one another. Personal space . . . has been likened to a snail shell, a soap bubble, an aura, and "breathing room." (26)

✤ MLA FORMAT ALERT: When a quotation is longer than four handwritten or typed lines, do not put quotation marks around the quoted words. Instead, set the quoted words off from your own words by indenting each line of the quotation. In a typed paper, use a 10-space indent for each line of a quotation longer than four lines. If you are handwriting or using a computer, indent each line of the quotation one inch. Put one space after the last punctuation mark of the quotation, and then put in the parenthetical citation. For other examples of long quotations, of prose and of poetry, see Amy Brown's research paper in Chapter 34. ✤

4. CITING ONE AUTHOR—MLA

Give an author's name as it appears on the source: for a book, the title page; for an article, directly below the title or at the end of the article. Many nonprint sources also name an author: for a CD, cassette, tape, or software, for example, check the printed sleeve or cover. For an online source, identify an author as he or she is identified online.

Males in Germany and the United States stand farther apart and touch less when they talk to other males than when they talk to females (Shuter 305).

5. Citing Two or Three Authors—MLA

Give the names in the order they have in the source. Spell out *and*. For three authors, use a comma between the first- and second-named authors.

As children get older, they become more aware of standards for personal space (Worchel and Cooper 536).

Personal space gets larger or smaller depending on the circumstances of the social interaction (Fisher, Bell, and Baum 149).

6. Citing More than Three Authors—MLA

With three or more authors, you can name them all or use the first author's name only, followed by *et al.*, either in a parenthetical reference or in your sentence. Do not underline *et al.* No period follows *et*, but do use a period after *al*.

❖ USAGE ALERT: The abbreviation *et al.* stands for "and others"; when an author's name followed by *et al.* is a subject, use a plural verb. ❖

Fisher et al. have found that personal space gets larger or smaller depending on the circumstances of the social interaction (158).

Personal space gets larger or smaller depending on the circumstances of the social interaction (Fisher et al. 158).

7. Citing More than One Source by an Author—MLA

When you use two or more sources by an author, include the relevant title in each citation. In parenthetical citations, use a shortened version of the title. For example, in a paper using as sources Edward T. Hall's *The Hidden Dimension* and "Learning the Arabs' Silent Language," parenthetical citations use *Hidden* and "Learning." Shorten the titles as much as possible, keeping them unambiguous to readers and starting them with the word by which you alphabetize the works in Works Cited. Separate the author's name and the title with a comma, but do not use punctuation between the title and page number.

Although most people are unaware that interpersonal distances exist and contribute to people's reactions to one another (Hall, Hidden 109),
Arabic males seem to understand the practicality of close conversational distances (Hall, "Learning" 41).

When you incorporate the title into your own sentences, you can omit a subtitle, but do not shorten it more than that.

TEACHING TIP
Asking students to make up a title and citation for their imaginary autobiography, perhaps published this year by Prentice Hall/Simon & Schuster, may inject a little fun into learning to cite a book.

8. Citing Two or More Authors with the Same Last Name—MLA

Use each author's first and last name in each citation, whether in your sentences or in parenthetical citations.

According to British zoologist Desmond Morris, conversational distances vary between people from different countries (131). If an American backs away from an Arab, the American is considered cold, the Arab pushy (Charles G. Morris 516).

9. Citing a Work with a Group or Corporate Author—MLA

When a corporation or other group is named as the author of a source you want to cite, use the corporate name just as you would an individual's name.

In a five-year study, the Boston Women's Health Collective reported that these tests are usually unreliable (11).

A five-year study shows that these tests are usually unreliable (Boston Women's Health Collective 11).

10. Citing a Work by Title—MLA

If no author is named, use the title in citations. In your own sentences, use the full main title and omit a subtitle, if any. For parenthetical citations, shorten the title as much as possible (making sure the shortened version refers unambiguously to the correct source), and always make the first word the one by which you alphabetize it. The following citation is to an article fully titled "Are You a Day or Night Person?"

The "morning lark" and "night owl" connotations typically are used to categorize the human extremes ("Are You" 11).

11. Citing a Multivolume Work—MLA

When you cite more than one volume of a multivolume work, include the relevant volume number in each citation. (In the Works Cited list, list the multivolume work once and give the total number of volumes; see item 9 in the Works Cited examples in 33c-3.) Give the volume number first, followed by a colon and one space, followed by the page number(s).

By 1900, the Amazon forest dwellers had been exposed to these viruses (Rand 3: 202).

Rand believes that forest dwellers in Borneo escaped illness from
retroviruses until the 1960s (4: 518-19).

12. Citing Material from a Novel, Play, or Poem—MLA

When you cite material from literary works, part, chapter, act, scene, canto, stanza, or line numbers usually help readers trying to locate what you refer to more than page numbers do. Unless your instructor tells you not to, use arabic numerals for these references, even if the literary work uses roman numerals.

For novels that use them, give part and/or chapter numbers after page numbers. Use a semicolon after the page number but a comma to separate a part from a chapter.

Flannery O'Connor describes one character in <u>The Violent Bear It Away</u> as
"divided in two—a violent and a rational self" (139, pt. 2, ch. 6).

For plays that use them, give act, scene, and/or line numbers. Use periods between these numbers.

Among the most quoted of Shakespeare's lines is Hamlet's soliloquy
beginning "To be, or not to be: that is the question" (3.1.56).

For poems and plays that use them, give canto, stanza, and/or line numbers. Use periods between these numbers.

In "To Autumn," Keats's most melancholy image occurs in the lines "Then
in a wailful choir the small gnats mourn / Among the river swallows"
(3.27-28).

♣ MLA ABBREVIATION ALERT: The *MLA Handbook* advises spelling out the word *Line* (or *Lines*) the first time you cite a line reference because the abbreviation for line (l., plural ll.) can so easily be misread as the numeral 1. After the first citation, you can omit the word.♣

13. Citing a Work in an Anthology or Other Collection—MLA

You may want to cite a work you have read in a book that contains many works by various authors and that was compiled, written, or edited by someone other than the person you are citing. For example, suppose you want to cite "When in Rome" by Mari Evans, which you have read in a literature text by Pamela Annas and Robert Rosen. Use Evans's name and the title of her work in the in-text citation and as the first block of information for the entry in the Works Cited list (see item 10 in the list of MLA Works Cited examples).

QUOTATION ABOUT WRITING

Beginning to write, you discover what
you have to write about.

—Kit Reed

In "When in Rome," Mari Evans uses parentheses to enclose lines
expressing the houseworker's thoughts as her employer offers lunch, as
in the first stanza's "(an egg / or soup / . . . there ain't no meat)"
(688-89).

14. Citing an Indirect Source—MLA

When you want to quote words that you found quoted in someone else's
work, put the name of the person whose words you are quoting into
your own sentence. Indicate the work where you found the quotation
either in your sentence or in a parenthetical citation beginning with
"qtd. in."

✤ RESEARCH ALERT: When it is possible to do so, find the primary
source for words that you want to quote rather than taking a quotation
from a secondary source. ✤

Martin Scorsese acknowledges the link between himself and his films: "I
realize that all my life, I've been an outsider. I splatter bits of
myself all over the screen" (qtd. in Giannetti and Eyman 397).

Giannetti and Eyman quote Martin Scorsese as acknowledging the link
between himself and his films: "I realize that all my life, I've been an
outsider. I splatter bits of myself all over the screen" (397).

15. Citing Two or More Sources in One Reference—MLA

If more than one source has contributed to an idea, opinion, or fact in
your paper, acknowledge all of them. In a parenthetical citation, separate each block of information with a semicolon followed by one space.

Once researchers agreed that these cultural "distance zones" existed,
their next step was to try to measure or define them (Hall 110-20;
Henley 32-33; Fisher, Bell, and Baum 153).

Because long parenthetical citations can disturb the flow of your paper,
consider using an endnote or footnote for citing multiple sources; see
33c-4.

16. Citing an Entire Work—MLA

References to an entire work usually fit best into your own sentences.

In The Clockwork Sparrow, Sue Binkley analyzes studies of circadian
rhythms undertaken between 1967 and 1989.

17. CITING AN ELECTRONIC SOURCE WITH A NAME OR TITLE AND PAGE NUMBERS—MLA

The principles that govern in-text citations of electronic sources are exactly the same as the ones that apply to books, articles, letters, interviews, or any other source you get information from on paper or in person. You put in your own sentences or in parenthetical references enough information for a reader to be able to locate full information about the source in the Works Cited list.

When an electronically accessed source identifies its author, use the author's name for in-text citations. If an electronic source does not name the author, use its title for in-text citations and for the first block of information in that source's Works Cited entry. (See item 10 above for an example of a work cited by its title and for advice about shortening a title for an in-text citation.)

When an electronic source has page numbers, use them exactly as you would the page numbers of a print source.

18. CITING AN ELECTRONIC SOURCE THAT NUMBERS PARAGRAPHS—MLA

When an electronic source has numbered paragraphs (instead of page numbers), use them for in-text references as you would page numbers, with two differences: (1) Use a comma followed by one space after the name (or title); and (2) use the abbreviation *par.* for a reference to one paragraph or *pars.* for a reference to more than one paragraph, followed by the number(s) of the paragraphs you are citing.

```
Artists seem to be haunted by the fear that psychoanalysis might destroy
creativity while it reconstructs personality (Francis, pars. 22-25).
```

19. CITING AN ELECTRONIC SOURCE WITHOUT PAGE OR PARAGRAPH NUMBERS—MLA

Many online sources do not number pages or paragraphs. In the Works Cited entry for such a source, include the abbreviation *n. pag.* ("no pagination"). This abbreviation serves to explain to readers why in-text references to this source do not cite page numbers. Here is an example from an online source without page numbers or paragraph numbers.

```
From March to April in 1994, violations of this important disclosure
regulation increased 123 percent (Pessan).
```

33c-2

Compiling an MLA-Style Works Cited List

In MLA documentation, in-text citations must be accompanied by a list of all the sources referred to in your paper. In a Works Cited list, include only the sources from which you quote or paraphrase or summarize. Do not include sources that you have consulted but do not refer to in the paper unless your instructor asks for a Works Consulted list (which follows the same format as a Works Cited list). Chart 142 gives general information about a Works Cited list.

GUIDELINES FOR COMPILING AN MLA-STYLE WORKS CITED LIST 142

■ **TITLE**

Works Cited

■ **PLACEMENT OF LIST**

Start a new page numbered sequentially with the rest of the paper, after Notes pages, if any.

■ **CONTENTS AND FORMAT**

Include all sources quoted from, paraphrased, or summarized in your paper. Start each entry on a new line and at the regular left margin. If the entry uses more than one line, indent all lines but the first five spaces (or one-half inch) from the left margin. Double-space all lines.

■ **SPACING AFTER PUNCTUATION**

In the Fourth Edition of the MLA Handbook, examples of Works Cited entries use one space after a period at the end of an information unit such as the author name(s), the title of the cited source, and the publication information. (In the past, MLA specified two spaces after these periods.) Unless your instructor tells you to use two spaces after a period, one space is acceptable.
Put one space after a comma.
Put one space after a colon.

■ **ARRANGEMENT OF ENTRIES**

Alphabetize by author's last name. If no author is named, alphabetize by the title's first significant word (not *A*, *An*, or *The*).

■ **AUTHORS' NAMES**

Use first names and middle names or middle initials, if any, as given in the source. Do not use initials for any name that is given in full. For one author or the first-named author in multiauthor works, give the last name first. Use the word *and* with two or more authors. List multiple authors in the order given in the source. Use a comma between the first author's last and first names and after each complete author name except the last. After the last author name, use a period: Fein, Ethel Andrea, Bert Griggs and Delaware Rogash.

GUIDELINES FOR COMPILING AN MLA-STYLE WORKS CITED LIST (continued)

142

Include *Jr., Sr., II, III,* but do not include other titles and degrees before or after a name. For example, an entry for a work by Edward Meep, III, M.D., and Sir Feeney Bolton, would start like this: `Meep, Edward, III, and Feeney Bolton.`

■ **CAPITALIZATION OF TITLES**

Capitalize all major words in titles.

■ **SPECIAL TREATMENT OF TITLES**

Use quotation marks around titles of shorter works (poems, short stories, essays, articles). Underline titles of longer works (books, names of newspapers or journals containing cited articles). For underlining, <u>use an unbroken line like this</u> (unless you use software that underlines only with a <u>broken</u> <u>line,</u> <u>like</u> <u>this</u>).

When a book title includes the title of another work that is usually underlined (such as a novel, play, or long poem), do not underline the incorporated title: <u>Decoding</u> Jane Eyre.

If the incorporated title is usually enclosed in quotation marks (such as a short story or short poem), keep the quotation marks and underline the complete title of the book (do not underline the period): <u>Theme and Form in "The Waste Land</u>."

Drop *A, An,* or *The* as the first word of a periodical title.

■ **PLACE OF PUBLICATION**

If several cities are listed for the place of publication, give only the first. If a U.S. city name alone would be ambiguous, also give the state's two-letter postal abbreviation. For an unfamiliar city outside the United States, include an abbreviated country name or an abbreviated Canadian province name.

■ **PUBLISHER**

Use shortened names as long as they are clear: *Prentice* for *Prentice Hall, Simon* for *Simon & Schuster*. For university presses, use the capital letters *U* and *P* (without periods): for *Oxford University Press* and the *University of Chicago Press*, respectively, `Oxford UP`; `U of Chicago P`.

■ **PUBLICATION MONTH ABBREVIATIONS**

Abbreviate all publication months except *May, June,* and *July.* Use the first three letters followed by a period: `Dec., Feb.`

■ **PARAGRAPH NUMBERS IN ELECTRONIC SOURCES**

For electronic sources that number paragraphs instead of pages, give the total number of paragraphs followed by the abbreviation pars.: `77 pars.` ➡

33c–2
cont.

GUIDELINES FOR COMPILING AN MLA-STYLE WORKS CITED LIST (continued)

GUIDELINES FOR COMPILING AN MLA-STYLE WORKS CITED LIST (continued)

142

■ INCLUSIVE PAGE NUMBERS

Use inclusive page numbers to give the starting page number and the ending page number of any paginated electronic source and any paginated print source that is part of a longer work (for example, a chapter in a book, an article in a journal). Inclusive page numbers signal that the cited work is on those pages and all pages in between. If that is not the case, use the style shown below for discontinuous page numbers. In either case, give numerals only, without the words *page* or *pages* or the abbreviations *p.* or *pp.*

Use the full second number through 99. Then use only the last two digits for the second number unless unclear: 103-04 is clear, but 567-602 requires full numbers.

■ DISCONTINUOUS PAGES

Use the starting page number followed by a plus sign (+): 32+.

■ WORKS CITED ENTRIES: BOOKS

Citations for books have three main parts: author, title, and publication information (place of publication, publisher, and date of publication).

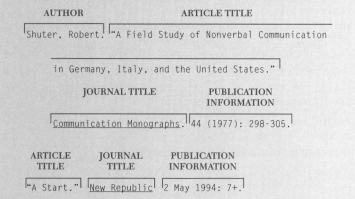

AUTHOR	TITLE	PUBLICATION INFORMATION
Didion, Joan.	Salvador.	New York: Simon, 1983.

■ WORKS CITED ENTRIES: PRINT ARTICLES

Citations for periodical articles contain three major parts: author, title of article, and publication information (usually the periodical title, volume number, year of publication, and inclusive page numbers).

AUTHOR   ARTICLE TITLE

Shuter, Robert. "A Field Study of Nonverbal Communication

in Germany, Italy, and the United States."

JOURNAL TITLE   PUBLICATION INFORMATION

Communication Monographs. 44 (1977): 298-305.

ARTICLE TITLE   JOURNAL TITLE   PUBLICATION INFORMATION

"A Start." New Republic 2 May 1994: 7+.

GUIDELINES FOR COMPILING AN MLA-STYLE WORKS CITED LIST (continued)

142

■ WORKS CITED ENTRIES: ELECTRONIC SOURCES

Citations for electronic sources contain at least six major parts: author, publication information, title of database, publication medium, name of vendor or computer service, electronic publication date or access date. Electronic versions of sources that also appear in print start with information about the print version. Here is an entry for a journal article accessed through a computer service; it also has a print version.

ARTICLE TITLE	TITLE OF PRINT JOURNAL	PUBLICATION INFORMATION FOR PRINT JOURNAL
"A Start."	New Republic	(2 May 1994): n. pag.

ELECTRONIC PUBLICATION MEDIUM	COMPUTER NETWORK	ACCESS DATE
Online.	America Online.	21 Apr. 1996.

Here is an entry for an article from a CD-ROM encyclopedia.

ARTICLE AUTHOR	ARTICLE TITLE	CD-ROM TITLE
Regan, Robert.	"Poe, Edgar Allan."	Academic American

ELECTRONIC PUBLICATION MEDIUM	CD-ROM PUBLICATION INFORMATION
Encyclopedia. CD-ROM.	Grolier Electronic Publishing, 1993.

Following models for an MLA-style Works Cited list

Directory

PRINT SOURCES: BOOKS
1. Book by One Author—MLA
2. Book by Two or Three Authors—MLA
3. Book by More than Three Authors—MLA
4. Two or More Books by the Same Author(s)—MLA

33c-3

MLA MLA

MLA

QUOTATION ABOUT WRITING
Whatever machine you use, however sophisticated your technology, it's ideas that count. In the beginning was the idea. No machine will give you the ability to spot an opening, take a new idea, and see it through to profitable fruition.
—Tom Crabtree

PRINT SOURCES: BOOKS

1. BOOK BY ONE AUTHOR—MLA

Schaller, George B. <u>The Last Panda</u>. Chicago: U of Chicago P, 1993.

2. BOOK BY TWO OR THREE AUTHORS—MLA

Smith, Richard J., and Mark Gibbs. <u>Navigating the Internet</u>.
     Indianapolis: Sams, 1994.

3. BOOK BY MORE THAN THREE AUTHORS—MLA

Cameron, Deborah, et al. <u>Researching Language: Issues of Power and</u>
     <u>Method</u>. London: Routledge, 1992.

4. TWO OR MORE BOOKS BY THE SAME AUTHOR(S)—MLA

Waller, R. J. <u>The Bridges of Madison County</u>. New York: Warner, 1992.

---. <u>Old Songs in a New Cafe</u>. New York: Warner, 1994.

---. <u>Slow Waltz in Cedar Bend</u>. New York: Warner, 1993.

QUOTATION ABOUT WRITING

When I sit at my table to write, I never know what it's going to be till I'm under way. I trust in inspiration, which sometimes comes and sometimes doesn't. But I don't sit back waiting for it. I work *every* day.

—Alberto Moravia

TEACHING TIP

In the list of Works Cited or References, the place of publication is given. The name of the city alone is sufficient if it is well known. If, however, the state in which the city is located might not be known to the reader, the name of the state should also be included. A list of abbreviations of the names of states and territories of the United States appears in section 30j.

Students sometimes list the state without the city of publication in citations when they do not recognize the city's name and are unsure about where to find the city's name on title pages and copyright pages or in library catalog entries.

5. Book by Group or Corporate Author—MLA

Environmental Defense Fund. <u>Recycling and Incineration: Evaluating the Choice</u>. Washington: Island, 1990.

American Psychological Association. <u>Publication Manual of the American Psychological Association</u>. 4th ed.. Washington: APA, 1994.

6. Book with No Author Named—MLA

<u>The Chicago Manual of Style</u>. 14th ed. Chicago: U of Chicago P, 1993.

7. Book with an Author and an Editor—MLA

If your focus is on Eudora Welty as the author of the reviews in *A Writer's Eye* and your paper refers to her and/or her words, put her name first in the Works Cited entry:

Welty, Eudora. <u>A Writer's Eye: Collected Book Reviews</u>. Ed. Pearl A. McHaney. Jackson: UP of Mississippi, 1994.

If your focus is on Pearl A. McHaney's work as the editor of this collection of reviews and your paper refers to her and/or her words, put her name first in the Works Cited entry:

McHaney, Pearl A. ed. <u>A Writer's Eye: Collected Book Reviews</u>. By Eudora Welty. Jackson: UP of Mississippi, 1994.

8. Translation—MLA

Dostoevsky, Fyodor. <u>Devils</u>. Trans. Michael R. Katz. Oxford: Oxford UP, 1992.

9. Work in Several Volumes or Parts—MLA

When you use more than one volume of a multivolume work, after the title give the total number of volumes. In each parenthetical citation, give both volume and page numbers (see item 11 in 33c-2).

Rand, Enid. <u>Virology</u>. 5 vols. Philadelphia: Lippincott, 1979.

When you use only one volume, instead of the total number of volumes, give the number of the volume you used. In parenthetical citations, give page numbers only; do not repeat the volume number.

Rand, Enid. <u>Virology</u>. Vol. 2. Philadelphia: Lippincott, 1979.

When you use only one volume of a multivolume work in which each volume is titled separately, you can list it as you would any book, using its individual title and not referring to the rest of the volumes.

Goldman, L. H., Cloria L. Cronin, and Ada Aharoni. <u>Saul Bellow: A</u>

    <u>Mosaic</u>. New York: P. Lang, 1992.

    If you want to include information about the set of volumes, put it after the basic information about the volume you used.

Goldman, L. H., Cloria L. Cronin, and Ada Aharoni. <u>Saul Bellow: A</u>

    <u>Mosaic</u>. New York: P. Lang, 1992. Vol. 2 of <u>Twentieth Century</u>

    <u>American Jewish Writers</u>. 14 vols.

10. ANTHOLOGY OR COLLECTION—MLA

    When your paper is about a collection of works rather than about the individual selections in an anthology or collection, use this form. Also see item 15 below.

Elliott, Emory, et al., eds. <u>American Literature: A Prentice Hall</u>

    <u>Anthology</u>. Concise ed. Englewood Cliffs, NJ: Prentice, 1991.

11. ONE SELECTION FROM AN ANTHOLOGY OR COLLECTION—MLA

Franklin, Benjamin. An Address to the Public. <u>American Literature: A</u>

    <u>Prentice Hall Anthology</u>, Concise ed. Ed. Emory Elliott et al.,

    Englewood Cliffs, NJ: Prentice, 1991. 173-74.

12. MORE THAN ONE SELECTION FROM AN ANTHOLOGY OR COLLECTION—MLA

    When you use more than one selection from one anthology, in the Works Cited list you can give one entry for the anthology and separate brief entries for each selection cited from the anthology. This plan is more efficient than using the form shown in item 10 for each selection you use. Give full details about the anthology or edited collection, with the editor's name as the first item of information. For each selection cited in your paper, give the name of the selection's author and title. End this information with a period, and then give the name that starts the entry for the anthology and inclusive pages on which the specific selection falls. For citations in your paper, use the name of the author of the selection, not the editor of the anthology. The following entries show first an entry for an anthology followed by entries for two selections in the anthology. Readers who look at the Glück and Ortiz entries are directed to the Elliott entry for full information about the anthology and see that the cited material is on pages 1952 and 1944, respectively.

Elliott, Emory, et al., eds. American <u>Literature: A Prentice Hall</u>

    <u>Anthology</u>, Concise ed. Englewood Cliffs, NJ: Prentice, 1991.

QUOTATION ABOUT WRITING

My task—which I am trying to achieve— is by the power of the written word to make you hear, to make you feel. It is, before all, to make you see.

—Joseph Conrad

Glück, Louise. "Elms." Elliott et al. 1952.

Ortiz, Simon J. "Dry Root in a Wash." Elliott et al. 1944.

13. SIGNED ARTICLE IN A REFERENCE BOOK—MLA

Sax, Joseph L. "Environmental Law." <u>Encyclopedia Americana</u>. 1994 ed.

Alphabetically arranged collections such as the encyclopedias in this model and the next one do not contain page numbers.

14. UNSIGNED ARTICLE IN A REFERENCE BOOK—MLA

"Russia." <u>Encyclopaedia Britannica</u>. 1994 ed,

15. EDITION—MLA

When a book is in some edition other than the first, the edition number appears on the title page. Include this information after the title. Use *2nd ed., 3rd ed., Rev. ed.* (for *Revised edition*), and so on. Put a period after **ed.**, which also acts as the period at the end of the information block.

Walker, Robert S. <u>AIDS Today, Tomorrow: An Introduction to the HIV</u>
　　　<u>Epidemic in America</u>. 2nd ed. Atlantic Highlands, NJ: Humanities,
　　　1994.

Books are also "editions" when an editor has made an important contribution, such as in selecting works and writing background material about them for an anthology. In this sort of edition, the editor's name (or editors' names) come first. Also see item 10 above.

Lantolf, James P., and Gabriela Appel, eds. <u>Vygotskian Approaches to</u>
　　　<u>Second Language Research</u>. Norwood, NJ: Ablex, 1994.

Spear, Thomas, and Richard Waller, eds. <u>Being Masai: Ethnicity and</u>
　　　<u>Identity in East Africa</u>. Athens: Ohio UP. 1993.

16. INTRODUCTION, PREFACE, FOREWORD, OR AFTERWORD—MLA

Diamond, Jared. Foreword. <u>Wild Forests Conservation Biology and Public</u>
　　　<u>Policy</u>. By William S. Alverson, Walter Kuhlmann, and Donald M.
　　　Waller. Washington, DC: Island, 1994. iv.

Carter, Carol. Introduction. <u>Majoring in the Rest of Your Life</u>. By
　　　Carter. New York: Noonday-Farrar, 1990. 1-7.

When you cite an introduction, preface, foreword, afterword, or appendix, give first the name of the person who wrote it. Then give the name of the cited part, capitalizing it and using a period after it; do not underline it or put it in quotation marks. Then give the title of the book. If the preface, introduction, foreword, afterword, or appendix was written by someone other than the author of the book, give the word *By* and the name of the book's author(s), in normal order. If the book's author wrote the part you are citing, after *By* repeat only the last name or names. After publication information, give inclusive page numbers. If a cited preface or introduction uses roman numerals for page numbers, use roman numerals.

17. UNPUBLISHED DISSERTATION—MLA

```
Black, Laurel Johnson. "Language, Power, and Gender in Student-Teacher
     Conferences." Diss. Miami U, 1993.
```

18. REPRINT OF AN OLDER BOOK—MLA

```
Melville, Herman. Moby Dick, or The Whale. 1851. New York: Modern
     Library, 1992.
```

A republished book may be the paperback version of a book originally published as a hardbound, or it may be the reissue of a book. Republishing information can be found on the copyright page. Give the date of the original version before the publication information for the version you used.

19. BOOK IN A SERIES—MLA

```
Rothman, Hal. On Rims and Ridges: The Los Alamos Area since 1880.
     Twentieth-Century American West. Lincoln: U of Nebraska P, 1992.
```

Give the book title, underlined, after the author name. Put the series title, neither underlined nor in quotation marks, after the book title.

20. BOOK WITH A TITLE WITHIN A TITLE—MLA

```
Hayes, Kevin J., ed. The Critical Response to Herman Melville's Moby
     Dick. Westport, CT: Greenwood, 1994.
```

When a book title includes the title of another work that is usually underlined (such as a novel, play, or long poem), do not underline the incorporated title. When a book title includes a title enclosed in quotation marks (such as of a short story or most poems), keep the quotation marks and underline the entire title.

21. GOVERNMENT PUBLICATIONS—MLA

For most government publications, use the name of the government as the first information unit (such as United States). If no author is named, give the name of the branch of government or the government agency next (such as Dept. of State or Cong. House).

United States. Dept. of the Interior. Minerals Management Service. _Minerals Revenues, 1992: Report on Receipts from Federal and Indian Leases_. Washington: GPO, 1993.

United States. Dept. of Commerce. National Oceanic and Atmospheric Administration. _COSPAS-SARSAT Search and Rescue Satellite System_. Washington: GPO, 1988.

United States. Dept. of Labor. Bureau of Labor Statistics. _Consumer Expenditure Survey, 1990-91_ (Bulletin 2425). Washington: GPO, 1993.

For citations from the _Congressional Record,_ just give the abbreviation _Cong. Rec.,_ the date, and page numbers.

Cong. Rec. 26 Nov. 1993: 3050-3051.

22. PUBLISHED PROCEEDINGS OF A CONFERENCE—MLA

Pavlyshyn, Marko, and J. E. M. Clarke, eds. _Ukraine in the 1990s. Proc. of the First Conference of the Ukrainian Studies Association of Australia_. Melbourne: Monash University, 1992.

If the title of the publication of the conference proceedings includes the name and location of the conference, do not repeat that information after the title. Just give author(s), title, and publication details.

PRINT SOURCES: ARTICLES AND OTHER SHORT DOCUMENTS

23. SIGNED ARTICLE FROM A DAILY NEWSPAPER—MLA

Steinberg, Jacques. "Love, Peace, Money, Lawsuits." _New York Times_ 12 May. 1995: B1.

24. EDITORIAL, LETTER TO THE EDITOR, REVIEW—MLA

"Patching up Health Care." Editorial. _New York Times_ 17 July 1994: E16.

Turkel, Stanley. Letter. _New York Times_ 3 July 1993: L18.

Doniger, Wendy. "Shackled to the Past." Rev. of _Gerald's Game_ by Stephen King. _New York Times Book Review_ 16 Aug. 1992: 3.

25. UNSIGNED ARTICLE FROM A DAILY NEWSPAPER—MLA

"Gene Is Shown to Block the Spread of Prostate Cancer in Mice." _New York Times_ 12 May 1995: A17.

26. Signed Article from a Weekly or Biweekly Magazine or Newspaper—MLA

Rosen, Jeffrey. "Is Affirmative Action Doomed?" <u>New Republic</u> 17 Oct.

    1994: 25+.

The Rosen article runs on pages 25-30 and 34-35; the + sign is sufficient to show that it runs past page 25.

27. Signed Article from a Monthly or Bimonthly Periodical—MLA

Came, Barry. "Policing Haiti." <u>Maclean's</u> Oct. 1994: 20-22.

Bell, Jim. "Kingdom Come: Canada's Inuit Finally May Be Getting Their

    Own Homeland, But at What Price?" <u>Earthwatch</u> Sept./Oct.: 10-11.

28. Unsigned Article from a Weekly or Monthly Periodical—MLA

"The March Almanac." <u>Atlantic Monthly</u>. 16 Mar. 1994: 16.

29. Article from a Collection of Reprinted Articles—MLA

Brumberg, Abraham. "Russia after Perestroika." <u>New York Review of Books</u>

    27 June 1991: 53-62. Rpt. in <u>Russian and Soviet History</u>. Ed.

    Alexander Dallin. Vol. 14, The Gorbachev Era. New York: Garland,

    1992. 300-320.

30. Article from a SIRS Collection of Reprinted Articles—MLA

Curver, Philip C. "Lighting in the 21st Century." <u>Futurist</u> Jan./Feb.

    1989: <u>Energy</u>. Ed. Eleanor Goldstein. Vol. 4. Boca Raton: SIRS,

    1990. Art. 84.

Social Issues Resources Series (SIRS) articles are looseleaf collections of reprints from many sources. Give information about the original publication before the information about the article's publication in SIRS. Use the abbreviation *Art.* before the SIRS article number.

31. Article in a Journal with Continuous Pagination—MLA

A journal that pages continuously throughout a volume (usually one year's publications) does not begin each issue with page 1. If the first issue in the volume ends on page 160, for example, the second issue starts on page 161. A reader who has the volume number, the year, and the page numbers can locate the correct issue of a continuously paged journal. Give the volume number in arabic numerals (without an abbreviation before it such as *vol.* or *Vol.*) immediately after the journal name. Include the year in parentheses. Give inclusive page numbers unless the article is not printed on consecutive pages; in that case, give the article's first page number followed by a plus sign (+).

LaFollette, M. C. "The Politics of Research Misconduct: Congressional
    Oversight, Universities, and Science." <u>Journal of Higher Education</u>
    65 (1994): 261-85.

32. ARTICLE IN A JOURNAL THAT PAGES EACH ISSUE SEPARATELY—MLA

If each issue in a year's issues of a scholarly journal starts on page 1, give an issue number after the volume number. Use arabic numerals. Separate the two numbers with a period but with no space before or after the period. For example, in the model, 30.10 signifies that the Hancock article is in volume 30, number 10 of *IEEE Spectrum*.

Hancock, D. "Prototyping the Hubble Fix." <u>IEEE Spectrum</u> 30.10 (1993):
    34-39.

If a journal uses issue numbers but not volume numbers, give the issue number after the journal name.

33. AN ABSTRACT FROM A COLLECTION OF ABSTRACTS

To cite an abstract, first give information for the full work: the author's name, the title of the article, and publication information about the full article. If a reader could not know that the cited material is an abstract, give the word *Abstract,* not underlined, followed by a period. Give publication information about the collection of abstracts. For abstracts identified by item numbers rather than page numbers, use the word *item* before the item number.

Marcus, Hazel R. and Shinobu Kitayamo. "Culture and the Self:
    Implications for Cognition, Emotion, and Motivation. <u>Psychological</u>
    <u>Review</u> 88 (1991): 224-53. <u>Psychological Abstracts</u> 78: item 23878.

34. PUBLISHED AND UNPUBLISHED LETTERS—MLA

If you cite a letter from a published source, name the author of the letter first. Identify the letter as such, and give its date, if available. Then give publication information.

Lapidus, Jackie. Letter to her mother. 12 Nov. 1975. <u>Between Ourselves:</u>
    <u>Letters Between Mothers and Daughters</u>. Ed. Karen Payne. Boston:
    Houghton, 1983. 323-26.

If you cite a personal letter that is not in a published source, give the letter writer's name as author, and put *Letter to the author* after the letter writer's name. Then give the date on the letter.

Reilly, Gary Edward. Letter to the author. 26 Dec. 1994.

You can document electronic mail in a similar way.

```
Putnam, Christopher. E-mail to the author. 6 June 1996.
```

35. MAP OR CHART—MLA

```
Russia and Post-Soviet Republics. Map. Moscow: Mapping Production
    Association, 1992.
```

NONPRINT SOURCES

36. INTERVIEW—MLA

```
Friedman, Randi. Telephone interview. 30 June 1992.
```

For a face-to-face interview, use `Personal interview` instead of `Telephone interview`. For a published interview, give the name of the interviewed person first, identify the source as an interview, and then give details as for any published source: author (preceded by the word *By*), title, publication details.

For a radio or television interview, give the name of the interviewed person first, the name of the interviewer next, and then information about the program on which the interview was broadcast.

```
Kennan, George F. Interview with Robert MacNeil. MacNeil/Lehrer News
    Hour. PBS. WGBH, Boston. 22 Aug. 1991.
```

37. LECTURE, SPEECH, ADDRESS—MLA

```
Clinton, William J. Address. World Youth Day conference. Denver, 12 Aug.
    1993.
```

38. FILM OR VIDEOTAPE—MLA

```
A World of Gestures: Cultural and Nonverbal Communication. Writ./Dir.
    David Archer. Berkeley: U of Cal. Extension Media Center, 1992.
```

39. RECORDING—MLA

In a citation of a recording, put first the information important to your use of the source. Here is an entry with the focus on the director of the choral group.

```
De la Cuesta, Ismael Fernando, dir. Benedictine Monks of Santo Domingo
    de Silos. Chant. Angel, 1994.
```

If the use of this source in the paper focused on the performers and the music, the entry would look like this:

```
Benedictine Monks of Santo Domingo de Silos. Chant. Dir. Ismael Fernando
    De la Cuesta. Angel, 1994.
```

If you are citing a recording in some medium other than a compact disk, name the medium. To cite a specific song, give the song title in quotation marks before the title of the recording.

```
Springsteen, Bruce. "Local Hero." Lucky Town. Audiocassette. Columbia,
     1992.
```

40. Live Performance—MLA

```
Song of a Mockingbird. By Susan J. Whitenight. Prod. Randal King. Utah
     Valley State College Theater, Orem. 28 Nov. 1994.
```

41. Work of Art or Musical Composition

```
Cassatt, Mary. Five O'Clock Tea. Museum of Fine Arts, Boston.

Gershwin, George. Porgy and Bess.

Schubert, Franz. Symphony no. 8 in B minor.

Schubert, Franz. Unfinished Symphony.
```

For musical compositions, give composer and title of work. Underline the title of an opera, ballet, or descriptive word title for music. But if a composition is identified only by musical form, number, and key, do not underline it and do not put it in quotation marks. See the entries for Schubert, which show two ways of identifying the same composition.

42. Radio or Television Program—MLA

For programs that title both the series and each episode, give the episode title first in quotation marks, and then give the series title underlined. If your use of the program focuses on a participant (such as a performer, writer, or director), give that name first, an abbreviated indication of that person's role (perf., writ., dir.), and then the programming information. Include the network, the local station and its city, and the date of the broadcast.

```
"The Homecoming." Frontline. PBS. WNYC, New York. 25 Apr. 1995.
```

ELECTRONIC SOURCES

The objectives for documenting electronic sources are the same as those for print sources: giving information so that a reader understands what sources you have used and can find those sources that are generally available. The 1995 edition of the *MLA Handbook for Writers of Research* makes two major distinctions that affect the information you put in a Works Cited entry for an electronic source. One is whether the database is "portable," such as those on CD-ROM or diskette, or online; each Works Cited entry names the electronic medium, and the ones you are most likely to encounter are portable databases on CD-ROM and online databases. The second is whether the source has a print version or exists only in an electronic version; each Works Cited entry for a source that also has a print version starts out with information about the print version. For such sources, follow the information in the entries above for printed documents, and then add the necessary information about your electronic access of the source.

In general, the basic information needed for an electronic source is name of author (if any), publication information for a print version (if any), database title, publication medium, name of the producer (for "portable" databases) or computer network or service (for online databases), electronic publication date ("portable") or date of access (online).

To see the differences in an entry for a portable and an online source, compare items 43 and 44. They show a Works Cited entry for the same abstract from *Psychological Abstracts.* Item 43 documents the source accessed through PsycLIT, a CD-ROM version, and item 44 documents online access.

43. CD-ROM Database: Abstract with a Print Version—MLA

```
Marcus, Hazel R. and Shinobu Kitayamo. "Culture and the Self:
     Implications for Cognition, Emotion, and Motivation." Psychological
     Abstracts 78 (1991): item 23878. PsycLIT. CD-ROM. SilverPlatter.
     Sept. 1991.
```

This model shows a portable database of information that also appears in a print version and that is updated from time to time. The information units for such a source start with the print version, followed by information about the electronic version. This source is an abstract from *Psychological Abstracts.* The information following the title *Psychological Abstracts* is the volume number and year and the item number of the abstract in the print version. PsycLIT is the name of the CD-ROM database, and SilverPlatter is the name of the producer of the CD-ROM. The database was issued in September 1991. Compare this entry with item 44, for this source accessed online.

44. Online Database: Abstract with a Print Version—MLA

```
Marcus, Hazel R. and Shinobu Kitayamo. "Culture and the Self:
     Implications for Cognition, Emotion, and Motivation." Psychological
     Abstracts 78 (1991): item 23878. PsycINFO. Online. DIALOG. 10 Oct.
     1991.
```

This entry is for the same abstract from *Psychological Abstracts* shown in item 43 but accessed online. This model notes PsycINFO, the

EXTRA EXERCISE B
Using the following information, compile a Works Cited list following MLA style.

1. *Abraham Lincoln: The Man Behind the Myths*, by Stephen B. Oates. Harper & Row, Publishers, New York, Cambridge, Philadelphia, San Francisco, London, Mexico City, Sao Paulo, and Sydney, 1984.

2. Barbara W. Tuchman. *Practicing History*. Alfred A. Knopf, Inc. Copyright 1936, 1959, 1966, 1974, 1981. Introduction copyright 1981. New York.

3. *Time's Arrow, Time's Cycle: Myth and Metaphor in the Discovery of Geological Time*. Stephen Jay Gould. Harvard University Press, Cambridge, Massachusetts. 1987.

4. T. C. Smout. *A Century of the Scottish People, 1830–1950*. New Haven and London. 1986, Yale University Press.

5. Thomas J. Peters and Robert H. Waterman, Jr. *In Search of Excellence*. Harper & Row, Publishers, New York, 1982.

6. *The Man Who Mistook His Wife for a Hat, and Other Clinical Tales*. Oliver Sacks. New York. Summit Books. "The Autist Artist." No year of publication listed. Pages 204 through 223.

7. *The Rise and Fall of the House of Medici*. 1974. Penguin Books. New York. Christopher Hibbert.

8. *Capote: A Biography*. 1988. Simon & Schuster. New York. Gerald Clarke.

name of the online database, where item 43 notes PsycLIT, the name of the CD-ROM database. It uses Online where the model in item 43 uses CD-ROM. Access was through a computer service, so this model uses DIALOG where item 43 uses SilverPlatter. In both entries, *78* is the volume number of the print version of *Psychological Abstracts*, and *item 23878* is the abstract number in the print version. The date on which the abstract was accessed is October 10, 1991.

45. CD-ROM: ARTICLE FROM A MAGAZINE WITH A PRINT VERSION—MLA

"The Price Is Right." <u>Time</u>. 20 Jan. 1992: 38. <u>Time Man of the Year</u>.
    CD-ROM. Compact Publishing, Inc. 1993

The information common to both the CD-ROM version and the print version comes first. After the publication date for the print version comes a colon followed by the page number for the print version, 38. The title of the CD-ROM is Time Man of the Year, its producer is Compact Publishing, Inc., and its copyright year is 1993. Underline both the title of the print publication and the title of the CD-ROM.

46. CD-ROM: SELECTION FROM A BOOK WITH A PRINT VERSION—MLA

"Prehistoric Humans: Earliest Homo Sapiens." <u>The Guinness Book of</u>
    <u>Records</u> 1994. Guinness Publishing, Ltd. 1994. The <u>Guinness</u>
    <u>Multimedia Disk of Records</u>, 1994 Edition. Version 2.0. CD-ROM.
    Grolier Electronic Publishing, 1994.

The information about the book version ends after the publisher and year and information about the CD-ROM version begins. Version 2.0 signals that this CD-ROM is updated periodically; the producer changes version numbers rather than giving update dates.

47. CD-ROM: MATERIAL WITH NO PRINT VERSION—MLA

"Spanish Dance." <u>Encarta</u> 1994. CD-ROM. Redmond, WA: Microsoft, 1993

Encarta is a CD-ROM encyclopedia with no print version. "Spanish Dance" is the title of an article in this encyclopedia.

48. CD-ROM: NONPERIODICAL PUBLICATION—MLA

Wick, James, and Dave Jackson. <u>Wayzata World Factbook</u> 1993 Edition.
    CD-ROM. Wayzata Technology, 1992.

When authors are named, treat the name(s) as for a print publication.

<u>World Atlas MPC</u>. Version 3.2. CD-ROM. Novato: Software Toolworks, 1992.

49. Work in More than One Publication Medium—MLA

Some sources come in more than one medium: a book and a CD, a disk and a video, a CD and a laserdisk. As for other electronic sources, give as much information as available, separating it into information blocks for each medium.

```
Clarke, David James, IV. Novell's CNE Study Guide. Book. Network Support
     Encyclopedia. CD-ROM. Alameda: Sybex, 1994.
```

This book and CD-ROM come together. The book and the CD-ROM have different titles, but the publication information—Alameda: Sybex, 1994—applies to both.

Diskettes and magnetic tape are two other "portable" electronic mediums. For them, use the same kinds and patterns of information shown for CD-ROMs, except list *Diskette* or *Magnetic tape* for the publication medium.

The next section shows Works Cited entries for online sources.

50. Online: Article from a Newspaper with a Print Version—MLA

```
Kapor, Mitchell, and Jerry Berman. "A Superhighway Through the
     Wasteland?" New York Times. 24 Nov. 1993: Op-ed page. New York
     Times Online. 5 May 1995.
```

Information applying to the print version of this article in the *New York Times* ends at Op-ed page. Online is the publication medium and *New York Times Online* is the name of the database. The date 5 May 1995 tells when the article was accessed.

51. Online: Article from a Magazine with a Print Version—MLA

```
"Homeowners Insurance." Consumer Reports. October 1993: n. pag. Online.
     CompuServe. 5 May 1995.
```

When an online source does not show page numbers even though a source has a print version, at the end of the information about the print version, put *n. pag.*, an abbreviation meaning "no pagination." This abbreviation in a Works Cited entry signals readers why page numbers are not given in parenthetical references to the source in your paper.

52. Online: Material with No Print Version—MLA

```
"Athenian-Spartan Rivalry." Academic American Encyclopedia. Online.
     CompuServe. 3 Feb. 1995.
```

ANSWERS: EXTRA EXERCISE B
Works Cited

Clarke, Gerald. *Capote: A Biography.* New York: Simon, 1988.

Gould, Stephen Jay. *Time's Arrow, Time's Cycle: Myth and Metaphor in the Discovery of Geological Time.* Cambridge: Harvard UP, 1987.

Hibbert, Christopher. *The Rise and Fall of the House of Medici.* New York: Penguin, 1974.

Oates, Stephen B. *Abraham Lincoln: The Man Behind the Myths.* New York: Harper, 1984.

Peters, Thomas J., and Robert H. Waterman, Jr. *In Search of Excellence.* New York: Harper, 1982.

Sacks, Oliver. "The Autist Artist." *The Man Who Mistook His Wife for a Hat, and Other Clinical Tales.* New York: Summit, n.d.

Smout, T. C. *A Century of the Scottish People, 1830–1950.* New Haven: Yale UP, 1986.

Tuchman, Barbara W. *Practicing History.* New York: Knopf, 1981.

MLA MLA MLA MLA MLA MLA MLA

53. ONLINE: MATERIAL FROM AN ELECTRONIC NEWSLETTER—MLA

"Microsoft Licenses OSM Technology from Henter-Joyce." _Microsoft®_
    WinNews Electronic Newsletter. 2:6 (1 May 1995): n. pag. Online.
    Internet. 15 May 1995.

The numerals 2:6 mean volume 2, number 6 of this electronic newsletter.

54. ONLINE: AN ELECTRONIC TEXT—MLA

Herodotus. _The History of Herodotus_. Trans. George Rawlinson. Online.
    Book Stacks Unlimited. Internet. 1 Jun. 1995.

Book Stacks Unlimited is where the electronic text "resides." You access this "location" through the Internet network. Here is an entry for the same source showing how to include an electronic address, in this case for a location on the Internet. Start an electronic address with Available FTP (which stands for "file transfer protocol") followed by a colon and the address.

Herodotus. _The History of Herodotus_. Trans. George Rawlinson. Online.
    Book Stacks Unlimited. Internet. 1 Jun. 1995. Available FTP: books.
    com.

55. ONLINE: A PUBLIC MESSAGE—MLA

Be skeptical about using an online posting as a source. Some of them contain cutting-edge information from experts; some of them contain trash. To cite one, give the author name (if any), document title, and then Online posting. Then give location information, network name, and the date that you accessed the message.

33c-4

Using Content or Bibliographic Notes in MLA Style

In MLA style, footnotes or endnotes serve two specific purposes: (1) You can use them for content (ideas and information) that does not fit into your paper but is still worth relating; and (2) you can use them for bibliographic information that would intrude if you were to include it in your text.

TEXT OF PAPER

Eudora Welty's literary biography, _One Writer's Beginnings_, shows us how both the inner world of self and the outer world of family and place form a writer's imagination.[1]

CONTENT NOTE—MLA

[1] Welty, who values her privacy, has resisted investigation of her life. However, at the age of 74, she chose to present her own autobiographical reflections in a series of lectures at Harvard University.

TEXT OF PAPER

Barbara Randolph believes that enthusiasm is contagious (65).[1] Many psychologists have found that panic, fear, and rage spread more quickly in crowds than positive emotions do, however.

BIBLIOGRAPHIC NOTE—MLA

[1] Others who agree with Randolph include Thurman 21, 84, 155; Kelley 421-25; and Brookes 65-76.

❖ MLA FORMAT ALERT: Place a note number at the end of a sentence, if possible. Put it after any punctuation mark except the dash. Do not put any space before a note number, and put one space after it. In typed papers, raise the note number a little above the line of words. In word processing programs, use superscript numbers. ❖

For more examples of MLA-style content notes and to see page format for endnotes, see the student research paper in section 34b.

33d

Using APA-style documentation

The American Psychological Association (APA) endorses a name-year parenthetical reference documentation system that is used in its journals and has come to be used by students in the social sciences and some other disciplines. APA in-text citations alert readers to material you have used from outside sources. These citations function with an alphabetical **References list** at the end of your paper containing information that enables readers to retrieve the sources you have quoted from (see 31c), paraphrased (see 31d), or summarized (see 31e).

33d-1

Citing sources in the body of a paper in APA style

In-text citations identify a source by a name (usually an author name) and a year (for copyrighted sources, usually the copyright year). You can often incorporate the relevant name, and sometimes the year, into your sentence. Otherwise, put this information in parentheses, placing the parenthetical reference so that a reader knows exactly what it refers to and is distracted by it as little as possible.

The APA *Publication Manual* recommends that if you refer to a work more than once in a paragraph, you give the author name and date

QUOTATION ABOUT WRITING

We do not write in order to be understood; we write in order to understand.

—C. Day-Lewis

33d–1
cont.

the first time that you mention the work, and then give only the name after that. There is one exception: If you are citing two or more works by the same author, each citation must include the date so that a reader knows which work is being cited.

APA style requires page numbers for direct quotations* only (not for paraphrases or summaries). However, some instructors expect page references for any use made of sources, so find out your instructor's preference. Put page numbers in parentheses, using the abbreviation *p.* before a single page number and *pp.* when the material you are citing falls on more than one page.

1. CITING A PARAPHRASED OR SUMMARIZED SOURCE—APA

People from the Mediterranean prefer an elbow-to-shoulder distance from each other (Morris, 1977). [Name and date cited in parentheses.]

Desmond Morris notes that people from the Mediterranean prefer an elbow-to-shoulder distance from each other (1977, p. 131). [Name cited in text, date and page cited in parentheses.]

2. CITING THE SOURCE OF A SHORT QUOTATION—APA

A recent report of reductions in SAD-related "depression in 87 percent of patients" (Binkley, 1990, p. 203) reverses the findings of earlier studies. [Name, date, and page reference in parentheses immediately following the quotation.]

Binkley reports reductions in SAD-related "depression in 87 percent of patients" (1990, p. 203). [Name incorporated into the words introducing the quotation and date and page number in parentheses immediately following the quotation.]

3. FORMATTING A LONG QUOTATION AND CITING ITS SOURCE—APA

Incorporate a direct quotation of fewer than 40 words into your own sentence(s) and enclose it in quotation marks. Place the parenthetical citation after the closing quotation mark and, if the quotation falls at the end of the sentence, before the sentence-ending punctuation. When you use a quotation longer than 40 words, set it off from your words by starting it on a new line and by indenting each line of the quotation 5 spaces from the left margin. Do not enclose it in quotation marks. Place the parenthetical citation 2 spaces after the end punctuation of the last sentence.

* When a source is no more than one page long, the page number is included in information about the source in the References list. Therefore, it is unnecessary to repeat the page number in in-text citations.

DISPLAYED QUOTATION (40 OR MORE WORDS)

Jet lag, with its characteristic fatigue and irregular sleep patterns, is a common problem among those who travel great distances by jet airplane to different time zones:

> Jet lag syndrome is the inability of the internal body rhythm to rapidly resynchronize after sudden shifts in the timing. For a variety of reasons, the system attempts to maintain stability and resist temporal change. Consequently, complete adjustment can often be delayed for several days—sometimes for a week—after arrival at one's destination. (Bonner, 1991, p. 72).

Interestingly, this research shows that the number of flying hours is not the cause of jet lag.

The following examples show how to handle parenthetical citations for various sources. Remember, though, that you often can introduce source names, including titles when necessary, and sometimes even years in your own sentences.

5. CITING ONE AUTHOR—APA

One of his questions is "What binds together a Mormon banker in Utah with his brother, or other coreligionists in Illinois or Massachusetts?" (Coles, 1993, p. 2)

In a parenthetical reference in APA style, a comma and a space separate a name from a year and a year from a page reference. (Examples 1 through 4 above also show citations of works by one author.)

2. CITING TWO AUTHORS—APA

If a work has two authors, give both names in each citation.

One report describes 2,123 occurrences (Krait & Cooper, 1994).

The results Krait and Cooper (1994) report would not support the conclusions Davis and Sherman draw in their review of the literature (1992).

When citing two (or more) authors, use an ampersand (&) between the (final) two names for parenthetical references, but use the word *and* for references in your own sentence.

3. CITING THREE, FOUR, OR FIVE AUTHORS—APA

For three, four, or five authors, use all the authors' last names in the first reference. In all subsequent references, use only the first author's last name followed by *et al.*

FIRST REFERENCE

In one anthology, 35 percent of the selections had not been anthologized
before (Elliott, Kerber, Litz, & Martin, 1992).

SUBSEQUENT REFERENCE

Elliott et al. (1992) include 17 authors whose work has never been
anthologized.

4. CITING SIX OR MORE AUTHORS—APA

For six or more authors, use the name of the first author followed
by *et al.* for all references, including the first.

5. CITING AUTHOR(S) WITH TWO OR MORE WORKS IN THE SAME YEAR—APA

If you use more than one source written in the same year by the
same author(s), alphabetize the works by their titles for the References
list, and assign letters in alphabetical order to the years—(1996a),
(1996b), (1996c). Use the year-letter combination in parenthetical references. Note that a citation of two or more of such works lists the years
in alphabetical order.

Most recently, Jones (1996c) draws new conclusions from the results of
17 sets of experiments (1996a, 1996b).

6. CITING TWO OR MORE AUTHORS WITH THE SAME LAST NAME—APA

Use first- and middle-name initials for every in-text citation of
authors who share a last name.

R. A. Smith (1997) and C. Smith (1989) both confirm these results.

These results have been confirmed independently (C. Smith, 1989; R. A.
Smith, 1997).

7. CITING A GROUP OR CORPORATE AUTHOR—APA

If you use a source in which the "author" is the name of a corporation, agency, or group, an in-text reference gives that name as author.
Use the full name in each citation unless an abbreviated version of the
name is likely to be familiar to your audience. In that case, use the full
name and give its abbreviation at the first citation; then use the abbreviation for subsequent citations.

This exploration will continue into the 21st century (National
Aeronautics and Space Administration [NASA], 1996).

In subsequent citations, you can then use the abbreviated form.

8. Citing Works by Title—APA

If no author is named, use a shortened form of the title in citations. Ignoring *A*, *An*, or *The*, make the first word the one by which you alphabetize the title in References. The following citation is to an article fully titled "Are You a Day or Night Person?"

```
The "morning lark" and "night owl" connotations typically are used to
categorize the human extremes ("Are You," 1989).
```

9. Citing More than One Source in a Parenthetical Reference—APA

If more than one source has contributed to an idea or opinion in your paper, cite the sources alphabetically in one set of parentheses; separate each block of information with a semicolon.

```
Conceptions of personal space vary among cultures (Morris, 1977; Worchel
& Cooper, 1983).
```

10. Citing a Personal Communication—APA

Telephone calls, personal letters, and interviews are "personal communications" that your readers do not have access to. Acknowledge personal communications in parenthetical references but do not include them in your References list.

```
Recalling his first summer at camp, one person said, "The proximity of
12 other kids made me—an only child with older, quiet parents—frantic
for the entire eight weeks" (A. Weiss, personal communication, January
12, 1996).
```

11. Citing Graphics—APA

If you include in your paper a graphic from another source, give a note in the text at the bottom of the table or graphic crediting the original author and the copyright holder. Here are examples of two source lines, one for a graphic from an article, the other for a graphic from a book. (If you plan to publish your document, you will need copyright permission from the copyright holder in order to reproduce the table or graphic. You will also have to add a line such as *Reprinted* [or *Adapted*] *with permission.*)

GRAPHIC FROM AN ARTICLE

```
Note. From "Bridge over troubled waters? Connecting research and
pedagogy in composition and business/technical communication" by J.
Allen, 1992, Technical Communication Quarterly, 1(4), p. 9. Copyright
1992 by the Association of Teachers of Technical Writing.
```

QUOTATION ABOUT WRITING

I have long since decided if you wait for the perfect time to write, you'll never write. There is no time that isn't flawed somehow.

—Margaret Atwood

APA

APA

33d-2

GRAPHIC FROM A BOOK

```
Note. From How to lower your fat thermostat: The no-diet reprogramming
plan for lifelong weight control (p. 74) by D. Remington, M.D., A. G.
Fisher, Ph.D., and E. Parent, Ph.D., 1983, Provo: Vitality House
International. Copyright 1983 by Vitality House International.
```

Compiling an APA-style References list

In APA documentation, in-text citations must be accompanied by a list of sources referred to in your paper. Include in this References list the "recoverable" sources that you quote from, paraphrase, or summarize. A recoverable source is one that another person could retrieve with reasonable effort. Do not include in the References list any source not available to others, such as personal letters and other personal communications. (To alert readers to your use of such sources, you use a parenthetical citation marking the source as a personal communication; see, for example, item 34 about personal interviews.) Chart 143 summarizes information about the References list.

GUIDELINES FOR COMPILING AN APA-STYLE REFERENCES LIST 143

■ **TITLE**

References

■ **PLACEMENT OF LIST**

Start a new page numbered sequentially with the rest of the paper, after Notes page(s), if any.

■ **CONTENTS AND FORMAT**

Include all quoted, paraphrased, or summarized sources in your paper that are not personal communications, unless your instructor tells you to include all the references you have consulted, not just those you have referred to. Start each entry on a new line, and double-space all lines. Check which of the following indent styles your instructor wants you to use:

1. First line of each entry indented, other lines full width.

   This style is shown in the APA Manual. Indent the first line of each entry 5 to 7 spaces (or 1 default tab, which is about an inch in most word-processing programs). If an entry has more than one line, make all lines after the first full width.

```
    Shuter, R. (1977). A field study of nonverbal communica-
tion in Germany, Italy, and the United States. Communication
Monographs, 44, 298-305.
```

GUIDELINES FOR COMPILING AN APA-STYLE REFERENCES LIST (continued)

143

2. First line of each entry full width, other lines indented.

This "hanging indent" style makes source names and dates prominent. Type the first line of each entry full width, and indent an entry's subsequent lines 5 to 7 spaces (or 1 tab).

Shuter, R. (1977). A field study of nonverbal communication in
    Germany, Italy, and the United States. <u>Communication
    Monographs, 44,</u> 298-305.

■ SPACING AFTER PUNCTUATION

The 1994 *APA Manual* calls for one space after most punctuation marks: periods at the ends of information units in references (and at the ends of sentences in your paper), commas, semicolons, and colons (except in ratios in your paper [2:1, 100:1]).

■ ARRANGEMENT OF ENTRIES

Alphabetize by author's last name. If no author is named, alphabetize by the first significant word (not *A*, *An*, or *The*) in the title of the work.

■ AUTHORS' NAMES

Use last names, first-name initials, and middle initials if any. Reverse the order for all author names, and use an ampersand (&) between the second-to-last and last authors: Mills, J. F., & Holahan, R. H.

Give names in the order used on the work (title page of book, usually under title of article or other printed work). Use a comma between the first author's last name and first initial and after each complete author name except the last. After the last author name, use a period.

■ DATE

Put date information after name information, enclosing it in parentheses and using a period followed by one space after the closing parenthesis.

For books, articles in journals that have volume numbers, and many other print and nonprint sources, the year of publication or production is the date to use. For articles from most magazines and newspapers, use the year followed by a month and sometimes day-date. Individual entries later in this chapter show how much information to give for various sources.

■ CAPITALIZATION OF TITLES

For books, capitalize the first word, the first word after a colon between a title and subtitle, and any proper nouns. For names of journals and proceedings of meetings, capitalize the first word, all nouns and adjectives, and any other words five or more letters long. ➜

QUOTATION ABOUT WRITING

. . . most writing is done away from the typewriter, away from the desk. I'd say it occurs in the quiet, silent moments.

—Henry Miller

QUOTATION ABOUT WRITING

This forward motion is also carried by the sounds. When I write, I write out loud. It's very important to me how the consonants click off against one another and how the vowels move into one another and out again. I also like the sounds of a line to move in an interesting and logical way through the mouth.

—Miller Williams

GUIDELINES FOR COMPILING AN APA-STYLE REFERENCES LIST (continued)

143

■ **SPECIAL TREATMENT OF TITLES**

Use no special treatment for titles of shorter works (poems, short stories, essays, articles). Underline titles of longer works (books, names of newspapers or journals containing cited articles). For underlining, use an unbroken line if possible.

Do not drop *A, An,* or *The* from the titles of periodicals (such as newspapers, magazines, and journals).

■ **FORM DESCRIPTION**

When a source is not a book or an article, a statement about its form is often useful for a reader who wants to retrieve the source. Enclose "form" information in brackets, and include it after a title and before a period at the end of the block of title information. Do not underline it. Electronically accessed sources should always have a form statement: for example, [On-line] or [CD-ROM]. Also see items 36-43.

■ **PUBLISHER**

Use the full name of a publisher, but drop *Co., Inc., Publishers,* and the like.

■ **PLACE OF PUBLICATION**

For publishers in the United States, give city and state (use 2-letter postal abbreviations) for all but the largest U.S. cities (such as Boston, Chicago, Los Angeles, and New York). For other countries, give city and country.

■ **PUBLICATION MONTH ABBREVIATIONS**

Do not abbreviate publication months.

■ **PAGE NUMBERS**

Use the full second number. Use *p.* and *pp.* before page numbers. List all discontinuous pages, with numbers separated by commas: pp. 32, 44-45, 47-49, 53.

■ **REFERENCES ENTRIES: BOOKS**

Citations for books have four main parts: author, date, title, and publication information (place of publication and publisher).

AUTHOR	DATE	TITLE	PUBLICATION INFORMATION
Didion, J.	(1977).	A book of common prayer.	New York: Simon & Schuster.

GUIDELINES FOR COMPILING AN APA-STYLE REFERENCES LIST (continued)

■ REFERENCES ENTRIES: ARTICLES

Citations for periodical articles contain four major parts: author, date, title of article, and publication information (usually the periodical title, volume number, and page numbers).

AUTHOR	DATE	ARTICLE TITLE

Shuter, R (1977). A field study of nonverbal communication in

PERIODICAL TITLE

Germany, Italy, and the United States Communication Monographs

VOLUME NUMBER | PAGE NUMBERS

44, 298-305

■ REFERENCES ENTRIES: ELECTRONIC SOURCES

Because standards for citing electronic sources are still being developed, APA recommends giving information for print forms of sources when print and electronic forms are the same. For widely available online sources, include path information. The basic elements of an electronic reference include author(s), date, title and form description (such as [*On-line*] or [*CD-ROM*]), periodical title and other information about a print version, location information (such as an availability statement and path for an online source or the producer and database name for a CD source). Here is an entry for an abstract on CD-ROM.

AUTHORS	DATE	ARTICLE TITLE

Marcus, H. F. & Kitayamo, S. (1991). Culture and the self:

FORM DESCRIPTION | JOURNAL TITLE AND PUBLICATION INFORMATION

Implications for group dynamics. [CD-ROM]. Psychological Review,

LOCATION INFORMATION

88(2), 224, 253. Abstract from: SilverPlatter File: PsycLIT

Item: 78-23878

QUOTATION ABOUT WRITING

How can you sit down to write until you have stood up to live?
—Henry David Thoreau

QUOTATION ABOUT WRITING

I have the words already. What I am seeking is the perfect order of words in the sentence. You can see for yourself how many different ways they might be arranged.

—James Joyce

Following models for an APA-style References list

Directory

PRINT SOURCES: BOOKS

1. Book by One Author—APA
2. Book by Two Authors—APA
3. Book by Three or More Authors—APA
4. Two or More Books by the Same Author(s)—APA
5. Book by Group or Corporate Author—APA
6. Book with No Author Named—APA
7. Book with an Author and an Editor—APA
8. Translation—APA
9. Work in Several Volumes or Parts—APA
10. Anthology or Edited Book—APA
11. One Selection from an Anthology or an Edited Book—APA
12. Two Selections from One Anthology or an Edited Book—APA
13. Signed Article in a Reference Book—APA
14. Unsigned Article in a Reference Book—APA
15. Edition—APA
16. Introduction, Preface, Foreword, or Afterword—APA
17. Unpublished Dissertation or Essay—APA
18. Reprint of an Older Book—APA
19. Book in a Series—APA
20. Book with a Title Within a Title—APA
21. Government Publications—APA
22. Published Proceedings of a Conference—APA

PRINT SOURCES: ARTICLES AND OTHER SHORT DOCUMENTS

23. Article from a Daily Newspaper—APA
24. Editorial, Letter to the Editor, or Review—APA
25. Unsigned Article from a Daily Newspaper—APA
26. Article from a Weekly or Biweekly Magazine or Newspaper—APA
27. Article from a Monthly or Bimonthly Periodical—APA
28. Unsigned Article from a Weekly or Monthly Periodical—APA
29. Article from a SIRS Collection of Reprinted Articles—APA
30. Article in a Journal with Continuous Pagination—APA
31. Article in a Journal that Pages Each Issue Separately—APA
32. Letters—APA
33. Map or Chart—APA

NONPRINT SOURCES

34. Interview—APA
35. Lecture, Speech, Address—APA
36. Film or Videotape—APA

33

APA
APA
APA
APA
APA
APA
APA
APA
APA
APA
APA

PRINT SOURCES: BOOKS

1. BOOK BY ONE AUTHOR—APA

Schaller, G. B. (1993). <u>The last panda</u>. Chicago: University of Chicago Press.

2. BOOK BY TWO AUTHORS—APA

Smith, R. J., & Gibbs, M. (1994) <u>Navigating the Internet.</u> Indianapolis, IN: Sams.

3. BOOK BY THREE OR MORE AUTHORS—APA

McMahan, E., Day, S., & Funk, R. (1993). <u>Nine short novels by American women.</u> New York: St. Martin's.

Cameron, D., Frazer, E., Harvey, P., Rampton, M. B. H., & Richardson, K. (1992). <u>Researching language: Issues of power and method.</u> London: Routledge.

In an APA References list, include the last names and initials of all authors, even though in your paper you use only the first author's name when a work has six or more authors.

4. TWO OR MORE BOOKS BY THE SAME AUTHOR(S)—APA

Waller, R. J. (1992). <u>The bridges of Madison County</u>. New York: Warner Books.

Waller, R. J. (1993). <u>Slow waltz in Cedar Bend</u>. New York: Warner Books.

Waller, R. J. (1994). <u>Old songs in a new cafe</u>. New York: Warner Books.

EXTRA EXERCISE C
Using the same sources that appeared in Extra Exercise B, compile a References list, following APA style.

ANSWERS: EXTRA EXERCISE C
References
Clarke, G. (1988). *Capote: A biography*. New York: Simon & Schuster.

Gould, S. J. (1987). *Time's arrow, time's cycle: Myth and metaphor in the discovery of geological time*. Cambridge: Harvard University Press.

Hibbert, C. (1974). *The rise and fall of the House of Medici*. New York: Penguin Books.

Oates, S. B. (1984). *Abraham Lincoln: The man behind the myths*. New York: Harper & Row.

Peters, T. J., & Waterman, R. H., Jr. (1982). *In search of excellence*. New York: Harper & Row.

Sacks, O. (n.d.). The autist artist. In *The man who mistook his wife for a hat, and other clinical tales* (pp. 204–223). New York: Summit Books.

Smout, T. C. (1986). *A century of the Scottish people, 1830–1950*. New Haven: Yale University Press.

Tuchman, B. W. (1981). *Practicing history*. New York: Alfred A. Knopf.

Repeat the author name(s) for each entry. Arrange the entries by date, from least recent to most recent. To cite two or more works by the same author(s) in the same year, arrange those entries in alphabetical order by title, and then assign a letter to each year (for example, 1993a, 1993b, 1993c). In parenthetical citations, the letter following the year distinguishes one same-year source from another.

5. BOOK BY GROUP OR CORPORATE AUTHOR—APA

Environmental Defense Fund. (1990). <u>Recycling and incineration: Evaluating the choice</u>. Washington, DC: Island.

American Psychological Association. (1994). <u>Publication manual of the American Psychological Association</u> (4th ed.). Washington, DC: Author.

When a book is in an edition other than the first, include the edition number in parentheses after the title. Put the period at the end of the block of title information after the closing parenthesis (also see item 6).

6. BOOK WITH NO AUTHOR NAMED—APA

<u>The Chicago manual of style</u> (14th ed.). (1993). Chicago: University of Chicago Press.

In your paper, use a shortened version of the title in parenthetical references (drop *A*, *An*, or *The* from a shortened title). Underline the words you use for a book title, and capitalize each significant word, even ones that start with lowercase letters in the References list: (Chicago Manual, 1993).

7. BOOK WITH AN AUTHOR AND AN EDITOR—APA

Welty, E. (1994). <u>A writer's eye: Collected book reviews</u> (P. A. McHaney, Ed.). Jackson, MI: University Press of Mississippi.

In an APA References list, always capitalize the abbreviation *Ed.* when it stands for the word *Editor* (or *Editors*). (Use a lowercase letter when *ed.* stands for "*edition*," as in *Rev. ed.* or *2nd ed.*)

8. TRANSLATION—APA

Dostoevsky, F. (1992). <u>Devils</u> (M. R. Katz, Trans.). Oxford, England: Oxford University Press.

9. Work in Several Volumes or Parts—APA

Goldman, L. H., Cronin, C. L., & Aharoni, A. (1992). <u>Saul Bellow: A mosaic: Vol 2. Twentieth century American Jewish writers</u>. New York: P. Lang.

10. Anthology or Edited Book—APA

Lantolf, J. P., & Appel, G. (Eds.). (1994). <u>Vygotskian approaches to second language research</u>. Norwood, NJ: Ablex.

Spear, T., & Waller, R. (Eds.). (1993). <u>Being Masai: Ethnicity and identity in East Africa</u>. Athens, OH: Ohio University Press.

11. One Selection from an Anthology or an Edited Book—APA

Savitch, W. J. (1991). Infinity is in the eye of the beholder. In C. Georgopoulos, & R. Ishihara (Eds.), <u>Interdisciplinary approaches to language: Essays in honor of S. Y. Kuroda</u> (pp. 487-500). Boston: Klumer Academic.

12. Two Selections from One Anthology or an Edited Book—APA

Blank, C. (Ed.). (1992). <u>Language and civilization: A concerted profusion of essays and studies in honor of Otto Hietsch</u>. Frankfort-on-Main, Germany: P. Lang.

Middleton, M. (1992). A note on computer jargon. In C. Blank (Ed.), <u>Language and civilization: A concerted profusion of essays and studies in honor of Otto Hietsch</u> (pp. 732-739). Frankfort-on-Main, Germany: P. Lang.

Give full publication information in each entry, whether for a selection or for the whole work. In selection entries, after the title of the main work, enclose page numbers for the selection in parentheses, followed by a period. In the main entry, the first information unit is the name of the editor or compiler of the collection. In an entry for each selection entry, the first unit is the name of the author of the selection.

13. Signed Article in a Reference Book—APA

Sax, J. L. (1994). Environmental Law. In <u>The encyclopedia Americana</u> (International ed.)(Vol. 10, p. 488). Danbury, CT: Grolier.

QUOTATION ABOUT WRITING

No tears in the writer, no tears in the reader. No surprise for the writer, no surprise for the reader.

—Robert Frost

QUOTATION ABOUT WRITING

As late as 1806 I was waiting for genius to descend upon me so that I might write. . . . If I had spoken around 1795 of my plan to write, some sensible man would have told me "to write every day for an hour or two." Genius or no genius. That advice would have made me use ten years of my life that I spent stupidly waiting for genius.

—Stendhal

14. UNSIGNED ARTICLE IN A REFERENCE BOOK—APA

> Russia. (1994). In <u>The new encyclopedia Britannica</u> (15th ed.) (Vol. 10, pp. 253-255). Chicago: Encyclopedia Britannica.

15. EDITION—APA

> Walker, R. S. (1994). <u>AIDS today, tomorrow: An introduction to the HIV epidemic in America</u> (2nd ed.). Atlantic Highlands, NJ: Humanities Press.

16. PART OF A BOOK—APA

If the part of the book you are citing was written by the person who wrote the book, do the entry as you would for the entire work with these exceptions. If the part you are citing has a title, give it, without quotation marks or underlining, after the year (for example, a chapter title or the words *Preface, Foreword, Introduction, Afterword,* and *Appendix*). Then, give the title of the book, followed by parentheses enclosing the page numbers of the cited part and ending with a period after the closing parenthesis. Then give publication information.

> Troyka, Lynn Quitman. (1996). Preface for ESL students. In <u>Simon & Schuster Handbook for Writers</u> (4th ed., pp. 738-740). Englewood Cliffs, NJ: Prentice Hall.

Page numbers can follow an edition number or a volume number in one set of parentheses; use a comma between the sets of information.

If the part you are citing does not have a special title, do the entry as you would for any book, but include page numbers in parentheses after the title. If the part you are citing was written by someone other than the person(s) who wrote the book, first give the name of the person who wrote the part, then give the date, then give the title of the part. Then put the word *In* followed by the name(s) of the book's author(s) or editor(s) in normal order, not reversed. Then give the title of the book, page numbers in parentheses of the relevant part, and publication information.

> Diamond, J. (1994). Foreword. In W. S. Alverson, W. Kuhlmann, & D. M. Waller, <u>Wild Forests Conservation Biology and Public Policy</u>. Washington, DC: Island Press.

17. UNPUBLISHED DISSERTATION OR ESSAY—APA

> Black, L. J. (1993). <u>Language, power, and gender in student-teacher conferences</u>. Unpublished doctoral dissertation, Miami University, Miami.

Stafford, K. M. (1993, January). <u>Trapped in death and enchantment:</u> <u>The liminal space of women in three classical ballets</u>. Paper presented at the annual meeting of the American Comparative Literature Association Graduate Student Conference, Riverside, CA.

18. Reprint of an Older Book—APA

Melville, H. (1851/1992). <u>Moby Dick, or The whale</u>. New York: Modern Library.

19. Book in a Series—APA

Rothman, H. (1992). <u>On rims and ridges: The Los Alamos area since</u> <u>1880. Twentieth-Century American West</u>. Lincoln: University of Nebraska Press.

The abbreviation NE (for Nebraska) does not follow Lincoln in this entry because University of Nebraska Press identifies the state.

20. Book with a Title Within a Title—APA

Hayes, K. J.(Ed.). (1994). <u>The critical response to Herman</u> <u>Melville's</u> Moby Dick. Westport, CT: Greenwood Press.

21. Government Publications—APA

Calvert, Ken. (1993, November 26). <u>Speech to the 103rd Congress</u>. Congressional Record, 139 (168) 3050-3051.

National Oceanic and Atmospheric Administration. (1988). <u>COSPAS-</u> <u>SARSAT search and rescue satellite system</u>. Washington, DC: U.S. Government Printing Office.

National Education Association. (1992). <u>1991-92 estimates of school</u> <u>statistics as provided by the state Departments of Education</u>. West Haven, CT: NEA Professional Library.

22. Published Proceedings of a Conference—APA

Pavlyshyn, M., & Clarke, J. E. M. (Eds.). (1992). <u>Ukraine in the</u> <u>1990s: Proceedings of the first conference of the Ukrainian Studies</u> <u>Association of Australia</u>. Melbourne: Monash University.

PRINT SOURCES: ARTICLES AND OTHER SHORT DOCUMENTS

23. ARTICLE FROM A DAILY NEWSPAPER—APA

Broad, W. J. (1994, November 21). Nuclear roulette for Russia: Burying uncontained waste. <u>The New York Times</u>, p. A1.

24. EDITORIAL, LETTER TO THE EDITOR, OR REVIEW—APA

Patching up health care. (1994, July 17). [Editorial]. <u>The New York Times</u>, p. E16.

Turkel, Stanley. (1993, July 3). [Letter to the editor]. <u>The New York Times</u>, p. L18.

Doniger, Wendy. (1992, August 16). Shackled to the past. [Review of Gerald's Game]. <u>New York Times Book Review</u>, p. 3.

Form descriptions—[Editorial], [Letter to the editor], and [Review of Gerald's Game]—are enclosed in brackets because they are form descriptions given in the words of the person who used the sources and inserted into the blocks of title information (see 29c-1). Descriptions of form are not titles; do not put titles of special documents or of parts of works in brackets (see item 16).

25. UNSIGNED ARTICLE FROM A DAILY NEWSPAPER—APA

"Gene Is Shown to Block the Spread of Prostate Cancer in Mice." (1995, May 12). <u>The New York Times</u>, p. A17.

26. ARTICLE FROM A WEEKLY OR BIWEEKLY MAGAZINE OR NEWSPAPER—APA

Rosen, J. (1994, October 17). Is affirmative action doomed? <u>The New Republic</u>, pp. 25-30, 34-35.

When material is not on consecutive pages, give all page numbers.

27. ARTICLE FROM A MONTHLY OR BIMONTHLY PERIODICAL—APA

Came, B. (1994, October). Policing Haiti. <u>Maclean's</u>, pp. 20-22.

Bell, J. (1992, September/October). Kingdom come: Canada's Inuit finally may be getting their own homeland, but at what price? <u>Earthwatch</u>, pp. 10-11.

28. Unsigned Article from a Weekly or Monthly Periodical—APA

The March almanac. (1994, March 16). <u>Atlantic Monthly</u>, p. 16.

29. Article from a SIRS Collection of Reprinted Articles—APA

Curver, P. C. (1990). Lighting in the 21st century. In Social issues resources series. <u>Energy</u> (Vol. 4, Article 84). Boca Raton, FL: Social Issues Resources.

30. Article in a Journal with Continuous Pagination—APA

LaFollette, M. C. (1994). The politics of research misconduct: Congressional oversight, universities, and science. <u>Journal of Higher Education, 65</u>, 261-85.

31. Article in a Journal that Pages Each Issue Separately—APA

Hancock, D. (1993). Prototyping the Hubble Fix. <u>IEEE Spectrum, 30</u> (10), 34-39.

32. Letters—APA

Orlyansky, V. (1991). Letter to the Soviet President. In R. McKay (Ed.), <u>Letters to Gorbachev: Life in Russia through the postbag of "argumenty i fakty"</u> (pp. 120-121). London: Michael Joseph.

An *unpublished* letter is not available to your readers. Treat it as a personal communication, acknowledging it in a parenthetical reference in your paper but not including it in the References list.

33. Map or Chart—APA

<u>Russia and Post-Soviet Republics</u> [Map]. (1992). Moscow: Mapping Production Association.

NONPRINT SOURCES

34. Interview—APA

A personal interview is not available to your readers. Treat it as a personal communication, acknowledging it in a parenthetical reference in your paper but not including it in the References list.

Randi Friedman (personal communication, June 30, 1992) endorses this view.

35. LECTURE, SPEECH, ADDRESS—APA

Clinton, W. J. (1993, August 12). Address. Speech presented to students at World Youth Day conference, Denver, CO.

36. FILM OR VIDEOTAPE—APA

Archer, D. (Writer/Director). (1992). A world of gestures: Cultural and nonverbal communication [Videotape]. Berkeley: Univ. of Cal. Extension Media Center.

37. RECORDING—APA

De la Cuesta, I. F. (Director). (1994). Chant [CD]. The Benedictine Monks of Santo Dimingo de Silos. (Recording No. CDC 724355513823). Madrid, Spain: Angel Records.

38. LIVE PERFORMANCE—APA

Whitenight, S. J. (Author/Director), & King, R. (Producer). (1994, November 28). Song of a Mockingbird [Live performance]. Orem, UT: Utah Valley State College Theater.

39. WORK OF ART OR MUSICAL COMPOSITION—APA

Hatcher, B. Seer [Art work]. Provo, UT: Brigham Young University Art Museum.

40. RADIO OR TELEVISION PROGRAM—APA

MacNeil, R. (Interviewer). (1991, August 22). Interview with G. F. Kennan. The MacNeil/Lehrer news hour (Show #4144) [Television program]. Washington, DC: Public Broadcasting Service.

ELECTRONIC SOURCES

For electronic sources not covered here, the APA Manual suggests consulting Li and Crane's (1993) *Electronic Style: A Guide to Citing Electronic Information.*

41. ONLINE DOCUMENT WITHOUT A PRINT VERSION—APA

Wallach, D. S. (1993, September 22). FAQ: Typing injuries (2/5): General Info. [Online]. Available FTP: rtfm.mit.edu Directory: pub/usenet/news.answers File: typing-injury-faq/general.z

Keep capitalization the same as you find it in the source. Avoid punctuating the availability, directory, and file statements to separate the information units because extra punctuation marks can be mistaken as part of the address. In the example, end punctuation has been omitted for that reason.

42. COMPUTER SOFTWARE—APA

<u>Transparent Language Presentation Program</u> (Ver. 2.0 for Windows) [Computer software]. (1994). Hollis, NH: Transparent Language.

43. ABSTRACT ON CD-ROM—APA

Marcus, H. F. & Kitayamo, S. (1991). Culture and the self: Implications for group dynamics [CD-ROM]. <u>Psychological Review,</u> <u>88</u>(2), 224, 253. Abstract from: SilverPlatter File: PsycLIT Item: 78-23878

44. INFORMATION SERVICES: ERIC AND NEWSBANK—APA

Chiang. L. H. (1993). Beyond the Language: Native Americans' Nonverbal Communication. (ERIC Document Reproduction Service No. ED 368 540).

Wenzell, R. (1990). Businesses prepare for a more diverse work force. (NewsBank Document Reproduction Service N. EMP 27:D12).

Writing an abstract and using notes in APA style

     33d-4

You may be asked to include an abstract at the start of a paper you prepare in APA style. An abstract, as described in the 1994 edition of the APA *Publication Manual*, is "a brief, comprehensive summary" (p. 8). Make this summary accurate, objective, and exact.

❖ APA FORMAT ALERT: If you include an abstract in an APA-style paper, put it on page 2, a separate page after the title page. For an example of an abstract, see the student paper on biological clocks in section 35b. ❖

Content notes can be used in APA-style papers for additional relevant information that cannot be worked effectively into a text discussion. Use consecutive arabic numerals for note numbers, both within your paper and on a separate page following the last text page of your paper. Use the heading *Notes* on this page, number it with your paper, and double-space the notes themselves.

BACKGROUND

Until the middle of the fifteenth century, the only books available to Europeans were handwritten manuscripts, which were costly and often inaccurate. The development of printing made books available to the common people for the first time.

The major breakthrough in the history of printing was the invention of movable type, the making of a stamp for each letter on a separate base so that the letters could be assembled to form a page. Although this system was already known in China and Korea (where it was little used because of the large number of Chinese characters and the lack of suitable ink), its discovery in Europe was made independently. Credit for the European development is given to Johann Gutenberg (c. 1400–1468). Although his "Gutenberg Bible," printed in 1455, was not his first printed work, it is his most famous one.

Today it is often remarked that the world is going through another printing revolution. With the availability of copying machines, memory typewriters, word processing computer programs, and a variety of desktop printers, methods of producing printed material have undergone another major shift. Whereas only a few years ago having a document printed meant handing it over to a professional printer, today it is likely to be produced on equipment readily available in most offices and many homes.

33e

Using CM-Style Documentation

The style manual of the University of Chicago Press endorses two styles of documentation. One is a "name-year" style, similar to APA's system, using in-text citations that direct readers to an alphabetical References list containing full bibliographic details about each source. Parenthetical references commonly contain an author name and a publication year, separated by a space but no punctuation: `(English 1995)`.

The other style of CM (for *Chicago Manual*) documentation is a note system often used in the disciplines of English, humanities, and history. The CM note system gives complete bibliographic information within a footnote or endnote the first time a source is cited. If that source is cited again, less information is given because the source has already been fully described. A separate bibliography is usually unnecessary.

TEXT

`Welty also makes this point.`[1]

NOTE

`   1. Eudora Welty, One Writer's Beginnings (Cambridge: Harvard University Press, 1984), 17.`

Notes may be either at the end of a paper (endnotes) or at the foot of the page on which a citation falls (footnotes). Endnotes are usually easier to format, especially if you are handwriting or typing your paper. Popular word processing programs can format either endnotes or footnotes easily.

Section 33e focuses primarily on the CM bibliographic note system of documentation. Several of the models in section 33e-2 show References list entries as well as bibliographic note entries.

33e-1

Creating CM-Style Bibliographic Notes

Chart 144 gives general guidelines for the content and format of CM-style bibliographic notes.

GUIDELINES FOR COMPILING CM-STYLE BIBLIOGRAPHIC NOTES 144

■ **TITLE**

For endnotes, Notes, on a new page numbered sequentially with the rest of the paper, after the last text page of the paper. (Footnotes appear at the bottom of pages where sources are cited.)

144

■ FORMAT

Place endnotes after the text of your paper, on a separate page entitled Notes. Center the word Notes about an inch from the top of the page. Double space after the word Notes. Single-space the notes themselves. Indent each note's first line about 3 characters (or 1 tab space in your word-processing program); do not indent a note's subsequent lines.

In the body of your paper, use raised (superscript) arabic numerals for the note numbers. Note numbers should be positioned after any punctuation marks except the dash, preferably at the end of a sentence. On the Notes page, superscript and note should be the same type size, and a period should follow the superscript. (Not all word-processing programs allow you to observe these guidelines.)

■ SPACING AFTER PUNCTUATION

No special requirements.

■ ARRANGEMENT OF NOTES

Numerical order

■ AUTHORS' NAMES

Give the name in standard (not inverted) order, with names and initials as given in the original source. Use the word *and* between (the last) two authors.

■ CAPITALIZATION OF TITLES

Capitalize the first word and all major words.

■ SPECIAL TREATMENT OF TITLES

Underline the titles of long works, and use quotation marks around the titles of shorter works.

Omit *A, An,* and *The* from the titles of newspapers and periodicals. For an unfamiliar newspaper title, in parentheses, give the city (and state, if the city is not well known): for example, (*Newark, New Jersey*) *Star-Ledger.*

■ PUBLICATION INFORMATION

Enclose publication information in parentheses. Use a colon and one space after the city of publication. Give complete publishers' names or abbreviate them according to standard abbreviations in *Books in Print.* Omit *Co., Inc.,* and *Ltd.* Use *Press* (spelled out, not abbreviated). Use *Univ.* for University.

Do not abbreviate publication months.

→

BACKGROUND

Nicolás Antonio (1617–1684) is credited with the creation of modern bibliography and the shaping of literary history into a scholarly discipline. His *Bibliotheca Hispana* is an index in Latin of Old World and New World Spanish writers after 1500. It also contains a history of earlier Spanish literature.

All you need is a room without any particular interruptions.

—John Dos Passos

■ **PAGE NUMBERS**

In inclusive page numbers, give the full second number for 2 through 99. For 100 and beyond, give the full second number if a shortened version is ambiguous.

List all discontinuous page numbers.

Use a comma to separate page numbers for a cited part of a book from the parenthetical publication information.

Use the abbreviations *p.* and *pp.* with page numbers for material from journals that do not use volume numbers.

■ **SECOND CITATIONS**

After giving full bibliographic information in the first note citing a source, subsequent citations can be brief. In short papers, author name(s) and a page reference is usually sufficient information. If you have used more than one work by the author(s), give a shortened title as well.

■ **CONTENT NOTES**

Try to avoid using content notes. If you must use one or two, make them footnotes and use symbols (* and † are standard) rather than numbers. You can repeat these footnote symbols on every page.

■ **BIBLIOGRAPHIC NOTES: BOOKS**

Citations for books include the author, title, publication information, and page numbers if applicable. Note 1 is for the first citation of a book; note 2 is for its second citation in a paper that cites two works by Welty, *One Writer's Beginnings* and "A Worn Path."

AUTHOR	TITLE	PUBLICATION INFORMATION

1. Eudora Welty, *One Writer's Beginnings* (Cambridge: Harvard

PAGE
NUMBERS

University Press, 1984), 15.

2. Welty, *One*, 21.

■ **BIBLIOGRAPHIC NOTES: ARTICLES**

Citations for articles include the author, article title, journal title, volume number, year, and page numbers. Note 1 shows the first

GUIDELINES FOR COMPILING CM-STYLE 144
BIBLIOGRAPHIC NOTES (continued)

citation of an article, and note 2 shows the second citation for the article in a paper citing only one work by these authors.

AUTHORS

1. D. D. Cochran, W. Daniel Hale, and Christine P. Hissam,

ARTICLE TITLE

"Personal Space Requirements in Indoor versus Outdoor Locations."

JOURNAL TITLE	VOLUME NUMBER	YEAR	PAGE NUMBERS
Journal of Psychology	117	(1984):	132-33.

2. Cochran, Hale, and Hissam, 133.

Following models for CM-style documentation

Directory

PRINT SOURCES: BOOKS

1. Book by One Author—CM
2. Book by Two or Three Authors—CM
3. Book by More than Three Authors—CM
4. Multiple Citation of a Single Source—CM
5. Book by Group or Corporate Author—CM
6. Book with No Author Named—CM
7. Book with an Author and an Editor—CM
8. Translation—CM
9. Work in Several Volumes or Parts—CM
10. One Selection from an Anthology or an Edited Book—CM
11. Two Selections from One Anthology or an Edited Book—CM
12. Signed Article in a Reference Book—CM
13. Unsigned Article in a Reference Book—CM
14. Edition—CM
15. Anthology or Edited Book—CM
16. Introduction, Preface, Foreword, or Afterword—CM
17. Unpublished Dissertation or Essay—CM
18. Reprint of an Older Book—CM
19. Book in a Series—CM

33e–2

PRINT SOURCES: BOOKS

1. BOOK BY ONE AUTHOR—CM

1. George B. Schaller, <u>The Last Panda</u> (Chicago: The University of Chicago Press, 1993).

2. Giuliana Prata, M.D., <u>A Systematic Harpoon into Family Games: Preventive Interventions in Therapy</u> (New York: Brunner/Mazel Publishers, 1990).

Here are References list forms for books by one author:

Prata, Giuliana, M.D. <u>A Systematic Harpoon into Family Games: Preventive Interventions in Therapy</u>. New York: Brunner/Mazel, 1990.

Schaller, George B. <u>The Last Panda</u>. Chicago: The University of Chicago Press, 1993.

2. BOOK BY TWO OR THREE AUTHORS—CM

1. Elizabeth McMahan, Susan Day, and Robert Funk, <u>Nine Short Novels by American Women</u> (New York: St. Martin's Press, 1993).

2. Richard J. Smith and Mark Gibbs, <u>Navigating the Internet</u>, (Indianapolis: Sams Publishing, 1994).

Here are References list entries. A parenthetical citation lists two or three authors: (McMahan, Day, and Funk 1993).

McMahan, Elizabeth, Susan Day, and Robert Funk. 1993. <u>Nine short novels by American women</u>. New York: St. Martin's.

Smith, Richard J., and Mark Gibbs. 1994. <u>Navigating the Internet</u>. Indianapolis: Sams Publishing.

3. BOOK BY MORE THAN THREE AUTHORS—CM

1. Deborah Cameron et al., <u>Researching Language: Issues of Power and Method</u> (London: Routledge Publishers, 1992).

Here is a References list entry. A parenthetical citation also uses et al. for more than three authors: (Cameron et al. 1992).

Cameron, Deborah, et al. 1992. <u>Researching language: Issues of power and method</u>. London: Routledge.

4. MULTIPLE CITATION OF A SINGLE SOURCE—CM

Second and subsequent notes use shortened forms (see Chart 144). *Ibid.* can be used when the information in a note is exactly the same as the information in the immediately preceding note. If only the page references differ in two successive notes, you can use *Ibid.* with the respective pages.

2. Schaller, 33.

3. Ibid., 37.

5. BOOK BY GROUP OR CORPORATE AUTHOR—CM

1. Environmental Defense Fund, <u>Recycling and Incineration: Evaluating the Choices</u> (Washington: Island Press, 1990).

2. American Psychological Association, <u>Publication Manual of the American Psychological Association</u>, 4th ed. (Washington: American Psychological Association, 1994).

Here are References list entries. A parenthetical citation uses the group name as though it were an individual's name: (Environmental Defense Fund 1990).

Environmental Defense Fund. 1990. <u>Recycling and incineration: Evaluating the choice</u>. Washington: Island Press.

American Psychological Association. 1994. <u>Publication manual of the American Psychological Association</u>, 4th ed. Washington: A.P.A.

TEACHING TIP

Older documentation styles often called for the use of abbreviations, many of them in Latin. Although current style manuals have dropped most of the abbreviated terms, your students may need to know what the terms mean when they appear in articles encountered in the course of doing research. Students should be cautioned not to use them in their own papers unless you, another instructor, or their style manual asks them to do so. Some of the more common ones appear in section 30j.

6. Book with No Author Named—CM

> 1. The Chicago Manual of Style, 14th ed. 1993. Chicago: University of Chicago Press.

7. Book with an Author and an Editor—CM

When the focus in your paper is on Welty and her reviews, use this form:

> 1. Eudora Welty, <u>A Writer's Eye: Collected Book Reviews</u>, ed. Pearl Amelia McHaney (Jackson, Mississippi: University Press of Mississippi, 1994).

When your focus is on McHaney's work as editor, use this form:

> 1. Pearl Amelia McHaney, ed., <u>A Writer's Eye: Collected Book Reviews</u>, by Eudora Welty (Jackson, Mississippi: University Press of Mississippi, 1994).

Here are the References list entries for each focus, first on Welty as author and second on McHaney as editor. Parenthetical citations use the name that begins the References entry.

> Welty, Eudora. 1994. <u>A writer's eye: Collected book reviews</u>. Edited by P. A. McHaney. Jackson: University Press of Mississippi.
>
> McHaney, P. A., ed. 1994. <u>A writer's eye: Collected book reviews</u>, by Eudora Welty. Jackson: University Press of Mississippi.

8. Translation—CM

> 1. Fyodor Dostoevsky, <u>Devils</u>, trans. Michael R. Katz (Oxford: Oxford University Press, 1992).
>
> Dostoevsky, Fyodor. 1992. <u>Devils</u>. Translated by M. R. Katz. Oxford: Oxford UP.

9. A Work in Several Volumes or Parts—CM

> 1. L. H. Goldman, Cloria L. Cronin, and Ada Aharoni, <u>Saul Bellow: A Mosaic</u>, vol. 3 of <u>Twentieth Century American Jewish Writers</u> (New York: P. Lang Publishers, 1992).

10. One Selection from an Anthology or an Edited Book—CM

> 1. Walter J. Savitch, "Infinity Is in the Eye of the Beholder," in <u>Interdisciplinary Approaches to Language: Essays in Honor of S. Y. Kuroda</u>, ed. Carol Georgopoulos and Roberta Ishihara (Boston: Klumer Academic, 1991), 487-500.

11. Two Selections from One Anthology or an Edited Book—CM

If you cite two or more selections from the same anthology or edited book, give complete bibliographical information in the first note for each selection.

12. Signed Article in a Reference Book—CM

1. Joseph L. Sax, "Environmental Law" in <u>Encyclopedia Americana</u>, International ed., 1994.

13. Unsigned Article in a Reference Book—CM

1. <u>Encyclopedia Britannica</u>, 15th ed., s.v. "Russia."

14. Edition—CM

1. Robert Searles Walker, <u>AIDS Today, Tomorrow: An Introduction to the HIV Epidemic in America</u>, 2nd ed. (Atlantic Highlands, New Jersey: Humanities Press, 1994).

15. Anthology or Edited Book—CM

1. James P. Lantolf, and Gabriela Appel, ed., <u>Vygotskian Approaches to Second Language Research</u> (Norwood, New Jersey: Ablex Publishing Corporation, 1994).

16. Introduction, Preface, Foreword, or Afterword—CM

1. Jared Diamond, foreword to <u>Wild Forests Conservation Biology and Public Policy</u>, by William S. Alverson, Walter Kuhlmann, and Donald M. Waller (Washington: Island Press, 1994).

17. Unpublished Dissertation or Essay—CM

1. Laurel Johnson Black, "Language, Power, and Gender in Student-Teacher Conferences" (Ph.D. diss., Miami University, 1993), 122-34.

State the author's name first, the title in quotation marks (not underlined), then a description of the work (such as *Ph.D. diss.* or *master's thesis*), then the degree-granting institution, and the date.

18. Reprint of an Older Book—CM

1. Herman Melville, <u>Moby Dick, or The Whale</u> (1851; reprint, New York: Modern Library, 1992).

19. Book in a Series—CM

1. Hal Rothman, <u>On Rims and Ridges: The Los Alamos Area since 1880</u>, Twentieth-Century American West (Lincoln: University of Nebraska Press, 1992).

20. Book with a Title Within a Title—CM

1. Kevin J. Hayes, ed., <u>The Critical Response to Herman Melville's</u> Moby Dick (Westport, Connecticut: Greenwood Press, 1994).

21. SECONDARY SOURCE—CM

1. Mary Wollstonecraft, <u>A Vindication of the Rights of Woman</u> (1792), 90, quoted in Caroline Shrodes, Harry Finestone, and Michael Shugrue, <u>The Conscious Reader</u>, 4th ed. (New York: Macmillan Publishing, 1988), 282.

When you quote one person's words, having found them in another person's work, give information as fully as you can about both sources. Note 1 shows the form when the focus of your citation is Mary Wollstonecraft's words. If your focus is on what Shrodes, Finestone, and Shugrue have to say about Wollstonecraft's words, handle the information as shown in note 2.

2. Caroline Shrodes, Harry Finestone, and Michael Shugrue, <u>The Conscious Reader</u>, 4th ed. (New York: Macmillan Publishing, 1988), 282, quoting Mary Wollstonecraft, <u>A Vindication of the Rights of Woman</u> (1792), 90.

22. GOVERNMENT PUBLICATIONS—CM

1. House, Representative Ken Calvert speaking on <u>Resentment to the Endangered Species Act</u>, 103rd Cong., 1st sess., Congressional Record (26 November 1993), 139, pt. 168: 3050-1.

2. House, Subcommittee on Housing and Community Development of the Committee on Banking, Finance, and Urban Affairs, <u>Basic Laws on Housing and Community Development</u>, revised through September 30, 1991, Pub L 102-109 (Washington, D.C: GPO, 1991).

3. U.S. Department of Commerce, National Oceanic and Atmospheric Administration, COSPAS-SARSAT Search and Rescue Satellite System, pamphlet (Washington, D.C.: GPO, 1988).

4. National Education Association, <u>1991-92 Estimates of School Statistics as Provided by the State Departments of Education</u>, developed under contract with N.I.E., U.S. Department of Education (West Haven, Connecticut: NEA Professional Library, 1992).

When a government department, bureau, agency, or committee produces a document, cite that group as the author. GPO stands for Government Printing Office.

23. PUBLISHED PROCEEDINGS OF A CONFERENCE—CM

1. Marko Pavlyshyn, and J. E. M. Clarke, eds., <u>Ukraine in the 1990s: Proceedings of the First Conference of the Ukrainian Studies Association of Australia</u> (Melbourne: Monash University, Slavic Section, 1992).

Pavlyshyn, M., and J. E. M. Clarke, eds. 1992. <u>Ukraine in the 1990s: Proceedings of the first conference of the Ukrainian Studies Association of Australia</u>. Melbourne: Monash University.

24. ARTICLE FROM A DAILY NEWSPAPER—CM

1. William J. Broad, "Nuclear Roulette for Russia: Burying Uncontained Waste," New York Times 21 November 1994, sec. A, p. 1.

Here is the References list entry. A parenthetical citation uses name and year: (Broad 1994).

Broad, W. J. 1994. Nuclear roulette for Russia: Burying uncontained waste. New York Times, 21 November.

25. EDITORIAL, LETTER TO THE EDITOR, OR REVIEW—CM

1. "Patching Up Health Care," editorial, New York Times 17 July 1994, sec. E, p. 16.

2. Stanley Turkel, letter, New York Times 3 July 1993, sec. L, p. 18.

3. Wendy Doniger, "Shackled to the Past," review of Gerald's Game, by Stephen King, New York Times Book Review 16 Aug. 1992, p. 3.

Here are References list entries:

Patching up health care. 1994. Editorial in New York Times. 17 July.

Turkel, Stanley. 1993. Letter. New York Times. 3 July.

Doniger, Wendy. 1992. Shackled to the past. Review of Gerald's Game, by Stephen King. New York Times Book Review. 16 August.

26. UNSIGNED ARTICLE FROM A DAILY NEWSPAPER—CM

1. "Gene Is Shown to Block the Spread of Prostate Cancer in Mice," New York Times 12 May 1995, sec. A, p. 17.

27. ARTICLE FROM A WEEKLY OR BIWEEKLY MAGAZINE OR NEWSPAPER—CM

1. Jeffrey Rosen, "Is Affirmative Action Doomed?" New Republic, 17 October 1994, 25-30, 34-35.

Here is the References list entry.

Rosen, J. 1994. Is affirmative action doomed? New Republic. 17 October.

28. ARTICLE FROM A MONTHLY OR BIMONTHLY PERIODICAL—CM

1. Jim Bell, "Kingdom Come: Canada's Inuit Finally May Be Getting Their Own Homeland, But at What Price?" Earthwatch, September/October 1992, 10-11.

Here is the References list entry:

Bell, J. 1992. Kingdom come: Canada's Inuit finally may be getting their own homeland, but at what price? Earthwatch. September/October.

QUOTATION ABOUT WRITING

Some authors type their works, but I cannot do that. Writing is tied up with the hand, almost with a special nerve.

—Graham Greene

29. Unsigned Article from a Weekly or Monthly Periodical—CM

1. "The March Almanac," <u>Atlantic Monthly</u>, March 1994, 16.

30. Article from a Collection of Reprinted Articles—CM

1. Abraham Brumberg, "Russia after Perestroika," <u>The Gorbachev Era</u>, Articles on Russian and Soviet History, vol. 14 (New York: Garland Publications, 1992).

31. Article in a Journal with Continuous Pagination—CM

1. Marcel C. LaFollette, "The Politics of Research Misconduct: Congressional Oversight, Universities, and Science," <u>Journal of Higher Education</u> 65 (1994): 261-85.

Here is the References list entry:

LaFollette, Marcel C. 1994. The politics of research misconduct: Congressional oversight, universities, and science. <u>Journal of Higher Education</u>. 65: 261-85.

32. Article in a Journal that Pages Each Issue Separately—CM

1. Dennis Hancock, "Prototyping the Hubble Fix," <u>IEEE Spectrum</u>, 30, no. 10 (1993): 34-39.

NONPRINT SOURCES

33. Personal Interview—CM

1. Randi Friedman, interview by author, Ames, Iowa, 30 June 1992.

For an unpublished interview, give the name of the interviewee, identify the interviewer, and then give location and date.

34. Letters—CM

Treat a published letter like any other published document. For an unpublished letter, give the name of the writer, the name of the recipient, and the date of the letter.

1. Gary Edward Reilly, letter to author, 26 December 1994.

35. Film or Videotape—CM

1. Dane Archer, <u>A World of Gestures: Cultural and Nonverbal Communication</u> (Berkeley: The University of California Extension Media Center, 1992), videocassette.

Here is the References list entry:

Archer, Dane. 1992. <u>A world of gestures: Cultural and nonverbal
communication</u>. Berkeley: Univ. of Cal. Extension Media Center.
Videocassette.

36. Recording—CM

1. Ismael Fernandes de la Cuesta, <u>Chant</u>, Benedictine Monks of Santo
Domingo de Silos, Angel CDC 724355513823.

ELECTRONIC SOURCES

37. Computer Software—CM

1. Transparent Language Presentation Program, ver. 2.0 for Windows,
Transparent Language, Inc., Hollis, New Hampshire.

Here is the References list entry:

Transparent Language Presentation Program Ver. 2.0 for Windows.
Transparent Language, Inc., Hollis, New Hampshire.

38. ERIC Information Service—CM

1. Linda H. Chiang. <u>Beyond the Language: Native Americans' Nonverbal
Communication</u> (Anderson, IN: Midwest Association of Teachers of
Educational Psychology, 1993) ERIC ED 368540.

Here is the References list entry:

Chiang. Linda H. 1993. <u>Beyond the Language: Native Americans' Nonverbal
Communication</u>. Anderson, IN: Midwest Association of Teachers of
Educational Psychology, ERIC, ED 368540.

39. Electronic Documents—CM

Until uniform standards for documenting electronic sources exist,
the *Chicago Manual* recommends following documentation guidelines
of the International Standards Organization *(ISO)*. Follow the source
for capitalizing and punctuating, since these usually mechanical operations can affect the ability to locate material. In general, the information
units are author(s) if any; title; database medium; information about a
print version; access or update dates; item or access numbers, if any;
paging or other description of length, if any; and location information.
The ISO recommends putting information about the database medium,
access dates, and length in brackets.

1. Dan S. Wallach, "FAQ: Typing Injuries (2/5): General Info.," in
typing-injury-faq/general.z [USENET newsgroup], 1993_[cited 14 Nov.
1993]: available from mail-server @ rtfm.mit.edu; INTERNET

33f   Using CBE-style documentation

In its 1994 style manual, *Scientific Style and Format*, the Council of Biology Editors (**CBE**) endorses two documentation systems widely used in mathematics and the physical and life sciences. The first system uses name-year parenthetical citations in the text of a paper together with a References list that gives full bibliographic information for each source. The second system uses numbers to mark references to sources in the paper. These numbers correlate with a numbered References list that gives full bibliographic information for each source.

Each of these styles uses a slightly different format for entries in the References list. With the name-date parenthetical system, a name and a date are the first two units of information in each References entry. When in-text citations are numbers referring to the numbered entries in the References list, the first two units of information in References entries are usually a name and title.

This handbook focuses mainly on CBE's numbered reference system. Here is the way it works:

- The first time you cite each source in your paper, assign it a number in sequence, starting with 1.

- In your References list, list and number each entry in the order of its appearance in your paper, starting with 1.

CBE recommends using superscript numbers for marking source citations in your paper, although numbers in parentheses are also acceptable. Here is a brief example showing two sources cited in a paper and a References list arranged in citation sequence.

IN-TEXT CITATIONS

Sybesma[1] insists that this behavior occurs periodically, but Crowder[2] claims never to have observed it.

REFERENCES LIST

1. Sybesma C. An introduction to biophysics. New York: Academic Press; 1977. 648 p.

2. Crowder. W. Seashore life between the tides. New York: Dodd, Mead & Co.; 1931. New York: Dover Publications Reprint; 1975. 372 p.

Each citation of Sybesma's *Introduction to Biophysics* is followed by a superscript 1, and each citation of Crowder's *Seashore Life* is followed by a superscript 2 in this paper.

Compiling a CBE-style References list

GUIDELINES FOR COMPILING A CBE-STYLE REFERENCES LIST   145

■ **TITLE**

References **or** Cited References

■ **PLACEMENT OF LIST**

Start a new page numbered sequentially with the rest of the paper.

■ **CONTENTS AND FORMAT**

Include all sources quoted from, paraphrased, or summarized in your paper.

Center the title about 1 inch from the top of the page.

Start each entry on a new line. Put the number followed by a space at the regular left margin. If an entry takes more than one line, indent the second and all other lines. Double-space each entry and between entries.

■ **SPACING AFTER PUNCTUATION**

Follow the spacing shown in the models in 33f-2.

■ **ARRANGEMENT OF ENTRIES**

Sequence the entries in the order that you cite the sources in your paper.

■ **AUTHORS' NAMES**

Invert all author names, giving the last name first. You can give first names or use only initials of first and middle names. If you use initials, do not use a period or a space between first and middle initials. If you use full first names, separate the names of multiple authors with a semicolon (without the word or symbol for *and*) Use a period after the last author's name.

■ **CAPITALIZATION OF TITLES**

Capitalize a book or an article title's first word and any proper nouns. Do not capitalize the first word of a subtitle unless it is a proper noun.

Capitalize the titles of academic journals. If the title of a periodical is one word, give it in full; otherwise, abbreviate it according to recommendations established by the *American National Standard for Abbreviations of Titles of Periodicals.*

Capitalize a newspaper title's major words, giving the full title, including a beginning *A, An,* or *The.*

→

GUIDELINES FOR COMPILING A CBE-STYLE REFERENCES LIST (continued)

145

■ **SPECIAL TREATMENT OF TITLES**

Do not underline titles or enclose them in quotation marks.

■ **PLACE OF PUBLICATION**

Use a colon after the city of publication. Add a state postal abbreviation or a country name to a city that might be ambiguous (Springfield, VA, and Springfield, VT, for example).

■ **PUBLISHER**

Give publishers' names in full, including *Co., Inc., Press, Ltd.,* and so on. Use a semicolon after the publisher's name.

■ **PUBLICATION MONTH ABBREVIATIONS**

Abbreviate publication months.

■ **INCLUSIVE PAGE NUMBERS**

Shorten the second number as much as possible while keeping it unambiguous: for example, 233-4 for 233 to 234; 233-44 for 233 to 244; 233-304. Use the abbreviation *p* without a period or underlining with designations of pages. Follow the guidelines in the models.

■ **DISCONTINUOUS PAGE NUMBERS**

Give the full numbers of all discontinuous pages, preceding the first number with the *p* abbreviation.

■ **TOTAL PAGE NUMBERS**

When citing an entire book, for the last information unit give the total pages followed by the abbreviation *p* and a period to end the information unit.

■ **REFERENCES ENTRY: BOOK**

Citations for books usually list author(s), title, publication information, and pages (either total pages when citing an entire work or inclusive pages for citing part of a book). Each unit of information ends with a period.

1. Stacy RW, Williams DT, Worden RE, McMorris RO. Essentials of biological and medical sciences. New York: McGraw-Hill Book Company, Inc.; 1955. 727 p.

■ **REFERENCES ENTRY: ARTICLE**

Citations for articles usually list author(s), article title, journal name and publication information, each section followed by a period. Sci Am is the abbreviated form of Scientific American. The volume number is 269, and the issue number, in parentheses, is (3).

```
1. Weissman IL, Cooper MD. How the immune system develops. Sci Am
   1993 Mar;269(3):65-71.
```

Following models for a CBE-style References list   33f-2

Directory

PRINT SOURCES: BOOKS

PRINT SOURCES: ARTICLES

OTHER SOURCES

PRINT SOURCES: BOOKS

1. BOOK BY ONE AUTHOR—CBE

1. Hawking SW. Black holes and baby universes and other essays. New
   York: Bantam Books; 1993. 320 p.

Use one space but no punctuation between an author's last name
and the initial of the first name. Do not put punctuation or a space
between a first and a middle initial.

2. BOOK BY MORE THAN ONE AUTHOR—CBE

1. Wegzyn S, Gille J-C, Vidal P. Developmental systems: at the
   crossroads of system theory, computer science, and genetic
   engineering. New York: Springer-Verlag; 1990. 595 p.

3. BOOK BY GROUP OR CORPORATE AUTHOR—CBE

1. Chemical Rubber Company. Handbook of laboratory safety. 3rd ed. Boca
   Raton (FL): CRC Press; 1990.

Use a two-letter postal abbreviation enclosed in parentheses after
the name of a city that might be unfamiliar to your readers.

4. ANTHOLOGY OR EDITED BOOK—CBE

1. Heermann B, Hummel S, editors. Ancient DNA: recovery and analysis of
   genetic material from paleontological, archeological, museum,
   medical, and forensic specimens. New York: Springer-Verlag; 1994.
   1029 p.

5. ONE SELECTION OR CHAPTER FROM AN ANTHOLOGY OR EDITED BOOK—CBE

1. Basov NG, Feoktistov LP, Senatsky YV. Laser driver for inertial
   confinement fusion. In: Brueckner, KA, editor. Research trends in
   physics: inertial confinement fusion. New York: American Institute of
   Physics; 1992: p 24-37.

6. ALL VOLUMES OF A MULTIVOLUME WORK—CBE

1. Crane FL, Morre DJ, Low HE, editors. Oxidoreduction at the plasma
   membrane: relation to growth and transport. Boca Raton (FL): Chemical
   Rubber Company Press; 1991. 2 vol.

7. Unpublished Dissertation or Thesis—CBE

1. Baykul MC. Using ballistic electron emission microscopy to
   investigate the metal-vacuum interface. [dissertation]. Orem (UT):
   Polytechnic University; 1993. 111 p.

PRINT SOURCES: ARTICLES

8. Published Article from Conference Proceedings—CBE

1. Tsang CP, Bellgard MI. Sequence generation using a network of
   Boltzmann machines. In: Tsang CP, editor. Proceedings of the 4th
   Australian Joint Conference on Artificial Intelligence; 1990 Nov 8-
   11; Perth, Australia. Singapore: World Scientific; 1990: p 224-33.

9. Signed Newspaper Article—CBE

1. Hoke F. Gene therapy: clinical gains yield a wealth of research
   opportunities. Scientist 1993 Oct 4;Sect A:1, 5, 7.

Sect stands for Section.

10. Unsigned Newspaper Article—CBE

1. [Anonymous]. Irish urge postgame caution. USA Today 1993 Nov 12; Sect
   C:2.

11. Article in a Journal with Continuous Pagination—CBE

1. Scott ML, Fredrickson RJ, Moorhead BB. Characteristics of old-growth
   forests associated with northern spotted owls in Olympic National
   Park. J Wildlf Mgt 1993;57:315-21.

Give only the volume number before the page numbers.

12. Article in a Journal that Pages Each Issue Separately—CBE

1. Weissman IL, Cooper MD. How the immune system develops. Sci Am 1993
   Mar;269(3):65-71.

Give both the volume number and the issue number (here, 269 is the
volume number and 3 is the issue number). *Sci Am* is the abbreviation
for *Scientific American* based on the standards established by the
American National Standard for Abbreviations of Titles of Periodicals.

13. Journal Article on Discontinuous Pages—CBE

1. Richards FM. The protein folding problem. Sci Am 1991 Nov;246(1):54-
   7. 60-6.

14. Entire Issue of a Journal—CBE

1. Whales in a modern world: a symposium held in London, November 1988.
   Mamm Rev 1990 Jan;20(9).

November 1988, the date of the symposium, is part of the title of
the issue in this case.

OTHER SOURCES

15. Slide Set—CBE

1. Human parasitology [slides]. Chicago (IL): American Society of
   Clinical Pathologists Press; 1990: color. Accompanied by: guide.

16. Electronic Sources—CBE

In general, to cite electronic sources, start with a statement of the
type of document, and then give the information you would give for a
print version. Then give information that would help a reader to locate
the electronic source. End with a date: your access date for online
sources or the date of the update you used for CD-ROM databases that
are updated periodically.

34 *Case Study: A Student Writing an MLA Research Paper*

This chapter presents a case study of a student, Amy Brown, going through the processes of conducting research and writing a paper based on her findings. Section 34a narrates the processes. Section 34b shows the final draft of Brown's paper, along with commentary on the paper's key elements. The commentary includes Process Notes explaining many of Brown's decisions during her writing process.

REFERENCE TO SUPPLEMENTS

For additional help with writing a successful research paper, refer students to *The Research Organizer: Prentice Hall Resources for Composition* by S. Hopke.

Amy Brown was given this assignment for a research paper: Write a research paper on the general subject of communication. The paper should be 1,800 to 2,000 words long and should be based on a variety of sources. The final paper is due in six weeks. Interim deadlines for parts of the work will be announced. To complete this assignment, you need to engage in three interrelated processes: conducting research, understanding the results of that research, and writing a paper based on the first two processes. Consult the *Simon & Schuster Handbook for Writers*, Fourth Edition, especially Chapter 32, which gives you practical, step-by-step guidance on what this assignment entails.

Observing the processes of researching and writing an MLA-style research paper

34a

Amy Brown faced many challenges as she worked on her assignment. Some decisions did not come easily, especially in the early stages of her research process. Brown expected the process to lead to a few puzzles and frustrations, and she resolved to remain patient with herself and the project.

Narrowing the subject of communication to a more **suitable topic** proved the most difficult challenge. Because the idea of unspoken

34a
cont.

messages among people interested her, Brown decided to concentrate on *nonverbal communication.* She used that term to start compiling a list of **headings and key words** (see 32i). Making her first trip to the library for this research project, she looked for the term *nonverbal communication* in the Library of Congress Subject Headings (LCSH). *Nonverbal communication* was there, listed with its call number— BF637.N66—which Brown copied down immediately. The letters *BF* would help her locate sources on nonverbal communication in any library using the Library of Congress (LC) system to catalog its materials.

One of the LCHS subdivisions under nonverbal communication was especially meaningful to Brown: *personal space.* She knew that personal space concerns the physical distance people expect to maintain between themselves and others. Brown had become aware of the concept when a cousin who was job hunting lived with Brown and her family for three weeks. Although Brown and her cousin liked each other, Brown became cranky toward her as time went on, feeling that she had lost her "space." Discovering the idea of personal space as a part of communication intrigued Brown. Here was a topic she wanted to research.

Brown then browsed the general encyclopedia collection. Most discussed nonverbal communication in their entries on communication. In the *Encyclopaedia Britannica,* Brown found an entry for *personal space,* but it was about the biological topic of distances between plants. Afraid she might have come to a dead end, she decided to look in one more general encyclopedia, the 1993 edition of *Academic American.* It was a lucky choice: She found a very short article on nonverbal communication with a bibliography at the end. It listed the book *Body Language* by Julius Fast. Brown began an Author Names section in her **research log,** making Fast the first entry.

Heading next for specialized encyclopedias, Brown discovered that her library shelved all specialized reference materials by call number. She located the reference books with the *BF* call letters she had copied down from LCSH. Looking first in *The Encyclopedia of Psychology,* Brown found an article "Nonverbal Behavior" that summarized various aspects of nonverbal communication and introduced two pieces of information that turned out to be crucial: the term *proxemics,* a synonym for personal space, and the name of an early researcher into personal space, Edward T. Hall. Hall's book *The Hidden Dimension* was cited in the bibliography of the article. Brown now had the name of an **authority** and of a book that ultimately turned out to be a **major source** on her topic.

Pleased with her discovery, Brown wrote about it in her research log, including all the information that she might need to find Hall's *The Hidden Dimension.* She also added Hall to her Author Names list, along with the names of two other experts mentioned in the encyclopedia article: Desmond Morris for studies of multicultural aspects and Judith Hall for research on gender differences in personal space. Brown made a bibliography card in MLA format for the "Nonverbal Behavior" article in *The Encyclopedia of Psychology* and then photocopied the article.

In a second specialized encyclopedia, *The Encyclopedic Dictionary of Psychology*, Brown found an article on proxemics, which named Edward T. Hall as the main authority on the subject and defined proxemics in detail.

Brown next used her **library catalog.** This computerized system let her search by author, title, and subject. Using the names in her Author Names list, she located books by Morris, Fast, Edward Hall, and Judith Hall. When she searched by subject, her library's system accepted only *nonverbal communication* (rather than *proxemics* or *personal space*). From the 25 or 30 listings that appeared on the screen, Brown chose works whose titles or authors she recognized from the research she had done so far. Using the key word *personal space* during the title search, Brown discovered an important title that would also turn out to be a key source: *Personal Space* by Robert Sommer. The catalog also listed several other works by Edward Hall, including a 1990 book written with Mildred Hall.

Over the next few days, Brown skimmed the books she had checked out. She felt that they provided her with a solid foundation. She also watched two videos that had been on the printout from her catalog searches but, deciding that they were too general to be useful, returned them.

The next challenge Brown faced was to find the most **current information** about personal space. Because *nonverbal communication* was cataloged under a social science call number, Brown chose the *Social Science Periodical Index* to find current scholarly articles. *Proxemics* was listed with the cross-reference "See personal space." Brown found numerous articles exploring personal space, many of them with bibliographies that listed her older sources. Seeing their names reassured her that she had uncovered some of the authorities on her topic. Brown decided to read several articles. Because some of them were unavailable in her college library, she arranged to get them through interlibrary loan.

As a last step in gathering current sources, Brown consulted a **periodicals database** her library had recently acquired. She took a few minutes to learn the computer access codes and then searched using the narrower key term *personal space,* as well as the more general key term *nonverbal communication.* Under nonverbal communication she found 68 listings, many of them available in full-text print form (available for complete versions to be called up onscreen or printed out). Being familiar with the names of credible authorities in the field and

QUOTATION ABOUT WRITING

There mark what ills the scholar's life
    assail:
Toil, envy, want, the patron, and the gaol.
           —Samuel Johnson

34a

cont.

keeping her narrowed topic of personal space in mind, Brown felt she was equipped to choose worthwhile articles from the database. She scanned the available articles onscreen and printed out those that she felt fairly sure would be relevant.

During this search for materials, Brown was slowly formulating a **research question** that would help to focus her use of the sources she had gathered. Because Edward Hall's discussion of differing standards for personal space in different cultures interested her, Brown brainstormed by posing research questions related to that aspect. "What is personal space?" was too broad and lacked focus. "How do North Americans' and Arabs' standards for personal space differ?" was too narrow for the resources available in her college library. Widening this too specific idea to "How do standards for personal space differ among cultures?" Brown was now ready to focus her exploration of her sources. (For a flow chart that shows Brown's narrowing process, see page 544.)

Now Brown was ready to think about her purpose and audience (see 1b, 1c, and 32e). For an audience, she chose a **general reader**—rather than a specialized reader—because she wanted to assume that the audience would know little about the topic of personal space. Deciding on a purpose proved more complicated. Brown started by wanting to write with a persuasive purpose, but she soon switched to an informative purpose. At first, she wanted to argue that people from different countries have serious trouble with crosscultural communication unless they are aware of varying expectations concerning personal space. While reading and taking notes to answer her research question, however, Brown realized that she could not explain basic crosscultural concepts and argue a position within the time and length limits of the assignment. She settled on an informative purpose.

Brown now had a working bibliography. Using MLA documentation style (see section 33c), she had made bibliography cards (see 33b) on key books and articles. It was time to read closely and take notes. Brown carefully headed each index card with the author of the source. Making sure to avoid plagiarism, she paraphrased, summarized, and copied quotations according to the techniques described in Chapter 31. Whenever she copied an author's exact words, Brown enclosed them in oversized quotation marks to alert herself to be especially careful to avoid plagiarism when writing from these notes.

While taking notes, Brown rejected a few sources that duplicated what she already had. Later, as she was writing her paper, she dropped a few other sources that were related to personal space but not to her paper. Her final version uses 15 sources.

In organizing her paper, Brown looked through her notes and saw that they fell into two piles: standards for personal space in North America and standards in other countries. She tried to outline the material and quickly realized that she would need to start with a definition of personal space. Going back through her cards, she created a third pile for definitions.

Composing her thesis statement was next. Brown wanted her thesis statement to be the last sentence of her introductory paragraph. She drafted a preliminary thesis statement to use as she wrote the first full draft of her paper. Later she revised the thesis statement (for a description of the evolution of her final thesis statement, see 32r). Here is an early draft of Brown's introductory paragraph; the last sentence contains the preliminary thesis statement.

```
People know unconsciously what close is when they stand
near other people during conversations. This relates to the
concept of personal space—the amount of physical distance
people expect during social interaction. Standards for
personal space vary among cultures.
```

Brown knew that this early draft was flawed. It lacked interest, the word "this" was a vague pronoun reference, and the thesis statement did not give a full picture of the paper. She showed her draft to three friends and asked them to react. One friend, a major in psychology, had a newspaper clipping in his files that Brown thought would be a good source to draw on for introducing her essay. For Brown's final draft, see page 1 of her paper in 34b.

In writing her paper, Brown composed three drafts. In addition to rewriting her opening paragraph, Brown made other improvements as she revised. Her first draft lacked clear signals to readers about the material's organization. In her second draft, Brown worked hard to craft topic sentences to start many of her paragraphs, realizing that these sentences showed the structure she had imposed on the topic as she synthesized what she had learned from her various sources. Also, Brown felt that her first draft relied too much on quotations, and so she paraphrased (see 31d) and summarized (see 31e) some of the material for the second draft. She kept quotations only when an author's language carried some special significance (see, for example, Brown's third and fourth paragraphs) or helped establish the credibility of the information. In the third draft, Brown polished her word choice, corrected her grammar and spelling, and reworked her conclusion. She decided that the conclusion should be a call to action (see 4g), urging people to become sensitive to the concept of personal space and thereby avoid intercultural misunderstandings. Brown's first draft of a concluding paragraph was only one sentence long, so she knew it needed work.

Brown's final draft appears in 34b. A commentary explaining elements of the paper accompanies each page of this final draft. Process Notes, a special feature of the commentary, narrate Brown's thinking and writing processes as she made choices and decisions.

QUOTATION ABOUT WRITING

Of making many books there is no end; and much study is a weariness of the flesh.

Bible, *Ecclesiastes*

34b

QUOTATION ABOUT WRITING
A title page is like a tray of hors d'oeuvres; it suggests what is to come.
—Susie R. Rambo

BACKGROUND
A direct title tells exactly what the essay will be about. An indirect title hints at the essay's topic. In either case, it stands alone, not as part of the body of the essay. (See 3c-2.)

Analyzing an MLA-style research paper
Amy Brown follwed MLA style for format decisions on this paper.

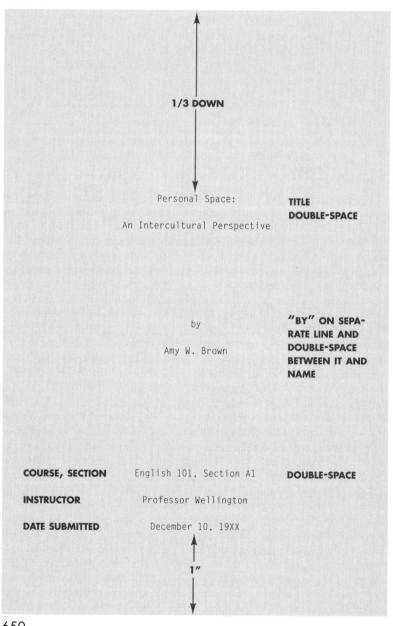

1/3 DOWN

Personal Space:

An Intercultural Perspective

TITLE
DOUBLE-SPACE

by

Amy W. Brown

"BY" ON SEPARATE LINE AND DOUBLE-SPACE BETWEEN IT AND NAME

COURSE, SECTION   English 101, Section A1

INSTRUCTOR   Professor Wellington

DATE SUBMITTED   December 10, 19XX

DOUBLE-SPACE

1"

Title page and first page of essay with a title page. If your instructor requires a title page, you can use the format and types of information shown on page 650 for Amy Brown's title page. Then, on page 1 of your paper, put your last name followed by a space followed by the numeral 1 in the upper right corner 1/2 inch below the top edge of the page. Double-space below this heading, and then type the paper's title, centering it. Double-space after the title, and then start your paper, indenting the first line of each paragraph 5 characters. Double-space after the title, and begin your paper. The first page of Amy Brown's paper, on page 654, follows this format.

First page without a title page. If your instructor does not require a title page, follow MLA format style, shown below, for the first page of your paper.

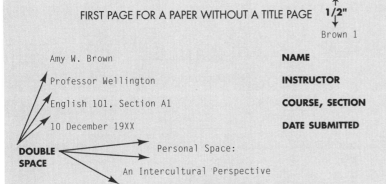

FIRST PAGE FOR A PAPER WITHOUT A TITLE PAGE   **1/2"**

Brown 1

Amy W. Brown   **NAME**

Professor Wellington   **INSTRUCTOR**

English 101, Section A1   **COURSE, SECTION**

10 December 19XX   **DATE SUBMITTED**

DOUBLE   Personal Space:
SPACE
                        An Intercultural Perspective

When she returned home after a year in South America, U.S. writer Judith Martin began to have a problem. People kept interpreting her behavior as flirtatious, but she was not flirting. Fairly soon she figured out what was happening. When most South Americans talk to each other face-to-face, they stand closer together than do most people from the United States or Canada. Martin had not readjusted from South American distances (9). Apparently, she had forgotten about the phenomenon known as personal space--the amount of physical distance people expect during social interaction. Everyone has expectations concerning the use of personal space, but

QUOTATION ABOUT WRITING
The wastepaper basket is the writer's best friend.

—Isaac B. Singer

BACKGROUND

A formal outline (see 2o) follows conventions concerning content and format that ensure that relationships among ideas are clear and that the content is orderly. If it is a topic outline, each item in it is only a word or a phrase. If it is a sentence outline, each item is a complete sentence.

34b
cont.

DOUBLE-SPACE 1" 1/2"

Brown i

Outline

<u>Thesis statement</u>: Everyone has expectations concerning the use of personal space, but accepted distances for that space are determined by each person's culture.

I. Research on personal space began in the 1960s.

   A. Most people are unaware that interpersonal distances exist.

   B. Personal space depends on invisible boundaries.

   C. Personal space moves with people as they interact.

   D. People do not like anyone to trespass on their personal space.

II. Research reveals North Americans' expectations for personal space.

   A. Hall identifies four zones for personal space.

   B. Subcultures help determine expectations for personal space.

   C. Gender influences people's use of personal space.

III. Research reveals standards for personal space in countries other than the United States.

   A. Conversational distances vary by cultures.

      1. Western Europeans use fingertip-to-shoulder distance.

      2. Eastern Europeans use wrist-to-shoulder distance.

      3. Mediterraneans use elbow-to-shoulder distance.

   B. Amounts of touching vary in different cultures.

   C. Arabs prefer close interpersonal distances.

   D. Japanese do not prefer close interpersonal distances.

Name and page-number heading. Except for a title page, give each page of a paper you prepare according to MLA format guidelines a heading in the upper right corner 1/2 inch below the top edge of the paper. Use your last name, followed by a space, followed by the page number. Number pages that come before your essay begins, such as outline pages, with lowercase roman numerals (see Amy Brown's outline). Use arabic numeral 1 on the page on which your essay begins, and then number each page consecutively through to the last page of Works Cited. Double-space below the name and page number to whatever comes next on the page.

Outline. Brown's instructor required a formal outline in the final draft of each student's research paper. To format her outline, Brown referred to sections 2o and 32s in this handbook. In the upper right corner heading consisting of her last name and the page number, she used lowercase roman numerals for the page numbers, a conventional way of showing that the outline comes before the first page of the essay itself. She double-spaced below the name-number heading and then centered the word "Outline," using a capital letter to start it. She double-spaced and then typed the words "Thesis statement" at the left margin, underlining them. The thesis statement matches the last sentence of the first paragraph of her paper.

Brown used a **sentence outline,** not a topic outline (see 2o). To reflect the organization of her paper, she divided the material in the outline into three major parts, numbered I, II, and III. Each item in the three major parts she numbered A, B, etc. Part III-A needed more detail, so the added items are numbered 1, 2, and 3. The items in the outline are in parallel form: Each starts with a subject followed by a verb in the PRESENT TENSE.

QUOTATION ABOUT WRITING

Sometimes writer's block is no more than a signal that you have not done enough research.

—Sophy Burnham

34b

cont.

Brown 1

A

Personal Space:

An Intercultural Perspective

1   When she returned home after a year in South America, B
U.S. writer Judith Martin began to have a problem. People
kept interpreting her behavior as flirtatious, but she was
not flirting. Fairly soon she figured out what was
happening. When most South Americans talk to each other
face-to-face, they stand closer together than do most
people from the United States or Canada. Martin had not
readjusted from South American distances (9). Apparently,
she had forgotten about the phenomenon known as personal
space--the amount of physical distance people expect during social interaction. Everyone has expectations concern- C
ing the use of personal space, but accepted distances for
that space are determined by each person's culture.

2   Observations about personal space began about thirty
years ago. Anthropologist Edward T. Hall was a pioneer in D
the field. He became very interested in how interpersonal
distances affected communication between people. In his
aptly titled book The Hidden Dimension, Hall coined the
word "proxemics" to describe people's use of space as a
means of communication (1). When The Hidden Dimension was E
published in the 1960s, most people were unaware that
interpersonal distances existed and contributed to
people's reactions to one another. Today, even though
people may be generally more sensitive to multicultural
issues, the cultural differences and expectations Hall
described (109) can still be misunderstood and can still E
affect people's reactions to one another.

COMMENTARY

A. **Title.** Brown's title prepares readers for her paper by giving the paper's major term (personal space) and the focus of her paper's discussion (more than one culture). ❖ PROCESS NOTE: In an earlier draft, Brown's title was "Proxemics: An Intercultural Perspective on the Need for Space." She rejected it because "space" was too general and "proxemics" was too technical. She then tried "Being Close: An Intercultural Perspective," but she revised the first half to avoid multiple meanings. ❖

B. **Introductory device.** Brown uses an anecdote. (See 4g.) She wanted it to serve four functions: to make the abstract concept of personal space concrete and familiar; to tie into the paper's title; to lead into the thesis statement; and to capture readers' interest. ❖ PROCESS NOTE: For an early draft of this paragraph, see page 649. ❖

C. **Thesis statement.** The last sentence of Brown's introductory paragraph is her thesis statement. Emerging from the paper's title and opening anecdote, the thesis prepares readers for what to expect. Brown's thesis developed from her synthesis of the information and ideas she encountered as she conducted her research. ❖ PROCESS NOTE: For the evolution of Brown's thesis statement, see 32r. ❖

D. **Evaluation of source.** Brown establishes Edward T. Hall as an expert by identifying him as an anthropologist and as a pioneer on the subject of personal space. ❖ PROCESS NOTE: Brown confirmed that Hall was an authoritative, reliable source by finding his name and his work, mentioned in articles and listed in bibliographies with articles in reference works such as *The Encyclopedia of Psychology* and *The Encyclopedic Dictionary of Psychology* (see 34a). ❖

E. **Parenthetical page reference for author and book named in the text.** Brown uses two sources by Edward T. Hall in her paper. (His other work is cited in paragraph 10.) Also, she uses a source by Judith Hall (see paragraph 7). To identify the source here unmistakably, she uses Hall's name and the work title here; the parenthetical references include only the page numbers. (Brown also uses a work by Edward T. Hall and Muriel Reed Hall, but that source is always cited as Hall and Hall.) Brown uses quotation marks for the coined word "proxemics." Also, she inserts the first parenthetical reference before the period, at the end of the sentence, because the entire sentence refers to information in Hall. She inserts the second parenthetical reference after "Hall described," not before the sentence-ending period, signaling to readers that Hall's description of cultural differences and expectations is the material on page 109. Brown, not Hall, is saying that "even today" misunderstandings can still occur and "can still affect people's reactions to one another."

BACKGROUND

In "Scoring Peers' Papers: Teaching Audience Awareness and Generating Enthusiasm," (*Teaching English in the Two Year College*, 20:4, Dec. 1993, 300–305) Sharon Albert and Kathryn Ring explain a teaching process that asks students from two classes to grade each others' papers. While the identity of individual graders and writers remain anonymous, students develop the sense of writing to a real audience rather than simply to their instructor.

BACKGROUND

An ellipsis is a set of three spaced dots used to show that some of the original writer's words have been left out of a quotation. If an omission occurs at the beginning of a quotation, an ellipsis is not needed to show the omission. Also, an ellipsis is not necessary at the end of a quotation as long as it ends in a complete sentence. (See 29d.)

Brown 2

3   Personal space depends on invisible boundaries. Those boundaries move with people as they interact. Personal space gets larger or smaller depending on the circumstances of the social interaction at any moment (Fisher, Bell, and Baum 149). Robert Sommer, an environmental psychologist, uses literary and visual analogies to describe personal space:

> Like the porcupines in Schopenhauer's
> fable, people like to be close enough to
> obtain warmth and comradeship but far
> enough away to avoid pricking one
> another. Personal space . . . has been
> likened to a snail shell, a soap bubble,
> an aura, and "breathing room." (26)

4   People can react strongly to trespassers on their personal space. In a textbook, social psychologists Stephen Worchel and Joel Cooper supplied one literary version. Poet W. H. Auden describes his own personal space and threatens a uniquely negative reaction to intrusions in his space:

> Some thirty inches from my nose
> The frontier of my person goes
> And all the untilled air between
> Is private pagus or demesne
> Stranger, unless with bedrooms eyes
> I beckon you to fraternize
> Beware of rudely crossing it
> I have no gun but I can spit.

> (qtd. in Worchel and Cooper 539)

F

G

H

I

J

J

K

COMMENTARY

F. **Topic sentence.** Brown uses a topic sentence (see 4a) to start many of her paragraphs. ❧ PROCESS NOTE: Brown's topic sentences in this paper emerged from her reflecting on what she learned about personal space as she conducted her research and came to understand what she read. Her topic sentences are the result of her thinking critically, most especially by making connections among ideas as she synthesized all her material (see 5b and 5f). ❧

G. **Paraphrase of original source.** ❧ PROCESS NOTE: In an earlier draft, Brown quoted the material and worked it into her prose. In her final draft, she used a paraphrase because it was not worded memorably enough to warrant quotation. ❧

H. **Parenthetical reference to authors not named in the text.** Authors' names and source page are in parentheses.

I. **A long quotation.** A quotation of more than four typewritten lines is set off from the rest of the text. Brown introduces it with a colon because she has written a complete sentence (compare with paragraph 12). She indents the material (10 characters or 1 inch) on the left and does not paragraph-indent the first line. In the fifth line, Brown uses a three-dot ellipsis where she omitted words (the full original source is shown in 32j–2). The words "breathing room" are in quotation marks because they appear this way in the original source. The parenthetical page reference is placed after the punctuation that ends the quotation.

J. **Use of an unusual source.** ❧ PROCESS NOTE: Although W. H. Auden is not a likely expert on personal space, Brown was delighted to use his poem. Because she had found the poem quoted in a discussion of personal space by social psychologists, she felt justified in using it. Also, it expressed a truth about personal space in exceptionally memorable language. She decided that this poem would be especially meaningful to the nonspecialist readers in her freshman English class. ❧

K. **Parenthetical reference for an indirect source.** Brown had to rely on an indirect source because her efforts to locate the poem in Auden's collected works were unsuccessful. (Brown found that for his later collections, Auden revised and even removed some poems from earlier collections.) She wanted to include the poem (see comment H above). In her parenthetical reference, she used *qtd. in,* the abbreviation for "quoted in," to show the quoted words are Auden's and can be found on page 539 of a work by Worchel and Cooper.

TEACHING TIP
Students sometimes think they are the only readers who skip over long quotations. You may want to assure them that they are not alone. The implication for students as writers, of course, is that when they feel they must include a lengthy quotation, in order to present a complicated idea in detail, for example, it is helpful to prepare the reader by explaining its importance. To make it as brief as possible, all irrelevant material should be deleted so that every word counts.

TEACHING TIP

You may want to point out to students that symbols, such as # % ə + and =, should not be used in the body of a paper, although they often appear in graphs and tables. The dollar sign can be used anywhere when accompanied by figures.

Brown 3

5   Research provides information about the distances that people living in the United States prefer when interacting. The pioneering work was done by Edward T. Hall. He observed the behavior of a group of middle-class adults in business and professions in the northeastern United States. He saw four zones of personal space; they are summarized and explained in Table 1.

Table 1

Hall's "Distance Zones"[a]   L

	Intimate	Personal	Social	Public
Close	0 to 6"	$1\frac{1}{2}'$ to $2\frac{1}{2}'$	4' to 7'	12' to 25'
Far	6" to $1\frac{1}{2}'$	$2\frac{1}{2}'$ to 4'	7' to 12'	25' +

Source: Discussion in Edward T. Hall, <u>Hidden</u> 110-20; also   M
Stewart 4-5; Fisher, Bell, and Baum 153.

[a]Selected illustrations of each zone are: <u>Close</u>   N
<u>Intimate</u>: lovers, children with parents; <u>Far Intimate</u>: strangers in crowds; <u>Close Personal</u>: husband and wife talking on the street; <u>Far Personal</u>: friends talking on the street; <u>Close Social</u>: boss and subordinate at a meeting; <u>Far Social</u>: receptionist and people in a waiting room; <u>Close Public</u>: teacher and students in a classroom; <u>Far Public</u>: actors or public speakers with audiences.

6   Researchers working with Edward T. Hall's data found that accepted interpersonal distances in the United States also depend on other factors. For example, subcultures help determine expectations concerning personal space. Fisher, Bell, and Baum report that groups of Hispanic-Americans generally interact more closely within their subculture than Anglo-Americans do within theirs.

COMMENTARY

L. **Table.** A table is an excellent way to summarize complex or extensive information that involves numbers and/or repeated categories. In MLA STYLE, a table should be placed as close as possible to the paragraph in which it is first mentioned. If a table cannot fit in the space remaining on the page, it can be placed on the next page after the end of the first paragraph on that page. Some instructors permit students to put tables on a separate page, titled Appendix, at the end of the paper, but before pages for notes (if any) and the Works Cited list. Brown uses the format suggested in the *MLA Handbook for Writers of Research Papers*, 4th edition: table number and title at the left margin above the body of the table, lowercase letter to signal a note, source information immediately below the data, and note below source information. In MLA style, table notes are indicated by lowercase letters, and text notes by numbers (see paragraphs 9 and 10). ✤ PROCESS NOTE: In an early draft, Brown wrote sentences to present the information now in this table. She did not think of using a table until she showed her early draft to a friend who said that the material was hard to follow and boring. She then tried to condense the material and, as she was writing, decided that a table would be clearer and more concise. ✤

M. **Source identification.** Because Brown uses two works by Edward T. Hall, she includes a shortened title *(Hidden)* here so that readers will know which of his works she is referring to. (She uses his first name to distinguish him from Judith Hall, author of another source Brown uses; see paragraph 7. The other work by Edward T. Hall is cited in paragraph 10.) Brown uses semicolons to separate each item in a series of multiple references.

N. **Choice of examples.** ✤ PROCESS NOTE: In writing the footnote to the table, Brown had many choices of illustrations for each zone. She chose the ones that seemed to her the most familiar and therefore effective examples. ✤

QUOTATION ABOUT WRITING

And sometimes the work is so boring you think you'll scream. For one book, I made up a game. I would look through the dictionary until I found an obscure and magnificent word, then use it in the text. I remember once constructing an entire chapter of the book I was working on around one word (*autochthons*), and the puzzle was to do it in such a way that no one knew the word came first.
—Sophy Burnham

34b
cont.

Brown 4

They further explain that "in general subcultural groups tend to interact at closer distances with members of their own subculture than with nonmembers" (158).   O

7   Gender also influences people's sense of personal space. In her book <u>Nonverbal Sex Differences</u>, Judith Hall   P   Q says that women stand closer to another person than men do. In general, two women stand closest to each other, a woman and a man stand somewhat farther apart than two women, and two men stand farthest apart from each other (85-105). The effect of gender can produce the opposite   R result, however. A study of taxicab passengers in Australia found that 86 percent of women passengers riding alone sat in the back left seat of the taxi, as far from the driver as possible. (The driver sits on the right side in Australia.) Ninety-five percent of men riding alone, on the other hand, chose to ride in the front left seat, next to the driver (Kenner and Katsimaglis 625). Gender also seems to affect people's decisions to trespass on others' personal space. If two women are talking to each other while standing on opposite sides of a corridor, both men and women tend to walk between them. In contrast, both men and women walk around a pair of men or a man and a woman conversing (Lomax et al. 3).

8   Expectations concerning personal space exist in all   S cultures, but such expectations vary greatly from culture to culture (Fast 29). Research reveals standards for personal space in countries other than the United States. For example, conversational distances vary between people from different countries, according to Desmond Morris, a British zoologist. He notes that when people from Western Europe stand on the street and talk, the space between

COMMENTARY

O. **Quotation within sentence.** Brown fits a quotation into her prose, using quotation marks to avoid plagiarism. The parenthetical reference goes immediately after the end of the material from the source (after a closing quotation mark, not before it). ❧ PROCESS **!** NOTE: Brown used a quotation because she felt that the material comparing one subgroup with another might be sensitive. She wanted her readers to have particular confidence in her presentation of the information. This is the third quotation in Brown's paper; the other two (paragraphs 3 and 4) are long quotations, which are displayed. This is a short run-in quotation, which Brown felt covered the material well and offered a change of pace in ways to integrate quotations. ❧

P. **Word choice.** Brown uses *gender,* not *sex* here. ❧ PROCESS **!** NOTE: As Brown read journal articles, she noted that most of them used "gender" rather than "sex," although Judith Hall uses both "sex" and "gender" in *Nonverbal Sex Differences.* Brown chose "gender" because it was used by a greater number of the sources she consulted. ❧

Q. **Author with same last name as another source author.** Brown uses the full name Judith Hall to distinguish this citation of a source from references to Edward T. Hall, who is cited in paragraphs 2, 5, 10, and 12.

R. **Paraphrase of an original source.** ❧ PROCESS NOTE: As Brown **!** paraphrased her source, she did not include all the data in the original. She paraphrased the general observations about men and women mentioned in the article by Kenner and Katsimaglis, but she did not include all their specific details. Brown chose details relating to her focus on men and women riding alone. In choosing, she checked carefully that her choices did not distort the source's meaning and the overall conclusions of the study. ❧

S. **Summary of original source.** Brown uses a summary to condense a source. ❧ PROCESS NOTE: Although Brown liked the informal **!** tone of Morris's material, she did not quote it. She found it easy to summarize. Here is the original: ❧

> Unfortunately, different countries have different ideas about exactly how close is close. It is easy enough to test your own "space reaction": When you are talking to someone in the street or in any open space, reach out with your arm and see where the nearest point on his body comes. If you hail from western Europe, you will find

➡

34b

cont.

Brown 5

them is the distance it would take one person's fingertip to reach the other's shoulder. People from Eastern Europe converse at a wrist-to-shoulder distance. People from the Mediterranean, however, prefer elbow-to-shoulder distance (131).

9   Permitted amounts of touching also illustrate intercultural differences in standards for personal space. Touching while conversing differs in Germany, France, and the United States. Hall and Hall report that Germans keep eye contact but avoid any deliberate or unintentional touching (39). They describe the French, in contrast, as gesturing, handshaking, and embracing, although the intensity of touching in France varies from region to region (92). Americans, like the French, shake hands when greeting people and indicate their openness by smiling frequently, but they seem to prefer a comfortable conversational distance without any physical contact (142).[1]

10   Arabs prefer close interpersonal distances. Polhemus explains that Arab students move close together more often, confront each other directly, and touch each other more frequently when talking than do American students (21). In an interview called "Learning the Arabs' Silent Language," Edward T. Hall claims that Arabs know the practicality of close conversational distances: "If you are interested in something, your pupils dilate; if I say something you don't like, they tend to contract" (47).[2] Hall goes on to explain that conversational distances of two feet—preferred by many Arabs—permit people to see each other's pupils better than does the typical North American distance of five feet (48).

11   The Japanese traditionally do not prefer close interpersonal distances. Because the island of Japan is

T

T

T,U

V

W

X

COMMENTARY

(S continued)

that he is at roughly fingertip distance from you. In other words, as you reach out, your fingertips will just about make contact with his shoulder. If you come from eastern Europe you will find you are standing at "wrist distance." If you come from the Mediterranean region you will find that you are much closer to your companion, at little more than "elbow distance."

T. **Use of sources.** ✣ PROCESS NOTE: Brown wondered whether she needed to use three separate parenthetical references (after the second, third, and fourth sentences). Her instructor explained that naming the source of all the cited information cited—Hall and Hall—is required only once as long as Brown mentions these authors in her own sentence. Because the details about German, French, and American behavior are in three different places in Hall and Hall, however, three parenthetical citations give the page references. ✣

U. **Related information in a note.** Brown uses a content note (see 33c-4) for related information here and in paragraph 10. A note number is raised slightly above the line after the period ending the sentence. (These raised numbers are called superscripts in word processing programs.) Endnotes are placed at the end of a paper, on a separate sheet of paper titled Notes; see Brown's page 8 for her two content notes.

V. **Word choice.** ✣ PROCESS NOTE: In an early draft, Brown used the words "says" and "say" in most places where she presented information from a source. When she revised, Brown wanted to vary her word choice. She looked at Chart 133 in section 31f to get ideas for different words. In her final draft Brown varies the verbs she uses to include *claim, describe, explain, note, report,* and *observe.* ✣

W. **Quotation from an interview.** Brown quotes what Hall said at an interview. She can be sure of the exact wording because the interview is reported in a respected magazine. In general, professional writers check the wording of a quotation before they use it in print. When material is even slightly controversial, professional writers usually also reconfirm all paraphrases and summaries with the source. Some of the most highly respected publications have a staff whose sole job is to verify information and reconfirm quoted material. Some instructors require students to follow these practices. Also, some instructors prefer that material from an interview be paraphrased or summarized, unless a student has tape-recorded the

➜

QUOTATION ABOUT WRITING
The desire to write grows with writing.
—Erasmus

QUOTATION ABOUT WRITING

I think we must quote whenever we feel that the allusion is interesting or helpful or amusing.

—Clifton Fadiman

34b

cont.

Brown 6

quite small for its population, public places are often very crowded. To cope, the people remain formal and aloof even when in very close proximity to one another (Fast 38). More recently, however, many Japanese have lived and worked in Western countries, as well as having seen Western movies and television programs in Japan. As a result, the younger Japanese are beginning to perceive personal space more as Westerners do. Sometimes, conflicts arise between younger and older Japanese, whose cultural experiences have been much less modified by exposure to western perceptions of personal space (Herlivi).

Y

12   Anyone can easily be misunderstood who is insensitive to the ways that people from other cultures-- or, as Herlivi suggests, within a changing culture--use personal space. Clearly, what is considered obnoxious in one culture might be considered polite in another (Fisher, Bell, and Baum 167). As Edward T. Hall says, virtually everything people are and do

> is associated with the experience of
> space.... Therefore, people from differ-
> ent cultures, when interpreting each
> other's behavior, often misinterpret the
> relationship, the activity, or the
> emotions. This leads to alienation in
> encounters or distorted communications.
> (Hidden 171)

Z

COMMENTARY

interview. ❖ PROCESS NOTE: While reading her sources, Brown repeatedly was impressed with Edward T. Hall's language. She kept feeling that her paraphrases and summaries could not possibly do justice to Hall. But she resisted the temptation to quote him extensively. She was aware that a student research paper is, in one sense, an exercise in which a student is expected to demonstrate the ability to paraphrase and summarize well. She quoted Hall here and in paragraph 12 because he is a major reference for her paper and Brown felt that this material helped establish the credibility of her information. ❖

X. **Word choice.** Brown originally wrote "Hall explains that," but when she was revising, she changed the verb to "goes on to explain." This change creates a link to the preceding sentence, helping readers to know that Edward T. Hall (not Judith Hall) is the source.

Y. **Summary of a personal interview.** Brown interviewed Kyoko Herlivi, a student at her college, who was born and had lived most of her life in Japan and who had recently married an American. ❖ PROCESS NOTE: Brown relies on Fast, a respected authority, for the background information about Japanese behavior regarding personal space. Although Herlivi confirmed the general information that Brown had read in Fast about Japanese attitudes in the past, what Brown summarizes from the interview is Herlivi's insights into changing behavior and a plausible reason for the change. ❖

Z. **Combined quotation from two paragraphs in original sources.** Brown combines into one quotation material from two paragraphs in Edward T. Hall. She needs no punctuation to lead into the quotation (compare with the lead-in to the poem quoted after paragraph 4, where a colon is used) because her lead-in is an incomplete sentence. She uses a four-dot ellipsis to show that the quotation is taken from two paragraphs. Here is the original source (Hall, *Hidden* 171):

> This book emphasizes that virtually everything that man is and does is associated with the experience of space. Man's sense of space is a synthesis of many sensory inputs: visual, auditory, kinesthetic, olfactory, and thermal. Not only does each of these constitute a complex system—as, for example, the dozen different ways of experiencing depth visually—but each is molded and patterned by culture. Hence, there is no alternative to accepting the fact that people reared in different cultures live in different sensory worlds.
>
> We learn from the study of culture that the patterning of perceptual worlds is a function not only of culture but of *relationship*, *activity*, and *emotion*. Therefore, people from different cultures, when interpreting each other's behavior, often misinterpret the relationship, the activity, or the emotions. This leads to alienation in encounters or distorted communications.

QUOTATION ABOUT WRITING

It's as hard to get from almost finished to finished as to get from beginning to almost done.

—Elinor Fuchs

QUOTATION ABOUT WRITING

34b
cont.

Each paragraph almost discovers the paragraph it precedes. When I end one paragraph I know it must lead to another.
—Roger Rosenblatt

Brown 7

13   In the next few years, more studies should be undertaken to uncover information about cultural differences in matters of personal space. Such information will be important to help us understand personal space in all cultures (Remland, Jones, and Brinkman 215-17, 30). International understanding cannot thrive unless people recognize and accept such cultural disparities.

AA

14   As international travel and commerce increase, intercultural contact is becoming commonplace. Soon, perhaps, cultural variations in expectations for personal space will be as familiar to everyone as are cultural variations in food and dress. Until then, people need to make a special effort to learn one another's expectations concerning personal space. Once people are sensitive to such matters, they can stop themselves from taking the wrong step: either away from or toward a person from another culture.

BB

COMMENTARY

AA. **Concluding device.** In paragraphs 13 and 14, Brown concludes her paper with a call for action (for concluding devices, see 4g). ❖ PROCESS NOTE: In early drafts, Brown's concluding paragraph was quite long. In her final draft, Brown divided it into two paragraphs and added a relevant quotation.(See also Comment BB.) ❖

BB. **Revising a concluding paragraph.** ❖ PROCESS NOTE: Brown rewrote her paragraph 14 almost as many times as she did her introductory paragraph. She wanted to get some punch into the ending. After many revisions, she wrote a last sentence that delivered the impact she was searching for. She also consulted Chart 27 in section 4g to remind herself what to avoid in conclusions and then decided to get rid of the phrase "of the sort discussed in this paper." The idea of using steps as a metaphor came to her nearly at the last minute, and she quickly worked it into her final draft. Here is one early draft of paragraph 14. ❖

> Contact between cultures is happening more frequently. After all, international travel and commerce increase daily. It is urgent, therefore, that everyone knows that there are lots of variations among cultures in personal space. That means there are more differences than those in food and dress. Researchers' observations of the sort discussed in this paper help people understand more about the wide variety of expectations concerning proper amounts of interpersonal closeness and distance.

QUOTATION ABOUT WRITING
A writer who waits for ideal conditions under which to work will die without putting a word on paper.
—E. B. White

34b
cont.

Sometimes I organize a piece so carefully that I will not only know the general thought I want to end with, I will write the last sentence before having written anything else. This sentence will contain all of the feeling of a piece unwritten, but I know it will be there and almost always I'm right.

—Roger Rosenblatt

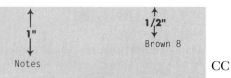

1″

1/2″
Brown 8

Notes

CC

DD

double-space

    [1] Hall and Hall point out that "space is sacred" to Germans, and privacy is extremely important. Americans often feel lonely when they live and work in Germany. They miss the close association with next-door neighbors, and they often feel that Germans are aloof and inhospitable.

    [2] This might explain why some Arab leaders wear sunglasses indoors.

COMMENTARY

CC. **Endnotes.** On a separate numbered page titled Notes, Brown provides commentary that does not fit into the text of her paper. Content notes in MLA style comment upon, explain, or clarify material written in the text. Each note starts with a number raised slightly (or a superscript number in word-processing programs) and indented five spaces or one-half inch. Double spacing is used within and between all notes. The format of the page is the same as for other pages: The name-number page line is one-half inch from the top edge of the page, in the upper right corner. The word *Notes,* with the first letter capitalized, is centered a double-space below the name/page line.

DD. **Comments in endnotes.** ✤ PROCESS NOTE: Brown used notes to include this material. She found the information in the first note, about the loneliness of Americans living in Germany, very interesting and decided that her readers would, too. She used a note for this detail because it did not fit neatly into the logic of her paragraphs. The second note developed when Brown was thinking about the information she had read in the Edward T. Hall interview. A picture flashed into her mind of a man in Arab dress wearing sunglasses. Her insight makes an appropriate and interesting comment in a note. ✤

QUOTATION ABOUT WRITING
There are no dull subjects. There are only dull writers.
—H. L. Mencken

!

QUOTATION ABOUT WRITING

In every real sense, the writer writes in order to teach himself, to understand himself, to satisfy himself; the publishing of the ideas is a curious anticlimax.
—Alfred Kazin

34b
cont.

Brown 9

Works Cited

Fast, Julius. <u>Body Language</u>. New York: Evans, 1970.　　　EE

Fisher, Jeffrey D., Paul A. Bell, and Andrew Baum.　　　FF
　　　<u>Environmental Psychology</u>. 2nd ed. New York: Holt,
　　　1984.

Hall, Edward T. <u>The Hidden Dimension</u>. New York: Doubleday,
　　　1966.

---. Interview. "Learning the Arabs' Silent Language."　　　GG,
　　　With Kenneth Friedman. <u>Psychology Today</u> Aug. 1979:　　　HH
　　　44-54.

Hall, Edward T., and Mildred Reed Hall. <u>Understanding</u>
　　　<u>Cultural Differences: Germans, French, and</u>
　　　<u>Americans</u>. Yarmouth ME: Intercultural Press, 1990.

Hall, Judith. <u>Nonverbal Sex Differences: Communication</u>　　　II
　　　<u>Accuracy and Expressive Style</u>. Baltimore: Johns
　　　Hopkins UP, 1984.

Herlivi, Kyoko. Personal interview. 2 Jan. 1995.　　　JJ

Kenner, Andrew N., and George Katsimaglis.
　　　"Gender Differences in Proxemics: Taxie Seat
　　　Choices." <u>Psychological Reports</u> 72 (1993): 625-26.

Lomax, Crystal M., et al. "Proxemics in Public: Space　　　KK
　　　Violations as a Function of Dyad Composition." ERIC
　　　ED 367 940.

Martin, Judith. "Here's Looking at You." <u>Newsday</u> 27 Jan.　　　LL
　　　1981, sec. 2: 9+.

Morris, Desmond. <u>Manwatching: A Field Guide to Human</u>
　　　<u>Behavior</u>. New York: Abrams, 1977.

Polhemus, Ted. "Social Bodies." <u>The Body as a Medium of</u>　　　MM
　　　<u>Expression</u>. Ed. Jonathan Benthall and Ted Polhemus.
　　　New York: Dutton, 1975. 13-35.

COMMENTARY

General Format. An alphabetically arranged list of all the sources referred to in the paper, called Works Cited, is used; it follows MLA documentation style (see 33c). Entries are alphabetized by each author's last name; if no author's name is given, the work's title is the first information unit and is alphabetized by its first word (excluding *A, An,* or *The*). Any entry more than one line long has a five-space (or one-half inch) indent for each line after the first. Double spacing is used within and between entries, including after the name/page line to the title, Works Cited.

EE. **Entry for a book by one author.**

FF. **Entry for book by three authors.** Inverted order (last name, first name) for name of first author, but regular order for others. *Second edition* abbreviated to *2nd ed.* Publisher abbreviated from *Holt, Rinehart and Winston* to *Holt*. (*Note:* In a work with three or fewer authors, all names are listed; see the Lomax entry for a work by four or more authors.)

GG. **Second work by same author.** Three hyphens and a period stand for the repetition of the preceding author's name. (*Note:* In such instances, works by the same author are listed alphabetically by title, not chronologically according to date of publication.)

HH. **Entry for an interview published in a magazine.** Entry listed by person interviewed, not by the person doing the interviewing. The page numbers are not preceded by *pp.*

II. *University Press* abbreviated *UP.*

JJ. **Entry for a personal (face-to-face) interview.** The date given is the date on which the interview took place.

KK. **Entry for material from an information service.** ERIC stands for Educational Resources Information Center. The number is the ERIC document number.

LL. **Entry for an article in a daily newspaper.** Title of article in quotation marks. Name of newspaper, *Newsday,* underlined. Date of newspaper in this order: day, month (abbreviation permitted), year. Then newspaper section and page numbers without *pp.* The + symbol is used only for newspaper articles when material continues on another page.

MM.**Entry for article in a book.** Author of article heads the entry. Editors of book, with names in regular order, follow book title. Title of article in quotation marks. Title of book underlined. Page numbers—without *pp.*—after city of publication and publisher.

Brown 10   NN

Remland, Martin S., Tricia S. Jones, and Heidi Brinkman.
    "Proxemic and Haptic Behavior in Three European
    Countries." Journal of Nonverbal Behavior 15 (1991):
    215-32.

Sommer, Robert. Personal Space: The Behavioral Bases of   OO
    Design. Englewood Cliffs: Prentice, 1969.

Stewart, Susan. "Too Close for Comfort?" Current Health 2
    Dec. 1992: 4-5.

Worchel, Stephen, and Joel Cooper. Understanding Social   PP
    Psychology. 3rd ed. Homewood, IL: Dorsey, 1983.

COMMENTARY

NN. **Entry for an article in a journal with continuous pagination.** Article title in quotation marks. Journal title underlined. Then volume number, year in parentheses, and page numbers without the abbreviation *pp*.

OO. Publisher abbreviated from *Prentice Hall* to *Prentice*.

PP. **Entry for book by two authors.** Inverted order (last name, first name) for name of first author, but regular order for second name. Place of publication includes city *and* two-letter postal abbreviation for state because many readers might not know that Homewood is in Illinois.

35 *Case Study: A Student Writing an APA Research Paper*

REFERENCE TO SUPPLEMENTS
For additional help with writing a successful research paper, refer students to *The Research Organizer: Prentice Hall Resources for Composition* by S. Hopke.

This chapter presents a student research paper written in the DOCUMENTATION STYLE of the American Psychological Association (APA). Section 35a discusses the researching (see Chapter 32), planning (see Chapter 2), drafting (see 3b and 32t), and revising (see 3c and 32t) processes of the student, Carlos Velez. Section 35b shows the final draft of the paper, including its abstract.

Carlos Velez was given this assignment for a research paper in a course called Introduction to Psychology: Write a research paper of 1,800-2,000 words about an unconscious process in humans. For guidance, refer to the *Simon & Schuster Handbook for Writers,* Fourth Edition, Chapters 31 through 33. Use the documentation style of the American Psychological Association (APA) explained in Chapter 33. Your topic and working bibliography are due in two weeks. An early draft of your paper is due two weeks later (try to get it close to what you hope will be your last draft, so that comments from me and your peers can concretely help you write an excellent final draft). Your final draft is due one week after the early draft is returned to you with comments.

35a Observing the processes of researching and writing an APA-style research paper

After Carlos Velez read his assignment, he started **planning** by listing various unconscious processes in humans so that he could pick one most interesting to him. Referring to his class notes and the textbook from his psychology course, he found these topics: sleep, dreams, insomnia, biological clocks, daydreams, hypnosis, and meditation. He favored biological clocks because of his experiences with jet lag whenever he traveled between his home in California (in the Pacific Time Zone) and his grandparents' home in Puerto Rico (in the Eastern Time Zone).

Velez then checked to see whether the library at his college had enough sources useful for research on biological clocks. He was pleased to find books, journal articles, magazine and newspaper articles, and even a videotape of a Public Broadcasting System program on the subject. So that he could compile a working bibliography (see 33b) and, at the same time, try to find an approach to the topic suitable for a paper of 1,800-2,000 words, Velez began to read and take notes (see 32j). He saw entire books about biological clocks, so he realized that he would need to narrow the topic (see 32d) sufficiently to shape a THESIS STATE-MENT (see 32r and 2n). The narrowing process worried him because he had been told in other college courses that his topics for research papers were too broad. He was determined this time to avoid that same problem.

The working bibliography that Velez submitted consisted of twenty-two sources, though he had read and rejected about six others as inadequate (he knew that this represented real progress for him). He did not intend to use them all in his paper, but he wanted them available as he wrote his early drafts. Not surprisingly, his instructor urged him to reduce the list by half once drafting began; otherwise Velez would risk writing too little about too much. He redoubled his efforts to read even more critically to evaluate his sources (see 32f-3) and weed out material. He got his list down to nineteen sources, took detailed notes (see 32j) on each, and began to group his material into emerging subtopics.

To start **drafting** his paper, Velez spread his note cards around him for easy reference, but he felt somewhat overwhelmed by the amount of information at hand, and he wrote only a few sentences. To break through, he decided to write a "discovery draft" (see 3b) to see what he had absorbed from his reading and note-taking. That very rough draft became his vehicle for many things, including creating an effective THESIS STATEMENT, inserting source information according to APA documentation style, and checking the logical arrangement of his material.

Revising for Velez started with his THESIS STATEMENT, a process that helped him further narrow his focus. He started with "Biological clocks are fascinating," which expressed his feelings but said nothing of substance. His next version served well as he revised his discovery draft into a true first draft: "Biological clocks, our unconscious time keepers, affect our lives in many ways including compatibility in marriage, family

TEACHING TIP
You might want to explain that formats are of major importance in many disciplines other than English composition. The formats constitute "genres" that readers expect. The formats ease communication because readers know where to look for specific information: background, data, conclusions.

QUOTATION ABOUT WRITING

Writing represents a unique mode of learning—not merely valuable, not merely special, but unique. . . . Writing serves learning uniquely because writing as process-and-product possesses a cluster of attributes that correspond uniquely to certain powerful learning strategies.
—Janet Emig,
"Writing as a Mode of Learning"

life, jet travel, work schedules, illnesses, medical treatments, and the space program." That version proved to Velez that he was covering too much for an 1,800–2,000-word research paper, and he wanted to drop material. He decided first to inform his readers about the phenomenon of biological clocks and then to discuss the effects of those clocks on people's alertness in the morning and later in the day, on travelers on jet airplanes, and on workers' performance. For his final draft, Velez used this more focused thesis statement: "Biological clocks, which are a significant feature of human design, greatly affect personal and professional lifestyles."

Using APA documentation style made Velez attend very closely to the details of correct parenthetical references (see 33d-1) within his paper and a correct References list (see 33d-2 and 33d-3) at the end. Because he had used MLA DOCUMENTATION STYLE in other courses, he made sure not to confuse the two styles. For example, he saw that APA-style parenthetical citations require a page reference for a quotation but not for a paraphrase or summary (whereas MLA style requires a page reference for all three). For format and style details of the References list at the end of his paper, he found Chart 143 in section 33d-2 especially helpful.

As Velez checked the logical arrangement of his material, he realized that because he had dropped some aspects of biological clocks when he finally narrowed his topic sufficiently, he needed a little more depth about those aspects that he was retaining. A few hours back in the library gave him what he needed. Having to retrace his steps had a dramatic impact on Velez: Now he saw the difference between researching a topic too broadly (and therefore gathering too many sources for the assignment) and researching a few aspects of a topic in depth by focusing on selected sources. His final draft, which appears in 35b, draws on thirteen sources, a number that is down drastically from the twenty-two with which he started.

On page 677, part of Velez's title page and abstract page are shown. For guidelines on writing an abstract, see section 33d–4.

Looking at the final draft of an APA-style research paper

```
                          Biological Clocks⟵— 1"—⟶
                                  1



                    Biological Clocks:
              The Body's Internal Timepieces


                       Carlos Velez
```

APA - Style Title Page

```
                              ⟵— 1"—⟶
       1"          Biological Clocks
                          2
                       DOUBLE SPACE
               Abstract
       Circadian rhythms, which greatly affect human
       lives, often suffer disruptions in technologi-
       cal societies, resulting in such disorders as
 ⟵ 1"⟶ jet lag syndrome and seasonal affective disor-
       der (SAD). With growing scientific awareness of
       both natural circadian cycles and the effects
       of disturbances of these cycles, individuals
       are learning how to control some negative
       effects.
```

APA - Style Abstract Page

35b
cont.

Biological Clocks:

The Body's Internal Timepieces

Life in modern, technological societies is built around timepieces. People set clocks on radios, microwave ovens, VCRs, and electric coffee makers. Students respond to bells that start and end the school day as well as dividing it into blocks of time. Almost everyone relies on clocks to manage time well. While carefully managing the minutes and hours each day, individuals are often encouraged or forced by current styles of family and work life to violate another kind of time: their body's time. Biological clocks, which are also known as circadian cycles, are a significant feature of human design that greatly affect personal and professional lifestyles.

The term "circadian," which is Latin for "about a day," describes the rhythms of people's internal biological clocks. Circadian cycles are in tune with external time cycles such as the 24-hour period of the earth's daily rotation as signaled by the rising and setting of the sun. Usually, humans set their biological clocks by seeing these cycles of daylight and darkness. Carefully designed studies conducted in caves or similar environments that let researchers control light and darkness have shown that most people create cycles slightly over 24 hours when they are not exposed to natural cycles of day and night (Allis & Haederle, 1989; Enright, 1980). Human perception of the external day-night cycle affects the production and release of a brain hormone, melatonin, which is important in initiating and regulating the sleep-wake cycle, as Alfred Lewy and other scientists at the National Institute of Health in Bethesda, Maryland, have found (Winfree, 1987). During the winter, female melatonin secretion increases at night. However, the amount of

Biological Clocks

4

melatonin secreted by females during the night decreases once summer arrives (Angier, 1995).

An individual's lifestyle reflects that person's own circadian cycle. Scientists group people as "larks" or "owls" based on whether individuals are more efficient in the morning or at night. The idea behind the labels is that "in nature certain animals are diurnal, active during the light period; others are nocturnal, active at night. The 'morning lark' and 'night owl' connotations typically are used to categorize the human extremes" ("Are You," 1989, p. 11).

"Larks" who must stay up late at night and "owls" who must awaken early in the morning experience mild versions of the disturbances, called "jet lag," that time-zone travelers often encounter. Jet lag, which is characterized by fatigue and irregular sleep patterns, results from disruption of circadian rhythms, a common problem among those who travel great distances by jet airplane to different time zones:

> Jet lag syndrome is the inability of the
> internal body rhythm to rapidly resynchronize
> after sudden shifts in the timing. For a
> variety of reasons, the system attempts to
> maintain stability and resist temporal change.
> Consequently, complete adjustment can often be
> delayed for several days—sometimes for a
> week—after arrival at one's destination.
> (Bonner, 1991, p. 72)

Interestingly, research shows that the number of flying hours is not the cause of jet lag. Rather, "the number, rate, and direction of time-zone changes are the critical factors in determining the extent and degree of jet lag symptoms," according to Richard Coleman (1986, p. 67) in <u>Wide Awake at 3 a.m.: By Choice or by Chance?</u> Eastbound travelers find it harder than westbound travelers to adjust, because traveling

35b
cont.

Biological Clocks

5

east forces people to go to bed before their biological clocks are ready for them to do so (Coleman).

Another group that suffers greatly from biological clock disruptions consists of people whose livelihoods depend on erratic schedules. This situation affects 20- to 30-million U.S. workers whose work schedules differ from the usual morning starting time and afternoon or early evening ending time (Weiss, 1989). Charles Czeisler, director of the Center for Circadian and Sleep Disorders at Brigham and Woman's Hospital in Boston, reports that 27 percent of the U.S. workforce does shift work (Binkley, 1990). Shift work can mean, for example, working from 7:00 a.m. to 3:00 p.m. for six weeks, from 3:00 p.m. to 11:00 p.m. for six weeks, and from 11:00 p.m. to 7:00 a.m. for six weeks. Many shift workers endure stomach and intestinal-tract disorders, and, on average, they have a three times higher risk of heart disease than non-shift workers (Bingham, 1989). In a 1989 report to the American Association for the Advancement of Science, Czeisler states that "police officers, [medical] interns, and many others who work nights perform poorly and are involved in more on-the-job accidents than their daytime counterparts" (Binkley, p. 26).

Other researchers confirm that safety is at risk during late-shift hours (Chollar, 1989). In a study of 28 medical interns observed during late night shifts over a one-year period, 25 percent admitted to falling asleep while talking on the phone, and 34 percent had at least one accident or near-accident during that period (Weiss, 1989). Investigations into the Challenger Shuttle explosion and the nuclear-reactor disasters at Three-Mile Island and Chernobyl reveal critical errors made by people undergoing the combined stresses of lack of sleep and unusual work schedules (Toufexis, 1989).

Biological Clocks

6

One especially negative effect of an upset biological clock is a syndrome increasingly recognized as a medical problem: the disorder known as Seasonal Affective Disorder (SAD). Dr. Thomas A. Wehr of the National Institutes of Mental Health, who first discovered the circadian rhythm differences between genders, is conducting further research to explain why more women than men suffer from SAD (Angier, 1995). Table 1 lists some of the major symptoms of SAD.

Table 1

Common Symptoms of Seasonal Affective Disorder

Sadness	Later waking
Anxiety	Increased sleep time
Decreased physical	Interrupted,
activity	unrefreshing sleep
Irritability	Daytime drowsiness
Increased appetite	Decreased sexual drive
Craving for carbohydrates	Menstrual problems
Weight gain	Work problems
Earlier onset of sleep	Interpersonal problems

Note. From The Clockwork Sparrow (p. 204) by S. Binkley, 1990, Englewood Cliffs, NJ: Prentice Hall. Copyright 1990 by Prentice Hall, Inc.

SAD appears to be related to the short daylight (photoperiod) of winter in the temperate zones of the northern and southern hemispheres. The phenomenon of SAD not

QUOTATION ABOUT WRITING
It is by sitting down to write every morning that one becomes a writer. Those who do not do this remain amateurs.
—Gerald Brenan

35b
cont.

Biological Clocks

7

only illustrates the important role of circadian rhythms, but also it dramatically proves that an understanding of circadian principles can help scientists to improve the lives of people who experience disruptions of their biological clocks. Binkley claims that exposure to bright light for periods of up to two hours a day during the short photoperiod days of winter reduces SAD-related "depression in 87 percent of patients...within a few days; relapses followed" (pp. 203-204) when light treatment ended.

Exposure to long periods of bright light is not, however, an appropriate solution for people whose safety is at risk because of continual assaults on their circadian cycles by shift schedules at work. Establishing work schedules more sensitive to biological clocks could reduce certain safety hazards. A group of police officers in Philadelphia were studied while on modified shift schedules (Locitzer, 1989; Toufexis, 1989). These officers changed between day shifts and night shifts less frequently than they had on former shift schedules; they rotated forward rather than backward in time; and they worked four rather than six consecutive days. Officers reported 40 percent fewer patrol-car accidents and decreased use of drugs or alcohol to get to sleep. Overall, the police officers preferred the modified shift schedules. Charles Czeisler, who conducted the study, summarizes the importance of these results: "When schedules are introduced that take into account the properties of the human circadian system, subjective estimates of work schedule satisfaction and health improve, personnel turnover decreases, and worker productivity increases" (Locitzer, 1989).

Scientists like Charles Czeisler are beginning to help individuals live harmoniously with their biological clocks.

Biological Clocks

8

Growing awareness of the effects of such situations as shift work and travel across time zones is one significant step toward control. The use of light to manipulate the body's sense of time is another. As more people become aware of how circadian rhythms affect lifestyles, the day might soon come when we can fully control our biological clocks instead of their controlling us.

35b
cont.

Biological Clocks

9

References

Allis. T., & Haederle, M. (1989, June 12). Ace in the hole: Stefania Follini never caved in. <u>People</u>, p. 52.

Angier, N. (1995, March 14). Modern life suppresses an ancient body rhythm. <u>The New York Times</u>, pp. C1, C3.

Are you a day or night person? (1989, March). <u>USA Today Magazine</u>, p. 11.

Bingham, R. (Writer & Director). (1989). <u>The time of our lives</u> [Television production]. KCET Commercial Television of Southern California, PBS.

Binkley, S. (1990). <u>The clockwork sparrow.</u> Englewood Cliffs, NJ: Prentice Hall.

Bonner, P. (1991, July). Travel rhythms. <u>Sky Magazine</u>, pp. 72-73, 76-77.

Chollar, S., (1989, November). Safe solutions for night work. <u>Psychology Today,</u> p. 26.

Coleman, R. (1986). <u>Wide awake at 3:00 a.m.: By choice or by chance?</u> New York: W. H. Freeman.

Enright, J. T. (1980). <u>The timing of sleep and wakefulness</u>. Berlin: Springer-Verlag.

Locitzer, K. (1989, July/August). Are you out of sync with each other? <u>Psychology Today</u>, p. 66.

Toufexis, A. (1989, June 5). The times of your life. <u>Time</u>, pp. 66-67.

Weiss, R. (1989, January 21). Safety gets short shrift on long night shift. <u>Science News</u>, p. 37.

Winfree, A. (1987). <u>The timing of biological clocks</u>. New York: W. H. Freeman.

Writing Across the Curriculum

When you write for the different disciplines that you encounter during your college years, you become familiar with the perspectives and assumptions that underlie each discipline. Part Eight compares and contrasts the various disciplines so that you can respond effectively to the major types of writing assignments in each discipline. As you use Chapters 36 through 40, be aware that the information in this handbook serves as a resource for your entire college career and beyond.

36 *Comparing the Different Disciplines*

REFERENCE TO SUPPLEMENTS

For guidelines on establishing and maintaining a successful collaborative writing classroom, see P. Kelvin/S. Leonard, "Teaching Collaborative Writing," in L. Julian, et al., *Strategies and Resources for Teaching Writing with the Simon & Schuster Handbook for Writers*.

BACKGROUND

In an article entitled "Defining Writing Across the Curriculum" (*WPA: Writing Program Administration* 11 [Fall 1987]: 19–24), Susan McLeod outlines two philosophical bases for WAC programs: cognitive and rhetorical. The first, associated with Janet Emig and James Britton, assumes that writing is a mode of thinking and learning. It emphasizes the use of journals and other ungraded writing assignments to assist learning. The latter, developed by Ken Bruffee, Elaine Maimon, and others, emphasizes the contextual and social constraints of writing. Because the discourse community is considered important to learning the conventions expected in a finished product, classes are likely to employ collaborative learning strategies and writing-response groups.

36a   ## Recognizing similarities and differences among the disciplines

The humanities, the social sciences, and the natural sciences each have their own perspectives on the world and their own philosophies about academic thought and research. To understand some of the differences among the disciplines, consider these three quite different paragraphs about a mountain.

HUMANITIES

The mountain stands above all that surrounds it. Giant timbers—part of a collage of evergreen and deciduous trees—conceal the expansive mountain's slope, where cattle once grazed. At the base of the mountain, a cool stream flows over rocks of all sizes, colors, and shapes. Next to the outer bank of the stream stands a shingled farmhouse, desolate, yet suggesting its active past. Unfortunately, the peaceful scene is interrupted by billboards and chairlifts, landmarks of a modern, fast-paced life.

SOCIAL SCIENCES

Among the favorite pastimes of American city dwellers is the "return to nature." Many outdoor enthusiasts hope to enjoy a scenic trip to the mountains, only to be disappointed. They know they have arrived at the mountain that they have traveled hundreds of miles to see because huge billboards are directing them to its base. As they look up the mountain, dozens of people are riding over the treetops in a chairlift, littering the slope with paper cups and food wrappers. At the base of the mountain stands the inevitable refreshment stand, found at virtually all American tourist attractions. Land developers consider such commercialization a way to preserve and utilize natural resources, but environmentalists are appalled.

NATURAL SCIENCES

The mountain is approximately 5,600 feet in height. The underlying rock is igneous, of volcanic origin, composed primarily of granites and feldspars. Three distinct biological communities are present on the mountain. The community at the top of the mountain is alpine in nature, dominated by very short grasses and forbs. At middle altitudes, a typical northern boreal coniferous forest community is present, and at the base and lower altitudes, deciduous forest is the dominant community. This community has, however, been highly affected by agricultural development along the river at its base and by recreational development.

These examples illustrate that each discipline has its writing traditions and preferences. The paragraph written for the humanities describes the mountain from the individual perspective of the writer—a perspective both personal and yet representative of a general human response. The paragraph written for the social sciences focuses on the behavior of people as a group. The paragraph written for the natural sciences reports observations of natural phenomena.

As you study and write in each of the academic disciplines, you become familiar with alternative ways of thinking. As you come to know the habits of mind that characterize each discipline, you develop specialized vocabularies that allow you to participate in the conversations of each discipline. As your perspectives are broadened, you gain lifelong access to the pleasures of informed insight—among the major benefits of a college education.

No matter what differences exist among the academic disciplines, all subject areas interconnect and overlap. Chart 162 lists similarities and differences.

SIMILARITIES AND DIFFERENCES IN WRITING ACROSS THE DISCIPLINES	162

SIMILARITIES

1. Consider your purpose, audience, and tone.	Chapters 1–2
2. Use the writing process to plan, shape, draft, revise, edit, and proofread.	Chapters 2–3
3. Develop a thesis.	Chapters 2–3
4. Arrange and organize your ideas.	Chapter 2
5. Use supporting evidence.	Chapters 2–4
6. Develop paragraphs thoroughly.	Chapter 4
7. Critically think, read, and write, and use correct reasoning and logic.	Chapter 5
8. Argue well.	Chapter 6
9. Write effective sentences.	Chapters 16–19

➔

SIMILARITIES AND DIFFERENCES IN WRITING ACROSS THE DISCIPLINES

BACKGROUND
Susan McLeod speculates about the future of WAC programs as she traces their development in colleges and universities through the past decade ("Writing Across the Curriculum: The Second Stage and Beyond," *College Composition and Communication* 40 [October 1989]: 337–342).

BACKGROUND
Many writing-across-the-curriculum programs offer support for instructors interested in developing new teaching techniques that involve writing. Such support often takes the form of workshops led either by a resident faculty member or by an outside consultant. At the workshops, instructors from varied disciplines discuss writing-to-learn-strategies, evaluation methods, journal keeping, and related matters. One successful format is an off-campus "retreat" where instructors spend several days working on such issues. Many schools also have a director of writing who serves as a resource person for faculty members looking for help in introducing writing into their assignments and classroom activities.

QUOTATION ABOUT WRITING
Problem solving is common ground for all the disciplines and fundamental to all human activities. . . . The discovery function of writing in the content areas, particularly in the scientific and technological fields, can help students become aware of the processes they use to solve problems.

—Carol Berkenkotter,
"Writing and Problem Solving"

BACKGROUND

Commenting that "there's almost no subject that can't be made accessible in good English," William Zinsser (*Writing to Learn* [New York: Harper & Row, 1988]) defines jargon as "the lingo of people in specialized fields who have infected each other with their private terminology and don't think there's any other way to say what they mean" (p. 66). He divides jargon into two main forms: buzzwords and special occupational terms. The first group is, for Zinsser, particularly objectionable because it is composed of words that "make the insider feel important when he uses them but that don't really mean anything" (p. 67). The second category consists of terms that some field has found it necessary to invent, terms that serve a particular need when professional people talk together. One proof of their value is that nonprofessionals quickly adopt them if they become important. The problem, according to Zinsser, arises when "jargon becomes a crutch—when its users become so dependent on their private terminology that they claim they can't express themselves in any other way" (p. 68).

BACKGROUND

To those teachers in other disciplines who fear that using writing to teach their course will be a waste of time or that they will not be able to evaluate students' work, Ruth Couch provides answers and suggestions for making writing-to-learn strategies work ("Dealing with Objections to Writing Across the Curriculum," *Teaching English in the Two-Year College* 16 [October 1989]: 193–196).

36b cont.

SIMILARITIES AND DIFFERENCES IN WRITING ACROSS THE DISCIPLINES (continued)

36a-1

SIMILARITIES AND DIFFERENCES IN WRITING ACROSS THE DISCIPLINES (continued) 162

10. Choose words well. Chapters 20–21
11. Use correct grammar. Chapters 7–15
12. Spell correctly. Chapter 22
13. Use correct punctuation and mechanics. Chapters 23–30

DIFFERENCES

1. Conduct research and select sources according to each discipline (see 36a-1).
2. Select a style of documentation appropriate to each discipline (see 36a-2 and Chapter 33).
3. Follow manuscript format requirements, if any, in each discipline (see 36a-3).
4. Use specialized language, when needed, in each discipline (see 36a-4).

For example, in a humanities class you might read *Lives of a Cell*, by Lewis Thomas, a collection of essays about science and nature written by the late noted physician and prize-winning author. As you consider the art of the writer, you will also be thinking deeply about biology and other sciences.

The four differences listed in Chart 162 are discussed in detail here.

Conducting research and selecting sources according to each discipline

Primary sources offer you first-hand exposure to information. No one comes between you and the exciting experience of discovering and confronting material on your own. Research methods differ among the disciplines when primary sources are used. In the humanities, existing documents are primary sources; the task of the researcher is to analyze and interpret these primary sources. Typical primary-source material for research could be a poem by Dylan Thomas, the floor plans of Egyptian pyramids, or early drafts of music manuscripts. In the social and natural sciences, primary research entails the design and undertaking of experiments involving direct observation. The task of the researcher in the social and natural sciences is to conduct the experiments or to read the first-hand reports of experiments and studies written by people who conducted them.

Secondary sources—articles and books about a primary source—are also important in all disciplines. In the humanities, you can learn much from the examples of others who have analyzed and interpreted primary sources. In the social and natural sciences, secondary sources can usefully synthesize findings in many areas and draw parallels that offer new insights.

Selecting a style of documentation appropriate to each discipline

Writers use **documentation** to give credit to the sources they have used. A writer who does not credit a source is guilty of **plagiarizing**—a serious academic offense (see 31a). Styles of documentation differ among the disciplines.

In the humanities, many fields use the documentation style of the Modern Language Association (MLA). MLA documentation style is explained and illustrated in section 33c. The student research paper in Chapter 34 and the student literary analysis in Chapter 37 use MLA documentation style. CM (Chicago Manual) style, also used in the humanities, is described in 33e. In the social sciences, most fields use the documentation style of the American Psychological Association (APA). APA documentation style is explained and illustrated in 33d. The student research paper in Chapter 35 uses APA documentation style. In the natural sciences, documentation styles vary, as is explained in 33f and 38g.

Following manuscript format requirements, if any, in each discipline

As a reflection of the differences among academic disciplines, different formats are sometimes expected for presentation of material. These special formats have evolved to communicate a writer's purpose, to emphasize content by eliminating distracting variations in format, and to make the reader's work easier. Writing in the humanities is less often subject to set formats, although writing is expected to be well organized and logically presented. Writing in the social and natural sciences often calls for set formats for specific types of writing.

Using specialized language, when needed, in each discipline

Specialized language is often referred to as **jargon**. Jargon is useful when it helps people who are specialists communicate easily with each other in a kind of "verbal shorthand." When specialized material is communicated to the general reading public, however, any jargon has to

36a-2

36a-3

36a-4

TEACHING TIP

Because the differences in documentation styles are easier to see from actual papers than to understand from a description, you may want to bring examples of research papers that use different documentation systems to class. The papers will make students aware that there is no single right way to cite sources; there is, instead, a way that is appropriate for a particular writing task and audience. The demonstration has the added benefit of showing students in various disciplines what is expected of them in their fields of study.

BACKGROUND

In *Programs That Work: Models and Methods for Writing Across the Curriculum* (Portsmouth, NH: Boynton/Cook, 1989), Toby Fulwiler and Art Young examine fourteen successful college and university WAC programs.

QUOTATION ABOUT WRITING

In schools where the lessons taught in English classes are not repeated and emphasized in the student's other classes, the knowledge and skills learned in those lessons tend to atrophy. We believe language skills deserve more conscious attention from teachers in all academic disciplines, and that teachers who recognize the role played by these "elementary" skills can help students increase their learning ability, improve their communication skills, and enhance their cognitive and emotional growth.

—Toby Fulwiler and Art Young,
Language Connections

TEACHING TIP

You might ask students to write contrastive paragraphs in the humanities, social sciences, and sciences using one of these topics:

a river	a sport	an illness
a car	the *Titanic*	an insect

36

TEACHING TIP

One way for students to demonstrate mastery of a subject is to be able to explain it in several different ways rather than parroting the textbook or the professor. This technique is useful in any discipline. For example, an engineering student might be asked to explain to a variety of audiences how radar works. In a series of short written assignments, the student explains radar to (1) a classmate who has missed several lectures but shares the same science background; (2) his nonscientist parents, who want to know what he is learning; (3) a group of sixth-graders.

REFERENCE TO SUPPLEMENTS

For using collaborative writing in a computer classroom, see *Computers and Writing: Prentice Hall Resources for Composition* by D. Rodrigues.

BACKGROUND

New Visions of Collaborative Writing, (Janis Forman, ed., Portsmouth, NH: Boynton-Cook, 1992) provides nine essays that prompt teachers to understand, evaluate, and use collaborative approaches in the writing classroom. Of particular interest are the articles that explore ways of collaborating through electronic writing and ways of addressing ethical questions related to collaboration.

36a-4
cont.

be defined so that everyone can understand the message. Jargon is not useful when it is unnecessarily obscure and overblown (see 21e-2).

All disciplines use specialized language to some extent. The specialized terms in the social and natural sciences are generally more technical and less accessible to nonspecialists than are those in the humanities. The more important that exactness is to a discipline, the more likely that many words will have specialized meanings. For example, consider the word *niche*. It has two generally known meanings: "a place particularly suitable to the person or thing in it," and "a hollowed space in a wall for a statue or vase." *Niche* in the natural sciences, however, has a very specialized meaning: "the set of environmental conditions—climate, food sources, water supply, enemies—that permit an organism or species to survive."

! ❖ USAGE ALERT: Many writers in scientific disciplines make a habit of writing in the passive voice. Yet style manuals for scientific writing agree with the advice you will find in 8o: Use the active voice except for purposes best fulfilled by the passive.* ❖

36b ## Using collaborative writing in various disciplines

If you are told to engage in **collaborative writing**, you will be expected to work with others in your class on a project. A collaborative writing group consists of two or more people, according to the instructor's directions. (Be aware that in many classes your instructor might prefer that you work alone on projects. To avoid any risk of charges of cheating or plagiarism, get permission from your instructor if you want to work collaboratively on your own with other students.)

Many professions require people to serve on committees, to reach general agreement, and to write reports of their deliberations and recommendations. Many businesses and academic fields require people to work together on reports or papers that draw upon the different skills and information each person in the group can contribute. Some college courses incorporate the experience of writing collaboratively. For example, in a marketing course, each of several groups might be expected to develop a new product, conduct research for marketing the product, and write a paper explaining their plan. Similarly, in a science course, a collaborative project might consist of jointly conducting an experiment, assessing its results, and writing a report.

*You may want to look at section 2.06 in the *Publication Manual of the American Psychological Association*, Fourth Edition (36).

Collaborative writing gives you the advantage of being able to share your knowledge and hear what others know. "Two heads are better than one" often proves true. Still, working with others on writing projects demands patience and graciousness. You have to work along with the pace of the group, listen carefully as you consider closely what others are saying, and contribute your part to the endeavor. Chart 163 gives guidelines. Here are guidelines to help you function productively when writing collaboratively. Use them in conjunction with Guidelines for Being an Effective Peer Critic, given in Chart 18 in section 3c-5.

GUIDELINES FOR COLLABORATIVE WRITING 163

GETTING UNDERWAY

1. Get to know each other's names. If you exchange phone numbers, you can be in touch outside of class.
2. Participate in the group process. During discussions help to set a tone that encourages everyone to participate, including people who do not like to interrupt, who want time to think before they talk, or who are shy. If you are not used to contributing in a group setting, try to take a more active role.
3. Facilitate the collaboration. As a group, assign work to be done between meetings. Distribute the responsibilities as fairly as possible. Also, decide whether to choose one discussion leader or to rotate leadership.

PLANNING THE WRITING

4. After discussing the project, brainstorm (see 2g) or use other techniques to think of ideas (see 2d through 2j).
5. As a group, choose the ideas that seem best. Incubate (see 2k), if time permits, and discuss the choices again.
6. As a group, divide the project into parts and distribute assignments as fairly as possible.
7. As you work on your part of the project, take notes so that you can be ready to report to the group.
8. As a group, sketch an overview (if you choose to outline, see 2n) of the paper to get a preliminary idea of how best to use the material contributed by individuals.

TEACHING TIP

For students who are initially resistant to the idea of collaborative writing, it is sometimes helpful to point out that many products in today's world are the result of group efforts, even those that are considered "art." You might call attention, for instance, to the credits that run after a feature-length movie or television show to make students aware of the many individuals who are needed to produce one film. Examples from other fields of work, such as assembly plants, shops, libraries, and construction projects, are easy to cite. You might ask them to name instances in other courses where learning takes place in groups, such as labs and study sessions.

TEACHING TIP

College students need to make connections, to see relationships among the ideas and data they meet in their various courses if they are to develop their skills in critical thinking. This chapter is designed, therefore, as a resource for students who want to apply what they have learned in composition classes to their writing in other courses. The material in this chapter is offered to help students see that what they learn in "writing class" is related to what they need to do as they write throughout their college careers and beyond.

QUOTATION ABOUT WRITING

But liberal learning does not permit us to hold on to any single answer for too long. As soon as you find one answer, you discover that that answer leads to other questions. Liberal learning can be unsettling. People like certainty, the right answer, the only way. Because of this desire for certainty and security, people can find themselves living with answers that other people have imposed upon them. In a free society, people learn to cultivate inquiring minds. They see that in broad areas of life there are no single right answers, that knowledge has a peculiar way of generating more questions, and that the world is more ambiguous than it appears. Liberal learning frees the mind to experience a sense of wonder at this ambiguous and fascinating world. F. Scott Fitzgerald writes, "The test of a first-rate intelligence is the ability to hold two opposed ideas in the mind at the same time, and still retain the ability to function." A liberally educated person learns to use this first-rate intelligence to function—even to prevail—in the midst of ambiguity.

—Elaine P. Maimon, et al.,
Writing in the Arts and Sciences

GUIDELINES FOR COLLABORATIVE WRITING (continued) 163

DRAFTING THE WRITING

9. DRAFT* a first paragraph or two. This material sets the direction for the rest of the paper. Each member of the group can draft a version, but agree on one draft for these paragraphs before getting too far into the rest of the draft. Your group might rewrite once the whole paper has been drafted, but a preliminary beginning helps to focus everyone.

10. Work on the rest of the paper. Decide whether each member of the group should write a complete draft or a different part of the whole. Use photocopies to share work.

REVISING THE WRITING

11. Read over the drafts. Check that everything useful has been incorporated into the draft.

12. Use the Revision Checklists in section 3c-3 to decide on revisions. Work as a group, or assign sections to subgroups. Use photocopies to share work.

13. Agree on a final version. Assign someone to prepare it in final form and make photocopies.

EDITING THE WRITING

14. As a group, review photocopies of the final version. Do not leave the last stages to a subgroup. Draw on everyone's knowledge of grammar, spelling, and punctuation. And use everyone's eyes to proofread.

15. Use the Editing Checklist in section 3d to make sure that the final version has no errors. If necessary, retype. No matter how well the group has worked collaboratively, or how well the group has written the paper, a sloppy final version reflects negatively on the entire group.

---

* You can find the definitions of a word printed in small capital letters (such as DRAFT) in the Glossary of Terms toward the end of this handbook.

37 *Writing About Literature*

Literature, which includes **fiction** (novels and stories), **drama** (plays and scripts), and **poetry** (poems and lyrics), has developed from age-old human impulses to discover and communicate meaning by telling stories, reenacting events, and singing or chanting. Reading and then writing about literature can deliver a related satisfaction: You have the chance to think about meaning and to tell others what you have found.

Understanding methods of inquiry into literature

All questions about literature require you to read a work closely. Some questions then ask you to deal with the material on a literal level (see 5d-1). You might be asked to explain the meaning of a passage in a novel or to find out what historical events were going on when the work was written or what other scholars have said about some element of the work.

Other questions call for inferential reasoning (see 5d-2) and evaluative thinking (see 5d-3). You might be asked to discuss the effect of sound or rhythm or rhyme in a poem or to compare characters in two plays by a particular playwright. Unlike inquiry in many other disciplines, you might also be asked to describe your response or reaction to a work of literature after a close, careful reading.

In each case, your answers must be thorough, well-reasoned, well-supported with evidence, and informed by knowledge of the work.

REFERENCE TO SUPPLEMENTS

For a thorough discussion of methods of inquiry into a literary work, see E. V. Roberts, "Reading and Writing about Literature: A Brief Manual," in L. Julian, et al., *Strategies and Resources for Teaching Writing with the Simon & Schuster Handbook for Writers.*

Understanding purposes and practices in writing about literature

The general purposes of writing about literature are to inform and to persuade (see 1b). **Informative writing** includes explaining what a passage means or what constitutes a particular work's key elements. **Persuasive writing** includes arguing the merits of an evaluation or an interpretation. Reaction papers (see 37d-1) often combine informative

REFERENCE TO SUPPLEMENTS

For a thorough discussion of purposes and practices in writing about literature, see E. V. Roberts, "Reading and Writing About Literature: A Brief Manual," in L. Julian, et al., *Strategies and Resources for Teaching Writing with the Simon & Schuster Handbook for Writers.*

BACKGROUND
The March 1995 *College English* offers a "Symposium: Literature in the Composition Classroom" (265–318). This lively debate includes the following articles: "Imaginative Literature in Composition Classrooms?" (Erwin R. Steinberg); "Fictionalizing the Disciplines: Literature and the Boundaries of Knowledge" (Michael Garner); "Three Views of English 101" (Erika Lindemann); "Notes on the Dying of a Conversation" (Gary Tate); "Through the Looking-Glass: A Response" (Jane Peterson). The editor's introduction notes that this symposium "challenges us to rethink our assumptions about teaching or not teaching literary works in Freshman English and to continue the dialogue over developing a unified theory that will take into account the demands of our students, our institutions, and our society at large, as we redefine what it means to teach writing."

37b
cont.

and persuasive purposes. All writing about literature calls for you to analyze, synthesize, and assess critically (see Chart 28 in section 5a).

37b-1

Using first and third person appropriately

Instructors usually have students use the FIRST PERSON (*I, we, our*) to write about their points of view or personal evaluations, and the *third person* (*he, she, it, they*) for other assignments. Be sure to inquire about and adapt to your instructor's requirements. In research papers, the first person is usually acceptable only when you present your personal experience, your own conclusions, or your personal views contrasted with those of the sources that you have consulted and DOCUMENTED.

37b-2

Using verbs in the present tense and the past tense correctly when writing about literature

When you describe or discuss a literary work or any of its elements, use the PRESENT TENSE: *George Henderson **takes** control of the action and **tells** the other characters when to speak and when not to.* The present tense is also correct for discussing what the author has done in a specific work: *Because Susan Glaspell* [the author] ***excludes** Minnie and John Wright from the stage as speaking characters, she **forces** us to learn about them through the words of others.*

If you are discussing events that take place before the action of a literary work begins, a PAST-TENSE VERB is correct: *The characters **have** gathered* [before the action starts] *at the Wright farmhouse when the play begins.* Also use past tenses, as appropriate, to discuss historical events or biographical information: *Susan Glaspell **was** a social activist who **was** strongly **influenced** by the chaotic events of the early twentieth century.*

37b-3

Using your own ideas and using secondary sources

Some assignments call only for your own ideas about the subject of your essay. Other assignments ask you to support your analysis with **secondary sources**. Secondary sources include books and articles in which an expert discusses material related to your topic. You can locate secondary sources by using the research process discussed in Chapter 32.

Whenever you use secondary sources, **avoid plagiarism** (see 31a). So that no reader thinks that the ideas of another person are yours, always document your sources (see 31b and Chapter 33). Also, to work material from secondary sources skillfully and gracefully into your writing, use the techniques of quotation (see 31c), paraphrase (see 31d), and summary (see 31e).

Using documentation style for writing about literature

37c

If you use SECONDARY SOURCES when you write about literature, you are required to credit your sources by using DOCUMENTATION. Many college instructors require their students to use the documentation style of the Modern Language Association (MLA), an organization of scholars and teachers of language and literature. MLA documentation style is described in Section 33c. Two other documentation styles sometimes required in the humanities are APA (American Psychological Association), presented in Section 33d, and CM (Chicago Manual), presented in Section 33e.

Writing different types of papers about literature

37d

Before you write a paper in which you refer or react to a literary work, be sure to read the work closely. To read well, use your understanding of the reading process (see 5b) and engage in critical reading (see 5d).

Writing reaction papers

37d-1

In a paper in which you react to a work of literature, you might ask and try to answer a central question that the work made you think about, criticize a point of view in the work, or present a problem that you see in the work. For example, if you are asked to respond to a play, you might write about why you did or did not enjoy reading the play, how the play does or does not relate to your personal experience or to your view of life, what the play made you think about and try to puzzle through. You can focus on the entire play or on a particular scene, character, or set of lines.

Writing book reports

37d-2

A book report informs readers about the content of a book—by summarizing its plot and its theme and by discussing (1) the significance and purpose of the book, (2) how the book presents its content, and (3) who might be most interested in the book. When you discuss the significance of the book, try to relate it to your field of study. For example, if the book is a classic in children's literature, your focus for a literature class would differ somewhat from your focus for a course in psychology or education.

BACKGROUND

The relatively new school of literary theory known as Reader Response Criticism came about as a challenge to the Formalists, who had held sway in classrooms and journals for several decades. The Reader Response theorists, such as David Bleich, Norman Holland, Wolfgang Iser, Stanley Fish, and Jonathan Culler, rejected the affective fallacy of the New Critics, and asked whether it is the reader or the text that determines interpretation. Although the Reader Response critics vary widely in their theoretical assumptions, critical strategies, and pedagogical practices, they all conclude that understanding and evaluation are based on subjective opinion. There is no such thing as an unbiased, objective reading of a text.

A number of useful articles and books that address the various theories of Reader Response have recently been published. In addition to such primary sources as Iser's *The Implied Reader* (Baltimore: Johns Hopkins UP, 1974) and Fish's *Is There a Text in This Class?* (Cambridge: Harvard UP, 1980), there are helpful explanations in Steven Lynn's "A Passage into Critical Theory" (*College English* 52 [March 1990]: 258–269) and in Reed Way Dasenbrock's "Do We Write the Text We Read?" (*College English* 53 [January 1991]: 7–17). Charles Moran and Elizabeth Penfield have collected a number of readable essays on contemporary critical theory and assessed their use for teachers in *Conversations* (Urbana: NCTE, 1990).

QUESTIONS FOR AN INTERPRETATION PAPER

MAJOR ASPECTS OF LITERARY WORKS TO ANALYZE

37d-3

Writing interpretations

An interpretation discusses either what the author means by the work or what the work means personally to the reader. When you are writing an interpretation paper, always consider the questions in Chart 164.

QUESTIONS FOR AN INTERPRETATION PAPER   164

1. What is the theme of the work?
2. How are particular parts of the work related to the theme?
3. If patterns exist in various elements of the work, what do they mean?
4. What message does the author convey through the use of major aspects of the work, listed in Chart 165?
5. Why does the work end as it does?

37d-4

Writing analyses

Analysis is the examination of the relationship of a whole to its parts. In a **literary analysis**, you are expected to discuss your well-reasoned ideas about a work of fiction, poetry, or drama. To get to know the work well and to gather ideas for your analysis, read the work thoroughly, again and again. Watch for patterns in the aspects of literary analysis listed in Chart 165. Write notes as you go along so that you have a record of two important resources for your writing: the patterns you find in the material and your reactions to the patterns and to the whole work.

MAJOR ASPECTS OF LITERARY WORKS TO ANALYZE   165

PLOT	The events and their sequence
THEME	Central idea or message
STRUCTURE	Organization and relationship of parts to each other and to the whole
CHARACTERIZATION	Traits, thoughts, and actions of the people in the plot
SETTING	Time and place of the action

MAJOR ASPECTS OF LITERARY WORKS TO ANALYZE (continued) 165

POINT OF VIEW	Perspective or position from which the material is presented—sometimes by a narrator or a main character
STYLE	How words and sentence structures present the material
IMAGERY	The pictures created by the words (similes, metaphors, figurative language) [for a list and definitions, see Chart 100 in section 21c]
TONE	The attitude of the author toward the subject of the work—and sometimes toward the reader—expressed through the choice of words and through the imagery
FIGURES OF SPEECH	Includes metaphor and simile
SYMBOLISM	The meaning beneath the surface of the words and images
RHYTHM AND RHYME	Beat, meter, repetition of sounds, and the like.

Three case studies of students writing about literature

37e

This section includes three student essays of LITERARY ANALYSIS. Two do not use SECONDARY SOURCES (see 37e-1 and 37e-2) and one does use them (see 37e-3). All three essays use MLA documentation style (see sections 33c and 37c).

Student essay interpreting a plot element in a short story

37e-1

The following essay interprets a plot element in Edgar Allan Poe's story "The Tell-Tale Heart."

Born in 1809, Edgar Allan Poe was an important American journalist, poet, and fiction writer. In his short, dramatic life, Poe gambled, drank, lived in terrible poverty, saw his young wife die of tuberculosis, and died himself under mysterious circumstances at age 40. He also created the detective novel and wrote brilliant, often bizarre short stories that still stimulate the reader's imagination.

When Valerie Cuneo read Poe's "The Tell-Tale Heart," first published in 1843, she was fascinated by one of the plot elements: the

QUOTATION ABOUT WRITING

[Over her desk hangs a yellow cardboard with the words:] "Will the reader turn the page?"

—Catherine Drinker Bowen

BACKGROUND

In *Writing Themes About Literature*, 8th ed. (Prentice Hall, 1995), Edgar V. Roberts considers the objection that too much literary analysis "spoils" appreciation of a work. Pointing out that the purpose is not to "cut up literature like a frog and leave it in pieces," he explains that literary analysis should make it possible to see more in a work, to find greater appreciation of its literary excellence. To that end, he suggests four broad areas that literary analysis explores: (1) meaning, (2) structure, (3) style, and (4) background and influences.

REFERENCE TO SUPPLEMENTS

For a process approach to writing different types of literary papers, see E. V. Roberts, "Reading and Writing about Literature: A Brief Manual," in L. Julian, et al., *Strategies and Resources for Teaching Writing with the Simon & Schuster Handbook for Writers*.

BACKGROUND

In "Fostering Audience Awareness Through Interpretive Communities," (*Teaching English in the Two Year College*, 19:2, May 1992, 148–155), R.J. Willey suggests ways of using reader-response strategies to encourage students' interaction with literary texts and thus to become more aware of the audience for their own writing.

sound of a beating heart that compels the narrator of the story to commit a murder and then to confess it to the police. In the following paper, Cuneo discusses her interpretation of the source of the heartbeat.

```
          The Sound of a Murderous Heart
     In Edgar Allan Poe's short story "The Tell-Tale
Heart," several interpretations are possible as to the
source of the beating heart that causes the
narrator-murderer to reveal himself to the police. The
noise could simply be a product of the narrator's
obviously deranged mind. Or perhaps the murder victim's
spirit lingers, heart beating, to exact revenge upon
the narrator. Although each of these interpretations is
possible, most of the evidence in the story suggests
that the inescapable beating heart that haunts the
narrator is his own.
     The interpretation that the heartbeat stems from
some kind of auditory hallucination is flawed. The
narrator clearly is insane--his killing a kind old man
because of an "Evil Eye" demonstrates this--and his
psychotic behavior is more than sufficient cause for
readers to question his truthfulness. Even so, nowhere
else in the story does the narrator imagine things
that do not exist. Nor is it likely that he would
intentionally attempt to mislead us since the narrative
is a confessional monologue through which he tries to
explain and justify his actions. He himself describes
his "disease" as a heightening of his senses, not of
his imagination. Moreover, his highly detailed account
of the events surrounding the murder seems to support
this claim. Near the end of the story, he refutes the
notion that he is inventing the sound in his mind when
he says, "I found that the noise was not within my
ears" (792). Although the narrator's reliability is
questionable, there seems to be no reason to doubt this
particular observation.
```

Interpreting the heartbeat as the victim's ghostly retaliation against the narrator also presents difficulties. Perhaps most important, when the narrator first hears the heart, the old man is still alive. The structure of the story also argues against the retaliation interpretation. Poe uses the first-person point of view to give readers immediate access to the narrator's strange thought processes, a choice that suggests the story is a form of psychological study. If "The Tell-Tale Heart" were truly a ghost story, it would probably be told in the third person, and it would more fully develop the character of the old man and explore his relationship with the narrator. If the heartbeat that torments the narrator is his own, however, these inconsistencies are avoided.

The strongest evidence that the tell-tale heart is really the narrator's is the timing of the heartbeat. Although it is the driving force behind the entire story, the narrator hears the beating heart only twice. In both of these instances, he is under immense physical and psychological stress--times when his own heart would be pounding. The narrator first hears the heartbeat with the shock of realizing that he has accidentally awakened his intended victim:

> Meantime the hellish tattoo of the heart
> increased. It grew quicker and quicker, and
> louder every instant. The old man's terror
> must have been extreme! It grew louder, I
> say, louder every moment!--do you mark me
> well? I have told you that I am nervous: so
> I am. And now at the dead hour of the night,
> amid the dreadful silence of that old house,
> so strange a noise as this excited me to
> uncontrollable terror. (791)

As the narrator's anxiety increases, so does the volume and frequency of the sound, an event easily

➡

BACKGROUND

In "The Reading-Writing Connection: What's Process Got to Do with It?" Cheryl Glenn demonstrates the many ways she integrates the teaching of writing into the teaching of literature. She argues that it is essential for English instructors to understand the theory and practice of the writing classroom and to use that knowledge as they plan and teach their literature courses. (In *When Writing Teachers Teach Literature*, Toby Fulwiler and Art Young, eds., Portsmouth, NH: Boynton-Cook, 1995)

QUOTATION ABOUT READING

There is more treasure in books than in all the pirates' loot on Treasure Island . . . and best of all, you can enjoy these riches every day of your life.
—Walt Disney

QUOTATION ABOUT TITLES

A good title should be like a good metaphor: It should intrigue without being too baffling or too obvious.
—Walker Percy

QUOTATION ABOUT WRITING

People need books with an epic background. They are bored with books that tell only one story on one level. They need something fantastic, something that gives them a sense of living in history. As it is, most novels aren't giving readers a chance to use their sense of history.
—Günter Grass

QUOTATION ABOUT LITERATURE

All good books are alike in that they are truer than if they had really happened.
—Ernest Hemingway

QUOTATION ABOUT LITERATURE

The cultivation of literary pursuits forms the basis of all sciences, and in their perfection consist the reputation and prosperity of kingdoms.

—Marques de Pombal,
Portuguese statesman

QUOTATION ABOUT WRITING

Literature is the art of writing something that will be read twice.

—Cyril Connolly

QUOTATION ABOUT LITERATURE

Why *shouldn't* truth be stranger than fiction? Fiction, after all, has to make sense.

—Mark Twain

QUOTATION ABOUT WRITING

When I'm near the end of the book, I sleep in the same room with it. Somehow the book doesn't leave you when you're asleep right next to it.

—Joan Didion

explained if the heartbeat is his own. Also, the sound of the heart persists even after the old man is dead, fading slowly into the background, as would the murderer's own heartbeat after his short, violent struggle with the old man. This reasoning can also explain why the narrator did not hear the heart on any of the seven previous nights when he looked into the old man's bedchamber. Because the old man slept and the "Evil Eye" was closed, no action was necessary (according to the narrator-murderer's twisted logic), and therefore he did not experience the rush of adrenaline that set his heart pounding on the fatal eighth visit.

The heart also follows a predictable pattern at the end of the story when the police officers come to investigate a neighbor's report of the dying old man's scream. In this encounter the narrator's initial calm slowly gives way to irritation and fear. As he becomes increasingly agitated, he begins to hear the heart again. The narrator clearly identifies it as the same sound he heard previously, as shown by the almost word-for-word repetition of the language he uses to describe it, calling it "a low, dull, quick sound--much such a sound as a watch makes when enveloped in cotton" [Poe's italics] (792). As the narrator-murderer focuses his attention on the sound, which ultimately overrides all else, his panic escalates until, ironically, he is betrayed by the very senses that he boasted about at the start of the story.

Work Cited

Poe, Edgar Allan. "The Tell-Tale Heart." American Literature: A Prentice Hall Anthology. Vol. 1. Ed. Emory Elliott, Linda K. Kerber, A. Walton Litz, and Terence Martin. Englewood Cliffs: Prentice, 1991. 789-792.

Student essay analyzing the characters in a drama

The following essay analyzes actions and interactions of the male and female characters in *Trifles*, a one-act play written by Susan Glaspell. Glaspell (1882-1948) was a feminist and social activist who wrote many plays for the Provincetown Players, a theater company she cofounded in Cape Cod, Massachusetts. She wrote *Trifles* in 1916, four years before women were allowed to vote in the United States. In 1917, Glaspell rewrote *Trifles* as the short story "A Jury of Her Peers." In both versions of the work, two married couples and the county attorney gather at a farmhouse where a taciturn farmer has been murdered, apparently by his wife. The five characters try to discover a motive for the murder. In doing so, they reveal much about gender roles in marriage and in the larger society.

After reading *Trifles*, Peter Wong said to his instructor, "No male today could get away with saying some of the things the men in that play say." The instructor encouraged Wong to analyze that reaction.

```
            Gender Loyalties: A Theme in Trifles
        Susan Glaspell's play Trifles is a study of
    character even though the two characters most central
    to the drama never appear on stage. By excluding Minnie
    and John Wright from the stage as speaking characters,
    Glaspell forces us to learn about them through the
    observations and recollections of the group visiting
    the farmhouse where the murders of Minnie Wright's
    canary and of John Wright took place. By indirectly
    rounding out her main characters, Glaspell invites us
    to view them not merely as individuals but also as
    representatives in a conflict between the sexes. This
    conflict grows throughout the play as characters'
    emotions and sympathies become increasingly polarized
    and oriented in favor of their own gender. From this
    perspective, each of the male characters can be seen to
    stand for the larger political, legal, and domestic
    power structures that drive Minnie Wright to kill her
    husband.
        George Henderson's speaking the first line of the
    play is no accident. Although his power stems from his
    position as county attorney, Henderson represents the
```
➡️

QUOTATION ABOUT WRITING
I finished my first book seventy-six years ago. I offered it to every publisher on the English-speaking earth I had ever heard of. Their refusals were unanimous and it did not get into print until, fifty years later, publishers would publish anything that had my name on it.
—George Bernard Shaw

QUOTATION ABOUT LITERATURE
Shakespeare was a dramatist of note:
He lived by writing things to quote.
—H. C. Bunner

QUOTATION ABOUT LITERATURE
Critics of literature have the same essential function as teachers of literature: this is not to direct the judgment of the audience, but to assist the audience in those disciplines of reading on which any meaningful judgment must rest.
—Mark Schorer

QUOTATION ABOUT WRITING

The actual writing of a book never takes more than six months. I don't care which book it is. People who are writing on a book for five years, six years, have often said they're "writing a book." Writing a book doesn't take that long. They're doing a dance around the book. I used to do that myself. The term "work in progress" means "haven't started."

—Tom Wolfe

QUOTATION ABOUT WRITING

I always write the end of everything first. I always write the last chapters of my books before I write the beginning. . . . Then I go back to the beginning. I mean, it's always nice to know where you're going is my theory.

—Truman Capote

QUOTATION ABOUT READING

I suggest that the only books that influence us are those for which we are ready, and which have gone a little farther down our particular path than we have yet gone ourselves.

—E. M. Forster

37e-2
cont.

political, more than the legal, sphere. With a job similar to a district attorney's today, he is quite powerful even though he is the youngest person present. He takes control of the action, telling the other characters when to speak and when not to and directing the men in their search for evidence that will establish a motive for the murder. As the person in charge of the investigation, George Henderson orders the other characters about. Mrs. Peters acknowledges his skill at oratory when she predicts that Minnie Wright will be convicted in the wake of his "sarcastic" cross-examination (speech 63).

Glaspell reveals much of the conflict in the play through the heated (but civil) exchanges between George Henderson and Mrs. Hale. His behavior (according to the stage directions, that of a gallant young politician) does not mask his belittling of Minnie Wright and of women in general:

> COUNTY ATTORNEY. I guess before we're through she may have something more serious than preserves to worry about.
>
> HALE. Well, women are used to worrying over trifles. [The two women move a little closer together.]
>
> COUNTY ATTORNEY. [With the gallantry of a young politician.] And yet, for all their worries, what would we do without the ladies? [The women do not unbend. He goes to the sink, takes a dipperful of water from the pail and pouring it into a basin, washes his hands. Starts to wipe them on the roller-towel, turns it for a cleaner place.] Dirty towels! [Kicks his foot against the pans under the sink.] Not much of a housekeeper, would you say, ladies?
>
> (speeches 29-31)

As this excerpt shows, George Henderson seems to hold that a woman's place is in the kitchen, even when she is locked up miles away in the county jail. He shows so much emotion at the discovery of dirty towels in the kitchen that it is almost as if he has found a real piece of evidence that he can use to convict Minnie Wright, instead of an irrelevant strip of cloth. It is apparent that his own sense of self-importance and prejudicial views of women are distracting him from his real business at the farmhouse.

Sheriff Henry Peters, as his title suggests, represents the legal power structure. Like the county attorney, Henry Peters is also quick to dismiss the "trifles" that his wife and Mrs. Hale spend their time discussing while the men conduct a physical search of the premises. His response to the attorney's asking whether he is absolutely certain that the downstairs contains no relevant clues to the motive for the murder is a curt "Nothing here but kitchen things" (speech 25). Ironically, the women are able to reconstruct the entire murder, including the motive, by beginning their inquiries with these same "kitchen things." Sheriff Peters and the other men all completely miss the unfinished quilt, the bird cage, and the dead bird's body. When the sheriff overhears the women talking about the quilt, his instinctive reaction is to ridicule them, saying, "They wonder if she was going to quilt it or just knot it!" (speech 73). Of course, the fact that Minnie Wright was going to knot the quilt is probably the single most important piece of evidence that the group could uncover, since John Wright was strangled with what we deduce is a quilting knot. Although he understands the law, the sheriff seems to know very little about people, and this prevents him from ever cracking this case. His blindness is made clear when he chuckles his assent to the county

➡️

QUOTATION ABOUT WRITING

. . . before I begin to write I "see" a story completely, often down to the very length and rhythm of paragraphs and sentences. I visualize the characters completely: I have heard their dialogue, I know how they speak, what they want, who they are, nearly everything about them that touches upon the central crisis in their lives. Then, when I write the story or the scene, I am only remembering, re-constructing an event that has already taken place. I don't make it up as I write. Never. I spend a great deal of time simply walking around, sitting, day-dreaming, going through the motions of an ordinary life with—I suspect—an abstracted, dreamy, rather blank expression on my face.

—Joyce Carol Oates

QUOTATION ABOUT WRITING

I suppose that some writers begin with a phrase, an idea, or a concept. I always begin with an image. The starting point of *Leaf Storm* is an old man taking his grandson to a funeral, in *No One Writes to the Colonel* it's an old man waiting, and in *One Hundred Years*, an old man taking his grandson to the fair to find out what ice is.

—Gabriel Garcia Márquez

37e-2
cont.

QUOTATION ABOUT WRITING

I used to think that in mysteries or thrillers the action and intrigue were important and not the characters. The truth is that the action and intrigue don't count for anything unless the reader cares about and likes the characters. So in a suspense novel, the most important thing—the first consideration—is that the characterization has to be good.

—Ken Follett

QUOTATION ABOUT READING

It is not true that we have only one life to live; if we can read, we can live as many more lives and as many kinds of lives as we wish.

—S. I. Hayakawa

attorney's observation that Mrs. Peters is literally "married to the law" (speech 145) and therefore beyond suspicion of trying to hinder the case against Minnie Wright. This assumption is completely wrong, for Mrs. Peters joins Mrs. Hale in suppressing the evidence and lying to the men.

Rounding out the male characters is Lewis Hale, a husband and farmer who represents the domestic sphere. Although Lewis Hale may not be an ideal individual, he provides a strong foil for John Wright's character. We might expect Lewis Hale, as Mrs. Hale's spouse, to be a good (or at least a tolerable) person, and, on the whole, he is. Although he too misses the significance of the "trifles" in the kitchen and mocks the activities of his wife and Mrs. Peters, he seems less eager than the other men to punish Minnie Wright—possibly because he knew John Wright better than they did. Lewis Hale is clearly reluctant to provide evidence against Minnie Wright when he speaks of her behavior after he discovers the body:

> HALE. She moved from that chair to this one over here [Pointing to a small chair in the corner.] and just sat there with her hands held together and looking down. I got a feeling that I ought to make some conversation, so I said I had come in to see if John wanted to put in a telephone, and at that she started to laugh, and then she stopped and looked at me--scared. [The county attorney, who has had his notebook out, makes a note.] I dunno, maybe it wasn't scared. I wouldn't like to say it was . . .
>
> (speech 23)

Lewis Hale is the only man who tries to bring up the incompatibility of the Wrights' marriage, citing John Wright's dislike for conversation and adding, "I didn't know if what his wife wanted made much difference to John--" (speech 9), but George Henderson cuts him off before he can pursue this any further. Lewis Hale is a personable and talkative man--not at all like John Wright, whom Mrs. Hale likens to "a raw wind that gets to the bone" (speech 103). Lewis Hale is a social being who wants to communicate with the people around him, as his desire for a telephone party line indicates. The Hales' functional marriage shows that gender differences need not be insurmountable, but it also serves to highlight the truly devastating effect that a completely incompatible union can have on two people's lives. Mrs. Hale reminds us that even a marriage that "works" can be dehumanizing:

> MRS. HALE. I might have known she needed
> help! I know how things can be--for
> women. I tell you it's queer, Mrs.
> Peters. We live close together and we
> live far apart. We all go through the
> same things--it's all just a different
> kind of the same thing.
>
> (speech 136)

The great irony of the drama is that the women are able to accomplish what the men cannot: They establish the motive for the murder. They find evidence suggesting that John Wright viciously killed his wife's canary--her sole companion through long days of work around the house. More important, they recognize the damaging nature of a marriage based upon the unequal status of the participants. Mrs. Hale and Mrs. Peters decide not to help the case against Minnie Wright, not because her husband killed a bird, but because he isolated her, made her life miserable for years, and cruelly destroyed her one source of comfort. Without hope of help from the various misogynistic, paternalistic, and uncomprehending political, legal,

➜

QUOTATION ABOUT WRITING

All fiction writers work by indirection: to show, not to tell; not to make statements about a character, but to demonstrate it in his actions or his conversations or by suggesting his thoughts, so that the reader understands for himself. Because fiction accomplishes its ends by using the oblique.

—Eudora Welty

QUOTATION ABOUT WRITING

The two most engaging powers of an author are to make new things familiar, familiar things new.

—William Makepeace Thackeray

QUOTATION ABOUT READING

When I get a little money, I buy books; and if any is left, I buy food and clothes.
—Erasmus

QUOTATION ABOUT LITERATURE

Great Literature is simply language charged with meaning to the utmost possible degree.
—George Orwell

QUOTATION ABOUT WRITING

Fame is a bee
It has a song—
It has a sting—
Ah, too, it has a wing.
—Emily Dickinson

37e-2
cont.

37e-3

and domestic power structures surrounding her, Minnie Wright took the law into her own hands. As the characters of George Henderson, Henry Peters, and Lewis Hale demonstrate, she clearly could not expect understanding from the men of her community.

Work Cited

Glaspell, Susan. <u>Trifles. Literature: An Introduction to Reading and Writing</u>. 4th ed. Edgar V. Roberts and Henry E. Jacobs. Englewood Cliffs: Prentice, 1995. 1038-48.

Student research paper analyzing two poems

The following essay is a literary analysis that uses SECONDARY SOURCES.

Born in 1889 on the Caribbean island of Jamaica, Claude McKay moved to the United States in 1910 and became a highly respected African-American poet.

Paule Cheek chose to write about Claude McKay's nontraditional use of a very traditional poetic form, the sonnet. A sonnet has fourteen rhyming lines and develops one idea. In secondary sources Cheek found information about McKay's life that she felt gave her further insights into both the structure and the meaning of McKay's sonnets "The White City" and "In Bondage." Cheek used MLA documentation style (see sections 33c and 37c) in her paper.

Words in Bondage: Claude McKay's
Use of the Sonnet Form in Two Poems
The sonnet has remained one of the central poetic forms of Western tradition for centuries. This fourteen-line form is easy to learn but difficult to master. With its fixed rhyme schemes, number of lines, and meter, the sonnet form forces writers to be doubly creative while working within it. Many poets over the years have modified or varied the sonnet form, playing

upon its conventions to keep it vibrant and original. One such writer was Jamaican-born Claude McKay (1889-1948).

The Jamaica of McKay's childhood was very different from turn-of-the-century America. Slavery had ended there in the 1830s, and McKay was able to grow up "in a society whose population was overwhelmingly black and largely free of the overt white oppression which constricted the lives of black Americans in the United States during this same period" (Cooper, The Passion of Claude McKay 5-6). This background could not have prepared McKay for what he encountered when he moved to America in his twenties. Lynchings, still common at that time, were on the rise, and during the Red Scare of 1919 there were dozens of racially motivated riots in major cities throughout the country. Thousands of homes were destroyed in these riots, and several African-Americans were tortured and burned at the stake (Cooper, Claude McKay: Rebel Sojourner in the Harlem Renaissance 97). McKay responded to these atrocities by raising an outraged cry of protest in his poems. In two of his sonnets from this period, "The White City" and "In Bondage," we can see McKay's mastery of the form, and his skillful use of irony in the call for social change.

McKay's choice of the sonnet form as the vehicle for his protest poetry at first seems strange. Since his message was a radical one, we might expect that the form of his poetry would be revolutionary. Instead, McKay gives us sonnets--a poetic form that dates back to the early sixteenth century and that was originally intended to be used exclusively for love poems. Critic James R. Giles notes that this choice

  is not really surprising, since McKay's
  Jamaican education and reading had been
  based firmly upon the major British poets.

➜

QUOTATION ABOUT WRITING

Once I was riding on a plane and I saw, as we were coming down, the man sitting next to me take the wedding ring off his finger and put it into his pocket. All I had to do was to imagine what might be happening there, what might be going through his mind, or what he was up to, to give me the idea for a story.

     —Raymond Carver

QUOTATION ABOUT WRITING

Writing's not terrible, it's wonderful. I keep my own hours, do what I please. When I want to travel, I can. But mainly I'm doing what I most wanted to do all my life. I'm not into the agonies of creation.

     —Raymond Carver

QUOTATION ABOUT WRITING

Before I write down one word, I have to have the character in mind through and through. I must penetrate into the last wrinkle of his soul. I always proceed from the individual; the stage setting, the dramatic ensemble, all of that comes naturally and does not cause me to worry, as soon as I am certain of the individual in every aspect of his humanity. But I have to have his exterior in mind also, down to the last button, how he stands and walks, how he conducts himself, what his voice sounds like. Then I do not let him go until his fate is fulfilled.

—Henrik Ibsen

QUOTATION ABOUT LITERATURE

Literature always anticipates life. It does not copy it, but molds it to its purpose. The nineteenth century, as we know it, is largely an invention of Balzac.

—Oscar Wilde

From the point quite early in his life when he began to think of himself as a poet, his models were such major English writers as William Shakespeare, John Milton, William Wordsworth. He thus was committed from the beginning to the poetry which he had initially been taught to admire. (44)

McKay published both "The White City" and "In Bondage" in 1922, and they are similar in many ways. Like most sonnets, each has fourteen lines and is in iambic pentameter. The diction is extremely elevated. For example, this quatrain from "In Bondage" is almost Elizabethan in its word choice and order:

> For life is greater than the thousand wars
> Men wage for it in their insatiate lust,
> And will remain like the eternal stars,
> When all that shines to-day is drift and dust.
>
> (8-12)

If this level of diction is reminiscent of Shakespeare, it is no accident. Both poems employ the English sonnet rhyme scheme (a b a b c d c d e f e f g g) and division into three quatrains and a closing couplet. McKay introduces a touch of his own, however. Although the English sonnet form calls for the "thematic turn" to fall at the closing couplet, McKay defies convention. He incorporates two turns into each sonnet, instead of one. This allows him to use the first "mini-turn" to further develop the initial theme set forth in the first eight lines while dramatically bringing the poem to a conclusion with a forcefully ironic turn in the closing couplet. Specifically, in "The White City," McKay uses the additional turn to interrupt his description of his "Passion" with a vision of "a mighty city through the mist" (9). In "In Bondage" he uses the additional turn to justify his desire to escape the violent existence that society has imposed upon his people.

McKay also demonstrates his poetic ability through his choice of words within his customized sonnets. Consider the opening of "In Bondage":

I would be wandering in distant fields
Where man, and bird, and beast, lives leisurely,
And the old earth is kind, and ever yields
Her goodly gifts to all her children free;
Where life is fairer, lighter, less demanding,
And boys and girls have time and space for play
Before they come to years of understanding--
Somewhere I would be singing, far away. (1-8)

The conditional power of "would" in the first line, coupled with the alliterative "wandering," subtly charms us into a relaxed, almost dreamlike state, in which the poet can lead us gently through the rest of the poem. The commas in the second line force us to check our progress to a "leisurely" crawl, mirroring the people and animals that the line describes. By the time we reach the eighth line, we are probably ready to join the poet in this land of "somewhere ... far away."

Then, this optimistic bubble is violently burst by the closing couplet:

But I am bound with you in your mean graves,
O black men, simple slaves of ruthless
  slaves. (13-14)

In "The White City," McKay again surprises us. This time, he does so by turning the traditional love sonnet upside down: instead of depicting a life made unendurable through an overpowering love, McKay shows us a life made bearable through a sustaining hate:

I will not toy with it nor bend an inch.
Deep in the secret chambers of my heart
I muse my life-long hate, and without flinch
I bear it nobly as I live my part.
My being would be a skeleton, a shell,
If this dark Passion that fills my every mood,

➜

QUOTATION ABOUT WRITING

My characters always take shape first; they wander around my mind looking for something to do. I know I'm ready to put them in a story when an ending comes to mind. The ending always comes first.
—S. E. Hinton

QUOTATION ABOUT WRITING

Don't put anything in a story that does not reveal character or advance the action.
—Kurt Vonnegut, Jr.

QUOTATION ABOUT TITLES

I'm terrible about titles; I don't know how to come up with them. They're the one thing in the story I'm really uncertain about.
—Eudora Welty

QUOTATION ABOUT WRITING
The characters don't really live in my head; they come alive as I start to write about them; then I am never sure what is going to happen. I'm always surprised.
—Judy Blume

QUOTATION ABOUT WRITING
I try to envision the story as a silent movie before I start adding dialogue.
—John Sayles

QUOTATION ABOUT READING
Reading is to the mind what exercise is to the body.
—Sir Richard Steele

37e-3
cont.

And makes my heaven in the white world's hell,
Did not forever feed me vital blood. (1-8)

If it were not for the presence of "life-long hate" in line three, this opening would easily pass as part of a conventional love sonnet. The emotion comes from "deep in the secret chambers" of the speaker's heart (2), it allows him to transcend "the white world's hell" (7), and it is a defining "Passion." Once again, however, McKay uses the couplet to defy our expectations by making it plain that he has used the form of the love sonnet only for ironic effect: "The tides, the wharves, the dens I contemplate, / Are sweet like wanton loves because I hate" (13-14).

McKay's impressive poetic ability made him a master of the sonnet form. His language could at times rival even Shakespeare's, and his creativity allowed him to adapt the sonnet to his own ends. His ironic genius is revealed in his use of one of Western society's most elevated poetic forms in order to critique that same society. McKay once described himself as "a man who was bitter because he loved, who was both right and wrong because he hated the things that destroyed love, who tried to give back to others a little of what he had got from them ... " (Barksdale and Kinnamon, 491). As these two sonnets show, McKay gave back very much indeed.

Works Cited

Barksdale, Richard, and Kenneth Kinnamon, eds. <u>Black Writers of America: A Comprehensive Anthology.</u> New York: Macmillan, 1972.

Cooper, Wayne F. <u>Claude McKay: Rebel Sojourner in the Harlem Renaissance.</u> Baton Rouge: Louisiana State UP, 1987.

---, ed. <u>The Passion of Claude McKay.</u> New York: Schocken Books, 1973.

Giles, James R. <u>Claude McKay.</u> Boston: Twayne, 1976.

McKay, Claude. "In Bondage." <u>Literature: An Introduction to Reading and Writing.</u> 4th ed. Edgar V. Roberts and Henry E. Jacobs. Englewood Cliffs: Prentice, 1995. 772-73.

---,"The White City." <u>Literature: An Introduction to Reading and Writing.</u> 4th ed. Edgar V. Roberts and Henry E. Jacobs. Englewood Cliffs: Prentice, 1995. 967.

QUOTATION ABOUT WRITING

Dialogue has to show not only something about the speaker that is its own revelation, but also maybe something about the speaker that he doesn't know but the other character does know. You've got to show a two-way revelation between speaker and listener, which is the fascination of writing dialogue. Dialogue is action.

—Eudora Welty

QUOTATION ABOUT WRITING

As for my next book, I am going to hold myself from writing it till I have it impending in me: grown heavy in my mind like a ripe pear; pendant, gravid, asking to be cut or it will fall.

—Virginia Woolf

38 *Writing in the Social Sciences and Natural Sciences*

38a   Understanding methods of inquiry in the social sciences

Disciplines in the **social sciences** include subject areas such as economics, education, geography, political science, psychology, and sociology. At some colleges, history is included in the social sciences; at others it is included in the humanities. The social sciences focus on the behavior of people as individuals and in groups.

Observation is a common method for inquiry in the social sciences. To make observations, take along whatever tools or equipment you might need: writing or sketching materials, and perhaps recording or photographic equipment. As you make observations, take very accurate and complete notes. If you use abbreviations to speed your note-taking, make sure you will later understand them when you need to write up your observations. In a report of your observations, tell what tools or equipment you used, because your method might have influenced what you saw (for example, your taking photographs may make people act differently than usual).

Interviewing is another common technique that social scientists use. Interviews are useful for gathering people's opinions and impressions of events. If you interview, remember that interviews are not always a completely reliable way to gather factual information, because people's memories are not precise. If your only source for facts is interviews, try to interview as many people as possible so that you can cross-check the information. Before you interview anyone, practice with whatever note-taking tools you might need, so that they do not intrude on the interview process (see also 32h-1).

Questionnaires can be useful for gathering information in the social sciences. When you administer a questionnaire, be sure that you ask a sufficient number of people to respond, so that you do not reach conclusions based on too small a sample of responses. To write questions for a questionnaire, use the guidelines in Chart 166.

GUIDELINES FOR WRITING QUESTIONS FOR A QUESTIONNAIRE 166

1. First, define what you want to find out, and then write questions that will elicit the information you seek.
2. Phrase questions so that they are easy to understand.
3. Use appropriate language (see 21a), and avoid artificial language (see 21e).
4. Be aware that how you phrase your questions will determine whether the answers that you get truly reflect what people are thinking. Make sure that your choice of words does not imply what you want to hear.
5. Avoid questions that invite one-word answers about complex matters that call for a range of responses.
6. Test a draft of the questionnaire on a small group of people before you use it. If any question is misinterpreted or hard to understand, revise and retest it.

GUIDELINES FOR WRITING QUESTIONS FOR A QUESTIONNAIRE

Understanding writing purposes and practices in the social sciences

38b

Social scientists write to inform readers by presenting and explaining information (see 1b-1) or to persuade readers by arguing a point of view (see 1b-2).

Analysis (see 4f-6 and 5a) helps social scientists write about problems and their solutions. For example, an economist writing about a major automobile company in financial trouble might first break the situation into parts, analyzing employee salaries and benefits, the selling price of cars, and the costs of doing business. Next, the economist might show how these parts relate to the financial status of the whole company. Then the economist might speculate about how specific changes would help solve the company's financial problems.

Social scientists are particularly careful to **define their terms** when they write, especially when they discuss complex social issues. For example, if you are writing a paper on substance abuse in the medical profession, you first have to define what you mean by the terms *substance abuse* and *medical profession*. By *substance* do you mean alcohol

---

TEACHING TIP

All academic writing falls from time to time into language that is at best unnecessarily complex and at worst misleading. The social sciences are particularly prone to using jargon and inflated language that is likely to pose problems for the reader. Students can be asked to rewrite obscure sentences or passages from published articles and reports in their discipline so that the ideas and research are more readily comprehended.

BACKGROUND

In her book *Good Writing: A Guide and Sourcebook for Writing Across the Curriculum*, (New York: St. Martin's Press, 1988), Linda Simon advises that although essays for social science courses usually follow the form of a general expository essay, students should be able to deal with the presentation of data gathered from interviews, questionnaires, and surveys. They need to know how to formulate a strong and workable thesis, then choose evidence to support it from their collected information. Presentation of concrete details gives validity to the writer's generalizations.

QUOTATION ABOUT HISTORIANS

The first quality [of a historian] is to be true and impartial; the next is to be interesting.

—David Hume

QUOTATION ABOUT HISTORIANS

A historian is a prophet in reverse.

—Friedrich von Schlegel

QUOTATION ABOUT ECONOMISTS

If all economists were laid end to end, they would not reach a conclusion.

—George Bernard Shaw

Some social scientists divide research papers into two categories: the qualitative and the quantitative. Qualitative research, as the name implies, investigates human values, patterns, or other characteristics that cannot be described numerically. It usually includes the personal involvement of the researcher with the subject being studied through interviews, observation, and, in some cases, participation. Throughout the study, the researcher is looking for meaning and patterns, moving progressively towards formulation of a hypothesis, and ultimately, a theory. A major problem for students who attempt to do qualitative research is time. Because the researcher must suit his or her schedule to the availability of the subject, sometimes the semester (or quarter) is not long enough to compile sufficient data to formulate significant conclusions. Also, the student may on occasion find it impossible to be present when important events occur. The quantitative research paper, on the other hand, follows a more structured (and predictable) process. Dealing with subjects that can be tested and expressed numerically, it is appropriate for comparing situations or examining frequency of occurrence. In many cases the researcher begins with a hypothesis, designs a means of testing it, then goes on to prove or disprove it. It requires some skill and knowledge on the part of the researcher in the use of graphs, statistics, and other techniques of quantitative expression.

I learned more about economics from one South Dakota dust storm than I did in all my years in college.
—Hubert Humphrey

38b
cont.

and drugs or only drugs? How are you quantifying *abuse*? When you refer to the medical profession, are you including nurses and lab technicians or only doctors? Without defining these terms, you can confuse your readers or lead them to wrong conclusions.

Social scientists often use **analogy** (see 4f-8) to make unfamiliar ideas clear. When an unfamiliar idea is compared to one that is more familiar, the unfamiliar idea becomes easier to understand. For example, sociologists may talk of the "culture shock" that some people feel when they enter a new society. The sociologists might compare this "shock" to the reaction that someone living today might have if suddenly moved hundreds of years into the future or the past.

In college courses in the social sciences, some instructors ask students to write their personal reactions to information or experiences, in which case the first person (*I, we, our*) is acceptable. In most writing for the social sciences, however, writers use the third person (*he, she, it, one, they*). Also, because the emphasis is on people or groups being observed rather than on the person doing the observing, some social scientists use the PASSIVE VOICE (see 8n-8o) rather than the ACTIVE VOICE. The *Publication Manual of the American Psychological Association*, the most commonly used style manual in the social sciences (see 38c), however, recommends the active voice whenever possible.

38c

Using documentation style in the social sciences

If you use SECONDARY SOURCES when you write about the social sciences, you are required to credit these sources by using DOCUMENTATION. The most commonly used DOCUMENTATION STYLE in the social sciences is that of the American Psychological Association (APA). The APA documentation style uses parenthetical references in the body of a paper and a References list at the end of a paper. APA documentation style is described in section 33d. For an example of a student research paper that uses APA documentation style, see Chapter 35.

The *Chicago Manual* (*CM*) style of documentation is sometimes used in the social sciences. *CM* bibliographic note style is described in section 33e.

38d

Writing different types of papers in the social sciences

Two major types of papers in the social sciences are case studies and research papers.

Writing case studies in the social sciences

38d-1

A **case study** is an intensive study of one group or individual. It is usually presented in a relatively fixed format, but the specific parts and order of case-study formats vary. Most case studies contain the following components: (1) basic identifying information about the individual or group; (2) a history of the individual or group; (3) observations of the individual's or group's behavior; and (4) conclusions and perhaps recommendations as a result of the observations.

In writing a case study, describe situations; do not interpret them unless your assignment allows you to interpret *after* you report. Be sure to differentiate between fact and opinion (see 5d-3). For example, you may observe nursing-home patients lying in bed on their sides facing the door. Describe exactly what you see; do not interpret this observation as, say, patients watching for visitors. Perhaps medicines are injected in the right hip, and patients are more comfortable lying on their left side, thus facing the door.

Writing research papers in the social sciences

38d-2

You may be assigned a **research paper** in the social sciences for which you must consult SECONDARY SOURCES. (See 32l on using specialized reference books and 32m-2 on using specialized indexes.) These sources are usually articles and books that report, summarize, and otherwise discuss the findings of other people's research. For an example of a student research paper written for an introductory psychology course, see Chapter 35.

Understanding methods of inquiry in the sciences

38e

Disciplines in the **natural sciences** include astronomy, biology, chemistry, geology, and physics. The sciences focus on natural phenomena. The purpose of scientific inquiry is discovery. Scientists formulate and test hypotheses in order to explain cause and effect (see 5f) systematically and objectively.

The **scientific method,** commonly used in the sciences to make discoveries, is a procedure for gathering information related to a specific hypothesis. The scientific method is the cornerstone of all inquiry in the sciences. Guidelines for using the scientific method are shown in Chart 167.

BACKGROUND

In his discussion of scientific discourse, James Kinneavy, in *A Theory of Discourse* (New York: W. W. Norton, 1971) asserts that it "consists in a consideration of one facet of an object and the making of certain kinds of assertions about this facet." Because its primary concern is with subject matter, all descriptive, narrative, classificatory, and evaluative statements are about the reality under consideration. In short, science is "thing" oriented, not person-oriented. Thus, the assertions must concern the subject of the research, exclude the feelings and emotions of the writer, and only indirectly involve the reader as an object of persuasion. The writing avoids literary effects, for it does not seek to call attention to itself as an object of pleasure. . . . The encoder and decoder are less evident in scientific writing than in informative or exploratory discourse. A newspaper or the Platonic dialogues, for example, reflect the writer or speaker much more strongly than does a scientific report. A second difference is probability. Exploratory discourse, says Kinneavy, asks a question; informative discourse answers it; and scientific discourse proves it. "The presence in the discourse of proof, is, therefore, one distinguishing attribute of scientific discourse."

BACKGROUND

Steve Trombulak and Sallie Sheldon report in "The Real Value of Writing to Learning Biology" (*Journal of College Science Teaching* 18 [May 1989]: 384–388), that writing not only improves students' performance, but also increases their appreciation of science.

QUOTATION ABOUT SCIENCE

The great tragedy of science—the slaying of a beautiful theory by an ugly fact.
—T. H. Huxley

GUIDELINES FOR USING THE SCIENTIFIC METHOD   167

1. Formulate a tentative explanation—known as a **hypothesis**—for a scientific phenomenon. Be as specific as possible.
2. Read and summarize previously published information related to your hypothesis.
3. Plan and outline a method of investigation to uncover the information needed to test your hypothesis.
4. Experiment, exactly following the investigative procedures you have outlined.
5. Observe closely the results of the experiment, and write notes carefully.
6. Analyze the results. If they prove the hypothesis to be false, rework the investigation and begin again. If the results prove the hypothesis to be true, say so.
7. Write a report of your research. At the end, you might suggest additional hypotheses that might be investigated.

38f   Understanding writing purposes and practices in the natural sciences

Scientists usually write to inform their audiences about factual information.

Exactness is extremely important in scientific writing. Readers expect precise descriptions of procedures and findings, free of personal biases. Scientists expect to be able to *replicate*—repeat step-by-step—the experiment or other process and get the same outcome as the writer.

Completeness is also essential in scientific writing. Without complete information, the reader might come to wrong conclusions. For example, a researcher may investigate how different types of soil affect plant growth. The researcher should report not only the analysis of each soil type, but also the amount of daylight each plant receives, the moisture content of the soil, the amount and type of fertilizer used, and all other related facts. Having all this information may lead the researcher to unexpected insights. For instance, plant growth may be less dependent on soil type than on a combination of soil type, fertilizer, and watering. This observation could be made only if the researcher had carefully noted all the facts.

The sciences generally focus on the experiment rather than the experimenter and on objective observation rather than subjective interpretation. Unless you are writing a personal-reaction paper, generally avoid using the first person (*I, we, our*) in writing science papers.

When writing for the sciences, often you are expected to follow fixed formats, which are designed to summarize a project and present its results efficiently. In your report, organize the information to achieve clarity and precision. Writers in the sciences sometimes use charts, graphs, tables, diagrams, and other illustrations to present material. In fact, illustrations can sometimes explain complex material more clearly than words can.

Using documentation style in the natural sciences   38g

If you use SECONDARY SOURCES when you write about the sciences, you are required to credit your sources by using DOCUMENTATION. DOCUMENTATION STYLES in the various sciences differ somewhat. Ask your instructor which style you should use. If your instructor has no preference, consult 33g for a list of available style manuals in the sciences, and try to locate the manual you need. If you cannot locate the manual, or if the science you are writing in does not have a style manual, find a journal that publishes research in that science and imitate its documentation style.

The Council of Biology Editors (CBE) has compiled style and documentation guidelines for the life sciences, the physical sciences, and mathematics in *Scientific Style and Format: The CBE Manual for Authors, Editors, and Publishers*, 6th edition (1994). CBE documentation guidelines are described in section 33f.

Writing different types of papers in the natural sciences   38h

Two major types of papers in the sciences are reports and reviews.

Writing science reports   38h-1

Science reports tell about observations and experiments. Such reports may also be called "laboratory reports" when they describe laboratory experiments. Formal reports include the eight sections (including the title) described in Chart 168. Less formal reports, which are sometimes assigned in introductory college courses, might not include an abstract or a review of the literature. Ask your instructor which sections to include in your report.

717

QUOTATION ABOUT WRITING IN THE NATURAL SCIENCES

With the rise of experimental methods in the eighteenth century, science has developed increasingly sophisticated methods of data collection, observation, and verification. Using carefully controlled laboratory environments, natural scientists must observe reactions, detail materials and procedures, and repeat experiments—all of which call for written records. They must immediately record observations, make entries for all reactions, and specify all facets of a procedure. The concern for methods suggests how pivotal to scientific training is the laboratory notebook and the laboratory report.

—Diane Bennett Durkin, *Writing in the Disciplines*

BACKGROUND

In "Implementing Writing Across the Curriculum: Strategies in the Biological Sciences" (*Dissertation Abstracts International* 50 [August 1989]: 339A), Joanna Theresa Ambron reports on the use of various heuristic devices and writing-to-learn strategies in biology courses. She discusses journal writing, freewriting, microthemes, and clustering.

QUOTATION ABOUT WRITING

The universe is full of magical things, patiently waiting for our wits to grow sharper.

—Eden Phillpotts

QUOTATION ABOUT EDUCATION

Education is an admirable thing, but it is well to remember from time to time that nothing that is worth knowing can be taught.

—Oscar Wilde

38h-1
cont.

PARTS OF THE SCIENCE REPORT

PARTS OF THE SCIENCE REPORT 168

1. **Title.** This is a precise description of what your report is about.
2. **Abstract.** This is a short overview of the report.
3. **Introduction.** This section states the purpose behind your research and presents the hypothesis. Any needed background information and a review of the literature appear here.
4. **Methods and material.** This section describes the equipment, material, and procedures used.
5. **Results.** This section provides the information obtained from your efforts. Charts, graphs, and photographs help present the data.
6. **Discussion.** This section represents your interpretation and evaluation of the results. Did your efforts support your hypothesis? If not, can you suggest why not? Use concrete evidence in discussing your results.
7. **Conclusion.** This section lists conclusions about the hypothesis and the outcomes of your efforts, with particular attention to any theoretical implications that can be drawn from your work. Be specific in suggesting further research.
8. **References cited.** This list presents references cited in the review of the literature, if any. Its format conforms to the requirements of the documentation style in the particular science.

SAMPLE SCIENCE REPORT (Excerpts)

An Experiment to Predict Vestigial Wings in an F2
Drosophila Population

INTRODUCTION
The purpose of this experiment was to observe second
filial generation (F2) wing structures in Drosophila.
The hypothesis was that abnormalities in vestigial wing
structures would follow predicted genetic patterns.

METHODS AND MATERIALS
On February 7, four Drosophila (P1) were observed.
Observation was made possible by etherizing the parents

(after separating them from their larvae), placing them on a white card, and observing them under a dissecting microscope. The observations were recorded on a chart.

On February 14, the larvae taken from the parents on February 7 had developed to adults (F1), and they were observed using the same methods as on February 7. The observations were recorded on the chart.

On February 19, the second filial generation (F2) was supposed to be observed. This was impossible because they did not hatch. The record chart had to be discontinued.

RESULTS

No observations of F2 were possible. For the F1 population, according to the prediction, no members should have had vestigial wings. According to the observations, however, some members of F1 did have vestigial wings.

[DISCUSSION SECTION OMITTED]

CONCLUSIONS

Two explanations are possible to explain vestigial wings in the F1 population. Perhaps members from F2 were present from the F1 generation. This is doubtful since the incubation period is 10 days, and the time between observations was only 8 days. A second possible explanation is that the genotype of the male P1 was not WW (indicating that both genes were for normal wings) but rather heterozygous (Ww). If this were true the following would be the first filial products in a 1:1 ratio:

$$P_1 \quad Ww \; X \; ww$$
$$F_1 \quad Ww \; ww$$

Thus, the possibility for vestigial wings would exist. The problem remains, however, that the ratio

Bad scientific writing involves more than stylistic inelegance; it is often the outward and visible form of an inward confusion of thought.

—Peter F. Woodford, "Sounder Thinking through Clearer Writing"

QUOTATION ABOUT SCIENCE

The most incomprehensible thing about the world is that it is comprehensible.

—Albert Einstein

QUOTATION ABOUT SCIENCE

I seem to have been only a boy playing on the seashore, and diverting myself in now and then finding a smoother pebble or a prettier shell than ordinary, whilst the great ocean of truth lay all undiscovered before me.

—Sir Isaac Newton

QUOTATION ABOUT GEOGRAPHY

Anybody who believes that the way to a man's heart is through his stomach flunked geography.

—Robert Byrne

QUOTATION ABOUT GEOGRAPHY

To travel is to discover that everyone is wrong about other countries.

—Aldous Huxley

QUOTATION ABOUT EDUCATION

The primary purpose of a liberal education is to make one's mind a pleasant place in which to spend one's time.

—Sydney J. Harris

38h-1
cont.

```
was not 1:1 2:1 (i.e., 24 normal to 12 abnormal).
One explanation could be that the total number was not
large enough to extract an average.

    The hypothesis concerning predicted genetic
patterns in F2 could not be confirmed because the F2
generation did not hatch.  This experiment should be
repeated to get F2 data.  A larger F1 sample should be
used to see if the F1 findings reported here are
repeated.
```

38h-2

Writing science reviews

A **science review** is a paper discussing published information on a scientific topic or issue. The purpose of the review is to gather together for readers the current knowledge about the topic or issue.

Sometimes the purpose of a science review is to suggest a new interpretation of the old material. Any reinterpretation is based on a synthesis of old information with new, more complete information. In such reviews, the writer must marshal evidence to persuade readers that the new interpretation is valid.

If you are required to write a science review, (1) choose a very limited scientific issue currently being researched; (2) use information that is current—the more recently published the articles, books, and journals you consult, the better; (3) accurately summarize and paraphrase material—as explained in 31e and 31d; (4) document your sources (see Chapter 33). If your review is more than two or three pages, you might want to use headings to help your reader understand the organization and idea progression of your paper. See Chapter 32 for advice on finding sources.

39 *Business Writing*

Business writing requires of you what other kinds of writing call for: understanding your audience and your purpose. This chapter explains how to write business letters (see 39a), job application letters (see 39b), and résumés (see 39c). As you write for business, use the guidelines listed in Chart 169.

GUIDELINES FOR BUSINESS WRITING   169

- Consider your audience's needs and expectations.
- Show that you understand the purpose for a business communication and the context in which it takes place.
- Put essential information first.
- Make your points clearly and directly.
- Use conventional formats.

Writing and formatting a business letter   39a

Business letters are written to give information, to build good will, or to establish a foundation for discussions or transactions. Experts in business and government agree that the letters likely to get results are short, simple, direct, and human. Here is good, basic advice: (1) Call the person by name; (2) tell what your letter is about in the first paragraph; (3) be honest; (4) be clear and specific; (5) use correct English; (6) be positive and natural; (7) edit ruthlessly.

For business letters, use the guidelines in Chart 170 and the format on page 723. To avoid sexist language in the salutation of your letter, use the guidelines in Chart 171. For a business envelope, see page 727.

REFERENCES TO SUPPLEMENTS

See transparency 9-3 for memo writing in the *Prentice Hall/Simon & Schuster Transparencies for Writers* by D. Carter.

For more on teaching students to write successful letters, memos, resumes, and job applications, see L. Julian, "Workplace Writing: Teaching Skills to Willing Learners," in L. Julian, et al., *Strategies and Resources for Teaching Writing with the Simon & Schuster Handbook for Writers.*

BACKGROUND

In "Real World Writing and the English Curriculum," Margaret A. Mansfield explains what professional writing can offer the writing classroom. She suggests that completing professional writing assignments provides students with a complex, authentic audience and, in addition, can encourage fuller understanding of the way collaboration works in "real world" writing situations. (*College Composition and Communication*, 44:1, Feb. 1993, 69–83)

BACKGROUND

Margaret Ann Smith examined students' sense of audience in a beginning management class. She also studied how their perceptions of writing changed and developed (*Dissertation Abstracts International* 50 [August 1989]: 330A).

TEACHING TIP

Some students expect business writing to involve rules about margins, indentations, and abbreviations. While such concerns do matter, they should take only a small part of your time. Format can be taught in just a few lessons; the emphasis in business writing is on audience, tone, and organization.

Audience. Business writers need to be acutely aware of their audiences. Since business correspondence is aimed at a particular individual or a limited group of individuals rather than the general audience essays are aimed at, in certain aspects business writing differs markedly from essay writing. The most obvious difference is that the use of *you* and *I/we* is preferable to the third person often used in essays.

Tone. The tone of business correspondence needs to be adjusted to suit the actual relationship between author and audience. It is perfectly conceivable that a businessperson might write a very formal memo to the staff of one department about lax security and a minute later write a relatively friendly memo to another department congratulating it for exceeding production goals. The key word in deciding on the appropriate tone is *relationship*. Your students can judge the nature of the relationship by asking themselves a few questions as they prepare to write: Who is the person I am writing to? How long and under what circumstances have we known one another? What do I want him or her to do? No matter what the relationship, correspondence should be written in standard, clear, and honest English. See Chapter 21 for discussions of levels of formality and artificial language.

Organization. The organization of a business document will vary with its pur-

➜

LETTERHEAD	If printed stationery is not available, type the company name and address centered at top of white paper, $8\frac{1}{2} \times 11''$.
DATE	Put the date at the left margin under the letterhead, when typing in block form as shown in the example. When using paragraph indentations, type the date so that it ends at the right margin.
INSIDE ADDRESS	Direct your letter to a specific person. Be accurate in spelling the name and the address. If unsure of your information, telephone and ask questions of a secretary or other assistant.
SUBJECT LINE	Place at the left margin. In a few, concise words state the letter's subject.
SALUTATION	Use a first name only if you personally know the person. Otherwise, use *Mr.* or *Ms.* or whatever title is applicable with the person's last name. Avoid sexist language.
CLOSING	*Sincerely* or *Sincerely yours* are generally appropriate, unless you know the person very well and wish to use *Cordially*. Leave about four lines for your signature.
NAME LINES	Type your full name and title below your signature. The title can be on the same or the next line as your name.
SECOND PAGE	Head a second page with three items of information: the name of the person or company to which your letter is addressed, the number *2* or *page 2*, and the date. Place the information on three lines at the top left margin or on one line spaced across the top of the page.

BUSINESS LETTER FORMAT

LETTERHEAD	**ALPHAOMEGA INDUSTRIES, INC.** 123456 Motor Parkway Fresh Hills, CA 55555
DATE	December 28, 19XX
INSIDE ADDRESS	Ron R. London, *Sales Director* **Seasonal Products Corp.** 5000 Seasonal Place Wiscasset, ME 00012
SUBJECT LINE	Subject: ***Spring Promotional Effort***
SALUTATION	Dear Ron:
MESSAGE	Since we talked last week, I have completed plans for the Spring promotion of the products that we market jointly. AlphaOmega and Seasonal Products should begin a direct mailing of the enclosed brochure on January 28. I have secured several mailing lists that contain the names of people who have a positive economic profile for our products. The profile and the outline of the lists are attached. Do you have additional approaches for the promotion? I would like to meet with you on January 6 to discuss them and to work out the details of the project. Please call me and let me know if a meeting next week at your office accommodates your schedule.
CLOSING	Sincerely,
NAME, TITLE	*Alan Stone* Alan Stone *Director of Special Promotions*
writer's/ typist's initials	AS/kw
copies	PC: Yolanda Lane, *Vice President, Marketing*
enclosures	ENC: Brochure; Mailing Lists; Customer Profile

TEACHING TIP, cont'd.

pose. To help students become familiar with the conventional forms of business letters, résumés, and memos, some examples are provided in this chapter.

TEACHING TIP

Some people are fascinated by those initials and abbreviations they see in letters, at the left margin a few lines below the signature. Few of our students have any need to use these on a regular basis, but in case you are asked about these symbols, here's a quick review.

AS/kw The writer's initials followed by the typist's initials (known as reference initials). Practice varies in the use of capital and lowercase letters. Sometimes a colon is used: *AS:kw*.

Enclosures: Typed below the reference initials, a numeric notation alerts the opener of the mail to the presence of additional material: brochures, résumés, photographs. A multi-page enclosure counts as one. Sometimes the notation is written out as "Enc.: résumé and letter of reference."

cc: Ken Lane Typed below the reference initials, the abbreviation *cc* indicates that a carbon copy has been sent. Carbon paper is passé, but the abbreviation lingers. The notation is followed by a name or initials.

P.S. A postscript may be added after everything else to highlight a point made within the letter or to add a brief personal message. Do not use a postscript to add important information that you forgot to include in the letter; rewrite the letter. Strings of postscripts (P.P.S., etc.) are definitely not suitable for business writing.

QUOTATION ABOUT BUSINESS

No nation was ever ruined by trade.
—Benjamin Franklin

TEACHING TIP: SALUTATIONS

The salutation is the first thing a reader sees, so it must be suitable if the letter is to be taken seriously. In most situations the salutation presents no problem, but sometimes the writer has to make a difficult decision. Here are some guidelines:

1. When the recipient's name is known: *Dear Mr. _____ ;*
Dear Ms. _____ ; Dear Mrs. _____ ;
Dear Miss _____ .

2. When the writer normally calls the recipient by his or her first name and when the letter is relatively informal: *Dear Heidi; Dear Elliot.*

3. When the letter is going to a position within an organization and the writer has not been able to get an individual's name: *Manager, Customer Service Department; Dear Manager.*

4. When the writer does not know the sex of the recipient: *Dear Mr. or Ms. Gery; Dear Director; Dear Mr. or Ms. Director.*

5. When the recipient is a group: *Dear Members of _____ ; Dear Committee Members.*

6. When there will be many anonymous recipients: *Dear Homeowners; Dear Student, Dear Customer.*

GUIDELINES FOR WRITING A NONSEXIST SALUTATION 171

You may want to send a business letter when you do not have a specific person to whom it should be addressed. Use the following steps to prepare a salutation.

1. Telephone the company to which you are sending the letter. State your reason for sending the letter, and ask for the name of the person who should receive it.

2. Use a first name only if you know the person. Otherwise, use *Mr.* or *Ms.* or an applicable title. Avoid a sexist title such as *Dear Sir.*

3. If you cannot find out the name of the person who should read your letter, use a generic title.

NO

Dear Sir: [obviously sexist]

Dear Madam/Sir or Dear Sir/Madam:
[few women want to be addressed as "Madam"]

YES

Dear Personnel Officer:

Dear IBM Sales Manager:

In addressing an envelope, remember that the best-written letter means nothing if it does not reach its destination. In the illustration on page 727, you will see the U.S. Postal Service guidelines for addressing envelopes so that they can be processed by machine. (Envelopes that must be sorted by hand add three days or more to mail-delivery time.)

39b Writing and formatting a job application letter

Chart 172 gives guidelines for a job application letter. A sample job application letter appears on page 726.

GUIDELINES FOR JOB APPLICATION LETTERS 172

YOUR ADDRESS	Type your address in block style as you would on an envelope. Use as your address (with a zip code) a place where you can be reached **by letter.**
DATE	Put the date below your address. Make sure that you mail the letter on either the same day or the next day; a delayed mailing can imply lack of planning.
INSIDE ADDRESS	Direct your letter to a specific person. Telephone the company to find out the name of the person to whom you are writing. Be accurate. A misspelled name can offend the receiver. A wrong address usually results in a lost letter.
SALUTATION	Be accurate. No one likes to see his or her name misspelled. In replying to an ad that gives only a post-office box number, omit the salutation and start your opening paragraph directly below the inside address. To avoid sexist language, use Chart 171.
INTRODUCTORY PARAGRAPH	State your purpose for writing and your source of information about the job.
BODY PARAGRAPH(S)	Interest the reader in the skills and talents you offer by mentioning whatever experience you have *that relates to the specific job.* Mention your enclosed résumé, but do *not* summarize it.
CLOSING PARAGRAPH	Suggest an interview, stating that you will call to make arrangements.
CLOSING	*Sincerely* or *Sincerely yours* is generally appropriate.
NAME LINES	Type your full name below your signature. Leave about four lines for your signature.
NOTATION	If you are enclosing any material with your letter, type *ENC:* and briefly list the items.

TEACHING TIP

Few letters are as difficult for students to write as those they send in hopes of getting a job interview. The following suggestions can be adapted to any job-seeking situation.

Before writing a letter of application, the student should already have prepared a stock résumé, one that can be used for any job in the student's area of interest. A properly written résumé will be good for six months to a year or more. As it lists the basics of a career to date, it should not have to be redone for each job sought.

In the cover letter, students should tell a prospective employer what they can bring to the job, why they feel they are qualified—not why they want the job. This is the place to expand upon the information listed in the résumé. Do not, however, summarize or repeat large parts of the résumé.

In paragraph 1, students should tell how they found out about the job (ad, friend with the company). In paragraphs 2 to 4, students should pick three skills or personal qualities that they know are needed for the job. These may include, but are not limited to, using office machines, driving a delivery truck, preparing a payroll, speaking a second language, being available for night shifts or out-of-town travel.

In the next paragraph, students should discuss their specific qualifications. They can draw upon work experience, education, volunteer work, family responsibilities, and hobbies. In the final paragraph, students should thank the reader for taking the time to consider the application. They should also express a wish for an interview at the employer's convenience and include a phone number and address.

JOB APPLICATION LETTER

UNIVERSITY OF TEXAS AT ARLINGTON
422 Broward
Arlington, Texas 75016

May 15, 19XX

Rae Clemens, *Director of Human Resources*
Taleno, Ward Marketing, Inc.
1471 Summit Boulevard
Houston, Texas 78211

Dear Ms. Clemens:

I am answering the advertisement for a marketing trainee that Taleno, Ward placed in today's <u>Houston Chronicle</u>.

Marketing has been one of the emphases of my course work here at the University of Texas, Arlington, as you will see on my enclosed résumé. This past year, I gained some practical experience as well, when I developed marketing techniques that helped to turn my typing service into a busy and profitable small business.

Successfully marketing the typing service (with flyers, advertisements in college publications, and even a two-for-one promotion) makes me a very enthusiastic novice. I can think of no better way to become a professional than working for Taleno, Ward.

I will be here at the Arlington campus through August 1. You can reach me by phone at (713) 555-1976. Unless I hear from you before, I'll call on May 25 about setting up an interview.

Sincerely yours,

Lee Franco

LEE FRANCO

ENC: Résumé

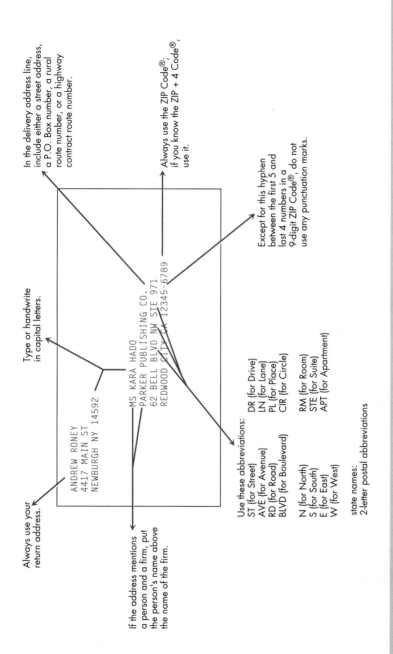

In the delivery address line, include either a street address, a P.O. Box number, a rural route number, or a highway contract route number.

Always use the ZIP Code®, if you know the ZIP + 4 Code®, use it.

Except for this hyphen between the first 5 and last 4 numbers in a 9-digit ZIP Code®, do not use any punctuation marks.

Type or handwrite in capital letters.

Always use your return address.

If the address mentions a person and a firm, put the person's name above the name of the firm.

ANDREW RONEY
4417 MAIN ST
NEWBURGH NY 14592

MS KARA HADO
PARKER PUBLISHING CO.
62 BELL BLVD NW STE 971
REDWOOD CITY CA 12345-6789

Use these abbreviations:
ST (for Street)
AVE (for Avenue)
RD (for Road)
BLVD (for Boulevard)

DR (for Drive)
LN (for Lane)
PL (for Place)
CIR (for Circle)

RM (for Room)
STE (for Suite)
APT (for Apartment)

N (for North)
S (for South)
E (for East)
W (for West)

state names:
2-letter postal abbreviations

U.S. Postal Service Guidelines for Business Envelope Format

QUOTATION ABOUT BUSINESS

The propensity to truck, barter and exchange one thing for another . . . is common to all men, and to be found in no other race of animals.

—Adam Smith

39c Writing and formatting a résumé

A **résumé** is an easy-to-read, factual document that presents your qualifications for employment. All résumés cover certain standard items: name, address, phone number; education; past experience; skills and talents; publications, awards, honors, membership in professional organizations; list of references or a statement that they are "available upon request."

A résumé gives you an opportunity to present a positive picture of yourself to a prospective employer. Employers understand that college students may have limited experience in the business world. Think of headings that allow you to emphasize your strengths. For example, if you have never done *Business Experience*. You can use *Work Experience* for volunteer or other unpaid work. If the experience shows that you have run school or social events, *Organizational Experience*. If your greatest strength is your educational achievements first.

You may choose to arrange in emphatic order with the most important information and the least important last. Or you may choose to arrange in chronological (time) order, a sequence that is good for steady work history or solid progress in a particular field. Lee Franco's résumé, which was sent with the job application letter on page 720, is on page 729. It uses emphatic order. Stephen Schmit's résumé, on page 730, uses chronological order.

When you are applying for a specific job, modify your basic résumé to emphasize your qualifications for that job. Lee Franco added the *Marketing Trainee* heading and the statement about relevant experience for becoming a marketing trainee to her basic résumé and positioned the *Marketing Experience* section first. These modifications help to send a message that Franco's qualifications for the marketing trainee position are better than other applicants'. If you keep your résumé on computer, you can easily tailor it to specific job opportunities.

Your résumé usually has to fulfill only one purpose: It has to convince the person who first looks at it to put it into the "Call for an interview" pile rather than into the wastebasket. To do that best, a résumé should be eye-catching and informative, and it should make its readers think, "We should talk to this person; seems like someone who would be an asset to our business."

EMPHATIC RÉSUMÉ

MARKETING TRAINEE

LEE FRANCO
University of Texas at Arlington
422 Broward
Arlington, Texas 75016
713-555-1976

The experience I acquired marketing my typing service provided me with a good practical background for a position as a marketing trainee.

MARKETING EXPERIENCE (program for campus typing service)

> Evaluated typing-service capabilities; analyzed market for service; drew up and implemented marketing plan; produced 2-color flyer, designed print ads and wrote copy, developed and ran special promotion. August 19XX to February 19XX

BUSINESS EXPERIENCE

> Type-Right Typing Service: Ran campus typing service for two years. Duties included word processing (Word, Wordperfect, Displaywrite), proofreading, billing and other financial record-keeping (Excel), and customer contact. August 19XX to present.

> Archer & Archer Advertising: Worked as general assistant in the copy department under direct supervision of John Allen, Director. Duties included proofreading, filing, direct client contact. June 19XX to August 19XX.

ADDITIONAL EXPERIENCE

> Coordinated student-employment service at Hawthorne High School, Baton Rouge, Louisiana. Duties included contacting students to fill jobs with local employers, arranging interviews, and writing follow-up reports on placements.

EDUCATION

> University of Texas, Arlington
> B.A. May 19XX, Psychology, Marketing

EXTRACURRICULAR

> Marketing Club, Computer Graphics Society

> *References available upon request.*

QUOTATION ABOUT WRITING
I aim to be content with what I produce. It's an aim I never achieve, but I go over my work word by word, time and again, so as to be as little dissatisfied as possible.
—Graham Greene

QUOTATION ABOUT WRITING

Ever tried? Ever failed? No matter. Try again. Fail again. Fail better.

—Samuel Beckett

QUOTATION ABOUT BUSINESS

The selfish spirit of commerce knows no country, and feels no passion or principle but that of gain.

—Thomas Jefferson

CHRONOLOGICAL RÉSUMÉ

STEPHEN L. SCHMIT
5230 St. Stephens Street
Boston, Massachusetts 02188
(617) 555-8165

CAREER QUALIFICATIONS   Technical writer trained in preparation of manuals, catalogues, and instructional materials. Experiences in writing computer documentation containing syntax formats.

WORK EXPERIENCE   *Northeastern University, Boston, MA,* Reading and Writing Specialist, English Language Center, March-July 19XX, January-March 19XX.

Created individual lesson plans for each student assigned to the Reading and Writing Laboratory and developed materials for use in Laboratory programs. Ran the Laboratory for approximately 100 students 20 hours a week. Kept all records of students' work and prepared written and oral reports on student progress and laboratory operations.

Tutor of Foreign Students, September 19XX-present. Integrated foreign students into a large urban school and community and was a positive role model educationally and socially.

W. M. Mercer, Inc., Boston, MA, September-December 19XX.
Data processing and general office duties. Created and implemented a CRT search system for office personnel.

SPECIAL SKILLS C programming language; WORD, WordPerfect, Lotus 1–2–3, Excel.

EDUCATION Northeastern University, Boston, MA, Bachelor of Arts, June 19XX.

Concentration: English with minors in Economics and Technical Communications.

Activities: Selected to serve on the Residence Judicial Board, a faculty-staff-student group adjudicating residence-hall disputes; Northeastern News reporter; Northeastern Yearbook staff.

40 *Writing Under Pressure*

When you write under the pressure of time constraints, you are expected to write as completely and clearly as possible. The demands of writing under pressure can sometimes seem overwhelming, but if you break the challenge into small, sequential steps and then focus on each step in turn, you can succeed. If you tend to freeze under pressure, force yourself to take some slow, deep breaths and use a relaxation technique such as counting backwards from ten. When you turn to the task, remember to break the whole into parts so that the process is easier to work through.

Writing answers for essay tests is one of the most important writing tasks that you face in college. Common in the social sciences and humanities, essay tests are becoming increasingly common in the natural sciences as well. Essay tests give you the chance to synthesize and apply your knowledge, thereby helping your instructor determine what you have learned. Essay tests demand that you recall information and also put assorted pieces of that information into contexts that lead to generalizations you can support.

Understanding cue words and key words 40a

Most essay questions contain what is sometimes called a **cue word**, a word of direction that tells what the content of your answer is expected to emphasize. Knowing the major cue words and their meanings can increase your ability to plan efficiently and to write effectively. Be guided by the list of cue words and sample essay-test questions in Chart 173.

Each essay question also has one or more **key words** that tell you the information, topics, and ideas you are to write about. For example, in the question "Criticize the architectural function of the modern football stadium," the cue word is "criticize," and the key words are "archi-

REFERENCES TO SUPPLEMENTS

For more on handling essay exams, see *Teaching Writing: Prentice Hall Resources for Composition* by P. Hastings, ch. 5, "Impromptu Writing: Essay Tests."

See transparency 9-2 for essay test strategies in the *Prentice Hall/Simon & Schuster Transparencies for Writers* by D. Carter.

BACKGROUND

Diane Durkin (*Writing in the Disciplines* [New York: Random House, 1987]) warns that students often go wrong in writing papers or answers to essay questions on tests because they spend too little time analyzing the task they are given. She suggests several steps that can help students understand assignments more clearly and thoroughly. She advises them to do the following:

1. Find the key verb in the assignment. Does it ask you to analyze? explain? define? summarize? If the verb is vague— e.g., *consider*—you must substitute another verb that is indicated by the question as a whole.

2. Determine the subject of the writing task. What is the topic?

3. Rewrite the assignment in a form that tells you precisely what you are to do.

TEACHING TIP

Some essay questions ask students to respond to a quotation. Here are some suggestions you can give your students to help them formulate their answers.

The quotation may come from a familiar source, such as the text for the course, or from an unfamiliar source. Whether the student is working with a familiar or unfamiliar source, the following guidelines can be helpful:

1. Read the quotation carefully.

2. Paraphrase the quotation on scratch paper to be as sure as possible of its meaning.

3. Ask the professor to explain any words that are unfamiliar, if that is permitted.

4. Determine what you are supposed to do with the quotation. Argue against it? Support it? Compare it with another idea in your course readings or lectures?

5. If you use language from the quotation in your answer, use quotation marks. Follow the guidelines for using quotations in section 31e.

TEACHING TIP

Many students feel anxious about writing under time limits, as in an exam, for instance. In addition to following the strategies for writing essay tests, they may find it helpful to have the following suggestions to follow.

1. Allow yourself enough time to arrive at least ten minutes before the exam is scheduled to begin so that you can easily find a chair and desk.

2. Bring all the materials you will need to write comfortably, including extra paper for jotting notes, extra pens, and any books that you are permitted to use for reference.

→

tectural function" and "football stadium." To answer the question successfully, you must define "architectural function," then describe the typical modern football stadium (mentioning major variations when important), and then discuss how well the typical modern football stadium fits your definition of "architectural function."

CUE WORDS FOUND IN QUESTIONS FOR ESSAY TESTS   173

- **Analyze** means to separate something into parts and then discuss the parts and their meanings.

  Analyze Socrates's discussion of "good life" and "good death."

- **Clarify** means to make clear, often by giving a definition of a key term and by using examples to illustrate it.

  Clarify T. S. Eliot's idea of tradition.

- **Classify** means to arrange into groups on the basis of shared characteristics.

  Classify the different types of antipredator adaptations.

- **Compare and contrast** means to show similarities and differences.

  Compare and contrast the reproductive cycles of a moss and a flowering plant.

- **Criticize** means to give your opinion concerning the good points and bad points of something.

  Criticize the architectural function of modern football stadiums.

- **Define** means to give the definition of something and thereby to separate it from similar things.

  Define the term "yellow press."

- **Describe** means to explain features to make clear an object, procedure, or event.

  Describe the chain of events that constitutes the movement of a sensory impulse along a nerve fiber.

- **Discuss** means to consider as many elements as possible concerning an issue or event.

  Discuss the effects of television viewing on modern attitudes toward violence.

CUE WORDS FOUND IN QUESTIONS FOR ESSAY TESTS (continued)

173

- **Evaluate** means to give your opinion about the value of something.

  Evaluate Margaret Mead's contribution to anthropology studies.

- **Explain** means to make clear or intelligible something that needs to be understood or interpreted.

  Explain how the amount of carbon dioxide in the blood regulates rates of heartbeat and breathing.

- **Illustrate** means to give examples of something.

  Illustrate the use of symbolism in Richard Wright's novel *Native Son*.

- **Interpret** means to explain the meaning of something.

  Give your interpretation of Maxine Kumin's poem "Beans."

- **Justify** means to show or prove that something is valid or correct.

  Justify the existence of labor unions in today's economy.

- **Prove** means to present evidence that cannot be refuted logically or with other evidence.

  Prove that smoking is a major cause of lung cancer.

- **Relate** means to show the connections between two or more things.

  Relate increases in specific crimes in 1932–33 to the prevailing economic conditions.

- **Review** means to reexamine, summarize, or reprise something.

  Review the structural arrangements in proteins to explain the meaning of the term *polypeptide*.

- **Show** means to point out or demonstrate something.

  Show what effects pesticides have on the production of wheat.

- **Summarize** means to repeat briefly the major points of something.

  Summarize the major benefits of compulsory education.

- **Support** means to argue in favor of something.

  Support the position that destruction of rain forests is endangering the planet.

TEACHING TIP, cont.

3. While you are waiting for the exam to begin, clear your mind by thinking about something other than the material you have studied. Mentally reviewing details at the last minute is likely to make you panic. Some people bring a pleasure book to read while they wait for the exam to be distributed.

TEACHING TIP

In *Helping Students Write Well* Barbara E. Walvoord lists six guidelines for students taking essay exams. Pointing out that "the race goes not to the swiftest writers but to those who best organize and present what they know," she suggests that the student taking an essay test follow these general procedures.

1. Organize around a clear focus, one that is limited enough to cover in the time allotted and that allows inclusion of all the material the teacher will expect to find. This focus should be expressed in a thesis sentence.

2. Outline the answer. Know the three or four points to be covered to be sure that they all develop, explain, or prove the thesis sentence.

3. Come to the point quickly, perhaps even beginning with the thesis sentence.

4. Stick to the subject. Telling everything isn't expected. The test is to select, organize, and analyze major points.

5. Be thorough. Do not leave out anything important to the defense of the thesis sentence.

6. Support generalities with specific and relevant evidence.

TEACHING TIP

Here are two responses to an essay question in a course on criminal justice. It includes a quotation. The first answer is successful; the second is not. The sentences are numbered for your reference.

Essay Question: In his book *The Hidden Dimension,* Edward T. Hall says that "people from different cultures, when interpreting each other's behavior, often misinterpret the relationship, the activity, or the emotions. This leads to alienation or distorted communications" (171). Explain how Hall's observations might be important to a law enforcement professional. Use an example from lectures and reading in this course.

Answer 1

Successful Response

(1) Edward T. Hall believes that individuals whose cultural backgrounds differ may have trouble understanding each other. (2) This semester we learned that in some cultures it is considered rude to look another person in the eye when responding to an accusation or reprimand. (3) In the United States, on the other hand, many people believe that an individual who does not make eye contact is lying or feeling guilty. (4) Law enforcement professionals who are aware of Hall's findings may be less apt to make incorrect assumptions about the guilt or innocence of a person from a different culture. (5) Avoiding "alienation or distorted communications" (Hall 171) may prevent cases of false arrest and will almost certainly make for better relationships between members of the community and law enforcement professionals.

Answer 1 is successful because:

(1) Sentence 1 demonstrates that the student understands Hall's point.

➔

Writing effective responses to essay-test questions

An effective response to an essay-test question is complete and logically organized. Here are two answers to the question "Classify the different types of antipredator adaptations." The first one is successful; the second is not. The sentences are numbered for your reference, and they are explained at the bottom of this page and the top of p.735.

ANSWER 1

(1) Although many antipredator adaptations have evolved in the animal kingdom, they all can be classified into four major categories according to the prey's response to the predator. (2) The first category is hiding techniques. (3) These techniques include cryptic coloration and behavior in which the prey assumes characteristics of an inanimate object or part of a plant. (4) The second category is early enemy detection. (5) The prey responds to alarm signals from like prey or other kinds of prey before the enemy can get too close. (6) Evasion of the pursuing predator is the third category. (7) Prey that move erratically or in a compact group are displaying this technique. (8) The fourth category is active repulsion of the predator. (9) The prey kills, injures, or sickens the predator, establishing that it represents danger to the predator.

ANSWER 2

(1) Antipredator adaptations are the development of the capabilities to reduce the risk of attack from a predator without too much change in the life-supporting activities of the prey. (2) There are many different types of antipredator adaptations. (3) One type is camouflage, hiding from the predator by cryptic coloration or imitation of plant parts. (4) An example of this type of antipredator adaptation is the praying mantis. (5) A second type is the defense used by monarch butterflies, a chemical protection that makes some birds ill after eating the butterfly. (6) This protection may injure the bird by causing it to vomit, and it can educate the bird against eating other butterflies. (7) Detection and evasion are also antipredator adaptations.

Here is an explanation of what happens, sentence by sentence, in the two answers to the question about antipredator adaptations.

	ANSWER 1	**ANSWER 2**
Sentence 1	Sets up classification system and gives number of categories based on key word	Defines key word

	ANSWER 1	**ANSWER 2**
Sentence 2	Names first category	Throwaway sentence— accomplishes nothing
Sentence 3	Defines first category	Names and defines first category
Sentence 4	Names second category	Gives an example for first category
Sentence 5	Defines second category	Gives an example for second (unnamed) category
Sentence 6	Names third category	Continues to explain example
Sentence 7	Defines third category	Names two categories
Sentence 8	Names fourth category	
Sentence 9	Defines fourth category	

Answer 1 sets about immediately answering the question by introducing a classification system as called for by the cue word *classify*. Answer 2, on the other hand, defines the key word, a waste of time on a test that will be read by an audience of specialists. Answer 1 is tightly organized, easy to follow, and to-the-point. Answer 2 rambles, never manages to name the four categories, and says more around the subject than on it.

Using strategies when writing under pressure

40c

If you use specific strategies when writing under pressure, you can be more comfortable and your writing will likely be more effective. As you use the strategies listed in Chart 174, remember that your purpose in answering questions is to show what you know in a clear, direct, and well-organized way.

The more you use the strategies in the chart and adapt them to your personal needs, the better you will use them to your advantage. Try to practice them, making up questions that might be on your test and timing yourself as you write the answers. Doing this offers you another benefit: If you study by anticipating possible questions and writing out the answers, you will be very well prepared if one or two of them show up on the test.

TEACHING TIP, cont.

(2) Sentences 2 and 3 provide what the question asks: an example from the course readings and lectures.

(3) Sentences 4 and 5 address the purpose of the question: to relate the quotation from Hall's book to the law enforcement profession.

(4) Sentence 5 contains a direct quotation from Hall that is appropriately used and correctly punctuated.

Answer 2
Unsuccessful Response
(1) Edward T. Hall thinks we might encounter alienation. (2) Why should law enforcement professionals have to worry about whether or not someone else can understand their culture? (3) There are too many other issues that are more important, like stopping drug traffic and preventing gang wars. (4) I am against Hall's idea and what he says about alienation and in encounters or distorted communication.

Answer 2 is unsuccessful because:

(1) Sentence 1 shows that the student does not understand what Hall is saying. The student uses words from the quotation but distorts their meaning.

(2) Sentences 2, 3, and 4 give the student's opinion, but do not address the purpose of the question: to apply the quotation to the law enforcement profession.

(3) No sentence in this answer gives an example from the course readings or lectures, although the question asks for one.

(4) Sentence 4 uses a direct quotation from Hall, but the quotation does not fit grammatically or logically with the rest of the sentence, nor is it properly punctuated.

TEACHING TIP

Some students have a harder time than others writing under a time limit. For those who have serious difficulty in pacing themselves, and thus suffer greater anxiety about the process, a few suggestions may help. Making an outline at the outset, or at least jotting down the major points to be covered, can save the student time by charting the direction of the answer. Leaving a few minutes at the end for quick editing will produce more polished copy. Some students leave blank space at the beginning of an answer so that an accurate introduction can be inserted after the answer is written. The student who has problems working efficiently under a time limit can improve his or her performance with practice. Before an examination, such a student should compose several questions an instructor is likely to ask, then, with a timer running, practice writing answers to them. A familiar process is always less threatening than an unfamiliar one.

TEACHING TIP

Any instructor with more than a few weeks of classroom experience knows that making good essay questions for an examination is not a simple matter. Considerations regarding adequate coverage of material, clarity of instructions, and availability of time must play a part in what is asked and how it is asked as well. As a way to understand the students' task, and how one can reasonably expect it to be carried out, an instructor can always write the answers to the questions he or she poses. The results are often gratifying, but sometimes they reveal gaps in what is being tested, ambiguous directions, or unreasonable length.

STRATEGIES FOR WRITING ESSAY TESTS   174

1. Do not start writing immediately.
2. If the test has two or more questions, read them all at the start. Determine whether you are supposed to answer all the questions. Doing this gives you a sense of how to budget your time either by dividing it equally or by allotting more for some questions. If you have a choice, select questions about which you know the most and can write about most completely in the time limit.
3. Analyze each question that you answer by underlining the cue words and key words (see 40a) to determine exactly what the question asks.
4. Use the writing process as much as possible within the constraints of the time limit. Try to allot time to plan and revise. For a one-hour test of one question, take about 10 minutes to jot down preliminary ideas about content and organization, and save 10 minutes to reread, revise, and edit your answer. If you suddenly are pressed for time—but try to avoid this—consider skipping a question that you cannot answer well or a question that counts less toward your total score. If you feel blocked, try free writing (see 2f) to get your hand and your thoughts moving.
5. Support any generalizations with specifics (see 4c about using the formula RENNS for being specific).
6. Beware of "going off the topic." Respond to the cue words and key words (see 40a) in the question, and do not try to reshape the question to conform to what you might prefer to write about. Remember, your reader expects a clear line of presentation and reasoning that answers the given question.

EXERCISE 40-1

Look back at an essay that you have written under time pressure. Read it over and decide whether you would change the content of your answer or the strategies you used as you were writing under pressure. List these specific strategies, and, if you think they were useful, add them to Chart 174.

Writing When English Is a Second Language

When English is your second language, you face the special challenge of needing to learn characteristics of English that native-born writers take for granted. Part Nine begins with a special ESL Preface to set the context for your using the rest of Part Nine, which explains the features of English that tend to give nonnative writers the most trouble. As you use Chapters 41 through 46, remember that learning to write English involves much more than studying separate features. As for writers in any language, the more time you spend actually writing, the faster you can become a fluent writer.

Preface for ESL Students

REFERENCE TO SUPPLEMENTS

For more on the special needs of some ESL students, see C. Myers, "ESL Writers in the Composition Class," in L. Julian, et al., *Strategies and Resources for Teaching Writing With The Simon & Schuster Handbook for Writers*.

Do you sometimes worry when you write in English? If you ever do worry about your English writing, let me assure you that you have much in common with me and with many U.S. college students. But as an ESL writer, you face a special challenge because you must attend to every word, every phrase, every sentence, and every paragraph in a way that native speakers of English do not.

You may be reassured to know that any errors you make as an ESL writer indicate that you are progressing through necessary stages of second-language development. Eventually, when you have passed through all the stages that all language learners must, you should be a proficient writer of English.

Unfortunately, there are no shortcuts. As with progress in speaking, listening, and reading comprehension in a new language, passing through the various stages of language development takes time. Some students have more available time than others, and some students have a home or study environment that enables faster learning of a new language. However, no matter how fast a language skill is learned, all the stages of language development must be experienced. Just as most adults make mistakes when they learn to play a new sport, few people write fluently and without error when they compose a first draft of a piece of writing. In fact, only rarely have even the most noted and experienced writers ever written something perfectly the first time.

What can you do to progress as quickly as possible from one writing stage to another? You might start by trying to remember what the typical school writing is like in your first language. Try to recall how ideas are presented in writing in your native language, especially when information has to be explained and when a matter of opinion has to be argued.

In recalling the typical style of school writing in your native language, compare it with what you are learning about writing style in American English. For example, most college writing in the United States has a very direct, straightforward basic structure. In a typical essay or research paper, the reader expects to find a THESIS STATEMENT,* which clearly states the overall message of the piece of

*You can find the definition of a word printed in small capital letters (such as THESIS STATEMENT) in the Glossary of Terms toward the back of this handbook.

writing, by the end of the first or second paragraph. Usually, each paragraph that follows relates directly to the thesis statement and starts with a sentence, called a TOPIC SENTENCE, that tells the point of the paragraph. The rest of each paragraph usually supports the point by using reasons, examples, and other specific details. The final paragraph brings the essay or research paper to a reasonable, logical conclusion.

This handbook contains many examples of writing by U.S. college students. For essays, see sections 3f, 6h, and 37e. For research papers, see Chapters 34 and 35 and section 37e. Also, this handbook explains paragraph structures typically expected in U.S. college writing; see Chapter 4. By the way, these typical academic structures do not apply to novels, plays, poems, or articles in most newspapers and magazines published in the United States.

Writing structures typical of your native language probably differ from those in the United States. Always honor your culture's writing traditions and structures, for they reflect the richness of your heritage. At the same time, try to adapt to and practice the academic writing style characteristic of the United States. Later, when you are writing fluently, your college instructors likely will encourage you to practice other American English writing styles that are less common and that allow greater liberty in organization and expression.

Over the past twenty years, many interesting observations have been made about the distinctive variations in school writing styles among people of different cultures and language groups. Research about these contrasts is ongoing, so scholars hesitate to generalize about them. Even so, interesting differences seem to exist. For example, many Spanish-speaking students feel that U.S. school writing lacks the sort of traditional introductory background observations that Spanish-language writing usually includes, yet U.S. composition teachers will often mark such introductory material as wordy or not sufficiently relevant to the central point of an essay or research paper. Traditional French school essays usually begin with a series of points that are discussed in the body of the essay and then repeated in reverse order in the conclusion. Japanese school writing customarily begins with references to nature. In some African nations, a ceremonial, formal opening is expected to start school writing as an expression of respect for the reader. As a person, I greatly enjoy discovering the rich variations in the writing traditions of the many cultures of the world. As a teacher, however, my responsibility is to explain the expectations in the United States.

The ESL chapters following this special ESL preface are designed to help you focus on errors that many ESL writers make. I hope that Chapters 41 through 46 can be of great use to you.

I hope also that the rest of this handbook will become your trusted companion. Throughout its pages, ESL Notes (signaled by the letters **ESL** in the access bar on the outside of this book's pages) and

BACKGROUND

To set a context for Part IX, the *Annotated Instructor's Edition* of this handbook includes the specially commissioned bibliographic essay "Teaching Composition to Speakers of Other Languages: An Overview" by Joy Reid, University of Wyoming, who has written extensively about ESL. This essay represents the theoretical and practical stance toward students and teaching that underlies the ESL material in this handbook.

Joy Reid's essay also explains differences between international students and residents, which can be significant. Depending on how long they have lived in the United States, residents may be very fluent orally and yet have rather serious literacy problems. International students, on the other hand, are often excellent readers with impressive vocabularies, but may have deficiencies in writing and speaking. Reid's essay also provides an overview of cultural and rhetorical patterns that will help instructors understand their ESL students' preconceptions and needs. Finally, the discussion of the relationship of accuracy-fluency to error is valuable to instructors trying to help students master the rules and patterns of English.

TEACHING TIP: ESL

Many ESL students are used to a style of pedagogy different from what they encounter in the United States. For example, U.S. colleges tend to be more test-oriented than those in other countries. Students may be surprised to find out that their placement or course grade depends heavily on only one or two tests. Also, U.S. colleges are more "student-responsible" than those in some other countries. In the United States, students are responsible for asking questions if they do not understand or if they want to question a point. In many other countries, it is considered disrespectful to question or interrupt the instructor, so some ESL students may prefer to leave class confused rather than appear rude. You many want to help ESL students feel comfortable about asking their professors questions. (Usually, this takes more than a one-time invitation.)

One especially troublesome manifestation of ESL students' reluctance to question instructors occurs when assignments or directions are given to a class. ESL students often say that they understand an assignment only to ask another student to explain it to them later. Misunderstandings are easily spread. One way to anticipate this problem is to give students clear, concise written instructions, whether handed out or written on the board with ample time for students to copy them.

various kinds of Alerts (signaled by ! in the access bars) present information in related contexts that can help you as you acquire American English-language writing skills. A directory of selected ESL Notes and Alerts follows this Preface to help you locate ones that may be especially useful to you.

Lynn Quitman Troyka

Lynn Quitman Troyka

DIRECTORY OF ESL NOTES AND SELECTED ALERTS

- Recognizing noun suffixes: ESL Note, page 170
- Recognizing adjective suffixes: ESL Note, page 174
- Not repeating a subject with a personal pronoun in the same clause: ESL Note, page 181
- Using *to* and *for* with indirect objects: ESL Note, page 183
- Phrasing indirect questions: ESL Note, page 191
- Changing verb form in only one verb in a verb phrase: ESL Note, page 206
- Not omitting pronoun subjects: ESL Note, page 239
- Not omitting *it* included in an expletive (subject filler): ESL Note, page 243
- Revising long sentences: ESL Note, page 348
- Using computerized thesauruses cautiously: Computer Alert, page 388
- Using only one end-punctuation mark: Punctuation Alert, page 425

41 Singulars and Plurals
ESL

HOW TO USE CHAPTER 41 ESL EFFECTIVELY

1. Use this chapter together with these handbook sections:
   - 7a NOUNS
   - 8c -*s* form of VERBS
   - 11a–11l SUBJECT-VERB AGREEMENT
   - 12f nouns as MODIFIERS
2. Remember that throughout this handbook, you can find the definitions of words printed in SMALL CAPITAL LETTERS in the Glossary of Terms.
3. Use any **cross-references** (often given in parentheses) to find full explanations of key concepts.

   This chapter can help you choose between using SINGULARS (one) and PLURALS (more than one). Section 41a discusses the concept of COUNT and NONCOUNT NOUNS. Section 41b discusses DETERMINERS and nouns. Section 41c discusses particularly confusing instances of the choice between singular and plural. Section 41d discusses some nouns with irregular plural forms.

Understanding the concept of count and noncount nouns
41a

Count nouns name items that can be counted: *radio, street, idea, fingernail.* Count nouns can be SINGULAR or PLURAL (*radios, streets*).

Noncount nouns name things that are thought of as a whole and not separated into separate, countable parts: *rice, knowledge, traffic.* Two important rules to remember about noncount nouns are that (1) they are never preceded by *a* or *an*, and (2) they are never plural. Chart 159 lists eleven categories of uncountable items, giving examples in each category.

BACKGROUND
In "Toward an Understanding of the Distinct Nature of L2 Writing: ESL Research and Its Implications," Tony Silva sorts the main distinctions between L1 and L2 writing into two useful categories: composing processes and written text features (*TESOL Quarterly* 27, 1993, 657–677).

TEACHING TIP
To help students understand countable and uncountable nouns, you may want to write a few sentences on the board or in a handout illustrating the use of the ones that even advanced students often have problems with: *advice, homework, information, jewelry, news, vocabulary, weather.* Ways to count them should be included (*a piece of advice/information/jewelry, ten vocabulary words, two homework assignments, a news story/item,* and so on).

TEACHING TIP: ESL

Many nouns have both countable and uncountable forms, particularly food items
such as cake/cakes, chicken/chickens,
chocolate/chocolates, fruit/fruits, meat/
meats, but many others as well: life/lives,
liberty/liberties, love/loves, beauty/beau-
ties, water/waters, and so on. Often the
countable form is part of an idiom. Usually, the uncountable meaning is general
and the countable meaning specific. To
count uncountable nouns that do not
have countable forms, measure-words or
the names of containers are often used.

General: We bought some <u>food</u>, including <u>meat</u>.

Specific: We bought *two* <u>chickens</u>, a
pound of <u>hamburger</u>, a *loaf* of <u>bread</u>, a
box of <u>chocolates</u>, and a *carton* of <u>milk</u>.

General: <u>Life</u> is precious.

Specific: Cats have nine <u>lives</u>.

41a
cont.

UNCOUNTABLE ITEMS

UNCOUNTABLE ITEMS

159

- ■ **Groups of similar items making up "wholes":** *clothing, equipment, furniture, jewelry, junk, luggage, mail, money, stuff, traffic, vocabulary, etc.*
- ■ **Abstractions:** *advice, equality, fun, health, ignorance, information, knowledge, news, peace, pollution, respect, etc.*
- ■ **Liquids:** *blood, coffee, gasoline, water, etc.*
- ■ **Gases:** *air, helium, oxygen, smog, smoke, steam, etc.*
- ■ **Materials:** *aluminum, cloth, cotton, ice, wood, etc.*
- ■ **Food:** *beef, bread, butter, macaroni, meat, pork, etc.*
- ■ **Particles or grains:** *dirt, dust, hair, rice, salt, wheat, etc.*
- ■ **Sports, games, activities:** *chess, homework, housework, reading, sailing, soccer, etc.*
- ■ **Languages:** *Arabic, Chinese, Japanese, Spanish, etc.*
- ■ **Fields of study:** *biology, computer science, history, literature, math, etc.*
- ■ **Events in nature:** *electricity, heat, humidity, moonlight, rain, snow, sunshine, thunder, weather, etc.*

Some nouns can be countable or uncountable depending on their
meaning in a sentence. Most of these nouns name things that can be
meant either individually or as "wholes" made up of individual parts.

COUNT	You have a **hair** on your sleeve. [In this sentence, *hair* is meant as an individual, countable item.]
NONCOUNT	Kioko has black **hair.** [In this sentence, *hair* is meant as a whole.]
COUNT	The **rains** were late last year. [In this sentence, *rains* is meant as individual, countable occurrences of rain.]
NONCOUNT	The **rain** is soaking the garden. [In this sentence, parti- cles of *rain* are meant as a whole.]

When you are editing your writing (see Chapter 4), be sure that
you have not added a plural *-s* to any noncount nouns, for they are
always singular in form.

! ❖ VERB ALERT: Be sure to use a singular verb with any noncount noun
that functions as a subject in a clause. ❖

To check whether a noun is count or noncount, look it up in a dictionary such as the *Longman Dictionary of American English.* In this

dictionary, count nouns are indicated by [C], and noncount nouns are indicated by [U] (for uncountable). Nouns that have both count and noncount meanings are marked [C;U].

Using determiners with singular and plural nouns

41b

Determiners, also called *expressions of quantity,* are used to tell "how much" or "how many" about nouns. Other names for determiners include LIMITING ADJECTIVES, *noun markers,* and ARTICLES. (For information about articles—the words *a, an,* and *the*—see Chapter 42ESL.)

Choosing the right determiner with a noun can depend on whether the noun is NONCOUNT or COUNT (see 41a). For count nouns, you must also decide whether the noun is singular or plural. Chart 160 lists many determiners and the kinds of nouns that they can accompany.

DETERMINERS TO USE WITH COUNT AND NONCOUNT NOUNS 160

GROUP 1: DETERMINERS FOR SINGULAR COUNT NOUNS

With every **singular count noun,** always use one of the determiners listed in Group 1.

a, an, the

> **a house**   **an egg**   **the car**

one, any, some, every, each, either, neither, another, the other

> **any house**   **each egg**   **another car**

my, our, your, his, her, its, their, nouns with *'s or s'*

> **your house**   **its egg**   **Connie's car**

this, that

> **this house**   **that egg**   **this car**

one, no, the first, the second, etc.

> **one house**   **no egg**   **the fifth car**

GROUP 2: DETERMINERS FOR PLURAL COUNT NOUNS

All the determiners listed in Group 2 can be used with **plural count nouns.** Plural count nouns can also be used without determiners, as discussed in section 42b.

the

> **the bicycles**   **the rooms**   **the ideas**   ➡

BACKGROUND

Many expressions of quantity, such as <u>all</u>, <u>(a) few</u>, <u>(a) little</u>, <u>many</u>, <u>most</u>, <u>some</u>, can be used along or with <u>of the</u>. When used alone, they are general in meaning: with <u>of the</u>, they are specific: *Some students/Some of the students in my classes* are interested in extracurricular activities.

TEACHING TIP: ESL

You might want to suggest that ESL students try to watch the news on TV, then listen to the same news on the radio, and then read about some of the same events in the newspaper. The repetitions, along with the variations in medium and language, can be instructive and reinforcing.

When learning a new language, teachers and classes help, but if students try to write a few sentences in English and then the next day read a newspaper, they might see a word or sentence similar to the one they tried to write the day before. It jumps at them from the page. They see written what they had been trying to say, and the next time that they try to write the same thing, they can do it.

DETERMINERS TO USE WITH COUNT AND NONCOUNT NOUNS (continued)

160

some, any, both, many, more, most, few, fewer, the fewest, a number of, other, several, all, all the, a lot of

some bicycles	**many rooms**	**all ideas**

my, our, your, his, her, its, their, nouns with 's or s'

our bicycles	**her rooms**	**students' ideas**

these, those

these bicycles	**those rooms**	**these ideas**

no, two, three, four, etc., the first, the second, the third, etc.

no bicycles	**four rooms**	**the first ideas**

GROUP 3: DETERMINERS FOR NONCOUNT NOUNS

All the determiners listed in Group 3 can be used with noncount nouns (always singular). Noncount nouns can also be used without determiners, as discussed in section 42b.

the

the rice	**the rain**	**the pride**

some, any, much, more, most, other, the other, little, less, the least, enough, all, all the, a lot of

enough rice	**a lot of rain**	**more pride**

my, our, your, his, her, its, their, nouns with 's or s'

their rice	**India's rain**	**your pride**

this, that

this rice	**that rain**	**this pride**

no, the first, the second, the third, etc.

no rice	**the first rain**	**no pride**

! ❖ USAGE ALERT: The phrases *a few* and *a little* convey the meaning "some": *I have **a few** rare books* means "I have *some* rare books." *They are worth **a little** money* means "They are worth *some* money."

Without the word *a*, the words *few* and *little* convey the meaning "almost none": *I have **few** [or very few] books* means "I have *almost no* books." *They are worth **little** money* means "They are worth *almost no* money." ❖

Using correct forms in *one of* constructions, for nouns used as adjectives, and with *States* in names or titles

41c

One of constructions

One of constructions include *one of the* and a NOUN or *one of* followed by an ADJECTIVE-noun combination (*one of my hats, one of those ideas*). Always use a plural noun as the OBJECT when you use *one of the* with a noun or an adjective-noun combination.

NO   One of the **reason** to live here is the beach.

YES   One of the **reasons** to live here is the beach.

NO   One of her best **friend** has moved away.

YES   One of her best **friends** has moved away.

The VERB in these constructions is always singular because it agrees with the singular *one*, not with the plural noun: *One of the most important inventions of the twentieth century **is** [not *are*] television.*

For advice about verb forms that go with *one of the . . . who* constructions, see section 11k.

Nouns Used as Adjectives

ADJECTIVES in English do not have plural forms. When you use an adjective with a plural noun, make the noun plural but not the adjective: *the **green** [not *greens*] leaves.* Be especially careful when you use as an adjective a word that can also function as a noun.

The bird's wingspan is ten **inches.** [*Inches* is functioning as a noun.]

The bird has a ten-**inch** wingspan. [*Inch* is functioning as an adjective.]

Do not add *-s* (or *-es*) to the adjective even when it is modifying a plural noun or pronoun.

NO   Many **Americans** students are basketball fans.

YES   Many **American** students are basketball fans.

Names or Titles that Include the Word States

States is a plural word. However, names such as the *United States* or the *Organization of American States* refer to singular things—one

TEACHING TIP: ESL
Many ESL students find closed-captioning on television helpful. Some new TV sets are equipped with this capability. Watching news, soap operas, and other programs with English captions helps students develop their fluency, listening comprehension, vocabulary, knowledge of idioms, and reading comprehension. The captioning is not always entirely accurate; spelling errors and omissions are rather common. Nonetheless, the advantage of being able to *see* the language while listening to it outweighs the disadvantages.

41
ESL

41c
cont.

country and one organization, even though made up of many states. When *States* is part of a name or title referring to one thing, the name is a singular noun and therefore requires a singular verb.

NO   The United **States have** a large entertainment industry.
         The United **State has** a large entertainment industry.

YES   The United **States has** a large entertainment industry.

41d   ## Using nouns with irregular plurals

Some English nouns have irregular spellings. In addition to those discussed in Chart 101 in section 22c, here are others that often cause difficulties.

Plurals of Foreign Nouns and Other Irregular Nouns

Whenever you are unsure whether a noun is plural, look it up in a dictionary. If no plural is given for a singular noun, add an *-s*.

Many nouns from other languages that are used unchanged in English have only one plural. If two plurals are listed in the dictionary, look carefully for differences in meaning. Some words, for example, keep the plural form from the original language for scientific usage and have another English-form plural for nonscientific contexts: *formula, formulae, formulas; appendix, appendices; appendixes; index, indices, indexes; medium, media, mediums; cactus, cacti, cactuses; fungus, fungi, funguses.*

Words from Latin that end in *-is* in their singular form become plural by substituting *-es: parenthesis, parentheses; thesis, theses; oasis, oases;* for example.

Other Words

Medical terms for diseases involving an inflammation end in *itis: tonsillitis, appendicitis.* They are always singular.

The word *news,* although it ends in *s,* is always singular: *The **news** is* encouraging. The words *people, police,* and *clergy* are always plural even though they do not end in *s: The **police are** prepared.*

EXERCISE 41-1

Consulting Chapter 41, select the correct choice from the words in parentheses and write it in the blank.

Example   In the United States, the (popularities, popularity) **popularity** of cats as pets (are, is) **is** rapidly outstripping that of dogs.

746

1. One of the main (reason, reasons)_____ may be the recent change in (American, Americans) _____ lifestyles.
2. Many people in the (United State, United States) _____ are moving from big houses with large yards to small apartments with (ten-feet, ten-foot) _____ balconies.
3. Dogs must be walked, even in (rain, rains) _____ and (snow, snows) _____
4. People also are spending (many, much) _____ time away from home.
5. As long as they have sufficient (food, foods) _____ and (waters, water) _____ , cats can safely be left alone for a few days.

ANSWERS & COVERAGE: EXERCISE 41–1

1. reasons [41c, plural obj. with *one of*] American [41c, singular for noun used as adj]
2. United States [41c, *States* plural in *United States*] ten-foot [41c, singular for noun used as adj]
3. rain, snow [41a, singular for noncount nouns]
4. much [41b, *much* the correct determiner with noncount noun *time*]
5. food, water [41a, noncount nouns always singular]

42 *Articles*

ESL

BACKGROUND

In "Assessment of ESL Students in Mainstream College Composition," Lisa Hillenbrand offers alternatives and insights for non-ESL trained composition instructors who must assess compositions written by ESL students. (*Teaching English in the Two Year College*, 22:2, May 1994, 125–129)

HOW TO USE CHAPTER 42ESL EFFECTIVELY

1. Use this chapter together with these handbook sections:
   - 7a ARTICLES and NOUNS
   - 41a SINGULARS and PLURALS with COUNT and NONCOUNT NOUNS
   - 41b DETERMINERS with count and noncount nouns

2. Remember that throughout this handbook, you can find the definitions of words printed in SMALL CAPITAL LETTERS in the Glossary of Terms.

3. Also, use any **cross-references** (usually given in parentheses) to find full explanations of key concepts.

This chapter gives you guidelines for using articles. Section 42a discusses using articles with singular count nouns. Section 42b discusses using articles with plural count nouns and with noncount nouns (which are always singular). Section 42c discusses using articles with proper nouns and with GERUNDS.

42a Using *a, an,* or *the* with singular count nouns

The words *a* and *an* are called **indefinite articles.** The word *the* is called a **definite article.** Articles are one type of determiner. (For other determiners, see Chart 160 in 41b.) Articles signal that a noun will follow and that any modifiers between the article and the noun refer to that noun.

a chair	**the** computer
a cold, metal chair	**the** lightning-fast computer

Every time you use a singular count noun, a common noun that names one countable item, the noun requires some kind of determiner; see Group 1 in Chart 160 (in Chapter 41) for a list. To choose between *a* or *an* and *the,* you need to determine whether the noun is **specific** or **nonspecific.** A noun is considered specific when anyone who reads your writing can understand from the context of your message exactly and specifically to what the noun is referring.

For nonspecific singular count nouns, use *a* (or *an*). When the singular noun is specific, use *the* or some other determiner. Chart 161 can help you decide when a singular count noun is specific and therefore requires *the*.

✤ ALERT: Use *an* before words that begin with a vowel sound. Use *a* before words that begin with a consonant sound. Words that begin with *h* or *u* can have either a vowel or a consonant sound. Make the choice based on the sound of the first word after the article, even if that word is not the noun.

an idea	**a g**ood idea
an umbrella	**a u**seless umbrella
an honor	**a h**istory book ✤

WHEN A SINGULAR COUNT NOUN IS SPECIFIC AND REQUIRES *THE* 161

- **Rule 1: A noun is specific and requires *the* when it names something unique or generally known.**

  The sun has risen above **the horizon**. [Because *sun* and *horizon* are generally known nouns, they are specific nouns in the context of this sentence.]

- **Rule 2: A noun is specific and requires *the* when it names something used in a representative or abstract sense.**

  Benjamin Franklin favored **the turkey** as **the national bird** of the United States. [Because *turkey* and *national bird* are representative references rather than references to a particular turkey or bird, they are specific nouns in the context of this sentence.]

- **Rule 3: A noun is specific and requires *the* when it names something defined elsewhere in the same sentence or in an earlier sentence.**

  The ship *Savannah* was the first steam vessel to cross the Atlantic Ocean. [The word *Savannah* names a specific ship.]

  The carpet in my bedroom is new. [*In my bedroom* defines exactly which carpet is meant, so *carpet* is a specific noun in this context.]

  I have **a computer** in my office. **The computer** is often broken. [*Computer* is not specific in the first sentence, so it uses *a*. In the second sentence, *computer* has been made specific by the first sentence, so it uses *the*.] ➡

QUOTATION ABOUT READING

Books had instant replay long before televised sports.

—Bern Williams

BACKGROUND: COLLABORATION

In "Peer Response in the Multicultural Classroom: Dissensus—A Dream (Deferred)," Carrie Shively Leverenz suggests that, while the traditional goal of much classroom collaboration has been to reach consensus, in fact the preservation of differences may be more valuable. Especially within the multicultural classroom, Leverenz champions "dissensus" (the encouragement of open-ended questioning, challenging, and delaying the rush to judgment). (*Journal of Advanced Composition,* 14:1, Winter 1994, 167–187)

TEACHING TIP: ESL

Understanding Rule 4 may be particularly difficult for some ESL students since the context is partly extralingual. That is, the *situation* makes the noun definite; it is familiar to both speaker and listener, who understand the office or company policies regarding computer repairs. Here are other examples from the context of a home; in each case, the noun is definite because the situation in which it occurs is familiar:

I'm going to walk <u>the</u> dog in <u>the</u> park. When I get back, I'll set <u>the</u> VCR for the movie.

WHEN A SINGULAR COUNT NOUN IS SPECIFIC AND REQUIRES *THE* (continued)   161

■ **Rule 4: A noun is specific and requires *the* when it names something that can be inferred from the context.**
Monday, I had to call **the technician** to fix it. [If this sentence follows the two sentences about a computer in Rule 3 above, *technician* is specific in this context.]

One common exception affects Rule 3 in Chart 161. A noun may still require *a* (or *an*) after the first use if one or more descriptive adjectives come between the article and the noun: *I bought **a sweater** today. It was **a** [not *the*] **red sweater**.* Other information may make the noun specific so that *the* is correct. For example, *It was **the red sweater that I saw in the store yesterday*** uses *the* because the *that* clause makes specific which red sweater is meant.

42b

Using articles with plural nouns and with noncount nouns

With plural nouns and noncount nouns, you must decide whether to use *the* or to use no article at all. (For guidelines about using DETERMINERS other than articles with nouns, see Chart 160 in 41b.)

What you learned in section 42a about nonspecific and specific nouns can help you make the choice between using *the* or using no article. Chart 161 in section 42a explains when a singular count noun's meaning is specific and calls for *the*. Plural nouns and noncount nouns with specific meanings usually use *the* in the same circumstances. However, a plural noun or a noncount noun with a general or nonspecific meaning usually does not use *the*.

Geraldo grows **flowers** but not **vegetables** in his garden. He is thinking about planting **corn** sometime.

Plural Nouns

A plural noun's meaning may be specific because it is widely known.

The oceans are being damaged by pollution. [Because the meaning of *oceans* is widely understood, *the* is correct to use. This example is related to Rule 1 in Chart 161.]

A plural noun's meaning may also be made specific by a word, PHRASE, or CLAUSE in the same SENTENCE.

Geraldo sold **the daisies from last year's garden** to the florist. [Because the phrase *from last year's garden* makes *daisies* specific, *the* is correct to use. This example is related to Rule 3 in Chart 161.]

A plural noun's meaning usually becomes specific by being used in an earlier sentence.

Geraldo planted **tulips** this year. **The tulips** will bloom in April. [*Tulips* is used in a general sense in the first sentence, without *the*. Because the first sentence makes *tulips* specific, *the tulips* is correct in the second sentence. This example is related to Rule 3 in Chart 161.]

A plural noun's meaning may be made specific by the context.

Geraldo fertilized **the bulbs** when he planted them last October. [In the context of the sentences about tulips, *bulbs* is specific and calls for *the*. This example is related to Rule 4 in Chart 161.]

Noncount Nouns

Noncount nouns are always singular in form (see 41a). Like plural nouns, noncount nouns use either *the* or no article. When a noncount noun's meaning is specific, use *the* before it. If its meaning is general or nonspecific, do not use *the*.

Kalinda served **rice** to us. She flavored *the rice* with curry. [*Rice* is a noncount noun. This example is related to Rule 3 in Chart 161: By the second sentence, *rice* has become specific, so *the* is used.]

Kalinda served us **the rice that she had flavored with curry.** [*Rice* is a noncount noun. This example is related to Rule 3 in Chart 161: *Rice* is made specific by the clause *that she had flavored with curry*, so *the* is used.]

Generalizations with Plural or Noncount Nouns

Rule 2 in Chart 161 tells you to use *the* with singular count nouns used in a general sense. With generalizations using plural or noncount nouns, omit *the*.

NO	**The tulips** are **the flowers** that grow from **the bulbs.**
YES	**Tulips** are **flowers** that grow from **bulbs.**
NO	**The dogs** require more care than **the cats** do.
YES	**Dogs** require more care than **cats** do.

TEACHING TIP: ESL

Cultural bias can intrude on ESL students' ability to grasp a point because of philosophies and ideas that are specific to U.S. culture. For example, an ESL student may have difficulty with an assignment on flag-burning because few nations hold their flag in the same regard as the United States does. Another rather extreme example concerns one in-class essay prompt that directed students to argue whether they believed great individuals were born great or "became" great because of the times and the circumstances of their lives. Individualism is highly valued in U.S. culture, but many others do not revere the "great individual." Socialist or communist societies value the group over the individual, in some cases to the extent of suppressing the individual in favor of the group. Students who have lived in such societies may not know enough specific details about "great individuals" to adequately support an essay on the topic.

TEACHING TIP: ESL
You might want to show some of your ESL writers a few of the published letters of Bartolomeo Vanzetti, the Italian immigrant to the United States who was sentenced to death in the 1920s for murders that he and many supporters insisted he did not commit. Vanzetti wrote from prison, in imperfect English that sometimes seems halfway between English and Italian. Even so, his letters are full of human passion and of love of humanity and nature. Frankly, I have read some writers in English who write more "correctly" than Vanzetti, but rarely have I encountered anything as beautiful as his letters.

42c

Using *the* with proper nouns and with gerunds

Proper Nouns

Proper nouns name specific people, places, or things (see 7a). Most proper nouns do not require ARTICLES: *We visited **Lake Mead** with **Asha** and **Larry.*** As shown in Chart 162, however, certain types of proper nouns do require *the*.

PROPER NOUNS THAT USE *THE*

PROPER NOUNS THAT USE *THE*	162

■ Nouns with the pattern *the* . . . *of* . . .

the United States of America   **the** fourth **of** July

the President of Mexico   **the** University **of** Paris

■ Plural proper nouns

the United Arab Emirates

the Johnsons

the Rocky Mountains [but Mount Fuji]

the Chicago Bulls

the Falkland Islands [but Long Island]

the Great Lakes [but Lake Louise]

■ Collective proper nouns (nouns that name a group)

the Modern Language Association

the Society of Friends

■ Some (but not all) geographical features

the Amazon   **the** Gobi Desert   **the** Indian Ocean

■ Two countries and one city

the Congo   **the** Sudan   **the** Hague [capital of the Netherlands]

Gerunds

Gerunds are present participles (the *-ing* form of VERBS) used as nouns: ***Skating** is challenging*. Gerunds usually are not preceded by *the*.

NO	**The constructing** new bridges is necessary to improve traffic flow.
YES	**Constructing** new bridges is necessary to improve traffic flow.

Use *the* before a gerund when two conditions are met: (1) the gerund is used in a specific sense (see 42a) and (2) the gerund does not have a DIRECT OBJECT.

NO	**The designing** fabric is a fine art. [*Fabric* is a direct object of *designing,* so *the* should not be used.]
YES	**Designing** fabric is a fine art. [*Designing* is a gerund, so *the* is not used.]
YES	**The designing** of fabric is a fine art. [*The* is used because *fabric* is the OBJECT OF THE PREPOSITION *of* and *designing* is meant in a specific sense.]

EXERCISE 42-1

Consulting Chapter 42, select the correct choice from the words in parentheses and write it in the blank.

EXAMPLE   For centuries, (a, an, the) **the** heart was regarded with awe by physicians.

1. As (a, an, the) _____ result, (a, an, the) _____ first surgeon to cut into (a, an, the) _____ human heart had to overcome many fears and superstitions.
2. Asked to guess when this surgery was first tried, most people would say in (a, an, the) _____ middle of (a, an, the) _____ twentieth century.
3. Heart surgery actually was first performed in 1893 by (a, an, the) _____ African-American surgeon named Daniel Hale Williams.
4. (A, An, The) _____ injured young man was brought to (a, an, the) _____ Chicago hospital with (a, an, the) _____ knife wound in (a, an, the) _____ heart.
5. Surgeon Williams cast aside age-old taboos and dared to operate— successfully—on (a, an, the) _____ heart.

ANSWERS & COVERAGE: EXERCISE 42–1

1. *a* result [nonspecific use of singular count noun]; *the* first surgeon to cut into [singular count noun made specific by the word *first* and the phrase *to cut into . . . ,* Rule 3 in Chart 161]; *the* human heart [representative use of singular count noun, Rule 2]

2. *the* middle of *the* twentieth century [widely understood meaning of singular count nouns, Rule 1]

3. *an* African-American surgeon [first use of noun, *an* before vowel sound]

4. *An* injured young man, *a* Chicago hospital, *a* knife wound [first use of nouns, *an* or *a* depending on vowel or consonant sound]; *the* heart [wide comprehension of noun's meaning and the context make use specific, Rules 1 & 4]

5. *the* heart [wide comprehension, context, Rules 1 & 4]

43 *Word Order*
ESL

HOW TO USE CHAPTER 43 ESL EFFECTIVELY

1. Use this chapter together with these handbook sections:
    - 7k–7o SENTENCE patterns
    - 7e ADJECTIVES
    - 7p sentence types
    - 7f ADVERBS
    - 7m MODIFIERS
    - 11f VERBS in inverted word order
    - 7o CLAUSES
2. Remember that throughout this handbook, you can find the defini-
    tions of words printed in SMALL CAPITAL LETTERS in the Glossary of
    Terms.
3. Also, use any **cross-references** (usually given in parentheses) to
    find full explanations of key concepts.

    This chapter can help you with several issues of word order in
sentences. Section 43a discusses standard word order for English sentences and important variations. Section 43b discusses the placement of
adjectives. Section 43c discusses the placement of adverbs.

43a   **Understanding standard and inverted
word order in sentences**

    In **standard word order,** the most common pattern for declara-
tive sentences in English, the SUBJECT comes before the VERB. (To better understand these concepts, review sections 7k–7o.)

       SUBJECT   VERB

       That book   was heavy.

With **inverted word order,** the MAIN VERB or an AUXILIARY VERB comes before the subject. The most common use of inverted word order in English is forming **direct questions.** Questions that can be answered with "yes" or "no" begin with a form of *be* used as a main verb, or with an auxiliary verb (*be, do, have*), or with a modal auxiliary (*can, should, will,* and others—see Chapter 46 ESL).

QUESTIONS THAT CAN BE ANSWERED WITH YES OR NO

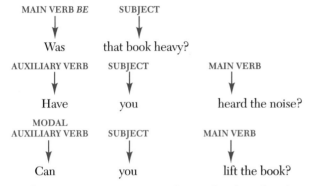

MAIN VERB *BE*	SUBJECT	
Was	that book heavy?	

AUXILIARY VERB	SUBJECT	MAIN VERB
Have	you	heard the noise?

MODAL AUXILIARY VERB	SUBJECT	MAIN VERB
Can	you	lift the book?

To form a yes/no question with a verb other than *be* as the main verb and when there is no auxiliary or modal as part of a verb phrase, use the appropriate form of the auxiliary verb *do.*

AUXILIARY VERB	SUBJECT	MAIN VERB
Do	you	want me to put the book away?

A question that begins with a **question-forming word** like *why, when, where,* or *how* cannot be answered with "yes" or "no": **Why did** *the book fall?* Some kind of information must be provided to answer such a question; the answer cannot be "yes" or "no." Information is needed: for example, *It was too heavy for me.*

Most information questions follow the same rules of inverted word order as yes/no questions.

INFORMATION QUESTIONS: INVERTED ORDER

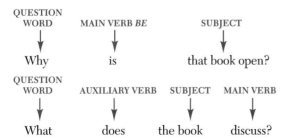

QUESTION WORD	MAIN VERB *BE*	SUBJECT	
Why	is	that book open?	

QUESTION WORD	AUXILIARY VERB	SUBJECT	MAIN VERB
What	does	the book	discuss?

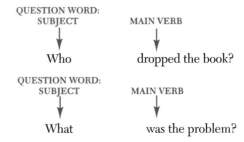

When *Who* or *What* functions as the subject in a question, however, use standard word order.

INFORMATION QUESTIONS: STANDARD ORDER

QUESTION WORD: SUBJECT	MAIN VERB
↓	↓
Who	dropped the book?

QUESTION WORD: SUBJECT	MAIN VERB
↓	↓
What	was the problem?

! ✤ ALERT: When a question has more than one auxiliary verb, put the subject after the first auxiliary verb.

The same rules apply to emphatic exclamations: ***Was** that book heavy!* ***Did** she enjoy that book!*

Also, when you use negatives such as *never, hardly ever, seldom, rarely, not only,* or *nor* to start a clause, use inverted order. These sentence pairs show the differences.

I have never seen a more exciting movie. [standard order]

Never have I seen a more exciting movie. [inverted order]

She is not only a talented artist **but also** an excellent musician.

Not only is she a talented artist, but **she is also** an excellent musician.

I didn't like the book, and **my husband didn't either.**

I didn't like the book, and **neither did my husband.**

! ✤ USAGE ALERT: With indirect questions, use standard word order: *She asked **how I dropped the book*** (not *She asked **how did I drop the book***). ✤

❖ STYLE ALERT: Word order deliberately inverted can be effective, when used sparingly, to create emphasis in a sentence that is neither a question nor an exclamation (also see 19f). ❖

Understanding the placement of adjectives

43b

Adjectives modify—that is, they describe or limit—NOUNS, PRO-NOUNS, and word groups that function as nouns (see section 7e). In English, an adjective comes directly before the noun it describes. However, when more than one adjective describes the same noun, several sequences may be possible. Chart 163 shows the most common order for positioning several adjectives.

WORD ORDER FOR MORE THAN ONE ADJECTIVE   163

1. **Determiners, if any:** *a, an, the, my, your, Jan's, this, that, these, those,* and so on

2. **Expressions of order, including ordinal numbers, if any:** *first, second, third, next, last, final,* and so on

3. **Expressions of quantity, including cardinal (counting) numbers, if any:** *one, two, three, few, each, every, some,* and so on

4. **Adjectives of judgment or opinion, if any:** *pretty, happy, ugly, sad, interesting, boring,* and so on

5. **Adjectives of size and/or shape, if any:** *big, small, short, round, square,* and so on

6. **Adjectives of age and/or condition, if any:** *new, young, broken, dirty, shiny,* and so on

7. **Adjectives of color, if any:** *red, green blue,* and so on

8. **Adjectives that can also be used as nouns, if any:** *French, Protestant, metal, cotton,* and so on

9. **The noun**

1	2	3	4	5	6	7	8	9
A		few		tiny		red		ants
The	last	six					Thai	carvings
My			fine		old		oak	table

QUOTATION ABOUT WRITING

There are, of course, basic principles to be observed: Adjectives are to be avoided unless they are strictly necessary; adverbs too, which is even more important. When I open a book and find that so and so has "answered sharply" or "spoken tenderly," I shut it again: It's the dialogue itself which should express the sharpness or the tenderness without any need to use adverbs to underline them.

—Graham Greene

TEACHING TIP: ESL

Often, students for whom English is a second language ask instructors to suggest ways to increase fluency in the writing of English. Given their varied backgrounds (culture, age, gender, and facility with language—both the first language and English), not all ESL students respond equally well to the same suggestion, so this idea has to be tailored accordingly.

Here is a variation on keeping a journal that can help ESL students think and express themselves somewhat more freely than they might be used to, at least compared with expectations in U.S. colleges. This variation starts where many ESL students are most comfortable: writing down facts and other types of information.

I suggest that students buy a thick notebook to keep a daily ESL journal. On the left side of each page, they should write a few sentences of information to help them easily recall the day's events. On the right side, they should write any kind of creative thought about those events: perhaps a story they recall, an interesting word to discuss, a mood to describe, or even a poem or dialogue. If they see a movie or read a book or a newspaper or magazine article, they should write down on the left side the title, the actors' or characters' names, and a factual summary of the material. On the right side, they should give their comments about what they liked or didn't. They might even try to write part of a movie script or a novel or a memory, just to practice and enjoy writing.

An added bonus is that students who keep an ESL journal are likely to find that they have done some work for many assignments even before the assignments have been given. Their journals can provide them with many subjects and examples to use when they are asked to write. Also, their practice with ideas in writing can make it easier for them to talk in class about their ideas.

43c Understanding the placement of adverbs

Adverbs modify—that is, describe or limit—VERBS, ADJECTIVES, other adverbs, or entire sentences (see section 7f). Adverbs are usually positioned first, in the middle, or last in clauses. Chart 164 summarizes adverb types, what they tell about the words they modify, and where each type can be placed.

TYPES OF ADVERBS AND WHERE TO POSITION THEM   164

■ **Adverbs of manner**
- describe *how* something is done
- usually are in middle or last position

> Nick **carefully** groomed the dog
> Nick groomed the dog **carefully.**

■ **Adverbs of time**
- describe *when* or *how long* about an event
- usually are in the first or last position

> *First*, he shampooed the dog.
> He shampooed the dog *first*.

- include *just, still,* and *already,* and similar adverbs, which usually are in the middle position

> He had **already** brushed the dog's coat.

■ **Adverbs of place**
- describe *where* an event takes place
- usually are in the last position

> He lifted the dog **into the tub**

■ **Adverbs of frequency**
- describe *how often* an event takes place
- usually are in the middle position

> Nick has **never** been bitten by a dog.

- are in the first position when they modify an entire sentence (see Sentence adverbs below)

> **Occasionally,** he is scratched while shampooing a cat.

TYPES OF ADVERBS AND WHERE TO POSITION THEM (continued)   164

■ **Adverbs of degree or emphasis**
- describe *how much* or *to what extent* about other modifiers
- are directly before the word they modify

> Nick is **extremely** calm around animals. *[Extremely* modifies *calm.]*

- include *only*, which is easy to misplace (see 15b-1)

■ **Sentence adverbs**
- modify the entire sentence rather than just one word or a few words
- include transitional words and expressions (see 4d-1) as well as *maybe, probably, possibly, fortunately, unfortunately, incredibly,* and others
- are in the first position

> **Incredibly,** he was once asked to groom a rat.

TYPES OF ADVERBS AND WHERE TO POSITION THEM (continued)

❖ PUNCTUATION ALERT: Unless they are very short (fewer than five letters), adverbs in the first position are usually followed by a comma. ❖

❖ USAGE ALERT: Do not let an adverb in a middle position separate a verb from its DIRECT OBJECT or INDIRECT OBJECT (see section 15b-3). ❖

!

!

EXERCISE 43-1

Consulting Chapter 43, find and correct any errors in word order.

1. The antique glass beautiful vase shattered on the floor.
2. Lu Mi had not meant to break her favorite mother's jar.
3. She was so upset that almost she cried.
4. When Lu Mi's mother heard the sound of shattering glass, she ran into the room asking, "You are all right?"
5. Knowing that Lu Mi had broken accidentally the vase, her mother was not angry extremely.

ANSWERS & COVERAGE: EXERCISE 43–1

1. The **beautiful antique glass** vase [43b: adjective of judgment precedes adjective of age; adjective of age precedes adjective derived from noun]
2. her **mother's favorite jar** [43b: determiner precedes descriptive adjective]
3. that **she almost** cried [43c, adverb of degree is positioned before word it modifies, *cried*]
4. **"Are you** all right?" [43a, inverted word order for questions, form of *be* precedes subject]
5. had **accidentally broken,** was **not extremely angry** [43c, adverbs of degree precede the word they modify]

44 Prepositions
ESL

1. Use this chapter together with these handbook sections.
    - 7g PREPOSITIONS
    - 21a using appropriate language

2. Remember that throughout this handbook, you can find the definitions of words printed in SMALL CAPITAL LETTERS in the Glossary of Terms.

3. Also, use any **cross-references** (usually given in parentheses) to find full explanations of key concepts.

Prepositions function with other words in PREPOSITIONAL PHRASES. Prepositional phrases usually indicate **where** (direction or location), **how** (by what means or in what way), or **when** (at what time or how long) about the words they modify.

This chapter can help you with several uses of prepositions, which function in combination with other words in ways that are often idiomatic. An idiom's meaning differs from the literal meaning of each individual word (see 20a). For example, *Yao-Ming **broke into** a smile* means that a smile appeared on Yao-Ming's face. However, the dictionary definitions of *break* and *into* imply that *broke into a smile* means "shattered the form of" a smile. Knowing which preposition to use in a specific context takes much experience reading, listening to, and speaking the language. A dictionary like the *Longman Dictionary of Contemporary English* or the *Oxford Advanced Learner's Dictionary* can be especially helpful when you need to find the correct preposition to use in cases not covered by this chapter. Section 44a lists many common prepositions. Section 44b discusses prepositions with some expressions of time and place. Section 44c discusses combinations of verbs and prepositions called PHRASAL VERBS. Section 44d discusses common expressions using prepositions.

TEACHING TIP: ESL

The use of prepositions in any language is idiomatic, so prepositions can be especially difficult for ESL students. In practice, the closer a first language is to English in structure and derivation, the fewer problems a speaker of that language will have with prepositions. Students who speak an Indo-European language (French, German, Spanish, etc.) usually have fewer problems. One important exception is Spanish speakers and the English prepositions *in, on,* and *at*. Spanish uses a single preposition, *en*, for all the meanings covered by *in, on,* and *at*. Consequently, Spanish speakers often need help in distinguishing among the three English prepositions.

Students who speak languages that are not related to English at all (Japanese, Korean, Chinese, Arabic, etc.) have the most difficulty with prepositions. These students need to understand that prepositions are idiomatic and that patience and practice are needed to learn them. (Vietnamese students who have studied French in school may benefit more by referring to a French-English dictionary for meanings and uses of prepositions rather than a Vietnamese-English dictionary.)

Recognizing prepositions

44a

Chart 165 shows many common prepositions.

COMMON PREPOSITIONS				165
about	before	except for	near	through
above	behind	excepting	next	throughout
according to	below	for	of	till
across	beneath	from	off	to
after	beside	in	on	toward
against	between	in addition to	onto	under
along	beyond	in back of	on top of	underneath
along with	but	in case of	out	unlike
among	by	in front of	out of	until
apart from	by means of	in place of	outside	up
around	concerning	inside	over	upon
as	despite	in spite of	past	up to
as for	down	instead of	regarding	with
at	during	into	round	within
because of	except	like	since	without

COMMON PREPOSITIONS

Using prepositions with expressions of time and place

44b

Chart 166 shows how to use the prepositions *in, at,* and *on* to deliver some common kinds of information about time and place. The chart, however, does not cover every preposition that indicates time or place, nor does it cover all uses of *in, at,* and *to.* For example, it does not explain the subtle difference in meaning delivered by the prepositions *at* and *in* in these two correct sentences: *I have a checking account **at** that bank* and *I have a safe-deposit box **in** that bank.* Also, the chart does not include expressions that operate outside the general rules. (Both these sentences are correct: *You ride **in** the car* and *You ride **on** the bus.*)

QUOTATION ABOUT WRITING

Not to have an audience is a kind of death.

—Tillie Olsen

QUOTATION ABOUT WRITING

I think I am a verb instead of a personal pronoun. A verb signifies to be, to do, to suffer. I signify all these.

—Ulysses S. Grant

TIME

- ■ *in* a year or a month (*during* is also correct but less common)

    in 1995   **in** May

- ■ *in* a period of time

    in a few months (seconds, days, years)

- ■ *in* a period of the day

    in the morning (afternoon, evening)

    in the daytime (morning, evening) but **at** night

- ■ *on* a specific day

    on Friday   **on** my birthday

- ■ *at* a specific time or period of time

    at noon   **at** 2:00   **at** dawn   **at** nightfall

    at takeoff (the time a plane leaves)

    at breakfast (the time a specific meal takes place)

PLACE

- ■ *in* a location surrounded by something else

    in the province of Alberta   **in** the kitchen

    in Utah   **in** the apartment

    in downtown Bombay   **in** the bathtub

- ■ *at* a specific location

    at your house   **at** the bank

    at the corner of Third Avenue and Main Street

- ■ *on* the top or the surface of something

    on page 20

    on the second floor, but **in** the attic or **in** the basement

    on Washington Street

    on the mezzanine

    on street level

44c   Using prepositions in phrasal verbs

Phrasal verbs, also called *two-word verbs* and *three-word verbs,* are VERBS that combine with prepositions to deliver their meaning.

In some phrasal verbs, the verb and the preposition should not be separated by other words: **Look at** the moon [not **Look** the moon **at**]. In **separable phrasal verbs,** other words in the sentence can separate the verb and the preposition without interfering with meaning: *I **threw away** my homework* is as correct as *I **threw** my homework **away**.*

Here is a list of some common phrasal verbs. The ones that cannot be separated are marked with an asterisk (*).

LIST OF SELECTED PHRASAL VERBS

ask out	get along with*	look into
break down	get back	look out for*
bring about	get off*	look over
call back	go over*	make up
drop off	hand in	run across*
figure out	keep up with*	speak to*
fill out	leave out	speak with*
fill up	look after*	throw away
find out	look around	throw out

Position a PRONOUN OBJECT between the words of a separable phrasal verb: *I threw **it** away.* Also, you can position an object phrase of several words between the parts of a separable phrasal verb: *I threw **my research paper** away.* However, when the object is a clause, do not let it separate the parts of the phrasal verb: *I threw away **all the papers that I wrote last year.***

Many phrasal verbs are informal and are used more in speaking than in writing. For academic writing, a more formal verb may be more appropriate than a phrasal verb. In a research paper, for example, *propose* or *suggest* might be better choices than *come up with.* For academic writing, acceptable phrasal verbs include *believe in, benefit from, concentrate on, consist of, depend on, dream of* (or *dream about*), *insist on, participate in, prepare for,* and *stare at.* None of these phrasal verbs can be separated.

EXERCISE 44-1

Consulting Chapter 44 and using the list of phrasal verbs in section 44b, write a one- or two-paragraph description of a typical day at work or school in which you use at least five phrasal verbs. After checking a dictionary, revise your writing, substituting for the phrasal verbs any more formal verbs that you think may be more appropriate for academic writing.

ANSWER: EXERCISE 44–1

Answers will vary.

TEACHING TIP: ESL

Some of the most obvious errors that ESL students make are with idiom. Idiomatic errors stand out in a sentence and can distract the reader from what is being said. However, many of the more glaring idiomatic errors, such as misuse of articles and prepositions, are actually rather trivial in terms of meaning and grammar. In many cases, "proper" idiom varies from state to state, even from city to city. In addition, most idiomatic errors are not going to disappear in a single semester; students have to work them out over time with more exposure to idiomatic English and more experience with English idiom. How, then, are teachers to judge what idiomatic errors are worth correcting? The following three criteria can be helpful: (1) Is the meaning of the sentence obscured or confused by the error? (2) Does the idiomatic error excessively distract the reader from the meaning of the sentence? (3) Is the idiomatic phrase common enough to cause the student trouble in the future?

ESL students can become frustrated because their problems with English idiom sometimes stubbornly persist despite extensive effort to make them "go away." Some ESL students can become obsessed with sentence-level errors, often to the point of overlooking major issues of logic, organization, and support. Instructors can help such students maintain a proper perspective by reminding them that grammar and idiom are only a small part of the overall writing process and that eliminating idiomatic errors is a matter of practice rather than knowledge.

44d ## Using prepositions in common expressions

In many common expressions, different prepositions convey great differences in meaning. For example, four prepositions can be used with the verb *agree* to create five different meanings.

agree to = to give consent [I cannot **agree to** buy you a new car.]

agree about = to arrive at a satisfactory understanding [We **agree about** your needing a car.]

agree on = to arrive at a satisfactory understanding [You and the seller must **agree on** a price for the car.]

agree with = to have the same opinion [I **agree with** you that you need a car.]

agree with = be suitable or healthful [The idea of having such a major expense does not **agree with** me.]

You can find entire books filled with English expressions that include prepositions. The list below shows a few that you are likely to use often.

LIST OF SELECTED EXPRESSIONS WITH PREPOSITIONS

ability in	different from	involved with [*someone*]
access to	faith in	knowledge of
accustomed to	familiar with	made of
afraid of	famous for	married to
angry with *or* at	frightened by	opposed to
authority on	happy with	patience with
aware of	in charge of	proud of
based on	independent of	reason for
capable of	in favor of	related to
certain of	influence on *or* over	suspicious of
confidence in	interested in	time for
dependent on	involved in [*something*]	tired of

45
ESL
Gerunds, Infinitives, and Participles

HOW TO USE CHAPTER 45 ESL EFFECTIVELY

1. Use this chapter together with these handbook sections:
   - 7d VERBALS
   - 11a SUBJECT-VERB AGREEMENT
   - 7k–7l SUBJECTS and OBJECTS
   - 18a–18c parallelism
   - 8b PRINCIPAL PARTS of verbs

2. Remember that throughout this handbook, you can find the definitions of words printed in SMALL CAPITAL LETTERS in the Glossary of Terms.

3. Also, use any **cross-references** (usually given in parentheses) to find full explanations of key concepts.

   Participles are verb forms (see 8b). A verb's *-ing* form is its present participle. The *-ed* form of a regular verb is its past participle; irregular verbs form their past participles in various ways (for example, *bend, bent; eat, eaten; think, thought*—for a complete list, see Chart 59 in section 8d). Participles can function as ADJECTIVES (*a **smiling** face, a **closed** book*).
   A verb's *-ing* form can also function as a NOUN (***Sneezing** spreads colds*), which is called a **gerund.** Another verb form, the infinitive, can also function as a noun. An **infinitive** is a verb's simple or base form usually preceded by the word *to* (*We want everyone **to smile***). Verb forms—participles, gerunds, and infinitives—functioning as nouns or modifiers are called ***verbals,*** as explained in section 7d.

QUOTATION ABOUT WRITING
I am a completely horizontal author. I can't think unless I'm lying down, either in bed or stretched on a couch.
—Truman Capote

QUOTATION ABOUT WRITING
The First Chapter Law is, "Don't spend much time on it. You're going to have to rewrite it."

—Tony Hillerman

This chapter can help you make the right choices among verbals. Section 45a discusses gerunds and infinitives used as subjects. Section 45b discusses verbs that are followed by gerunds, not infinitives. Section 45c discusses verbs that are followed by infinitives, not gerunds. Section 45d discusses meaning changes depending on whether certain verbs are followed by a gerund or by an infinitive. Section 45e explains that meaning does not change for certain sense verbs no matter whether they are followed by a gerund or an infinitive. Section 45f discusses differences in meaning between the present-participle form and the past-participle form of some modifiers.

45a Using gerunds and infinitives as subjects

Gerunds are used more commonly than infinitives as subjects. Sometimes, however, either is acceptable.

Choosing the right health club is important.

To choose the right health club is important.

! ❖ VERB ALERT: When a gerund or an infinitive is used alone as a subject, it is singular and requires a SINGULAR verb. When two or more gerunds or infinitives create a COMPOUND SUBJECT, they require a plural verb. (See sections 7k and 11d.) ❖

45b Using a gerund, not an infinitive, as an object after certain verbs

Some VERBS must be followed by GERUNDS used as DIRECT OBJECTS. Other verbs must be followed by INFINITIVES. Still other verbs can be followed by either a gerund or an infinitive. (A few verbs can change meaning depending on whether they are followed by a gerund or an infinitive; see 45d.) Chart 167 lists common verbs that must be followed by gerunds, not infinitives.

Yuri **considered** *calling* [not *to call*] the mayor.

He **was having trouble** *getting* [not *to get*] a work permit.

Yuri's boss **recommended** *taking* [not *to take*] someone who speaks English and Russian to the agency that issues the permits.

VERBS AND EXPRESSIONS THAT USE GERUNDS AFTER THEM 167

acknowledge	detest	mind
admit	discuss	object to
advise	dislike	postpone
anticipate	dream about	practice
appreciate	enjoy	put off
avoid	escape	quit
cannot bear	evade	recall
cannot help	favor	recommend
cannot resist	finish	regret
complain about	give up	resent
consider	have trouble	resist
consist of	imagine	risk
contemplate	include	suggest
defer from	insist on	talk about
delay	keep (on)	tolerate
deny	mention	understand

Gerund After go

Go is usually followed by an infinitive: *We can **go to see** [not* go *seeing] a movie tonight.* Sometimes, however, *go* is followed by a gerund in phrases such as *go swimming, go fishing, go shopping,* and *go driving: I will **go shopping** [not* go to shop] *after work.*

Gerund After be + *Complement* + *Preposition*

Many common expressions use a form of the verb *be* plus a COMPLEMENT plus a preposition. In such expressions, use a gerund, not an infinitive, after the preposition. Here is a list of some of the most frequently used expressions in this pattern.

LIST OF SELECTED *BE* + COMPLEMENT + PREPOSITION EXPRESSIONS

be (get) accustomed to	be interested in
be angry about	be prepared for
be bored with	be responsible for
be capable of	be tired of
be committed to	be (get) used to
be excited about	be worried about

We **are excited about *voting*** [not *to vote*] in the next election.

Who will **be responsible for *locating*** [not *to locate*] our polling place?

45
ESL

!

45b
cont.

♣ USAGE ALERT: Always use a gerund, not an infinitive, as the object of a preposition. Be especially careful when the word *to* is functioning as a preposition in a phrasal verb (see 44c): *We are committed **to changing*** [not *to change*] *the rules.* ♣

45c

Using an infinitive, not a gerund, as an object after certain verbs

Chart 168 lists selected common VERBS and expressions that must be followed by INFINITIVES, not GERUNDS, as OBJECTS.

She **wanted *to go*** [not *wanted going*] to the lecture.

Only three people **decided *to question*** [not *decided questioning*] the speaker.

VERBS AND EXPRESSIONS THAT USE INFINITIVES AFTER THEM			168
afford	claim	hope	promise
agree	consent	intend	refuse
aim	decide	know how	seem
appear	decline	learn	struggle
arrange	demand	like	tend
ask	deserve	manage	threaten
attempt	do not care	mean	volunteer
be left	expect	offer	vote
beg	fail	plan	wait
cannot afford	give permission	prepare	want
care	hesitate	pretend	would like

Infinitives After be + Complement

Gerunds are common in constructions that use forms of the verb *be*, a COMPLEMENT, and a PREPOSITION (see 45b). However, use an infinitive, not a gerund, when *be* plus a complement is not followed by a preposition.

We **are eager *to go*** [not *going*] camping.

I **am ready *to sleep*** [not *sleeping*] in a tent.

Infinitives to Indicate Purpose

Use an infinitive in expressions that indicate purpose: *I read a book **to learn** more about Mayan culture.* This sentence means "I read a book for the purpose of learning more about Mayan culture." *To learn* delivers the idea of purpose more concisely (see Chapter 16) than expressions such as "so that I can" or "in order to."

Infinitives with *the first, the last, the one*

Use an infinitive after the expressions *the first, the last,* and *the one: Soon-yi is **the first to arrive** [not arriving] and the last **to leave** [not leaving] every day.*

Unmarked Infinitives

Infinitives used without the word *to* are called **unmarked infinitives** or **bare infinitives.** An unmarked infinitive may be hard to recognize because it is not preceded by *to.* Some common verbs followed by unmarked infinitives are *feel, have, hear, let, listen to, look at, make* (meaning "compel"), *notice, see,* and *watch.*

Please let me **take** [not *to take*] you to lunch. [unmarked infinitive]

I want **to take** you to lunch. [marked infinitive]

I can have Kara **drive** [not *to drive*] us. [unmarked infinitive]

I will ask Kara **to drive** us. [marked infinitive]

The verb *help* can be followed by either a marked or an unmarked infinitive. Either is correct: *Help me **put** [or **to put**] this box in the car.*

♣ USAGE ALERT: Be careful to use parallel structure (see Chapter 18) correctly when you use two or more gerunds or infinitives after verbs. If two or more VERBAL OBJECTS follow one verb, put the verbals into the same form.

NO	We went **sailing** and **to scuba dive.**
YES	We went **sailing** and **scuba diving**.
NO	We heard the wind **blow** and the waves **crashing.**
YES	We heard the wind **blow** and the waves **crash.**
YES	We heard the wind **blowing** and the waves **crashing.**

Conversely, if you are using verbal objects with COMPOUND PREDICATES, be sure to use the kind of verbal that each verb requires.

NO	We enjoyed **scuba diving** but do not plan **sailing** again. [*Enjoyed* requires a gerund object and *plan* requires an infinitive object; see Charts 166 and 167.]
YES	We enjoyed **scuba diving** but do not plan **to sail** again. ♣

QUOTATION ABOUT WRITING
I write the big scenes first, that is, the scenes that carry the meaning of the book, the emotional experience.
—Joyce Cary

QUOTATION ABOUT WRITING
Wearing down seven number two pencils is a good day's work.
—Ernest Hemingway

45d **Knowing how meaning changes when certain verbs are followed by a gerund or an infinitive as an object**

With stop

The verb *stop* followed by a GERUND means "finish, quit." *Stop* followed by an infinitive means "stop or interrupt one activity to begin another."

We **stopped eating.** [We finished our meal.]

We **stopped to eat.** [We stopped another activity, such as driving, in order to eat.]

With remember *and* forget

The verb *remember* followed by an infinitive means "not to forget to do something": *I must **remember to talk** with Isa. Remember* followed by a gerund means "recall a memory": *I **remember talking** in my sleep last night.*

The verb *forget* followed by an infinitive means "to not do something": *If you **forget to put** a stamp on that letter, it will be returned. Forget* followed by a gerund means "to do something and not recall it": *I **forget having put** the stamps in the refrigerator.*

With try

The verb *try* followed by an infinitive means "make an effort": *I **tried to find** your jacket.* Followed by a gerund, *try* means "experiment with": *I **tried jogging** but found it too difficult.*

45e **Understanding that meaning does not change whether a gerund or an infinitive follows certain sense verbs**

Sense VERBS include words such as *see, notice, hear, observe, watch, feel, listen to,* and *look at.* The meaning of these verbs is usually not affected whether they are followed by a GERUND or by an INFINITIVE as an OBJECT. *I **saw** the water **rise** and I **saw** the water **rising** both have the same meaning in American English.

EXERCISE 45-1

Consulting sections 45b, 45c, 45d, and 45e, write the correct form of verbal object (either a gerund or an infinitive) for each verb in parentheses.

EXAMPLE

Everyone would like (find) <u>to find</u> easier ways to use computers.

1. Think about (hold) _____ a computer on your lap and (write) _____ on its screen with a pen.
2. Several new computers will let you (do) _____ just that.
3. Engineers have developed these new machines, called "pen-based" computers, (replace) _____ pencil and paper.
4. No bigger than spiral notebooks and called electronic notebooks, pen-based computers have a special stylus for (write) _____ directly onto the flat screen.
5. No (train) _____ or (type) _____ is required.
6. Manufacturers hope (open) _____ up whole new markets.
7. Pen-based computers will help (revive) _____ slow sales of computers.
8. Many people who never considered (buy) _____ a computer before are starting (look) _____ seriously at the pen-based computer.
9. People who cannot be tied to a desk by a computer cord can now enjoy the convenience and power of a computer simply by (put) _____ down their clipboard and (pick) _____ up an electronic notebook.
10. I remember (wish) _____ for a notebook computer myself.

Choosing between -*ing* forms and -*ed* forms for adjectives

45f

Deciding whether to use the -*ing* form (PRESENT PARTICIPLE) or the -*ed* form (PAST PARTICIPLE of a regular VERB) as an ADJECTIVE in a specific sentence can be difficult. For example, *I am* **amused** and *I am* **amusing** are both correct in English, but their meanings are very different. To make the right choice, decide whether the modified NOUN or PRONOUN is causing or experiencing what the participle describes.

Use a present participle (-*ing*) to modify a noun or pronoun that is the agent or the cause of the action.

Mica described your **interesting** plan. [The noun *plan* causes what its modifier describes—interest; so *interesting* is correct.]

I find your plan **exciting.** [The noun *plan* causes what its modifier describes—excitement; so *exciting* is correct.]

Use a past participle (-*ed* in regular verbs) to modify a noun or pronoun that experiences or receives whatever the modifier describes.

An **interested** committee wants to hear your plan. [The noun *committee* experiences what its modifier describes—interest; so *interested* is correct.]

Excited by your plan, I called a board meeting. [The pronoun *I* experiences what its modifier describes—excitement; so *excited* is correct.]

Here are frequently used participles that convey very different meanings, depending on whether the -*ed* or the -*ing* form is used.

amused, amusing	frightened, frightening
annoyed, annoying	insulted, insulting
appalled, appalling	offended, offending
bored, boring	overwhelmed, overwhelming
confused, confusing	pleased, pleasing
depressed, depressing	reassured, reassuring
disgusted, disgusting	satisfied, satisfying
fascinated, fascinating	shocked, shocking

EXERCISE 45-2

Consulting section 45f, choose the correct participle.

EXAMPLE   It can be a (satisfied, satisfying) <u>satisfying</u> experience to learn about the lives of artists.

1. Artist Frida Kahlo led an (interested, interesting) _____ life.
2. When she was 18, (horrified, horrifying) _____ observers saw Kahlo (injured, injuring) _____ in a streetcar accident.
3. A (disappointed, disappointing) _____ Kahlo had to abandon her plan to study medicine.
4. Instead, she began to create paintings filled with (disturbed, disturbing) _____ images.
5. Some art critics consider Kahlo's paintings to be (fascinated, fascinating) _____ works of art even though many people find them (overwhelmed, overwhelming) _____ .

ANSWERS: EXERCISE 45-2

1. *interesting* (life conveys rather than experiences interest)
2. *horrified* (observers experience rather than convey horror); *injured* (Kahlo experiences rather than causes injury)
3. *disappointed* (Kahlo experiences rather than causes disappointment)
4. *disturbing* (images cause rather than experience disturbance)
5. *fascinating* (works of art cause rather than experience fascination); *overwhelming* (paintings overwhelm rather than experience being overwhelmed—*overwhelming* modifies the pronoun *them*, for which the referent is *paintings*)

46
ESL

Modal Auxiliary Verbs

HOW TO USE CHAPTER 46ESL EFFECTIVELY

1. Use this chapter together with these handbook sections.
   - ■ 7c recognizing VERBS
   - ■ 8j PROGRESSIVE FORMS
   - ■ 8e AUXILIARY VERBS
   - ■ 8g VERB TENSE
   - ■ 8l-8m SUBJUNCTIVE MOOD

2. Remember that throughout this handbook, you can find the definitions of words printed in SMALL CAPITAL LETTERS in the Glossary of Terms.

3. Also, use any **cross-references** (usually given in parentheses) to find full explanations of key concepts.

Auxiliary verbs are known as *helping verbs* because adding an auxiliary verb to a MAIN VERB helps the main verb convey additional information (see 8e). For example, the auxiliary verb *do* is important in turning sentences into questions. *You have to sleep* becomes a question when *do* is added: *Do you have to sleep?* The most common auxiliary verbs are forms of *be, have,* and *do.* Charts 60 and 61 in section 8e list the forms of these three verbs.

Modal auxiliary verbs are one type of auxiliary verb. They include *can, could, may, might, should, had better, must, will, would,* and others discussed in this chapter. They have only two forms: the present future and the past. Modals differ from *be, have,* and *do* used as auxiliary verbs in the ways discussed in Chart 169.

TEACHING TIP: ESL

It may help ESL students to realize that the extensive auxiliary verb system of English is linguistically quite unusual. Most languages alter the single verb form for conjugation instead of adding one or more auxiliary verbs. For this reason auxiliary verbs can present special difficulties, particularly the use of *do* in questions and negative statements. ESL students who try to translate into their first language can become confused by this "extra" word that carries no meaning in a question (*Do* you like pizza?) or a negative statement (I *do* not like pizza). To further complicate matters, forms of *do* can have an emphatic function in declarative sentences (I *do* like pizza; I *do* have time to eat some pizza).

QUOTATION ABOUT WRITING

I know very dimly when I start what's going to happen. I just have a very general idea, and then the thing develops as I write.

—Aldous Huxley

SUMMARY OF MODALS AND THEIR DIFFERENCES FROM OTHER AUXILIARY VERBS

169

■ Modals in the present or future are always followed by the simple form of a main verb: *I might **go** tomorrow.*

■ One-word modals have no *-s* ending in the third-person singular: *She **could** go with me, you **could** go with me, they **could** go with me.* (The two-word modal *have to* changes form to agree with its subject: *I **have to** leave, she **has to** leave.*) Auxiliary verbs other than modals usually change form for third-person singular: *I **have** talked with her, he **has** talked with her.*

■ Some modals change form in the past. Others (*should, would, must,* which convey probability, and *ought to*) use *have* + a past participle. *I **can** do it* becomes *I **could** do it* in past-tense clauses about ability. *I **could** do it* becomes *I **could have** done it* in clauses about possibility.

■ Modals convey meaning about ability, advisability, necessity, possibility, and other conditions: For example, *I can go* means "I am able to go." Modals do not indicate actual occurrences.

This chapter can help you use modals to convey shades of meaning. Section 46a discusses using modals to convey ability, necessity, advisability, possibility, and probability. Section 46b discusses using modals to convey preferences, plans or obligations, and past habits. Section 46c introduces modals in the PASSIVE VOICE.

46a Conveying ability, necessity, advisability, and possibility, and probability with modals

Conveying Ability

The modal *can* conveys ability now (in the present) and *could* conveys ability before (in the past). These words deliver the meaning of "able to." For the future, use *will be able to.*

> We **can** work late tonight. [*Can* conveys present ability.]
> I **could** work late last night, too. [*Could* conveys past ability.]
> I **will be able to** work late next Monday. [*Will be able* is future; *will* here is *not* a modal.]

Adding *not* between a modal and the main verb makes the CLAUSE negative: *We* **can not** (or **cannot**) *work late tonight;* **I could not** *work late last night;* **I will not be able to** *work late next Monday.*

❧ USAGE ALERT: You will often see negative forms of modals turned into CONTRACTIONS: *can't, couldn't, won't, wouldn't,* and others. Because contractions are considered informal usage by some instructors, you will never be wrong if you avoid them in academic writing except for reproducing spoken words. ❧

Conveying Necessity

The modals *must* and *have to* convey the message of a need to do something. Both *must* and *have to* are followed by the simple form of the main verb. In the present tense, *have to* changes form to agree with its subject.

> You **must** leave before midnight.
> She **has to** leave when I leave.

In the past tense, *must* is never used to express necessity. Instead, use *had to.*

PRESENT TENSE
> We **must** study today.
> We **have to** study today.

PAST TENSE
> We **had to** [not *We must*] take a test yesterday.

The negative forms of *must* and *have to* also have different meanings. *Must not* conveys that something is forbidden; *do not have to* conveys that something is not necessary.

> You **must not** sit there. [Sitting there is forbidden.]
> You **do not have to** sit there. [Sitting there is not necessary.]

Conveying Advisability or the Notion of a Good Idea

The modals *should* and *ought to* express the idea that doing the action of the main verb is advisable or is a good idea.

> You **should** go to class tomorrow morning.

In the past tense, *should* and *ought to* convey regret or knowing something through hindsight. They mean that good advice was not taken.

> You **should have** gone to class yesterday.
> **I ought to have** called my sister yesterday.

!

The modal *had better* delivers the meaning of good advice or warning or threat. It does not change form for tense.

You **had better** see the doctor before your cough gets worse.

Need to is often used to express strong advice, too. Its past-tense form is *needed to*.

You **need to** take better care of yourself.

Conveying Possibility

The modals *may, might,* and *could* can be used to convey an idea of possibility or likelihood.

We **may** become hungry before long.
We **could** eat lunch at the diner next door.

The past-tense forms for *may, might*, and *could* use these words followed by *have* and the past participle of the main verb.

I **could have studied** French in high school, but I studied Spanish instead.

Conveying Probability

In addition to conveying the idea of necessity (see Conveying Necessity, p. 775), the modal auxiliary verb *must* also can convey probability or likelihood. It means that a well-informed guess is being made.

Marisa **must** be a talented actress. She has been chosen to play the lead role in the school play.

When *must* conveys probability, the past tense is *must have* plus the past participle of the main verb.

I did not see Boris at the party; he **must have left** early.

EXERCISE 46-1

Consulting section 46a, fill in the blanks with the past-tense modal that expresses the meaning given in parentheses.

EXAMPLE   I (advisability) **should have** gone to bed at the regular time last night.

1. I (advisability) _____ learned my lesson after what happened in class today.
2. Because I (necessity, no choice) _____ finish writing a paper, I stayed up until 3:00 a.m.
3. In class today, I (ability) _____ not stay awake.

ANSWERS & COVERAGE:
EXERCISE 46–1

1. should have *or* ought to have [46a, past-tense form of auxiliary]
2. had to *or* needed to [46a, past-tense form of auxiliary]
3. could [46a past-tense form of auxiliary]

→

4. The instructor (making a guess) _____ seen my eyes close.
5. I woke up instantly when I heard him say, "You (advice, good idea) _____ stayed in bed if you (necessity, no choice) _____ sleep, Mr. Lee."

Conveying preferences, plans, and past habits with modals

46b

Conveying Preferences

The modals *would rather* and *would rather have* express a preference. *Would rather* (PRESENT TENSE) is used with the SIMPLE FORM of the MAIN VERB and *would rather have* (PAST TENSE) is used with the PAST PARTICIPLE of the main verb.

> We **would rather see** a comedy than a mystery.
> Carlos **would rather have stayed** home last night.

Conveying Plan or Obligation

A form of *be* followed by *supposed to* and the simple form of a main verb delivers a meaning of something planned or of an obligation.

> I **was supposed to meet** them at the bus stop.

Conveying Past Habit

The modals *used to* and *would* express the idea that something happened repeatedly in the past.

> I **used to** hate going to the dentist.
> I **would** dread visiting the dentist each time.

♣ USAGE ALERT: Both *used to* and *would* can be used to express repeated actions in the past, but *would* cannot be used for a situation that lasted for a duration of time in the past.

!

> **NO**   I **would** live in Arizona.
> **YES** I **used to** live in Arizona. ♣

Recognizing modals in the passive voice

46c

Modals use the ACTIVE VOICE, as shown in sections 46a and 46b. In the active voice, the subject does the action expressed in the MAIN VERB (see 8m-8o).

Modals can also use the PASSIVE VOICE. In the passive voice, the doer of the main verb's action is either unexpressed or is expressed as an OBJECT in a PREPOSITIONAL PHRASE starting with the word *by*.

PASSIVE	The waterfront **can be seen** from my window.
ACTIVE	I **can see** the waterfront from my window.
PASSIVE	The tax form **must be signed by** the person who fills it out.
ACTIVE	The person who fills out the tax form **must sign** it.

EXERCISE 46-2

Consulting Chapter 46, select the correct choice from the words in parentheses and write it in the blank.

EXAMPLE   I (would, used to) **used to** collect stamps.

1.   Devi (should have, should have been) _____ hired by the bookstore manager.
2.   The plane (must be landed, must have landed) _____ on time.
3.   You (ought not to have, ought not have) _____ said that.
4.   I am going to have some ice cream even though I (cannot, should not) _____ .
5.   You (might not have been, might not have) _____ left your checkbook at home.

1.   should have been [46c, passive modal auxiliary verb with *Devi* receiving the action of the verb]
2.   must have landed [46a, correct form for past-tense modal auxiliary verb expressing likelihood]
3.   ought not to have [46a, correct form for modal auxiliary verb expressing advisability]
4.   should not [46a, correct modal for expressing negative advisability rather than negative ability]
5.   might not have [46a, correct form for active modal auxiliary verb expressing likelihood or possibility]

Usage Glossary

This usage glossary presents the customary manner of using particular words and phrases. *Customary manner*, however, is not as firm in practice as the term implies. Usage standards change. If you think a word's usage might differ from what you read here, consult a dictionary published more recently than this book.

As used here, *informal* indicates that the word or phrase occurs commonly in speech but should be avoided in academic writing. Nonstandard indicates that the word or phrase should not be used in standard spoken English and in writing.

Some commonly confused words appear in this Usage Glossary. For an extensive list of homonyms and other commonly confused words, see 22b. Parts of speech, sentence structures, and other grammatical terms mentioned in this Usage Glossary are defined in the Terms Glossary, which starts on page TG-1.

a, an Use *a* before words beginning with consonants (*a **d**og*, *a **g**rade*, *a **h**ole*) or consonant sounds (*a **o**ne-day sale*, *a **E**uropean*). American English uses *a*, not *an*, with words starting with a pronounced *h*: *a* [not an] *historical event*.

accept, except *Accept* means "agree to; receive." As a verb, *except* means "exclude, leave out"; as a preposition, *except* means "leaving out": ***Except*** [preposition] *for one detail, the workers were ready to* ***accept*** [verb] *management's offer: They wanted the no-smoking rule* ***excepted*** [verb] *from the contract.*

advice, advise *Advice*, a noun, means "recommendation"; *advise*, a verb, means "recommend; give advice": *My* ***advice*** *is to do what your physician* ***advises***.

affect, effect As a verb, *affect* means "cause a change in; influence" (*affect* also functions as a noun in the discipline of psychology). As a noun, *effect* means "result or conclusion"; as a verb, it means "bring about": *Many groups* ***effected*** [verb] *amplification changes at their concerts after discovering that high decibel levels* ***affected*** [verb] *their hearing. Many fans still choose to ignore sound's harmful* ***effects***.

aggravate, irritate *Aggravate* is used colloquially to mean "irritate." Use *aggravate* to mean "intensify; make worse." Use *irritate* to mean "annoy; make impatient."

ain't Nonstandard contraction for *am not*, *is not*, and *are not*.

all ready, already *Already* means "before; by this time"; *all ready* means "completely prepared": *The ballplayers were **all ready**, and the manager had **already** given the lineup card to the umpire.*

all right Two words, never one (not *alright*).

all together, altogether *All together* means "in a group, in unison"; *altogether* means "entirely, thoroughly": *The judge decided it was **altogether** absurd to expect the jurors to stay **all together** in one hotel room.*

allude, elude *Allude* means "refer to indirectly or casually"; *elude* means "escape notice": *They were **alluding** to budget cuts when they said that "constraints beyond our control enabled the suspect to **elude** us."*

allusion, illusion An *allusion* is an indirect reference to something; an *illusion* is a false impression or idea.

a lot Informal for *a great deal* or *a great many*; avoid it in academic writing.

a.m., p.m. Use only with numbers, not as substitutes for the words *morning, afternoon*, or *evening*: *We will arrive in the **afternoon*** [not *in the p.m.*].

among, between Use *among* for three or more items and *between* for two items: *My roommates and I discussed **among** ourselves the choice **between** staying in school and getting full-time jobs.*

amount, number Use *amount* for uncountable things (*wealth, work, corn, happiness*); use *number* for countable items: *The **amount** of rice to cook depends on the **number** of dinner guests.*

and/or Appropriate in business and legal writing when either or both items it connects can apply: *This process is quicker if you have a modem **and/or** a fax machine.* In the humanities, usually express alternatives in words: *This process is quicker if you have a modem, a fax machine, or both.*

anymore Use *anymore* with the meaning "now, any longer" in negations or questions only: *No one knits **anymore**.* For positive statements, use an adverb such as *now*: *Summers are so hot **now*** [not *anymore*] *that holding yarn is unbearable.*

anyplace Informal for any place or anywhere.

anyways, anywheres Nonstandard for anyway, anywhere.

apt, likely, liable *Apt* and *likely* are used interchangeably. Strictly, *apt* indicates a tendency or inclination: *Allen is **apt** to leave early on Friday. Likely* indicates a reasonable expectation or greater certainty than *apt: I will **likely** go with him to the party. Liable* denotes legal responsibility or implies unpleasant consequences: *Maggy and Gabriel are* **liable** *to be angry if neither of us shows up.*

as, like, as if, as though Use *as*, not *like*, as a subordinating conjunction introducing a clause: *This hamburger tastes good,* **as** [not *like*] *a hamburger should.* Use *as if* (or *as though*), not *like*, to introduce a subjunctive or other conditional clause: *That hamburger tastes* **as if** [not *like*] *it had been grilled all day. As* and *like* can both function as prepositions in comparisons. Use *like* to suggest a point of similarity or an area of resemblance, but not complete likeness, between nouns or pronouns: *Mexico,* **like** [not *as*] *Argentina, belongs to the United Nations.* Use *as* to show equivalence: *Beryl acted* **as** [not *like*] *the moderator of our panel.* Also, if the items are in prepositional phrases, use *as* even if you are suggesting only one point of similarity: *In Mexico,* **as** [not *like*] *in Argentina, Spanish is the main language.*

assure, ensure, insure *Assure* means "promise, convince"; *ensure* means "make certain or secure"; *insure* means "indemnify or guarantee against loss" and is reserved for financial or legal certainty, as in insurance: *The agent* **assured** *me that he could* **insure** *my rollerblades but that only I could* **ensure** *that my elbows and knees would outlast the skates.*

as to Avoid as a substitute for *about: They answered questions* **about** [not *as to*] *their safety record.*

awful, awfully The adjective *awful* means "causing fear." Avoid it as a substitute for intensifiers such as *very* or *extremely.* In academic writing, also avoid the informal usage of the adverb *awfully* for *very* or *extremely.*

a while, awhile As two words, *a while* is an article and a noun that can function as a subject or object. As one word, *awhile* is an adverb; it modifies verbs. In a prepositional phrase, the correct form is *a while: for a while, in a while, after a while.*

bad, badly *Bad* is an adjective; use it after linking verbs. (Remember that verbs like *feel* and *smell* can function as either linking verbs or action verbs.) *Badly* is an adverb and is nonstandard after linking verbs; see 12d: *Farmers feel* **bad** *because a* **bad** *drought has* **badly** *damaged the crops.*

been, being *Been* is the past participle of the verb *be; being* is the present participle of *be*, used in the progressive form: *You* **are being** [not *been*] *silly if you think I believe you* **have been** [not *being*] *to Sumatra.*

being as, being that Nonstandard for *because* or *since: We forfeited the game* **because** [not *being as* or *being that*] *our goalie has appendicitis.*

beside, besides *Beside* is a preposition meaning "next to, by the side of": *She stood* **beside** *the new car, insisting that she would drive.* As a preposition, *besides* means "other than, in addition to": *No one besides her had a driver's license.* As an adverb, besides means "also, moreover": *Besides, she owned the car.*

better, had better Used in place of *had better, better* is informal: *We had better* [not *We better*] *be careful.*

breath, breathe Breath is a noun; breathe is a verb.

bring, take Use *bring* for movement from a distant place to a near place or to the speaker; use *take* for movement from a near place or from the speaker to a distant place: *If you bring a leash when you come to my house, you can take Vicious to the vet.*

but, however, yet Use *but, however,* or *yet* alone, not in combination with each other: *The economy is strong, but* [not *but yet* or *but however*] *unemployment is high.*

calculate, figure, reckon Informal or regional for *estimate, imagine, expect, think,* and similar words.

can, may *Can* signifies ability or capacity; *may* requests or grants permission. In negations, however, *can* is acceptable in place of *may*: *You cannot* [or *may not*] *leave yet.*

can't hardly, can't scarcely Nonstandard; double negatives.

censor, censure The verb *censor* means "delete objectionable material; judge"; *censure* means "condemn; reprimand officially."

chairman, chairperson, chair Many writers and speakers prefer the gender-neutral terms *chairperson* and *chair* to *chairman*; *chair* is more common than *chairperson.*

choose, chose *Choose* is the simple form of the verb; *chose* is the past-tense form: *I chose the movie last week, so you choose it tonight.*

cloth, clothe *Cloth* is a noun meaning "fabric"; *clothe* is a verb meaning "cover with garments or fabric; dress."

complement, compliment *Complement* means "bring to perfection, go well with; complete"; *compliment* means "praise; flatter": *They complimented us on the design of our experiment, saying that it complemented work done twenty years ago.*

conscience, conscious The noun *conscience* means "a sense of right and wrong"; the adjective *conscious* means "being aware or awake."

consensus of opinion Redundant; use *consensus* only.

continual(ly), continuous(ly) *Continual* means "occurring repeatedly"; *continuous* means "going on without interruption": *Intravenous fluids were given continuously for three days after surgery; nurses were continually hooking up new bottles of saline.*

couple, couple of Nonstandard for *a few* or *several*: *Rest for **a few*** [not *a couple* or *a couple of*] *minutes.*

data Plural of *datum*, a rarely used word. Usage commonly treats *data* as a singular, using a singular verb.

different from, different than *Different from* is preferred for formal writing; *different than* is common in speech.

disinterested, uninterested *Disinterested* means "impartial"; *uninterested* means "indifferent; not concerned with."

don't A contraction for *do not*, but not for *does not* (*doesn't*): *She **doesn't*** [not *don't*] *like crowds.*

emigrate from, immigrate to *Immigrate to* means "enter a country to live there"; *emigrate from* means "leave one country to live in another."

enthused Nonstandard substituting for the adjective *enthusiastic*: *Are you **enthusiastic*** [not *enthused*] *about seeing a movie?*

etc. Abbreviation for the Latin *et cetera*, meaning "and the rest." For writing in the humanities, avoid in-text use of *etc.*; acceptable substitutes are *and the like, and so on, and so forth.*

everyday, every day The adjective *everyday* means "daily" and modifies nouns; *every day* is an adjective-noun combination, which functions as a subject or object: *I missed the bus **every day** last week. Being late for work has become an **everyday** occurrence.*

everywheres Nonstandard for everywhere.

explicit, implicit *Explicit* means "directly stated or expressed"; *implicit* means "implied, suggested": *The warning on cigarette packs is **explicit**: "Smoking is dangerous to health." The **implicit** message is "Don't smoke."*

farther, further Although many writers reserve *farther* for geographical distances and *further* for all other cases, current usage treats them as interchangeable.

fewer, less Use *fewer* for anything that can be counted (with count nouns): ***fewer** dollars, **fewer** fleas, **fewer** haircuts.* Use *less* with collective or other noncount nouns: ***less** money, **less** scratching, **less** hair.*

fine, find *Fine* can be a noun or an adjective: *She risked a $100 **fine** for parking in a reserved space when she ran into Sears to buy a **fine** electric drill. Find* is the simple form of the verb: *We **find** new evidence each day.*

former, latter When two items are referred to, *former* signifies the first one and *latter* signifies the second. Do not use *former* and *latter* for references to more than two items.

go, say *Go* is nonstandard for *say, says*, or *said: After he stepped on my hand, he **said*** [not *he goes*], *"Your hand was in my way."*

gone, went *Gone* is the past participle of *go*; *went* is the past tense of *go: They **went*** [not *gone*] *to the concert after Ira **had gone*** [not *had went*] *home.*

good and Nonstandard intensifier: *They were exhausted* [not *good and tired*].

good, well *Good* is an adjective (***good idea***). Using it as an adverb is nonstandard. *Well* is the equivalent adverb: *run well* [not *run good*].

got, have *Got* is nonstandard in place of *have: What do we **have*** [not *got*] *for supper?*

have, of Use *have*, not *of*, after such verbs as *could, should, would, might, must: You should **have*** [not *should of*] *called first.*

have got, have got to Avoid using *have got* when *have* alone delivers your meaning: *I **have*** [not *have got*] *two more sources to read.* Avoid *have got to* for *must: I **must*** [not *have got to*] *turn in a preliminary thesis statement by Monday.*

hopefully An adverb meaning "with hope, in a hopeful manner" or "it is hoped that," *hopefully* can modify a verb, an adjective, or another adverb: *They waited **hopefully** for the plane to land. Hopefully* is commonly used as a sentence modifier with the meaning "I hope," but you should avoid this usage in academic writing: *I hope* [not *Hopefully*] *the plane will land safely.*

if, whether Use either *if* or *whether* at the start of a noun clause: *I don't know **if*** [or *whether*] *I want to dance with you.* In conditional clauses, use *whether* (or *whether or not*) when alternatives are expressed or implied: *I will dance with you **whether or not** I like the music.* Similarly: *I will dance with you **whether** the next song is fast or slow.* Use *if* in a conditional clause that does not express or imply alternatives: ***If*** *you promise not to step on my feet, I will dance with you.*

imply, infer *Imply* means "hint at or suggest without stating outright"; *infer* means "draw a conclusion from what is being expressed." A writer or speaker implies; a reader or listener infers: *When the governor **implied** that she would not seek reelection, reporters **inferred** that she hoped to run for Vice President.*

incredible, incredulous *Incredible* means "extraordinary; not believable"; *incredulous* means "unable or unwilling to believe." A person would be incredulous in response to finding something incredible: *Listeners were **incredulous** as the freed hostages described the **incredible** hardships they had experienced.*

inside of, outside of Nonstandard for *inside* or *outside: She waited **outside*** [not *outside of*] *the dormitory.* Also, *inside of* meaning "in less than" in time references is an Americanism inappropriate for academic writing: *I changed clothes **in less than*** [not *inside of*] *ten minutes.*

irregardless Nonstandard for *regardless*.

is when, is where Avoid these constructions in giving definitions: *Defensive driving **involves drivers' staying alert** [not is when drivers stay alert] to avoid accidents that other drivers might cause.*

its, it's *Its* is a personal pronoun in the possessive case: *The dog buried **its** bone. It's* is a contraction of *it is* or *it has*: ***It's** a hot day; **it's** seemed hotter than usual because the humidity is high.*

kind, sort Use *this* or *that* with these singular nouns; use *these* or *those* with the plural nouns *kinds* and *sorts*. Also, do not use *a* or *an* after *kind of* or *sort of*: *Drink **these kinds** of fluids* [not this kind of fluids] *on **this sort** of* [not sort of a] *day.*

kind of, sort of Informal as adverbs meaning "in a way; somewhat": *The hikers were **somewhat** [not kind of] dehydrated by the time they got back to camp.*

later, latter *Later* means "after some time; subsequently"; *latter* refers to the second of two: *The college library stays open **later** than the town library; also, the **latter** is closed on weekends.*

lay, lie *Lay (laying, laid)* means "place or put something, usually on something else" and needs a direct object; *lie (lying, lay, lain)*, meaning "recline," does not take a direct object; see 8f. Substituting *lay* for *lie* is nonstandard: ***Lay** [not lie] the blanket down, and then **lay** the babies on it so they can **lie** [not lay] in the shade.*

leave, let *Leave* means "depart"; *let* means "allow, permit." *Leave* is nonstandard for *let*: ***Let** [not Leave] me use your car tonight.*

lots, lots of, a lot of Informal for *many, much, a great deal*: ***Many** [not A lot of] bees were in the hive.*

may be, maybe *May be* is a verb phrase; *maybe* is an adverb: *Our team **may be** tired, but **maybe** we can win anyway.*

media Plural of *medium*, but common usage pairs it with a singular verb. In most cases, a more specific word is preferable: ***Television reporters** offend* [not The media offends] *viewers by shouting questions at grief-stricken people.*

morale, moral *Morale* is a noun meaning "a mental state relating to courage, confidence, or enthusiasm." As a noun, *moral* means "ethical lesson implied or taught by a story or event"; as an adjective, *moral* means "ethical": *One **moral** to draw from corporate downsizings is that overstressed employees suffer from low **morale**. Under such stress, sometimes even employees with high **moral** standards steal time, supplies, or products from their employers.*

most Nonstandard for *almost*: ***Almost** [not Most] all the dancers agree. Most* is correct as the superlative form of an adjective (*some, more,* *most*): ***Most*** *dancers agree*. It also makes the superlative form of adverbs and some adjectives: ***most*** *suddenly*, ***most*** *important*.

Ms. A woman's title free of reference to marital status, equivalent to *Mr.* for men.

nowheres Nonstandard for *nowhere*.

off of Nonstandard for *off*: *Don't fall* **off** [not off of] *the piano*.

OK, O.K., okay All three forms are acceptable in informal writing. In academic writing, try to express meaning more specifically: *The weather was* **satisfactory** [not okay] *for the race*.

on account of Wordy; use *because* or *because of*: ***Because of*** [not On account of] *the high humidity, paper jams occur in the photocopier*.

percent, percentage Use *percent* with specific numbers: *two percent, 95 percent*. Use *percentage* when descriptive words accompany amounts that have been expressed as percentages: *About **47 percent** of the eligible U.S. population votes regularly; but when presidential elections are excluded, the **percentage** [not percent] of voters in the population drops sharply*.

plus Nonstandard as a substitute for *and*: *The band will do three concerts in Hungary,* **and** [not plus] *it will tour Poland for a month*. Nonstandard as well as a substitute for *also, in addition, moreover*: **Also** [not Plus], *it may be booked to do one concert in Vienna*.

precede, proceed *Precede* means "go before"; *proceed* means "advance, go on, undertake, carry on": ***Preceded*** *by elephants and tigers, the clowns* ***proceeded*** *into the tent*.

pretty Informal qualifying word; use *rather, quite, somewhat,* or *very* in academic writing: *The flu epidemic was* **quite** [not pretty] *severe*.

principal, principle *Principle* means "a basic truth or rule." As a noun, *principal* means "chief person; main or original amount"; as an adjective, *principal* means "most important": *During assembly, the* **principal** *said, "A* **principal** *value in this society is the* **principle** *of free speech."*

raise, rise *Raise (raised, raising)* needs a direct object; *rise (rose, risen, rising)* does not take a direct object. Using these verbs interchangeably is nonstandard: *What if the mob* **rises** [not raises] *up and runs amok?*

rarely ever Informal; in academic writing, use *rarely* or *hardly ever*: *The groups* **rarely** [not rarely ever] *meet, so they* **hardly ever** *interact*.

real, really Nonstandard intensifiers.

reason is because Redundant; use *reason is that*: *One* **reason** *we moved away* **is that** [not is because] *we changed jobs*.

reason why Redundant; use either *reason* or *why*: *I still do not know* **the reason that** [or I still do not know **why**, not the **reason** why] *they left home*.

regarding, in regard to, with regard to Too stiff or wordy for most writing purposes; use *about, concerning,* or *for: What should I do **about*** [not *with regard to*] *dropping this course?*

respective, respectively The adjective *respective* relates the noun it modifies to two or more individual persons or things; the adverb *respectively* refers to a second set of items in a sequence established by a preceding set of items: *After the fire drill, Dr. Pan and Dr. Moll returned to their **respective** offices, on the second and third floors, **respectively**.* (Dr. Pan has an office on the second floor; Dr. Moll has an office on the third floor.) Do not confuse *respective* and *respectively* with *respectful* and *respectfully*, which refer to showing regard for or honor to something or someone.

right Colloquial intensifier; use *quite, very, extremely,* or a similar word for most purposes: *You did **very** * [not *right*] *well on the quiz.*

seen Past participle of *see (see, saw, seen), seen* is a nonstandard substitute for the past-tense form, *saw.* As a verb, *seen* must be used with an auxiliary verb: *Last night, I **saw*** [not *seen*] *the show that you **had seen** in Florida.*

set, sit *Set (set, setting)* means "put in place, position, put down" and must have a direct object. *Sit (sat, sitting)* means "be seated." *Set* is nonstandard as a substitute for *sit: Sue **set*** [not *sat*] *the sandwiches beside the salad, made Spot **sit*** [not *set*] *down, and then **sat*** [not *set*] *on the sofa.*

shall, will *Shall* was once used with *I* or *we* for future-tense verbs, and *will* was used with all other persons (*We **shall** leave Monday, and he **will** leave Thursday*); but *will* is commonly used for all persons now. Similarly, distinctions were once made between *shall* and *should.* *Should* is much more common with all persons now, although *shall* is used about as often as *should* in questions asking what to do: ***Shall*** [or *Should*] *I get your jacket?*

should, would Use *should* to express condition or obligation: *If you **should** see them, tell them that they **should** practice what they preach.* Use *would* to express wishes, conditions, or habitual actions: *If you **would** buy a VCR for me, I **would** tape all the football games for you.*

sometime, sometimes, some time The adverb *sometime* means "at an unspecified time"; the adverb *sometimes* means "now and then"; *some time* is an adjective-noun combination meaning "an amount or span of time": ***Sometime** next year we have to take qualifying exams. I **sometimes** worry about finding **some time** to study for them.*

stationary, stationery *Stationary* means "not moving"; *stationery* refers to paper and related writing products.

such Informal intensifier; avoid it in academic writing unless it precedes a noun introducing a *that* clause: *That play got terrible* [not *such bad*] *reviews. It was* **such** *a dull drama that it closed after one performance.*

supposed to, used to The final *-d* is essential: *We were* **supposed to** [not *suppose to*] *leave early. I* **used to** [not *use to*] *wake up as soon as the alarm rang.*

sure Nonstandard for *surely* or *certainly: I was* **certainly** [not *sure*] *surprised at the results.*

than, then *Than* indicates comparison: *One is smaller* **than** *two. Then* relates to time: *I tripped and* **then** *fell.*

that there, them there, this here, these here Nonstandard for *that, them, this,* and *these,* respectively.

that, which Use *that* with restrictive (essential) clauses only; *which* can be used with both restrictive and nonrestrictive clauses, but many writers use *which* for nonrestrictive clauses only: *The house* **that** [or *which*] *Jack built is on Beanstalk Street,* **which** [not *that*] *runs past the reservoir.*

their, there, they're *Their* is a possessive; *there* means "in that place" or is part of an expletive construction; *they're* is a contraction of *they are:* **They're** *going to* **their** *accounting class in the building* **there** *behind the library.* **There are** *twelve sections of Accounting 101.*

theirself, theirselves, themself Nonstandard for *themselves.*

them Nonstandard for *these* or *those: Buy* **those** [not *them*] *strawberries.*

thusly Nonstandard for *thus.*

till, until Both are acceptable; except in expressive writing, avoid the contracted form *'til* in academic writing.

to, too, two *To* is a preposition; *too* is an adverb meaning "also; more than enough"; *two* is the number: *When you go* **to** *Chicago, visit the Art Institute. Go* **to** *Harry Caray's for dinner,* **too**. *It won't be* **too** *expensive because* **two** *people can share an entree.*

toward, towards Both are acceptable; *toward* is somewhat more common.

try and, sure and Nonstandard for *try to* and *sure to: If you* **try to** [not *try and*] *find a summer job, be* **sure to** [not *sure and*] *list on your resumé all the software programs you can use.*

type Nonstandard for *type of: Use that* **type of** [not *type*] *glue on plastic.*

unique An absolute adjective; use it without *more, most,* or other qualifiers, or use a different adjective: *Solar heating is* **uncommon** [not *rather unique*] *in the northeast. In only one home in Vermont, a* **unique** [not *very unique*] *heating system uses hydrogen for fuel.*

wait on Informal for *wait for*; appropriate in the context of persons giving service to others: *I had to **wait** a half hour for that clerk to **wait on** me.*

where Nonstandard for *that: I read **that** [not *where*] Michael Jordan might retire from basketball again.*

where . . . at Redundant; drop *at*: ***Where** is your **house** [not *house at*]?*

-wise The suffix *-wise* means "in a manner, direction, or position." Be careful not to attach *-wise* indiscriminately to create new words rather than using good words that already exist. When in doubt, check your dictionary to be sure that a *-wise* word you want to use is acceptable.

your, you're *Your* is a possessive; *you're* is the contraction of *you are*: ***You're** generous to share **your** Internet time with us.*

Terms Glossary

This glossary defines important terms used in this handbook, including the ones that are printed in SMALL CAPITAL LETTERS. Many of these glossary entries end with parenthetical references to the handbook section(s) or chapter(s) where the specific term is most fully discussed.

absolute phrase A phrase containing a subject and a participle that modifies an entire sentence: ***The semester*** [subject] ***being*** [present participle of *be*] ***over,*** *the campus looks deserted.* (7n)

abstract noun A noun that names things not knowable through the five senses: *idea, respect.* (7a)

active voice An attribute of verbs showing that the action or condition expressed in the verb is done by the subject, in contrast with the passive voice, which conveys that the action or condition of the verb is done to the subject. (8n–8o)

adjective A word that describes or limits (modifies) a noun, a pronoun, or a word group functioning as a noun: *silly, three.* (12)

adjective clause A dependent clause also known as a *relative clause*. An adjective clause modifies a preceding noun or pronoun and begins with a relative word (such as *who, which, that,* or *where*) that relates the clause to the noun or pronoun it modifies. Also see *clause.* (7o–2)

adverb A word that describes or limits (modifies) verbs, adjectives, other adverbs, phrases, or clauses: *loudly, very, nevertheless, there.* (12)

adverb clause A dependent clause beginning with a subordinating conjunction that establishes the relationship in meaning between the adverb clause and its independent clause. An adverb clause modifies the independent clause's verb or the entire independent clause. Also see *clause, conjunction.* (7o–2)

agreement The required match of number and person between a subject and verb or a pronoun and antecedent. A pronoun that expresses gender must match its antecedent in gender also. (11)

analogy An explanation of the unfamiliar in terms of the familiar. Like a simile, an analogy compares things not normally associated with each other; but unlike a simile, an analogy does not use *like* or *as* in making the comparison. Analogy is also a rhetorical strategy for developing paragraphs. (21c, 4f–8)

analysis A process of critical thinking that divides a whole into its component parts in order to understand how the parts interrelate. Sometimes called *division*, analysis is also a rhetorical strategy for developing paragraphs. (5, 4f–6)

antecedent The noun or pronoun to which a pronoun refers. (10, 11m–11r)

antonym A word opposite in meaning to another word. (20a)

APA style See *documentation style*.

appositive A word or group of words that renames a preceding noun or noun phrase: *my favorite month*, **October**. (7m–3)

argument A rhetorical attempt to convince others to agree with a position about a topic open to debate. (1b, 6)

articles Also called *determiners* or *noun markers*, articles are the words *a*, *an*, and *the*. *A* and *an* are indefinite articles, and *the* is a definite article; also see *determiner*. (7a, 42)

assertion A statement. In developing a thesis statement, an assertion is a sentence that makes a statement and expresses a point of view about a topic. (2n)

audience The readers to whom a piece of writing is directed. (1c)

auxiliary verb Also known as a *helping verb*, an auxiliary verb is a form of *be*, *do*, *have*, *can*, *may*, *will*, and others, that combines with a main verb to help it express tense, mood, and voice. Also see *modal auxiliary verb*. (8e)

base form See *simple form*.

bibliography A list of information about sources. (33)

brainstorming Listing all ideas that come to mind on a topic, and then grouping the ideas by patterns that emerge. (2g)

case The form of a noun or pronoun in a specific context that shows whether it is functioning as a subject, an object, or a possessive. In modern English, nouns change form in the possessive case only (*city* = form for subjective and objective cases; *city's* = possessive-case form). Also see *pronoun case*. (9)

cause and effect The relationship between outcomes (effects) and the reasons for them (causes). Cause-and-effect analysis is a rhetorical strategy for developing paragraphs. (5i, 5k, 4f–9)

chronological order Also called *time order*, an arrangement of information according to time sequence; an organizing strategy for sentences, paragraphs, and longer pieces of writing. (4e)

citation Information to identify a source referred to in a piece of writing. Also see *documentation*. (31, 33)

clause A group of words containing a subject and a predicate. A clause that delivers full meaning is called an *independent* (or *main*) *clause*. A clause that lacks full meaning by itself is called a *dependent* (or *subordinate*) *clause*. Also see *adjective clause, adverb clause, nonrestrictive element, noun clause, restrictive element*. (7o)

cliché An overused, worn-out phrase that has lost its capacity to communicate effectively: *flat as Kansas, ripe old age*. (21d)

climactic order Sometimes called *emphatic order*, climactic order is an arrangement of ideas or information from least important to most important. (4e)

clustering See *mapping*.

coherence The clear progression from one idea to another using transitional expressions, pronouns, selective repetition, and/or parallelism to make connections between ideas. (4d)

collective noun A noun that names a group of people or things: *family, committee*. (11h, 11r)

comma fault See *comma splice*.

comma splice The error that occurs when only a comma connects two independent clauses. (13)

common noun A noun that names a general group, place, person, or thing: *dog, house*. (7a)

comparative The form of a descriptive adjective or adverb that expresses a different degree of intensity between two: *bluer, less blue; more easily, less easily*. Also see *positive, superlative*. (12e)

comparison and contrast A rhetorical strategy for organizing and developing paragraphs by discussing a subject's similarities (comparison) and differences (contrast). (4f–7)

complement An element after a verb that completes the predicate, such as a direct object after an action verb or a noun or adjective after a linking verb. Also see *object complement, predicate adjective, predicate nominative, subject complement*.

complete predicate See *predicate*.

complete subject See *subject*.

complex sentence See *sentence types*.

compound predicate See *predicate*.

compound sentence See *sentence types*.

compound subject See *subject*.

concrete noun A noun naming things that can be seen, touched, heard, smelled, or tasted: *smoke, sidewalk*. (7a)

conjunction A word that connects or otherwise establishes a relationship between two or more words, phrases, or clauses. Also see *coordinating conjunction, correlative conjunction,* and *subordinating conjunction.*

coordinating conjunction A conjunction that joins two or more grammatically equivalent structures: *and, or, for, nor, but, so, yet.*

coordination The use of grammatically equivalent forms to show a balance or sequence of ideas. (17a–17d)

correlative conjunction A pair of words that joins equivalent grammatical structures, including *both . . . and, either . . . or, neither . . . nor, not only . . . but (also).*

count noun A noun that names items that can be counted: *radio, street, idea, fingernail.* (41a–41b, 42a–42b)

critical response Formally, an essay summarizing a source's central point or main idea and then presenting the writer's synthesized reactions in response. (5g)

cumulative sentence The most common structure for a sentence, with the subject and verb first, followed by modifiers adding details; also called a *loose sentence.* (19e)

dangling modifier A modifier that attaches its meaning illogically, either because it is closer to another noun or pronoun than to its true subject or because its true subject is not expressed in the sentence. (15c)

declarative sentence A sentence that makes a statement: *Sky diving is exciting.* Also see *exclamatory sentence, imperative sentence, interrogative sentence.*

deduction The process of reasoning from general claims to a specific instance. (5j–2)

definite article See *articles.*

demonstrative pronoun A pronoun that points out the antecedent: *this, these; that, those.*

denotation The dictionary definition of a word. (20a)

dependent clause A clause that cannot stand alone as an independent grammatical unit. Also see *adjective clause, adverb clause, noun clause.*

descriptive adjective An adjective that describes the condition or properties of the noun it modifies and (except for a very few such as *dead* and *unique*) has comparative and superlative forms: *flat, flatter, flattest.*

descriptive adverb An adverb that describes the condition or properties of whatever it modifies and that has comparative and superlative forms: *happily, more happily, most happily.*

determiner A word or word group, traditionally identified as an adjective, that limits a noun by telling "how much" or "how many" about it. Also called *expression of quantity, limiting adjective,* or *noun marker.* (41b, 42)

diction Word choice. (20, 21)

direct address Words naming a person or group being spoken to; written words of direct address are set off by commas: *The answer,* **my friends,** *lies with you. Go with them,* **Gene.** (24f)

direct discourse In writing, words that repeat speech or conversation exactly and so are enclosed in quotation marks.

direct object A noun or pronoun or group of words functioning as a noun that receives the action (completes the meaning) of a transitive verb. (7l)

direct question A sentence that asks a question and ends with a question mark: *Are you going?*

direct quotation See *quotation.*

documentation The acknowledgment of someone else's words and ideas used in any piece of writing by giving full and accurate information about the person whose words were used and where those words were found; for example, for a print source, documentation usually includes author name(s), title, place and date of publication, and related information. (31, 33)

documentation style Any of various systems for providing information about the source of words, information, and ideas quoted, paraphrased, or summarized from some source other than the writer. Documentation styles discussed in this handbook are MLA, APA, CM, and CBE. (33)

double negative A nonstandard negation using two negative modifiers rather than one. (12c)

drafting A part of the writing process in which writers compose ideas in sentences and paragraphs. (3b)

edited American English English language use that conforms to established rules of grammar, sentence structure, punctuation, and spelling; also called *standard English.* (21a–2)

editing A part of the writing process in which writers check the technical correctness of grammar, spelling, punctuation, and mechanics. (3d)

elliptical construction A sentence structure that deliberately omits words expressed elsewhere or that can be inferred from the context.

euphemism Language that attempts to blunt certain realities by speaking of them in "nice" or "tactful" words. (21e)

evidence Facts, data, examples, and opinions of others used to support assertions and conclusions.

exclamatory sentence A sentence beginning with *What* or *How* that expresses strong feeling: *What a ridiculous statement!*

expletive The phrase *there is (are)*, *there was (were)*, *it is*, or *it was* at the beginning of a clause, changing structure and postponing the subject: ***It is** Mars that we hope to reach* (compare *We hope to reach Mars*).

expository writing See *informative writing*.

expression of quantity See *determiner*.

faulty predication A grammatically illogical combination of subject and predicate. (15d–2)

finite verb A verb form that shows tense, mood, voice, person, and number while expressing an action, occurrence, or state of being.

first person See *person*.

freewriting Writing nonstop for a period of time to generate ideas by free association of thoughts. Focused freewriting may start with a set topic or may build on one sentence taken from earlier freewriting. (2f)

fused sentence The error of running independent clauses together without the required punctuation that marks them as complete units. (14)

future perfect progressive tense The form of the future perfect tense that describes an action or condition ongoing until some specific future time: *they will have been talking*.

future perfect tense The tense indicating that an action will have been completed or a condition will have ended by a specified point in the future: *they will have talked*.

future progressive tense The form of the future tense showing that a future action will continue for some time: *they will be talking*.

future tense The form of a verb, made with the simple form and either *shall* or *will*, expressing an action yet to be taken or a condition not yet experienced: *they will talk*.

gender Concerning languages, the classification of words as masculine, feminine, or neutral. In English, a few pronouns show changes in gender in third-person singular: *he, him, his*; *she, her, hers*; *it, its, its*. A few nouns naming roles change form to show gender difference: *prince, princess*, for example. (11q, 21b)

gerund A present participle functioning as a noun: ***Walking** is good exercise*. Also see *verbal*.

gerund phrase A gerund, its modifiers, and/or object(s), which functions as a subject or an object. (7n)

helping verb See *auxiliary verb*.

homonyms Words spelled differently that sound alike: *to, too, two.* (22b)

idiom A word, phrase, or other construction that has a different meaning from its usual meaning: *He lost his head. She hit the ceiling.*

illogical predication See *faulty predication.*

imperative mood The mood that expresses commands and direct requests, using the simple form of the verb and often implying but not expressing the subject, *you: Go.* (8l)

imperative sentence A sentence that gives a command: *Go to the corner and buy me a newspaper.*

indefinite article See *articles, determiner.*

indefinite pronoun A pronoun, such as *all, anyone, each,* and *others,* that refers to a nonspecific person or thing. (11p)

independent clause A clause that can stand alone as an independent grammatical unit. (7o–1)

indicative mood The mood of verbs used for statements about real things or highly likely ones: *I think Grace is arriving today.* (8l)

indirect discourse Reported speech or conversation that does not use the exact structure of the original and so is not enclosed in quotation marks. (15a-4)

indirect object A noun or pronoun or group of words functioning as a noun that tells to whom or for whom the action expressed by a transitive verb was done. (7l)

indirect question A sentence that reports a question and ends with a period: *I asked if you are going.*

indirect quotation See *quotation.*

induction The reasoning process of arriving at general principles from particular facts or instances. (5j–1)

infinitive A verbal made of the simple form of a verb and usually, but not always *to,* that functions as a noun, adjective, or adverb.

infinitive phrase An infinitive, its modifiers, and/or object, which functions as a noun, adjective, or adverb.

informal language Word choice that creates a tone appropriate for casual writing or speaking. (21a–1)

informative writing Writing that gives information and, when necessary, explains it; also known as *expository writing.* (1b)

intensive pronoun A pronoun that ends in *-self* and that intensifies its antecedent: *Vida **himself** argued against it.*

interjection An emotion-conveying word that is treated as a sentence, starting with a capital letter and ending with an exclamation point or a period: *Oh! Ouch!*

interrogative pronoun A pronoun, such as *whose* or *what*, that implies a question: **Who** *called*?

interrogative sentence A sentence that asks a direct question: *Did you see that?*

intransitive verb A verb that does not take a direct object. (8f)

invention techniques Ways of gathering ideas for writing. (2)

inverted word order In contrast to standard order, the main verb or an auxiliary verb comes before the subject in inverted word order. Most questions and some exclamations use inverted word order. (19f)

irony Words used to imply the opposite of their usual meaning. (21c)

irregular verb A verb that forms the past tense and past participle in some way other than by adding *-ed* or *-d*. (8d)

jargon A particular field's or group's specialized vocabulary that a general reader is unlikely to understand. (21e)

levels of formality The degree of formality of language reflected by word choice and sentence structure. A highly formal level is used for ceremonial and other occasions when stylistic flourishes are appropriate. A medium level, which is neither too formal nor too casual, is acceptable for most academic writing. (21a–1)

levels of generality In grouping information or ideas, moving from the most general to the most specific. (2l)

limiting adjective See *determiner*.

linking verb A main verb that links a subject with a subject complement that renames or describes the subject. Linking verbs convey a state of being, relate to the senses, or indicate a condition. (8a)

logical fallacies Flaws in reasoning that lead to illogical statements. (5k)

loose sentence See *cumulative sentence*.

main clause See *independent clause*.

main verb A verb that expresses action, occurrence, or state of being and that shows mood, tense, voice, number, and person. (8)

mapping An invention technique based on thinking about a topic and its increasingly specific subdivisions; also known as *clustering* and *webbing*. (2i)

mechanics Conventions governing matters such as the use of capital letters, italics, abbreviations, and numbers. (30)

metaphor A comparison implying similarity between two things; a metaphor does not use words such as *like* or *as*, which are used in a simile and which make a comparison explicit: *a mop of hair* (compare the simile *hair like a mop*). (21c)

misplaced modifier Describing or limiting words that are wrongly positioned in a sentence so that their message is either illogical or relates to the wrong word(s). (15b)

mixed construction A sentence that unintentionally changes from one grammatical structure to another, incompatible one, thus garbling meaning. (15d)

mixed metaphors Incongruously combined images. (21c)

MLA style See *documentation style*.

modal auxiliary verb A group of auxiliary verbs that add information such as a sense of needing, wanting, or having to do something or a sense of possibility, likelihood, obligation, permission, or ability. (46)

modifier A word or group of words functioning as an adjective or adverb to describe or limit another word or word group. (12, 19e)

mood The attribute of verbs showing a speaker's or writer's attitude toward the action by the way verbs are used. English has three moods: imperative, indicative, and subjunctive. Also see *imperative mood, indicative mood, subjunctive mood*. (8l–8m)

noncount noun A noun that names "uncountable" things: *water, time*. (41, 42)

nonessential element See *nonrestrictive element*.

nonrestrictive element A descriptive word, phrase, or dependent clause that provides information not essential to understanding the basic message of the element it modifies and so is set off by commas. Also see *restrictive element*. (24e)

nonsexist language See *sexist language*.

nonstandard Language usage other than edited American English. Also see *edited American English*. (21a–2)

noun A word that names a person, place, thing, or idea. Nouns function as subjects, objects, or complements.

noun clause A dependent clause that functions as a subject, object, or complement. (7o–2)

noun complement See *complement*.

noun determiner See *determiner*.

noun phrase A noun and its modifiers functioning as a subject, object, or complement. (7n)

number The attribute of some words indicating whether they refer to one (singular) or more than one (plural).

object A noun, pronoun, or group of words functioning as a noun or pronoun that receives the action of a verb (direct object); tells to whom or for whom something is done (indirect object); or completes the meaning of a preposition (object of a preposition). (7l)

object complement A noun or adjective renaming or describing a direct object after a few verbs including *call, consider, name, elect*, and *think: I call joggers **fanatics***.

objective case The case of a noun or pronoun functioning as a direct or indirect object or object of a preposition or of a verbal. A few pronouns change form to show case (*him, her, whom*). Also see *case*. (9)

paragraph A group of sentences that work together to develop a unit of thought. (4)

paragraph development Using specific, concrete details (RENNS) to support a generalization in a paragraph; rhetorical strategies for arranging and organizing paragraphs. (4f)

parallelism The use of equivalent grammatical forms or matching sentence structures to express equivalent ideas. (18)

paraphrase A restatement of someone else's ideas in language and sentence structure different from that of the original. (31d)

parenthetical documentation See *parenthetical reference*.

parenthetical reference Information enclosed in parentheses following quoted, paraphrased, or summarized material from a source to alert readers to the use of material from a specific source. Parenthetical references function together with a list of bibliographic information about each source used in a paper to document the writer's use of sources. (33c–1, 33d–1)

participial phrase A phrase that contains a present participle or a past participle and any modifiers and that functions as an adjective. Also see *verbal*.

passive construction See *passive voice*.

passive voice The form of a verb in which the subject is acted upon; if the subject is mentioned in the sentence, it usually appears as the object of the preposition *by: I was frightened by the thunder* (compare the active-voice version *The thunder frightened me*). The passive voice emphasizes the action, in contrast to the active voice, which emphasizes the doer of the action. (8n–8o)

past participle The third principal part of a verb, formed in regular verbs, like the past tense, by adding *-d* or *-ed* to the simple form. In irregular verbs, it often differs from the simple form and the past tense: *break, broke, **broken.*** (8b)

past perfect progressive tense The past perfect tense form that describes an ongoing condition in the past that has been ended by something stated in the sentence: *I had been talking.*

past perfect tense The tense that describes a condition or action that started in the past, continued for a while, and then ended in the past: *I had talked.*

past progressive tense The past tense form that shows the continuing nature of a past action: *I was talking.*

past tense form The second principal part of a verb, in regular verbs formed by adding *-d* or *-ed* to the simple form. In irregular verbs, the past tense may change in several ways from the simple form. (8b, 8d)

perfect tenses The three tenses—the present perfect (*I have talked*), the past perfect (*I had talked*), and the future perfect (*I will have talked*)—that help to show complex time relationships between two clauses. (8i)

periodic sentence A sentence that begins with modifiers and ends with the independent clause, thus postponing the main idea—and the emphasis—for the end; also called a *climactic sentence*. (19e)

person The attribute of nouns and pronouns showing who or what acts or experiences an action. First person is the one speaking (*I, we*); second person is the one being spoken to (*you, you*); and third person is the person or thing spoken about (*he, she, it; they*). All nouns are third person.

personal pronoun A pronoun that refers to people or things, such as *I, you, them, it.*

persuasive writing Writing that seeks to convince the reader about a matter of opinion. (1b)

phrasal verb A verb that combines with one or more prepositions to deliver its meaning: *ask out, look into.* (44c)

phrase A group of related words that does not contain a subject and predicate and thus cannot stand alone as an independent grammatical unit. A phrase functions as a noun, verb, or modifier. (7n)

plagiarism A writer's presenting another person's words or ideas without giving credit to that person. Documentation systems allow writers to give proper credit to sources in ways recognized by scholarly communities. Plagiarism is a serious offense, a form of intellectual dishonesty that can lead to course failure or expulsion. (31)

planning An early part of the writing process in which writers gather ideas. Along with shaping, planning is sometimes called *prewriting.* (2)

plural See *number*.

positive The form of an adjective or adverb when no comparison is being expressed: *blue, easily*. Also see *comparative, superlative*. (12e)

possessive case The case of a noun or pronoun that shows ownership or possession. Also see *case*. (9, 27a–27d)

predicate The part of a sentence that contains the verb and tells what the subject is doing or experiencing or what is being done to the subject. A *simple predicate* contains only the main verb and any auxiliary verb(s). A *complete predicate* contains the verb, its modifiers, objects, and other related words. A *compound predicate* contains two or more verbs and their objects and modifiers, if any. (7k)

predicate adjective An adjective used as a subject complement: *That tree is **leafy***.

predicate nominative A noun or pronoun used as a subject complement: *That tree is a **maple***.

premises In a deductive argument expressed as a syllogism, statements presenting the conditions of the argument from which the conclusion must follow. (5j)

preposition A word that conveys a relationship, often of space or time, between the noun or pronoun following it and other words in the sentence. The noun or pronoun following a preposition is called its *object*. (7g, 44)

prepositional phrase See *phrase, preposition*.

present participle A verb's *-ing* form. Used with auxiliary verbs, present participles function as main verbs. Used without auxiliary verbs, present participles function as nouns or adjectives. (8b, 7d)

present perfect progressive tense The present perfect tense form that describes something ongoing in the past that is likely to continue into the future: *I have been talking*.

present perfect tense The tense indicating that an action or its effects, begun or perhaps completed in the past, continue into the present: *I had talked*.

present progressive tense The present tense form of the verb that indicates something taking place at the time it is written or spoken about: *I am talking*.

present tense The tense that describes what is happening, what is true at the moment, and what is consistently true. It uses the simple form (*I **talk***) and the *-s* form in the third person singular (*he, she, it **talks***). (8h)

prewriting A term for all activities in the writing process before drafting. See *planning* and *shaping*. (2)

primary sources "Firsthand" work: write-ups of experiments and observations by the researchers who conducted them; taped accounts, interviews, and newspaper accounts by direct observers; autobiographies, diaries, and journals; expressive works (poems, plays, fiction, essays); also known as *primary evidence*. Also see *secondary source*. (5h, 32g)

progressive forms Verb forms made in all tenses with the present participle and forms of the verb *be* as an auxiliary. Progressive forms show that an action, occurrence, or state of being is ongoing. (8j)

pronoun A word that takes the place of a noun and functions in the same ways that nouns do. Types of pronouns are *demonstrative, indefinite, intensive, interrogative, personal, reciprocal, reflexive,* and *relative*. The word (or words) a pronoun replaces is called its *antecedent*. (9, 10, 11m–11r)

pronoun-antecedent agreement The match in expressing number and person, and for personal pronouns, gender as well, required between a pronoun and its antecedent. (11m–11r)

pronoun case The way a pronoun changes form to reflect its use as the agent of action (subjective case), the thing being acted upon (objective case), or the thing showing ownership (possessive case). (9)

pronoun reference The relationship between a pronoun and its antecedent. (10)

proofreading Reading a final draft to find and correct any spelling or mechanics mistakes, typing errors, or handwriting illegibility; the final step of the writing process. (3e)

proper adjective An adjective formed from a proper noun: *Victorian, American*.

proper noun A noun that names specific people, places, or things and is always capitalized: *Michael Stipe, Buick*.

purpose The goal or aim of a piece of writing: to express oneself, to provide information, to persuade, or to create a literary work. (1b)

quotation Repeating or reporting another person's words. *Direct quotation* repeats another's words exactly and encloses them in quotation marks. *Indirect quotation* reports another's words without quotation marks except around any words repeated exactly from the source. Both direct and indirect quotation require documentation of the source to avoid plagiarism. Also see *indirect discourse*. (28a, 31c)

reciprocal pronoun The pronouns *each other* and *one another* referring to individual parts of a plural antecedent: *We respect **each other***.

References In many documentation styles, including APA, the title of a list of sources cited in a research paper or other written work. (33d, 33e, 33f)

reflexive pronoun A pronoun that ends in -*self* and that reflects back to its antecedent: *They claim to support* **themselves**.

regular verb A verb that forms its past tense and past participle by adding -*ed* or -*d* to the simple form. Most English verbs are regular. (8d)

relative adverb An adverb that introduces an adjective clause: *The lot* **where** *I usually park my car was full.*

relative clause See *adjective clause.*

relative pronoun A pronoun, such as *who, which, that, who, whom, whoever,* and a few others, that introduces an adjective clause or sometimes a noun clause.

restrictive clause A dependent clause that gives information necessary to distinguish whatever it modifies from others in the same category. In contrast to a nonrestrictive clause, a restrictive clause is not set off with commas. (24e)

restrictive element A word, phrase, or dependent clause that provides information essential to the understanding of the element it modifies. In contrast to a nonrestrictive element, a restrictive element is not set off with commas. (24e)

revision A part of the writing process in which writers evaluate their rough drafts and, based on their assessments, rewrite by adding, cutting, replacing, moving, and often totally recasting material. (3c)

rhetoric The area of discourse that focuses on arrangement of ideas and choice of words as a reflection of the writer's purpose and sense of audience. (1)

rhetorical strategies In writing, various techniques for presenting ideas to deliver a writer's intended message with clarity and impact. Reflecting typical patterns of human thought, rhetorical strategies include arrangements such as chronological and climactic order; stylistic techniques such as parallelism and planned repetition; and patterns for organizing and developing writing such as description and definition. (4)

Rogerian argument An argument technique adapted from the principles of communication developed by psychologist Carl Rogers. (6c)

run-on (run-together) sentence See *fused sentence.*

secondary source A source that reports, analyzes, discusses, reviews, or otherwise deals with the work of someone else, as opposed to a primary source, which is someone's original work or firsthand report. A reliable secondary source should be the work of a person with appropriate credentials, should appear in a respected publication or other medium, should be current, and should be well-reasoned. (5h, 32g)

second person See *person*.

sentence See *sentence types*.

sentence fragment A portion of a sentence that is punctuated as though it were a complete sentence. (13)

sentence types A grammatical classification of sentences by the kinds of clauses they contain. A *simple sentence* consists of one independent clause. A *complex sentence* contains one independent clause and one or more dependent clauses. A *compound-complex sentence* contains at least two independent clauses and one or more dependent clause. A *compound sentence* contains two or more independent clauses joined by a coordinating conjunction. Sentences are also classified by their grammatical function; see *declarative sentence, exclamatory sentence, imperative sentence*, and *interrogative sentence*. (7j, 7p)

sexist language Language that unfairly or unnecessarily assigns roles or characteristics to people on the basis of gender. Language that avoids gender stereotyping is called *nonsexist language*. (21b, 11q)

shaping An early part of the writing process in which writers consider ways to organize their material. Along with planning, shaping is sometimes called *prewriting*. (2)

simile A comparison, using *like* or *as*, of otherwise dissimilar things. (21c)

simple form The form of the verb that shows action, occurrence, or state of being taking place in the present. It is used in the singular for first and second person and in the plural for first, second, and third person. It is also the first principal part of a verb. The simple form is also known as the *dictionary form* or *base form*. (8b)

simple predicate See *predicate*.

simple sentence See *sentence types*.

simple subject See *subject*.

simple tenses The present, past, and future tenses, which divide time into present, past, and future. (8h)

singular See *number*.

slang Coined words and new meanings for existing words, which quickly pass in and out of use; not appropriate for most academic writing. (21a-3)

source A book, article, document, other work, or person providing information. (1e, 31, 32, 33)

split infinitive One or more words coming between the two words of an infinitive. (15b-2)

standard English See *edited American English*.

standard word order The most common order for words in English sentences: the subject comes before the predicate.

subject The word or group of words in a sentence that acts, is acted upon, or is described by the verb. A *simple subject* includes only the noun or pronoun. A *complete subject* includes the noun or pronoun and all its modifiers. A *compound subject* includes two or more nouns or pronouns and their modifiers. (7k)

subject complement A noun or adjective that follows a linking verb, renaming or describing the subject of the sentence; also called a *predicate nominative*. (7m–1)

subjective case The case of the noun or pronoun functioning as a subject. Also see *case*. (9)

subject-verb agreement The required match between a subject and verb in expressing number and person. (11a–11l)

subjunctive mood The verb mood that expresses wishes, recommendations, indirect requests, speculations, and conditional statements: *I wish **you were** here*. (8l-8m)

subordinate clause See *dependent clause*.

subordinating conjunction A conjunction that introduces an adverbial clause and expresses a relationship between the idea in it and the idea in the independent clause. (7h)

subordination The use of grammatical structures to reflect the relative importance of ideas. A sentence with logically subordinated information expresses the most important information in the independent clause and less important information in dependent clauses or phrases. (17a-17d)

summary An extraction of the main message or central point of a passage or other discourse; a critical thinking activity preceding synthesis. (5f, 31e)

superlative The form of an adjective or adverb that expresses comparison among three or more things: *bluest, least blue; most easily, least easily*. (12e)

syllogism The structure of a deductive argument expressed in two premises and a conclusion. The *first premise* is a generalized assumption or statement of fact. The *second premise* is a different assumption or statement of fact based on evidence. The *conclusion* is also a specific instance that follows logically from the premises. (5j)

synonym A word that is close in meaning to another word. (20a)

synthesis A component of critical thinking in which material that has been summarized, analyzed, and interpreted is connected to what is already known (one's prior knowledge). (5b, 5f)

tag question An inverted verb-pronoun combination added to the end of a sentence, creating a question, that "asks" the audience to agree with the assertion in the first part of the sentence: *You know what a tag question is,* ***don't you?*** A tag question is set off from the rest of the sentence with a comma. (24f)

tag sentence See *tag question*.

tense The time at which the action of the verb occurs: in the present, the past, or the future. (8g–8k)

tense sequence In sentences that have more than one clause, the accurate matching of verbs to reflect logical time relationships. (8k)

thesis statement A statement of an essay's central theme that makes clear the main idea, the writer's purpose, the focus of the topic, and perhaps the organizational pattern. (2n)

third person See *person*.

tone The writer's attitude toward his or her material and reader, especially as reflected by word choice. (1d)

topic The subject of discourse.

topic sentence The sentence that expresses the main idea of a paragraph. (4b–3)

Toulmin model for argument A model that defines the essential parts of an argument as the *claim* (or *main point*), the *support* (or *evidence*), and the *warrants* (or *assumptions behind the main point*). (6e)

transition The connection of one idea to another in discourse. Useful strategies for creating transitions include transitional expressions, parallelism, and planned repetition of key words and phrases. (4d)

transitional expressions Words and phrases that signal connections among ideas and create coherence. (4d–1)

transitive verb A verb that must be followed by a direct object. (8f)

unity The clear and logical relationship between the main idea of a paragraph and the evidence supporting the main idea. (4b)

usage A customary way of using language. (21, Usage Glossary)

valid A term applied to a deductive argument when the conclusion follows logically from the premises. Validity describes the structure of an argument, not its truth. (5j)

verb A class of words that shows action or occurrence or describes a state of being. Verbs change form to show time (tense), attitude (mood), and role of the subject (voice). Verbs occur in the predicate of a clause and can be in verb phrases, which may consist of a main verb, any auxiliary verbs, and any modifiers. Verbs can be described as transitive or intransitive depending on whether they take a direct object. (8)

verbal A verb part functioning as a noun, adjective, or adverb. Verbals include *infinitives*, *present participles* (functioning as adjectives), *gerunds* (present participles functioning as nouns), and *past participles*. (7d)

verbal phrase A group of words that contains a verbal (an infinitive, participle, or gerund) and its modifiers.

verb phrase A main verb, any auxiliary verb(s), and any modifiers.

voice An attribute of verbs showing whether the subject acts (active voice) or is acted upon (passive voice). (8n–8o)

webbing See *mapping*.

Works Cited In MLA documentation style, the title of a list of all sources cited in a research paper or other written work. (33c-2–33c-3)

writing process Stages of writing in which a writer gathers and shapes ideas, organizes material, expresses those ideas in a rough draft, evaluates the draft and revises it, edits the writing for technical errors, and proofreads it for typographical accuracy and legibility. The stages often overlap. See *planning, shaping, drafting, revision, editing,* and *proofreading*. (1, 2, 3)

Index

All entries in boldface italics (***advice, advise,*** for example) are discussed in the Usage Glossary and any other place listed. Section numbers are in boldface type and page numbers in regular type. The listing "**30m:** 515" thus refers you to page 515, which is in section 30m.

CHARTS IN TINTED BOXES

CHARTS IN TINTED BOXES *(continued)*

Response Symbols

Here are two lists of symbols your instructor might write on your papers. The first list shows traditional cvorrection symbols; the second list shows complimentary symbols. You can find material related to each item by consulting the handbook sections or chapters given.

Correction Symbols

ab	abbreviation error, **23b, 30h-30k**		*pl*	plural error, **22c**
ad	adjective or adverb error, **12**		*pro ref*	pronoun reference error, **10**
agr	agreement error, **11**		*pro agr*	pronoun agreement error, **11m-11r**
ca	case error, **9**		*pe/*	punctuation error, **23-29**
cap	needs capital letter, **30a-30e**		*ref*	pronoun reference error, **10**
cl	avoid cliché, **21d**		*rep*	repetitious (redundant), **16c**
coh	needs coherence, **4d**		*ro*	run-on sentence, **14**
coord	faulty coordination, **17a-17d**		*shift*	shift, **15a**
cs	comma splice, **14**		*sl*	avoid slang, **21a-3**
dev	needs development, **4a, 4c, 4f**		*sp*	spelling error, **22**
dm	dangling modifier, **15c**		*subord*	faulty subordination, **17e-17h**
e	needs exact language, **20b**		*sxt*	sexist language use, **11q, 21b**
emph	needs emphasis, **19**		*t*	verb tense error, **8g-8k**
frag	sentence fragment, **13**		*trans*	needs transition, **4d-1, 4d-5**
fs	fused sentence, **14**		*u*	needs unity, **4b, 4c**
hyph	hyphenation error, **22d**		*us*	usage error, **Usage Glossary**
inc	incomplete sentence, **15e**		*v*	verb form error, **8b-8f**
ital	italics (underlining) error, **30f-30g**		*v ag*r	verb agreement error, **11a-11l**
k	awkward construction, **15, 16, 21e**		*var*	needs sentence variety, **19**
			w	wordy, **16**
lc	needs lowercase letter, **30a-30e**		*wc*	word choice error, **20, 21**
mixed	mixed construction, **15d**		*ww*	wrong word, **20, 21**
mm	misplaced modifier, **15b**		∧	insert
num	number use error, **30l-30m**		ℛ	delete
¶	start new paragraph, **4**		∼	transpose
no ¶	do not start new paragraph, **4**		#	space needed
//	parallelism, **18**		⌣	close up
			?	meaning unlcear

Complimentary Symbols

gd coh	good coherence, **4d**		*gd th*	good thesis statement, **2n, 3c-2, 6b, 32r**
gd coord	good coordination, **17a-17c**		*gd trans*	good transitions, **4d-1, 4d-5**
gd dev	good development, **4c, 4f**		*gd ts*	good topic sentence, **4a, 4b**
gd log	good logic, **5j-5k**		*gd u*	good unity, **4b, 4c**
gd //	good parallelism, **18**		*gd var*	good sentence variety, **19**
gd rea	good reasoning, **5i-5k**		*gd wc*	good word choice, **20, 21**
gd rev	good revising, **3c**		*gd wp*	good writing process, **1, 2, 3**
gd sub	good subordination, **17e-17g**			

How to Find Information in Your *Simon* & *Schuster Handbook for Writers*

You can use your *Simon and Schuster Handbook for Writers* as a reference book, just as you use a dictionary or an encyclopedia. At each step, use one or more suggestions to find the information you want.

STEP 1: Use lists to decide where to go.

- Overview of Contents (on inside front cover)
- Scan the longer Contents that starts on page iii.
- Scan the Index at the back of the book for a detailed alphabetical list of all major and minor topics.
- Scan the list of Charts in Tinted Boxes that highlight and summarize all major subjects.

STEP 2: Locate the number that leads to the information you seek.

- Find a chapter number.
- Find a number-letter combination for a subsection of a chapter for a rule or guiding principle.
- Find a chart number.
- Find a page number.

STEP 3: Check elements on each page to confirm where you are in the book. (See the opposite page.)

- Look for the shortened title at the top of each page (left page for chapter title and right page for section title).
- Look for a chapter number at the top of the tan "access bar" that runs down the outer edge of each page.
- Look down the tan access bar for a subsection's number-letter combination.
- Look for a chart number and title in the tan access bar.
- Look for a page number at the bottom of the page.

STEP 4: Locate and read the information you need. Use special features, illustrated on the opposite page, to help you.

- Use cross-references (usually given in parentheses) to related key concepts.
- Find the definition for any word printed in small capital letters in the Terms Glossary at the back of the book.
- Use ❖ ALERT ❖ notes, signaled by an exclamation point in the tan access bar that runs down the edge of the page, for computer tips and for pointers about related matters of usage, grammar, punctuation, and writing.